WORD ASSOCIATIONS
of Young Children

WORD ASSOCIATIONS
of Young Children

by

Doris R. Entwisle

THE JOHNS HOPKINS PRESS   •   Baltimore, Maryland

To
Nathan and Edith Entwisle

Preface

At a time when research in language acquisition is more versatile and widespread than ever before, it is hard to bring oneself to the brink of publication. Each month sees important new material coming into print. This makes the author's task difficult, but undoubtedly it has also made this monograph richer and more interesting than it would have been five years ago. The recent attention of Miller and McNeill to a theory of language acquisition has been very timely, and certainly the application of modern linguistic theory to language acquisition is as welcome as it is overdue. It makes the data collected here more serviceable and also helps to unify the findings.

Mostly observational data are presented here. High speed computing equipment has been an absolute necessity from the start. But data reductions actually employ computers in a banal way and for the most part only sorting programs were required. More imaginative uses of computers hopefully will aid in building up a backlog of experimentation so that the language acquisition process can be studied more thoroughly and more experimentally.

This research began formally in September, 1961, with some informal and casual investigation before that time. It is an impossibility to include all the analyses and fragments of data from four years of research in a single volume. For one thing, some approaches led up blind alleys, although considerable time and effort were expended before they were abandoned. Our purpose here is to present a central core of data, word associations of Maryland urban children of kindergarten, first, third, and fifth grades, very much in the tradition of the norms presented by the Minnesota group. We hope that these detailed associative data will be of service to other investigators. In addition we present analyses of a much greater fund of data that is not included because it is too specialized or too redundant to be worth publishing in detail. The data generally are analyzed in a quasi-experimental frame. The urban data fall into two main socioeconomic groups, and at present there is no lower-lower-class urban (slum) group. This gap is being filled in during 1965–66 and will be reported separately later. Other supplementary analyses may also be published in the future.

A word is needed about the chronological sequence of this work, particularly since some attempts at data-gathering and analysis proved futile and are therefore not discussed in the book. Originally a sample of hard-of-hearing children was planned. We had hoped that hard-of-hearing children might form a provocative contrast with the Amish (whose exposure to speech was also presumably reduced, but for other reasons, namely cultural customs). It turned out that children with moderate hearing deficiencies in the age groups needed were just not available in sufficient numbers in the Baltimore City area. Children of school age with uncompensated hearing deficiencies of the conduction type are now unusual because they are seen and treated early. This research path is therefore closed. Although there are no data reported on hard-of-hearing children, we are grateful to Ruth Diaz-Plaja, who interviewed many children with hearing impairments, and who searched for children who might be included in this study. We are also grateful to Dr. William Hardy of The Johns Hopkins Hospital Hearing and Speech Clinic for his help with this same effort.

I am indebted to many colleagues for assistance and advice. Daniel Forsyth, now at the Center for Cognitive Studies, Harvard University, supervised the gathering of much of the data in the first year of the project and aided in the initial planning of the research. Rolf Muuss of Goucher College fulfilled a similar role in the second year of the research, making contact with school personnel and supervising the data-gathering. In addition Dr. Muuss supervised the gathering of some German samples and aided in their translation and reduction. These will be reported on separately at a later time. He also obtained some of the data from Goucher College students. Peter Houts, now of Stanford Medical School, interviewed some Goucher College students individually and contributed valuable suggestions.

Through the good offices of John Hostetler it was possible to interview Amish respondents, and Mrs. Sadie Lapp procured these data. Our debt to these two persons is very great, for without their help study of the Amish would have been impossible. The cultural customs of this group make it very difficult for those who are not Amish to be received.

Several persons have contributed in a less direct, but very important, way by reading preliminary drafts of portions of the manuscript, and also by supplying me with drafts of their own work on closely related matters. David McNeill, formerly of Harvard University and now at the University of Michigan, has provided many insights. Chapter 8 particularly attests to the extent of his influence upon the present work. James Deese encouraged me to begin this research in the first place, has made many valuable suggestions over the entire period of the project, and has permitted me to read the manuscript of his book, *The Structure of Associations in Language and Thought*, to be published in the spring of 1966 by The Johns Hopkins Press. To a large extent Dr. Deese's and John Stephens' interest in this area were my initial stimulus. Iris Rotberg, Susan Ervin, and Roger Brown have generously supplied me with many papers in advance of publication, and have also criticized preliminary versions of some portions of the book. Others who have generously made suggestions about parts of the manuscript are James Coleman and Robert Gordon.

It is a pleasure to acknowledge the co-operation of the Board of Education, Baltimore County, Maryland, whose Research Bureau has made possible the gathering of the data over a three-year period. In particular, we are grateful to Loyal Joos, Director of Research, during the period this study was being carried out. Without exception the staffs of the Baltimore County schools have been outstanding in their willingness to participate and in their general helpfulness. Records have been furnished and other aid extended to a degree that is remarkable. The staffs of several privately-run kindergartens, Kiddy Kollege, Mrs. Dorff's Kindergarten, and Towson Presbyterian Kindergarten, also were outstanding in their co-operation. We are also grateful to volunteers at Goucher College and The Johns Hopkins University who provided data for adults.

Many persons served as interviewers, and their assistance is gratefully acknowledged: Marjorie Berson, Edith Brown, Barbara Bush, Janet Deacon, Rachel Flavelle, Betty Habach, Susan Hewlett, Betty Hildum, Mayan Lau, Elizabeth Lawless, Janet McLanaghan, Janet Pearson, Betsey Southerland, Allegra Terrien.

The analysis of the data has been long and extensive. A number of persons have aided in this: Patricia Durrett, Barbara Bricks, Kenneth Munzert, Veronica Evering, and Joyce Norris. Their diligence has been indispensable. A particular debt is owing to the Homewood Computing Center and its Director, M. Patricia Powers. Doris Stude and Helen Wirtz have aided in preparing the manuscript. Their careful work has done much to bring this project to its final stage. Very special thanks are due to Barbara Bricks who has helped with every phase of this research. Her conscientious work has done much to improve the whole project.

Grateful acknowledgment is made to the *Journal of Verbal Learning and Verbal Behavior; Psychological Reports;* and *Sociometry* for permission to reproduce material previously incorporated in articles published in these journals.

Finally, I am particularly grateful to the National Institutes of Health, which has provided the continuous support that makes research of this kind possible and to The Johns Hopkins University Department of Electrical Engineering for the facilities needed.

Baltimore, Maryland   Doris Entwisle
September, 1965

Contents

WORD ASSOCIATIONS
of Young Children

Chapter One

The Scope of This Book and
Its Relation to Other Research

The study of association is an ancient one, dating back to Aristotle. The first free association experiment, tried by Galton with himself as subject, rapidly led to similar studies by the German experimentalists, but it was the clinicians who gave the strongest impetus in this field. In this context Kent and Rosanoff (1910) sampled associations of 1,000 normal adults of various educations and occupations to establish a "normal" base line with which they could compare their psychiatric patients. For many years their sample was the authoritative one. The particular list of words they selected set the pattern for several research generations. Unfortunately, their list was mostly made up of very common nouns and adjectives, the least interesting kinds of words for modern workers. Only since the beginning of this decade have other kinds of words been used as stimuli in word association studies.

This break with the past, signals an entirely new interest in word association, i.e., as a method for gathering data relevant to verbal habits and linguistic development. Whereas, formerly, word association studies were inspired by clinical hypotheses, now interest is generally directed toward other goals. Associations are relevant to problems of verbal learning and concept formation, to efficiency in problem solving and to creativity, and also, since Brown and Berko's (1960) experiment, to patterns of linguistic development. The outlook is now more experimental or quasi-experimental than psychometric. It is in this frame that the present book rests.

Other Studies of Children's Word Associations

Until now there has been a gap in our knowledge of word associations. For adults and college level students there are several large samples (Russell and Jenkins, 1954;

1

Palermo and Jenkins, 1964; Jones and Fillenbaum, 1964), and recently there has been extensive sampling of school-age children at grades four, five, six, eight, ten, and twelve (Palermo and Jenkins, 1964). But before this book, there has been nothing available on younger children (below fourth grade) except for small samples of children employed in experiments by Brown and Berko (1960), and Ervin (1961). These small samples of younger children led directly to the present study, for they revealed some remarkable things. Ervin demonstrated striking changes in children's word associations concomitant with age. Syntagmatic responses gave way to paradigmatic ones. (Syntagmatic associates are those echoing syntactic orders ["deep"—"hole"], whereas, paradigmatic associates are those matching form class ["deep"—"shallow"].) Brown and Berko also presented convincing data of a sharp rise in paradigmatic word associations in middle childhood and showed this to be highly correlated with the acquisition of grammar.

One other study was directly instrumental in leading to the present work. Many years ago Woodrow and Lowell (1916) gathered associations from 1,000 Minneapolis school children using essentially the Kent-Rosanoff stimulus list. (Theirs were the only data available for children until the work of Ervin and that of Brown and Berko, and are the only extensive data on children's associations prior to 1964.) They compared children's associations with those of adults (procured by Kent and Rosanoff), and showed that associations of adults and children differed markedly. In very few instances was the most popular adult response also the most popular child response. Even more interesting was their observation that the character of responses changed from childhood to adulthood, with child responses following a sequential (syntagmatic) pattern and adult responses following a replacement pattern (paradigmatic).

These several studies, reviewed briefly here, are the main ones leading to the research reported in this book and they will be treated more fully later on. They suggest the kinds of changes with age that occur, changes that the present work documents in considerable detail. Furthermore, the discrepancies between the Woodrow and Lowell data and the later data are provocative and lead to interesting hypotheses about mechanisms of word association development. Some casual experimentation by the author, together with the realization that no data on young children were available to test speculations generated by modern notions of verbal learning, led directly to the research reported in this book.

Overview of the Book

The work here deals with word associations of young children, ages four to eleven. It differs from previous efforts in providing *large* groups of young children and also in studying IQ, SES, and other characteristics of respondents that can be related to associations. Such variables have never been investigated previously for subjects of any age. It differs from previous work also in using a stimulus list composed of words drawn from different form classes and possessing different degrees of familiarity (frequency). Several methodologic inquiries, conducted more or less parenthetically, have relevance not only for this study, but for many kinds of studies of verbal behavior.

A major purpose of this work is to study language acquisition over elementary school ages through the medium of association data. Part of the riddle of language acquisition stems from a paucity of evidence concerning what language capability children of various ages actually do possess. Some evidence, although it is fragmentary and indirect, can be obtained through word association procedures. The chief finding is that paradigmatic responses—responses matching the form class of the stimulus—increase over the years of middle childhood, but at different rates. There is a surprising orderliness even in four-year-olds' associations, and this orderliness continues to increase up to age eleven, the upper limit of our samples. Another major purpose of this work is to present association data so that other investigators can calibrate stimulus materials for verbal learning experiments. No association values of English words have heretofore been available for young children of elementary school age.

The entire research effort has been geared to high-speed computing equipment. Such equipment made it possible to incorporate background variables like IQ and socioeconomic status for the first time. Modern data-processing methods are essential, for each division on each variable requires an individual sort and print-out. Also, as the number of subjects increases, the difficulty of the tabulation increases disproportionately. The present study would have been impossible without electronic computers.

Early chapters of the book describe the samples of children, the sample of word stimuli, and the method of collecting and sorting the data. Later chapters discuss the various main results, such as how associations vary with the age of the child or with the form class of the stimulus. Often, as will be seen, the major variables interact. For instance, changes with form class proceed more rapidly for more intelligent children. Theoretical implications of the results, particularly in relation to other research and in relation to language acquisition broadly considered, are discussed in the final two chapters.

The same ninety-six stimulus words are used with many different kinds of subjects. Our list contains thirty words from the Kent-Rosanoff (K-R) list. The other sixty-six words consist of verbs, adverbs, prepositions, pronouns, low-frequency adjectives and low-frequency nouns, in order to provide a broad sample of language. Appendices C and D present alphabetical tabulations of associations to these ninety-six stimuli by kindergarten, first-grade, third-grade, and fifth-grade children who reside in urban areas of Maryland. Appendix A gives the three most common responses for these same groups of children (plus an adult comparison group). Appendix B tabulates parallel information on children obtained by other workers (Palermo and Jenkins, 1964; Woodrow and Lowell, 1916) for the Kent-Rosanoff words on our list, and some parallel data for adults collected by Fillenbaum and Jones (1965).

To sum up, this book differs from previous work in studying associations of large samples of young children. It also differs in studying associative responses according to characteristics of the subjects, such as IQ and residential locus, never previously investigated. It attempts to place the empirical findings in context with other previous empirical work and in a theoretical setting, to the extent that theory is available. It also attempts to account for why associative patterns change and what significance this phenomenon may have for language acquisition.

Language Learning

Language learning is coming under closer and closer scrutiny, partly as a consequence of developments made possible by high-speed computers, and partly because of rapid strides in research on thinking and concept formation. The striking fact about a human being's use of language is the lack of repetition. To use Miller's (1964) statement, productivity sets the central problem for the psycholinguist. A fluent speaker, even a young child, produces and understands sentences that he has never heard (or seen) in exactly the same form before. This fact pushes the learning of language outside the associationistic frame so comfortable for many learning theories. In the author's view, and also in Moore's (1964), learning theory of any school is least satisfying when applied to the two chief accomplishments of early childhood—learning to walk and learning to talk. Many others have also expressed the conviction that contemporary learning theory has little to contribute to the analysis of language acquisition (Deese, 1964a; Chomsky, 1959; Lenneberg, 1964; Miller, 1964). In short, there has as yet been no general fusion of psychological theory and linguistic analysis.

Association-by-contiguity has many weaknesses as far as language learning is concerned. It is awkward to use in accounting for the learning of "black" as a response to "white," although Ervin (1961) has offered the hypothesis of "erroneous anticipation" to explain such associates. She suggests that, as one listens to speech, the sentence environments that have been shared in the past elicit either word by covert anticipation. For instance, as a person listens to the sentence "A cat is ———," he may covertly anticipate the ending as either "black" or "white." If he anticipates "black" when "white" occurs, this puts "black" and "white" in apposition with one another. The apposition provides the contiguity necessary for an associationistic explanation. Some ingenious experiments by McNeill (1963) tended to support Ervin's hypothesis, but later work (McNeill, 1965) shows that the number of erroneous anticipations, when these are made overt, is unrelated to production of paradigmatic associates. Also, of course, it is hard to see why errors would not lead to extinction of the covert response. The erroneous anticipation hypothesis does not now appear adequate to account for the known facts.

Association by contiguity has other weaknesses. It cannot explain the lack of association between words at the end of one sentence and "the" at the beginning of the next, as Bruner and Olver (1963) point out. As an alternative to an S-R formulation, many are drawn toward Piaget's (1932) assumptions of sensorimotor patterning on the basis of action, with gradual development of representation and reversibility. After passing through a stage of concrete operations, the child finally develops a set of rules governing "generation of the possible." In language behavior the last stage is reached when the child is capable of spinning out the allowable permutations and combinations. Piaget's formulation, insofar as it is pertinent to our problems and our data, is unfortunately too vague and nonspecific to have any power. It seems more a short description of what happens rather than an explanation of why things happen, or how they happen, or why some things happen rather than others.

So far, simple models have proved inadequate for explaining the child's acquisition of language. The limitations of a Markov model have been succinctly stated by Miller and Chomsky (1963):

> A K-limited Markov source cannot serve as a natural grammar of English no matter how large K may be. Increasing K does not isolate the set of grammatical sentences for, even though the number of high-probability grammatical sequences included is thereby increased, the number of low-probability sequences excluded is also increased. Moreover, for any finite K there would be ungrammatical sequences longer than K symbols that a stochastic user could not reject.

No one actually teaches a child to talk, and yet, as our data and other data show, even by the age of four there is definite evidence of concept formation denoting the principal word classes. Davis (1937) found that *all* grammatical constructions used by adults appear in the speech of eight-year-olds, at least in rudimentary form. These facts that are so easy to overlook are not so easy to explain. Some of our data bear on aspects of the problem of language acquisition, and in the latter part of the book considerable attention is paid to the evolution of form class concepts. Naturally, our evidence is by its nature only fragmentary, although it does give rise to descriptions of several phenomena that would have to be covered in any comprehensive theory of language acquisition. The evolution of the various form classes is one of the contributions of the present research. Language behavior evolves together with great exposure to spoken language, so interaction with the environment influences the development of response patterns. Some of our data highlight the manner in which reduced exposure slows the pace of development.

It is remarkable that children's learning of language has not led to the accumulation of more empirical evidence. In explaining language acquisition "It is first necessary to know *what* is acquired and used," Katz and Fodor (1963, p. 172). Many sources, including Davis' work cited above, suggest that children before age ten have accomplished the most important steps in language acquisition. Yet the only extensive word association data for children have been the very early data of Woodrow and Lowell. We therefore have tried to supply some empirical data, by gathering word associations from young children, but the piling up of relevant observations is bound to be a slow process. Chomsky (1964) warns that observational data alone are unlikely to be sufficient. He feels that ingenious experiments are needed to reveal language competence as opposed to language performance. We have no quarrel with his position. Ingenious experiments are more likely to be generated from a solid empirical base, however—McNeill's work being an example in point. We hope that one outcome of the present book will be to provide observations that will generate more experimental work. The data presented suggest some provocative hypotheses to investigate, and they also provide methodologic clues and materiel for experimental maneuvers.

Associations and Language Learning

One approach to the study of language behavior of very young children has been to record lengthy samples of speech. Then the child's use of vocabulary, grammatical structures, and so on, is deduced from this corpus. The task is not easy, and a large corpus may be required. Uhrbrock (1936) found with a girl almost five years old who dictated 24,000 words, that fifty-two *new* words appeared in the twenty-fourth thousand. With this strategy the number of subjects is relatively few, the sample of language large. Such studies made with children of different ages tell when the consistent use of question-forms, irregular verbs, and the other signals of a mature speaker occur.

An alternate approach is to get a small sample of language, via word association techniques, but to sample many children. This study is one of the first attempts to exploit this approach, an approach not feasible before high-speed computing equipment was available. Factorial designs have been used that employ altogether over 1,700 subjects.

The validity of word associations as indicators of linguistic development has only recently been established and other links between word associations and conceptual tasks are also recent. We know, for instance, that persons producing more relevant associations are superior problem-solvers (Johnson, 1964.) We also know that word associations influence concept formation, with relevant associations facilitating and irrelevant associations hindering concept manipulation (Thysell and Schulz, 1964). One might inquire why children's word associations indicate their stage of linguistic development. If a child responds "car" or "moon" to "slow," what evidence is this that he even knows the meanings of these words? Actually there are very few associations, even those of five-year-olds, that fail to have a strong semantic or syntactic relation to the stimulus. The examples of "car" or "moon" in response for "slow" are typical responses of young children (5 years old). Consistent responses of a different kind, for instance "fast" and "quick" to the stimulus "slow," become very common by age eight. A clear change has intervened. Somehow children between the ages of five and eight come to understand the substitution privileges of adjectives. This does not mean that children can define the word "adjective," or necessarily even have any notion of the existence of parts of speech. Rather they seem to have built a new classification system for words based on usage of these words in contexts.

As will be seen, association data for children possess a striking degree of internal consistency. The patterns typical of average children are repeated, for example, in low-IQ children at later ages, or are repeated in children from culturally deprived groups of average intelligence at later ages. Another kind of consistency is found in the parallel patterns of different samples procured by different investigators in very different geographical areas, and even in children speaking different languages. There are also correlations that exist between associations and usage. Kindergarten children use three to four times as many nouns in speech as college freshmen (Horn, 1927). This is paralleled by a preponderance of nouns in the associates of young children four and five, and many fewer noun responses (except to noun stimuli) in college age adults.

But Brown and Berko (1960) have provided the major rationale to support the study of children's word associations as a way of studying linguistic development. They used artificial verbal materials to study emergence of grammatical concepts in children, and obtained word associations from the same children. They found that the linguistic skills required to correctly perceive and use a part of speech were highly correlated with the frequency of paradigmatic responses. This provides the best and most direct evidence available of the validity of associations as indicators of linguistic development during middle childhood, over the ages of main concern to us.[1]

Our data mainly pertain to lexical words (nouns, adjectives, verbs), and, as previously mentioned, the chief finding is that paradigmatic responses increase strikingly over the childhood years, but at different rates for different words. Adult responses to the same words, and data from other sources, suggest that an evolutionary pattern for word associations may be invariant but may unfold more rapidly for some words than for others. This pattern will be more fully described later, and its delineation is a major outcome of our research.

Word association data tend to reveal the formation of word classes or concepts and so they forecast the individual's potential ability to emit different combinations of words from those he has heard. They provide indirect evidence of knowledge of "rules" that make possible the generation of new, but permissible combinations of words. To generate sentences one must learn sets of rules: concepts with exceptions. The child must somehow become aware of the constraints that operate on successive words in the language so that as he attempts to understand a spoken sentence he can process the received acoustic signals efficiently. Rules reduce the uncertainty in the system. Our data suggest that the child first learns what-follows-what (the phase of syntactic responding), and then what-substitutes-for-what (the phase of paradigmatic responding). Paradigmatic classes have some properties that are entirely semantic and other properties determined from both grammar and semantics. (These two stages may correspond to learning sets of grammatical rules and semantic rules, two sets of rules mentioned by Miller and Isard [1963].)

Some linguistic concepts can be plainly seen in the process of discovery and consolidation in our data. Form class comprehension is observed long before "parts-of-speech" are studied in school. Much hinges on the "syntagmatic" (syntactic) or "paradigmatic" designation of associates. (This is classification of associates as following sequential patterns ["deep"—"hole"] or as following substitution patterns ["deep"—"shallow"].) When a child gives a paradigmatic associate, he indicates that he knows something of the rules governing a particular form class, that he knows what-substitutes-for-what. He may deduce this after hearing a word in many contexts, with different words preceding and following. Even four- and five-year-olds know many properties of nouns and other form classes, abstractly and without regard for usage in a specific context.[2]

---

[1] Earlier, Howes (1957) produced evidence that the average probability that a given word will be emitted as a response in a word association experiment is the same as its probability in general discourse for *adults*.

[2] By concentrating on word associations, and the linguistic concepts that may be studied through them, we can provide some information about language learning, and this is naturally emphasized in this book. On the other hand, we do not wish to deny the importance or the necessity of other linguistic concepts even though we will pay them scant attention.

Quite independent of research in psycholinguistics, clinicians studying aphasic syndromes have adopted a twofold classification for speech disorders (Osgood and Miron, 1963). There seems to be a *more-than-superficial resemblance* between our syntactic-paradigmatic dichotomy and the aphasic categories, especially the clinical differences in aphasic patients labeled "similarity disorders" and "contiguity disorders" (Jakobson and Halle, 1956). Patients with a similarity disorder have little difficulty completing sentences, in carrying on conversation, or in doing other things that depend on context and organization, but they do have trouble in labeling. Patients with a contiguity disorder are able to understand and produce lexical words, to categorize and label, but they cannot maintain a flow of speech. Some clinicians feel that the essential features of the classical sensory and motor aphasic types can be better defined in terms of disturbances in word-finding vs. disturbances in syntactics. This suggestion of an organic or functional parallel to the paradigmatic-syntactic shifts noted in child development is provocative.

Word Association and Learning

It seems rather paradoxical, considering the vast literature on learning, that learning of the kind that goes on between the ages of five and eighteen has received scant attention from experimentalists in America until fairly recently. (The same is not true in Russia.) A possible exception to this general inattention is the area of concept formation. Interest here springs partly from newly-possible experimental approaches to thinking and concept formation, and partly from a growing conviction that tackling such problems in the laboratory with infra-human animals is not productive. Word association research overlaps concept formation research because associations can be viewed as being generated by (or generating) mediating responses ("mediators" and "concepts" being identical by some definitions). Association seems to be the simplest process involved in concept formation. Brown and Berko (1960), and especially McNeill (1963, 1965) have pointed the way to study language acquisition via strategies employed in other kinds of concept formation studies.

This brings up the issue of "nonsense" syllables vs. actual words in verbal learning experiments. Nonsense syllables have many drawbacks, the chief being that they tend to be resolved by the learner into discrete letter units. As Deese (1961) points out, they are encoded letter by letter. As stimuli, then, they do not have the unitary quality of words, and for this reason they call forth different kinds of learning performances from words. Also, real language habits are built up over a long span of time and it is impossible to duplicate this learning with a few hours laboratory practice.

A favorite method of science, and one that has had unqualified success in the physical sciences, is the splitting of a process into components which can be studied or measured separately. Then the over-all process is described when the descriptions of each of its parts are added together. (The ismorphism between this descriptive process and the mathematical operation of integration gives some idea of the popularity of this approach.) Application of similar strategies to many psychological problems has been disappointing. The wait for basic problems of language learning to be elucidated by molecular studies in the laboratory may be not only long but futile. The divide-and-conquer tactic fails because verbal learning problems cannot be pared down and split up without changing the problem, as was made clear in the earlier comments about nonsense syllables. Piaget's research style has had considerable appeal exactly because of its molar approach. In a way the concern of behavioral theorists for mediating symbols and Piaget's emphasis on maturational stages of cognitive organization find a meeting ground in the present work.

Individual and group differences in cognitive functioning have received little attention from any group so far (see Kagan, *et al.*, 1963), and some of the present work helps fill this gap, for we sample children systematically at several ages, at several intelligence levels, and also in several distinct subcultural groups. In a way this work presents an epidemiology of word associations for middle childhood and represents a fusion between a purely descriptive study and an experimental attack on problems of word associations. Although no experimental maneuvers are possible (we cannot alter a child's exposure to language over long periods of time) several studies are quasi-experimental. Replication and careful descriptions of samples, plus the use of several control variables to partition variance, make it possible to implicate, at least temporarily, some factors not previously studied in relation to word associations.

This assemblage of young children's word associations was originally prompted by the need for materials to use in verbal learning experiments with grade school children. Children are often preferable as subjects in learning experiments because of their shorter and less complex previous learnings (see Eisman, 1955; Norcross and Spiker, 1958; and Spiker, 1960, for typical experiments). It is tedious, however, to calibrate meaningful verbal materials for use in experiments. In studying paired associate learning, for instance, Casteneda, *et al.* (1961) had to tabulate associations to sixty-three adjectives prior to the start of an experiment because the association value of the learning materials was unknown. This study gives distributions of associates for some verbal stimuli at several ages so other investigators can carry out experiments more easily.

There is an extensive literature showing the influence of word associations upon learning. Deese (1959a) reports a correlation of .88 between interitem associative strength and the number of words on a list that could be recalled, and also a negative correlation between extra-list intrusions in recall and interitem associative strength. Other studies (Jenkins, *et al.*, 1958; Deese, 1959b) attest to the importance of simple associative processes in recall. At the same time, a number of imaginative experiments directed to topics in verbal learning required the filling in of what might be described as a more qualitative background. They are not so directly concerned with the influence of association value upon learning as with reverberations of associative mechanisms in other kinds of problems. For instance, what mechanism explains Cohen's (1964) observation that items in exhaustive categories are more easily recalled than nonexhaustive items? Many experiments on verbal learning with adults demand replication in children, yet without a background of tabulated associations such experiments are extremely difficult to perform.

Associations and Concept Formation

A large part of the language acquisition process takes place prior to the ages with which we are concerned (Miller and McNeill, 1965). For children ages four to eleven the development of concepts of form class and the enrichment of semantics seem to predominate. Children begin to distinguish generalized concepts like superordinate and subordinate categories, contrasts, apposites and so on. Our data suggest that the semantic enrichment continues past age eleven and it is a particularly difficult accomplishment because of the similarities and ambiguities of English words.

One way to study relationships among semantic concepts is exemplified in a study by Deese (1962a) using factor analysis where the structure of associative meaning is revealed via associations among clusters of words. Some similar work of ours (Chapter 7) suggests that factorial structure changes with age and may differ from one cultural group to another.

The hypothesis-validating possibilities of factor analysis are more promising with these data than is usually true, because adding words to a list is much simpler, and also more straightforward, than adding tests to a battery. That is, if a factor, say "flight," emerges for a group of words containing names of insects, it is possible to add another winged creature to the list and see if it also is heavily loaded on the same factor. Some replications of factor analytic studies of similar but not identical lists of words were in surprisingly close agreement. This approach seems promising, and Russian workers (Berlyne, 1963), who have studied semantic generalization intensively, in all cases find the degree of generalization corresponding to the closeness of semantic relation defined in word association experiments.

Cross-cultural research in cognition has excited much interest lately, with anthropologists, linguists, mathematicians, and others contributing. Osgood (1964) provides evidence for a universal framework underlying certain affective or connotative aspects of language, but there may also be cultural (innate) differences in cognition. Studies of mathematical concept learning in children in California and in Acora, Ghana, suggest that there are different "natural" concepts (Hill, 1964). (Ordered sets are easier for American children to learn first.) In our research linguistic concepts formed by children from different American subcultures are not identical, although our evidence on this point is neither as firm nor as extensive as we should like. More reliance can be placed upon our finding that linguistic development proceeds more slowly in some subcultures than in others.

Present Status of Word Associations vis-à-vis Linguistic Development

For all its popularity as a topic of inquiry, word association work prior to 1950 led to the forging of very little theory. Early studies were motivated by different questions from those we now contemplate,[3] and the earlier empirical studies are

---

[3] From time to time, associations of children have been examined in the hope that they might clarify mental processes of schizophrenia with its regression of the individual to primitive modes of responding. There seems to be little resemblance between the language of schizophrenics and that of children, however (Fairbanks, 1944), and this study takes no notice of such possible applications.

useful now mostly by accident. (Those that cite data only in summary, or reduced form, are of little use.) The contrast between old and recent interests is highlighted by the divergent analytical rubrics employed, the tendency now being to emphasize grammatical properties of associates, or contextual and substitution probabilities of words. The area of semantics is being restudied from the standpoint of modern linguistic theory.

At present there is no disagreement about the importance of linguistic behavior, but there is wide disagreement about how associations are established. In the association-by-contiguity view, associations are formed because the constituents are perceived close together in space, in time, or close in some other way. Often mediating responses are posited as theoretical constructs, although mediators have serious weaknesses (see Fodor, 1965). Bruner and Olver (1963) also find mediators unsatisfying and prefer a grammatical approach. They hold that "most grouping is determined by gradually emerging, learned *rules* of morphemic and syntactic ordering of the speech flow, aided and abetted by the formation of conceptual rules for grouping classes of objects in the world of experience and memory." They feel that developmental evolution proceeds so as to reduce the strain of information processing.

There is considerable evidence that mediating responses or "rules for grouping classes of objects" come with advancing age, but the bases of grouping are not necessarily constant. Superordinate responses increase between grades four and six and decrease thereafter (Palermo and Jenkins, 1963). This is consistent with our observation that syntactic responses at ages five and six gradually give way to paradigmatic responses, but that some paradigmatic responses *decrease* in frequency between fifth grade and college as syntactic responses increase in popularity.

A fresh look at the nature of associations has been taken recently by McNeill (1965) as a consequence of two ingenious experiments. He proposes that associations are not based on recall, as is tacitly assumed, but rather that associations are generated much as the individual words in a sentence are generated by a speaker. Rather than grouping words on lists, a process beyond the presumed power of memory, the individual assigns properties to words. Words are contrasted in terms of properties, and paradigmatic associates flow from a minimal contrast between words. This is a view that we will examine at length, and one that resolves a good many, but not all, of the major findings in our data. It seems to represent a workable synthesis of the S-R position and the position of more cognitively oriented theorists.

The only theory of linguistic development that attempts to be comprehensive is that of Miller and McNeill (1965). This account of linguistic development assumes basic grammatical relations are not learned but are part of innate endowment. Their presentation draws from empirical data gathered by many investigators, and is buttressed by a few experiments at critical points. Our concern is with language acquisition that occurs between ages five and ten, the period when they point to development of semantics. Much of our data is pertinent to this portion of their theory, as will be brought out in Chapter 8.

The reader, then, should be forewarned that this book does not revolve around a unitary theme. Rather it revolves around a mass of empirical information and naturally some parts of this information are more enlightening than other parts. Because so little is known, every attempt has been made to reduce the data to a comprehensible form and to relate them to other bits of information. An earnest effort is made to point up gaps in the data. At the same time, because information is so scarce, no opportunity is lost to try to make the data comprehensible in terms of what is already known.

Chapter Two

The Design of the Survey

The data were gathered over a three-year period, starting about November 1, 1961, and continuing through June, 1964. The composition of the sample population is given in Table 2.1. Children from Baltimore County, Maryland, were studied in 1961–63. Other subjects (Amish and adult samples) were studied in 1963–64. All subsamples are equally divided by sex within any other category. For instance the third-grade, urban, high-SES, high-IQ subsample consists of seventy children, of whom thirty-five are male and thirty-five female.

The Maryland Sample

The basic normative group consists of prekindergarten, kindergarten, first-, third-, and fifth-grade students from Baltimore County, numbering 1,160 altogether, with 20, 200, 340, 340, and 260 in the respective grade divisions. These 1,160 students were interviewed individually. Eighty additional fifth-graders were interviewed by a group method, making a total of 340 in fifth grade, also.

Appendix D summarizes responses for the first-, third-, and fifth-grade *urban* samples. (The 80 fifth-grade students who were tested under group procedures are included with the 200 individually tested fifth-grade students.) The urban samples at each grade thus consist of a total of 280 students, so numbers in the various columns of Appendix D are directly comparable. Appendix C gives responses for 200 kindergarten children. Rural respondents are not included in these appendices.

The normative groups form an incomplete factorial design (see Table 2.1). Control variables are grade, sex, IQ, and place of residence. Residential locus defined high-SES (socioeconomic status) urban, low-SES urban, and rural subsamples with boundaries that conform roughly to certain boundaries used by the U.S. Census. Table 2.2 gives background data for the various socioeconomic groups and compares these data with census data.

13

TABLE 2.1.   Composition of Total Sample—Number of Subjects by Strata—Each Stratum Equally Divided by Sex

| | Grand total | Subjects from Baltimore County, Maryland | | | | | | | | | |
| Grade | | High-SES urban | | | Low-SES urban | | | Rural | | | |
		High IQ[b]	Med. IQ[b]	Total	Med. IQ[b]	Low IQ[b]	Total	High IQ[b]	Med. IQ[b]	Low IQ[b]	Total
Individual administration											
Prekindergarten	20										
Kindergarten	200	100[a]			100[a]						
First grade	340	70[a]	70[a]	140	70[a]	70[a]	140	20	20[a]	20[a]	60
Third grade	340	70[a]	70[a]	140	70[a]	70[a]	140	20[a]	20[a]	20	60
Fifth grade	260	50[a]	50[a]	100	50[a]	50[a]	100	20[a]	20[a]	20[a]	60
Group administration											
Third grade	20	20									
Fifth grade	80	20[a]	20[a]	40	20[a]	20[a]	40				
Total	1,260										

Amish subjects from Lancaster County, Pennsylvania

		IQ
First grade	20	85.3
Second grade	20	108.2
Third grade	20	92.8
Fifth grade	20	101.1
Sixth grade	20	96.6
TOTAL	100	

College subjects

		Median Score CEEB Verbal Aptitude
The Johns Hopkins University, Baltimore, Maryland	100 males	624
Goucher College, Towson, Maryland	100 females	617
Total	200	

[a] Sample contains 20 *S*s studied in 1961–62 with remainder studied in 1962–63.

[b] High IQ, 122, or higher. Medium IQ, 95–105, inclusive. Low IQ, 85, or less. Most IQ's were determined from California Test of Mental Maturity, except first-graders, who had the SRA Test of Primary Mental Abilities.

TABLE 2.2.   Definitions of Socioeconomic Strata from Baltimore County

Locale (see Fig. 2.1)	U.S. census— average schooling of father, in yrs.[a]	Computed average schooling of father, in years	U.S. census— median annual family income[a]
High-urban: (Towson, Timonium, Lutherville, Ruxton)	14.1	14.7	$9,171
Low-urban: (Edgemere, Sparrow's Point, Dundalk)	9.7	10.3	$6,219
Rural: (Upper Baltimore County—Parkton, Hereford) (Communities with less than 2,500 persons)	10.2	9.9	$7,049

[a] U.S. Census of Population, 1960. Maryland, General Social and Economic Characteristics, U.S. Dept. of Commerce, Bureau of the Census.

Maryland contains twenty-three counties plus the City of Baltimore, and these political subdivisions are also school districts. In the United States such large school districts are rare. They have obvious advantages for research because within a single school system curriculum and school practices tend to be constant. All Maryland elementary students in this study were enrolled in schools under the jurisdiction of the Baltimore County Board of Education, a school district embracing approximately 600 square miles with over 105,000 children. Figure 2.1 shows the geographic distribution of the Baltimore County schools whose pupils participated in this research.

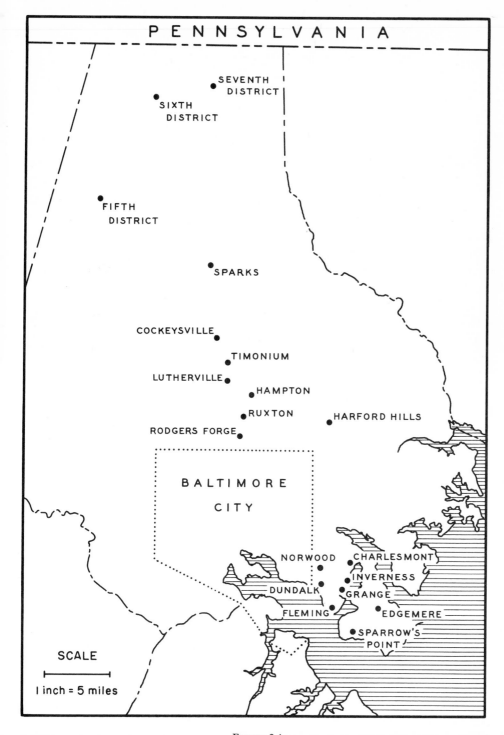

FIGURE 2.1

System-wide IQ tests are given every two years, and IQ scores in pupil folders were used by us. (These were California Tests of Mental Maturity for all but first-graders, who take the SRA Test of Primary Mental Abilities.) Three IQ strata were formed. These IQ subgroups are as disparate as possible, with (1) "High IQ" defined as 122, or more (2) "Medium IQ" as 95 to 105, inclusive, and (3) "Low IQ" as 85, or less.

No IQ data are available for kindergarten or prekindergarten groups. Fathers' education, a good index of intelligence for young children, suggests that the high-SES kindergarten children are probably comparable in IQ to high-SES, high-IQ, first-grade children in our sample. Similarly the low-SES kindergarten children are probably comparable in IQ to the low-SES, medium-IQ, first-grade children.

Descriptive data for the normative sample are summarized in Table 2.3. The sampling by grades gave a fairly even progression by chronological age. High-IQ students, particularly boys, are more rare in the first grade than in the third or fifth grades. This probably implies that the first-grade sample, with tested IQ of 122 or better, is more highly selected than high-IQ groups for later grades.

Socioeconomic status (SES) is a difficult variable to manipulate. We sampled clusters of schools which enroll children from homogeneous neighborhoods and there are three main clusters. (See Fig. 2.1.) One cluster of schools (the "District" schools) is located in a rural area of Baltimore County about thirty-five miles north of Baltimore City. These schools serve a large geographic area of low-density stable population. A second cluster of schools, just north of the city line in Baltimore County, draws many pupils from one-family residences in the $15–30,000 range, and some pupils from homes of greater value, up to $50,000 or more. This forms a high-SES urban cluster. There is extensive geographic and social mobility in this group because of transfer of professional parents (engineers, scientists, etc.). A third cluster, the low-SES urban group, is located in a highly industrialized area around Sparrows Point, about three miles southeast of the Baltimore City line. This section of Baltimore is noted for its shipbuilding and heavy steel industries and the residences there are predominantly multiple-family or "row" houses. Row-houses can be individually owned, but are attached on either side to other identical dwellings. They sell new in the $6–10,000 range in that section. Houses in the Sparrows Point area are occasionally in poor condition. Migration into this area is limited and migrants often come from the rural south, particularly from Appalachia. The 1960 census data for Maryland presented in Table 2.4 confirm that income level and type of employment of father are very different for the two urban clusters.

All children were selected *in advance* from school records to fill the quotas of the sample (equal numbers of each sex, grade, and IQ level). Repeat visits were made in case predesignated subjects could not be interviewed. Of the 500 subjects designated in advance for samples drawn in 1961–62, only 10 had to be replaced later (extended absences because of broken legs, rheumatic fever, etc.). The selection procedure was not random in the strict meaning of the term but should tend to minimize bias.

Every student was classified as white or colored, but the number of nonwhite is negligible. All schools in Baltimore County are integrated, but during the period of this research considerable *de facto* segregation existed because of residential segre-

TABLE 2.3. Characteristics of Subjects

	Kindergarten	
	High-SES High-IQ	Low-SES Med.-IQ
Average age	5.6	5.6
Average IQ	125	100
Average father's education (highest grade completed)	16.6[a]	12.5[b]

	Grade 1						
	High-SES Urban		Low-SES Urban		Rural		
	High-IQ	Med.-IQ	Med.-IQ	Low-IQ	High-IQ	Med.-IQ	Low-IQ
Average age	6.4	6.6	6.5	6.7	6.6	6.7	6.9
Average IQ	129.9	102.6	102.8	75.0	128.1	99.8	77.4
Average father's education (highest grade completed)	15.5	13.8	10.5	9.6	12.9	10.4	7.5

	Grade 3						
	High-SES Urban		Low-SES Urban		Rural		
	High-IQ	Med.-IQ	Med.-IQ	Low-IQ	High-IQ	Med.-IQ	Low-IQ[c]
Average age	8.5	8.7	8.7	9.0	8.6	8.8	9.2
Average IQ	131.5	100.5	100.4	79.8	131.9	99.6	78.3
Average father's education (highest grade completed)	15.6	13.4	9.9	8.7	12.2	9.0	8.5

	Grade 5						
	High-SES Urban		Low-SES Urban		Rural		
	High-IQ	Med.-IQ	Med.-IQ	Low-IQ	High-IQ	Med.-IQ	Low-IQ
Average age	10.4	10.7	10.6	10.11	10.4	10.7	11.7
Average IQ	131.0	100.8	100.1	79.7	131.9	100.1	77.1
Average father's education (highest grade completed)	14.7	13.0	10.1	9.7	12.3	9.7	7.8

	Amish				
	Grade 1	Grade 2	Grade 3	Grade 5	Grade 6
Average age	6.9	7.11	8.7	10.9	12.0
Average IQ	85.3[d]	108.3	92.8	101.1	96.6
Average father's education (highest grade completed)	8.0	8.0	8.0	8.0	8.0

	Rural matched to Amish	
	Grade 1	Grade 3
Average age	6.8	8.7
Average IQ	84.7	92.8
Average father's education (highest grade completed)	8.1	9.2

[a] For ninety-nine subjects.

[b] For eighty-eight subjects.

[c] Only nineteen subjects available.

[d] For two of the twenty children IQ scores were not available.

gation. There are only four colored students in the high-SES urban sample, and very small numbers in the rural and low-SES urban samples. The distribution of Negroes is shown in Table 2.5. In the low-SES neighborhoods from which our subjects are drawn the Negro population is much lower than the 10 to 12 per cent figure derived from census data. Also this is a much lower percentage of Negroes than is found in Baltimore City (34 per cent over-all).

TABLE 2.4.   Census Data on Social, Educational, and Economic Characteristics of Subsamples within Baltimore County, Maryland[a]

	Lutherville–Timonium, Md. (corresponds to our high-SES urban)	Sparrow's Pt.–Edgemere, Md. (corresponds to our low-SES urban)	Rural: (communities with less than 2,500 persons: Upper Baltimore County—Parkton, Hereford)
Per cent migrant persons over five yrs. (lived in different counties in 1955–60)	50.2	14.3	
Married women in labor force, husband present, own children under six, per cent	8.8	17.2	
Employment of father in manufacturing industry, per cent	33.0	66.2	
White-collar employment of father, per cent	70.5	25.7	
Per cent with incomes $10,000, and over	40.4	16.1	
Median annual family income	$9,171.00	$6,219.00	$7,049.00
Average schooling of father, in years	14.1	9.7	10.2

Race composition of sampled areas in Baltimore County	White	Negro
Rural Baltimore County	69,600	3,348
Timonium–Lutherville	11,990	275
Sparrow's Point–Edgemere	10,655	1,220

[a] U.S. Census of Population, 1960. Maryland, General Social and Economic Characteristics, U.S. Dept. of Commerce, Bureau of the Census.

TABLE 2.5.   Distribution of Negroes

Kindergarten

High-SES		Low-SES	
High-IQ		Med.-IQ	
M	F	M	F
		1	

Grade 1

High-SES				Low-SES				Rural					
High-IQ		Med.-IQ		Med.-IQ		Low-IQ		High-IQ		Med.-IQ		Low-IQ	
M	F	M	F	M	F	M	F	M	F	M	F	M	F
							3				1		2

Grade 3

High-SES				Low-SES				Rural					
High-IQ		Med.-IQ		Med.-IQ		Low-IQ		High-IQ		Med.-IQ		Low-IQ	
M	F	M	F	M	F	M	F	M	F	M	F	M	F
		1			2	8	4					2	

Grade 5

High-SES				Low-SES				Rural					
High-IQ		Med.-IQ		Med.-IQ		Low-IQ		High-IQ		Med.-IQ		Low-IQ	
M	F	M	F	M	F	M	F	M	F	M	F	M	F
	1	2		1	2	4	1				1	2	

Adult

Male	Female
1	

It was originally planned to tabulate the father's occupation. Father's occupation is recorded at the time a student enrolls in school, but no uniform recording scheme is followed. Occupations are frequently listed by company affiliation only, and we often found the occupation listed to be incompatible with educational status. For instance, the occupation "engineer" was frequently listed beside a less-than-college education. Therefore, "father's education—highest grade completed" replaced occupation as a datum. Cases where information was not recorded are omitted.

The Amish Sample

Just north of the Maryland-Pennsylvania line in an area near Lancaster, Pennsylvania, around a town called Intercourse (see Figure 2.2) are several Old Order Amish communities. Inhabitants are descended from Anabaptist immigrants of 200 years ago, and their religious beliefs cause them to eschew modern conveniences such as cars and telephones. They prefer to live without electricity and so their homes are without radios or television. Movies and other audio-visual aids are absent from the parochial elementary schools. Social customs tend to minimize conversational interchange between adult and child.

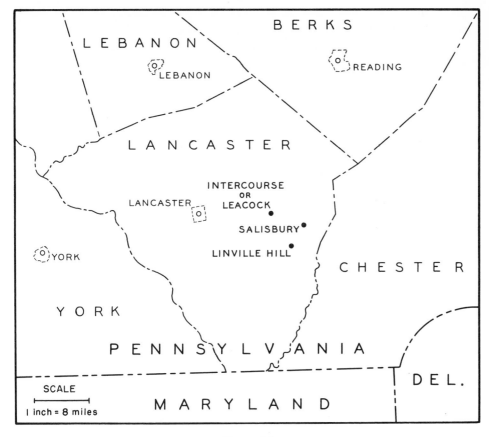

FIGURE 2.2

Besides lack of radio and TV, very few books and magazines are found in the Amish home. Very few non-Amish come to the door. Exceptions are the regular calls of the fruitman, breadman, pretzelman, and the milkman who hauls the farmer's milk. Pennsylvania Dutch is spoken in every home and many children starting the first grade are not able to speak or understand English. Most of the Amish are farmers, but some of the children interviewed said their father was a carpenter, blacksmith, mason, or warehouse worker in the city.

Farms are about one-quarter mile or one-half mile apart. The children play among themselves at home, and usually there are three or four preschool siblings. Very few, if any, have bedtime stories read to them. The attitude toward school is one of tolerance: "We go to school because we are required to." However, some parents are more concerned and may help their children with homework.

Dr. John Hostetler, a former member of this sect and now a sociologist, arranged for an Amish woman to secure word associations from Old Order Amish children. (He has published a very complete description of the customs and living conditions of this group, see Hostetler, 1963.) She secured samples at an Amish parochial school with eight grades and two teachers.

Our Amish informant gave the following description of an Amish child's day:

> The child, one of a family of six or even twelve children, will get up about 6:00 A.M. He may go to the barn to help with the chores assigned him, feeding cattle, horses or calves. Breakfast is served, usually as hearty as any other meal in the day, around the family table in the kitchen. He will get very little attention unless, of course, he misbehaves. He is ready when the school bus arrives and joins his non-Amish friends, who have accepted him long ago. He is now in the English world. At home everything was spoken in Dutch. The evening chores await him, after which he is free to play with his siblings or do his homework. He seldom plays with his parents. They are busy with the younger ones and the farm work. He goes to bed about 7:30 or 8:00 after a few reminders from his parents and without any stories or other attention. After he crawls into bed with another member of the family, he may tell about his experiences at school.
>
> Preschool children usually find their own entertainment. They often play outside or in the barn. Little boys follow their father around while the girls may play with their dolls. Endless amusements can be found on the farm with various tools, ropes, and odd scraps of chains, etc. Little ones sometimes fall asleep playing on a buggy or elsewhere in the barn. A visit to Grandmother is very common for she lives not far away. Family ties are close.

No data on median income like that for the rural Maryland sample are available for the Amish but their dollar income would not be a good index of real income in any case. Amish farms are well-run and prosperous, and community solidarity eliminates the need for insurance, shielding members against the perils of sickness and old age. Most garments and other necessities of life are manufactured on the farm, and there is little need for cash because automobiles and other "luxuries" are forbidden.

Samples of Amish children in the first, second, third, fifth, and sixth grades were interviewed by an Amish woman. Some IQ data for third, fifth, and sixth grades were available from school records. The Lorge-Thorndike test was used (see Table

2.3). The average IQ of Amish samples differs from the average IQ of the rural Maryland samples.[1]

The College Samples

Adult comparison data were gathered in 1963–64 from 100 undergraduates at The Johns Hopkins University (males) and 100 students at Goucher College (females). These data were procured by having students write associations to stimuli presented in a booklet. Although it is difficult to make comparisons between the college groups and the grade school groups on the basis of IQ, probably the college group is best compared to high-IQ, high-SES samples at lower ages.

The Sample of Word Stimuli

A total of ninety-six word stimuli was used with all subjects. These ninety-six words were selected to overlap as far as possible lists used previously by other investigators, but words were primarily selected to implement a factorial design with form class and frequency of usage as control variables. Frequency was determined from the Thorndike-Lorge (1944) J-Count. The factorial design of word stimuli is shown in Table 2.6. Nouns, adjectives, and verbs are sampled at three frequency ranges. Adverbs could not be divided on frequency. Eight pronouns, all of high frequency, and eight miscellaneous words (prepositions, conjunctions, and one adverb) complete the list.

TABLE 2.6. Design of Word Stimuli

Form class	Frequency (Thorndike-Lorge J-count)		
	Over 1,000	500–1,000	Less than 500
Nouns	8 words	8 words	8 words
Adjectives	8 words	8 words	8 words
Verbs	8 words	8 words	8 words
Others, not stratified on frequency	8 adverbs, 8 pronouns, 8 miscellaneous words		

Insofar as possible stimuli were selected from: (1) the original Kent-Rosanoff list, also used extensively by the Minnesota group, (2) words used in an experimental study with a small sample of children by Ervin (1961), (3) words used by Deese (1960, 1962) in studies of undergraduate males. The previous lists were exhausted successively in the order listed above. Before 1960 the original Kent-Rosanoff (1910) list was used almost exclusively in word association studies. This set of words therefore

---

[1] This will be discussed in detail in Chapter 6. Special samples of rural Maryland children were constructed that matched the Amish samples in IQ. Data for these samples are given in Table 6.10. These special rural samples consist of twenty subjects drawn from the pool of sixty subjects.

IQ tests (Draw-A-Man) were administered by us to the first- and second-graders.

has value for comparative purposes, despite the lack of form classes other than nouns and adjectives and the predominance of high frequency words. There are thirty words from the Kent-Rosanoff list (thirteen nouns, seventeen adjectives). In Table 2.7 the letters (K-R, E, etc.) following stimulus words identify their presence on earlier lists, and Thorndike-Lorge frequency information is presented there also.

Frequency is defined in terms of the Thorndike-Lorge J-count. Comparison of the J- and G-counts (Table 2.7) reveals that the distinction between high-frequency and medium-frequency nouns fades away for adults. This change in the definition of frequency is important in interpreting the adult data and will be referred to again. Our major interest was in young children so the stimulus list was designed using the J-count to produce frequency variance appropriate for young subjects.

TABLE 2.7.   Characteristics of the Stimulus Words

	Nominal form class[a]	Entwisle frequency category[b]	J-count[c]	G-count[d]	Used previously by[e]					
add	verb	High	M	AA	D					
allow	verb	Med.	700*	AA						
always	adverb		M	AA			P-J	E		
because	conjunction		M	AA			P-J		F-J	
bee	noun	Low	330*	A	D					
begin	verb	High	M*	AA						
belong	verb	Med.	600*	AA						
between	preposition		M	AA						
bird	noun	High	M*	AA	D					
bitter	adjective	Low	240*	A		K-R	R-J	P-J		
black	adjective	High	M*	AA	D	K-R	R-J	P-J		
bright	adjective	Med.	555*	AA	D					
bug	noun	Low	38	10	D					
butterfly	noun	Low	138	22	D	K-R	R-J	P-J		
carry	verb	High	M	AA			P-J			
chair	noun	Med.	700*	AA	D	K-R	R-J	P-J		
clean	adjective	Med.	615*	AA	D					
cocoon	noun	Low	25	3	D					
cold	adjective	High	M*	AA	D	K-R	B-B	R-J	P-J	
color	noun	High	M*	AA						
dark	adjective	High	?	AA		K-R	B-B	R-J	P-J	F-J
deceive	verb	Low	150*	33						
enjoy	verb	Med.	566*	AA						
examine	verb	Low	233*	A						
flower	noun	High	M*	AA	D					
fly	noun	High	?	AA	D					
fruit	noun	Med.	551*	AA		K-R	R-J	P-J		
gallop	verb	Low	177	25						
gently	adverb		145	46		B-B				
give	verb	High	M	AA				E		
hand	noun	High	M	AA	D	K-R	R-J	P-J	E	F-J
happen	verb	Med.	689*	AA						
hard	adjective	High	M*	AA	D	K-R	B-B	R-J	P-J	F-J
he	pronoun		M	AA			P-J		F-J	
her	pronoun		M	AA					F-J	
high	adjective	High	M	AA	D	K-R	R-J	P-J	F-J	
him	pronoun		M	AA			P-J	E	F-J	
inquire	verb	Low	230*	A						
insect	noun	Low	210*	40	D					
into	preposition		M	AA						
it	pronoun		M	AA			P-J		F-J	
join	verb	Med.	580*	AA	D					
listen	verb	Med.	700*	AA						
long	adjective	High	M	AA		K-R	R-J	P-J	F-J	
loud	adjective	Med.	560⁴	A		K-R	R-J	P-J		
loudly	adverb		140*	22						
maintain	verb	Low	260*	26						

TABLE 2.7.—Continued

	Nominal form class[a]	Entwisle frequency category[b]	J-count[c]	G-count[d]	Used previously by[e]						
man	noun	High	M	AA	D	K-R	B-B	R-J	P-J		F-J
mix	verb	Low	277*	A							
moth	noun	Low	34	9	D						
move	verb	High	M	AA							
music	noun	Med.	660*	AA		K-R		R-J	P-J		
needle	noun	Low	153*	34		K-R	B-B	R-J	P-J		
net	noun	Low	310*	A	D						
never	adverb		M	AA							
obey	verb	Low	237*	A	D						
ocean	noun	Med.	700*	AA		K-R		R-J	P-J		
off	preposition		M	AA							
on	preposition		M	AA					P-J		F-J
once	adverb		M	AA							
pleasant	adjective	Med.	610*	AA							
prepare	verb	Med.	700*	AA							
pretty	adjective	High	?	AA	D						
quiet	adjective	Low	352*	A		K-R		R-J	P-J		
restore	verb	Low	245*	49							
river	noun	High	M*	AA		K-R		R-J	P-J		
rough	adjective	Low	345*	A	D	K-R		R-J	P-J		
run	verb	High	M	AA	D						
sad	adjective	Med.	500*	A							
salt	noun	Med.	534*	AA		K-R		R-J	P-J		
seldom	adverb		290*	A	D						
sell	verb	Med.	500*	AA	D				P-J		
she	pronoun		M	AA							
sheep	noun	Med.	500*	A	D	K-R		R-J	P-J		
short	adjective	High	M*	AA		K-R		R-J	P-J		
since	conjunction		M	AA							
sit	verb	High	M*	AA	D				P-J		
slow	adjective	Low	450*	A		K-R		R-J	P-J	E[f]	
slowly	adverb		250*	A			B-B		P-J	E[f]	
smooth	adjective	Low	289*	A	D	K-R		R-J	P-J		
sometimes	adverb		700*	AA							
sour	adjective	Low	50	15		K-R		R-J	P-J		
square	noun	Med.	626*	AA		K-R		R-J	P-J		
swift	adjective	Low	216*	43		K-R		R-J	P-J		
table	noun	High	M*	AA		K-R	B-B	R-J	P-J	E	
tall	adjective	Med.	700*	AA	D						
tell	verb	High	M	AA	D				P-J		F-J
them	pronoun		M	AA							
they	pronoun		M	AA					P-J		F-J
thirsty	adjective	Low	34	11		K-R		R-J	P-J		
up	preposition		M	AA	D					E	F-J
us	pronoun		M	AA					P-J		
usually	adverb		583*	AA							
wild	adjective	Med.	622*	AA							
wing	noun	Med.	700*	AA	D						
yellow	adjective	Med.	526*	AA	D	K-R		R-J	P-J		

[a] This is defined to be the form class considered in our analysis (supposedly the most frequent usage of the word). For instance, "hand" is considered to be a noun, in spite of its usage as a verb.

[b] "High" means 1,000, or higher, on J-count; "medium" means from 500 to 999 on J-count; and low is below 500 on J-count.

[c] J-count column. M = 1,000 or more in 120 juvenile books. M* = probably 1,000 or more (see p. 253, *The Teacher's Word Book of 30,000 Words*).

[d] G-count column. A = 50–99 per million. AA = 100, or over, per million.

[e] "K-R" is Kent-Rosanoff (1910) plus Woodrow and Lowell (1916) except "bitter" was omitted by Woodrow and Lowell. "D" is Deese (1960, 1962). "B-B" is Brown and Berko (1960). "R-J" is Russell and Jenkins (1954). "P-J" is Palermo and Jenkins (1964). The words used by Palermo (1965) in a recent study of children in grades one through four are not reported. "E" is Ervin (1961). "F-J" is Fillenbaum and Jones (1964).

[f] "Slower" used by Ervin.

* Estimated, see Thorndike and Lorge (1944).

It is literally impossible to select stimulus words according to form class. Usage cannot be determined when words are given singly, without context. The single words that constitute the stimulus list can be classified only according to nominal form class membership, therefore. For some words agreement on form class is almost unanimous without imposing a context. The word "table" for example, will usually be perceived as a noun, although it can serve as a verb, "table a function," or as an adjective, "table land." Other words such as "fly" and "color" are more difficult to assign, and may change with age. For instance, children often use "color" as a verb, but this is a rare use for adults. Form class of the stimulus words has been assigned according to most common usage and our procedure resembles that used by Fillenbaum and Jones (1965).[2]

Frequency counts derived from juvenile books suitable for grades three to eight (the basis for the J-count) might be inappropriate for kindergarten, first grade, or prekindergarten children. To check this, responses of twenty four-year-old children were classified as relevant to the stimulus word either semantically or syntactically, or irrelevant (Table 2.8). (See Note at the end of Chapter 3 for criteria used in judging responses syntactically relevant.) With the exceptions of "cocoon," "swift," and "bitter," the nouns and adjectives appear to be fairly well understood by children four years of age. The remainder of the list, except for the most common verbs, yields from 25 to 50 per cent irrelevant responses. The J-count thus seems less appropriate for estimating comprehension of children below grade three than form class membership.[3]

Within the list of stimulus words is a set of semantically related words (for convenience termed the "butterfly" list): "bee," "bird," "black," "bright," "bug," "butterfly," "cocoon," "color," "flower," "fly," "insect," "moth," "pretty," "wing," "yellow." These words have been used extensively by Deese (1961, 1962a) and Rotberg (1964, 1965), and are often given as associates to one another. For instance, "bird" often begets "fly" or "wing." A study of the interrelationships of these words in adults (Deese, 1962a) by factor analytic techniques showed that certain aspects of associative meaning could be defined. For instance, the word "butterfly" has loadings on factors like "animate being," "wingedness," "belonging to insect category," etc. By analyzing associative meaning in the same way, using associations of children of various ages, it is possible to study semantic development over childhood (cf. Chapter 7).

Word Order on the Stimulus List[4]

It seems likely that associations to words appearing early on a list may affect associations to words that appear later on the same list, but little is known about

---

[2] This problem is discussed at length in Chapter 3 in connection with the classification of responses.

[3] Our sample of words, although representative, is extremely small compared to the vocabulary of use, estimated for six-year-olds to be from 8.5 to 14.4 thousand words, and by eight years of age to increase to as much as 24.8 thousand words (Davis, 1937).

[4] Since this work has been completed, Bilodeau and Howell (1965) have given much attention to the problem of order.

this. Bousfield's and Cohen's (1953, 1955) notions of clustering and relatedness-increments would suggest such an order effect, as would Cohen's (1964) finding that items in exhaustive categories are better remembered than items in nonexhaustive categories. A random order of stimulus words or any order that changed from one subject to the next would be extremely difficult to manage. Therefore, word order effects were investigated in a very limited way by using one order of stimulus words in the first year (1961–62) and a permutation of that order thereafter (1962–64). This permits comparisons holding many other variables (IQ, residential locus, etc.) constant for two large groups of urban subjects. Of course word order and year-to-year changes are completely confounded, but we doubt that year-to-year changes for cross-sectional sampling are large.

TABLE 2.8. Irrelevant and Syntactically Relevant Responses for Four-year-old Subjects (N = 20)
(The responses not tabulated are semantically relevant)

	Per cent of responses			Per cent of responses			Per cent of responses	
	Irrelevant	Syntactically relevant		Irrelevant	Syntactically relevant		Irrelevant	Syntactically relevant
table	15	25	music	—	20	moth	—	25
color	5	25	ocean	—	35	bug	—	20
hand	10	35	fruit	—	5	butterfly	—	20
bird	5	45	salt	—	15	bee	—	40
river	10	5	chair	—	5	needle	10	40
flower	5	50	wing	—	15	net	15	55
man	5	25	sheep	—	—	insect	30	20
fly	—	25	square	—	35	cocoon	55	—
	6.9	29.4		—	16.3		13.8	27.5
high	5	40	yellow	10	20	smooth	5	10
hard	—	15	clean	—	70	swift	80	—
long	5	45	tall	5	10	rough	—	15
pretty	10	20	sad	5	15	thirsty	—	10
black	—	5	bright	15	—	sour	20	10
cold	—	20	wild	10	25	quiet	5	35
dark	15	15	loud	15	35	slow	5	25
short	—	55	pleasant	10	30	bitter	70	—
	4.4	26.9		8.8	25.6		23.1	13.1
move	—	40	allow	25	30	gallop	10	35
give	—	65	enjoy	—	40	restore	50	5
sit	5	65	sell	15	10	mix	20	25
begin	25	20	listen	5	60	maintain	95	—
tell	5	65	prepare	70	—	obey	5	40
carry	5	35	happen	25	50	inquire	80	5
run	5	30	belong	20	35	deceive	85	—
add	35	20	join	45	10	examine	45	15
	10	42.5		25.6	29.4		48.8	15.6
usually	65	35	he	15	20	because	20	50
never	20	70	they	35	25	between	60	20
seldom	80	10	it	55	25	since	75	20
always	20	60	her	10	15	on	40	15
loudly	15	5	she	35	—	up	—	50
slowly	20	15	them	55	35	off	20	25
sometimes	25	60	him	15	10	into	25	30
gently	25	5	us	30	10	once	10	50
	33.8	32.5		31.3	17.5		31.3	32.5

One would expect that order effects would be most noticeable for related words—the cluster of "butterfly" words, for example. A previous association to the stimulus word "cocoon" might (a) make "cocoon" more likely as a response to subsequent words related semantically to cocoon, i.e., make "cocoon" more likely as a response to "moth," or (b) make the response given to "cocoon," say "butterfly," more likely as a response to other words of the cluster. It would also seem that order effects would be more pronounced for words of low frequency because relatively rare words occur in few contexts to compete with the experimental context. By the same reasoning, younger children might be more prone to word-order effects than older subjects, since their experience with language is limited.

Much the same point is made by Bousfield (1961) when he points out that a manifest response is not determined exclusively by its previously acquired strength. A stimulus occurs within whatever context is present at the time, and the context affects the probability of a particular response. Context can include previous associations. Bousfield believes context effects to be most potent for responses with low-habit strengths. Therefore, the "butterfly" subset of low-frequency nouns (see Table 2.9) was studied first to see if position of a word within the stimulus list was important.

TABLE 2.9.   Yearly Position Changes for Words on "Butterfly" List

	Serial position on list 1961–62	Serial position on list 1962–63
bee*	43	67
bird	50	26
black	51	27
bright	61	37
bug*	20	92
butterfly*	33	57
cocoon*	83	11
color	23	95
flower	70	46
fly	93	21
insect*	90	18
moth*	12	84
pretty	48	72
wing	26	50
yellow	17	89

* Words marked with asterisks are low-frequency nouns.

Table 2.9 gives the serial position of "butterfly" words within the total list of ninety-six words for the two successive years when data were gathered from urban children. For instance, "bee" was the forty-third stimulus word in 1961–62 and the sixty-seventh stimulus word in 1962–63. The important thing, of course, is not the actual position of the word, but its position with respect to related words. For instance, "bee" occurs before "insect" the first year, and after "insect" the second year. If order matters, one would expect "bee" to be given more often in response to "insect" the first year than in the second year. Having very recently heard "bee," children may have this response facilitated. Other facilitations may occur also, such as those produced by a previous response. For instance, if "beetle" is given as a

Table 2.10.   Changes in Response Related to Order-on-list of Stimulus Word

Stimulus word	Response word	Precedence by year[a]	Expected sign of difference in response percentages from 1961–62 to 1962–63	Observed sign of difference in response percentages		
				Grade 1	Grade 3	Grade 5
bee	bug	BA	−	*	+	−
	insect	AB	+	*	−	−
bug	bee	AB	+	−	+	*
	insect	AB	+	+	+	+
butterfly	bee	AA	0	−	*	*
	bug	BA	−	*	+	*
	insect	AB	+	*	−	+
	moth	BA	−	*	*	−
cocoon	butterfly	BA	−	−	−	+
insect	bee	BA	−	−	*	*
	bug	BA	−	−	+	+
	butterfly	BA	−	*	−	*
moth	bug	AA	0	−	*	−
	butterfly	AB	+	−	+	−
	insect	AB	+	*	+	+

Summary of changes attributable to order-on-list
for low-frequency nouns for fifth-grade children

		Expectation			
		+	−	0	
Observations	+	3	2	0	5
	−	2	2	1	5
		5	4	1	

[a] "A" means the response word given also appeared later in the stimulus list. "B" means the response word given had appeared earlier in the list of stimulus words. The order changed from one year to the next.

* The response not given by grade.

response to "bee," its appearance as a response to "insect" may be facilitated. These kinds of facilitations, depending upon responses that differ from person to person, are too complex for us to seek out here. We will attend only to responses that are also stimuli.[5]

Table 2.10 reports an analysis aimed at evaluating the effect of order-on-list for responses to the "butterfly" words with each grade examined separately. After each stimulus word responses selected from the "butterfly" group are listed. (Others not listed, i.e., "cocoon," were not given as responses.) Then, under "Precedence by year" the order of the words in the list in two successive years is coded. For instance, the stimulus word "bee" elicits "bug." The "BA" following "bug" means that "bug"

[5] Mutual relations among "butterfly" words are borne out by an examination of the three most popular responses to each word. Fifth-grade children give "insect" as a response to all other words on the list except "moth." Other stimulus words on the list also appear frequently as responses, and of course this is what led to their study by Deese in the first place.

occurred before (B) "bee" the first year, and after (A) "bee" the second year, so the order is Before-After (BA). In this case one would expect that "bug" would appear more often as a response to "bee" in the first year than in the second year because of its recent appearance before "bee" the first year. This expectation is coded in the next column as a minus sign. It is expected that the number of "bug" responses will *decrease* from the first year to the second, because of its relative position in the list with respect to "bee." To take another example, "insect" occurred *after* "bee" the first year (A), and *before* "bee" the second year (B). In this case the expectation is that more "insect" responses to "bee" will occur the second year, when "insect" precedes "bee" on the stimulus list. This expectation is coded as a plus sign.

The percentage of subjects at three grade levels who chose related responses in both years were listed, and the directions of change in percentages from the first year to the second year were noted. These constitute the observed directions of changes. For instance, fifth-grade subjects gave *fewer* "bug" responses to "bee" in the second year than in the first year. Since the percentage decreased from one year to the next, a minus sign appears opposite "bug" in the "bee" group.

For fifth-grade responses to "bee," then, one change agrees (the decrease in "bug" responses), but another disagrees (the decrease in "insect" responses).[6] Altogether the conformity of fifth-grade responses to expectation casts doubt on the importance of order. The distribution of expected changes and of observed changes is summarized at the bottom of Table 2.10 (zero signifies "no change"). Clearly there is no piling up in the corners (matches) between observation and expectation. Five cases conform to expectation while four do not.

Previous occurrence of a word as a stimulus thus appears to have no appreciable effect on evoking this same word later as a response for fifth-grade children. Similar analyses show essentially the same results for the other grades. The largest change observed from one year to the next is a little over 15 per cent, and changes of this magnitude occur in *both* positive and negative directions. Also for a stimulus where *no* change is predicted from one year to the next (the relative position of stimulus word and response word remain the same in the list of stimulus words) changes as large as 6 per cent are noted.

So far the discussion has concerned words of low commonality ("moth," "bee," "bug," etc.), and these may not show much change because all responses are of relatively low frequency in any case. Five additional words of higher commonality, "bird," "flower," "fly," "wing," "yellow," were therefore studied. The percentage changes from one year to the next, summarized in Table 2.11, are small, only one-third of them amounting to 5 per cent or more. For stimulus response pairs "fly"—"insect" and "fly"—"bird" changes of +5.4 per cent and −7.3 per cent are noted when the expectation is no change. These two cases account for two of the five

---

[6] The fifth-grade results were studied first. Later analyses will show that at times first-grade children associate on the basis of different attributes of stimulus words than fifth-grade children. First-grade children occasionally concentrate on syntactic or auditory characteristics of words. For instance, they give "raccoon" and "moon" as associates to "cocoon," and these responses are replaced by responses such as "animal" and "caterpillar" by the fifth grade.

TABLE 2.11.   Summary of High Commonality Words in Relation to Order Effects
(Fifth grade students)

Stimulus word	Response word	Precedence by year	Expectation	Percentage change observed
bird	fly	AB	+	+20.4
	wing	AB	+	+05.4
flower	bee	BA	−	+01.9
	bug	BA	−	−01.3
	butterfly	BA	−	−00.6
	yellow	BA	−	−00.5
fly	insect	BB	0	+05.4
	bird	BB	0	−07.3
	bug	BA	−	−00.4
	wing	BA	−	−01.5
wing	bird	BA	−	−02.1
	fly	AB	+	+12.1
	butterfly	BA	−	+00.2
yellow	butterfly	AB	+	+03.3
	flowers	AB	+	+02.5

changes that are greater than 5 per cent, and again equivocal directionality as well as small size of changes makes it appear that order effects are not large.

The response "fly" to "bird" and to "wing" is the only marked change associated with word order. Facilitation of significant degree occurs for this single response out of the many we have examined. This occurs for a word with a very high probability of response (see Appendix D)—apparently a strong tendency can be amplified. It is the only positive instance of an order effect that is large enough to be of practical significance. In the second list "fly" occurred very close to "wing"—only four words separated them. This may have contributed to the influence of position. Position on the list may be important only if the separation between two words is less than immediate memory span, or when a relatively strong tendency already exists.

The conclusion is that order-on-list is probably negligible for the words on our list of stimuli even for closely related words. Changes as high as 10 per cent are likely when the same order is maintained from one testing to another, and effects associated with order are of this magnitude. In fact, most are below this magnitude.

Our observation of negligible order effects is important if words on this list are to be used in experiments on verbal learning. In such an application, related words should be separated as far as possible as a precautionary measure. Order effects for adult subjects were *not* studied. They may be more pronounced because of the richer and stronger association patterns of adults.

Chapter Three

Procuring and Analyzing the Data

Over the years word associations have been obtained in a number of ways. Most commonly subjects have recorded their own associations in writing. Since young children cannot be expected to do this, we used an individual interview to gather data. An adult said stimulus words aloud and recorded the subject's response.

Method of Securing Associations

As mentioned previously, children of the desired sex, grade, and IQ were identified and predesignated students were interviewed. Repeat visits were made if a child was not available on the first visit. In a very few cases (less than 1 per cent) children could not be seen on repeat visits because of prolonged illness (cardiac disease, fractured legs, etc.). In no case was an interview terminated after it was begun.

Each child was escorted individually from his classroom to another place in the school. The interviewers were all female (mostly college students), and had practiced obtaining associations from adults and other children prior to gathering data for the study. Interviewers and teachers were careful to refer to the procedure as a "game," and the interviewer tried to create an atmosphere that was casual and relaxed.

Instructions were adapted from those used with adults (Palermo and Jenkins, 1964), rephrased slightly so the child could practice giving associations. Interviewers repeated the directions if necessary. The instructions were:

"Today I want to play a word game with you. You may not have played this game before, so let me explain it to you. I'm going to read you some words, one at a time. Each time I read a word, I want you to tell me the first word that you think of. When you tell me the word, I'll write it down and then read you another word. To make sure you understand the game, let's try a few practice words. I'll say a word, and then you tell me the first word you think of. O.K.? The first word is:

Cat_____

"That's fine. Now, let's try another practice word, and then we'll start the regular game. The next word is:

Grass_____

"That's right. Now we'll play the game, and see if you can think of a word to tell me for every word I read to you. All right?"

More examples were used if necessary, but were rarely required. All responses were recorded verbatim.

Young children often respond with more than one word, even though they understand the directions perfectly. With kindergarten and first-grade children this may happen because word boundaries are unclear or ambiguous. For instance, "upon "is a word and "up" and "on" are also words. Children who have not learned to read face a difficult task in determining word boundaries. A young child who hears a particular sequence often ("once-upon-a-time") may classify the sequence as a single word until further experience—hearing each word in other contexts—defines the separate words. A child may give many single word responses, *indicating he comprehends directions*, and yet respond to some stimulus words with a phrase. This behavior probably reflects a stage of language comprehension rather than confusion about directions.

Various forms of the same word have been kept distinct. For instance, "run" is tabulated separately from "running" or "ran." The reader can easily combine variants of the same word if he wishes. Separate recording may preserve important information. For instance, past tenses of *irregular* verbs appear frequently as responses to irregular verbs, but past tenses to regular verbs are rare.

The difficulties children have in placing boundaries on words, especially in separating words from phrases, have been noted before (Werner and Kaplan, 1952; Templin, 1957) and are not characteristic of only English-speaking children (see Ervin and Miller, 1963). Breaking phrases into individual words may be a persistent source of trouble for low-IQ children. We found two fifth-grade boys with IQ's below eighty-five who gave "apone" to the stimulus word "once" when they wrote their own responses (Entwisle, *et al.*, 1964). This appears to be the perseveration of "upon-a" in undifferentiated form.[1] Huttenlocher (1964) provides some direct evidence on this matter. She found that commonly encountered grammatical pairs, "he went" for example, cannot be learned easily backwards ("went he") whereas nongrammatical pairs ("black—white") can be reversed easily. Apparently the ability to separate the items in a pair governs the difficulty of reversal. Grammatical pairs that are uncommon sequences in English, for instance "table-goes," are as easily reversed as nongrammatical pairs.

Confusion about word boundaries may be least troublesome for nouns. Several

---

[1] Probably establishing grapheme-phoneme correspondences is hindered by failure to distinguish "apone" as two words when heard. This suggests that drill on word division might be fruitful in remedial reading programs.

children, ages four and five, were asked casually: "Tell me a word." Without exception the response given was a noun. The fact that often nouns have specific referents that may be pointed to (they permit ostensive definitions) must make it easier to establish boundaries for these words than for words like "lately" or "next."

Computer Tabulation of Responses

The factorial plan for the stimulus words (frequency and form class) and also for subjects (place of residence, IQ, sex, grade) was the basis for the first tabulation of results. Responses were sorted according to the smallest cell in the design. Responses were then re-sorted as various strata were combined. For example, fifth-grade results can be summarized for three IQ strata combined, for any one IQ stratum within any SES group, and so on. Any tabulation can be for the two sexes combined or separate. Because the data are lists of responses, results for a large group cannot be obtained easily by combining constituent subgroups. Each breakdown requires re-sorting. Such a tremendous sorting task, involving in all more than 170,000 data cards re-sorted in several different ways, could not have been done without high-speed electronic data-processing equipment. Several computers, the IBM's 1401, 7074, 7094, have been employed at various times in the analysis.

Raw data were transferred from test forms to IBM cards. Each response, together with information identifying the subject and his characteristics, was punched on a separate card. A thirty-eight column field (cols. 1–38) was reserved for subject's name, school, and classroom number, IQ score, sex, place of residence, birth date, highest grade completed by father, and race. In columns 39 and 40 the stimulus word was designated by a numeric code (1–96). Columns 41 to 79 contained the response in alphabetic form. Responses of more than thirty-nine characters were truncated at the thirty-ninth character. In the eightieth column was punched an alphabetic code designating the form class of the response word. A sample card is shown in Figure 3.1. Several procedures, including an IBM 1401 checking program, served to verify transcription of data from test forms to cards.

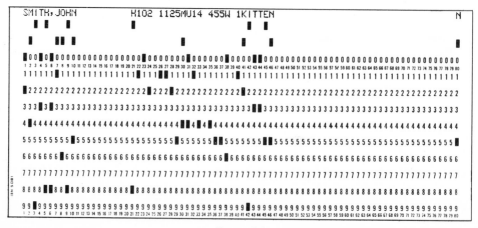

FIGURE 3.1

Appendices C and D are photographic reproductions of computer output for the total urban Maryland samples at kindergarten, first, third, and fifth grades. Breakdowns by IQ, SES, and sex, etc. and form class summaries are not reproduced.

Classification of Response Words

A difficulty that hampers word association research is lack of linguistically relevant and exhaustive categories to which response words may be assigned. In fact, not knowing the relevant dimensions of language-users hampers the entire study of language acquisition, including the development of mathematical models.

The most successful attempt to impose a schema inductively has been made by Fries (1952). Fries's major dichotomy is in terms of lexical vs. function words, a distinction that does not account for major variations in association. Our list does not have many function words, although some like "her" and "his" are included in our pronoun group. In addition, a few other words ("because," "since," "up," and others) represent the function word group. The stimulus list is mostly composed of lexical words and includes nouns, adjectives, verbs, and adverbs. Fries's analysis of these classes is what is most useful for us.

As Fries points out, the meaning of any utterance consists of the lexical meanings of the separate words plus the structural meanings. Certainly, even very young children have mastered many concepts of structural meaning, and the consensus is that by age four, or even earlier, this process is almost complete. Word orders signalling questions, plurals of nouns, and past tenses of verbs are all present in the speech of children younger than those in this study.

Structural meanings are hard to study using isolated words, and word association techniques yielding a single stimulus word paired with a single response word also have limitations for study of lexical meaning. But pairs of words (one stimulus word and one response word) do have advantages in terms of data-collection and analysis, however, particularly for large groups of subjects.

To classify word association responses we have mainly employed a form class division adapted from Fries and similar to that used by Ervin (1961), Fillenbaum and Jones (1965), Deese (1962b), and others. Some additional classifications in terms of commonality (the total frequency of the three most popular responses) are presented to permit easy comparison with previous work that has been summarized in this way (see Appendices A and B). For adjectives, contrast responses are tabulated in some cases. By and large, however, attention is directed mainly to the number of responses of the same form class as the stimulus (paradigmatic responses).

Sometimes it is hard to assign a word to a single form class. Lexical meaning, as mentioned in Chapter 2, is not sufficient basis for classification. Fries says: (p. 73)

> A part of speech in English, like the strike in baseball, is a functioning pattern. There is no single characteristic that all the examples of one part of speech must have in the utterances of English. All the instances of one part of speech are the "same" only in the sense that in the structural patterns of English each has the same functional significance.

Form class of a response word is often doubtful when only word pairs are available, and so we adopted some conventions for arbitrary assignments when necessary. When two scorers independently classify the same data using these rules, agreement is about 98.5 per cent. This is almost as high as the agreement for one scorer on two occasions. Essentially, our method of classification, although different in details from those of Ervin (1961) and Deese (1962b), resembles schemas used by these authors, the main difference being that they discard doubtful cases. To implement a factorial design (to assess variables such as IQ and SES) we could not discard any responses. We felt that the advantages of studying IQ and SES outweighed the disadvantages of possibly misclassifying a few responses.

The classification is made in terms of the *first* word of a response if more than one word is given, with one exception. If the stimulus word is repeated in the midst of a response phrase, that word following the stimulus word, *as repeated*, is used. For example, if to "it" a child responds "That's it, folks," then the word "folks" is classified according to form class, and taken as the response form class used in the analysis. Multiple word responses are frequent at the youngest ages and also become more numerous again at the fifth grade.

Most decisions were easy. Thus "chair," "car," "horse," and many other words are commonly used as nouns, and so were classified as nouns. The specialized usages that put these words in a different class ("chair a session," "car sickness," "horse around") were ignored, because these usages are so rare as to be safely overlooked with young children. Other words belonging to more than one form class could be easily excluded on the bases of contextual clues. For instance, "mean" can be a noun, an adjective, or a verb, and even with young children the adjectival and verb usages are frequent. But "pleasant" followed by "mean" suggests that "mean" in this instance be classified as an adjective. Similarly "drink" in response to "mix" is classified as a noun. If no reliable clues could be found to suggest the proper form class ("flower"—"plant" can be either a noun or a verb), the first, and presumably most common, designation in a standard dictionary (*The American College Dictionary*, Random House, 1962) was used. The "C" category (greetings, nonsense words, conjunctions, etc.) was kept as small as possible.

A few arbitrary rules were heeded. They are listed below:

	Form Class
Color names (red, brown, etc.)	Adjectives
Numbers (one, two, etc.)	Adjectives
Please, yes, no, hi, bye, no response	Residual category (C)
Fly	Noun in all cases except as response to "bird" and "wing"
Flies	Verb when indicated by context

What has been said about classifying response words reflects back also upon the stimulus words. Clearly if it is difficult to classify response words by form class, this difficulty applies also to stimulus words. It is impossible to select a set of stimulus words to represent form classes except after the fact, but such *post hoc* selection would lead to enormous problems in data-collection. It would cause protocols to exist in various stages of completeness and overlap in ways that would make analysis very difficult. Again, sacrificing certain interests to others, we chose to designate the form class of the stimulus words arbitrarily and proceed from there.[2] Responses summarized for broad categories of stimulus words are bound to be distorted to the degree that "nouns," for example, include words not reacted to as nouns by all the subjects. The principal form class for a given word may even vary from one age to another. We suspect this to be infrequent. (The word "color" is an exception, because "color" is interpreted as a verb frequently by young children.)

One may lament the ambiguity of the language and yet to invent words or select words with no ambiguities may not be as desirable as might first appear. Deese (1961) presents cogent experimental reasons for studying real words, and Melton (1961) emphasizes the methodologic folly in trying to invent pristine verbal materials. As far as linguistic development is concerned, it may be in developing resources adequate to cope with this ambiguity that a child faces his most difficult tasks in learning a language. The ambiguities may stimulate concept formation efforts. Semantic ambiguities may follow after early acoustic ambiguities are resolved. "Cocoon" at first elicits "moon" and "raccoon," and later we find associates to "cocoon" ("butterfly" and "moth") grouped with "insects" and "bugs." Still later they fall into a smaller subclass "lepidoptera." In resolving confusions a child may be forced to notice distinctions that contribute very positively to understanding of language and to systematizing it.

Administration Procedures

It has been pointed out that most children included were too young either to read a stimulus word or to write a response. This necessitated an individual-oral (I-O) administration procedure with an adult interviewer saying a word aloud and then recording the subject's oral response.

Although there are exceptions (Clousing, 1927; and Woodrow and Lowell, 1916), previously word associations have mostly been gathered using written procedures. Groups of subjects hear the stimuli, or read them from slides or booklets, and then write their own responses. Variants of this procedure will be called the group-written (G-W) method. Preliminary analyses (Entwisle and Forsyth, 1963) comparing the I-O procedure with the more usual G-W procedure suggested that high-SES children give more common responses than low-SES children when interviewed by an adult.

The consensus of early work is that administration procedures are relatively unimportant. With adults (college students) Clousing (1927) found essentially no difference between written and oral response methods. Woodrow and Lowell (1916), after reviewing the literature antedating their study, noted that written responses did not appear to differ from oral responses, except that "no response" occurred more

---

[2] Requiring subjects to use words in sentences as associations are being gathered may tend to disrupt the associative task and cause subjects to depart from instructions. If done later, there is no guarantee that the usage given subsequently is the usage the subject had in mind at the time the association was emitted.

frequently with written responses. Their subjects, of course, aged nine to twelve, could read and write. Woodworth and Schlosberg (1958) suggest that the I-O form yields more popular associates than the written method, perhaps because of time pressure. Noting an interaction between commonality gain scores and "social sensitivity," Jenkins (1959) confirmed the hypothesis that method of administration, particularly the instructions, is related to commonality. Also, Jenkins and Russell (1960) feel that time pressure and test wiseness do much to explain systematic changes in word association between 1910 and 1952. This line of research has been elaborated by Horton, *et al.* (1963) who found an interrelation between instructional set and need for social approval. The need for social approval was differentially related to commonality in college students under relaxed, but not under speed conditions.

With young children we find that method of administration per se produces relatively small differences in commonality for those of low SES. Differences that do exist can be explained by misspellings or rhyming, both obvious products of the method used (Entwisle and Forsyth, 1963). The same cannot be said for high-SES children, who show much higher average commonality under I-O conditions (66 per cent vs. 55 per cent). High-SES children apparently carry out the task of emitting associations rather differently, depending upon whether they are saying responses aloud to an adult or writing responses "alone." These children are highly motivated to win esteem from adults. This may cause them to try to emit "correct" associations even though the interview is supposed to be a "game" and not a "test."

Since our research is directed toward uncovering age patterns in word associations, the discontinuity between our data for young children procured by the I-O method and data on older subjects, procured by us and by others using a G-W method, commands attention. A preliminary study of differences in commonality associated with SES was undertaken for two parallel fifth-grade samples (Entwisle and Forsyth, 1963). Positive results prompted several further analyses, and also prompted the gathering of some additional small samples (third-grade, high-IQ children under G-W conditions, college females under two varieties of I-O conditions). These various small surveys, all related to administration procedures, will now be summarized.

Fifth-grade Samples, Form Class Analysis

Close to 60 per cent paradigmatic responses (for all form classes combined) are given under G-W procedures for *both* the high-SES and low-SES urban groups. Under I-O conditions, the high-SES groups give 75 per cent paradigmatic responses on the average. The low-SES group also gives more paradigmatic responses under I-O conditions, mostly because the lowest-IQ children give more paradigmatics to stimuli of all form classes. The patterns reproduced below (Table 3.1) suggest that matching responses to verbs increase for both SES groups under I-O conditions. The face-to-face interaction seems to exert equal pressure on both groups as far as verbs are concerned. Nouns remain very much the same under both conditions, except for the lowest-IQ group. But adjectives yield many more paradigmatics for the high-SES sample, and also for the low-IQ portion of the low-SES sample.

TABLE 3.1. Percentages of Paradigmatic Responses for Fifth-Grade SES Groups under Two Administration Conditions

(1961–62 data)

| | Group-Written (G-W) | | | | Individual-Oral (I-O) | | | |
| | High-SES | | Low-SES | | High-SES | | Low-SES | |
	High-IQ	Med.-IQ	Med.-IQ	Low-IQ	High-IQ	Med.-IQ	Med.-IQ	Low-IQ
Nouns	81.0	76.0	71.0	70.2	80.0	75.2	73.1	78.1
Adjectives	55.6	59.6	71.9	63.3	86.7	76.5	70.4	74.0
Verbs	56.1	58.3	51.7	55.0	66.9	63.8	59.8	58.5

The over-all increase in paradigmatic responding from one administration condition to the other is mostly owing to the adjectives and verbs. The analysis of variance in Table 3.2 supports this assertion, for besides a highly significant difference between the two administration methods ($p < .001$), there is an interaction between form class and administration method that borders on significance ($p \cong 0.10$). This comes about because responses to adjectives differ from one administration condition to the other, while other form classes do not.[3]

TABLE 3.2. Analysis of Variance, Matching Responses to Nouns, Adjectives, and Verbs for Two Urban SES Groups, Fifth Grade, under G-W and under I-O Administration

Source of variation	d.f.	MS	F	P(F)
Form Class (FC)	2	4498	19.22	$< .001$
Group vs. Individual Administration (G vs. IA)	1	2763	11.81	$< .001$
SES and IQ (pooled)	3	218	—	—
FC X G vs. IA	2	577	2.46	$\cong .10$
FC X SES-IQ	6	18	—	—
G vs. IA X SES-IQ	3	223	—	—
Residual	54	234		

Deese (1962b, 1964b) has studied the adjectival responses of adults, and finds that paradigmatic responses to high-frequency adjectives are much more likely to be contrasts than paradigmatic responses to low-frequency adjectives. Under his definitions almost all our adjectives are "high frequency" and have popular contrast responses. (Few contrast responses are possible with the nouns and verbs in our list.) What has elsewhere been termed an opposite-evoking set, OES (Carroll, *et al.*, 1962) is apparently activated in high-SES urban children by I-O conditions.

Some contrast responses appear in our data that are the same as those cited by Carroll. Additional ones include "pretty-ugly," "clean-dirty," "sad-happy," "bright-dark, dull," "wild-tame," "pleasant-unpleasant," "quiet-loud." The contrast pairs are listed below:

[3] SES and IQ are partially confounded and the numbers of subjects here are small. Tables 3.3 and 3.4 pinpoint the differences between SES groups under the two administration conditions.

Contrast Responses for Adjectives

High-frequency	Med.-frequency	Low-frequency
black—white	bright—dark, dull	bitter—sweet
cold—hot, warm	clean—dirty	quiet—loud, noisy
dark—light	loud—quiet, soft	rough—smooth
hard—easy, soft	pleasant—unpleasant	slow—fast
high—low	sad—happy	smooth—rough
long—short	tall—short, small	sour—sweet
pretty—ugly	wild—tame	swift—slow
short—long, tall	yellow—	thirsty—

Table 3.3 shows the percentages of contrast responses to adjectives. It is clear that the increase in paradigmatic responses to adjectives is largely owing to an increase in contrast responses by the high-SES groups. The number of contrasts almost doubles for both high-IQ and medium-IQ students. The puzzling difference between the two low-SES urban groups is resolved, because under both forms of administration the low-IQ component gives the same number of contrast responses. The increase in paradigmatic responses for the low-SES, low-IQ sample under individual administration, noted earlier, is thus made up of noncontrast responses. The paradigmatic responses of the low-SES, medium-IQ group, which remain the same under both administration conditions, consist of *fewer* contrast responses under individual administration (46 per cent vs. 36 per cent). Therefore, the paradigmatic responses to adjectives that are not contrasting must increase, as in the low-IQ, low-SES sample. For low-SES children, then, paradigmatic responding increases for both IQ segments if *only* noncontrast responses are considered. Contrast responses decrease in the medium-IQ group to about the same level as in the low–IQ group, and the low-IQ group gives about 35 per cent contrast responses under both conditions.

TABLE 3.3.   Percents of Contrast[a] Responses Given to Adjectives under Group and Individual Administrations by Fifth-Grade Students

(1961–62 data)

Stimuli (adjectives)	High-SES				Low-SES			
	High-IQ		Med.-IQ		Med.-IQ		Low-IQ	
	Group	Indiv.	Group	Indiv.	Group	Indiv.	Group	Indiv.
High-frequency	40.0	71.9	41.3	63.8	62.5	42.5	49.4	52.5
Med.-frequency	27.1	50.0	27.9	42.1	37.1	30.7	28.6	30.0
Low-frequency	24.3	50.0	23.6	57.1	37.9	35.0	27.1	26.4
Total	30.5	57.3	30.9	54.3	45.8	36.1	35.0	36.3

[a] See Table 3.7 for specific words.

For high-SES children contrast responses to adjectives almost double irrespective of IQ level. This rise is almost sufficient to account for the differences in paradigmatics to adjectives under the two forms of administration.

The giving of contrast responses by high-SES children has been observed subsequently by Palermo and Jenkins (1965a) with oral and written administration.

Since they used different stimulus words it is impossible to make direct comparisons, but they note 25 per cent contrast responses with a written procedure and 48 per cent contrast responses when stimuli are presented orally. Their subjects are from middle- to high-socioeconomic levels.

The next question is, of course, what replaces contrast adjectives for the high-SES children under group conditions. The answer is nouns (see Table 3.4). The high-SES children replace contrast (paradigmatic) responses with noun (syntactic) responses under group administration conditions. The low-SES group does not do this.

TABLE 3.4. Percents of Noun Responses Given by Fifth-Grade Students to Adjective Stimuli under G-W and I-O Administration

(1961–62 data)

| Stimulus (adjectives) | High-SES | | | | Low-SES | | | |
| | High-IQ | | Med.-IQ | | Med.-IQ | | Low-IQ | |
	Group	Indiv.	Group	Indiv.	Group	Indiv.	Group	Indiv.
High-frequency	41.9	5.0	28.1	12.5	18.8	22.5	16.9	15.0
Med.-frequency	41.3	14.4	31.3	34.4	28.1	31.3	25.6	18.1
Low-frequency	36.9	9.4	29.4	6.9	10.0	8.1	26.3	14.4
Total	40.0	9.5	29.6	17.9	19.0	20.6	22.9	15.8

These results are anticipated in a study by Siipola, *et al.* (1955), where associations were obtained under "free" and under "pressure" conditions and then classified by grammatical categories. College students served as subjects. Only noun and adjective stimuli were used, and classifications of paradigmatic responses were further divided into contrast and noncontrast categories. The number of adjective-adjective pairs where the response was noncontrast was the same under pressure or free conditions. The contrast adjective-adjective pairs more than doubled under pressure conditions (176 to 442), and the contrast noun-noun pairs also more than doubled (46 to 99), even though not many of the nouns possess antonyms. For adjectives there is a startling shift to syntactic (adjective-noun) pairing under free conditions (392 to 705). All these changes are significant beyond the 1 per cent level and were confirmed on replication.

The existence of antonyms, and thus the possibility for contrast responses, obviously differs from one form class to another. Relatively few nouns have strong opposites, whereas adjectives, especially the common ones, as a rule do have a popular contrast ("good"—"bad," "high"—"low," etc.). Responses to adjectives consequently are greatly affected by administration procedures. In assembling data in different age groups it is probably wise to use group-procured data for adjectives. In Chapter 4, where age and form class are studied, fifth-grade data procured under group procedures are included in tables along with individual data. This factor is important in comparing fifth-grade responses with adult responses because all adult samples have been procured using group procedures.

Third-Grade Group Administration

To see how early the tendency to give contrast responses developed, data were secured from high-SES, high-IQ third-grade children using a written method. Success was surprising when misspellings are edited. Menyuk (1963) found that different methods of obtaining a language sample did not influence the structures to be found in the grammar of four- to five-year-old children, so it seemed possible that administration effects might be smaller for younger children. Commonalities are shown in Table 3.5. In seven of nine comparisons the G-W sample displays *greater* commonality and the total is considerably larger, amounting to 59 per cent vs. 54 per cent. The reverse was true for fifth-grade children, where I-O administration yielded higher commonality for high-SES children. Individual administration then, produces *smaller* commonalities than group administration for third-grade children.

TABLE 3.5.   Commonalities in Per Cents for Third-Grade High-IQ Samples under Two Administration Conditions

(160 responses possible for each entry)

Stimuli grouped by form class and frequency categories	G-W administration	I-O administration
High-frequency nouns	56.9	55.0
Med.-frequency nouns	65.0	55.6
Low-frequency nouns	62.5	56.3
Average Nouns	61.5	55.6
High-frequency adjectives	70.0	76.3
Med.-frequency adjectives	56.9	61.3
Low-frequency adjectives	66.3	60.6
Average Adjectives	64.4	66.0
High-frequency verbs	63.8	55.6
Med.-frequency verbs	49.4	37.5
Low-frequency verbs	40.0	30.0
Average Verbs	51.0	41.0

This reversal in administration effects between the third- and the fifth-grade is puzzling. The IQ's of children in the G-W sample are exactly comparable to those in the I-O sample, the mean IQ in both groups being 130, so an IQ difference cannot be invoked. The point in the school year at which the G-W and I-O samples were tested differed, the G-W sample being tested about three months later. Commonality does increase with age, but not at a rate fast enough to account for this difference. (Also commonalities observed for these third-grade groups are very close to the maximal levels noted at any age level.) Again we turn to a summary of paradigmatic response tendencies (Table 3.6). The individual figures exceed the group administration results, but the differences are not large. There is very little difference between adjectives and verbs. In addition, the number of contrast responses to adjectives is about equal under I-O or G-W conditions. When these highly intelligent third-graders write their own associations, they appear to be relatively unaffected by the test-taking attitudes that apparently influence fifth-graders of the same SES level.

TABLE 3.6.   Percentages of Paradigmatic Responses for Third-Grade High-IQ High-SES Students under Two Administration Conditions

Stimuli grouped by form class and frequency categories	G-W administration	I-O administration
	(N = 20)	(N = 70)
High-frequency nouns	67.5	65.7
Med.-frequency nouns	75.0	73.9
Low-frequency nouns	80.0	85.0
Average Nouns	74.2	74.8
High-frequency adjectives	77.5	81.1
Med.-frequency adjectives	62.5	71.6
Low-frequency adjectives	70.0	69.8
Average Adjectives	70.0	74.2
High-frequency verbs	66.3	68.6
Med.-frequency verbs	46.9	51.1
Low-frequency verbs	57.5	51.8
Average Verbs	56.9	57.1

These results suggest that a response set, or test-wiseness, develops sometime after the third-grade. Probably age patterns based on individual data, to be presented in the next chapter, are relatively unaffected except for adjectives at the fifth-grade level. The paradigmatic response rate to adjectives at the third-grade level can be as high as 70 per cent; at college level it is about 66 per cent. At intermediate ages it can rise to 78 per cent (with individual administration) or fall to 55 per cent (with group procedures).

College Sample under Individual Administration (Females)

As a further check upon the appearance of contrast responses under different administration procedures, two parallel samples of female college students were studied. One sample of college girls gave associations under a G-W procedure, and another sample gave associations to an interviewer who was also a student at the same college. The numbers of contrast responses for the two groups are almost identical. Under G-W conditions the girls gave 41 per cent contrast to adjectives, and under I-O conditions with a college girl as interviewer they gave 42 per cent contrasts. This result is surprising because Siipola's data, cited earlier, show that different test conditions affected college girls' associations.

The discrepancy between our data and Siipola's emphasizes the specific factor affecting the interview situation: the role relationships between interviewer and interviewee. When college girls serve as interviewers for their classmates, the situation is not comparable to an adult interviewing a child.

To try to duplicate the role-relations of the adult-child dyad, data were gathered from female college students with a male professor (authority figure) serving as interviewer. The same instructions were given under both conditions. There were noticeably more contrast responses when an authority figure administered the stimulus list (see Table 3.7). It is thus *not* the written vs. oral aspects of the task that are important in producing different responses, but the social relations involved. The high-SES, fifth-grade children are sensitive to such relationships, whereas apparently such relations have less impact upon lower-SES children or upon third-grade children.

TABLE 3.7.   Percentages of Contrast Responses to Adjectival Stimuli:[a] Peer vs. Authority Figure as Interviewer

Stimulus word	Contrast word	Interviewed by	
		Peer	Authority
black	white	52	45
cold	hot, warm	44	70
dark	light	40	55
hard	easy, soft	80	85
high	low	64	90
long	short	56	75
pretty	ugly	16	15
short	long, tall	60	75
Average high-frequency		52	64
bright	dark, dull	8	15
clean	dirty	48	65
loud	quiet, soft	56	70
pleasant	unpleasant	12	35
sad	happy	36	65
tall	small, short	64	75
wild	tame	20	25
Average med.-frequency		35	50
bitter	sweet	52	70
quiet	loud, noisy	44	50
rough	smooth	60	45
slow	fast	68	75
smooth	rough	24	20
sour	sweet	40	35
swift	slow	16	10
Average low-frequency		43	44

[a] "Yellow" and "thirsty" are omitted because they do not have contrast responses.

Conclusions about Administration Conditions

Several pieces of evidence, all emerging in the last decade, suggest that administration procedures may have greater impact upon word associations than has previously been suspected. One example is our finding that administration effects can exceed those produced by sizable differences in IQ. Other examples are studies of creativity (Hills, 1958), showing that commonness of response swings widely depending upon instructions, and the data of Siipola, *et al.* (1955) showing that form class of response varies greatly under relaxed or "pressure" conditions. Closely related also are studies showing that effectiveness of reinforcers depends on social class (Zigler and Kanzer, 1961) because, of course, some kind of reinforcement is necessary if a child is to participate as a subject.

Sensitivity of word associations to administration procedures concerns us for three major reasons: (1) the mapping of trends over age since adult data are procured by group procedures impossible to use with young children, (2) the appropriateness of using the percentage of paradigmatic responses as an index of linguistic development, (3) the methodological problems raised, especially in connection with studies of cultural deprivation.

In later chapters word associations have been assumed to reflect development of grammatical or semantic concepts over middle childhood. If the number of paradigmatic responses changes with variables other than age, its usefulness as a developmental measure is limited. We therefore have pursued several lines of investigation, reported above, to throw light on this matter, including the form class analysis of fifth-grade responses gathered under two administration conditions, the comparison of two administration procedures with third-grade children, and the analysis of college girls' associations gathered in several different ways.

Data from other investigators is also relevant. Woodrow and Lowell (1916) analyzed two administration procedures and conclude: "The agreement between the children's oral data and their written data is so close that there can be little doubt but that all our conclusions would hold as well for the one as for the other. It is interesting to note, however, that *orally the children give nearly twice as many associations by contrast . . .*" (italics ours). Contrast responses are more than twice as common under the oral procedure for the adjectives used by Woodrow and Lowell, even though total percentages are low:

	Written	Oral
dark (light)	3.8	9.8
deep (shallow)	.6	1.6
soft (hard)	2.7	6.3

Their subjects display much weaker tendencies to match form class of the response to form class of the stimulus than modern children of the same age. That some paradigmatic responses are replaced by syntactic responses under written conditions is therefore of minor impact in their work, because relatively few responses are affected. In our data, where paradigmatic responses are 60 to 70 per cent or even higher, contrasts assume much greater importance. Nevertheless, the Woodrow and Lowell data corroborate the increase in contrast responses with oral (authority figure) presentation.

All these results can be further considered in the same frame with data of Siipola, *et al.* (1955) showing that paradigmatic responses to adjectives decrease under "free" conditions. She used two sets of instructions with college girls, and those intended to produce time pressure were like the standard instructions of the Minnesota group. She found 58 per cent paradigmatics to adjectives under pressure conditions and 62 per cent noun responses given to adjectives under free conditions. The discrepancy is accounted for by contrast responses which more than double for *both* nouns and adjectives under pressure conditions. The instructions emphasized speed. Her conclusion was that the associative process is not merely slowed down, but undergoes a fundamental change. Our work suggests that role relations can induce pressure as well as instructions.

The same kind of explanation also extends to Rosenzweig's (1964) findings with French construction workers and French students. He notes, for primary responses only, that the students are much more likely to give opposite responses. He attributes the difference more to social class than to years of schooling, and finds a similar but smaller difference between American workmen and students. Again, sensitivity to role-relations would account for such findings, since social class distinctions are stronger in France than in this country.

The matter of role-relations raises an interesting point concerning the origin of sex differences in word associations. Generally, females give more common responses than males, and our college data show more paradigmatics for females (by definition the paradigmatics include contrast responses). Data reported in Chapter 5 show fifth-grade girls give 50.2 per cent contrast responses to adjectives vs. 46.8 per cent for boys. The total number of contrast responses given by college students is smaller, but the sex differential is of approximately the same size (44.7 per cent vs. 40.9 per cent). It may be that females, being generally more suggestible and sensitive to role-relations of authority, produce more contrast responses than males in word association procedures because they react more strongly to the "pressure" applied.

The pitfalls of assigning causal relationships are illustrated by the data on administration conditions. It has been shown that an individual interview causes high-SES children to give different responses from those given when children are seen in a group. Suppose, for a moment, that no study of administration conditions had been undertaken. Then if the two SES groups were compared, with IQ held constant, it would turn out (as an analysis of variance corroborates) that there is no over-all SES effect, but there is an SES × grade interaction. The conclusion from this observation alone might be that SES has no effect at the first grade, but its effect becomes manifest by the fifth grade. In other words, the schooling (or home conditions) of low-SES children are such as to cause them to fall progressively behind high-SES children as they progress through elementary school, even though the two groups are equal at first grade. But the administration data make it clear that the two SES levels are responding very similarly when tested in groups. More detailed study of the actual responses given reveals the tendency to give contrasts (a response-set type of phenomenon) is the factor responsible for differences between high-SES and low-SES children.

This possible confounding of SES and an administration-procedure interaction is emphasized because it has wide implications, particularly now when great effort is being channeled into the study of culturally deprived children, or children from minority groups. In the present research we intentionally included many variables and first tried a pilot study with about 500 children to see what variables seemed important. It turned out that every variable included had significant impact. Thus, one cannot help but wonder what other variables, not included, also would account for significant variance, or interact substantially with variables already included. The fact that very little variance is left unaccounted for is no guarantee that crucial variables have not been omitted.

Another methodologic point is brought out by the comparison with Siipola's data. Her instructions appear to produce differences, but if our conclusions about role relations are correct, under either instruction condition pressure may be high. Our data suggest that role-relations become more important with older subjects.

NOTE: CRITERIA FOR SYNTACTIC ASSOCIATIONS

In all cases in which the stimulus word was repeated with a word preceding, the association was classified as syntactic. In some cases the *preceding* word, if it had been given alone, would not have been judged syntactic. For instance,

Stimulus word	Response
hard	hard letter
table	baby table

In all cases where the negative of a word was given it was judged paradigmatic ("happen"—"unhappen").

A. NOUN STIMULI.

1. Often a noun followed by another noun clearly represents a syntactic association even though the nominal form class of the stimulus and response are the same. For example,

Stimulus word	Response
flower	pot
flower	garden
table	cloth
color	picture

Such examples were classified as syntactic.

2. A verb following a noun may or may not represent a syntactic association. The test is whether the verb could be the predicate in a simple sentence with the noun as subject. For example,

hand	look

is *not* taken as syntactic, because "hand" could not be the subject of a simple sentence with the verb "look," but

hand	pick

is taken as a syntactic association since "hand" and "pick" could form a sentence.

3. Adjectives associated with nouns may also represent syntactic associations. There seem to be many backward associations for young children so we have judged a noun followed by an adjective to be syntactic if (a) the response adjective normally *precedes* the stimulus noun, for example:

Stimulus word	Response
hand	second
hand	left

or (b) the response word would make a meaningful simple sentence if "is" were inserted between the stimulus word and the response word.
For example,

river	rocky

but not

river	light

All conjunctions and articles were judged syntactic, as were possessive pronouns.

In several cases the stimulus word belongs to more than one form class. Some usages are so rare that no real classification problem exists. For instance, "table a motion" makes "table" a verb, but we did not encounter this usage with the young subjects in our sample. On the other hand "color" which probably would be used very rarely by adults as a verb, was used often as a verb by our subjects.

color	with crayons
color	picture

In these cases, where the stimulus was obviously interpreted as belonging to a different form class from the one assigned, rules for syntactic associations to the form class assumed by the subject were applied.

B. Adjectives.

For adjective stimuli, the criteria are less difficult. Most nouns following adjectives are syntactic, but here semantics again determine the classification. For instance, "cloud" in response to "high" is syntactic, but "milk bottles" or "pie" in response to "high" is not. Again the criterion is whether the adjective can follow "*noun* is" and make a simple meaningful sentence. Thus some nouns, some pronouns, prepositions, and prepositional phrases are judged as syntactic.

Because stimulus words were spoken by the experimenter, "high" was interpreted in some instances as the greeting "Hi." Therefore, "say," and other verbs, are syntactic for this usage. Again, the assumed form class was used in making judgments. "Pretty" presented special problems because it is used so often adverbially to modify other adjectives: "pretty horrible," "pretty awful," etc. All suitable adjectives following "pretty" were judged as syntactic.

C. Verbs.

Adverbs, prepositions, and conjunctions are taken as syntactic. For transitive verbs, nouns (objects) are taken as well as pronouns if they make simple meaningful sentences. For instance, "grass" in response to "give" is *not* taken as syntactic, but "flower" is taken as syntactic. Verbs preceded by "to" ("begin" as stimulus, and "to eat" as response) are clearly syntactic. Many backward associations probably exist for intransitive verbs (as "boy" in response to "run"), but these presented such difficult classification problems they had to be overlooked.

The reliability of the syntactic classification has not been investigated. It should be pointed out, however, that interest attaches principally to the *difference* in syntactic associations with age. As long as the same criteria are applied across ages and the same responses at various age levels are classified in the same way, differences are probably reliable. The first-grade responses were classified initially because commonalities are much smaller at this level, and then third-grade and fifth-grade responses were checked back against the first-grade responses. Even more important, many analyses are based on primary responses only. There is little room for disagreement with primary responses, and, of course, many fewer decisions are involved. As was true in assigning form classes to stimuli or responses, a moderate amount of ambiguity is unavoidable, but the positive value of the information obtained seems to outweigh the drawbacks associated with subjective judgments.

Chapter Four

Changes with Age

The major purpose of this research is to study how word associations of children change with increasing age. The associations given by urban Maryland children of kindergarten, first, third, and fifth grades to the set of ninety-six stimulus words are tabulated alphabetically in Appendices C and D. The three most common responses at each grade level are identified for individual stimulus words in Appendix A and compared with data procured by others in Appendix B. Adult data are given for comparison.[1]

In this chapter and the next two chapters the data from the appendices are analyzed in relation to the parameters of the design and resummarized in many ways. For instance, commonality differences associated with age are examined. Results are presented from two major points of view: in terms of variables describing the stimuli (form class and frequency) and in terms of the variables characterizing samples of subjects (grade, IQ, SES, residential locus, sex). There are interactions between subject and stimulus variables as well: for example, commonality increases with age at different rates for the different form classes. Association data are so bulky that a reader cannot reduce raw data himself, and for this reason great effort has been put into presenting the data in summary form and reducing them in several different ways. Major conclusions about age of the respondents and properties of the stimulus words are given in this chapter. Chapter 5 reports results related to intelligence and sex, and Chapter 6 discusses residential locus.

Results from individual administration have been used except when noted other- wise. The kindergarten and fifth-grade samples, each consisting of 200 subjects, have

---

[1] As indicated in Table 2.1, samples of rural Maryland children and Amish children have also been studied. In addition some four-year-olds and college subjects were studied for comparative purposes. A few other specialized samples were gathered (see Chapter 3, p. 36), mostly to study administration conditions. Space prevents listing associations fully except for the urban Maryland grade school groups.

been adjusted when necessary in age-trend analyses, to be equivalent to the first- and third-grade samples (N = 280).

Preliminary data (Entwisle, *et al.*, 1964) on the word associations of young children to high-frequency nouns, adjectives, and verbs revealed a striking increase in paradigmatic responding between kindergarten children and fifth-graders. Other evidence documents this paradigmatic shift (Brown and Berko, 1960; Ervin, 1961), but heretofore there have not been enough data to define the shift precisely. Our earlier data show increases in paradigmatic responding that vary by form class of the stimulus. Noun stimuli yielded many noun responses, even at the earliest ages, and the increase in the noun-noun pattern from kindergarten to fifth grade was relatively slight. With adjectival stimuli there was an accelerating increase between kindergarten and third grade in the number of adjectival responses, altogether amounting to a jump of 500 per cent. There was a further slight increase from the third to the fifth grade in adjective-adjective pairs. Changes in responses for verbs proceeded at a slower pace than for other form classes, but paradigmatic responding was strongly established by the fifth grade.

The age patterns just described are based on a preliminary sample of 500 children, and on responses to twenty-four stimulus words. Now there are data on associations to ninety-six stimuli, with responses from 1,040 children in an urban Maryland sample, and from several hundred other children (rural, Amish, etc.). Also, 200 college students responded to the same stimuli and so provide comparable adult data. The present chapter will describe age patterns more fully on the basis of these larger samples.

The sample design of neither the subjects nor the word stimuli is a complete factorial. This complicates both the analyses and the presentation of results. Often we will confine attention to the seventy-two stimulus words (twenty-four nouns, twenty-four adjectives, and twenty-four verbs) that can be further subdivided into three frequency levels for each form class. The urban Maryland sample includes two socioeconomic levels, with high- and medium-IQ strata in the high-SES group, and medium- and low-IQ strata in the low-SES group. Each urban SES level can thus be considered separately and IQ differences studied within one SES level. Or re-using a portion of these data and combining them in another way, one may hold IQ constant (at medium level) and examine SES differences, as in Chapter 6. These smaller complete factorial designs cannot be combined into a single large design because there is no low-IQ high-SES stratum nor high-IQ low-SES stratum. Such subjects were not available in sufficient numbers.

Because of the incomplete design, parts of the information summarized in one table may be summarized again in another table in a different context. These redundancies are noted. As would be expected, major conclusions are corroborated from one place to another whenever independent analyses are possible. The principal disadvantage is that some interactions (IQ × SES, for instance) cannot be isolated because these two factors are partially confounded. It will be shown that there are clear differences associated with IQ, for instance, but it is impossible to show that differentials associated with IQ are not constant from one status level to another.

The stimulus words *are* a complete factorial in terms of form class and frequency divisions if one eliminates 25 per cent of the words (adverbs, pronouns, and miscellaneous) and considers the remaining seventy-two words. Many analyses which follow are based on this reduced stimulus list, including only nouns, adjectives, and verbs. Frequency at three levels is also an orthogonal variable for the seventy-two-word list. The reader is referred to Table 2.1 for a recapitulation of the sample designs.

Scoring Measures

Several different measures are available to express changes in associative responding. Commonality, defined here as the total frequency of the three most popular responses, is useful for several reasons. It is almost perfectly reliable, and it has often been used by others. Commonality data facilitate comparison between our work and that of others.

The most frequently used measure is the frequency count of responses by form class. For any stimulus word, one can classify response words exhaustively in terms of their presumptive form classes (adjectives, verbs, etc.),[2] and this turns out to be very useful in studying behavioral changes correlated with age. An earlier study (Entwisle, *et al.*, 1964) compares the classification of responses by form class with a classification based on a "syntactic" vs. "nonsyntactic" dichotomy.[3] The latter distinction is often difficult to make, but it focuses on a salient characteristic of children's language. Our earlier study shows that the syntactic-paradigmatic dichotomy is highly correlated with the form class division for elementary school children. The form class division is preferable because it requires fewer subjective judgments. Most analyses are based on form class, but occasionally a syntactic classification for the most popular response is used.

The form class division includes paradigmatic responses. Paradigmatic responses, the form class of the response matching the form class of the stimulus, are very useful for studying language development, particularly if a few other combinations (adjective-noun, noun-verb, verb-adverb, or verb-preposition) are also examined.[4] As we noted earlier (Entwisle, *et al.*, 1964) and also as others have noted (see Ervin, 1961, for relevant citations) matching responses increase remarkably with age, but the complete evolution of paradigmatics, particularly as regards age characteristics and form class variations, has not been described previously.

Commonality Analysis of the Normative Tables

Table 4.1 summarizes commonality data on individual stimulus words by age, IQ, and SES subgroups. Commonalities for the fifth grade are given separately for

---

[2] In Chapter 3 the relation between form class categories and traditional grammatical classes was discussed.

[3] Criteria for this dichotomy are summarized in a Note following Chapter 3.

[4] This is essentially the dichotomy used by Brown and Berko (1960). They labeled it Heterogeneous (Htg.) vs. Homogeneous (Hmg.).

individually administered tests (N = 200) and group administered tests (N = 80) since matched samples showed differences in commonality (see Chapter 3).

TABLE 4.1. Commonalities in Per Cent

(Sum of frequencies of the three most popular responses)

	Kindergarten			First grade				
	High-SES	Low-SES	Combined	High-SES		Low-SES		Combined
				High-IQ	Med.-IQ	Med.-IQ	Low-IQ	
Sample size	100	100	200	70	70	70	70	280
bird	31.0	38.0	35.0	54.3	42.9	55.7	41.4	45.7
color	18.0	25.0	19.5	30.0	25.7	38.6	31.4	27.9
flower	15.0	18.0	14.0	21.4	24.3	14.3	18.6	16.8
fly	24.0	28.0	23.0	31.4	27.1	30.0	24.3	25.7
hand	9.0	14.0	9.5	30.0	18.6	17.1	11.4	16.1
man	14.0	26.0	20.0	40.0	27.1	31.4	20.0	27.1
river	33.0	51.0	41.5	35.7	31.4	38.6	35.7	32.5
table	38.0	50.0	44.5	64.3	38.6	41.4	42.9	45.4
Total nouns High-frequency	22.8	31.3	25.9	38.4	29.5	33.4	28.2	29.7
chair	34.0	44.0	37.5	58.6	44.3	64.3	38.6	48.9
fruit	25.0	28.0	26.5	32.9	22.9	30.0	27.1	25.0
music	22.0	35.0	27.5	57.1	35.7	37.1	22.9	29.6
ocean	23.0	37.0	29.0	41.4	31.4	44.3	35.7	34.6
salt	37.0	53.0	44.5	68.6	48.6	44.3	45.7	51.8
sheep	19.0	26.0	22.5	40.0	28.6	25.7	17.1	24.6
square	21.0	24.0	22.0	45.7	25.7	31.4	11.4	27.1
wing	33.0	42.0	36.0	52.9	51.4	45.7	32.9	43.9
Total nouns Med.-frequency	26.8	36.1	30.7	49.6	36.1	40.3	28.9	35.7
bee	18.0	17.0	17.0	20.0	20.0	14.3	11.4	14.3
bug	24.0	24.0	26.5	50.0	30.0	27.1	20.0	28.9
butterfly	33.0	25.0	27.5	32.9	30.0	47.1	32.9	33.6
cocoon	16.0	13.0	12.0	25.7	17.1	14.3	11.4	14.6
insect	31.0	19.0	25.0	48.6	42.9	24.3	15.7	31.8
moth	13.0	15.0	23.5	41.4	28.6	18.6	8.6	20.0
needle	34.0	33.0	32.5	48.6	32.9	27.1	22.9	31.1
net	28.0	27.0	27.5	31.4	22.9	25.7	28.6	26.1
Total nouns Low-frequency	24.6	21.6	21.7	37.3	28.0	24.8	18.9	25.0

	Third grade					Fifth grade				
	High-SES		Low-SES		Com- bined	High-SES		Low-SES			Com- bined
	High- IQ	Med.- IQ	Med.- IQ	Low- IQ		High- IQ	Med.- IQ	Med.- IQ	Low- IQ	Group	
Sample size	70	70	70	70	280	50	50	50	50	80	280
bird	54.3	47.1	57.1	44.3	48.2	56.0	48.0	60.0	44.0	30.0	46.1
color	51.4	38.6	38.6	44.3	41.4	46.0	48.0	44.0	34.0	48.8	42.1
flower	34.3	37.1	40.0	25.7	34.6	44.0	44.0	42.0	48.0	30.0	40.0
fly	47.1	35.7	31.4	34.3	36.8	68.0	56.0	44.0	40.0	33.8	45.0
hand	50.0	32.9	35.7	25.7	34.3	62.0	42.0	58.0	40.0	36.3	43.2
man	70.0	68.6	51.4	65.7	61.8	64.0	68.0	74.0	68.0	32.5	57.1
river	75.7	68.6	54.3	48.6	57.9	76.0	74.0	54.0	46.0	52.5	59.3
table	67.1	60.0	68.6	54.3	62.9	68.0	60.0	58.0	66.0	67.5	62.9
Tot. noun High-freq.	56.3	48.6	47.1	42.9	47.2	60.5	55.0	54.3	48.3	37.7	49.5

TABLE 4.1. (cont.)

	Third grade					Fifth grade					
	High-SES		Low-SES			High-SES		Low-SES			
	High IQ	Med. IQ	Med. IQ	Low IQ	Com-bined	High IQ	Med. IQ	Med. IQ	Low IQ	Group	Com-bined
Sample size	70	70	70	70	280	50	50	50	50	80	280
chair	54.3	67.1	72.9	42.9	58.9	78.0	68.0	66.0	68.0	65.0	68.6
fruit	58.6	44.3	61.4	41.4	49.6	60.0	62.0	68.0	58.0	61.3	61.8
music	32.9	37.1	31.4	34.3	30.1	36.0	30.0	34.0	40.0	33.8	30.7
ocean	74.3	68.6	75.7	74.3	73.6	70.0	74.0	66.0	72.0	76.3	71.1
salt	68.6	72.9	78.6	75.7	73.9	74.0	60.0	56.0	64.0	53.8	60.0
sheep	42.9	44.3	48.6	44.3	45.4	50.0	54.0	46.0	50.0	38.8	43.6
square	60.0	55.7	65.7	44.3	50.4	62.0	58.0	56.0	58.0	45.0	52.9
wing	62.9	72.9	64.3	62.9	62.9	68.0	78.0	64.0	58.0	56.3	62.5
Tot. noun Med.-freq.	56.8	57.9	62.3	52.5	55.6	62.3	60.5	57.0	58.5	53.8	56.4
bee	34.3	45.7	37.1	22.9	33.2	60.0	46.0	44.0	44.0	52.5	48.6
bug	70.0	71.4	74.3	41.4	63.6	70.0	78.0	70.0	74.0	43.8	63.2
butterfly	45.7	45.7	44.3	40.0	41.7	56.0	60.0	48.0	50.0	40.0	45.7
cocoon	58.6	50.0	28.6	38.6	40.4	60.0	44.0	34.0	54.0	33.8	40.7
insect	64.3	64.3	67.1	54.3	62.5	72.0	68.0	68.0	70.0	60.0	66.1
moth	61.4	50.0	32.9	22.9	38.6	58.0	64.0	38.0	52.0	47.5	50.7
needle	71.4	55.7	61.4	58.6	60.4	68.0	68.0	56.0	52.0	50.0	58.2
net	52.9	32.9	37.1	34.3	36.8	62.0	50.0	52.0	40.0	22.5	41.8
Tot. noun Low-freq.	57.3	52.0	47.9	39.1	47.1	63.3	59.8	51.3	54.5	43.8	52.9

	Kindergarten			First grade				
	High-SES	Low-SES	Combined	High-SES		Low-SES		Combined
				High-IQ	Med.-IQ	Med.-IQ	Low-IQ	
Sample size	100	100	200	70	70	70	70	280
black	15.0	20.0	15.5	47.1	24.3	28.6	25.7	28.9
cold	24.0	32.0	24.5	65.7	41.4	41.4	25.7	41.8
dark	38.0	26.0	30.5	64.3	38.6	44.3	31.4	42.9
hard	18.0	19.0	18.5	57.1	18.6	38.6	24.3	32.1
high	18.0	22.0	19.0	48.6	24.3	34.3	17.1	28.6
long	15.0	20.0	16.0	55.7	27.1	24.3	10.0	26.1
pretty	31.0	17.0	22.5	27.1	22.9	28.6	28.6	24.6
short	28.0	20.0	23.5	52.9	34.3	27.1	21.4	30.7
Total adjectives High-frequency	23.4	22.0	21.3	52.3	28.9	33.4	23.0	32.0
bright	34.0	40.0	36.0	52.9	44.3	38.6	28.6	41.1
clean	18.0	22.0	17.5	42.9	25.7	24.3	17.1	24.6
loud	19.0	17.0	15.5	52.9	27.1	34.3	15.7	29.3
pleasant	15.0	15.0	14.5	20.0	17.1	14.3	14.3	11.4
sad	23.0	29.0	26.5	50.0	41.4	38.6	25.7	38.9
tall	26.0	27.0	26.5	62.9	40.0	48.6	31.4	33.2
wild	33.0	33.0	31.0	34.3	22.9	31.4	20.0	23.2
yellow	26.0	26.0	23.5	34.3	27.1	25.7	31.4	25.7
Total adjectives Med.-frequency	24.3	26.1	20.6	43.8	30.7	32.0	23.0	28.3

TABLE 4.1. (cont.)

	Kindergarten			First grade				
	High-SES	Low-SES	Combined	High-SES		Low-SES		
				High-IQ	Med.-IQ	Med.-IQ	Low-IQ	Combined
Sample size	100	100	200	70	70	70	70	280
bitter	20.0	15.0	15.0	40.0	14.3	17.1	11.4	17.9
quiet	19.0	15.0	15.0	54.3	20.0	30.0	22.9	27.9
rough	22.0	16.0	19.0	24.3	22.9	28.6	24.3	20.4
slow	33.0	27.0	29.0	60.0	38.6	50.0	27.1	43.2
smooth	11.0	15.0	12.5	42.9	20.0	25.7	20.0	26.1
sour	17.0	22.0	19.5	31.4	25.7	18.6	18.6	21.1
swift	10.0	12.0	10.0	15.7	10.0	12.9	10.0	8.9
thirsty	41.0	56.0	47.0	64.3	44.3	62.9	55.7	56.4
Total adjectives Low-frequency	21.6	22.3	20.9	41.6	24.5	30.7	23.8	27.7

	Third grade					Fifth grade					
	High-SES		Low-SES		Com-bined	High-SES		Low-SES			Com-bined
	High-IQ	Med.-IQ	Med.-IQ	Low-IQ		High-IQ	Med.-IQ	Med.-IQ	Low-IQ	Group	
Sample size	70	70	70	70	280	50	50	50	50	80	280
black	75.7	70.0	68.6	58.6	65.4	78.0	82.0	78.0	76.0	52.5	71.1
cold	75.7	72.9	80.0	77.1	75.0	80.0	68.0	64.0	84.0	53.8	68.2
dark	84.3	80.0	87.1	81.4	82.5	94.0	94.0	76.0	82.0	75.0	83.2
hard	74.3	78.8	77.1	67.1	73.6	76.0	78.0	68.0	90.0	53.8	70.4
high	74.3	70.0	70.0	65.7	68.6	78.0	84.0	74.0	74.0	76.3	73.9
long	68.6	70.0	78.6	67.1	67.5	78.0	70.0	62.0	80.0	56.3	65.0
pretty	87.1	67.1	75.7	62.9	73.5	82.0	80.0	76.0	78.0	52.5	70.0
short	84.3	81.4	77.1	65.7	77.5	90.0	84.0	58.0	88.0	63.8	78.9
Total adj. High-freq.	78.0	73.8	76.8	68.2	72.8	82.0	80.0	69.5	81.5	53.9	72.6
bright	60.0	64.3	70.0	60.0	62.5	50.0	58.0	48.0	60.0	36.3	47.9
clean	71.4	54.3	61.4	55.7	58.6	86.0	60.0	52.0	66.0	50.0	55.0
loud	68.6	61.4	42.9	44.3	51.8	76.0	72.0	54.0	48.0	46.3	56.1
pleasant	42.9	44.3	30.0	20.0	32.9	66.0	58.0	54.0	50.0	33.8	50.4
sad	80.0	80.0	81.4	81.4	78.6	84.0	80.0	84.0	92.0	68.8	78.9
tall	75.7	65.7	74.3	68.6	68.9	80.0	74.0	70.0	72.0	51.3	66.4
wild	47.1	30.0	32.9	27.1	33.2	58.0	50.0	56.0	48.0	38.8	47.5
yellow	54.3	51.4	44.3	45.7	44.3	76.0	58.0	50.0	54.0	52.5	55.0
Total adj. Med.-freq.	62.5	56.4	54.6	50.4	53.8	72.0	63.8	58.5	61.3	47.2	57.1
bitter	60.0	44.3	48.6	35.7	44.3	82.0	74.0	58.0	54.0	42.5	58.2
quiet	61.4	67.1	52.9	54.3	58.9	70.0	58.0	56.0	66.0	40.0	53.6
rough	47.1	47.1	52.9	35.7	44.6	64.0	76.0	54.0	62.0	48.8	59.6
slow	85.7	84.3	82.9	88.6	83.2	86.0	88.0	78.0	94.0	75.0	82.1
smooth	60.0	65.7	72.9	52.9	63.2	66.0	74.0	66.0	72.0	58.8	66.1
sour	62.9	54.3	50.0	42.9	51.1	82.0	62.0	72.0	56.0	32.5	57.1
swift	50.0	20.0	27.1	15.7	25.4	82.0	62.0	62.0	54.0	63.8	63.2
thirsty	65.7	67.1	67.1	74.3	68.9	74.0	74.0	76.0	66.0	58.8	66.8
Total adj. Low-freq.	61.6	56.3	56.8	50.0	50.5	75.8	71.0	65.3	65.5	52.5	63.3

TABLE 4.1. (cont.)

	Kindergarten			First grade				
	High-SES	Low-SES	Combined	High-SES		Low-SES		Combined
				High-IQ	Med.-IQ	Med.-IQ	Low-IQ	
Sample size	100	100	200	70	70	70	70	280
add	8.0	14.0	10.0	18.6	10.0	11.4	10.0	8.2
begin	8.0	9.0	7.5	24.3	14.3	14.3	12.9	10.4
carry	23.0	20.0	20.5	14.3	37.1	22.9	24.3	19.3
give	15.0	14.0	12.5	12.9	17.1	17.1	14.3	12.9
move	12.0	12.0	11.0	21.4	15.7	12.9	15.7	12.9
run	21.0	24.0	21.5	47.1	38.6	38.6	34.3	35.7
sit	48.0	46.0	46.5	57.1	51.4	67.1	51.4	55.7
tell	16.0	14.0	13.0	21.4	15.7	24.3	12.9	15.4
Total verbs High-frequency	18.9	19.1	17.8	27.1	25.0	26.1	22.0	21.3
allow	9.0	8.0	6.5	14.3	12.9	17.1	8.6	8.9
belong	9.0	14.0	10.5	20.0	15.7	17.1	15.7	13.2
enjoy	14.0	14.0	12.0	17.1	20.0	12.9	15.7	13.2
happen	14.0	10.0	10.5	17.1	12.9	10.0	17.1	12.9
join	14.0	14.0	12.0	18.6	14.3	22.9	11.4	13.9
listen	18.0	17.0	14.0	24.3	18.6	31.4	15.7	20.0
prepare	9.0	12.0	10.0	14.3	11.4	11.4	11.4	9.3
sell	12.0	16.0	11.5	14.3	15.7	14.3	12.9	10.7
Total verbs Med.-frequency	12.4	13.1	10.9	17.5	15.2	17.1	13.6	12.7
deceive	7.0	8.0	7.5	11.4	18.6	12.9	10.0	9.6
examine	14.0	15.0	13.0	24.3	17.1	22.9	14.3	18.6
gallop	49.0	58.0	52.5	64.3	60.0	52.9	30.0	49.6
inquire	21.0	16.0	17.0	25.7	18.6	18.6	15.7	15.1
maintain	10.0	6.0	5.5	10.0	11.4	14.3	8.6	7.9
mix	21.0	31.0	24.5	22.9	20.0	28.6	21.4	20.4
obey	10.0	10.0	8.5	24.3	21.4	17.1	8.6	13.6
restore	22.0	27.0	24.5	34.3	32.9	25.7	22.9	26.4
Total verbs Low-frequency	19.3	21.4	19.1	27.1	25.0	24.1	16.4	20.1

	Third grade					Fifth grade				
	High-SES		Low-SES		Com-bined	High-SES		Low-SES			Com-bined
	High-IQ	Med.-IQ	Med.-IQ	Low-IQ		High-IQ	Med.-IQ	Med.-IQ	Low-IQ	Group	
Sample size	70	70	70	70	280	50	50	50	50	80	280
add	77.1	72.9	72.9	68.6	70.4	74.0	70.0	74.0	72.0	56.3	64.6
begin	75.7	44.3	44.3	30.0	46.4	96.0	82.0	72.0	68.0	61.3	73.9
carry	28.6	21.4	30.0	27.1	23.6	38.0	48.0	34.0	36.0	35.0	35.0
give	55.7	44.3	47.1	31.4	42.5	64.0	56.0	52.0	52.0	47.5	53.6
move	30.0	30.0	40.0	20.0	27.5	32.0	54.0	26.0	32.0	30.0	29.3
run	72.9	68.6	72.9	60.0	68.9	62.0	76.0	68.0	64.0	62.5	66.1
sit	71.4	64:3	72.9	61.4	66.4	82.0	82.0	68.0	64.0	52.5	67.5
tell	41.4	27.1	31.4	20.0	26.4	32.0	34.0	36.0	26.0	30.0	28.9
Tot. verb High-freq.	56.6	46.6	51.4	39.8	46.5	60.0	62.8	53.8	51.8	47.0	52.4

TABLE 4.1. (cont.)

	Third grade					Fifth grade					
	High-SES		Low-SES			High-SES		Low-SES			
	High IQ	Med. IQ	Med. IQ	Low IQ	Combined	High IQ	Med. IQ	Med. IQ	Low IQ	Group	Combined
Sample size	70	70	70	70	280	50	50	50	50	80	280
allow	21.4	14.3	25.7	14.3	15.0	40.0	22.0	26.0	16.0	31.3	23.9
belong	30.0	18.6	22.9	20.0	18.6	44.0	30.0	26.0	38.0	22.5	25.4
enjoy	42.9	44.3	38.6	27.1	38.2	64.0	50.0	56.0	50.0	55.0	54.6
happen	18.6	20.0	20.0	20.0	14.6	18.0	20.0	16.0	22.0	18.8	14.6
join	37.1	35.7	32.9	25.7	30.0	40.0	54.0	34.0	40.0	30.0	35.4
listen	58.6	40.0	37.1	48.6	43.9	70.0	68.0	58.0	52.0	33.8	52.1
prepare	48.6	37.1	27.1	14.3	29.3	50.0	52.0	46.0	48.0	32.5	44.3
sell	50.0	27.1	34.3	14.3	30.7	48.0	52.0	50.0	42.0	40.0	42.9
Tot. verb Med.-freq.	38.4	29.6	29.8	23.0	27.5	46.8	43.5	39.0	38.5	33.0	36.7
deceive	25.7	22.9	14.3	10.0	16.1	30.0	26.0	34.0	30.0	13.8	22.9
examine	32.9	25.7	40.0	25.7	26.8	56.0	56.0	40.0	28.0	31.3	38.6
gallop	62.9	58.6	44.3	50.0	50.7	78.0	70.0	62.0	48.0	56.3	61.4
inquire	14.3	27.1	20.0	21.4	16.4	44.0	28.0	12.0	20.0	25.0	20.7
maintain	11.4	11.4	10.0	11.4	5.4	24.0	16.0	18.0	24.0	11.3	12.9
mix	34.3	37.1	31.4	37.1	35.0	46.0	42.0	52.0	38.0	33.8	40.0
obey	28.6	30.0	25.7	22.9	20.7	58.0	44.0	48.0	36.0	46.3	42.5
restore	28.6	24.3	24.3	37.1	28.2	30.0	26.0	34.0	38.0	22.5	28.9
Tot. verb Low-freq.	29.8	29.6	26.3	27.0	24.9	45.8	38.5	37.5	32.8	30.0	33.5

	Kindergarten			First grade				
	High-SES	Low-SES	Combined	High-SES		Low-SES		Combined
				High-IQ	Med.-IQ	Med.-IQ	Low-IQ	
Sample size	100	100	200	70	70	70	70	280
always	7.0	11.0	7.0	25.7	14.3	12.9	10.0	10.0
gently	13.0	16.0	13.0	31.4	18.6	14.3	10.0	15.7
loudly	15.0	12.0	13.0	47.1	30.0	21.4	14.3	11.1
never	21.0	13.0	15.5	30.0	21.4	24.3	14.3	19.6
seldom	11.0	9.0	9.0	14.3	12.9	11.4	12.9	11.1
slowly	24.0	23.0	22.0	58.6	37.1	50.0	34.3	42.9
sometimes	7.0	12.0	9.5	17.1	11.4	17.1	10.0	10.4
usually	7.0	9.0	6.0	18.6	8.6	11.4	10.0	7.1
Total adverbs	13.1	13.1	11.9	30.4	19.3	20.4	14.5	17.5
he	20.0	22.0	19.5	54.3	35.7	44.3	21.4	38.9
her	23.0	29.0	26.0	52.9	27.1	32.9	21.4	33.2
him	24.0	17.0	20.0	44.3	22.9	20.0	11.4	23.2
it	12.0	8.0	8.5	34.3	22.9	30.0	27.1	24.6
she	31.0	26.0	28.5	57.1	35.7	28.6	18.6	31.8
them	8.0	14.0	10.0	25.7	14.3	14.3	10.0	12.5
they	12.0	16.0	11.0	21.4	11.4	11.4	14.3	10.4
us	20.0	24.0	21.5	37.1	31.4	22.9	18.6	25.0
Total pronouns	18.8	19.5	18.1	40.9	25.2	25.5	17.9	25.0
because	18.0	21.0	19.0	25.7	27.1	35.7	27.1	26.8
between	14.0	15.0	11.0	12.9	14.3	17.1	10.0	12.1
into	15.0	17.0	15.0	27.1	12.9	17.1	20.0	15.4
off	17.0	19.0	16.0	61.4	38.6	28.6	11.4	32.5
on	20.0	14.0	15.5	42.9	30.0	27.1	12.9	24.6
once	13.0	12.0	12.0	31.4	30.0	20.0	18.6	22.9
since	8.0	9.0	6.5	18.6	8.6	12.9	10.0	7.5
up	29.0	32.0	29.0	68.6	60.0	61.4	48.8	56.1
Total misc.	16.8	17.4	15.5	36.1	27.7	27.5	19.8	24.7

TABLE 4.1. (cont.)

	Third grade				Fifth grade					
	High-SES		Low-SES		Com-bined	High-SES		Low-SES			Com-bined
	High-IQ	Med.-IQ	Med.-IQ	Low-IQ		High-IQ	Med.-IQ	Med.-IQ	Low-IQ	Group	
Sample size	70	70	70	70	280	50	50	50	50	80	280
always	48.6	27.1	28.6	21.4	30.0	58.0	40.0	42.0	34.0	40.0	42.1
gently	52.9	51.4	38.6	30.0	42.5	58.0	62.0	62.0	58.0	30.0	50.0
loudly	57.1	54.3	40.0	37.1	43.2	66.0	70.0	54.0	38.0	40.0	48.9
never	47.1	37.1	41.4	37.1	40.4	58.0	48.0	36.0	48.0	48.8	45.0
seldom	28.6	24.3	14.3	17.1	18.2	40.0	42.0	40.0	26.0	40.0	35.7
slowly	75.7	67.1	68.6	72.9	71.1	68.0	66.0	62.0	74.0	52.5	62.1
sometimes	41.4	38.6	28.6	28.6	32.1	44.0	36.0	48.0	32.0	26.3	32.8
usually	28.6	25.7	30.0	21.4	24.6	44.0	42.0	40.0	36.0	30.0	37.1
Total adverbs	45.9	40.7	36.3	33.2	37.8	54.5	50.8	48.0	43.3	38.4	44.2
he	70.0	68.6	68.6	70.0	67.5	76.0	72.0	78.0	72.0	76.3	74.3
her	57.1	72.9	81.4	67.1	74.3	78.0	80.0	64.0	76.0	71.3	72.1
him	67.1	70.0	60.0	64.3	62.5	82.0	78.0	68.0	74.0	65.0	71.4
it	48.6	38.6	35.7	45.7	40.4	56.0	48.0	44.0	38.0	37.5	42.9
she	74.3	72.9	74.3	75.7	73.6	86.0	82.0	76.0	80.0	76.3	76.4
them	47.1	41.4	40.0	38.6	40.0	66.0	46.0	46.0	52.0	56.3	52.9
they	47.1	42.9	38.6	24.3	35.4	82.0	60.0	52.0	62.0	61.3	60.0
us	62.9	48.6	52.9	50.0	52.5	64.0	54.0	54.0	58.0	57.5	56.1
Total pronouns	61.6	57.0	56.4	54.1	55.8	73.8	65.0	60.8	64.0	62.7	63.3
because	31.4	21.4	22.9	22.9	21.1	38.0	24.0	44.0	28.0	36.3	33.6
between	37.1	24.3	38.6	32.9	29.6	58.0	46.0	58.0	54.0	37.5	45.0
into	57.1	48.6	60.0	57.1	52.5	54.0	64.0	56.0	58.0	56.3	55.0
off	87.1	84.3	84.3	71.4	79.3	90.0	82.0	80.0	84.0	81.3	82.1
on	72.9	62.9	72.9	62.9	65.7	70.0	80.0	54.0	78.0	52.5	64.3
once	47.1	35.7	30.0	27.1	34.6	58.0	58.0	54.0	58.0	23.8	44.6
since	32.9	22.9	20.0	22.9	22.9	28.0	26.0	18.0	24.0	12.5	18.9
up	91.4	95.7	94.3	94.3	93.9	86.0	94.0	82.0	92.0	78.8	83.6
Total misc.	57.1	49.5	52.9	49.1	50.0	60.3	59.3	55.8	59.5	47.3	53.4

Commonality increases strikingly with grade, and this finding is generally noted (Woodrow and Lowell, 1916; Palermo and Jenkins, 1964). In Table 4.2 commonality data are summarized by grade. For *every* form class and frequency division of stimulus words, commonality increases from kindergarten to fifth grade. There are some reversals from individual fifth-grade data to college. There are no reversals when fifth-grade group data are used. The number of anomalous responses given by kindergarten children decreases with age. Familiarity of the word is an important consideration here; 5 to 10 per cent anomalous responses are given by kindergarteners to common words. As remarked in Chapter 2, a few words ("cocoon," "inquire," etc.) yield a fairly high percentage of responses that are neither syntactically nor semantically related to the stimulus word for kindergarteners, but these drop out rapidly.

A particular result of the present study is the *differential* rate of increase in commonality for stimulus words of different form classes. In Table 4.3 two analyses of variance for the two different SES groups reveal that grade, form class, and frequency are highly significant as sources of variance, and that the form class × grade interaction is significant.

TABLE 4.2. Commonality Summary in Percentages

	Grade					
				Fifth		
	Kindergarten	First	Third	Indiv.	Group	College
High-freq. nouns	25.9	29.7	47.2	54.5	37.7	52.8
Med.-freq. nouns	30.7	35.7	55.6	59.6	53.8	53.4
Low-freq. nouns	21.7	25.0	47.1	57.2	43.8	49.8
Total nouns	26.1	30.1	50.0	57.1	45.1	52.0
High-freq. adjectives	21.3	32.0	72.8	78.2	53.9	65.4
Med.-freq. adjectives	20.6	28.3	53.8	63.9	47.2	51.8
Low-freq. adjectives	20.9	27.7	50.5	69.4	52.5	61.8
Total adjectives	20.9	29.3	59.0	70.5	51.2	59.7
High-freq. verbs	17.8	21.3	46.5	57.1	47.0	52.8
Med.-freq. verbs	10.9	12.7	27.5	42.0	33.0	52.8
Low-freq. verbs	19.1	20.1	24.9	38.7	30.0	48.6
Total verbs	15.9	18.0	33.0	45.9	36.6	51.4
Adverbs	11.9	17.5	37.2	49.1	38.4	61.8
Pronouns	18.1	25.0	55.6	65.9	62.7	72.3
Miscellaneous	15.5	24.7	49.7	58.7	47.3	62.9

TABLE 4.3. Analysis of Variance for Commonality, Data Summarized Separately by SES Level (Form classes are nouns, adjectives, and verbs; grades are first, third, and fifth)

		High-SES			Low-SES		
Source of variation	d.f.	MS	F	P(F)	MS	F	P(F)
Form class	2	67,593	52.15	< .001	55,755	40.73	< .001
Frequency	2	9,586	7.40	< .01	11,568	8.45	< .01
Grade	2	127,017	98.01	< .001	126,463	92.38	< .001
IQ	1	17,138	13.22	< .01	8,042	5.87	< .05
Form class × grade	4	3,089	2.38	n.s.[b]	5,603	4.09	< .01
IQ interactions	6	2,811	—	—	2,871	—	—
Residual	36[a]	1,296			1,369		

[a] All interaction terms except IQ × G, IQ × FC, IQ × F totaled in preceding line of table are included in this residual.

[b] n.s. = not significant.

Palermo (1962) reports percentages based on the five most common responses. His data were recombined to give frequencies of the three most common responses for fifth grade and college so that they might be directly compared with the data in Table 4.2. He finds 46.1 per cent of fifth-grade children and 52.0 per cent of college persons giving the three most popular responses (for all 200 stimuli, without separation by form class). Our fifth-grade commonalities for data obtained by individual administration (Table 4.2) exceed his with the exception of medium- and low-frequency verbs but our group administration results are very close to his, the over-all commonality being 45.6 per cent. All his data were procured via group administration. Palermo's fifth-grade results are very close to his fourth-grade results (45.5 per cent), and both resemble our third-grade results obtained by individual administration. It can be seen from Table 4.2 that commonality differs markedly from one form class to another but that individual and group-procured data differ even more. Palermo's list contains about 40 per cent nouns, 19 per cent adjectives, 17 per cent verbs, 9 per cent adverbs, 7 per cent pronouns, and 9 per cent miscellaneous words. Our list is roughly equivalent in terms of adverbs, pronouns, and miscellaneous words, but contains fewer nouns (25 per cent) and more adjectives and verbs (25 per cent each) than his list.

An over-all commonality rate of 52 per cent for Palermo's college sample appears consonant with our rates for nouns and verbs, but not with our rates for adjectives and adverbs. Our college sample resembles Palermo's college sample more closely than the two grade-school groups resemble one another, especially in terms of administration, but again the list composition should be taken into account. Altogether, the degree of correspondence between Palermo's results and our own is good, and suggests that regional or geographic differences within the United States may not be large.

An additional report by Palermo (1965) summarizes results obtained by individual interview from 100 children, grades one to four inclusive, for 100 words selected from the longer list used previously with older children. Again the composition of the list (fifty-one nouns, eighteen adjectives, fourteen verbs, five adverbs, seven pronouns, five prepositions) differs from ours. When frequency of the three most popular responses is computed, there is a reversal in Palermo's figures between second and third grades (60.7 per cent vs. 58.2 per cent for girls, and 57.5 per cent vs. 55.5 per cent for boys, at second and third grades, respectively). In Table 4.2, giving commonality data by form classes for our samples over the same age range with samples matched on IQ and SES, there are no reversals. It seems likely that the reversal found by Palermo reflects the heterogeneity of his samples at various ages rather than a genuine decline between second and third grades.

To aid the reader in making commonality comparisons among various sets of data, Appendix B gives the frequency of the three most common responses to stimuli on our list that have also been used as stimuli by other workers. Specifically, data for adults and for children are given for thirty words taken from the Kent-Rosanoff list and rates from other studies are given parallel to our own. For adults three sets of data in addition to our own are given: Kent-Rosanoff (1910); Russell and Jenkins (1954); Palermo and Jenkins (1964). The correspondence is good, especially between the Palermo and Jenkins data and our own, although agreement is best for words with strong contrast responses. Also, for adults complete form class analyses are compared with data gathered by Fillenbaum and Jones (1964) for sixteen identical stimulus words. For children there are data from Woodrow and Lowell (1916), data for fourth-, fifth-, and sixth-grade samples of Palermo and Jenkins (1964), and our own data for kindergarten, first-, third-, and fifth-grade samples. Differences in the three most common responses are confined to words with low frequencies, for the most part, although commonalities in our data are much higher, no doubt because of individual administration.

Form Class Analysis of the Normative Tables

A more sensitive approach to age changes is by way of the number of matching or paradigmatic responses. This measure mirrors changes in response that are closely linked to linguistic development (Brown and Berko, 1960). In Table 4.4 percentages of matching responses (nouns in response to nouns, adjectives in response to adjectives, etc.) are given for four age levels, and an adult (college) sample is added for comparison. It is clear that matching responses increase remarkably with age over childhood. This fact has been noted before (see Ervin, 1961, for relevant citations), although previous conclusions have been based on small samples of subjects and limited samples of stimulus words.[5]

TABLE 4.4. Percentage of Paradigmatic Responses[a]

	Kinder- garten	First grade	Third grade	Fifth grade (indiv. admin.)	Fifth grade (group admin., high-IQ)	College
High-freq. nouns	56.6	59.7	65.7	72.0	72.5	69.2
Med.-freq. nouns	65.7	63.8	72.8	77.0	83.1	76.9
Low-freq. nouns	61.3	64.5	80.3	85.4	87.5	85.1
Total nouns	61.2	62.7	72.9	78.1	81.0	77.1
High-freq. adjectives	17.5	34.2	78.9	83.0	53.1	70.7
Med.-freq. adjectives	19.2	33.3	68.2	73.4	56.9	60.9
Low-freq. adjectives	13.7	27.6	64.6	79.2	56.9	65.9
Total adjectives	16.8	31.7	70.6	78.5	55.6	65.8
High-freq. verbs	18.8	22.6	60.5	68.6	60.0	58.1
Med.-freq. verbs	17.5	18.8	40.4	51.5	48.8	59.6
Low-freq. verbs	13.6	19.7	41.6	58.6	59.4	62.3
Total verbs	16.6	20.4	47.5	59.6	56.1	60.0
Adverbs	8.6	17.9	51.2	62.1	57.5	78.9
Pronouns	16.5	29.8	65.4	65.2	60.0	78.0

[a] Responses per entry are: 1,600 for kindergarten, fifth grade individual, and college samples; 2,240 for first and third grade samples; 160 for fifth-grade high-IQ group administration sample.

Table 4.4 reveals a rather startling fact: college figures are *less* than fifth-grade figures for nouns and high-frequency verbs, whether group or individual fifth-grade data are examined. (Other reversals are only seen with individual fifth-grade data.) This observation contradicts a statement often made—that adult associations are more often paradigmatic than children's—and suggests that comparing children's responses with adult responses may not be meaningful except when form classes are

[5] Palermo (1965) reports the numbers of paradigmatic responses to six form classes of stimuli for the five most frequent responses. There again is a reversal at third grade that we do not corroborate. In our Amish data, to be discussed in Chapter 6, a similar reversal at second grade was directly traced to a sample of children whose IQ's were higher on the average than samples at other ages. We suspect this accounts for Palermo's finding also.

examined separately and when due notice is taken of differences in administration procedures. Some categories do increase from fifth grade to college, particularly the less common verbs, adverbs, and pronouns. These appear to be still in the process of consolidation at ages eleven–twelve, because paradigmatics increase sharply between fifth grade and college.

A recapitulation of some other data suggests how verbs may evolve after the fifth-grade. Responses reported by Palermo and Jenkins (1964) to eight verbs of high frequency ("carry," "come," "find," "make," "see," "sit," "take," "tell"), were categorized by form class using our criteria. The percentages of paradigmatic responses are:

			Grade		
5th	6th	8th	10th	12th	College
38	40	50	47	45	50

These data suggest that verbs continue to develop until about the eighth grade. The reversal between high school and college may come from varying IQ composition of samples at these ages.

Form class of responses appears to be affected by administration procedure, especially contrast responses to adjectives, (see Chapter 3), and so both individual and group-procured data for the fifth grade have been presented in Table 4.4. When individual fifth-grade data are compared with college data for adjectives, there is a 12 per cent drop (78.5 vs. 65.8). Group fifth-grade data, on the other hand, are *below* the college figures for adjectives, and there is a 10 per cent increase from group fifth-grade data to college data. It appears that the same kind of administration procedure must be used for various age groups in forming conclusions with respect to adjectives. But, as was made clear in Chapter 3, "same kind of administration" may mean putting respondents under the same pressures. "Pressure" may differ for different kinds of respondents even though the situation is objectively the same.

Except for nouns, fifth-grade group figures for paradigmatics are surprisingly homogeneous over all form classes: 55.6 per cent, 56.1 per cent, 57.5 per cent, and 60.0 per cent for adjectives, verbs, adverbs, and pronouns, respectively. College figures do not possess the same degree of homogeneity: 65.8 per cent, 60.0 per cent, 78.9 per cent, 78.0 per cent, for the same form classes.

There is some similarity between Table 4.2 (commonality) and Table 4.4 (matching responses) for fifth-grade and college data. The two different measures display a rather similar developmental pattern. Form classes acquired late in terms of substitution-property knowledge (adverbs and pronouns) are those where the response repertoire is most restricted.

McNeill (1965) has hypothesized that a syntactic pattern appears for adults that is different from the syntactic patterns for young children. Our data are consistent with this statement, and the falling off of paradigmatic responses to nouns and high-frequency verbs between the fifth grade and college may be an indication of it. When syntactic pairs in the fifth-grade, high-IQ, group administration data are compared with the college data, verbs account for 8.3 per cent of the fifth-grade responses to nouns and 9.9 per cent of the college responses to nouns. There are also more adjective responses to nouns for college students (11 per cent vs. 8.4 per cent). For high-frequency verbs, where the developmental pattern indicates maturity by the fifth grade, there are over twice as many (18.6 per cent vs. 8.8 per cent) adverbial responses at college as at fifth grade.

It appears that new meanings continue to be attached to words long after they are firmly laid down in terms of form class. The potential pool of such meanings is huge, of course, and could support further changes along these lines throughout adulthood. To our knowledge, no one has studied changes over the adult age range, although it might be profitable to do so, since it is known that vocabulary and other verbal skills increase. (Some more complete syntactic analyses are presented in Chapter 8.)

Table 4.5 includes the data of Table 4.4 and adds the distribution of responses for form classes not matching the stimulus. Some combinations strongly suggest syntactic patterns. For instance, few adverbs are given in response to nouns and adjectives at any age (the maximum is 3.6 per cent), but adverb responses to verbs amount to 10 per cent for high-frequency verbs over the entire childhood range, and for medium-frequency verbs there are increases in adverb responses with age. The number of adverb responses is smaller for low-frequency verbs, but doubles between kindergarten and fifth grade. There is also a noticeable difference between verbs and nouns-and-adjectives as far as prepositional responses are concerned. The response rate to verbs wanes, but accounts for significant fractions of responses at kindergarten and first-grade levels.

TABLE 4.5.   Per Cents of Responses in Various Form Classes According to Stimulus Characteristics Summarized for Urban Samples

(Fifth-grade data procured by individual interview)

	N[a]	A[a]	V[a]	B[a]	P[a]	R[a]	C[a]
High-freq. nouns							
Kind.	56.6	7.8	22.2	1.9	3.4	1.9	6.2
1	59.7	9.6	20.4	2.5	2.1	1.1	4.5
3	65.7	15.0	15.2	1.8	1.3	.2	.9
5	72.0	14.6	11.7	.7	.4	.4	.2
College	69.2	14.8	12.3	2.4	.4	.3	.6
Med.-freq. nouns							
Kind.	65.7	5.0	18.8	1.0	1.8	1.6	6.1
1	63.8	8.0	19.6	.7	1.9	1.4	4.6
3	72.8	9.6	15.9	.4	.6	.1	.5
5	77.0	9.7	12.2	.2	.4	.1	.4
College	76.9	13.0	9.0	.1	.3	.1	.6
Low-freq. nouns							
Kind.	61.3	4.4	21.4	.9	2.0	1.4	8.6
1	64.5	7.7	16.9	1.2	2.0	1.4	6.4
3	80.3	5.7	9.6	1.2	1.4	.5	1.3
5	85.4	5.4	7.5	.4	.6	.2	.6
College	85.1	5.2	8.4	.0	.8	.0	.5
High-freq. adjectives							
Kind.	61.9	17.5	6.9	3.6	1.5	2.2	6.3
1	46.5	34.2	7.8	2.7	1.8	2.0	5.0
3	14.8	78.9	2.5	1.1	.5	.8	1.3
5	13.2	83.0	1.4	1.0	.0	.5	.9
College	24.5	70.7	2.6	1.4	.0	.3	.6

TABLE 4.5.   (cont.)

	N[a]	A[a]	V[a]	B[a]	P[a]	R[a]	C[a]
Med.-freq. adjectives							
Kind.	57.1	19.2	12.8	2.5	2.5	.9	5.0
1	45.5	33.3	12.1	1.9	2.2	1.0	4.0
3	22.2	68.2	6.3	1.6	.6	.3	.9
5	19.1	73.4	6.3	.8	.0	.1	.3
College	34.1	60.9	3.5	.7	.2	.1	.5
Low-freq. adjectives							
Kind.	52.2	13.7	20.5	2.8	2.4	.9	7.5
1	40.4	27.6	19.2	3.3	1.7	1.2	6.6
3	17.9	64.6	12.2	2.4	1.0	.2	1.8
5	11.5	79.2	5.6	3.0	.1	.1	.4
College	25.4	65.9	6.1	2.1	.0	.1	.4
High-freq. verbs							
Kind.	52.8	4.0	18.8	9.0	6.3	3.8	5.3
1	43.6	4.5	22.6	13.1	7.7	3.6	4.9
3	15.6	4.7	60.5	12.8	3.5	1.4	1.5
5	15.0	3.9	68.6	9.2	1.3	1.2	.8
College	17.0	1.9	58.1	18.6	2.1	2.0	.4
Med.-freq. verbs							
Kind.	49.9	5.8	17.5	3.3	6.6	9.7	7.2
1	43.5	9.9	18.8	6.6	7.4	7.3	6.5
3	23.8	12.7	40.4	9.5	6.2	4.5	2.8
5	18.8	12.0	51.5	10.0	4.1	1.9	1.7
College	20.4	4.9	59.6	7.8	2.4	4.0	.9
Low-freq. verbs							
Kind.	63.4	4.6	13.6	2.0	3.8	2.1	10.4
1	57.1	7.3	19.7	2.3	4.1	1.7	7.9
3	39.0	7.6	41.6	3.4	2.7	1.6	4.1
5	26.4	5.0	58.6	3.7	1.3	1.1	3.9
College	30.1	2.3	62.3	3.9	.5	.5	.4
Adverbs							
Kind.	35.1	8.2	31.9	8.6	8.2	1.4	6.6
1	28.1	12.1	27.8	17.9	6.3	1.5	6.5
3	10.5	19.0	15.0	51.2	1.8	.8	1.8
5	6.6	19.2	9.7	62.1	1.0	.2	1.2
College	5.1	7.3	7.2	78.9	.2	.2	1.1
Pronouns							
Kind.	43.8	3.5	27.2	1.6	16.5	.8	6.6
1	30.6	5.5	24.7	3.0	29.8	1.6	4.7
3	15.9	2.0	11.5	2.6	65.4	1.7	.8
5	21.4	2.2	6.6	3.1	65.2	.7	.8
College	14.1	1.8	4.3	1.2	78.0	.5	.2

[a] N = Nouns, A = Adjectives, V = Verbs, B = Adverbs, P = Pronouns, R = Prepositions, C = All others.

A further clue concerning the prevalence of syntactic responding can be obtained by comparing the verb responses to nouns and to adjectives (recapitulated for convenience in Table 4.6). There are many noun-verb sequences for high- and medium-frequency stimuli even at fifth-grade level, but adjective-verb combinations are unlikely. Syntactic responses decrease, then, but are *not absent* by fifth grade. One principle or the other, paradigmatic or syntactic, is governing the production of most responses by the fifth grade. Very little "random pairing" is seen. Above 93 per cent of responses to adjectives are either nouns or adjectives, representing syntactic and paradigmatic tendencies respectively. The syntactic principle appears to exert a stronger and stronger effect as time elapses between the consolidation of the form class (taken as the peak of paradigmatic responding) and the counting of syntactic responses. For high-frequency nouns, which should be consolidated earliest, adjective and verb responses together account for a little less than one-quarter of total responses at the fifth grade. Paradigmatic responses predominate in the remaining three-quarters.

TABLE 4.6.   Verb Responses to Nouns and Adjectives in Per Cents
(Based on 2,240 responses in each category—taken from Table 4.5)

	To noun stimuli			To adjective stimuli		
	High-freq.	Med.-freq.	Low-freq.	High-freq.	Med.-freq.	Low-freq.
Kindergarten	22.2	18.8	21.4	6.9	12.8	20.5
First grade	20.4	19.6	16.9	7.8	12.1	19.2
Third grade	15.2	15.9	9.6	2.5	6.3	12.2
Fifth grade	11.7	12.2	7.5	1.4	6.3	5.6

Responses to nouns are hard to interpret. The high number of noun responses to noun stimuli at kindergarten and first grade should probably not be construed as a paradigmatic response pattern, because a verb stimulus or an adjective stimulus is very likely to elicit a noun response also. A noun response is by far the most likely type of response *to any stimulus word* for preschool children. A *selective* increase in syntactic responding to high frequency nouns coincides with the increase in paradigmatic responding. From kindergarten to third grade, the number of adjectival responses to high-frequency nouns doubles. The increase in adjectival responses occurs jointly with the increase in noun responses, but both increments are modest. In contrast, verbs and all other responses to high-frequency nouns decrease steadily from the kindergarten level. The total pattern, consisting of a gradual increase in paradigmatic responses, a decrease in one kind of syntactic response (verb), and an increase in another kind of syntactic response (adjective), hints strongly of an adult syntactic pattern beginning to manifest itself, as suggested by McNeill.

There are many patterns visible in Table 4.5. At kindergarten level responses are already beginning to show strong differentiation with respect to form class. Noun responses predominate no matter what the form class of the stimulus, but the strength of this tendency varies. While over 61 per cent of responses to nouns are nouns, only 35 per cent of responses to adverbs are nouns. There is some syntactic responding to verbs, as judged from adverb, pronoun, and preposition responses. The clearest illustration of the presence of paradigmatic responses for kindergarten children is the pattern for high-frequency adjectives and verbs, as shown below:

		Response Word	
		Adj.	Verb
	Adj.	17.5	6.9
Stimulus Word			
	Verb	4.0	18.8

The nonmatching responses are probably good indicators of a basal level for unpredictable responses, and the number of matching responses (17.5 and 18.8) is much greater.[6] Even though noun responses predominate (over 50 per cent for both adjective and verb stimuli), there is a strong tendency for the remaining responses to be paradigmatic. Undoubtedly, some of the noun responses are syntactic, but these are hard to separate from the remaining noun responses. Noun responses to high-frequency adjectives are more numerous than noun responses either to high-frequency nouns or verbs (61.9 vs. 55.6 or 52.8).

Verb responses (22.2) to nouns slightly exceed verb responses to verbs (18.8) and greatly exceed verb responses to adjectives (6.9)(all high-frequency). Verb responses to adverbs are at a surprisingly high rate (31.9). In fact, the degree of patterning in the kindergarten data is altogether remarkable. Although there are many noun responses to low-frequency verbs (63.4 per cent), there are still three times as many verb responses to low-frequency verbs as there are adjective responses (13.6 vs. 4.6).

No IQ data are available for kindergarten subjects, but probably they are above average. The kindergarten group is evenly divided on SES, as are the other urban groups. The children attending kindergarten generally are favored in terms of income, because kindergartens are privately run, tuition institutions. Children attending kindergarten seemed to come from families of higher status than first-graders in the same areas. The data show great changes occurring in the year between kindergarden and first grade, but differences between kindergarteners and first-graders are probably underestimated because of the kindergarten selection.

The most striking changes between kindergarten and first grade are the increases in paradigmatic responding to adjectives and adverbs. The rate for both form classes doubles. There are also increases in matching responses to nouns and verbs, although that for nouns is minimal (from 61.2 per cent to 62.6 per cent). Adverbs begin to show a pattern that persists over the childhood period, with fewer verb responses and more adjective responses as age advances. Responses to adverbs are frequently related through a root word—"gentle" in response to "gently," for instance. The reverse is not true. Adverb responses to adjectives are exceedingly rare, and *fewer* than verb responses to adjectives in all instances. This points to an asymmetric pattern involving the root word. Adverbs in response to verbs increase by about the same factor as paradigmatic responses to verbs.

The increase in paradigmatic responses to adjectives is countered by an equal and opposite tendency in the noun responses to adjectives. All other categories of response for adjectives are fairly stable over the kindergarten-first-grade range.

These large changes between kindergarten and first grade in word categorization may partially explain Menyuk's (1964) observation that there is comparatively little growth in the use of transformations during this age period. She observes a plateau in the production of syntactic structures just at the time we observe an upsurge in appreciation of form class properties of words. It may be that progress in one phase

---

[6] The "C" responses (no response, nonsense words, etc.) for kindergarten are inversely related to frequency, and are correlated with comprehensibility of the stimulus word. They drop off sharply as age increases. Even though commonality of response at kindergarten is low, a word like "cocoon" yields a surprising number of responses that are semantically related to the stimulus.

of language development temporarily lessens progress in another phase, in the same way that a younger child, when learning to walk, may make relatively little progress in talking.

The number of noun responses to adverbs is less at every grade than the number of noun responses to adjectives, again pointing to a syntactic linkage of adjectives and nouns. Syntactic responding is *at its childhood peak* around the first- to third-grade level for most words on our list, but is still present at fifth grade. The decline in noun-verb sequences between kindergarten and first grade suggests that this combination may be a popular one at younger ages. This is, of course, impossible to observe.

The majority of responses by the fifth grade are paradigmatic, and almost all the remainder appear syntactic. There are practically no anomalous responses at this level in contrast to 5–10 per cent anomalous responses even for common words noted with kindergarteners. Response distributions by form class are extremely orderly by fifth grade.

Four-year-olds

It is hard to get associations from children under five years of age, but a small sample of four-year-olds (N = 20) was obtained (see Table 4.7). The degree of orderliness in responses is surprising. Even at this age there are 6 per cent adverb responses to verbs, and less than 1 per cent adverb responses to nouns or adjectives. Also, there are about 18 per cent adjective responses to adjectives, compared to 10 per cent adjective responses to verbs. Many sophisticated responses are already in the subjects' repertoires. For instance, to "she," "girl" is given by 20 per cent, "he" is given by 25 per cent, and these responses are the two preferred responses of older children and adults.

TABLE 4.7. Form Class of Responses in Per Cents for Four-year-old Children (N = 20)

	N[a]	A[a]	V[a]	B[a]	P[a]	R[a]	C[a]
High-freq. nouns	63.1	13.1	18.8	1.3	1.9	.6	1.3
Med.-freq. nouns	62.5	9.4	19.4	.0	1.3	3.1	4.4
Low-freq. nouns	61.3	6.9	21.3	.6	.6	3.1	6.3
Total nouns	62.3	9.8	19.8	.6	1.3	2.3	4.0
High-freq. adjectives	63.1	18.1	8.8	1.9	2.5	3.1	2.5
Med.-freq. adjectives	58.8	21.3	10.0	.6	3.1	3.8	2.5
Low-freq. adjectives	48.1	16.3	26.9	.6	1.9	1.9	4.4
Total adjectives	56.7	18.6	15.2	1.0	2.5	2.9	3.1
High-freq. verbs	35.0	9.4	20.0	10.0	13.8	9.4	2.5
Med.-freq. verbs	40.6	10.0	13.8	.6	15.6	11.9	7.5
Low-freq. verbs	41.9	10.0	16.3	7.5	8.1	3.1	13.1
Total verbs	39.2	9.8	16.7	6.0	12.5	8.1	7.7
Adverbs	26.9	13.1	41.3	4.4	6.9	1.9	5.6
Pronouns	44.4	2.5	24.4	.0	17.5	.6	10.6

[a] N = Nouns, A = Adjectives, V = Verbs, B = Adverbs, P = Pronouns, R = Prepositions, C = All others.

The data on four-year-olds may not be typical of four-year-olds generally. The twenty children in the four-year-old sample are a highly selected group, enrolled in prekindergarten in an affluent suburban area, and their parents, without exception, had at least a college education. There is also selection within the prekindergarten group on co-operativeness. Several children began the word association procedure but could not be induced to complete it. These records were discarded and replaced by records secured from more co-operative children. The four-year-old data thus must represent an extreme in development for this age, and they actually match the entire kindergarten sample rather closely.

The most obvious difference between four- and five-year-old responses and later responses is the presence of multiple word replies (see Table 7.2). There is certainly ambiguity concerning word boundaries with very young children (see Chapter 3). Another salient characteristic of four-year-old responses and responses of children in kindergarten and first grade is their obvious relation to the acoustical properties of words. Much more than older children, four-year-olds generate associations from the sound of a stimulus word. For instance, "inquire" yields "in church," probably because it is heard as "in choir"; other responses are "restore"— "building a store," "seldom"—"sell beds," "sell ice," "celery," etc. It is more surprising that the same type of response occurs to words that are very common and well understood. To "she," for instance, 35 per cent of the four-year-olds respond with "sheep" or "sheet." There is no question but what "she," "sheep" and "sheet" are contained in their vocabularies and that "she" is a word often used by four-year-olds, although it is doubtful if many understand "inquire." The tendency to generalize on an inappropriate dimension (the phonetic one) may be a troublesome phase, and may seriously interfere with central "dictionaries."

Inappropriate generalization may interfere with acquisition of language to a greater degree than is commonly suspected. For instance, to "her" one child responded "herricane," and then asked: "How come there are no himmicanes?" Another child assumed that any man called "Mr." was married, apparently because "Mrs.," a similar title, designates married women.

Another dimension along which inappropriate generalization occurs is the directional one. For instance, to "it" one child replied "That's it, folks," where the first associate is a word *preceding* the stimulus word. Rather frequently responses of young children consist of a phrase in which the stimulus word is embedded. Backward associations, aside from those occurring in phrases, are hard to identify. Syntactic responses from adults tend to move in a forward direction: "fruit"—"fly," "high"— "noon," "soft"—"sell," to take words for which there are counter examples. We do not have reverse responses: "fruit" in response to "fly" or "soft" in response to "sell" from adults. The association, besides having strength as measured by frequency, has also directionality. This forward directionality is not nearly so dominant in the four-year-old data, and responses appear to move in both directions.

It is unlikely that associations are first established in both directions and then the backward ones eliminated. Rather, we believe, that as language chunks are being internalized, instead of single words, phrases or longer segments of language may constitute a language unit. Until the word groups have been broken down into separate words, any part of the phrase elicits the remainder, whether backward or forward, and the response is like a representational response.

There is another problem that needs brief mention even though the present data do not bear on it. Besides coping with inappropriate dimensions of generalization, a child must establish constancies. Gibson (1963) points out that when children learn to recognize letters, some differences between printed letters must not be allowed to interfere with the discrimination of sameness. A capital must be recognized as such in various styles of type, when printed slightly out of position, rotated some-what around a longitudinal axis, etc. Similar perceptions of constancies, hearing the same word no matter what the pitch of the speaker's voice, or disregarding regional accents, must also be required to learn spoken language. In addition to making appropriate generalizations, the child must inhibit inappropriate generalizations.

Frequency of the Stimulus Words

Frequency is a significant source of variance in all analyses, but compared to form class its impact is small and unpredictable. Before synthesizing the findings with respect to age, we must consider the impact of familiarity (frequency) of the stimulus words.

Frequency has not been an explicit topic of study in previous normative assemblages of word associations, although it is known (Noble, 1952; Cofer and Shevitz, 1953) that high-frequency words tend to elicit more associations than low-frequency words, and that frequency is related to learning parameters (Hall, 1954; Sumby, 1963). In the analysis of Table 4.8, as in previous analyses based on commonality (Table 4.3), frequency is shown to be significant. In later analyses it turns out to be significant also.

Frequency interacts with both other major variables extracted in Table 4.8 (grade and form class), and the form-class-by-frequency breakdown and the fre-quency-by-grade breakdown are given in Table 4.9. The interactions with frequency are complex and there is no consistent trend within form classes. This is probably because the frequency dimension is not unitary. For instance, at first grade frequency must be equivalent to "comprehensibility of the stimulus," but this would not hold for

TABLE 4.8.   Analysis of Variance, Matching Responses for Frequency and Form Class Categories at Three Grade Levels
(Urban Maryland data—indiv. adminis. only—fifth-grade values adjusted)

Source of variation	d.f.	MS	F	P(F)
Grade	2	345,406	1354.5	<.001
Form class	2	234,580	919.9	<.001
Frequency	2	7,367	28.9	<.001
G × form class	4	30,750	120.6	<.001
G × frequency	4	2,940	11.5	<.001
Form class × frequency	4	15,610	61.2	<.001
Grade × form class × frequency	8	9,606	37.7	<.001
Residual	81	255		

TABLE 4.9.   Per Cents of Matching Responses Showing Frequency Interactions
(Individual administration—fifth-grade values adjusted)

Frequency of stimulus	Form class of stimulus			Frequency of stimulus	Grade		
	Nouns	Adjectives	Verbs		1	3	5
High	65.4	65.5	50.4	High	39.0	68.2	74.1
Medium	70.8	58.3	36.9	Medium	38.6	60.3	67.1
Low	76.6	57.0	40.1	Low	37.2	62.1	74.4

the higher two grades. By fifth grade, both high- and low-frequency words are producing about the same number of matching responses, whereas medium-frequency words are producing fewer than either. The modest differences associated with frequency at first grade are an indication of the relative unimportance of this variable.

Sumby (1963) speculates that high-frequency words will be associated semantically and low-frequency words associated phonetically. Insofar as our data are appropriate, this hypothesis is not borne out except for children age six and younger who give some Klang associations to words like "cocoon." Paradigmatic associates, which are semantically determined for the most part, are slightly more common with low-frequency than with high-frequency stimuli in our adult data. This is the opposite of Sumby's prediction, but our low-frequency words may not be rare enough to test his hypothesis, and our low-frequency nouns are interrelated.

With form class and frequency, the situation also seems amorphous. Low-frequency nouns elicit more paradigmatic responses than other nouns, but this word group has special properties (the "butterfly" constellation). The low-frequency nouns in this particular list will beget nouns to a greater extent than nouns from other frequency categories, because the nouns in the cluster tend to elicit one another ("moth"— "cocoon"). For verbs both comprehensibility of the stimulus and the developmental lag contaminate any simple pattern. Again variation with frequency is not linear (50 per cent, 37 per cent, 40 per cent) and no simple conclusion emerges.

Deese (1962b) states that association to nouns and high-frequency adjectives are mainly schematic (paradigmatic) while associates to adverbs, low-frequency adjectives, and verbs are more likely to be sequential (syntactic). Our data do not agree with his assertions, since adverbs *exceed* both verbs and adjectives in stimulating paradigmatic responses (see Table 4.4) at the college level, and rates are rather different for adjectives and verbs. The explanation for the contradictions between Deese's data and our own hinges on frequency. Deese sampled words at different frequency levels, divided by form class into 253 nouns, 118 adjectives, 101 verbs, and 32 adverbs. He found the frequency of syntagmatic associates (roughly the complement of our paradigmatic responses) to be smallest for nouns, largest for adverbs, and intermediate for adjectives and verbs, with all mean differences significant except that for the adjective-verb comparison.

These results do not coincide with our observations. This disagreement provokes curiosity, particularly since both Deese and the author have sampled Johns Hopkins undergraduates. In the first place, our frequency categories are much narrower than his, partly as a consequence of using the J-count rather than the G-count. Thus, a word of "A" Thorndike-Lorge frequency (his second most frequent category) sometimes by our criteria is "low-frequency." His list to be used with adults contains many relatively rare words, whereas our sampling of frequency had to be appropriate for young children and our words are mostly "high-frequency" by his criteria. The correlation that he observes between the frequency of syntagmatic associates and frequency of usage for adjectives would thus not be expected in our data.

We note the highest rate (79 per cent) of paradigmatic responding to adverbs, and this is in direct contrast to Deese's observation that adverbs yield largely syntagmatic associates. Again, this is probably a direct consequence of constriction on the frequency dimension; all our adverbs except "gently," and "loudly" are of high frequency. The root words "gentle" and "loud" are both of high frequency and have strong contrast responses, so in some ways the adverbs derived from them are high frequency too. Most low-frequency adverbs are too rare to be used with young children, i.e., "amazingly." A realistic frequency stratification for children is inappropriate for adults, and therefore our adult data are comparable only to Deese's high-frequency data.

A further classification made by Deese is of direct relevance. He classified paradigmatic associates into those in direct contrast with the stimulus and those that were not. He found that paradigmatic associates to high-frequency adjectives are much more likely to be contrasts than paradigmatic associates to low-frequency adjectives. On our list of adjectives, all but two ("yellow," "thirsty") have strong contrast responses. For this reason it is not surprising that our rates of paradigmatic responding to adjectives are higher than rates for verbs.

Our adult data are more interesting from the standpoint of changes in responses over age than in terms of absolute levels of paradigmatic responding for adults. The most provocative finding is that paradigmatic responding is *higher* for some categories of stimuli at fifth grade than at college. Concomitantly, at college level there is an increase in syntactic responses. (See noun responses to verbs and adjectives at college level.)

The amount of variance that frequency accounts for, although statistically significant far beyond conventional limits, is small compared to that accounted for by other variables. Frequency, as defined here, has little practical significance. Interactions of other variables with frequency are also statistically significant, but seem to reflect the influence of incidental variables. Since frequency has not been included before in normative studies, its inclusion deserves emphasis. It turns out, however, that very little information is gained by its inclusion.

Contrast Responses Changing with Age[7]

One of the most noticeable age changes is that involving contrasts. As stated, all adjectives but two have strong contrasts, and some nouns, verbs, and adverbs have contrasts also. This is a property of the present list of stimulus words that seems to affect results strongly.

[7] See Chapter 5 for data on contrast response changes between fifth grade and college.

Church (1961) says that very bright children may be able to give antonyms at age five, and this speculation is confirmed even in our four-year-old data. Commonality is low for such young subjects, but Table 4.10 reveals that a considerable portion of commonality in the four-year-old data is attributable to antonymic responses. Other common responses besides antonyms are syntactic responses ("long"—"pants," "quiet"—"mouse," etc.). The five-year-old sample (N = 100) reveals much the same patterns. Syntactic responses were tabulated for this same set of adjectives (Table 4.11), and with one exception these decrease from prekindergarten to kindergarten. This represents some of the most clear-cut evidence available of the appearance and then disappearance of an early syntactic phase. It suggests that a considerable part of associative development may occur prior to the ages of our youngest samples. Since the stimuli are mostly very common words, much of the phase of early syntactic responding may already have taken place prior to the time when children are old enough to be interviewed.

TABLE 4.10.   Contrast Responses to Adjectives in Per Cents for Four-year-old and Five-year-old High-SES Samples

Stimulus word	Contrast word	% Four-year-old responses (N = 20)	% Five-year-old responses (N = 100)
black	white	10	3
cold	{ hot / warm	15	15
dark	light	5	12
hard	{ easy / soft	10	6
high	low	10	10
quiet	{ noisy / loud	5	11
sad	happy	20	11
short	long	5	10
slow	fast	10	21
tall	{ little / small	25	14

TABLE 4.11.   Syntactic Responses to Adjectives in Per Cents for Four-year-old and Five-year-old High-SES Samples

Stimulus word	Four-year-olds Syntactic word	Per cent	Five-year-olds Syntactic word	Per cent
black	pencil	10	{ crayon / bird	5 / 5
cold	winter	10	winter	9
dark	night	30	night	19
hard	heart	10	{ rock / word	8 / 7
high	sky	10	sky	5
quiet	mouse	10	mouse	1
sad	cry	10	cry	7
short	pants	30	pants	15
slow	{ poke / motion / walk	10 / 10 / 10	{ poke / motion / walk	6 / 1 / 6
tall	man	15	man	10

Persons differ in their style of responding to opposite-evoking stimuli, and Carroll, *et al.* (1962) show that persons responding with opposites to opposite-evoking stimuli respond differently to nonopposite-evoking stimuli than persons resistant to the "opposite" set. Table 4.12 gives the percentages of opposite responses for three grade levels for all high-frequency words on our list that duplicate Carroll's words. It is apparent that there is a great increase in the tendency to give opposites as responses from the first to the third grade. From the third to the fifth grades there are as many decreases as increases.[8] For some adjectives, the increase between the first and third grade is about fourfold. This increase is larger than the increase in commonality noted over the same ages. All high-frequency nouns increase in total commonality from 30 per cent to 47 per cent from first to third grade, and all high-frequency adjectives increase in total commonality from 32 per cent to 73 per cent for the same age span. Actually seven of the eight high-frequency adjectives overlap Carroll's list, and these seven adjectives increase on the average from 17 per cent to 48 per cent in commonality when only contrast responses are counted. *Almost the entire increase in commonality or in paradigmatics for adjectives between ages six and eight is accounted for by the increase in contrast responses.* The three most popular responses increase 41 per cent while the opposite responses increase 31 per cent. Thus only about 10 per cent of the increased commonality is due to factors other than an increased use of opposites.

TABLE 4.12.   Contrast Responses in Per Cents According to Age

Stimulus word	Response word	Kindergarten	First grade	Third grade	Fifth grade
black	white	3.0	12.1	49.6	45.4
cold	{ hot	12.5	26.4	49.6	42.5
	{ warm	6.0	9.6	20.7	21.1
dark	light	12.5	30.4	66.1	64.3
hard	{ soft	5.0	19.7	53.2	47.9
	{ easy	2.5	3.9	14.3	19.3
high	low	8.5	21.8	63.2	63.2
long	short	4.5	20.0	63.2	58.6
man	woman	10.0	12.9	43.6	45.4
short	{ long	7.0	16.8	56.8	46.4
	{ tall	3.5	4.6	9.6	22.1

The concept of "oppositeness" is less appropriate generally for the other form classes (verbs, adverbs, etc.). Responses to adverbs suggest that often multiple word responses are given because there are no opposites that are single words. "Sometimes," for instance, can generate the response "always," but some children respond "no times."

The developmental patterns in paradigmatic responding *together* with developmental patterns in contrastive responding suggest that the evolutionary form class pattern may be more complex than has been assumed up to now. The development

[8] In Chapter 3 where administration conditions were studied, it was found that contrasts were more frequent under oral than under written conditions for fifth-grade, high-SES students, but not for a third-grade, high-IQ, high-SES sample.

of paradigmatic responses by form class is confounded with the antonymic properties of responses to adjectives.

Adjectives appear to develop more rapidly than verbs in terms of children's learning of substitution privileges, but this may reflect the fact that the concept "oppositeness" has been learned and is applied where appropriate, rather than that substitution properties of adjectives are learned sooner than substitution properties of verbs. Children *may* group words together that have similar privileges of occurrence, but they may group on the basis of other cues that are not uniformly available for all words. For an adjective which does not have a readily available contrast response the paradigmatic frequency is low, i.e., for "thirsty" the rate is 3.5 per cent, 13.9 per cent, 36.4 per cent, and 40.5 per cent for kindergarten, first, third, and fifth grades, respectively. This looks very different from "tall," with 31.0 per cent, 49.3 per cent, 89.3 per cent, and 92.0 per cent, for the same ages. This hypothesis is further strengthened by comparing two verbs, "add" which has the strong contrast response "subtract," and "move" which does not have available a strong contrast response:

	K	1st	3rd	5th
Add	15.0%	18.2%	72.5%	77.5%
Move	19.5%	22.1%	49.3%	55.5%

The change for verbs is not as early as that for adjectives, but there is a large difference in paradigmatic responses by third grade, with the verb that possesses an antonym clearly surpassing.

The assignment of form classes as an aid to analysis should not lead one to assume that *children* are using form class properties as the basis for word categorizations. The variance within any frequency and form class category is considerable. Paradigmatic responding may be a good index of development, but it may tell little about the actual process of language growth. Words within any form class category do not necessarily resemble each other in ability to call forth a paradigmatic response, even though some trends appear when responses to many words are pooled. These points will be considered again in Chapter 8.

The Pattern with Age

Clearly the development of paradigmatic response patterns does *not* begin at the same time for all words. Different form classes develop at different rates, and within a form class some words develop more rapidly than others.

It may be that every word goes through an orderly sequence of development, with the rate of progression through the sequence depending on frequency of the word and modified by a "confusion index." For instance, irregular verbs are very frequent, but must interfere with one another dreadfully, as confusion between "bring," "brang," "bringed," and "brought" testifies. Perhaps, as associations mature, a word elicits first a noun, second a syntactic response, third a paradigmatic response, and fourth a different syntactic response. An infrequent word may evolve only part of the way through this four-part sequence. Only the most frequent words may go through the entire sequence. Our data taken as a whole, together with hints from data gathered by others, suggest such an evolutionary pattern for the development of word associations. Every word appears to evolve through roughly the same stages but rates of evolution differ. Some words may evolve so slowly that they appear to be arrested at some intermediate stage of development.

Our speculation is that the rate depends on exposure modified by at least two other factors, both related to stimulus discriminability. (Frequency counts, as provided in the Lorge-Thorndike list and elsewhere, are rough measures of exposure, but may bear little relation to frequency in spoken discourse, the chief avenue of exposure for young children.) Exposure by itself is necessary but not sufficient to hasten evolution. Consider a word like "once" that appears in the phrase "once upon a time." Unless "once" is encountered in other contexts[9] there will be no opportunity to infer its meaning apart from this rather specialized context. In this case an association is likely to be the remainder of the phrase. It may be difficult under such conditions for the preliterate child to know whether a word is "once" or "onceupon." Another factor which must govern speed of evolution is the ease with which one word can be confused with another. This is partly a matter of confusion between stimuli ("they" and "them" differ by only one letter). Words like "he"—"him," "he"—"she," and "her" as object or possessive, are obviously difficult to distinguish for young children. At first grade "can" and "come" account for 6 per cent of the responses to the word "them," but disappear by the fifth grade. Often sentences in conversation take the form pronoun-verb or pronoun-verb-pronoun. No adjectives precede pronouns (unlike nouns) and this makes the context of the verb confusing.

Estimates of exposure for preliterate children (perhaps prior to the third grade) should be based on oral language. With television and radio it is likely that exposure now is much less closely related to frequency counts from written sources than was true formerly.

Our data indicate that the earliest and most primitive kind of association is a noun, no matter what the form class of the stimulus word. It may be a mistake to call these "associations" at all, however. If a four-year-old co-operative child is told to say a word after he hears an adult say a word, he emits a word that often has no semantic or other relation to the stimulus. In fact, when very young children are asked to "say a word" with no stimulus word preceding, they are very prone to say a noun. (McCarthy (1930) found nouns constituting 47 per cent of the words of eighteen-month-old children.) But even in data from four-year-olds there are some clear matching responses and some syntactic responses. It might be better, then, to regard four-year-old responses as a display of associations for some words and lack of association for others. Those that have bona fide associates are those of high frequency in terms of previous exposure. As Brown and Fraser's (1964) data for much younger children show, there may be surprisingly little overlap in the vocabularies of use of young children.

---

[9] Ervin's notion of contextual variety, closely related to this discussion, will be fully treated in Chapter 8.

At ages five and six there is considerable syntactic responding. A peak in syntactic responding is observed at these ages *for our stimulus words*, but there is still considerable syntactic responding at age ten or eleven, and there is some syntactic responding at age four. Also at first grade there is more paradigmatic responding than would be presumed on the basis of earlier reports, from 18 per cent to 60 per cent for form classes in our sample.

The tendency to give paradigmatic responses varies by form class in our data but does not seem related to any distinction between lexical and function words. For adjectives where exposure is great and which possess antonyms, there are many paradigmatics by third grade using individual interviews, but college students do not give as many paradigmatics. For less frequent adjectives, too rare to be used with young children, other investigators show many syntactic associates are given at adulthood.

These facts suggest that there may be a constant pattern for evolution of associates that is concealed by cross-sectional age sampling and by the particular words constituting the stimulus list. Suppose that associations to a word evolve as shown below:

INCREASING EXPOSURE

--→

| Anomalous (noun) | Early syntactic | Paradigmatic | Late syntactic |

All words may go through similar stages of development at a rate that depends on exposure but is modified both by discriminability of stimulus and by contextual clues. The syntactic-paradigmatic shift, pointed to by us (Entwisle, *et al.*, 1964) and others (Brown and Berko, 1960; Ervin, 1961) is thus reinterpreted. A word acquired very early like "chair" yields paradigmatics even though the subject may be four years old. Thus it is *not* that associations are a function of age of the subject, with four-year-olds giving anomalous responses, six- to eight-year-olds giving syntactic responses, and older subjects giving paradigmatics. Instead at any age all kinds of responses are found because at all ages words are being acquired and consolidated linguistically. An example of a word where the evolution is rapid is the word "hand." At first grade there is no response "give" to this word even though syntactic responses to other words are common at this age, but by fifth grade "give" appears. At adulthood, "give" accounts for 2.8 per cent of the responses. A similar pattern occurs for "flow" in response to "river." These very common nouns we presume are already well along in the paradigmatic portion of the continuum and so begin to evolve some adult type syntactic responses. But these so-called adult syntactics are of a different genre from the early syntactics based on grammatical contiguity. They are enlargements in meaning, a more flexible and richer interpretation of a concept. Thus, "bright" appears in response to "color," and "yellow" appears in response to "butterfly" for adults. The meaning of a word is interpreted less rigidly and the associative structure seems to be undergoing an enrichment process.

Additional experimental evidence indicating that associations evolve to different words at different rates is cited by Jenkins and Palermo (1964). With rare adjectives as stimuli, most responses from adults were nouns. They suggest that progressions observed with children are still proceeding with adults, although at a very advanced level. Deese's adult data, already mentioned, are also consistent with this view.

This evolution of associations will be discussed more fully and placed in theoretical context in Chapter 8.

Chapter Five

The Effects of Intelligence and Sex

In this chapter variations of word associations with intelligence will be studied. This topic has not been reported on explicitly before, although very early (Rosanoff and Rosanoff, 1913) there was evidence that association was related to mental capacity. Not surprisingly there turn out to be interactions between IQ and age and also between IQ and form class, i.e., the impact of IQ is not the same from one age to another or from one form class to another. Sex differences and the interactions between sex and IQ will also be discussed.

There are several samples matched on age and SES but of different average IQ, the largest and most important being two main urban SES groups. The numbers of subjects in various groups are recapitulated here for convenience, and only those interviewed individually will be considered. Each group is equally divided by sex.

	High-SES		Low-SES	
	High-IQ (122, or above)	Medium-IQ (95–105)	Medium-IQ (95–105)	Low-IQ (85, or less)
1st grade	70	70	70	70
3rd grade	70	70	70	70
5th grade	50	50	50	50

With marked changes in paradigmatic responses by age, it is not surprising that IQ can be related to orderly patterns in paradigmatic responding.[1] Table 5.1 summarizes

---

[1] Some measures of linguistic maturity, i.e., the number of grammatical transformations used (Menyuk, 1963), do *not* show differences associated with IQ, even when differences by age appear. This may be partly a consequence of the metric used.

76

analyses of variance *within* each main urban SES group, based on numbers of match-ing responses. For the high-SES group, subjects of high- and medium-IQ are in-cluded; for the low-SES group, subjects of medium- and low-IQ. It was impos-sible to obtain[2] three IQ levels within each SES grouping. The parallel analyses yield very similar results, with IQ accounting for significant variance within each group. The IQ difference attains a somewhat higher significance level in the high-SES group. This finding accords with intuition (IQ differences in the high-SES group are larger on the average [30 points] than in the low-SES group [20 points]). There is no way, therefore, to determine whether a specific IQ difference, say twenty points, exerts more influence on children of one SES grouping than on another.

TABLE 5.1. Analysis of Variance, Matching Responses, for High- and Low-SES Groups of First, Third, and Fifth Grades

(Individual administration)

Source of variance	d.f.	High-SES			Low-SES		
		MS	F	P(F)	MS	F	P(F)
IQ	1	10,330	7.03	≈.01	8,066	4.99	<.05
Grade	2	157,622	107.30	<.001	188,113	116.26	<.001
Form class	2	104,483	71.12	<.001	130,699	80.78	<.001
IQ × G	2	713	—	—	2,199	1.36	—
IQ × FC	2	1,487	1.01	—	1,328	—	—
G × FC	4	16,030	10.91	<.01	16,709	10.33	<.01
IQ × G × FC	4	1,672	1.14	—	838	—	—
Residual	36	1,469			1,618		

Some notion of the magnitude of differences associated with IQ can be obtained from Table 5.2, showing percentages of matching responses for all the form classes by IQ-SES groups. Because of the grade × form class interaction (see Table 5.1), the influence of IQ is most noticeable at points of change. Consider adjectives, where perhaps the grade distribution is optimal for revealing changes. At kindergarten roughly the same number of matching responses is observed for both adjective and verb stimuli (about 17 per cent), probably a basal level for paradigmatic responding to stimuli of both these form classes. That the figure does not change from four-year-old to kindergarten level is another indication that this is a minimum. By first grade there is a noticeable increase in paradigmatic responses to adjectives that is very orderly by IQ strata. The lowest IQ group shows an increase from about 17 per cent to about 22 per cent. The average IQ groups show much greater increases in para-digmatic responding to adjectives, to a rate of about 30 per cent, nearly doubling in one year. For the highest IQ group the change is even larger, being 46 per cent by first grade. Almost exactly the same trends prevail for pronouns between IQ strata at first grade.

---

[2] The correlation between the neighborhood of a school and the IQ level of its population was remarkable. In one school with about 200 children in fifth grade, we could not locate ten boys with IQ's in the 95–105 range. Most were much higher than this. The same correlation was noticeable in schools of low-SES neighborhoods, but in the opposite direction, high-IQ children being rare.

TABLE 5.2.   Percentage of Paradigmatic Responses Summarized for Age × IQ × SES Groups[a]

| | Kindergarten | | First grade | | | | Third grade | | | | Fifth grade[b] | | | |
| | High-SES | Low-SES | High-SES | | Low-SES | | High-SES | | Low-SES | | High-SES | | Low-SES | |
			High IQ	Med. IQ	Med. IQ	Low IQ	High IQ	Med. IQ	Med. IQ	Low IQ	High IQ	Med. IQ	Med. IQ	Low IQ
HFN	52.0	61.4	62.0	63.0	56.6	57.2	65.7	64.1	65.4	65.9	70.5	73.8	72.3	68.8
MFN	59.8	71.4	68.2	65.5	61.8	59.6	73.9	71.4	71.6	72.5	78.0	74.5	76.1	77.0
LFN	57.1	65.4	70.2	66.6	58.7	62.3	85.0	80.0	82.3	73.8	89.3	86.3	83.0	83.0
Tot. noun	56.3	66.1	66.8	65.1	59.0	59.7	74.8	71.8	73.1	70.7	79.3	78.2	77.1	76.3
HFA	17.3	17.9	46.3	32.7	35.0	23.0	81.1	79.1	83.2	72.3	86.8	81.3	78.6	85.5
MFA	19.1	19.5	47.1	30.7	30.3	25.0	71.6	69.1	69.6	62.3	75.0	73.2	74.3	71.3
LFA	13.8	13.4	43.8	24.5	25.0	17.1	69.8	65.9	67.0	53.7	81.1	80.0	81.4	74.5
Tot. adj.	16.7	16.9	45.7	29.3	30.1	21.7	74.2	71.4	73.3	62.8	81.0	78.2	78.1	77.1
HFV	17.9	19.8	25.5	22.1	21.4	21.3	68.6	60.5	63.0	49.8	71.8	69.8	64.5	66.1
MFV	19.1	16.1	21.1	19.3	16.8	18.2	51.1	37.3	42.1	31.1	60.7	51.4	48.6	45.2
LFV	13.2	13.9	20.7	22.0	17.9	18.2	51.8	44.5	44.6	25.5	67.3	59.5	58.0	49.5
Tot. verb	16.7	16.6	22.4	21.1	18.7	19.2	57.1	47.4	49.9	35.5	66.6	60.2	57.0	53.6
Adverbs	9.8	7.3	30.9	15.5	16.4	8.8	63.0	50.2	49.1	42.7	70.0	65.2	59.8	53.6
Pronouns	16.6	16.4	43.0	30.2	27.0	19.1	64.6	67.3	64.8	64.6	72.0	63.6	57.5	67.7

[a] See Tables 2.2, 2.3, and 2.4 for definitions of socioeconomic and IQ sample divisions.

[b] Data from group and individual administration are combined here.

During the year between kindergarten and first grade, then, at about the time the child passes his sixth birthday, there is rapid development of paradigmatics to adjectives and pronouns, and the rate of development is highly correlated with the general intelligence of the child. For children of high intelligence the rate of paradigmatic responding to adjectives increases from 17 per cent to 46 per cent in one year. Instead of responding to words on the basis of syntactic linkages, on basis of sound alone, or most primitively, by giving a noun, these children have advanced rapidly in understanding similar privileges of occurrence and in semantics, particularly contrasts. The filing system for adjectives seems to be reorganized at about this age.

By third grade, IQ differences no longer are associated with large differences in paradigmatic responding to adjectives. The rate of paradigmatic responding is 63 per cent for the lowest-IQ group and escalates to 74 per cent for the highest-IQ group. Both these percentages exceed that noted for the high-IQ first-graders (46 per cent). The medium-IQ groups are in between, at about 70 per cent. By fifth grade, the lowest-IQ group has surpassed the highest-IQ group of third grade, and an asymptote close to 80 per cent appears to be the rule. Changes from the third to fifth grade are much smaller than from first to third grade.

The strong relation between adjectival paradigmatic responding and IQ over a restricted age range is hardly surprising. It is an example of the kind of phenomenon which allows intelligence scales to be developed in terms of age changes. To see correlates of intelligence in linguistic development, one must analyze data over a suitable age range. Children sampled before or after a change takes place may contribute only "noise" to the data. The matter of looking in an appropriate place for differences will be further pointed up in the sex analysis.

The trends in paradigmatic responses to verbs are similar to trends for adjectives but occur at later ages. The pace of verb development is slower and the ultimate asymptote is lower. There is a small increase in paradigmatic responding to verbs from kindergarten to first grade, and as noted earlier, paradigmatic responses to verbs are about equal to paradigmatic responses to adjectives at kindergarten level (17 per cent). At first grade paradigmatic responses to verbs vary only slightly with IQ, from 19 per cent for the lowest group to 22 per cent for the highest group.

From the first to the third grade there is a marked increase in paradigmatics to verbs, and, as was true for adjectives, IQ differences are accentuated at the phase of most rapid change. More specifically, Table 5.2 indicates paradigmatic responding to verbs at rates of 36 per cent for the lowest group, 48 per cent for the average group, and 57 per cent for the high-IQ group. The rate at third grade for high-IQ students is *not* attained by the low-IQ group at fifth grade (as was true for adjectives). One interpretation is that an IQ differential of fifty points (130 vs. 78) is equivalent to more than two developmental years at this age. Compared to adjectives, changes associated with verbs are less dramatic and more widely spaced, and the differences between the various IQ groups persist longer. Again differences associated with IQ are not uniform across all ages, but are much greater around the third-grade level than elsewhere. The low-SES, medium-IQ group at fifth grade is at about the same stage of development for verbs as the high-SES, high-IQ, third-grade group.

It is possible that the rate for verbs continues to increase substantially over the next two to three years, say to ages twelve or thirteen. Our data here are equivocal. When fifth-grade group administered data are compared with college data (see Table 4.4) there is almost no difference between percentages for high- and low-frequency verbs. The medium-frequency verbs change by 10 per cent. Probably a maximum of about 60 per cent is reached for all verbs at some age intermediate between fifth grade and college, and earlier some data of Palermo and Jenkins (1964) were cited that lead to this conclusion.

Noun responses generally show the least change, and so it is not surprising that nouns also show the least variation concomitant with IQ. The ubiquity of noun responses (see Entwisle, *et al.*, 1964) makes it difficult to evaluate paradigmatic responding to nouns, and as mentioned earlier, for young children the most frequent form class for responses to any stimulus word is the noun class. Anomalous responses, bearing neither a syntactic nor a semantic relation to the stimulus word, are almost always nouns if they have no acoustic similarity. For instance, with four-year-olds "book," "breakfast," "dress," "light," are responses to "swift." There is a regular increase in paradigmatic responding to nouns from kindergarten to fifth grade (Table 4.5), but the change, from about 60 to about 80 per cent over the six-year age span, is the smallest change for any form class. Differences associated with IQ are orderly and in the anticipated direction, but small (7 per cent at first grade, 5 per cent at third grade, and 3 per cent at fifth grade). In terms of linguistic information, nouns are the least interesting of the form classes, and the preoccupation of association research over many years with the Kent-Rosanoff list, so heavily loaded with high-frequency nouns, is unfortunate.

In a different kind of language study Chotlos (1944) found significant differences associated with IQ. Large written samples procured from pairs of children of different IQ levels showed that type-token ratios for nouns, adjectives, verbs, and adverbs vary with IQ. Usage of adjectives and adverbs, but not nouns and verbs, continued to increase with age. His subjects ranged in age from ten years ten months to fifteen years and ten months, ages just above those included in the present study. Thus, although IQ differences in associative responses to the particular words on our list may tend to decrease or be eliminated with advancing age, other kinds of differences in language associated with IQ may persist.

Commonality most often, but not always, increases with age. For example, the percentage of individuals responding "chair" to "table" increases from 30 per cent at age four to 58 per cent at the fifth-grade level, but for other words commonality may *decrease*. Commonality data show a marked trend related to intelligence, with higher IQ associated with larger commonalities (summarized in Table 5.3). This association is most noticeable at lower ages and diminishes by the fifth-grade. Within SES groups, there is noticeably higher commonality for children of higher IQ (Table 5.3).[3] Because of the correlation between SES and IQ, what are commonly called "status differences" in language usage may actually reflect IQ differences. Commonality has been linked to cognitive tasks such as problem solving (Johnson, 1964) and concept manipulation (Thysell and Schultz, 1964), with higher commonality associated with superior performance.

TABLE 5.3.　　Commonality Comparisons in Per Cents for IQ and SES Groups
(Rates are combined for nouns, adjectives, and verbs of all frequencies)

	First grade		Third grade		Fifth grade	
	(N=280)		(N=280)		(N=200)	
	High-IQ	Med.-IQ	High-IQ	Med.-IQ	High-IQ	Med.-IQ
High-SES	37.2	26.7	55.2	50.1	63.1	59.4
	Med.-IQ	Low-IQ	Med.-IQ	Low-IQ	Med.-IQ	Low-IQ
Low-SES	29.1	22.0	50.3	43.7	54.0	54.7

Palermo and Jenkins (1963) find increasing commonality in a wide variety of association studies carried out with many kinds of subjects over a wide span of years. In general modern groups have much higher commonality of response than early groups. The most noticeable difference between data of Woodrow and Lowell (1916) gathered fifty years ago from children ages nine to twelve, and modern data for children the same age, is the late appearance (or lack) of paradigmatic responses, but also commonality for modern groups is higher. Mass media and other accompaniments of modern life may be responsible for this, although it is hard to see why "salt" should elicit "pepper" only 3 per cent of the time in 1916, and 44 per cent now in subjects of the same age. The "chair" response to "table" appears in the Kent-Rosanoff data (1910) for adults at a rate of 29 per cent, approximately the same rate as for modern four-year-olds. These differences will be discussed more fully in Chapter 7.

[3] In Chapter 6 SES differences will be discussed.

Sex

To simplify the presentation, analyses so far have not included a sex breakdown. The chief finding in terms of sex (Tables 5.4 and 5.5) is that boys lag behind girls in verbal development, a fact widely documented in other sources and from other kinds

TABLE 5.4. Analysis of Variance, Urban Samples, Matching Responses—First, Third, and Fifth Grades—for Nouns, Adjectives, and Verbs

(1962–63 data)

Source of variation	d.f.	MS	F	P(F)
Form class	2	64,500	449.79	< .001
Grade	2	85,693	597.98	< .001
IQ plus SES[a]	3	5,628	39.28	< .001
Sex	1	28	—	—
F × G	4	7,013	48.90	< .001
F × Sex	2	144	—	—
G × IQS	6	598	4.17	< .001
G × Sex	2	111	—	—
IQS × Sex	3	185	1.29	—
F × G × Sex	4	240	1.67	—
G × IQS × Sex	6	144	—	—
Residual	180	143.40		

[a] High and medium IQ at high SES, medium and low IQ at low SES. This variance is extracted to increase the precision of this analysis, but analyses in terms of these two variables are presented elsewhere. (See Table 5.1 and Chapter 6.)

TABLE 5.5. Sex Differences in Paradigmatic Responses of First-Grade Children—Analysis of Variance. Urban First Grade Samples, Matching Responses for Nouns, Adjectives, and Verbs

(1962–63 data)

Source of variation	d.f.	MS	F	P(F)
Form class	2	43,673	713.49	< .001
IQ plus SES[a]	3	2,668	43.59	< .001
Sex	1	177	2.89	.10
F × IQS	6	815	13.31	< .001
F × Sex	2	232	3.79	< .05
IQS × Sex	3	254	4.15	< .05
Form Class × IQS × Sex	6	56	—	—
Residual	48	61		

| | First grade, matching responses in percentages | | | |
| | High-SES | | Low-SES | |
	High-IQ	Med.-IQ	Med.-IQ	Low-IQ
Males	44.4	39.8	34.4	31.8
Females	49.7	36.4	35.4	35.2

| | First grade, matching responses in percentages | | |
	Nouns	Adjectives	Verbs
Males	63.0	31.1	18.7
Females	61.3	33.2	23.0

[a] High and medium IQ at high SES, medium and low IQ at low SES. This variance is extracted to increase the precision of this analysis, but analyses in terms of these two variables are presented elsewhere. (See Table 5.1 and Chapter 6.)

of data. This lag in terms of our measures is *temporary*, however, and surprisingly slight. Table 5.4 presents an analysis of variance based on the number of matching (paradigmatic) responses given to nouns, adjectives, and verbs at three grade levels. Principal interest here attaches to sex, other variables having been discussed previously. There is no effect attributable to sex, either by itself or in interaction with other variables.

Since sex differences are usually more noticeable the younger the child, first-grade data were further examined. Within SES and IQ groups, sex differences are prominent (see lower part, Table 5.5). Except for the high-SES, high-IQ sample, females show a remarkable constancy in terms of matching responses, with a rate close to 35 per cent. Males, on the other hand, show a decreasing rate across the SES-IQ groupings. An analysis of variance based on only first-grade results shows that this sex × subsample interaction is significant (Table 5.5). There is also a form class × sex interaction, manifesting itself in a manner that could be guessed from trends noted earlier—females are somewhat accelerated compared to males in giving adjectival responses, and considerably accelerated in giving verb responses.

At ages four and five sex differences appear that are large in relative terms, but small in absolute magnitude. At these ages primitive noun responses tend to mask other trends. Percentages of matching responses for ages four (N = 20) and five (N = 160) are summarized separately by sex in Table 5.6. A difference of eight percentage points, as in the kindergarten data for adjectives, is relatively large. In the four-year-old responses, males are giving more paradigmatics to adjectives and verbs than females. In fact, four-year-old males exceed the kindergarten females. Very few subjects were tested at this age, however (only ten), so it seems hazardous to press conclusions from these data.

TABLE 5.6.   Percentages of Matching Responses

(1962–63 data)

| | Age 4 (N = 20) | | Kindergarten (N = 160) | |
	Male	Female	Male	Female
Nouns	60.8	63.8	59.8	59.1
Adjectives	22.5	14.6	13.8	21.6
Verbs	21.7	11.7	15.9	18.6

Effects attributable to sex are surprisingly small. Our results are consistent with Menyuk's (1964) report of negligible sex differences in the usage of all grammatical structures for preschool and first-grade children and Berko's (1958) finding that kinds of grammatical structures (adding "s" to form the third person singular of verbs, the possessive, and the plurals of nouns) show age trends, but no differences between boys and girls. Paradigmatic responding may be a more sensitive measure than use of grammatical transformations because so many more data-units can be generated from a given number of emitted words. These small sex differences at the youngest ages suggest that the form class developmental sequence is the same for boys and girls of similar IQ and SES level, except for a slight acceleration just before first grade.

Sex differences are not entirely absent for older subjects, however. Palermo (1962) notes consistent sex differences in commonality recalculated to include the three most popular responses (Table 5.7). Females give more common responses, and males give a greater number of different responses. The difference between the sexes is one based on idiosyncratic responses rather than one based on males giving a relatively larger number of moderately popular responses, as both his data and our data show. The differences in paradigmatic responses occur only at first grade, but there is *greater commonality* displayed by females at all ages. Table 5.8 shows (for high-frequency nouns, adjectives, and verbs) how consistently females exceed males in commonality. The differences by fifth grade, however, are small, especially in terms of percentages, varying from about 1 per cent for nouns to about 4 per cent for adjectives.

TABLE 5.7.   Commonality Percentages from Palermo (1962), for the Three Most Common Responses

	Fourth grade	Fifth grade	College
Male	43.8	44.5	50.2
Female	47.1	47.8	53.8

TABLE 5.8.   Commonality for High-Frequency Words for the Two Sexes Separately

(1961–62 data)

	Male	Female
First grade (N = 80)		
High-frequency nouns	28.5	33.1
High-frequency adjectives	28.5	34.2
High-frequency verbs	20.8	26.0
Third grade (N = 80)		
High-frequency nouns	41.7	49.6
High-frequency adjectives	63.8	75.6
High-frequency verbs	44.8	49.4
Fifth grade (N = 160)		
High-frequency nouns	46.9	47.8
High-frequency adjectives	66.8	70.8
High-frequency verbs	50.3	51.9

What is more interesting is that the shape of the distribution for the two sexes appears to differ and this difference is *maintained* at least through the fifth grade. Even though differences in commonality for the two sexes decrease with age, the boys continue to give many more unique responses. One might think that a common response for girls would be a less common response for boys, but that boys would have their own favorite response. This does not seem to be true—rather the common responses are equally favored by the two sexes, but for boys there is less commonality for relatively infrequent words. To give an example: for fifth grade "table" elicits fourteen responses from girls that are not selected by boys. However, "table" elicits twenty-one responses from boys that are not selected by girls. With only high-frequency words being considered, there is no reason to think lack of comprehension is causing this difference.

There is considerably more information on sex differences in association responses for adults (mostly college students), than for children (Schellenberg, 1930; Wyatt, 1932; Terman and Miles, 1936; Tresselt, Leeds, and Mayzner, 1955; Palermo and Jenkins, 1965b). The consensus is that females tend to give more common responses, and that differences are most noticeable for low-frequency responses. Palermo and Jenkins report statistically significant sex differences in paradigmatic responding as far as *primary* responses are concerned. We find (Table 5.9) that college females exceed college males in paradigmatic responding for every form class except pronouns, although the differences are not large. (Palermo and Jenkins' analysis is confined to popular responses only.) Thinking that sex differences might be less noticeable for high-frequency words, we compared low-frequency nouns, adjectives, and verbs separately. The figures, males given first, are: nouns, 86 per cent, 84 per cent; adjectives, 64 per cent, 68 per cent; verbs, 60 per cent, 63 per cent. The differences here (except for nouns) are somewhat less pronounced, but as noted earlier (Chapter 4), the frequency categories are probably not suitable for adult respondents. Sex differences in paradigmatic responding may be accentuated for rare words, but the present stimulus list does not contain words suitable for investigating this.

TABLE 5.9.   Sex Differences in College Responses

(Percentages)

Syntactic responses	Hopkins (male) students	Goucher (female) students
Nouns in response to adjectives	81.0	84.0
Adverbs in response to verbs	28.0	22.0
Paradigmatic responses		
Nouns	76.9	77.2
Adjectives	63.4	68.2
Verbs	57.0	62.9
Adverbs	75.9	82.0
Responses to pronouns		
Nouns in response to pronouns	8.0	20.1
Pronouns in response to pronouns	82.0	74.0

There are some *increases* in syntactic responding between fifth grade and college, but no consistent sex trends in the syntactic responses of adults. Table 5.9 shows that pronouns are reversed in sex dominance compared with other form classes. This reversal perhaps implies a more sophisticated categorization of pronouns by females, but the exact interpretation is not clear. Besides giving fewer pronoun responses to pronouns, females give many more noun responses to pronouns than males.

As mentioned in Chapter 3, there are sizable sex differences in contrast responses to adjectives, shown for fifth grade and college in Table 5.10. On the average, females give 50.2 per cent (fifth grade) and 44.7 per cent (college) contrast responses to adjectives, while males give 46.8 per cent and 40.9 per cent at the same respective ages. This difference favoring females is sufficient to account for the differences in paradigmatic percentages by sex (see Table 5.9) for adjectives. This suggests again that the same instructions generate more "pressure" for females than for males.

TABLE 5.10. Contrast Responses to Adjectives in Per Cents, Males vs. Females, at Fifth Grade and College Levels

Stimulus	Response	Fifth grade (Indiv. admin.)		College (Group admin.)	
		M	F	M	F
bitter	sweet	19	25	64	57
black	white	53	53	62	54
bright	dark, dull	28	34	16	19
clean	dirty	46	48	36	37
cold	hot, warm	66	69	59	50
dark	light	66	70	58	58
hard	easy, soft	76	71	58	65
high	low	60	68	51	67
long	short	61	67	51	59
loud	quiet, soft	40	46	48	44
pleasant	unpleasant	17	19	5	14
pretty	ugly	32	46	12	26
quiet	loud, noisy	56	54	31	32
rough	smooth	30	26	23	33
sad	happy	61	64	45	48
short	long, tall	73	73	58	67
slow	fast	74	81	59	71
smooth	rough	37	38	32	47
sour	sweet	31	46	38	42
swift	slow	5	7	8	7
tall	short, small	64	67	72	67
wild	tame	34	32	14	19
Average		46.8	50.2	40.9	44.7

In summary, the differences associated with sex are small, and for this list of words the developmental rate for boys and girls is the same except for a slight acceleration at kindergarten—first grade. The same cannot be said for IQ. It exerts a strong influence continuing even to the fifth grade for verbs and adverbs, the form classes consolidated last. Differences for adverbs are six percentage points within one SES level, and five percentage points within the other. Differences for verbs are similar. Other form classes are strongly affected by intelligence at earlier ages. The size of the effects attributable to IQ makes it clear that associates gathered from young children cannot be studied in relation to age unless the IQ composition of cross-sectional samples is known. The differences associated with intelligence are large enough to distort or obscure age differences. In comparing the present data with adult data gathered from college students, it is probably wise to use the high-IQ, fifth-grade, group administration data.

Chapter Six

Socioeconomic, Rural-Urban, and Subcultural Differences[1]

A perennial concern of the social scientist is the extent to which findings may be generalized. Are observations of college sophomores typical also for adults more generally? Are measurements made on children in suburban schools applicable to slum children, rural children, Negro children, or others? Easily accessible persons may not be representative of populations of interest or of larger populations. Little attention has so far been paid to this matter in word association research.

Our finding that administration procedures affect middle- and lower-class children differently (Entwisle and Forsyth, 1963, Chapter 3) underscores the danger in casual generalization over sociologic groups. One of the principal aims of this research has been to try to supply evidence on the extent to which children's word associations vary between different subcultures or with different places of residence. Sociolinguistics, a "nascent interdisciplinary pursuit" (Pietrzyk, 1964), is less than a decade old and so far relatively little attention has been paid to sociological differences in language development. (See also, Useem, 1963.)

Evidence about word associations for different sociologic groups is sparse, and it is also equivocal. A very early study (Mitchell, *et al.*, 1919) reports that Negro children lag behind white children when age trends in responses are compared, and John and Goldstein (1964) report lags, for lower class Negro children (age four) in action words and in words related to rural living. Yet John elsewhere (1963) reports minimal differences in word associations between middle class and lower-lower class Negroes in somewhat older children. (The improvement in Negro educational opportunity over forty-five years may explain the difference between John's recent finding and Mitchell's earlier findings.) Differences by social class *are* found on other measures of

---

[1] Portions of this chapter have appeared in *Sociometry*, see Entwisle (1965b).

conceptual development, however (John, 1963), and by fifth grade, being a member of the lower class is associated with poor performance.

In countries where class demarcations are more rigid, language differences by social class have been reported and appear larger than those in the United States. For instance, in England, Bernstein (1960, 1962) finds differences in language between upper and lower class children. In France Rosenzweig (1964) finds large differences between French construction workers and French students, but much smaller differences between Americans of similar occupations. There are methodologic questions, too numerous and too complicated to enumerate here, that one can raise with respect to all these studies. The most obvious is lack of control of some kind of IQ measure, because large differences associated with intelligence are found in all our samples of children. Often in sampling populations, intelligence and social status are confounded, and this could lead to attributing differences to social class that are at least partly owing to differences in intellectual level. Nevertheless, social class, or race membership, or national origin plus social class, seem to have some impact on language development, because data to be described in this chapter show that there is considerable variation in linguistic development between American subcultures when IQ is held constant.

Practically nothing is known about the transmission of linguistic habits from one generation to the next. In some societies there is a formalized system of baby talk (Ervin and Miller, 1963). The wide differences in linguistic usage between social classes must be initiated early in life, and recent research already cited (John, Bernstein) sheds some light on this. As will be seen, our data support the conclusion that some subcultural groups within the United States may be retarded in basic language development by as much as two years. This is not a matter of an enhanced vocabulary or a more elegant and grammatical manner of speaking. It is a matter of acquiring fundamental concepts about words that will permit simple communication—in knowing that substitution properties are possessed by adjectives and verbs, for instance.

In an attempt to broaden the base of word association studies in the United States in terms of specific target populations, we have sought out and studied several groups of children who depart in some respect from the suburban prototypical subject: children of blue-collar workers, rural children, Amish children. A future project will study Negro and white slum children. Sampling these groups also helps outline the natural process of linguistic development because, as will be seen, children from different places develop at different rates. Development of associative patterns is so rapid in some groups, like the high-SES, high-IQ groups already described, that the importance of a particular developmental phase or its pattern over time might be clouded. For instance, the childhood syntactic phase appears and then disappears so rapidly that it is hard to study. With children whose language development is not so rapid the phases are more prolonged and are thus more clearly visible.

We will first describe differences in word association development according to socioeconomic level (SES) of two large Maryland urban groups. Later appropriate fractions of these urban groups are compared with rural samples matched on average

IQ. Rural samples will be further compared with samples of Old Order Amish children, who live in a subculture apart from the mainstream of modern America.

Two Maryland Urban Groups of Different Socioeconomic Status

The two main urban samples, whose place of residence puts them in different socioeconomic classes, each contain 210 children of average IQ (95–105) who attend schools under the same jurisdiction. On several measures the higher-SES sample may be contrasted with the lower: median family income, $9,171 vs. $6,219; highest grade completed by father 14.7 vs. 10.3; percentage of fathers employed in manufacturing industry, 33.0 per cent vs. 66.2 per cent; per cent migrant persons, 50.2 per cent vs. 14.3 per cent (for details see Chapter 2). In brief, the comparison is roughly between high white-collar and blue-collar groups. We have already pinpointed differences in language development associated with different intelligence levels when SES is held constant. Now we are about to look for language differences in children from socioeconomic groups whose social customs or child-rearing practices may vary.

The percentages of paradigmatic responses given by students from three grade levels, all of *average IQ*, but from different SES groups are presented in Table 6.1. If one considers only the *direction* of the difference for totals (total nouns, total adjectives, etc.) associated with the five form classes, there are ten out of fifteen comparisons in which the high-SES children exceed the low-SES children (a one-tailed sign test with continuity correction indicates this difference is not significant).

TABLE 6.1.   Percentage of Paradigmatic Responses—Two Maryland Urban Groups of Differing SES, Matched on IQ (At middle level, 95–105, inclusive—taken from Table 5.2)

Form class of stimulus word	Grade 1		Grade 3		Grade 5	
	High-SES	Low-SES	High-SES	Low-SES	High-SES	Low-SES
High-freq. nouns	63.0	56.6	64.1	65.4	73.8	72.3
Med.-freq. nouns	65.5	61.8	71.4	71.6	74.5	76.1
Low-freq. nouns	66.6	58.7	80.0	82.3	86.3	83.0
Total nouns	65.1	59.0	71.8	73.1	78.2	77.1
High-freq. adjectives	32.7	35.0	79.1	83.2	81.3	78.6
Med.-freq. adjectives	30.7	30.3	69.1	69.6	73.2	74.3
Low-freq. adjectives	24.5	25.0	65.9	67.0	80.0	81.4
Total adjectives	29.3	30.1	71.4	73.3	78.2	78.1
High-freq. verbs	22.1	21.4	60.5	63.0	69.8	64.5
Med.-freq. verbs	19.3	16.8	37.3	42.1	51.4	48.6
Low-freq. verbs	22.0	17.9	44.5	44.6	59.5	58.0
Total verbs	21.1	18.7	47.4	49.9	60.2	57.0
Total adverbs[a]	15.5	16.4	50.2	49.1	65.2	59.8
Total pronouns[a]	30.2	27.0	67.3	64.8	63.6	57.5

[a] Based on eight stimulus words.

The differences associated with SES are small, moreover, except perhaps for nouns at first grade, adverbs at fifth grade, and pronouns generally. The low-frequency nouns ("cocoon," "bee," "bug," "insect," etc.) are used in specialized situations, the kinds of situations higher-SES children may encounter and lower-SES children may not. (John and Goldstein [1964] note that words encountered in rural environments are difficult for children of this age.)

A parametric analysis (Table 6.2) of paradigmatic responses given to nouns, adjectives, and verbs re-emphasizes the conclusion that SES effects are very small. SES by itself, or in interaction with any other variable, is not significant.[2] There may be slightly accelerated language development for children from upper middle class homes compared to lower middle or lower class homes when intelligence is held constant, but this is probably an *acceleration* only. At fifth grade the only differences greater than 5 per cent are for adverbs and pronouns. The particular words included in this study are common words that are learned early. Evidence already presented shows that the nouns and adjectives, as well as some verbs, are fully developed in terms of paradigmatic responses prior to fifth grade. Use of complex grammatical structures, or other skills not considered here, might show SES differences. Differences do remain at fifth-grade level for verbs, adverbs, and pronouns, the form classes more slowly developed. With children two to three years older, we suspect that these small differences would not persist because by then asymptotic levels of paradigmatic responding are probably reached for all form classes.

TABLE 6.2. Analysis of Variance for Two Urban SES Groups Matched on IQ. Paradigmatic Responses for Nouns, Adjectives, and Verbs.

Source of variation	d.f.	Mean square	F	P(F)
Form class	2	114,921	254.25	< .001
Frequency	2	4,606	10.19	< .01
Grade	2	183,399	405.75	< .001
SES	1	389	—	—
Fo × Fr	4	7,231	16.00	< .01
Fo × G	4	16,726	37.00	< .01
Fo × S	2	146	—	—
Fr × G	4	1,792	3.96	< .05
Fr × S	2	132	—	—
G × S	2	489	1.08	—
Residual	29	452		

These negative results in terms of SES require cautious interpretation, with due notice taken of the children who were sampled. None of the subjects resembles slum dwellers in terms of cultural deprivation. The median salary for fathers in the lower-SES group is about $6,200 (estimated from 1960 census), a figure far above a bare subsistence level. Incomes of the urban Negro families in Maryland, by contrast, average about $3,300. We have no data for groups experiencing this degree of economic deprivation. The slight differences here linked to SES do not necessarily imply that only slight differences would be found if children from the lowest-SES

[2] Note that five out of six differences for adverbs and pronouns favor the higher status group. Adverbs and pronouns are not included in the analysis given in Table 6.2.

levels were tested. In other words, a slight difference in language development may accompany what is a relatively slight degree of cultural and economic deprivation.

When middle and lower-lower class Negroes are compared (John, 1963) consistent class differences in language skills emerge between groups of children from the same subculture but of different socioeconomic class. A serious warning must be given here, however, for it is problematic whether differences recorded in performance represent true deficits or reflect instead methodologic factors. We have already seen with fifth-grade students from two SES levels that it was not SES level per se which was directly linked to higher rates of paradigmatic responding or to higher commonality figures. Rather it was the differing reaction to the test situation on the part of children from different social backgrounds that produced the difference. (John points to the fact middle class children seem to have mastered the skill of choosing the most appropriate single response.) If administration procedures had not been studied as a variable in themselves, the difference would have (erroneously) been ascribed to SES. This kind of confounding is particularly troublesome in studies of different racial groups, because social situations in all respects objectively the same may nevertheless have widely differing impact on children of different cultural backgrounds.

Rural Maryland Sample

Maryland is unusual in that school districts coincide with counties, and are very large. The state is divided into twenty-three counties plus the City of Baltimore. All our grade school Maryland subjects were enrolled in schools under the jurisdiction of the Baltimore County Board of Education (see Fig. 2.1), and the County is so large (over 600 square miles) that it contains truly rural as well as urban areas. The advantages of studying children in the same school system are legion—curriculum, testing programs, basal salary of teachers, and many other factors are the same within one system. Rural communities usually spend considerably less per pupil than urban areas, and ordinarily comparisons involve students from schools in different systems. Often a large part of any rural-urban difference must be attributed to differences between systems. Even within one system there is undoubtedly bias favoring the more urban schools. Field trips to points of interest are easier for suburban schools, the PTA is better supported and contributes more to school furnishing and equipment, and so on. But the major yardsticks one uses to evaluate schools tend to be fairly uniform within a single system and it is therefore hoped that the rural and urban children of this study manifest differences that can be attributed mainly to variations in residential locus rather than to differences between schools.

Children from rural areas of Baltimore County, drawn from three grades and with three IQ strata in each grade, were studied in 1961–62. (These data, an additional sixty subjects for each grade, are not included in Appendix D.) In rural-urban comparisons IQ level can be held constant. Since differences between two urban SES levels have already been shown to be small, it should make little difference whether the rural group is compared to the high- or low-SES urban groups. Actually, the rural samples are compared with *both* urban SES groups, because both are needed to cover the entire IQ range. Analyses comparing rural and urban subjects are based on data gathered in 1961–62. Results are unchanged if 1962–63 urban data are added in also.

Analyses of variance, summarized in Table 6.3, are based on the numbers of paradigmatic responses given to nouns, adjectives, and verbs by rural and urban groups. The medium-IQ rural group is a part of both comparisons. Form class, frequency, grade, and IQ are significant, as in all previous analyses. Place-of-residence, the variable of major interest here, is significant beyond the 1 per cent level when medium- and low-IQ rural subjects are compared with low-SES urban subjects of the same IQ levels. Place-of-residence is also significant when rural and high-SES urban subjects are compared (medium- and high-IQ).

TABLE 6.3. Analysis of Variance, Numbers of Paradigmatic Responses Given to Nouns, Adjectives, and Verbs by Rural and Urban Subjects Matched on IQ

(Data for 1961–62)

Source of variation	d.f.	Rural vs Low-SES Urban			Rural vs High-SES Urban		
		MS	F	P(F)	MS	F	P(F)
Form class	2	21,005	335.01	<.001	17,766	345.57	<.001
Frequency	2	631	10.06	<.01	596	11.59	<.01
Grade	2	31,502	502.42	<.001	27,200	529.07	<.001
IQ	1	1,115	17.78	<.01	2,297	44.68	<.01
Place of residence							
(rural vs urban)	1	1,168	18.63	<.01	262	5.01	<.05
Form × frequency	4	1,090	17.63	<.01	1,409	27.41	<.01
Form × grade	2	6,264	99.90	<.001	6,318	122.89	<.01
Form × IQ	2	192	3.06	=.05	55	1.07	—
Form × place	2	193	3.08	=.05	58	1.13	—
Grade × IQ	2	19	—	—	424	8.25	<.01
Grade × place	2	221	3.52	<.05	186	3.62	<.05
IQ × place	1	89	1.42	—	168	3.27	<.05
Form × grade × IQ	4	278	4.43	<.01	162	3.15	<.05
Form × grade × place	4	159	2.54	=.05	41	—	—
Grade × IQ × place	2	221	3.52	<.05	154	3.00	=.05
Residual	74	62.70			51.41		

A rural-urban difference contrasts with the finding of no SES differences when two urban groups were compared in a parallel analysis (see Table 6.2). The rates of paradigmatic responding differ, by as much as 10 per cent in some instances, between rural and urban children of the same IQ. Living in rural or urban surroundings appears to have considerable impact, then, on the rate of linguistic development. This difference is the more interesting because one would think that the upper and lower urban SES groups would have cultural milieus as disparate as the rural and urban groups.

Form class and grade and place interact triply in the *low*-IQ groups but not in the high-IQ groups. Some insight into this is gained by examining numbers of matching responses for the low urban and rural groups given in Table 6.4. Rural children lag behind low-SES urban children of the same IQ in the development of adjective and verb responses. This lag is characteristic *only* of the medium and low-IQ children however. When rural and high-SES children who have average or above average IQ's (right half of Table 6.3) are compared, there is no such form class × grade × place interaction. The bottom half of Table 6.4 suggests that there is a lag for rural children at first grade, but it has disappeared by third grade. One implication is that rural residence is a modest handicap for language development, one easily compensated for by higher intelligence.

TABLE 6.4.   Percentage of Paradigmatic Responses Given by Rural and Urban Subjects Matched on IQ
(Each entry based on 960 responses, 1961–62; med.-IQ rural sample is part of both comparisons)

Form class of stimulus word	Rural vs. low-SES urban					
	(Medium- [95–105] and Low- [below 86] IQ)					
	First grade		Third grade		Fifth grade	
	Rural	Low-SES urban	Rural	Low-SES urban	Rural	Low-SES urban
Total nouns	60.0	62.0	68.9	72.9	79.3	75.6
Total adjectives	17.6	28.9	64.5	71.1	74.3	74.1
Total verbs	17.3	18.1	40.0	50.0	53.0	59.2

Form class of stimulus word	Rural vs. high-SES urban					
	(Medium- [95–105] and High- above 122 IQ)					
	First grade		Third grade		Fifth grade	
	Rural	High-SES urban	Rural	High-SES urban	Rural	High-SES urban
Total nouns	67.0	67.6	74.7	73.1	77.9	79.2
Total adjectives	30.8	38.8	68.4	65.6	81.0	84.8
Total verbs	19.8	24.2	50.7	51.5	62.1	65.3

Note: These data were gathered at about the same time in the school year (Jan. through April) and by the same interviewers. Data gathered in 1962–63 from low-SES subjects was obtained from late October through the first half of December. The composite figures for low-SES subjects (see Table 5.2) show the low-SES subjects not quite as far advanced as the 1961–62 data alone. This stems at least partly from the different testing times in the school year.

The rural-urban difference found for children of average or below average IQ is a retardation in terms of the form class developmental sequence. The age analyses for the urban samples showed that adjectives generally arouse as many paradigmatic responses at third grade as they do at fifth grade. Verbs are developing by third grade, but have not developed as far as adjectives. The timing of these developmental patterns is a function not only of age and IQ (and to a slight degree of sex), then, but also of place-of-residence, especially for less intelligent children.

Rural residence apparently impedes language development somewhat during the preschool period so that first-graders who live in the country are retarded compared to first-graders who live in the city.[3] This is true irrespective of IQ level. Rural children

[3] No kindergartens are available to rural dwellers.

of superior endowment quickly compensate, however, and by the third-grade the difference in adjectives is abolished. Rural children of lesser endowment still lag at third grade. At fifth grade there is still some indication of a slower trend for verbs, the last form class to develop.

The words on the stimulus list are all relatively common words. The ability to generate paradigmatic associates to these words probably implies ability to generate sentences containing these words and others of their class that are associates (McNeill, 1965). This is a kind of minimum performance necessary for communication in our culture, because words like "man," "high," and "tell" recur many times every day within the hearing of children. It does not necessarily follow that *all* language skills are eventually learned to the same degree by different groups of children, i.e., that subcultural differences in other measures would also become negligible with advancing age. There is evidence, for instance, that some higher level language skills are possessed by highly educated adults (graduate students) but not by the less well educated (average two years of high school) (Werner and Kaplan, 1950; Kaplan, 1950).

Both analyses in Table 6.3 emphasize once more the importance of IQ in language development. Only the higher-IQ group displays a place $\times$ IQ interaction, and this happens because there is *no* effect attributable to place-of-residence at the top IQ stratum. Paradigmatic response rates are identical for the high-IQ groups (63 per cent), but differ at the middle-IQ level (55 per cent for rural and 59 per cent for urban). Again, rural residence may be completely camouflaged if IQ is sufficient, but children of average or below average IQ are handicapped by rural locus, at least through middle childhood.

The locus differences are about 2 per cent for higher-IQ groups and 4 per cent for lower-IQ groups when all grades are combined. (Differences by grade have already been discussed in detail.) The IQ differences run from 4–5 per cent, the larger difference being noted for the higher-IQ groups. These differences are statistically significant, but of course, much smaller than differences associated with age or form class.

TABLE 6.5. The IQ and Father's Educational Level for Children in Rural and Urban Samples[a]

| | Urban | | | | | | Rural | | | |
| | High-SES | | Total high-SES | Low-SES | | Total low-SES | High-IQ | Med.-IQ | Low-IQ | Total rural |
	High-IQ	Med.-IQ		Med.-IQ	Low-IQ					
First grade										
Mean IQ	127.3	101.1		101.4	76.9		128.1	99.8	77.4	
Mean grade completed by father	15.1	12.6	13.9	11.3	9.0	10.2	12.9	10.4	7.5	10.3
Third grade										
Mean IQ	131.3	100.4		100.3	79.9		131.9	99.6	78.3	
Mean grade completed by father	15.7	14.8	15.3	9.6	8.9	9.3	12.2	9.0	8.5	9.9
Fifth grade										
Mean IQ	130.3	100.3		100.3	78.8		131.9	100.1	77.1	
Mean grade completed by father	14.1	13.7	13.9	9.5	10.4	10.0	12.3	9.7	7.8	9.9

[a] Differences between urban data and that cited in Table 2.3 stem from the fact that the present comparison is based only on 1961–62 urban data.

What cultural factors can account for the rural-urban differences? Table 6.5 reveals that sample strata are closely matched in terms of average IQ, rural and urban means all being within two points of one another. Because of the well-known correlation between intelligence of parents and children, it is not surprising to see that in all subgroups but one, father's educational level parallels exactly the IQ patterns in the urban children's samples.

Father's educational level varies by SES level and for children of medium IQ it is 13.7 vs. 10.1 for high and low SES respectively. But we have already seen that urban children of the same IQ manifest minimal differences in paradigmatic responding when SES groups are compared, in spite of this rather large difference in father's educational level favoring the high-SES group. The rural children come from homes where the educational background of parents is about the same as that of urban low-SES children of similar IQ (9.7 vs. 10.1 for medium-IQ children, and somewhat lower for low-IQ children). But the importance of this factor in explaining rural-urban differences seems questionable since large differences (over three years) between urban groups were not associated with language differences in the urban children.

The rural-to-urban difference thus seems better explained by other facts than father's educational level or cultural background in the home. Most obvious is exposure to language. Opportunities for verbal interaction may be limited for the rural preschooler because of isolation of dwellings, lack of kindergartens, lower exposure to television and radio. (This will be emphasized again when the Amish results are considered.) John and Goldstein (1964) suggest that comprehension of words with shifting and complex referents (labels and action words) may be impeded when adult-child interaction is insufficient or lacking. In their studies where social class differences have been found, they feel it is the use of language rather than its quality that differentiates the familial settings.

Some additional information is available to describe the exact nature of the lag noticed for rural children. For high-frequency nouns, adjectives, and verbs the most frequent response was judged to be syntactic or non-syntactic, and a score computed on this measure. A syntactic response was one that the experimenter classified as having a high transitional probability on subjective grounds.[4] Thus, many responses of different form class ("high"—"school," "dark"—"night," etc.) are classified as syntactic. In addition certain pairs like "table"—"spoon" or "table"—"cloth" would be syntactic even though of the same form class. Kindergarteners have a strong tendency toward syntactic responses (46 per cent and 30 per cent for the two SES groups) considering only the primary response to high-frequency nouns, adjectives, and verbs (see Table 6.6). No rural kindergarten samples were obtainable. Syntactic responses have *decreased* from kindergarten to first grade for urban children to an average rate of about 23 per cent for all IQ levels. The rural first-grade subjects, on the other hand, give syntactic responses at a rate surpassing that noted for urban kindergarten groups (over 35 per cent). This is further corroboration of the relative immaturity of rural subjects when IQ is controlled. The high-IQ rural child is giving

---

[4] See Entwisle, *et al.* (1964), for details of this procedure; also Note at end of Chapter 3.

syntactic responses at about the same rate as the low-IQ urban child at first grade (primary responses only). Syntactic responses fall off rapidly from first to third grade for rural children and have become almost completely absent in high-IQ fifth-graders. There is a definite association between syntactic responses and IQ level, lower-IQ subjects giving more syntactic responses.

TABLE 6.6. Numbers[a] of Syntactic Response, Based on only the Primary Response to High-Frequency Nouns, Adjectives, and Verbs

(1961–62 data)

	Kindergarten				Total	Per cent
	High-SES	Low-SES				
High-freq. nouns	0	2/70			2/70	2.9
High-freq. adjectives	24/51	19/57			43/108	39.8
High-freq. verbs	23/52	3/48			26/100	26.0
Per cent for samples	45.6	13.7			25.5	

	First grade								
	High-SES		Low-SES		Rural				
	High-IQ	Med.-IQ	Med.-IQ	Low-IQ	High-IQ	Med.-IQ	Low-IQ	Total	Per cent
High-freq. nouns	7/42	7/57	3/71	10/61	20/71	16/57	16/49	79/408	19.4
High-freq. adjectives	4/93	8/59	13/75	15/47	17/78	15/56	23/45	95/453	21.0
High-freq. verbs	14/56	31/55	27/56	26/50	28/61	29/51	12/41	167/370	45.1
Per cent for samples	13.1	26.9	21.3	32.3	31.0	36.6	37.8	27.7	

	Third grade								
	High-SES		Low-SES		Rural				
	High-IQ	Med.-IQ	Med.-IQ	Low-IQ	High-IQ	Med.-IQ	Low-IQ	Total	Per cent
High-freq. nouns	14/88	6/75	13/90	11/84	6/96	11/74	9/73	70/580	12.1
High-freq. adjectives	0/106	0/118	8/120	9/125	0/126	8/112	2/95	27/802	3.4
High-freq. verbs	6/82	5/83	11/93	7/75	7/97	16/76	17/68	69/574	12.0
Per cent for samples	7.2	4.0	10.6	9.5	4.1	13.4	11.9	8.5	

	Fifth grade								
	High-SES		Low-SES		Rural				
	High-IQ	Med.-IQ	Med.-IQ	Low-IQ	High-IQ	Med.-IQ	Low-IQ	Total	Per cent
High-freq. nouns	4/97	5/94	10/94	6/79	8/96	14/99	4/78	51/637	8.0
High-freq. adjectives	0/144	11/135	7/95	6/119	0/29	13/33	10/114	47/669	7.0
High-freq. verbs	0/107	7/108	6/90	10/90	0/116	0/98	0/74	23/683	3.4
Per cent for samples	1.1	6.8	8.2	7.6	3.3	11.7	5.3	6.1	

[a] Fractions given are the number of syntactic responses in the numerator divided by the total frequency. The most common response to each of eight high-frequency words was classified as syntactic or nonsyntactic. Then of these *primary* responses, the frequency of the syntactic responses is added to give the numerator, while the denominator is the sum of the frequencies of primary responses to each group of eight stimuli, whether it was syntactic or not.

The Amish Sample

Discrepancies between modern data and the data of Woodrow and Lowell (1916), as well as the need to sample different modern subcultures, prompted the study of Amish children. The IQ composition of the Amish sample is crucial in making comparisons, because of the strong association between IQ and some phases of language development. For Amish children in grades three through six, school records furnished IQ scores. First- and second-graders were given Draw-A-Man tests. The Amish (20 children at grades 1, 2, 3, 5, and 6) turned out to have mean IQ scores that differ from rural Maryland groups in some instances, so composite samples were made up from the rural Maryland data that matched the IQ of the Amish groups.[5] The average IQ's for the Amish samples and the specially constructed rural Maryland samples are given in Table 6.7. The Amish fifth-grade sample was within one point of the average IQ rural Maryland fifth-grade sample, and so it was not necessary to construct a matching sample.

TABLE 6.7.   Average IQ of Samples of Twenty Students

Grade	Amish	Rural Maryland matched to Amish	Rural Maryland medium-IQ
First	85.3	84.7	99.8
Third	92.8	92.8	99.6
Fifth	101.1	—	100.1

Rates of paradigmatic responding, in percentages, are given in Table 6.8 for the Amish and two rural Maryland groups. In addition figures are presented for a sixth-grade Amish sample (average IQ equal to 96.6). Several conclusions follow immediately from Table 6.7, the most obvious being that the Amish lag behind both rural Maryland groups for all form classes at every grade. The data for the Amish

TABLE 6.8.   Paradigmatic Responses (Per Cents) for Amish and Two Rural Samples at First, Third, and Fifth Grades

(Each entry is based on 160 responses)

	First grade			Third grade			Fifth grade		Sixth grade
	Amish (Dutch responses omitted)	Match-ing rural	Average rural	Amish	Match-ing rural	Average rural	Amish	Average rural[a]	Amish
High-freq. nouns	50.0	55.6	58.1	61.9	63.8	62.5	64.4	71.9	75.6
Med.-freq. nouns	47.5	58.8	65.6	68.8	71.3	69.4	70.0	76.9	79.4
Low-freq. nouns	45.6	62.5	63.1	68.1	75.6	76.3	85.6	88.1	85.6
Total nouns	47.7	59.0	62.3	66.3	70.2	69.4	73.3	79.0	80.2
High-freq. adjectives	16.9	18.1	26.3	51.3	64.4	73.8	71.3	81.9	87.5
Med.-freq. adjectives	11.9	21.3	21.9	52.5	62.5	62.5	71.9	76.3	84.4
Low-freq. adjectives	17.5	16.9	15.6	42.5	66.9	66.3	73.1	80.6	83.8
Total adjectives	15.4	18.8	21.3	48.8	64.6	67.5	72.1	79.6	85.2
High-freq. verbs	18.1	23.1	16.3	42.5	56.3	51.3	67.5	71.9	76.3
Med.-freq. verbs	14.4	15.0	17.5	33.8	43.1	33.8	48.8	51.9	48.1
Low-freq. verbs	17.5	21.3	8.8	30.6	41.3	39.4	51.9	56.3	67.5
Total verbs	16.7	19.8	14.2	35.6	46.9	41.5	56.0	60.0	64.0

[a] The average IQ of this group was within one point of the average IQ for the Amish fifth-grade sample.

[5] The composite samples were made by finding a rural subject with an IQ close to that of an Amish child. The averages of the specially constructed rural samples differ by less than 0.6 points from the Amish averages.

and the matching rural sample were subjected to an analysis of variance (Table 6.9).[6] In addition to grade, form class, and the grade $\times$ form class interaction again being highly significant as in all previous analyses, there is a highly significant difference between the Amish and the matched rural sample. (Frequency is not a significant source of variance, so it and all its interactions are included in the residual term.) The developmental sequence is *not* different (no AR $\times$ FC $\times$ G interaction) but the Amish lag behind at every grade.

TABLE 6.9. Analysis of Variance, Numbers of Paradigmatic Responses, Amish and Matching Rural Maryland Samples (Nouns, adjectives, verbs; first, third and fifth grades)[a]

Source of variation	d.f.	MS	F	P(F)
Amish vs. matched rural	1	1,850	19.87	<.001
Form class	2	8,345	89.63	<.001
Grade	2	19,334	207.65	<.001
AR $\times$ FC	2	23	—	—
AR $\times$ G	2	79	—	—
FC $\times$ G	4	1,322	14.20	<.001
AR $\times$ FC $\times$ G	4	105	1.13	—
Residual	36	93.11		

[a] An analysis of only the third- and fifth-grade responses, when no Dutch responses are given, leads to the same outcome as this analysis.

In the last column of Table 6.8 figures are given for sixth-grade children from the same schools as the younger children. In every instance the sixth-grade Amish sample exceeds the fifth-grade rural Maryland sample, so the difference between the Amish and rural fifth-grade samples is clearly less than one developmental year. At earlier ages the differences are probably larger, and probably third-grade Amish groups are at a level close to that of second-grade rural groups.[7] As with IQ deficits and the rural-to-urban deficit noted earlier, however, these differences favoring non-Amish groups appear to be lags. The final level of paradigmatic responding attained by the Amish (suggested by the sixth-grade Amish sample) is probably indistinguishable from the level attained by the rural Maryland children.

Before discussing further the general subcultural patterns, we must briefly consider the impact of bilingualism on the language development of Amish children. In most Amish homes, Pennsylvania Dutch (a German dialect with many English importations) is spoken predominantly. English is spoken in school, and this requires that Amish children substitute English for Pennsylvania Dutch when they start school. This bilingualism does not account for the retardation of Amish children in paradigmatic responses, however, because the number of paradigmatic responses is constant whether English or Dutch responses are counted. First-grade Amish

[6] Some Dutch responses were given by Amish first-graders. No Dutch responses were given by other Amish children. In the analysis of Table 6.9, Dutch responses are not included. An identical analysis, for only the third and fifth grades, leads to exactly the same results. It thus appears that the factor of Dutch responses has little bearing on this language measure.

[7] A second-grade Amish group was procured but unfortunately happened to be of much higher average IQ (108.3) than the other Amish groups. Comparisons with this group are inappropriate and so no firm conclusion can be reached about the lag at earlier ages.

children gave Dutch responses to about 19 per cent of the stimuli but *no* Dutch responses were given by either third- or fifth-grade Amish children. About 5 per cent of the Dutch responses are representational—Dutch equivalents of the English stimulus word. Of the remainder, the paradigmatic patterns match very closely patterns observed with English responses by the same subjects (see Table 6.10). Thus differences between form classes are maintained whether English *or* Dutch responses are analyzed. This makes it appear immaterial, in terms of this measure, whether an English *or* a Dutch response is given. The similarity of analyses based on all grades compared to analyses based on only third- and fifth-grade data, when no Dutch responses are given, has already been pointed out.

TABLE 6.10.   Per Cent Paradigmatic Responses
(Representational responses excluded—5 per cent)

	English (81 per cent)	Dutch (14 per cent)
Nouns	59	63
Adjectives	39	38
Verbs	28	30

Another piece of evidence to suggest the relative unimportance of bilingualism *for this analysis* can be gleaned from commonality summaries given in Table 6.11. In all cases commonality differences are greater at fifth grade than at first grade. In fact, differences are rather small at first grade, even though IQ favors the rural group. One would expect that effects of bilingualism would be most pronounced at first grade, the entire preschool period consisting of exposure to Dutch. This does not seem to be the case because commonalities become less similar over the elementary school period. It is probably not bilingualism then, but other factors that operate to produce the differences between Amish and rural children, because the differences occur when one would expect the impact of bilingualism to be least.

TABLE 6.11.   Commonality at Three Grade Levels (in Per Cents) for Amish and Medium-IQ Rural Groups
(Each entry based on 480 responses)

	First grade		Third grade		Fifth grade	
	Amish	Rural	Amish	Rural	Amish	Rural
Nouns	31.5	35.6	45.8	48.8	55.8	64.4
Adjectives	31.0	31.9	52.9	64.6	68.9	76.3
Verbs	27.1	29.8	33.8	38.1	47.7	51.5

The most provocative data relate to syntactic patterns on the Amish data. In Table 6.12 verb responses to nouns and noun responses to adjectives are tabulated for Amish and rural Maryland respondents (average IQ). Syntactic patterns seem to persist longer in Amish subjects. For instance, noun-verb and adjective-noun combinations are slightly more frequent in rural than in Amish respondents at first grade. By the third grade there is a striking reversal, for Amish adjective-noun pairs greatly exceed rural adjective-noun pairs (32 per cent vs. 19 per cent, respectively). Referring back to Table 6.8 one can see that paradigmatic adjectival responses at the third-grade level are much more numerous for rural subjects (65 per cent vs. 49 per cent). The difference in this case, 16 per cent, is of about the same magnitude, but in the opposite direction from the syntactic adjective-noun difference at third-grade for the same two groups. Adjective-noun pairs are less numerous by the fifth-grade, accounting for about 13 per cent of the rural and about 20 per cent of the Amish responses. There are only small differences, Amish exceeding rural, in the noun-verb pairs.[8]

TABLE 6.12. Selected Syntactic Responses Compared for Rural Maryland (Medium-IQ) and Amish Respondents

(Each cell entry is based on 160 responses)

| Stimulus word type | Verb responses | | | | | |
| | First | | Third | | Fifth | |
	Amish	Rural	Amish	Rural	Amish	Rural
High-freq. nouns	17.5	16.9	12.5	11.9	15.0	11.9
Medium-freq. nouns	13.1	18.1	15.0	16.9	15.0	15.6
Low-freq. nouns	16.3	16.3	13.8	8.1	6.9	6.9
Total	15.6	17.1	13.8	12.3	12.3	11.5
	Noun responses					
High-freq. adjectives	47.5	51.3	31.9	18.7	23.8	12.5
Medium-freq. adjectives	45.0	48.7	31.3	23.1	21.9	16.9
Low-freq. adjectives	45.6	45.6	32.5	16.3	15.6	8.8
Total	46.0	48.5	31.9	19.4	20.4	12.7

The perseveration of syntactic response patterns after first grade in the Amish is of the greatest theoretical interest. For kindergarten and first-grade responses of urban subjects, a syntactic peak of short duration between kindergarten and first grade is quickly overwhelmed by paradigmatic changes. By third grade the syntactic pattern has died out and been replaced by large increases in paradigmatic responding. There is no doubt of the existence of a definite phase of syntactic responding for urban children, but its importance might be underrated if only the urban data were examined. Syntactic responding is also of interest in relation to the early data of Woodrow and Lowell, since their subjects were developmentally behind modern urban respondents. This will be discussed in Chapter 7.

Subcultural Differences

The broad pattern of linguistic development along an age continuum for paradigmatic responding to the words on our list was described in Chapter 4. This pattern

---

[8] The noun-adjective linkage cannot be attributed to administration method because it occurs at early ages, ages that previously (see Chapter 3) did not show changes linked to method.

is replicated, but displaced, for various subgroups. Lowered IQ may cause a slight lag, best seen via differences in responses to adjectival stimuli at third grade and to verb stimuli at fifth grade. Although relatively large differences in background characterize the high-SES urban and low-SES urban groups, only very mild differences appear in language development. For the major lexical parts of speech, nouns, adjectives, and verbs, differences are not significant even when a very precise analysis is made. It should be remarked that slight differences in practical terms turn out to be statistically significant in most analyses since the factorial designs and large sample sizes are bound to produce high precision.

Because of the minimal differences associated with urban SES levels, it is all the more surprising to note strong rural-urban differences. Differences in family conditions between rural and urban groups are no larger than between the two urban groups (in some cases smaller) and all the children, urban or rural, are enrolled in highly similar schools and carefully matched on IQ. One is therefore led to believe that residential locus itself is the factor responsible. Isolation of houses must tend to discourage verbal interaction with peers. Exposure to language may also be reduced because of difficulty in TV reception. Most rural areas are remote from major TV broadcasters, and rather elaborate antenna facilities are required for adequate reception. Rural children may also have less leisure available for TV-watching because of long bus rides and more home chores.

The above line of reasoning seems even more plausible when the Amish data are added to the picture. Residential locus is different geographically from the rural Maryland groups, but in other respects, especially that of isolation, very similar. The greatest difference between the Amish children and rural Maryland children is in subcultural customs tending to discourage verbal interchanges between adults and children, and also, of course, a drastic reduction in exposure to mass media. A socially determined learning condition of great importance in language learning may be opportunities (direct, or vicariously via TV) for the child to participate in dialogues involving adult speakers. The educational level of Amish parents (eighth grade) is not very different from that of fathers of rural children of average intelligence (between nine and ten years).

It is tempting to conclude that the four samples (two urban Maryland groups of different SES, the rural Maryland, and the Amish) are comparable except for exposure to spoken and written language. In urban settings, where one presumes high exposure to language because of mass media, crowded dwellings, large numbers of easily accessible peers, and proximity of movies, theaters, and other recreational facilities, there are negligible differences in language associated with income level, father's educational status, and other measures of social class. Rural Maryland children of intelligence comparable to urban Maryland children develop language facility more slowly with exposure to educational facilities held constant. Conditions of life in rural areas other than schooling appear to be responsible for the difference. This presumption is reinforced by the fact that Amish children display further deficits in language development compared to rural Maryland children, again with intelligence controlled. Here the educational opportunities are not as well equated, to be sure. Lack of opportunities for verbal interaction, including covert interactions with radio and television speakers, seem a possible cause of this slowed development for Amish children.

These findings related to subcultural differences in language development have some bearing on Ervin and Miller's (1963) speculation that different language structures condition different learning patterns. They note, for instance, that Navaho children are somewhat retarded in language development. This retardation would be predicted from our results, quite apart from any differences between the Navaho and English languages, because of residential locus and/or subcultural customs. Since non-Navaho children who live in rural areas are relatively retarded in linguistic development, a similar retardation in Navaho children who reside in rural settings would be predicted.

A little data for Navaho adults suggests that the Navaho subculture as well as rural locus may influence language development, however. Twenty-eight adult residents within the Navaho reservation gave associations to nouns and nominal compounds, verbs, modifiers, and special stem verbs (Ervin and Landar, 1963). Although low commonalities (17 per cent) are found, about half the words elicit the same primary response in Navaho that is found for the same words in English, a surprising degree of consistency with such vast differences between languages. (Commonality for Amish children is less, but not commonality for rural Maryland children [see Table 6.11].) The differences between modern Navahos and modern English-speaking Americans are reminiscent of the differences between adults sampled by Kent and Rosanoff in 1910 and those sampled by Russell and Jenkins in 1960. Again, the impact of mass media and other trappings of modern life loom large. The actual proportions of paradigmatics in Navaho adults, however, are surprisingly close to our adult figures for nouns and verbs: 59 per cent and 52 per cent, respectively. The figure of 42 per cent for modifiers is low. Brown and Berko (1960) found over 81 per cent paradigmatic responses for modifiers with adults and our rate for adjectives is high, but of course is based on words with strong contrast responses. Rates of paradigmatic responding in Navahos did not appear to be related to education.

Some data of Rosenzweig (1964) which, at first thought seems contradictory, actually may be consistent with data already cited. Using the Kent-Rosanoff list with French construction workers and French students he finds more paradigmatics for the students, *but only the primary responses are used in this analysis.* The two sets of data may actually be entirely compatible if all responses are assigned to form classes, as in Ervin's Navaho data, for although the Navaho's primaries account for a smaller percentage of responses than American adults' generally, the total rate of paradigmatic responding to nouns and verbs is similar. Rosenzweig's finding of a difference in paradigmatics may thus be entirely owing to lower commonalities for the less educated group. Again, however, it is hard to compare different sets of data based on different stimulus lists.

Miller and Ervin (1963) predicted that as knowledge of significant properties of children's language increases, more attention would be paid to the evolving differential usage of children, particularly to features of the environment which alter the rate of change. Our data confirm this prediction. The Amish are at an extreme with respect to two factors mentioned by Miller and Ervin, cultural customs and number of siblings. Speech development may be affected by reading to children (Irwin, 1960), and children in towns with television come to school with larger vocabularies than do children in comparable towns without television (Schramm, *et al.*, 1961). Neither reading by adults nor exposure to television are characteristic of the Amish. With regard to another environmental factor, it has been suggested that older children are the most important environmental force in shaping younger children's speech habits (Hockett, 1950) and Amish are known for their large families. But there is a negative correlation between verbal ability and family size, intelligence held constant (Nisbet, 1961), presumably because of fewer opportunities to interact with adults, so the large Amish family may militate against accelerated verbal development. Both cultural customs and conditions of family life, then, do not favor language development of Amish children, to the extent that research on these topics is applicable here.

It should be borne in mind that comparisons of the Amish and rural Maryland children (unlike the urban-rural comparisons made earlier) are not as clear-cut because they attend schools under different jurisdictions.

Genetic differences in mental factors related to verbal ability cannot be entirely ruled out. The Amish and rural Maryland children are from different stocks, the Amish being a particularly clean-cut group from a genetic standpoint. Yet migration away from the Amish group and away from rural locations may be encouraged by similar abilities and conditions. Persons of greater verbal ability and inclination may find it easier to leave the farm and obtain employment in the city, so that depletion of both groups over the last half-century would be selective in the same manner. Thus instead of exposure to language, innate endowment could be at least partly responsible for the differences in rates of development. The fact that all groups apparently attain the same level of development by about the sixth grade poses no real difficulty for a genetic explanation. The best counterargument is provided by John's finding that lower-lower class urban individuals did not show differences in word association from their more favored counterparts in urban settings and our similar finding for different SES urban groups. One would expect selection in terms of verbal ability to operate between social classes as well as between subcultural groups.

Chapter Seven

Relation to Other Studies

In this chapter major points of contact between this research and other research will be identified. Often this will take the form of a detailed comparison of our data with that of another study, i.e., the Woodrow and Lowell (1916) data, or the Palermo and Jenkins (1964) data. The intent is to point up findings that replicate, contradict, or supplement observations of other workers. Data in Appendices A and B are provided so the reader can make comparisons independently.

The process of language acquisition has been studied sporadically over the years and research has not proceeded within any unified theoretical frame. Points of contact between our work and previous work are therefore not easy to establish, and sometimes it is hard to interpret the joint findings. For example, discrepancies between our observations and Woodrow and Lowell's observations suggest that linguistic development of young children today proceeds at an accelerated pace compared to fifty years ago. But relative acceleration by itself does not explain all the differences between the two sets of data. Administration procedures, our research suggests, have greater impact upon modern data because their effects are felt mostly on paradigmatic responses which appear at earlier ages now than formerly. This is a kind of interactive effect that is difficult to interpret with only a single sample of early data. Jenkins and Russell (1960) similarly note that attitudes toward test-taking and time pressure go far in explaining differences occurring in adult associations from 1910 to 1952.

To try to tell a complete story about linguistic development over ages four to ten would be both presumptuous and unwarranted on the basis of information currently at hand. What we attempt in this chapter is to interpret our data in the light of data gathered by others.

One of the major problems facing research in any underdeveloped area is that of measurement. What indices or scales should be used? How can one establish the reliability and validity of instruments and choose among data reduction techniques?

Association data are unbelievably bulky, even when reduced to alphabetic tabulations such as those in the Appendices. The reader should be reminded that tabulations on each variable (IQ, SES, etc.) yield as much data as are given in the Appendices, and many groups (rural, Amish) are not listed. With such masses of data, it is difficult to see patterns that may emerge as one age group is compared with another, or as one IQ group is compared with another. By adopting such measures as rate of paradigmatic responding and commonality, some patterns emerge for individual words or for classes of words (high-frequency nouns, low-frequency verbs, etc.), but certainly the particular patterns seem to depend on what measures are chosen. It has become more and more apparent as the present research has progressed that patterns are dependent on the particular sample of stimulus words.

A Developmental Scale

The stimulus words used in this study have now been used extensively with large groups of children. Variations with IQ are large over the kindergarten to third-grade range, and sizable even up to fifth grade. Other co-variations have already been discussed in detail. The detailed information now available concerning this word list permits its use as a developmental scale, and it is particularly well-suited for use with groups of children. Little special training is required for the interviewers, and the list can be administered rapidly.

Such a word association list might serve as a rough test of intelligence if further validating work were done. Since the task can be accomplished quickly in a casual setting, without there being any "wrong responses" possible, it might be useful when text anxiety is a problem. Further validation might also make the scale useful for children with handicaps of various kinds.

The Development of Associative Meaning

Measures used so far, whether the syntactic-paradigmatic or form class divisions, or commonality, pertain to individual words. Stimulus words have been grouped into categories, as high-frequency nouns or low-frequency verbs, and these categories emphasize grammar more than semantics. The way in which meanings overlap and the structure of meaning among word clusters, i.e., semantics, cannot be studied by strategies like those employed so far. Factor analysis of the patterns of overlapping response to related stimulus words as proposed by Deese (1962a) is a technique for studying the structure of associative meaning. Associations are not classified as heretofore in terms of logical or grammatical relations, but according to the relationships associations have with one another.

To explore the development of conceptual clusters relating different words to one another, a "butterfly" group of words was incorporated in the stimulus list (Chapter 3). The emergence of an associative structure with advancing age can be studied if the same set of stimulus words is used to obtain responses from various age groups.

Deese has already demonstrated that associative meaning can be highly structured for college students. By mapping a structure using responses to the same list at successive ages one can study the *development* of associative meaning. To do this, the stimulus list included fifteen words from Deese's (1961, 1962a) "butterfly" cluster: "bee," "bird," "black," "bright," "bug," "butterfly," "cocoon," "color," "flower," "fly," "insect," "moth," "pretty," "wing," "yellow." As mentioned earlier, ninety-six stimuli, including the above words, were administered to 200 kindergarten children, to 280 first-, third-, and fifth-grade urban Maryland children, and also to 200 college students (at Johns Hopkins University and Goucher College). The list was also given to some rural Maryland children and to some Amish children.

Responses to the fifteen "butterfly" words were tabulated separately for five urban groups (kindergarten to college) and then overlap matrices were formed.[1] Overlap coefficients were factor analyzed using the principal factor method separately for each age group. The number of factors to be rotated was arbitrarily specified for all age groups as equal to the number of eigenvalues greater than unity. (Rotation of all factors yields very similar results.) The sign attached to factors have been changed in some instances to preserve homogeneity between groups.[2]

Rotated factor loadings for kindergarten, first, third, and fifth grade, and adult samples are shown in Table 7.1.

There are many small loadings for kindergarten and first grade that tend to approach zero with advancing age. This pattern was evident also in the original overlap matrices, for with the younger children almost every cell of a matrix contains an entry, whereas with the older children more empty cells appear. Very young children have flat distributions of associations and tend to give many idiosyncratic responses, so that some overlap stems from accidental factors that would tend to produce overlap within any set of words, even a set chosen at random. As children mature, overlaps are more predictable and patterned.

The arrangement of the factors in Table 7.1 is arbitrary, since factors vary somewhat in dominance over the various age groups. To facilitate discussion the factors are named, although no particular significance should attach to this.

The first factor has high loadings on the words "bird," "fly," and "wing." The common concept here appears to be "flight." The loading on this factor for "bird" and "wing" remains high across all ages. The loading on "fly" decreases modestly during the grade school ages (probably because "fly" is related to other categories of insects, to be discussed below). The loading on "butterfly" drops precipitously from .50 to .11. The fading out of "butterfly," especially noticeable between first and third grades, can be interpreted as a diminution of the significance of the "fly" syllable in "butterfly." Young children attend to the acoustic properties of words (this tendency produces *Klang* associations, "cocoon"—"moon," for example). The early inclusions of "butterfly" in the flight cluster is probably not based so much on semantic generalization as on acoustic similarities of words. These nonsemantic pairs drop out rapidly after the first grade.

---

[1] The procedure used to compute overlap coefficients is described by Deese (1962a).

[2] The principal factor solution (Harman, 1960) assumes the matrix to be positive, semi-definite. When this condition is not always fulfilled, as in our data, the first factor will not always be positive.

TABLE 7.1.   Rotated Factor Loadings for "Butterfly" Words at Five Age Levels

| | Factor I (flight) | | | | | Factor II (bugs) | | | |
	K	First	Third	Fifth	Adult	K	First	Third	Fifth	Adult
bee	−.04	.04	.10	.03	.18	.66	.32	.33	.43	.34
bird	.76	.69	.73	.75	.77	−.02	−.01	.00	−.01	.01
black	.06	.04	.00	.00	−.01	.00	.01	.00	.00	.03
bright	−.04	.00	.00	.00	−.03	−.10	−.01	−.01	.00	.01
bug	.07	.08	.07	.05	.05	.44	.71	.84	.81	.83
butterfly	.50	.50	.32	.18	.11	.07	.23	.17	.46	.04
cocoon	−.15	.06	−.09	−.02	−.08	−.05	.05	−.16	−.09	−.06
color	−.01	−.02	.00	.00	−.05	.02	−.01	.00	.00	.00
flower	−.01	.01	.00	.00	.00	.19	.14	.01	.05	.05
fly	.34	.68	.63	.54	.54	.23	.16	.17	.31	.17
insect	.05	−.06	.02	.02	.02	.55	.72	.84	.81	.84
moth	.04	.16	.05	.02	.13	.40	.34	.19	.44	.18
pretty	.03	.00	.00	.00	−.05	−.12	−.06	.00	.00	−.02
wing	.74	.63	.75	.77	.73	.06	−.02	−.01	−.02	−.01
yellow	−.01	.00	.00	.00	.17	.03	.01	.02	.01	.00

| | Factor III (lepidoptera) | | | | | Factor IV (color) | | | |
	K	First	Third	Fifth	Adult	K	First	Third	Fifth	Adult
bee			.33	.08	.08	.03	.01	−.01	−.01	.03
bird			.02	−.01	.00	.03	−.01	.01	.01	.02
black			.00	−.02	.01	.57	.50	.53	.55	.32
bright			.01	.02	−.02	.12	.14	.15	.09	.43
bug			.07	−.04	.05	.01	.00	.00	.01	.00
butterfly			.57	.45	.72	.00	.11	.06	.05	.14
cocoon			.69	.85	.75	.02	.14	.00	.00	−.03
color			−.01	.00	.03	.64	.62	.70	.73	.69
flower			.05	−.01	.01	−.01	.02	.05	−.01	.14
fly			.19	.10	.11	−.04	.00	−.01	−.01	−.05
insect			.06	−.04	.04	.01	.02	.00	.00	.01
moth			.64	.48	.62	.01	.00	−.01	−.01	−.05
pretty			−.03	−.01	.01	.01	.00	.01	−.05	−.18
wing			−.01	−.01	.03	.01	.01	.00	.00	.02
yellow			.00	.02	.03	.58	.64	.70	.72	.57

| | Factor V (prettiness and residual) | | | | |
	K	First	Third	Fifth	Adult
bee	.05	.08	.04	.08	.24
bird	−.02	−.03	.02	.00	.02
black	−.10	−.06	−.07	.01	−.22
bright	.16	.11	.04	.15	−.05
bug	.00	−.05	−.01	−.05	−.03
butterfly	.07	.10	.10	.09	.14
cocoon	−.05	.12	−.05	−.01	−.05
color	.00	−.04	.03	.04	.04
flower	.67	.68	.72	.71	.60
fly	.06	.02	.00	.01	−.02
insect	.08	−.05	.00	−.04	−.02
moth	−.17	.06	.01	−.02	−.03
pretty	.72	.73	.74	.72	.70
wing	−.02	−.01	−.02	.00	.00
yellow	.14	.07	−.03	.06	.27

The second and third factors are related. Interpreted together they suggest how a verbal concept may be developed and refined. Several words in the list belong to a category that might be designated "Bugs": "bee," "bug," "butterfly," "fly," "insects," "moth" and indirectly, "cocoon" (the larval stage of "butterfly" and "moth"). By first grade high loadings (.71 to .72) on this factor characterize "bug" and "insect" and moderate loadings are found for "bee," "butterfly," "fly," and "moth." Adult loadings on Factor II for "moth" and "butterfly" are markedly reduced compared to other ages. This decrease is associated with an increase in Factor III (Lepidoptera). There appears to be a subcategory developing that consists of the lepidoptera sub-group of insects—high loadings for "butterfly," "cocoon," and "moth," and loadings close to zero on other words belonging to the broad category of insects. Through the fifth grade, "butterfly" and "moth" have moderate loadings on Factor II, but these diminish in the adult group. In a complementary way, loadings on Factor III for the lepidoptera group are high for adults. At grade three, Factor III might be named "specific kinds of insects." "Bug" and "insect" are not included, but subordinates of both these words have moderate loadings. One interpretation is that a list of sub-ordinates from the bug-insect grouping are separated out and the lepidoptera portion assumes a tighter structure. Probably another cluster centering around "bee" ("bee"—"wasp") would also emerge if words suitable for revealing this had been included in the list.

What appears to be a vague general rubric at third grade, "bugs," undergoes gradual sharpening and tightening with increasing age. "Bugs" and "insects" appear to develop as a superordinate class, with specific instances in a subordinate position. Then there is further differentiation when clusters within the subordinate list crystal-lize.

Factor IV, "color," reveals a developmental change that is qualitatively different and linguistically of different significance from changes discussed above. Kinder-garten and first-grade loadings are high for "black," "color," and "yellow," and these loadings are maintained with age, or even become slightly larger, up to fifth grade. Throughout childhood the loadings on "bright" are small but appear to be more consistent than other small loadings, ranging from .09 to .15. At adulthood the composition of this factor appears to have undergone some metamorphosis. There are lower loadings on "black" and "yellow" while "color" remains about the same. (It is tempting to conclude that this break again represents the establishment of a subordinate-superordinate relation.) But of greater interest are the loadings of .43 on "bright" and −.18 on "pretty," the only two adjectives on the list aside from color names. These adjectives have now been incorporated in a loose structure with "color" at the core. "Pretty" which was absent throughout childhood appears for the first time, and "bright," which remained at low values during childhood, now has a sizable loading. Words of different form classes sharing loadings on the same factor suggest an enlargement of the semantic space. The adjective loadings may be directly related to our earlier observation that syntactic responses of one kind, namely adjectives in response to nouns, increase, while syntactic responses of another kind (verbs to nouns) decrease between first and third grade.[3]

The factor analyses seem to indicate tight structures within form class divisions (paradigmatic categories) that become differentiated during childhood into more and more precise groups. The appearance of other form classes within the structure at adulthood suggests that the structure of the groups has changed—perhaps it has become multidimensional. "Yellow" in response to "butterfly" occurs at fifth grade,

---

[3] Probably not much attention should be paid to Factor V, since by definition it contains a high proportion of residual variance. There does appear to be some relation to ideas of prettiness.

and more strongly with adults, but it is not present at first grade. This is evidence of semantic enrichment.

In the next chapter the relation between our data and a theory of linguistic development outlined by Miller and McNeill (1965) will be discussed. They postulate that "semantic markers" are added by a child to his mental dictionary of words, and that these markers are added slowly. The emergence of a new factor (lepidoptera) could be taken to signify the adding of a semantic marker to the words "butterfly," "moth," and "cocoon," that permits them to be distinguished by a minimal contrast from the broader category of insects.

Another kind of evidence bearing on this same point at first appears to be almost paradoxical. Multiple-word responses,[4] so common at kindergarten and first grade, decrease by third grade. But then they *increase again* at fifth grade, particularly for girls, who generally are advanced in linguistic development compared to boys (see Table 7.2). (These totals are based on approximately 10,000 responses at grade five.) Examination of the multiple-word responses reveals that the early ones are predominantly syntactic sequences ("once"—"upon a time") whereas those appearing for fifth-graders are definitions—("ocean"—"a body of water"). The strength of this tendency at fifth grade is remarkable. It seems to indicate an active categorization process, with the child making direct efforts to classify words and distinguish among them on semantic grounds.

TABLE 7.2.   Number of Multiple Word Responses by Grade

	Kindergarten	First	Third	Fifth
Male	21.3	10.9	5.9	7.1
Female	20.6	10.0	3.4	7.5
Total	20.9	10.4	4.7	7.3

Another kind of evidence suggesting active efforts at word categorization are the games played by elementary school children with balls or jump ropes. It is very common to hear them go through naming sequences ("The names of five vegetables are: —— —— —— —— ——") with names produced in rhythm with the bounce of a ball or the swing of a jump rope. Another popular game is one where a category is named, and then subordinates within the category are produced alternately by two children as they face one another and slap hands rhythmically. In both games the names must be produced rather rapidly.[5] Bruner and Olver (1963) call attention to the same phenomenon, when they note the increase in functional groupings between grades one and six. Children attend more to the *uses* of things rather than the apparent qualities of objects.

The percentages of variance accounted for by the several factors give a succinct

---

[4] These were tabulated for the entire list of ninety-six stimulus words.

[5] Overt practice may occur much more than is commonly realized throughout all of childhood. Weir (1962) in studying a two-and-one-half-year-old boy noted that the word "go" was practiced by adding other expressions to it ("for glasses," "for man," etc.).

summary of the changes in structure at various ages (see Table 7.3). The first three rows of the table show, first, the bifurcation as insects become distinct from other flying things between first and third grade, and second, the further division within this category as lepidopterous insects are separated from the general insect category between fifth grade and adulthood. The distinction between insects and other flying things appears to be a very clear example of the process identified over a decade ago by Werner and Kaplan (p. 102, 1952): ". . . many childish words are subjected to the process of conventionalization till their meanings are fairly congruent with the word content of adults." The factor loadings show that "bugs" differs in meaning depending upon the age of the person to whom one may be speaking. Thus, to name a factor with the same term at various ages is in some ways inappropriate.

TABLE 7.3. Proportions of Variance Attributable to Factors

Factor	K	First	Third	Fifth	Adult
I (flight)	.29	.35	.19	.19	.19
II (insects)	.19	.23	.31	.32	.20
III (lepidoptera)	—	—	.16	.15	.29
IV (color)	.18	.21	.18	.19	.17
V (prettiness and residual)	.17 .17	.20	.15	.15	.15

Factors that appear in any analysis are naturally a function of words on the list. Thus in a similar list used by Deese which also included "summer," "sky," "garden," and other words, the first factor emerges as a dichotomy between animate and inanimate things. In terms of our list factor is irrelevant.

Word association studies are often difficult to interpret because of the subjectivity of classification schemes for reducing the data. For instance, a superordinate-subordinate classification is usually empirically derived but there is no guarantee that a dimension perceived by a group of people bears any relation to fundamentals of language categorization. Factor analysis has the advantage of being replicable and nonsubjective when the principal factor method together with a rotation procedure are specified. (The centroid procedure used by Deese will not necessarily compare closely with a principal factor solution.) The replicability of factor analysis for word association data is borne out by comparing our results with Rotberg's (1965) (see Table 7.4). The "butterfly" list (plus other words) was administered independently by Rotberg to a population of fifty Hopkins undergraduates and the data were factor analyzed exactly as ours. Our adult population consisted of 100 (mostly different) Hopkins undergraduates plus 100 Goucher (female) undergraduates. There are comparable data for twelve words from the same general population on two different occasions. The two samples differ in the inclusion of females in the Entwisle data. The factor analytic results are very similar, especially in assignment of high loadings. Some interesting similarities emerge, even though the two sets of "butterfly" words were imbedded in different longer lists which of course would be expected to change the picture. Also Rotberg (1964) finds "airplane" has a high loading on

TABLE 7.4. Rotberg's Factor Analysis Compared to Entwisle Data (Loadings below .10 Omitted) (Twelve "butterfly" words administered separately to college students)

	I (flight)		II (bugs)		III (lepidoptera)		IV (color)	
	R	E	R	E	R	E	R	E
bee			.14	.34				
bird	.77	.77						
bug			.83	.83				
butterfly	.10	.11			.72	.72		.14
cocoon					.75	.75		
color							.80	.69
flower							.11	.14
fly	.57	.54	.22	.17		.11		
insect	.10		.82	.84				
moth		.13	.10	.18	.74	.62		
wing	.80	.73						
yellow	.11	.17					.72	.57

Factor I when she administers her list to her sample. This gives considerable credence to the assignment of the name "flight" to the first factor.

This suggests that association data from different investigators can be compared after being reduced via factor analysis. Lack of a uniform set of measures is a great hindrance in making comparisons between various sets of association data. In fact, it is often necessary to reanalyze data (see Appendices A and B) before even the most elementary comparisons are possible.

Clusters of word meanings are naturally occurring concepts. By eliciting associations and then performing the kind of analysis described here, one may view the accrual of meanings to words directly. This offers several advantages for the study of concept formation. For one thing, naturally occurring concepts possess direct relevance to verbal learning. This approach can also be taken in cross-cultural settings, somewhat as Osgood (1964) and Hill (1964) use other methods, and some preliminary data of this kind are given next.

Another encouraging fact bearing on the factor analytic approach is that not much associative overlap may be needed to prove the existence of a definite structure. Extremely weak associates can effectively mediate paired-associate learning (see Jenkins, 1963). Altogether there is considerable evidence pointing to the validity of factor analytic methods (Deese, 1964b).

Factor Analytic Approach to Subcultural Differences

The data in Chapter 6 suggest that linguistic development differs for rural and urban Maryland children, and that Amish children develop more slowly than any of the non-Amish groups. The close correspondence between our data and Rotberg's for adults prompted a comparison of children in the various subcultural groups via factor analyses of the "butterfly" list. An outstanding question was whether different rates of development, obtained by studying paradigmatic responses, would also be mirrored in the factor loadings. This tactic also offers a way to investigate semantics for the various subcultural groups and ages. There is no reason to think, for instance, that the word "butterfly" means exactly the same thing to a city as to a country child, or to a third-grader and an adult. The same word at different ages may carry different meanings and, of course, the very fact that associations change so much over age attests to this. The Amish samples consist of twenty subjects at each age, a small number for this kind of analysis. This limitation should be kept in mind. The other samples are much larger (rural, 60 per grade; urban, 200 and 280 per grade).

In Table 7.5 factor loadings (over 0.10 in absolute value) are given for factor analyses of various samples of children, with data of Table 7.1 reiterated. For all

TABLE 7.5. Rotated Factor Loadings for Various Cultural Groups on Words Taken from the "Butterfly" List

	Kindergarten	First grade			Third grade			Fifth grade		
		Urban	Rural	Amish	Urban	Rural	Amish	Urban	Rural	Amish
Factor I (flight)										
bee				.18			−.12		.13	.46
bird	.76	.69	.68	.61	.73	.72	.77	.75	.66	.64
bug			.30	.20						
butterfly	.50	.50	.50	.64	.32	.25	.24	.18	.32	.31
cocoon							−.12			−.11
flower							.13			
fly	.34	.68	.66	.73	.63	.54	.25	.54	.68	.63
moth		.16								.29
wing	.74	.63	.60		.75	.73	.78	.77	.80	.69
Factor II (bugs)										
bee	.66	.32	.47	−.50	.33	.35	−.07	.43	.47	.13
bird			−.12							
bug	.44	.71	.63	.57	.84	.81	.77	.81	.79	.83
butterfly		.23	.21		.17		.17	.46	.39	.34
flower	.19									
fly	.23				.17	.36	.18	.31	.23	.11
insect	.55	.72	.74	.65	.84	.80	.79	.81	.78	.82
moth	.40				.19	.28		.44	.46	.24
pretty	−.12									
wing			.11							
Factor III (lepidoptera)[a]										
bee			.17		.33					.12
bright		.25								
butterfly			.21		.57	.57	.60	.45	.53	.42
cocoon			.65		.69	.70	.62	.85	.89	.85
flower										−.14
fly					.19					
moth			.67		.64	.60	.74	.48	.42	.34
pretty										.18
Factor IV (color)										
black	.57	.50	.58	.61	.53	.57	.66	.55	.56	.47
bright[b]	.12	.14	.36		.15	.21			.24	
butterfly			.11							
cocoon			.14							
color	.64	.62	.58	.57	.70	.71	.67	.73	.70	.79
pretty			.14							
yellow	.58	.64	.55	.64	.70	.71	.49	.72	.68	.82

[a] The Amish at first grade do not have the "flight" factor defined in the same way as other children, because "wing" is low. "Moth" and "wing" both have high loadings on a third factor which simultaneously is negative for "butterfly."

[b] This word was not included for the Amish groups because it did not overlap any other words in the list. The Amish samples, 20 at each grade, are much smaller than the rural (60 per grade), or the urban (280 per grade).

groups at all ages first factor loadings on "bird" are large, varying from .61 to .77. The pattern for "wing" is very much the same except for first grade Amish. The distribution of loadings for "fly" is also similar except for kindergarten and third-grade Amish. The scattered small loadings for other words in the Amish sample give the impression that the concept represented by this factor is not well crystallized for the Amish.

The most interesting word as far as the first factor is concerned is "butterfly." At kindergarten and first grade all groups display sizable loadings (.50 or higher). By third grade there is a falling off, and this diminution continues at fifth grade *only* for the urban children. One possibility is that the "fly" syllable in "butterfly" still occupies the attention of the rural and Amish children, as seems to be the case for urban children at younger ages. Attention to acoustic properties rather than semantic properties is characteristic of young or linguistically immature children.

The second factor has high loadings on "bug" and "insect" for all groups at all ages. The rural and urban groups look very similar. The loadings for "bee," "butterfly," and "moth" are fairly large for the non-Amish groups by fifth grade, ranging between .39 and .47. The Amish display smaller loadings on these words altogether and even a negative one $(-.50)$ for "bee" at first grade. The superordinate category of "bugs" seems much less developed for the Amish, and this may be an example of relative retardation. This is suggested also by the figures for the Amish in Factor III.

On the fourth factor (color) the various groups display very similar loadings, except that "bright" has no overlap for the Amish group. This may stem from the small size of the Amish sample.

"Yellow" has many more paradigmatic associates at first grade than other adjectives, perhaps indicating an earlier development compared to other adjectives. Colors are certainly given much attention by four- and five-year-olds. The factor analysis suggests that Amish children may pay similar attention to color at these same ages.

The small sample sizes of both words and persons are limitations, but the results here shed some light on the relative retardation of the Amish pointed to in other analyses. With longer lists of words it might be feasible to explore the development of various kinds of categories, especially to see on what attributes they are distinguished. For instance Brown and McNeill (1965) have studied semantic attributes experimentally by pairing nonsense words with kinship terms. A kinship term denotes (1) sex, (2) direct vs. lateral relationship, and (3) age in relation to ego. For instance "grandmother" denotes female, direct, and older than ego. They find that errors are predictable in terms of these attributes. For kinship words and a few other kinds of words, there can be *a priori* assignment of attributes, but usually this is not the case. Factor analyses of the kind reported here may permit one to identify attributes for other kinds of words with less obvious interrelations.

Old and Modern Association Data

Results for Amish respondents have been compared with results for rural Maryland respondents via form class measures and factor analyses, and Amish children are apparently retarded in linguistic development. The Amish results are also relevant to comparisons between old and modern data, because the Amish choose to live under conditions more like those of fifty years ago than those of today. As mentioned at the beginning of the chapter, we hoped that the Amish respondents might provide a modern counterpart for data collected by Woodrow and Lowell from Minneapolis school children half-a-century ago.

Two independent lines of word association research (Palermo and Jenkins, 1963; Entwisle, *et al.*, 1964), using different measures and somewhat different conceptual frameworks, have independently led to the same conclusion: modern children are accelerated in language development compared to children of fifty years ago (Woodrow and Lowell, 1916). The acceleration may be considerable, as much as four or five years.

This acceleration is further documented by Templin's (1957) comparison of sentence length between children in Minneapolis sampled twenty years apart (Davis, 1937). These two samples were matched on sex, intelligence, age, and socioeconomic status, and so are much more appropriate to compare than our sample (or Palermo and Jenkins' sample) with the Woodrow and Lowell sample. It was found that at ages three and three-and-one-half years, sentences on the average were half a word longer in 1957. At four and four-and-one-half years of age, the sentences were one word longer, and at age six, the mean sentence length was approximately equal to the sentence length used by nine-and-one-half-years-olds in Davis' sample. This finding points to cultural rather than educational factors as being important, for these remarkable changes occur in children prior to school entrance or before formal language instruction in school.

Many factors conspire to hasten language development in modern children. Elementary school curricula have evolved with the primary aim of helping children to learn to read rapidly and efficiently. Supplementary exercises are designed specifically to exploit verbal habits and skills already in a child's repertoire. For instance, even very young children match number of pronouns and verbs when speaking, and these habits can be drawn upon to aid in setting up the grapheme-phoneme correspondences needed for reading. Audio-visual aids funnel information into several sensory channels at once and link them in new ways. Mass media are probably the most potent force, however, when considering conditions of life now, compared to 1910. The ubiquitous audio-visual aid, television, undoubtedly pushes language development in the toddler as well as the school-age child. The preschool child now spends many hours listening to speech that is correlated with pictures, via the TV set. In the United States it is estimated that three-year-old children already average about forty-five minutes of TV a day. Average daily watching time increases to a peak of three hours at ages twelve to thirteen. The cumulative statistics are staggering: during the span of thirteen years of school attendance the total time spent watching television ranges between 6,000 and 12,000 hours. The latter figure equals the total number of hours spent attending school (Schramm, 1964).

The flow of language from the TV set is almost continuous. Exposure to spoken discourse, mainly emanating from *adult* speakers, may be multiplied many times over compared to its level early in the century for preschool children. In the 1910–20 period working hours separating parents from children were longer, and there was less emphasis on parent-child interaction in the family. One also gets the impression that there was considerably less verbalization in the school, although this is hard to check. As anyone who has tried to converse with three- or four-year-old children knows, the feedback for adults from such conversations is insufficient to support continuous discourse, even if the attention span of the child should be long enough. Verbal interchanges with playmates or siblings, although perhaps more continuous than face-to-face interchanges with adults, do not offer the variety of vocabulary and syntax contained in an adult conversion. The TV set, and the radio, both with unin- terrupted spoken signals of an adult variety, may offer an unprecedented opportunity for language learning. A socially determined learning condition of central importance for language development is the willingness of adults to engage the child in dialogue, or for the child to overhear dialogue. Modern home conditions provide for a kind of pseudo-adult-child interaction.

Theoretical interest attaches to the 1916–64 difference since so little is known about specific learning mechanisms in language acquisition. This difference in some ways represents an *ex post facto* experiment. Changes in verbal behavior have come about and the task is now to identify the particular causes. The enhancement of linguistic development is a question not only of theoretical interest, but of possible wide applica- tion. Without here mentioning various explanations proposed (this will be the topic of Chapter 8) we suggest that whatever is abstracted that speeds linguistic develop- ment must be possible only after considerable exposure. Conditions of exposure must interact with maturation.

Palermo and Jenkins (1965a) point out that in the Woodrow and Lowell (1916) data the frequency of most popular responses was about the same for children and adults, but for only 39 per cent of the words was the first response the same for the two groups. They also report that between fourth grade and college 107 words (out of 200) held corresponding first ranks—this is over 53 per cent.

They find less overlap between the two children's samples in 1916 and now than between modern fourth grade and college data.

Other work (Palermo, 1962) shows that popular responses, diversity of responses, number of idiosyncratic responses, contrast responses, and paradigmatic responses have increased from 1916 to 1961. The responses of children in grades four and five obtained by Woodrow and Lowell using an oral method of presentation were com- pared to responses obtained from 1,000 children by written presentation, and to those from 200 children using oral presentation. The findings parallel ours for con- trast responses in written and oral presentation methods (see pp. 42ff.). There are more contrast responses under oral conditions (29.2 per cent vs. 22.2 per cent), but the difference is insufficient to account for differences between Woodrow and Lowell findings (2.5 per cent) and modern data.[6] Similarly, in classifying paradigmatic responses, he notes some differences associated with administration procedure but

---

[6] Absolute levels are not comparable in our data and the data of Palermo for several reasons. Definitions of contrast responses and paradigmatic responses are not identical, but more important he considers the five most common responses only in classifying paradigmatic responses, whereas we use all responses.

these differences are smaller than those noted between old and modern data. His data suggest that administration procedure is responsible for some minor fraction of the discrepancy, especially contrast responses, but in general this factor cannot account for the wide differences observed.

The differences between old and modern data provoke curiosity in another way, for besides displaying greater frequency of popular responses, modern data show a greater number of different responses. These observations are almost antithetical to one another and suggest that changes over the years in associative patterns involve changes in the distribution parameters. A sample, like Woodrow and Lowell's, taken at one age, does not allow any assessment of changes in associative patterns[7] with age, and change-over-time, if it could be isolated in their data, would of course be exceedingly useful in trying to evaluate their data or to explain differences between their data and modern data.

The Woodrow and Lowell data are puzzling. The degree of association development in their children ages nine to twelve resembles closely the developmental level we find with five- or six-year-olds. (It is here that the limitations of the Kent-Rosanoff stimulus list are felt most keenly.) In table 7.6 the Woodrow and Lowell data are re-summarized. Our data for the twenty-nine matching stimulus words only, and also for our entire list of adjectives and nouns, are included in Table 7.6.

The first conclusion from Table 7.6 is that verb responses are much more frequent for the Woodrow and Lowell sample, and the percentages of verb responses exceed those we find even with five-year-old modern children. In our data verb responses to nouns decrease sharply with age over the first- to fifth-grade range. Adjectival responses increase with age in modern data. Neither kind of response at any age is as large as the percentages noted by Woodrow and Lowell. Verb responses included among the three most popular responses in their data amount to 17 per cent at both age nine and age twelve. This evidence, although very scanty, suggests that verb responses *do not* decrease with age. Here of course, the evidence is tenuous because twelve-year-olds in the same grade as nine-year-olds probably are less intelligent. Intelligence has already been shown to be correlated with association data, so a decrease might be obscured with systematic bias in IQ. The three most common responses for adults, listed by Woodrow and Lowell, reveal only three verb responses for the twenty-nine stimulus words that overlap our list. This *does* suggest that verb responses to nouns and adjectives decrease sharply with age. There is no single age group in our data with patterns exactly resembling the Woodrow and Lowell data patterns. Only for the five–six-year age range (kindergarten and first grade) however, is there an appreciable number of verb responses, so this age level seems most like the Woodrow and Lowell data.

One explanation for the presence of so many verb responses on the Woodrow and Lowell data may be that fifty years ago children heard more speech from other children and less adult speech than now. Average family size has declined in the interval and on television and radio adult speakers predominate. A socially determined learning condition of great importance may be the availability of adults for

[7] Age data are given only for the three most common responses with no frequencies listed.

TABLE 7.6.   Woodrow and Lowell Data, Reclassified by Form Class of Response, Compared to Entwisle Data

	W. & L.[a]	Entwisle Same stimulus words					Entwisle Complete list of words				
		K	First	Third	Fifth	Adult	K	First	Third	Fifth	Adult
Stimulus High-freq. nouns											
Responses											
Adjectives	13.6	4.4	4.9	3.8	3.6	4.1	7.8	9.6	15.0	14.6	14.8
Adverbs	.1	1.0	1.1	.5	.1	.1	1.9	2.5	1.8	.7	2.4
Nouns	54.6	62.5	68.4	84.6	88.1	85.0	56.6	59.7	65.7	72.0	69.2
Verbs	31.1	21.0	17.1	8.4	7.0	8.0	22.2	20.4	15.2	11.7	12.3
Stimulus Med.-freq. nouns											
Responses											
Adjectives	18.6	5.4	8.3	10.5	11.0	14.4	5.0	8.0	9.6	9.7	13.0
Adverbs	1.1	1.1	.8	.5	.2	.1	1.0	.7	.4	.2	.1
Nouns	63.1	66.5	65.4	76.5	78.3	76.9	65.7	63.8	72.8	77.0	76.9
Verbs	17.6	18.4	17.5	11.5	9.9	7.4	18.8	19.6	15.9	12.2	9.0
Stimulus Low-freq. nouns											
Responses											
Adjectives	16.5	3.3	7.3	8.4	13.0	10.3	4.4	7.7	5.7	5.4	5.2
Adverbs	.0	1.0	.4	.0	.3	.0	.9	1.2	1.2	.4	.0
Nouns	39.1	60.3	64.6	81.3	77.5	80.0	61.3	64.5	80.3	85.4	85.1
Verbs	44.3	25.0	20.5	8.0	8.3	8.8	21.4	16.9	9.6	7.5	8.4
Stimulus High-freq. adjectives											
Responses											
Adjectives	29.7	17.7	34.3	77.8	81.6	71.4	17.5	34.2	78.9	83.0	70.7
Adverbs	1.7	3.8	3.0	1.2	1.1	1.4	3.6	2.7	1.1	1.0	1.4
Nouns	61.3	60.9	46.2	15.5	14.1	23.6	61.9	46.5	14.8	13.2	24.5
Verbs	7.3	7.4	8.3	2.9	1.6	3.0	6.9	7.8	2.5	1.4	2.6
Stimulus Med.-freq. adjectives											
Responses											
Adjectives	16.1	24.5	42.0	67.5	58.0	52.0	19.2	33.3	68.2	73.4	60.9
Adverbs	.5	3.5	1.4	1.1	1.8	.0	2.5	1.9	1.6	.8	.7
Nouns	54.9	49.0	36.4	23.8	32.5	46.0	57.1	45.5	22.2	19.1	34.1
Verbs	27.9	15.5	14.8	7.0	7.3	1.8	12.8	12.1	6.3	6.3	3.5
Stimulus Low-freq. adjectives											
Responses											
Adjectives	37.5	13.1	27.5	64.0	77.6	63.0	13.7	27.6	64.6	79.2	65.9
Adverbs	.7	3.1	3.5	2.7	3.4	2.4	2.8	3.3	2.4	3.0	2.1
Nouns	43.2	52.0	39.9	17.7	12.5	27.1	52.2	40.4	17.9	11.5	25.4
Verbs	17.9	21.0	19.3	12.5	5.9	6.9	20.5	19.2	12.2	5.6	6.1

[a] In recalculating the Woodrow and Lowell response percentages some frequencies are found to be in error by as much as 20 (responses to "hard"). These errors cause some total percentages not to add exactly to 100 per cent when all responses are classified.

conversation. Earlier in analyzing the Amish data this matter has been discussed. Our data for rural and Amish groups suggests that form class development is retarded when opportunities for exposure are reduced, and the verb response may represent a prolongation of a syntactic phase like that found with the Amish. It is somewhat puzzling that noun-verb combinations are not much more frequent in the Amish data, since adjective-noun sequences are.

Palermo compares form classes of five most popular responses (fourth and fifth grades combined) for his data and the data of Woodrow and Lowell:

	W. and L.	Palermo
Nouns	62.6	73.6
Adjectives	51.1	62.1

Our nouns are close to his—71.3 per cent and 76.4 per cent (all his nouns are of A or AA frequency in the Thorndike-Lorge count). Adjectives are not very close to his (83 per cent, 73 per cent, 79 per cent for three frequency levels) but this is where there are large differences attributable to administration conditions. Palermo selected high status fourth- and fifth-grade respondents so they could write their own responses. Our data (Table 4.2) comparing commonality for fifth grade and college suggest that the correspondence between popular responses for children and adults may be characteristic only of the form classes sampled by Woodrow and Lowell. For instance, we note the same commonality (52.8 per cent) for high-frequency nouns, but differences close to 15 per cent on medium- and low-frequency verbs and adverbs. The Woodrow and Lowell stimulus list may not have provided an opportunity for child-adult differences to reveal themselves.

All in all, the Woodrow and Lowell data suggests a greatly prolonged syntactic phase, extending as much as five or six years beyond the time we note a syntagmatic phase for common words. Unfortunately, their data contain so few form classes that it is hard to make comparisons. The observation of a prolongation of the syntactic phase in the Amish suggests why some of the differences may exist, but in terms of syntagmatic responses the children of fifty years ago are far behind the Amish. In particular, the numerous verb responses to adjectives, even more than the slowness of paradigmatic development, suggest great retardation compared to modern children. In kindergarten children we find 7 per cent of responses to adjectives are verbs. They note this same figure for high-frequency adjectives, but much higher rates for medium- and low-frequency adjectives (28 per cent and 18 per cent). The adjective-verb linkage strikes one as a very immature pattern.

Chapter Eight

The Data in Perspective

Two traditions underlie work with word associations, the experimental and the psychometric. This book fits under both rubrics. Most of our observations are from quasi-experiments or *ex post facto* experiments. For instance, the Amish samples, or the samples at various IQ levels, represent attempts to study variables in a more systematic way than can usually be done by surveys. And yet, since age of subjects is the major variable, the work is psychometric, but in a different sense from word association research dealing wholly with the classification of the relations between stimuli and their responses. It is psychometric in the sense of deriving a developmental scale that supposedly has a significant relation to the natural process of language acquisition.

The modest success attained by this study is reflected in several areas rather than a single area, and the areas are not closely related. One outcome is a surprisingly good developmental scale for language with considerable sensitivity over the elementary school age range. Variations in paradigmatics are sharp enough to discriminate among children of different IQ and between children of various ages. Although considerable further study would be necessary to establish validity and reliability, such a scale might have some usefulness in specialized situations where anxiety could be held to lower levels than it is in standard testing situations. Another outcome is fairly precise documentation of subcultural variations in verbal development, together with some notion about how these variations may arise. In addition, the importance of role relations in gathering language data is pointed up. Role relations may be especially significant for research methodology in studies of cultural deprivation.

As far as verbal learning is concerned, there is some reason to think that study of associations in children will be more fruitful than similar studies with adults. The dimensionality of the semantic space is probably less, for one thing, and our factor analytic studies give partial confirmation of this. Jenkins (1962) found a high degree of sensitivity to normative associative strength in paired-associate learning tasks with fourth-grade subjects, contrary to the earlier findings of the Minnesota investigators with college populations.

Perhaps the most significant outcome of this research is the light shed on language acquisition over the period of middle childhood, from kindergarten to fifth grade.

Empirical work over the past few years has filled in our knowledge of early language acquisition considerably even though many gaps remain. Outstanding longitudinal studies are those by Brown and Ervin and their co-workers (Brown and Fraser, 1964; Brown, Fraser, and Bellugi, 1964; Brown and Bellugi, 1964; Ervin, 1964, Miller and Ervin, 1964). These analyses are reminiscent of analyses performed by an anthropologist in the field who attempts to produce a grammar for an exotic language. The consensus is that a fairly complete grammar is laid down by age four. For a child to accomplish this feat seems to demand that there be an inherited predisposition to accept certain word orders and to derive meaning from given sequences, and to ignore the more numerous possibilities that do not occur (Miller, 1964; Lenneberg, 1964; Miller and McNeill, 1965, and others).[1] Attempts to account for acquisition in terms of formal teaching by parents or in terms of abstractions drawn by the child from his own experience have been unsuccessful. The rapidity of the process, and particularly the nesting patterns of English, rule out a contiguity-type model. This implies that conventional learning theory cannot explain the acquisition of grammar.

Our concern is not with this age period, however, for our work begins after age four, when the major rudiments of grammar have already been laid down. Our interest is in linguistic development over ages five to ten. Although a genetic explanation may be required for the early stages of language learning, conventional learning theory may nevertheless account for later development occurring over the period of middle childhood, particularly acquisition of semantics. In fact, both Brown and Fraser (1963) and Cofer (1963) make the point that one kind of learning theory may be needed to account for early linguistic accomplishments while a very different theory is demanded by later stages of development.

Several investigations of syntax have been carried out under the general influence of contemporary linguistic theory, but there is little research of this sort as yet on semantic development. McNeill's (1964) experiments show that five-year-old children know very little about semantics even though they are relatively sophisticated in grammar. Thus, most semantics must be learned later. Conventional learning theory may give a fairly good accounting of the semantic embellishments, refinements, and additions *subsequent* to the consolidation of the basic structure of language. Language learning during middle childhood seems to offer many opportunities for retroactive and proactive inhibition to come into play, for instance. One need only look at responses to pronouns and strong verbs, where similarity can yield confusion, to be impressed with the potential predictive power of transfer theory in certain areas of language learning.

---

[1] Werner and Kaplan (1950) anticipated this conclusion by more than a decade, stating, "the close correspondence of the developmental curves . . . between two seemingly independent aspects of language lends support to those theories that assume a genetic interdependence of meaning and structure" (pp. 256–57).

The Findings

Before attempting to place the data in a theoretical setting, it is first necessary to give a brief review of the chief empirical findings. There are several facts about word associations that emerge unequivocally from our data, and a theory of developmental psycholinguistics should account for them.

The primary finding is the great increase in paradigmatics and the shift (for some words) from a syntactic to a paradigmatic type of response. Although this shift was discovered long ago (Woodrow and Lowell, 1916), its exact nature has not been defined until now. Previously the implication has been that this shift affects all words and occurs sometime after school entrance, even though the data in hand were insufficient to support such broad statements. Our data suggest that only a small portion of the vocabulary may evolve through this pattern at any particular age, and perhaps the description of the shift has been oversimplified. In particular, the timing of the shift may be more a function of the particular words used than has been realized heretofore. The potential for producing syntactic responses seems to vary greatly from word to word, even within the same form class. This may be partly a function of the number of different usages and meanings a word has.

Secondly, the present data show an unmistakable displacement by age of the paradigmatic shift depending upon the form class of the stimulus word. The data for verbs and adjectives which show the displacement most clearly (from Table 4.4) are reproduced here for convenience:

	Per cent of Paradigmatic Responses				
	K	1	3	5 (Indiv.)	5 (Group)
Adjective stimulus	16.8	31.7	70.6	78.5	55.6
Verb stimulus	16.6	20.4	47.5	59.6	56.1

Between kindergarten and first grade there is a decided increase in paradigmatics to common adjectives, particularly those possessing antonyms.[2] This adjectival pattern is most clearly seen in the highly intelligent group, where increases from 17 to over 40 per cent are noted within a single year. The pattern heralded by the very intelligent at first grade develops strongly over all IQ levels between the first and third grades. By age eight, in fact, paradigmatic responding to adjectives is over 70 per cent. The increase in paradigmatics to verbs starts more slowly, continues longer, and attains a lower final level than is the case for adjectives.

Both adjectives and verbs start at the same level, but the rate of development for verbs is much slower. The level for verbs at third grade (48 per cent) is considerably below that found for adjectives. There is an even slower evolution of adverbs with age.[3]

---

[2] There is a similar increase for pronouns which is temporarily being ignored.

[3] All these data were procured by individual administration, but the comparison of group-procured and individually-procured data for third-grade students (Table 3.6) showed no difference associated with method.

It is noteworthy that the shift does not seem to depend on any simple contrast between lexical and function words. This echoes the results of Fillenbaum and Jones (1965) in terms of varying degrees of paradigmatic responding with adults.

The third fact that any theory should encompass concerns the asymmetries in response. Adverbs often yield adjectives as responses, but the reverse is seldom true. The number of adjectival responses to nouns increases, even though the total number of heterogeneous responses decreases from first to fifth grade, and in particular the number of verb responses to nouns decreases.

The fourth finding is that syntactic responses of young children differ in kind from those of adults, with children's reflecting grammatical pairings (noun-verb sequences, for instance), and adults' reflecting semantic refinement (adjective-nouns or combinations of words that signal newly acquired meanings).

Another finding, whose paradoxical nature is easy to overlook because it is so familiar, is that children give many more different associations than adults. In fact, the younger the child the more various the associations are, even though the vocabulary of a young child is smaller than an older child's or an adult's. The distributions of word associations (frequency ranks plotted against number of words with a particular frequency) change with age. The number of *different* associations diminishes as children grow older and the popularity of some associates increases. Attempts to summarize these statements in mathematical form have been frequent, and not long ago a stochastic model was proposed and applied to data obtained from adults (Horvath, 1963). Using one parameter, the ratio of the number of different response words to the total number of response words, this model fits data from adults for a few individual words very well, and predicts the frequency of the primary response especially well. Several attempts were made to fit similar or identical one-parameter models to our data for children's associative distributions. This was not fruitful, perhaps because the samples of children are not large enough. But subsequent work suggests that such efforts may be doomed to failure no matter how large the sample of subjects. The models tend to fit responses of *intermediate frequency*, neither the very frequent responses nor the idiosyncratic responses, but these middle-of-the-road responses are both the least interesting psychologically and also the most scarce. It is our feeling that empirical data used to provide good fits for single words is probably fortuitous, and that efforts at model-building may be premature. When more is known about associative structure, classes of words that are homogeneous on some fundamental dimension may emerge. At this stage it might be possible to attain more success with simple models.

This point of view is reminiscent of one set forth by Carroll, *et al.* (1962) in connection with another facet of word association work. He calls attention to the multi-dimensionality of word association schema commonly employed, which certainly is a fatal handicap for measurement. Also much to the same point is Mandlebrot's (1959) statement that laws of the Zipf-type, despite their practical importance, have defied explanation even though they provide one of the best defined and most conspicuous challenges to those interested in statistical laws of nature.

Ervin's Theory of Contextual Variety

Explicit explanations of how word associations develop are few. Since paradigmatics by definition never occur together—they involve understanding "what-substitutes-for-what"—they have been puzzling, especially from the viewpoint of contiguity theory. Ervin (1963) has suggested that they are learned via contiguity brought about by erroneous anticipation. Some experiments by McNeill (1963) aimed directly at testing Ervin's notion seemed at first to produce results consonant with her theory. Later and more precise experiments (McNeill, 1965) tend to negate this notion, however, because when subjects make their anticipations overtly, the anticipations do not correlate with paradigmatic response strength. Also, of course, this explanation is undermined by the same facts that Miller and Chomsky (1963) marshall to show the limitations of a Markov model in explaining language development. There probably is insufficient opportunity for exposure to a great many similar contexts, with the probability of any particular context being small.

Ervin (1963) has also discussed contextual variety as a factor in the development of word association patterns, and this can be considered separately from the erroneous anticipation hypothesis. It is suggested that a word appearing in many different contexts will develop paradigmatic responses more rapidly than another word appearing in few contexts. Presumably the relative strength of syntagmatics is reduced when contextual variety is great, and the paradigmatics' competitive position thereby improved.

It is very hard to provide data relevant to the contextual variety hypothesis because somehow words would have to be matched in terms of other attributes as well as varying contexts. One possibility is to compare responses to pronouns ("he," "him"; "she," "her"; "they," "them"). [4] These words should all be of approximately the same difficulty, their chief difference within pairs ("he"—"him," etc.) consisting of position in sentences. At fifth grade these pairs of pronouns elicit almost exactly the same amount of paradigmatic responding. At kindergarten, first, and third grades, however, the nominative form has fewer paradigmatics in seven of nine instances. This provides some weak support for greater contextual variety resulting in more rapid development of paradigmatics.

There are no direct data on the extent of contextual variety related to occurrences of words of various form classes. Reflection suggests, however, that contextual variety for either adjectives or verbs comes about through nouns that surround them, particularly in the case of children who tend to use short sentences of simple structure. We should expect to see as sequences of words in sentences:

	(1) adjective	noun	verb	(adv.)
or				
	(2) noun	verb	adjective	noun

or variations of these. The variety of contexts for adjectives and verbs in such arrangements is hard to judge, but probably is roughly equivalent for the two paradigms, except that a leading adjective might achieve greater variety by way of

---

[4] This kind of test was suggested by Ervin, 1961.

apposition with ends of preceding sentences. But adjectives occurring in the initial position in sentences may be balanced by verbs occurring in the initial position in commands.

There must be a large difference in terms of context for adjectives and verbs, however, when pronouns are present in sentences. The crucial characteristic of pronouns, as far as the present discussion is concerned, is that they frequently precede and follow verbs, but they almost never are contiguous with adjectives. For example, one cannot say "little he," or "tall him," or "good her," but one very often says "he went," "tell him," or "get her." Particularly in conversation, the form of language most available to preliterate children, are pronouns plentiful. In telephone conversations pronouns exceed all other tokens, even articles, in terms of occurrence, and constitute almost one-quarter of the words uttered (French, *et al.*, 1930). The percentage of pronouns used by preschoolers may even exceed this.

How does this relate to the differential development of adjectives and verbs over time? Conjugations with pronouns would seem to vastly reduce contexts of verbs compared to adjectives even though other common kinds of sentences, without pronouns, produce varieties of context that appear to be roughly comparable. Contextual variety for verbs, then, especially the common ones, may be reduced compared to adjectives, especially for young children. If so, Ervin's contextual variety notion is consonant with the kind of form class displacement we observe, because verbs seem to develop later even when some allowance is made for the antonymic property affecting displacement. (See discussion of antonyms below.)

Contextual variety also is consonant with other word association phenomena beside the adjective-verb displacement. It may account for why the Woodrow and Lowell data show fewer paradigmatics than modern data, because exposure to language was considerably less before the days of mass media. Contextual variety also suggests why paradigmatics increases with age, and why exposure to adult conversation might hasten development. Greater exposure is bound to lead to more variety only when the exposure increases variety. The slow development of adverbs, shown in our data and Brown and Berko's (1960) data, can be accounted for by contextual variety. They typically appear in final position, suggesting that variety rather than order is the important factor (see Ervin and Landar, 1963).

It is our opinion that the adjective-verb displacement we observe may be exaggerated in our data, however. Much of it seems to depend on whether or not a word possesses antonyms. Among the adjectives on the stimulus list only two ("yellow" and "thirsty") do not possess strong antonyms. Even the less frequent adjectives, i.e., "bitter," have strong contrast responses. "Yellow," a color name, and "thirsty" with the apposite "hungry" are not very good examples of words with nonantonymic properties either, but they are the only two available. The percentages of paradigmatic responses to these two words at various grades are shown below:

	K	1	3	5
yellow	33	47	66	46
thirsty	4	14	36	40
Average for both words	18	30	51	43
Average for 24 adjectives on list	17	32	71	79

These average figures show a 20 per cent increase for "yellow" and "thirsty" between first and third grades, which compares with a 30 per cent increase for verbs as a whole. The increase in paradigmatic responses to these two adjectives is much smaller than the increases for other adjectives over the same ages (40 per cent).

The same idea seems to be applicable to verbs. Three of the verbs on the list have antonymic responses: "add"—"subtract," "give"—"take," and "sell"—"buy." The percentage of paradigmatic responses increases much more rapidly between first and third grades for these three verbs (46 per cent) than for the remainder of the verbs (30 per cent):

	K	1	3	5
add	15	18	72	72
give	11	14	61	74
sell	10	17	52	63
Average for three verbs	12	16	62	70
Average for 24 verbs on list	17	20	47	59

It seems likely that the same explanation underlies both the departure of "yellow", and "thirsty" from the general pattern for adjectives, and the departure of "add," "give," and "sell" from the general verb pattern. Much of the displacement of age changes by form class must be owing to the specific words chosen, then, particularly the adjectives. Those that have contrasts seem to develop much more rapidly than others of their class. In fact, the differences between the two kinds of adjectives exceed the form class differentials.

Considering the total pattern of our data, together with bits of pertinent information from other sources, suggests that each word, or word group, goes through an evolutionary process (perhaps sparked by contextual variety). This evolution has already been outlined in some detail in Chapter 4. But the age patterns in children's word associations suggest that the emphasis in some common generalizations about word associations may be misplaced. The true state of affairs may be distorted by over-attention to some details and a neglect of others. For instance, the statement that adult associations tend to be more paradigmatic than children's has to be qualified—adult paradigmatics for nouns and adjectives are *fewer* than fifth-grade paradigmatics, and some new syntagmatics appear. Or, to take another example, low-frequency adverbs supposedly elicit a clear majority of syntagmatic responses, but this pattern may be typical only for certain adverbs (those without antonyms) and not others. Generalizations over form class categories, or even over groups of words within a category, are perilous.

Statements that hinge on the age of subjects rather than on properties of words themselves may be in error. In this connection cross-cultural comparisons are very informative. As pointed out previously, for common words, Navaho adults emit the same per cent of paradigmatics to nouns and verbs as Johns Hopkins undergraduates (Ervin and Landar, 1963).[5]

[5] Other cross cultural comparisons (Rosenzweig, 1964) based only on primaries may be misleading in this connection.

It seems that all words evolve through a fixed sequence with most familiar words being the first to go through the various stages. For very young children there may be marked idiosyncrasies in usage that alter familiarity to a great extent. For this reason some paradigmatics are given even by four-year-olds. The syntactic-paradigmatic shift, supposedly characteristic of middle childhood, actually occurs at many different ages throughout childhood, over every age for which we have data. More words on our list go through this metamorphosis around ages six to eight than any other time, but already it has been shown that particular words may possess paradigmatic responses at age four or syntagmatic responses at adult ages. The fact that the shift occurs between ages six and eight appears to depend on the words themselves. With a different set of stimulus words, particularly with different adjectives, we could find the shift displaced. For the adjectives on our list there are relatively few changes in syntactic responses between first and fifth grades, but many changes between fifth grade and adulthood.

Miller and McNeill's Theory

This capsule summary of the evolution of word associations is consonant with a theory proposed by Miller and McNeill (1965). Of the many persons who have been challenged to explain the process of language acquisition, so far they are the only ones to develop a comprehensive theory, which includes a section on development of word associations and which delineates the roles of semantics and syntax. Heretofore, linguistic theory and studies of language acquisition have mainly evolved separately and had little influence upon one another. They point out that to say that a need for precision and cognitive economy motivate the developmental sequence is not to explain how a child meets these needs. They appeal to the child's innate *faculté de langage*. Their theory is not in contradiction to Ervin's notion of contextual variety. Rather her notions supplement their theory and suggest a mechanism by which some of the changes they point to could occur.

Where we can cite evidence relevant to statements made by Miller and McNeill our observations are generally consonant with their position. They believe that starting at about eighteen months of age the child's language needs increase, forcing him to compile a word dictionary. His previously adequate sentence dictionary is now conceptually awkward. Entries for a word in the dictionary consist of selection restrictions plus a series of semantic markers. Markers are economical because a single marker may affect a large group of words. This minimizes the burden on memory.[6] An example given by Miller and McNeill of a hypothetical set of markers for the word "flower" includes: "physical object," "living," "small," "plant," etc. They assume that dictionary entries are built up sequentially, and the addition of a

---

[6] The parallel state of affairs for the earlier development of the sound system was independently proposed by Jakobson (1956) in a very influential hypothesis. It is predicted that the development of the sound system can be described in terms of successive contrasts between features that are maximally different, the number of contrasting features being much smaller than the number of phonemes. Thus changes can come about suddenly.

semantic marker introduces a distinction that separates one entire class of words from another. For instance, "living" vs. "nonliving" is a marker that could affect a very broad class of words.

Because children have fewer markers than adults, they will tend to have much broader classes of words. This would account for our observation, and the observations of many others, that many more different responses are given by young children to a stimulus word than by older children or by adults. To the word "table," for example, 200 kindergarten children give 87 different responses, while 200 college students give 28 different responses. Selection restrictions depend on syntax. A child with few (or no) markers may produce an association by using selection restrictions that embody his knowledge of grammatical rules. This is the picture in the early syntactic phase when many noun-verb and sentence completions or phrase completions are common. Since nouns have relatively fewer selection restrictions they may rapidly proceed to the marker-development phase. This is consistent with our observation that nouns develop paradigmatics earlier than other words.

It is hypothesized that all lexical words pass through the same set of steps but at different rates. With low exposure a word might appear to be at an intermediate stage because its evolutionary rate is extremely slow. There is no way, of course, to assess the validity of Miller and McNeill's constructs (selection restrictions and semantic markers), but the assumptions and rationale of their theory appear to fit well with our data.

As already stated in considerable detail, the differential rate of paradigmatic development for various form classes shown in our data may be misleading in some ways, for it suggests that the properties attaching to form class membership somehow cause, or are associated with, different rates of word development. There is apparently a syntactic-paradigmatic shift for each word and some words show this sooner than others but, generally speaking, form class membership seems to have little effect on the rate. Other attributes could be used to group words that might yield more homogeneous groups. As already mentioned, we believe the displacement observed for adjectives and verbs may be to some extent a distortion brought about by the particular sample of words selected. We think that each word evolves through an orderly associative patterning sequence, where the rate of evolution depends upon exposure, perhaps modified by some kind of confusion parameter. Adult syntagmatics could thus be examples of words that have only partly evolved, or words that have evolved all the way.

As an adult it is difficult to appreciate the confusion inherent in one's native tongue, but it must be considerable, and this is why a confusion parameter may be required. For instance, in tracing specific responses over age, it was found that a common response to "swift" at third grade is "cheese," but this response is absent by fifth grade. Although at first this may seem merely anomalous, probably "swift" is being interpreted as "Swiss" and the response is part of "Swiss cheese." Also, "swim," a popular response to "swift" at third grade, drops out by fifth grade. Other popular responses at first grade that drop off sharply thereafter are "care" to "chair," "hide" to "high," "lawn" to "long," "short" to "belong," "church" to "inquire," "cough" and "mop" to "moth," "moon" to "move," to mention a few of the common ones that appear to be most confusing. One can only guess at the amount of unlearning that must go on as markers are reassigned to words, and the words entered properly in the dictionary. There is direct evidence that an interfering word list of high acoustic similarity to an original list produces more inhibition than a list with very different pronunciation (Wickelgren, 1965).

The anomalies just cited arise from acoustic similarities. Other words that are very similar in terms of pronunciation and meaning, with relatively minor distinctions in usage, are the strong verbs. In Table 8.1 responses which are the past tense of the eight most common verbs on our stimulus list are summarized in percentages over different age groups. The verbs that are regular ("add," "carry," "move") generally have no responses of the regular past tense at any age—one exception being a rate of 1.4 per cent for "carried" in response to "carry" at third grade. The strong verbs, on the other hand, elicit many responses of the irregular past tense, and these vary with age so as to suggest that the irregular past tenses are being laid down as separate entries in the dictionary. In fact, at the college level, particularly for males, these responses still occur with surprising frequency. These facts suggest that sheer exposure differences alone are incapable of explaining differences in developmental rate.

TABLE 8.1.   Responses to Verbs in the Past Tense   (Per cents)

Stimulus: Response:	add added	begin began	carry carried	give gave	move moved	tell told	run ran	sit sat
First grade N = 280	0	0	0	0	0	1.8	2.5	2.1
Third grade N = 280	0	3.9	1.4	19.3	0	6.4	13.2	12.5
Fifth grade N = 200	0	3.0	0	9.5	0	9.5	9.0	6.0
College N = 200	0	2.0	0	4.5	0.5	2.0	1.5	6.5

The S-P shift *appears* to occur at a particular age because many words are at a particular stage of development. The first meaningful associative stage exists when syntactic responses begin to occur. They indicate knowledge of selection restrictions. For the very common nouns and other words in the primitive vocabulary, early knowledge of selection restrictions cannot be observed via association data because of the age of the child, but it is observed indirectly in the pairing of pivot words with other words. Most selection restrictions may be laid down by age four *for a limited, somewhat idiosyncratic vocabulary*. At age four we see already the presence of considerable paradigmatic responding. Between ages five and six we see syntactic responding at its peak for *this sample of words*, but many words yield paradigmatic responses and many other words do not yield either pattern of response. The sample of words is arbitrary, however, and at ages five and six there is still a high percentage of responses that bear no relation, either syntactic or semantic, to the stimulus (up to 50 per cent for some words). Responses that occur with fairly high frequency at first grade but that disappear later are "bitter"—"litter," "join"—"party," "into"—"Indian," etc. (see Table 8.2). Paradigmatics begin to develop strongly after first grade, and this corresponds to the laying down of semantic markers, which then determine associations, rather than selection restrictions as previously.

TABLE 8.2. Nonparadigmatic Responses of at least 2.5 Per Cent Frequency That Drop out at Successive Ages

Stimulus word	Responses present grade 1, not grade 5[a]	Responses present grade 3, not grade 5[a]
Nouns		
bee	good	
bug	crawl	
butterfly	catch, flies	
chair	care	
flower		pink
fly		down, go, run
man	can, work	
music	loud	loud
wing	sing	
Adjectives		
bitter	litter	
bright	might, morning	
clean	clothes, floor, the house, table	
cold	coat, water, weather	
dark	dog, mark, sun, moon	morning
hard	heart	
high	bye, down, hide	bye
long	hair	
loud	mouth	
pleasant	present	street
pretty	dress	
quiet	be, be quiet, house, down	
rough	bark	play
short	man, mort, shorts, pants	
slow	down, go, sled	
sour	food, kraut	
swift	broom, swim	cheese, swim
tall	man	man
thirsty	drink of water, glass	
wild	cat	
Verbs		
add	one	
allow	allowance	him, you
begin	work	again, now
belong	here, home, short, house	
carry		me
enjoy	boy, me, party	good
gallop	horsie	
give	the, you	them
happen	here, what	
inquire	church, wire	
join	party, game	game
listen	to me, to	to
maintain	man	
mix	butter, mixer	
obey	okay, your mother	orders
prepare	man	
sell		store, things
sit	quiet	
tell	mell, mother, you	

TABLE 8.2.   (cont.)

Stimulus word	Responses present grade 1, not grade 5[a]	Responses present grade 3, not grade 5[a]
Adverbs		
always	go	
gently	baby, good, jet	
loudly	hear, slow, water	low
never		go
seldom	celery	
slowly	car	
sometimes	sun, I	
usually	I	
Pronouns		
he	man	
it	bit, can, pit	bit
she	sheep, sheet	
them	can, come	
they	can, hay	
us	bus	
Miscellaneous		
because		be, it, not, they
between	me, two, meals	
into	house, Indian	house
off	car	
on		no
once		last
since	you	after, money
up	jump, stairs	

[a] 1962–63 data.

Ervin's notion of contextual variety could embrace both an exposure factor (related to frequency) and a confusion factor. Exposure is related to semantic marker development, and the generality of a marker, i.e., the size of various word classes, must influence the rate at which the words enter the dictionary. Thus, perhaps the rapid development of paradigmatics to adjectives, occurring between first grade and third grade, and even earlier between kindergarten and first grade, reflects the laying down of *one* marker, the contrast marker. Evidence presented earlier has already made clear that the contrast evoking adjectives *and* verbs are the ones that develop rapidly. This may be because the laying down of a single marker is what is required. It is possible that factor analytic methods, discussed in Chapter 7, provide a way to identify markers.

Another observation to be explained is the reappearance of syntagmatics between childhood and adulthood. Those that occur with frequency of 2.5 per cent or more are listed in Table 8.3. McNeill (1965) points out that these syntagmatics are different from those of childhood, and terms them "pseudo-syntagmatics." We have some rather precise data on the actual nature and extent of these syntagmatics that disappear and reappear. To get the data in Tables 8.2 and 8.3, all responses of the same form class as the stimulus word were discarded and then the syntagmatics with frequency higher than five were cross-tabulated.[7] This identifies responses that were fairly common at first grade but not at fifth grade, and so on. The reverse situation, responses common for adults but not for children, was also investigated. Aside from anomalous acoustical associates, already mentioned, other associates present at first grade and not at fifth grade are predominantly based on grammatical contiguities. For instance, "bug" yields "crawl"; "clean" yields "clothes," "floor," "the house," "table," and so on.

TABLE 8.3.   Nonparadigmatic Adult Responses with Frequency of at least 2.5 Per Cent Not Present at First and Fifth Grades

Stimulus word[a]	Responses present at adult, not grade 1[b]	Responses present at adult, not grade 5[b]
Nouns		
bug		me
butterfly	yellow	
color	bright	
fly	away, soar, swim	away, soar, swim
hand	give	
insect		bite
music	soft	
river	flow	
salt	bitter, sour	thirsty
Adjectives		
bitter	taste	
clean	Mr., room	Mr., room, up
cold	shower	shower
dark	alley	alley
hard	sell	sell
high	noon	noon
long	day	day, hair
loud		mouth
pleasant	smile	smile, day
quiet	hospital	peace
rough	sandpaper	sandpaper
slow		down
smooth	silk, skin	skin
sour	grape	cream
swift		bird, run
tall		boy, man
wild	geese, goose	geese, goose
yellow		bird
Verbs		
add	sum	up
begin	beguine, now	again, beguine, now
belong	group, member, together, with	member, with
carry	away, back, burden, load, off, out	away, off, out
deceive	deception, false	deception, false
enjoy	pleasure	
give		up
happen	event, often	again, event

[7] These tabulations were carried out with 1962–63 data, so N = 200 at each age.

TABLE 8.3. (cont.)

Stimulus word[a]	Responses present at adult, not grade 1[b]	Responses present at adult, not grade 5[b]
Verbs		
inquire	about, into, question	into, question
join	group	
listen		music, to
mix	drink, master	batter, master, up
move	motion, over, quickly	over
obey	command	orders
prepare	meal	meal
restore	antique, order	antique, order
sell	out, short	out, short
sit	on	
tell	him	him, tale
Adverbs		
loudly	noise	
Pronouns		
he		man
it	neuter, object, thing	neuter, object
them	group	
they	group	
Miscellaneous		
because	of, reason	therefore
between	them	them
into	room	enter, house, room
on	top	
since	before, once, time	
up		stairs

[a] For stimulus words not given, there were no adult nonparadigmatic responses with frequency at least 2.5 per cent that did not occur at least with 1 per cent frequency at the earlier ages.
[b] 1962–63 data.

For adults the nonparadigmatic associations also are based on grammatical contiguities, but some of them seem qualitatively different from the syntagmatics of young children: "bug"—"me," "cold"—"shower," "dark"—"alley," "hard"—"sell," and so on. One very appealing explanation for many of these responses is that they represent actually *different* words, although homonyms, from the same words when presented to children. Thus, "hard sell" and "bug me" are clear examples of new meanings acquired for old familiar words. We also see semantic enrichment where "yellow" and "butterfly" are linked together in adults but not in children. Adults seem to give less stereotyped responses than fifth-graders to many words. This corresponds to the laying down of more and more markers. Brown (1957) has suggested that the number of differentiated elements that belong to a category or class may be a critical attribute of level of development. The present study suggests that perhaps the number of elements in a class is inversely related to development, but both statements could be included by using markers.

The factor analyses of the butterfly cluster suggest a way to get at semantic markers more directly. The replicability of these analyses is very encouraging. Other data reduction techniques (latent structure analysis or cluster analysis of a kind like that used by Coleman and Macrae, 1960) may be even more appropriate. The variation in results with age and with different subcultural groups provides an economical summary of complex relationships.

The intransitivity of certain associations (adjectives in response to adverbs, but not the reverse) is hard to subsume under Miller and McNeill's theory. For instance, "gently" yields "gentle," but "soft" does not yield "softly," nor does "hard" yield "hardly." It has already been remarked that regular verbs ("add," "carry," etc.) do not yield their past tense—"added," "carried." This suggests why adjectives do not yield adverbs—perhaps adverbs of the "gently," "softly" variety are stored as inflected adjectives. Thus the adjective will not yield an adverbial derivative, but the inflection will be removed to yield the root word. At first grade "sell" yields "seldom" and "celery," two semantically unrelated but acoustically similar words. These inappropriate responses do not appear at later ages. Many words that have identical first syllables are *not* related, and this fact may inhibit generalization of the add-a-syllable kind. Such inhibition may make the adjective-adverb response unlikely.

Summary

Altogether the data are remarkably consistent with Miller and McNeill's theory in accounting for changes in semantics that occur over the period of middle childhood. Form classes do not appear to be a particularly useful categorization, and some more fundamental basis for classifications, perhaps based on minimal contrastive properties like markers, is needed. More work is needed to see if the evolutionary pattern for individual words is correct.

More work is in progress to outline social class differences, especially of slum groups. Also at the same time interviewer interactions will be studied.

The difference between IQ levels and cultural groups found in this research become less prominent with advancing age. This suggests that for equally common words adults will respond rather similarly no matter what their educational or social background. (Bilodeau and Howell (1965) do not find differences between airmen whom they tested and earlier samples of Russell and Jenkins on forty-five words from the Kent-Rosanoff list.) The variations in response of young children are large, however, and further work on association or on other facets of verbal learning with children ages four to eleven will need to take account of these variables.

The importance of administration conditions generally, for adults as well as for children, is stressed, and much data besides our own testifies to this. Since administration conditions appear to affect mainly certain kinds of words (contrast-evoking adjectives), this variable can be at least partly controlled by the composition of word lists. It is possible that other classes of words in addition to contrast evoking words may be sensitive, however, and more work is needed to investigate this.

Bibliography

The American College Dictionary. C. L. BARNHART (ed.), New York: Random House, 1962.

BERKO, J. "The child's learning of English morphology," *Word*, 1958, *14*, 150–77.

BERLYNE, D. E. "Soviet research on intellectual processes in children," *Monog. Soc. Res. Child Develpm.*, 1963, *28*, 165–83.

BERNSTEIN, B. "Language and social class (research note)," *Brit. J. Soc.*, 1960, *11*, 271–76.

————. "Linguistic codes, hesitation phenomena, and intelligence," *Language and Speech*, 1962, *5*, 31–46.

BILODEAU, E. A. and HOWELL, D. C. *Free Association Norms By Discrete and Continued Methods.* Technical Report No. 1, Contract Nonr-475(10) Tulane University and the Office of Naval Research, 1965.

BOUSFIELD, W. A. "The problem of meaning in verbal learning," *Verbal Learning and Verbal Behavior*, C. N. COFER (ed.), New York: McGraw Hill, 1961.

BOUSFIELD, W. A. and COHEN, B. H. "The effects of reinforcement on the occurrence of clustering in the recall of randomly arranged associates," *J. Psychol.*, 1953, *36*, 67–81.

————. "The occurrence of clustering in the recall of randomly arranged words of different frequencies of usage," *J. gen. Psychol.*, 1955, *52*, 83–95.

BROWN, R. *Words and Things*, Glencoe, Ill.: The Free Press, 1957.

BROWN, R. and BELLUGI, U. "Three processes in the child's acquisition of syntax," *Harvard educ. Rev.*, 1964, *34*, 133–51.

BROWN, R. and BERKO, J. "Word association and the acquisition of grammar," *Child Develpm.*, 1960, *31*, 1–14.

BROWN, R. and FRASER, C. "The acquisition of syntax," *Verbal Behavior and Learning*, C. N. COFER and B. S. MUSGRAVE (eds.), New York: McGraw-Hill, 1963.

————. "The acquisition of syntax," *The Acquisition of Language*, U. BELLUGI and R. BROWN (eds.), *Monog. Soc. Res. Child Develpm.*, 1964, *29*, 43–79.

BROWN, R., FRASER, C., and BELLUGI, U. "Explorations in grammar evaluation," *The Acquisition of Language*, U. BELLUGI and R. BROWN (eds.), *Monog. Soc. Res. Child Develpm.*, 1964, *29*, 79–92.

BROWN, R. and McNEILL, D. Personal communication, 1965.

BRUNER, J. B. and OLVER, R. R. "Development of equivalence transformations in children," *Monog. Soc. Res. Child Develpm.*, 1963, *28*, 125–141.

CARROLL, J. B., KJELDERGAARD, P. M. and CARTON, A. S. "Number of opposites vs. number of primaries as a response measure in free association tests," *J. verb. Learn. verb. Behav.*, 1962, *1*, 1–13.

CASTANEDA, A., FAHEL, L. S., and ODOM, R. "Associative characteristics of sixty-three adjectives and their relation to verbal paired-associate learning in children," *Child Develpm.*, 1961, *32*, 297–304.

CHOMSKY, N. "A review of *Verbal Behavior* by B. F. Skinner," *Language*, 1959, *35*, 26–58.

———. Formal discussion of the paper by Miller and Ervin, in *The Acquisition of Language*, U. BELLUGI and R. BROWN (eds.), *Monog. Soc. Res. Child Develpm.*, 1964, *29*, 35–39.

CHOTLOS, J. W. "A statistical and comparative analysis of individual written language samples," *Psychol. Monog.*, 1944, *56*, 77–111.

CHURCH, J. *Language and the Discovery of Reality*, New York: Random House, 1961.

CLOUSING, J. "The relation between personality trait ratings and free association responses." Unpublished master's thesis, Univ. of Minnesota, 1927.

COFER, C. N., Comments on the Paper by Brown and Fraser, in *Verbal Behavior and Learning*, C. N. COFER and B. S. MUSGRAVE (eds.), New York: McGraw-Hill, 1963.

COFER, C. N. and SHEVITZ, R. "Word association as a function of the Thorndike-Lorge frequency of the stimulus words." ONR Contract N70-NE-397, TR, 1953.

COHEN, B. H. "All-or-none characteristic of coding behavior." Presented at APA Meetings, Los Angeles, September, 1964.

COLEMAN, J. S. and MACRAE, D. "Electronic processing of sociometric data for groups up to 1000 in size," *Amer. soc. Rev.*, 1960, *25*, 722–27.

DAVIS, E. A. "The development of linguistic skill in twins, singletons with siblings, and only children from age five to ten years," *Inst. Child Welfare Monog.*, No. 14, Minneapolis: Univ. of Minnesota Press, 1937.

DEESE, J. "On the prediction of occurrence of particular verbal intrusions in immediate recall," *J. exp. Psychol.*, 1959a, *58*, 17–22.

———. "Influence of inter-item associative strength upon immediate free recall," *Psychol. Rep.*, 1959b, *5*, 305–12.

———. Personal communications, 1960, 1962.

———. "From the isolated verbal unit to connected discourse," in *Verbal Learning and Verbal Behavior*, C. N. COFER (ed.), New York: McGraw-Hill, 1961.

———. "On the structure of associative meaning," *Psychol. Rev.*, 1962a, *69*, 161–75.

———. "Form class and the determinants of association," *J. verb. Learn. verb. Behav.*, 1962b, *1*, 79–84.

———. "Comments and conclusions," in *The Acquisition of Language*, U. BELLUGI and R. BROWN (eds.), *Monog. Soc. Res. Child Develpm.*, 1964a, *29*, 177–81.

———. "The associative structure of some common English adjectives," *J. verb. Learn. verb. Behav.*, 1964b, *3*, 347–57.

———. *The Structure of Associations in Language and Thought*, in press, Baltimore: The Johns Hopkins Press, 1966.

EISMAN, B. S. "Attitude formation. The development of a color preference response through mediated generalization," *J. abnorm. soc. Psychol.*, 1955, *50*, 321–26.

ENTWISLE, D. R. "Form class of children's word associations," *J. verb. Learn. verb. Behav.*, in press, 1965a.

———. "Sociolinguistics: A developmental and comparative study in four subcultural settings," *Sociometry*, in press, 1965b.

ENTWISLE, D. R. and FORSYTH, D. F. "Word associations of children: Effect of method of administration," *Psychol. Rep.*, 1963, *13*, 291–99.

ENTWISLE, D. R., FORSYTH, D. F., and MUUSS, R. "The syntactic-paradigmatic shift in children's word associations," *J. verb. Learn. verb. Behav.*, 1964, *3*, 19–29.

ERVIN, S. M. "Changes with age in the verbal determinants of word association," *Amer. J. Psychol.*, 1961, *74*, 361–72.

———. "Correlates of associative frequency," *J. verb. Learn. verb. Behav.*, 1963, *1*, 422–31.

————. "Imitation and structural change in children's language," in *New Directions in the Study of Language*, E. LENNEBERG (ed.), Cambridge: Massachusetts Institute of Technology Press, 1964.

ERVIN, S. M. and LANDAR, H., "Navaho word-associations," *Amer. J. Psychol.*, 1963, *76*, 49–57.

ERVIN, S. M. and MILLER, W. R. "Language development," in *Child Psychology*, H. W. STEVENSON (ed.), *62nd Yearbook of the Nat'l. Soc. for the Study of Educ.*, Chicago: Univ. of Chicago Press, 1963.

FILLENBAUM, S. and JONES, L. V. "Grammatical contingencies in word association," *J. verb. Learn. verb. Behav.*, 1965, *4*, 248–55.

FODOR, J. A. "Could meaning be an r$_m$?," *J. verb. Learn. verb. Behav.*, 1965, *4*, 73–81.

FRENCH, N. R., CARTER, C. W., and KOENIG, E. W. "The words and sounds of telephone conversations," *Bell Syst. tech. J.*, 1930, *9*, 290–324.

FRIES, C. C. *The Structure of English. An introduction to the construction of English sentences*, New York: Harcourt, Brace and Co., 1952.

GIBSON, E. J. "Perceptual Development," in *Child Psychology*, H. W. STEVENSON (ed.), *62nd Yearbook of Nat'l. Soc. for the Study of Educ.*, Chicago: Univ. of Chicago Press, 1963.

HALL, J. F. "Learning as a function of word frequency," *Amer. J. Psychol.*, 1954, *67*, 138–40.

HARMAN, H. H. *Modern Factor Analysis*, Chicago: Univ. of Chicago Press, 1960.

HILL, S. "Cultural differences in mathematical concept learning," in *Transcultural Studies in Cognition. Amer. Anthrop. Spec. Publ.*, 1964, *66*, No. 3.

HILLS, J. R. "Controlled association scores and engineering success," *J. appl. Psychol.*, 1958, *42*, 10–13.

HOCKETT, C. F. "Age-reading and linguistic continuity," *Language*, 1950, *26*, 449–55.

HORN, M. D. "An investigation of the vocabulary of kindergarten children." Unpublished master's thesis, University of Iowa, 1927.

HORTON, D. L., MARLOWE, D., and CROWNE, D. P. "The effect of instructional set and need for social approval on commonality of word association responses," *J. abnorm. soc. Psychol.*, 1963, *66*, 67–72.

HORVATH, W. J. "A stochastic model for word-association tests," *Psychol. Rev.*, 1963, *70*, 361–64.

HOSTETLER, J. *Amish Society*, Baltimore: The Johns Hopkins Press, 1963.

HOWES, D. "On the relation between the probability of a word as an association and in general linguistic usage," *J. abnorm. soc. Psychol.*, 1957, *54*, 75–85.

HUTTENLOCHER, J. "Children's language: Word-phrase relationships," *Science*, 1964, *143*, 264–65.

IRWIN, O. C. "Language and Communication," in *Handbook of Research Methods in Child Development*, P. H. MUSSEN (ed.), New York: John Wiley and Sons, 1960.

JAKOBSON, R. and HALLE, M. *Fundamentals of Language*, S' Gravenhage: Mouton, 1956.

JENKINS, J. J. "Effects on word-association of the set to give popular responses," *Psychol. Rep.*, 1959, *5*, 94.

————. "First California Conference," *J. verb. Learn. verb. Behav.*, 1962, *1*, 312–20.

————. "Mediated associations: Paradigms and situations," in *Verbal Behavior and Learning*, C. N. COFER and B. J. MUSGRAVE (eds.), New York: McGraw Hill, 1963.

JENKINS, J. J., MINK, W. D., and RUSSELL, W. A. "Associative clustering as a function of verbal association strength," *Psychol. Rep.*, 1958, *4*, 127–36.

JENKINS, J. J. and PALERMO, D. S. "Mediation processes and the acquisition of linguistic structure," in *The Acquisition of Language*, U. BELLUGI and R. BROWN (eds.), *Monog. Soc. Res. Child Develpm.*, 1964, *29*, No. 1, 141–69.

JENKINS, J. J. and RUSSELL, W. A. "Systematic changes in word association norms, 1910–1952," *J. abnorm. soc. Psychol.*, 1960, *60*, 293–304.

JOHN, V. P. "The intellectual development of slum children: Some preliminary findings," *Amer. J. Orthopsychiat.*, 1963, *33*, 813–22.

JOHN, V. P. and GOLDSTEIN, L. S. "The social context of language acquisition," *Merrill Palmer Quart.*, 1964, *10*, 265–75.

JOHNSON, P. E. "Associative meanings of concepts in physics," *J. educ. Psychol.*, 1964, *55*, 84–88.

JONES, L. V. and FILLENBAUM, S. *Grammatically Classified Word Associations*, Research Memorandum No. 15, The Psychometric Laboratory, University of North Carolina, 1964.

KAGAN, J., MOSS, H. A., and SIGEL, I. E. "Psychological significance of styles of conceptualization," *Monog. Soc. Res. Child Develpm.*, 1963, *28*, 73–111.

KAPLAN, B. "A comparative study of acquisition of meanings in low educated and high educated adults." Unpublished thesis, Clark University, 1950.

KATZ, J. J. and FODOR, J. A. "The structure of a semantic theory," *Language*, 1963, *39*, 170–210.

KENT, G. H. and ROSANOFF, A. J. "A study of association in insanity," *Amer. J. Insanity*, 1910, *67*, 1 and 2.

LENNEBERG, E. H. *New Directions in the Study of Language*, Cambridge: Massachusetts Institute of Technology Press, 1964.

MANDLEBROT, B. "A note on a class of skew distribution functions: Analysis and critique of a paper by H. A. Simon," *Information and Control*, 1959, *2*, 90–99.

McCARTHY, D. "Language development of the preschool child," *Inst. Child Welfare Monog.*, Minneapolis: Univ. of Minnesota Press, No. 4, 1930.

McNEILL, D. "The origin of association within the same grammatical class," *J. verb. Learn. verb. Behav.*, 1963, *2*, 250–62.

———. "Is Child Language Semantically Consistent?" Mimeo., "Word Association and Semantic Consistency," Mimeo., Harvard University, 1964.

———. "A Study of association," *J. verb. Learning verb. Behav.*, 1966, in press.

MELTON, A. W. "Comments on Professor Peterson's paper," in *Verbal Behavior and Learning*, C. N. COFER and B. S. MUSGRAVE (eds.), New York: McGraw-Hill, 1963.

MENYUK, P. "Syntactic structures in the language of children," *Child Develpm.*, 1963, *34*, 407–22.

———. "Syntactic rules used by children from preschool through first grade," *Child Develpm.*, 1964, *35*, 533–46.

MILLER, G. A. "The psycholinguists: On the new scientists of language," *Encounter*, 1964, *23*, 29–37.

MILLER, G. A. and CHOMSKY, N. "Finitary models of language users," in *Handbook of Mathematical Psychology*, R. D. LUCE, R. R. BUSH, and E. GALANTER (eds.), New York: John Wiley and Sons, 1963.

MILLER, G. A. and ISARD, S. "Some perceptual consequences of linguistic rules," *J. verb. Learn. verb. Behav.*, 1963, *2*, 217–28.

MILLER, G. A. and McNEILL, D. "Developmental Psycholinguistics." Mimeo., Harvard University Center for Cognitive Studies, 1965 (in preparation for publication).

MILLER, W. and ERVIN, S. M. "The development of grammar in child language," in *The Acquisition of Language*, U. BELLUGI and R. BROWN (eds.), *Monog. Soc. Res. Child Develpm.*, 1964, *29*, 9–34.

MITCHELL, I., ROSANOFF, I. R., and ROSANOFF, A. J. "A study of association in Negro children," *Psychol. Rev.*, 1919, *26*, 354–59.

MOORE, O. K. "Comments and conclusions," in *The Acquisition of Language*, U. BELLUGI and R. BROWN (eds.), *Monog. Soc. Res. Child Develpm.*, 1964, *29*, 181–84.

NISBET, J. "Family environment and intelligence," in *Education, Economy, and Society*, A. H. HALSEY, J. FLOUD and C. A. ANDERSON (eds.), New York: Free Press, 1961.

NOBLE, C. R. "The role of stimulus meaning (m) in serial verbal learning," *J. exp. Psychol.*, 1952, *43*, 437–46.

NORCROSS, K. J. and SPIKER, C. C. "Effects of mediated associations on transfer in paired-associate learning," *J. exp. Psychol.*, 1958, *55*, 129–34.

OSGOOD, C. E. "Semantic differential technique in the conservative study of cultures," *Transcultural Studies in Cognition, Amer. Anthrop. Spec. Publ.*, 1964, *66*, No. 3.

OSGOOD, C. E. and MIRON, M. S. (eds.), *Approaches to the Study of Aphasia*, Urbana: University of Illinois Press, 1963.

PALERMO, D. S. "Cross-sectional comparisons of word-association norms collected from fourth grade to college." Presented at Amer. Psychol. Assoc. Meeting, St. Louis, 1962.

———. "Characteristics of word association responses obtained from children in grades one through four." Presented at Society for Research in Child Development Meeting, at Minneapolis, Minn., Spring, 1965.

PALERMO, D. S. and JENKINS, J. J. "Frequency of superordinate responses to a word association test as a function of age," *J. verb. Learn. verb. Behav.*, 1963, *1*, 378–83.

———. *Word Association Norms Grade School through College*, Minneapolis: Univ. of Minnesota Press, 1964.

———. "Changes in the word associations of fourth and fifth grade children from 1916 to 1961," *J. verb. Learn. verb. Behav.*, 1965a, *4*, 180–87.

———. "Sex differences in word associations," *J. gen. Psychol.*, 1965b, *72*, 77–84.

PIAGET, J. *The Language and Thought of the Child*, New York: Harcourt, Brace, 1932.

PIETRZYK, A. "Bibliographer's comment," in *Selected Titles in Sociolinguistics*, Center for Applied Linguistics of the Modern Language Assoc. of Amer., Washington, D.C., 1964.

ROSANOFF, I. R. and ROSANOFF, A. J. "A study of association in children," *Psychol. Rev.*, 1913, *20*, 43–89.

ROSENZWEIG, M. R. "Word associations of French workmen: Comparisons with associations of French students and American workmen and students," *J. verb. Learn. verb. Behav.*, 1964, *3*, 57–69.

ROTBERG, I. Personal communication, 1964.

———. "A method for developing comprehensive categories of meaning," in preparation, 1965.

RUSSELL, W. A. and JENKINS, J. J. *The Complete Minnesota Norms for Responses to 100 words from the Kent-Rosanoff Word Association Test*. Technical Report No. 11, ONR Contract N* onr-66216, August, 1954.

SCHELLENBERG, P. E. "A group free-association test for college students." Unpublished doctoral dissertation, University of Minnesota, Minneapolis, 1930.

SCHRAMM, W. (ed.), *The Effects of Television on Children and Adolescents*, New York: UNESCO, 1964.

SCHRAMM, W., LYLE, J., and PARKER, E. B. *Television in the Lives of Our Children*, Stanford, Calif.: Stanford Univ. Press, 1961.

SIIPOLA, E., WALKER, W. N., and KOLB, D. "Task attitudes in word association, projective and nonprojective," *J. Pers.*, 1955, *23*, 441–59.

SPIKER, C. C. "Associative transfer in verbal paired-associate learning," *Child Developm.*, 1960, *31*, 73–88.

SUMBY, W. H. "Word frequency and serial position effects," *J. verb. Learn. verb. Behav.*, 1963, *1*, 443–50.

TEMPLIN, M. C. *Certain Language Skills in Children*, Minneapolis: University of Minnesota Press, 1957.

TERMAN, L. M. and MILES, C. C. *Sex and Personality: Studies in Masculinity and Femininity*, New York: McGraw-Hill, 1936.

THORNDIKE, E. L. and LORGE, I. *The Teacher's Word Book of 30,000 Words*, New York: Bureau of Publications, Teachers College, Columbia University, 1944.

THYSELL, R. V. and SCHULZ, R. W. "Concept-utilization as a function of the strength of relevant and irrelevant associations," *J. verb. Learn. verb. Behav.*, 1964, *3*, 203–8.

TRESSELT, M. E., LEEDS, D. S., and MAYZNER, M. S. "The Kent-Rosanoff word associations: II. A comparison of sex differences in response frequencies," *J. genet. Psychol.*, 1955, *87*, 149–53.

UHRBROCK, R. S. "Words most frequently used by a five-year-old girl," *J. educ. Psychol.*, 1936, *27*, 155–58.

USEEM, J. "Notes on the sociological study of language," *Social Science Research Council ITEMS*, 1963, *17*, 29–31.

WEIR, R. *Language in the Crib*, The Hague: Mouton, 1962.

WERNER, H. and KAPLAN, B. "Development of word meaning through verbal context: An experimental study," *J. Psychol.*, 1950, *29*, 251–57.

WERNER, H. and KAPLAN, B. "The acquisition of word meanings: A developmental study," *Soc. Res. Child Develpm. Monogr.*, 1952, *15*, No. 51.

WICKELGREN, W. A. "Acoustic similarity and retroactive interference in short-term memory," *J. verb. Learning verb. Behav.*, 1965, *4*, 53–61.

WOODROW, H. and LOWELL, F. "Children's association frequency tests," *Psychol. Monogr.*, 1916, No. 22, 1–110.

WOODWORTH, R. S. and SCHLOSBERG, H. *Experimental Psychology*, New York: Holt, 1958.

WYATT, H. G. "Free word association and sex differences," *Amer. J. Psychol.*, 1932, *44*, 454–72.

ZIGLER, E. and KANZER, P. "The effectiveness of two classes of verbal reinforcers on the performance of middle- and lower-class children." Paper presented at Soc. Res. Child Develpm. Symposium, March, 1961.

Appendix A:

Three Most Common Responses

Three most common responses of Entwisle data—kindergarten, first, third, fifth and adult—includes all ninety-six stimulus words in alphabetical order followed by three most common responses of male and female in per cents. In case of a tie in responses the first word alphabetically was placed first in the response column.

Stimulus Words Classified by Form Class and Frequency

Frequency	Nouns	Adjectives	Verbs	Other words
				Adverbs
	bird	black	add	always
	color	cold	begin	gently
	flower	dark	carry	loudly
High	fly	hard	give	never
	hand	high	move	seldom
	man	long	run	slowly
	river	pretty	sit	sometimes
	table	short	tell	usually
				Pronouns
	chair	bright	allow	he
	fruit	clean	belong	her
	music	loud	enjoy	him
	ocean	pleasant	happen	it
Medium	salt	sad	join	she
	sheep	tall	listen	them
	square	wild	prepare	they
	wing	yellow	sell	us
				Miscellaneous
	bee	bitter	deceive	because
	bug	quiet	examine	between
	butterfly	rough	gallop	into
Low	cocoon	slow	inquire	off
	insect	smooth	maintain	on
	moth	sour	mix	once
	needle	swift	obey	since
	net	thirsty	restore	up

Characteristics of the urban Maryland samples summarized earlier in Chapter 2 are given here again for the reader's convenience. For more data, consult Chapter 2. All samples consist of equal numbers of boys and girls.

Characteristics of the Urban Maryland Samples

		Grade K N = 200				
		Average age				
High-SES (N = 100)		5.6				
Low-SES (N = 100)		5.6				

		Grade 1 N = 280		Grade 3 N = 280		Grade 5 N = 280	
		Mean IQ	Av. Age	Mean IQ	Av. Age	Mean IQ	Av. Age
High-SES	High-IQ (N = 70)	130	6.4	131	8.5	131	10.4
	Med.-IQ (N = 70)	103	6.6	100	8.7	101	10.7
Low-SES	Med.-IQ (N = 70)	103	6.5	100	8.7	100	10.6
	Low-IQ (N = 70)	75	6.7	80	9.0	80	10.11

APPENDIX A: Three Most Common Responses: Kindergarten, First Grade, Third Grade, Fifth Grade, and Adult*

Kindergarten

Stimulus word	Response (male)		Response (female)	
add	numbers	06.0	water	05.0
	paper	06.0	number	03.0
	bad	05.0	ant	02.0
allow	allowance	04.0	not	03.0
	people	04.0	bow	02.0
	cloud	03.0	paper	02.0
always	do	04.0	all	03.0
	be good	03.0	be good	02.0
	not	02.0	do	02.0
because	why	17.0	because	13.0
	don't	02.0	he	03.0
	he	02.0	dog	02.0
bee	sting	11.0	sting	06.0
	bumble bee	04.0	bumble bee	05.0
	honey	04.0	bumble	04.0
begin	start	04.0	story	05.0
	starting	03.0	with	04.0
	a song	02.0	end	02.0
belong	to	07.0	to you	04.0
	to me	03.0	house	03.0
	to you	03.0	be	02.0
between	me	05.0	each other	05.0
	meals	04.0	us	05.0
	you	03.0	me	04.0
bird	fly	22.0	fly	22.0
	flying	07.0	wing	09.0
	wing	06.0	wings	05.0
bitter	bit	07.0	better	05.0
	butter	07.0	cold	05.0
	better	05.0	bit	03.0
black	crayon	07.0	brown	06.0
	bird	06.0	color	06.0
	cat	05.0	crayon	06.0
bright	sun	20.0	sun	18.0
	light	13.0	light	11.0
	brown	03.0	sky	07.0
bug	fly	06.0	bee	10.0
	insect	06.0	fly	08.0
	bee	05.0	insect	08.0
butterfly	fly	16.0	fly	16.0
	butter	06.0	butter	08.0
	flies	06.0	flying	05.0
carry	carrot	07.0	baby	15.0
	baby	06.0	me	06.0
	hurry	04.0	bag	04.0

* Rounding errors in Appendix A are ±0.2 per cent or less

Stimulus word	Response (male)		Response (female)	
chair	sit	19.0	sit	20.0
	table	10.0	table	18.0
	bear	05.0	sit down in chair	04.0
clean	house	10.0	house	08.0
	the house	04.0	floor	06.0
	vacuum cleaner	04.0	dirty	05.0
cocoon	raccoon	07.0	raccoon	07.0
	baboon	03.0	tree	05.0
	moon	03.0	animal	03.0
cold	hot	08.0	hot	17.0
	water	07.0	warm	10.0
	winter	07.0	water	05.0
color	red	09.0	coloring book	07.0
	book	06.0	red	07.0
	picture	06.0	blue	06.0
dark	night	12.0	light	15.0
	light	10.0	night	15.0
	moon	07.0	morning	05.0
deceive	a letter	02.0	chair	04.0
	clock	02.0	see	04.0
	me	02.0	receive	03.0
enjoy	boy	04.0	fun	06.0
	fun	04.0	party	05.0
	party	04.0	love	03.0
examine	doctor	14.0	doctor	04.0
	picture	03.0	eyes	04.0
	ham	02.0	baby	02.0
flower	grow	08.0	grass	05.0
	plant	05.0	leaf	05.0
	rose	05.0	bee	04.0
fly	bird	13.0	bird	17.0
	butterfly	07.0	birds	04.0
	airplane	06.0	wings	04.0
fruit	apple	13.0	apple	13.0
	eat	06.0	eat	09.0
	banana	05.0	banana	07.0
gallop	horse	45.0	horse	46.0
	on a horse	05.0	a horse	03.0
	horsey	04.0	on a horse	03.0
gently	soft	07.0	cat	04.0
	jet	06.0	soft	04.0
	baby	03.0	jet	03.0
give	live	04.0	present	14.0
	away	03.0	gift	03.0
	people	03.0	presents	03.0
hand	shake	05.0	arm	06.0
	egg	03.0	finger	04.0
	fingers	03.0	foot	03.0
happen	what	04.0	hurt	05.0
	accident	03.0	something happened	05.0
	to	03.0	what	05.0

Stimulus word	Response (male)		Response (female)	
hard	rock	09.0	soft	08.0
	work	05.0	rock	07.0
	steel	04.0	work	06.0
he	she	08.0	boy	09.0
	man	06.0	she	09.0
	key	04.0	her	08.0
her	girl	09.0	him	15.0
	she	08.0	girl	09.0
	him	06.0	she	05.0
high	sky	08.0	low	10.0
	low	07.0	sky	05.0
	tree	04.0	tree	04.0
him	boy	05.0	her	15.0
	her	04.0	boy	09.0
	you	04.0	she	07.0
inquire	sing	06.0	church	08.0
	wire	06.0	wire	06.0
	church	03.0	quiet	05.0
insect	bug	12.0	bug	12.0
	bee	07.0	bee	06.0
	fly	07.0	fly	06.0
into	house	08.0	house	07.0
	to	05.0	the house	04.0
	door	03.0	to	04.0
it	is	05.0	is	04.0
	sit	03.0	was	03.0
	bit	02.0	bit	02.0
join	club	09.0	game	04.0
	party	05.0	club	03.0
	fun	04.0	coin	03.0
listen	learn	05.0	hear	08.0
	be quiet	04.0	to me	05.0
	hear	04.0	be quiet	04.0
long	grass	07.0	grass	09.0
	short	06.0	lawn mower	03.0
	time	06.0	short	03.0
loud	scream	06.0	quiet	07.0
	quiet	05.0	low	05.0
	holler	04.0	noise	05.0
loudly	scream	04.0	quiet	08.0
	door	03.0	scream	05.0
	holler	03.0	softly	05.0
maintain	cane	03.0	glass	03.0
	canteen	03.0	bird	02.0
	lion	03.0	chair	02.0
man	lady	06.0	woman	13.0
	walk	06.0	lady	07.0
	woman	06.0	hand	05.0
mix	cake	13.0	cake	24.0
	a cake	03.0	a cake	05.0
	cement	03.0	bowl	04.0

Stimulus word	Response (male)		Response (female)	
moth	fly	07.0	fly	05.0
	ball	04.0	ball	04.0
	cloth	04.0	bug	03.0
move	car	10.0	over	04.0
	walk	04.0	away	03.0
	cow	03.0	door	03.0
music	piano	17.0	piano	17.0
	play	07.0	dance	10.0
	play a piano	03.0	play	03.0
needle	pin	13.0	thread	22.0
	thread	11.0	pin	07.0
	shot	06.0	sew	07.0
net	fish	22.0	fish	13.0
	catch	05.0	catch	09.0
	butterfly	03.0	catfish	03.0
never	ever	12.0	again	05.0
	again	05.0	touch	05.0
	do	03.0	do	04.0
obey	boy	04.0	baby	03.0
	your mother	04.0	door	03.0
	be good	02.0	the law	03.0
ocean	water	11.0	water	17.0
	boat	10.0	city	07.0
	city	10.0	fish	07.0
off	on	10.0	on	14.0
	light	03.0	dog	02.0
	car	02.0	in	02.0
on	off	12.0	off	12.0
	gone	04.0	with the snow	03.0
	lawn mower	03.0	bon	02.0
once	twice	05.0	twice	06.0
	two	03.0	upon a time	04.0
	upon a time	03.0	again	03.0
pleasant	nice	06.0	nice	07.0
	living	05.0	living	06.0
	day	04.0	happy	03.0
prepare	car	04.0	food	05.0
	repair	03.0	pear	05.0
	eat	02.0	dinner	03.0
pretty	girl	11.0	girl	14.0
	dress	06.0	dress	08.0
	lady	04.0	beautiful	04.0
quiet	be quiet	07.0	loud	10.0
	loud	04.0	noisy	07.0
	be	03.0	noise	05.0
restore	food	12.0	food	13.0
	store	06.0	buy	08.0
	door	03.0	store	07.0
river	water	21.0	water	19.0
	boat	20.0	boat	11.0
	stream	06.0	ocean	07.0

Stimulus word	Response (male)		Response (female)	
rough	dog	12.0	tough	08.0
	fight	05.0	dog	06.0
	tough	05.0	rug	03.0
run	fast	12.0	skip	08.0
	play	08.0	walk	07.0
	skip	05.0	fast	06.0
sad	cry	11.0	happy	18.0
	happy	07.0	crying	09.0
	mad	05.0	cry	05.0
salt	pepper	35.0	pepper	40.0
	water	07.0	egg	03.0
	food	03.0	food	03.0
seldom	sell	06.0	sell	05.0
	cellar	03.0	fork	04.0
	bell	02.0	button	02.0
sell	food	07.0	food	08.0
	clothes	04.0	cellar	02.0
	something	03.0	door	02.0
she	girl	12.0	he	14.0
	sheep	10.0	girl	11.0
	he	05.0	him	06.0
sheep	dog	08.0	wool	10.0
	lamb	08.0	lamb	07.0
	wool	08.0	horse	06.0
short	pants	17.0	long	09.0
	long	05.0	pants	09.0
	cut	04.0	baby	04.0
since	bince	02.0	I	04.0
	boat	02.0	bottle	02.0
	butter	02.0	chair	02.0
sit	down	29.0	down	29.0
	chair	16.0	chair	14.0
	on a chair	04.0	on a chair	04.0
slow	fast	13.0	fast	23.0
	poke	07.0	walk	08.0
	go	04.0	walking	05.0
slowly	fast	06.0	fast	16.0
	walk	06.0	walk	11.0
	quiet	03.0	walking	05.0
smooth	road	07.0	hard	09.0
	soft	04.0	baby	06.0
	baby	02.0	soft	04.0
sometimes	I	06.0	I	03.0
	do	03.0	sun	03.0
	sun	03.0	I play	02.0
sour	kraut	14.0	milk	06.0
	lemon	07.0	kraut	04.0
	milk	05.0	drink	03.0
square	triangle	11.0	triangle	09.0
	block	08.0	box	08.0
	box	06.0	circle	06.0

Stimulus word	Response (male)		Response (female)	
swift	lift	05.0	sweep	05.0
	swim	04.0	broom	04.0
	cheese	03.0	cheese	03.0
table	chair	21.0	chair	43.0
	floor	10.0	chairs	04.0
	eat	08.0	eat	03.0
tall	man	12.0	small	15.0
	small	08.0	man	06.0
	big	07.0	big	05.0
tell	me	08.0	me	05.0
	secret	06.0	people	03.0
	a secret	04.0	show and tell	03.0
them	people	06.0	people	04.0
	him	04.0	stem	03.0
	then	03.0	they	02.0
they	hay	04.0	are	07.0
	are	03.0	him	03.0
	bay	03.0	pay	03.0
thirsty	water	25.0	drink	24.0
	drink	20.0	water	22.0
	I want a drink	04.0	get a drink	03.0
up	down	17.0	down	28.0
	airplane	05.0	sky	07.0
	hill	03.0	baby	02.0
us	bus	08.0	people	11.0
	people	07.0	me	07.0
	we	06.0	bus	06.0
usually	play	03.0	sometimes	04.0
	happen	02.0	fun	03.0
	house	02.0	never	03.0
wild	animal	18.0	animal	18.0
	animals	07.0	horse	09.0
	horse	06.0	animals	04.0
wing	bird	20.0	bird	23.0
	fly	15.0	fly	09.0
	plane	04.0	sing	03.0
yellow	crayon	12.0	sun	09.0
	green	09.0	red	08.0
	sun	07.0	color	06.0

First Grade

add	numbers	04.2	and	03.6
	adding machine	02.2	something	03.6
	now	02.2	numbers	02.8
allow	me	03.6	loud	05.0
	you	03.6	quiet	02.8
	cow	02.8	soft	02.8
always	not always	05.8	never	06.4
	come	02.2	go	02.8
	do	02.2	again	02.2

Stimulus word	Response (male)		Response (female)	
because	why	20.0	why	21.4
	I	03.6	I	03.6
	he	02.2	he	02.8
bee	good	05.8	sting	07.2
	sting	04.2	fly	05.0
	fly	03.6	see	03.6
begin	end	03.6	start	04.2
	here	03.6	work	03.6
	not begin	03.6	end	02.8
belong	here	06.4	here	05.8
	to	05.0	long	05.0
	home	04.2	in	03.6
between	me	05.0	middle	06.4
	middle	04.2	after	03.6
	you	03.6	meals	02.8
bird	fly	27.2	fly	47.2
	nest	07.2	nest	05.0
	sing	02.8	sing	02.8
bitter	butter	06.4	bit	07.2
	sweet	06.4	butter	07.2
	better	02.8	sweet	05.8
black	white	11.4	white	12.8
	blue	08.6	blue	10.8
	brown	05.0	brown	09.2
bright	light	15.0	sun	16.4
	sun	13.6	dark	15.0
	dark	10.8	light	11.4
bug	insect	11.4	fly	15.8
	fly	07.8	insect	12.8
	spider	04.2	bee	6.4
butterfly	fly	20.0	fly	23.6
	butter	08.6	butter	07.2
	bee	04.2	bird	04.2
carry	baby	06.4	baby	13.6
	carrot	05.0	carrot	05.8
	carriage	02.8	carriage	05.0
chair	sit	25.0	table	25.8
	table	15.8	sit	25.0
	desk	03.6	bear	02.8
clean	dirty	11.4	house	13.6
	house	07.2	dirty	09.2
	floor	04.2	vacuum cleaner	05.0
cocoon	moon	06.4	raccoon	04.2
	caterpillar	04.2	animal	03.6
	bird	03.6	caterpillar	03.6
cold	hot	27.2	hot	25.8
	warm	07.2	warm	12.2
	ice	04.2	winter	06.4
color	red	11.4	red	12.8
	blue	07.2	crayon	10.0
	crayon	07.2	blue	07.2

Stimulus word	Response (male)		Response (female)	
dark	light	28.6	light	32.2
	night	08.6	night	09.2
	black	03.6	moon	06.4
deceive	leave	03.6	see	07.8
	see	02.8	cat	02.2
	door	02.2	good	02.2
enjoy	fun	07.8	fun	07.8
	me	04.2	party	02.8
	boy	03.6	boy	02.2
examine	doctor	10.0	doctor	11.4
	eyes	05.8	eyes	05.8
	man	02.8	can	02.2
flower	water	05.0	pretty	08.6
	grow	04.2	rose	08.6
	rose	04.2	grass	07.2
fly	bird	10.8	bird	20.0
	high	07.2	butterfly	06.4
	butterfly	06.4	bug	05.0
fruit	apple	07.8	apple	03.6
	eat	07.8	eat	10.8
	orange	05.8	banana	04.2
gallop	horse	42.2	horse	46.4
	ride	03.6	fast	02.8
	pony	02.8	horsey	02.8
gently	hard	05.0	hard	07.8
	soft	05.0	soft	07.2
	softly	03.6	baby	04.2
give	me	05.8	me	04.2
	present	05.0	present	03.6
	you	03.6	something	03.6
hand	fingers	06.4	arm	07.2
	man	05.0	fingers	07.2
	foot	04.2	finger	05.8
happen	happy	04.2	what	07.8
	now	04.2	happy	07.2
	house	02.8	not happen	02.2
hard	soft	17.2	soft	22.2
	work	07.8	work	08.6
	rock	06.4	easy	05.0
he	she	17.2	she	20.0
	me	12.8	her	11.4
	her	07.8	me	08.6
her	him	13.6	him	14.2
	he	10.8	she	12.8
	girl	06.4	he	10.0
high	low	18.6	low	25.0
	down	03.6	bye	05.0
	sky	03.6	sky	03.6
him	her	07.2	her	19.2
	me	04.2	she	08.6
	he	03.6	boy	05.0

Stimulus word	Response (male)		Response (female)	
inquire	quiet	08.6	church	05.8
	sing	03.6	sing	05.8
	church	02.8	quiet	03.6
insect	bug	21.4	bug	22.2
	bee	07.2	fly	03.6
	fly	07.2	in	03.6
into	house	05.8	out	07.2
	out	05.0	house	04.2
	to	05.0	in	03.6
it	is	15.8	is	17.8
	at	03.6	at	07.2
	mitten	02.8	can	02.8
join	club	10.0	fun	04.2
	coin	04.2	party	04.2
	party	03.6	coin	03.6
listen	hear	10.0	hear	13.6
	to	05.8	quiet	06.4
	now	02.8	here	03.6
long	short	18.6	short	21.4
	grass	05.8	hair	03.6
	big	03.6	little	02.8
loud	soft	10.8	soft	13.6
	quiet	10.0	quiet	11.4
	low	06.4	low	06.4
loudly	softly	12.8	softly	15.8
	loud	05.0	quiet	05.0
	quiet	05.0	scream	04.2
maintain	water	04.2	can	04.2
	can	02.2	light	02.8
	car	02.2	door	02.2
man	woman	10.0	woman	15.8
	lady	07.2	lady	12.2
	can	03.6	father	05.8
mix	cake	15.0	cake	15.0
	butter	02.8	stir	04.2
	cook	02.2	mixer	03.6
moth	fly	08.6	fly	08.6
	cloth	06.4	butterfly	05.8
	butterfly	05.8	cloth	05.0
move	stop	07.2	fast	05.0
	car	05.8	still	05.0
	go	02.8	go	04.2
music	piano	12.2	piano	15.0
	sing	07.8	sing	15.0
	teacher	07.8	play	05.0
needle	thread	12.2	thread	19.2
	shot	09.2	pin	10.8
	sew	06.4	sew	07.8
net	fish	15.8	fish	11.4
	catch	08.6	bird	07.2
	bird	04.2	catch	05.0

Stimulus word	Response (male)		Response (female)	
never	ever	10.0	ever	10.0
	again	05.0	again	06.4
	always	04.2	always	03.6
obey	rules	05.8	rules	05.8
	me	05.0	bad	05.0
	law	03.6	mother	05.0
ocean	water	15.8	water	22.2
	sea	09.2	sea	10.8
	boat	06.4	boat	05.0
off	on	25.8	on	30.8
	light	03.6	go	02.8
	car	02.2	car	02.2
on	off	16.4	off	25.0
	light	02.8	in	02.8
	me	02.8	come	02.2
once	twice	12.2	twice	11.4
	two	05.8	two	07.8
	time	04.2	time	04.2
pleasant	living	05.0	present	06.4
	nice	03.6	nice	04.2
	time	03.6	unpleasant	03.6
prepare	food	05.8	pear	04.2
	dinner	04.2	dinner	02.8
	apple	02.2	floor	02.2
pretty	girl	07.2	ugly	14.2
	ugly	07.2	dress	09.2
	dress	05.0	girl	06.4
quiet	loud	16.4	loud	17.8
	be quiet	07.2	noisy	07.8
	down	05.0	be	03.6
restore	food	12.8	store	17.2
	store	06.4	food	10.0
	more	03.6	buy	03.6
river	water	15.0	water	22.2
	stream	09.2	ocean	07.8
	boat	07.2	boat	07.2
rough	dog	07.8	dog	09.2
	tough	07.8	fight	05.8
	fight	05.0	hard	05.0
run	fast	15.0	fast	17.8
	walk	12.2	walk	10.8
	jump	05.8	jump	10.0
sad	happy	20.8	happy	27.2
	mad	10.8	cry	09.2
	bad	05.0	mad	07.2
salt	pepper	40.0	pepper	48.6
	water	07.8	hot	03.6
	eat	02.2	sugar	03.6
seldom	sell	05.0	sell	07.8
	celery	02.8	celery	02.2
	door	02.2	selling	02.2

Stimulus word	Response (male)		Response (female)	
sell	food	03.6	food	07.8
	fruit	03.6	candy	02.8
	cellar	02.8	something	02.8
she	he	20.0	he	22.8
	me	07.2	girl	06.4
	girl	04.2	sheep	05.8
sheep	lamb	12.2	lamb	19.2
	wool	06.4	wool	05.0
	white	03.6	she	04.2
short	long	20.0	long	13.6
	pants	09.2	big	09.2
	big	05.0	little	07.2
since	mince	02.8	when	03.6
	not since	02.8	then	02.8
	now	02.2	you	02.8
sit	down	36.4	down	33.6
	chair	14.2	chair	15.8
	stand	05.8	stand	05.8
slow	fast	35.0	fast	36.4
	car	02.8	walk	05.8
	down	02.8	sled	05.0
slowly	fast	30.8	fast	28.6
	walk	09.2	walk	09.2
	car	06.4	fastly	05.0
smooth	hard	09.2	soft	14.2
	soft	08.6	hard	09.2
	rough	04.2	rough	06.4
sometimes	I	04.2	sun	05.0
	you	03.6	I	03.6
	not sometimes	02.8	never	02.8
sour	kraut	09.2	milk	10.0
	sweet	07.2	lemon	06.4
	milk	05.0	sweet	05.8
square	box	15.0	round	10.0
	circle	06.4	box	09.2
	hair	05.8	circle	07.8
swift	soft	04.2	swim	04.2
	fast	03.6	fast	02.8
	broom	02.2	wind	02.8
table	chair	31.4	chair	40.8
	eat	05.0	eat	07.8
	mad	04.2	sit	02.8
tall	short	13.6	small	13.6
	little	08.6	little	12.2
	small	07.8	short	10.8
tell	me	05.0	me	11.4
	you	04.2	something	04.2
	not tell	02.8	you	03.6
them	me	04.2	me	04.2
	us	04.2	they	04.2
	people	03.6	us	04.2

Stimulus word	Response (male)		Response (female)	
they	people	04.2	can	05.8
	are	03.6	the	03.6
	went	02.8	we	03.6
thirsty	water	28.6	water	20.0
	drink	21.4	drink	12.2
	hungry	05.0	hungry	11.4
up	down	46.4	down	56.4
	airplane	03.6	sky	02.8
	elevator	02.8	stairs	02.8
us	we	09.2	you	10.0
	me	07.2	we	09.2
	you	07.2	me	07.2
usually	help	02.8	sometimes	03.6
	me	02.8	do	02.8
	sometimes	02.8	something	02.8
wild	animal	10.8	animal	13.6
	horse	07.8	animals	05.8
	lion	05.0	horse	04.2
wing	fly	20.8	fly	24.2
	bird	13.6	bird	16.4
	swing	06.4	swing	06.4
yellow	green	09.2	blue	10.8
	blue	07.8	red	09.2
	red	07.8	color	07.2

Third Grade

Stimulus word	Response (male)		Response (female)	
add	subtract	62.8	subtract	66.4
	numbers	05.0	plus	02.8
	take away	02.8	arithmetic	02.2
allow	not allowed	07.8	let	05.0
	let	04.2	not	05.0
	cannot	02.8	me	04.2
always	never	15.0	never	17.2
	sometimes	10.0	sometimes	08.6
	not always	05.0	all the time	05.0
because	why	08.6	why	13.6
	something	06.4	he	04.2
	he	05.0	so	04.2
bee	sting	17.8	sting	12.8
	fly	09.2	bug	10.0
	insect	07.2	fly	09.2
begin	start	27.2	start	21.4
	end	15.0	end	20.8
	after	03.6	finish	06.4
belong	to	11.4	to	10.0
	own	04.2	me	05.0
	yours	04.2	mine	03.6
between	middle	17.8	middle	21.4
	in the middle	06.4	together	05.0
	together	04.2	under	04.2

Stimulus word	Response (male)		Response (female)	
bird	fly	37.2	fly	32.8
	animal	09.2	animal	08.6
	dog	03.6	nest	05.8
bitter	sour	21.4	sour	20.0
	sweet	17.8	sweet	19.2
	better	07.2	bit	04.2
black	white	45.8	white	52.8
	color	10.8	dark	09.2
	blue	07.2	cat	05.8
bright	dark	30.0	dark	30.8
	light	19.2	light	30.0
	sun	09.2	sun	05.0
bug	insect	44.2	insect	40.8
	fly	11.4	fly	14.2
	bee	08.6	bee	07.8
butterfly	fly	22.2	fly	17.8
	insect	15.0	insect	12.2
	bug	07.2	bird	09.2
carry	heavy	08.6	hold	12.8
	hold	07.8	baby	08.6
	drop	07.2	drop	07.8
chair	sit	27.2	sit	31.4
	table	16.4	table	21.4
	selfish	10.0	dish	13.6
clean	dirty	47.2	dirty	47.8
	wash	06.4	house	07.8
	house	02.8	wash	04.2
cocoon	butterfly	18.6	animal	19.2
	animal	08.6	butterfly	13.6
	raccoon	07.2	raccoon	12.8
cold	hot	45.0	hot	53.6
	warm	20.0	warm	21.4
	freezing	05.8	freezing	05.0
color	red	15.0	red	22.8
	blue	13.6	blue	12.8
	black	11.4	black	07.2
dark	light	62.2	light	69.2
	night	12.2	night	10.0
	black	05.0	black	05.8
deceive	receive	10.8	receive	07.8
	give	04.2	get	03.6
	bad	02.8	decide	02.8
enjoy	fun	15.0	happy	12.8
	happy	14.2	fun	12.2
	like	09.2	like	12.2
examine	doctor	13.6	test	09.2
	test	09.2	doctor	08.6
	operate	05.8	eyes	08.6
flower	pretty	11.4	rose	15.8
	plant	10.0	pretty	14.2
	rose	10.0	plant	07.2

Stimulus word	Response (male)		Response (female)	
fly	walk	17.2	walk	17.2
	bird	06.4	bird	16.4
	bug	06.4	bug	10.0
fruit	apple	21.4	apple	24.2
	vegetable	20.8	vegetable	12.8
	eat	07.8	orange	11.4
gallop	horse	25.8	horse	30.8
	trot	12.2	run	13.6
	ride	10.0	trot	09.2
gently	soft	24.2	soft	21.4
	hard	08.6	softly	11.4
	softly	07.8	hard	10.8
give	take	21.4	gave	27.8
	gave	10.8	take	17.8
	something	05.0	me	04.2
hand	arm	18.6	arm	17.8
	finger	07.8	fingers	12.2
	foot	05.8	finger	06.4
happen	happy	07.2	happy	05.0
	didn't	06.4	not happen	04.2
	didn't happen	05.8	something	04.2
hard	soft	48.6	soft	57.8
	easy	16.4	easy	11.4
	rock	07.2	rock	05.0
he	she	27.2	she	36.4
	her	22.2	her	25.0
	me	12.8	him	12.8
her	him	28.6	him	33.6
	she	23.6	she	22.2
	he	18.6	he	21.4
high	low	56.4	low	69.2
	bye	03.6	up	03.6
	sky	02.8	by	02.8
him	her	33.6	her	55.0
	she	12.2	she	10.0
	me	08.6	boy	08.6
inquire	sing	07.2	sing	11.4
	not inquire	04.2	quiet	04.2
	quiet	04.2	singing	02.8
insect	bug	44.2	bug	50.0
	fly	10.8	animal	07.2
	animal	07.2	fly	05.0
into	out	32.8	out	44.2
	out of	09.2	in	07.8
	outside	08.6	outside	05.8
it	is	16.4	is	32.8
	that	10.0	that	09.2
	bit	05.0	at	07.8
join	together	12.8	together	17.2
	club	11.4	club	12.2
	gang	02.8	come	03.6

Stimulus word	Response (male)		Response (female)	
listen	hear	30.0	hear	30.0
	quiet	09.2	quiet	10.8
	talk	04.2	not listen	05.0
long	short	59.4	short	66.4
	far	03.6	large	02.2
	grass	03.6	wide	02.2
loud	soft	25.0	soft	36.4
	quiet	17.2	quiet	09.2
	noisy	07.2	noisy	07.8
loudly	softly	27.2	softly	32.8
	noisy	09.2	soft	08.6
	soft	06.4	noisy	06.4
maintain	not maintain	02.8	can	02.8
	hold	02.2	contain	02.8
	retain	02.2	begin	02.2
man	woman	37.8	woman	49.2
	boy	08.6	lady	11.4
	lady	07.2	men	10.8
mix	cake	15.0	stir	15.8
	stir	10.8	cake	15.0
	fix	07.2	fix	06.4
moth	butterfly	15.8	butterfly	18.6
	fly	12.2	insect	10.8
	insect	12.2	fly	07.2
move	go	10.0	still	12.8
	stay	08.6	stay	10.0
	still	08.6	away	05.8
music	sing	10.8	sing	15.0
	song	08.6	song	11.4
	sound	05.8	sound	09.2
needle	thread	25.8	thread	36.4
	pin	24.2	pin	21.4
	sharp	07.2	sharp	05.0
net	fish	20.0	fish	22.8
	catch	12.8	catch	10.0
	string	03.6	hair	04.2
never	ever	20.0	always	15.0
	always	13.6	ever	13.6
	again	06.4	again	11.4
obey	listen	07.2	listen	08.6
	rules	07.2	disobey	07.8
	law	06.4	good	07.2
ocean	sea	37.2	sea	42.8
	water	22.2	water	21.4
	river	10.8	river	12.2
off	on	72.2	on	79.2
	of	02.2	down	02.8
	gone	01.4	go	02.2
on	off	55.0	off	60.8
	go	05.8	top	03.6
	no	02.8	go	02.8

Stimulus word	Response (male)		Response (female)	
once	twice	21.4	twice	20.8
	one	06.4	one	07.8
	time	05.8	upon	07.2
pleasant	nice	16.4	nice	20.8
	unpleasant	07.8	unpleasant	08.6
	happy	04.2	happy	07.2
prepare	fix	13.6	ready	15.8
	ready	10.8	fix	09.2
	get ready	04.2	get ready	04.2
pretty	beautiful	31.4	beautiful	40.8
	ugly	29.2	ugly	33.6
	nice	06.4	cute	02.8
quiet	loud	32.2	loud	32.8
	noisy	21.4	noisy	20.0
	noise	05.0	noise	05.8
restore	store	10.8	store	16.4
	keep	07.8	food	09.2
	food	07.2	keep	05.0
river	water	24.2	lake	19.2
	stream	23.6	stream	19.2
	ocean	11.4	water	19.2
rough	soft	15.0	hard	21.4
	smooth	12.8	soft	18.6
	hard	10.0	smooth	10.8
run	walk	35.0	walk	32.8
	fast	23.6	fast	19.2
	ran	13.6	ran	12.8
sad	happy	67.2	happy	67.2
	unhappy	06.4	mad	07.2
	mad	05.0	glad	03.6
salt	pepper	55.0	pepper	57.8
	water	13.6	water	07.8
	sugar	06.4	sugar	06.4
seldom	always	06.4	often	10.0
	sell	06.4	always	04.2
	often	05.0	sell	04.2
sell	buy	17.2	buy	10.0
	sold	13.6	sold	08.6
	give	05.8	give	05.8
she	he	32.8	he	41.4
	her	18.6	her	21.4
	him	14.2	him	18.6
sheep	lamb	20.8	lamb	24.2
	wool	15.8	animal	09.2
	animal	11.4	wool	08.6
short	long	55.8	long	57.2
	tall	10.8	small	12.2
	small	10.0	tall	08.6
since	then	10.0	then	10.0
	when	07.8	when	10.0
	now	05.8	money	02.8

Stimulus word	Response (male)		Response (female)	
sit	stand	29.2	stand	31.4
	down	22.2	down	23.6
	chair	15.0	sat	17.2
slow	fast	77.8	fast	79.2
	not fast	04.2	walk	02.2
	turtle	02.8	go	01.4
slowly	fast	47.8	fast	56.4
	fastly	15.8	faster	06.4
	faster	08.6	fastly	06.4
smooth	soft	27.2	soft	35.0
	rough	16.4	hard	21.4
	hard	14.2	rough	11.4
sometimes	always	20.0	always	25.0
	all the time	06.4	something	06.4
	somewhere	04.2	all the time	03.6
sour	sweet	31.4	sweet	36.4
	bitter	10.0	good	09.2
	good	06.4	bitter	07.8
square	round	23.6	round	22.8
	circle	13.6	circle	17.8
	triangle	12.8	box	12.8
swift	fast	20.0	fast	12.8
	soft	05.8	soft	04.2
	cheese	04.2	swim	04.2
table	chair	44.2	chair	58.6
	desk	06.4	desk	05.8
	eat	06.4	leg	03.6
tall	short	44.2	short	47.2
	small	14.2	small	17.8
	high	10.0	big	05.8
tell	ask	15.0	talk	09.2
	talk	07.8	told	08.6
	well	05.0	ask	07.2
them	they	19.2	they	19.2
	us	12.2	us	11.4
	him	11.4	people	08.6
they	them	11.4	them	27.2
	are	10.8	people	07.2
	people	08.6	are	05.8
thirsty	water	26.4	drink	28.6
	drink	22.2	water	22.8
	hungry	17.8	hungry	19.2
up	down	86.4	down	88.6
	high	03.6	high	05.8
	fly	01.4	stairs	01.4
us	you	28.6	you	27.2
	them	12.8	them	15.8
	me	10.8	we	12.2
usually	always	10.8	always	10.0
	sometimes	09.2	sometimes	08.6
	often	05.0	often	05.8

Stimulus word	Response (male)		Response (female)	
wild	tame	17.2	animal	16.4
	animal	11.4	tame	14.2
	not wild	04.2	horse	05.0
wing	fly	40.8	fly	37.2
	bird	17.8	bird	21.4
	sing	05.0	arm	05.0
yellow	color	23.6	color	22.8
	black	12.8	blue	11.4
	red	10.0	red	11.4

Fifth Grade

add	subtract	67.0	subtract	60.0
	put together	04.0	numbers	04.0
	multiply	03.0	take away	03.0
allow	let	12.0	let	12.0
	not allowed	07.0	can	04.0
	permission	05.0	permission	04.0
always	never	26.0	never	23.0
	sometimes	10.0	all the time	11.0
	forever	08.0	sometimes	09.0
because	reason	15.0	cause	16.0
	why	12.0	why	12.0
	excuse	06.0	reason	06.0
bee	sting	21.0	sting	20.0
	insect	19.0	insect	19.0
	honey	07.0	bug	09.0
begin	start	58.0	start	43.0
	end	20.0	end	25.0
	began	04.0	stop	09.0
belong	own	10.0	own	15.0
	yours	09.0	mine	13.0
	mine	07.0	join	10.0
between	middle	39.0	middle	41.0
	in the middle	05.0	in the middle	07.0
	together	05.0	in	06.0
bird	fly	27.0	fly	26.0
	animal	15.0	animal	19.0
	robin	09.0	robin	07.0
bitter	sour	41.0	sour	32.0
	sweet	19.0	sweet	25.0
	cold	07.0	cold	05.0
black	white	53.0	white	53.0
	color	18.0	color	15.0
	dark	06.0	dark	12.0
bright	dark	22.0	dark	28.0
	light	16.0	light	23.0
	smart	11.0	dull	06.0
bug	insect	64.0	insect	55.0
	beetle	06.0	fly	10.0
	ant	05.0	animal	07.0

Stimulus word	Response (male)		Response (female)	
butterfly	insect	35.0	insect	32.0
	bug	08.0	fly	12.0
	moth	08.0	animal	10.0
carry	hold	19.0	hold	21.0
	heavy	08.0	drop	11.0
	walk	07.0	heavy	07.0
chair	sit	37.0	sit	27.0
	desk	15.0	table	26.0
	table	15.0	desk	20.0
clean	dirty	46.0	dirty	48.0
	wash	08.0	neat	07.0
	not dirty	07.0	wash	04.0
cocoon	animal	16.0	animal	23.0
	butterfly	14.0	butterfly	15.0
	caterpillar	09.0	caterpillar	11.0
cold	hot	42.0	hot	46.0
	warm	24.0	warm	23.0
	freezing	07.0	freezing	06.0
color	red	22.0	red	18.0
	black	12.0	blue	12.0
	yellow	10.0	crayon	10.0
dark	light	66.0	light	70.0
	black	10.0	black	11.0
	night	08.0	night	08.0
deceive	receive	23.0	receive	18.0
	give	04.0	received	04.0
	get	03.0	forget	02.0
enjoy	like	19.0	like	23.0
	happy	16.0	happy	21.0
	fun	15.0	fun	15.0
examine	test	17.0	test	18.0
	look	14.0	check	12.0
	check	11.0	doctor	12.0
flower	rose	18.0	pretty	17.0
	plant	15.0	rose	16.0
	pretty	08.0	plant	14.0
fly	insect	23.0	insect	24.0
	walk	18.0	walk	16.0
	airplane	07.0	bird	12.0
fruit	apple	30.0	apple	30.0
	vegetable	24.0	vegetable	14.0
	orange	14.0	orange	12.0
gallop	horse	26.0	horse	32.0
	trot	22.0	trot	30.0
	ride	12.0	hop	05.0
gently	soft	37.0	soft	41.0
	hard	11.0	softly	13.0
	softly	08.0	hard	06.0
give	take	40.0	take	32.0
	receive	10.0	gave	10.0
	gave	09.0	receive	10.0

Stimulus word	Response (male)		Response (female)	
hand	arm	23.0	arm	24.0
	fingers	19.0	finger	10.0
	finger	09.0	fingers	10.0
happen	did	06.0	happy	06.0
	unhappen	05.0	now	06.0
	does	04.0	done	05.0
hard	soft	55.0	soft	56.0
	easy	21.0	easy	15.0
	rock	05.0	rough	04.0
he	her	35.0	she	29.0
	she	22.0	her	28.0
	boy	15.0	boy	18.0
her	him	33.0	him	44.0
	she	29.0	girl	19.0
	he	14.0	he	15.0
high	low	60.0	low	68.0
	tall	09.0	tall	08.0
	up	04.0	hello	05.0
him	her	56.0	her	61.0
	boy	10.0	boy	11.0
	he	07.0	man	05.0
inquire	ask	13.0	ask	13.0
	tell	04.0	sing	07.0
	not inquire	03.0	tell	05.0
insect	bug	53.0	bug	49.0
	animal	08.0	animal	12.0
	ant	07.0	fly	10.0
into	out	44.0	out	36.0
	go	09.0	go	09.0
	out of	07.0	inside	07.0
it	is	21.0	is	22.0
	that	13.0	that	14.0
	thing	10.0	thing	10.0
join	together	30.0	together	29.0
	club	06.0	club	04.0
	army	04.0	group	04.0
listen	hear	45.0	hear	54.0
	quiet	08.0	talk	06.0
	obey	05.0	heard	04.0
long	short	61.0	short	67.0
	wide	05.0	grass	02.0
	grass	03.0	length	02.0
loud	soft	40.0	soft	46.0
	noise	11.0	noisy	11.0
	low	06.0	noise	06.0
loudly	softly	32.0	softly	44.0
	noisy	09.0	soft	10.0
	noise	07.0	noisy	08.0
maintain	contain	06.0	tain	06.0
	hold	06.0	have	04.0
	keep	04.0	hold	04.0

Stimulus word	Response (male)		Response (female)	
man	woman	51.0	woman	54.0
	person	07.0	lady	11.0
	boy	04.0	person	08.0
mix	stir	16.0	stir	21.0
	cake	11.0	cake	16.0
	together	09.0	together	12.0
moth	insect	23.0	insect	20.0
	butterfly	20.0	bug	19.0
	bug	10.0	butterfly	12.0
move	go	13.0	stay	11.0
	still	11.0	walk	09.0
	stay	08.0	still	08.0
music	song	11.0	sing	11.0
	sound	10.0	instrument	10.0
	sing	08.0	sound	09.0
needle	thread	23.0	thread	39.0
	pin	22.0	pin	09.0
	sharp	21.0	sharp	08.0
net	fish	37.0	fish	33.0
	catch	12.0	catch	10.0
	rope	05.0	hair	08.0
never	always	20.0	always	20.0
	ever	19.0	ever	17.0
	again	07.0	not	05.0
obey	disobey	22.0	disobey	20.0
	listen	14.0	listen	17.0
	do	06.0	desire	04.0
ocean	sea	33.0	sea	39.0
	water	29.0	water	22.0
	lake	06.0	river	11.0
off	on	70.0	on	79.0
	not on	07.0	not on	05.0
	in	04.0	go	03.0
on	off	56.0	off	58.0
	top	07.0	top	07.0
	go	04.0	go	06.0
once	twice	42.0	twice	38.0
	one	09.0	upon	08.0
	one time	05.0	time	07.0
pleasant	nice	23.0	nice	20.0
	happy	17.0	unpleasant	19.0
	unpleasant	17.0	happy	18.0
prepare	ready	18.0	ready	24.0
	fix	16.0	get ready	17.0
	get ready	13.0	fix	10.0
pretty	beautiful	36.0	ugly	46.0
	ugly	32.0	beautiful	33.0
	cute	07.0	handsome	03.0
quiet	loud	33.0	loud	33.0
	noisy	23.0	noisy	21.0
	silent	07.0	soft	09.0

Stimulus word	Response (male)		Response (female)	
restore	keep	10.0	store	14.0
	store	09.0	keep	11.0
	put away	08.0	put away	11.0
river	stream	31.0	stream	29.0
	water	19.0	water	18.0
	lake	11.0	lake	16.0
rough	smooth	30.0	hard	27.0
	hard	16.0	smooth	26.0
	soft	13.0	soft	16.0
run	walk	35.0	walk	35.0
	fast	24.0	fast	23.0
	ran	08.0	ran	10.0
sad	happy	61.0	happy	64.0
	unhappy	13.0	unhappy	23.0
	not happy	05.0	mad	03.0
salt	pepper	43.0	pepper	51.0
	sugar	10.0	food	10.0
	water	07.0	water	10.0
seldom	often	18.0	often	25.0
	always	09.0	never	07.0
	hardly	06.0	always	04.0
sell	buy	36.0	buy	24.0
	give	06.0	sold	12.0
	sale	06.0	give away	05.0
she	her	32.0	he	45.0
	he	27.0	her	17.0
	girl	17.0	him	16.0
sheep	animal	18.0	lamb	28.0
	lamb	15.0	animal	19.0
	goat	11.0	dog	07.0
short	long	47.0	long	51.0
	tall	27.0	tall	22.0
	small	11.0	small	13.0
since	then	14.0	then	11.0
	before	06.0	when	07.0
	long ago	04.0	last time	05.0
sit	stand	31.0	stand	42.0
	down	26.0	down	18.0
	chair	16.0	chair	14.0
slow	fast	74.0	fast	81.0
	turtle	06.0	not fast	04.0
	not fast	04.0	pokey	02.0
slowly	fast	42.0	fast	52.0
	fastly	13.0	fastly	13.0
	faster	07.0	not fast	05.0
smooth	rough	37.0	rough	38.0
	soft	18.0	soft	25.0
	hard	08.0	hard	12.0
sometimes	always	21.0	always	17.0
	all the time	08.0	often	13.0
	something	08.0	once	07.0

Stimulus word	Response (male)		Response (female)	
sour	sweet	31.0	sweet	46.0
	bitter	28.0	bitter	22.0
	not sweet	04.0	lemon	04.0
square	round	39.0	circle	22.0
	circle	11.0	round	18.0
	triangle	11.0	box	14.0
swift	fast	58.0	fast	48.0
	slow	05.0	slow	07.0
	quick	04.0	quickly	06.0
table	chair	47.0	chair	47.0
	desk	06.0	eat	09.0
	eat	06.0	desk	07.0
tall	short	55.0	short	59.0
	small	09.0	high	09.0
	large	07.0	small	08.0
tell	talk	12.0	told	13.0
	say	08.0	talk	11.0
	ask	07.0	ask	08.0
them	they	24.0	they	30.0
	people	14.0	us	15.0
	us	11.0	people	09.0
they	them	40.0	them	42.0
	people	13.0	people	11.0
	we	06.0	us	08.0
thirsty	water	34.0	water	40.0
	drink	19.0	drink	18.0
	hungry	13.0	hungry	16.0
up	down	79.0	down	83.0
	high	03.0	high	04.0
	airplane	02.0	in the air	02.0
us	you	18.0	you	27.0
	them	16.0	we	25.0
	we	14.0	them	11.0
usually	often	17.0	often	21.0
	unusually	12.0	sometimes	15.0
	always	09.0	unusually	12.0
wild	tame	34.0	tame	32.0
	animal	19.0	animal	10.0
	tamed	05.0	calm	05.0
wing	fly	27.0	bird	40.0
	bird	24.0	fly	29.0
	feather	06.0	airplane	02.0
yellow	color	41.0	color	44.0
	red	09.0	green	09.0
	green	07.0	blue	07.0

Adult Data

add	subtract	69.0	subtract	77.0
	up	06.0	math	04.0
	multiply	05.0	sum	04.0

Stimulus word	Response (male)		Response (female)	
allow	let	30.0	permit	45.0
	permit	26.0	let	34.0
	him	03.0	give	06.0
always	never	49.0	forever	30.0
	forever	14.0	never	30.0
	ever	03.0	sometimes	11.0
because	since	21.0	since	27.0
	why	21.0	why	24.0
	of	16.0	reason	12.0
bee	sting	14.0	sting	19.0
	hive	12.0	honey	15.0
	honey	12.0	buzz	10.0
begin	start	31.0	start	47.0
	end	21.0	end	19.0
	stop	10.0	again	07.0
belong	to	25.0	join	14.0
	join	16.0	to	11.0
	together	11.0	together	10.0
between	among	35.0	among	44.0
	in	15.0	us	12.0
	them	11.0	in	05.0
bird	fly	33.0	fly	32.0
	wing	07.0	wing	10.0
	dog	05.0	robin	08.0
bitter	sweet	64.0	sweet	57.0
	sour	09.0	sour	16.0
	taste	03.0	taste	04.0
black	white	62.0	white	54.0
	dark	06.0	dark	08.0
	blue	04.0	night	08.0
bright	light	26.0	light	25.0
	dark	12.0	dull	10.0
	star	09.0	shiny	10.0
bug	insect	29.0	insect	39.0
	fly	13.0	beetle	11.0
	bee	09.0	bee	05.0
butterfly	cocoon	15.0	cocoon	16.0
	moth	12.0	wings	09.0
	insect	09.0	moth	08.0
carry	on	09.0	hold	09.0
	out	09.0	burden	08.0
	back	06.0	load	06.0
chair	table	30.0	table	26.0
	sit	25.0	sit	21.0
	seat	07.0	seat	16.0
clean	dirty	36.0	dirty	37.0
	wash	07.0	room	08.0
	dirt	03.0	house	07.0
cocoon	butterfly	28.0	butterfly	31.0
	moth	12.0	caterpillar	16.0
	caterpillar	06.0	moth	11.0

Stimulus word	Response (male)		Response (female)	
cold	hot	47.0	hot	37.0
	warm	12.0	warm	13.0
	frigid	03.0	snow	07.0
color	red	25.0	red	24.0
	blue	17.0	blue	20.0
	black	10.0	yellow	16.0
dark	light	58.0	light	58.0
	black	08.0	night	16.0
	night	07.0	black	09.0
deceive	trick	14.0	lie	25.0
	lie	12.0	trick	12.0
	receive	10.0	cheat	11.0
enjoy	like	24.0	like	31.0
	fun	12.0	love	09.0
	love	08.0	fun	08.0
examine	test	24.0	test	32.0
	look	15.0	look	11.0
	doctor	07.0	doctor	10.0
flower	rose	15.0	rose	22.0
	petal	08.0	petal	07.0
	bud	07.0	garden	06.0
fly	plane	09.0	plane	17.0
	away	08.0	bird	09.0
	airplane	07.0	airplane	07.0
fruit	apple	29.0	apple	36.0
	fly	08.0	orange	15.0
	orange	07.0	eat	05.0
gallop	horse	40.0	horse	60.0
	run	14.0	trot	13.0
	trot	11.0	run	11.0
gently	softly	30.0	softly	34.0
	soft	07.0	tenderly	14.0
	caress	04.0	soft	08.0
give	take	41.0	take	58.0
	gave	09.0	donate	09.0
	up	06.0	gift	04.0
hand	foot	20.0	foot	24.0
	arm	11.0	arm	10.0
	finger	11.0	finger	10.0
happen	occur	35.0	occur	54.0
	event	06.0	event	09.0
	to	06.0	once	04.0
hard	soft	36.0	soft	60.0
	sell	05.0	difficult	05.0
	work	04.0	work	03.0
he	she	55.0	she	61.0
	her	18.0	her	10.0
	him	11.0	him	06.0
her	him	47.0	him	51.0
	she	24.0	she	16.0
	his	06.0	girl	06.0

Stimulus word	Response (male)		Response (female)	
high	low	51.0	low	67.0
	noon	05.0	tall	04.0
	above	03.0	jump	03.0
him	her	78.0	her	72.0
	he	06.0	man	04.0
	me	02.0	song	04.0
inquire	ask	61.0	ask	71.0
	about	07.0	question	06.0
	into	04.0	ask about	02.0
insect	bug	50.0	bug	48.0
	bite	07.0	bite	10.0
	fly	06.0	bee	09.0
into	out	28.0	out of	23.0
	out of	18.0	out	16.0
	onto	06.0	enter	07.0
it	that	18.0	that	19.0
	is	13.0	thing	16.0
	thing	12.0	is	08.0
join	together	17.0	together	18.0
	group	15.0	group	11.0
	army	05.0	unite	11.0
listen	hear	49.0	hear	59.0
	talk	07.0	music	07.0
	to	06.0	quiet	03.0
long	short	51.0	short	59.0
	day	04.0	ruler	03.0
	hair	04.0	after	02.0
loud	soft	48.0	soft	44.0
	noise	14.0	noise	19.0
	mouth	06.0	noisy	15.0
loudly	softly	51.0	softly	50.0
	noise	03.0	noisily	09.0
	noisily	03.0	noise	07.0
maintain	keep	31.0	keep	43.0
	hold	05.0	hold	08.0
	continue	04.0	keep up	07.0
man	woman	86.0	woman	78.0
	girl	03.0	boy	04.0
	wife	02.0	wife	02.0
mix	cake	11.0	cake	13.0
	stir	09.0	stir	13.0
	together	06.0	batter	7.0
moth	butterfly	14.0	butterfly	19.0
	ball	12.0	ball	07.0
	fly	10.0	bug	06.0
move	away	10.0	fast	07.0
	fast	08.0	run	07.0
	stop	08.0	stop	07.0
music	listen	06.0	sound	10.0
	soft	06.0	song	09.0
	song	05.0	piano	08.0

Stimulus word	Response (male)		Response (female)	
needle	pin	27.0	thread	38.0
	thread	24.0	pin	16.0
	haystack	07.0	point	11.0
net	fish	39.0	fish	40.0
	catch	12.0	catch	10.0
	tennis	07.0	hair	08.0
never	always	41.0	always	39.0
	again	10.0	ever	14.0
	ever	10.0	again	07.0
obey	command	21.0	command	21.0
	disobey	18.0	disobey	13.0
	follow	06.0	follow	09.0
ocean	sea	43.0	sea	44.0
	water	10.0	water	06.0
	city	05.0	waves	06.0
off	on	84.0	on	78.0
	color	02.0	light	05.0
	of	02.0	beat	02.0
on	off	52.0	off	57.0
	top	12.0	top	10.0
	in	07.0	upon	05.0
once	twice	53.0	twice	58.0
	upon	10.0	again	04.0
	again	05.0	always	04.0
pleasant	nice	13.0	nice	29.0
	sweet	09.0	unpleasant	14.0
	good	08.0	happy	06.0
prepare	fix	19.0	fix	14.0
	make	10.0	ready	13.0
	ready	10.0	make	11.0
pretty	girl	27.0	ugly	26.0
	beautiful	14.0	girl	16.0
	ugly	12.0	beautiful	09.0
quiet	loud	26.0	loud	20.0
	noise	10.0	soft	17.0
	soft	10.0	noisy	12.0
restore	fix	13.0	fix	15.0
	renew	05.0	maintain	06.0
	repair	05.0	replace	06.0
river	stream	21.0	stream	37.0
	flow	08.0	water	17.0
	lake	07.0	flow	09.0
rough	smooth	25.0	smooth	33.0
	tough	14.0	tough	14.0
	soft	08.0	harsh	04.0
run	walk	41.0	walk	39.0
	fast	14.0	fast	12.0
	jump	04.0	skip	11.0
sad	happy	45.0	happy	48.0
	glad	06.0	unhappy	17.0
	unhappy	05.0	cry	04.0

Stimulus word	Response (male)		Response (female)	
salt	pepper	28.0	pepper	36.0
	water	21.0	water	10.0
	sugar	08.0	thirsty	08.0
seldom	never	41.0	often	30.0
	often	20.0	never	26.0
	always	09.0	rarely	08.0
sell	car	53.0	car	52.0
	sold	05.0	vend	06.0
	hard	03.0	short	03.0
she	he	38.0	he	52.0
	her	30.0	her	21.0
	him	07.0	him	06.0
sheep	lamb	17.0	wool	19.0
	wool	16.0	lamb	19.0
	dog	14.0	dog	13.0
short	long	31.0	long	44.0
	tall	27.0	tall	23.0
	thin	05.0	fat	10.0
since	then	39.0	then	28.0
	when	16.0	when	13.0
	because	07.0	because	10.0
sit	down	35.0	down	36.0
	stand	19.0	stand	22.0
	sat	10.0	chair	17.0
slow	fast	59.0	fast	71.0
	down	17.0	down	04.0
	stop	04.0	car	02.0
slowly	fast	35.0	quickly	29.0
	quickly	20.0	fast	13.0
	rapidly	04.0	lazy	04.0
smooth	rough	32.0	rough	47.0
	soft	17.0	soft	13.0
	curve	05.0	skin	04.0
sometimes	always	44.0	always	33.0
	never	16.0	often	26.0
	often	12.0	never	13.0
sour	sweet	38.0	sweet	42.0
	bitter	12.0	cream	11.0
	cream	10.0	bitter	10.0
square	round	32.0	round	41.0
	circle	17.0	circle	18.0
	cube	11.0	box	08.0
swift	fast	39.0	fast	42.0
	slow	08.0	slow	07.0
	quick	07.0	quick	05.0
table	chair	62.0	chair	69.0
	top	09.0	top	06.0
	cloth	06.0	cloth	05.0
tall	short	72.0	short	66.0
	man	04.0	man	05.0
	thin	04.0	boy	04.0

Stimulus word	Response (male)		Response (female)	
tell	talk	09.0	relate	14.0
	say	08.0	story	14.0
	story	07.0	say	12.0
them	us	37.0	us	32.0
	they	24.0	they	26.0
	we	08.0	we	06.0
they	them	35.0	them	36.0
	we	18.0	we	16.0
	us	15.0	us	13.0
thirsty	water	26.0	water	42.0
	drink	18.0	drink	18.0
	dry	16.0	hungry	18.0
up	down	73.0	down	67.0
	high	03.0	stairs	12.0
	above	02.0	high	03.0
us	we	76.0	we	64.0
	them	07.0	you	12.0
	you	06.0	together	08.0
usually	always	25.0	often	29.0
	often	22.0	always	18.0
	never	21.0	sometimes	13.0
wild	animal	16.0	tame	19.0
	tame	14.0	animal	08.0
	free	06.0	geese	07.0
wing	bird	24.0	bird	53.0
	fly	22.0	fly	16.0
	plane	10.0	plane	10.0
yellow	bird	22.0	green	14.0
	blue	07.0	color	08.0
	green	07.0	sun	08.0

Appendix B:

Comparisons of Three Most Common Responses Obtained by Various Investigators

Thirty selected words from the Kent-Rosanoff list in alphabetical order. (Part I) Comparisons of three most common responses (in per cents) by Woodrow and Lowell (no grade breakdown) and Palermo and Jenkins (fourth, fifth, and sixth grades). Responses to the same thirty words obtained by Entwisle at kindergarten, first, third, and fifth grades. (Part II) Comparisons of three most common responses (no sex divisions) obtained by various investigators (in per cents). For adults only—investigators include Kent-Rosanoff, Russell-Jenkins, Palermo-Jenkins, and Entwisle. (Part III) Sixteen selected words used in Fillenbaum and Jones data, reclassified according to form class and compared with Entwisle data for the same words (in per cents, using adult data only).

Part I: Children

Stimulus word	Woodrow and Lowell N = 1,000		Palermo and Jenkins					
			Fourth N = 500		Fifth N = 500		Sixth N = 500	
bitter			sour	21.2	sour	24.2	sour	29.8
			sweet	14.2	sweet	14.4	sweet	15.6
			taste	5.0	taste	6.8	taste	7.2
black	dark	31.5	dark	35.6	dark	36.2	dark	40.0
	color	10.4	white	24.8	white	25.0	white	22.0
	dress	6.3	color	11.0	color	9.8	color	12.2
butterfly	fly	17.9	insect	16.0	insect	15.0	insect	17.2
	wings	11.4	fly	15.4	fly	13.4	fly	13.0
	pretty	8.9	pretty	9.4	bird	10.8	bird	11.4
chair	sit	43.0	table	34.8	table	32.6	table	34.4
	seat	13.1	sit	31.8	sit	32.0	sit	26.0
	set	3.8	soft	3.4	seat	30.0	seat	4.2
cold	winter	10.3	hot	20.8	hot	21.8	warm	23.0
	ice	8.4	warm	18.8	warm	21.4	hot	16.4
	freeze	6.8	snow	11.4	snow	9.4	snow	9.8
dark	night	42.1	light	40.2	light	40.4	light	37.4
	black	8.0	night	20.4	night	22.8	night	20.8
	light	5.7	black	16.8	black	13.8	black	19.0
fruit	apples	17.4	apple	25.4	apple	26.2	apple	29.6
	eat	15.3	eat	14.0	eat	14.8	eat	10.6
	apple	13.1	food	10.0	good	9.8	food	10.6
hand	fingers	13.0	arm	12.4	arm	12.8	arm	16.0
	work	11.3	finger	9.4	fingers	10.8	fingers	11.4
	clock	6.5	foot	9.4	finger	10.6	finger	8.2
hard	stone	11.3	soft	37.6	soft	34.2	soft	35.0
	rock	9.2	work	10.2	work	11.0	rock	10.2
	work	8.9	easy	7.0	easy	8.0	work	6.8
high	mountain	12.0	low	51.2	low	46.4	low	43.0
	hill	9.2	tall	8.6	tall	8.8	tall	8.0
	up	6.0	up	4.8	mountain	7.4	mountain	7.8
long	far	9.0	short	42.6	short	47.0	short	42.8
	grass	7.5	far	5.6	far	3.4	far	6.0
	big	5.5	tall	5.4	tall	3.4	length	3.0
loud	noise	20.1	soft	26.6	soft	25.6	soft	25.6
	holler	19.0	noise	16.6	noise	17.4	noise	18.4
	talk	13.0	shout	6.8	shout	5.4	noisy	6.2
man	work	16.8	woman	16.6	woman	18.8	woman	20.0
	hat	8.2	women	15.2	women	11.4	boy	11.2
	person	4.5	boy	10.0	person	10.6	women	9.4
music	piano	19.8	sing	14.2	sing	13.2	song	12.6
	sing	15.3	song	11.6	song	12.6	sing	11.8
	sweet	7.9	notes	8.4	sound	10.0	sound	10.4
needle	sew	16.0	thread	30.4	thread	28.4	thread	35.6
	sewing	15.2	pin	16.4	sharp	15.8	sharp	16.0
	thread	14.7	sharp	14.8	pin	15.0	pin	10.4
ocean	water	41.3	water	38.6	water	43.6	water	45.8
	sea	8.8	sea	28.0	sea	26.0	sea	22.4
	waves	8.8	lake	7.4	lake	7.4	blue	5.2
quiet	still	30.0	loud	19.8	loud	24.4	loud	24.2
	sleep	7.2	noise	12.8	noise	11.4	noise	8.2
	noise	7.0	soft	6.0	noisy	5.2	noisy	6.6

		Entwisle					
Kindergarten N = 200		First N = 280		Third N = 280		Fifth N = 200	
better	5.0	butter	6.8	sour	20.7	sour	36.5
bit	5.0	sweet	6.1	sweet	18.6	sweet	22.0
butter	5.0	bit	5.0	better	4.6	cold	6.0
crayon	6.5	white	12.1	white	49.3	white	53.0
cat	5.0	blue	9.6	color	8.2	color	16.5
dark	4.5	brown	7.1	dark	7.5	dark	9.0
fly	16.0	fly	21.8	fly	20.0	insect	33.5
butter	7.0	butter	7.9	insect	13.6	fly	8.0
wings	4.5	bird	3.9	bug	7.5	animal	7.0
sit	19.5	sit	25.0	sit	29.3	sit	32.0
table	14.0	table	20.7	table	18.9	table	20.5
bear	4.0	bear	3.2	desk	10.4	desk	17.5
hot	12.5	hot	26.4	hot	49.3	hot	44.0
warm	6.5	warm	9.6	warm	20.7	warm	23.5
water	6.0	winter	5.7	freezing	4.6	freezing	6.5
night	13.5	light	30.4	light	65.7	light	68.0
light	12.5	night	8.9	night	11.1	black	10.5
moon	4.5	moon	3.6	black	5.4	night	8.0
apple	13.0	apple	10.7	apple	23.2	apple	30.0
eat	7.5	eat	9.3	vegetable	16.8	vegetable	19.0
banana	6.0	orange	5.0	orange	9.6	orange	13.0
arm	4.0	fingers	6.8	arm	18.2	arm	23.5
shake	3.5	arm	4.6	fingers	8.6	fingers	14.5
finger	2.5	foot	4.6	finger	7.1	finger	9.5
rock	8.0	soft	19.6	soft	53.2	soft	55.5
work	5.5	work	8.2	easy	13.9	easy	18.0
soft	5.0	rock	4.3	rock	6.1	rock	3.5
low	8.5	low	21.8	low	62.9	low	64.0
sky	6.5	sky	3.6	up	3.2	tall	8.5
tree	4.0	down	3.2	bye	2.1	Hello	4.0
grass	8.0	short	20.0	short	62.9	short	64.0
short	4.5	grass	3.9	grass	2.5	wide	3.5
time	3.5	big	2.1	big	1.9	grass	2.5
quiet	6.0	soft	12.1	soft	30.7	soft	43.0
scream	5.0	quiet	10.7	quiet	13.2	noise	8.5
soft	4.5	low	6.4	noisy	7.5	noisy	8.5
woman	9.5	woman	12.9	woman	43.6	woman	52.5
lady	6.5	lady	9.6	lady	9.3	person	7.5
hand	4.0	father	4.6	men	8.9	lady	7.0
piano	17.0	piano	13.6	sing	12.9	sing	10.5
dance	6.0	sing	11.4	song	10.0	song	9.5
play	5.0	teacher	4.6	sound	7.5	sound	9.5
thread	16.5	thread	15.7	thread	31.1	thread	31.0
pin	10.0	shot	7.9	pin	22.9	pin	15.5
shot	6.0	pin	7.5	sharp	6.1	sharp	14.5
water	14.0	water	18.9	sea	40.0	sea	36.0
city	8.5	sea	10.0	water	21.8	water	25.5
boat	6.5	boat	5.7	river	11.4	river	7.5
loud	7.0	loud	17.1	loud	32.5	loud	33.0
be quiet	4.5	noisy	6.4	noisy	20.7	noisy	22.0
noise	4.5	be quiet	4.3	noise	5.4	silent	5.0

Part I: Children—continued

Stimulus word	Woodrow and Lowell N = 1,000		Palermo and Jenkins					
			Fourth N = 500		Fifth N = 500		Sixth N = 500	
river	water	43.3	water	29.8	water	32.0	water	33.8
	swim	7.2	lake	27.4	lake	22.4	lake	17.8
	lake	4.2	stream	18.8	stream	13.2	stream	14.6
rough	hard	14.4	smooth	17.6	hard	20.2	smooth	18.6
	boy	8.9	hard	16.2	smooth	18.0	hard	17.4
	mean	7.1	bumpy	7.0	tough	7.4	tough	8.6
salt	bitter	11.0	pepper	38.0	pepper	35.8	pepper	38.3
	meat	9.9	food	7.8	food	8.8	sugar	8.4
	white	9.7	sugar	6.2	sugar	7.0	food	7.0
sheep	wool	41.1	lamb	17.4	lamb	19.8	wool	18.8
	animal	11.7	animal	17.0	animal	17.4	animal	16.6
	lamb	7.9	wool	14.8	wool	17.0	lamb	15.6
short	small	21.4	long	34.8	long	30.6	long	30.6
	little	15.7	small	14.8	small	19.8	small	18.0
	long	5.4	tall	14.4	tall	16.4	tall	15.4
slow	lazy	13.8	fast	50.4	fast	51.6	fast	51.2
	walk	10.7	stop	5.8	walk	5.4	stop	4.4
	fast	6.5	turtle	4.2	stop	5.0	turtle	3.8
smooth	soft	13.2	soft	30.6	soft	31.6	soft	31.2
	even	7.0	rough	16.2	rough	17.0	rough	14.6
	nice	6.8	hard	10.0	hard	8.8	flat	8.6
sour	milk	12.4	sweet	21.8	sweet	24.6	sweet	24.2
	pickles	8.9	lemon	6.0	lemon	6.4	bitter	6.6
	sweet	7.5	milk	4.8	bad	4.8	cream	5.2
square	block	30.0	round	20.0	round	20.8	round	17.8
	oblong	9.5	circle	14.4	circle	12.2	circle	11.0
	corner	8.3	box	13.6	block	9.6	box	7.2
swift	fast	39.1	fast	49.2	fast	52.0	fast	58.6
	run	20.2	slow	6.2	slow	6.2	slow	6.0
	horse	12.4	run	4.0	smooth	3.6	run	3.4
table	eat	35.8	chair	43.2	chair	39.2	chair	39.6
	dishes	12.6	eat	14.0	eat	13.4	food	12.8
	legs	7.0	food	9.0	food	10.2	eat	9.2
thirsty	water	37.7	water	39.4	water	42.6	water	46.6
	drink	36.4	drink	24.6	drink	23.2	drink	25.0
	dry	13.2	hungry	5.2	hungry	7.2	dry	6.2
yellow	color	32.0	color	39.2	color	42.4	color	38.6
	dress	12.9	red	11.8	red	9.4	red	7.4
	flower	10.5	blue	7.6	black	7.6	black	5.6

	Entwisle						
Kindergarten N = 200		First N = 280		Third N = 280		Fifth N = 200	
water	20.0	water	18.6	water	21.8	stream	30.0
boat	15.5	boat	7.1	stream	21.4	water	18.5
ocean	6.0	stream	6.8	lake	14.3	lake	13.5
dog	9.0	dog	8.6	soft	16.8	smooth	28.0
tough	6.5	tough	6.4	hard	15.7	hard	21.5
fight	3.5	fight	5.4	smooth	11.8	soft	14.5
pepper	37.5	pepper	44.3	pepper	56.4	pepper	47.0
water	4.5	water	5.4	water	10.7	water	8.5
food	3.0	sugar	2.1	sugar	6.4	sugar	7.0
wool	9.0	lamb	15.7	lamb	22.5	lamb	21.5
lamb	7.5	wool	5.7	wool	12.1	animal	18.5
dog	6.0	white	3.2	animal	10.4	dog	8.0
pants	13.0	long	16.8	long	56.4	long	49.0
long	7.0	big	7.1	small	11.1	tall	24.0
tall	3.5	pants	6.8	tall	9.6	small	12.0
fast	18.0	fast	35.7	fast	78.6	fast	77.5
walk	6.0	walk	4.3	not fast	2.9	not fast	4.0
poke	5.0	car	3.2	turtle	1.8	turtle	3.5
hard	4.5	soft	11.4	soft	31.1	rough	37.5
road	4.0	hard	9.3	hard	17.9	soft	21.5
soft	4.0	rough	5.4	rough	13.9	hard	10.0
kraut	9.0	milk	7.5	sweet	33.9	sweet	38.5
milk	5.5	kraut	7.1	bitter	8.9	bitter	25.0
lemon	5.0	sweet	6.4	good	7.9	lemon	3.5
triangle	10.0	box	12.1	round	23.2	round	28.5
box	7.0	round	7.9	circle	15.7	circle	16.5
block	4.5	circle	7.1	box	11.1	box	11.0
sweep	4.0	fast	3.2	fast	16.4	fast	53.0
cheese	3.0	swim	3.2	soft	5.0	slow	6.0
wind	3.0	soft	2.5	slow	3.6	smooth	4.0
chair	32.0	chair	36.1	chair	51.4	chair	47.0
food	6.5	eat	6.4	desk	6.1	eat	7.5
eat	5.5	sit	2.9	eat	4.6	desk	6.5
water	23.5	water	24.3	drink	25.4	water	37.0
drink	22.0	drink	23.9	water	24.6	drink	18.5
glass	2.0	hungry	8.2	hungry	18.6	hungry	14.5
crayon	8.5	blue	9.3	color	23.2	color	42.5
sun	8.0	red	8.6	red	10.7	green	8.0
green	7.5	green	7.9	blue	10.4	red	6.5

Part II: Adults

Stimulus Word	Kent-Rosanoff N = 1,000		Russell and Jenkins N = 1,000		Palermo and Jenkins N = 1,000		Entwisle N = 200	
bitter	sweet	30.5	sweet	65.2	sweet	54.4	sweet	60.5
	sour	22.2	sour	12.5	sour	15.2	sour	12.5
	taste	6.6	taste	4.3	taste	4.3	taste	3.5
black	white	33.9	white	75,1	white	58.5	white	58.0
	dark	17.2	dark	5.4	dark	9.4	dark	7.0
	color	12.9	cat	2.6	night	5.0	night	5.5
butterfly	insect	26.1	moth	14.4	moth	12.4	cocoon	15.5
	bird	6.4	insect	11.7	insect	9.6	moth	10.0
	fly	4.4	wing	10.4	yellow	7.3	net	7.0
chair	table	19.1	table	49.8	table	32.8	table	28.0
	seat	12.7	sit	20.5	sit	22.4	sit	23.0
	sit	10.7	leg	4.5	seat	4.8	seat	11.5
cold	warm	16.6	hot	34.8	hot	32.9	hot	42.0
	hot	15.1	snow	21.8	snow	20.9	warm	12.5
	winter	12.0	warm	16.8	warm	16.5	snow	5.0
dark	light	42.7	light	82.9	light	61.8	light	58.0
	night	22.1	night	5.5	night	17.9	night	11.5
	black	7.6	room	3.3	black	5.0	black	8.5
fruit	apple	15.7	apple	37.8	apple	44.9	apple	32.5
	apples	10.2	vegetable	11.4	fly	9.1	orange	11.0
	vegetable	7.5	orange	9.4	orange	6.2	fly	5.0
hand	foot	20.4	foot	25.5	foot	22.8	foot	22.0
	fingers	8.3	fingers	23.7	arm	14.8	arm	10.5
	arm	6.8	arm	13.1	finger	12.4	finger	10.5
hard	soft	36.7	soft	67.4	soft	58.5	soft	58.0
	stone	10.2	rock	4.8	rock	6.3	difficult	3.5
	wood	6.6	easy	2.4	egg	4.6	easy	3.5
high	low	32.8	low	67.5	low	56.8	low	59.0
	mountain	15.7	school	4.9	mountain	6.8	noon	2.5
	tall	5.7	mountain	3.2	tall	4.4	tall	2.5
long	short	41.3	short	75.8	short	63.4	short	55.0
	distance	8.1	fellow	1.1	road	2.4	day	3.0
	length	5.0	narrow	1.0	tall	1.9	hair	3.0
loud	noise	20.5	soft	54.1	soft	42.3	soft	46.0
	soft	16.5	noise	21.0	noise	23.1	noise	16.5
	noisy	11.2	quiet	6.8	quiet	4.3	noisy	9.0
man	woman	39.4	woman	76.7	woman	62.4	woman	82.0
	male	9.9	boy	6.5	boy	8.1	boy	2.5
	boy	4.4	girl	3.1	women	4.8	wife	2.0
music	piano	18.0	song	18.3	song	16.4	song	7.0
	sound	9.5	note	16.8	sound	16.1	sound	7.0
	song	6.8	sound	12.4	note	9.4	piano	6.0
needle	thread	16.0	thread	46.4	thread	45.7	thread	31.0
	sharp	15.2	pin	14.0	sharp	12.1	pin	21.5
	pin	14.7	eye	7.2	sew	8.7	haystack	7.5

Part II: Adults

Stimulus Word	Kent-Rosanoff N = 1,000		Russell and Jenkins N = 1,000		Palermo and Jenkins N = 1,000		Entwisle N = 200	
ocean	water	42.7	water	31.4	water	36.2	sea	43.5
	deep	8.7	sea	23.3	sea	15.5	water	8.0
	sea	7.5	blue	11.1	blue	10.1	river	4.5
quiet	still	13.6	loud	34.8	loud	26.3	loud	23.0
	noisy	11.3	noisy	11.3	noise	8.7	soft	13.5
	rest	6.8	noise	9.8	noisy	8.7	noisy	8.5
river	water	39.3	water	24.6	water	28.6	stream	29.0
	stream	11.7	stream	21.1	stream	15.4	water	11.0
	lake	6.5	lake	10.5	Mississippi	8.9	flow	8.5
rough	smooth	34.6	smooth	43.9	smooth	30.4	smooth	28.0
	hard	3.8	hard	6.9	hard	7.0	tough	14.0
	uneven	3.8	road	4.4	sandpaper	6.9	soft	6.0
salt	pepper	14.2	pepper	43.0	pepper	30.8	pepper	32.0
	sugar	8.8	sugar	8.3	taste	5.9	water	16.0
	taste	8.7	water	7.6	sugar	5.3	sugar	6.5
sheep	animal	22.5	wool	20.1	wool	18.7	lamb	17.5
	lamb	15.1	lamb	19.8	lamb	18.0	wool	17.5
	wool	14.3	animal	7.5	animal	10.5	dog	13.0
short	long	27.9	tall	39.7	tall	41.1	long	37.5
	tall	16.8	long	33.6	long	20.5	tall	25.0
	small	13.6	fat	7.6	fat	13.5	fat	7.5
slow	fast	31.6	fast	75.2	fast	63.4	fast	65.0
	easy	6.3	car	2.3	turtle	3.6	down	10.5
	snail	6.2	stop	2.2	car	2.7	rapid	2.5
smooth	rough	27.7	rough	32.8	rough	24.3	rough	39.5
	soft	7.9	soft	20.6	soft	23.7	soft	15.0
	glass	5.6	hard	13.6	hard	10.8	hard	3.5
sour	sweet	34.9	sweet	56.8	sweet	48.7	sweet	40.0
	vinegar	9.1	grapes	9.1	lemon	10.5	bitter	11.0
	lemon	7.8	lemon	6.3	cream	7.7	cream	10.5
square	round	25.0	round	37.2	round	31.5	round	36.5
	block	7.1	circle	21.1	circle	14.3	circle	17.5
	table	4.7	block	6.5	block	9.4	cube	8.0
swift	fast	22.2	fast	36.9	fast	45.2	fast	40.5
	slow	19.0	slow	23.8	slow	15.5	slow	7.5
	quick	11.7	river	3.3	river	3.9	quick	6.0
table	chair	26.7	chair	84.0	chair	69.1	chair	65.5
	wood	7.6	food	4.1	food	5.9	top	7.5
	furniture	7.5	desk	2.1	desk	3.3	cloth	5.5
thirsty	water	34.1	water	34.8	water	43.2	water	34.0
	dry	21.8	drink	29.6	drink	24.9	drink	18.0
	drink	20.6	dry	12.1	dry	10.5	hungry	16.5
yellow	color	30.1	blue	15.6	color	9.2	bird	14.0
	water	7.0	red	11.5	blue	7.5	green	10.5
	orange	4.7	color	10.6	red	6.9	blue	7.0

Fillenbaum and Jones (1965) have gathered associations to 109 stimulus words, mostly those appearing with greatest frequency in the spoken responses to TAT pictures. The subjects were 466 male college students. Directions emphasized speed, and subjects wrote their own responses. Their data are compared with our data for college students below. It was necessary to combine some of their categories to be able to compare form class of the responses directly with our data.

Our data agrees well with the Fillenbaum and Jones data, the principal exceptions being the pronouns. This is puzzling because pronouns was the only category in our data where males consistently exceeded females in paradigmatic responding. Thus since Fillenbaum and Jones's data are derived entirely from males, one would expect that their data would show a higher rate of paradigmatics to pronouns than our data. Also since their instructions emphasized speed probably more than ours, one would expect more pronoun responses ("he"—"her," "him"—"her," etc.) Although the general agreement between the two sets of data is good, the discrepancy for pronouns is puzzling and there seems no obvious way to resolve it.

Comparison of Form Class of Responses for Fillenbaum and Jones Data[a] and Entwisle Data

	N	A	V	B	P	R	C	Other
because	16.0	1.0	2.0	5.0	10.0	24.0	14.0	28.0
dark	32.0	65.0	1.0					1.0
hand	79.0	6.0	3.0		1.0	6.0		5.0
hard	23.0	65.0	1.0			3.0		7.0
he	9.0	1.0	20.0		69.0			
her	30.0	2.0		1.0	65.0			1.0
high	18.0	71.0	1.0			8.0		2.0
him	9.0	1.0	3.0	1.0	83.0	1.0		2.0
it	18.0	3.0	41.0	2.0	29.0	1.0		5.0
long	26.0	62.0	4.0	5.0		1.0		2.0
man	85.0	4.0	4.0		2.0	1.0		3.0
on	28.0	4.0	2.0	1.0	11.0	51.0		4.0
she	15.0	2.0	17.0		64.0			1.0
tell	16.0	1.0	45.0		31.0	1.0		6.0
they	8.0	2.0	25.0	1.0	62.0			2.0
up	7.0	5.0	2.0	4.0		81.0		1.0
Entwisle Data								
because	12.0	1.0	4.0	29.0	5.0	12.0	37.0	
dark	25.0	72.0	3.0					
hand	77.0	5.0	12.0	4.0	2.0	1.0		
hard	23.0	73.0	1.0	1.0		1.0	1.0	
he	9.0	1.0	3.0		87.0		1.0	
her	14.0	2.0	1.0	1.0	81.0	1.0		
high	24.0	66.0	5.0	4.0			1.0	
him	9.0	1.0			89.0	1.0		
it	35.0	4.0	20.0	1.0	37.0	3.0		
long	27.0	65.0	4.0	3.0		1.0		
man	97.0	2.0	1.0	1.0				
on	18.0	2.0	5.0	2.0	1.0	72.0		
she	14.0	1.0	2.0		83.0			
tell	32.0	1.0	57.0	2.0	8.0			
they	11.0	2.0	6.0	3.0	77.0	1.0		
up	15.0	1.0	2.0	5.0		74.0	2.0	

[a] Fillenbaum and Jones (1965) determine form class somewhat differently. We have re-grouped some of their categories (see below) to make them comparable to our classificatory scheme, and rounded to the nearest whole per cent:

Entwisle	Fillenbaum and Jones
N	N
A	A, T, Q
V	V, X
B	D
P	P, I
R	O
C	C
Other	R, J, U

Appendix C:

Response Frequencies of Urban Maryland Kindergarten Children (N=200)

Entwisle Urban Maryland Data. Computer printout of all kindergarten responses to ninety-six stimulus words, divided by sex, in alphabetical order.

RESPONSE WORD	KINDERGARTEN M	F	T	RESPONSE WORD	KINDERGARTEN M	F	T

1. ADD

RESPONSE WORD	M	F	T	RESPONSE WORD	M	F	T
A CUP OF WATER.	1	–	1	MISTER ED	1	–	1
A HORSE.	1	–	1	MOUSE	–	1	1
A LETTER.	1	–	1	MR ED	1	1	2
A PLUS.	1	–	1	NAD	1	–	1
ADD WORDS.	–	1	1	NAME.	–	1	1
ADDING MACHINE.	1	–	1	NEWSPAPER	1	–	1
ADDRESS.	–	1	1	NINETY NINE	1	–	1
ALL OVER.	1	2	3	NUMBER.	1	3	4
ANT.	1	2	3	NUMBERS	6	1	7
APPLE.	–	1	1	NUT	–	1	1
APPLES.	–	1	1	ONE	–	1	1
AUNT.	1	–	1	ONE MILLION DOLLARS	1	–	1
BAD.	5	1	6	ONTO A BUILDING	1	–	1
BEAR.	–	1	1	OUR AUNT.	–	1	1
BLUE.	1	–	1	PAD	1	1	2
BOOK.	–	1	1	PAPER	6	1	7
BOOTS.	–	1	1	PENCIL.	1	–	1
BREATH.	1	–	1	PIECE OF PAPER.	–	1	1
BUTTONS	–	1	1	PLANT	–	1	1
CAD.	3	–	3	POCKETBOOK.	1	–	1
CAKE.	–	1	1	POINT	1	1	2
CANT.	1	–	1	POINTS.	1	–	1
CHAIR	2	–	2	POISON.	1	–	1
CHALK	–	1	1	PUPPY	–	1	1
CHEER	1	–	1	PUT SOMETHING NEW IN.	–	1	1
COOK DINNER	–	1	1	RAD.	–	1	1
COOKIES	1	–	1	READ.	1	–	1
CRAYON.	–	1	1	RUN	–	1	1
CROSS	–	1	1	RUNNING	–	1	1
DAD	1	1	2	SAD.	1	1	2
DO LONG	1	–	1	SAID.	1	–	1
DONKEY.	–	1	1	SAT.	1	–	1
DOOR.	1	2	3	SCHOOL.	–	1	1
DRESS.	–	1	1	SHEEP	–	1	1
EAGLE	1	–	1	SING.	–	1	1
ED THE HORSE.	1	–	1	SOCK.	1	–	1
EGG.	–	2	2	SOME BRICKS TO A HOUSE.	1	–	1
EGGS.	1	–	1	SOMEONE IS COOKING.	–	1	1
ELEPHANT.	1	–	1	SOMETHING	4	–	4
FAD	–	2	2	SOMETIMES	–	1	1
FAN	1	1	2	SUBTRACT.	1	1	2
FIFTY	1	–	1	TAD	1	1	2
FILL YOUR WHOLE PAPER	–	1	1	TADPOLE	–	1	1
FLOUR	1	–	1	TAPE.	–	1	1
FLOWER.	–	2	2	TEETH.	–	1	1
FLYING SAUCER	–	1	1	THE AD ON TELEVISION.	1	–	1
GIRL.	1	–	1	THE WORDS	–	1	1
GIVE ME THE PAD	1	–	1	THIRD	–	1	1
GLAD.	–	1	1	THIS.	–	1	1
GO SHOPPING	1	–	1	TIGER	–	1	1
GO TO THE BATHROOM.	–	1	1	TO ADD	1	–	1
GROW	1	–	1	TOYS.	1	–	1
GUESS	–	1	1	TREE.	2	–	2
HAD	1	–	1	TREES GROWING	–	1	1
HE.	–	1	1	TWO AND TWO	–	1	1
HORSE	–	1	1	TWO CARDS	1	–	1
I ADD	–	1	1	TWO PEOPLE.	–	1	1
IM GOING TO ADD PICTURES.	–	1	1	TWO PLUS TWO.	1	–	1
IN.	–	1	1	TYPEWRITER.	–	1	1
IN YOUR PAPER	–	2	2	WALK.	–	1	1
INSECT.	–	1	1	WALL.	1	–	1
JACK.	1	–	1	WATER	1	5	6
KNEE.	–	1	1	WE ADDED SOME ICE CREAM.	–	1	1
LAD.	1	–	1	WHEN PEOPLE ADD SOMETHING	–	1	1
LEAVES.	–	1	1	WINDOW.	–	1	1
LETTERS	2	–	2	WINDY	–	1	1
LIKE YOU ADD A PAPER.	–	1	1	WITH PAPER.	1	–	1
MACHINE	–	1	1	WORD.	–	1	1
MAD	–	2	2	WRITE	1	1	2
ME.	–	1	1	WRITING	2	2	4
MEDICINE.	1	1	2	YOU	–	1	1
MILK.	2	1	3	ZOO	–	1	1

2. ALLOW

RESPONSE WORD	M	F	T	RESPONSE WORD	M	F	T
A	1	–	1	BE GOOD	–	1	1
A LADDER.	2	–	2	BE QUIET.	–	1	1
A LION.	–	1	1	BE QUIET, PLEASE.	–	1	1
A T V	–	1	1	BEAR.	1	–	1
ALASKA.	–	1	1	BEGIN	1	–	1
ALLOWANCE	4	1	5	BELL.	1	–	1
ALLOWED	2	1	3	BIKE.	–	1	1
ALLOWED NOT GO DOWN THE STREET				BOAT.	–	1	1
ALLOWED NOT TO GO THERE	1	–	1	BOW	–	2	2
ALLOWED OUTSIDE	1	–	1	BOYS.	1	–	1
ALLOWED TO GO ACROSS THE STREET				CAN I	–	1	1
	–	1	1	CANT COME IN.	1	–	1
AMOUNT.	1	–	1	CHAIR	–	1	1
BABY.	–	1	1	CHOIR	–	1	1
BARBERSHOP.	1	–	1	CLIMB	–	1	1
				CLOUD	3	1	4

RESPONSE WORD	KINDERGARTEN M	F	T	RESPONSE WORD	KINDERGARTEN M	F	T

2. ALLOW

RESPONSE WORD	M	F	T	RESPONSE WORD	M	F	T
COME IN	1	–	1	OWL	–	1	1
COW	1	1	2	PAPER	–	2	2
CURTAIN	–	1	1	PEN	–	1	1
DO IT	1	–	1	PEOPLE	4	–	4
DOG	2	–	2	PEOPLE ARE ALLOWED	1	–	1
DOGS	–	1	1	PEOPLE TO COME IN	1	–	1
DONT	–	1	1	PERMISSION	1	–	1
DONT ALLOW YOU TO DO THAT	1	–	1	PERSON	–	1	1
DONT DO IT	1	–	1	PIG	–	1	1
EAT	1	–	1	PLAY	1	–	1
ELEPHANT	1	–	1	POCKET	1	–	1
ENGINEERS ARE LOUD	1	–	1	POLICE	–	1	1
FATHER	–	1	1	POOL	–	1	1
FEMALE	–	1	1	POT	–	1	1
FLOWER	1	–	1	QUIET	1	2	3
FOULED	–	1	1	RABBIT	–	1	1
G	–	1	1	REAL	–	1	1
GARDEN	–	1	1	ROPE	1	–	1
GIRL	–	1	1	SALLY	1	–	1
GLASSES	1	–	1	SAY	1	–	1
GO OUTISDE	–	1	1	SCREAM	2	–	2
GRASS	1	–	1	SEAGULL	1	–	1
HIGHCHAIR	–	1	1	SING	–	1	1
HIM	1	–	1	SLIDING GLASS DOORS	–	1	1
HIM TO GO IN MY YARD	1	–	1	SLOW	–	1	1
HIT	–	1	1	SNOW PLOW	–	1	1
HORSE	–	1	1	SOFT	–	1	1
HOUD	1	–	1	SOFTLY	1	–	1
HOUSE	2	–	2	SOMEBODY	1	–	1
HOW	–	1	1	SOMEBODY IN	1	–	1
HOWD	1	–	1	SOMEBODYS PLAYING REAL			
I ALLOWED YOU TO GO				LOUD	–	1	1
OUTSIDE	1	–	1	SOMETHING	1	–	1
I DONT KNOW	–	1	1	STAIRS	–	1	1
I PLAY WITH A OWL	–	1	1	STAY OUT	–	1	1
IF YOUR PARENTS SAY TO				SUN	–	1	1
SWING IN YOUR OW	–	1	1	SWIMMING	1	–	1
IN A HOUSE	1	–	1	TALKING	1	1	2
IN THE HOUSE	1	1	2	TELL	1	–	1
ITS ALLOWED. STAY IN				THAT	1	–	1
THE HOUSE	1	–	1	THE LAW	–	1	1
JANE	–	1	1	THEM	–	1	1
L	–	1	1	THEY LOVE EACH OTHER	–	1	1
LAMB	–	1	1	TO	2	2	4
LEAVES	1	–	1	TO CATCH BUTTERFLIES	1	–	1
LIGHT	–	1	1	TO CROSS STREET	–	1	1
LIKE YOU SCREAM	–	1	1	TO DO	1	–	1
LIPSTICK	1	–	1	TO DO THINGS	–	1	1
LOLLIPOP	–	1	1	TO GO IN THE WOODS	–	1	1
LOUD	2	1	3	TO GO OUTSIDE	–	1	1
LOUD BOYS	1	–	1	TO GO OUTSIDE WHEN ITS			
LOUD LION	1	–	1	DARK	1	–	1
LOWAGE	1	–	1	TO GO OVER	–	1	1
MACHINE	1	–	1	TO HAVE	–	1	1
ME	1	–	1	TO PAY	–	1	1
ME TO GO IN THE KITCHEN	1	–	1	TO PLAY	1	–	1
ME TO INTRODUCE MYSELF	–	1	1	TO WALK TO SCHOOL	–	1	1
MOM	–	1	1	TOO ALLOWED	1	–	1
MONEY	1	–	1	TOO LOUD	1	1	2
MOUTH	1	–	1	TOWED	1	–	1
MY PROPERTY	1	–	1	TOWEL	–	1	1
NEVER	–	1	1	TREE	–	1	1
NO	–	1	1	US TO	–	1	1
NOISE	–	1	1	USE	1	–	1
NOT	–	3	3	VOICE	–	1	1
NOT ALLOW	–	2	2	WE ALLOW CATS NEAR	–	1	1
NOT ALLOWED	–	2	2	YELL	1	–	1
NOT LOUD	1	–	1	YOU	1	2	3
NOT TO DO THINGS BAD	1	–	1	YOU ARE ALLOWED	1	–	1
OW	2	–	2	YOU TO DO SOMETHING	1	–	1

3. ALWAYS

RESPONSE WORD	M	F	T	RESPONSE WORD	M	F	T
A BEE	–	1	1	BIRDIE	1	–	1
A CAR	–	1	1	BLANKET	1	1	1
A STORY	1	–	1	BLOCKS	1	–	1
AIRPLANE	–	1	1	BOAT	1	–	1
ALL	–	3	3	BRICKS	1	–	1
ALONE	1	–	1	BRUSH YOUR TEETH	1	1	2
BALLS	–	1	1	BUSY DAYS	–	1	1
BE	1	–	1	BUTTERFLY FLY AROUND	1	–	1
BE GOOD	3	2	5	CALL	1	–	1
BE GOOD MANNERS	–	1	1	CALLING	1	–	1
BE HERE	–	1	1	CAR	1	–	1
BE MY WAY	1	–	1	CARROT	–	1	1
BE NICE	1	–	1	CARRY YOUR BIKE	1	–	1
BEAR	–	1	1	CHAIR	–	2	2
BEE	1	–	1	CHILD	1	–	1
BEGINS	1	–	1	CHIMNEY	–	1	1
BEHAVE	1	–	1	CHOOSE	1	–	1
BIG	1	–	1	COME	1	1	2

RESPONSE WORD	M	F	T
3. ALWAYS			
COUNT	1	–	1
COW	1	–	1
CUP	–	1	1
DID	1	–	1
DINOSAUR	1	–	1
DISH	–	1	1
DO	4	2	6
DO IT	–	1	1
DO NOT	–	1	1
DO SOMETHING GOOD	1	–	1
DO THINGS RIGHT	–	1	1
DO WHAT YOU RE SUPPOSED TO DO	1	–	1
DOING	–	1	1
DOING SOMETHING	1	–	1
DOLWAYS	–	1	1
DONT DO SOMETHING BAD	–	1	1
DONT FORGET	–	1	1
DONT FORGET ME	1	–	1
DONT TOUCH FILL	–	1	1
EAT FRUIT	1	–	1
ELEPHANT	–	1	1
FAN	1	–	1
FEEL IT	–	1	1
FIRE	1	–	1
FISH	1	1	2
FLOWERS	–	1	1
FLY	–	1	1
FRUIT	1	–	1
GET A DRINK OF WATER	–	1	1
GLAD	–	1	1
GLASSES	–	1	1
GO	1	1	2
GO HOME	1	–	1
GO TO KINDERGARTEN	–	1	1
GOOD	–	1	1
GRASS	1	–	1
GROWING	1	–	1
GUN	–	1	1
HAD TO HAPPEN	1	–	1
HALLWAYS	–	1	1
HAPPEN	–	1	1
HASTE	1	–	1
HELP MOMMY	–	1	1
HERE	–	1	1
HIGHWAY	1	–	1
HOME	–	2	2
HOOK	–	1	1
HORSY	1	–	1
HOSE	–	1	1
HOUSE	1	2	3
I ALWAYS DO A PUZZLE	1	–	1
I ALWAYS EAT	–	1	1
I HAVE TO FALL	1	–	1
I HAVE TROUBLE WITH MY CAR	–	1	1
I MAKE UP MY BED	1	–	1
IN	1	–	1
INDIANS	–	1	1
JEWELRY BOX	–	1	1
KEEP	1	–	1
KINDERGARTEN	–	1	1
KNOWED SOMETHING	–	1	1
LALWAYS	1	–	1
LAWAYS	1	–	1
LOVE	–	1	1
MATCHES	1	–	1
MAYBE	–	1	1
ME	–	2	2
NEVER	1	1	2
NO	1	–	1
NONE	–	1	1
NOT	2	–	2
OBEY MOTHER AND FATHER	1	–	1
ON	–	1	1
ORANGE	1	–	1
OUT	1	–	1
PAINT	–	1	1
PAY YOUR ORDERS	–	1	1
PIN	1	–	1
PLANE	1	–	1
PLAY	2	–	2
PLAY WITH THE TRAIN	1	–	1
POCKET BOOK	–	2	2
POLWAYS	1	–	1
PRETEND	1	–	1
READING A BOOK	1	–	1
REMEMBER	2	–	2
REMEMBER TO OBEY THE LAW	1	–	1
RIDE A HORSE	1	–	1
ROAD	–	1	1
ROOF	–	1	1
RUG	1	1	2
SCHOOL	1	1	2
SHADE	1	–	1
SHOVELING	–	1	1
SICK	–	1	1
SOLDIER	–	1	1
SOMEPLACE	1	–	1
SOMETHING	1	–	1
SOMETHING HAPPENS	1	–	1
SOMETHING HURTS	–	1	1
SOMETIMES	–	2	2
STAY	–	1	1
STORM	1	–	1
SUPPERTIME	1	–	1
TALKING	–	1	1
TALL	–	1	1
TALWAYS	1	–	1
TAPE	–	1	1
THE APPLE FALLS DOWN	1	–	1
THE FLOUR GOES STALE	–	1	1
THE PEOPLE SHOUT	–	1	1
THE SAME	1	–	1
THE WAY	1	–	1
THIS	–	1	1
TIE	–	1	1
TIME	1	–	1
TONGUE	1	–	1
TOY	1	–	1
VACUUM	–	1	1
WE ALWAYS GO TO THE STORE	–	1	1
WE GET ON THE SWINGS	–	1	1
WE GO THIS WAY AND THAT WAY	–	1	1
WENT	–	1	1
WERE GOING TO PLAY	–	1	1
WHAT	1	–	1
WHEN ITS ALWAYS SOMEBODYS BIRTHDAY	–	1	1
WHEN PEOPLE GET ALWAYS	1	–	1
WILL BE THERE	–	1	1
WITH ME	–	1	1
WORK	1	–	1
YOU ALWAYS DO IT	1	–	1
YOU DO SOMETHING	1	–	1
YOU GO DO	1	–	1
YOU GO OUT TO PLAY	–	1	1
YOU RIDE A BICYCLE SOMETIMES ALWAYS	1	–	1
YOURE BEING GOOD	1	–	1
4. BECAUSE			
A RABBIT	–	1	1
ALL LADIES WEAR BRACELETS	–	1	1
ALLOW	1	–	1
AN ACCIDENT HAPPENED	1	–	1
ANIMAL	–	1	1
ASH TRAY	1	–	1
BE	1	–	1
BE QUIET	1	–	1
BETAUS	–	1	1
BIRDIE	1	–	1
BIRDS ARE OUT SWIMMING INTO THE SEA	–	1	1
BOY	–	1	1
BUZ	–	1	1
CAN	1	–	1
CANNON	1	–	1
CAR	–	1	1
CARD	–	1	1
CAT	1	–	1
CAUSE	–	1	1
CHAIR	1	–	1
CIGARETTES	–	1	1
CRIB	–	1	1
CURTAIN	1	–	1
CUZ	1	–	1
DID	–	1	1
DOG	–	2	2
DON T	1	–	1
DONT	1	–	1
DONT DO IT	1	–	1
DRAPERIES	–	1	1
F	–	1	1
FLOWER	1	–	1
FLY	1	–	1

RESPONSE WORD	KINDERGARTEN M	F	T

4. BECAUSE

RESPONSE WORD	M	F	T
FURNACE	1	–	1
GARDEN	–	1	1
GROW	–	1	1
HE	2	3	5
HE IS HOT	1	–	1
HEARTY LOVE	–	1	1
HES GOOD	–	1	1
HORSE	2	–	2
HOT	–	1	1
HOUSE STARTS ON FIRE	1	–	1
I AM GOING TO HAVE TO HAVE MY TONSILS O	–	1	1
I CANT COME OVER	–	1	1
I DID SOMETHING	1	–	1
I DON T KNOW	–	1	1
I DON T KNOW WHY	–	1	1
I DON T LIKE YOU	1	1	2
I DON T WANT TO	–	1	1
I DON T WANT YOU TO	–	1	1
I GET TO WRITE ON THE BOARD	–	1	1
I HATE YOU	–	1	1
I LIKE YOU	1	2	3
I LOVE HIM	1	1	1
I LOVE YOU	–	2	2
I MADE SOMETHING	–	1	1
I NEED TO	1	1	2
I SAID SO	1	1	2
I SAID SOMETHING	–	1	1
I WANT TO GO ACROSS THE STREET	–	1	1
I WANTED TO	1	1	2
I WISH	–	1	1
I WONT PLAY WITH YOU	–	1	1
IM THINKING	–	1	1
INDIAN	1	–	1
IT	–	1	1
IT IS	–	1	1
JIM	1	–	1
JUST	1	–	1
JUST BECAUSE	–	1	1
JUST WHY BECAUSE	1	–	1
KNIFE	1	–	1
KNOW	1	–	1
KNOW WHY	–	1	1
LAWS	1	–	1
LIKE YOU	–	1	1
LIPSTICK	–	1	1
LOVE	–	2	2
MELAUSE	1	–	1
MI-AUSE	1	–	1
MOMMIE SAID	1	–	1
MOMMY	1	1	2
MUSE	1	–	1
MUSIC	1	–	1
MY	–	1	1
MY DADDY SAID SO	1	–	1
MY MOTHER HAD TO GO INTO THE STORE	–	1	1
NAIL	–	1	1
NICE	1	–	1
NO	1	–	1
NO RESPONSE	1	–	1
NOBODY CARES	–	1	1
NOT	–	2	2
NOT BECAUSE	–	1	1
OF FIRE	1	–	1
OF YOU	–	1	1
OUT	–	1	1
PACAUSE	1	–	1
PEAS	1	–	1
PECAN	1	–	1
PENCIL	–	1	1
PENCILS	–	1	1
PEOPLE SAY BECAUSE	1	1	2
PERSONS	–	1	1
PICTURES	–	1	1
PUMPKIN	–	1	1
RED PAINT	1	–	1
RIDE	–	1	1
SAWS	–	1	1
SHELF	–	1	1
SHOES	1	–	1
SITTING DOWN	–	1	1
SOMETHING	2	–	2
STEP	1	–	1
STICK	1	–	1
TABLE	1	–	1
TALK	1	–	1
TEMPERATURE	1	–	1
THAT	1	–	1
THE BABYS SLEEPING	–	1	1
THEY WANT A DRINK OF WATER	1	–	1
THEY WANT TO	1	–	1
THIS	–	1	1
THIS IS WHY	–	1	1
TOO CAUSE	1	–	1
TROUBLE	–	1	1
UPSTAIRS	–	1	1
WAS	1	–	1
WAVES	–	1	1
WE ARE DONE	1	–	1
WE DONT LIKE YOUR PEOPLE	–	1	1
WE HAD TO	1	–	1
WE LIKE YOU	1	–	1
WHAT	2	1	3
WHY	17	13	30
WHY DONT YOU DRINK	1	–	1
WITH YOU	–	1	1
WORD	–	1	1
WORRY ME	1	–	1
WRONG	1	–	1
YOU	2	–	2
YOU ARE	1	–	1
YOU CAN DO SOMETHING	1	–	1
YOU CAN T THROW ROCKS	1	–	1
YOU DON T DO ANYTHING WRONG	1	–	1
YOU DON T LISTEN	1	–	1
YOU HIT ME	1	–	1
YOU RE NOT ALLOWED TO DO THAT	1	–	1
YOU RE NOT SUPPOSED TO	1	–	1
YOU RE TIRED	–	1	1

5. BEE

RESPONSE WORD	M	F	T
A	1	1	2
A B	1	1	2
A BEE MAKE HONEY	1	–	1
A BRACELET	–	1	1
A BUTTERFLY	1	–	1
A GOOD GIRL	–	2	2
A LIGHT	1	–	1
A THING THAT FLIES	1	–	1
ARE	–	1	1
B FOR BUMBLEBEE	–	1	1
BALL	1	–	1
BE A HOUSE	–	1	1
BE A PERSON	1	–	1
BE GOOD	–	1	1
BEAD	1	–	1
BEAK	1	–	1
BEANS	–	1	1
BEGAN	1	–	1
BELT	–	1	1
BEWARE	2	–	2
BILLY	1	–	1
BIT	–	1	1
BIT ME	–	1	1
BOAT	1	–	1
BOOKS	–	1	1
BOOT	–	1	1
BOY	1	–	1
BRUCE	1	–	1
BUG	2	3	5
BUMBLE	3	3	6
BUMBLE BEE	4	2	6
BUMBLE BEE STING	1	–	1
BUMBLEBEE	1	5	6
BUTTERFLY	1	1	2
BUY	1	–	1
BUZZES	1	–	1
C	2	2	4
CLIMB	–	1	1
CLOCK	1	–	1
COAT	1	–	1
D	2	–	2
DEBBIE	–	1	1
DEE	–	2	2
DO YOU WANT ANOTHER	–	1	1
DOG	–	1	1
DOOR	–	1	1
E	1	1	2
EAR	–	1	1

5. BEE

RESPONSE WORD	M	F	T
EAT	1	–	1
FARM	–	1	1
FATHER	–	1	1
FLIES	–	1	1
FLIES IN THE AIR	–	1	1
FLOWER	–	1	1
FLOWERS	–	2	2
FLY	3	2	5
FLYING	–	1	1
FLYING AROUND THE HOUSE	1	–	1
FUNNY	–	1	1
GEE	1	–	1
GIRLS	–	1	1
GOOD	1	2	3
HAT	1	–	1
HAW	1	–	1
HE	1	1	2
HELLO	1	1	2
HIDE	1	1	2
HIVE	1	1	2
HOLD	1	–	1
HONEY	4	1	5
HONEY-BEE	2	–	2
I	1	1	2
I BE WITH YOU	–	1	1
INSECT	1	–	1
IS	1	–	1
JACKET	–	1	1
KEE	1	–	1
KIND	1	–	1
LEAVE	–	1	1
LEAVES	1	–	1
LEE	1	–	1
LETTER	–	2	2
LIGHT	–	1	1
LION	1	–	1
LONG	–	2	2
ME	1	1	2
MOSQUITO	1	–	1
MOTHER BEES	–	1	1
MY VALENTINE	1	–	1
NAME STARTS WITH B	–	1	1
NEST	1	–	1
NEST OR HIVE	1	–	1
O	1	2	3
OW	–	1	1
PAPER	–	1	1
PEA	1	1	2
POCKETBOOK	–	1	1
POLICEMAN	1	–	1
R	–	1	1
RIBBON	–	1	1
SEE	2	2	4
SNOW	1	–	1
SOMEBODY BELONGS TO A LADY			
STING	10	6	16
STING YOU	–	1	1
STINGER	–	1	1
STINGING	–	1	1
STONE	–	1	1
STRONG	–	1	1
STUNG	1	1	2
STUNG ME	2	1	3
STUNG YOU	–	1	1
SWEATER	1	–	1
T	2	–	2
TABLE	–	1	1
TACK	1	–	1
TEA	–	1	1
TO	–	1	1
TREE	3	1	4
VASE	1	–	1
WE	1	–	1
WHEN BEES STING YA	1	–	1
WHEN IT STINGS YOU	1	–	1
WING	–	1	1

6. BEGIN

RESPONSE WORD	M	F	T
A BOOK	1	–	1
A COW	–	1	1
A SNOWMAN	–	1	1
A SONG	2	–	2
A WATCH BEGINS WHEN YOU WIND IT UP	1	–	1
AGAIN	–	1	1
ALL OVER	1	–	1
ALWAYS BEGIN	–	1	1
AT THE STARTING LINE OF A RACE	1	–	1
BABIES	–	1	1
BAND	1	–	1
BE	1	–	1
BECAUSE MY MOTHER DONT LET ME DO THAT	–	1	1
BEGINNER	2	–	2
BEGINNERS	1	–	1
BEGINNING BALLET	–	1	1
BEGINNING SOMETHING	1	–	1
BEGUN	1	–	1
BOAT	–	1	1
BOOK	1	–	1
BOX	–	1	1
BRANCH	1	–	1
BUBBLES	1	–	1
BUILDING A HOUSE	1	–	1
BUTTER	1	–	1
CALENDAR	–	1	1
CANDLE	–	1	1
CAR	1	–	1
CAT	1	1	2
CAUSE	–	1	1
CHALK	1	–	1
CHIN	1	–	1
CLOSE	–	1	1
DID	1	–	1
DOOR	1	–	1
DOUGH	1	–	1
DRESS	–	1	1
END	–	2	2
FINISH	–	1	1
FIREPLACE	1	–	1
FOR YOUR WORK	1	–	1
FORGOT	–	1	1
FRIENDS	–	1	1
FROM YOUR POCKETBOOK	1	–	1
FUN	2	–	2
GAME	–	1	1
GINNY	–	1	1
GIRL	–	1	1
GIVE FOOD	1	–	1
GLASS	–	1	1
GO	1	1	2
GOD	1	–	1
GROWING	–	1	1
HAIR	–	1	1
HEAVE	–	1	1
HIM	2	–	2
HORSE	–	1	1
HOT THING	1	–	1
I BEGIN MY SONG	–	1	1
I COME OUT OF SCHOOL	–	1	1
I JUST BEGIN ON MY PUZZLE	1	–	1
IN	2	–	2
KNIFE	–	1	1
LAMP	–	1	1
LEARN	1	–	1
LEGIN	1	–	1
LETS BEGIN THE GAME NOW	1	–	1
LETTER	2	–	2
LIFE	–	1	1
LIGHT	1	–	1
LIGHT SWITCH	–	1	1
LIKE A BEAR	1	–	1
LONG	1	–	1
LYN	1	–	1
MIRROR	–	1	1
MOPPING THE FLOOR	–	1	1
MOVIE	–	1	1
MOVIES	–	1	1
NEEDLE	1	–	1
NICE	–	1	1
NO	–	1	1
OH	–	1	1
ONCE	1	–	1
ONCE UPON A TIME	1	–	1
ONE	1	–	1
PAGIN	1	–	1
PEARL	1	–	1
PEN	–	1	1
PENCIL	1	–	1
PIANO	1	–	1
PICK	–	1	1
PICTURE	–	1	1
PIN	–	1	1
PLASTER	–	1	1
PLAY	1	–	1

RESPONSE WORD	KINDERGARTEN M	F	T

6. BEGIN

RESPONSE WORD	M	F	T
POCKETBOOK	1	–	1
PRETEND	–	1	1
PUPPY	–	1	1
PUZZLE	–	1	1
RACE	–	1	1
RACING CAR	1	–	1
RAIN	–	1	1
REACH IN	1	–	1
READERS	–	1	1
RECORDS	1	–	1
SCHOOL	1	1	2
SEEKING	–	1	1
SHEEP	–	1	1
SINGING LESSONS	–	1	1
SKATE	1	–	1
SOMETHING	2	1	3
STAGE	–	1	1
START	4	1	5
START AT THE BEGINNING	1	–	1
STARTING	3	–	3
STOP	1	1	2
STORY	–	5	5
STOVE	–	1	1
SWITCH	2	–	2
TALK	–	1	1
THE DAY OF HALLOWEEN	–	1	1
THE MOVIE BEGINS	–	1	1
THE PARADES BEGINNING	1	–	1
THE STORY	1	1	2
THREE	1	–	1
TO	1	2	3
TO A PICTURE	1	–	1
TO BEHAVE	1	–	1
TO CHALK	–	1	1
TO CRY	1	1	2
TO EAT	1	–	1
TO GET READY	1	–	1
TO GO HOME	1	–	1
TO GO TO SCHOOL	1	1	2
TO PLAY BALL	–	1	1
TO SING	–	1	1
TO SOMETHING HAPPEN	1	–	1
TO START A SHOW	–	1	1
TO WORK THE TRACTOR	1	–	1
TO WRITE	–	1	1
TRY	–	1	1
UP IN THE END	1	–	1
VIOLIN	1	–	1
WALL	1	1	2
WERE GOING TO BEGIN GOING TO OUR MOTHER	–	1	1
WHALE	–	1	1
WHEN	–	1	1
WHEN BEGIN A STORY	–	1	1
WHITE	–	1	1
WIFE	–	1	1
WIND	1	–	1
WIRE	–	1	1
WITH	1	4	5
WITH B	–	2	2
WITH O	1	–	1
WITH THAT	–	1	1
WITH THE A	1	–	1
WORK	2	–	2
WORKING	–	1	1
WRITING	–	1	1
YEAR	–	1	1
YOU	1	–	1
YOUR HOMEWORK	1	–	1
YOUR TROUBLES	–	1	1

7. BELONG

RESPONSE WORD	M	F	T
A CLUB	1	–	1
A DANCE	–	1	1
A POCKETBOOK	–	1	1
AND IN	1	–	1
AT HOME	1	1	2
AT MY HOUR	–	1	1
AT MY HOUSE	–	1	1
BACK	–	1	1
BE	1	2	3
BE TALL	–	1	1
BE WIDE	1	–	1
BE-TWICE	1	–	1
BEAR	–	1	1
BED	1	–	1
BEETLE	1	2	3
BEHAVE	–	1	1
BEHIND	1	–	1
BELONGS TO HIM	1	–	1
BELOW	–	1	1
BLOCKS	–	1	1
BUMBLEBEE	1	–	1
BUY	1	–	1
CAR	1	–	1
CARPET	–	1	1
CHAIR	–	1	1
CHEW	1	–	1
CHILDREN BELONG WITH THEIR MOTHER	–	1	1
CHURCH	1	–	1
CLUB	2	–	2
COFFEE POT	–	1	1
COW	1	1	2
DARKNESS	–	1	1
DEBBY	–	1	1
DOG	2	1	3
DONT	1	–	1
DONT BE TOO LONG	–	1	1
DONT GIVE	–	1	1
DRYER	1	–	1
EACH	–	1	1
FISH	1	1	2
FLY	1	1	2
FRIENDS	1	–	1
GARAGE	1	–	1
GIVE	–	1	1
GLASSES	–	1	1
GO	1	–	1
GONE	2	–	2
GRASS	–	2	2
GROW LONG	1	–	1
HAIR	–	1	1
HARD	1	–	1
HAT	–	1	1
HE BELONGED HERE	–	1	1
HEAT	–	1	1
HERE	2	1	3
HILL	1	–	1
HOME	2	2	4
HONG	1	–	1
HORSE	–	1	1
HOUSE	2	3	5
I BELONG TO YOU	1	–	1
IN	–	1	1
IN A CORNER	1	–	1
IN A FAMILY	1	–	1
IN A HOUSE	–	2	2
IN THE FAMILIES	1	–	1
IN THE HOUSE	–	1	1
IN THE ZOO	–	1	1
IN TOILET	–	1	1
IN YOUR HOUSE	–	1	1
IT BELONGS TO SOMEONE ELSE	1	–	1
JAIL	1	–	1
KEEP	1	–	1
KEEP MY HAIR LONG	–	1	1
LADDER	–	1	1
LAMP	–	1	1
LAWN MOWER	1	1	2
LIGHT	1	–	1
LITTLE GIRL	–	1	1
LIVE	–	1	1
LOAN SOMETHING	–	1	1
LONG	2	1	3
LOST	1	–	1
LOW	–	1	1
ME	–	1	1
MOMMY	1	–	1
MOTHER	1	–	1
NELONG	1	–	1
ON THE SHELF	–	1	1
PAPER	1	–	1
PELONG	1	–	1
PENCIL	1	–	1
PEOPLE	–	1	1
PEOPLE BELONG SOMEWHERE	1	–	1
PICTURE	1	–	1
POCKETBOOK	1	–	1
PUPPY	1	–	1
PUT	–	1	1
ROOM	1	–	1
RUN	1	–	1
SCREEN	1	–	1
SEE	1	–	1
SELONG	1	1	2
SHORT	–	2	2

RESPONSE WORD	KINDERGARTEN M	F	T	RESPONSE WORD	KINDERGARTEN M	F	T

7. BELONG

RESPONSE WORD	M	F	T	RESPONSE WORD	M	F	T
SITTING IN CHAIR	1	—	1	TO YOU	3	4	7
SKY	—	1	1	TO YOUR MOTHER AND FATHER	1	—	1
SOME AUGS JOIN OTHER AUGS	—	1	1	TO YOUR OWN FAMILY	1	—	1
SOMETHING IS LONG	—	1	1	TOYS	—	2	2
SOMEWHERE ELSE	1	—	1	UNDERWEAR	—	1	1
SONG	1	—	1	US	1	—	1
SPELL	—	1	1	WALK	1	—	1
TABLE	—	2	2	WE BELONG TO EACH OTHER	—	1	1
TAKE	—	1	1	WE BELONGED IN THE CABIN	—	1	1
TAKE IT AWAY	1	—	1	WHERE YOU ARE	1	—	1
THIS	—	1	1	WILL	1	—	1
TO	7	2	9	WINDOW	1	—	1
TO A FAMILY	1	—	1	WITH	—	1	1
TO A HOUSE	1	1	2	WITH ME	—	1	1
TO CLUB	—	1	1	WOOD	1	—	1
TO DOG	—	1	1	WRONG	1	—	1
TO HIM	—	1	1	YOU	1	2	3
TO ME	3	2	5	YOU BELONG IN YOUR PLACE	—	1	1
TO ONE ANOTHER	—	1	1	YOU BELONG TO YOUR OWN			
TO SOMEBODY	1	2	3	HOUSE	1	—	1
TO THE CLUB	—	1	1	YOUR HOUSE	—	1	1
TO THE HOSPITAL	1	—	1	YOUR PLACE	1	—	1
TO THE WIZARD	1	—	1				

8. BETWEEN

RESPONSE WORD	M	F	T	RESPONSE WORD	M	F	T
A BLOCK UNDER THE CHAIR	1	—	1	KEEP	1	—	1
A BOOK	—	1	1	KETEEN	1	—	1
A CIRCLE	1	—	1	KNIFE	—	1	1
A HOUSE	2	—	2	LITTLE	—	2	2
A LINE	1	—	1	LUNCH	1	—	1
A S	1	—	1	MAN	1	—	1
B	2	—	2	ME	4	4	8
BE	1	1	2	ME AND YOU	1	—	1
BE GOOD	1	—	1	ME-EEN	1	—	1
BEAN	—	3	3	MEAL	—	1	1
BEAR	—	1	1	MEAL SNACKS	—	1	1
BETEEN	—	1	1	MEALS	4	1	5
BETWEEN	—	1	1	MEALTIME	1	—	1
BETWEEN ME	1	—	1	MEAN	1	—	1
BIG	—	1	1	MELEAN	1	—	1
BIRD	1	—	1	MIDDLE	1	—	1
BLUE	—	2	2	MOON	1	—	1
BOAT	—	1	1	MOTHER	—	2	2
BOOK	—	1	1	MUSIC	—	1	1
BOTH	—	1	1	NEVER	—	1	1
BOTTLE	—	1	1	NOT	—	1	1
BOY	1	—	1	ON THE SIDE	—	1	1
BRICKS	—	1	1	ONE ANOTHER	—	1	1
BUILDING	—	1	1	OUR LEGS	1	—	1
CAMEL	1	—	1	OUT	—	1	1
CANDLE	—	1	1	PANTS	1	—	1
CARS	—	2	2	PEOPLE	1	—	1
CAUTION	1	—	1	PEOPLE SAY BETWEEN	1	1	2
CHAIR	2	—	2	PICTURE	1	—	1
CRACKS	1	—	1	PIN	1	—	1
CRAYON	1	—	1	PRETZEL	1	—	1
CRIB	—	1	1	PURPLE	2	—	2
CURTAIN	—	1	1	RED	2	—	2
DINNER	—	1	1	ROCKS	—	1	1
DOG	—	1	1	ROOM	—	1	1
EACH OTHER	2	5	7	RUG	—	1	1
EACH OTHERS	1	—	1	SANTA WON T COME UNLESS			
EVERYBODY	—	1	1	YOU RE GOOD	—	1	1
EVERYTHING	—	1	1	SCHOOL BUS	1	—	1
EYE	—	1	1	SKIRT	—	1	1
FINGER	—	1	1	SKY	—	1	1
FINGERS	1	—	1	SNOW	1	—	1
FISH	—	1	1	SOMEBODY	1	—	1
FLOOR	—	1	1	SOMETHING ELSE	—	1	1
GLASSES	1	—	1	STOP LIGHT	1	—	1
GLEAN	1	—	1	SUNGLASSES	—	1	1
GREY	1	—	1	SWEATER	—	1	1
HE	—	1	1	TEDDY BEAR	—	1	1
HE HURT MY FOOT	1	—	1	TEETH	—	3	3
HIDE	—	1	1	TEN	1	—	1
HIDE-AND-SEEK	1	—	1	THE BOY	1	—	1
HIM	1	—	1	THE CARS THERE IS A BOY			
HIT	—	1	1	SMASHED	1	—	1
HOME	—	1	1	THE COLORS	1	—	1
HOUSE	2	1	3	THE TABLE	—	1	1
HOUSES	1	—	1	THEM	—	1	1
I BETWEEN THE TWO PEOPLE	1	—	1	THERE IS A STOP SIGN	—	1	1
I WAS BETWEEN MY TWO				THEY	1	—	1
FRIENDS	—	1	1	THIS	—	1	1
IM CUTTING IT OUT NOW.				TIRES	1	—	1
YOU CAN NEVER F	1	—	1	TO ANOTHER	1	—	1
IN BETWEEN	—	1	1	TOGETHER	2	1	3
IN THE MIDDLE	2	—	2	TREES	—	1	1
INK	—	1	1	TULIP	—	1	1
KEEN	1	—	1	TWEEN	1	—	1

RESPONSE WORD	KINDERGARTEN M	F	T	RESPONSE WORD	KINDERGARTEN M	F	T

8. BETWEEN

RESPONSE WORD	M	F	T	RESPONSE WORD	M	F	T
TWEEZERS	1	–	1	WHITE CRAYON	1	–	1
TWINS	2	–	2	WHO	1	–	1
TWO CATS	–	1	1	WIND	1	–	1
TWO LITTLE FRIENDS	–	1	1	WINDOW	1	–	1
US	2	5	7	WITH YOU	–	1	1
WE TWINS	–	1	1	YELLOW	1	1	2
WEAN	–	1	1	YOU	3	3	6
WEEN	–	1	1	YOU AND I	–	1	1
WEEN MIDEEN	1	–	1	YOUR FEET	1	–	1
WHAT	1	–	1	YOUR FINGERS	–	1	1
WHITE	–	1	1	YOUR LEGS	1	–	1
WHITE AND GREY	1	–	1				

9. BIRD

RESPONSE WORD	M	F	T	RESPONSE WORD	M	F	T
A BIRD FLEW ON MY HEAD	1	–	1	HURT	–	1	1
A SEAGULL	1	–	1	HURT WINGS	–	1	1
ANIMAL	1	–	1	HURTS HIS WING	1	–	1
BABIES	1	–	1	I SAW A BIRD FLY	1	–	1
BELL	1	–	1	IM HAPPY	–	1	1
BIRD'S HEAD	–	1	1	IN A TREE	1	–	1
BIRDS	–	1	1	IS FLYING	–	2	2
BLUE	1	2	3	JURD	1	–	1
BOAT	–	1	1	LERD	1	–	1
BOY	–	1	1	MAKE NOISE	–	1	1
BUTTERFLY	1	–	1	NEST	3	2	5
CAGE	1	–	1	NURD	1	–	1
CAN	–	1	1	OWL	–	1	1
CANDLE	1	–	1	PAPER	–	1	1
CAT	2	1	3	PARROT	–	1	1
CHAIR	1	1	2	PELICAN	1	–	1
COAT	–	1	1	PET	–	1	1
CRACKED EGGS	1	–	1	PICTURE	–	1	1
DEAD	1	–	1	PIGEON	–	1	1
DOG	2	–	2	PIRD	1	–	1
EAGLE	3	–	3	PUMPKIN SEEDS	–	1	1
EGYPT	–	1	1	PURRED	–	1	1
FALL	–	1	1	RACING	–	1	1
FATHER BIRD	–	1	1	ROBIN	2	2	4
FEATHER	1	1	2	SEE	–	3	3
FIRE	1	–	1	SING	–	3	3
FISH	–	1	1	SINGING	1	2	3
FLIES	3	1	4	SKY	–	3	3
FLOWER	–	1	1	SOME BIRDS FLY	–	1	1
FLY	23	22	45	STAR	1	–	1
FLY IN THE SKY	–	1	1	SWIMMING POOL	1	–	1
FLY UP IN THE AIR	1	1	2	SWING	–	2	2
FLYING	7	3	10	SWINGING	1	–	1
FLYING AROUND	1	–	1	TEETH	1	–	1
FLYING BIRD	1	–	1	THE BIRD IS FLYING IN			
FLYING UP IN THE AIR	–	1	1	THE AIR	–	1	1
FLYS	1	–	1	THE BIRD LOST HIS WINGS	1	–	1
FOOD	1	–	1	THREAD	1	–	1
FRIENDS	–	1	1	TREE	–	2	2
GIRD	–	1	1	TURD	–	1	1
GRASS	1	–	1	TWEET	1	1	2
GUN	–	1	1	WIND	–	1	1
HAPPY	1	–	1	WING	6	9	15
HAVE A BAD LEG	–	1	1	WINGS	4	5	9
HE FLIES	1	–	1	WIRE	1	–	1
HEARD	2	–	2	WORD	1	–	1
HER	1	–	1	WORK	1	–	1
HOUSE	1	–	1				

10. BITTER

RESPONSE WORD	M	F	T	RESPONSE WORD	M	F	T
A DOG BIT ME	–	1	1	BITTER	–	1	1
A DOG BITING A BOYS HAND	1	–	1	BLACK	1	–	1
A MONKEY	1	–	1	BLOUSE	–	1	1
ALLIGATOR	–	1	1	BOAT	–	1	1
AWFUL	–	1	1	BOOK	–	1	1
BABY	1	–	1	BOX	–	1	1
BAD	1	1	2	BUTTER	7	3	10
BALL	–	1	1	BUY	–	1	1
BAT	2	–	2	CAKE	1	–	1
BATTER	2	1	3	CAT	1	1	2
BEAR	1	–	1	CHEESE	–	1	1
BEATER	–	1	1	CHOCOLATE	–	2	2
BEE	–	1	1	CHURNING	–	1	1
BEER	–	1	1	CLOCK	1	–	1
BELLS	–	1	1	COKE	1	–	1
BETTER	5	5	10	COLD	3	5	8
BIB	–	1	1	COUGH DROP	–	1	1
BIRD	1	–	1	CRAB	1	–	1
BIT	7	3	10	CRIED	–	1	1
BIT HIM	1	–	1	DITTER	1	–	1
BIT US	1	–	1	DOESNT TASTE GOOD	1	1	2
BIT YOU	–	1	1	DOG	1	1	2
BITE	2	1	3	DOOR	–	1	1
BITS SOMEBODY	–	1	1	DRINK	1	1	2

RESPONSE WORD	KINDERGARTEN M	F	T	RESPONSE WORD	KINDERGARTEN M	F	T

10. BITTER

RESPONSE WORD	M	F	T	RESPONSE WORD	M	F	T
DRINK OF BITTER	–	1	1	PILL	1	–	1
EAT	3	1	4	PITCHER	–	1	1
EAT YOUR FOOD BETTER	1	–	1	PUMPKIN	–	1	1
EVERY LITTER BUG HURTS	1	–	1	RAIN	–	1	1
FAN	1	–	1	RASH	–	1	1
FISH	–	1	1	REFRIGERATOR	1	–	1
FITTER	1	–	1	RUN	2	–	2
FLAG	1	–	1	SHEEP	–	1	1
FLOWER	–	1	1	SICKER	1	–	1
FOOD	1	–	1	SISTER	–	1	1
GET OUT THE BUTTER	–	1	1	SITTER	1	–	1
GIRAFFE	–	1	1	SKIN	–	1	1
GLASS	–	1	1	SMASHING	1	–	1
GRASS	1	–	1	SMITHER	–	1	1
HAT	–	1	1	SNOW	2	–	2
HIT HER	1	2	3	SOFT	1	–	1
HITTER	3	–	3	SOME MOSQUITOES BIT	–	1	1
HONEY	3	–	3	SOMEONE IS GOING TO EAT YOU UP	–	1	1
HORSE	1	–	1	SOUR	2	1	3
HOUSE	2	3	5	SPIDER	–	1	1
I DONT LIKE IT	–	1	1	SUIT	1	–	1
INSECT	–	1	1	SWEET	–	3	3
IT HURTS	–	1	1	TABLE	–	1	1
ITCH	1	–	1	TEETH	1	–	1
JEEP	–	1	1	THE BITTER WAS GOOD	–	1	1
KEY	1	–	1	THE PICTURE	–	1	1
KITTER	1	1	2	THIRD	–	1	1
LEMON	1	–	1	TOO BITTER	1	–	1
LIKE THAT BOY BIT YOU	–	1	1	TOWEL	1	–	1
LITTER	1	–	1	TRAIN	–	1	1
LITTLE GIRL	–	1	1	TREE	1	1	2
MIT	–	1	1	TWENTY	1	–	1
MITTER	1	–	1	UGH	1	–	1
MR	–	1	1	WATER	1	1	2
NOW	1	–	1	WET	1	–	1
OUCH	–	1	1	WIFE	1	–	1
PAINT	1	–	1	WIRE	–	1	1
PATTER	1	2	3	WIZARD	–	1	1
PENCIL	–	1	1	WOOD	–	1	1
PEOPLE	1	–	1	ZOOM	1	–	1
PICKLES	–	1	1				
PICTURE	1	1	2				

11. BLACK

RESPONSE WORD	M	F	T	RESPONSE WORD	M	F	T
AT	1	–	1	GREY	1	–	1
B	2	1	3	HAT	3	1	4
BACK	1	–	1	HORRIBLE	1	–	1
BEAR	1	–	1	HORSE	–	1	1
BEAUTY	1	–	1	HOUSE	1	–	1
BEE	–	1	1	I HAVE A BLACK SHOE	–	1	1
BIRD	6	2	8	I SEE YOU BLACKIE	–	1	1
BLACKEN	–	1	1	ITS GETTING DARK	–	1	1
BLACKY	–	1	1	JEAN	–	1	1
BLUE	3	2	5	K	–	1	1
BOARD	–	1	1	LACK	2	–	2
BOAT	1	–	1	LAUGH	1	–	1
BOOK	1	1	2	LEOTARDS	–	1	1
BREAK	–	1	1	LICORICE	–	1	1
BRIGHT	–	1	1	LIGHT	–	1	1
BROWN	1	6	7	LIGHTS OFF	1	–	1
BUTTERFLY	–	1	1	LOBSTER	–	1	1
CANDY	–	1	1	MAN	–	1	1
CAR	1	–	1	MONKEY	–	1	1
CAT	5	5	10	NIGHT	4	1	5
CATS	–	1	1	NIGHT TIME	2	1	3
CEMENT	1	–	1	NO RESPONSE	1	–	1
CHAIR	–	1	1	ORANGE	–	1	1
CHILDREN COLOR WITH A BLACK CRAYON	–	1	1	PACK	–	1	1
CHIMNEY	1	–	1	PAINT	1	1	2
CIRCLE	1	–	1	PAPER	1	–	1
CLOUDS	–	1	1	PAT	1	–	1
COAT	–	1	1	PEOPLE	1	–	1
COLD	–	2	2	PICTURE	–	1	1
COLOR	3	6	9	PILLOW	1	–	1
COLOR CRAYON	1	–	1	PINK	–	1	1
CRAYON	6	6	12	PLACE	–	1	1
CURTAIN	1	–	1	PUMPKIN	–	1	1
DARK	5	4	9	PURPLE	–	1	1
DIRT	1	–	1	RAT	–	1	1
DOG	3	3	6	RED	2	3	5
DOOR HANDLE	1	–	1	ROUND	–	1	1
FISH	–	1	1	SACK	2	–	2
FLY	–	1	1	SANTA CLAUS	–	1	1
FOG	1	–	1	SAT	–	1	1
FROG	–	1	1	SHACK	–	1	1
GIRL	–	1	1	SHEEP	1	–	1
GO STOP	–	1	1	SHIP	1	–	1
GORILLA	1	–	1	SHOE	3	–	3
GREEN	3	–	3	SKY	1	–	1
				SKYSCRAPER	–	1	1

RESPONSE WORD	KINDERGARTEN M	F	T

11. BLACK

RESPONSE WORD	M	F	T
SLACK	1	–	1
SMACK	1	1	2
SOME TREE TRUNKS ARE BLACK.	1	–	1
SPIDER.	–	1	1
SUN	–	1	1
SWING	–	1	1
TACK.	2	1	3
TELEPHONES.	1	–	1
TOO BLACK	1	–	1
TOO DARK.	1	–	1
TRAIN	1	–	1
TREE.	–	1	1
WACK.	1	–	1
WALL PAPER.	–	1	1
WHITE	2	4	6
WINDOW.	1	–	1
YAK.	1	–	1
YELLOW.	1	1	2

12. BRIGHT

RESPONSE WORD	M	F	T
BEE	–	1	1
BREAKFAST	1	–	1
BROWN	3	–	3
CAR	1	–	1
CHAIR	–	2	2
CLOUD	–	1	1
CLOUDY.	1	–	1
COLOR	1	–	1
CURTAINS.	–	1	1
CUTTING	–	1	1
DARK.	3	4	7
DAY	1	1	2
DO.	–	1	1
DOG	–	1	1
DOG FOOD.	1	–	1
DRESS	–	1	1
FLASHLIGHT.	1	–	1
FLOWER.	1	–	1
FUN	1	–	1
GAS STATION	–	1	1
GAY	–	2	2
GIRL.	–	1	1
GLASS	–	1	1
GLASSES	–	1	1
HIGH.	1	–	1
HOUSE.	1	–	1
I WRITE A CARD TO MY GRANDMA.	1	–	1
IN THE SKY.	–	1	1
INDIAN.	–	1	1
ITS MORNING	–	1	1
ITS SHINY	–	1	1
ITS SUNNY	1	–	1
ITS TOO BRIGHT.	1	–	1
JIM	–	1	1
KID	1	–	1
KITE.	1	–	1
LAMB.	–	1	1
LETTER.	1	–	1
LIGHT	13	11	24
LIGHT SWITCH.	1	–	1
LITTLE GIRL	1	–	1
MAYONNAISE.	–	1	1
MIGHT	1	–	1
MOON.	–	1	1
MORNING	2	3	5
NIGHT	1	–	1
OUTSIDE	1	1	2
PAPER	1	2	3
PEN	1	–	1
PENCIL.	2	1	3
PICTURE	1	–	1
PIECE	–	1	1
PIG	–	1	1
PIPE.	1	–	1
PITE.	1	–	1
PLANT	1	–	1
PLAY OUTSIDE.	–	1	1
PRETTY.	1	–	1
RIGHT	2	2	4
SHEEP	1	–	1
SHINY	1	1	2
SIGHT	1	1	2
SKIRT	1	1	2
SKITE.	1	–	1
SKY	2	7	9
SPRITE.	2	–	2
STAR.	1	2	3
STARS	1	–	1
SUN	21	18	39
SUN BRIGHT.	–	1	1
SUN COMES OUT	1	–	1
SUN IS BRIGHT	1	–	1
SUN OUT	–	1	1
SUNNY	1	2	3
SUNNY DAY	2	1	3
SUNSHINE.	3	4	7
SWAY.	1	–	1
SWITCH.	1	–	1
THE SUN	1	–	1
THE SUN IS BRIGHT	–	1	1
THE SUN SHINING	–	1	1
THE SUNSHINES BRIGHT.	–	1	1
TIGHT	–	1	1
TOWEL	–	1	1
WHEN THE SUN SHINES	–	1	1
WHITE PEOPLE.	–	1	1
WHITEY.	–	1	1
WIPE.	2	–	2
WIRE.	–	1	1
WOOD.	1	–	1
WRITE ON THE PIECE OF PAPER.	1	–	1
YELLOW.	1	–	1

13. BUG

RESPONSE WORD	M	F	T
A BUG FLYING AROUND	1	–	1
A BUGGY	–	1	1
A FLY	2	–	2
A SPIDER.	1	–	1
ANT	1	3	4
AROUND YOU.	–	1	1
BEACH BUGGY	1	–	1
BEE	5	10	15
BEE ATE IT UP	1	–	1
BEETLE.	1	–	1
BIT	1	–	1
BIT ME ON THE SHOULDER.	1	–	1
BITE.	1	–	1
BITE ME	1	–	1
BLACK BUG	1	–	1
BLACK WIDOW SPIDER.	1	–	1
BLOOD	1	–	1
BUG	–	1	1
BUGGY	2	2	4
BUILDING.	–	1	1
BUSHES.	–	1	1
BUTTERFLY	4	3	7
BUY	–	1	1
CAR	1	–	1
CATCH	–	1	1
CATS KILL BUG	–	1	1
CHASE	–	1	1
CLIMB	–	1	1
CLOUD	–	1	1
COME.	1	–	1
COWBOY.	–	1	1
CRAWL	4	3	7
CRAWLING.	1	–	1
CRAWLS.	–	1	1
CRIB.	1	–	1
DOES.	–	1	1
DOG.	1	1	2
DOOR.	1	–	1
DRESS	–	1	1
DUG.	–	1	1
DUMB.	–	1	1
FAN	–	1	1
FLIES	4	1	5
FLOOD.	1	1	2
FLOWER.	1	–	1
FLY	6	8	14
FLYING.	–	1	1
FROG.	1	–	1
GALAXIE	1	–	1
GALLOP.	1	–	1
GET	–	1	1
GET AWAY.	–	1	1

RESPONSE WORD	KINDERGARTEN M	F	T

13. BUG

RESPONSE WORD	M	F	T	RESPONSE WORD	M	F	T
GLASSES	–	1	1	NO	–	1	1
GRASSHOPPER	2	–	2	ON YOUR CLOTHES	–	1	1
GROUND	–	1	1	OUTSIDE	1	–	1
HAIR SO LONG	–	1	1	PENCIL	–	1	1
HE GETS ON US	–	1	1	PICK	–	1	1
HONEY	–	1	1	PILLOW	–	1	1
HORSE	1	–	1	POISON	–	1	1
HOUSE	–	1	1	RAT, KILL IT	1	–	1
HUG	1	–	1	SCARE ME	–	1	1
I SAW A BUG	1	–	1	SKIES	1	–	1
IM A JOLLY GOOD FELLOW	1	–	1	SNUG	–	1	1
IN MY HOUSE	–	1	1	SPIDER	3	1	4
INSECT	6	8	14	SPIDER WEB	1	–	1
IS COMING IN	1	–	1	STEP ON HIM	–	1	1
IS FLYING	–	1	1	STING	5	1	6
IT CRAWLS	1	–	1	STING YOU	–	1	1
JUG	1	–	1	STINGER	1	–	1
JUMP	1	–	1	SUG	–	1	1
KILL	1	4	5	THERES A BUG OUTSIDE	–	1	1
KILLED	1	–	1	TRAINING	–	1	1
LIGHT	–	1	1	TUG	2	2	4
LIKE A BUG IS IN A HOUSE	–	1	1	UGG	1	–	1
LITTERBUG	1	–	1	US	–	1	1
LUG	1	–	1	WALK	3	1	4
LUGGAGE	1	–	1	WALL	1	–	1
ME	1	–	1	WATER SPIDER	1	–	1
MOSQUITO	2	1	3	WINDOW	1	–	1
MOTH	1	–	1	WING	–	1	1
MOVING	1	–	1	WORLD	1	–	1
MUG	2	1	3	YELLOW	–	1	1

14. BUTTERFLY

RESPONSE WORD	M	F	T	RESPONSE WORD	M	F	T
A BUG	–	1	1	I FLIED ON A BUTTERFLY	1	–	1
A BUTTERFLY FLIES	1	–	1	I FLY BUTTERFLY	–	1	1
A CAT	1	–	1	IN THE FIELD	–	1	1
AIR	2	–	2	INK PEN	1	–	1
AIRPLANE	–	1	1	IS FLYING	1	–	1
AN ANGEL IS FLYING	–	1	1	IT FLIES	–	1	1
ANGEL	–	1	1	IT GIVES BUTTER TO YOU	1	–	1
BABY DOLL	–	1	1	IT MAKE BUTTER	1	–	1
BEAR	–	1	1	KEEP FOOD INSIDE A REFRIGERATOR	1	–	1
BEE	–	1	1	KILL IT	–	1	1
BILLY GOAT	–	1	1	LAND	–	1	1
BIRD	3	2	5	LIGHTNING BUG	–	1	1
BOARD	–	1	1	LIPSTICK	–	1	1
BUSHES	–	1	1	LIVES IN ROSES	1	–	1
BUTTER	6	8	14	LOOKS SO PRETTY	–	1	1
BUTTER HIGH	1	–	1	LUTTER	1	–	1
CATCH	3	2	5	MAN	–	1	1
CATCHING	–	1	1	MOSQUITO	1	1	2
CATERPILLAR	1	1	2	NET	3	2	5
CHASE EM	1	–	1	OUTSIDE	2	–	2
COAL	1	–	1	PAPER	1	–	1
COCOON	–	2	2	PRETTY	1	2	3
COW	1	–	1	PUFF-FLY	1	–	1
CUT OFF HIS WINGS	–	1	1	RED LIGHT	1	–	1
DINOSAUR	1	–	1	SHEEP	–	1	1
DISHES	–	1	1	SHOE	–	1	1
DOG	1	–	1	SHOES	1	–	1
EGG	1	–	1	SIDEWALK	–	1	1
FEATHER	1	–	1	SITTING ON THE TREE	1	–	1
FLEE	–	1	1	SKY	–	2	2
FLIES	6	2	8	SNAIL	–	1	1
FLIES IN THE AIR	–	1	1	STINGS	–	1	1
FLOWER	1	–	1	SUMMER	–	2	2
FLUTTER	1	1	2	THATS THE NAME OF MY DOG	1	–	1
FLY	16	16	32	THE BUTTERFLIES FLYING UP	–	1	1
FLY AWAY	–	1	1	THEYRE REAL PRETTY	1	–	1
FLYING	3	5	8	TOO MUCH OF A BUTTERFLY	1	–	1
FLYING AROUND	1	–	1	TREE	1	–	1
FLYING IN THE AIR	1	–	1	TUTTERFY	–	1	1
GETTERFLY	–	1	1	UP IN THE AIR	1	–	1
GLASS	–	1	1	WALKS	–	1	1
GO AWAY	1	–	1	WE EAT BUTTER	–	1	1
GOES THRU A WINDOW	1	–	1	WHEN PEOPLE CATCH A BUTTERFLY	–	1	1
HAWK	1	–	1	WIFE	1	–	1
HE FLIES	1	–	1	WIND	1	–	1
HE FLY	–	1	1	WINDOW	1	–	1
HEART	–	1	1	WING	5	2	7
HER	–	1	1	WINGS	4	5	9
HID	–	1	1	WUTTERFLY	1	–	1
HIGH	1	1	2	YELLOW	1	2	3
HONEY	–	1	1				
HOUSE	–	1	1				

RESPONSE WORD	KINDERGARTEN M	F	T	RESPONSE WORD	KINDERGARTEN M	F	T

15. CARRY

RESPONSE WORD	M	F	T	RESPONSE WORD	M	F	T
A BABY	3	2	5	HARD	–	1	1
A BAG	–	1	1	HARRY	4	–	4
A BASKET	1	–	1	HEAVY	1	2	3
A BOX	1	–	1	HIGH	–	1	1
A CARRIAGE WITH A BABY IN IT	1	–	1	HIM	–	1	1
A CARROT	–	1	1	I CARRIED MY BABY IN THE STORE	1	–	1
A PACKAGE	1	–	1	I CARRY MY DOGGIE	–	1	1
A PACKAGE OF FOOD	–	1	1	IM CARRYING STUFF	1	–	1
A PICNIC BASKET	1	–	1	IN A BIKE	1	–	1
A PIGGYBACK RIDE	–	1	1	IN A CAR	–	1	1
A PLUG	1	–	1	IT DROPS OVER	1	–	1
A TRAIN	–	1	1	ITS TOO HEAVY	1	–	1
BABIES	–	2	2	JERRY	1	–	1
BABY	6	15	21	KAREN	1	–	1
BABY CARRIAGE	2	–	2	LARRY	1	1	2
BABY DOLL	–	1	1	LOUDLY	1	–	1
BAG	2	4	6	LUGGAGE	1	–	1
BAGS	1	–	1	MAN	1	–	1
BARREN	1	–	1	MARRY	1	–	1
BARRY	–	1	1	ME	3	6	9
BASKET	–	4	4	ME ON A HORSIE	1	–	1
BAY	–	1	1	MOUSE	1	–	1
BEAR	1	–	1	MY BABY	–	1	1
BIG	1	–	1	MY BAG	–	1	1
BIKE	–	1	1	NET	1	–	1
BOX	3	2	5	PACKAGES	1	–	1
BOXES AND STUFF	1	–	1	PAPER	1	–	1
BRIDE	–	1	1	PARRY	1	–	1
BUG	1	–	1	PEOPLE CARRY A BABY	–	1	1
BUGGY	1	–	1	PERSON	1	–	1
CAMEL	1	–	1	PIANO	–	1	1
CARE	1	–	1	PICTURE	1	–	1
CARED	1	–	1	PIECE OF A CHURCH	1	–	1
CAROL	–	1	1	POCKETBOOK	–	1	1
CARRIAGE	3	4	7	PUT IT DOWN	–	1	1
CARROT	7	4	11	RABBIT	1	–	1
CARROTS	–	2	2	RIDING UP IN THE AIR WITH A PLANE	–	1	1
CARRY BABY	–	1	1	SHOP	–	1	1
CARRYING A BABY	1	–	1	SOME GROCERIES	–	1	1
CARRYING A BOX	1	–	1	SOME PEOPLE ARE THAT NAME	1	–	1
CARRYING SOMEBODY	1	–	1	SOMEONE	–	1	1
CAT	2	–	2	SOMETHING	2	–	2
CHAIR	–	2	2	STONES	1	–	1
CHERRY	1	–	1	STOOP	1	–	1
COLOR	–	1	1	STREAM	1	1	2
DIRT	1	–	1	SUITCASE	1	2	3
DO NOT	–	1	1	TABLE	1	–	1
DOG	1	–	1	THAT	–	1	1
DOLL	–	2	2	THE CLOTHES	1	–	1
DONKEY	1	–	1	THIS BAG	–	1	1
DOOR	–	1	1	TRAIN	–	1	1
DROP	1	1	2	TRUCK	1	–	1
DUMP TRUCK	1	–	1	TRUNK	1	–	1
EAT	–	1	1	WALKING	1	–	1
EGG	1	–	1	WARRY	1	–	1
FLOOR	–	1	1	WERE GOING TO SOMEWHERE	–	1	1
FOOD	1	1	2	WINDOW	–	1	1
FURNITURE	2	–	2	WITH	–	1	1
GO CARRY	1	–	1	YOU	–	1	1
GRAPES	–	1	1	YOURE TOO HEAVY	–	1	1
HANDS	1	–	1				

16. CHAIR

RESPONSE WORD	M	F	T	RESPONSE WORD	M	F	T
AIR	–	1	1	HORSE	1	–	1
AND BENCH	1	–	1	HOUSE	–	1	1
BEAR	5	3	8	HURTS	–	1	1
BLUE	–	1	1	I SIT DOWN ON MY CHAIR	1	–	1
BOAT	–	1	1	I SIT IN MY CHAIR	–	1	1
BOOK	–	1	1	IM SITTING	1	–	1
BREAD	1	–	1	IM SITTING DOWN ON A CHAIR	–	1	1
BROKEN	1	–	1	IM SITTING ON ONE	1	–	1
CARE	1	1	2	KINDERGARTEN	–	1	1
CHAIRY	–	1	1	KITE	–	1	1
CHEAP	–	1	1	LAIR	–	1	1
CHERRY	–	1	1	LAYER	1	–	1
CHURCH	–	1	1	LION	–	1	1
COUCH	–	2	2	MAN	3	–	3
DARE	–	1	1	MAN SITTING IN IT	2	1	3
DOWN	1	–	1	MARE	2	1	3
FAIR	–	1	1	MOTHER	1	–	1
FALLS DOWN	1	–	1	MOVE	1	–	1
FEET	–	1	1	NO CHAIR	–	1	1
FISH	1	–	1	NUMBER	–	1	1
FUN TO SIT IN A CHAIR	1	–	1	OCTOPUS	–	1	1
GIRL	–	1	1	PAIR	1	–	1
HAIR	4	1	5	PAPER	1	1	2
HALL	1	–	1	PARED	1	1	2
HANDLE	1	–	1				

RESPONSE WORD	KINDERGARTEN M	F	T

16. CHAIR

RESPONSE WORD	M	F	T
PEAR.	–	2	2
PENCIL.	–	1	1
PEOPLE.	2	–	2
PEOPLE SIT IN A CHAIR	–	1	1
PEOPLE SIT ON CHAIR	1	–	1
PERSON.	–	1	1
PIECES.	–	1	1
PRESENT	1	–	1
ROCK.	1	2	3
ROCK WITH THE CHAIR	1	–	1
ROCKER.	1	–	1
ROCKING	1	1	2
SEAT.	2	–	2
SEW	–	1	1
SIT.	19	20	39
SIT DOWN.	2	4	6
SIT DOWN IN CHAIR AND EAT	–	1	1
SIT DOWN ON A CHAIR	1	–	1
SIT IN.	–	1	1
SIT IN A CHAIR.	1	–	1
SIT IN CHAIR.	–	1	1
SIT IN IT	1	–	1
SIT IN THE CHAIR.	1	–	1
SIT ON.	1	–	1
SIT ON A CHAIR.	–	1	1
SIT ON THE CHAIR AND WRITE.	1	–	1

RESPONSE WORD	M	F	T
SITS.	1	–	1
SITTING	3	2	5
SITTING ON.	1	–	1
SMOCK	1	–	1
SOFA.	2	1	3
SOMEBODY SITTING IN THE CHAIR.	–	1	1
SOMEONE IS SITTING IN A CHAIR.	–	1	1
SOMETHING TO DRINK.	1	–	1
SQUARE.	1	–	1
STEEL	1	–	1
TABLE	10	18	28
TEAR.	1	–	1
TO SIT DOWN IN.	–	1	1
TO SIT IN.	–	2	2
TOO BIG OF A CHAIR.	1	–	1
WALL.	1	1	2
WE SIT ON IT.	–	1	1
WHERE	1	–	1
WILD DEER	1	–	1
WINDOW.	1	–	1
WRIST WATCH	–	1	1
YOU SIT IN.	–	1	1
YOU SIT ON THE CHAIR.	1	–	1

17. CLEAN

RESPONSE WORD	M	F	T
A HOUSE	1	–	1
ALL DONE.	1	–	1
BACK MACHINE.	1	–	1
BATH.	–	1	1
BATHROOMS	1	–	1
BEAN.	1	2	3
BEAR.	–	1	1
BEES.	–	1	1
BOAT.	–	1	1
BRIDE	–	1	1
BRUSH	1	–	1
CAGE.	–	1	1
CAT	1	–	1
CELLAR.	1	1	1
CLEANER	1	1	2
CLEANING.	–	1	1
CLEANING SOMETHING.	1	–	1
CLEANING THE DISHES	–	1	1
CLEAR	–	1	1
CLOTH	–	1	1
CLOTHES	–	2	2
CRAYON.	1	–	1
CRIB.	1	–	1
DEAN.	–	1	1
DIRTY	1	6	7
DISHES.	2	1	3
DUST.	2	–	2
DUST CLOTH.	–	1	1
DUSTER.	–	1	1
FARM.	–	1	1
FILL.	1	–	1
FIRE ENGINE	1	–	1
FISHES.	1	–	1
FLOOR.	3	7	10
FLOWER.	–	1	1
FOOD.	1	–	1
FOR WATER FALL.	–	1	1
FRESH	–	2	2
GARBAGE CAN	–	1	1
GO.	1	–	1
GO TO BED	–	1	1
GOOD.	–	1	1
HANDS	1	1	2
HEAN.	1	–	1
HELP.	–	1	1
HORSE	–	2	2
HOUSE	10	8	18
I CAN CLEAN	1	–	1
I CLEAN MY POT.	1	–	1
I CLEAN WITH YOU.	–	1	1
ICE BOX	1	–	1
INSECT.	–	1	1
ITS NOT DIRTY	1	–	1
KITCHEN	–	1	1
LADY.	1	1	2
LARK.	1	–	1
LAUNDRY	1	–	1
LEAN.	4	–	4
LIKE YOU CLEAN THE HOUSE.	–	1	1
LIQUID.	1	–	1

RESPONSE WORD	M	F	T
MAID CLEANS	–	1	1
MEAN.	3	2	5
MOP	–	3	3
MR. CLEAN	1	–	1
MY PLATE.	–	1	1
MY SUITS CLEAN.	1	–	1
NAME.	1	–	1
NAPKIN.	–	1	1
NICE AND CLEAN.	1	–	1
OUR FLOOR.	1	–	1
OUT THE HOUSE	1	–	1
PAPER	–	1	1
PEOPLE.	1	–	1
PEOPLE CLEAN THEIR HOUSE.	–	1	1
PLATE	1	1	2
PLATE CLEANER	1	–	1
PLEASE.	1	1	2
PRETTY.	–	1	1
Q.	–	1	1
ROCK.	1	–	1
ROOM.	1	2	3
RUG	–	1	1
SCRUB	1	–	1
SEEN.	1	–	1
SHINE	1	–	1
SHINY	–	1	1
SHOES	1	1	2
SOMETHING	1	1	2
STORE	1	–	1
SWEEP	1	1	2
TABLE	–	2	2
TEETH	2	–	2
THAT YOU CLEAN UP THE HOUSE.	1	–	1
THE CLOTHES	1	–	1
THE FLOOR	–	1	1
THE FLOORS.	1	–	1
THE HOUSE	4	3	7
THE RUGS.	–	1	1
THE TABLE	–	1	1
THINGS.	–	1	1
TIRED	1	–	1
TOO CLEAN	1	–	1
TOOTHPASTE.	1	–	1
UP.	3	2	5
UP A HOUSE.	1	–	1
UP PLACE.	1	–	1
UP THE HOUSE.	1	–	1
UP THE WHOLE YARD IN TIME TO GO IN.	1	–	1
UP YOUR HOUSE.	4	2	6
VACUUM CLEANER.	4	2	6
WASH.	3	–	3
WASHER.	–	1	1
WASHING MACHINE	–	1	1
WASHRAG.	–	1	1
WATER	2	1	3
WAX	–	1	1
WE CLEANED THE HOUSE.	–	1	1

RESPONSE WORD	KINDERGARTEN M	F	T	RESPONSE WORD	KINDERGARTEN M	F	T

17.   CLEAN

RESPONSE WORD	M	F	T	RESPONSE WORD	M	F	T
WHERE YOU CLEAN THE BATHTUB.	1	–	1	YOUR BREATH IS CLEAN.	–	1	1
WINDOW.	–	1	1	YOUR PLATE.	1	–	1

18.   COCOON

RESPONSE WORD	M	F	T	RESPONSE WORD	M	F	T
A FLOWER.	1	–	1	HOW	1	–	1
A LOOM.	1	–	1	I SEE A COCOON.	–	1	1
A LOON.	1	–	1	IN PETER PAN STORY.	–	1	1
A WORM.	–	1	1	INDIAN.	1	–	1
A WORM IS IN A COCOON AND COMES OUT A.	1	–	1	INSECT.	1	–	1
ALLIGATOR	–	1	1	IS PLAYING WITH THE RABBIT	1	–	1
ANIMAL.	2	3	5	IT GROWS AND LITTLE BUGS LIVE IN.	1	–	1
BABOON.	3	1	4	IT HAS FUR.	1	–	1
BABY.	1	–	1	IT S BROWN.	–	1	1
BAGOON.	1	–	1	JUMP.	1	–	1
BALLOON	2	1	3	JUMP IN THE GROUND.	1	–	1
BEAR.	1	–	1	JUNE.	1	–	1
BEES LIVE IN IT	1	–	1	KA.	1	–	1
BIRD.	1	1	2	LADY.	1	–	1
BLACK	1	–	1	LEAF.	–	1	1
BOON.	1	–	1	LIGHT SWITCH.	1	–	1
BOY	–	1	1	LIKE A ANIMAL	–	1	1
BRACELET.	–	1	1	LOON.	–	1	1
BUCKLE.	–	1	1	MAKING HIS HOUSE.	–	1	1
BUTTERFLIES GO IN IT.	–	1	1	MAN	1	–	1
BUTTERFLY	2	3	5	MILK.	1	–	1
BUTTERFLY NEST.	–	1	1	MOON.	3	–	3
BUTTERFLY SLEEPS IN THE COCOON.	–	1	1	MOUSE	–	1	1
BUTTON.	1	–	1	NEEDLES	–	1	1
BZZZZZ.	–	1	1	NOISY	–	1	1
CAR	1	–	1	OCTOPUS	–	1	1
CATERPILLAR	2	3	5	OUCH.	1	–	1
CHAIR	–	2	2	OWL	1	1	2
CHOO CHOO TRAIN	1	–	1	PAPER	–	2	2
CLIMBING UP A TREE.	1	–	1	PEANUT.	1	–	1
CLOCK.	–	1	1	PIECE OF TRUCK ON A CAR	1	–	1
COCA-COLA	1	–	1	PINE CONE	–	1	1
COCOA	1	–	1	PLAY.	1	–	1
COCOANUT.	1	–	1	RABBIT.	2	1	3
COCOON.	–	1	1	RACCOON	11	7	18
COKE.	–	2	2	RAT	2	3	5
COMB.	1	–	1	READING	–	1	1
COOCOO CLOCK.	–	1	1	RUNS.	1	–	1
COOK.	–	3	3	SEA HORSE	–	1	1
COOKIES	–	1	1	SHACOON	1	–	1
COON.	1	1	2	SILLY	–	1	1
COON HAS BABIES	–	1	1	SKIRT	–	1	1
COONS MILK.	1	–	1	SKY	–	1	1
COTEEN.	–	1	1	SNAIL	–	1	1
COW	–	1	1	SNAKE	1	–	1
CRACK	–	1	1	SODA.	1	–	1
CROW.	–	1	1	SOFA.	–	1	1
CUCKOO CLOCK.	1	–	1	SOON.	–	1	1
DAY	–	1	1	SPOON.	1	–	1
DEER.	–	1	1	SQUARE.	–	1	1
DISH.	–	1	1	SQUIRREL.	1	–	1
DOG	–	1	1	STICKERS.	1	–	1
DOOM.	–	1	1	STINK	1	–	1
DOON.	1	1	2	SWITCH.	1	–	1
DOOR.	1	–	1	SYMBOL.	–	1	1
EAT THE TREES	1	–	1	TABLE	–	3	3
EATING.	–	1	1	TAIL.	1	–	1
EIGHT	–	1	1	THATS SOMETHING THAT LIVES IN THE WOODS	1	–	1
ELEPHANT.	–	1	1	THEYRE NOT DOGS	–	1	1
FEELING	–	1	1	TREE.	–	5	5
FLY	1	–	1	WALK.	1	1	2
FOOD.	–	1	1	WALL.	–	1	1
FUN	–	1	1	WANT TO GO SOMEWHERE.	1	–	1
GAGOON.	–	1	1	WHITE	1	–	1
GET AFTER HIM	1	–	1	WHO	1	–	1
GO UP IN THE MOON	–	1	1	WIND.	–	1	1
GOON.	2	–	2	WINDOW.	–	1	1
GREEN	1	–	1	WITH BLACK CIRCLES.	–	1	1
HAVE.	–	1	1	WORM.	–	1	1
HEAR.	1	1	2				
HORSE	1	–	1				

19.   COLD

RESPONSE WORD	M	F	T	RESPONSE WORD	M	F	T
A CAT	1	–	1	BE WARM	1	–	1
A WALL	2	2	4	BETTER NOT GO OUTSIDE	–	1	1
AIR	2	2	4	BIRD.	1	–	1
AND THEN YOU GET YOUR COAT ON.	1	–	1	BLACK	1	–	1
BABY.	1	1	2	BLOW.	1	–	1
BAG	–	1	1	BOLD.	–	1	1
				BOWLED.	1	–	1

RESPONSE WORD	KINDERGARTEN M	F	T	RESPONSE WORD	KINDERGARTEN M	F	T

19. COLD

RESPONSE WORD	M	F	T	RESPONSE WORD	M	F	T
BUNDLE UP	–	1	1	KNOLD	1	–	1
CAR	2	–	2	LEAF	1	–	1
CATCH COLD	1	–	1	LIKE ICE	–	1	1
CHILDREN	–	1	1	LIPSTICK	–	1	1
CHILLY	–	1	1	LOLD	1	–	1
CLOCK	1	–	1	MILK	3	–	3
COAL	1	–	1	MOLD	1	1	2
COAT	2	–	2	NAIL	1	–	1
COKE	1	–	1	NOSE DROPS	1	–	1
COLD THINGS	–	1	1	OUT IN THE SNOW	1	–	1
COLOR CRAYONS	–	1	1	OUTSIDE	4	2	6
COLTS	1	–	1	PAPER	–	1	1
COUGH	1	–	1	PEOPLE HAVE A COLD	1	–	1
COVER	–	1	1	PERSON	–	1	1
DASH	–	1	1	POLE	1	–	1
DAY	–	1	1	RAINY	–	1	1
DOG	1	–	1	REAL COLD	–	1	1
DOLED	–	1	1	SHIRT	1	–	1
DON T GO OUTSIDE	–	1	1	SHIVERING	–	1	1
DRESS	1	–	1	SICK	–	1	1
DRINK	–	1	1	SNEEZE	–	2	2
FIRE	1	–	1	SNOW	1	3	4
FORT	1	–	1	SNOWY DAY	–	1	1
FOUL	–	1	1	SOLD	–	1	1
FREEZING	4	2	6	SOMEONE IS COLD	–	1	1
FROZE	–	1	1	STEAM ENGINE	1	–	1
FURNACE	2	–	2	STREET	1	–	1
GET A COLD	1	–	1	SUMMERTIME	1	–	1
GLASSES	–	1	1	SUN	–	1	1
GRIEF	1	–	1	SUNNY	–	1	1
HOLD	2	–	2	TEACHER	1	–	1
HORSE	–	2	2	THE OUTSIDE IS REAL COLD	–	1	1
HOT	8	17	25	TOO COLD	–	1	1
HOUSE	–	1	1	TREE	–	1	1
ICE	1	–	1	WARM	2	10	12
IM	–	1	1	WATER	7	5	12
IM COMING IN	1	–	1	WE SHAKE COLD	–	1	1
IN	1	–	1	WEATHER	2	1	3
IN THE WINTERTIME	–	1	1	WET	1	–	1
IT GETS WARM	–	1	1	WHEN WE PUT ON JACKETS	–	1	1
IT IS COLD OUTISDE	1	–	1	WHEN YOU COME OUT OF THE WATER	1	–	1
IT WAS COLD INTO THE WINTER	1	–	1	WIND	5	3	8
IT WAS COLD OUTSIDE	–	1	1	WINDOW	1	–	1
ITS COLD OUTSIDE	–	1	1	WINDS BLOWING	1	–	1
ITS TOO COLD	1	–	1	WINTER	7	5	12
ITS WINDY	1	–	1	WINTERS COLD	1	–	1
JACKET	–	2	2	YOURE FREEZING	1	–	1

20. COLOR

RESPONSE WORD	M	F	T	RESPONSE WORD	M	F	T
A BOOK	1	1	2	FLOWERS	–	1	1
A PICTURE	3	2	5	GOLD	1	–	1
ANY COLOR	1	–	1	GREEN	1	1	2
BACK	–	1	1	GREY	–	1	1
BALL	1	–	1	HOUSE	–	1	1
BLACK	3	2	5	I COLOR IN MY COLORING BOOK	–	1	1
BLUE	2	6	8	I COLOR MY PICTURE	1	–	1
BLUISH	–	1	1	I GET TO COLOR	–	1	1
BOOK	6	6	12	ICE CREAM	1	–	1
BOOKS	1	–	1	IM COLORING	1	–	1
BOY	1	–	1	IN THE COLORING BOOK	2	–	2
BROWN	2	1	3	IT	1	–	1
BUG	–	1	1	IT RED	1	–	1
BULOR	–	1	1	KEY	1	–	1
BUTTER	–	1	1	LOLOR	1	–	1
BUTTERFLY	–	1	1	MAN	1	–	1
BY NUMBER	–	1	1	MOTHER	–	1	1
CAT	1	–	1	MUSTARD	1	–	1
CHILDREN COLOR IN THEIR COLORING BOOK	–	1	1	ON PAPER	–	1	1
CIGARETTES	1	–	1	ON PAPERS	–	1	1
CLOCK	–	1	1	ORANGE	–	2	2
COLORING	–	1	1	PAINT	1	1	2
COLORING A COLORING BOOK	–	1	1	PAPER	4	3	7
COLORING A PICTURE	1	–	1	PARP	2	–	2
COLORING BOOK	4	7	11	PENCIL	2	–	2
COLORING ON THE COLORING BOOK	–	1	1	PICTURE	6	3	9
COLORS	1	–	1	PICTURES	1	1	2
CRAYON	5	4	9	PINK	1	1	2
CRAYONS	5	4	9	PLAY	–	1	1
CUDDLE	1	–	1	POLICE DOG	–	1	1
DECORATED XMAS TREE	1	–	1	PRETTY	–	3	3
DOLOR	–	1	1	PRETTY PICTURE YOU COLORED	1	–	1
DRAW	–	1	1	PURPLE	1	1	1
DRAW PICTURES	1	–	1	PUTHOR	1	–	1
DRESS	–	1	1	RAINBOW	–	1	1
ELLOR	1	–	1	RECEIVE	–	1	1
EYES	–	1	1	RED	9	7	16

RESPONSE WORD	KINDERGARTEN M	F	T	RESPONSE WORD	KINDERGARTEN M	F	T

20. COLOR

RESPONSE WORD	M	F	T	RESPONSE WORD	M	F	T
RIGHT	1	–	1	THIS RED	–	1	1
ROACH	1	–	1	TV	4	–	4
ROAD	–	1	1	TV COLOR	1	–	1
SELF	–	1	1	WE ARE COLORING	–	1	1
SIT	–	1	1	WE COLOR PAGE	–	1	1
SQUIRREL	1	–	1	WHITE	2	1	3
TABLE	1	–	1	WITH A COLORING BOOK	1	–	1
TEETH	1	–	1	WITH A CRAYON	–	1	1
THE	–	1	1	WRITE	–	3	3
THE COLOR MAP	1	–	1	YELLOW	4	1	5
THE COLOR RED	–	1	1	YOU COLOR WITH A CRAYON	1	–	1
THE FOOD WE EAT	–	1	1				

21. DARK

RESPONSE WORD	M	F	T	RESPONSE WORD	M	F	T
ANIMAL	–	1	1	ITS SCARY	1	–	1
ANIMALS	1	–	1	KID	–	1	1
AT NIGHT	–	1	1	LARK	3	–	3
BAD	1	–	1	LIGHT	10	15	25
BARK	2	2	4	LIGHT OFF	1	–	1
BAT	1	–	1	LIGHTS OFF	1	–	1
BED	2	1	3	LIKE ITS THE NIGHT TIME	1	–	1
BED TIME	2	1	1	LITTLE	–	1	1
BLACK	6	1	7	MARK	–	1	1
BLACK OUT	–	1	1	MIRROR	1	–	1
CANT SEE	1	–	1	MOON	7	2	9
CAT	–	2	2	MOONS OUT	–	1	1
CHAIR	1	–	1	MORNING	4	5	9
CLAY	–	1	1	NIGHT	12	15	27
CLOCK	1	–	1	NIGHT TIME	–	1	1
CLOSET	1	–	1	NOON	–	1	1
CLOUDS	1	–	1	OUT	–	1	1
D	1	–	1	PARK	–	1	1
DARK HOUSE	–	1	1	PLACE	–	1	1
DAY	1	2	3	PLANE	–	1	1
DAYLIGHT	1	–	1	RARK	–	1	1
DAYTIME	1	1	2	RAT	–	1	1
DOG	1	3	4	REAL DARK	1	1	2
DOGS EATING A BONE	–	1	1	ROOM	1	1	2
DONT PLAY OUTSIDE	–	1	1	RUN	1	–	1
FARK	–	1	1	SAND	1	–	1
FLASHLIGHT	1	–	1	SHARK	1	–	1
FOG	1	–	1	SKY	–	2	2
GHOST	2	1	3	SLEEP	3	1	4
GO TO BED	–	1	1	SLEEPING	–	1	1
GO TO SLEEP	–	2	2	SPOOKY	2	–	2
GUN	2	–	2	STAR	–	1	1
HAIR	–	1	1	STARS	–	3	3
HARK	1	–	1	START	–	1	1
HEART	2	–	2	STEAM ENGINE	1	–	1
HOME	–	1	1	STORE	1	–	1
HOUSE	1	1	2	SUN	1	3	4
HURRY	1	–	1	THROW	1	–	1
IN	1	–	1	TONIGHT	1	–	1
IN THE NIGHT	–	2	2	TOO	1	–	1
IN THE NIGHT TIME	–	1	1	TREE	–	2	2
IT S DARK OUT	1	–	1	WALK	–	1	1
IT S DARK OUTSIDE	–	1	1	WALKING	1	–	1
IT S DARK TONIGHT	–	1	1	WE GO TO SLEEP	–	1	1
IT S GETTING DARK	–	1	1	WHEN THE MOON GOES DOWN	1	–	1
IT S NIGHT	1	–	1	WOODS	1	–	1
IT S NIGHT TIME	1	–	1	YOU SLEEP IN THE DARK	1	–	1

22. DECEIVE

RESPONSE WORD	M	F	T	RESPONSE WORD	M	F	T
A	–	1	1	BOOK	–	1	1
A CITY	1	–	1	BOX	1	1	2
A GIFT	1	–	1	BOY	1	–	1
A HORSE	–	1	1	BROWN	–	1	1
A LETTER	2	–	2	BUTTER	1	–	1
A PACKAGE	–	1	1	CAR	1	–	1
A SEED	1	–	1	CAT	–	2	2
AN KNEES	1	–	1	CEIVE	1	–	1
ANIMAL	1	–	1	CHAIR	1	4	5
ANOTHER BOX	–	1	1	CHRISTMAS	–	1	1
ANY	–	1	1	CHRISTMAS EVE	–	1	1
APPLE	–	1	1	CHURCH	1	–	1
ASK	–	1	1	CLOCK	2	–	2
BE QUIET	1	–	1	COLD	1	–	1
BEAD	–	2	2	D	1	–	1
BEAVE	–	1	1	DAKEEVE	1	–	1
BEAVER	1	–	1	DC	1	1	2
BECEIVE	1	–	1	DECEIVELY	1	–	1
BECIEVED	1	–	1	DEE	1	–	1
BEE	1	1	2	DEEP	1	–	1
BEES	1	–	1	DEER	1	–	1
BIRD	–	1	1	DEPEEVE	1	–	1
BLOCK	–	1	1	DISEASE	–	1	1
BOAT	1	1	2	DONT	–	2	2

RESPONSE WORD	KINDERGARTEN M	F	T	RESPONSE WORD	KINDERGARTEN M	F	T

22. DECEIVE

RESPONSE WORD	M	F	T	RESPONSE WORD	M	F	T
DOOR	–	1	1	POLO SHIRT	1	–	1
DRESS	–	1	1	PRESENT	1	–	1
DUNK	1	–	1	RADIO	1	–	1
EGG	1	–	1	RAIN	–	1	1
EVE	1	–	1	RECEIVE	2	3	5
EVIL	1	–	1	RECEIVE PRESENT	–	1	1
FAN	–	1	1	RECEIVE YOUR HOLY COMMUNION	–	1	1
FIRE DEPT	1	–	1	RECEIVING SOMETHING	1	–	1
FIRE ENGINE	1	–	1	REMEMBER	–	1	1
FLOWER	–	2	2	RETREAT	1	–	1
FREEZE	1	–	1	ROOF	1	–	1
FUN	1	–	1	RUN AND PLAY	–	1	1
GEEB	–	1	1	SAND	–	1	1
GELEASE	–	1	1	SANTA CLAUS	–	1	1
GIVE	–	1	1	SAUCE	–	1	1
GO	–	1	1	SAVING SELF	1	–	1
GOLD	1	–	1	SEASON	1	–	1
GRASS	1	–	1	SEE	1	4	5
HAIR	–	1	1	SEED	1	–	1
HAY	1	–	1	SHIRT	–	1	1
HE	1	1	2	SHOCK	1	–	1
HEATER	1	–	1	SICK	–	2	2
HOOK	1	–	1	SIGN	1	–	1
HORSE	–	1	1	SIT DOWN	–	1	1
HOSPITAL	1	–	1	SNEEZE	–	1	1
HOUSE	1	2	3	SOMETHING	1	–	1
I DONT KNOW	1	–	1	STARS	1	–	1
I HAVE A DISEASE	–	1	1	SURRENDER	1	–	1
I SEE YOU	–	1	1	T	1	–	1
KEY	1	–	1	TABLE	–	1	1
KNOB	–	1	1	TAKE BACK	–	1	1
LEAVE	1	–	1	TEETH	1	–	1
LEOPARD	–	1	1	TELEPHONE	–	1	1
LETTER	1	2	3	TELEVISION	–	1	1
LIGHT	1	1	2	TENDER	1	–	1
LIKE A DOGS NAME	–	1	1	THAT HOW YOU GET MESSAGE	1	–	1
LOVING	–	1	1	THE BALL	1	–	1
MAIL	1	–	1	THE SIGN	1	–	1
MAN	1	–	1	THINK OF SOMETHING	–	1	1
ME	2	–	2	THIS	–	1	1
MEAN	1	–	1	TO TALK	–	1	1
MESSAGES	1	–	1	TRAIN	–	1	1
MOTOR	1	–	1	TREE	–	1	1
MY HOME	1	–	1	UNDECEIVE	–	1	1
NEW YEARS EVE	–	1	1	US	–	1	1
NOT DECEIVE	–	1	1	WASHINGTON	2	–	2
NUTS	–	1	1	WASHINGTON D C	1	1	2
OCEAN	1	1	2	WATER	1	–	1
OFFICE	–	1	1	WE ALL DECEIVED	–	1	1
ON ME	1	–	1	WEEDS	1	–	1
PACKAGE	1	–	1	WHEN PEOPLE SELL SOMETHING	–	1	1
PANTS	1	–	1	WHERE	–	1	1
PAPER	1	1	2	WIDE	1	–	1
PEA	1	–	1	WINDOW	–	2	2
PEEVE	–	1	1	WORK	–	1	1
PERSON	1	–	1	YOUR LETTER	1	–	1
PHONE	–	1	1	ZEBRA	1	–	1
PIECE OF THE DOOR	1	–	1				
PLAY	1	–	1				
POCKETBOOK	–	1	1				

23. ENJOY

RESPONSE WORD	M	F	T	RESPONSE WORD	M	F	T
A MOVIE STAR	–	1	1	ENJOIN	–	1	1
A PARTY	1	2	3	ENJOY	1	–	1
BEAUTIFUL	–	1	1	ENJOYFULLY	–	1	1
BEER	1	–	1	ENLOY	1	–	1
BEGIN	1	–	1	FARMER	1	–	1
BEING AT ATLANTIC CITY	1	–	1	FIFTEEN	1	–	1
BIRTHDAY PARTY	1	–	1	FIRE	1	–	1
BOBBY PIN	–	1	1	FLOWERS	–	1	1
BOTTLE	–	1	1	FLY	1	1	2
BOY	4	2	6	FOOD	2	–	2
BURN IT	1	–	1	FUN	4	6	10
BUTTON	–	1	1	FURNACE	–	1	1
CHRISTMAS	–	1	1	GIMME THE CRAYONS	–	1	1
CHURCH	1	–	1	GLASS	–	1	1
CIRCUS	1	1	2	GOING OUT FOR DINNER	–	1	1
COLOR IT BLUE	–	1	1	GOLD	–	1	1
COON	1	–	1	GOOD	–	1	1
DANCING	–	1	1	GREEN	1	–	1
DAY	–	1	1	HAPPY	2	–	2
DINNER	1	–	1	HAPPY BIRTHDAY	–	1	1
DOING SOMETHING	1	–	1	HAVE YOU ENJOYED YOURSELVES	1	–	1
DONUTS	1	–	1	HAVING	–	1	1
DRINK	–	1	1	HAVING YOU	–	1	1
EAR	–	1	1	HORSE	–	1	1
EAT	–	1	1	HOUSE	1	1	2
EATING FOOD	–	1	1	HOY	1	–	1
EMPOY	–	1	1				

23. ENJOY

RESPONSE WORD	M	F	T	RESPONSE WORD	M	F	T
I AM ENJOYING THIS CROWD.	–	1	1	SANDWICH.	1	–	1
I ENJOY MY CAKE	–	1	1	SCHOOL.	–	1	1
I ENJOY MY PICTURE.	1	–	1	SHIRT	–	1	1
I LIKE IT.	1	1	2	SINGING	1	–	1
I LIKE THIS	–	1	1	SIT DOWN.	1	–	1
I THINK	–	1	1	SITTING AT THE TABLE.	–	1	1
IN.	1	2	3	SMOKING	1	–	1
INSIDE.	1	–	1	SNOW.	1	–	1
JEWELRY	–	1	1	SODA.	2	–	2
JOIN A BIRTHDAY	1	–	1	SOME FOOD	1	–	1
JOINING A MEETING	1	–	1	SOME PERSON	–	1	1
KIMONO.	1	–	1	SOMETHING	1	–	1
LAST.	–	1	1	STOOL	–	1	1
LIFE.	–	2	2	SUPPER.	1	–	1
LIKE.	1	1	2	SUSAN	–	1	1
LOVE.	1	3	4	SWAN.	–	1	1
LOY	1	–	1	TABLE	–	1	1
MAN	–	1	1	TEA	–	1	1
ME.	1	–	1	THE BREEZE.	–	1	1
ME-OY	1	–	1	THE FAMILY.	–	1	1
MEETING	–	1	1	THE FUN	1	1	2
MOTHER.	–	1	1	THE PARTY	2	2	4
MOUSE	1	–	1	THE PEOPLE.	1	1	2
MOVIE	1	–	1	THE PICTURE ON TV	1	1	2
MUSIC	1	–	1	THIS.	–	1	1
NAME.	–	1	1	TIME.	1	–	1
NOT HAVE ANY FUN.	1	–	1	TINJOY.	1	–	1
OBOY.	1	–	1	TO A PARTY.	–	1	1
ONE PARTY	1	–	1	TODDLE.	–	1	1
OWL.	1	–	1	TOY	2	–	2
OYSTER.	1	–	1	TV.	3	–	3
PARTY	3	5	8	US.	2	–	2
PEACE	1	–	1	WALL.	–	1	1
PEOPLE.	4	1	5	WE ENJOYING SOME FOOD	–	1	1
PEOPLE ENJOY.	1	–	1	WHEN THEY ENJOY A PARTY	–	1	1
PICTURE	1	–	1	WHITE	–	1	1
PIPE.	–	1	1	YELLOW.	–	1	1
PLAY.	2	1	3	YOU	2	1	3
PLAYING	1	2	3	YOUR FRIENDS.	–	1	1
PLAYING OUTSIDE	1	–	1	YOUR FUN.	1	–	1
PROGRAM	–	1	1	YOUR PICNIC	–	1	1
PURPLE.	–	1	1	YOUR PICTURE.	1	–	1
RECORD.	1	–	1	YOURSELF.	3	–	3
RIDE.	2	–	2	YOURSELF AT THE PARTY	–	1	1
RING.	–	1	1				

24. EXAMINE

RESPONSE WORD	M	F	T	RESPONSE WORD	M	F	T
A DOCTOR.	1	–	1	DOOR KNOB	1	–	1
A FIRE.	1	–	1	DRAPE	1	–	1
A PAPER	–	1	1	DUSAMINE.	1	–	1
A PILL.	1	–	1	EAT	–	1	1
A PLAN.	–	1	1	ELAMINE	1	–	1
ABRASION.	1	–	1	EXAM.	–	1	1
ARM	–	1	1	EXAMINATE	1	–	1
BABY.	–	2	2	EXAMINATION	–	1	1
BED	1	1	2	EXAMINED.	1	–	1
BEFORE SCHOOL	1	–	1	EXPERIMENT.	1	–	1
BLOOD PRESSURE.	–	1	1	EYE	1	–	1
BOW	–	1	1	EYES.	1	4	5
BOX	–	1	1	FAMINE.	1	–	1
BOY	–	1	1	FASCINATION	1	–	1
BUS	–	1	1	FEEL	–	1	1
CAMPER.	–	1	1	FENCE	1	–	1
CANNON.	1	–	1	FIX	–	1	1
CAR	–	1	1	FLOWER.	–	2	2
CAT	–	1	1	FOOT.	1	–	1
CELLAR.	1	–	1	FOX	1	–	1
CHAIR	–	1	1	FRAMIN.	1	–	1
CHECK-UP	–	1	1	FROG.	–	1	1
CHEST	–	1	1	FUN	–	1	1
CHILDREN.	–	1	1	FURNACE	–	1	1
CHILDREN GO TO DOCTORS.	–	1	1	GAMIN	–	1	1
CHURCH.	1	–	1	GET SICK.	1	–	1
CLOCK	1	–	1	GIRL.	–	1	1
COAT.	–	1	1	GLASSES	–	1	1
COMB.	–	1	1	GO HOME	1	1	2
COOK.	1	–	1	HAM	2	–	2
COUNTRY	–	1	1	HEAD.	–	1	1
COWS.	–	1	1	HELP.	–	1	1
DADDY	1	–	1	HERE.	–	1	1
DAM	1	1	2	HES WRITING HIS CAZAMINE.	1	–	1
DENTIST	1	1	2	HORSE	–	1	1
DIG	1	–	1	HOSPITAL.	2	1	3
DOCTOR.	13	5	18	HOUSE	1	1	2
DOCTOR CASE	1	–	1	HURT.	–	1	1
DOCTOR USES WHEN YOU'RE SICK	–	1	1	I DONT KNOW	1	–	1
DOES THAT MEAN GOOD	1	–	1	IM EXAMINE THE BIRD	1	–	1
DOG	1	–	1	IN SCHOOL	1	–	1
				INHAMIN	1	–	1

RESPONSE WORD	KINDERGARTEN M	F	T	RESPONSE WORD	KINDERGARTEN M	F	T

24. EXAMINE

RESPONSE WORD	M	F	T	RESPONSE WORD	M	F	T
IT FAMINE	–	1	1	SHOT	–	1	1
JEALOUS	1	–	1	SHOULDER	–	1	1
LAMB	1	–	1	SICK	1	1	2
LAMINE	1	–	1	SMACK	1	–	1
LAMP	–	1	1	SNOW	–	1	1
LEG	1	–	1	SOME BOATS	–	1	1
LEMON	1	–	1	SOME EXAMINE JOIN OTHERS	–	1	1
LION	1	–	1	SOMETHING	1	–	1
ME	–	2	2	SOMETHINGS THE MATTER	1	–	1
MOTHER	–	1	1	STETHOSCOPE	–	1	1
NEEDLE	1	–	1	STOVE	–	1	1
NEEDLES	1	–	1	SWEEP	1	–	1
NO EXAMINE	1	–	1	TE	–	1	1
NOT EXAMINE	–	1	1	THAT GOT HURT	–	1	1
NOTHING	–	1	1	THE BOY	1	–	1
NURSE	1	–	1	THE HEART	–	1	1
OPERATE	1	1	2	THE PERSON	–	1	1
OVEN	1	–	1	THEY EXAMINED THEIR SHEEP	1	–	1
PAMINE	1	–	1	THIS PAPER	1	–	1
PAN	1	–	1	TIME	–	1	1
PASTE	–	1	1	TO THE EXAMS ON FOOD	–	1	1
PENCIL	–	1	1	TOILET	1	–	1
PEOPLE	2	1	3	TOOTHPICK	–	1	1
PERSON	1	2	3	TOWEL	1	–	1
PICTURE	3	–	3	TRAIN	1	–	1
PIG	1	–	1	TREE	2	–	2
PLANE	1	–	1	TRUCK	1	–	1
PURPLE	1	–	1	VICKS	–	1	1
PUTTING	–	1	1	WASHING MACHINE	1	–	1
QUIET	–	1	1	WE ALL DID SOME EXAMINE	–	1	1
RAT	–	1	1	WORK	–	1	1
REINDEER	–	1	1	WRITING	1	1	2
RINGS	–	1	1	X-RAYS	–	1	1
SEE	–	1	1	XAMINE	1	–	1
SELF	–	1	1	YOU	1	2	3
SHED	1	–	1	YOU HAVE AN EXAM	1	–	1
SHEEP	1	–	1	YOUR A DAY	–	1	1
SHOE	–	1	1	YOUR EYES	1	–	1

25. FLOWER

RESPONSE WORD	M	F	T	RESPONSE WORD	M	F	T
A ROSE	1	–	1	GROWS IN THE GROUND	1	–	1
A TREE	1	–	1	GUM	–	1	1
AIR	1	–	1	HAIR	–	1	1
BAT	1	–	1	HONEY	2	2	4
BED	1	–	1	HOUSE	–	1	1
BEE	4	4	8	HOWER	–	1	1
BEES	–	1	1	I LIKED MY FLOWER	1	–	1
BIG	–	1	1	IN THE GARDEN	1	–	1
BLOOM	–	1	1	IN YOUR GARDEN	–	1	1
BLOOMING	–	1	1	INSECT	1	1	2
BOUQUET	1	–	1	IS GROWING	1	–	1
BOWER	–	1	1	IS PLANTING	–	1	1
BOWL	–	1	1	IT GROWS ON A STEM	1	–	1
BOX	–	1	1	IT SMELLS PRETTY	–	1	1
BOY	–	1	1	KITCHEN	1	–	1
BRANCH	1	–	1	KNIFE	–	1	1
BUSHES	1	–	1	LAMB	1	–	1
BUTTERFLY	1	–	1	LEAF	1	5	6
CAUGHT A INSECT	1	–	1	LEAVES	–	1	1
CAULIFLOWER	1	–	1	LOWER	2	–	2
CHAIR	1	1	2	MOMMY	–	1	1
COLOR	1	–	1	MOWER	1	–	1
CORN	–	1	1	NEVER	–	1	1
DAISY	4	4	8	NOT NO GOOD	–	1	1
DAISY LION	1	–	1	ON THE GREEN	–	1	1
DIE	–	1	1	OUR FLOWERS ARE GETTING DEAD	–	1	1
DIRT	1	1	2	PANSY	–	1	1
DOG	1	–	1	PART OF A STICK	1	–	1
DOLL	1	–	1	PETUNIA	1	–	1
DOOR HANDLE	1	–	1	PICK	2	3	5
FEEL	–	1	1	PICK FLOWER	–	1	1
FENCE	–	1	1	PICK UP	–	1	1
FLAG	1	–	1	PINK	–	1	1
FLOW	–	1	1	PLANT	4	–	4
FLOWERS	1	–	1	PLOWER	–	1	1
FRUIT	–	1	1	POT	2	2	4
GARDEN	1	2	3	POT,WATER,DIRT	1	–	1
GIVE	1	–	1	POWER	–	1	1
GIVING IT A DRINK	–	1	1	PRETTY	4	3	7
GOWER	–	1	1	RAIN	–	1	1
GRASS	2	5	7	ROOT	1	–	1
GROW	8	4	12	ROSE	5	3	8
GROWED	1	–	1	ROSE BUSH	1	–	1
GROWING IN A PIECE OF GRASS	–	1	1	ROSEBUD	–	1	1
GROWING IN THE GARDEN	1	–	1	ROSES	–	1	1
GROWS	–	1	1	SCOOTER	1	–	1
GROWS BIG	1	–	1	SEED	1	2	3
GROWS FROM THE GROUND	–	1	1	SEEDS	–	1	1

RESPONSE WORD	KINDERGARTEN M	F	T	RESPONSE WORD	KINDERGARTEN M	F	T

25.   FLOWER

RESPONSE WORD	M	F	T	RESPONSE WORD	M	F	T
SHIRT	–	1	1	SUN	1	–	1
SHOE	1	–	1	THEYRE REAL PRETTY	1	–	1
SHOWER	1	–	1	TOWER	2	–	2
SMELL	3	2	5	TULIP	–	2	2
SMELL GOOD	–	1	1	TWIN	1	–	1
SMELL IT	1	–	1	TYPEWRITER	–	1	1
SMELLS PRETTY	1	–	1	VASE	–	1	1
SNEEZE	–	1	1	WAS GROWING ON THE GROUND	–	1	1
SOME BEES GET HONEY FROM A FLOWER	–	1	1	WATER	2	2	4
SOUR	2	–	2	WATER FLOWER	1	–	1
STEM	1	1	2	WHAT PUT ON MEAL	–	1	1
				WIRE	1	–	1

26.   FLY

RESPONSE WORD	M	F	T	RESPONSE WORD	M	F	T
A BAD LEG	–	1	1	I FLY	1	–	1
A BEE	–	1	1	I WITH YOU	–	1	1
A BIRD	3	–	3	IM GOING TO FLY	–	1	1
A BUTTERFLY	–	1	1	IN AIR	1	–	1
AIR	1	–	1	IN BED	1	–	1
AIRPLANE	6	–	6	IN THE AIR	1	–	1
AROUND	2	–	2	IN THE IAR	–	1	1
AROUND A PLACE	1	–	1	INSECT	4	2	6
AWAY	1	2	3	JET	1	–	1
BEE	4	1	5	KIE	–	1	1
BEETLE	–	1	1	KITE	–	2	2
BIRD	13	17	30	LAND	1	–	1
BIRDIES	1	–	1	LIE	1	–	1
BIRDS	1	4	5	LIP	–	1	1
BIRDS FLY	–	1	1	MOSQUITO BITE	–	1	1
BLOCKS	–	1	1	MY	1	–	1
BOARD	–	1	1	NIGH	1	–	1
BRICK	–	1	1	NO RESPONSE	–	1	1
BUG	1	2	3	NUMBER	1	–	1
BUMBLE BEE	1	1	2	ON THE SLIDING BOARD	–	1	1
BUTTERFLIES	1	–	1	PANTS	1	–	1
BUTTERFLY	7	3	10	PIE	1	1	2
BUZZES	1	–	1	REFRIGERATOR	–	1	1
BY	1	–	1	ROOF	1	–	1
CARPET	–	1	1	SCHOOL BUS	–	1	1
CRASH	1	1	2	SHOE	1	–	1
CRYING	–	1	1	SKY	–	3	3
CUPBOARD	–	1	1	SLEEP	1	–	1
DEAD	1	–	1	SLIDE DOWN A SLIDING BOARD	–	1	1
DIE	–	1	1	SLIDE DOWN THE SLIDING BOARD	1	–	1
DINOSAUR	1	–	1	SLIDING BOARD	1	1	2
DISH	–	1	1	SLOW	1	–	1
DOG	–	1	1	SLY	1	–	1
DONT FLY	1	–	1	SOCK IN	1	–	1
DOWN	2	1	3	SORE	–	1	1
EAGLE	–	1	1	SPIDER	1	–	1
FAIRY	1	–	1	SQUIRREL	1	–	1
FALL	–	1	1	STOP	–	3	3
FAST	4	1	5	SWATTER	–	1	1
FLEW	–	1	1	THE BIRD FLIES	–	1	1
FLIES	1	1	2	THE BIRDS ARE FLYING	–	1	1
FLIES AROUND	1	–	1	THEY GO REAL HIGH	–	1	1
FLOCK	–	1	1	THRU THE AIR	–	1	1
FLOWER	–	1	1	TIGER	1	–	1
FLOWERS	–	1	1	TURTLE	1	–	1
FLY AIRPLANE	1	–	1	UMBRELLA	–	1	1
FLYING IN AN AIRPLANE	–	1	1	UP IN THE AIR	1	1	2
FROM HOME	–	1	1	UP IN THE SKY	1	–	1
GLASSES	–	1	1	WALK	2	1	3
GO	–	1	1	WATER	1	–	1
GOOD BYE	1	–	1	WING	–	1	1
GUY	–	1	1	WINGS	1	4	5
HANDLE	–	1	1	WOLF	–	1	1
HIGH	4	1	5	YELLOW	1	–	1
HORSE	1	–	1				
HOW	–	1	1				

27.   FRUIT

RESPONSE WORD	M	F	T	RESPONSE WORD	M	F	T
A DIET	1	–	1	CHERRY	–	1	1
APPLE	13	13	26	CIRCLE	1	–	1
APPLES	1	2	3	COCKTAIL	5	2	7
BABY FOOD	1	–	1	COLOR	1	–	1
BANANA	5	7	12	COTTON	1	–	1
BANANAS	1	–	1	DISH	–	1	1
BELL	1	–	1	DO SOMETHING	1	–	1
BOOT	3	1	4	DOLLY	–	1	1
BOWL	–	2	2	DOOT	–	1	1
BOX	–	2	2	DRINK	–	1	1
BROTHER	–	1	1	DRINKING	1	–	1
BUTTON	–	1	1	DROPPED ON THE FLOOR	1	–	1
CANDY	–	1	1	EAT	6	9	15
CAR	1	–	1	EAT IT	1	1	2
CAT	–	1	1	EAT THE FRUIT	1	–	1

RESPONSE WORD	KINDERGARTEN M	F	T	RESPONSE WORD	KINDERGARTEN M	F	T

27. FRUIT

RESPONSE WORD	M	F	T	RESPONSE WORD	M	F	T
EATING.	2	1	3	PART OF A HOUSE	1	–	1
EATING SOME FRUIT	1	1	2	PEACHES	1	–	1
EATING THE FRUIT.	–	1	1	PEAR.	3	1	4
FISH.	–	1	1	PEARS	2	2	4
FLAVOR.	–	1	1	PEARS AND APPLES	1	–	1
FLOOR.	–	1	1	PINEAPPLE AND JUICES.	–	1	1
FLORIDA	1	–	1	QUOOT.	–	1	1
FLOWER.	–	1	1	ROOTIN TOOTIN	–	1	1
FOOD.	2	–	2	RUG	1	–	1
GET	–	1	1	SALAD	1	–	1
GO IN SWIMMING IN THE WATER.	1	–	1	SANTA CLAUS	1	–	1
GOOD.	1	3	4	SCOOT	1	–	1
GRAPEFRUIT.	1	–	1	SHOOT	–	1	1
GRAPES.	–	2	2	SNOW.	1	–	1
GUM	–	1	1	SOUP.	–	1	1
HOOF.	1	–	1	SPOON	–	1	1
HOOT.	–	1	1	STEM.	1	–	1
I ATE MY FRUIT.	1	–	1	SUGAR	–	1	1
I ATE SOME FRUIT.	–	1	1	SUIT.	1	–	1
I WANT TO EAT SOME.	1	–	1	SWEETS.	–	1	1
ICEBOX.	–	1	1	TABLE	–	1	1
IS GOOD	1	1	2	TASTE	–	1	1
IS NICE AND FRESH TO EAT.	–	1	1	TASTE GOOD.	1	–	1
JUICE.	3	–	3	TOMATO.	1	–	1
KITCHEN	–	1	1	TOOT.	1	–	1
KNOB.	–	1	1	TOOTER.	–	1	1
LEMON	2	1	3	TREE.	–	1	1
LIGHT	–	1	1	VEGETABLE	2	2	4
LOOP.	1	–	1	VEGETABLES.	–	1	1
LOOT.	2	–	2	WAS	–	1	1
MOTHER.	–	1	1	WATERMELON.	1	–	1
MOTHER FIX A FRUIT COCKTAIL	–	1	1	WE.	1	1	2
NUT	1	–	1	WE EAT FRUIT.	–	1	1
OATMEAL	1	–	1	WHAT I EAT.	–	1	1
ON.	–	1	1	WHAT YOU EAT.	1	–	1
ORANGE.	7	1	8	WHEN PEOPLE EAT FRUIT	1	–	1
ORANGES	1	–	1	WHITE	–	1	1
				YOU EAT FRUIT	1	–	1

28. GALLOP

RESPONSE WORD	M	F	T	RESPONSE WORD	M	F	T
A HORSE	2	3	5	LIGHT	–	1	1
A HORSE GALLOPS	2	–	2	LIKE ON A HORSE	1	–	1
A PONY.	–	1	1	NOW	1	–	1
AFTER	–	1	1	OCEAN	–	1	1
ALONG	1	–	1	OFF YOUR HORSE.	1	–	1
APPLE	1	–	1	ON A HORSE.	5	3	8
AROUND ON A HORSE	1	–	1	ON HORSES	1	–	1
AWAY.	2	2	4	ON THE HORSE.	1	–	1
BALLOP.	–	1	1	ON YOUR HORSEY.	–	1	1
BED	–	1	1	ONE	–	1	1
BLOCKS.	–	1	1	OVER THE RIVER.	–	1	1
BLUE.	–	1	1	PALLOP.	1	–	1
BOOK.	–	1	1	PONY.	2	2	4
CANTER	1	–	1	RADIATOR.	–	1	1
CAR.	–	1	1	REIN.	–	1	1
COWBOY	–	1	1	RIDE.	1	1	2
DONKEY	1	–	1	RUN	2	1	3
DONT	–	1	1	SADDLE.	1	–	1
FAST.	1	–	1	SALLOP.	–	1	1
FURNITURE	–	1	1	SANTA CLAUS	–	1	1
GAL	–	1	1	SKIDDY UP	–	1	1
GALLON.	–	1	1	SKIP.	1	–	1
GALLOPING	1	1	2	SKY	1	–	1
GALLOPING ON A HORSE.	1	–	1	SPIDER.	1	–	1
GALLOPING ON THE HORSE.	–	1	1	STICK HORSE	1	–	1
GITTA UP.	1	–	1	STOP GALLOPING.	–	1	1
GITTY UP.	1	–	1	STUPID.	–	1	1
GREEN	–	1	1	TALLOP.	–	1	1
GROW.	1	–	1	THE GALLANT MEN	1	–	1
HALLOP.	1	–	1	THE HORSE	2	–	2
HALLUP.	–	1	1	THE HORSES.	–	1	1
HEAD.	1	–	1	TOO FAST.	1	–	1
HOP	1	–	1	WALLOF.	1	–	1
HORSE	46	46	92	WAY	–	1	1
HORSES	1	–	1	WE ON THE HORSE THATS GALLOPING.	–	1	1
HORSES GALLOP	–	1	1	WE RIDE ON A HORSIE	–	1	1
HORSEY.	3	2	5	WHITE HORSE	–	1	1
HORSIE.	1	1	2	YELLOW.	1	–	1
HORSY	1	2	3				
LALLOP.	2	–	2				

29. GENTLY

RESPONSE WORD	M	F	T	RESPONSE WORD	M	F	T
A JET	1	–	1	BE CAREFUL WITH THE BABY.	–	1	1
AIR	1	–	1	BE GENTLE	1	–	1
AIRPLANE.	–	1	1	BE NICE	1	–	1
BABY.	3	1	4	BED	1	–	1

29. GENTLY

RESPONSE WORD	M	F	T
BEHAVE NICE	–	1	1
BENT	–	1	1
BENTLY	1	–	1
BET	1	–	1
BLACKS	1	–	1
BOAT	1	–	1
BRICKS	–	1	1
BUBBLES	–	1	1
CALENDAR	1	–	1
CAR	–	1	1
CARRY	1	–	1
CAT	2	4	6
CHAIR	–	2	2
CHILD	–	1	1
COAT	1	–	1
COMFORTABLE	–	1	1
COW	1	–	1
DEAD TREE	1	–	1
DEAFLY	–	1	1
DOG	1	1	2
DOLL	1	1	2
DONT PUSH	1	–	1
DOOR	1	–	1
DOWN	2	–	2
DOWN THE STREAM	–	1	1
DUCK	1	–	1
EYE	–	1	1
FAST	1	–	1
FENTLY	–	1	1
FLOWERS	–	1	1
FUZZ	1	–	1
GENT	1	1	2
GENTLE	–	1	1
GENTLENS	1	–	1
GENTLY	–	1	1
GO ON A JET	–	1	1
GOES WITH THE SKY	–	1	1
GOOD	–	1	1
GRAB	–	1	1
GRASS	2	–	2
GREEN	1	–	1
GRILL	1	–	1
HAIR	–	1	1
HANDS	1	2	3
HAPPY	1	–	1
HARD	2	–	2
HARDLY	–	2	2
HAT	1	–	1
HIT	–	1	1
HOLD	–	1	1
I TURN	1	–	1
I WILL WALK	–	1	1
IT S SOFT	–	1	1
JACK	1	–	1
JET	6	3	9
JET AIRPLANE	1	–	1
JET LANDS	1	–	1
JET PLANE	1	–	1
JETS FLY OFF IN THE SKY	–	1	1
JETSONS	–	1	1
JIMMY	–	1	1
JUGGLE	–	1	1
JUGGLER	–	1	1
JUMP	–	1	1
KENTLY	1	–	1
KEY	–	1	1
KIND	2	1	3
KISS	–	1	1
LAMB	1	–	1
LOVE	–	1	1
LYING DOWN	1	–	1
MAN	1	–	1
MANNERS	–	1	1
MET	–	1	1
METLY	1	–	1
NENTLY	1	1	2
NICE	1	–	1
NO RESPONSE	–	1	1
NOISY	1	–	1
NOT	1	–	1
OKAY	–	1	1
ON	–	1	1
PAT	1	2	3
PEOPLE	–	1	1
PERFECT	–	1	1
PERFUME	1	–	1
PET	2	2	4
PET THE DOG	1	–	1
PETTING	–	1	1
PICK	–	1	1
PICK UP CAREFULLY	1	–	1
PLANE	–	1	1
PLAY	–	1	1
PLAYING	1	–	1
PLEASE	1	–	1
POT	1	–	1
PRESS-ENTLY	1	–	1
PRETTY NICE	1	–	1
PUSH	1	–	1
QUICK	1	–	1
QUIET	1	2	3
RABBIT	1	–	1
RAT	–	1	1
RENTLY	–	1	1
RING	–	1	1
SENT	1	–	1
SIT	–	1	1
SLEEP	1	–	1
SLOW	1	–	1
SOFT	7	4	11
SOFTLY	–	1	1
SOMETHINGS GENTLY	1	–	1
STILL	–	1	1
SWEET	–	1	1
SWING	1	–	1
TABLE	1	–	1
TAKE	1	–	1
TALK	1	–	1
THE JETSONS	1	–	1
THINK	1	–	1
TOO GENTLY	1	–	1
TOUCH	–	1	1
TOUCH BABIES	–	1	1
TOUCH IT GENTLY	1	–	1
TREE	1	2	3
TRY TO WALK	–	1	1
TURN	1	–	1
TURNIP GREENS	–	1	1
WALK	2	2	4
WALK GENTLY	–	1	1
WALK HOME	–	1	1
WALL	–	2	2
WHEN PEOPLE BE GENTLY TO SOMEBODY	–	1	1
WITH THE BABY	–	1	1
WOOD	–	1	1
YELLOW	1	–	1
YOU	1	–	1
YOU FEEL PEOPLE GENTLY	1	–	1
YOU RUN AND PLAY	–	1	1
YOURE NICE	–	1	1

30. GIVE

RESPONSE WORD	M	F	T
A BABY	–	1	1
A BIRD TO A MOMMIE BIRD	1	–	1
A BULB	1	–	1
A PENANCE	–	1	1
A PRESENT	2	2	4
A TOY	1	–	1
A VISIT TO PEOPLE	–	1	1
ALWAYS	–	1	1
ANIMALS	1	–	1
APPLE	1	–	1
ARE	1	–	1
ARM	–	1	1
AWAY	3	2	5
AWAY SOMETHING	1	–	1
BANDAID	–	1	1
BIG CHICKEN	–	1	1
BIRDY	1	–	1
BIS	–	1	1
BOAT	1	1	2
BOOK	1	1	2
CAKE	1	1	2
CANDY	2	1	3
CARS	–	1	1
CHRISTMAS TREE	–	1	1
COW	–	1	1
CURTAIN	–	1	1
DARK	1	–	1
DIV	–	1	1
DO NOT	–	1	1
DO SOMETHING	1	–	1
DO YOU WANT ANOTHER	–	1	1
DOLL	–	1	1

RESPONSE WORD	KINDERGARTEN M	F	T	RESPONSE WORD	KINDERGARTEN M	F	T

30. GIVE

RESPONSE WORD	M	F	T	RESPONSE WORD	M	F	T
DOOR.	1	1	2	PAN.	–	1	1
DRAW BRIDGE	1	–	1	PENCIL.	–	1	1
DUST.	–	1	1	PEOPLE.	3	–	3
E.	–	1	1	PEOPLE STUFF.	1	–	1
EARS.	–	1	1	PEOPLE THE THINGS YOU DONT WANT.	1	–	1
FENCE	1	–	1	PICTURE A FELLING	1	–	1
FISH.	–	1	1	PIVE.	1	–	1
FOOD.	2	1	3	PLEASANT.	1	–	1
FOOD TO EACH OTHER.	1	–	1	PRESENT	1	14	15
FOUR.	–	1	1	PRESENTS.	2	3	5
FRUIT	1	–	1	RING.	–	1	1
GAVE.	–	1	1	SCREW	1	–	1
GET A DRINK OF WATER.	–	1	1	SHAKE HANDS	1	–	1
GIFT.	1	3	4	SHARE	–	1	1
GIVE UP	–	1	1	SHOE.	1	–	1
GIVING OUT SOME LITTLE PLAYHOUSES	–	1	1	SHOES.	1	–	1
GLASSES	1	–	1	SIT.	1	–	1
GOOFY	–	1	1	SIVE.	1	1	2
HALF AN APPLE TO SOMEBODY	1	–	1	SOMEBODY A DRINK.	–	1	1
HAND A DIAPER	–	1	1	SOMEBODY GIVES SOMETHING TO SOME OTHER.	1	–	1
HE GAVE ME.	1	–	1	SOMEBODY SOMETHING.	1	–	1
HEATER.	1	–	1	SOMEONE A TOY	–	1	1
HELP.	1	1	2	SOMETHING	2	–	2
HIM	2	–	2	SOMETHING AWAY.	–	1	1
HORN.	1	–	1	STOP.	–	1	1
HORSE	2	–	2	TABLE	1	–	1
I	–	1	1	TAKE.	1	1	2
I GAVE MY DOG AWAY.	1	–	1	THANK YOU	–	1	1
I GIVE THINGS TO POOR PEOPLE	–	1	1	THANKS.	3	2	5
I GIVE YOU A PRESENT.	–	1	1	THANKS TO GOD	–	1	1
I SHARE MY TOYS	–	1	1	THANKSGIVING.	–	2	2
I WILL.	–	1	1	THE PEOPLE.	1	–	1
IM GIVING SOMETHING TO A PERSON	1	–	1	THINGS TO PEOPLE.	1	–	1
IT TO ME.	–	1	1	THIS BACK TO ME	–	1	1
KIND.	–	1	1	TO.	–	1	1
LAY	–	1	1	TO ME.	1	–	1
LIGHTER	1	–	1	TO THE POOR	1	–	1
LIMB.	1	–	1	TO THE UNITED STATES.	1	–	1
LIPSTICK.	–	1	1	TO YOUR AMERICAN SOCIETY.	1	–	1
LIVE.	4	1	5	TOY	1	2	3
LOST.	1	–	1	TOYS.	1	1	2
LOVE.	–	1	1	TRACTOR	1	–	1
MAN	1	–	1	TREE.	–	1	1
ME.	1	1	2	US.	1	2	3
ME THAT	1	–	1	US A PRESENT.	1	–	1
ME THAT TOY BAG	1	–	1	US BACK.	–	1	1
MINE.	1	1	2	VACUUM CLEANER.	1	–	1
MIVE.	1	–	1	WATER TO SOMEBODY ELSE.	1	–	1
MONEY	–	1	1	WE GIVE TRULY	1	–	1
MONEY TO THE BANK	1	–	1	WELL.	–	1	1
MORE MONEY.	–	1	1	WHEN PEOPLE ARE GIVING SOMETHING TO	–	1	1
MY SISTER	1	–	1	WIVE.	1	–	1
NICE.	1	–	1	X.	1	–	1
NOT	1	–	1	YOUR MOTHER AND FATHER A KISS	1	–	1
P.	–	1	1				
PAINT	–	1	1				

31. HAND

RESPONSE WORD	M	F	T	RESPONSE WORD	M	F	T
A PEN TO SOMEBODY	–	1	1	DO SOMETHING.	1	–	1
ACHE.	1	–	1	EAT	1	1	2
AMBULANCE	1	–	1	EGG	3	–	3
ARM	1	6	7	ELEVATOR.	–	1	1
BABY CHICKEN.	–	1	1	FACE.	–	1	1
BAND.	2	2	4	FAN.	1	1	2
BEAUTIFUL	1	–	1	FEET.	1	2	3
BEETLE.	–	1	1	FINGER.	1	4	5
BLEEDING.	1	–	1	FINGERNAIL.	1	–	1
BOAT.	1	–	1	FINGERNAILS	1	–	1
BONES	1	–	1	FINGERS	3	2	5
BOOK.	–	1	1	FLY	1	–	1
BOOKS	–	1	1	FOOD.	–	2	2
BORROW.	1	–	1	FOOT.	2	3	5
BUMBLEBEE	1	–	1	FOR PICKING UP THINGS	–	1	1
BUNNY RABBIT.	1	–	1	FRY	–	1	1
CAKE.	–	1	1	GET WITH.	–	1	1
CAR	1	–	1	GIVE.	–	1	1
CARRY	2	–	2	GIVE ME BACK.	–	1	1
CAT	–	1	1	GIVING SOMEBODY SOMETHING TO EAT	–	1	1
COAT.	1	–	1	GOOD.	–	1	1
COOK WITH HANDS	1	–	1	GROWS	1	–	1
COUCH	1	–	1	HAM	1	1	2
COW	1	–	1	HAMMER.	1	–	1
CUT OFF HAND.	–	1	1	HANDLE.	1	1	2
DAN	–	1	1	HEAD.	2	–	2
DISHES.	–	1	1	HEN	3	–	3
DO.	1	–	1				

RESPONSE WORD	KINDERGARTEN M	F	T

31. HAND

RESPONSE WORD	M	F	T
HENS ARE LAYING AN EGG.	1	–	1
HOLD.	–	1	1
HOLDING SOMEBODYS HAND.	1	–	1
HOUSE	–	1	1
HURT	–	2	2
I HAVE A HAND	–	1	1
I PAT THE HAND.	–	1	1
I WANT A CANDLE	1	–	1
IT.	–	1	1
JAGUAR.	1	–	1
KISS.	–	1	1
LAND.	2	–	2
LETS SHAKE HANDS.	1	–	1
LIGHT	–	1	1
LIPSTICK.	–	1	1
LITTLE FINGER	1	–	1
LITTLE ONE.	–	1	1
MAN	1	1	2
ME.	–	1	1
ME THAT	1	–	1
ME THAT QUARTER	1	–	1
MINE.	1	–	1
MITTEN.	–	1	1
MONEY	–	1	1
MOUTH	–	1	1
NEEDLE.	–	1	1
NO RESPONSE	2	–	2
NOW	–	1	1
ON.	1	1	2
ON A MAN.	–	1	1
ON AN ARM	–	1	1
ORANGES	–	1	1
OUT THINGS.	1	–	1
OVER THE MONEY.	1	–	1
PACKAGE	1	–	1
PACKAGES.	–	1	1
PAN	3	–	3
PATTER-KILLER	1	–	1
PEACH	–	1	1
PEN	1	1	2
PENCIL.	1	2	3
PEOPLE.	–	1	1
PEOPLE HAVE HANDS	–	1	1
PIANO	1	–	1
PICK.	1	–	1
PICK UP WITH HANDS.	1	–	1
PICKING UP A HAND	1	–	1
PICTURE	1	–	1
POND.	1	–	1
PRINT	1	–	1
PUT	–	1	1
PUT OUT YOUR HAND	1	–	1
REACH	1	–	1
REACH UP TO THE ICE CREAM	1	–	1
RING.	1	2	3
SELL.	–	1	1
SEWING.	–	1	1
SHAKE	5	2	7
SHAKE HAND.	1	–	1
SHAKE HANDS	2	–	2
SHELLS.	–	1	1
SOMEBODYS HAND.	–	1	1
SOMETHING	1	1	2
SQUEEZING	–	1	1
STICKS.	–	1	1
STIR.	–	1	1
TAKE.	1	1	2
THAT YOU PICK UP YOUR POCKETBOOK	1	–	1
THE BABY.	–	1	1
THE CLOCK HAND.	1	–	1
THE HANDS	1	–	1
THEM.	–	1	1
THEM TO ME.	1	–	1
THINGS.	–	1	1
THIS.	–	1	1
TO WRITE WITH	–	1	1
TOOLS	–	1	1
TOUCH	–	1	1
TWO	–	1	1
TWO HANDS	–	1	1
WE PICK SOMETHING UP AND EAT IT	–	1	1
WHIP KIDS	1	–	1
WORK.	1	1	2
WRIST	–	1	1
WRITE	3	–	3
YOU HAVE A HAND	–	1	1
YOUR FINGERS.	1	–	1

32. HAPPEN

RESPONSE WORD	M	F	T
A BABY BIRD FALL OUT OF A TREE	–	1	1
A BUILDING GOT BUILDED AND WE DONT KNOW	1	–	1
A DAY AGO.	2	–	2
A LONG TIME AGO	1	–	1
ACCIDENT.	3	–	3
AND WE ALL FALL DOWN.	1	–	1
APPLE	1	–	1
ASH TRAY.	1	–	1
BACKEL.	–	1	1
BAD	2	–	2
BALL.	1	–	1
BASEBOARD	1	–	1
BED	–	1	1
BEE	–	1	1
BEGIN	1	–	1
BIG	–	1	1
BIKE	1	–	1
BOAT.	–	1	1
BRUISE.	1	–	1
BUTTON.	–	1	1
CABIN	1	–	1
CAP	1	–	1
CAPPEN.	–	1	1
CAPTAIN	1	–	1
CAR	2	–	2
CAT	1	1	2
CAT FOOD.	1	–	1
CAUGHT IN A MOUSETRAP	1	–	1
CHAIR	–	1	1
CLAPPING.	1	–	1
COME HOME	1	–	1
COULD	–	1	1
CRIB.	–	1	1
CRY	–	1	1
CRYING.	–	1	1
CUT	–	2	2
CUT YOURSELF.	1	–	1
DAMN.	1	–	1
DAY	1	–	1
DREAM	–	1	1
EAT	1	–	1
FALL.	2	3	5
FALLING	1	–	1
FATTENED.	1	–	1
FELL DOWN	–	1	1
FELL OFF HER BIKE	–	1	1
FIRE.	1	–	1
FIRED OFF A JOB	–	1	1
FISH.	–	1	1
FLAP	1	–	1
FLOWERS	–	1	1
GET MUD THROWNED IN MY FACE	1	–	1
GLAD.	–	1	1
GO IN THE HOUSE WHEN IT RAINS.	–	1	1
GOD	–	1	1
GOT KILLED.	1	–	1
GRAPES.	–	1	1
GREEN	–	1	1
GROUND.	–	1	1
HAIR.	–	1	1
HAMMER.	1	–	1
HANGER.	–	1	1
HAPPY	1	3	4
HAT.	1	1	2
HAVE.	1	–	1
HE FELL	1	–	1
HOOK.	–	1	1
HORN.	1	–	1
HOSPITAL.	–	1	1
HOW CAN THAN THAT HAPPEN.	–	1	1
HURT.	1	5	6
HURT KNEE	–	1	1
I FELL DOWN	–	1	1
IN.	1	–	1
IN 1940	1	–	1
IT.	–	1	1
IT HAPPENED	–	1	1
IT HAPPENED ONE DAY WHEN SOMEBODY STOLE	1	–	1
JAPPEN.	1	–	1

RESPONSE WORD	KINDERGARTEN			RESPONSE WORD	KINDERGARTEN		
	M	F	T		M	F	T

32. HAPPEN

RESPONSE WORD	M	F	T	RESPONSE WORD	M	F	T
JUMP ROPE	–	1	1	SOMETHING TERRIBLE HAPPENS	–	1	1
KNEE	1	–	1	SOMETHING TO DRINK	–	1	1
LAMP	–	1	1	SOMETIMES	1	1	2
LAP	1	–	1	SPOT	1	–	1
LAPPENED	1	–	1	STREAM	1	–	1
LAUGHING	1	–	1	SUGAR	1	–	1
LOCKER	1	–	1	SWING	–	1	1
MAPPEN	1	–	1	TAPPEN	1	–	1
ME	–	1	1	THERE	1	–	1
MEND	1	–	1	THERE IS	–	1	1
MILK	–	1	1	THIS HAPPENED	1	–	1
NICE	1	–	1	TO	3	–	3
NOW	1	–	1	TO ME	–	1	1
ONCE	1	–	1	TO ME A LONG TIME AGO	–	1	1
ONCE MORE	1	–	1	TO YOU	–	1	1
ONE	–	1	1	TRAP	–	1	1
ONE DAY	1	–	1	TRASH	1	–	1
PAPPEN	–	1	1	TV	–	1	1
PEN	–	1	1	UM GOING TO HOP	–	1	1
PLANE CRASHED	1	–	1	WAPPENED	1	–	1
POLICEMAN	1	–	1	WE GET HURT	–	1	1
RAPID	1	–	1	WHAT	4	5	9
REAL	–	1	1	WHAT ARE YOU DOING	–	1	1
REFRIGERATOR	1	–	1	WHAT HAPPEN	–	1	1
SACK	1	–	1	WHAT HAPPEN TO MY STOCKING	1	–	1
SAD	–	2	2	WHAT HAPPENED	3	3	6
SCHOOL	1	–	1	WHAT HAPPENED TO THE BOY	1	–	1
SHIRT	–	1	1	WHAT HAPPENED TO THE MAN	1	–	1
SHOE	–	1	1	WHEN SOMETHING HAPPEN	–	1	1
SIDEWALK	–	1	1	WHEN WE DO SOMETHING	1	–	1
SING SOFTLY	–	1	1	WINDOW	1	2	3
SOMEBODY FALLS AND SOMEBODY MIGHT NOT K	1	–	1	WRECK	1	–	1
SOMEBODY GOT HURT	1	–	1	YEAR	–	1	1
SOMETHING	1	1	2	YESTERDAY	–	1	1
SOMETHING BAD	1	–	1	YOU	2	1	3
SOMETHING HAPPENED	1	5	6	YOU FALL	–	1	1
SOMETHING HAPPENED TO ME	–	1	1	YOU GET SPANKED	1	–	1

33. HARD

RESPONSE WORD	M	F	T	RESPONSE WORD	M	F	T
A HARD DONUT	1	–	1	ITS	1	–	1
A ROCK IS HARD	–	1	1	ITS TOO HARD. DONT EAT IT	1	–	1
ACE	1	–	1	LARD	2	–	2
ACHE	1	–	1	LARGE	1	–	1
APPLE	1	–	1	LIPSTICK	–	1	1
BABY	–	1	1	LIVING	1	–	1
BANG	1	–	1	LOVE	–	1	1
BARD	–	1	1	MANNERS	1	–	1
BARN	1	–	1	MARBLE IS HARD	1	–	1
BEAR	1	–	1	MARD	2	–	2
BITE	–	1	1	MARRED	–	1	1
BLOCK	1	–	1	MATERIAL	–	1	1
BOAT	1	–	1	METAL	2	1	3
BOOK	–	1	1	MOUSE	–	1	1
BRACELET	–	1	1	MUD	1	–	1
BRICKS	1	–	1	NAIL	–	1	1
BUTTER	1	–	1	NINE	1	–	1
CANDY	1	–	1	NO	–	1	1
CARD	2	–	2	NOSE	–	1	1
CARDS GET MAILED	1	–	1	ORANGE	–	1	1
CEMENT	3	1	4	PEOPLE	–	1	1
CHAIR	2	–	2	PLAY DOUGH	1	–	1
CHRISTMAS CAROL	–	1	1	POCKET BOOK	1	–	1
CLARK	–	1	1	POLE	–	1	1
COKE	–	1	1	PRESENT	1	–	1
CRAYON	–	1	1	PRICK	–	1	1
DARD	–	1	1	R	–	1	1
DAY	1	–	1	RIGHT	–	1	1
DEER	–	1	1	RING	–	1	1
DOING HOMEWORK	–	1	1	ROCK	9	7	16
EASY	2	3	5	ROCKS	2	–	2
FEED ANIMALS	1	–	1	ROUGH	1	1	2
FEET	1	–	1	SALT	1	–	1
GET OFF	–	1	1	SAND	–	1	1
GIRL	–	1	1	SEND	–	1	1
GO AWAY	–	1	1	SHARE	–	1	1
HAND	–	1	1	SIT ON	1	–	1
HARRE	1	–	1	SMASH UP THE HOUSE	1	–	1
HEAD	–	3	3	SNOW	–	1	1
HEADED	1	–	1	SOFT	2	8	10
HEART	1	4	5	SOMETHING HARD	–	1	1
HIT SOMEBODY HARD	1	–	1	SOMETHING IS HARD	1	1	2
I BLOW MY HORN	–	1	1	SQUISH	–	1	1
I CAN STOP ON IT	1	–	1	STEEL	4	–	4
I HIT MY HEAD ON THE HARD WATER	1	–	1	STREAM	–	1	1
ICE	1	–	1	SUBMIT	1	–	1
ICE SKATES	1	–	1	TABLE	–	2	2

RESPONSE WORD	KINDERGARTEN M	F	T	RESPONSE WORD	KINDERGARTEN M	F	T

33. HARD

RESPONSE WORD	M	F	T	RESPONSE WORD	M	F	T
TARRED	1	–	1	TOYS FOR CHRISTMAS	1	–	1
TEETH	1	–	1	TRAIN	1	–	1
TELEPHONE	–	1	1	TREE	1	2	3
THINGS	–	2	2	TV	–	1	1
THINKING	1	–	1	VALENTINE HEART	1	–	1
THIS CANDY IS HARD	–	1	1	WALK	1	1	2
THIS IS A HARD ROCK	1	–	1	WALL	1	1	2
THIS IS HARD TO DO	–	1	1	WASHING	–	1	1
TIME	1	–	1	WATER	1	1	2
TO	1	1	2	WE PULL HARD	–	1	1
TO DO	1	–	1	WEAPON	–	1	1
TO MAKE SOMETHING	–	1	1	WHEEL	1	–	1
TO SELL	–	1	1	WILL SQUEEK MY EARS OUT	1	–	1
TO WORK	–	1	1	WOOD	4	1	5
TO WRITE	–	1	1	WORK	5	6	11
TOO HARD	1	1	2	WORKING	1	–	1
TOYS	1	–	1	YOU	–	1	1

34. HE

RESPONSE WORD	M	F	T	RESPONSE WORD	M	F	T
A BOYS GOING TO ANOTHER BOYS BIRTHDAY	–	1	1	I PLAY WITH HIM	–	1	1
A HE BABY	–	1	1	INDIAN	–	1	1
ACTION	1	–	1	IS	2	1	3
AND HER	–	1	1	IS A BOY	1	–	1
AND HIS FRIENDS ARE GOING OUT	1	–	1	IS GOING TO HURT YOU	–	1	1
ARMS	1	–	1	IS HANDSOME	–	1	1
BABY	–	1	1	JACK	–	1	1
BE	–	1	1	JUMP	1	–	1
BE NICE	1	–	1	KEY	4	–	4
BEACH	1	–	1	LAUGH	1	–	1
BEAR	1	–	1	LEE	3	–	3
BEGAN	1	–	1	LIKE A BOY	–	1	1
BELONGS IN A ZOO	1	–	1	LOVE	–	1	1
BIG	1	–	1	LOVES	–	1	1
BIRD	–	1	1	LOVES ME	1	–	1
BLACK	–	1	1	MADE	–	1	1
BLANKET	1	–	1	MAN	6	4	10
BOAT	2	1	3	ME	2	1	3
BOOKS	–	1	1	MINK	1	–	1
BOY	3	9	12	MONKEY	–	1	1
BROKE	1	–	1	MOUNTAIN	1	–	1
CHRISTMAS	1	–	1	NEEDLE	–	1	1
CLIMB	–	1	1	OUR CATS A HE	1	–	1
COWGIRL	–	1	1	PANTS	1	–	1
D	3	–	3	PEA	–	1	1
DEE	–	1	1	PEOPLE	–	2	2
DID	1	–	1	PERSON	–	1	1
DID A BAD THING	–	1	1	PLAYED	1	–	1
DID IT	–	1	1	PUT HIS CLOTHES ON	1	–	1
DID SOMETHING	1	–	1	REINS	1	–	1
DINING ROOM	–	1	1	SAID	–	1	1
DIRT	–	1	1	SAIL	1	–	1
DOLL	–	1	1	SAW ME	–	1	1
DONE SOMETHING	1	–	1	SEA	–	1	1
DOOR	–	1	1	SEE	–	1	1
E	–	1	1	SHE	8	9	17
EAT ICE CREAM	1	–	1	SHEEN	1	–	1
ELEVATOR	–	1	1	SHOE	1	–	1
FARM	1	–	1	SHOVEL	1	–	1
FELL DOWN	1	–	1	SIGN	1	–	1
FISHED	–	1	1	SIT	1	–	1
FRESH WATER	1	–	1	STING	1	–	1
FURNACE	–	1	1	SWAM	1	–	1
GIRL	1	–	1	SWIMMING	–	1	1
GIVE AWAY	1	–	1	THE ROCKING CHAIR	–	1	1
GLASS	–	1	1	THREE	–	1	1
GO	–	1	1	TOOK	–	2	2
GRASS	1	2	3	TOOK MY TOYS	1	–	1
GREEN	–	1	1	TOOK THIS	–	1	1
GRETCHEN	–	1	1	TRUCK	1	–	1
HAS A RAKE	1	–	1	US	1	–	1
HE IS MY FATHER	–	1	1	WAS	–	1	1
HEAR	–	1	1	WAVES	1	–	1
HEAT	3	1	4	WE HAD A HE DOG	–	1	1
HEATER	1	–	1	WE LIKE	1	–	1
HEEL	1	–	1	WE PICK UP HE	–	1	1
HER	1	8	9	WENT	1	1	2
HERE	1	–	1	WENT OUT	1	–	1
HIM	3	1	4	WENT OUT TO DINNER	–	1	1
HIT ME	1	1	2	WENT TO THE BATHROOM	1	–	1
HOLY	1	–	1	WHEN ARE YOU GOING TO PAY GROCERIES	1	–	1
HORSE	2	1	3	WHO IS HE	–	1	1
HOT	–	2	2	WINDOW	1	1	2
				YOU	1	1	2

35. HER

RESPONSE WORD	M	F	T	RESPONSE WORD	M	F	T
A BABY	–	1	1	A BEAR	1	–	1
A BABY HER	–	1	1	A GIRL	2	2	4

35. HER

RESPONSE WORD	M	F	T
A WOMAN	1	-	1
AM	-	1	1
BACK	-	1	1
BAKING	-	1	1
BAR	1	-	1
BAT	1	-	1
BIRD	1	2	3
BIRDIE	1	-	1
BIRDIE WING FELL OFF	1	-	1
BLONDE	-	1	1
BOAT	-	2	2
BOY	1	1	2
BROKE	1	-	1
BURP	1	-	1
BURR	2	2	4
BUTTON	-	1	1
BUTTONS	1	-	1
CAR	-	1	1
CAT	-	1	1
CHAIR	-	1	1
CHIMNEY	1	-	1
COOK	1	-	1
CRIB	1	-	1
CUR	1	-	1
CURL	1	-	1
CURT	1	-	1
CURVE ON A ROAD	-	1	1
DARTS	1	-	1
DIAMOND	-	1	1
DID	2	-	2
DIRD	1	-	1
DOG	1	-	1
DOGGY	-	1	1
DOING	1	-	1
DOLL BABY	-	1	1
DONALD	-	1	1
DONT	1	-	1
DOOR	1	2	3
DRESS	2	-	2
EGG	1	-	1
FEMALE	-	1	1
FLA	-	1	1
FLOOR	1	-	1
FLOWERS	-	1	1
FOR A WALK	-	1	1
FUR	-	2	2
GIRL	9	9	18
GLASS	-	1	1
GLASSES	1	1	2
GO	1	-	1
GO HOME	1	-	1
GOAT	1	-	1
GOOD	-	1	1
HE	1	4	5
HIM	6	15	21
HIS	2	-	2
HORSE	1	-	1
HOT	1	-	1
HURRY	-	1	1
HURT	1	-	1
HURT MY KNEE	-	1	1
HURT YOU	-	1	1
I LIKE HER	1	-	1
ICE CREAM	1	-	1
IRON	-	1	1
IS A BEE	1	-	1
IS A GIRL	-	1	1
IS IN THE BATHROOM	1	-	1
IS WRITING	-	1	1
LADY	1	-	1
LAMB	1	-	1
LER	1	-	1
LIGHT	-	1	1
LOOK AT HER	1	-	1
LOVE	-	1	1
LUR	1	-	1
MADE A MESS AGAIN	1	-	1
MAN	1	-	1
ME	1	1	2
MEN	1	-	1
MER	-	1	1
MILK	1	-	1
MOUSE	-	1	1
MOVIE BEN HUR	1	-	1
MY SISTER	1	-	1
NICE	1	-	1
NICKEL	1	-	1
PAINT	-	1	1
PAPER	-	1	1
PATCH	-	1	1
PEARLS	-	1	1
PEOPLE	-	1	1
PERSON	-	1	1
PICKS UP LEAVES	-	1	1
PIGEON	-	1	1
PLAY	2	-	2
POCKETBOOK	1	-	1
PUPPY	-	1	1
PURR	3	1	4
RING	-	1	1
SHE	8	5	13
SHE WAS FIGHTING AGAINST A DOG	1	-	1
SHE WAS PLAYING	1	-	1
SHE WENT TO THE BATHROOM	-	1	1
SHELF	-	1	1
SOLDIER	1	-	1
SOME HERS MEET OTHER HERS	-	1	1
SPEAK TO HER	-	1	1
STAMP	-	1	1
STORY	1	-	1
TAPE	-	1	1
THATS A GIRL	1	-	1
THIRD	1	-	1
TREE	1	-	1
WANTED TO GET A BRAND NEW WATCH	-	1	1
WANTS SOME FOOD	-	1	1
WANTS TO PLAY WITH MY TOYS	1	-	1
WAS MAKING A NOISE	-	1	1
WENT	1	-	1
WHEN A GIRLS COMING TO ANOTHER LITTLE G	-	1	1
WHOS SHE	-	1	1

36. HIGH

RESPONSE WORD	M	F	T
ABOVE	-	2	2
AIR	1	-	1
AIRPLANE	3	-	3
AND GO SEEK	-	1	1
ANGELS	1	1	2
BE HIGH	1	-	1
BEE	-	2	2
BEEHIVE	1	1	2
BIG	-	1	1
BIKE	1	-	1
BILLS	1	-	1
BLOUSE	-	1	1
BOO	1	-	1
BOOKS	-	1	1
BOX	-	2	2
BOY	1	-	1
BUILDINGS ARE HIGH	1	-	1
BUY	1	2	3
BY	1	-	1
BYE	3	4	7
CHAIR	-	1	1
CHICKEN	1	-	1
CLIMB	1	-	1
CLOCK	-	1	
COLD	-	1	1
COW	-	1	1
DESK	-	1	1
DIE	-	1	1
DONT FALL	1	-	1
DOOR	1	-	1
DOWN	2	-	2
FRIEND	1	1	2
GET	-	1	1
GIANT	1	-	1
GLAD TO SEE	-	1	1
GLASS	-	1	1
GO JUMP UP IN THE AIR	1	-	1
GOLD	1	-	1
GOOD	-	1	1
GOOD NEIGHBOR	-	1	1
GOOD-BYE	1	3	4
GUY	1	-	1
HEIGHT	1	-	1
HELLO	2	3	5
HI	1	-	1
HI PAL	1	-	1
HI, ME	-	1	1

RESPONSE WORD	M	F	T
36. HIGH			
HIDE.	2	–	2
HIDE AND GO SEEK.	1	1	2
HIDE FROM PEOPLE.	–	1	1
HIGH CHAIR.	1	–	1
HIGHS	1	–	1
HILL.	1	–	1
HOT	1	–	1
HOUSE HIGH.	1	–	1
I CLIMB UP MY LADDER HIGH	–	1	1
I HIDE IT ON THE STOVE.	1	–	1
IM SAYING HI TO SOMEONE	–	1	1
IN A TREE	1	–	1
IN THE AIR.	2	2	4
IN THE SKY.	1	–	1
IN THE TREE	–	1	1
ITS TOO HIGH UP HERE.	1	–	1
JUMPING	1	–	1
KITE.	1	–	1
LETTER.	–	1	1
LIFT.	–	1	1
LIPSTICK.	–	1	1
LOVE.	–	1	1
LOW	7	10	17
LYE	1	–	1
MAN	1	–	1
ME-IGH.	1	–	1
MOON.	–	1	1
MOTHER.	–	1	1
MOUNTAIN.	2	1	3
MOUNTAINS	1	–	1
MY.	–	1	1
NICE.	–	1	1
NO MORE	1	–	1
PAPER	1	–	1
PEOPLE.	1	1	2
PEOPLE SAY HOP.	1	–	1
PERSON.	–	1	1
PICTURE	1	–	1
READING A BOOK.	–	1	1
REAL HIGH	–	1	1
ROCKETS	1	–	1
SAYING HI TO THE GRANDPARENTS	–	1	1
SHELF	–	1	1
SHOVEL.	1	1	2
SIDEWALK.	–	1	1
SKY	8	5	13
SLIDE	–	1	1
SO VERY, VERY HIGH.	1	–	1
SOMEBODY CAME HOME AND I SAID HI	1	–	1
SOMETHING IS HIGH	–	1	1
SPANK	1	–	1
SUN	1	–	1
SWING	1	1	2
TALL.	–	1	1
TELEPHONE	–	1	1
THE FLYING TRAPEZE.	1	–	1
THE SKY SO HIGH	–	1	1
THE WIND.	1	–	1
THERE	–	1	1
THINK	–	1	1
TIE.	1	–	1
TISSUE.	1	–	1
TO.	–	1	1
TO GRAMMA	1	–	1
TO YOU.	–	1	1
TOO HIGH.	1	–	1
TOY	–	1	1
TRANSPARENCE.	–	1	1
TREE.	4	4	8
TREE TOP.	1	–	1
UP.	1	–	1
UP IN AIR	–	1	1
UP IN SKY	1	–	1
UP IN THE AIR	–	1	1
UP IN THE AIR JUMPING	1	–	1
UP IN THE SKY	–	1	1
UP ON THE SWING	1	–	1
WALLET.	1	–	1
WE GROW UP HIGH	–	1	1
WHATS UP DOC.	1	–	1
WHEN PEOPLE SAY HI.	–	1	1
WINDOWS	–	1	1
WINGS	–	1	1
WITH ME UP THERE.	–	1	1

RESPONSE WORD	M	F	T
37. HIM			
A HILL.	–	1	1
A PERSON.	1	–	1
BABY.	–	1	1
BEAR.	–	1	1
BEHAVE.	1	–	1
BELOW	1	–	1
BIB	1	–	1
BIG	1	–	1
BIKE.	1	–	1
BOY.	5	9	14
BUTTER.	1	–	1
CANDLE.	–	1	1
CAT	–	1	1
CHAIR	1	–	1
CHIMNEY	1	–	1
CHRISTMAS	1	–	1
COME.	1	–	1
COME HERE	–	1	1
COME TO DINNER.	–	1	1
COMING.	–	1	1
COON.	–	1	1
DAVID	–	1	1
DEE	1	–	1
DID	1	–	1
DIM	2	2	4
DOG.	1	–	1
DONKEY.	–	1	1
DOOR.	–	1	1
DORN.	–	1	1
DRESS	2	2	4
DRIVE	1	–	1
ENDS THE STORY.	1	–	1
EYE	2	–	2
FARMER.	–	1	1
FATHER.	–	1	1
FENCE	1	–	1
G	1	–	1
GATE.	–	1	1
GIRL.	1	2	3
GLASSES	1	–	1
GLIN.	1	–	1
GO.	1	1	2
HAM	1	–	1
HE.	1	–	1
HE BEATS HIM.	–	1	1
HE IS WORKING	1	–	1
HE WENT TO THE BATHROOM	1	–	1
HEATER.	1	–	1
HEM	1	1	2
HEN	1	–	1
HER	4	15	19
HIDE.	1	–	1
HIM IS.	–	1	1
HISSELF	1	–	1
HIT	–	1	1
HOUSE	2	–	2
HUM	1	–	1
HURRY	1	–	1
I HEM YOUR SKIRT.	–	1	1
I LIKE HIM.	1	–	1
IN.	–	2	2
INCH.	1	–	1
IS GOING OUT TO THE STORE	–	1	1
IS PLAYING.	1	–	1
IS TALL	1	–	1
JIM	1	–	1
JOHN.	1	–	1
KID	1	–	1
KIM	3	2	5
KIN	1	–	1
KLIM.	–	1	1
LIM	1	–	1
LIMB.	1	–	1
LIN	1	–	1
LITTLE.	1	2	...
MAN.	2	2	4
ME.	2	3	5
MOTHERS	–	1	1
MR.	1	–	1
NEST.	–	1	1
NOW	1	–	1
ONE	–	1	1
ONE, TWO.	–	1	1
PANTS	2	–	2
PARROT.	1	–	1
PIG.	1	–	1
PLAY WITH HIM	–	1	1
POCKET.	1	–	1

RESPONSE WORD	KINDERGARTEN M	F	T	RESPONSE WORD	KINDERGARTEN M	F	T

37. HIM

RESPONSE WORD	M	F	T	RESPONSE WORD	M	F	T
PRESENT	1	–	1	TALKING	–	1	1
RABBIT	–	1	1	THEM	–	1	1
ROOSTER	–	1	1	THIN	1	–	1
SCHOOL	1	–	1	TIM	1	–	1
SELF	1	–	1	TIMMY	1	–	1
SEW	1	1	2	TIN	1	–	1
SEWING	–	1	1	TO	1	–	1
SHE	–	7	7	TREE	1	1	2
SHOES	–	1	1	TRIM	–	1	1
SHOULDER	1	–	1	WALK	1	–	1
SIGN	1	–	1	WALKING	1	–	1
SIM	–	1	1	WALLPAPER	–	1	1
SKIRT	–	1	1	WEAR	1	–	1
SLIM	–	1	1	WEARS A SHIRT	1	–	1
SMALL	1	–	1	WEARS HAT	1	–	1
SOMEBODY	1	–	1	WENT	–	1	1
STEAL	1	–	1	WENT FOR A WALK	–	1	1
STEEL	1	–	1	WENT TO THE STORE	–	1	1
SWING	–	1	1	WHEN MEN VISIT OTHER MEN	–	1	1
SWITCH	–	1	1	WIND	–	2	2
TABLE	–	1	1	WINDOW	–	1	1
TAKES ME	–	1	1	YOU	4	–	4

38. INQUIRE

RESPONSE WORD	M	F	T	RESPONSE WORD	M	F	T
A CHOIR	1	–	1	LIAR	1	1	2
A WORD	1	–	1	LIGHT	–	3	3
ANIMAL	1	–	1	LOT	1	–	1
AT CHURCH	–	1	1	MANAGER	1	–	1
BACK	1	–	1	MAT	–	1	1
BARREL	1	–	1	MIRE	1	–	1
BE QUIET	2	1	3	MIRROR	–	1	1
BEAR	1	–	1	NET	–	1	1
BIRD	–	2	2	NIGHT	–	1	1
BIRDS	–	1	1	NO CHOIR	–	1	1
BIRTHDAY	1	–	1	NOISE	–	1	1
BOAT	2	–	2	NOISY	1	–	1
BOOK	1	–	1	NOW	1	–	1
BOTTLE	–	1	1	OUTQUIRE	1	–	1
BOYS ARE IN THE CHOIR	1	–	1	PARACHUTE	1	–	1
BROTHER	1	–	1	PENCIL	1	–	1
BRUSH YOUR TEETH	–	1	1	PEOPLE	1	1	2
BUTTER	1	–	1	PICTURE	–	1	1
CAR	1	–	1	PILLOW	–	1	1
CARRY IT	1	–	1	POCKETBOOK	1	–	1
CHAIR	1	–	1	POLE	1	–	1
CHILD	1	–	1	POLICEMAN	1	–	1
CHIRE	1	–	1	PULL OUT A PLUG	–	1	1
CHOIR	2	1	3	QUIET	3	5	8
CHOIR FROM XMAS PLAY	1	–	1	QUIRY	–	1	1
CHOIR SING	–	1	1	RADIATOR	1	–	1
CHURCH	3	8	11	RAISE YOUR HAND	–	1	1
COURSE	1	–	1	SCHOOL	–	1	1
COURT	1	–	1	SEAT	–	1	1
DISHES	–	1	1	SELFISH	1	–	1
DOG	2	1	3	SERVANT	1	–	1
DOOR	2	1	3	SILENT	1	–	1
EARS	–	1	1	SING	6	5	11
ELECTRIC	1	–	1	SING CHOIR	1	–	1
ELEPHANT	–	1	1	SING IN CHOIR	–	2	2
ENTIRE	1	–	1	SING IN THE CHOIR	1	–	1
FATHER	1	1	2	SINGING	1	4	5
FIRE	1	–	1	SIRE	1	–	1
FLOOR	–	1	1	SIT	1	–	1
FLOWER	–	1	1	SKY	–	1	1
FLOWERS	–	1	1	SLEEP	1	–	1
GAME	1	–	1	SLOW	–	1	1
GIRL	–	1	1	SONG	1	1	2
GO TO CHOIR	–	1	1	SPRING	–	1	1
HARD WORK	–	1	1	STRIKE	1	–	1
HIGH	–	1	1	TABLE	–	1	1
HIGHER	3	–	3	TABLE WHEEL	–	1	1
HORSE	–	2	2	TAKE	–	1	1
I DONT KNOW	1	1	2	TELEPHONE	–	1	1
I INQUIRED MY MOTHER	1	–	1	TELEPHONE POLE	1	–	1
I SING IN CHOIR	–	1	1	TELEVISION	–	1	1
IF TO MARRY YOU	1	–	1	THE DEFENDERS	–	1	1
IM GOING TO BE IN CHAIR	–	1	1	THE PEOPLE	–	1	1
IN	2	–	2	THEY	–	1	1
IN CHOIR PRACTICE	1	–	1	THINK	–	1	1
IN LIAR	1	–	1	TIRE	–	1	1
IN QUIRE CHURCH	–	1	1	TIRED	1	–	1
IN SPEAK	1	–	1	TO BE IN PEOPLES HOUSE	–	1	1
IN THE CHOIR	–	1	1	TO BE QUIET	–	1	1
IN THE SKY	–	1	1	TOO CHOIR	1	–	1
INBIRED	–	1	1	TREES	1	–	1
INQUIRY	–	1	1	US	–	1	1
IRON	1	–	1	VOICES	1	–	1
JAIL	1	–	1	WASH	1	–	1
LEG	1	–	1	WE PUT THE WIRE UP	–	1	1

RESPONSE WORD	KINDERGARTEN M	F	T	RESPONSE WORD	KINDERGARTEN M	F	T

38. INQUIRE

RESPONSE WORD	M	F	T	RESPONSE WORD	M	F	T
WE SING	1	–	1	WINDOW	1	–	1
WE WERE ALL IN CHOIR	–	1	1	WIRE	6	6	12
WHEN ARE THEY GOING TO FIX THE INQUIRE	1	–	1	WIRE GOING THROUGH ELECTRICITY	1	–	1
WHY	1	–	1	WORK	1	–	1

39. INSECT

RESPONSE WORD	M	F	T	RESPONSE WORD	M	F	T
A BEE	1	–	1	HURTED	1	–	1
A BUG	1	–	1	I GOT KILLED	–	1	1
A BUMBLEBEE	–	1	1	I WATCH YOU INSECT	–	1	1
ANIMAL	1	–	1	IN	6	–	6
ANT	2	1	3	IN TECT	–	1	1
BAD	–	1	1	INBECK	1	–	1
BALL	1	–	1	INDECT	1	–	1
BEE	7	6	13	INRET	–	1	1
BEES	–	1	1	INSECTS JOIN OTHER INSECTS	–	1	1
BEETLE	1	–	1	INSIDE	–	2	2
BET	1	1	2	KILL	–	1	1
BINSECT	1	–	1	KILL INSECT	–	1	1
BIRD	1	1	2	KILL IT	1	–	1
BITE	3	4	7	LAMP	–	1	1
BITE FROM	1	–	1	LIGHT	1	1	2
BITE ME	–	1	1	LIKE YOURE GOING IN A HOUSE	–	1	1
BITES	–	1	1	LIP	–	1	1
BITTEN	1	–	1	LIPSTICK	–	1	1
BLOCKS	–	1	1	MAN	1	–	1
BOAT	1	–	1	MIDDLE-SECT	1	–	1
BOOK	1	–	1	MONSTER	1	–	1
BOW	–	1	1	MOSQUITO	1	–	1
BUG	12	12	24	MOTHER	–	1	1
BUGS	3	2	5	MOTOR	1	–	1
BUMBLEBEE	–	1	1	NET	1	–	1
BUS	–	1	1	NOT	1	–	1
BUTTERFLY	–	1	1	NOW	1	–	1
BUY	–	1	1	OUTSECT	1	–	1
CANNON	1	–	1	PAPER	1	–	1
CATERPILLAR	–	1	1	PASSWORD	1	–	1
CHAIR	–	2	2	PEOPLE	–	1	1
CLOCK	–	1	1	PIG	1	–	1
COAT	–	1	1	PRAYING	1	–	1
COLLECT	1	–	1	PUMPKIN	1	–	1
COUCH	–	1	1	RAID	1	–	1
COVERED	–	1	1	RUN AND PLAY	–	1	1
CROSS	–	1	1	SECRETARY	1	–	1
DEAD	–	1	1	SECT	1	–	1
DIGSET	–	1	1	SHEEPS	1	–	1
DO SACHED	1	–	1	SHIP	1	–	1
DOCTOR	–	1	1	SIGN	1	–	1
DOG	1	–	1	SMALL	1	–	1
DOLL	–	1	1	SPIDER	2	1	3
DRESS	–	1	1	STINGS	1	–	1
EAT	1	1	2	STOP	–	1	1
EGG	–	1	1	STUNG ME	–	1	1
END	–	1	1	SUNSET	1	–	1
EVIL	–	1	1	TABLE	–	1	1
EXAMINE	–	1	1	TERMITE	–	1	1
FINK	1	–	1	THE WIRE WENT OFF	–	1	1
FLOWER	1	1	2	THERE NO INSECTS ON	–	1	1
FLY	7	6	13	THEYRE LITTLE	1	–	1
FLY AROUND	1	–	1	THREE	–	1	1
FOX	1	–	1	TINSECTS	1	–	1
GIRL	–	1	1	VAPORIZE	1	–	1
GO TO DOCTOR S	1	–	1	WE ALL DID SOME INSECT	–	1	1
GRASS	–	1	1	WHEN PEOPLE GO IN A HOUSE	–	1	1
GRASSHOPPER	2	1	3	WHEN THE INSECT BITES THE TAILOR	1	–	1
HAT	1	–	1	WINTER	1	–	1
HERE	–	1	1	WOMAN	–	1	1
HILL	–	1	1	WOODS	–	1	1
HOUSE	–	1	1				
HURRY	–	1	1				
HURT	–	1	1				

40. INTO

RESPONSE WORD	M	F	T	RESPONSE WORD	M	F	T
A BOAT	1	–	1	ANT	1	–	1
A CAVE	–	1	1	BAG	–	1	1
A DRAWER	1	–	1	BARREL	1	–	1
A HOLE	1	–	1	BAT	1	–	1
A HOUSE	1	2	3	BATHTUB	–	1	1
A MAN CHOPS WOOD IN TWO	–	1	1	BEEN TO	1	–	1
A MESS	–	1	1	BETTER NOT GO IN THERE	–	1	1
A MONKEY	1	–	1	BLACK	1	–	1
A NEST	1	–	1	BOAT	–	1	1
A PLACE	–	1	1	BOOK	1	–	1
A TRUMPET	–	1	1	BOON	–	1	1
A TUNNEL	–	1	1	BOX	1	–	1
A WINDOW	–	1	1	BROKE	1	–	1
ACORN	1	–	1	BUILDING	1	–	1

RESPONSE WORD	KINDERGARTEN M	F	T

40. INTO

RESPONSE WORD	M	F	T
BUTTERFLY	-	2	2
BUTTONS	-	1	1
CAR	1	-	1
CAVE	-	1	1
CHAIR	-	1	1
CHOO CHOO	-	1	1
CHRISTMAS TREE	1	-	1
CLOCK	-	2	2
COLD	1	-	1
COME	1	-	1
COME INTO ROOM	-	1	1
COMING	-	1	1
CRIME	-	1	1
CUP	2	-	2
CUT	-	1	1
CUT BREAD INTO	-	1	1
DINTO	-	1	1
DIS INTO	-	1	1
DOES IT GROW FROGS	-	1	1
DON T EAT CANDY	-	1	1
DONALD DUCK	-	1	1
DOOR	2	-	2
FAN	1	-	1
FINGER	-	1	1
FINISH	1	-	1
FLOWER	-	2	2
FOOD	1	-	1
FOR ALL	-	1	1
FOREST	-	2	2
FRAME	1	-	1
FUN	-	1	1
GET INTO SOMETHING	1	-	1
GETTING SOMETHING TO EAT	-	1	1
GIRAFFE	1	-	1
GIRL	-	1	1
GOT INTO A FIGHT	1	-	1
HARD WORK	-	1	1
HAT	-	1	1
HEART	-	1	1
HEAVEN	1	-	2
HIVE	1	-	1
HOLE	-	2	2
HORSE	1	-	1
HOUSE	8	7	15
I INTO WITH YOU	1	1	1
IN	1	-	1
IN A HOUSE	1	-	1
IN THE MOON	-	1	1
IN TROUBLE	1	-	1
INDIAN	2	3	5
INDOORS	-	2	2
INFUSED	1	-	1
INNERTUBE	1	-	1
INSIDE	1	1	2
INTERRUPT	-	1	1
IT	-	1	1
JAW	1	-	1
JUNK	-	1	1
LAMB	-	1	1
LETTER	1	1	2
LIGHT	1	-	1
ME	-	2	2
MESS	1	-	1
MINTO	1	-	1
MODERN	1	-	1
MONKEY	1	-	1
MOON	1	-	1
MY GABLE CAN	-	1	1
MY WAY	-	1	1
NINCOMPOOP	1	-	1
NO TO	-	1	1
NOSE	1	-	1
NOTHING	-	1	1
NUMBER	-	1	1
ONE OF THE SQUARE	1	-	1
OPENER	1	-	1
OUT	-	1	1
OUT TO	2	-	2
PAIL	-	1	1
PERSON	-	1	1
PICTURE	1	2	3
PLANT	-	1	1
PLAY INTO	1	-	1
PURPLE	1	-	1
RIGHT	-	1	1
ROUGH	1	-	1
SHADE	-	1	1
SHOUT	1	-	1
SIDE	1	-	1
SKY	1	-	1
STRAP	-	1	1
SWIM	1	-	1
SWIMMING	1	-	1
SWITCH	1	-	1
TENT	1	-	1
THE CAVE	-	1	1
THE DOG	2	-	2
THE HOUSE	2	4	6
THE TRUCK	-	1	1
THE TUNNEL	-	1	1
THE WORLD	-	1	1
THIS ROOM	1	-	1
TO	5	4	9
TOOTH PICK	-	1	1
TOOTHPASTE	-	1	1
TREE	2	1	3
TROUBLE	1	-	1
TUBE	2	-	2
TUNE	1	-	1
TWO	2	-	2
TWO NETS	1	-	1
TWO SHOES	1	-	1
WALL	-	1	1
WATER	1	-	1
WE	-	1	1
WE ALL INTO	-	1	1
WRISTWATCH	-	1	1
YOU BLOW	1	-	1
YOUR ROOM	1	-	1
YOURE SITTING THERE	1	-	1

41. IT

RESPONSE WORD	M	F	T
A LIGHT	1	-	1
A NEW TOY	1	-	1
A WALL	1	-	1
ADD	-	1	1
ANIMAL	1	-	1
AT	-	1	1
BALL	1	1	2
BASE	1	-	1
BASEBALL	1	-	1
BAT	1	-	1
BEE	1	-	1
BELIEVE ME	-	1	1
BENCH	-	1	1
BIT	2	2	4
BITE	1	1	2
BITTER	-	1	1
BOARD	1	-	1
BROKE DOWN	1	-	1
BUTTERFLY	1	-	1
CALL	-	1	1
CAR	1	-	1
CAT	1	-	1
CATCH	-	1	1
CHAIR	-	2	2
CHASE	1	-	1
CLOCK	1	-	1
COAT	-	1	1
COLOR	1	-	1
COME	1	-	1
COOL	1	-	1
COW	-	1	1
DID	1	-	1
DID DO SEEN THOSE FLOWERS	-	1	1
DIT	-	1	1
DO IT	1	-	1
DOES WE WILL DO THIS THING	1	-	1
DOG	1	-	1
DOOR	1	1	2
FETCH	-	1	1
FIGHT	-	1	1
FLIES	1	1	2
FLY	-	1	1
FLYING	-	1	1
FREEZE	1	-	1
GAME	1	-	1
GET	1	-	1
GET INTO THE CAKE	-	1	1
GIVE ME IT	1	-	1
GLASSES	-	1	1
GO	-	1	1
GRASS	1	1	2
GUN	1	1	2
HAPPENED	-	1	1

RESPONSE WORD	M	F	T	RESPONSE WORD	M	F	T

41.   IT

RESPONSE WORD	M	F	T	RESPONSE WORD	M	F	T
HAPPENED ONE DAY	1	–	1	PEOPLE SAY IT	1	–	1
HAS ELECTRICITY TO IT	–	1	1	PERSON	–	1	1
HE ATE	1	–	1	PICTURE	1	2	3
HEART	–	1	1	PIT	1	1	2
HIDE	1	–	1	PLASTIC	1	–	1
HIGH	1	–	1	PRICK	1	–	1
HIT	2	1	3	RAT	–	1	1
HIT BALL	1	–	1	RHYTHMS	–	1	1
HIT ME	–	1	1	RING	–	1	1
HIT YOU	1	–	1	RIT	1	–	1
HIT YOURSELF	–	1	1	ROUGH	1	–	1
HORSIE	–	1	1	RUN	1	–	1
HOUSE	–	1	1	SAW ME	–	1	1
I GET IT	–	1	1	SHIRT	1	–	1
I HIT MY KITTY	1	–	1	SIP	1	–	1
I SEE IT	1	–	1	SIT	3	1	4
ICE CAPADES	1	–	1	SMART	–	1	1
ICE CREAM	–	1	1	SOCK	1	–	1
IDIOT	–	1	1	SOMEBODY HIT ME	1	–	1
IF	–	2	2	SOMEPLACE	–	1	1
IS	5	4	9	SOMETHING	1	–	1
IS A BABY	–	1	1	SPIT	1	–	1
IS A LIGHT	1	–	1	STAR	1	–	1
IS A RACOON	–	1	1	STRONG	–	1	1
IS FOR SOMETHING LIKE A GUN	–	1	1	SUN	–	1	1
IS GOOD	–	1	1	TABLE	–	1	1
IS PRETTY	–	1	1	TELLS ME SOMETHING	1	–	1
IS ROLLING DOWN THE HILL	1	–	1	THAT	–	1	1
ITCH	–	1	1	THAT WILL BE IT	–	1	1
JIT	1	–	1	THEY SAY ITS A DOG	–	1	1
KICK	1	–	1	TIT	–	1	1
KIT	–	1	1	TOO MUCH OF IT	1	–	1
KITTEN	1	–	1	TOOTHBRUSH	–	1	1
LAMP	–	2	2	TOWER	–	1	1
LEE	1	–	1	TREES	1	–	1
LICK	1	–	1	TRICKS	1	–	1
LID	1	–	1	TURN THE LIGHT	1	–	1
LOVES ME	1	–	1	TV	1	–	1
MAID	–	1	1	TWEET	–	1	1
MIT	1	–	1	US	1	1	2
MITT	–	1	1	WAS	1	3	4
MUST BE	1	–	1	WAS A LION	1	–	1
MUSTARD	–	1	1	WE BIT	–	1	1
NET	–	1	1	WE DO SOMETHING	1	–	1
NICE	–	1	1	WENT	–	1	1
NOT	–	2	2	WENT SO HIGH	–	1	1
NOT IT	–	1	1	WENT TO TOWN	1	–	1
NOTE	1	–	1	WHEEL	–	1	1
OH	1	–	1	WHITE PAPER	1	–	1
ON	–	1	1	WINDOW	–	1	1
ON THE CHAIR	1	–	1	WITH	–	1	1
OUT	1	–	1	WOOD	–	1	1
PARROT	1	–	1	YOU IT SOMETHING	1	–	1
PEARL	1	–	1	YOU RE IT	–	1	1
PENCIL	–	1	1	YOUR	–	1	1
PEOPLE	–	1	1	YOURE	–	1	1
				YOURE IT	1	–	1

42.   JOIN

RESPONSE WORD	M	F	T	RESPONSE WORD	M	F	T
A CLUB	1	–	1	EAT SUPPER	–	1	1
ALICE	–	1	1	ELEPHANT	–	1	1
ALONG	–	1	1	ENJOY	1	–	1
BALL	–	1	1	EVERYBODY COMES	–	1	1
BALL GAME	1	–	1	FEEL	–	1	1
BASEBALL BAT	1	–	1	FLOOR	–	1	1
BE GOOD	–	1	1	FOIN	–	1	1
BEAR	1	–	1	FOOD	–	1	1
BEER	1	–	1	FOR SOME FUN	–	1	1
BENCH	–	1	1	FUN	4	1	5
BIRD	–	1	1	GAME	1	4	5
BIRTHDAY PARTY	1	–	1	GAMES	–	1	1
BIT	–	1	1	GANG	1	–	1
BOIN	1	1	2	GIRL SCOUTS	–	1	1
BOOK	–	1	1	GLAD TO SEE YOU	–	1	1
BOOT	1	–	1	GO	–	1	1
BOY	–	1	1	GO HOME	1	–	1
BUILDING	1	–	1	GOING	1	–	1
CAT	1	–	1	GOOD	–	1	1
CIRCUS	1	–	1	GROUP	1	–	1
CLUB	9	3	12	HAPPY	2	–	2
COIN	3	3	6	HELPING	–	1	1
COMB	–	1	1	HERE	–	2	2
COOKIE	–	1	1	HOIN	1	–	1
CRIB	–	1	1	HOME	1	–	1
CROWD	1	1	2	HORN	–	1	1
DE	1	–	1	HOUSE	2	1	3
DOG	1	–	1	I JOIN YOU	–	1	1
DUST	1	–	1	I KNOW SOMETHING IM GOING TO JOY ABOUT	1	–	1
EARRINGS	–	1	1				

RESPONSE WORD	KINDERGARTEN M	F	T

42. JOIN

RESPONSE WORD	M	F	T
IF YOU BE GOOD TO PERSONS	-	1	1
IN.	1	2	3
IN THE PARTY.	1	-	1
INTO THE PARTY.	-	1	1
JACK.	1	1	2
JAW.	-	1	1
JOIN A GAME	-	1	1
JOINING	1	-	1
JOINING TO THE PARTY.	-	1	1
JOINT	2	-	2
JOY	-	2	2
LETTER.	1	-	1
LIGHT	-	1	1
LIKE A PARADE	1	-	1
LIKE YOU GO TO A PARTY.	-	1	1
LOIN.	2	-	2
ME.	1	1	2
MEETING	-	1	1
MICKEY MOUSE CLUB	1	-	1
MOTHER.	-	1	1
MURGATROYD.	-	1	1
MY FOLKS.	1	-	1
NAVY.	2	-	2
NO RESPONSE	-	1	1
NOIN.	1	-	1
NOT JOIN.	-	1	1
OF.	1	-	1
OUR NEW CLUB.	-	1	1
OUT AT THE MOVIES	-	1	1
PALM.	-	1	1
PAN	1	-	1
PAPER	-	1	1
PARADE.	-	1	1
PARTY	4	2	6
PEOPLE.	-	1	1
PEOPLE COME TO YOUR HOUSE	1	-	1
PEOPLE COME VISIT PEOPLE.	-	1	1
PEOPLE COMING	-	1	1
PERSON.	2	-	2
PIANO	2	-	2
PICTURE	-	1	1
PLAY PAT BALL	-	1	1
POINT	2	-	2
POLITE.	-	1	1
POWDER.	1	-	1
RACE.	-	1	1
ROBBER.	1	-	1
SAW	1	-	1
SCHOOL.	-	1	1
SCOUTS.	-	1	1
SHOW.	-	1	1
SOME PEOPLES JOIN SOME OTHERS	-	1	1
SOMEBODY.	-	1	1
SWEATER	-	1	1
SWIMMING.	-	1	1
SWIMMING CLASS.	1	-	1
TABLE.	1	1	2
THANK YOU	1	1	2
THE CLUB.	1	1	2
THE FAIR.	-	1	1
THE FUN	-	1	1
THE NICE THINGS YOU HAVE.	-	1	1
THE PARADE.	2	-	2
THE PARTY.	2	2	4
THE PEOPLE.	1	-	1
THE WHOLE FAMILY.	-	1	1
THINK	-	1	1
TO A MOVIE.	1	-	1
TO THE WORLD.	1	-	1
TOGETHER.	1	1	2
TOIN.	1	-	1
TOY	-	1	1
TREE.	-	1	1
UP.	-	1	1
US.	-	1	1
VISIT	1	-	1
WALK.	1	-	1
WIFE.	-	1	1
WITH ME	-	1	1
WOIN.	-	1	1
WOOD.	1	-	1
WORLD	1	1	2
YMCA.	1	1	2
YOU	1	-	1
YOU IN.	1	-	1

43. LISTEN

RESPONSE WORD	M	F	T
AND LEARN	1	-	1
ATTENTION	1	-	1
BABY.	-	1	1
BAD	-	1	1
BARKS	-	1	1
BE NICE	1	-	1
BE QUIET.	4	4	8
BEGIN	1	-	1
BIRD.	2	1	3
BISSEN.	1	-	1
BOWL.	-	1	1
BROWN	-	1	1
BUS	1	-	1
CAREFULLY	1	-	1
CHAIR	1	2	3
CHOIR	-	1	1
CLOCK	-	1	1
CLOSE	-	1	1
CLOSE YOUR EARS	1	-	1
COME.	1	-	1
COME DOWN	1	-	1
COW	1	-	1
DISSEN.	1	-	1
DISTEN.	-	1	1
DONKEY.	1	-	1
DONT DO THAT.	-	1	1
DONT LISTEN	-	1	1
DONT TALK	1	-	1
DOOR.	-	1	1
DOOR KNOB	1	-	1
EAR	1	-	1
FLAG.	1	-	1
FLOOR	-	1	1
FOR A BIRDIE.	-	1	1
FOR A BUTTERFLIES	1	-	1
FOR A DOG	1	-	1
GARDEN.	-	1	1
GET DRESSED	1	-	1
GISTEN.	-	1	1
GO DO SOMETHING	1	-	1
GOOD.	-	1	1
GUN	-	1	1
HEAR.	4	8	12
HEAR SOMETHING.	1	-	1
HELLO	-	1	1
HERE.	1	-	1
HORSE	-	1	1
I CANT HEAR	-	1	1
I DONT TALK	-	1	1
I FEAR A FIRE ENGINE.	-	1	1
KISS.	1	-	1
KISSIN.	1	-	1
KISSING	1	-	1
LEARN	5	2	7
LID.	1	-	1
LISTEN TO SOMETHING	1	-	1
LOOK.	1	2	3
MAN	-	1	1
ME.	2	1	3
MOTHER.	1	-	1
MOUSE	-	1	1
MUSIC	1	2	3
MY HOME	-	1	1
NO.	-	2	2
NOT LISTENING	-	1	1
NOT TO SAY ANYTHING	1	-	1
NOTHING	1	-	1
PAPER	1	1	2
PAY ATTENTION	1	-	1
PEOPLE.	1	-	1
PEOPLE HEAR SOMETHING	1	-	1
QUESTION.	-	1	1
QUIET.	4	4	8
RECORD.	1	-	1
ROCK.	1	-	1
ROOF.	1	-	1
RUN AND DANCE	-	1	1
SAD	-	1	1
SIT	1	1	2
SIT DOWN.	-	1	1
SOMETHING	1	-	1
SOUND	2	2	4
SOUR.	-	1	1
STAR.	1	-	1
STORY	1	-	1
SWEET	-	1	1
TALKING	-	2	2
TEACHER	1	1	2

RESPONSE WORD	M	F	T	RESPONSE WORD	M	F	T

43. LISTEN

RESPONSE WORD	M	F	T	RESPONSE WORD	M	F	T
TISSEN.	1	–	1	TO THE TEACHER.	1	1	2
TO.	1	4	5	TO THIS.	–	1	1
TO A BEE.	1	–	1	TO WHAT IM SAYING.	1	–	1
TO A BIRD.	–	1	1	TO WHAT YOUR MOTHERS			
TO A BIRDS MOUTH.	1	–	1	SAYING TO YOU.	1	–	1
TO A CALL.	1	–	1	TO YOUR MOTHER.	4	1	5
TO A RECORD.	1	–	1	TO YOUR STORY.	1	–	1
TO FIRE TRUCKS.	1	–	1	TOO.	–	1	1
TO I WILL TELL YOU.	–	1	1	TOO LISTEN.	1	–	1
TO ME.	3	5	8	TRAIN.	–	1	1
TO MOMMY.	1	–	1	WAIT YOUR TURN.	–	1	1
TO MOTHER.	–	1	1	WATCH.	–	1	1
TO MUSIC.	–	1	1	WE LISTENED TO THE BIRDIE	–	1	1
TO PERSON.	–	1	1	WELL.	1	–	1
TO RADIO.	–	1	1	WENT.	–	1	1
TO SOUNDS.	1	–	1	WHAT YOUR MOTHER SAYS	–	1	1
TO THE BELL	1	–	1	WHAT YOURE DOING.	1	–	1
TO THE BIRD SING.	1	–	1	WHEN A LITTLE GIRLS			
TO THE MUSIC.	1	–	1	LISTENING.	–	1	1
TO THE OTHER PEOPLE	1	–	1	WINDOW.	1	–	1
TO THE PEOPLE	–	1	1	WONDER.	2	–	2
TO THE RECORD	–	1	1	WOOD.	2	1	3
TO THE STORY.	–	1	1	WORD.	1	–	1

44. LONG

RESPONSE WORD	M	F	T	RESPONSE WORD	M	F	T
A BANANAS KINDA LONG.	1	–	1	MIDNIGHT.	–	1	1
A CANNON.	1	–	1	MOMMY	–	1	1
A LOG IS REAL LONG.	–	1	1	MOTOR	1	–	1
A LONG MAN.	1	–	1	MOWER	2	–	2
AWAY.	–	1	1	MR SMITHS LAWN.	1	–	1
BANANA.	1	1	2	NAP	–	1	1
BAR.	–	1	1	ONLY DOOR CLOSE	–	1	1
BEAN.	1	–	1	ORANGE.	–	1	1
BELL.	1	–	1	PAN	–	1	1
BIG.	1	–	1	PAPER	–	1	1
BIRD.	–	2	2	PASTURE	1	–	1
BLACK.	1	–	1	PEOPLE.	2	–	2
BOARD.	1	1	2	PIECE OF STRING	1	–	1
BONG.	1	–	1	PLANT	1	–	1
BOOK.	–	2	2	PLAY.	–	1	1
BUILDING.	2	–	2	POCKETBOOK.	1	–	1
CLOCK.	–	1	1	PONG.	1	–	1
CONG.	1	–	1	REAL LONG	–	1	1
COOKIE.	1	–	1	RIDE.	3	1	4
CUT	–	2	2	ROAD.	1	1	2
CUTTING THE GRASS	1	–	1	ROPE.	2	3	5
DAY	1	–	1	RUBBER.	1	–	1
DOG	–	2	2	RUBBERBAND.	1	–	1
DONT BE LONG.	–	1	1	RUN	1	1	2
DOOR.	–	1	1	SCREAM.	1	–	1
DRESS	–	1	1	SHAWN	1	–	1
DUCK.	–	1	1	SHORT.	6	3	9
FATHER.	–	2	2	SHORTY-LONG	1	–	1
FIELD	1	–	1	SKINNY.	–	2	2
FISH.	1	1	2	SKIRT	–	1	1
FISHING RIDE.	1	–	1	SLOWLY.	1	–	1
FREE.	–	1	1	SNAKE.	–	1	1
GIANT	1	–	1	SO LONG	1	–	1
GIRAFFE	1	–	1	SOMETHING IS LONG	–	1	1
GIRL.	1	–	1	SOMETHINGS LONG	1	–	1
GONE.	–	1	1	SONG.	1	1	2
GONG.	–	1	1	SPIDER.	–	1	1
GOOD.	–	1	1	STORY	–	1	1
GRASS	7	9	16	STRETCH	1	–	1
GRASS LAWNMOWER	1	–	1	STRING.	1	1	2
GREEN	1	2	3	SUPPER.	1	–	1
GRONG	1	–	1	SWING	1	–	1
HAIR.	–	1	1	TABLE	1	1	2
HELLO	–	1	1	TAIL.	1	–	1
HERE.	–	2	2	TAKE LONG	–	1	1
HIGH.	–	1	1	THING	–	1	1
HOME.	–	1	1	THIS IS A LONG STORY.	–	1	1
HONG.	1	–	1	TIME.	6	1	7
HOOP.	–	1	1	TIME AGO.	1	–	1
HOSE.	–	1	1	TOO LONG.	1	–	1
HOUSE.	–	1	1	TRAIL	–	1	1
I TAKE A LONG WALK.	–	1	1	TREE.	2	1	3
IT WAS A LONG MOVIE	–	1	1	UP.	1	–	1
ITS A LONG BRIDGE	1	–	1	WAIT.	–	1	1
LAWN.	2	–	2	WALK.	3	–	3
LAWN MOWER.	2	1	3	WATER.	1	–	1
LAWNMOWER	2	3	5	WAY.	–	1	1
LIGHT.	–	1	1	WE MOW LAWN	–	1	1
LITTLE.	–	2	2	WELL.	1	–	1
LOG.	1	–	1	WHEN PEOPLE CUT THE GRASS	1	–	1
LOGS.	–	1	1	WHERE.	–	1	1
LONG RIDE	1	–	1	WINDOW.	–	1	1
LONG TONG	–	1	1	WOOD.	3	1	4
LONK.	1	–	1	WORD.	1	–	1
LOW.	–	1	1				

RESPONSE WORD	KINDERGARTEN M	F	T

45. LOUD

RESPONSE WORD	M	F	T
ALLOWED	–	1	1
AND CLEAR	1	–	1
BABY	–	1	1
BANG	1	–	1
BAT	1	–	1
BEAR	–	1	1
BELT	1	–	1
BIRDIES	–	1	1
BLACK	1	–	1
BOLD	–	1	1
BOUD	–	1	1
BOW	1	–	1
BOWED	1	1	2
BOYS	1	–	1
CALL	–	1	1
CHARGE	–	1	1
CHILDREN PLAY REAL LOUD	–	1	1
CLOUD	4	2	6
COME IN	1	–	1
COUD	1	–	1
COUNT	1	–	1
COWED	1	–	1
CROWD	1	–	1
CRY	1	–	1
CRYING	–	3	3
DISH	–	1	1
DOG RUN FASTER	–	1	1
DOGGIE	1	–	1
DONT SHOUT OUT LOUD	1	–	1
DRAFT	1	–	1
DRINK	–	1	1
EARACHE	1	–	1
ELEPHANT	1	–	1
FACE	1	–	1
FOUD	–	1	1
GENTLY	–	1	1
GIANT	–	1	1
GIVE	–	1	1
GRASS	–	1	1
HEAR	1	–	1
HERE	–	1	1
HOLD YOUR EARS	1	–	1
HOLLER	4	1	5
HOLLERING	1	–	1
HORN	1	–	1
HOUD	1	–	1
HOW	2	–	2
HOW DO YOU DO THAT	–	1	1
HURTS MY EARS	1	–	1
I SPEAK TO MOTHER LOUD	–	1	1
IM SINGING OUT LOUD	–	1	1
LADDER	2	–	2
LADY	–	1	1
LIGHT	–	1	1
LIKE YOURE SCREAMING	–	1	1
LION	1	–	1
LITTLE	–	1	1
LOG	1	–	1
LOLLIPOP	1	–	1
LOUD US	1	–	1
LOUDLY	–	2	2
LOUK	–	1	1
LOW	2	5	7
MONEY	1	–	1
MOTHERS	–	1	1
MOUTH	4	1	5
MUSIC	2	–	2
NO NOISE	1	–	1
NOISE	3	5	8
OUT	1	–	1
OW	1	–	1
PART OF A BUILDING	1	–	1
PEOPLE	1	1	2
PERSON	–	1	1
PICTURE	–	1	1
PIPE	1	–	1
PLAY	–	2	2
PLOW	1	–	1
PLUG	–	1	1
QUIET	5	7	12
RACKET	1	–	1
REAL LOUD	–	1	1
RUN	–	1	1
SCOUT	1	–	1
SCREAM	6	4	10
SCREAM YOUR HEAD OFF	–	1	1
SCREAMING	2	–	2
SEW	–	1	1
SHOUD	1	–	1
SHOUT	4	3	7
SHOUTING	–	1	1
SHUT UP	–	1	1
SLOW	1	1	2
SOFT	4	5	9
SOFTLY	–	1	1
SOMETHING TALL	–	1	1
SOUND	–	1	1
STOP	–	2	2
SUN	1	–	1
SWEATER	1	–	1
TABLE	–	2	2
TALK	2	3	5
TALK LOUD	–	1	1
TALKING	1	–	1
TOO LOUD	2	1	3
TOO MUCH NOISE	–	1	1
TOUD	1	–	1
TROUSERS	–	1	1
VOICE	2	–	2
WALL	–	1	1
WARM	1	–	1
WE CLOSE OUR EARS	–	1	1
WHAT YOU HEAR SOMETHING	–	1	1
YARD	1	–	1
YELL	3	2	5
YOU TALK TOO MUCH	–	1	1

46. LOUDLY

RESPONSE WORD	M	F	T
A LOUD VOICE	1	–	1
AIRPLANE	1	–	1
ALOUD	–	1	1
AND CLEARLY	1	–	1
BE QUIET	–	1	1
BEADS	1	–	1
BIRDS	–	1	1
BLANKET	1	–	1
BOARD	–	1	1
BORED	1	–	1
BOUVELY	1	–	1
BOYS	1	–	1
BREAK	1	–	1
CANT HEAR	1	–	1
CAR	1	1	2
CARE	–	1	1
CHAIN	–	1	1
CHAIR	1	1	2
CHILD	–	1	1
CHILDREN	1	–	1
CHIMNEY	1	–	1
CLAD	–	1	1
CLOTHES	–	1	1
CLOUD	2	–	2
COAT	1	1	2
COME NOW	1	–	1
COUDLY	–	1	1
COW	1	–	1
CROSS	–	1	1
CRYING	–	1	1
DON T DO IT	–	1	1
DONT TALK SO LOUDLY	–	1	1
DOOR	3	–	3
DOWLY	–	1	1
EAR	1	–	1
EYES	–	1	1
FARM	–	1	1
FIGHTING	–	1	1
FLOWER	2	–	2
FLOWERS	–	1	1
FOUDLY	1	–	1
GIRL	–	1	1
GO SWIMMING	–	1	1
GOUDLY	1	–	1
GRASS	–	1	1
HAVE TO BE QUIET WHEN DADDYS SLEEPING	–	1	1
HEAR	1	1	2
HEARING	–	2	2
HOLD YOUR EARS ITS TOO LOUD	–	1	1
HOLLER	3	1	4
HOUDLY	1	–	1
HOUSE	1	–	1
HURTS MY EARS	1	–	1
I DONT WANT TO HEAR IT	1	–	1
I SPEAK LOUD	–	1	1
I TALK LOUD	–	1	1

RESPONSE WORD	KINDERGARTEN M	F	T	RESPONSE WORD	KINDERGARTEN M	F	T

46. LOUDLY

RESPONSE WORD	M	F	T	RESPONSE WORD	M	F	T
IM VERY LOUD.	1	–	1	SHOUTED	1	–	1
INDIAN.	–	1	1	SIDEWALK.	–	1	1
JUMP.	1	–	1	SILENT.	–	1	1
LAY	–	1	1	SING.	–	1	1
LIGHT	–	1	1	SKIP.	–	1	1
LION.	1	–	1	SLOW.	–	1	1
LIPSTICK.	–	1	1	SLOWLY.	1	2	3
LISTEN.	1	–	1	SMOOTH.	1	–	1
LOUD.	2	2	4	SNOW.	1	–	1
LOUD MOUTH.	1	–	1	SOFT.	–	3	3
LOVE.	1	–	1	SOFTLY.	2	5	7
LOVELY.	1	–	1	SOMETHING IS LOUD	–	1	1
LOW	–	1	1	SOUND	–	1	1
LYING	1	–	1	SOUTH	1	–	1
MAN	1	–	1	SPEAK	3	–	3
MOUTH	2	–	2	STOP.	–	1	1
MUSIC	1	–	1	SWEET	–	1	1
NOISE	–	3	3	TALK.	3	3	6
OUT	1	–	1	TALK TOO MUCH	–	1	1
PART OF A TREE.	1	–	1	TALKING	–	1	1
PARTIES	1	–	1	TELEVISION.	1	–	1
PENCIL.	–	1	1	TOO LOUD.	3	1	4
PEOPLE.	2	–	2	TOVELY.	1	–	1
PEOPLE WILL SHOUT	–	1	1	TOWEL	1	–	1
POUDLY.	1	–	1	VOICE	–	1	1
PRETTY.	2	–	2	WALK.	1	2	3
PUSSIES	1	–	1	WALL.	1	–	1
QUIET	2	8	10	WATER	–	1	1
QUIETLY	1	3	4	WE DON T GO TO.	–	1	1
RECORD.	1	–	1	WE LOUDLY WENT TO THE			
ROOSTER	1	–	1	STORE.	–	1	1
SAIL.	–	1	1	WE SCREAM	1	–	1
SAY	–	2	2	WHEN CHILDREN PLAY LOUD	–	1	1
SCREAM.	4	5	9	WHEN PEOPLE HOLLER.	1	–	1
SCREAM OUT LOUD	1	–	1	WORK.	–	1	1
SCREAMING	–	1	1	YELL.	3	–	3
SCREECH	–	1	1	YELLING	1	–	1
SEE	–	1	1	YOU TALK.	1	–	1
SHOUT	3	2	5				

47. MAINTAIN

RESPONSE WORD	M	F	T	RESPONSE WORD	M	F	T
A HORSE NAMED MAINTAIN.	–	1	1	FOOD.	1	–	1
A LION.	1	–	1	FOR SOMETHING	–	1	1
A MAN TAMES THE LION.	1	–	1	FOUND	–	1	1
A MOO COW	–	1	1	FOX	1	–	1
A RECORD.	–	1	1	FRUIT	–	1	1
A TANK.	–	1	1	G	–	1	1
BACTINE	–	1	1	GET BROWN	–	1	1
BASEBALL.	1	–	1	GLASS	1	3	4
BIRD.	1	2	3	GLASSES	–	1	1
BOOK.	–	1	1	HAM	1	–	1
BOTTLE.	1	–	1	HANDLE.	–	1	1
BOX	–	1	1	HANE.	–	1	1
BRIDGE.	–	1	1	HAT	1	–	1
BUCKET.	1	–	1	HEAVENLY.	–	1	1
BUILDING.	1	–	1	HEN.	–	1	1
BUTTER.	1	–	1	HORSE	1	2	3
BUTTON.	1	–	1	HOUSE	–	1	1
CALINTAIN	1	–	1	HOUSES.	–	1	1
CAME.	1	1	2	I DONT KNOW	1	–	1
CAMPING	–	1	1	I MAINTAIN MY GASSER.	1	–	1
CAN.	1	1	2	I PLAY IN THE SAND.	–	1	1
CANE.	3	–	3	JESUS	–	1	1
CANTEEN	3	–	3	KAY	–	1	1
CARDBOARD	–	1	1	KITE.	1	–	1
CAT	–	1	1	KITTEN.	1	–	1
CHAIR	1	2	3	LAT	1	–	1
CHAMPAGNE	1	1	2	LAWNMOWER	1	–	1
CHANGE.	–	1	1	LEAF.	1	–	1
CHOCOLATE	–	1	1	LEMONADE.	–	1	1
CLAMP	–	1	1	LIGHT	1	–	1
COLD.	–	1	1	LIGHTING.	1	–	1
COLORING BOOK	–	1	1	LION.	3	–	3
CONTAINER	–	2	2	LION TAMER.	–	1	1
COOK.	1	–	1	LION TRAINER.	1	–	1
COWBOY.	–	1	1	LITTLE.	–	1	1
DEAR.	–	1	1	LITTLE TREE	1	–	1
DOG.	2	1	3	LOST.	–	1	1
DOOR.	1	1	2	LOTS OF	–	1	1
DOOR HANDLE	–	1	1	MADE FOR EVERYBODY.	–	1	1
DRINK.	1	1	2	MAIN.	3	–	3
EAT HAM	1	–	1	MAIN IN TAINT	1	–	1
EGG	–	1	1	MAINCHAIN	1	–	1
ENTAINED.	1	–	1	MAKE A CHAIN.	1	–	1
ENTERTAIN	–	1	1	MAN	1	2	3
FAIRY	–	1	1	MAN–MAN	1	–	1
FATHER DRINK.	–	1	1	MANAGER	1	–	1
FINGERNAIL.	–	1	1	MANE ON HORSES BACK	–	1	1
FLOWER.	–	2	2	MANGER.	–	2	2

RESPONSE WORD	KINDERGARTEN M	F	T

47. MAINTAIN

RESPONSE WORD	M	F	T
MATING.	–	1	1
MAYONNAISE.	1	1	2
ME.	1	–	1
MEAN.	1	–	1
MEND.	1	–	1
MORE FAT.	1	–	1
MOTORCYCLE.	1	–	1
MUSIC.	–	1	1
MY NAME IS MAN TAY.	1	–	1
NAIL.	1	–	1
NUMBER.	1	1	2
ONE.	1	–	1
ONE GARBAGE CAN.	1	–	1
ORANGE JUICE.	–	1	1
OWL.	1	–	1
PEACE.	–	1	1
PEOPLE.	2	1	3
PICTURE.	1	–	1
PLUG.	1	–	1
RECEIVE.	–	1	1
REST.	1	–	1
RIDE.	–	1	1
RIVERBOAT.	–	1	1
SALT.	1	–	1
SEE.	1	–	1
SHE.	1	–	1
SNOW.	1	–	1
STABLE.	1	–	1
STAIN.	1	–	1
STAIN FURNITURE.	1	–	1
STING.	1	–	1
SUGAR.	2	–	2
SUN FLOWER.	1	–	1
SWEEP.	–	1	1
TABLE.	–	1	1
TAIN.	–	2	2
TAME A DOG.	–	1	1
TAME HORSES.	–	1	1
TAMER.	1	–	1
TANE.	–	1	1
TEEN.	1	–	1
TENGKANE.	–	1	1
THAINFAIN.	1	–	1
THAT YOU USE WITH.	–	1	1
THE AMMUNITION.	1	–	1
THE ANIMALS.	1	–	1
THE BOX.	–	1	1
THE MAINTAIN RAN AWAY.	–	1	1
THIS.	1	1	2
TIE.	1	–	1
TIGERS.	1	–	1
TOO TAIN.	1	–	1
TRAIN.	4	–	4
TRASH CAN.	1	–	1
TRYING.	–	1	1
WANT TO DANCE.	–	1	1
WATER.	2	1	3
WHEN A MANS TAMING AN ANIMAL.	–	1	1
WHISKEY.	–	1	1
WINDOW.	–	1	1
WINE.	1	–	1
WORD.	–	1	1
WRISTWATCH.	–	1	1

48. MAN

RESPONSE WORD	M	F	T
A GIRL.	–	1	1
A LADY.	–	1	1
AND WOMAN.	–	1	1
AT OFFICE.	1	–	1
BAD.	1	–	1
BIG.	1	1	2
BOOK.	–	1	1
BOY.	4	–	4
BRAIN.	1	–	1
BUCKET.	1	–	1
BUSY.	–	1	1
BUYING.	1	–	1
CAN.	2	–	2
CANTEEN.	1	–	1
CAR.	3	1	4
CEMENT.	–	1	1
CHURCH.	1	–	1
CLOTHES.	–	2	2
COME IN.	1	–	1
COMING.	–	1	1
COUSIN.	–	1	1
CUT.	1	–	1
DAD.	1	–	1
DADDY.	2	–	2
DAN.	–	1	1
DANCE.	1	–	1
DANGER.	1	–	1
DOG.	–	3	3
DRIT.	–	1	1
DUMPTRUCK.	1	–	1
EAT.	–	1	1
FACE.	–	1	1
FAN.	–	1	1
FARMER.	1	–	1
FATHER.	3	3	6
FENCE.	1	–	1
FOOD.	3	–	3
GET MAD.	1	–	1
GIANT.	1	–	1
GIRL.	2	1	3
GOD.	–	1	1
GOES TO THE STORE.	–	1	1
GOING INTO THE FOREST.	1	–	1
GOING TO HIS OFFICE.	–	1	1
GOING TO WORK.	–	1	1
GROWN-UP.	1	–	1
HAIR.	–	2	2
HAND.	3	5	8
HANDS.	1	–	1
HAS ARM.	1	–	1
HAT.	4	1	5
HEAD.	2	–	2
HI DADDY.	–	1	1
HORSE.	–	1	1
HORSIE.	–	1	1
HOT.	1	–	1
HUSBAND.	–	1	1
I LIKE THE MAN.	1	–	1
IS GOING OUT TO WORK.	–	1	1
IS GOING TO WORK.	1	–	1
IT.	–	1	1
JAN.	–	1	1
JOIN THE MEN.	1	–	1
JOINS SOME OTHER MANS.	–	1	1
KISSING.	–	1	1
LADY.	5	7	12
LAND.	2	–	2
LUNCH BOX.	1	–	1
MAD.	2	–	2
MARRY.	1	–	1
MEAN.	–	1	1
MONKEY.	–	1	1
MOTH.	1	–	1
MOTHER.	1	2	3
MR.	–	1	1
MY FATHER.	–	1	1
OFFICE.	1	–	1
OH.	–	1	1
ONE ANOTHER.	–	1	1
PAN.	–	1	1
PEOPLE.	–	3	3
PIANO.	1	–	1
PICTURE.	1	–	1
PLAY BALL.	–	1	1
POP GEORGE.	–	1	1
RAN.	–	1	1
READING A BOOK.	–	1	1
ROAD.	–	1	1
RUN.	1	–	1
SCOOT.	1	–	1
SEE THE MAN.	–	1	1
SHAKE HANDS.	–	1	1
SHAN.	1	–	1
SHOE.	1	–	1
SICK.	–	1	1
SKIN.	1	–	1
SLAN.	1	–	1
SOME MAN ARE IN JOBS.	1	–	1
STATUE.	1	–	1
STICK.	–	1	1
STORY.	1	–	1
STRONG.	1	–	1
SWING.	–	1	1
TABLE.	–	1	1
TALK.	1	–	1
TALL.	1	2	3
TAN.	1	–	1
WALK.	6	1	7
WALKING.	1	1	2
WALKING HOME.	–	1	1

RESPONSE WORD	M	F	T	RESPONSE WORD	M	F	T

48. MAN

RESPONSE WORD	M	F	T	RESPONSE WORD	M	F	T
WEARS HAT	1	–	1	WHITE	1	–	1
WENT	–	1	1	WIFE	1	1	2
WHEN SOMEBODYS SAYING MAN	–	1	1	WOMAN	7	13	20
WHEN YOU GO ON TRAIN	1	–	1	WORK	1	2	3

49. MIX

RESPONSE WORD	M	F	T	RESPONSE WORD	M	F	T
A BOWL	–	1	1	LIPS	1	–	1
A CAKE	3	5	8	MAKE CAKE	–	1	1
A DRINK	1	–	1	MAKING CAKE	–	1	1
A RAT	1	–	1	MIK	1	–	1
AT	1	–	1	MILK	2	–	2
BABY	1	–	1	MITCH MILLER	–	1	1
BAKE	–	1	1	MITTENS	1	1	2
BAKE A CAKE	1	–	1	MIX-UP	–	1	1
BATTER	2	1	3	MIXER	2	2	4
BEAR	–	1	1	MIXING A CAKE	1	1	2
BEATER	1	2	3	MIXING SOUP	–	1	1
BEATERS	1	–	1	MIXMASTER	–	1	1
BELLS	–	1	1	MIXTURE	–	1	1
BIRDIE FEET	1	–	1	NESTLES QUICK	1	–	1
BITTER CAKE	–	1	1	NEXT	1	–	1
BOWL	1	4	5	ORANGE	1	–	1
BOX	–	1	1	PAN	–	1	1
BUTTER	2	–	2	PANCAKE	1	–	1
CAKE	13	23	36	PENCIL	–	1	1
CAKE MIX	1	–	1	PRETTY	–	1	1
CARE	1	–	1	PUT BUTTER IN IT	1	–	1
CAT	1	–	1	PUT SOME FLOUR IN, THEN MIX THE EGGS IN	1	–	1
CEMENT	3	–	3	SALAD	1	–	1
CEMENT MIXER	1	–	1	SAND BOX	–	1	1
COOK	–	1	1	SAUCE	1	1	2
COOKIE	1	1	2	SAUCES	–	1	1
CREAM	–	1	1	SICK	1	–	1
DIX	1	1	2	SIP	–	1	1
DOG	1	1	2	SITS	1	–	1
DOUGH	–	1	1	SIX	1	–	1
DRINK	–	1	1	SOIL	–	1	1
DYNAMITE	1	–	1	SOME LIQUID	1	–	1
EGG	–	2	2	SOMEONE IS MAKING SOMETHING	–	1	1
EGG NOG	1	–	1	SOMETHING	2	–	2
EGG-BEATER	1	–	1	SOUP	1	–	1
EGGS	1	–	1	SPOON	–	3	3
FEATHERS	1	–	1	STEER	1	–	1
FENCE	1	–	1	STEW	1	1	2
FIX	1	–	1	STICKS	1	–	1
FLOUR	1	–	1	STIR	2	–	2
FLOUR MIX	1	–	1	SUGAR	1	1	2
FLYER	–	1	1	TABLE	–	2	2
FOOD	1	–	1	THAT YOU PUT ON FROSTING	–	2	2
GIX	–	1	1	THE CAKE	–	2	2
GLASS	1	–	1	THE MILK	1	–	1
GLOVES	–	1	1	THE MIXTURE	–	1	1
HEAD	1	–	1	TICKS	–	3	3
HEATER	1	–	1	TICS	1	–	1
HIC	1	–	1	TOO OF A MIXTURE	1	–	1
HIP	1	–	1	TRUCK	1	–	1
HORSE	–	1	1	TWO WINDOWS	–	1	1
I MIXED IT WITH SOIL	1	–	1	UP	2	2	4
I WAS MIXING SOME THINGS UP TOGETHER	–	1	1	UP THIS	–	1	1
ICING	1	–	1	UP WITH ONIONS	–	1	1
IM MIXING SOMETHING FOR MY SON	1	–	1	WASHING MACHINE	1	–	1
IT WITH CONCRETE	1	–	1	WATER	1	–	1
JIX	1	–	1	WHITE STUFF	–	1	1
KICK	1	–	1	WITH A SPOON	–	1	1
KISS	–	1	1	WITH FLOURS	–	1	1
KNIT	1	–	1	WITH THE FROSTING BOWL	1	–	1
LICKS	1	–	1	YOURE MIXED UP	–	1	1
LIGHT	–	1	1				

50. MOTH

RESPONSE WORD	M	F	T	RESPONSE WORD	M	F	T
A BUG THAT FLIES	–	1	1	BOTH	–	1	1
A MOSS IS GROWING IN THE WINDOW	1	–	1	BRIDGE	–	1	1
A RAT	1	–	1	BROOM	–	1	1
A WASP	1	–	1	BROTH	1	–	1
ANT EATER	–	1	1	BRUSH	1	–	1
ARE SO THE BEES WONT GET IN	–	1	1	BUG	2	3	5
BABY	1	–	1	BUTTERFLIES HAVE MOTHS	1	–	1
BALL	4	4	8	BUTTERFLY	4	2	6
BALLS	–	1	1	CAT	–	1	1
BAND	–	1	1	CATCH	–	2	2
BAR	–	1	1	CATCH THE MOTH	1	–	1
BENT	1	–	1	CHAIR	1	–	1
BIRD	–	1	1	CHILD	–	1	1
				CHOCOLATE	–	1	1
				CHURCH	1	–	1

RESPONSE WORD	M	F	T	RESPONSE WORD	M	F	T

50. MOTH

RESPONSE WORD	M	F	T	RESPONSE WORD	M	F	T
CLOTH	4	3	7	NEW SHOES	1	–	1
CLOTHES	1	1	2	NIGHT	1	–	1
COAT	1	1	2	NOTH	1	–	1
COUGH	–	2	2	NOTHING	–	1	1
COW	1	–	1	OFF	1	–	1
CUP	–	1	1	ON THE FLOOR	–	1	1
DOFF	–	1	1	ON THE WINDOW	1	–	1
DOG	–	1	1	ON TV	1	–	1
DRINK	1	–	1	ONE DAY	–	1	1
DUMPLINGS	1	–	1	ORANGE PAINT	1	–	1
DUST	1	1	2	PEN	1	–	1
EAT	1	1	2	PETE	1	–	1
FLY	7	5	12	PICTURE	–	1	1
FLY SWATTER	1	–	1	POCKETBOOK	–	1	1
FLYING	–	1	1	POFF	1	–	1
FLYS	–	1	1	POTH	1	1	2
FOR SPIDER	1	–	1	POTTY	–	1	1
FRAME	–	1	1	RADIO	1	–	1
FUR	1	–	1	RAT	1	–	1
FURNITURE	–	1	1	RING	1	–	1
GARDEN	1	–	1	RUNS AND DANCE	–	1	1
GET	–	1	1	SAND	–	1	1
GETTING IT WITH A NET	–	1	1	SILLY	–	1	1
GOLF	–	1	1	SINK	–	1	1
GOTH	–	1	1	SLAP	1	–	1
GREEN	1	1	2	SMOKE	1	–	1
HAIR	–	1	1	SNOW	–	1	1
HE CLIMBS ON WINDOWS	–	1	1	SOFT	–	2	2
HOLES	–	1	1	SOMETHING THAT FLIES	1	–	1
HOME	1	–	1	SPIDER	1	1	2
HORSE	1	–	1	SPRAYING	–	1	1
HOUSE	–	1	1	STEPS	1	–	1
I MOTHED OUT THE HOUSE	1	–	1	STING	2	–	2
I PLAY WITH MY MOTHER	–	1	1	STONE	–	1	1
ICE CREAM	1	–	1	STORM	–	1	1
IM DRYING THE FLOOR WITH A MOTH	1	–	1	STUPID	1	–	1
IS FLYING	–	1	1	SWINGING AROUND	–	1	1
ITCHES ME	1	–	1	TABLE	–	1	1
K	–	1	1	TAUGHT YOU	–	1	1
KILL	–	2	2	TELEPHONE	–	1	1
LADYBUG	1	–	1	THAT FLIES IN THE AIR	1	–	1
LAID	–	1	1	THOUGHT	–	1	1
LIGHT	–	1	1	TOO MUCH OF MOTH	1	–	1
LIKE A SEALS NAME	–	1	1	TOSS	1	–	1
LOST	1	–	1	TOWEL	–	1	1
LOVE	–	1	1	TREE	–	1	1
MARBLE	1	–	1	TROUGH	1	1	2
MARTHA	1	–	1	TRUCK BROKE DOWN	1	–	1
ME	–	1	1	TURNS INTO A BUTTERFLY	1	–	1
MEN	–	1	1	WALK	1	–	1
MOF	1	–	1	WALL	–	1	1
MOMMY	–	1	1	WASHCLOTH	1	–	1
MOON	1	–	1	WASP	1	–	1
MOOSH	1	–	1	WATCH	1	–	1
MOP	–	1	1	WATER	–	1	1
MOP THE FLOOR	2	–	2	WERE	1	–	1
MOPH	1	–	1	WHEN THEYRE PUTTING A TABLECLOTH ON	–	1	1
MOSS	1	–	1	WINDOW	–	1	1
MOTH BALL	1	–	1	WING	1	–	1
MOTHER	–	1	1	WITH	1	–	1
MUFFIN PAN	–	1	1	WORM	1	–	1
MY MOTHER WAS CLEANING WITH THE MOTH	–	1	1	ZERO	1	–	1

51. MOVE

RESPONSE WORD	M	F	T	RESPONSE WORD	M	F	T
ACROSS STREET	1	–	1	CLOUD	–	1	1
ALONG	–	1	1	COON	–	1	1
ANIMAL	1	–	1	COW	3	2	5
ARM	–	1	1	COW MOOS	–	1	1
AROUND	–	1	1	D	1	–	1
AWAY	–	3	3	DIRT	2	–	2
AWAY FROM A HOUSE TO ANOTHER ONE	1	–	1	DO	1	–	1
BABY	–	2	2	DOCTOR	–	1	1
BALL	1	–	1	DOG	1	–	1
BEARS	1	–	1	DON T MOVE SIT NICE	–	1	1
BIKE	1	–	1	DONT	1	1	2
BOARD	1	–	1	DONT MOVE	–	2	2
BODY	1	–	1	DOOR	1	3	4
BOOK	1	–	1	FAST	1	–	1
BOOKS	–	1	1	FATHER	–	1	1
BOVE	–	1	1	FEET	3	1	4
BOY	–	1	1	FRIEND	1	–	1
BUFFALO	–	1	1	FROOVE	1	–	1
BUREAU	–	1	1	FROZEN	–	1	1
CAR	10	2	12	GET OUT OF THE WAY	–	1	1
CHAIR	–	1	1	GET UP	1	–	1
CLOCK	1	–	1	GET YOUR SHOES	1	–	1
				GO BACKWARDS	1	–	1

RESPONSE WORD	KINDERGARTEN M	F	T	RESPONSE WORD	KINDERGARTEN M	F	T

51. MOVE

RESPONSE WORD	M	F	T	RESPONSE WORD	M	F	T
GOING ON A VACATION	1	–	1	RING	–	1	1
GRASSHOPPER	1	–	1	RUN	–	2	2
HAT	1	–	1	SELL	–	1	1
HIVE	1	–	1	SHOES	–	2	2
HONEY	1	–	1	SIT	1	1	2
HORSE	1	1	2	SKIN	–	1	1
HOUSE	3	–	3	SKIRT	–	1	1
I CAN MOVE THAT	1	–	1	SLOW	1	1	2
I DARE YOU TO	1	–	1	SMOOTH	–	1	1
ICE	–	1	1	SOFT	–	1	1
JEW	1	–	1	SOMEWHERE	1	–	1
LAWN	1	–	1	STAY	–	1	1
LEGS	2	1	3	STEAMROLLER	1	–	1
LIKE YOURE MOVING A BIKE	–	1	1	STEP	–	1	1
LUVE	1	–	1	STILL	1	2	3
MAN	–	1	1	STOP	–	2	2
ME	–	1	1	SUET	1	–	1
MOO	2	–	2	SUN	–	1	1
MOON	1	2	3	SUNNY	1	–	1
MOON ON THE MAN	–	1	1	SWEEPER	1	–	1
MOUSSE	–	1	1	TABLE	–	3	3
MOVE OVER	–	1	1	THAT TRUCK	1	–	1
MOVELY	1	–	1	THAT YOU MOVE SOMETHING	1	–	1
MOVIE	–	1	1	THE CAR	1	–	1
MOVING	–	2	2	THE CHAIR	1	–	1
MOVING A COW	–	1	1	THE COW MOOS	–	1	1
MOVING VAN	–	1	1	THE FLYING SAUCER	1	–	1
MOW	–	1	1	THE HOUSE	1	–	1
MULE	–	1	1	THE TRAIN	1	–	1
MUSCLE	1	–	1	THE TURTLE	–	1	1
MY FURNITURE	–	1	1	THIS	1	–	1
NEVER MOVE,YOU GOT A BROKEN LEG	–	1	1	THIS TRAIN	1	–	1
NEW	–	1	1	TO ANOTHER HOUSE	–	1	1
NEW HOUSE	–	1	1	TO HOLLYWOOD	1	–	1
NICE MOVE	1	–	1	TO NEW YORK	1	–	1
ON	1	–	1	TOUCH	–	1	1
OUT	1	1	2	TRUCK	–	1	1
OUT OF A HOUSE	1	–	1	US	–	1	1
OUT OF HOUSE	1	–	1	WALK	4	1	5
OUT OF MY WAY	1	–	1	WALK OR RUN	1	–	1
OUT OF THE WAY	1	–	1	WALKING	–	2	2
OVER	–	4	4	WALL	1	1	2
PEOPLE MOVE	1	–	1	WATER	–	1	1
PICTURE	–	1	1	WHEN SOMEBODY MOVES	–	1	1
PLEASE	–	2	2	WORM	1	–	1
POOVE	1	–	1	YOU WALK	–	1	1
PUNISH	1	–	1	YOUR BONES	1	–	1
PUSHED	1	–	1	YOUR HEAD	1	1	2
RESTORE	1	–	1	YOUR HOUSE	1	–	1
				YOURSELF	–	1	1

52. MUSIC

RESPONSE WORD	M	F	T	RESPONSE WORD	M	F	T
A BAND	1	–	1	IS GOOD	1	–	1
A SLEIGH	1	–	1	IS PLAYING	1	–	1
AIR	–	1	1	KUSIC	1	–	1
ASH TRAY	1	–	1	LAMB	–	1	1
BANJO	2	1	3	LAND	–	1	1
BEAUTIFUL	–	1	1	LAUGHING	1	–	1
BOARDS	1	–	1	LIKE	–	1	1
BOX	2	–	2	LIKE PLAYING A SONG	–	1	1
BOY	1	–	1	LOOP	1	–	1
BUSIC	–	1	1	LOUD	1	–	1
CAR	1	–	1	LOVING	–	1	1
CAR PLUGS	1	–	1	LUSIC	1	–	1
CHAIR	1	1	2	MAN	1	–	1
CHAIRS	–	1	1	ME	1	–	1
CHANNEL	1	–	1	MOO	1	–	1
CLASS	–	1	1	MOTHER	–	2	2
COMES OUT OF PIANO	1	–	1	MOVE OVER SO I CAN PLAY	–	1	1
DANCE	2	10	12	MUSE	–	1	1
DESK	–	1	1	MUSICIAN	1	–	1
DOONIT	–	1	1	MUSICIANS	1	–	1
DRUM	2	1	3	ORCHESTRA	1	1	2
DUSIC	1	–	1	ORGAN	2	–	2
FOR SINGING	1	–	1	OUT OF WINDOW	–	1	1
FUN	2	3	5	PEOPLE ARE PLAYING A RECORD PLAYER	–	1	1
GIVE ME MY HORN BACK	1	–	1	PIANO	16	17	33
GLASS	–	1	1	PICTURE	1	–	1
GOING TO MUSIC SCHOOL	1	–	1	PLAY	7	3	10
HALL	1	–	1	PLAY A PIANO	3	–	3
HAVE A MOON	–	1	1	PLAY MUSIC	–	1	1
HIGH CHAIR	–	1	1	PLAY PIANO	1	–	1
HORN	1	–	1	PLAYING	–	1	1
HURTS MY EARS	1	–	1	PLAYING A ORGAN	–	1	1
I PLAY MY PIANO	–	1	1	PLUS MUSIC	1	–	1
IM DANCING TO MUSIC	1	–	1	PRACTICE	–	1	1
IN THE HI FI	–	1	1	PRETTY	3	1	4
INSTRUMENT	2	–	2	PUSIC	1	–	1
INSTRUMENTS	1	1	2				

RESPONSE WORD	KINDERGARTEN M	F	T

52. MUSIC

RESPONSE WORD	M	F	T	RESPONSE WORD	M	F	T
RADIO	–	1	1	SWIM	–	1	1
RECORD	5	4	9	TABLE	–	1	1
RECORD PLAYER	2	2	4	TEACHER	2	–	2
RECORDS	3	–	3	THATS PRETTY	1	–	1
ROCK	1	–	1	THERE WAS MUSIC AT MY			
SHOE	1	–	1	HOUSE	–	1	1
SILVER	–	1	1	TO A PARTY	–	1	1
SING	2	6	8	TOAD	–	1	1
SINGING	1	3	4	TOO	–	1	1
SOMEONE IS PLAYING THE				TOO LOUD MUSIC	–	1	1
PIANO	–	1	1	TROMBONE	–	2	2
SONG	–	1	1	VIOLIN	1	1	2
STACK	–	1	1	WE PLAY IT	–	1	1
STOP	–	1	1	WORD	1	–	1
STOP PLAYING THE MUSIC	–	1	1	YOU HEAR US SING	–	1	1
SWEATER	–	1	1				

53. NEEDLE

RESPONSE WORD	M	F	T	RESPONSE WORD	M	F	T
A NEEDLE STUCK ME	–	1	1	NEED	–	1	1
A PIN	1	–	1	NEETY	–	1	1
A STICK PIN IN MY THROAT	1	–	1	PEEDLE	1	1	2
AND PINS	1	–	1	PEN	1	–	1
AND THREAD	1	1	2	PENICILLIN	2	–	2
ARM	1	–	1	PICK	1	–	1
BARRETTE	–	1	1	PIN	13	7	20
BEEDLE	1	–	1	POCKETBOOK	1	–	1
BEETLE	1	–	1	POINT	1	–	1
BETTER NOT TOUCH IT YOU				POP THE BALLOONS	1	–	1
MIGHT STICK YOU	–	1	1	PRICK	1	1	2
BIRD	1	–	1	PRICKING	–	1	1
BOAT	1	–	1	PULLING THREAD	1	–	1
BOOK	1	–	1	RECORD	1	–	1
BOX	1	–	1	RECORD PLAYER	–	1	1
BUG	1	–	1	SEAGULL	1	–	1
BUMBLE BEE	–	1	1	SEW	4	7	11
CHAIR	1	–	1	SEW YOUR SHOES UP	–	1	1
CHILDREN	1	–	1	SEWING	1	4	5
CLOTH	–	1	1	SEWING CLOTHES	1	–	1
CLOTHES	1	–	1	SEWING MACHINE	–	1	1
CRY	1	–	1	SEWING UP CLOTHES	–	1	1
DOCTOR	3	2	5	SHARP	2	1	3
DOCTOR HAVE A NEEDLE	1	–	1	SHOT	6	6	12
DOG	–	1	1	SHOT BY A NEEDLE	1	–	1
DONT HURT	1	–	1	SOME DOCTORS HURT	–	1	1
DONT TOUCH	–	1	1	SOMEONE WITH A NEEDLE	–	1	1
DOWN	–	1	1	SOMETHINGS TELLED	1	–	1
DRESS	–	1	1	STICK	1	4	5
DUCK	1	–	1	STICK A NEEDLE IN			
EAT	1	–	1	SOMEBODYS TOE	1	–	1
FINGER	1	–	1	STICK THE NEEDLE IN THE			
GEEDLE	–	1	1	CUSHION	1	–	1
GIVES US A NEEDLE	–	1	1	STICK YOU	–	1	1
GLASS	–	1	1	STICKED	–	1	1
HAIR	–	1	1	STICKS YOU	–	1	1
HAT	–	1	1	STRING	–	2	2
HEEL	1	–	1	STUCK	–	1	1
HOSPITAL	–	1	1	SUNSET	1	–	1
HOT	1	–	1	TABLE	–	1	1
HURT	4	4	8	TEEDLE	1	–	1
HURTS	2	–	2	THAT HURTS PEOPLE	1	–	1
I SEW	–	1	1	THREAD	11	22	33
IN YOUR HAND	–	1	1	THROW UP	1	–	1
IT HURTS	–	1	1	TO TAKE CARE OF YOU AT			
LEEDLED	1	–	1	DOCTORS	1	–	1
MAKES HOLE AND MAKES				TOO SHARP	1	–	1
BLOOD	–	1	1	TRAIN	–	1	1
MAN	1	–	1	WHAT YOU PUT IN YOUR ARM	–	1	1
MEDICINE	1	1	2	WHEEL	1	–	1
MEEDLE	1	–	1	WHEN PEOPLE ARE SEWING	–	1	1
MENDING	–	1	1	WILD CAT	1	–	1
NEAT	–	1	1				

54. NET

RESPONSE WORD	M	F	T	RESPONSE WORD	M	F	T
A BOAT	–	1	1	BLACK	1	–	1
A BOY	1	–	1	BOAT	1	–	1
A CHAIR	1	–	1	BREAD	–	1	1
A DRESS	–	1	1	BULLDOZER KNOCKING DOWN			
A HAIR NET	–	1	1	TREE	1	–	1
BALL	1	2	3	BUTTERFLIES	1	–	1
BASKETBALL	1	–	1	BUTTERFLY	3	2	5
BASKETBALL NET	1	–	1	CAT	2	–	2
BATHINETTE	–	1	1	CATCH	5	9	14
BED	2	–	2	CATCH A FISH	1	–	1
BET	–	2	2	CATCH BUTTERFLIES	1	1	2
BIRD	2	–	2	CATCH BUTTERFLIES WITH			
BIRDS	–	1	1	NET	1	–	1
BIT	–	1	1	CATCH CRABS	2	–	2

RESPONSE WORD	KINDERGARTEN M	F	T	RESPONSE WORD	KINDERGARTEN M	F	T

54. NET

RESPONSE WORD	M	F	T	RESPONSE WORD	M	F	T
CATCH FISH	2	3	5	MITTEN	–	1	1
CATCH HIM	1	–	1	MY MOTHER KNITTED ME SOME GLOVES	1	–	1
CATCH THE NET	1	–	1	NECKLACE	–	1	1
CATCHES	1	–	1	NEST	2	3	5
CATCHING	–	1	1	NETS	1	–	1
CATCHING FISH	1	–	1	PAPER	1	–	1
CAUGHT A FISH	1	–	1	PENCIL	–	1	1
CAUGHT MY DOG	–	1	1	PEOPLE	1	–	1
CHURCH	1	–	1	PERSON	–	1	1
CLAP	–	1	1	PET	1	1	2
CRAB	3	1	4	PIN	1	1	2
CRABS IN	1	–	1	PLATE	1	–	1
CUPBOARD	–	1	1	PLAY NET	–	1	1
DAVID HAS A NET	–	1	1	PLUG	1	–	1
DOG CATCHER	–	1	1	PUMPKIN	–	1	1
DONET	–	1	1	RAT	–	1	1
FALL	1	1	2	RIGHT	1	–	1
FALL IN A NET	–	1	1	ROPE	–	1	1
FET	–	1	1	SANTA CLAUS	1	–	1
FIREMAN	1	1	2	SCAT	–	1	1
FISH	23	13	36	SET	–	1	1
FISHING	1	–	1	SEW	–	1	1
FISHING NET	1	–	1	SHEEP	–	1	1
FISHING POLE	1	–	1	SOCK	1	–	1
FISHING WITH A NET	–	1	1	SPIDER	–	1	1
FLY	1	1	2	STARFISH	–	1	1
FOOD	–	1	1	STRING	–	1	1
GOLDFISH	1	–	1	SUN	–	1	1
HAIR	–	3	3	TEDDY BEAR	1	–	1
HAT	–	2	2	TENNIS	–	1	1
HET	–	1	1	TET	1	1	2
HOUSE	–	1	1	THE FISH IS IN THE NET	1	–	1
I CAUGHT A FISH IN A NET	1	–	1	THROW A BALL	–	1	1
I PUT THE BALL IN THE NET	–	1	1	TOO MUCH OF A NET	1	–	1
IM CATCHING SOMETHING	–	1	1	TOUCH	–	1	1
INSECT	–	1	1	WALK	–	1	1
JET	1	–	1	WASH HAIR	–	1	1
JUMP	1	–	1	WE ALL FELL INTO THE NET	–	1	1
KILL	–	1	1	WE SQUEEZE OUR NECK	–	1	1
KNIT A SWEATER	1	–	1	WET	1	1	2
KNITTING	1	1	2	WHAT YOU PUT OVER YOUR HAIR	1	–	1
LADY	–	1	1	WINDOW	–	1	1
LIKE A BIRD IS BUILDING HIS HOUSE	–	1	1	WIPING A BROOM	1	–	1
MAN	1	–	1	YARD	–	1	1
MATTRESS	1	–	1	YOU CATCH FISH	1	–	1
MET	1	–	1				
MINE	–	1	1				

55. NEVER

RESPONSE WORD	M	F	T	RESPONSE WORD	M	F	T
AGAIN	5	5	10	DON T	1	–	1
ALPHABET	1	–	1	DONT	1	1	2
AM	–	1	1	DONT DO IT	1	1	2
ANYTHING	1	–	1	DONT NEVER DO THAT AGAIN	1	–	1
BAD	1	–	1	DONT STEP UP TO WAKE YOUR MOTHER	1	–	1
BE BAD	1	–	1	EAT POISON	–	1	1
BEAT	–	1	1	EVER	11	3	14
BELONG	–	1	1	EVER TOUCH ME	1	–	1
BIRD	2	–	2	FEVER	–	1	1
BIRD NEST	–	1	1	FLY	–	1	1
BOOKS	–	1	1	FOOD	–	1	1
BUTTERFLY	–	2	2	FURNITURE	–	1	1
CAT	2	–	2	GET SICK	–	1	1
CHAIN	1	–	1	GETTING PANTS	–	1	1
CLEVER	2	–	2	GO	–	2	2
COLD	–	1	1	GO ACROSS THE STREET WITHOUT YOUR MOTHE	–	1	1
COME	1	1	2	GO AGAIN	–	1	1
COME AWAY FROM ME	1	1	2	GO BARE FOOTED	–	1	1
COME BACK	2	1	3	GO HOME	1	–	1
COME BACK HERE AGAIN	1	–	1	GO IN THE FIELD WITHOUT ASKING MY MOTHE	–	1	1
COME TO YOUR HOUSE	1	–	1	GO NOWHERE	1	–	1
COMPLETE	–	1	1	GOOD BYE	1	–	1
COWBOY	–	1	1	GROW UP	–	1	1
DEVER	–	2	2	HAPPEN	–	1	1
DID SOMETHING	1	–	1	HATE PEOPLE	–	1	1
DISHES	–	1	1	HAY STACK	–	1	1
DO	3	4	7	HEAL	1	–	1
DO ANYTHING	1	–	1	HIT ME	1	–	1
DO BAD THINGS	–	1	1	HOUSE	1	1	2
DO IT	–	2	2	I NEVER, NEVER DO A PUZZLE	1	–	1
DO SOMETHING	–	1	1	I WILL COME BACK	–	1	1
DO SOMETHING BAD	1	–	1	I WONT DO THIS AGAIN	–	1	1
DO SOMETHING WRONG	–	1	1	I WONT SEE YOU NEVER	1	–	1
DO THAT	2	–	2	IN	2	–	2
DO THINGS BAD	1	–	1	IN A FISH FAIR	1	–	1
DO THINGS THATS BAD	1	–	1				
DO WHAT YOU ARE SUPPOSED TO DO	1	–	1				
DOCTOR	1	–	1				

RESPONSE WORD	KINDERGARTEN M	F	T

55. NEVER

RESPONSE WORD	M	F	T	RESPONSE WORD	M	F	T
INSECT	1	–	1	SIGN	–	1	1
KEVIN	–	1	1	SINGING	–	1	1
KILL	1	–	1	SOMETHING	1	–	1
KILLED	1	–	1	SPONGE	1	–	1
KNIFE	1	–	1	STEAL	1	–	1
LAND	2	2	4	STICKS	1	–	1
LAUGH	–	1	1	STOPPER	–	1	1
LEAVE	–	2	2	STREET LIGHT	–	1	1
LEAVE THAT BUG ALONE	–	1	1	SWING SET	1	–	1
LET BUGS GET ON MY RUG	–	1	1	TAKE ANY TOYS AWAY	–	1	1
LEVER	2	1	3	TEVER	–	1	1
LOVE	–	1	1	TIGHTS	–	1	1
ME	–	1	1	TOOK MY TOY	–	1	1
MESSAGE	1	–	1	TOUCH	2	5	7
MORE	1	–	1	TOUCH A BUMBLE BEE	1	–	1
MOTHER	–	1	1	TOUCH FIRE	–	1	1
NEST	1	–	1	TOUCH MATCHES	1	–	1
NO	1	–	1	TOUCH THAT	1	–	1
NOT	–	1	1	TOUCH THE STOVE	1	–	1
NOT ALLOWED	1	–	1	TOUCH THIS	–	1	1
PENCIL	1	–	1	TOY	–	1	1
PEOPLE SAY NEVER TOUCH IT	1	–	1	TREE	–	1	1
PEVER	1	–	1	TURN	–	1	1
PICK UP CHAIR	1	–	1	WATER	–	1	1
PLANE	1	–	1	WE	–	1	1
PLAY	2	1	3	WE NEVER GO OUT	–	1	1
PLAY WITH MY TOYS	–	1	1	WE RE NEVER GOING TO HAVE			
RECORD	1	–	1	THE RUG AGAIN	1	–	1
RIDE A HORSE	1	–	1	WEVER	1	–	1
SAND	–	1	1	WHEN PEOPLE SAY NEVER	–	1	1
SANTA CLAUS COME AGAIN	–	1	1	WHY	–	2	2
SCOTCH TAPE	–	1	1	YES	–	1	1
SEE	–	2	2	YOU NEVER DIE	1	–	1
SHOE	–	1	1	YOU NEVER RUN AWAY	–	1	1
SHOULDNT GO OUTSIDE ON A							
RAINY DAY	1	–	1				

56. OBEY

RESPONSE WORD	M	F	T	RESPONSE WORD	M	F	T
A BOOK	–	1	1	HE	–	1	1
A BOY	1	–	1	HER AND HIM	–	1	1
A CAT	1	–	1	HOUSE	1	–	1
A DOG	1	1	2	I	–	1	1
A HORSE	–	1	1	I OBEYED MY MOTHER CAUSE			
ANSWERS	1	–	1	I WANTED SOME	1	–	1
APPLE	1	–	1	ILL GO	–	1	1
BABIES	–	1	1	IN MY WAY	–	1	1
BABY	–	3	3	INDIAN	1	–	1
BAD	1	–	1	JAIL	1	–	1
BANQUET	1	–	1	KAY	–	1	1
BAY	4	1	5	LADY	–	1	1
BE	–	1	1	LAMB	–	1	1
BE BAD	1	–	1	LAST	–	1	1
BE GOOD	2	–	2	LAW	1	2	3
BEAR	–	1	1	LISTEN	–	1	1
BED	1	2	3	LOB	1	–	1
BELL	1	–	1	MAKE SOMETHING	1	–	1
BELLS	–	1	1	MASTER	1	–	1
BIRD	–	1	1	MAY	–	1	1
BOAT	1	–	1	ME	1	2	3
BOW	1	–	1	MOMMY	–	1	1
BOY	–	1	1	MOMMY AND DADDY	–	1	1
BRICKS	–	1	1	MONEY	–	1	1
BUTTERFLY	–	1	1	MOTHER	1	1	2
CAGE	–	1	1	MY MOTHER	1	–	1
CANDY	–	1	1	MY ORDERS	–	1	1
CHAIR	–	1	1	NAUGHTY	1	–	1
CHESAPEAKE	1	–	1	NICE	–	1	1
CHILDREN	1	–	1	NIGHT	–	1	1
CHURCH	–	1	1	NOT	1	1	2
CLAY	1	–	1	NOT DO IT	–	1	1
COFFEE	1	–	1	NOT OBEY	–	1	1
CRACKER	1	–	1	O	1	1	2
DO WHAT YOURE TOLD	1	–	1	OK	2	1	3
DOG	1	–	1	OKAY	1	–	1
DOOR	–	3	3	ONEY	1	–	1
DOOR HANDLE	1	–	1	OPAY	1	–	1
FAINT	1	–	1	ORDERS	2	1	3
FETCH	1	–	1	OTEY	–	1	1
FISH	1	1	2	OVERALLS	–	1	1
FLY	–	1	1	PAINT	1	–	1
FOOD	–	1	1	PARENTS	1	1	2
FOR HAY	1	–	1	PICTURE	2	–	2
FRAID	–	1	1	PLASTIC	–	1	1
GET MAD	1	–	1	PLEASE	–	1	1
GO	–	1	1	PLUG	–	1	1
GO TO BED	–	1	1	POBEY	1	–	1
GOD	–	1	1	POLICEMAN	–	1	1
GOOD	1	2	3	RECORD	–	1	1
GROWNUPS	1	–	1	RECTANGLES	1	–	1

RESPONSE WORD	M	F	T	RESPONSE WORD	M	F	T
				56. OBEY			
RIGHT	–	1	1	THIS	–	1	1
ROSE DAY	–	1	1	THREE	1	–	1
RULES	1	2	3	TO YOU	–	1	1
RUN	1	–	1	TO OBEY	1	–	1
SAY	1	1	2	TRAFFIC	2	–	2
SAY PLEASE	–	1	1	TRASH CAN	1	1	2
SEAL	–	1	1	WAIT	1	1	2
SHAME	1	–	1	WALL	1	1	2
SHEEP	–	1	1	WARD	1	–	1
SLEEP	1	–	1	WATER	–	1	1
SOME OBEYS JOIN OTHERS	–	1	1	WATER BAY	–	1	1
SOMEBODY	1	–	1	WAY	1	–	1
SOMETHING	1	–	1	WE ALL OBEYED	–	1	1
STOP IT	1	–	1	WHEN ITS A BAY	–	1	1
SURE	1	–	1	WHITE	1	–	1
SWIMMING POOL	1	–	1	YEA	1	–	1
TABLE	1	1	2	YELL	–	1	1
TELEPHONE	–	1	1	YES MAM	–	1	1
THANK YOU	1	–	1	YOU	1	1	2
THE BAY BRIDGE	1	–	1	YOUR MASTER	1	–	1
THE LAW	2	3	5	YOUR MOTHER	4	3	7
THE LORD	–	1	1	YOUR MOTHER AND FATHER	1	–	1
THE PEOPLE	1	–	1	YOUR ORDERS	–	1	1
THE TEACHER	1	–	1	YOUR PARENTS	2	2	4
THEY	1	–	1	YOURSELF	–	1	1
				57. OCEAN			
BANDAID	–	1	1	P	–	1	1
BEACH	–	1	1	PADDLE	1	–	1
BED	1	–	1	PAGE	1	–	1
BIRD	–	1	1	PEARL	1	–	1
BLUE	1	1	2	PEOPLE GO TO A BIG OCEAN	–	1	1
BOAT	10	3	13	PIPE	1	–	1
BOATS ON OCEAN	1	–	1	POOL	–	2	2
BOATS SWIMMING INTO THE OCEAN	–	1	1	POTION	–	1	1
BOCEAN	1	–	1	PRETTY	–	1	1
BOX	1	–	1	RIVER	2	2	4
BUMP	1	–	1	ROCKS	2	1	1
CAR	–	1	1	ROUGH	1	–	1
CAT	–	1	1	RUN IN THE OCEAN	–	1	1
CHAIR	1	–	1	SAIL	–	1	1
CITY	10	7	17	SALT	1	1	2
COAT	1	–	1	SALT WATER	1	–	1
COCEAN	1	–	1	SAND	1	–	1
DEEP	1	–	1	SEA	7	5	12
DOCEAN	–	1	1	SHARK	1	1	2
DOG	–	1	1	SHELL	1	1	2
FENCE	1	–	1	SHELLS	1	–	1
FISH	4	7	11	SHIP	1	–	1
FISHING	1	–	1	SHORE	1	–	1
FOCEAN	–	1	1	SIGN	–	1	1
FUNNY	1	–	1	SIT UP	–	1	1
HAMMER	–	1	1	SLEIGH	–	1	1
HANDLE	1	–	1	SOFA	1	–	1
I GO OVER THE OCEAN	–	1	1	SOMETHING AGAIN WAVE	–	1	1
I SWAM INTO THE OCEAN AND DROWNED	1	–	1	STOP	–	1	1
ICE	1	–	1	STREAM	–	1	1
IM PLAYING IN THE OCEAN	1	–	1	SWEATER	–	1	1
IRON	–	1	1	SWIM	4	5	9
IS DEEP	–	1	1	SWIM IN THE OCEAN	1	–	1
KITCHEN	–	1	1	SWIMMING	1	–	1
KNIFE	–	1	1	TEETH	–	1	1
LAKE	1	1	2	THE ATLANTIC OCEAN	–	1	1
LIKE YOU GO ON A BOAT	–	1	1	THE BOAT WAS IN THE OCEAN	–	1	1
LINER	1	4	5	THE CHESAPEAKE BAY	–	1	1
LIQUID	1	–	1	THE WATER	–	1	1
LOTION	1	–	1	THE WAVES ARE MOVING	1	–	1
MOTION	1	–	1	TOTION	1	–	1
NEWS	1	–	1	TRAIL	1	–	1
NO OCEAN	1	–	1	TREE	2	–	2
NOW	–	1	1	WATER	11	17	28
O	–	1	1	WAVE	1	–	1
OCEAGE	1	–	1	WAVES	4	3	7
OCEAN CITY	1	–	1	WHALE	3	–	3
				WINDOWS	–	1	1
				58. OFF			
A SWING	–	1	1	BROWN	–	1	1
APARTMENT HOUSE	–	1	1	BUS STOFF	1	–	1
AWFUL	1	–	1	CALIFORNIA	1	–	1
BACK	–	1	1	CAR	2	–	2
BIBLE	–	1	1	CAUGHT	1	–	1
BITE	–	1	1	CHAIR	1	1	2
BOAT	1	–	1	CHAIRS	–	1	1
BOFF	1	–	1	CHRISTMAS TREE	–	1	1
BORE	1	–	1	CIGARETTE	1	–	1

RESPONSE WORD	KINDERGARTEN M	F	T

58. OFF

RESPONSE WORD	M	F	T
COFFEEPOT	–	1	1
COME HOME	1	–	1
COUGH	2	–	2
CRAYONS	–	1	1
DARK	–	1	1
DAY	1	–	1
DECK	–	1	1
DOFF	–	1	1
DOG	2	2	4
DOOR	–	1	1
DRAWER	–	1	1
DUST	1	–	1
EAGLE	1	–	1
F	1	–	1
FALL	2	1	3
FIELD	–	1	1
FIRED	–	1	1
FLY	–	1	1
GET OFF	1	–	1
GLOFF	1	–	1
GO	2	1	3
GO OFF	–	1	1
GOING	–	1	1
GOOD BYE	–	1	1
GOT OFF THE SEE SAW	1	–	1
GREEN	–	1	1
GROUND	–	1	1
I TURNED ON THE LIGHT	–	1	1
I WENT OFF WITH YOU	–	1	1
IM TAKING A TRIP	1	–	1
IN	–	2	2
IN THE DAY	–	1	1
INSECT SPRAY	–	1	1
INTO	–	1	1
JET	1	–	1
JOFF	1	–	1
LAMP	1	–	1
LEAVE	1	–	1
LIGHT	3	1	4
LIGHTS	1	–	1
LOFF	–	1	1
LOFT	1	–	1
LOST	1	–	1
MAYBE	–	1	1
ME	1	–	1
MOFF	1	–	1
MOTH	1	1	2
MOUTH	1	–	1
MY PROPERTY	1	–	1
NIGHT	–	1	1
OF WORK	–	1	1
OF WORK TODAY	1	–	1
OFF	1	–	1
OFF WE GO	–	1	1
OFFICE	–	2	2
OFFY	–	1	1
OFTEN	1	2	3
OFTEN NO	–	1	1
ON	10	14	24
ON A TRIP	–	1	1
ON FRIDAYS	1	–	1
ON VACATION	1	–	1
ORANGE	1	–	1
PAPER	1	–	1
PAW	–	1	1
PEOPLE TURN THE LIGHT OFF	1	–	1
PICTURE	1	–	1
PLANE	1	–	1
RAT	1	–	1
READ	1	1	1
RED	1	–	1
RIDE	–	1	1
RING	–	1	1
ROCKET	1	–	1
RUSH	–	1	1
SAW	1	–	1
SCARY	1	–	1
SCHOOL	1	1	2
SEAT	1	–	1
SHOE	–	1	1
SLIDING BOARD	–	2	2
SLOW	1	–	1
SOFA	–	1	1
SOMEWHERE	1	–	1
STORE	1	–	1
SWITCH	1	–	1
TABLE	–	1	1
TAKE	1	–	1
TAKE-OFF	1	–	1
TALK	1	–	1
TEETH	–	1	1
THE DAY	1	–	1
THE FURNITURE	1	–	1
THE ROAD WE GO	1	–	1
THE SIDEWALK	1	–	1
THE STAIRS	–	1	1
THE STOVE	1	–	1
THE TRACK	1	–	1
THE WORLDS SO SWEET	–	1	1
TO A TRIP	1	–	1
TO JOIN SOMEBODY	–	1	1
TO SCHOOL	1	1	2
TO THE BALL GAME	–	1	1
TO THE MOVIES	1	–	1
TO THE SOUTH	1	–	1
TO THE STORE	1	–	1
TO THE WOODS	–	1	1
TO THE ZOO	–	1	1
TOO OFF	1	–	1
TOWN	–	1	1
TRAIN	–	1	1
TREE	1	1	2
TROUGH	1	–	1
TRUCK	–	1	1
TURN	1	1	2
TURN OFF LIGHT	–	1	1
TURN OFF THE CAR	1	–	1
TURN OFF THE LIGHT	–	1	1
TURN THE HEATER OFF	–	2	2
TURN THE WATER OFF	1	–	1
TV	1	–	1
US	1	1	2
WATCH	1	1	1
WE	1	–	1
WE GO TO SCHOOL	–	1	1
WENT AWAY	–	1	1
WERE GOING TO TURN THE LIGHTS OFF NOW Y	1	–	1
WHISCH	1	–	1
WING	–	1	1
WITH THAT THING	–	1	1
WIZARD	–	1	1
WOOD	1	–	1
WORK	–	1	1
YOUR SWING	–	1	1

59. ON

RESPONSE WORD	M	F	T
A GIANT S LONG	1	–	1
A MOUNTAIN	1	–	1
A PIPE	1	–	1
AGAIN WE GO	1	–	1
AND OFF	–	1	1
ARE	1	–	1
AWNING	–	1	1
BABY	–	1	1
BARREL	–	1	1
BEAR	2	–	2
BEGIN	–	1	1
BIKE	1	–	1
BIRD	–	1	1
BOAT	–	1	1
BON	1	2	3
BOY	1	–	1
BUILDING	1	–	1
CAR	–	2	2
CARN	1	–	1
CHAIR	–	1	1
CHAIRS	1	–	1
CHURCH	1	1	2
CLOCK	1	–	1
CLOTHES	2	1	3
COAT	–	1	1
COLD	1	–	1
COME ON GET ON YOUR BIKE	1	–	1
DAWN	–	1	1
DID	1	–	1
DOG	–	2	2
DONG	–	1	1
DONKEY	–	1	1
ELEVATOR	1	–	1
EYE	1	1	2
FAN	1	–	1
FENCE	1	–	1
FINGER	–	1	1
FLOOR	–	1	1

RESPONSE WORD	KINDERGARTEN M	F	T	RESPONSE WORD	KINDERGARTEN M	F	T

59. ON

RESPONSE WORD	M	F	T	RESPONSE WORD	M	F	T
FLY	-	1	1	SANTA CLAUS	-	1	1
FRESH	1	-	1	SEAT	1	-	1
GAME	-	1	1	SHIP	1	-	1
GASOLINE	-	1	1	SHOE	-	1	1
GET ON HORSEY	-	1	1	SHOW	1	1	2
GET YOUR SHOES ON	1	-	1	SLIDING DOORS	-	1	1
GLASSES	1	-	1	SNOW	1	-	1
GO	-	2	2	SOME	1	-	1
GO ON	1	-	1	SOMEPLACE	-	1	1
GO ON TO THE STORE	-	1	1	SOMETHING	1	-	1
GOES THE LIGHT	1	-	1	SOMETHING ON	-	1	1
GOING	-	1	1	SOMEWHERE	1	-	1
GOING ON	-	1	1	STAGE	-	1	1
GOLD	1	-	1	STICK	1	1	2
GONE	4	-	4	STOP	-	2	2
GRASS	1	1	2	SUPPER	1	-	1
HORSE	-	1	1	SWEEPER	1	-	1
I GO ON TODAY	-	1	1	SWITCH	-	1	1
IN	1	-	1	T V	1	-	1
JUMP	1	-	1	TABLE	1	1	2
LAWN	1	2	3	THE	-	1	1
LAWNMOWER	3	-	3	THE LINE	1	-	1
LETS GO ON TO THE GAME	1	-	1	THE SWING	1	-	1
LIGHT	-	1	1	THE TRAIL	-	1	1
LIGHT IS ON	-	1	1	THE TV	1	-	1
LIGHT SWITCH	1	-	1	THE TV IS ON	-	1	1
LIGHTS	1	-	1	THE TV WENT ON	-	1	1
MAYBE	-	1	1	THIS	1	-	1
ME	1	1	2	TIME	1	-	1
ME-ON	1	-	1	TO	1	-	1
MOTOR	1	-	1	TOO ON	1	-	1
MY WAY OUT	1	-	1	TOWEL	-	1	1
MY WORK	-	1	1	TRAIN	1	-	1
NO RESPONSE	1	-	1	TROMP	-	1	1
NOW	1	-	1	TRUCK	-	1	1
NURSERY SCHOOL	-	1	1	TURN	-	1	1
OCEAN	-	1	1	TURN A LIGHT ON	1	-	1
OFF	12	12	24	TURN IT ON	-	1	1
ON IT	-	1	1	TURN ON THE CAR	1	-	1
ON WITH THE SHOW	1	-	1	TV	1	1	2
ORANGE	1	1	2	TV SET	1	-	1
OUR ROAD	-	1	1	WALK	-	1	1
OVER	-	1	1	WALKING	-	1	1
PAPER	1	1	2	WALL	-	1	1
PENCIL	-	1	1	WALLS	-	1	1
PERFUME	-	1	1	WASHING MACHINE IS ON	1	-	1
PERSON	1	-	1	WAY (ON OUR WAY)	-	1	1
PING PONG	1	-	1	WHEN SOMEBODYS TURNING			
PIPE	-	1	1	THE LIGHT ON	-	1	1
PLAY	-	1	1	WITH THE PICTURE	-	1	1
POCKETBOOK	-	1	1	WITH THE SHOW	3	-	3
PUT ON THE TV	1	-	1	WORD	-	1	1
RADIO	1	-	1	YAWN	-	1	1
RUN	1	-	1	YOU	-	1	1
RUN IN SOMETHING	1	-	1	YOU GO SOMEWHERE	1	-	1
RUNNING AWAY	-	1	1	YOUR TRUCK	-	1	1

60. ONCE

RESPONSE WORD	M	F	T	RESPONSE WORD	M	F	T
A BABY	-	1	1	CHRISTMAS	-	1	1
A DAY	1	-	1	CHURCH	1	-	1
A DAY GO TO DENTIST	1	-	1	CIGARETTE	-	1	1
A LITTLE TIME THERE WAS				COUCH	-	1	1
A BUNNY RABBIT	1	-	1	CUNCE	1	-	1
A STORY	-	1	1	DAY	1	-	1
A WEEK	1	-	1	DECEMBER	1	-	1
AFTER ALL	-	1	1	DID	2	-	2
AGAIN	-	3	3	DOG	-	1	1
AIRPLANE	-	1	1	DONT	-	1	1
ALL	2	1	3	DUNCE	1	1	2
AND FOR ALL	-	1	1	EAT	-	1	1
ANOTHER	1	-	1	FLOWER	-	1	1
ANTENNA	-	1	1	FLOWERS	-	1	1
ART A SECOND	1	-	1	FRONT	1	-	1
BABY	-	1	1	GLASS	1	-	1
BATHTUB	-	1	1	GO	1	2	3
BEAR	-	1	1	GONE	-	1	1
BLOCK	-	1	1	GRASS	-	1	1
BOOK	-	2	2	GUN	1	-	1
BOY	2	-	2	GUNCE	1	-	1
BUCKET	1	-	1	HATE	1	-	1
BUMPS	-	1	1	HE WAS A TAILOR	1	-	1
BUNCE	1	2	3	HOLE	-	1	1
BUT	1	-	1	HORSES	1	-	1
CAN I USE IT ONCE	1	-	1	HOUSE	1	-	1
CAN PUSH THE BALL ONCE	1	-	1	HUNTS	1	-	1
CANDY	1	-	1	I	-	1	1
CARDBOARD	1	-	1	I HAD A TOY	1	-	1
CHEWING	-	1	1	I HURT MYSELF	1	-	1
CHOPPING DOWN TREE	1	-	1	I PLAY BALL	-	1	1

RESPONSE WORD	KINDERGARTEN M	F	T	RESPONSE WORD	KINDERGARTEN M	F	T

60. ONCE

RESPONSE WORD	M	F	T	RESPONSE WORD	M	F	T
I PLAYED IN A BASEBALL FIELD.	1	-	1	SEE.	1	-	1
I SAW A KANGAROO.	1	-	1	SHEEP.	1	1	2
I SEE YOU ONE DAY	-	1	1	SHUNCE.	-	1	1
I WANT IT	1	-	1	SOMETHING	1	-	1
I WAS WALKING TO THE ZOO ONCE	1	-	1	SPEAK	1	-	1
I WENT.	-	1	1	STAR.	1	-	1
IN LOVE	-	1	1	STORY	2	3	5
LAST.	-	1	1	TAKE A TURN	-	1	1
LEAF.	1	-	1	TALK.	-	1	1
LETS.	1	-	1	TATTOO.	1	-	1
LITTLE GIRL	-	1	1	THE TIME.	-	1	1
LONG TIME	1	-	1	THERE ISNT.	-	1	1
LOST.	-	1	1	THERE WAS A BIRDIE UP HIGH	-	1	1
LOVE.	-	3	3	THING	-	1	1
LUMPS	1	-	1	THREE	-	1	1
LUTZ.	1	-	1	THREE BEARS	-	1	1
MORE.	2	-	2	TIME.	2	1	3
MORE TIME	-	1	1	TO.	1	-	1
MOUSE	1	-	1	TUNCE	-	1	1
MOVIE	1	-	1	TWICE	5	6	11
NO.	-	1	1	TWO	3	3	6
NOSE.	-	1	1	TWO TIMES	2	-	2
NOW	1	-	1	TWOS.	-	1	1
O	1	-	1	UP.	2	-	2
ONE	2	2	4	UPON.	2	2	4
ONE ANSWER.	1	-	1	UPON A.	1	-	1
ONE CHANCE.	-	1	1	UPON A TIME	3	4	7
ONE MOVE.	-	1	1	USE FOR A DESK.	-	1	1
ONE TIME.	1	1	2	WALL.	1	-	1
ONLY ONE TIME	1	-	1	WANT SOMETHING.	1	-	1
OPEN.	1	-	1	WE.	-	1	1
OR TWICE.	1	-	1	WE GO THERE ONCE.	-	1	1
PEOPLE SAY ONCE	1	-	1	WE STARTED ONCE	1	-	1
PERSON.	-	1	1	WHAT.	1	-	1
PIECE OF A BARNYARD	1	-	1	WHEN IT STARTS OFF WITH A STORY.	-	1	1
PLAY.	1	-	1	WHEN YOU GO SOMEWHERE	1	-	1
PLAYTIME.	1	-	1	WHITE	-	1	1
POUNCE.	-	1	1	WINDOW.	1	-	1
PURSE.	-	1	1	WOULD	-	1	1
READ BOOK	-	1	1	WRITE	-	1	1
RED	1	-	1	YEAR.	1	-	1
RUN IN HOUSE ONCE	-	1	1	YOU CHEW UP LUNCH	1	-	1
RUN OUT INTO THE FOREST	-	1	1	YOU WONT LET YOU DO IT.	-	1	1
SECOND.	-	1	1				

61. PLEASANT

RESPONSE WORD	M	F	T	RESPONSE WORD	M	F	T
A BILLY GOAT.	1	-	1	FRIEND.	1	-	1
AIRPORT	-	1	1	GIRL.	1	-	1
ALONE	-	1	1	GIVE A PRESENT.	1	-	1
AND SOFT.	-	1	1	GIVING.	-	1	1
BAD	-	1	1	GO.	1	-	1
BALL.	1	-	1	GOAL.	1	-	1
BE CAREFUL.	2	-	2	GOOD.	1	2	3
BE GOOD	2	-	2	GOOD MORNING.	1	-	1
BE NICE	1	1	2	GUM	1	-	1
BE NICE TO YOUR FRIENDS	-	1	1	GUY	-	1	1
BE PLEASANT	1	-	1	HANDLE.	1	-	1
BE PLEASANT TO EVERYBODY.	-	1	1	HAPPY	2	3	5
BE PLEASANT TO THE ANIMALS.	1	-	1	HAT	-	1	1
BEASANT	-	1	1	HAVE A PLEASANT TIME.	-	1	1
BEING	-	1	1	HEALTHFUL	-	1	1
BICYCLE	1	-	1	HEART	-	1	1
BIRD.	-	1	1	HEASANT	1	-	1
BOARD	-	1	1	HELP.	1	-	1
BOOK	1	1	2	HERE.	-	2	2
BOOKS	-	1	1	HOUSE.	-	2	2
BREAKFAST	1	-	1	I DONT KNOW	1	-	1
CANT BE BAD AT SOMEBODYS HOUSE.	-	1	1	I PLEASANT YOU.	-	1	1
CARE.	-	1	1	IM GOING TO PLEASANT.	-	1	1
CAT	1	-	1	IT S DARK	1	-	1
CLOCK	-	1	1	ITS PLEASANT.	1	-	1
COMPANY COMES	-	1	1	ITS PLEASANT TO BE AT HOME	1	-	1
DAY.	4	1	5	KEVIN	1	-	1
DESSERT	1	-	1	KNITTING.	1	-	1
DONT.	-	1	1	LAWN MOWER.	1	-	1
DOOR.	-	1	1	LEASEMT	1	-	1
DRAPES.	1	-	1	LEAVES.	-	1	1
DREAMS.	-	2	2	LESSENT	1	-	1
DRIVE	1	-	1	LESSIT.	1	-	1
EACH OTHER.	1	-	1	LIKE.	1	1	2
ENJOY YOURSELF.	-	1	1	LIVING.	5	6	11
FLUTE	1	-	1	LOVE.	1	1	2
FOOD.	1	-	1	MAN	1	-	1
FOR MEETING YOU	1	-	1	MANNERS	1	-	1
FOR YOU	1	-	1	ME.	1	1	2
				MEET.	-	1	1

RESPONSE WORD	KINDERGARTEN M	F	T	RESPONSE WORD	KINDERGARTEN M	F	T

61. PLEASANT

RESPONSE WORD	M	F	T	RESPONSE WORD	M	F	T
MIGHT	1	–	1	SHUT UP	1	–	1
MILES	1	–	1	SIGN	1	–	1
MOOSE	–	1	1	SIT DOWN	1	–	1
MORNING	–	1	1	SKY	–	1	1
MOTHER	1	1	2	SOMETHING IS PLEASANT	–	1	1
NICE	6	7	13	STOP IT	–	1	1
NOISY	–	1	1	SUN	1	–	1
NOT PLEASANT	1	–	1	SURPRISE	–	1	1
PAPER	–	1	1	SWIM	1	–	1
PEA	–	1	1	SWIMMING	2	–	2
PEACEFUL	1	1	2	TEASANT	–	1	1
PEOPLE	3	2	5	THANKSGIVING	–	1	1
PEOPLE BE NICE TO EACH OTHER	–	1	1	THINGS	1	–	1
PHEASANT	–	2	2	TIME	–	2	2
PICNIC	–	1	1	TO MET SOMEBODY	–	1	1
PIPE	1	–	1	TOGETHER	1	–	1
PLACE	–	1	1	TRUCK	–	1	1
PLANES	1	–	1	TV	–	1	1
PLAY	–	2	2	VISIT	1	–	1
PLAYING	–	1	1	VISITING PEOPLE	–	1	1
PLEASE	1	–	1	WALKING	–	1	1
PLEDGENCE	1	–	1	WALL	1	–	1
PLENTY	–	1	1	WAY	–	1	1
PRESENT	3	1	4	WE	–	1	1
PRESENT FOR YOU	–	1	1	WE ALL PLEASANT CLOSE OUR HANDS	–	1	1
PRESENTS	1	–	1	WE ARE	1	–	1
PRESS	1	–	1	WE TALK QUIET	–	1	1
PRETTY	–	1	1	WESSENT	1	–	1
PUSSENT	1	–	1	WISH	1	–	1
QUIET	1	–	1	WOOD	1	–	1
READING	1	–	1	WORK IN SCHOOL	1	–	1
REAL PLEASANT	–	1	1	YOU	1	–	1
REASENT	–	1	1	YOU MAY GO TO BED	–	1	1
RED	–	1	1				

62. PREPARE

RESPONSE WORD	M	F	T	RESPONSE WORD	M	F	T
A LOG HOUSE	1	–	1	HANDLE	–	1	1
A PEAR	1	1	2	HOT	2	–	2
A SINK	1	–	1	HOUSE	2	–	2
AIRPLANE	–	1	1	I PREPARE MY CAR	1	–	1
ANIMALS	–	1	1	ICE	1	–	1
APPLE	1	2	3	IT	1	–	1
APPLES	–	1	1	JOY	–	1	1
ATTACK	1	–	1	KEY	1	–	1
BEAR	–	1	1	LAIR	1	–	1
BICYCLE	1	–	1	LAMPS	1	–	1
BOOKLET	–	1	1	LAST	–	1	1
BOOTS	–	1	1	LEPE	1	–	1
BOY	–	1	1	LIGHT	1	1	2
BRAND NEW	1	–	1	LIGHT SWITCH	1	1	2
CAMPING	–	1	1	LIKE A GIRLS NAME	–	1	1
CAR	4	–	4	LIPS	–	1	1
CAT	1	–	1	MADE	–	1	1
CHAIR	–	1	1	MAN	2	–	2
CHILDREN	1	–	1	ME	–	1	1
CLEANERS	–	1	1	MORE	1	–	1
COLD	–	1	1	MOTORCYCLE	1	–	1
COOKING	–	1	1	MOVE	–	1	1
CORNER	1	–	1	MOVING	–	1	1
CRIB	1	–	1	MY HAIR	–	1	1
DARE	–	1	1	NANCY	–	1	1
DINNER	–	3	3	NO	–	1	1
DOG	–	1	1	NO PREPARE	–	1	1
DONT	1	–	1	NOW	1	–	1
DRESSES	–	1	1	PALE	1	–	1
DRINK	–	1	1	PANTS	1	–	1
EAT	2	3	5	PARE	1	1	2
ECLAIR	1	–	1	PARE A PRESENT	1	–	1
EGG NOG	1	–	1	PARE SOMETHING	1	–	1
EQUIPMENT	1	–	1	PARE TOO MUCH	1	–	1
EYE	1	–	1	PARROT	1	–	1
FEATHER	–	1	1	PEAR	2	5	7
FIRE	1	–	1	PENCIL	1	–	1
FIX	1	–	1	PERFUME	–	1	1
FLOOR	–	1	1	PERSON	1	–	1
FLOWER	–	1	1	PICTURE	–	1	1
FOOD	2	5	7	PILL	–	1	1
FREE	1	–	1	PIPE	1	–	1
FURNACE	–	1	1	PLACE	–	1	1
GIVE	–	1	1	POCKETBOOK	1	–	1
GLASS	–	1	1	PRAYER	2	–	2
GLASSES	–	2	2	PREAPARE THE CAR	–	1	1
GLOVES	–	1	1	PUT TOGETHER	–	1	1
GROCERIES	1	–	1	RAIN	–	1	1
GROCERY	1	–	1	RAT	1	–	1
GROW	1	–	1	READY	1	–	1
HAIR	1	–	1	REAPAIR	–	1	1
HAMMER	2	–	2	RED	–	1	1

RESPONSE WORD	KINDERGARTEN M	F	T	RESPONSE WORD	KINDERGARTEN M	F	T

62. PREPARE

RESPONSE WORD	M	F	T	RESPONSE WORD	M	F	T
REESE	-	1	1	THE HOUSE	-	1	1
RELAIR	1	-	1	TIGER	-	1	1
REPAIR	3	3	6	TIRE	1	-	1
REPAIR FOOD	1	-	1	TO WORK	1	-	1
REPAIR ME	1	-	1	TOOLS	1	-	1
REPAIR MY TIRE	1	-	1	TOY	1	-	1
REPAIR THE CAR	1	-	1	TRAIN	-	2	2
ROCK	1	-	1	TREE	1	-	1
SAT	-	1	1	TRUCK	1	-	1
SCISSORS	1	-	1	TV SET	-	1	1
SHOE	1	-	1	US	-	1	1
SING	-	1	1	WALL	1	-	1
SIX	-	1	1	WALLPAPER	-	1	1
SLATE	1	-	1	WARM	-	1	1
SNOWFALL	1	-	1	WAS OUTSIDE	-	1	1
SOME	-	1	1	WE EAT PEARS	-	1	1
SOME PAPER	1	-	1	WERED	1	-	1
SOUR	-	1	1	WHAT	1	-	1
SPIDER CAUGHT ON TABLE	1	-	1	WHEELS	-	1	1
STAND IN CORNER	1	-	1	WHEN SOMEBODYS EATING A PEAR	-	1	1
STUFF	-	1	1	WINTER	1	-	1
SUN	-	1	1	WITH	-	1	1
SUPPER	1	1	2	YOU DONT WANT ANYTHING TO EAT	-	1	1
SWEATERS	-	1	1	YOUR SHOES	1	-	1
TABLE	-	2	2	YOUR TREE	1	-	1
TAKE OFF	1	-	1	YOURSELF	2	-	2
TEETARE	-	1	1				
TELEPHONE	-	1	1				
THAT YOU USE WITH	-	1	1				

63. PRETTY

RESPONSE WORD	M	F	T	RESPONSE WORD	M	F	T
A PRETTY PRINCESS	1	-	1	KITTY CAT	1	-	1
APPLE	1	-	1	KNIFE	1	-	1
AT PARTY	-	1	1	LADY	4	1	5
AWFUL	-	2	2	LIGHTNING	-	1	1
BABY	-	1	1	LOVE	1	-	1
BALLET	-	1	1	LOVELY	2	1	3
BALLS	-	1	1	LUTTY	1	-	1
BE NICE	1	-	1	MAN	1	-	1
BEAUTIFUL	1	4	5	MITTEN	-	1	1
BECAUSE I M GOING SOMEWHERE	-	1	1	MITTY	1	-	1
BIRD	2	-	2	MY MOTHER IS PRETTY	-	1	1
BLUE	1	1	2	MY PRETTY DRESS	-	1	1
BOOK	-	1	1	NECKLACE	-	1	1
BOW	-	1	1	NICE	2	2	4
BOY	3	-	3	NOT	-	1	1
BUCKLES	1	-	1	ORANGE	1	-	1
BUILDING	-	1	1	PAPPER	-	1	1
CAR	1	-	1	PARTY	-	1	1
CAT	1	-	1	PEOPLE	1	-	1
CHAIR	1	1	2	PERFUME	1	1	2
CHRISTMAS	-	1	1	PERSON	-	1	1
CITY	1	-	1	PETE	1	-	1
CLOTHES	1	-	1	PITY	1	-	1
COAT	-	1	1	PRETTY	-	1	1
COLOR	-	1	1	PUSS	-	1	1
CROCODILE	1	-	1	REAL PRETTY	-	1	1
D	1	-	1	RIBBON	1	-	1
DANCE	1	-	1	ROOSTER	1	-	1
DECORATE	1	-	1	SANTA CLAUS	-	1	1
DIAMOND	1	-	1	SHE IS A PRETTY GIRL	-	1	1
DIRTY	2	1	3	SMOKE STACK	1	-	1
DOLL	1	-	1	SOFT	-	1	1
DRESS	6	8	14	SOLDIER	1	-	1
DRESS UP FOR YOUR BOYFRIEND	-	1	1	SOME GIRLS ARE PRETTY	1	-	1
FACE	2	1	3	SOMEBODYS PRETTY	1	-	1
FLOWER	3	3	6	STRAIGHT BUTTERFLY	1	-	1
FLOWERS	1	3	4	SUN	1	-	1
GARDEN	-	1	1	SUNNY	-	1	1
GIRL	11	14	25	SWEET	-	1	1
GIRLS	1	1	2	TABLE REAL	-	1	1
GIRLS ARE PRETTY	1	-	1	THATS NICE	-	1	1
GLASS	1	-	1	TOO PRETTY	1	-	1
GO	1	-	1	TREE	1	-	1
GOOD	-	1	1	TREES ARE PRETTY	-	1	1
GRASS	-	1	1	UGLY	1	4	5
HAIR	2	3	5	VELVET	-	1	1
HAIRDO	-	1	1	WALL	1	-	1
HANDSOME	-	1	1	WATER	2	-	2
HERE	1	-	1	WE DRESS UP PRETTY	-	1	1
HOLES	1	-	1	WEAR CLOTHES	1	-	1
HORSES	-	1	1	WHEN A GIRL IS PRETTY	-	1	1
HOUSE	2	2	4	WICKY	1	-	1
I SAW A LADY THAT WAS PRETTY	1	-	1	WOMAN	1	-	1
INK	-	1	1	YOU	-	1	1
ITS NICE	1	-	1	YOU ARE PRETTY	1	-	1
KIND	-	1	1	YOU HAVE EARRINGS ON	-	1	1
KITTY	1	2	3	YOU LOOK PRETTY	1	-	1
				YOUR	-	1	1
				YOURE GETTING PEAS	1	-	1

RESPONSE WORD	KINDERGARTEN M	F	T	RESPONSE WORD	KINDERGARTEN M	F	T

64. QUIET

RESPONSE WORD	M	F	T
A HOUSE	1	–	1
A NAP	1	–	1
A RUGS QUIET	1	–	1
AFTERNOON	–	1	1
AS A MOUSE	1	–	1
ATTENTION	1	–	1
BABY	3	–	3
BABY ASLEEP	–	1	1
BE	3	3	6
BE QUIET	7	2	9
BE QUIET AT SCHOOL TIME	1	–	1
BE QUIET THE BABYS ASLEEP	1	–	1
BECAUSE I AM SLEEPING	–	1	1
BED	1	3	4
BEING QUIET	1	–	1
CANNON	1	–	1
CAUSE SOMEBODY IS TAKING A NAP	1	–	1
CHURCH	–	1	1
CLOCK	1	–	1
CREEP	1	–	1
CRIB	1	–	1
DECEMBER	1	–	1
DESIGN	–	1	1
DIET	–	2	2
DOG	–	1	1
DOGGIE	1	–	1
DONT	1	–	1
DONT BE LOUD	–	1	1
DONT MATTER A NOISE	1	–	1
DONT TALK	–	2	2
DOOR	1	–	1
DOOR KNOB	–	1	1
DOWN	–	1	1
FAST	1	–	1
FEET	1	–	1
FIGHT	–	1	1
FLOOR	–	1	1
FOR SINGING	–	1	1
GHOST	1	–	1
GIRL	1	–	1
GO TO SLEEP	–	2	2
HAIR	1	–	1
HEAR TV	–	1	1
HORSE	–	1	1
I DONT TALK ANYMORE	–	1	1
I WILL SING	–	1	1
IM GOING TO	–	1	1
IN HOUSE	–	1	1
IN THE HOUSE	1	–	1
ITS NIGHT AND SOMEONE IS SLEEPING	–	1	1
JESUS	1	–	1
KEEP YOUR MOUTH LOW	–	1	1
KITTY	–	1	1
KWIET	1	–	1
LADY	–	2	2
LIET	1	–	1
LIGHT	–	1	1
LOUD	4	10	14
MACHINE	1	–	1
MAP	–	1	1
MEANS TO SHUT UP	1	–	1
MIET	1	–	1
MOMMY	–	1	1
MONTH	–	1	1
MOTOR	1	–	1
MOUSE	1	1	2
MOUTH	1	–	1
MOUTH CLOSED	–	1	1
NIGHT	1	–	1
NO NOISE	1	–	1
NO RESPONSE	1	–	1
NO SCREAMING	–	1	1
NO TALKING	–	1	1
NOISE	2	5	7
NOISY	–	7	7
NONE-NOTHING	–	1	1
NOT QUIET	–	1	1
PAN	–	1	1
PAPER	1	2	3
PEACE AND QUIET	2	–	2
PEACEFUL	2	–	2
PEOPLE	1	1	2
PEOPLE SAY QUIET	1	–	1
PICK UP	–	1	1
PIG	1	–	1
PILOT	1	–	1
PIN	–	1	1
PLEASE	1	–	1
POCKET	1	–	1
QUIET ROOM	–	1	1
READ	1	–	1
READING	–	1	1
REAL QUIET	1	1	2
RIDING	–	1	1
RIGHT	1	–	1
RIOT	1	–	1
ROCKET	1	–	1
SHHH	1	2	3
SHOES	–	1	1
SHUT	1	–	1
SHUT UP	1	–	1
SIET	–	1	1
SILENT	–	1	1
SIT	2	–	2
SIT DOWN	–	1	1
SIT IN OFFICE	–	1	1
SLEEP	3	1	4
SLEEPING	–	2	2
SLOW	1	–	1
SMILE	–	1	1
SOMETIMES	–	1	1
SOUND	1	1	2
STEAL	1	–	1
STREET	1	–	1
STUPID, BE QUIET	1	–	1
TABLE	1	1	2
TALK	1	1	2
TERRY (HIS DOG)	1	–	1
THINK	1	–	1
TIET	1	–	1
TOO QUIET	1	–	1
TV	1	–	1
UP	1	–	1
WATCH	1	–	1
WATER	1	–	1
WE WERE QUIET	–	1	1
WHEN	1	–	1
WHEN CHILDREN ARE PLAYING QUIET	–	1	1
WHEN THE BABYS SLEEPING	1	1	2
WHY	1	–	1
WIET	1	1	2
WITH NOBODY MAKING A NOISE	1	–	1
XYLOPHONE	–	1	1
YELL	1	–	1
YOU RUN	1	–	1

65. RESTORE

RESPONSE WORD	M	F	T
A	1	–	1
A CART	–	1	1
A CHIMNEY	1	–	1
A MAN	1	–	1
A STORE GROCERY	1	–	1
ATTIC	1	1	2
BED	1	–	1
BEE	1	–	1
BESORE	1	–	1
BOARD	–	1	1
BOAT	1	–	1
BRIDGE	1	–	1
BUY	3	8	11
BUY FOOD	–	1	1
BUY THINGS	1	–	1
BY	1	–	1
CAN	1	–	1
CANDY	1	1	2
CANS	1	–	1
CAR	1	–	1
CARROTS	–	1	1
CHAIR	1	2	3
CHRISTMAS	1	–	1
CIGARETTE	1	–	1
CLOCK	–	1	1
CORD	1	1	2
COVERED	1	–	1
DISHES	–	1	1
DOG	–	1	1
DONUT	1	–	1
DOOR	3	1	4
EAT	1	–	1
FOOD	12	13	25
FOOD MARKET	–	1	1

RESPONSE WORD	KINDERGARTEN M	F	T

65. RESTORE

RESPONSE WORD	M	F	T	RESPONSE WORD	M	F	T
FOODS	2	—	2	PRETTY HOUSE	1	—	1
FOR REFRIGERATOR	—	1	1	R	—	1	1
FOR STORE	1	—	1	RACING	—	1	1
FOR YOUR TOUCH	1	—	1	RAIN	—	1	1
FRUIT	2	—	2	REACH	1	—	1
GET	—	1	1	READ S	1	—	1
GIVE	1	—	1	RELORE	1	—	1
GLASSES	—	1	1	REPAIR	1	—	1
GOING TO THE STORE	1	1	2	RESTORED	1	—	1
GOOD	—	1	1	ROBBER	—	1	1
GORE	—	1	1	ROBIN	—	1	1
GREEN	—	1	1	SCRATCHES	1	—	1
GROCERIES	—	1	1	SELL STUFF IN STORE	—	1	1
HE	—	1	1	SELLS FOOD	1	—	1
HEN	1	—	1	SHELF	1	—	1
HOME	1	—	1	SHELTER	1	—	1
HORSE	—	1	1	SHOP	—	1	1
I DONT KNOW	—	1	1	SIGN	2	—	2
I GET SOMETHING AT THE STORE	—	1	1	SIT	1	—	1
I HAVE A STORE	—	1	1	SOMETHING	—	2	2
I RESTORED MY HOUSE	1	—	1	STORAGE	—	1	1
IN CUPBOARD	—	1	1	STORE	6	7	13
JAY	1	—	1	STORE BURNT DOWN AND HAS TO BE BUILT OV	—	1	1
LADDER	1	—	1	STORE CLOTHES	—	1	1
LAMP SHADE	1	—	1	STORE FOOD	1	1	2
LAY	1	—	1	STORE GET STUFF AT	—	1	1
LETS GO TO THE STORE	1	1	2	STORE HIM	1	—	1
LIKE YOU BUY FOOD	—	1	1	STORE MAN	—	1	1
LORE	1	—	1	STOREKEEPER	—	1	1
LUGGAGE	—	1	1	STORES	—	1	1
MAKE STUFF	1	—	1	STORM	1	1	2
MAN	—	1	1	STORY	—	1	1
MILK	1	—	1	THE CABBAGE	1	—	1
MONEY	—	1	1	THE RESTORE WAS ON THE FLOOR	—	1	1
MORE	1	—	1	THEY	—	1	1
MOUNTAIN	—	1	1	THINGS	—	1	1
MOVE	—	1	1	TOYS	1	—	1
MY SAIL	1	—	1	TREE	1	—	1
MY TOYS	1	—	1	TRUCK	1	—	1
NO RESTORE	—	1	1	VACUUM CLEANER	—	1	1
OR	1	—	1	WALL	—	1	1
OUR OTHER FOOD	—	1	1	WATCH	1	—	1
OUT OF ORDER	1	—	1	WE GO TO STORE	—	1	1
PACKAGES	—	1	1	WEASEL	1	—	1
PAPER	1	—	1	WERE GOING TO A STORE	—	1	1
PENCIL	—	1	1	WHAT YOU BUY FROM	—	1	1
PEOPLE	1	—	1	WHEN A STORE IS MOVING	—	1	1
PEOPLE GO IN A STORE	1	—	1	WHERE YOU STORE THE FOOD	1	—	1
PESTORE	1	—	1	WIND	—	1	1
PICK UP THE ROOM	—	1	1	WINDOW	—	1	1
PLATE	1	1	2	XMAS TREE	1	—	1
POCKETBOOK	—	1	1				

66. RIVER

RESPONSE WORD	M	F	T	RESPONSE WORD	M	F	T
A BIG RIVER WHICH YOU GO OVER A BRIDGE	—	1	1	I GO SWIMMING IN THE RIVER	—	1	1
A BOAT GOES INTO THE RIVER	—	1	1	I JUMPED INTO THE RIVER	1	—	1
AT THE BEACH	—	1	1	IM SAILING A BOAT	1	—	1
BANK	—	1	1	INDIAN BOAT	1	—	1
BEACH	—	2	2	JIVER	1	—	1
BIB	1	—	1	LAKE	—	1	1
BLOCKS	—	1	1	LIGHT	—	1	1
BOAT	21	11	32	LIVER	3	—	3
BOAT IN THE RIVER	—	1	1	MONEY	1	—	1
BOATS	—	1	1	MOVE THE BOAT	—	1	1
BOX	1	—	1	NIGHT OVER THE RIVER	—	1	1
BRIDGE	2	—	2	NIVER	1	—	1
CHURCH	—	1	1	NUMBERS	1	—	1
CRASH	1	—	1	OCEAN	5	7	12
DEE	1	—	1	OLD BOOTS	1	—	1
DIVER	—	1	1	PAINT	1	—	1
DOWN THE STREAM	1	—	1	PENGUINS	—	1	1
DRINK	—	1	1	PIVER	1	—	1
DUCK	1	—	1	PRETTY	1	—	1
FATHER	3	1	4	RIBBON	1	1	2
FISH	3	2	5	RIBS	—	1	1
FISHING	1	1	2	RIDING IN CARS	—	1	1
FLOW	1	1	2	ROCK	—	1	1
FROM AN ANIMAL	—	1	1	ROCKS IN THE RIVER	1	—	1
GIVER	—	1	1	RUNNING	—	1	1
GO	—	1	1	SALLY	—	1	1
GO FISHING	1	—	1	SCREEN	1	—	1
GO INTO ATLANTIC OCEAN	—	1	1	SEA	1	1	2
GONE	—	1	1	SEAL	—	1	1
GOT LOTS OF WATER	1	—	1	SHEEP	—	1	1
GREEN	—	1	1	SHIVER	2	—	2
I GO OVER THE RIVER	—	1	1	SILENT	1	—	1
				SNAKE	—	1	1

RESPONSE WORD	M	F	T	RESPONSE WORD	M	F	T

66. RIVER

RESPONSE WORD	M	F	T	RESPONSE WORD	M	F	T
SNAKES.	1	–	1	VALLEY.	–	1	1
SOME PEOPLE SAIL ON RIVERS.	1	–	1	WALL.	1	–	1
SOME SHIPS COME INTO THE DOCK.	1	–	1	WATER.	20	19	39
STREAM.	6	6	12	WAVE.	–	1	1
SWIM.	2	6	8	WAVES.	–	2	2
SWIM IN.	–	1	1	WEED.	–	1	1
SWIMMING.	1	1	2	WHALE.	–	1	1
TIVER.	1	–	1	WHERE WATER IS.	–	1	1
TOO BIG OF A RIVER.	1	–	1	WHERE YOU GO FISHING.	–	1	1
TOOFY.	–	1	1	WHERE YOU SWIM.	–	1	1
				WOODS THAT HAVE A CREEK.	1	–	1
				YOU SWIM IN.	1	–	1

67. ROUGH

RESPONSE WORD	M	F	T	RESPONSE WORD	M	F	T
A DOG.	2	–	2	MEAN.	–	1	1
A ROCKS ROUGH.	1	–	1	MEN.	–	1	1
ANIMAL.	1	–	1	MEOW.	–	2	2
AWFUL.	1	–	1	MY BROTHER IS ROUGH.	–	1	1
BABY.	–	1	1	NASTY.	1	–	1
BABY CRIB.	–	1	1	NECK.	2	–	2
BAD.	1	1	2	NEVER.	–	1	1
BANDAGE.	–	1	1	NICKEL.	–	1	1
BARK.	1	1	2	NOISE.	–	1	1
BARKS.	–	1	1	PAPER.	–	1	1
BE NICE.	1	–	1	PENCIL.	–	1	1
BIG.	–	1	1	PEOPLE.	1	–	1
BIT.	1	–	1	PLAY.	–	2	2
BOAT.	–	1	1	PLAY NICE.	–	1	1
BOY.	–	1	1	PLAY ROUGH.	–	1	1
BOYS.	–	1	1	PLAYING ROUGH.	1	–	1
BUFF.	1	–	1	PLAYING WITH BABY.	–	1	1
BUMP.	–	1	1	PUFF.	2	–	2
BUMPY ROAD.	1	–	1	QUIET DOWN.	–	1	1
CAT.	2	1	3	RAILROAD TRACK.	–	1	1
CHAIR.	2	–	2	READY.	1	1	2
CHRISTMAS TREE.	–	1	1	RIDE.	1	–	1
CUFF.	–	1	1	ROAD.	1	–	1
CURTAINS.	–	1	1	ROCK.	–	2	2
DAY.	1	–	1	ROCKS.	2	–	2
DIRT ROAD.	1	–	1	ROUGH.	1	–	1
DOG.	13	6	19	ROUGHLY.	1	–	1
DOG BARKING.	–	1	1	ROUGHNESS.	–	1	1
DOGGY.	–	1	1	RUBBER.	1	–	1
DOGS.	1	–	1	RUFFLES.	1	–	1
DOGS RUN.	–	1	1	RUFFY.	–	1	1
DONT DO THAT.	–	1	1	RUG.	1	3	4
DONT PLAY ROUGH.	1	–	1	SAIL.	1	–	1
DONT PLAY TOO ROUGH.	1	–	1	SING.	–	1	1
DUFF.	–	1	1	SLOW.	–	1	1
EAR PLUG.	1	–	1	SOFT.	–	2	2
FIELDS.	–	1	1	STOP.	–	1	1
FIGHT.	5	2	7	TASTING CIGARETTES.	1	–	1
FIGHTING.	1	3	4	TENDER.	1	–	1
FISH.	–	1	1	TERRIBLE.	–	1	1
FOX.	–	1	1	THAT A ROUGH.	1	–	1
FRANNIE.	–	1	1	THE DOG SAYS RUFF.	–	1	1
GENTLE.	–	1	1	TIGHTS.	–	1	1
GET ROUGH.	1	–	1	TOO.	1	–	1
GOD.	1	–	1	TOO ROUGH.	1	2	3
GOLD.	–	1	1	TOUGH.	4	8	12
GOLF.	1	–	1	TREE.	–	1	1
GORILLA.	–	1	1	TRUCK.	–	1	1
GROUND.	1	–	1	TWO PERSONS ARE FIGHTING.	–	1	1
GRUFF.	–	1	1	WAFFLES.	–	1	1
GUFF.	–	1	1	WATCH.	1	–	1
GUY.	–	1	1	WATER.	2	–	2
GYM.	1	–	1	WE PLAY ROUGH.	–	1	1
HANDLE OF A DRAWER.	1	–	1	WERF.	–	1	1
HARD.	1	2	3	WHALE.	1	–	1
HAVING A FIGHT.	–	1	1	WHEN A DOGS PLAYING ROUGH.	–	1	1
HI.	–	1	1	WHEN YOURE FIGHTING ROUGH.	1	–	1
HIS TAIL WAS WAGGING.	1	–	1	WILD HORSE.	–	1	1
HIT.	–	1	1	WIND.	1	–	1
HOLE IN THE SWEATERS.	–	1	1	WINDOW OPENED.	1	–	1
HORSE.	1	–	1	WIRE.	1	–	1
HOUSE.	1	–	1	WITH THE BABY.	–	1	1
HOUSING.	1	–	1	WOOFY.	1	–	1
HUFF.	1	–	1	WRESTLE.	2	–	2
HURRY.	–	1	1	YELLOW LIGHT.	1	–	1
I ROUGH WITH MY DOGGIE.	–	1	1	YOU.	–	1	1
I RUN AFTER YOU.	–	1	1	YOU WEAR CLOTHES.	–	1	1
IS TOUGH.	1	–	1	YOURE TOO ROUGH IN THE HOUSE.	1	–	1
LAMB.	1	–	1	YOURE VERY ROUGH.	1	–	1
LUD.	1	–	1				

68. RUN

RESPONSE WORD	M	F	T	RESPONSE WORD	M	F	T
A CAR.	–	1	1	AND GET THE BALL.	–	1	1
AFTER.	–	1	1	AND JUMP.	–	1	1
AFTER A BUNNY.	–	1	1	AND PLAY.	–	2	2

RESPONSE WORD	KINDERGARTEN M	F	T

68. RUN

RESPONSE WORD	M	F	T	RESPONSE WORD	M	F	T
AND SEE	1	–	1	IN THE CELLAR	1	–	1
AWAY	3	1	4	JUMP	1	2	3
BABY	–	1	1	LADY	–	1	1
BALL	1	–	1	LUND	1	–	1
BECAUSE MY CAT RUN AWAY	–	1	1	MACHINE	1	–	1
BILLY GOAT	–	1	1	MAN	–	1	1
BOY	3	2	5	MOUSE	–	1	1
BRUSHES	1	–	1	ONE	1	1	2
BUG	1	–	1	PEOPLE	1	–	1
BUN	1	2	3	PIG	1	–	1
CAR	–	1	1	PLAY	8	3	11
CAT	–	1	1	RACE	1	1	2
CHAIR	1	–	1	RAN	1	–	1
CHILDREN RUN	–	1	1	REPTILE	1	–	1
CHILDREN RUNNING	–	1	1	RING	–	1	1
CLAP YOUR HANDS	–	1	1	RINSE	1	–	1
COME	1	–	1	ROBIN	1	–	1
CRUN	–	1	1	RUG	2	–	2
DARK	1	–	1	RUN AND PLAY	–	1	1
DO	–	1	1	RUNNING DOWN THE SIDEWALK	–	1	1
DOG	2	1	3	RUNNING DOWN THE STREET	1	–	1
DONE	1	–	1	RUT	–	1	1
DOOR	–	1	1	SCHOOL TEACHER	1	–	1
DOWN AND PLAY	1	–	1	SCRIBBLE	–	1	1
DRUM	1	–	1	SHOES	3	–	3
DUN	–	1	1	SIDEWALK	1	–	1
EXCITEMENT	1	–	1	SKATE	1	–	1
FALL	4	2	6	SKIP	4	8	12
FALLING DOWN	1	–	1	SLIDING BOARD	–	1	1
FAST	12	6	18	SNEAKERS	–	1	1
FEEL	–	1	1	SOME PEOPLE RUN	–	1	1
FEET	3	1	4	STOP	3	3	6
FELL	1	1	2	SUN	2	1	3
FOOT	1	–	1	TELL	–	1	1
FUN	3	6	9	TENNIS SHOES	1	–	1
GETS YOU HEALTHY AND STRONG	–	1	1	TIRED	–	2	2
GIRL	–	1	1	TO A HOUSE	1	–	1
GO GET THAT STICK	–	1	1	TO CATCH THE BALL	1	–	1
GOING	–	1	1	TO OUR HOUSE	1	–	1
GOLF	1	–	1	TO THE MARKET	–	1	1
GRASS	–	1	1	TON	–	2	2
HIDE	–	2	2	WAGON	1	–	1
HOME	1	–	1	WALK	6	7	13
HOP	–	1	1	WAY	–	1	1
HOUSE	2	3	5	WHITE	1	–	1
HUM	1	–	1	WIND	1	–	1
				YOU FALL DOWN	–	1	1

69. SAD

RESPONSE WORD	M	F	T	RESPONSE WORD	M	F	T
A CAT	1	–	1	GO AT THE HOSPITAL	–	1	1
ADD	2	1	3	GO THIS AWAY	–	1	1
ANGEL	1	–	1	GOT	–	1	1
AWFUL	1	–	1	HAD	1	–	1
BABY	1	–	1	HAPPY	8	18	26
BAD	2	2	4	HIGHCHAIR	–	1	1
BE HAPPY	1	–	1	HURT	–	1	1
BECAUSE	–	1	1	I DONT HAVE ANY FRIENDS	1	–	1
BECAUSE NOBODY TO PLAY WITH	1	–	1	I WAS SAD WHEN I GOT IN THE CAR	1	–	1
BELT	1	–	1	IM CRYING	–	1	1
BOMB	1	–	1	IM SAD	2	1	3
BOY	2	–	2	INSIDE	1	–	1
BRICKS	–	1	1	JUMP	1	–	1
BRIGHT	1	–	1	KID	1	–	1
BUCKET	–	2	2	LAD	2	–	2
CAD	1	–	1	LETTER	–	1	1
CAT	1	–	1	LIKE YOURE SAD	–	1	1
CHIMNEY	–	1	1	LIVING	1	–	1
CRY	11	5	16	LOCK	1	–	1
CRYING	2	9	11	LONELY	–	1	1
CUZ MY DOG WON T COME TO ME	–	1	1	LONESOME	1	–	1
DAD	–	1	1	MAD	5	4	9
DID	1	–	1	MAN	–	1	1
DIRT	–	1	1	ME	1	–	1
DISHES	–	1	1	MEAN	–	2	2
DOG	1	–	1	MOTHER LOST HER CHILD	1	–	1
DONT	2	–	2	MOUTH	–	1	1
DONT WANT TO GO TO BED	1	–	1	MOVIE	1	–	1
FACE	3	1	4	NAME	1	–	1
FAD	–	1	1	NOBODY TO PLAY WITH	1	–	1
FALL OFF	1	–	1	NOBODY WANTS TO PLAY WITH YOU	–	1	1
FEELING	1	–	1	NOT HAPPY	1	–	1
FRIEND	–	1	1	NUMBER	–	1	1
FUNNY-FACE	–	1	1	PAD	–	1	1
GIRL	–	3	3	PENCIL	1	1	2
GIVE	–	1	1	PEOPLE	3	3	6
GLAD	3	2	5	PERSON	–	2	2
GLASS	–	1	1	PIPE	1	–	1

RESPONSE WORD	KINDERGARTEN M	F	T	RESPONSE WORD	KINDERGARTEN M	F	T

69. SAD

RESPONSE WORD	M	F	T	RESPONSE WORD	M	F	T
PLAY	1	–	1	SOUR	–	1	1
PLAYGROUND	–	1	1	STORIES	1	–	1
POOR	1	1	2	STORY	1	–	1
ROCKS	1	–	1	TABLE RIM	–	1	1
SAND	3	2	5	THATS WHAT HAPPENED	–	1	1
SEE	–	1	1	THINK	–	1	1
SHE SAT ON A HORSE	–	1	1	TONGUE	1	–	1
SHOVEL	–	1	1	TOO SAD	1	–	1
SISTERS GONNA BE POLICEMAN	1	–	1	UNHAPPY	1	–	1
SIT	–	1	1	WAD	1	–	1
SITS DOWN ON THE CHAIR	–	1	1	WALK	–	1	1
SMILE	2	–	2	WATER	–	1	1
SOMEONE IS SAD AND THEY FELL DOWN	–	1	1	WE CRY	–	1	1
SOMETHING	1	–	1	WHATS WRONG	–	1	1
SOMETIMES YOUR MOUTH IS ALL LIKE THAT A	1	–	1	WHEN PEOPLE ARE SAD	–	1	1
				YOU SAT DOWN	1	–	1
				YOURE CRYING	1	–	1

70. SALT

RESPONSE WORD	M	F	T	RESPONSE WORD	M	F	T
AND BUTTER ON YOUR EGGS	–	1	1	OCEAN	–	1	1
AND PEPPER	1	1	2	ON DINNER	–	1	1
BACK	1	–	1	ON HAMBURGER	1	–	1
BAD	1	–	1	PALT	1	–	1
BALL	1	1	2	PEOPLE PUT SALT ON THEIR PLATE	–	1	1
BED	1	–	1	PEPPER	34	40	74
BETTER	1	–	1	PEPPER IT	1	–	1
BEVERLY	–	1	1	PIN	1	–	1
BOAT	–	1	1	POTATO	1	–	1
BOTTLE	1	–	1	POTATOES	2	–	2
BOX	1	–	1	POUR	–	1	1
BUTTER	1	–	1	POWDER	–	1	1
CEMENT	–	1	1	PUT	–	1	1
CEREAL	1	–	1	PUT ON EGGS	–	1	1
COOK	–	1	1	PUT ON FOOD	–	1	1
CRACKERS	–	1	1	PUT ON SOMETHING	–	1	1
DALT	–	1	1	PUT ON YOUR FOOD	1	–	1
DAUGHTER	–	1	1	PUTTING ON YOUR EGG	–	1	1
DELICIOUS	1	–	1	RAIN	1	–	1
DOESNT TASTE VERY GOOD	–	1	1	SALAD	1	–	1
EAT	1	–	1	SALT WATER FOR FISH	1	–	1
EGG	1	3	4	SALTY	2	–	2
EGGS	–	1	1	SAND	1	–	1
FOOD	3	3	6	SANDY	–	1	1
FOUGHT	1	–	1	SEA	1	–	1
GIVE ME THE SALT	1	–	1	SHAKER	1	1	2
HALT	–	1	1	SHIRT	1	–	1
HAMBURGER	1	–	1	SKY	–	1	1
HOPE	1	–	1	SMOKE STACK	1	–	1
HOT	–	3	3	SNEEZE	1	–	1
I DONT IT TOO SALTY	1	–	1	SOFT	–	1	1
I DONT LIKE IT	–	1	1	SOMEBODYS EATING SALT	1	–	1
I DONT LIKE SALT	–	1	1	SPILLING	1	–	1
I GET IN THE SALT	–	1	1	STEAK	1	–	1
I PUT SOME SALT ON MY BUTTER	–	1	1	SUGAR	1	2	3
I SHAKE THE SALT SHAKER ON MY HEAD	1	–	1	SWEATING	–	1	1
IN HAM	1	–	1	THIRSTY	1	–	1
JARFUL	–	1	1	TOMATO	1	–	1
LALT	2	–	2	TOO MUCH SALT	1	–	1
LOVE YOU	–	1	1	WALK	–	1	1
MAKE ME DIE	1	–	1	WATER	7	2	9
MALT	3	1	4	WE SNEEZE	1	–	1
MEAT	1	2	3	WHITE	1	1	2
MILKSHAKES	–	1	1	WOOD	1	–	1
NEVER PUT TOO MUCH SALT ON ANY FOOD	–	1	1	WOULD YOU PUT IT ON MY EGGS	–	1	1
NEWSPAPER	–	1	1	WROUGHT	–	1	1
NOODLES	–	1	1	YOU PUT ON YOUR FOOD	1	–	1
				YOU SPRINKLE ON MEAT	1	–	1

71. SELDOM

RESPONSE WORD	M	F	T	RESPONSE WORD	M	F	T
A NAME	–	1	1	BELL	2	1	3
A TREE	–	1	1	BELLS ON	1	–	1
AIR	1	–	1	BIRD	–	1	1
ALLIGATOR	1	–	1	BOAT	1	–	1
AN	–	1	1	BOOK	–	1	1
ANIMAL	1	–	1	BREAKS	1	–	1
APPLE	1	–	1	BROOM	–	1	1
APPLES	1	–	1	BUMBLEBEE	–	1	1
ASH TRAY	–	1	1	BUTTON	–	2	2
AWFUL	1	–	1	CAN	1	–	1
BABY	1	–	1	CANTALOUPE	–	1	1
BATHROOM	–	1	1	CELERY	1	–	1
BEE	1	–	1	CELERY	2	1	3
BEEP	1	–	1	CELLAR	3	–	3
BELDOM	1	–	1	CHAIR	1	1	2

RESPONSE WORD	KINDERGARTEN M	F	T
71. SELDOM			

RESPONSE WORD	M	F	T	RESPONSE WORD	M	F	T
CHICKEN	1	–	1	PEOPLE	1	1	2
CHRISTMAS TREE	–	1	1	PEPPER	1	–	1
CLOSE	–	1	1	PILLER	1	–	1
CLOTHES	1	–	1	POT	1	–	1
COAT	–	1	1	QUIET	–	1	1
COLD	1	–	1	RING	–	2	2
COSTUME	–	1	1	SAILBOAT	1	–	1
COW	1	–	1	SALT	1	–	1
CRAYON	1	–	1	SARA JACQUA	1	–	1
CRYSANTHEMUMS	–	1	1	SAW	–	1	1
DID	1	–	1	SCHOOL	–	1	1
DISH	1	–	1	SEE A LOT OF THINGS	–	1	1
DO	1	–	1	SELL	6	5	11
DOG	–	1	1	SELL A DRESS	1	–	1
DONT SELL THEM	–	1	1	SELL A HOUSE	–	1	1
DOOR	1	–	1	SELL CLOTHES	1	–	1
DOORKNOB	–	1	1	SELL DOGGY	1	–	1
DUMB PERSON	–	1	1	SELL FOOD	1	1	2
DUMB-BELL	1	–	1	SELL FRUIT	1	–	1
DUMP	1	–	1	SELL FRUITS OF ALL KINDS	1	–	1
ED SULLIVAN	1	–	1	SELL PEOPLE	–	1	1
EGG MAN	1	–	1	SELL STUFF	1	–	1
ELDOM	2	–	2	SELL THEM	1	–	1
EYES	–	1	1	SELL THINGS	–	2	2
FARM	1	–	1	SELLED FOOD	1	–	1
FEET	–	1	1	SELM	1	–	1
FENDEN	–	1	1	SEWING	–	1	1
FILL	–	1	1	SH	1	–	1
FINGERNAILS	–	1	1	SHELF	1	–	1
FLAG	–	1	1	SHOES	1	–	1
FLOOR	–	1	1	SHOULDER	1	–	1
FLOWER	2	1	3	SILVER	–	1	1
FOOD	–	4	4	SILVERWARE	1	–	1
FORK	–	1	1	SOMEONE IS CUTTING A WIRE	–	1	1
FRUIT	–	1	1	SOUGHT	1	–	1
FUN	–	1	1	STONE	–	1	1
GELDOM	–	1	1	SUGAR	–	1	1
GIRL	–	1	1	SWEATER	–	1	1
GREEN EYES	–	1	1	TABLE	2	1	3
GROCERIES	–	1	1	TASTE SALTY	–	1	1
HAIR	–	1	1	TELL	1	1	2
HAMMER	1	–	1	TELLDEM	1	–	1
HANDSOME	–	1	1	THE BOX	–	1	1
HELD	–	1	1	THE CANS	1	–	1
HOT	–	1	1	THEM	1	–	1
HOUSE	–	1	1	THEY RE FOR SALE	1	–	1
I SAW A SELDOM	1	–	1	THROUGH	–	1	1
I SELL SOME BEADS	–	1	1	TO	–	1	1
I WANT IT	–	1	1	TO ME	–	1	1
INSULT	–	1	1	TO THEM	–	1	1
IRON	1	–	1	TOY	2	1	3
JAR	–	1	1	TRAIN	1	–	1
JUDGE	1	–	1	TREE	1	1	2
KILLED THEM	1	–	1	TRUCK	1	–	1
LAMB	2	–	2	TURKEY	1	–	1
LELDOM	1	–	1	TWO WINDOWS	–	1	1
LET HER	1	–	1	WAGON	–	1	1
LIKE YOURE SHOUTING	1	–	1	WALL	–	1	1
LIPS	–	1	1	WASH	–	1	1
LITTLE	–	1	1	WATER	–	1	1
MAIL THEM	–	1	1	WE SELL THE BUNNY RABBIT	–	1	1
MAKING A DRESS	1	–	1	WELDOM	1	–	1
MELDOM	1	–	1	WELL	–	1	1
MONEY	1	–	1	WHEN SOMEBODYS SELLING SOMETHING	–	1	1
NAME	–	1	1	WINDOW	1	–	1
OUT OF	–	1	1	YOU PUT ON THE ROAD	1	–	1
PAPER	1	1	2				
PEACHES	1	–	1				

72. SELL			

RESPONSE WORD	M	F	T	RESPONSE WORD	M	F	T
A COAT	1	–	1	CANDY	–	1	1
A HOUSE	–	1	1	CAR	1	–	1
A LIGHT BULB	1	–	1	CARS	–	1	1
ADVERTISEMENT	1	–	1	CELERY	1	1	2
AN APPLE	–	1	1	CELLAR	2	2	4
APPLE	2	1	3	CHAIR	1	–	1
APPLES	1	1	2	CLOTHES	4	–	4
AT A STORE	–	1	1	COOKIES	–	1	1
AT THE GROCERY STORE	–	1	1	COW	1	–	1
BANANAS	2	1	3	CRY	–	1	1
BARGAIN	–	1	1	CURTAINS	1	–	1
BASEMENT	–	1	1	DELL	1	1	2
BEAR	–	1	1	DOG	–	1	1
BELL	1	1	2	DOGS	–	1	1
BERRIES	–	1	1	DONT	–	1	1
BIRD	–	1	1	DONT SELL	–	1	1
BOAT	1	–	1	DOOR	–	2	2
BREAK	–	1	1	DOWN	–	1	1
BUY	–	1	1	EAT	–	1	1

RESPONSE WORD	KINDERGARTEN M	F	T	RESPONSE WORD	KINDERGARTEN M	F	T

72. SELL

RESPONSE WORD	M	F	T	RESPONSE WORD	M	F	T
EGGS	1	1	2	PEOPLE	–	1	1
ELL	1	–	1	PEOPLE SELLING SOMEBODY	–	1	1
EYE	–	1	1	PLAYING IN THE CELLAR	1	–	1
FELL	–	1	1	PRESENT	2	–	2
FLOWER	–	1	1	RABBIT	1	–	1
FLOWERS	1	1	2	RING	–	1	1
FOOD	7	8	15	ROSES	–	1	1
FRUIT	2	2	4	RUGS	–	1	1
GLASS	–	1	1	SALAD	1	–	1
GO ON, GO	–	1	1	SALT	–	1	1
GOOD	–	1	1	SAW	1	1	2
GRAPES	–	2	2	SELLER	1	–	1
GREEN	2	–	2	SELLING PAPERS	1	–	1
GROCERIES	1	1	2	SELLING TOYS	1	–	1
GROCERY	1	–	1	SELLY	–	1	1
GUN	1	–	1	SHAVE	1	–	1
HAMBURGER	–	1	1	SHELLS	1	–	1
HAMBURGERS	1	–	1	SHOE	–	2	2
HELL	–	1	1	SHOES	1	–	1
HORSE	–	1	1	SHOP	–	1	1
HOUSE	2	1	3	SKIN	–	1	1
I FELL	1	–	1	SMALL	1	–	1
I SELL SOME CLOTHES	–	1	1	SNAKE	1	–	1
I SELL SOME COOKIES	–	1	1	SOME XMAS TREES	1	–	1
I SOLD MY HORSE	1	–	1	SOMEBODY SELLS GLASSES	1	–	1
ICE CREAM	1	–	1	SOMETHING	3	–	3
JAIL	1	–	1	SORRY	1	–	1
JARS	1	–	1	STAND	–	1	1
KEEP	1	–	1	STORE	1	1	2
L	1	–	1	STRAWBERRIES	–	1	1
LELL	1	–	1	STUFF	–	1	1
LITTLE	–	1	1	TABLE	–	1	1
LOLLYPOP	1	–	1	TEAPOT	1	–	1
MAN	–	1	1	TELL	1	–	1
MAT	–	1	1	THE	1	–	1
MAYONNAISE	–	1	1	THE FRUITS	1	–	1
ME	–	1	1	THE POPCORN	1	–	1
ME AN APPLE	1	–	1	THINGS AT GROCERY	1	1	1
MEAT	1	–	1	THIS CAT	1	–	1
MELL	2	1	3	TOO LATE	–	1	1
MITT	–	1	1	TOO MUCH	1	–	1
MIX	1	–	1	TOY	2	–	2
MONEY	1	1	2	TOYS	1	–	1
MY FOOD	–	1	1	TOYS TO THE POOR CHILDREN	1	–	1
NAP	–	1	1	TRASH CAN	1	–	1
NO	–	1	1	WASHING MACHINE	–	1	1
NOSE	–	1	1	WATER	–	1	1
ON	–	1	1	WATERMELONS	–	1	1
ORANGE	1	–	1	WE SELL OUR HOUSE	–	1	1
ORANGES	1	–	1	WERE GOING TO HAVE A SPECIAL SALE TODAY	1	–	1
OWL	1	–	1	WINDOW	–	1	1
PANTS	1	–	1	WOOD	1	1	2
PAPER	–	1	1	YELL	1	–	1
PEACHES	1	–	1	YOUR	–	1	1
PEANUTS	1	1	2	YOUR HOUSE	1	–	1
PELL	1	–	1				

73. SHE

RESPONSE WORD	M	F	T	RESPONSE WORD	M	F	T
A BABY SHEEP	–	1	1	DOOR	1	–	1
A BED	1	–	1	DRESS	2	1	3
A GIRL	2	2	4	DROPPED THIS BAG	–	1	1
A MAN RUNNING A CEMENT TRUCK	1	–	1	FALL	–	1	1
AND HE	–	1	1	FINGER	–	1	1
AND HER FRIENDS	1	–	1	FLOWER	–	1	1
ANGELS	1	–	1	FOLLOWED ME TO SCHOOL	1	–	1
BABYSIT	1	–	1	G	1	1	2
BARN	1	–	1	GIRL	12	11	23
BEAT	–	1	1	GIRL DOG	–	1	1
BED	1	1	2	GLASS	–	1	1
BEE	2	1	3	GO	1	1	2
BIRDIE	1	–	1	GOATS	–	1	1
BLOWING	–	1	1	GOSH	–	1	1
BOY	1	1	2	HAD	–	1	1
BRIDGE	–	1	1	HAM	1	–	1
BROKE	1	–	1	HAS BANANA	–	1	1
BUNNY	–	1	1	HE	5	14	19
BUTTONS	–	1	1	HER	2	2	4
CAME	–	1	1	HIM	2	6	8
CAT	1	–	1	HOUSE	1	–	1
CHEESE	1	–	1	I	1	–	1
CLEAN SHEET ON	–	1	1	I WALK WITH HER	–	1	1
COMING	–	1	1	IS	1	–	1
CRAYONING ON THE TABLE	–	1	1	IS A GIRL	1	1	2
D	1	–	1	IS A LAMB	1	–	1
DEEP	–	1	1	IS A NICE GIRL	1	–	1
DID	2	1	3	IS A WOMAN	–	1	1
DIED	–	1	1	IS DOING SOMETHING	–	1	1
DOG	1	–	1	IS MY GIRLFRIEND	–	1	1
				IS OUTSIDE	1	–	1

RESPONSE WORD	M	F	T
73. SHE			
IS PRETTY	1	–	1
IS SITTING DOWN	1	–	1
IT	–	1	1
KEY	3	–	3
KICKED A BUCKET	1	–	1
LAMBS	1	–	1
LEAN	1	–	1
LIKE A GIRL	–	1	1
LOVE	1	1	2
LOVES	–	1	1
MA	–	1	1
MAN	–	2	2
MATCH	–	1	1
ME	2	1	3
MESSED	1	–	1
MET	–	1	1
MOTHER	–	1	1
NICE	1	–	1
PEA	3	–	3
PEDALS	1	–	1
PET	–	1	1
PICTURE	–	1	1
PICTURES	1	–	1
PLAY	1	–	1
PRETTY	2	–	2
SCHOOL	–	1	1
SHEEP	10	5	15
SHEEP DOG	1	–	1
SHEET	–	1	1
SHEETS RUN	–	1	1
SHEPHERD	1	–	1
SHES A GIRL	–	1	1
SHOES	1	1	2
THE EIGHTH	1	–	1
TOO BAD	1	–	1
TOO OF A SHE	1	–	1
TOOK A DOG	–	1	1
TURN	1	–	1
UNLOCK	1	–	1
WALKS	1	–	1
WANTED TO VISIT	–	1	1
WAS	–	1	1
WE	1	–	1
WENT	1	–	1
WENT TO THE BATHROOM	1	–	1
WHISPER	1	–	1
WHO	–	1	1
WINDOW	–	1	1
YOU	2	–	2

RESPONSE WORD	M	F	T
74. SHEEP			
A LAMB	–	1	1
A PAPER	1	–	1
ANIMAL	1	2	3
BAA	2	1	3
BARN	–	1	1
BED	1	1	2
BEEP	–	1	1
BLACK SHEEP	–	2	2
BLANKET	1	1	2
BOO	1	–	1
BOY	–	1	1
BUY	–	1	1
CHEE	1	–	1
COW	2	1	3
COWS	1	–	1
CRIB	–	1	1
CUB SCOUT	–	1	1
CURLY	–	1	1
DEEP	2	1	3
DOG	8	4	12
DOGGIE	1	–	1
EAR	–	1	1
EAT	1	–	1
EEP	–	1	1
FARM	1	–	1
FARMER	1	–	1
FARMERS HOUSE	1	–	1
FLOCK	–	1	1
FOX	2	–	2
FUR	–	1	1
GIRLS	–	1	1
GO SHEEP	1	–	1
GOAT	1	1	2
GOD	1	–	1
GONE	1	–	1
GRASSES	–	1	1
GUARD	1	–	1
HAIR	1	2	3
HAS FUR	–	1	1
HAVE A FEW	–	1	1
HAVE A LITTLE LAMB	1	–	1
HEAP	–	3	3
HEAPS	1	–	1
HEEP	1	–	1
HER	–	1	1
HORSE	1	6	7
HUNTER	1	–	1
I SEE A SHEEP	–	1	1
IM GOING TO PET THE SHEEP	–	1	1
IN THE DARK	1	–	1
IS WHITE	1	–	1
JESUS	–	1	1
KEEP	2	–	2
LADY	–	1	1
LAMB	8	7	15
LAMBS	1	1	2
LAUGHTER	1	–	1
LAYING DOWN	–	1	1
LEAP	3	–	3
LEG	1	–	1
LETTER	1	–	1
LIGHT	1	–	1
LION	–	1	1
MAA	1	–	1
MAD	–	1	1
MAN	–	2	2
MASTER	–	1	1
MAT	–	1	1
ME	1	–	1
MEADOW	1	1	2
MEN TAKE THE WOOL OFF SHEEP FOR WINTER	–	1	1
NOISE	1	–	1
NOISE-BAA-BAA	–	1	1
NUMBER	–	1	1
ON THE HILL	1	–	1
PANTS	–	1	1
PASTURE	–	1	1
PEEP	1	–	1
PET	1	–	1
PIANO	–	1	1
POCKETBOOK	–	1	1
RUN	1	–	1
RUN AWAY	1	–	1
SAYS BAA	1	1	2
SEW	1	–	1
SHARE	1	–	1
SHE	–	3	3
SHEET	2	3	5
SHEPHERD	2	1	3
SHOE	1	2	3
SKIN	1	2	3
SLEEP	1	–	1
SNOW	–	1	1
SOME SHEEP JOIN OTHER SHEEP	–	1	1
STICK	–	1	1
TABLE	1	–	1
TAKE CARE OF	2	–	2
TALK	1	–	1
TENDING	1	–	1
THEY GO BAA	1	–	1
THEY GOT SOME MORE SHEEP	1	–	1
TRUCK	1	–	1
WALK	–	2	2
WEEP	1	–	1
WHITE	1	6	7
WHITE HAIR	1	–	1
WINDOWS	1	–	1
WOLF	2	–	2
WOOL	8	10	18

RESPONSE WORD	M	F	T
75. SHORT			
BABY	1	4	5
BALL	1	–	1
BIG	1	3	4
BOARD	–	1	1
BOAT	1	1	2
BOWL	–	1	1

RESPONSE WORD	KINDERGARTEN M	F	T	RESPONSE WORD	KINDERGARTEN M	F	T

75. SHORT

RESPONSE WORD	M	F	T	RESPONSE WORD	M	F	T
BOX	-	1	1	PANT	1	-	1
BOY	2	1	3	PANTS	17	9	26
BOYS	-	1	1	PEOPLE	1	1	2
CALL	1	-	1	PEOPLE ARE SHORT	-	1	1
CALLING	1	-	1	PERSON	-	2	2
CAT	1	1	2	PICTURE	-	1	1
CHAIR	1	-	1	PIN	-	1	1
CHRISTMAS TREE	-	1	1	PLATE	-	1	1
CIRCUIT	1	-	1	PORK	2	-	2
CLOCK	-	1	1	PORT	2	1	3
CLOTHES	1	-	1	QUART	-	1	1
CLOTHES YOU WEAR	-	1	1	RAINBOW	-	1	1
CORK	1	-	1	REAL SHORT	-	1	1
COURT	1	-	1	RIDE	-	1	1
CUT	4	-	4	ROPE	-	1	1
CUT DOLL CLOTHES SHORT	-	1	1	RUBBER	1	-	1
DOG	1	-	1	RUN AND DANCE	-	1	1
DORT	-	1	1	SEE	1	1	2
DRESS	1	3	4	SHADE	-	1	1
DUMB	-	1	1	SHEEP	1	-	1
FAST	-	1	1	SHIRT	1	1	2
FAT	1	-	1	SHORE BEACH	1	-	1
FELLOW	1	-	1	SHORT CUT	-	1	1
FIVE	1	-	1	SHORTS	1	4	5
FLAT	1	-	1	SHORTY	1	-	1
FLOWER	-	2	2	SHORTY PANTS	1	-	1
FORCE	-	1	1	SHORTY-FACE	1	-	1
GIRL	-	1	1	SKINNY	2	-	2
GOT	1	-	1	SKIRT	-	1	1
GREEN	1	-	1	SKY	1	-	1
HAIR	-	4	4	SLACKS	-	1	1
HIGH	-	1	1	SLEEVES	1	-	1
HOLE	1	-	1	SMALL	-	2	2
HORSE	2	1	3	SOMETHING IS SHORT	-	1	1
HORT	-	1	1	SORE	-	1	1
HOUSE	-	1	1	STICK	1	-	1
I	-	1	1	STOP	1	-	1
IN	1	-	1	STRING	1	-	1
KNIFE	-	1	1	SUGAR	-	2	2
LAMB	1	-	1	TAIL	1	-	1
LAMP	1	-	1	TALL	3	4	7
LAWN MOWER	1	-	1	THIS IS A SHORT BLOUSE	-	1	1
LITTLE	2	1	3	TINY MOUSE	-	1	1
LONG	5	9	14	TOO SHORT	1	-	1
LORT	2	1	3	TOY	1	-	1
LOW	-	1	1	WALK	1	-	1
MAKE IT BE LONG	1	-	1	WART	1	-	1
MAN	2	-	2	WARTS	1	-	1
MEDIUM	-	1	1	WE WEAR	-	1	1
MOMMY	-	1	1	WOW	1	-	1
MONEY	1	-	1	WRITING	1	-	1
MORT	1	-	1	YOUD BETTER GET IT LONG	-	1	1
MOUSE	1	1	2	YOUR	1	-	1
NOT VERY LONG	1	-	1				

76. SINCE

RESPONSE WORD	M	F	T	RESPONSE WORD	M	F	T
A BICYCLES A CINCH TO RIDE	1	-	1	CINCINNATI	1	1	2
A FLOWER	-	1	1	COMPANY	1	-	1
A HOUSE	1	-	1	CUP	-	1	1
A SOLDIER	1	-	1	DANCE	-	1	1
AGAIN	-	1	1	DARK	-	1	1
AGE	1	-	1	DINCE	-	1	1
AGO	1	-	1	DIRT	-	1	1
AND THEN	-	1	1	DO SOMETHING	1	-	1
ASHTRAY	-	1	1	DONE	1	-	1
BAD	-	1	1	DOOR	-	1	1
BASKET	-	1	1	EEL	1	-	1
BEGIN	1	1	2	EVERY DAY	-	1	1
BELT	-	1	1	EYE	-	1	1
BEND	1	-	1	FAMILY	-	1	1
BINCE	2	1	3	FATHER	-	1	1
BIRD	1	-	1	FENCE	2	1	3
BOAT	2	-	2	FIX	1	-	1
BOTTLE	-	2	2	FLY	1	-	1
BOUGHT	1	-	1	FOR SOMEBODY	-	1	1
BOW	-	1	1	FRUIT	-	1	1
BOY	-	1	1	GATE	1	-	1
BOYS	-	1	1	GLIN	1	-	1
BRUSH YOUR TEETH	-	1	1	GO INSIDE	1	-	1
BUILDING	1	-	1	GO-ED	-	1	1
BUS	1	-	1	GOING ON VACATION	1	-	1
BUTTER	1	-	1	GONE TO SCHOOL	-	1	1
BUTTERFLY	1	-	1	GOOD	-	1	1
CANDY	-	1	1	GREEN LIGHT	1	-	1
CENT	-	1	1	GROUND	1	-	1
CENTS	-	1	1	HAY	-	1	1
CENTURY	-	1	1	HEAD	1	1	2
CHAIR	-	2	2	HINTS	1	1	2
				HONEY	2	-	2

RESPONSE WORD	KINDERGARTEN M	F	T	RESPONSE WORD	KINDERGARTEN M	F	T

76. SINCE

RESPONSE WORD	M	F	T
HORSE	–	2	2
HOUSE	–	1	1
I	2	4	6
I CAME	–	1	1
I CANT DO THAT ILL PLAY WITH THE TRAIN	1	–	1
I DID A GOOD JOB	1	–	1
I GOT SENSE	1	–	1
I M GOING	–	1	1
I SAT DOWN I GOT BETTER	1	–	1
I SAW MY GRANDMOTHER	–	1	1
I SIT DOWN WITH YOU	–	1	1
I WALKED ON A FENCE	1	–	1
I WAS GOING OUTSIDE	–	1	1
I WILL BE THERE	–	1	1
IM ALONE	1	–	1
IN	1	–	1
IN THE MEADOW	1	–	1
IT HAPPENED	1	–	1
KITTY CAT	1	–	1
LADY	–	1	1
LAST YEAR	–	1	1
LAWNMOWER	1	–	1
LIGHT	1	–	1
LIN	1	–	1
LINCE	1	–	1
LINT	–	1	1
LITTLE SENSE	1	–	1
LOVE	–	1	1
MAKE SENSE	–	1	1
ME	1	–	1
MINCE	1	–	1
MITTEN	1	–	1
MONEY	1	1	2
NO	1	–	1
NO SUCH THING	–	1	1
NUMBERS	1	–	1
OUTSIDE	1	–	1
PANCAKE	–	1	1
PAPER COLORS	1	–	1
PEARS	–	1	1
PEN	1	–	1
PENCIL	–	1	1
PEOPLE	–	2	2
PIECE OF A DRAWER	1	–	1
PIG	1	–	1
PIN	1	–	1
PINCE	–	1	1
PINCH	1	–	1
PURR	–	1	1
ROSES	–	1	1
SAND	–	1	1
SAT	–	1	1
SAW YOU AGAIN	–	1	1
SCHOOL	–	1	1
SEEDY	–	1	1

RESPONSE WORD	M	F	T
SEND A CARD	1	–	1
SENSITIVE	–	1	1
SIMPLE	–	1	1
SINK	1	–	1
SISTER	1	–	1
SIT	–	1	1
SIT DOWN	1	–	1
SIT ON A CHAIR	–	1	1
SKY	–	1	1
SOMETHING	2	–	2
SPENDING	–	1	1
STINKS	1	–	1
STREAM	1	–	1
SUDS	–	1	1
TABLE	1	–	1
THANKSGIVING	1	–	1
THAT	1	–	1
THE	–	1	1
THE YEARS	1	–	1
THEN	1	1	2
TINCE	1	–	1
TREE	–	2	2
TRUCK	–	1	1
VACATION	1	–	1
WALK	–	1	1
WATCH	1	–	1
WATER	1	1	2
WAY	–	1	1
WE	2	2	4
WE CAME	1	–	1
WE HAD A DOG	–	1	1
WE HAD A DOGGIE	1	–	1
WE HAD A TRIP	–	1	1
WE HAVE A CAR AGAIN	1	–	1
WE HAVE DONE	1	–	1
WE HAVE FALLEN FROM THE SKY	1	–	1
WE MET OUR GRANDMOTHER	1	–	1
WE WENT TO THE HOUSE	1	–	1
WE WENT TO THE STORE	–	1	1
WENT AWAY	1	–	1
WEVE MET	–	1	1
WHAT	1	1	2
WHEN	1	1	2
WHEN DO YOU GO OUT ON THE STREET	–	1	1
WHEN SOMEBODY SAYS MIND YOUR OWN BUSINE	–	1	1
WINDOWS	–	1	1
YEAR	–	2	2
YESTERDAY	1	–	1
YESTERDAY IVE BEEN THERE	1	–	1
YOU DO	1	–	1
YOU HAVE SEEN THAT BIRD	–	1	1
YOUVE BEEN DOING SOMETHING LIKE PLAYING	1	–	1

77. SIT

RESPONSE WORD	M	F	T
ALWAYS SIT	–	1	1
APPLE	1	–	1
BABYSITTER	1	–	1
BALL	1	–	1
BE	–	1	1
BEG	1	–	1
BEING QUIET	–	1	1
BIT	1	–	1
BOARDS	1	–	1
BULLET	1	–	1
CAT	1	1	2
CHAIR	16	14	30
COAT	1	–	1
COWBOYS	1	–	1
CRYING	–	1	1
DIT	–	1	1
DOWN	30	29	59
DOWN IN THE CHAIR	1	–	1
DOWN ON A CHAIR	1	1	2
DOWN ON THE BED	1	–	1
DOWN ON THE CHAIR	1	–	1
DUCK	–	1	1
DUST	–	1	1
EAT	1	1	2
FIX SOMETHING TO EAT	–	1	1
FLOOR	1	–	1
GET UP	1	2	3
GIRL	–	2	2
GIT	–	1	1
GOOD	–	1	1
HANDKERCHIEF	–	1	1

RESPONSE WORD	M	F	T
HELP	–	1	1
HERE	1	–	1
HIT	3	–	3
HOUSE	1	–	1
I SIT DOWN WITH YOU	–	1	1
I SITTED ON THE CHAIR	–	1	1
IM SITTING IN A CHAIR	1	–	1
IN A CHAIR	2	2	4
IN IT	1	–	1
IN THE CHAIR	1	1	2
INDIAN	–	1	1
IT	1	–	1
KEYS	–	1	1
KIT	1	–	1
KNIT	2	–	2
LAY	–	2	2
LEAN	–	1	1
LIGHT	–	1	1
LIT	1	–	1
LOOK	–	1	1
LOW	1	–	1
MAN	1	–	1
MITT	–	1	1
MOVIES	1	–	1
NET	–	1	1
NIGHT	–	1	1
ON A CHAIR	4	–	4
ON THE CHAIR	2	1	3
OUTSIDE	1	–	1
PAPER	–	1	1
PEOPLE	–	1	1

RESPONSE WORD	KINDERGARTEN M	F	T	RESPONSE WORD	KINDERGARTEN M	F	T

77. SIT

RESPONSE WORD	M	F	T	RESPONSE WORD	M	F	T
PINK	–	1	1	STAND UP	–	1	1
PIPE	1	–	1	STATUE	–	1	1
PIT	–	1	1	STILL	–	1	1
PLEASE	1	–	1	STOP	–	1	1
QUIETLY	–	1	1	SWING	1	–	1
ROCKING CHAIR	1	–	1	SWITCH	1	–	1
SAND	–	1	1	TREE	1	–	1
SAT	–	1	1	UP	1	–	1
SEAT	2	–	2	WATCH	–	1	1
SEATED	–	1	1	WEB	1	–	1
SEE	–	1	1	WHEN PEOPLE ARE SITTING DOWN	–	1	1
SIT DOWN	–	1	1	WHERE	–	1	1
SITTING ON THE FLOOR	1	–	1	WINDOW	–	1	1
SITTY	–	1	1	WIT	1	–	1
SOFA	–	1	1				
STAND	–	2	2				

78. SLOW

RESPONSE WORD	M	F	T	RESPONSE WORD	M	F	T
A GIRL	–	1	1	OVERFLOW	1	–	1
BIKE	–	3	3	PAPER	1	–	1
BOAT	–	1	1	PEOPLE	1	–	1
BOW	1	3	4	PIANO	–	2	2
CABINET	–	1	1	PICK UP	1	–	1
CAR	2	2	4	POCKET	–	1	1
CAR SEAT	–	1	1	POE	–	1	1
CAR SLOWS DOWN	1	–	1	POKE	7	3	10
CAREFUL	–	1	1	POKEY	1	–	1
CARS	1	–	1	QUIET	1	–	1
CARS GO SLOW WHEN THE LIGHTS RED	–	1	1	REAL SLOW	–	2	2
CATCH	–	1	1	RIDE	1	–	1
CHAIR	1	–	1	RIDE BIKE	–	1	1
CHIMNEY	1	1	2	RIDE YOUR BIKE SLOW	–	1	1
CRIB	–	1	1	RIDING	1	–	1
DANCE	–	1	1	ROW	1	–	1
DOG	1	–	1	ROWBOAT	1	–	1
DONT DRIVE FAST	1	–	1	ROWED	1	–	1
DOUGH	–	1	1	RUG	1	–	1
DOWN	3	1	4	RUN	–	1	1
DOWN THE CAR	–	1	1	RUN SLOW	–	1	1
DRIVE	1	–	1	RUNNING	1	1	2
EAT	1	–	1	SCHOOL	1	1	2
EYES	–	1	1	SHOE	1	–	1
FAST	13	23	36	SHOES	–	1	1
FEELING	–	1	1	SHORT	1	–	1
FIRST	–	1	1	SLED	1	–	1
FISH	1	–	1	SLIDE DOWN THE SLIDING BOARD	–	1	1
FISH STICK	1	–	1	SLOW-DOWN	1	–	1
FLOOD	1	–	1	SLOWLY	1	1	2
FLOW	–	1	1	SLOWPOKE	–	3	3
FLY	1	–	1	STOP	2	2	4
GET DRESSED	1	–	1	SWING	–	1	1
GO	4	–	4	TABLE	–	1	1
GO FAST	1	–	1	TALK	1	–	1
GO SLOW	1	1	2	THE BOAT GOES SLOW	1	–	1
HARD	1	–	1	THE CAR DOWN	1	–	1
HOE	1	–	1	THE CAR IS SLOWING DOWN	–	1	1
HOUSE	–	1	1	THINK	1	–	1
I GO SLOW	1	–	1	TOO SLOW	1	–	1
I WILL WALK	–	1	1	TRUCK	1	–	1
JUMP SLOW	–	1	1	TURTLE	1	–	1
KILL	1	–	1	TYPEWRITER	–	1	1
LINE	1	–	1	WALK	4	8	12
LONG	1	–	1	WALK SLOW	1	1	2
LOUDLY	–	1	1	WALKING	3	5	8
LOW	2	–	2	WALKING TINSEY,TINSEY SLOW,SLOW	1	–	1
ME	1	1	2	WALL	1	–	1
ME IN	–	1	1	WE DONT WANT YOU TO RUN	–	1	1
MOTION	1	–	1	WE HAVE TO GO SLOW	1	–	1
MOTOR	–	1	1	WE WALK	1	1	2
MOUSE HOLE	1	–	1	WHEELS	1	–	1
MOW	2	–	2	WRITING	1	–	1
MUSIC	1	–	1				

79. SLOWLY

RESPONSE WORD	M	F	T	RESPONSE WORD	M	F	T
A HOUSE	–	1	1	BURN	–	1	1
ANIMAL	1	–	1	CANOE	1	–	1
BAIT	–	1	1	CAR	1	2	3
BALL	1	–	1	CAR GOING SLOW	1	–	1
BE SLOWLY	1	–	1	CAT	–	1	1
BEANY	–	1	1	CHAIR	1	2	3
BICYCLES GO SLOW SOMETIMES	1	–	1	CHILDREN ARE PLAYING WITH BIKES	–	1	1
BOAT	2	1	3	CHURCH	1	–	1
BOW	1	–	1	COLY	1	–	1
BRICK	–	1	1	COME	–	1	1
BROWNIE	–	1	1	DO THINGS VERY SLOWLY	–	1	1

RESPONSE WORD	KINDERGARTEN M	F	T
79. SLOWLY			
DONALD DUCK	–	1	1
DONT RUN	1	–	1
DONT WALK FAST BUT SLOW	–	1	1
DOOR	–	1	1
DOWLY	–	1	1
DOWN	1	–	1
DOWN HILL	1	–	1
DOWN THE HILL	1	–	1
DOWN THE STREET	1	–	1
DRIVE	2	1	3
FALL	–	2	2
FAN	–	1	1
FAST	5	16	21
FASTER	–	1	1
FASTLY	2	2	4
FEATHER	1	–	1
FISH	1	–	1
FLOAT	1	–	1
FLOWER	1	1	2
GIRL	–	1	1
GO FAST	–	1	1
GO SLOW	1	–	1
GO SLOWLY	1	1	2
GO-LY	–	1	1
GREEN	1	–	1
HIT	–	1	1
HOLY	–	1	1
HOUSE	–	1	1
HURRY	1	–	1
I RUN FAST	–	1	1
I TURN	1	–	1
I WILL TALK	–	1	1
IM GOING SLOW	1	–	1
LADDER	–	1	1
LIGHT	1	–	1
LINE	1	–	1
LONELY	–	1	1
LONG	1	–	1
LOUDLY	–	1	1
LOWLY	1	–	1
MOUSE	–	1	1
MOVING	–	1	1
MOWLY	2	–	2
MY MOTHER WENT SLOWLY IN THE CAR	1	–	1
NOW	1	–	1
PAN	1	–	1
PAPER	1	1	2
PEOPLE	–	1	1
PEOPLE RUN SLOWLY	1	–	1
PICK UP	1	–	1
PINK	1	–	1
PLAY	–	2	2
POKE	2	–	2
POKEY	1	–	1
POLIO	–	1	1
PRETZEL	1	–	1
QUIET	3	1	4
REAL FAST	–	1	1
REAL SLOW	–	1	1
RIDE	–	1	1
RIDE A BIKE SLOWLY	1	–	1
ROWLY	1	–	1
RUN	2	3	5
RUNNING	2	–	2
SLIDE DOWN THE SLIDING BOARD	–	1	1
SLOW	1	1	2
SLOW DOWN	1	1	2
SLOW MOTION	1	–	1
SLOW THE TRAIN DOWN	1	–	1
SLOW WALKING	1	–	1
SLOW-UP	1	–	1
SLOWPOKE	–	3	3
SMOKE	1	–	1
SNOW	1	–	1
SODA	1	–	1
SPEED	1	–	1
STEPS	1	–	1
STOP	1	1	2
SWING	1	–	1
TABLE	1	–	1
TAKE ME A RIDE	1	–	1
TALK	2	–	2
TALKING	–	1	1
THE CAR IS GOING SLOWLY	–	1	1
THINK	–	1	1
TOE	1	–	1
TOO SLOW	1	–	1
TURN	1	–	1
TURTLE	3	2	5
WALK	6	11	17
WALK SLOWLY	1	–	1
WALKING	1	5	6
WALKING SLOW	1	–	1
WALKING SLOWLY	–	1	1
WATER	–	1	1
WE ALL WENT SLOWLY	–	1	1
WE RUN SLOW	–	1	1
WE TURN	1	–	1
WINDOW	1	–	1
WORM	1	–	1
YOU RUN	1	–	1

RESPONSE WORD	KINDERGARTEN M	F	T
80. SMOOTH			
AND SOFTLY	–	1	1
ASH TRAY	1	–	1
BABY	2	4	6
BAD	1	–	1
BED	1	1	2
BEE	1	–	1
BIRD	–	1	1
BLANKET	3	1	4
BLOUSE	–	1	1
BOARD	–	1	1
BOOTH	–	1	1
BREAD	2	–	2
BUMPY	2	1	3
BUNNY	–	1	1
CAKE	–	2	2
CANNON BALL	1	–	1
CAR	1	–	1
CARPET	1	–	1
CAT	2	–	2
CATALOGUE	–	1	1
CEMENT	2	2	4
CHAIR	1	1	2
CLOTH	–	1	1
COCOON	1	–	1
COTTON	1	–	1
COW	1	–	1
CREAMY	–	1	1
CUCUMBER	1	–	1
CURTAIN	–	1	1
DIAPERS	–	1	1
DIRT	1	1	2
DONUT	–	1	1
DOOVE	–	1	1
DOUGH	1	1	2
FACE	1	2	3
FEEL	–	1	1
FLAT	2	2	4
FLOOR	–	2	2
FLOWERS	1	–	1
FLY	1	–	1
FOOD	1	–	1
FUR	1	–	1
GENTLY	2	1	3
GO	–	1	1
GOING SMOOTH	–	1	1
GOOD	–	1	1
GREASY HAND	1	–	1
GROUND	2	–	2
HAND	–	1	1
HANDS	1	1	2
HARD	–	9	9
HOOK	–	1	1
HOOVE	1	1	2
HOT	–	2	2
HOUSE	–	2	2
I FEEL SMOOTH	–	1	1
I LOVE SWEET	–	1	1
I SMOOTH MY CAKE	1	–	1
IRON	–	2	2
IRONING BOARD	1	–	1
IRONING SOME CLOTHES	–	1	1
IT IS NICE AND SMOOTH	–	1	1
ITS SO SMOOTH	1	–	1
KNIFE	1	–	1
LAMB	–	1	1
LAY	1	–	1
LIGHT	1	1	2
LOSE	1	–	1
LOUD	–	1	1
MIX	–	1	1

RESPONSE WORD	M	F	T
80. SMOOTH			
MOUH	1	–	1
MOUSE	1	–	1
MOVE	–	1	1
MY BLANKET IS SMOOTH	–	1	1
NEW CAR	–	1	1
NICE CAKE	–	1	1
NOT ROUGH	1	–	1
OWL	–	1	1
PANCAKE	2	1	3
PANTS	1	–	1
PAPER	2	–	2
PAT	–	1	1
PENCIL	–	1	1
PLASTER	–	1	1
POOSE	1	–	1
POOVE	1	–	1
POVE	1	–	1
PRETTY	1	–	1
RACKET	1	–	1
READ HARD	1	–	1
RED	–	1	1
RIVER	1	–	1
ROAD	7	1	8
ROADS	1	–	1
ROCK	1	1	2
ROUGH	1	1	2
RUG	–	1	1
SAILING	1	–	1
SAND	–	1	1
SHARK	1	–	1
SHEET	–	1	1
SHINY	–	1	1
SIGN	1	–	1
SKY	–	1	1
SLEET	–	1	1
SMOOTHING SOMETHING OUT	1	–	1
SMOOTHLY	1	–	1
SOFT	4	4	8
SOFTLY	–	1	1
SOME ROCKS ARE SMOOTH	1	–	1
SOMETHING	–	1	1
SOMETHING IS SMOOTH	–	1	1
SPREAD	1	–	1
STAR	–	1	1
STONEY	1	–	1
TABLE	1	–	1
TEDDY BEAR	1	–	1
TELEVISION	–	1	1
TEXTURE	1	–	1
THE DOOR	–	1	1
THE ROAD DOWN	1	–	1
THE RUG	2	–	2
THICK	–	1	1
TIRE	1	–	1
TOO SMOOTH	1	1	2
TOUCHLY	1	–	1
TOWEL	1	–	1
TUB	1	–	1
TUNNEL	–	1	1
TWOS	–	1	1
UTH	1	–	1
VANILLA	1	–	1
WHEN SOMETHINGS REAL SMOOTH	–	1	1
WHO	–	1	1
WHOSE	–	1	1
WOOD	1	–	1

RESPONSE WORD	M	F	T
81. SOMETIMES			
A SHEEP	–	1	1
A STORY NOT BELIEVED	1	–	1
ALL THE TIME	–	1	1
ALL THE TIMES	1	–	1
ANT	1	–	1
BEAR CLIMBS UP TREE	1	–	1
BEE	–	1	1
BEHAVE	1	–	1
BEHAVE SOMETIMES	–	1	1
BLUE	–	1	1
BOARD	–	1	1
BYE	–	1	1
CANDY	1	–	1
CANT DO ANYTHING	–	1	1
CAR	1	–	1
CHAIR	1	–	1
CHECK THE TOILET PAPER AND SOAP	1	–	1
CHILDREN	–	1	1
CLOSET	1	–	1
COAT	–	1	1
COME	1	–	1
COME BACK	1	–	1
COME OVER	–	1	1
DO	3	–	3
DOG	–	1	1
DOOR	1	–	1
DOOR LOCKER	1	–	1
DOUBLE	–	1	1
DUMB	–	1	1
EASY	1	–	1
EGG	1	–	1
EVERYTIME	1	–	1
FLAG	–	1	1
FUN TIME	1	–	1
GO	2	1	3
GO AWAY	–	1	1
GO BYBYS	–	1	1
GO IN A CAR	1	–	1
GUESS	–	1	1
HAPPENS	1	1	2
HE	1	–	1
HE GIVES ME A RING	1	–	1
HERE	–	1	1
HITS	–	1	1
HOUSE	1	1	2
HUNTIME	1	–	1
HURT	–	1	1
I	6	3	9
I CAN	–	1	1
I COME TO YOUR HOUSE	1	–	1
I DID TREE	1	–	1
I DO	1	–	1
I DO SOMETHING	1	–	1
I DO WHAT	1	–	1
I GET AN ACCIDENT	–	1	1
I GO SHOPPING	1	–	1
I GO SOMEWHERE	–	1	1
I GO TO THE STORE	–	1	1
I LOVE TO RUN	1	–	1
I PLAY	–	2	2
I PLAY IN THE BASEBALL FIELD	–	1	1
I STAY UP	1	–	1
I WATCH TV	1	–	1
I WILL COME OVER	–	1	1
I WISH	–	2	2
I WISH I WOULD BE WITH THE SHEEP	1	–	1
ILL DO IT	1	–	1
IM ALWAYS AWAKE	–	1	1
IM GOING TO SLIDE DOWN SLIDING BOARD	–	1	1
IM NICE	–	1	1
IN	–	1	1
IT HAPPENS	1	–	1
LAMP	–	1	1
LASSIE	–	1	1
LINE	1	–	1
LION	1	–	1
LITTLE	–	1	1
LOOK	–	1	1
LOVE	–	1	1
LUM	1	–	1
LUMTIMES	1	–	1
MATCHES	–	2	2
MAYBE	2	1	3
MAYBE NOT	–	1	1
MEAN	–	1	1
MY FATHER GAVE ME A SPANKING	1	–	1
NAUGHTY	1	–	1
NEST	1	–	1
NEVER	–	1	1
NICE	–	1	1
NO TIMES	1	1	2
NOON	1	–	1
NOT	1	–	1
NOT ALL THE TIME	1	–	1
NURSE	–	1	1
ONE TIME	–	1	1
OTHER TIMES	–	1	1
PAPER	2	2	4
PICK	–	1	1
PICK UP THE TOYS	1	–	1
PIRATE	–	1	1
PLANE RIDE	1	–	1
PLAY	2	2	4

RESPONSE WORD	KINDERGARTEN M	F	T	RESPONSE WORD	KINDERGARTEN M	F	T

81.　SOMETIMES

RESPONSE WORD	M	F	T	RESPONSE WORD	M	F	T
PURPLE.	1	–	1	WALK.	1	1	2
RIMS.	1	–	1	WALLET.	–	1	1
RUN	1	–	1	WE.	–	1	1
SAD	–	1	1	WE ARE GOING TO DO			
SCHOOL.	1	1	2	SOMETHING.	1	–	1
SEED.	–	1	1	WE CAN GO OUT	–	1	1
SHOOT	1	–	1	WE DO	1	–	1
SOLDIER	1	1	2	WE DO SOMETHING	1	–	1
SOME.	1	1	2	WE GET STINGED.	1	–	1
SOMETHING HAPPENS	–	1	1	WE GO.	–	1	1
SOMETHINGS YOU DONT	1	–	1	WE GO PLACE	–	1	1
STORY BOOKS	–	1	1	WE GO TO DANCE.	–	1	1
SUN	3	3	6	WE GO TO GRANDMOTHERS	1	–	1
SUNSHINE.	1	–	1	WE SING	–	1	1
SWING	–	1	1	WE TAKE TURNS	–	1	1
TAKE A WALK	–	1	1	WELL PLAY SOMETHING	1	–	1
TAKING NAPS	–	1	1	WHEN.	–	1	1
TALL.	–	1	1	WHEN PEOPLE ARE SAYING			
THE BIRDS FLY	–	1	1	SOMETIMES.	–	1	1
THINGS.	–	1	1	WHEN PEOPLE SAY SOMETIMES	1	–	1
THINGS HAPPEN	1	–	1	WINDOW.	–	1	1
THREE	–	1	1	WISH.	1	–	1
TIME.	–	2	2	WOODS	–	1	1
TIME ON THE CLOCK	1	–	1	YOU ARE TOLD.	1	–	1
TO STORE.	1	–	1	YOU CAN GO OUTSIDE.	1	–	1
TOC	1	–	1	YOU D BETTER WATCH.	1	–	1
TOY.	1	–	1	YOU GO OUTSIDE.	–	1	1
TOYS.	–	1	1	YOU HAVE TO DO THIS	–	1	1
TRY IT.	1	–	1	YOU LIKE TO PLAY GAMES.	–	1	1
TUMTIMES.	–	1	1	YOU LOVE ME	–	1	1
TUSIMES.	1	–	1	YOU WASH DISHES	–	1	1
UNDERSTAND.	–	1	1				

82.　SOUR

RESPONSE WORD	M	F	T	RESPONSE WORD	M	F	T
A FLOWER.	–	1	1	KRAUT	14	5	19
A FOOD.	1	–	1	LEMON.	7	3	10
APPLE	2	–	2	LETTUCE	1	1	2
APPLES.	–	1	1	LIGHT	1	–	1
ARCH.	1	–	1	LIME.	1	–	1
AWFUL	1	–	1	LINEN	–	1	1
BABY FOOD	–	1	1	LITTLE.	–	1	1
BALL.	2	–	2	LOUD.	1	–	1
BANANA.	–	1	1	MAKE MILK SOUR.	1	–	1
BEEF.	–	1	1	MEAT.	1	–	1
BENCH	1	–	1	MILK.	5	6	11
BLOUSE.	–	1	1	MILK WHICH DOESNT TASTE			
BOTTLE.	1	1	2	GOOD	–	1	1
BOWER	1	–	1	MOWER	1	–	1
BRACELET.	–	1	1	MY FOOD IS TOO SOUR	–	1	1
BUTTER.	1	–	1	NOT SOUR.	–	1	1
CAKE.	1	–	1	NURSE	–	1	1
CEILING	1	–	1	ONION	–	1	1
CELERY.	1	1	2	ORANGE.	5	1	6
CHURCH.	1	–	1	ORANGE JUICE.	–	2	2
CRACKER	–	2	2	PANTS	–	1	1
CRAP.	–	1	1	PEANUTS	–	1	1
CUP	1	–	1	PENCIL	1	–	1
DOESNT TASTE GOOD	1	–	1	PEOPLE.	–	1	1
DON T LIKE.	–	1	1	PEPPER.	–	1	1
DONT TASTE GOOD	1	–	1	PEPPERMINT.	–	1	1
DRAPES.	1	–	1	PICKLE.	–	2	2
DRESSING.	1	–	1	PICKLES	1	–	1
DRINK	1	3	4	PIN	–	1	1
EAR	–	1	1	PINK.	1	–	1
EAT	–	2	2	PLAIN WATER	–	1	1
EGG	1	–	1	PLANT	1	–	1
FOOD.	2	1	3	POWER	–	2	2
FOR HEAD.	1	–	1	PUSH.	–	1	1
FRUIT	–	1	1	PUSS.	4	1	5
GET A DRINK OF WATER.	–	1	1	PUT CHEESE ON IT.	1	–	1
GLASS	–	1	1	REAL STIFF.	1	–	1
GOOD.	1	2	3	SALADS SOUR	1	–	1
GRAPEFRUIT.	–	1	1	SALT.	–	1	1
GRAPES.	–	2	2	SANDWICH.	–	1	1
GUN	1	–	1	SAUERKRAUT.	1	–	1
HAWER	1	–	1	SELF.	–	1	1
HOLDER.	–	1	1	SEWING BOX.	–	1	1
HONEY	1	–	1	SHIRT	1	–	1
HORSERADISH	–	1	1	SHOWER.	1	–	1
HOT	1	–	1	SIGN.	–	1	1
HOWARD.	1	–	1	SIT	–	1	1
I CUT	–	1	1	SOAP.	1	–	1
ICE CREAM	1	–	1	SOCK.	1	–	1
ICKY.	–	1	1	SOMETHING IS SOUR	–	1	1
IM NOT GOING TO EAT	1	–	1	SOURPUSS.	–	1	1
INSIDE.	–	1	1	STEM.	1	–	1
IT DONT TASTE GOOD.	–	1	1	STEVEN.	–	1	1
ITS TOO SOUR.	1	–	1	SUN	–	1	1
JUICE	4	3	7	SWEET	–	3	3

RESPONSE WORD	KINDERGARTEN M	F	T	RESPONSE WORD	KINDERGARTEN M	F	T

82. SOUR

RESPONSE WORD	M	F	T	RESPONSE WORD	M	F	T
TABLE	–	1	1	TOO SOUR	1	1	2
TARYL	–	1	1	TOWER	–	1	1
TASTE	1	1	2	VOMIT	–	1	1
TASTE GOOD	–	1	1	WATER	1	–	1
TASTES ECKY	1	–	1	WE EAT IT	–	1	1
TASTES LIKE A SOURKRAUT	–	1	1	WHEN THINGS ARE SOUR THEY'VE BEEN IN FR	1	–	1
THE LEMON IS SOUR	–	1	1	WHY	1	–	1
THE MILK STAYS OUT OF THE HOUSE TOO LON	–	1	1	WOODS	–	1	1
THROW AWAY	1	–	1				

83. SQUARE

RESPONSE WORD	M	F	T	RESPONSE WORD	M	F	T
A BOX IS KINDA SQUARE	1	–	1	NOT RECTANGLE	1	–	1
AIR	3	–	3	ON THE FLOOR	–	1	1
ARM	–	1	1	ON YOUR SHIRT	1	–	1
BALL	4	1	5	PAPER	1	1	2
BEAR	3	2	5	PEAR	–	2	2
BED	–	1	1	PLARE	–	1	1
BIG	1	2	3	PLAY WITH IT	–	1	1
BLACK	2	1	3	POINTED	–	1	1
BLOCK	8	1	9	RAREFOOT	–	1	1
BOAT	1	–	1	RAT	–	1	1
BOOK	–	1	1	REAL SQUARE	1	–	1
BOX	6	8	14	RECTANGLE	1	3	4
BRICK	1	–	1	ROCK	–	1	1
BROWN	1	–	1	ROUND	4	4	8
BUTTERFLY	1	–	1	ROUND CIRCLE	–	1	1
CARD	1	–	1	RULE	1	–	1
CAT	1	–	1	SAND	–	1	1
CHAIR	1	–	1	SARE	–	1	1
CHILDREN PLAY WITH SQUARE BLOCKS	–	1	1	SCARED	–	1	1
CIRCLE	3	6	9	SCHOOL	–	1	1
CLEAR	1	–	1	SEAT	1	–	1
CLOTHES	–	1	1	SHOE	–	1	1
COATS	1	–	1	SNAKE	–	1	1
CORNER	1	1	2	SOMETHING SQUARE	–	1	1
CORNERS	1	–	1	SPOT	–	1	1
DANCE	1	–	1	SQUEAL	–	1	1
DARE	1	1	2	SQUIRRELS	–	1	1
DOOR	1	–	1	STAND	–	1	1
DOT	1	–	1	STANDING IN SQUARE	1	–	1
FAIR	1	–	1	STEP	–	1	1
FINGER	–	1	1	SWIMMING POOL	–	1	1
FLOOR	1	–	1	TABLE	1	2	3
FLOWERS	–	1	1	TALL	–	1	1
FUN	1	–	1	TEAR	3	1	4
GIRLS	–	1	1	TEDDY BEAR	1	–	1
GOLD	–	1	1	TELEPHONE	1	–	1
HAIR	5	2	7	THERE	–	3	3
HERE	–	1	1	THIS SQUARE OUTSIDE	–	1	1
HOLE	1	–	1	TOY	–	1	1
HORSE	–	1	1	TREE	1	–	1
HOUSE	2	1	3	TRIANGLE	12	9	21
INSIDE	1	–	1	TRIANGLES	–	1	1
IT	1	–	1	WAGON	1	–	1
IT WAS TOO SMALL	1	–	1	WALL	–	1	1
JUMP OVER THE SQUARE	–	1	1	WANT TO DANCE	–	1	1
KNIT	–	1	1	WE PLAY GAME	–	1	1
LAIR	2	–	2	WE SIT DOWN ON A	1	–	1
LIKE A BOX	1	–	1	WHEATIES	–	1	1
LITTLE	–	1	1	WHERE	2	1	3
MAKE	1	–	1	WINDOW	–	2	2
MAN	1	–	1	WRITE	1	–	1
MEAN	1	–	1	YOU PLAY WITH IT	–	1	1

84. SWIFT

RESPONSE WORD	M	F	T	RESPONSE WORD	M	F	T
A	–	1	1	BUTTERFLY	–	1	1
AIR	–	1	1	CAR	1	–	1
ALASKA	–	1	1	CHAIR	1	1	2
ARM	–	1	1	CHEESE	3	3	6
BALL	1	–	1	CLOUD	–	1	1
BAT	1	1	2	COWBOY	–	1	1
BATTER	1	–	1	DADDY	–	1	1
BEAR	1	1	2	DIFT	–	1	1
BIBLE	–	1	1	DIRT	–	2	2
BIFF	1	2	3	DIRTY	–	1	1
BIFT	1	–	1	DO A DANCE	1	–	1
BIKE	1	–	1	DOESNT	1	–	1
BIRD	1	–	1	DOLLAR	1	–	1
BIRDIE NEST	1	–	1	DUST PAN	1	–	1
BLACK PAINT	1	–	1	EAR	–	1	1
BOAT	1	–	1	EXCUSE	1	–	1
BREAD	–	1	1	FAST	2	–	2
BROOM	–	4	4	FEATHERS	–	1	1
BUN	1	–	1	FIRE ENGINE	1	–	1
BUTTER	1	–	1	FISH	1	–	1

RESPONSE WORD	KINDERGARTEN M	F	T
84. SWIFT			

RESPONSE WORD	M	F	T	RESPONSE WORD	M	F	T
FLOOR	1	1	2	SHOO FLY AWAY	–	1	1
FLOWER	1	–	1	SIGN	–	1	1
FLY	–	1	1	SILLY	1	–	1
FLYING	–	1	1	SLAP	1	–	1
GIRL	–	1	1	SLEPT	1	–	1
GRASS	1	–	1	SNIFF	1	–	1
HAIR	–	1	1	SNIFFLE	1	–	1
HANDICAP	1	–	1	SNOW	–	1	1
HIP	–	1	1	SOFT	1	1	2
HOME	–	1	1	SOLDIER	1	–	1
HORSE	–	1	1	SPANK	1	–	1
HOT	1	–	1	STOOL	–	1	1
HOUSE	–	1	1	STREAM	1	1	2
I HIT YOU ON THE BOTTOM	1	–	1	SWEEP	3	5	8
I SAW A SWIFT	1	–	1	SWEEP A HOUSE	1	–	1
I SWIFT SOMETHING	–	1	1	SWEEP THE FLOOR	1	–	1
I SWIFT WITH YOU	–	1	1	SWEEP YOUR RUG	–	1	1
IF	1	–	1	SWEEPER	–	1	1
IFT	–	1	1	SWEPT	1	1	2
IN SOMEBODY ELSES CAR INTO A TRUCK	1	–	1	SWEPT AWAY	1	–	1
KICK	–	1	1	SWIFT HAM	1	–	1
KLEENEXES	–	1	1	SWIFTY	–	1	1
KNIFE	1	–	1	SWIM	3	1	4
LABORATORY	1	–	1	SWIM IN THE WATER	1	–	1
LAKE	–	1	1	SWIMMING	1	–	1
LEAF	–	1	1	SWIMMING-POOL	–	1	1
LIFT	5	–	5	SWING	–	1	1
LIKE YOU SWIFT SOMETHING	1	–	1	SWINGS	–	1	1
LIQUOR	1	–	1	SWIPSWOP	–	1	1
LOW	–	1	1	SWISH	–	1	1
ME	1	–	1	SWISS STEAK	1	–	1
MIFF	1	–	1	SWIST WAS ON THE FLOOR	–	1	1
MILK	–	1	1	SWITCH	1	2	3
MISSED	1	–	1	SWITCH THAT	1	–	1
MIX MASTER	1	–	1	SWIVEL CHAIR	1	–	1
NAP	–	1	1	TABLE	1	–	1
NEST	1	–	1	THE BUTTERFLY	1	–	1
NICE	–	1	1	THE WIND	–	1	1
NUMBERS	–	1	1	TIFT	2	–	2
OCEANS	–	1	1	TOO SWIFT	1	–	1
ON THE WATER-IN THE WAVES	1	–	1	TOOTHBRUSH	–	1	1
ORANGE	–	1	1	TREE	1	–	1
OUT GOES THE DIRT	–	1	1	TWIST	1	1	2
PAN	1	–	1	WASHER	1	2	3
PAPER	–	1	1	WATER	1	1	2
PEOPLE AROUND	1	–	1	WENT HARD	1	–	1
PEOPLE LIFT SOMETHING	1	–	1	WHAT	1	–	1
PEPPER	–	1	1	WHEN LEAVES GO	–	1	1
PIANO	1	–	1	WHIFFED	–	1	1
PIFF	–	1	1	WHISTLE	1	–	1
PUTTING SWIFTS	1	–	1	WIF	1	–	1
RADIATOR	1	–	1	WIND	3	3	6
REAL	–	1	1	WINDOW	–	1	1
RIP	–	1	1	WINE	1	–	1
RIVER BANK	–	1	1	WING	–	1	1
S	–	1	1	WINTER	1	–	1
SHOE	1	–	1	WITH	–	2	2
				YOU	–	1	1

85. TABLE			

RESPONSE WORD	M	F	T	RESPONSE WORD	M	F	T
A	–	1	1	GET YOUR TOYS OFF THE TABLE	1	–	1
ABLE	1	1	2	GIRL	–	1	1
AND CHAIRS	1	–	1	GOD HEARS	1	–	1
BABLE	–	1	1	GRASS	–	1	1
BOTTLES	–	1	1	HABLE	–	1	1
CABLE	1	–	1	HORSE	–	1	1
CAR	1	–	1	I SIT DOWN AT MY TABLE	–	1	1
CHAIR	22	43	65	I WAS SITTING AT THE TABLE	–	1	1
CHAIRS	–	4	4	ICE BOX	1	–	1
CLOTH	4	–	4	LABEL	2	1	3
CUP	2	–	2	LAMP	1	1	2
D	–	1	1	LEG	2	1	3
DABLE	–	1	1	LEGS	2	1	3
DESK	1	1	2	LIGHT	1	–	1
DO SOMETHING	1	–	1	LIKE YOU EAT ON A TABLE	–	1	1
DRINK	1	1	2	LITTLE	1	–	1
EAT	8	3	11	LUNCH	3	2	5
EAT FOOD ON IT	1	–	1	MABEL	–	1	1
EAT ON	1	2	3	ON	–	1	1
EATING	–	1	1	PANTS	–	1	1
EATING AT A TABLE	1	–	1	PEOPLE	1	1	2
EATING YOUR BREAKFAST	–	1	1	PEOPLE ARE EATING AT A TABLE	–	1	1
EGG	1	–	1	PEOPLE EAT AT TABLES	1	–	1
FALLING	1	–	1	PIANO	–	1	1
FISH	1	–	1	PLATE	–	1	1
FOOD	10	3	13	PRETTY	–	1	1
FOOD IS ON THE TABLE	1	–	1				
FOR CHAIRS AND TABLE	–	1	1				
FOR EATING	1	–	1				

RESPONSE WORD	KINDERGARTEN M	F	T

85. TABLE

RESPONSE WORD	M	F	T	RESPONSE WORD	M	F	T
PUT FOOD ON	1	–	1	TED	–	1	1
ROOM	1	–	1	TELEVISION	1	–	1
SET	–	1	1	THERES A TABLE	1	–	1
SHOES	1	1	2	THERES ONLY FOUR CHAIR	–	1	1
SIGN	1	–	1	TO EAT ON	–	1	1
SILLY	1	–	1	TOO BIG OF A TABLE	1	–	1
SIT	6	1	7	TWO TABLES	1	–	1
SIT DOWN	–	1	1	WABLE	1	–	1
SIT DOWN TO EAT	–	1	1	WE EAT ON IT	–	1	1
SOFA	–	1	1	WHAT YOU EAT OFF OF	–	1	1
SOMEONE IS EATING ON THE TABLE	–	1	1	WHITE	–	1	1
SPOON	1	–	1	WINDOW	1	–	1
STANDING UP	1	–	1	WRITE	–	1	1
TABLE MANNERS	1	–	1	YOU EAT ON	1	–	1
TEA	–	1	1	YOU EAT ON IT	1	–	1

86. TALL

RESPONSE WORD	M	F	T	RESPONSE WORD	M	F	T
A BOOK	–	1	1	LOW	1	4	5
A CASTLE	1	–	1	MALL	2	–	2
A LIGHT	1	–	1	MAN	12	6	18
BALL	2	2	4	MARY	1	–	1
BEAR	2	–	2	MINK	–	1	1
BEARS	–	1	1	MONSTER	1	–	1
BEAVER	–	1	1	MY DADDY IS TALL	–	1	1
BEE	–	1	1	MY DADDYS	1	–	1
BEING SO HIGH	–	1	1	MY MOMMY	1	–	1
BIG	7	5	12	NICE AND TALL	1	–	1
BOX	–	2	2	NO, MAKE IT SMALL	1	–	1
BOX IS TALL	1	–	1	OPENER	1	–	1
BOY	2	–	2	PAUL	2	–	2
BRACELET	–	1	1	PEOPLE	3	2	5
CALL	–	1	1	PEOPLE ARE TALL	–	1	1
CARRY	–	1	1	POCKET	–	1	1
CHAIR	–	1	1	REAL TALL	–	1	1
CHURCH	1	–	1	SAW	1	–	1
CRAWL	–	1	1	SAW WOOD	–	1	1
DADDY	–	1	1	SEE	1	–	1
DOG	–	1	1	SHADOW	–	1	1
DOWN	1	–	1	SHALL	1	–	1
FARM HOUSE	1	–	1	SHELF	–	1	1
FARMER	1	–	1	SHORT	3	3	6
FAT	–	2	2	SIGN	1	1	2
FATHER	1	–	1	SIT	–	1	1
FRANKENSTEIN	1	–	1	SKINNY	–	2	2
GIANT	8	2	10	SLED	1	–	1
GLASS	–	1	1	SLOW	–	1	1
GO TO SCHOOL	–	1	1	SMALL	8	15	23
GRASS	–	1	1	SOMEONE IS TALL	–	1	1
GROW UP	–	1	1	SPIDER	1	–	1
GROWING	–	1	1	STEAL	1	–	1
HALL	3	–	3	STICK	–	1	1
HES TALL	1	–	1	STRAIGHT	1	–	1
HIGH	–	1	1	TABLE	1	–	1
HIPPOPOTAMUS STUNG BY A BEE	1	–	1	TALK	–	2	2
HORSE	1	1	2	TALLY TIT	–	1	1
HOUSE	2	2	4	TAR	1	–	1
I AM BIG AND TALL	–	1	1	TINY	–	1	1
I SAW A TALL MAN	1	–	1	TO BE A NURSE	–	1	1
IM A TALL MAN	1	–	1	TOO TALL	1	–	1
IM GETTING TALL TODAY	–	1	1	TOY	–	1	1
JAY	1	–	1	TREE	1	2	3
JUMP	1	–	1	WALL	1	1	2
LALL	2	–	2	WE GROW UP TALL	–	1	1
LAW	–	1	1	WINDOW	1	–	1
LAWN	1	–	1	YOU	1	1	2
LITTLE	2	4	6	YOU RE TALL	1	–	1
LONG	–	1	1	YOUNG	–	1	1

87. TELL

RESPONSE WORD	M	F	T	RESPONSE WORD	M	F	T
A DOG	–	1	1	CAT	1	–	1
A SECRET	4	–	4	CLOCK	1	–	1
A STORY	1	–	1	CRY	1	–	1
A TOOL	1	–	1	DON T	1	–	1
ASH TRAY	–	1	1	DON T TELL	–	1	1
BABY	–	1	1	DON T WILD	1	–	1
BEDDLE	–	1	1	DONT	–	1	1
BELL	–	2	2	DONT DO IT	–	1	1
BIRD	2	–	2	DONT TELL	1	–	1
BLOCKS	–	1	1	DONT TELL HIM	–	1	1
BO	1	–	1	DONT TELL MY MOTHER	1	–	1
BOX	1	–	1	EGG	1	–	1
BUS	–	1	1	EM WHAT TO DO	1	–	1
CALL	–	1	1	EVER	–	1	1
CAR	–	1	1	FAN	–	1	1
CARNIVAL	–	1	1	FAT	–	1	1

RESPONSE WORD	KINDERGARTEN M	F	T	RESPONSE WORD	KINDERGARTEN M	F	T

87. TELL

RESPONSE WORD	M	F	T	RESPONSE WORD	M	F	T
FLOOR	–	1	1	SOMEBODY	2	–	2
FORETELL	–	1	1	SOMEBODY ELSE	–	1	1
GOLFBALL	–	1	1	SOMETHING	2	–	2
HEAR	1	–	1	SOMETHING HAPPENED	1	–	1
HEARDS	–	1	1	SONG	–	1	1
HEAVENLY	–	1	1	STOP	–	1	1
HELL	1	1	2	STORIES	1	–	1
HER	–	1	1	STORY	3	2	5
HIDE	1	–	1	SURPRISE	–	1	1
HIM	–	1	1	SUSAN TO TURN OFF AND ON THE LIGHTS	–	1	1
HOLE	1	–	1	SWELL	–	1	1
HORSE	–	1	1	SWITCH	1	–	1
HOTEL	1	–	1	TABLE	–	2	2
HOUSE	1	–	1	TALE	–	1	1
HOW	–	1	1	TALK OUT LOUD	1	–	1
I TELL YOU SOMETHING	–	1	1	TALKING	1	–	1
IM GOING TO TELL	–	1	1	TATTLE	–	3	3
IM TELLING YOU A SECRET	1	–	1	TATTLETALE	5	3	8
KNIFE	–	1	1	TATTLETALE ON PEOPLE	–	1	1
L	1	–	1	TEETH	–	1	1
LEAD	1	–	1	TELEPHONE	–	2	2
LELL	1	–	1	TELLING ON YOU	–	1	1
LIAR	1	–	1	TELLING SOMEONE	–	1	1
LIE	–	1	1	TELLING TIME	–	1	1
LIGHT	1	–	1	TELLY	–	1	1
LIPSTICK	–	1	1	TENT	–	1	1
MATTEL	1	–	1	THE DOLLY MOTEL	–	1	1
ME	8	5	13	THE RATS	1	–	1
ME A SECRET	–	1	1	THE TRUTH	1	–	1
ME A STORY	–	2	2	THEM	1	–	1
ME WHAT YOU THINK OF ME	1	–	1	TIME	1	–	1
MEAN	–	1	1	TOUCH	–	1	1
MELL	3	1	4	TOUCH AND TELL	1	–	1
MOMMY	1	–	1	TOWEL	1	–	1
MOTHER	1	1	2	TOY	1	–	1
MOTOR	1	–	1	TRUCK	–	1	1
NOT	–	1	1	TRUTH	–	1	1
ON	–	1	1	US	1	1	2
ON SOMEONE	1	–	1	US STORY ABOUT SEA MONSTER	1	–	1
ON YOU	–	2	2	VEL	1	–	1
OTHER PEOPLE	1	–	1	WELL	2	1	3
PEOPLE	1	3	4	WHAT YOURE GOING TO DO	1	–	1
PERSON	1	–	1	WHEN PEOPLE SAY I CAN TELL	–	2	2
PLANE	1	–	1	WHO	–	2	2
PLAY-PEN	–	1	1	WOOD	2	–	2
POTATO	1	–	1	WORD	–	1	1
RUN AND PLAY	–	1	1	WORLD	1	–	1
SCREAM	1	–	1	YOU	2	–	2
SECRET	6	2	8	YOU A STORY	–	1	1
SEE	–	1	1	YOUR MOTHER	1	1	2
SELL	1	1	2				
SHOW	3	–	3				
SHOW AND TELL	1	3	4				
SOME PEOPLE PULL CATS TAILS	–	1	1				

88. THEM

RESPONSE WORD	M	F	T	RESPONSE WORD	M	F	T
A PICTURE FELL OFF THE WALL	1	–	1	DID	1	–	1
ANIMALS	–	1	1	DINING ROOM	1	–	1
APPLES	1	–	1	DO	2	–	2
ARE	1	–	1	DOG	1	1	2
ARE GOING OUT	–	1	1	DOOR	–	1	1
ARE PLAYING	–	1	1	DRUM	1	–	1
ARE STUPID	1	–	1	FAMILY	1	–	1
BAD	–	1	1	FEM	1	–	1
BAD WORD	1	–	1	FILM	–	1	1
BASKET	–	1	1	FIRE ENGINE	1	–	1
BEN	–	1	1	FISH	–	1	1
BEND	1	–	1	FISHING	1	–	1
BETWEEN	1	–	1	FLOWERS	1	1	2
BIB	1	–	1	FRIEND	1	–	1
BIM	1	–	1	FUN	1	–	1
BLOUSE	–	1	1	GEN	–	1	1
BONNY	–	1	1	GIRLS	–	1	1
BOY	–	1	1	GIVE	–	1	1
BRUSH	–	1	1	GIVE IT	–	1	1
BUS	1	–	1	GLASS	–	1	1
CAN	1	1	2	GLASSES	–	1	1
CAR	1	–	1	GO	–	1	1
CAUGHT	1	–	1	GO HOME	–	1	1
CAUSE TROUBLE	–	1	1	GO SOMEWHERE	1	–	1
CEMETERY	1	–	1	GO TO BED	1	1	2
CHAIR	–	1	1	GONE	1	–	1
CHARLIE	1	–	1	GOOD	1	1	2
COLOR	1	–	1	GOT HURT	1	–	1
CROWDED	–	1	1	GOT KILLED	1	–	1
CUTTING	–	1	1	GRASS	–	1	1
DESK	–	1	1	HE	–	1	1
				HELLO	–	1	1

RESPONSE WORD	M	F	T
	KINDERGARTEN		

88. THEM

RESPONSE WORD	M	F	T
HEM	1	–	1
HES YOU	1	–	1
HIM	4	2	6
HOOK	–	1	1
HORSE	1	1	1
HURT ME	–	1	1
I	–	1	1
I GAVE THEM SOME CAKE	–	1	1
I SEE THEM	1	–	1
IM	1	–	1
IM LONELY	1	–	1
JOIN	–	1	1
KEEP YOUR CLOTHES CLEAN	–	1	1
KEN	1	–	1
KIM	–	1	1
LAY	–	1	1
LEM	1	–	1
LEMON	1	–	1
LIGHT	2	1	3
LIGHT SWITCH	1	–	1
LIM	1	–	1
LIMB	1	–	1
LIVE	1	–	1
LOCK	–	1	1
LOVE	–	1	1
LOVE ME AND I LOVE THEM	–	1	1
M+M	–	1	1
MAN	1	–	1
MASS	–	1	1
MPM	1	–	1
MY FRIENDS	–	1	1
NAZI	1	–	1
NOT BE SAD	1	–	1
OUT	–	1	1
PARENTS	1	–	1
PARTY	–	1	1
PEM	1	–	1
PEOPLE	6	4	10
PEOPLE SAY THEM	1	–	1
PEOPLE WALKING	1	–	1
PERSON	1	1	2
PIANO	1	–	1
PICKLES	–	1	1
PIM	1	–	1
PIN	–	1	1
PLACE	–	1	1
PLAY	1	–	1
PLAY BALL	–	1	1
PLAYED IN MY BASEBALL FIELD	1	–	1
PLAYING IN THE SANDBOX	–	1	1
POCKETBOOKS	–	1	1
RUN	–	1	1
SCISSORS	–	1	1
SEE	–	1	1
SEE SAW	–	1	1
SIT	–	1	1
SOUNDS LIKE A GRANDFATHER	–	1	1
STEM	1	3	4
STEP ON A THUMBTACK	1	–	1
SWEATER	–	1	1
TABLE	1	–	1
TABLET	1	–	1
THAT IS FOR PEOPLE	1	–	1
THE	–	1	1
THE LAST	–	1	1
THEE	–	1	1
THEN	3	–	3
THEN I JUMPED INTO THE WATER AGAIN	1	–	1
THEN WE HAD SOMETHING TO EAT	–	1	1
THEN WHAT HAPPENED	–	1	1
THEY	1	2	3
THEY HAVE A CLUB	–	1	1
THEY HURT THEIRSELVES	1	–	1
THINK	–	1	1
THOSE	–	1	1
THOSE ARE BIG	1	–	1
TIE	–	1	1
TIM	–	2	2
TIMMY	1	–	1
TOES	1	–	1
TREE	1	–	1
TREES	1	–	1
TRUCK	1	–	1
TYPEWRITER	1	–	1
UM A VAMPIRE	–	1	1
US	1	1	2
WANTED TO KNOW WHAT HAPPENED	–	1	1
WE	1	2	3
WE BEAT THEM	–	1	1
WENT	–	1	1
WENT TO THE ZOO	1	–	1
WHAT	1	–	1
WHAT HAPPENED	1	–	1
WHAT TO DO WITH	–	1	1
WHATS YOUR NAME	–	1	1
WHEN PEOPLE SAY THEM AT A FAMILY	–	1	1
WHO ARE THEY	–	1	1
WHO ARE YOU	–	1	1
WHOLE FAMILY	1	–	1
WHY	1	–	1
WONT	–	1	1
WUNDA	1	–	1
YOU	2	–	2

89. THEY

RESPONSE WORD	M	F	T
ACCORDIAN LESSONS	1	–	1
ARE	3	7	10
ARE BIG	1	–	1
ARE COMING	1	–	1
ARE DOING SOMETHING	1	–	1
ARE GOING OUT	–	1	1
ARE GOING OUT FOR A RIDE	1	–	1
ARE PLAYING	–	1	1
ARE WORKING	1	–	1
BABY	–	2	2
BATHE THE BABY	–	1	1
BAY	3	–	3
BED	–	1	1
BELONG	1	–	1
BIKE	1	–	1
BOAT	1	–	1
BOUGHT	1	–	1
BOYS	–	1	1
CAN PLAY	1	–	1
CAR	–	1	1
CASTLE	1	–	1
CHAIR	1	–	1
CHEST	–	1	1
CHILD	–	1	1
CLAY	1	–	1
CLIMBED A TREE	1	–	1
CLOCK	–	1	1
COLOR	1	–	1
COME	1	–	1
COW	1	–	1
CRIB	–	2	2
DATE	2	–	2
DAY	2	2	4
DESIGN	–	1	1
DID SOMETHING	1	1	2
DO	2	–	2
DRAWER	–	1	1
DRESS	–	2	2
EAT ICE CREAM	1	–	1
EDWARD	1	–	1
FACE	–	1	1
FRIDAY	1	–	1
GO	1	1	2
GOOD	–	1	1
GOT THEIR TV OUT	–	1	1
GREEN	1	–	1
HAD	1	1	2
HAD TOOK THIS	1	–	1
HAMMERS	1	–	1
HANDLEBAR	1	–	1
HAVE	–	2	2
HAVE MANY CRACKERS	–	1	1
HAY	4	2	6
HE	1	–	1
HELP	–	2	2
HIM	–	3	3
HIT	–	1	1
HIT ME	1	–	1
HIT ME ONE DAY	1	–	1
HORSE	2	–	2
I CAN SEE THEY	1	–	1
IN	–	1	1
INDIAN	–	1	1
INDIAN HEADDRESS	–	1	1
IS HERE	–	1	1
J	1	–	1

RESPONSE WORD	KINDERGARTEN M	F	T

89. THEY

RESPONSE WORD	M	F	T
JACKET	–	1	1
JOIN	–	1	1
KEEP	1	–	1
LAMP	–	1	1
LAY	2	–	2
LAY EGG	–	1	1
LIGHT	2	–	2
LION	–	1	1
LOVE	–	1	1
LOVE YOU	1	–	1
MAY	2	–	2
MOVE	–	2	2
MOVE YOUR HOUSE	1	–	1
NEVER LEFT	1	–	1
NIGHT	–	1	1
OBEY	–	1	1
ONE	–	1	1
PAPER	–	1	1
PARENTS	1	–	1
PAY	–	3	3
PEOPLE	3	3	6
PEOPLE SAY THEY	1	–	1
PICTURE	1	–	1
PLAY	2	2	4
PLEASED ME	1	–	1
PLUG	1	–	1
RULES	–	1	1
SAID	–	1	1
SAY GOOD-BYE TO US	1	–	1
SHADOW	1	–	1
SHOE	1	–	1
SICK	1	–	1
SIGN	–	1	1
SKIP	–	1	1
SLEEPY	–	1	1
SMEYED	–	1	1
SNOW FLAKE	1	–	1
STAND	1	–	1
STEPPED ON MY TOE	1	–	1
STICK	–	1	1
STOCK	–	1	1
STONES	1	–	1
STOVE	1	–	1
SUN	–	1	1
SWIM	1	–	1
TALK	–	1	1
TELEPHONE	–	1	1
THATS SOME PEOPLE	1	–	1
THEM	2	–	2
THEN THEY WILL HURT SOMEBODY	1	–	1
THERES PEOPLE WALKING ALONG	1	–	1
THEYRE PLAYING GAMES	1	–	1
THIS TOWN	–	1	1
TOGETHER	1	–	1
TOOK MY TOY	–	1	1
TRAIN	1	–	1
TRIP	1	1	2
WALK	1	–	1
WANT	1	–	1
WANT ME TO COME	–	1	1
WANT YOU	–	1	1
WANTED TO GO OUTSIDE	–	1	1
WATER	–	1	1
WAY	–	1	1
WE GO TO SCHOOL ON DAYS	–	1	1
WEIGH	–	1	1
WENT	3	3	6
WENT INTO MY BASEBALL FIELD	1	–	1
WENT OUT	1	1	2
WENT TO THE BATHROOM	1	–	1
WENT TO THE STORE	–	1	1
WERE	–	1	1
WERE CLOCKS	1	–	1
WHAT	1	–	1
WHEEL	1	–	1
WHEN CHILDREN SAY THEY RUN	–	1	1
WHERE	–	1	1
WING	1	–	1
YOU	–	2	2

90. THIRSTY

RESPONSE WORD	M	F	T
A DRINK	1	–	1
A DRINK OF WATER	–	1	1
AIRPLANE	1	–	1
CAMPING	–	1	1
COKE	–	2	2
COOL	–	1	1
COW	–	1	1
CUP	–	1	1
CUP OF WATER	1	–	1
DADDY	–	1	1
DAY	1	–	1
DENTIST	1	–	1
DIRSTY	–	1	1
DOG	1	–	1
DRINK	20	24	44
DRINK OF MILK	–	1	1
DRINK OF WATER	2	2	4
DRINK WATER	–	1	1
DRINKING	1	–	1
DRINKING MILK AND WATER AND JUICE	–	1	1
DRINKS WATER	–	1	1
EAT AND WATCH TV	1	–	1
FAT	1	–	1
FOOD	1	–	1
FOR A GLASS OF MILK	–	1	1
FOR MILK	–	1	1
FOR WATER	1	–	1
FOUNTAIN	–	1	1
GET	–	1	1
GET A DRINK	1	3	4
GET A DRINK OF WATER	1	1	2
GET ME A DRINK OF WATER	1	–	1
GET SOMETHING TO DRINK	1	–	1
GIVE ME A DRINK	–	1	1
GLASS	1	3	4
GLASS OF WATER	–	1	1
GO	–	1	1
GO GET A DRINK OF WATER	1	1	2
GUN	1	–	1
HIRSTY	–	1	1
HOT	1	1	2
HUNGRY	–	1	1
I AM THIRSTY	–	1	1
I GET THIRSTY	–	1	1
I M	1	–	1
I WANNA DRINK	1	–	1
I WANT A DRINK OF WATER	4	–	4
I WANT SOMETHING TO DRINK	1	–	1
IM THIRSTY	4	–	4
IM THIRSTY BECAUSE I WANT TO GET A	1	–	1
IM THIRSTY. I WANT A DRINK	–	1	1
JUICE	2	–	2
LACK	1	–	1
LADDER	–	1	1
LEMONADE	–	1	1
MERCY	1	–	1
MILK	1	1	2
MOMMY	1	–	1
MURSTY	1	–	1
NOT THIRSTY	–	1	1
ORANGE JUICE	1	–	1
PEOPLE	1	–	1
PERSON	–	1	1
PLEASE GET ME A DRINK OF WATER	–	1	1
POCKETBOOK	–	1	1
PURSE	1	–	1
PURSTY	1	–	1
SHEEP	–	1	1
SINK	1	–	1
SODA	–	1	1
SOMETHING TO DRINK	–	1	1
STEPS	–	1	1
TAKE A DRINK	1	–	1
THATS ALL	1	–	1
THINK	–	1	1
THIRSTY	1	–	1
THURSDAY WE GO SEE THE TRAIN	1	–	1
TOO THIRSTY	1	–	1
UM	–	1	1
WANT A DRINK OF WATER	1	–	1
WANT SOMETHING TO DRINK	1	–	1
WATER	24	22	46
WE DRINK A GLASS OF WATER	–	1	1
WE RE GETTING A DRINK	–	1	1
WHEN CHILDREN ARE THIRSTY	–	1	1

RESPONSE WORD	KINDERGARTEN M F T			RESPONSE WORD	KINDERGARTEN M F T		

90. THIRSTY

RESPONSE WORD	M	F	T	RESPONSE WORD	M	F	T
WHEN HUNTING	1	–	1	YOU ASK YOUR MOTHER FOR SOME WATER	–	1	1
WHENSTY	–	1	1	YOU HAVE NO WATER	–	1	1
WORSETY	1	–	1				
X-RAY	1	–	1				

91. UP

RESPONSE WORD	M	F	T	RESPONSE WORD	M	F	T
A BLOCK	1	–	1	ITS RAIN	1	–	1
A HILL	–	1	1	JUMP	1	–	1
A ROCKET GO UP	1	–	1	KIMMY	–	1	1
A SQUARE	1	–	1	LITTLE	–	1	1
AIRPLANE	5	–	5	LOOK UP IN THE SKY	–	1	1
AND DOWN	1	1	2	LUP	1	–	1
AND VISIT PEOPLE	–	1	1	MIDWAY	1	–	1
BABY	2	2	4	MUP	1	–	1
BALLOON	1	1	2	ON THE HOUSE	1	–	1
BIRD	1	2	3	ON THE SWING	1	–	1
BIRD IN THE SKY	–	1	1	OUT OF GAS	1	–	1
BLOW YOUR HOUSE DOWN	1	–	1	PLEASE GO UP	–	1	1
BOARD	–	1	1	PUP	1	1	2
BOAT	–	1	1	RAIN	1	1	2
BUGS BUNNY	–	1	1	ROCK	1	–	1
BUNK	1	–	1	ROCKET	2	–	2
BUT	–	2	2	ROUND	1	–	1
CATCH	–	1	1	RUN	–	1	1
CEILING	–	1	1	SHE	–	1	1
CHIMNEY	1	–	1	SHUT	1	–	1
COAL CAR	1	–	1	SKUP	1	–	1
CUP	2	–	2	SKY	2	7	9
DOG	–	1	1	SLEEP	–	1	1
DOWN	16	28	44	SLIDING BOARD	–	1	1
DOWNSTAIRS	–	1	1	STAIRS	3	2	5
DRIVE UP	–	1	1	STEEL	1	–	1
DUMP	1	–	1	STEPS	–	2	2
ELEVATOR	1	–	1	STRETCH	–	1	1
FAN	1	–	1	SUCK	1	–	1
FLY	2	–	2	SWING	2	1	3
FLY UP IN A BALLOON	1	–	1	TABLE	–	2	2
FLYING A HELICOPTER	1	–	1	THE	–	1	1
FOOD	1	–	1	THE ELEVATOR GOES	–	1	1
FRONT	1	–	1	THE HILL	1	2	3
GIRLS	–	1	1	THE ROAD WE GO	1	–	1
GO	1	–	1	THE STEPS	–	1	1
GO THE DUMP TRUCK	1	–	1	THE STREET	1	–	1
GO UP	1	–	1	THE TREE	–	1	1
GO UP HILL	1	–	1	TO THE AIR	–	1	1
GO UP IN THE ELEVATOR	1	–	1	TO THE MOON	1	–	1
GO UP ONTO A LADDER INTO AN ATTIC	1	–	1	TOO HIGH	1	–	1
GO UPSTAIRS	–	1	1	TREE	1	1	2
GOES BIRD	–	1	1	TWO BLOCKS	–	1	1
HEAVEN	–	1	1	UP IN THE SKY	–	1	1
HIGH	2	2	4	UPPER	1	–	1
HILL	3	2	5	UPRIGHT	1	–	1
HOUSE	1	2	3	UPS A DAISY	1	–	1
I WALK UP	–	1	1	UPSTAIRS	2	–	2
I WENT UP THE ELEVATOR	1	–	1	WALL	–	1	1
IN	1	–	1	WE GO	1	1	2
IN A BALLOON	–	1	1	WE RUN UP	–	1	1
IN A PLANE	–	1	1	WHUPS	1	–	1
IN A ROCKET	1	–	1	WUP	1	–	1
IN THE AIR	1	–	1	YOU GO UP THE STAIRS	–	1	1
IN THE SKY	–	2	2	7-UP	1	–	1

92. US

RESPONSE WORD	M	F	T	RESPONSE WORD	M	F	T
A PERSON	1	–	1	CUSS	3	–	3
ALL THE PEOPLE	–	1	1	CUT	1	–	1
ALL US ARE GOING TO THE PARK	–	1	1	DID	2	–	2
ALONE	–	1	1	DO	1	–	1
AND	–	1	1	DOORKNOB	1	–	1
ARE MOVING	1	–	1	DUS	–	1	1
BACK	1	–	1	DUST	1	2	3
BED	–	1	1	EAT FOOD	–	1	1
BEHAVE	1	–	1	EVERYBODY IS HERE	–	1	1
BICYCLE	1	–	1	FACE	–	1	1
BONES	1	–	1	FAMILY	2	1	3
BOX	–	1	1	FATHER	–	1	1
BOY	1	–	1	FENCE	–	1	1
BOYS	–	1	1	FLOWER	–	2	2
BUS	8	6	14	FUN	1	1	2
CAR	1	–	1	FUSS	3	–	3
CARRY	–	1	1	GO	1	2	3
CAT	1	1	2	GO TO SCHOOL	1	–	1
CHAIRS	1	–	1	GO TO THE FAIR	1	–	1
CHEESE	–	1	1	GO TOGETHER	–	1	1
CHILDREN	1	1	2	GOING SHOPPING	–	1	1
CLASS	–	1	1	GOING TO THE STORE	1	–	1
				GRASS	1	–	1

RESPONSE WORD	KINDERGARTEN M	F	T

92. US

RESPONSE WORD	M	F	T
GUS	1	1	2
HAIR CUT.	1	–	1
HAND.	–	1	1
HIM	–	1	1
HURRY	1	–	1
I LOVE US	–	1	1
IS PLAYING.	–	1	1
JOIN.	1	–	1
KIDS.	1	–	1
KITTEN.	–	1	1
LEG	–	1	1
LIGHT	1	–	1
LIKE TO PLAY.	1	–	1
LOVE.	–	1	1
LOVES	–	1	1
LUS	2	–	2
MAN	–	1	1
ME.	4	7	11
ME AND US ARE GOING TO SLEEP.	–	1	1
MIGHT	–	1	1
MOTHERS	–	1	1
MOTOR	1	–	1
MOUSE	–	1	1
MUST.	–	1	1
MUSTARD	–	1	1
NOW	1	–	1
OVER.	–	1	1
PAPER	1	–	1
PASTE	–	1	1
PEOPLE.	6	11	17
PICTURE	1	1	2
PIPES	1	–	1
PLAY.	2	1	3
PLAY BALL	–	1	1
PUS	1	–	1
RED	1	–	1
REMEMBER.	–	1	1
RIDE.	–	1	1
RIDING A BIKE	1	–	1
ROCK.	–	1	1
RUN	2	–	2
SCARED OF GHOSTS.	1	–	1
SCORE	1	–	1
SEAGULL	1	–	1
SHOVEL.	–	1	1
SNAKE	1	–	1
STAY.	1	–	1
STORM	–	1	1
SUN	1	–	1
SUS	–	1	1
TAKE A WALK	–	1	1
TALK.	1	–	1
TENDER.	–	1	1
THATS A FAMILY.	–	1	1
THE DOG	1	–	1
THE HUSKY	–	1	1
THEM.	2	2	4
IINCE	1	–	1
TOGETHER.	2	2	4
TUSS.	–	1	1
TWO	–	1	1
WANT TO COME.	–	1	1
WASHINGTON.	–	1	1
WE.	6	2	8
WE ARE GOING TO PLAY.	–	1	1
WE BELIEVE SOMETHING.	1	–	1
WE GO DOWNTOWN.	–	1	1
WE HAD FUN.	1	–	1
WE PLAY	1	–	1
WE WRITE WORDS.	–	1	1
WELL.	1	–	1
WHITE	2	–	2
WIDEN IT.	–	1	1
WOOD.	–	1	1
YOU	3	2	5
YOURSELF.	1	–	1

93. USUALLY

RESPONSE WORD	M	F	T
A	–	1	1
ATTIC	–	1	1
BLOCK	1	–	1
BOOK.	1	2	3
BOUNCE.	1	–	1
BROOM	–	1	1
BRUSH	–	1	1
BUILDING.	–	1	1
CAR	1	–	1
CAT	1	1	2
CHRISTMAS TREE.	–	1	1
CHURCH.	1	1	2
CLEAN	1	–	1
CLEAN UP YOUR HOUSE	1	–	1
CLEANING.	1	–	1
CLOCK.	–	1	1
COFFEE.	1	–	1
COME CHILDREN	–	1	1
CRIB.	1	–	1
CRY.	–	1	1
CURE.	1	–	1
CUT THE LAWN.	1	–	1
DANCE.	–	1	1
DISHWATER	–	1	1
DO.	1	–	1
DO AND YOU USUALLY DONT	1	–	1
DO SOMETHING.	1	–	1
DO WHAT YOU RE SUPPOSED TO DO.	1	–	1
DOG.	1	–	1
DOING.	–	1	1
DOOR KNOB	1	–	1
DUST.	1	–	1
EASY.	1	–	1
EAT	1	–	1
ELECTRIC.	–	1	1
FALL.	–	1	1
FEED THE BABY	–	1	1
FINE.	–	1	1
FIVE	1	–	1
FOOD.	–	1	1
FUN	–	3	3
GIRL.	1	–	1
GLASSES	–	1	1
GLEAN	1	–	1
GO.	1	2	3
GO OUT.	1	–	1
GO TO SLEEP	1	–	1
GROW.	1	–	1
HAIR.	–	1	1
HAPPENS	2	–	2
HAS TO HAPPEN	1	–	1
HAVE TO GO TO THE AIRPLANE	1	–	1
HORSE	1	–	1
HOUSE	2	2	4
HUGH.	1	–	1
I	1	2	3
I ALWAYS CLEAN MY HOUSE	1	–	1
I DO PICK UP MY TOYS.	–	1	1
I DO SOMETHING.	–	1	1
I DONT KNOW	–	1	1
I GET BUBBLE GUM.	–	1	1
I GO OUT IN THE BASEBALL FIELD AND PLAY	1	–	1
I GO OUTSIDE TO PLAY.	1	–	1
I HAVE TO GO THE BATHROOM	1	–	1
I LIKE TO PLAY.	1	–	1
I PLAY BALL	–	1	1
I PLAY MY FAVORITE RECORD	–	1	1
I PLAY OUTSIDE.	–	1	1
I RIDE MY BIKE.	1	–	1
I SEE	1	–	1
IF.	–	1	1
IM USING A USUALLY.	1	–	1
IS.	–	1	1
IT HAPPENS.	1	–	1
ITS A BUSY DAY.	–	1	1
LATER	1	–	1
LEAN.	–	1	1
LIE	1	–	1
LIKE.	1	–	1
LIKE A FLAG	1	–	1
LIKE YOU USE SOMETHING.	–	1	1
LOCK.	1	–	1
LOLLYPOP.	1	–	1
MAD	1	–	1
MAYBE	1	–	1
MEAN.	–	1	1
MELT.	–	1	1
MOP	–	1	1
MORE PAPER.	–	1	1
MOST OF THE TIME.	1	–	1
MUSUALLY.	1	–	1
MY MOTHER SAYS I CAN TAKE SOME ASPIRIN.	–	1	1

RESPONSE WORD	KINDERGARTEN M	F	T	RESPONSE WORD	KINDERGARTEN M	F	T

93. USUALLY

RESPONSE WORD	M	F	T	RESPONSE WORD	M	F	T
NEVER	–	3	3	TELEPHONE	1	–	1
NICE	1	1	2	THAT YOU WRITE WITH	–	1	1
OFTEN	–	1	1	TOYS	–	1	1
OK	–	1	1	TREE	1	–	1
ON	1	–	1	TRUCK	–	1	1
ORIOLES	1	–	1	TUESDAY	–	1	1
OUT	1	–	1	UPSTAIRS	1	–	1
PAPER	1	–	1	USE	2	2	4
PEA	1	–	1	USE A SPOON	1	–	1
PENCIL	1	–	1	USUALLY	1	2	3
PERSON	–	1	1	WALL	1	1	2
PIANO	1	–	1	WASH	–	1	1
PICK	–	1	1	WATCH	1	–	1
PIG	–	1	1	WE	–	1	1
PLAN	–	1	1	WE CLEAN UP	1	–	1
PLAY	3	–	3	WE CLEAN UP A TABLE	1	–	1
PLAY WITH MY FRIENDS	–	1	1	WE DO SOMETHING	1	–	1
PLAY WITH THE TRAIN	1	–	1	WE DRINK OUR MILK	–	1	1
POOL	1	–	1	WE GO OUT SOMEWHERE	–	1	1
PUSUALLY	2	–	2	WE RIDE OUR BIKES	–	1	1
QUIET	–	1	1	WE SIT DOWN	1	–	1
REMEMBER	–	1	1	WE USUALLY GO TO PEOPLES HOUSES	–	1	1
SANTA	–	1	1	WE WOULD DO THINGS	1	–	1
SHED	1	–	1	WEAR MY BELT	1	–	1
SINGING	–	1	1	WHAT	1	–	1
SINK	–	1	1	WHEN PEOPLE SAY USUALLY LIKE SOMETIMES	–	1	1
SLEEP	–	1	1	WHY	–	1	1
SOMETHING	2	–	2	WILL	–	1	1
SOMETIMES	–	4	4	WINDOW	1	–	1
STAY	–	1	1	WINDOW CLOCK	1	–	1
STICK	1	–	1	WITH YOU	–	1	1
STOVE	1	–	1	WRISTWATCH	–	1	1
SUNNY OUT	–	1	1	YES	1	–	1
SWEEP	–	1	1	YOU	1	1	2
SWEET	–	1	1	YOU BEGAN	1	–	1
SWIMMING POOL	–	1	1	YOU DONT DO THINGS	1	–	1
TABLE	–	2	2	YOURE MAD	–	1	1
TALK	–	1	1				
TALKS	1	–	1				

94. WILD

RESPONSE WORD	M	F	T	RESPONSE WORD	M	F	T
A ANIMAL IS WILD	1	–	1	HAIR	1	–	1
A LION IS WILD	–	1	1	HEAR	1	–	1
A TIGER IS WILD	–	1	1	HILD	2	–	2
ALLIGATOR	–	1	1	HORSE	6	9	15
ANIMAL	18	18	36	HORSES	–	2	2
ANIMALS	7	4	11	INDIAN	1	1	2
ANIMALS ARE REAL WILD	–	1	1	INDIANS	1	1	2
BABY BEAR	–	1	1	JUNGLE	1	–	1
BE WILD	1	–	1	KILL	2	–	2
BEAR	2	–	2	LIGHT	1	–	1
BEAST	1	–	1	LION	7	4	11
BETTY	–	1	1	MAN	1	–	1
BILE	–	1	1	MILD	1	–	1
BILL	–	1	1	MOTHER	–	1	1
BIRD	1	3	4	NECK	–	1	1
BOAT	–	1	1	ONE	–	1	1
BOY	–	1	1	PILED	1	2	3
BUFFALO	–	1	1	QUIET	–	1	1
BULL	5	1	6	QUIET DOWN	1	–	1
BYE	1	–	1	RABBIT	1	–	1
CAT	3	4	7	RIBBON	–	1	1
CAT FIGHT	–	1	1	RING	–	1	1
CHAIR	–	1	1	RING BELL	–	1	1
CIGARETTE	–	1	1	RUN	–	2	2
COYOTE	1	2	3	SHEEP	1	1	2
DIALED	1	1	2	SILD	1	1	2
DID	1	–	1	SOFT	–	1	1
DOG	–	2	2	SOMETHINGS WILD IN THE FOREST	–	1	1
DOGGIE	–	1	1	STALLION	1	1	2
DOGS	1	–	1	SWITCH	1	–	1
DONT BE WILD AROUND THE HOUSE	1	–	1	TAME	1	–	1
DRAPE	1	–	1	TELEVISION	–	1	1
DUCK	–	1	1	TIE	1	–	1
ELEPHANT	2	–	2	TIGER	6	3	9
FIGHT	–	1	1	TOO WILD	1	–	1
FIGHTING, THATS WILD	1	–	1	TOUGH	1	–	1
FOREST	–	1	1	WE	–	1	1
GO SOMEWHERE	1	–	1	WEEP	1	–	1
GO TO BED	1	–	1	WHY	1	1	2
GOD	–	1	1	WIRE	1	–	1
GOOD	–	1	1	WIT	–	1	1
GORILLA	3	–	3	WOMAN	–	1	1
GRASS	–	1	1	YMCA	–	1	1
GREEN	1	–	1	YOU BETTER GET BACK HOME	–	1	1
GUN	–	1	1	ZEBRA	–	1	1

RESPONSE WORD	KINDERGARTEN M	F	T

95. WING

RESPONSE WORD	M	F	T	RESPONSE WORD	M	F	T
A BIRD WING	1	–	1	GOD	–	1	1
A BIRDS WING	–	1	1	HAVE TO HAVE ON BIRDIES	1	–	1
A BUTTERFLY	1	–	1	HE	–	1	1
A MASS	1	–	1	HEATER	–	1	1
A WASP	–	1	1	HORSE	–	1	1
A WING OF A BIRD	1	–	1	I SEE YOU QUEEN	–	1	1
AIRPLANE	2	1	3	JING	1	–	1
AIRPLANE WING	1	–	1	KING	2	–	2
BARS	–	1	1	LIKE A BIRD	1	–	1
BEE	–	1	1	LING	3	–	3
BING	–	1	1	MAKE BIRDS FLY	1	–	1
BIRD	19	23	42	MOTH	–	1	1
BIRD SEED	1	1	2	NO RESPONSE	1	–	1
BIRDIE	1	1	2	NO WING	–	1	1
BIRDIE HURT HER WINGS	–	1	1	NOW	1	–	1
BIRDIES WINGS	2	–	2	OF A BIRD	1	2	3
BIRDS	1	–	1	OF AN AIRPLANE	1	–	1
BIRDS WIGGLE THEIR	–	1	1	OF THE BIRD	1	–	1
BOOT	1	–	1	PEAR	–	1	1
BOY	–	1	1	PINK	1	–	1
BRANCH	–	1	1	PLANE	4	1	5
BREAST	–	1	1	RING	1	–	1
BROKEN	–	1	1	SING	2	3	5
BUG	1	–	1	SINGING	–	1	1
BUMBLEBEE	1	–	1	SKELETON	1	–	1
BUT	–	1	1	SLING	–	1	1
BUTTERFLY	2	2	4	SNOW	1	–	1
CHAIR	–	1	1	SPARKLES	–	1	1
CHIMNEY	–	1	1	STOP	1	–	1
CHRISTMAS	–	1	1	SUN	1	–	1
CHURCH	–	1	1	SWING	2	3	5
CRAB	–	1	1	SWING ON THE BIRD	1	–	1
CROSS	1	–	1	THAT FLAP	–	1	1
CURTAINS	–	1	1	THE BIRD HAS A WING	–	1	1
DAVE	–	1	1	THING	–	1	1
DIAMOND	–	1	1	TING	1	2	3
DING	1	2	3	TO FLY	1	1	2
DOG	1	–	1	TO FLY WITH	1	1	2
EAGLE	2	–	2	TO THE BIRD	–	1	1
EAT	1	–	1	TREE	–	1	1
EIGHT	1	–	1	WAY	1	–	1
FAN	1	–	1	WE	–	1	1
FEATHER	1	1	2	WEEDS	–	1	1
FIX SWING	–	1	1	WHAT THE BIRDS HAVE ON THEM	1	–	1
FLIES	2	–	2	WHEN BIRDS FLY	1	–	1
FLIES WITH WINGS	1	–	1	WILD WING BOOK	1	–	1
FLOOR	–	1	1	WIN	1	–	1
FLY	16	9	25	WINDOW SILL	–	1	1
FLYING	–	1	1	WING MY	–	1	1
FROM A BIRD	–	1	1	WINGING	–	1	1
GARAGE	–	1	1	YOU EAT	1	–	1
GO HOME	1	–	1				

96. YELLOW

RESPONSE WORD	M	F	T	RESPONSE WORD	M	F	T
A COLOR	1	–	1	FLOWERS	1	–	1
BANANAS ARE YELLOW	1	–	1	FLY	1	–	1
BELL	–	1	1	FROWN	–	1	1
BELLOW	1	–	1	GIRL	1	1	2
BIRD	–	1	1	GLASS	–	2	2
BLACK	1	–	1	GLASSES	–	1	1
BLUE	5	4	9	GLOVE	1	–	1
BOOK	–	2	2	GO	1	–	1
BRIGHT	–	1	1	GOOD	–	1	1
BROWN	4	–	4	GRASS	1	–	1
BUT	–	1	1	GRAY	1	–	1
BUTTER	1	–	1	GREEN	9	6	15
BUTTERFLY	2	1	3	HAIR	–	2	2
CANNON	1	–	1	HELLO	2	–	2
CAR	1	–	1	HOUSE	1	–	1
CAT	–	2	2	HOUSES	1	–	1
CLOTHES	1	–	1	I SEE A YELLOW PERSON	1	–	1
COAT	–	2	2	INDIANS	–	1	1
COLOR	2	6	8	IS A PRETTY COLOR	–	1	1
COLOR CRAYON	1	–	1	JELLO	–	1	1
COLORING	–	1	1	KELLO	1	–	1
COLOW	1	–	1	KITTEN	1	–	1
CRAYON	11	5	16	LEG	1	–	1
CRAYON COLOR	–	1	1	LETTER	–	1	1
CRAYONS	–	1	1	LIKE A YELLOW DRESS	–	1	1
CUDDLE	1	–	1	MOTHER	1	–	1
DANCE	–	1	1	MOVIE	–	1	1
DEER	–	1	1	MUSIC BOX	–	1	1
DELLOW	–	1	1	MY DRESS IS YELLOW	–	1	1
DRESS	–	1	1	NICE	1	–	1
DRUM	–	1	1	ORANGE	6	5	11
EAT	–	1	1	PAPER	2	–	2
FELLOW	1	–	1	PELLOW	1	–	1
FLOWER	1	3	4	PENCIL	1	1	2

RESPONSE WORD	KINDERGARTEN M	F	T	RESPONSE WORD	KINDERGARTEN M	F	T
			96.	YELLOW			
PEOPLE	1	–	1	SOMEWHERE	1	–	1
PILLOW	2	2	4	STUFF	–	1	1
PINK	1	2	3	SUN	7	9	16
PRETTY	1	1	2	THUMBTACK	–	1	1
RADIATOR	1	–	1	TOOTHBRUSH	1	–	1
RED	5	8	13	TRAIN	1	–	1
REDNESS	–	1	1	TRUCK	1	–	1
SIGN	–	1	1	WE COLOR	–	1	1
SOCK	–	1	1	WHITE	2	3	5
SOME GLOVES	–	1	1	XMAS TREE	1	–	1
SOMEBODYS COLORING A				YELL	–	1	1
BANANA YELLOW	–	1	1	YELLOW	–	1	1
SOMETHING IS YELLOW	1	–	1				

Appendix D:

Response Frequencies of Urban Maryland Children: First Grade, Third Grade, and Fifth Grade (N=280)

Entwisle Urban Maryland Data. Computer printout of all responses divided by sex, at first, third, fifth grade and adult levels, in alphabetical order. Ninety-six stimulus words.

RESPONSE WORD	1ST M	F	T	3RD M	F	T	5TH M	F	T

1. ADD

RESPONSE WORD	1ST M	F	T	3RD M	F	T	5TH M	F	T
A	1	–	1	–	–	–	–	–	–
A BOOK	–	1	1	–	–	–	–	–	–
A JAR	1	–	1	–	–	–	–	–	–
A LITTLE SALT	–	1	1	–	–	–	–	–	–
A NUMBER	–	–	–	1	–	1	–	–	–
A WORD	1	–	1	–	–	–	–	–	–
AD IS A MANS NAME	1	–	1	–	–	–	–	–	–
ADD TWO TIMES	1	–	1	–	–	–	–	–	–
ADDING	1	1	2	1	–	1	–	–	–
ADDING MACHINE	3	–	3	–	–	–	–	–	–
ADDITION	–	–	–	2	1	3	1	2	3
ADDS	–	1	1	–	–	–	–	–	–
ADVERTISEMENT	–	–	–	–	–	–	–	1	1
AIRPLANE	2	–	2	–	–	–	–	–	–
ALSO	–	–	–	–	–	–	1	–	1
AMOUNT	–	–	–	–	–	–	1	–	1
AN	–	–	–	–	1	1	–	–	–
AN ARITHMETIC PROBLEM	–	–	–	–	–	–	–	1	1
AND	–	5	5	–	–	–	–	1	1
ANOTHER HORSE	–	1	1	–	–	–	–	–	–
ANSWER	–	–	–	–	–	–	1	–	1
ANYTHING	1	–	1	–	–	–	–	–	–
APPLE	–	1	1	–	–	–	–	–	–
ARITHMATIC	–	–	–	–	–	–	–	1	1
ARITHMETIC	2	2	4	1	3	4	9	7	16
AT	–	1	1	–	–	–	–	–	–
BAD	2	–	2	2	–	2	1	–	1
BAT	1	–	1	–	–	–	–	–	–
BED	–	1	1	–	–	–	–	–	–
BELONG	–	–	–	–	–	–	–	1	1
BEND	–	1	1	–	–	–	–	–	–
BENT	–	1	1	–	–	–	–	–	–
BID	1	–	1	–	–	–	–	–	–
BLUE	1	1	2	–	–	–	–	–	–
BOOK	–	1	1	–	1	1	–	–	–
BOOKS	–	1	1	1	–	1	–	–	–
BOY	1	–	1	–	–	–	–	–	–
BROFLEN	–	–	–	–	–	–	1	–	1
BUSHES	1	–	1	–	–	–	–	–	–
BUTTON	1	–	1	–	–	–	–	–	–
CAD	1	1	2	–	–	–	–	–	–
CALM	1	–	1	–	–	–	–	–	–
CAN	2	2	4	–	–	–	–	–	–
CANDY	–	1	1	–	–	–	–	–	–
CANT	–	–	–	1	–	1	–	–	–
CARDS	1	–	1	–	–	–	–	–	–
CATCH	1	–	1	–	–	–	–	–	–
COMBINE	–	–	–	–	–	–	1	–	1
COME	–	1	1	–	–	–	–	–	–
COOKIE	–	1	1	–	–	–	–	–	–
COPY BOOK	1	–	1	–	–	–	–	–	–
COUNT	–	1	1	–	1	1	–	1	1
CRAYON	–	1	1	–	–	–	–	–	–
DAD	–	1	1	1	–	1	–	–	–
DESK	1	–	1	–	–	–	–	–	–
DIVIDE	–	–	–	–	–	–	2	1	3
DIXIE CUP	1	–	1	–	–	–	–	–	–
DO	–	–	–	–	–	–	–	1	1
DOG	1	1	2	–	–	–	–	–	–
DOOR	1	–	1	–	–	–	–	–	–
DOWN	1	–	1	–	–	–	–	–	–
DRAG	1	–	1	–	–	–	–	–	–
DRAW	–	1	1	–	–	–	–	–	–
DRESS	1	–	1	–	–	–	–	–	–
EGG	1	1	2	–	–	–	–	–	–
EGGS	–	1	1	1	–	1	–	–	–
ELSE	–	–	–	1	–	1	–	–	–
END	–	–	–	1	–	1	–	–	–
ENDING	–	–	–	–	1	1	–	–	–
EYE	–	1	1	–	–	–	–	–	–
FACE	1	–	1	–	–	–	–	–	–
FAD	1	–	1	–	–	–	–	–	–

RESPONSE WORD	1ST			3RD			5TH		
	M	F	T	M	F	T	M	F	T

1. ADD

RESPONSE WORD	M	F	T	M	F	T	M	F	T
FAST	1	1	2	–	–	–	–	–	–
FATHER	1	–	1	–	–	–	–	–	–
FIGHT	–	–	–	–	1	1	–	–	–
FIGURE	–	–	–	–	1	–	1	–	1
FISH	–	–	–	–	1	1	–	–	–
FIVE	–	–	–	1	–	1	–	–	–
FLAVOR	–	1	1	–	–	–	–	–	–
FLY	1	–	1	–	–	–	–	–	–
FOOT	–	–	–	–	–	–	–	1	1
FOUND	–	–	–	–	–	–	1	–	1
FURNACE	–	1	1	–	–	–	–	–	–
GIRL	–	–	–	1	1	2	–	–	–
GLAD	–	1	1	–	–	–	–	–	–
GLUE	1	–	1	–	–	–	–	–	–
GRASS	1	–	1	–	–	–	–	–	–
HAD	–	1	1	–	–	–	–	–	–
HAND	–	1	1	–	–	–	–	–	–
HANDLE	1	–	1	–	–	–	–	–	–
HAPPY	–	1	1	–	–	–	–	–	–
HAT	–	1	1	–	–	–	–	–	–
HAVE	1	–	1	–	–	–	–	–	–
HAVE TO	–	1	1	–	–	–	–	–	–
HE	–	2	2	–	–	–	–	–	–
HELP	1	–	1	–	–	–	–	–	–
HERE	–	1	1	–	–	–	–	–	–
HID	–	–	–	–	–	–	–	1	1
HOMEWORK	–	1	1	–	–	–	–	–	–
HORSE	–	1	1	–	–	–	–	–	–
HUSH	–	1	1	–	–	–	–	–	–
I	–	1	1	–	–	–	–	–	–
ICE CREAM	1	–	1	–	–	–	–	–	–
IN	1	–	1	–	–	–	–	1	1
IN A PAPER	–	–	–	1	–	1	–	–	–
IN GERMAN	–	1	1	–	–	–	–	–	–
INNING	–	1	1	–	–	–	–	–	–
INSECT	1	1	2	1	–	1	–	–	–
IT	–	1	1	–	–	–	–	1	1
JACK	1	–	1	–	–	–	–	–	–
JANE	1	–	1	–	–	–	–	–	–
JET	1	–	1	–	–	–	–	–	–
LAD	1	–	1	–	–	–	–	–	–
LETS ADD SOME MILK	–	1	1	–	–	–	–	–	–
LIKE YOU WORK	1	–	1	–	–	–	–	–	–
LOOK	–	1	1	1	–	1	–	–	–
MAD	1	3	4	1	2	3	–	–	–
ME	1	2	3	–	–	–	–	–	–
MILK	–	2	2	–	–	–	–	–	–
MINER	–	–	–	–	–	–	1	–	1
MINUTES	–	1	1	–	–	–	–	–	–
MISTAKE	–	–	–	–	–	–	1	–	1
MISTER	–	1	1	–	–	–	–	–	–
MONEY	2	–	2	–	–	–	–	–	–
MORE	2	–	2	–	–	–	1	–	1
MORNING	–	1	1	–	–	–	–	–	–
MOTORCYCLE	1	1	2	–	–	–	–	–	–
MR. ANN	1	–	1	–	–	–	–	–	–
MULTIPLICATION	–	–	–	–	–	–	1	–	1
MULTIPLY	–	1	1	–	–	–	6	6	12
NAME	–	–	–	–	1	1	–	–	–
NEWSPAPER	1	1	2	–	–	–	1	1	2
NO	1	–	1	–	–	–	–	–	–
NOT	–	1	1	–	–	–	–	–	–
NOT ADD	2	–	2	–	–	–	–	–	–
NOW	3	–	3	–	–	–	–	–	–
NUMBER	1	–	1	2	3	5	–	3	3
NUMBERS	6	4	10	7	2	9	3	4	7
NUMERAL	–	1	1	–	–	–	–	–	–
NURSE	–	1	1	–	–	–	–	–	–
ON	–	–	–	–	–	–	–	1	1
ONE	3	3	6	–	1	1	–	–	–
ONE ADDS SOMETHING TO THING.	–	1	1	–	–	–	–	–	–

1. ADD

RESPONSE WORD	1ST M	F	T	3RD M	F	T	5TH M	F	T
ONE AND ONE	–	1	1	–	–	–	–	–	–
ONE AND TWO	–	–	–	–	–	–	1	–	1
ONE CAKE	–	1	1	–	–	–	–	–	–
ONE MORE	–	1	1	–	–	–	–	–	–
ONE NUMBER	1	–	1	–	–	–	–	–	–
ONE NUMBER TO ANOTHER NUMBER	1	–	1	–	–	–	–	–	–
ORANGE	1	1	2	–	–	–	–	–	–
OWE	1	–	1	–	–	–	–	–	–
PAD	2	1	3	–	1	1	–	–	–
PAPER	1	4	5	–	1	1	1	–	1
PAPERS	1	–	1	–	–	–	1	–	1
PAST TENSE	–	–	–	–	–	–	1	–	1
PENCIL	2	3	5	–	1	1	–	–	–
PERSON	1	–	1	–	–	–	–	–	–
PLATES	–	1	1	–	–	–	–	–	–
PLUS	–	–	–	2	4	6	1	1	2
PROBLEM	–	–	–	2	3	5	1	1	2
PROBLEMS	–	1	1	–	–	–	–	–	–
PUNCH	1	–	1	–	–	–	–	–	–
PUT	–	–	–	–	–	–	1	–	1
PUT IN WATER	1	–	1	–	–	–	–	–	–
PUT ON	–	–	–	–	–	–	1	–	1
PUT SUGAR	–	1	1	–	–	–	–	–	–
PUT TOGETHER	–	–	–	1	1	2	5	2	7
PUTTING TOGETHER	–	–	–	–	1	1	–	–	–
RADD	1	–	1	–	–	–	–	–	–
READ	1	2	3	–	–	–	–	–	–
RED	–	1	1	–	–	–	–	–	–
ROAD	–	–	–	–	1	1	–	–	–
ROY	–	–	–	–	–	–	–	1	1
RUN	–	–	–	–	–	–	1	–	1
SAD	2	–	2	–	–	–	1	1	2
SAID	–	1	1	–	–	–	–	–	–
SAVE SOME CHICKENS AND THE LITTLE BABY	–	1	1	–	–	–	–	–	–
SCHOOL	–	1	1	1	–	1	1	2	3
SCREENDOOR	–	1	1	–	–	–	–	–	–
SEE	1	1	2	–	–	–	–	–	–
SEW	–	1	1	–	–	–	–	–	–
SHARE	1	–	1	–	–	–	–	–	–
SHIRT	1	–	1	–	–	–	–	–	–
SIDEWALK	1	–	1	–	–	–	–	–	–
SKIRT	–	1	1	–	–	–	–	–	–
SMALL	–	–	–	–	–	–	–	1	1
SNOW	1	–	1	–	–	–	–	–	–
SOMETHING	2	5	7	1	–	1	–	2	2
SOMETHING TO SOMETHINGS	1	–	1	–	–	–	–	–	–
SOMETHING TOGETHER	–	–	–	–	–	–	1	–	1
SPELL	–	1	1	–	–	–	–	–	–
SPELLING	–	1	1	–	–	–	–	–	–
SPIDER	–	1	1	–	–	–	–	–	–
STAR	1	–	1	–	–	–	–	–	–
STEAL	–	–	–	1	–	1	–	–	–
STUFF	1	–	1	–	–	–	–	–	–
SUB	–	–	–	–	–	–	2	–	2
SUBRATCT	–	–	–	–	–	–	–	1	1
SUBTRACT	3	2	5	91	93	184	79	72	151
SUBTRACTION	1	–	1	1	2	3	3	1	4
SUBTRACTS	–	–	–	–	1	1	–	1	1
SUBTRAT	–	–	–	–	–	–	–	1	1
SUDTARK	–	–	–	–	1	1	1	3	4
SUM	–	–	–	–	1	1	1	–	1
SUN	–	–	–	–	1	1	1	–	1
SURTAT	–	–	–	–	–	–	1	–	1
SWEATER	1	–	1	–	–	–	–	–	–
T	–	1	1	–	–	–	–	–	–
TACK AWAY	–	–	–	–	–	–	–	1	1
TAD	–	1	1	–	–	–	–	–	–
TAKE	1	–	1	1	–	1	–	1	1
TAKE AWAY	2	1	3	4	3	7	1	5	6
TAKES	–	–	–	1	–	1	–	–	–

RESPONSE WORD	1ST M	F	T	3RD M	F	T	5TH M	F	T

1. ADD

RESPONSE WORD	M	F	T	M	F	T	M	F	T
TED	1	–	1	–	–	–	–	–	–
TEETH	1	–	1	–	–	–	–	–	–
TEN	–	1	1	–	–	–	–	–	–
THE	–	2	2	–	–	–	–	–	–
THEM	–	1	1	1	–	1	1	–	1
THEN	–	–	–	1	–	1	–	1	1
THERE	–	–	–	1	–	1	–	–	–
THINGS	–	1	1	–	–	–	–	–	–
THIRTY	1	–	1	–	–	–	–	–	–
THIS	–	–	–	1	–	1	–	–	–
THREE	–	1	1	–	1	1	–	–	–
TO	3	–	3	–	–	–	1	1	2
TO A BUILDING	1	–	1	–	–	–	–	–	–
TO HAVE	–	–	–	–	–	–	–	1	1
TO THE MONEY	1	–	1	–	–	–	–	–	–
TOGETHER	–	–	–	–	2	2	–	2	2
TRAP	1	–	1	–	–	–	–	–	–
TRUCK	–	1	1	–	–	–	–	–	–
TV	–	1	1	–	–	–	–	–	–
TWO	–	1	1	–	1	1	–	–	–
TWO AND TWO	–	–	–	2	–	2	1	–	1
TWO PAIR	1	–	1	–	–	–	–	–	–
TYPE	–	1	1	–	–	–	–	–	–
TYPEWRITER	–	1	1	–	–	–	–	–	–
UNADD	1	–	1	–	–	–	–	–	–
UP	–	1	1	–	–	–	–	–	–
US	1	–	1	–	–	–	–	–	–
WADD	–	1	1	–	–	–	–	–	–
WALL	1	1	2	–	–	–	–	–	–
WASH RAG	1	–	1	–	–	–	–	–	–
WATER	1	–	1	–	–	–	–	–	–
WEEDS	1	–	1	–	–	–	–	–	–
WHEN	–	–	–	1	–	1	–	–	–
WHEN YOU ADD IT	1	–	1	–	–	–	–	–	–
WINDOW	1	–	1	–	–	–	–	–	–
WITH	–	–	–	–	1	1	–	–	–
WORD	2	–	2	–	–	–	–	–	–
WORDS	2	1	3	–	1	1	–	–	–
WORK	–	1	1	–	–	–	–	2	2
WRACK	–	1	1	–	–	–	–	–	–
WRITE	–	1	1	1	–	1	–	–	–
WRITING	1	1	2	–	–	–	–	–	–
YOU	2	1	3	–	–	–	–	–	–
YOUR CHEMICALS	–	1	1	–	–	–	–	–	–
YOUR NAME	–	1	1	–	–	–	–	–	–

2. ALLOW

RESPONSE WORD	M	F	T	M	F	T	M	F	T
A	–	–	–	1	–	1	–	–	–
ABBOW	1	–	1	–	–	–	–	–	–
ABLE	–	–	–	1	–	1	4	3	7
ABLE TO	–	–	–	–	–	–	–	1	1
ADMITTED	–	–	–	–	1	1	–	–	–
ADOPT	–	–	–	1	–	1	–	–	–
AID	–	–	–	–	–	–	1	–	1
AIRPLANE	1	–	1	–	–	–	–	–	–
ALASKA	1	–	1	–	–	–	–	–	–
ALL	–	–	–	2	–	2	–	–	–
ALL RIGHT	–	–	–	–	–	–	1	1	2
ALLOWANCE	2	3	5	3	–	3	–	–	–
ALLOWED	–	3	3	2	3	5	1	1	2
ALLOWED TO GO TO STORE	–	–	–	–	–	–	–	1	1
ALONE	–	–	–	2	2	4	–	–	–
ALONG	–	–	–	1	–	1	1	–	1
ALOUD	1	–	1	–	–	–	–	–	–
ALWAYS	–	–	–	–	1	1	–	1	1
ANGRY	–	–	–	1	–	1	–	–	–
ANYBODY IN THE HOUSE	–	1	1	–	–	–	–	–	–
APPROACH	–	–	–	–	–	–	1	–	1
ARE	–	1	1	–	–	–	–	–	–
ARE YOU ALLOWED OVER TO MY HOUSE	–	1	1	–	–	–	–	–	–

2. ALLOW

RESPONSE WORD	1ST M	F	T	3RD M	F	T	5TH M	F	T
ASK	–	–	–	–	–	–	2	–	2
AT LOW	–	–	–	–	1	1	–	–	–
AWAY	–	–	–	–	1	1	–	–	–
BABY	–	2	2	–	–	–	–	–	–
BAD	–	–	–	–	–	–	–	1	1
BAH	–	1	1	–	–	–	–	–	–
BALL	–	1	1	–	–	–	–	–	–
BAT	–	–	–	1	–	1	–	–	–
BE ABLE	–	–	–	–	1	1	1	1	2
BEABLE	–	–	–	–	–	–	1	–	1
BELONG	–	–	–	–	–	–	–	1	1
BENCH	–	1	1	–	–	–	–	–	–
BITE	–	1	1	–	–	–	–	–	–
BOAT	–	–	–	–	1	1	–	–	–
BOW	1	1	2	–	–	–	–	–	–
BOY	–	1	1	–	–	–	–	–	–
BROTHER	–	–	–	1	–	1	–	–	–
CAN	–	2	2	4	6	10	7	6	13
CAN HAVE	–	–	–	–	–	–	1	–	1
CANNOT	–	–	–	–	1	1	–	–	–
CANT	–	–	–	–	1	1	–	–	–
CAR	–	1	1	–	–	–	–	–	–
CAREFUL	–	–	–	1	–	1	–	–	–
CARRY	1	–	1	–	–	–	–	–	–
CAT	1	–	1	–	–	–	–	–	–
CEILING	–	1	1	–	–	–	–	–	–
CHAIR	–	–	–	–	1	1	–	–	–
CHALK	1	–	1	–	–	–	–	–	–
CHILDREN	–	1	1	–	1	1	–	1	1
CLEANING	–	1	1	–	–	–	–	–	–
CLOCK	–	1	1	–	–	–	–	–	–
CLOUD	1	–	1	1	–	1	–	–	–
COME	1	–	1	1	–	1	1	1	2
COME IN	–	1	1	1	1	2	–	–	–
COMPANY	–	–	–	–	1	1	–	–	–
COULD	–	–	–	1	–	1	–	–	–
COW	4	1	5	2	1	3	–	–	–
CUB	–	–	–	–	–	–	1	–	1
DARK	1	–	1	–	–	–	–	–	–
DEAD	–	1	1	–	–	–	–	–	–
DESK	–	1	1	–	–	–	–	–	–
DID	–	–	–	–	–	–	1	–	1
DIDNT	–	–	–	1	–	1	–	–	–
DIRTY	–	–	–	–	–	–	–	1	1
DISAGREE	–	–	–	–	–	–	–	1	1
DISALLOW	–	–	–	–	1	1	–	2	2
DISOBEY	–	–	–	–	–	–	2	–	2
DO	1	–	1	2	1	3	4	2	6
DO IT	–	1	1	2	–	2	1	–	1
DO NOT	–	1	1	–	–	–	1	–	1
DO SOMETHING	1	–	1	–	1	1	–	1	1
DONE	–	–	–	–	–	–	–	1	1
DONT	–	–	–	2	3	5	1	1	2
DONT ALLOW	–	–	–	1	2	3	1	1	2
DONT DO	–	–	–	–	–	–	1	–	1
DONT GO NEAR LIONS CAUSE THEY MIGHT BIT	–	1	1	–	–	–	–	–	–
DOOR	2	–	2	–	–	–	–	–	–
DOUG	–	1	1	–	–	–	–	–	–
DOWN	1	1	2	–	–	–	–	–	–
DRESS	–	1	1	1	–	1	–	–	–
E	1	–	1	–	–	–	–	–	–
EMPTY	–	–	–	–	–	–	–	1	1
FACE	1	–	1	–	–	–	–	–	–
FALLOW	–	–	–	–	–	–	–	1	1
FAMILY	1	–	1	–	–	–	–	–	–
FAR AWAY	–	–	–	1	–	1	–	–	–
FARM	1	–	1	–	–	–	–	–	–
FATHER	–	1	1	–	–	–	–	–	–
FELLOW	–	–	–	–	–	–	–	1	1
FENCE	–	1	1	–	–	–	–	–	–
FIB	–	–	–	1	–	1	–	–	–

2.   ALLOW

RESPONSE WORD	1ST M	1ST F	1ST T	3RD M	3RD F	3RD T	5TH M	5TH F	5TH T
FILLED	-	-	-	-	-	-	-	1	1
FIND	-	-	-	-	1	1	-	1	1
FLOOR	1	-	1	-	-	-	-	-	-
FLOWER	-	1	1	-	-	-	-	-	-
FOLLOW	-	-	-	-	-	-	-	2	2
FOR	1	-	1	-	-	-	-	-	-
FORGET	-	-	-	1	1	2	-	-	-
FOUL	-	1	1	-	-	-	-	-	-
FOUND	-	1	1	-	-	-	-	-	-
FULL	-	-	-	-	-	-	1	-	1
GATE	1	-	1	-	-	-	-	-	-
GET	-	-	-	-	-	-	-	1	1
GHOST	1	-	1	-	-	-	-	-	-
GIRL	1	-	1	1	1	2	-	-	-
GO	-	-	-	2	1	3	2	2	4
GO AHEAD	-	-	-	-	2	2	-	-	-
GOING TO	-	-	-	1	-	1	-	-	-
GONE	-	-	-	-	1	1	-	-	-
GOVERNOR	-	1	1	-	-	-	-	-	-
GRANTED	-	-	-	-	-	-	1	-	1
GREEN	-	1	1	-	-	-	-	-	-
HALF	-	1	1	-	-	-	-	-	-
HAPPEN	-	-	-	-	-	-	1	-	1
HARD	-	1	1	-	-	-	-	-	-
HAT	-	1	1	-	-	-	-	-	-
HAVE	-	-	-	-	-	-	-	1	1
HE	-	1	1	-	-	-	-	-	-
HEAR	-	1	1	-	-	-	-	-	-
HELLOW	1	-	1	-	-	-	-	-	-
HELP	-	-	-	-	1	1	-	-	-
HER	-	2	2	1	2	3	-	-	-
HERE	2	1	3	-	-	-	-	-	-
HIM	1	-	1	-	5	5	-	-	-
HIM IN	1	-	1	-	-	-	-	-	-
HIM TO RIDE A BIKE ON THE ROAD	-	1	1	-	-	-	-	-	-
HOLLER	1	1	2	-	-	-	-	-	-
HOLLER OUT LOUD	-	-	-	1	-	1	-	-	-
HOME	-	1	1	-	-	-	-	-	-
HONOR	-	-	-	-	-	-	-	1	1
HOT WATER	-	-	-	1	-	1	-	-	-
HURT	-	1	1	-	-	-	-	-	-
HUSH	-	1	1	-	-	-	-	-	-
I	-	1	1	-	-	-	-	-	-
I CANT ALLOW YOU IN	-	1	1	-	-	-	-	-	-
IF YOUR MOTHER LETS YOU	-	1	1	-	-	-	-	-	-
IN	2	1	3	-	1	1	1	-	1
IN HERE	1	-	1	-	-	-	-	-	-
IN MY HOUSE	-	1	1	-	-	-	-	-	-
INSTRUCTIONS	-	-	-	-	-	-	-	1	1
INTO	-	-	-	3	-	3	-	-	-
ISNT ALLOWED	-	-	-	-	1	1	-	-	-
IT	-	-	-	1	1	2	-	-	-
JALLOW	-	-	-	1	-	1	-	-	-
KATHY	1	-	1	-	-	-	-	-	-
KNOWS	-	-	-	-	1	1	-	-	-
LAMP	-	1	1	-	-	-	-	-	-
LASSO	-	-	-	1	-	1	-	-	-
LAUGH	-	-	-	1	-	1	-	-	-
LAW	-	-	-	-	-	-	1	1	2
LEARN	1	-	1	1	-	1	-	-	-
LET	1	-	1	7	7	14	21	22	43
LET DO	-	-	-	-	-	-	1	2	3
LETTERS	-	1	1	-	-	-	-	-	-
LIGHT	1	2	3	-	-	-	-	-	-
LIKE	-	-	-	-	-	-	-	1	1
LIKE SLOW	-	1	1	-	-	-	-	-	-
LION	2	-	2	-	-	-	-	-	-
LOLLIPOP	-	1	1	-	-	-	-	-	-
LOOK	-	1	1	-	-	-	-	-	-
LOUD	4	7	11	2	3	5	3	3	6

RESPONSE WORD	1ST			3RD			5TH		
	M	F	T	M	F	T	M	F	T

2. ALLOW

RESPONSE WORD	M	F	T	M	F	T	M	F	T
LOUD HEAR	–	–	–	–	1	1	–	–	–
LOUD SOUND	–	1	1	–	–	–	–	–	–
LOUDLY	1	–	1	–	2	2	–	1	1
LOW	1	1	2	–	1	1	–	–	–
LOWER	–	1	1	–	–	–	–	–	–
MAIL	–	–	–	–	1	1	–	–	–
MAILBOX	1	–	1	–	–	–	–	–	–
MANY	–	–	–	–	–	–	–	1	1
MAY	–	–	–	2	2	4	2	–	2
MAY DO	–	–	–	1	–	1	–	–	–
MAYBE	–	–	–	–	–	–	1	–	1
ME	5	2	7	3	6	9	–	2	2
ME TO GO	1	–	1	–	–	–	–	–	–
MOMENT	–	–	–	1	–	1	–	–	–
MONEY	1	1	2	–	–	–	1	2	3
MONKEY	1	–	1	–	–	–	–	–	–
MOSTLY	–	–	–	–	1	1	–	–	–
MOTHER	–	–	–	1	–	1	–	–	–
MOUSE	1	–	1	–	–	–	–	–	–
MOUTH	1	1	2	–	–	–	–	–	–
MOW	1	–	1	1	–	1	–	–	–
MY MOTHER	–	–	–	–	1	1	–	–	–
NAIL	1	–	1	–	–	–	–	–	–
NAPKIN	1	–	1	–	–	–	–	–	–
NET	–	–	–	–	1	1	–	–	–
NEVER	–	–	–	1	2	3	–	–	–
NO	–	4	4	3	1	4	2	2	4
NO DOGS	–	1	1	–	–	–	–	–	–
NO RESPONSE	–	–	–	–	–	–	–	1	1
NOBODY IN HOUSE	–	1	1	–	–	–	–	–	–
NOISE	1	1	2	1	1	2	3	1	4
NOISY	1	–	1	–	1	1	–	–	–
NONE	–	–	–	1	–	1	–	–	–
NOT	4	2	6	4	7	11	6	3	9
NOT ABLE	–	–	–	–	–	–	–	1	1
NOT ALLOW	4	2	6	11	6	17	8	2	10
NOT ALLOWED	2	–	2	3	2	5	–	1	1
NOT IN HERE	1	–	1	–	–	–	–	–	–
NOT TO	–	–	–	–	–	–	–	1	1
NOTHING	–	–	–	–	1	1	–	1	1
NOW	1	1	2	2	–	2	–	–	–
O K	–	–	–	2	–	2	–	–	–
OBEY	1	–	1	1	4	5	2	4	6
OBEYED	–	–	–	–	1	1	1	–	1
OF	–	–	–	–	1	1	–	–	–
OFF	–	1	1	–	–	–	–	1	1
OK	–	–	–	–	–	–	1	1	2
OKAY	–	–	–	1	–	1	2	1	3
ONE	–	1	1	–	–	–	–	–	–
ONLY	–	–	–	1	–	1	–	–	–
ORAL	–	–	–	–	–	–	1	1	2
ORALLY	–	–	–	–	–	–	–	1	1
ORCHARD	–	–	–	1	–	1	–	–	–
ORDER	–	–	–	1	–	1	1	1	2
ORDERS	1	–	1	–	1	1	–	–	–
OUT	1	–	1	–	1	1	1	–	1
OUTSIDE	–	–	–	1	–	1	–	–	–
OVAL	–	–	–	–	1	1	–	–	–
OW	3	–	3	1	–	1	–	–	–
OWL	1	–	1	–	–	–	–	–	–
OWN	–	–	–	–	–	–	–	1	1
PAL	–	–	–	1	–	1	–	–	–
PAPER	1	–	1	–	–	–	–	–	–
PARK	1	–	1	–	–	–	–	–	–
PEOPLE	1	3	4	–	–	–	–	–	–
PERMISSION	–	–	–	2	2	4	6	5	11
PERMIT	–	–	–	1	–	1	4	1	5
PERMITTING	–	–	–	–	–	–	–	1	1
PERSON	–	–	–	–	–	–	–	1	1
PICTURE	1	–	1	–	–	–	–	–	–
PIG	–	–	–	–	–	–	1	–	1
PLAY	1	–	1	–	–	–	–	1	1

2. ALLOW

RESPONSE WORD	1ST M	1ST F	1ST T	3RD M	3RD F	3RD T	5TH M	5TH F	5TH T
PLOW	–	–	–	–	–	–	–	1	1
PLUG	1	–	1	–	–	–	–	–	–
POCKETBOOK	–	1	1	–	–	–	–	–	–
POLITE	–	–	–	1	–	1	–	–	–
POW	1	1	2	–	–	–	–	–	–
PRIVATE	–	1	1	–	–	–	–	–	–
QUIET	2	4	6	3	–	3	2	2	4
RALLOW	–	1	1	–	–	–	–	–	–
READ	–	–	–	–	1	1	–	1	1
READ LOUD	1	–	1	–	–	–	–	–	–
RED	–	1	1	–	–	–	–	–	–
REFUSE	–	–	–	–	–	–	1	–	1
ROW	–	1	1	–	–	–	–	–	–
RULE	–	–	–	1	–	1	1	–	1
RUN	1	–	1	–	–	–	–	–	–
SAID	–	–	–	–	–	–	1	–	1
SAUNTED	1	–	1	–	–	–	–	–	–
SAY YES	–	–	–	–	–	–	–	1	1
SCHOOL	–	–	–	1	–	1	1	–	1
SCREAM	2	1	3	–	–	–	1	–	1
SEE	–	1	1	–	–	–	–	–	–
SHE	–	1	1	1	–	1	–	–	–
SHOUT	–	–	–	1	–	1	1	1	2
SHOUT OUT	–	1	1	–	–	–	–	–	–
SILENT	–	–	–	–	–	–	1	2	3
SINK	–	1	1	–	–	–	–	–	–
SKOMP	–	–	–	–	–	–	1	–	1
SLOW	1	1	2	1	–	1	–	–	–
SLOWLY	–	–	–	–	1	1	1	–	1
SNAKE	1	–	1	–	–	–	–	–	–
SNOW	1	–	1	–	–	–	–	–	–
SOFA	–	1	1	–	–	–	–	–	–
SOFT	2	4	6	–	5	5	3	3	6
SOFTLY	1	2	3	4	2	6	2	2	4
SOMEONE	–	–	–	–	2	2	–	–	–
SOMEONE ALLOWS YOU TO GO SOMEPLACE	–	1	1	–	–	–	–	–	–
SOMETHING	–	–	–	1	–	1	1	–	1
SORRY	–	–	–	–	–	–	1	–	1
SOUND	–	–	–	–	1	1	–	–	–
SPEAK	–	–	–	–	1	1	1	1	2
STOP	–	2	2	1	1	2	–	–	–
SUN	–	–	–	1	–	1	–	–	–
SWEEP	–	–	–	1	–	1	–	–	–
TAKE	–	–	–	–	–	–	1	–	1
TALK	–	1	1	2	1	3	–	2	2
TALK LOUD	1	1	2	–	–	–	–	–	–
TEACHER WOULD ALLOW YOU TO DO SOMETHING	–	–	–	–	–	–	–	1	1
THANK YOU	–	–	–	1	–	1	–	–	–
THAT	1	–	1	–	1	1	–	–	–
THEM	1	–	1	1	–	1	–	–	–
THEY	1	–	1	–	–	–	–	–	–
THINK	–	–	–	–	–	–	–	1	1
THIS	1	–	1	–	–	–	–	–	–
TIGER	1	–	1	–	–	–	–	–	–
TIME	–	–	–	–	–	–	2	–	2
TO	3	4	7	1	3	4	1	2	3
TO DO	1	–	1	1	–	1	2	4	6
TO GO	1	1	2	–	–	–	–	–	–
TO GO FISHING	1	–	1	–	–	–	–	–	–
TO GO OUTSIDE	2	–	2	–	–	–	–	–	–
TO ME	1	–	1	–	–	–	–	–	–
TO OBEY	–	–	–	–	–	–	1	–	1
TO SWING	1	–	1	–	–	–	–	–	–
TOO NOISY	–	1	1	–	–	–	–	–	–
TOW	1	–	1	–	–	–	–	–	–
TOWEL	–	1	1	–	–	–	–	–	–
TREE	1	–	1	–	–	–	–	–	–
TRUST	–	–	–	–	1	1	–	–	–
TRUSTED	–	–	–	–	–	–	–	1	1
UNABLE	–	–	–	–	–	–	–	1	1

RESPONSE WORD	1ST M	F	T	3RD M	F	T	5TH M	F	T

2. ALLOW

RESPONSE WORD	1ST M	F	T	3RD M	F	T	5TH M	F	T
UNALLOW	1	–	1	1	–	1	1	1	2
UNALLOWED	–	–	–	1	–	1	–	1	1
UNLOW	–	–	–	–	2	2	–	–	–
UNTIL	–	–	–	–	1	1	–	–	–
UP	–	–	–	–	–	–	1	–	1
US	–	–	–	–	1	1	–	–	–
VOICE	–	–	–	–	–	–	–	1	1
WALK	1	–	1	–	–	–	–	–	–
WALL	–	1	1	–	–	–	–	–	–
WAY	1	–	1	–	–	–	–	1	1
WHEN	–	1	1	–	–	–	–	–	–
WHEN YOU HOLLER	1	–	1	–	–	–	–	–	–
WHISTLE	1	–	1	–	–	–	–	–	–
WILL YOU	1	–	1	–	–	–	–	–	–
WINDOW	–	–	–	–	1	1	–	–	–
WITH	–	–	–	–	–	–	1	–	1
WOMAN	–	–	–	–	–	–	1	–	1
WORD	–	–	–	–	1	1	–	–	–
WORK	1	–	1	–	–	–	–	–	–
YARD	–	1	1	–	–	–	–	–	–
YELL	–	1	1	–	–	–	–	–	–
YELLOW	1	1	2	–	–	–	–	–	–
YES	2	1	3	1	1	2	1	–	1
YOU	5	–	5	4	2	6	–	1	1
YOU ARE	–	1	1	–	–	–	–	–	–
YOU CAN	–	–	–	1	2	3	–	–	–
YOU MAY	1	–	1	–	–	–	–	–	–
YOUR	–	1	1	–	–	–	–	–	–
YOU RE ALLOWED IN MY HOUSE	–	–	–	1	–	1	–	–	–

3. ALWAYS

RESPONSE WORD	1ST M	F	T	3RD M	F	T	5TH M	F	T
A LOT	–	–	–	–	1	1	–	–	–
AFTER	1	–	1	3	1	4	–	–	–
AGAIN	2	1	3	3	3	6	2	3	5
ALL	1	3	4	3	3	6	1	–	1
ALL THE TIME	–	–	–	6	6	12	8	12	20
ALL TIMES	–	–	–	1	2	3	1	–	1
ALMOST	–	–	–	1	1	2	1	–	1
ALONG	–	–	–	1	–	1	–	–	–
ALWAYS	–	–	–	–	–	–	1	–	1
ANY	–	–	–	–	1	1	–	–	–
ANYTIME	–	–	–	–	1	1	–	–	–
ANYWAY	–	1	1	–	–	–	1	–	1
ASKING	–	–	–	1	–	1	–	–	–
AT A SCHOOL	–	1	1	–	–	–	–	–	–
AWAY	1	1	2	2	4	6	2	–	2
AWFUL	–	–	–	–	1	1	–	–	–
BAD	–	1	1	–	1	1	–	–	–
BALL	–	–	–	1	–	1	–	–	–
BALWAYS	1	–	1	–	–	–	–	–	–
BE	–	1	1	–	–	–	–	–	–
BE CAREFUL	–	1	1	–	–	–	–	–	–
BE THE SAME	–	–	–	–	–	–	1	–	1
BEANS	1	–	1	–	–	–	–	–	–
BEAR	1	–	1	1	–	1	–	–	–
BECAUSE	1	–	1	3	2	5	–	1	1
BECOME	–	–	–	–	1	1	–	–	–
BEFORE	–	1	1	–	1	1	–	1	1
BEGETHER	1	–	1	–	–	–	–	–	–
BEGIN	–	–	–	–	1	1	–	–	–
BEGINNING	–	–	–	–	–	–	–	1	1
BELIEVE	–	–	–	–	–	–	–	1	1
BELONG	–	–	–	1	–	1	–	1	1
BETWEEN MEALS	–	1	1	–	–	–	–	–	–
BIG	1	1	2	–	1	1	–	–	–
BOAT	1	–	1	–	–	–	–	–	–
BOOK	1	1	2	–	–	–	–	–	–
BOW	1	–	1	–	–	–	–	–	–
BOY	1	–	1	–	–	–	–	–	–

RESPONSE WORD	1ST M	F	T	3RD M	F	T	5TH M	F	T

3.   ALWAYS

RESPONSE WORD	1ST M	F	T	3RD M	F	T	5TH M	F	T
BOYS	2	—	2	—	—	—	—	—	—
BROTHER	1	—	1	—	—	—	—	—	—
BYE-BYES	—	1	1	—	—	—	—	—	—
CAKE	1	—	1	—	—	—	—	—	—
CALWAYS	2	—	2	—	—	—	—	—	—
CAN	1	1	2	—	—	—	—	2	2
CAN DO SOMETHING	—	1	1	—	—	—	—	—	—
CANDY	—	1	1	—	—	—	—	—	—
CANT	—	—	—	1	1	2	—	—	—
CAR	1	—	1	—	—	—	—	—	—
CAT	1	—	1	—	—	—	—	—	—
CATCH	1	—	1	—	—	—	—	—	—
CHALKBOARD	1	—	1	—	—	—	—	—	—
CHALWAYS	1	—	1	—	—	—	—	—	—
CHRISTMAS	—	—	—	—	—	—	1	—	1
CLEAN	—	—	—	1	—	1	—	—	—
COME	3	1	4	—	3	3	—	—	—
COME HERE	—	1	1	—	—	—	—	—	—
COMING	—	—	—	1	—	1	—	—	—
CONTINUE	—	—	—	—	—	—	1	—	1
CUT	—	—	—	—	1	1	—	—	—
DALWAYS	—	1	1	—	—	—	—	—	—
DARK	—	1	1	—	—	—	—	—	—
DAYS	1	—	1	—	—	—	—	—	—
DEAD	1	—	1	—	—	—	—	—	—
DIDNT	—	—	—	1	1	2	1	—	1
DIFFERENT	—	—	—	1	—	1	1	—	1
DO	3	3	6	2	2	4	—	3	3
DO NOT TALK	1	—	1	—	—	—	—	—	—
DO SOMETHING	1	—	1	—	—	—	—	—	—
DO THAT	—	—	—	1	—	1	—	—	—
DO THINGS	1	—	1	—	—	—	—	—	—
DOES	—	—	—	—	1	1	1	—	1
DOING	—	—	—	—	1	1	—	—	—
DONT	1	—	1	—	—	—	1	—	1
DONT DO IT	—	—	—	1	—	1	—	—	—
DONT PLAY IN THE GRASS EVERYDAY	—	1	1	—	—	—	—	—	—
DONT TOUCH THE FLOWER	1	—	1	—	—	—	—	—	—
DOOR	—	1	1	—	—	—	—	—	—
EARTH	—	—	—	—	—	—	1	—	1
EAT	—	1	1	—	—	—	—	—	—
ENDING	—	—	—	—	1	1	—	—	—
ENJOY	—	—	—	—	1	1	—	—	—
EVER	—	—	—	2	1	3	3	2	5
EVERMORE	—	—	—	—	—	—	—	1	1
EVERY	—	—	—	1	—	1	2	1	3
EVERY DAY	—	—	—	—	2	2	1	—	1
EVERY TIME	—	—	—	2	1	3	3	2	5
EVERYBODY	—	—	—	1	—	1	—	—	—
EVERYTHING	—	—	—	1	—	1	—	—	—
FALL	1	—	1	1	—	1	—	—	—
FAR	—	—	—	1	—	1	—	—	—
FAT	1	—	1	—	—	—	—	—	—
FIND	—	1	1	—	—	—	—	—	—
FIVE	1	—	1	—	—	—	1	—	1
FOOD	—	—	—	—	—	—	1	—	1
FOR	1	—	1	—	—	—	1	—	1
FOREVER	—	—	—	2	1	3	9	9	18
FORGET	—	—	—	—	2	2	—	—	—
FORGOT	—	—	—	—	1	1	—	—	—
FRUIT	—	—	—	1	—	1	—	—	—
FUN	—	1	1	—	—	—	—	—	—
FURNITURE	1	—	1	—	—	—	—	—	—
GANG	—	—	—	—	—	—	1	—	1
GAY	—	—	—	—	1	1	—	—	—
GENTLE	—	1	1	—	—	—	—	—	—
GEORGE	—	1	1	—	—	—	—	—	—
GIRL	1	—	1	1	1	1	—	1	1
GO	3	4	7	1	2	3	—	1	1

RESPONSE WORD	1ST			3RD			5TH		
	M	F	T	M	F	T	M	F	T

3. ALWAYS

RESPONSE WORD	M	F	T	M	F	T	M	F	T
GO OUTSIDE	—	1	1	—	—	—	—	—	—
GOES FAST	—	1	1	—	—	—	—	—	—
GOES TO STORE	1	—	1	—	—	—	—	—	—
GOING	—	1	1	—	—	—	—	—	—
GONE	—	2	2	—	—	—	—	—	—
GOOD	3	1	4	1	—	1	—	—	—
GRASS	1	—	1	—	—	—	—	—	—
GROWS	—	1	1	—	—	—	—	—	—
HALL	1	—	1	—	—	—	—	—	—
HALLOWEEN	1	—	1	—	—	—	—	—	—
HALLWAY	2	—	2	—	—	—	—	—	—
HALLWAYS	—	—	—	1	—	1	—	—	—
HAND	—	1	1	—	—	—	—	—	—
HAPPEN	1	—	1	1	1	2	1	1	2
HAPPENED	—	—	—	—	—	—	—	1	1
HAPPENS	2	—	2	—	—	—	—	—	—
HAPPY	—	2	2	1	1	2	1	1	2
HARDLY	—	1	1	—	1	1	—	—	—
HAVE	1	—	1	1	—	1	—	—	—
HE	—	—	—	—	—	—	2	—	2
HEALTHY	—	—	—	1	—	1	—	—	—
HEAR	—	—	—	1	—	1	—	—	—
HERE	—	2	2	2	—	2	—	—	—
HOME	—	1	1	—	1	1	—	—	—
HOT	1	—	1	—	—	—	—	—	—
HOUSE	1	—	1	1	—	1	—	—	—
HURT	—	1	1	—	—	—	—	—	—
HURTS	—	1	1	—	—	—	—	—	—
I	—	1	1	—	—	—	—	—	—
I ALWAYS BE GOOD TO MY DADDY	—	1	1	—	—	—	—	—	—
I RIDE MY BIKE	—	—	—	—	—	—	—	1	1
I WILL ALWAYS LIVE WITH YOU	—	1	1	—	—	—	—	—	—
I WILL BE ALWAYS WITH YOU	—	—	—	1	—	1	—	—	—
ICE CREAM	1	—	1	—	—	—	—	—	—
IN	2	—	2	—	—	—	—	—	—
IN TROUBLE	—	—	—	1	—	1	1	—	1
INCH	—	—	—	1	—	1	—	—	—
IT	1	—	1	—	—	—	—	—	—
IT ALWAYS BELONGS TO YOU	—	—	—	1	—	1	—	—	—
JUMP	—	—	—	—	1	1	—	—	—
KEEP	2	1	3	—	1	1	1	1	2
KNOB	—	1	1	—	—	—	—	—	—
LAW	—	—	—	—	—	—	—	1	1
LAWAYS	1	1	2	—	—	—	—	—	—
LET PLAY	—	1	1	—	—	—	—	—	—
LIKE	1	—	1	—	—	—	—	—	—
LISTEN	—	1	1	—	—	—	—	—	—
LISTEN TO MOTHER	1	—	1	—	—	—	—	—	—
LITTLE	—	—	—	1	—	1	—	—	—
LONELY	—	—	—	—	—	—	1	—	1
LONG	1	1	2	1	1	2	—	1	1
LONG TIME AGO	—	1	1	—	—	—	—	—	—
LOOK	1	—	1	—	—	—	—	—	—
LOSE	—	—	—	—	1	1	—	—	—
LOT	—	—	—	1	—	1	—	—	—
MAIL	1	—	1	—	—	—	—	—	—
MAIN	—	—	—	—	—	—	—	1	1
MALWAYS	1	—	1	—	—	—	—	—	—
MAURYS	1	—	1	—	—	—	—	—	—
MAY	—	1	1	—	—	—	—	1	1
MAYBE	—	—	—	1	—	1	—	—	—
ME	1	—	1	1	—	1	—	—	—
MELLOW	—	1	1	—	—	—	—	—	—
MICROPHONE	—	—	—	1	—	1	—	—	—
MINE	1	—	1	—	—	—	—	—	—
MISS RICKY	1	—	1	—	—	—	—	—	—
MORE THAN ONCE	—	—	—	1	—	1	—	—	—
MOST	—	—	—	—	1	1	2	1	3
MOST OF THE TIME	—	—	—	1	—	1	—	—	—

RESPONSE WORD	1ST			3RD			5TH		
	M	F	T	M	F	T	M	F	T

3. ALWAYS

RESPONSE WORD	M	F	T	M	F	T	M	F	T
MOSTLY	—	—	—	—	1	1	—	—	—
MOTHER	—	1	1	—	—	—	—	—	—
MUST	—	—	—	—	—	—	1	—	1
MY MOMMY	—	1	1	—	—	—	—	—	—
NAP	—	1	1	—	—	—	—	—	—
NAVER	—	—	—	—	—	—	1	—	1
NEARLY	—	—	—	—	—	—	—	1	1
NEAT	—	—	—	1	—	1	—	—	—
NECESSARY	—	—	—	—	—	—	—	1	1
NENT	—	—	—	—	—	—	—	1	1
NEVER	1	9	10	22	24	46	39	37	76
NEVER ENDING	—	—	—	—	—	—	—	1	1
NEVER MISSING	—	—	—	—	—	—	—	1	1
NEVERTHELESS	—	1	1	—	—	—	—	—	—
NICE	—	2	2	—	1	1	—	—	—
NO	1	1	2	—	1	1	—	1	1
NOT	1	2	3	6	2	8	—	—	—
NOT ALWAYS	8	3	11	7	5	12	3	3	6
NOT STOP	—	—	—	—	—	—	1	—	1
NOTHING	—	—	—	—	—	—	1	—	1
NOW	—	2	2	2	2	4	1	1	2
NOWAYS	—	—	—	1	—	1	—	—	—
NUMBER	1	1	2	—	—	—	—	—	—
NUT	1	—	1	—	—	—	—	—	—
OBEY	2	—	2	—	—	—	—	—	—
OBEYS	—	1	1	—	—	—	—	—	—
OFTEN	—	—	—	1	3	4	1	2	3
OLD	—	—	—	—	—	—	—	1	1
ON	—	1	1	—	—	—	—	—	—
ONCE	—	—	—	—	—	—	—	2	2
ONCEDT	—	—	—	1	—	1	—	—	—
OUT	—	1	1	—	—	—	—	—	—
PACKAGES	1	—	1	—	—	—	—	—	—
PAINT	1	—	1	—	—	—	—	—	—
PAIR	—	1	1	—	—	—	—	—	—
PANTS	—	1	1	—	—	—	—	—	—
PENCIL	—	1	1	—	—	—	—	—	—
PEP	—	1	1	—	—	—	—	—	—
PLAY	2	2	4	—	—	—	—	—	—
PLEASE	—	1	1	—	—	—	1	—	1
PONIES	1	—	1	—	—	—	—	—	—
POSSIBLE	—	—	—	—	—	—	—	1	1
PROMISE	1	—	1	—	1	1	—	—	—
PUT	—	1	1	—	—	—	—	—	—
PUZZLE	—	1	1	—	—	—	—	—	—
QUICK	—	—	—	1	—	1	—	—	—
QUIET	1	2	3	—	—	—	—	—	—
READ A BOOK	—	1	1	—	—	—	—	—	—
READY	—	—	—	2	—	2	—	—	—
REFRIGERATOR	1	—	1	—	—	—	—	—	—
REGULAR	—	—	—	—	—	—	—	1	1
REMEMBER	1	1	2	2	4	6	—	—	—
RESPONSIBILITY	—	—	—	—	—	—	—	1	1
RIBBON	—	—	—	1	—	1	—	—	—
RIGHT	1	—	1	—	—	—	2	2	4
ROOM	1	—	1	—	—	—	—	—	—
RUNNING	—	—	—	1	—	1	—	—	—
SAD	2	—	2	—	—	—	—	—	—
SAID	—	1	1	—	—	—	—	—	—
SALWAYS	1	—	1	—	—	—	—	—	—
SAME	—	—	—	—	1	1	1	—	1
SATISFIED	—	—	—	—	1	1	—	—	—
SAY	—	1	1	—	—	—	—	—	—
SCHOOL	—	1	1	—	—	—	—	—	—
SEE	—	1	1	—	—	—	—	—	—
SELDOM	—	—	—	—	—	—	1	—	1
SEVEN	—	—	—	—	1	1	—	—	—
SHE	1	—	1	—	—	—	—	—	—
SHIRT	1	1	2	—	—	—	—	—	—
SHOE	2	—	2	—	—	—	—	—	—
SHORT	—	—	—	—	—	—	1	—	1
SIGN	1	—	1	—	—	—	—	—	—

RESPONSE WORD	1ST			3RD			5TH		
	M	F	T	M	F	T	M	F	T

3. ALWAYS

RESPONSE WORD	M	F	T	M	F	T	M	F	T
SIX	1	–	1	–	–	–	–	–	–
SLEEP	–	1	1	–	–	–	–	–	–
SLOW	1	–	1	–	–	–	1	–	1
SOMEBODY	1	–	1	–	–	–	–	–	–
SOMEONE ALWAYS BUYS YOU SOMETHING	–	1	1	–	–	–	–	–	–
SOMETHING	–	3	3	1	1	2	–	2	2
SOMETIME	–	–	–	–	1	1	1	–	1
SOMETIMES	2	3	5	14	12	26	12	10	22
SONG	–	–	–	–	1	1	1	–	1
STATES	–	–	–	–	1	1	–	–	–
STAY	1	1	2	2	–	2	1	–	1
STEERT	–	–	–	–	–	–	–	1	1
STEPS	1	–	1	–	–	–	–	–	–
STOCKINGS	–	1	1	–	–	–	–	–	–
STONE	–	1	1	–	–	–	–	–	–
STOP	–	1	1	–	–	–	–	–	–
STORY	–	1	1	–	–	–	–	–	–
SURE	1	–	1	–	–	–	–	1	1
SWIM	–	–	–	–	–	–	–	1	1
TABLE	–	2	2	–	–	–	–	–	–
TAKE AWAY	–	–	–	–	1	1	–	–	–
TALK	–	1	1	1	–	1	–	1	1
TALL	–	–	–	1	–	1	–	–	–
TELL	–	–	–	–	1	1	–	–	–
THAT	1	–	1	–	1	1	–	–	–
THE	–	1	1	–	–	–	–	–	–
THE LIGHT GOES ON	1	–	1	–	–	–	–	–	–
THE SAME	1	–	1	–	–	–	–	1	1
THEM	–	–	–	–	–	–	–	1	1
THEN	–	1	1	–	–	–	–	–	–
THERE	–	–	–	–	–	–	1	–	1
THEY	–	–	–	–	1	1	–	–	–
THIS WAY	–	1	1	–	–	–	–	–	–
TIME	–	1	1	–	–	–	1	1	2
TOGATHER	–	–	–	–	–	–	–	1	1
TOGETHER	–	–	–	1	5	6	4	1	5
TOW	–	1	1	–	–	–	–	–	–
TRUE	–	–	–	–	–	–	1	–	1
TWO	–	–	–	1	1	2	–	–	–
UP	–	2	2	–	–	–	–	–	–
US	1	–	1	–	–	–	–	–	–
USALLY	–	–	–	–	–	–	–	1	1
USUALLY	–	–	–	1	–	1	–	3	3
WADE	–	1	1	–	–	–	–	–	–
WALK	2	1	3	–	–	–	1	–	1
WALL	1	–	1	–	1	1	–	–	–
WANT	–	1	1	–	–	–	–	–	–
WATER AROUND HERE	1	–	1	–	–	–	–	–	–
WAY	–	–	–	–	1	1	2	1	3
WAYS	–	–	–	–	1	1	2	4	6
WE	1	–	1	–	–	–	–	–	–
WE FLY IN THE AIR	1	–	1	–	–	–	–	–	–
WENT	–	–	–	–	–	–	1	–	1
WHEN	–	–	–	–	1	1	–	–	–
WHEN YOU CATCH MUMPS	–	1	1	–	–	–	–	–	–
WHEN YOURE ALWAYS DOING SOMETHING	1	–	1	–	–	–	–	–	–
WHITE	–	1	1	–	–	–	–	–	–
WHY	–	–	–	–	1	1	–	–	–
WILL	2	1	3	–	–	–	1	1	2
WITH ME	1	–	1	–	–	–	–	–	–
WITH YOU	1	–	1	–	–	–	–	–	–
WONDERFUL	–	–	–	1	–	1	–	–	–
X	–	1	1	–	–	–	–	–	–
YES	–	–	–	–	–	–	1	–	1
YOU	2	–	2	–	–	–	1	–	1
YOU COULD MAKE SOMETHING	–	1	1	–	–	–	–	–	–
YOURS	–	–	–	–	–	–	–	1	1

RESPONSE WORD	1ST M	F	T	3RD M	F	T	5TH M	F	T

4.   BECAUSE

RESPONSE WORD	1ST M	F	T	3RD M	F	T	5TH M	F	T
A CAUSE	-	-	-	-	-	-	-	1	1
A REASON	-	-	-	-	-	-	1	-	1
ADD	-	-	-	-	-	-	1	1	2
AFTER	-	-	-	1	-	1	-	-	-
AGAIN	1	-	1	-	-	-	-	-	-
AGO	-	1	1	-	-	-	-	-	-
AIRPLANE	1	-	1	-	-	-	-	-	-
ALIKE	-	-	-	-	-	-	1	-	1
ALL	-	1	1	-	-	-	-	-	-
ALLOW	-	-	-	1	-	1	-	-	-
ALSO	-	-	-	-	-	-	-	1	1
ALWAYS	-	-	-	1	-	1	-	2	2
AND	-	-	-	1	-	1	-	1	1
ANETTE	-	1	1	-	-	-	-	-	-
ANSWER	-	-	-	-	-	-	3	2	5
ANY	-	-	-	-	-	-	1	-	1
ANYWAY	-	-	-	2	-	2	-	-	-
APPLES	-	-	-	-	1	1	-	-	-
BAD	-	-	-	-	1	1	1	-	1
BALL	-	1	1	-	-	-	-	-	-
BE	-	-	-	5	3	8	-	-	-
BE QUIET	1	-	1	-	-	-	-	-	-
BE QUIET, YOU TWO	1	-	1	-	-	-	-	-	-
BE WITH	-	-	-	1	-	1	-	-	-
BEAK	1	-	1	-	-	-	-	-	-
BEAUTIFUL	-	-	-	1	-	1	-	-	-
BECAME	-	-	-	-	3	3	2	3	5
BECAUSE	-	-	-	-	-	-	1	-	1
BECAUSE NOT	-	-	-	1	-	1	-	-	-
BECOME	-	-	-	1	1	2	1	1	2
BEFORE	-	-	-	-	2	2	-	-	-
BEGIN	-	-	-	3	1	4	-	1	1
BEHAUSE	1	-	1	-	-	-	-	-	-
BEHIND	-	-	-	1	-	1	-	-	-
BELONG	-	-	-	-	1	1	-	-	-
BESIDE	-	-	-	1	-	1	-	-	-
BID	-	-	-	-	1	1	-	-	-
BLAME	-	-	-	-	-	-	1	-	1
BLUE	-	1	1	-	-	-	-	-	-
BOOK	1	-	1	-	-	-	-	-	-
BOX	1	1	2	-	-	-	-	-	-
BOY	1	1	2	-	-	-	-	-	-
BRAVE	-	-	-	-	1	1	-	-	-
BRICK	1	-	1	-	-	-	-	-	-
BUILDING	1	-	1	-	-	-	-	-	-
BURN	-	1	1	-	-	-	-	-	-
BUT	1	-	1	-	-	-	-	-	-
BY	-	1	1	-	-	-	-	-	-
CAME	-	-	-	-	1	1	-	1	1
CAN	-	1	1	-	1	1	1	1	2
CANNOT	-	-	-	1	-	1	-	-	-
CANT	2	1	3	1	-	1	1	5	6
CANT DO IT	-	-	-	1	-	1	-	-	-
CANT GO OUT	1	-	1	-	-	-	-	-	-
CAR	-	2	2	-	-	-	1	-	1
CARDS	-	1	1	-	-	-	-	-	-
CAT	-	-	-	-	1	1	-	-	-
CAUSE	-	-	-	3	4	7	8	20	28
CERTAIN	-	-	-	-	-	-	-	1	1
CHICKEN	1	-	1	-	-	-	-	-	-
CHIMNEY	1	-	1	-	-	-	-	-	-
CHRISTMAS	-	-	-	-	-	-	1	-	1
CLAWS	1	-	1	-	-	-	-	-	-
CLOTHES	-	1	1	-	-	-	-	1	1
COME	-	-	-	-	-	-	-	1	1
CONTRACTION	-	-	-	1	-	1	-	-	-
COULDNT	1	-	1	-	-	-	-	-	-
COUSIN	-	1	1	-	-	-	-	-	-
CUSHION	-	-	-	-	1	1	-	-	-
CUZ	-	1	1	-	2	2	-	-	-
DANGEROUS	1	-	1	-	2	2	-	-	-
DID	-	-	-	-	2	2	1	1	2

RESPONSE WORD	1ST			3RD			5TH		
	M	F	T	M	F	T	M	F	T

4. BECAUSE

RESPONSE WORD	M	F	T	M	F	T	M	F	T
DIDNT	–	–	–	1	–	1	–	–	–
DIDNT BECAUSE	–	–	–	1	–	1	–	–	–
DO	–	–	–	–	–	–	1	–	1
DO IT	–	–	–	1	–	1	–	–	–
DO THIS	1	–	1	–	–	–	–	–	–
DOESNT	–	–	–	1	–	1	–	–	–
DOG	1	–	1	–	–	–	–	–	–
DOING SOMETHING	–	1	1	–	–	–	–	–	–
DONT	–	–	–	1	–	1	1	–	1
DONT DO	–	–	–	–	–	–	–	1	1
DONT DO IT	–	1	1	–	–	–	–	–	–
DONT TELL STORIES ON ANYBODY	–	1	1	–	–	–	–	–	–
DOOR	–	1	1	–	–	–	–	–	–
DOOR HANDLE	1	–	1	–	–	–	–	–	–
EERAUSE	–	1	1	–	–	–	–	–	–
EFFECT	–	–	–	–	–	–	–	1	1
EMPTY	–	–	–	1	–	1	–	–	–
EVEN	–	–	–	–	–	–	1	–	1
EVERYTHING	–	–	–	1	–	1	–	–	–
EXCUSE	–	–	–	–	–	–	6	3	9
EXCUSED	–	–	–	–	–	–	1	–	1
EXPLAINING	–	–	–	–	–	–	1	–	1
EXPLANATION	–	–	–	–	–	–	2	–	2
FATHER	1	–	1	–	–	–	–	–	–
FATHER SAID SO	1	–	1	–	–	–	–	–	–
FIRE	–	–	–	1	–	1	–	–	–
FOR	–	–	–	–	–	–	2	2	4
FORGET	–	–	–	1	–	1	–	–	–
FRIENDLY	–	–	–	–	–	–	1	–	1
FUZZ	1	–	1	–	–	–	–	–	–
GARBAGE	–	–	–	1	–	1	–	–	–
GIVE	–	1	1	–	–	–	1	–	1
GLASSES	–	1	1	–	–	–	–	–	–
GO	–	1	1	–	–	–	–	–	–
GO OUT	–	1	1	–	–	–	–	–	–
GOT IN TROUBLE	1	–	1	–	–	–	–	–	–
HAIR	–	1	1	–	–	–	–	–	–
HALL	–	1	1	–	–	–	–	–	–
HAND	1	–	1	–	–	–	–	–	–
HANDLE	–	–	–	1	–	1	–	–	–
HAPPEN	1	–	1	–	1	1	–	4	4
HAPPENED	–	–	–	1	–	1	–	–	–
HAUS	1	–	1	–	–	–	–	–	–
HAVE	–	–	–	–	–	–	–	1	1
HAVE TO	–	–	–	–	–	–	1	1	2
HAVE TO CLEAN	1	–	1	–	–	–	–	–	–
HE	3	4	7	7	6	13	4	–	4
HE CANT	–	1	1	–	–	–	–	–	–
HE CROSSED	1	–	1	–	–	–	–	–	–
HE DID SOMETHING	–	–	–	–	–	–	1	–	1
HE DID THAT	–	–	–	–	–	–	–	1	1
HE DOESNT	–	–	–	–	1	1	–	–	–
HE IS TEN YEARS OLD	1	–	1	–	–	–	–	–	–
HE LIKES	1	–	1	–	–	–	–	–	–
HECAUSE	1	–	1	–	–	–	–	–	–
HER	–	–	–	–	1	1	–	–	–
HERE	1	1	2	–	–	–	–	–	–
HIM	–	–	–	1	1	2	2	–	2
HIS	–	–	–	1	–	1	–	–	–
HORSE	–	1	1	–	–	–	–	–	–
HOUSE	–	1	1	–	–	–	–	–	–
HOW	–	2	2	–	–	–	–	–	–
I	5	5	10	2	3	5	2	1	3
I AM	–	–	–	–	2	2	–	–	–
I AM SICK	–	1	1	–	–	–	–	–	–
I DID	–	–	–	1	–	1	–	–	–
I DID SOMETHING WRONG	1	–	1	–	–	–	–	–	–
I DON T	–	–	–	1	–	1	–	–	–
I DON T WANT YOU TO TALK TOO MUCH	1	–	1	–	–	–	–	–	–
I JUST WANT TO GO	–	1	1	–	–	–	–	–	–

RESPONSE WORD	1ST M	F	T	3RD M	F	T	5TH M	F	T

4. BECAUSE

RESPONSE WORD	1ST M	F	T	3RD M	F	T	5TH M	F	T
I LIKE YOU	1	1	2	2	–	2	–	–	–
I NEVER LIKE TO	–	1	1	–	–	–	–	–	–
I SAID	–	–	–	1	–	1	–	–	–
I SAID SO	2	1	3	–	–	–	–	–	–
I WANT	1	–	1	–	–	–	–	–	–
I WANT THAT	1	–	1	–	–	–	–	–	–
I WANT TO	1	–	1	–	–	–	–	–	–
I WANT YOU TO COME	–	1	1	–	–	–	–	–	–
I WANTED TO	1	–	1	–	–	–	–	–	–
IM ASLEEP	–	–	–	1	–	1	–	–	–
IN	–	–	–	1	–	1	–	–	–
IS	–	1	1	–	–	–	–	–	–
IS LIKE DRINKING	–	1	1	–	–	–	–	–	–
IS SOMETHING	1	–	1	–	–	–	–	–	–
IT	–	2	2	6	–	6	–	–	–
IT HAPPENS	1	–	1	–	–	–	–	–	–
IT IS	–	–	–	1	–	1	–	–	–
ITS NOISY	–	1	1	–	–	–	–	–	–
ITS OKAY	–	–	–	–	1	1	–	–	–
JUMP	–	–	–	–	–	–	1	–	1
JUST BECAUSE	1	–	1	–	–	–	–	–	–
KATHY	1	–	1	–	–	–	–	–	–
KITTENS	1	–	1	–	–	–	–	–	–
LAWS	1	1	2	–	–	–	–	–	–
LEARN	–	1	1	–	1	1	–	–	–
LET	–	–	–	–	–	–	1	–	1
LETS	–	–	–	–	1	1	–	–	–
LIKE	1	–	1	1	1	2	1	–	1
LIONS	–	1	1	–	–	–	–	–	–
LISTEN	–	1	1	–	1	1	–	–	–
LONELY	–	–	–	–	1	1	–	–	–
LOOK	–	–	–	–	–	–	1	–	1
LOST	–	1	1	–	–	–	–	1	1
LOVE	–	1	1	–	–	–	–	–	–
LUD	–	–	–	–	1	1	–	–	–
MAD	–	1	1	–	–	–	1	–	1
MAKE	–	–	–	–	–	–	–	1	1
MAN	1	–	1	–	–	–	–	–	–
MAYBE	–	–	–	–	–	–	1	2	3
ME	1	1	2	–	–	–	–	–	–
MEAN	–	1	1	–	–	–	–	–	–
MEANING	–	–	–	–	–	–	1	–	1
MEANING SOMETHING	–	–	–	–	1	1	–	–	–
MEANS	–	–	–	–	1	1	–	–	–
MILE	1	–	1	–	–	–	–	–	–
MILK	–	1	1	–	–	–	–	–	–
MINE	–	–	–	1	–	1	–	–	–
MISSISSIPPI	–	–	–	–	–	–	1	–	1
MOMENT	–	1	1	–	–	–	–	–	–
MOTHER	–	–	–	–	–	–	1	–	1
NAUGHTY	–	–	–	–	–	–	–	1	1
NEARLY	–	–	–	–	1	1	–	–	–
NECESSARY	–	–	–	–	–	–	–	1	1
NEVER	–	–	–	1	1	2	1	–	1
NICE	–	1	1	–	1	1	–	–	–
NO	2	4	6	2	4	6	1	1	2
NO MONEY	–	1	1	–	–	–	–	–	–
NOISY	–	1	1	–	–	–	–	–	–
NOT	–	–	–	4	1	5	3	2	5
NOT BECAUSE	1	1	2	4	4	8	2	2	4
NOT TO DO	–	–	–	1	–	1	–	–	–
NOTHING	1	–	1	1	–	1	–	–	–
NOW	2	–	2	1	1	2	–	–	–
O K	–	–	–	1	–	1	–	–	–
OBEY	–	–	–	1	–	1	–	–	–
OCEAN	1	–	1	–	–	–	–	–	–
OF	1	–	1	1	–	1	–	1	1
OF DINNER TABLE	–	1	1	–	–	–	–	–	–
OF SOMETHING	–	–	–	1	–	1	–	–	–
OF YOU	–	1	1	–	–	–	–	–	–
OFTEN	–	–	–	–	–	–	–	1	1
ONCE	–	–	–	–	–	–	1	–	1

RESPONSE WORD	1ST M	F	T	3RD M	F	T	5TH M	F	T

4. BECAUSE

RESPONSE WORD	1ST M	F	T	3RD M	F	T	5TH M	F	T
ONE	1	–	1	–	–	–	–	–	–
OPEN	–	–	–	–	–	–	1	–	1
ORDER	–	–	–	–	–	–	–	1	1
OUT	–	–	–	–	1	1	–	–	–
PAPERS	1	–	1	–	–	–	–	–	–
PAUSE	1	–	1	–	–	–	–	–	–
PEARL	1	–	1	–	–	–	–	–	–
PEOPLE	1	1	2	–	2	2	–	–	–
PERSON TALKING	–	–	–	1	–	1	–	–	–
PINT	1	–	1	–	–	–	–	–	–
PLAY	–	1	1	1	–	1	–	–	–
PLEASE	–	–	–	–	–	–	1	–	1
POCKETBOOK	1	–	1	–	–	–	–	–	–
Q	–	1	1	–	–	–	–	–	–
QUESTION	–	–	–	1	–	1	1	–	1
QUIET	–	–	–	–	1	1	–	–	–
REASON	–	–	–	–	1	1	19	12	31
REASON WHY	–	–	–	–	–	–	1	1	2
RECAUSE	–	1	1	–	–	–	–	–	–
REMEMBER	–	–	–	1	–	1	–	1	1
RIDE	–	1	1	–	–	–	–	–	–
ROOM	–	–	–	–	–	–	–	1	1
SAID	–	–	–	–	1	1	–	2	2
SAME	–	–	–	–	–	–	1	–	1
SAW	1	–	1	1	–	1	–	–	–
SAY	–	–	–	–	1	1	–	–	–
SENTENCE	–	–	–	–	2	2	1	–	1
SET	–	–	–	1	–	1	–	–	–
SHARPENER	1	–	1	–	–	–	–	–	–
SHE	–	–	–	1	3	4	–	–	–
SHE DID	–	–	–	–	1	1	–	–	–
SHE SAID	–	–	–	–	1	1	–	–	–
SHIP	1	–	1	–	–	–	–	–	–
SINCE	–	–	–	–	–	–	–	1	1
SINK	1	–	1	–	–	–	–	–	–
SIT	–	–	–	1	–	1	–	–	–
SIT IN CHAIR	1	–	1	–	–	–	–	–	–
SO	–	1	1	1	6	7	2	–	2
SOFT	–	–	–	–	1	1	–	–	–
SOME	–	–	–	–	–	–	1	–	1
SOMEBODY DID SOMETHING BECAUSE	–	1	1	–	–	–	–	–	–
SOMEONE	–	–	–	–	–	–	1	1	2
SOMETHING	–	2	2	10	5	15	–	3	3
SOMETHING HAPPENED	1	–	1	1	–	1	–	–	–
SOMETHING YOU CANT DO	–	–	–	–	–	–	–	1	1
SOMETIMES	–	–	–	1	3	4	2	1	3
STARS	–	1	1	–	–	–	–	–	–
START	–	–	–	–	–	–	1	–	1
STICK	1	–	1	–	–	–	–	–	–
SWEATER	–	1	1	–	–	–	–	–	–
SWIMMING	–	–	–	1	–	1	–	–	–
TABLE	–	1	1	–	–	–	–	–	–
TALK	1	–	1	–	–	–	–	–	–
TARZAN	1	–	1	–	–	–	–	–	–
TEACHER	–	–	–	–	–	–	–	1	1
TELEPHONE	–	–	–	–	–	–	1	–	1
TELL	–	–	–	–	–	–	2	3	5
TELLING	–	–	–	–	1	1	1	–	1
TEN	–	–	–	–	1	1	–	–	–
THANK	1	–	1	1	–	1	–	–	–
THAT	1	1	2	1	–	1	–	–	–
THAT IS IT	–	–	–	–	–	–	1	–	1
THAT WHY	–	–	–	–	–	–	–	1	1
THATS THAT	–	–	–	–	–	–	1	–	1
THATS WHY	–	–	–	1	–	1	–	–	–
THE	–	2	2	–	–	–	–	–	–
THE CAUSE	–	–	–	–	–	–	–	1	1
THE REASON	–	–	–	–	–	–	–	1	1
THEM	–	–	–	–	3	3	–	–	–
THEN	–	–	–	–	1	1	–	–	–
THEY	1	–	1	3	6	9	–	–	–

RESPONSE WORD	1ST M	F	T	3RD M	F	T	5TH M	F	T

4. BECAUSE

RESPONSE WORD	1ST M	F	T	3RD M	F	T	5TH M	F	T
THING	–	–	–	–	–	–	–	1	1
THINK	1	–	1	–	–	–	–	2	2
THIS	–	–	–	–	–	–	1	–	1
THOUGH	–	–	–	–	–	–	1	–	1
TO	–	–	–	–	1	1	–	–	–
TO DO	–	–	–	–	–	–	–	2	2
TO GIVE AN ANSWER	–	–	–	–	–	–	–	1	1
TODAY	–	–	–	–	1	1	–	–	–
TOLD	–	1	1	–	–	–	–	1	1
TOWEL	–	1	1	–	–	–	–	–	–
TREE	1	–	1	–	–	–	–	1	1
TREES	1	–	1	–	–	–	–	–	–
TROUBLE	–	–	–	–	1	1	1	1	2
UN	–	–	–	1	–	1	–	–	–
UNBECAUSE	1	–	1	–	–	–	1	–	1
UNCAUSE	–	–	–	–	–	–	–	1	1
UNUSUAL	–	–	–	–	–	–	1	–	1
USUALLY	–	–	–	–	–	–	1	–	1
WALK	1	–	1	–	–	–	–	–	–
WALLS	1	–	1	–	–	–	–	–	–
WANT	–	1	1	1	–	1	3	–	3
WANT SOMETHING	1	–	1	–	–	–	–	–	–
WANT TO	1	–	1	2	–	2	1	1	2
WANTS	–	–	–	1	–	1	–	1	1
WAS	–	1	1	1	–	1	–	–	–
WASH HANDS	–	1	1	–	–	–	–	–	–
WATER	1	–	1	1	–	1	–	–	–
WAY	–	–	–	–	–	–	2	–	2
WE	1	–	1	2	–	2	–	–	–
WE CAN	–	–	–	–	1	1	–	–	–
WE DONT WANT	–	1	1	–	–	–	–	–	–
WE DONT WANT YOU TO	1	–	1	–	–	–	–	–	–
WE WANT TO	–	1	1	–	–	–	–	–	–
WELL	–	–	–	1	–	1	–	–	–
WHAT	–	–	–	–	–	–	1	–	1
WHEN	–	–	–	–	2	2	1	–	1
WHEN YOU BECAUSE TO SOMEBODY	1	–	1	–	–	–	–	–	–
WHENEVER YOUR MOTHER SAYS BECAUSE OF SO	–	1	1	–	–	–	–	–	–
WHITE	1	–	1	–	–	–	–	–	–
WHY	28	30	58	12	19	31	16	19	35
WHY NOT	–	–	–	–	1	1	–	–	–
WINDOW	1	–	1	–	–	–	–	–	–
WINTER	1	–	1	–	–	–	–	–	–
WITH	1	–	1	–	–	–	–	–	–
WORDS	1	–	1	–	–	–	–	–	–
WRITE	–	–	–	–	–	–	–	1	1
WY	–	–	–	–	–	–	1	–	1
YARD	–	1	1	–	–	–	–	–	–
YES	–	2	2	3	1	4	–	2	2
YOU	3	4	7	4	7	11	1	1	2
YOU ARE GOOD	–	1	1	–	–	–	–	–	–
YOU ARE NOT A GOOD GIRL	–	1	1	–	–	–	–	–	–
YOU CAN	1	–	1	–	–	–	–	–	–
YOU CANT GO OUTSIDE BECAUSE YOURE SICK	–	–	–	–	–	–	–	1	1
YOU CANT PLAY	–	1	1	–	–	–	–	–	–
YOU DID	–	–	–	–	1	1	–	–	–
YOU DONE REAL BAD	1	–	1	–	–	–	–	–	–
YOU SEE	–	–	–	–	1	1	–	–	–
YOU WANT TO DO SOMETHING	–	–	–	–	–	–	–	1	1
YOURE HOT	1	–	1	–	–	–	–	–	–
YOURE WRONG	–	1	1	–	–	–	–	–	–

RESPONSE WORD	1ST			3RD			5TH		
	M	F	T	M	F	T	M	F	T

5. BEE

RESPONSE WORD	M	F	T	M	F	T	M	F	T
A	2	2	4	1	–	1	–	–	–
A RAINCOAT	1	–	1	–	–	–	–	–	–
ABC	1	1	2	–	–	–	–	–	–
AGAIN	–	–	–	–	–	–	–	1	1
AIRPLANE	1	–	1	–	–	–	–	–	–
ALONE	–	1	1	–	–	–	–	–	–
ALPHABET	–	1	1	1	–	1	–	–	–
ALWAYS	–	–	–	1	–	1	–	–	–
AN INSECT	–	–	–	–	–	–	1	1	2
AN OBJECT THAT WILL STING YOU	–	1	1	–	–	–	–	1	1
ANIMAL	–	1	1	2	4	6	4	4	8
APPLE	1	–	1	–	–	–	–	–	–
ARE	–	1	1	–	–	–	1	–	1
B	1	–	1	1	–	1	1	–	1
B TWO	–	1	1	–	–	–	–	–	–
B-A	1	–	1	–	–	–	–	–	–
BABY	–	1	1	–	–	–	–	–	–
BAG	–	–	–	1	–	1	–	–	–
BALL	1	2	3	–	–	–	–	–	–
BANISH	–	1	1	–	–	–	–	–	–
BAT	2	–	2	–	–	–	–	–	–
BE	–	–	–	1	3	4	5	5	10
BE GOOD	1	2	3	–	–	–	–	–	–
BE QUIET	–	1	1	–	–	–	–	–	–
BEAD	–	1	1	–	–	–	–	1	1
BEAN	1	–	1	–	–	–	–	–	–
BEAR	–	1	1	–	–	–	–	–	–
BEAST	–	–	–	–	–	–	–	1	1
BEAVER	–	1	1	–	–	–	–	–	–
BECAUSE	–	–	–	2	–	2	1	1	2
BECAUSE MY MOMMY IS SICK	–	1	1	–	–	–	–	–	–
BED	–	1	1	–	–	–	–	–	–
BEE	–	–	–	–	–	–	2	–	2
BEE FLIES IN	1	–	1	–	–	–	–	–	–
BEE-NESS	–	1	1	–	–	–	–	–	–
BEEHIVE	1	–	1	–	–	–	–	–	–
BEEN	–	1	1	–	1	1	–	1	1
BEES	–	1	1	–	–	–	1	–	1
BEET	–	1	1	–	–	–	–	–	–
BEETLE	–	–	–	–	1	1	–	–	–
BEFORE	–	–	–	1	2	3	–	–	–
BEGAN	–	–	–	1	–	1	–	–	–
BEGIN	–	–	–	1	–	1	–	–	–
BEHIND	–	–	–	–	1	1	–	–	–
BEND	–	–	–	–	1	1	–	–	–
BESIDE	–	–	–	1	–	1	–	–	–
BET	1	–	1	–	–	–	–	–	–
BIG	1	3	4	1	–	1	–	–	–
BIG BAD	–	1	1	–	–	–	–	–	–
BIKE	–	–	–	–	1	1	–	–	–
BINGS	1	–	1	–	–	–	–	–	–
BIRD	–	–	–	1	2	3	–	–	–
BIS	–	1	1	–	–	–	–	–	–
BIT	–	1	1	–	–	–	–	–	–
BIT BEE	1	–	1	–	–	–	–	–	–
BOAT	1	–	1	–	–	–	–	–	–
BOATS	1	–	1	–	–	–	–	–	–
BOTTLE	1	–	1	–	–	–	–	–	–
BOUGHT	–	–	–	–	–	–	–	1	1
BOW AND ARROW	1	–	1	–	–	–	–	–	–
BOWL	1	–	1	–	–	–	–	–	–
BOY	–	1	1	–	–	–	–	–	–
BREAD	–	–	–	–	1	1	–	–	–
BRING	–	–	–	1	–	1	–	–	–
BUG	1	2	3	9	14	23	12	20	32
BUMBLE	4	2	6	1	1	2	3	4	7
BUMBLE BEE	2	–	2	1	1	2	1	–	1
BUMBLEBEE	2	4	6	2	1	3	2	1	3
BUSY	–	–	–	1	–	1	–	–	–

5. BEE

RESPONSE WORD	1ST M	F	T	3RD M	F	T	5TH M	F	T
BUT	1	1	2	—	—	—	—	—	—
BUTTERFLY	3	2	5	5	6	11	2	—	2
BUZZ	3	2	5	6	3	9	3	3	6
BUZZER	—	—	—	1	—	1	—	—	—
BY	1	—	1	—	1	1	—	—	—
C	1	1	2	—	—	—	—	—	—
CALLS	—	—	—	1	—	1	—	—	—
CAN	1	1	2	—	—	—	1	—	1
CANT STING	1	—	1	—	—	—	—	—	—
CAROL	—	1	1	—	—	—	—	—	—
CAUSE	3	1	4	1	2	3	—	1	1
CHAIR	—	1	1	—	—	—	—	—	—
CHAIRS	2	—	2	—	—	—	—	—	—
COLD	—	1	1	—	—	—	—	—	—
COULD BE WHEN IT GETS DARK	—	1	1	—	—	—	—	—	—
COULD HAVE WINGS	—	1	1	—	—	—	—	—	—
D	2	—	2	—	—	—	—	—	—
DEBBIE	—	—	—	—	1	1	—	—	—
DEE	—	—	—	—	1	—	1	—	1
DEED	—	—	—	—	1	1	—	—	—
DID	1	—	1	—	—	—	—	—	—
DOG	2	1	3	—	—	—	—	—	—
DONT	—	1	1	1	—	1	—	—	—
E	—	3	3	—	—	—	—	—	—
EAT	1	—	1	—	—	—	—	—	—
EE	1	—	1	—	—	—	—	—	—
ELEPHANT	—	1	1	—	—	—	—	—	—
EYE	—	1	1	—	—	—	—	—	—
FEET	—	—	—	—	1	1	—	—	—
FINGER	—	—	—	—	—	—	1	—	1
FIRE	1	—	1	—	—	—	—	—	—
FLIES	—	1	1	1	2	3	1	—	1
FLIES AROUND AND SAYS BEEEE	1	—	1	—	—	—	—	—	—
FLIES IN THE AIR	—	1	1	—	—	—	—	—	—
FLOOR	—	—	—	1	—	1	2	1	3
FLOWER	—	—	—	1	3	4	2	1	3
FLY	5	7	12	14	13	27	5	4	9
FLYING	2	—	2	—	—	—	—	—	—
FOR	—	—	—	1	—	1	—	—	—
FOR BLOCK	1	—	1	—	—	—	—	—	—
FURNACE	—	1	1	—	—	—	—	—	—
GAN	—	—	—	1	—	1	—	—	—
GAVE	—	—	—	—	—	—	—	1	1
GET AWAY FROM YOU HONEY	1	—	1	—	—	—	—	—	—
GLASS	1	—	1	—	—	—	—	—	—
GLASSES	1	—	1	—	—	—	—	—	—
GO TO BATHROOM	1	—	1	—	—	—	—	—	—
GOOD	8	4	12	1	1	2	1	1	2
GOOD BYE	—	—	—	1	—	1	—	—	—
GRASS	1	—	1	1	1	2	—	—	—
GRIZZLY BEAR	—	1	1	—	—	—	—	—	—
HAND	—	1	1	—	—	—	—	—	—
HAS	—	1	1	—	—	—	—	—	—
HAYSTACK	—	—	—	1	—	1	—	—	—
HE	3	—	3	5	2	7	3	1	4
HELICOPTER	1	—	1	—	—	—	—	—	—
HER	—	1	1	—	—	—	—	—	—
HERE	—	—	—	—	1	1	—	—	—
HIDE	1	—	1	—	—	—	—	—	—
HIGH	2	—	2	1	—	1	1	1	2
HIMSELF	—	—	—	—	—	—	—	1	1
HIVE	2	—	2	3	3	6	5	3	8
HOLE	—	1	1	—	—	—	—	—	—
HONEY	2	3	5	3	4	7	8	8	16
HONEY BEE	—	—	—	1	—	1	1	—	1
HOT	—	1	1	—	—	—	—	—	—
HURT	1	—	1	—	1	1	—	—	—
I	—	2	2	—	—	—	—	—	—
ICE CREAM	1	—	1	—	—	—	—	—	—
IN	1	—	1	—	—	—	—	—	—

RESPONSE WORD	1ST M	F	T	3RD M	F	T	5TH M	F	T

5. BEE

RESPONSE WORD	1ST M	F	T	3RD M	F	T	5TH M	F	T
INK	–	1	1	–	–	–	–	–	–
INSECT	1	–	1	10	12	22	24	22	46
INSECTS	–	–	–	1	–	1	–	–	–
IS	–	–	–	–	1	1	–	–	–
IS NOT	–	–	–	1	–	1	–	–	–
ISLAND	–	–	–	–	–	–	–	1	1
IT	1	2	3	–	–	–	–	–	–
JANE	1	–	1	–	–	–	–	–	–
KEY	1	1	2	–	–	–	–	–	–
KEYS	1	–	1	–	–	–	–	–	–
KIND	–	2	2	–	–	–	–	–	–
LIGHT	–	1	1	–	–	–	–	–	–
LITTLE	–	1	1	–	1	1	–	–	–
LOCKER	1	–	1	–	–	–	–	–	–
LOW	–	–	–	1	–	1	–	–	–
MANY	–	–	–	1	–	1	–	–	–
MARBLE	–	–	–	–	–	–	–	–	–
ME	5	3	8	2	2	4	–	2	2
MEAN	–	1	1	–	–	–	–	–	–
MEMBER	–	–	–	1	–	1	–	–	–
MOTHER	1	–	1	–	–	–	–	–	–
MY	1	–	1	–	2	2	–	–	–
NEAR	–	1	1	–	–	–	–	–	–
NECKLACE	–	–	–	–	1	1	–	1	1
NEST	2	–	2	1	1	2	1	–	1
NIGHT	1	–	1	–	–	–	–	–	–
NINETY-NINE	1	–	1	–	–	–	–	–	–
NOT	1	–	1	–	–	–	–	1	1
NOT BE	–	2	2	–	–	–	–	–	–
NOW	–	–	–	–	1	1	1	–	1
O – IN B AND O RAILROAD	–	1	1	–	–	–	–	–	–
OH	3	1	4	–	–	–	–	–	–
OWE	1	–	1	–	–	–	–	–	–
PAPER	–	1	1	–	–	–	–	–	–
PART	–	–	–	–	–	–	–	1	1
PEA	–	–	–	–	1	1	–	–	–
PEAR	1	–	1	–	–	–	–	–	–
PEARL	–	–	–	–	1	1	–	–	–
PIANO	–	1	1	–	–	–	–	–	–
POLICEMAN	–	–	–	1	–	1	–	–	–
PRETTY	–	–	–	–	–	–	–	1	1
QUEEN BEE	–	–	–	2	–	2	–	–	–
QUIET	–	–	–	–	–	–	1	–	1
RABBIT	–	–	–	–	1	1	–	–	–
READ	1	–	1	–	–	–	–	–	–
READY	–	–	–	1	–	1	–	–	–
REE	–	1	1	–	–	–	–	–	–
RUBBER BAND	1	–	1	–	–	–	–	–	–
SALT	–	1	1	–	–	–	–	–	–
SAW	–	1	1	–	1	1	–	–	–
SCHOOL	–	1	1	–	–	–	–	–	–
SCISSORS	1	–	1	–	–	–	1	–	1
SEA	–	1	1	–	–	–	1	–	1
SEE	1	5	6	1	4	5	2	1	3
SHE	–	–	–	–	1	1	1	–	1
SIDE	–	–	–	–	–	–	1	–	1
SOMETHING	–	–	–	–	–	–	–	1	1
SOMETHING THAT CAN STING	–	–	–	–	–	–	1	–	1
SOUR	–	1	1	–	–	–	–	–	–
SPELLING	–	–	–	–	–	–	1	–	1
SPIDER	–	–	–	–	–	–	1	–	1
STICK	–	1	1	–	–	–	–	–	–
STICKER	–	–	–	–	1	1	–	–	–
STING	6	10	16	25	18	43	26	32	58
STINGER	1	–	1	1	–	1	4	2	6
STINGS	–	1	1	1	–	1	–	–	–
STOOD	1	–	1	–	–	–	–	–	–
STOP	1	–	1	–	–	–	–	–	–
STUNG	–	1	1	1	1	2	2	–	2
STUNG ME	1	–	1	–	–	–	–	–	–
SUN	1	–	1	–	–	–	–	–	–
SWEET	–	–	–	–	–	–	–	1	1
TABLE	–	1	1	–	–	–	–	–	–

RESPONSE WORD	1ST			3RD			5TH		
	M	F	T	M	F	T	M	F	T

5. BEE

RESPONSE WORD	M	F	T	M	F	T	M	F	T
TALL	1	–	1	–	–	–	–	–	–
TEA	1	–	1	–	–	–	–	–	–
THE	1	–	1	–	2	2	–	–	–
THEN	–	–	–	1	–	1	–	–	–
THERE	–	–	–	3	–	3	2	1	3
THEY	–	1	1	–	–	–	–	–	–
THING	–	–	–	–	–	–	–	1	1
THIS	–	–	–	–	1	1	–	–	–
TODAY	–	–	–	–	1	1	–	–	–
TREE	–	1	1	–	–	–	–	1	1
UP	1	1	2	–	–	–	–	–	–
WASH	–	1	1	–	–	–	–	–	–
WASP	1	–	1	2	2	4	–	–	–
WE	–	1	1	2	1	3	–	–	–
WHEN YOURE BEING SOMETHING	1	–	1	–	–	–	–	–	–
WHERE	–	1	1	–	1	1	–	–	–
WHY	–	1	1	–	–	–	–	–	–
WING	1	–	1	–	–	–	–	–	–
WINGS	–	1	1	–	–	–	–	2	2
WITH	–	1	1	–	–	–	–	–	–
WOOD	–	1	1	–	–	–	–	–	–
WORKER BEE	–	–	–	–	–	–	–	1	1
YELLOW JACK	–	–	–	–	–	–	1	–	1
YELLOW JACKET	–	–	–	–	2	2	–	1	1
YOU	1	1	2	–	–	–	–	–	–
YOU BE	–	1	1	–	–	–	–	–	–
YOURSELF	–	–	–	–	–	–	1	–	1
ZEE	1	–	1	–	–	–	–	–	–

6. BEGIN

RESPONSE WORD	M	F	T	M	F	T	M	F	T
A STORY	1	–	1	–	–	–	–	–	–
ADD	1	–	1	–	–	–	–	–	–
AFTER	3	–	3	5	5	10	3	2	5
AGAIN	1	1	2	2	3	5	1	1	2
ALL	–	1	1	–	–	–	–	–	–
ALL WERE	–	1	1	–	–	–	–	–	–
ALMOST	–	–	–	–	1	1	–	–	–
ALWAYS	–	–	–	2	1	3	–	–	–
ANY	–	–	–	–	–	–	–	1	1
AT	1	–	1	–	–	–	–	–	–
AT THE B	1	–	1	–	–	–	–	–	–
AT THE DAY	1	–	1	–	–	–	–	–	–
BACKWARDS	–	–	–	–	–	–	–	1	1
BAD	1	–	1	–	–	–	–	–	–
BALL	1	–	1	–	–	–	–	–	–
BE	–	1	1	–	1	1	–	–	–
BE LAST	–	–	–	1	–	1	–	–	–
BECAME	–	–	–	1	–	1	–	–	–
BECAUSE	–	–	–	1	1	2	–	–	–
BECOME	–	–	–	1	–	1	–	–	–
BEFORE	–	1	1	–	3	3	–	–	–
BEG	–	1	1	–	–	–	–	–	–
BEGAN	–	1	1	5	6	11	5	7	12
BEGINNER	–	–	–	1	–	1	1	–	1
BEGINNING	–	–	–	1	1	2	2	2	4
BEGINNING THE STORY	–	–	–	–	1	1	–	–	–
BEGUN	–	–	–	–	–	–	1	1	2
BEHIND	–	–	–	1	–	1	–	–	–
BETTY	1	–	1	–	–	–	–	–	–
BETWEEN	–	–	–	–	1	1	–	–	–
BIRTHDAY	1	–	1	–	–	–	–	–	–
BLACK	1	–	1	–	–	–	–	–	–
BLACKBOARD	1	–	1	–	–	–	–	–	–
BLOCKS	1	–	1	–	–	–	–	–	–
BOOK	1	1	2	–	–	–	–	–	–
BOOKS	–	1	1	–	–	–	–	–	–
BRIDGE	–	–	–	–	1	1	–	–	–
BUT	1	–	1	–	–	–	–	–	–
CAN	–	–	–	–	–	–	1	–	1

RESPONSE WORD	1ST M	F	T	3RD M	F	T	5TH M	F	T

6.   BEGIN

RESPONSE WORD	1ST M	F	T	3RD M	F	T	5TH M	F	T
CANT	–	–	–	1	–	1	–	–	–
CAR	3	–	3	–	–	–	–	–	–
CARDS	–	1	1	–	–	–	–	–	–
CEILING	–	1	1	–	–	–	–	–	–
CHALKBOARD	–	1	1	–	–	–	–	–	–
CIRCLE	–	–	–	–	–	–	–	1	1
CLASS	1	–	1	–	–	–	–	–	–
CLOCK	1	–	1	–	–	–	–	–	–
CLOWN	–	1	1	–	–	–	–	–	–
COLOR	–	–	–	–	–	–	–	1	1
COME	1	3	4	–	1	1	–	–	–
COUNTING	1	–	1	–	–	–	–	–	–
CURTAIN	1	–	1	–	–	–	–	–	–
DAN	1	–	1	–	–	–	–	–	–
DAY	–	–	–	–	1	1	–	–	–
DICK	1	–	1	–	–	–	–	–	–
DID	–	–	–	–	–	–	–	1	1
DIDNT	–	–	–	1	–	1	–	–	–
DO	1	1	2	–	–	–	–	–	–
DO IT	–	–	–	1	1	2	–	–	–
DO WORK	1	–	1	–	–	–	–	–	–
DOG	–	2	2	–	–	–	–	–	–
DOING	–	–	–	1	–	1	–	–	–
DONE	1	–	1	2	–	2	–	–	–
DONT	–	–	–	1	1	2	–	1	1
DONT BEGIN	–	–	–	1	–	1	–	1	1
DOWN	–	1	1	–	–	–	–	–	–
DRAW	1	1	2	–	–	–	–	–	–
DRESS	–	2	2	–	–	–	–	–	–
EAT	–	1	1	–	–	–	–	–	–
EIGHT	–	–	–	–	1	1	–	–	–
END	5	4	9	21	29	50	23	28	51
ENDED	–	–	–	1	–	1	–	–	–
ENDING	1	1	2	2	–	2	–	–	–
FAIR	–	1	1	–	–	–	–	–	–
FAST	1	1	2	–	1	1	–	–	–
FIGHT	–	1	1	–	–	–	–	–	–
FINISH	1	–	1	4	8	12	3	4	7
FINISHED	–	–	–	4	–	4	–	2	2
FIRED	–	–	–	–	–	–	1	–	1
FIRST	1	1	2	2	–	2	–	–	–
FOOT	1	–	1	–	–	–	–	–	–
FOR	1	–	1	–	–	–	–	–	–
FOR ME	1	–	1	–	–	–	–	–	–
GAME	1	–	1	–	–	–	–	–	–
GIN	2	–	2	–	–	–	–	–	–
GIRL	1	–	1	–	–	–	–	–	–
GLASSES	–	1	1	–	–	–	–	–	–
GO	–	1	1	1	1	2	2	–	2
GO AWAY	–	–	–	1	–	1	–	–	–
GOING SOMETHING	–	1	1	–	–	–	–	–	–
GREEN	–	–	–	1	–	1	–	–	–
GRIN	–	–	–	–	–	–	–	1	1
HAIR	1	–	1	–	–	–	–	–	–
HAPPEN	–	1	1	–	–	–	–	–	–
HAVE DONE	–	–	–	1	–	1	–	–	–
HAVENT	–	–	–	–	1	1	–	–	–
HAVING A RACE	–	1	1	–	–	–	–	–	–
HE	–	1	1	–	–	–	–	–	–
HELM	1	–	1	–	–	–	–	–	–
HEN	–	1	1	–	–	–	–	–	–
HER	–	–	–	1	–	1	–	–	–
HERE	5	2	7	2	–	2	–	–	–
HOUSE	–	1	1	–	–	–	–	–	–
IN	2	–	2	1	–	1	1	–	1
INTO	–	–	–	1	–	1	–	–	–
JUST	–	–	–	–	–	–	1	–	1
KEEP GOING	–	–	–	–	–	–	–	1	1
KIN	1	–	1	–	–	–	–	–	–
LAST	–	3	3	1	4	5	1	1	2
LATER	–	–	–	–	1	1	–	–	–
LEARN	–	1	1	–	–	–	–	–	–

RESPONSE WORD	1ST M	F	T	3RD M	F	T	5TH M	F	T

6. BEGIN

RESPONSE WORD	1ST M	F	T	3RD M	F	T	5TH M	F	T
LEAVE	–	1	1	–	–	–	–	–	–
LIGHT	2	–	2	–	–	–	–	–	–
LIKE	1	2	3	–	–	–	–	–	–
LISTEN	1	–	1	–	–	–	–	–	–
LONG	–	1	1	–	1	1	–	–	–
LOOK	–	1	1	–	–	–	–	–	–
LYNN	2	–	2	–	–	–	–	–	–
ME	2	–	2	–	–	–	–	–	–
MEGIN	1	–	1	–	–	–	–	–	–
MISTAKE	–	–	–	–	1	1	–	–	–
MOTHER	–	1	1	–	–	–	–	–	–
MOVIE	2	–	2	–	–	–	–	–	–
NECKLACE	–	1	1	–	–	–	–	–	–
NEVER END	1	–	1	–	–	–	–	–	–
NEW YORK	–	–	–	–	–	–	–	1	1
NOT BEGIN	5	2	7	1	1	2	1	1	2
NOT FINISHED	–	–	–	–	1	1	–	–	–
NOT START	–	–	–	1	–	1	–	–	–
NOW	–	3	3	4	2	6	1	–	1
ONE	–	1	1	–	–	–	–	–	–
OPPOSITE	–	–	–	–	–	–	–	1	1
ORDER	–	–	–	–	1	1	–	–	–
ORDERS	1	–	1	–	–	–	–	–	–
OUT	1	–	1	–	–	–	–	–	–
OVER	–	–	–	–	1	1	–	–	–
OVER AGAIN	–	–	–	1	–	1	–	–	–
OVER THERE	1	–	1	–	–	–	–	–	–
PAPER	1	2	3	–	1	1	–	–	–
PAPERS	–	1	1	–	1	1	–	–	–
PEAR	1	–	1	–	–	–	–	–	–
PEOPLE	1	–	1	–	–	–	–	–	–
PEOPLE MIGHT THINK THE TREE WOULD GROW	–	1	1	–	–	–	–	–	–
PICTURE	–	1	1	–	–	–	–	–	–
PLANT	–	–	–	1	–	1	–	–	–
POPSICLE	1	–	1	–	–	–	–	–	–
QUIET	–	1	1	–	–	–	–	–	–
RACE	1	–	1	–	–	–	1	–	1
RACING	2	–	2	–	–	–	–	–	–
READING	1	–	1	–	–	–	–	–	–
REGIN	–	1	1	–	–	–	–	–	–
RELIN	–	1	1	–	–	–	–	–	–
REMEMBER	–	–	–	–	–	–	1	–	1
RESIN	1	–	1	–	–	–	–	–	–
RIDE	–	1	1	–	–	–	–	–	–
RING	–	1	1	–	–	–	–	–	–
RUN	1	1	2	–	–	–	–	–	–
RUNNING	1	–	1	–	–	–	–	–	–
RUSTLES	1	–	1	–	–	–	–	–	–
SATER	–	–	–	–	–	–	1	–	1
SAW	–	1	1	–	–	–	–	–	–
SAY	–	1	1	–	–	–	–	–	–
SCHOOL	1	2	3	–	–	–	–	–	–
SEAT	–	1	1	–	–	–	–	–	–
SEE	–	1	1	1	–	1	–	–	–
SENTENCE	–	–	–	–	1	1	–	–	–
SET	1	–	1	–	–	–	–	–	–
SEW	1	–	1	–	–	–	–	–	–
SHE	–	–	–	–	–	–	1	–	1
SHEET	–	1	1	–	–	–	–	–	–
SHIRT	–	1	1	–	–	–	–	–	–
SHORT	–	–	–	–	1	1	–	–	–
SHORT WAVES	1	–	1	–	–	–	–	–	–
SHOW	–	2	2	–	–	–	–	–	–
SIN	1	–	1	–	–	–	–	–	–
SINGING	–	2	2	–	–	–	–	–	–
SLOW	–	–	–	–	1	1	–	–	–
SOFT	–	–	–	–	1	1	–	–	–
SOMETHING	1	5	6	–	1	1	1	–	1
SOMETIMES	–	–	–	1	–	1	–	–	–
SORRY	–	–	–	1	–	1	–	–	–
SOUND	1	2	3	–	–	–	–	–	–

RESPONSE WORD	1ST M	F	T	3RD M	F	T	5TH M	F	T

6. BEGIN

RESPONSE WORD	1ST M	F	T	3RD M	F	T	5TH M	F	T
STAR	–	–	–	–	–	–	1	–	1
STARED	–	–	–	–	–	–	1	–	1
START	4	6	10	38	30	68	77	62	139
START WITH A BECAUSE THATS IN THE ABCS	–	1	1	–	–	–	–	–	–
STARTED	–	–	–	–	4	4	1	1	2
STARTING	1	–	1	–	1	1	–	–	–
STEP	–	–	–	1	–	1	–	–	–
STICK	–	–	–	–	–	–	1	–	1
STICKS	–	1	1	–	–	–	–	–	–
STOP	3	4	7	1	3	4	5	12	17
STOPPED	–	–	–	1	–	1	–	–	–
STORE	1	–	1	–	–	–	–	–	–
STORY	–	1	1	–	1	1	–	–	–
STUFF	1	–	1	–	–	–	–	–	–
SWIMMING	1	1	2	–	–	–	–	–	–
TABLE	1	–	1	–	–	–	–	–	–
TALK	–	1	1	2	–	2	–	–	–
TEA	1	–	1	–	–	–	–	–	–
TEN	1	–	1	–	–	–	–	–	–
THAT	–	1	1	1	–	1	–	–	–
THATS THE BEGINNING OF THE STORY	–	1	1	–	–	–	–	–	–
THE GINNING	–	1	1	–	–	–	–	–	–
THE PLAY	1	–	1	–	–	–	–	–	–
THE RACE	1	–	1	–	–	–	–	–	–
THE SHOW	–	1	1	–	–	–	–	–	–
THE STORY	–	1	1	–	–	–	–	–	–
THEN	–	–	–	–	1	1	–	–	–
THINGS	–	1	1	–	–	–	–	–	–
THIS	2	–	2	–	–	–	–	1	1
TIM	1	–	1	–	–	–	–	–	–
TIN	–	2	2	–	–	–	–	–	–
TIRED	–	–	–	1	–	1	–	–	–
TO	3	–	3	3	1	4	–	1	1
TO EAT	–	1	1	–	–	–	–	–	–
TO GO	–	1	1	–	–	–	–	–	–
TO JUMP	–	1	1	–	–	–	–	–	–
TO PLAY WITH ME	1	–	1	–	–	–	–	–	–
TO START	–	–	–	–	–	–	–	1	1
TO WORK	1	1	2	1	–	1	–	–	–
TO WRITE	–	1	1	–	–	–	–	–	–
TOASTER	1	–	1	–	–	–	–	–	–
TODAY	–	–	–	–	1	1	–	1	1
TOGETHER	–	–	–	–	1	1	–	–	–
TOP	–	1	1	–	–	–	–	–	–
TRACK	1	–	1	–	–	–	–	–	–
TRASH	–	1	1	–	–	–	–	–	–
TRASHCAN	–	–	–	–	1	1	–	–	–
TREE	–	1	1	–	–	–	–	–	–
TRUCK	1	–	1	–	–	–	–	–	–
UNDER	–	–	–	1	–	1	–	–	–
VACUUM CLEANER	1	–	1	–	–	–	–	–	–
WAGON	–	1	1	–	–	–	–	–	–
WAIT	–	–	–	2	1	3	–	–	–
WAKE	–	1	1	–	–	–	–	–	–
WALL	1	–	1	–	–	–	–	–	–
WATER	1	–	1	–	–	–	–	–	–
WE BEGIN A STORY	–	–	–	–	–	–	–	1	1
WHEN YOU BEGIN SOMETHING	1	–	1	–	–	–	–	–	–
WINDOW	–	1	1	–	–	–	–	–	–
WISH	–	–	–	–	–	–	1	–	1
WITCH	1	–	1	–	–	–	–	–	–
WITH	1	4	5	2	1	3	–	–	–
WITH THE BEGINNING	1	–	1	–	–	–	–	–	–
WITH WORDS	1	–	1	–	–	–	–	–	–
WORD	–	1	1	–	1	1	–	–	–
WORK	5	5	10	–	4	4	–	–	–
WRITE	–	1	1	–	–	–	–	–	–
WRITING	–	2	2	2	–	2	–	–	–
YELLOW	–	1	1	–	–	–	–	–	–
YES	2	–	2	–	–	–	–	–	–

RESPONSE WORD	1ST			3RD			5TH		
	M	F	T	M	F	T	M	F	T

6. BEGIN

RESPONSE WORD	M	F	T	M	F	T	M	F	T
YOU	1	1	2	1	–	1	–	–	–
YOU BEGIN ON SOMETHING	–	1	1	–	–	–	–	–	–

7. BELONG

RESPONSE WORD	M	F	T	M	F	T	M	F	T
A	1	–	1	–	–	–	–	–	–
A BOMB	–	–	–	–	–	–	1	–	1
A LONG COW	–	1	1	–	–	–	–	–	–
ABOVE	–	–	–	–	1	–	–	1	1
AFTER	–	–	–	–	1	1	–	1	1
AGAIN	–	–	–	–	1	1	–	1	1
ALONE	–	–	–	2	1	1	1	–	1
ALONG	–	–	–	2	–	2	–	1	1
ANIMAL	–	–	–	–	–	–	1	–	1
AS	–	–	–	–	1	1	–	–	–
AWAY	–	–	–	1	1	2	–	–	–
BABY	2	1	3	–	–	–	–	–	–
BAILEY	–	–	–	–	1	1	–	–	–
BALL	2	–	2	–	–	–	–	–	–
BE	1	1	2	3	–	3	–	1	1
BE SHORT	1	–	1	1	–	1	1	–	1
BE SURE	1	–	1	–	–	–	–	–	–
BE WIDE	–	1	1	–	–	–	–	–	–
BECAUSE	–	–	–	1	–	1	–	–	–
BECOME	–	–	–	–	–	–	–	1	1
BEFORE	–	–	–	–	2	2	1	1	2
BEGAN	–	–	–	–	1	1	–	–	–
BEGIN	–	–	–	1	1	2	1	–	1
BEGONE	–	–	–	1	–	1	1	–	1
BEHAVE	–	–	–	1	–	1	–	–	–
BEHIND	–	–	–	1	1	2	–	–	–
BELONE	–	–	–	–	–	–	1	–	1
BELONG	1	–	1	–	–	–	–	–	–
BELONG TO YOU	1	–	1	–	–	–	–	–	–
BELONGS THERE	–	1	1	–	–	–	–	–	–
BELOW	–	–	–	1	–	1	–	–	–
BERRY	1	–	1	–	–	–	–	–	–
BESIDE	–	–	–	–	–	–	–	1	1
BETTY	1	–	1	–	–	–	–	–	–
BETWEEN	–	–	–	–	–	–	–	1	1
BIG	1	–	1	1	–	1	–	–	–
BIRD	–	–	–	1	–	1	–	–	–
BLOND	–	2	2	–	–	–	–	–	–
BLUE	–	1	1	–	–	–	–	–	–
BOLOGNA	–	1	1	–	–	–	–	–	–
BOO	1	–	1	–	–	–	–	–	–
BOOK	–	–	–	–	–	–	1	–	1
BOX	1	–	1	–	–	–	–	–	–
BOY	1	–	1	–	–	–	–	–	–
BROTHER	–	1	1	–	–	–	–	–	–
BUG	–	–	–	–	1	1	–	–	–
BUTTONS	1	–	1	–	–	–	–	–	–
CACLONG	–	1	1	–	–	–	–	–	–
CAGE	1	–	1	–	–	–	–	–	–
CANDY CANE	–	1	1	–	–	–	–	–	–
CAR	–	1	1	–	–	–	–	–	–
CARE	–	–	–	1	–	1	1	–	1
CAREFUL	–	–	–	1	–	1	–	–	–
CAT	–	1	1	–	–	–	–	–	–
CHAIR	–	1	1	–	–	–	–	–	–
CHILD	–	–	–	–	1	1	–	–	–
CINNAMON	1	–	1	–	–	–	–	–	–
CLOTHES	1	–	1	–	–	–	–	–	–
CLUB	2	–	2	4	2	6	4	1	5
COAT	1	–	1	–	2	2	–	–	–
COLOR	–	–	–	1	–	1	–	–	–
COME	–	1	1	2	1	3	–	1	1
COME HERE	1	–	1	–	–	–	–	–	–
CONTAIN	–	–	–	–	1	1	–	–	–
CORN	–	1	1	–	–	–	–	–	–
COUNTRY	–	–	–	1	–	1	–	–	–

RESPONSE WORD	1ST			3RD			5TH		
	M	F	T	M	F	T	M	F	T

7. BELONG

RESPONSE WORD	M	F	T	M	F	T	M	F	T
CRAYON BOX	–	–	–	1	–	1	–	–	–
CURTAIN	–	1	1	–	–	–	–	–	–
CUT	1	1	2	–	–	–	–	–	–
DECIDE	–	–	–	–	1	1	–	–	–
DELONG	–	1	1	1	–	1	–	–	–
DESK	1	1	2	–	–	–	–	–	–
DID	–	–	–	–	1	1	–	–	–
DINING ROOM	1	–	1	–	–	–	–	–	–
DISBELONG	–	–	–	–	–	–	1	1	2
DO YOU BELONG TO THE PARENTS	–	1	1	–	–	–	–	–	–
DOESNT BELONG	–	–	–	1	–	1	–	–	–
DOG	–	1	1	–	–	–	1	1	2
DONT	1	–	1	–	1	1	–	–	–
DONT BELONG	–	1	1	–	–	–	1	1	2
DOWN	–	–	–	–	1	1	–	–	–
DRAWER	–	1	1	–	–	–	–	–	–
DREAM	–	1	1	–	–	–	–	–	–
EARLY	1	–	1	–	–	–	–	–	–
END	–	–	–	–	1	1	–	–	–
FAMILY	–	1	1	2	–	2	–	1	1
FAR	–	–	–	1	–	1	–	–	–
FATHER	–	–	–	–	–	–	1	–	1
FAWN	–	1	1	–	–	–	–	–	–
FINE	1	–	1	–	–	–	–	–	–
FOG	–	–	–	1	–	1	–	–	–
FOOD	–	2	2	–	–	–	–	–	–
FOR	–	–	–	–	–	–	1	–	1
FOUND	–	–	–	–	1	1	1	–	1
FRIEND	–	–	–	–	–	–	1	–	1
FUN	–	1	1	–	–	–	–	–	–
GAVE	–	–	–	–	1	1	–	–	–
GIRL	–	–	–	–	–	–	1	–	1
GIVE	–	–	–	–	2	2	–	1	1
GO	–	1	1	2	–	2	–	–	–
GO THERE	–	–	–	1	–	1	–	–	–
GOES	–	–	–	–	–	–	–	1	1
GOOD	–	–	–	–	–	–	–	1	1
GOT	–	–	–	–	1	1	–	–	–
GRASS	2	1	3	–	–	–	–	–	–
GRAY	–	–	–	1	–	1	–	–	–
GREEN	–	1	1	–	–	–	–	–	–
GROUP	–	–	–	–	–	–	–	1	1
HAND	–	1	1	–	–	–	–	–	–
HAT	1	–	1	–	–	–	1	–	1
HAVE	–	–	–	2	3	5	2	2	4
HAVE THINGS WHERE ARE YOU	1	–	1	–	–	–	–	–	–
HE LOAN	–	–	–	1	–	1	–	–	–
HELONG	1	–	1	–	–	–	–	–	–
HEN	–	–	–	–	1	1	–	–	–
HER	–	–	–	–	1	1	1	–	1
HERE	9	8	17	2	–	2	1	–	1
HERS	–	–	–	–	1	1	1	1	2
HIM	–	1	1	2	–	2	3	1	4
HIMSELF	–	–	–	–	–	–	1	–	1
HIRE	–	–	–	–	–	–	1	–	1
HIS	–	–	–	2	1	3	5	1	6
HOLD	–	–	–	–	1	1	–	2	2
HOME	6	2	8	1	–	1	–	–	–
HONEY	–	–	–	–	–	–	–	1	1
HONG	1	–	1	–	–	–	–	–	–
HOT	–	1	1	–	–	–	–	–	–
HOUSE	3	4	7	–	1	1	–	–	–
HUG	–	–	–	–	–	–	1	–	1
I BELONG HOME	–	1	1	–	–	–	–	–	–
IN	1	5	6	1	–	1	1	–	1
IN IT	–	–	–	1	–	1	–	–	–
IN THE HOUSE	1	3	4	–	–	–	–	–	–
IN YOUR ROOM	1	–	1	–	–	–	–	–	–
IN YOUR SEAT	–	–	–	–	1	1	–	–	–
INSECT	–	–	–	–	–	–	1	–	1

RESPONSE WORD	1ST M	F	T	3RD M	F	T	5TH M	F	T

7. BELONG

RESPONSE WORD	1ST M	F	T	3RD M	F	T	5TH M	F	T
INSIDE	1	–	1	–	–	–	–	–	–
IS	–	1	1	–	–	–	–	1	1
IT	–	1	1	–	–	–	–	–	–
IT IS MINE	–	–	–	–	1	1	–	–	–
IT S SOMEBODY S	–	–	–	–	–	–	1	–	1
IT WILL BE LONG BEFORE YOUR BIRTHDAY	1	–	1	–	–	–	–	–	–
JEWELRY	–	–	–	–	1	1	–	–	–
JOIN	–	–	–	1	1	2	8	11	19
JOINED	–	–	–	–	–	–	–	1	1
JUMP	–	–	–	–	1	1	–	–	–
KEEP	–	–	–	1	1	2	–	3	3
KEPT	–	–	–	1	–	1	–	–	–
LATE	–	1	1	–	–	–	–	–	–
LAWN	3	1	4	–	1	1	–	–	–
LAWN MOWER	1	–	1	–	1	1	–	–	–
LET S GO ON A LONG TRIP	–	1	1	–	–	–	–	–	–
LETTER	–	–	–	1	–	1	–	–	–
LIGHT	1	–	1	1	–	1	–	–	–
LIKE YOU WOULD BELONG TO A CLUB	–	–	–	–	–	–	–	1	1
LINE	1	–	1	–	–	–	–	–	–
LIPS	–	1	1	–	–	–	–	–	–
LITTLE GIRL	–	1	1	–	–	–	–	–	–
LONG	2	7	9	–	4	4	4	5	9
LONG RIDE IN AN AIRPLANE	–	1	1	–	–	–	–	–	–
LONG TO	–	–	–	–	–	–	1	–	1
LONGER	–	–	–	–	–	–	1	–	1
LOOK	2	–	2	–	–	–	–	–	–
LOST	–	–	–	1	–	1	2	–	2
LOW	–	–	–	1	–	1	–	–	–
MAKE	1	–	1	–	–	–	–	–	–
MAN	1	–	1	–	–	–	–	–	–
ME	5	4	9	3	7	10	4	2	6
MEMBER	–	–	–	1	–	1	1	–	1
MIND	–	–	–	–	–	–	1	–	1
MINE	1	2	3	2	5	7	10	15	25
MISSING	1	–	1	–	–	–	–	–	–
MONEY	–	1	1	–	–	–	–	–	–
MOT	1	–	1	–	–	–	–	–	–
MOTHER	1	–	1	–	2	2	1	–	1
MOUTH	–	1	1	–	–	–	–	–	–
MY	1	–	1	–	–	–	–	–	–
NINE	–	–	–	1	–	1	–	–	–
NO	–	1	1	1	–	1	–	–	–
NOISE	–	–	–	1	–	1	–	–	–
NON-BELONG	–	1	1	–	–	–	1	–	1
NOT	–	1	1	–	3	3	–	1	1
NOT ABLE	–	–	–	–	–	–	1	–	1
NOT BELONG	4	2	6	5	3	8	–	2	2
NOT HIS	–	–	–	–	–	–	–	1	1
NOT LONG	–	1	1	–	–	–	–	–	–
NOT TO BELONG	–	–	–	–	–	–	1	–	1
NOT TOGETHER	–	–	–	1	–	1	–	–	–
NOT USED	–	–	–	1	–	1	–	–	–
NOW	–	1	1	–	–	–	–	1	1
ON	–	1	1	1	–	1	–	–	–
ONERSHIP	–	–	–	–	–	–	1	–	1
OTHERS	–	–	–	–	1	1	1	–	1
OUR	–	–	–	–	–	–	1	–	1
OURS	–	–	–	–	1	1	–	–	–
OUT	3	–	3	–	1	1	–	2	2
OUTSIDE	1	–	1	1	–	1	–	–	–
OVEN	–	–	–	–	–	–	–	1	1
OWN	–	–	–	7	5	12	11	15	26
OWNED BY	–	–	–	–	–	–	1	–	1
OWNER	–	–	–	–	–	–	1	1	2
OWNERSHIP	–	–	–	–	–	–	2	1	3
PAPER	1	–	1	–	–	–	–	–	–
PARENTS	–	–	–	–	1	1	–	1	1
PART	–	–	–	–	–	–	2	–	2

RESPONSE WORD	1ST M	F	T	3RD M	F	T	5TH M	F	T

7.   BELONG

RESPONSE WORD	1ST M	F	T	3RD M	F	T	5TH M	F	T
PAWN	1	–	1	–	–	–	–	–	–
PERSON	–	–	–	1	–	1	–	1	1
PICTURE	–	–	–	1	–	1	–	–	–
PIG	1	–	1	–	–	–	–	–	–
PLACE	1	1	2	3	1	4	–	1	1
POLE	1	–	1	–	–	–	–	–	–
POSSESS	–	–	–	–	–	–	–	1	1
POSSESSION	–	–	–	–	–	–	1	1	2
POSSESSIVE	–	–	–	–	–	–	–	1	1
PROPERTY	–	–	–	–	–	–	1	–	1
PUT	–	2	2	–	–	–	–	–	–
RECEIVE	–	1	1	–	–	–	–	1	1
RED	–	1	1	–	–	–	–	–	–
RELONG	–	1	1	–	–	–	–	–	–
ROOM	1	–	1	–	–	–	–	–	–
SADE	–	–	–	–	–	–	1	–	1
SAY	1	–	1	–	–	–	–	–	–
SCHOOL	–	1	1	–	–	–	–	–	–
SEAT	–	1	1	–	–	–	–	–	–
SEE	–	1	1	–	–	–	–	–	–
SEWING MACHINE	1	–	1	–	–	–	–	–	–
SHORT	5	2	7	3	1	4	–	1	1
SHOULDER	–	1	1	–	–	–	–	–	–
SING	1	–	1	–	–	–	–	–	–
SINK	–	1	1	–	–	–	–	–	–
SKY	–	1	1	–	–	–	–	–	–
SLOW	2	–	2	–	–	–	–	–	–
SOMEBODY	–	1	1	–	2	2	1	–	1
SOMEBODY S	–	–	–	1	–	1	–	–	–
SOMEONE	–	–	–	2	4	6	1	2	3
SOMEONES	–	–	–	–	–	–	–	1	1
SOMETHING	–	1	1	1	1	2	1	1	2
SOMETHING BELONGS TO YOU	–	1	1	–	–	–	–	1	1
SONG	1	1	2	2	–	2	–	1	1
SPORT	–	–	–	–	1	1	–	–	–
START	–	–	–	–	1	1	–	–	–
STAY	1	–	1	–	2	2	1	1	2
STEAL	1	–	1	1	–	1	–	–	–
STICK	–	–	–	–	1	1	–	–	–
STOLED	–	–	–	1	–	1	–	–	–
STOP	–	1	1	–	–	–	–	–	–
STRING	1	–	1	–	–	–	–	–	–
TABLE	–	1	1	–	–	–	–	–	–
TAKE	–	1	1	1	2	3	1	2	3
TAKE AWAY	–	–	–	–	–	–	1	–	1
TAKE CARE	–	–	–	–	1	1	–	–	–
TAKES YOU LONG	–	1	1	–	–	–	–	–	–
TALL	1	–	1	–	–	–	–	–	–
TELEVISION	–	1	1	–	–	–	–	–	–
THE	–	–	–	–	1	1	–	–	–
THEIR	–	–	–	1	2	3	–	–	–
THEIRS	–	–	–	–	4	4	3	1	4
THEM	–	–	–	–	4	4	–	–	–
THERE	–	1	1	–	1	1	1	1	2
THINGS	–	–	–	–	–	–	–	1	1
THINK	–	–	–	–	1	1	–	–	–
THIRD	–	–	–	1	–	1	–	–	–
THIS BELONGS THERE	–	1	1	–	–	–	–	–	–
THREE	1	–	1	–	–	–	–	–	–
TIGER	–	1	1	–	–	–	–	–	–
TILL	–	–	–	–	1	1	–	–	–
TIME	–	–	–	–	–	–	1	–	1
TO	7	4	11	16	14	30	8	12	20
TO A LION	1	–	1	–	–	–	–	–	–
TO A PERSON	1	–	1	–	–	–	–	–	–
TO HER	–	–	–	–	1	1	–	–	–
TO HIM	–	–	–	2	–	2	–	–	–
TO KEEP	–	–	–	–	–	–	1	–	1
TO ME	3	3	6	3	2	5	1	1	2
TO MOTHER	1	1	2	–	–	–	–	–	–
TO MOTHER AND FATHER	1	–	1	–	–	–	–	–	–
TO MYSELF	–	–	–	1	–	1	–	–	–

RESPONSE WORD	1ST M	F	T	3RD M	F	T	5TH M	F	T

7. BELONG

RESPONSE WORD	1ST M	F	T	3RD M	F	T	5TH M	F	T
TO OWN	–	–	–	–	–	–	–	1	1
TO SOMEBODY	1	–	1	2	–	2	–	–	–
TO SOMEONE	–	–	–	3	–	3	–	–	–
TO THE FAMILY	1	–	1	–	–	–	–	–	–
TO US	1	–	1	–	–	–	–	–	–
TO YOU	2	1	3	2	–	2	2	1	3
TOGETHER	–	–	–	1	3	4	2	6	8
TOO LONG	–	–	–	–	1	1	–	–	–
TOY	1	–	1	–	–	–	–	–	–
TOYS	–	1	1	–	–	–	–	–	–
TRAIN	1	–	1	–	–	–	–	–	–
TREE	1	–	1	–	–	–	–	–	–
UNABLE	–	–	–	–	–	–	–	1	1
UNBELONG	1	–	1	–	–	–	–	–	–
UNLONG	–	–	–	–	1	1	–	–	–
UP	–	–	–	1	–	1	–	–	–
UPON	–	–	–	–	1	1	–	–	–
WANT	–	1	1	–	–	–	–	–	–
WANTED	–	–	–	–	–	–	1	–	1
WATER	1	–	1	–	–	–	–	–	–
WELAWNED	–	1	1	–	–	–	–	–	–
WHEEL	1	–	1	–	–	–	–	–	–
WHERE	–	2	2	–	1	1	–	–	–
WHITE	–	1	1	–	–	–	–	–	–
WHO	–	1	1	–	–	–	–	–	–
WINDOW	1	1	2	–	–	–	–	–	–
WITH	–	1	1	1	–	1	–	–	–
WITH YOU	–	2	2	–	–	–	–	–	–
WITHOUT	–	–	–	–	–	–	1	–	1
WONT	1	–	1	–	–	–	–	–	–
WORDS	–	1	1	–	–	–	–	–	–
WRONG	–	–	–	1	–	1	–	–	–
YOU	1	3	4	2	4	6	2	–	2
YOU WEAR A PIN	1	–	1	–	–	–	–	–	–
YOUR	–	–	–	–	1	1	–	–	–
YOURS	–	–	–	6	1	7	10	6	16
YOURSELF	–	–	–	2	–	2	–	–	–

8. BETWEEN

RESPONSE WORD	1ST M	F	T	3RD M	F	T	5TH M	F	T
A BOY	1	–	1	–	–	–	–	–	–
A DUCK	1	–	1	–	–	–	–	–	–
A LEAF	1	–	1	–	–	–	–	–	–
ABOUT	–	–	–	–	–	–	–	1	1
AFTER	1	5	6	2	2	4	1	1	2
AGAINST EACH OTHER	1	–	1	–	–	–	–	–	–
AHEAD	–	–	–	–	2	2	–	–	–
AISLE	–	–	–	–	1	1	–	–	–
ALWAYS	–	–	–	–	–	–	1	–	1
AMONG	–	–	–	–	–	–	1	2	3
AND	1	–	1	–	–	–	–	–	–
ANGRY	–	–	–	–	1	1	–	–	–
ANOTHER	–	–	–	–	–	–	1	–	1
APART	–	–	–	1	1	2	–	1	1
APPLES	1	–	1	–	–	–	–	–	–
AROUND	–	–	–	–	1	1	–	–	–
AT THE END	–	–	–	1	–	1	–	–	–
BABIES	–	1	1	–	–	–	–	–	–
BABY	1	–	1	–	–	–	–	–	–
BACK	–	1	1	–	–	–	–	–	–
BALL	–	1	1	–	–	–	–	–	–
BAR	–	1	1	–	–	–	–	–	–
BARS	–	–	–	1	–	1	–	–	–
BE	1	1	2	3	1	4	–	–	–
BEAR	–	1	1	–	–	–	–	–	–
BECAUSE	–	–	–	2	–	2	–	–	–
BED	1	–	1	–	–	–	–	–	–
BEDSIDE	–	–	–	1	–	1	–	–	–
BEFORE	1	–	1	–	2	2	–	–	–
BEHIDE	–	–	–	–	–	–	1	–	1
BEHIND	–	–	–	1	4	5	2	1	3

RESPONSE WORD	1ST			3RD			5TH		
	M	F	T	M	F	T	M	F	T

8.   BETWEEN

RESPONSE WORD	1ST M	F	T	3RD M	F	T	5TH M	F	T
BEKEEN	1	–	1	–	–	–	–	–	–
BELOW	–	1	1	1	–	1	–	–	–
BENEATH	–	–	–	1	–	1	1	2	3
BENEEN	–	1	1	–	–	–	–	–	–
BESIDE	–	–	–	3	4	7	2	1	3
BETTY	1	–	1	–	–	–	–	–	–
BETWEEN SOMETHING	–	–	–	–	–	–	1	–	1
BIG	–	–	–	1	–	1	–	–	–
BLACK	1	1	2	–	–	–	–	–	–
BLOW	–	–	–	–	–	–	–	1	1
BLUE	1	3	4	–	1	1	–	–	–
BOARD	–	1	1	–	–	–	–	–	–
BOOK	1	–	1	–	–	–	–	–	–
BOOKS	–	1	1	–	–	–	–	–	–
BOTH	–	–	–	–	1	1	–	–	–
BOY	1	1	2	–	–	–	–	–	–
BRUSH	–	–	–	–	–	–	–	1	1
BUG	1	–	1	–	–	–	–	–	–
BUS	–	1	1	–	–	–	–	–	–
BUTTON	–	1	1	–	–	–	–	–	–
CAFETERIA	1	–	1	–	–	–	–	–	–
CAN	1	1	2	–	1	1	–	–	–
CAR	–	–	–	–	–	–	1	–	1
CARE	–	1	1	–	–	–	–	–	–
CARS	1	1	2	–	1	1	1	1	2
CAT	–	–	–	–	–	–	1	–	1
CAUGHT	–	–	–	–	–	–	–	2	2
CAVE	–	–	–	1	–	1	–	–	–
CEILING	–	–	–	1	–	1	–	–	–
CENTAL	–	–	–	–	–	–	1	–	1
CENTER	–	–	–	–	–	–	4	1	5
CHAIR	–	–	–	–	1	1	–	–	–
CHAIRS	–	1	1	–	–	–	–	–	–
CHALK	1	–	1	–	–	–	–	–	–
CIRCLE	–	–	–	–	–	–	1	–	1
CLEAN	–	1	1	–	–	–	–	–	–
CLOSE	–	–	–	–	–	–	–	1	1
COAT HANGER	1	–	1	–	–	–	–	–	–
COLOR WORDS	–	1	1	–	–	–	–	–	–
COOKIE	1	–	1	–	–	–	–	–	–
COOKIES	1	–	1	–	–	–	–	–	–
CORNER	–	–	–	–	1	1	–	–	–
COVERS	–	–	–	–	1	1	–	–	–
DANCED	–	1	1	–	–	–	–	–	–
DECEEN	–	–	–	1	–	1	–	–	–
DESK	–	–	–	–	–	–	1	–	1
DESKS	–	–	–	1	–	1	–	–	–
DIFFERENCE	–	–	–	–	1	1	–	1	1
DIFFERENT	–	–	–	–	1	1	–	–	–
DINNER	–	1	1	–	–	–	–	–	–
DIRECTLY	–	–	–	–	–	–	1	–	1
DIVIDE	–	–	–	–	1	1	–	–	–
DO	–	–	–	–	1	1	–	–	–
DOESNT	–	–	–	1	–	1	–	–	–
DOOR	2	1	3	1	–	1	–	–	–
EACH OTHER	1	2	3	–	–	–	1	–	1
EASY	–	–	–	–	–	–	–	1	1
EMPTY	–	–	–	1	–	1	–	–	–
END	–	–	–	1	3	4	1	1	2
FAR APART	–	1	1	–	1	1	–	–	–
FASTER	–	1	1	–	–	–	–	–	–
FIEND	–	1	1	–	–	–	–	–	–
FIGHT	–	–	–	1	–	1	–	–	–
FINGER IN BRUSH	–	1	1	–	–	–	–	–	–
FIRST	–	–	–	–	1	1	–	–	–
FOR	–	1	1	–	–	–	–	–	–
FOUR	–	1	1	–	–	–	–	–	–
FULL	1	–	1	–	–	–	–	–	–
GARBAGE	1	–	1	–	–	–	–	–	–
GET	1	–	1	–	–	–	–	–	–
GET OUT	–	–	–	–	–	–	–	1	1
GIRL	–	1	1	–	1	1	–	–	–

8. BETWEEN

RESPONSE WORD	1ST M	1ST F	1ST T	3RD M	3RD F	3RD T	5TH M	5TH F	5TH T
GO	–	1	1	–	–	–	–	–	–
GREEN	–	1	1	–	1	1	–	–	–
HALF AND HALF	–	–	–	–	1	1	–	–	–
HALF BETWEEN	1	–	1	–	–	–	–	–	–
HAND	–	1	1	–	–	–	–	–	–
HANDS	–	–	–	–	1	1	–	–	–
HAPPY	–	–	–	1	–	1	–	–	–
HE	–	–	–	1	–	1	–	–	–
HEEN	1	–	1	–	–	–	–	–	–
HER	1	–	1	–	–	–	1	–	1
HERE	1	–	1	1	1	2	–	–	–
HIGH	–	–	–	–	1	1	–	–	1
HIM	1	1	2	–	–	–	1	–	1
HOLE	–	–	–	1	–	1	–	–	–
HORN	1	–	1	–	–	–	–	–	–
HORSE	–	1	1	–	–	–	–	–	–
HOUSE	–	3	3	–	–	–	–	–	–
HOUSES	3	–	3	–	–	–	–	1	1
I	–	–	–	–	1	1	–	–	–
IN	–	–	–	3	3	6	4	8	12
IN BACK	–	–	–	–	–	–	–	1	1
IN BETWEED	–	–	–	–	–	–	–	1	1
IN BETWEEN	1	–	1	–	–	–	3	1	4
IN BETWEEN SOMETHING	–	–	–	1	–	1	–	–	–
IN FRONT	–	–	–	2	1	3	–	–	–
IN MIDDLE	–	–	–	–	–	–	1	1	2
IN THE MIDDLE	2	2	4	9	5	14	5	7	12
IN THE MIDDLE OF	–	–	–	–	–	–	–	1	1
IN THE MIDST	–	–	–	–	–	–	1	–	1
IN-BETWEEN	–	–	–	–	–	–	1	–	1
INBETWEEN	–	–	–	1	3	4	–	1	1
INBETWEEN MIDDLE	–	–	–	–	1	1	–	–	–
INFRANT	–	–	–	–	–	–	1	–	1
INSIDE	–	–	–	2	5	7	4	10	14
INSTRUMENT	–	1	1	–	–	–	–	–	–
INTO	–	–	–	1	–	1	1	2	3
INTWEEN	–	–	–	–	1	1	–	–	–
IT	–	1	1	2	1	3	–	–	–
JUMP ROPE	–	1	1	–	–	–	–	–	–
KEEN	1	–	1	–	–	–	–	–	–
KITTEN	1	–	1	–	–	–	–	–	–
LEEN	–	–	–	–	–	–	–	1	1
LEGS	1	–	1	–	–	–	–	–	–
LET GO	1	–	1	–	–	–	–	–	–
LET ME BE IN BETWEEN	1	–	1	–	–	–	–	–	–
LETTER	1	–	1	–	–	–	–	–	–
LIGHT	–	1	1	–	–	–	–	–	–
LIKE	1	–	1	1	–	1	–	–	–
LITTLE	–	–	–	–	1	1	–	–	–
LITTLE IN BETWEEN	–	–	–	–	1	1	–	–	–
LOOK BETWEEN THERE	–	1	1	–	–	–	–	–	–
LOVE	–	1	1	–	–	–	–	–	–
LUT	1	–	1	–	–	–	–	–	–
MAN	1	–	1	–	–	–	–	–	–
ME	7	3	10	2	2	4	–	–	–
MEAL	–	1	1	1	–	1	2	–	2
MEALS	4	4	8	–	2	2	–	–	–
MEAN	2	–	2	–	–	–	–	–	–
MEN	–	1	1	–	–	–	–	–	–
METWEEN	1	–	1	–	–	–	–	–	–
MIDDER	–	–	–	–	–	–	–	1	1
MIDDLE	6	9	15	26	30	56	48	50	98
MIDDLE SIZE	–	1	1	–	–	–	–	–	–
MIDDY	–	–	–	–	–	–	1	–	1
MIDWAY	–	–	–	–	–	–	1	–	1
MIGHT	1	–	1	–	–	–	–	–	–
MILLS	–	1	1	–	–	–	–	–	–
MOTHER	–	1	1	–	–	–	–	–	–
MOTORCYCLE	–	1	1	–	–	–	–	–	–
MUD	1	–	1	–	–	–	–	–	–
MUSHROOMS	–	1	1	–	–	–	–	–	–
MUSIC	–	1	1	–	–	–	–	–	–

RESPONSE WORD	1ST M	F	T	3RD M	F	T	5TH M	F	T

8.   BETWEEN

RESPONSE WORD	1ST M	F	T	3RD M	F	T	5TH M	F	T
MY	–	1	1	–	–	–	–	–	–
MY TOOTH	–	–	–	1	–	1	–	–	–
NAIL	–	1	1	–	–	–	–	–	–
NEAR	–	–	–	–	–	–	–	1	1
NERE	–	–	–	–	–	–	1	–	1
NEVER	–	–	–	–	1	1	–	–	–
NEXT	–	–	–	1	–	1	–	–	–
NIGHT	–	–	–	1	–	1	–	–	–
NOSIE	–	–	–	–	–	–	–	1	1
NOT BETWEEN	–	–	–	–	1	1	1	1	2
NOTHING	1	–	1	–	–	–	–	–	–
NOW	–	–	–	1	–	1	–	–	–
NUMBER	–	–	–	1	–	1	–	–	–
NUMBER 10	1	–	1	–	–	–	–	–	–
NURSE	–	1	1	–	–	–	–	–	–
OBJECT	–	–	–	–	–	–	1	–	1
ONE	–	–	–	–	1	1	–	–	–
OPEN	–	–	–	1	–	1	1	–	1
OTHER	–	–	–	–	–	–	1	–	1
OUR	–	1	1	–	–	–	–	–	–
OUT	2	1	3	2	1	3	–	3	3
OUTSIDE	–	–	–	4	1	5	1	3	4
OUTSIDES	1	–	1	–	–	–	–	–	–
OVER	–	–	–	1	1	2	–	–	–
OWN	1	–	1	–	–	–	–	–	–
PAN	1	–	1	–	–	–	–	–	–
PAPER	1	–	1	–	–	–	–	–	–
PART	–	–	–	–	1	1	–	–	–
PEAN	1	–	1	–	–	–	–	–	–
PENCIL	1	–	1	–	1	1	–	–	–
PEOPLE	1	1	2	–	–	–	1	1	2
PIG	–	–	–	1	–	1	1	–	1
PINK	–	1	1	1	–	1	–	–	–
PRESSING AGAINST	–	–	–	–	–	–	1	–	1
PURPLE	1	–	1	–	1	1	–	–	–
PUT PEANUT BUTTER BETWEEN THE SANDWICHE.	–	1	1	–	–	–	–	–	–
PUT TOGETHER	–	–	–	–	–	–	1	–	1
QUEEN	1	–	1	–	–	–	–	–	–
RABBIT	–	–	–	1	–	1	–	–	–
RECEIVE	1	–	1	–	–	–	–	–	–
RED	–	–	–	–	1	1	–	–	–
RETWEEN	–	1	1	–	–	–	–	–	–
RIVER GOES BETWEEN THE ROCKS.	–	–	–	–	–	–	–	1	1
ROCK	1	–	1	–	–	–	–	–	–
ROCKS	1	1	2	1	–	1	–	–	–
SANTA CLAUS	1	–	1	–	–	–	–	–	–
SCHOOL	–	1	1	–	–	–	–	–	–
SCREENED	1	–	1	–	–	–	–	–	–
SEE	1	–	1	–	–	–	–	–	–
SEEDS	–	–	–	–	–	–	1	–	1
SEEN	–	1	1	–	–	–	–	–	–
SENT	–	1	1	–	–	–	–	–	–
SEWING	1	1	2	–	–	–	–	–	–
SHEETS	1	–	1	–	–	–	–	–	–
SHELF	–	1	1	–	–	–	–	–	–
SIDE	–	2	2	3	–	3	1	1	2
SINK	–	1	1	–	–	–	–	–	–
SIT DOWN IN A CHAIR	1	–	1	–	–	–	–	–	–
SIZE	–	–	–	–	–	–	1	–	1
SKINNY	–	–	–	1	–	1	–	–	–
SMASH	–	–	–	1	–	1	–	1	1
SNACKS	1	–	1	–	–	–	–	–	–
SODA	–	1	1	–	–	–	–	–	–
SOMEBODY	–	–	–	1	–	1	–	–	–
SOMEONE	–	1	1	–	–	–	–	–	–
SOMETHING	–	2	2	1	2	3	1	–	1
SOMETHINGS BETWEEN	–	1	1	–	–	–	–	–	–
SPACE	–	–	–	–	1	1	1	–	1
SPEAKER	–	–	–	1	–	1	–	–	–
SPEAN	–	–	–	–	–	–	–	1	1

8.   BETWEEN

RESPONSE WORD	1ST M	1ST F	1ST T	3RD M	3RD F	3RD T	5TH M	5TH F	5TH T
SPLIT	–	–	–	1	–	1	–	–	–
SPREAD	–	1	1	–	–	–	–	–	–
SQUASHED	–	–	–	2	–	2	1	–	1
SQUEEZED IN	–	–	–	1	–	1	–	–	–
STAND	–	1	1	–	–	–	–	–	–
STANDING	1	–	1	–	–	–	–	–	–
STATION	–	–	–	1	–	1	–	–	–
STREET	–	–	–	–	–	–	1	–	1
STRING	2	–	2	–	–	–	–	–	–
SUN	–	1	1	–	–	–	–	–	–
SUPPER	–	–	–	–	1	1	–	–	–
SURROUNDED	–	–	–	2	–	2	–	–	–
TABLE	2	1	3	–	–	–	–	–	–
TALK	1	–	1	–	–	–	–	–	–
TALL	2	–	2	–	–	–	–	–	–
TEETH	–	1	1	–	–	–	–	–	–
THAT	1	–	1	–	–	–	–	–	–
THE	1	1	2	–	–	–	2	–	2
THE CARS	–	–	–	1	–	1	–	–	–
THE MIDDLE	1	1	2	–	–	–	–	–	–
THE TABLES	1	–	1	–	–	–	–	–	–
THEM	–	–	–	1	2	3	–	–	–
THEN	–	1	1	–	–	–	–	–	–
THERE	–	–	–	1	–	1	–	–	–
THEU	–	–	–	–	–	–	1	–	1
THEY	1	–	1	–	–	–	–	–	–
THIN	1	–	1	–	–	–	–	–	–
THING	–	–	–	–	–	–	–	1	1
THIS	–	–	–	1	–	1	–	–	–
THOSE	–	–	–	–	–	–	–	1	1
THREE	–	3	3	–	–	–	–	–	–
THREE PEOPLE	–	–	–	–	–	–	1	–	1
THROUGH	1	–	1	1	1	2	1	1	2
TIME	–	–	–	1	–	1	–	–	–
TO	–	–	–	–	–	–	1	1	2
TO MEET	1	–	1	–	–	–	–	–	–
TOES	–	1	1	–	–	–	1	–	1
TOGATHER	–	–	–	–	–	–	1	–	1
TOGETHER	2	3	5	6	7	13	7	6	13
TOO LATE	–	1	1	–	–	–	–	–	–
TOP	–	–	–	–	–	–	1	–	1
TRAIN	1	–	1	–	–	–	1	–	1
TRAP	–	–	–	–	–	–	1	–	1
TREE	–	1	1	–	–	–	–	–	–
TREES	1	–	1	–	–	–	–	–	–
TUCK	–	–	–	–	1	1	–	–	–
TWEEN	–	–	–	1	1	2	–	1	1
TWINS	–	1	1	–	1	1	–	–	–
TWO	3	3	6	1	3	4	2	1	3
TWO BEDS	–	–	–	–	–	–	–	1	1
TWO BLOCKS	1	–	1	–	–	–	–	–	–
TWO BOXES	1	–	1	1	–	1	–	–	–
TWO BOYS	1	1	2	–	–	–	–	–	–
TWO GIRLS	–	–	–	–	1	1	–	–	–
TWO GRASSES	1	–	1	–	–	–	–	–	–
TWO LINES	–	–	–	–	–	–	–	1	1
TWO OBJECTS	–	–	–	–	–	–	1	–	1
TWO PERSONS	1	–	1	–	–	–	–	–	–
TWO SIDES	–	–	–	–	–	–	–	1	1
UNDER	–	2	2	5	6	11	3	1	4
UNDERNEATH	–	–	–	–	–	–	1	–	1
UNDERSTAND	–	1	1	–	–	–	–	–	–
UNHAPPY	–	–	–	1	–	1	–	–	–
UNTWEEN	–	–	–	–	–	–	–	1	1
UP	–	1	1	–	–	–	–	–	–
US	2	3	5	2	1	3	1	1	2
WALK	–	1	1	–	–	–	–	–	–
WALL	1	–	1	–	–	–	–	1	1
WALLS	1	–	1	–	–	–	–	–	–
WASH YOURSELF GOOD	–	1	1	–	–	–	–	–	–
WHAT	–	–	–	–	1	1	–	–	–
WHEN YOU'RE BETWEEN SOMETHING	1	–	1	–	–	–	–	–	–

RESPONSE WORD	1ST			3RD			5TH		
	M	F	T	M	F	T	M	F	T

8. BETWEEN

RESPONSE WORD	M	F	T	M	F	T	M	F	T
WHITE	1	1	2	–	–	–	–	–	–
WOULD	–	1	1	–	–	–	–	–	–
YES	1	–	1	–	–	–	–	–	–
YOU	5	4	9	3	4	7	–	1	1
YOU AND ME	1	–	1	–	–	–	–	–	–
YOU RE BETWEEN THE HASSOCK	1	–	1	–	–	–	–	–	–
YOU RE NUTS	1	–	1	–	–	–	–	–	–
YOUR	–	–	–	1	–	1	–	–	–

9. BIRD

RESPONSE WORD	M	F	T	M	F	T	M	F	T
A BIRD THAT IS FLYING IN THE AIR	–	1	1	–	–	–	–	–	–
A CARDINAL	–	–	–	1	–	1	–	–	–
A FLYING CREATURE	–	–	–	1	1	2	2	1	1
AIRPLANE	1	–	1	1	1	2	2	–	2
AMINAL	–	–	–	–	–	–	–	1	1
AN ANIMAL	–	–	–	–	–	–	–	1	1
ANIMAL	–	–	–	13	12	25	22	19	41
ANIMALS	–	–	–	–	1	1	–	–	–
ANMAL	–	–	–	–	–	–	1	–	1
BABY	–	1	1	–	–	–	–	–	–
BAT	1	–	1	–	1	1	–	–	–
BEAK	–	1	1	–	–	–	–	–	–
BEAR	1	–	1	–	1	1	1	–	1
BEAST	–	–	–	–	–	–	1	1	2
BEAT	–	–	–	–	1	1	–	–	–
BED	1	–	1	–	–	–	–	–	–
BEE	2	1	3	1	–	1	–	1	1
BETTY	1	–	1	–	–	–	–	–	–
BIRD	–	1	1	–	–	–	–	–	–
BIRDS	–	1	1	–	–	–	–	1	1
BIRTHDAY	–	1	1	–	–	–	–	–	–
BLACK	–	–	–	–	1	1	3	–	3
BLUE	2	2	4	–	1	1	2	2	4
BLUE JAY	–	–	–	–	–	–	1	1	2
BLUEBIRD	–	2	2	3	–	3	–	–	–
BLUEJAY	1	–	1	–	1	1	2	1	3
BOBOLINK	–	–	–	–	–	–	1	–	1
BOOK	–	1	1	–	–	–	–	1	1
BOOKS	1	–	1	–	–	–	–	–	–
BRANCHES	1	–	1	–	–	–	–	–	–
BREAD	1	–	1	–	–	–	–	–	–
BUEJAY	–	–	–	1	–	1	–	–	–
BUG	–	–	–	–	1	1	–	1	1
BUT	1	–	1	–	–	–	–	–	–
BUTTERFLY	1	1	2	1	–	1	–	–	–
CACTUS	1	–	1	–	–	–	–	–	–
CAGE	–	–	–	–	–	–	1	–	1
CAN FLY	–	1	1	–	1	1	–	2	2
CARDINAL	–	–	–	–	1	1	4	2	6
CAT	–	–	–	5	7	12	12	3	15
CAT BIRD	–	–	–	1	–	1	–	–	–
CATCH	1	–	1	1	–	1	–	–	–
CHAIR	–	1	1	–	–	–	–	–	–
CHICK	–	–	–	–	1	1	–	–	–
CHICKEN	–	1	1	–	2	2	–	–	–
CHICKEN HAWK	–	–	–	1	–	1	–	–	–
CIGARETTES	1	–	1	–	–	–	–	–	–
CLASS	–	–	–	1	–	1	–	–	–
CLOUDS	–	–	–	–	–	–	1	–	1
COCKATOO	–	–	–	–	–	–	–	1	1
COME	–	1	1	–	–	–	–	–	–
CONE	1	–	1	–	–	–	–	–	–
COO	–	1	1	–	–	–	–	–	–
COULD FLY AROUND	–	1	1	–	–	–	–	–	–
CRANE	–	–	–	–	–	–	–	1	1
CREATURE	–	–	–	–	1	1	–	–	–

RESPONSE WORD	1ST			3RD			5TH		
	M	F	T	M	F	T	M	F	T

9.   BIRD

RESPONSE WORD	M	F	T	M	F	T	M	F	T
CROW	–	–	–	–	–	–	–	2	2
CURD	2	–	2	–	–	–	–	–	–
DEAD	1	–	1	–	–	–	–	–	–
DEAR	–	–	–	–	–	–	–	1	1
DEBT	–	1	1	–	–	–	–	–	–
DIRT	–	2	2	–	–	–	–	–	–
DOG	2	–	2	5	7	12	4	2	6
DUCK	–	1	1	3	–	3	–	–	–
EAGLE	2	–	2	4	1	5	3	2	5
EGG	1	–	1	–	–	–	–	–	–
FEATHER	1	1	2	–	–	–	1	2	3
FEATHERED FRIEND	–	–	–	–	–	–	1	–	1
FEATHERS	2	–	2	–	–	–	3	1	4
FEE	1	–	1	–	–	–	–	–	–
FEED	1	–	1	–	–	–	–	–	–
FISH	1	–	1	1	–	1	–	–	–
FLEW	1	–	1	–	1	1	–	–	–
FLICKER	–	–	–	–	–	–	1	–	1
FLIES	3	1	4	2	–	2	1	–	1
FLIES UP IN THE AIR	–	1	1	–	–	–	–	–	–
FLOCK	–	–	–	1	–	1	–	1	1
FLY	38	66	104	53	45	98	32	30	62
FLYING	3	3	6	–	1	1	2	3	5
FLYS	–	–	–	–	–	–	–	1	1
FOOD	–	3	3	–	–	–	–	–	–
FOWL	–	–	–	–	–	–	–	1	1
FOX	–	–	–	2	–	2	–	–	–
FRIEND	–	–	–	–	–	–	–	1	1
GIRD	–	–	–	1	–	1	–	–	–
GLAD	–	–	–	1	–	1	–	–	–
GLASS	1	–	1	–	–	–	–	–	–
GO	–	–	–	1	–	1	–	–	–
GOLD	–	–	–	–	1	1	–	–	–
GRASS	1	–	1	–	–	–	–	–	–
HAPPY	–	1	1	–	–	–	–	–	–
HAT	1	–	1	–	–	–	–	–	–
HAWK	–	–	–	1	–	1	2	–	2
HEAD	–	1	1	–	–	–	–	–	–
HEAR	1	–	1	–	–	–	–	–	–
HEARD	–	1	1	–	2	2	–	–	–
HERD	1	–	1	–	–	–	–	1	1
HIGH	–	–	–	–	1	1	–	1	1
HOBBY	–	–	–	–	–	–	–	1	1
HORSE	1	–	1	–	1	1	–	–	–
HOT	–	–	–	–	–	–	1	–	1
HOUSE	–	1	1	–	–	–	–	–	–
HUMMING	–	–	–	–	–	–	1	–	1
HUNT	–	–	–	–	–	–	1	–	1
IN TREE	1	–	1	–	–	–	–	–	–
INSECT	–	–	–	1	2	3	1	–	1
IS	–	–	–	–	1	1	–	–	–
JAY	–	–	–	1	–	1	–	–	–
KANGAROO	1	–	1	–	–	–	–	–	–
KILLED	–	–	–	1	–	1	–	–	–
KING	–	1	1	–	–	–	–	–	–
LANDED	1	–	1	–	–	–	–	–	–
LERD	2	–	2	–	–	–	–	–	–
LIKE	–	1	1	–	–	–	–	–	–
LIRD	–	1	1	–	–	–	–	–	–
LIVE	–	–	–	–	1	1	–	–	–
MAT	–	–	–	1	–	1	–	–	–
MIGHT CANT FLY	–	1	1	–	–	–	–	–	–
MOCKING BIRD	–	–	–	–	1	1	–	–	–
MONKEY	–	–	–	–	1	1	–	–	–
MOSQUITO	–	–	–	–	–	–	1	–	1
MOTHER	–	–	–	–	–	–	–	1	1
NATURE	–	–	–	–	1	1	–	–	–
NEST	10	7	17	3	8	11	1	6	7
NET	–	–	–	1	–	1	–	–	–
NIRD	–	2	2	–	–	–	–	–	–
NO BIRD	1	–	1	–	–	–	–	–	–
NOT GOOD	–	–	–	–	–	–	–	1	1

RESPONSE WORD	1ST M	F	T	3RD M	F	T	5TH M	F	T

9. BIRD

RESPONSE WORD	1ST M	F	T	3RD M	F	T	5TH M	F	T
ORIOLE	–	–	–	–	1	1	1	2	3
OWL	–	–	–	1	–	1	–	–	–
PAPER	2	–	2	–	–	–	–	–	–
PARAKEET	–	1	1	1	–	1	–	–	–
PET	–	–	–	–	–	–	1	1	2
PHEASANT	–	–	–	–	1	1	–	–	–
PIANO	1	–	1	–	–	–	–	–	–
PICTURE	1	–	1	–	–	–	–	–	–
PIGEON	1	1	2	–	–	–	1	2	3
PIPE	1	–	1	–	–	–	–	–	–
PLANE	–	–	–	2	–	2	1	–	1
PLAYGROUND	1	–	1	–	–	–	–	–	–
PLUG	1	–	1	–	–	–	–	–	–
PRETTY	–	–	–	2	2	4	–	–	–
RABBIT	–	–	–	1	1	2	–	1	1
RACOON	–	–	–	–	1	1	–	–	–
RAT	–	–	–	–	–	–	1	–	1
RED BIRD	–	–	–	–	–	–	–	1	1
ROBIN	1	–	1	3	6	9	13	13	26
SAW	–	–	–	1	–	1	–	–	–
SCARLET TANAGER	–	–	–	–	–	–	–	1	1
SCHOOL BUS	1	–	1	–	–	–	–	–	–
SEAGULL	–	–	–	1	–	1	–	–	–
SEEDS	–	–	–	–	–	–	–	1	1
SHOE	1	–	1	–	–	–	–	–	–
SHOT	1	–	1	–	–	–	–	–	–
SING	4	4	8	4	3	7	1	6	7
SINGING	–	1	1	–	–	–	–	1	1
SIRD	1	–	1	–	–	–	–	–	–
SKIRD	1	–	1	–	–	–	–	–	–
SKY	–	2	2	2	–	2	–	2	2
SMALL	1	–	1	–	–	–	–	1	1
SNIRD	1	–	1	–	–	–	–	–	–
SOMETHING THAT FLIES	–	–	–	–	–	–	–	1	1
SONG	–	–	–	–	–	–	–	1	1
SOUTH	–	–	–	–	–	–	1	–	1
SPARROW	–	–	–	–	–	–	2	–	2
SPIDER	–	1	1	–	–	–	–	–	–
SWALLOW	–	–	–	1	–	1	–	–	–
SWAN	–	–	–	–	–	–	1	–	1
TEETH	1	–	1	–	–	–	–	–	–
THAT	–	–	–	–	1	1	–	–	–
THING	–	–	–	1	–	1	–	–	–
TIGER	–	1	1	–	–	–	–	–	–
TOOTHBRUSH	1	–	1	–	–	–	–	–	–
TREE	1	4	5	–	2	2	1	4	5
TWEET	1	–	1	–	1	1	–	1	1
VERTEBRATE	–	–	–	–	–	–	1	–	1
WASP	–	–	–	1	–	1	–	–	–
WE	–	2	2	–	–	–	–	–	–
WERE	1	–	1	–	–	–	–	–	–
WHAT FLIES IN THE AIR	1	–	1	–	–	–	–	–	–
WHEN THE BIRDS IS FLYING	1	–	1	–	–	–	–	–	–
WHERE BIRDS GET IN THE NEST THEY GOT WI	1	–	1	–	–	–	–	–	–
WHISTLE	1	–	1	–	1	1	–	–	–
WIND	1	–	1	–	–	–	–	–	–
WING	3	4	7	4	8	12	2	3	5
WINGS	2	1	3	2	3	5	3	2	5
WOODS	–	1	1	–	–	–	–	–	–
WORD	2	1	3	1	–	1	–	–	–
WORM	1	–	1	–	1	1	–	1	1
YELLOW	–	1	1	–	–	–	–	–	–
YOU	1	–	1	–	–	–	–	–	–
YOU RE	1	–	1	–	–	–	–	–	–

RESPONSE WORD	1ST M	F	T	3RD M	F	T	5TH M	F	T

10.   BITTER

RESPONSE WORD	1ST M	F	T	3RD M	F	T	5TH M	F	T
A GLASS OF WATER TASTES BITTER	–	–	–	1	–	1	–	–	–
A PICKLE IS BITTER SOMETIMES	1	–	1	–	–	–	–	–	–
ANGRY	1	–	1	1	–	1	–	–	–
APPLE	2	–	2	–	–	–	–	–	–
ASK	–	–	–	–	1	1	–	–	–
AWFUL	–	1	1	–	2	2	4	4	8
B	1	–	1	–	–	–	–	–	–
BABY	–	3	3	–	–	–	–	–	–
BACK	–	–	–	–	1	1	–	–	–
BAD	2	3	5	5	4	9	6	2	8
BAD MAN	–	–	–	–	1	1	–	1	1
BAD TASTE	–	–	–	–	1	1	–	–	–
BALL	1	–	1	–	–	–	–	–	–
BARBARA	–	–	–	1	–	1	–	–	–
BAT	1	–	1	–	–	–	–	–	–
BATTER	–	1	1	–	2	2	–	–	–
BEATER	–	–	–	1	–	1	–	–	–
BEE	–	1	1	–	–	–	–	–	–
BEET	1	–	1	–	–	–	–	–	–
BELL	–	–	–	–	1	1	–	–	–
BET	–	–	–	–	1	1	–	–	–
BETTER	5	2	7	10	3	13	1	2	3
BID	–	1	1	–	–	–	–	–	–
BIG	–	1	1	1	–	1	–	–	–
BIGGER	–	1	1	–	–	–	–	–	–
BIKE	1	–	1	–	–	–	–	–	–
BIRD	1	1	2	–	–	–	–	–	–
BIT	4	10	14	5	6	11	2	2	4
BIT NOSE	1	–	1	–	–	–	–	–	–
BIT THINGS	1	–	1	–	–	–	–	–	–
BITE	3	4	7	2	5	7	–	2	2
BITTER	–	–	–	–	–	–	1	–	1
BITTERS	1	–	1	–	–	–	–	–	–
BLUE	–	–	–	–	–	–	1	–	1
BOARD	–	1	1	–	–	–	–	–	–
BOAT	2	–	2	–	–	–	–	–	–
BOY	1	–	1	–	–	–	–	–	–
BREAK	1	–	1	–	–	–	–	–	–
BRITTLE	–	–	–	1	–	1	–	–	–
BUG	–	–	–	–	1	1	–	–	–
BUTTER	9	10	19	4	3	7	1	3	4
BUTTERFLY	–	–	–	1	–	1	–	–	–
C	1	–	1	–	–	–	–	–	–
CAKE	–	1	1	–	–	–	–	–	–
CALL PEOPLE NAMES	–	1	1	–	–	–	–	–	–
CAN	1	–	1	–	–	–	–	–	–
CAR	1	–	1	–	–	–	–	–	–
CAT	2	2	4	–	–	–	1	–	1
CAT BITE	–	–	–	1	–	1	–	–	–
CHAIR	1	–	1	–	–	–	–	–	–
CHANGE	–	–	–	1	–	1	–	–	–
CHEESE	–	1	1	–	–	–	–	–	–
CHOCOLATE	–	–	–	2	–	2	–	1	1
CLEAN	–	–	–	1	–	1	–	–	–
CLOTHES	1	1	2	–	–	–	–	–	–
COFFEE	–	–	–	–	–	–	1	–	1
COLD	3	5	8	3	6	9	10	9	19
COLORS	–	1	1	–	–	–	–	–	–
COMB	–	–	–	–	1	1	–	–	–
COOK	1	–	1	–	–	–	–	–	–
CRY	1	–	1	–	–	–	–	–	–
CUP	1	–	1	–	–	–	–	–	–
DAYS	–	1	1	–	–	–	–	–	–
DEAD	1	–	1	–	–	–	–	–	–
DIE	–	1	1	–	–	–	–	–	–
DIFFERENT	–	–	–	–	1	1	–	–	–
DISHES	–	–	–	–	1	1	–	–	–
DO	–	–	–	–	–	–	1	–	1
DOESNT TASTE	–	–	–	1	–	1	–	–	–
DOESNT TASTE GOOD	1	1	2	–	–	–	–	1	1

RESPONSE WORD	1ST M	1ST F	1ST T	3RD M	3RD F	3RD T	5TH M	5TH F	5TH T

10. BITTER

RESPONSE WORD	1ST M	F	T	3RD M	F	T	5TH M	F	T
DOG	1	2	3	–	–	–	–	–	–
DOG BIT HER	–	1	1	–	–	–	–	–	–
DOG BITE	2	1	3	–	–	–	–	–	–
DONT BIT HER	1	–	1	–	–	–	–	–	–
DONT BITE HARD	–	1	1	–	–	–	–	–	–
DOOR	2	2	4	–	–	–	–	–	–
DRINK	–	1	1	–	–	–	–	–	–
DULL	–	–	–	–	–	–	–	1	1
EAT	2	–	2	1	–	1	–	–	–
EGG	1	–	1	–	–	–	–	–	–
EYES	–	–	–	–	1	1	–	–	–
FAT	–	–	–	–	1	1	–	–	–
FINE	–	1	1	–	–	–	–	–	–
FINER	–	–	–	1	–	1	–	–	–
FINGER	1	–	1	–	–	–	–	–	–
FITTER	1	1	2	–	–	–	–	–	–
FIX	1	–	1	–	–	–	–	–	–
FLOWER	–	–	–	–	–	–	–	1	1
FLY	–	–	–	–	–	–	–	1	1
FOOD	1	1	2	–	–	–	1	1	2
FRIGHTEN	–	–	–	–	1	1	–	–	–
FUNNY	–	–	–	–	1	1	–	–	–
FUNNY IDEA THOUGH	1	–	1	–	–	–	–	–	–
GARBAGE	–	–	–	–	1	1	–	–	–
GENTLE	–	–	–	1	–	1	–	–	–
GO	–	1	1	–	–	–	–	–	–
GOOD	4	3	7	3	5	8	5	1	6
GOODER	–	–	–	1	–	1	–	1	1
GRASS	1	1	2	–	–	–	–	–	–
GREEN	–	1	1	–	–	–	–	–	–
GROUCHY	–	–	–	–	–	–	1	–	1
HAND	–	1	1	–	–	–	–	–	–
HAPPY	–	–	–	–	–	–	1	1	2
HARD	1	1	2	2	4	6	5	3	8
HARSH	–	–	–	–	–	–	1	2	3
HASTILY	–	–	–	–	–	–	–	1	1
HAT	–	1	1	–	–	–	–	–	–
HE	–	1	1	–	1	1	–	–	–
HERE	–	1	1	–	–	–	–	–	–
HIGH	1	–	1	–	–	–	–	–	–
HIT	1	–	1	–	–	–	–	–	–
HITTER	1	–	1	–	–	–	–	1	1
HONEY	–	1	1	–	1	1	–	1	1
HORRIBLE	–	–	–	–	–	–	–	1	1
HOT	1	1	2	–	–	–	–	–	–
HOUSE	1	–	1	–	–	–	–	–	–
I CANT THINK	–	–	–	–	1	1	–	–	–
ICING	–	–	–	1	–	1	–	–	–
IT DOESNT GOT NO SUGAR	–	1	1	–	–	–	–	–	–
JIMMY	–	–	–	–	–	–	–	1	1
JUICY	–	–	–	1	–	1	–	–	–
JUMPER	–	1	1	–	–	–	–	–	–
KAY	1	–	1	–	–	–	–	–	–
KEEP YOUR BABY SISTER FROM GOING OUT IN.	–	1	1	–	–	–	–	–	–
KETTLE	1	–	1	–	–	–	–	–	–
KIND	–	–	–	–	2	2	–	–	–
KITTEN	–	1	1	–	–	–	–	–	–
KITTER	3	–	3	–	–	–	–	–	–
LEMAN	–	–	–	–	–	–	1	–	1
LEMON	–	1	1	–	–	–	1	–	1
LIGHT	–	1	1	–	–	–	–	–	–
LIP	1	–	1	–	–	–	–	–	–
LITTER	3	3	6	2	4	6	–	–	–
LITTERBUG	–	1	1	–	–	–	–	–	–
LITTLE	–	3	3	–	–	–	–	–	–
LITTLE PERSON	1	–	1	–	–	–	–	–	–
LOOK	–	1	1	–	–	–	–	–	–
MAD	–	–	–	–	–	–	–	1	1
MAIL	1	–	1	–	–	–	–	–	–
ME	–	–	–	–	–	–	1	–	1
MEAN	–	–	–	–	1	1	–	–	–

RESPONSE WORD	1ST M	F	T	3RD M	F	T	5TH M	F	T

10. BITTER

RESPONSE WORD	1ST M	F	T	3RD M	F	T	5TH M	F	T
MILK	1	–	1	–	–	–	–	–	–
MINE	–	–	–	1	–	1	–	–	–
MINT	–	1	1	–	–	–	–	–	–
MITTEN	1	–	1	–	–	–	–	–	–
MITTER	1	–	1	–	–	–	–	–	–
MIXING	1	–	1	–	–	–	–	–	–
MOCK	–	1	1	–	–	–	–	–	–
MOSQUITO	–	1	1	–	–	–	–	–	–
MOVE	–	–	–	1	–	1	–	–	–
MOVIE	–	–	–	–	–	–	1	–	1
NASTY	–	–	–	–	–	–	–	1	1
NEVER	–	–	–	–	1	1	–	–	–
NICE	1	1	2	–	1	1	–	1	1
NO	–	–	–	–	–	–	1	–	1
NO RESPONSE	–	–	–	–	1	1	–	–	–
NO TASTE	–	–	–	–	–	–	1	–	1
NOT	–	2	2	–	–	–	1	–	1
NOT BETTER	–	–	–	–	–	–	–	1	1
NOT BITTER	2	–	2	–	–	–	–	–	–
NOT GOOD	–	–	–	1	–	1	–	–	–
NOT NICE	–	–	–	1	–	1	–	–	–
NOT SWEET	–	–	–	1	–	1	–	2	2
NOT TASTE	–	–	–	–	–	–	1	–	1
NOT TASTING GOOD	–	–	–	–	–	–	2	–	2
NOW	–	1	1	–	–	–	–	–	–
OH	–	1	1	–	–	–	–	–	–
ORANGE	1	–	1	–	–	–	–	–	–
OUCH	1	–	1	–	–	–	–	–	–
PAPER	–	1	1	1	–	1	–	–	–
PAT A CAT	1	–	1	–	–	–	–	–	–
PEANUT BUTTER	–	–	–	–	1	1	–	–	–
PEOPLE	1	–	1	–	–	–	–	–	–
PEPPER	1	–	1	–	1	1	–	–	–
PICK-UP	–	2	2	–	–	–	–	–	–
PICKLE	–	–	–	–	1	1	–	–	–
PICTURE	1	–	1	–	–	–	–	–	–
PILL	–	–	–	–	–	–	1	–	1
PITTED	1	–	1	–	–	–	–	–	–
PUMP	–	1	1	–	–	–	–	–	–
PUT IN GLASS	1	–	1	–	–	–	–	–	–
RAT	–	–	–	–	1	1	–	–	–
RED	–	–	–	1	–	1	–	–	–
REFRIGERATOR	1	–	1	–	–	–	–	–	–
RICHARD	1	–	1	–	–	–	–	–	–
RITTER	–	2	2	–	–	–	–	–	–
ROUGH	–	–	–	–	–	–	1	–	1
ROUGHER	–	–	–	–	1	1	–	–	–
SAD	–	–	–	1	–	1	–	–	–
SALAD	1	–	1	–	–	–	–	–	–
SALT	1	–	1	–	–	–	–	–	–
SALTY	–	–	–	–	1	1	–	–	–
SANDWICH	–	–	–	1	–	1	–	–	–
SAWLER	–	–	–	–	–	–	–	1	1
SCHOOL	–	1	1	–	–	–	–	–	–
SHOR	–	–	–	–	–	–	1	–	1
SICK	–	1	1	–	1	1	–	–	–
SIDEWALK	1	–	1	–	–	–	–	–	–
SILKY	–	–	–	–	1	1	–	–	–
SIT BETTER	1	–	1	–	–	–	–	–	–
SITTER	1	–	1	3	–	3	–	–	–
SITTING	–	–	–	–	1	1	–	–	–
SKIPPER	–	–	–	–	–	–	–	1	1
SMALL	–	–	–	1	–	1	–	–	–
SNITTER	1	–	1	–	–	–	–	–	–
SOFT	1	–	1	–	1	1	1	–	1
SOFTY	–	–	–	–	1	1	–	–	–
SOMEBODY BIT A GIRL	–	1	1	–	–	–	–	–	–
SOMETHING	–	1	1	–	–	–	–	–	–
SONG	–	–	–	–	1	1	–	–	–
SOUR	4	7	11	32	27	59	47	36	83
SOWER	–	–	–	–	–	–	1	–	1
SPIDER	–	1	1	–	–	–	–	–	–

RESPONSE WORD	1ST M	F	T	3RD M	F	T	5TH M	F	T

10. BITTER

RESPONSE WORD	1ST M	F	T	3RD M	F	T	5TH M	F	T
STINK	–	–	–	1	–	1	–	–	–
STRONG	–	–	–	1	–	1	–	3	3
STUFF	1	–	1	–	–	–	–	–	–
SUN	1	–	1	–	–	–	–	–	–
SWEET	9	8	17	25	27	52	23	38	61
SWEETER	–	–	–	1	–	1	–	–	–
SWEETLY	–	–	–	–	–	–	–	1	1
TABLE	–	1	1	–	–	–	–	1	1
TALK	–	–	–	–	–	–	–	1	1
TARTY	–	–	–	–	–	–	–	1	1
TASTE	–	1	1	8	2	10	3	2	5
TASTES BAD	–	–	–	–	1	1	–	–	–
TASTING	–	–	–	1	–	1	1	1	2
TASTY	–	–	–	–	–	–	–	2	2
TATTER	1	–	1	–	–	–	–	–	–
TEA	–	1	1	–	–	–	–	–	–
TEACHER	–	–	–	–	–	–	1	–	1
TEETH	–	–	–	1	–	1	–	–	–
TERRIBLE	–	–	–	–	2	2	3	1	4
THE	1	–	1	–	–	–	–	–	–
THICK	–	1	1	–	–	–	–	–	–
THINK	–	–	–	1	–	1	–	–	–
TITTER	–	–	–	–	–	–	1	–	1
TONGUE	–	1	1	–	–	–	–	–	–
TOUCH	–	1	1	–	–	–	–	–	–
TREE	1	–	1	–	–	–	–	–	–
UGLY	–	–	–	–	–	–	1	–	1
UNTASTY	–	–	–	–	–	–	1	1	2
UP	–	1	1	–	–	–	–	–	–
VERY	–	–	–	–	–	–	–	1	1
VINEGAR	1	–	1	–	–	–	–	–	–
WAKE	–	1	1	–	–	–	–	–	–
WALL	1	–	1	–	1	1	–	–	–
WARM	1	1	2	–	–	–	–	–	–
WATER	1	–	1	–	–	–	–	–	–
WEATHER	–	–	–	1	–	1	–	–	–
WET	–	–	–	–	–	–	1	–	1
WHEN ITS MEAN	–	1	1	–	–	–	–	–	–
WHOLE	–	–	–	–	1	1	–	–	–
WINDOW	–	1	1	–	–	–	–	–	–
WINDOWS	1	–	1	–	–	–	–	–	–
WINTER	2	1	3	1	–	1	–	1	1
WORK	–	1	1	–	–	–	–	–	–

11. BLACK

RESPONSE WORD	1ST M	F	T	3RD M	F	T	5TH M	F	T
A COLOR	–	–	–	–	–	–	–	1	1
BACK	–	2	2	–	2	2	–	1	1
BALL	–	1	1	–	–	–	–	–	–
BAT	1	–	1	–	–	–	–	–	–
BEAR	–	–	–	–	1	1	–	–	–
BEARD	1	–	1	–	–	–	–	–	–
BECAUSE	–	–	–	1	–	1	–	–	–
BED	–	–	–	–	–	–	–	1	1
BEE	2	–	2	–	–	–	–	–	–
BIRD	5	2	7	–	–	–	–	–	–
BLACK	1	–	1	–	–	–	–	–	–
BLACK DOG	–	–	–	–	–	–	–	1	1
BLND	–	–	–	–	–	–	1	–	1
BLOCK	–	1	1	–	–	–	–	–	–
BLUE	12	15	27	10	6	16	5	2	7
BLUE-GREEN	–	–	–	1	–	1	–	–	–
BOARD	–	–	–	1	–	1	–	–	–
BOOK	1	–	1	–	–	–	–	–	–
BOY	–	1	1	–	–	–	–	–	–
BRIGHT	1	–	1	–	–	–	–	–	–
BRING	–	–	–	–	–	–	1	–	1
BROWN	7	13	20	1	4	5	5	–	5
BUBBLE	–	1	1	–	–	–	–	–	–
BUG	–	1	1	1	–	1	–	–	–
BUGGER	–	–	–	–	–	–	1	–	1

RESPONSE WORD	1ST M	1ST F	1ST T	3RD M	3RD F	3RD T	5TH M	5TH F	5TH T

11. BLACK

RESPONSE WORD	1ST M	1ST F	1ST T	3RD M	3RD F	3RD T	5TH M	5TH F	5TH T
BUN	–	1	1	–	–	–	–	–	–
CAKE	1	–	1	1	–	1	–	–	–
CAR	1	1	2	–	–	–	–	–	–
CAT	5	11	16	3	8	11	6	4	10
CHAIR	1	–	1	–	–	–	–	–	–
CLOUD	–	–	–	–	–	–	–	1	1
CLOUDS	1	–	1	–	–	–	–	–	–
COAL	1	–	1	–	–	–	–	–	–
COFFEE	–	–	–	–	–	–	1	–	1
COLAR	–	–	–	–	–	–	1	–	1
COLOR	3	3	6	16	7	23	29	22	51
COLOR YOUR PICTURE	–	1	1	–	–	–	–	–	–
COLORLESS	–	–	–	–	–	–	1	–	1
COMB	–	–	–	–	1	1	–	–	–
CRAYON	6	6	12	2	1	3	–	4	4
CRIB	–	1	1	–	–	–	–	–	–
CROW	1	–	1	–	–	–	1	–	1
CUT	–	1	1	–	–	–	–	–	–
DACK	–	1	1	–	–	–	–	–	–
DARK	6	6	12	8	13	21	6	14	20
DESK	1	–	1	–	–	–	–	–	–
DOG	2	2	4	2	1	3	–	–	–
DONT TOUCH IT	–	1	1	–	–	–	–	–	–
DOOR	1	–	1	–	–	–	–	–	–
DRESS	–	–	–	–	–	–	–	1	1
DUCK	–	1	1	–	–	–	–	–	–
EAGLE	2	–	2	–	–	–	–	–	–
FLAG	–	1	1	–	–	–	–	–	–
FLY	–	1	1	–	–	–	–	–	–
FRIGHT	–	1	1	–	–	–	–	–	–
FRONT	–	–	–	–	–	–	–	1	1
FROWN	–	–	–	1	–	1	–	–	–
GNAT	–	1	1	–	–	–	–	–	–
GOLD	–	–	–	–	1	1	–	–	–
GRAY	–	–	–	1	1	2	–	–	–
GREEN	4	3	7	2	1	3	–	1	1
GREY	1	–	1	–	–	–	1	–	1
HACK	4	–	4	–	–	–	–	–	–
HAIR	1	1	2	–	–	–	–	1	1
HALLOWEEN	–	–	–	1	–	1	–	–	–
HANGER	–	–	–	1	–	1	–	–	–
HAT	1	1	2	–	–	–	–	–	–
HEAR	–	1	1	–	–	–	–	–	–
HOUSE	1	–	1	–	–	–	–	–	–
ICE CREAM	1	–	1	–	–	–	–	–	–
IS A CRAYON	1	–	1	–	–	–	–	–	–
JACK	1	1	2	–	–	–	1	–	1
JET	1	–	1	–	–	–	–	–	–
KENT	1	–	1	–	–	–	–	–	–
KITTEN	–	–	–	–	–	–	–	1	1
KNACK	–	–	–	1	–	1	–	–	–
LIGHT	3	–	3	–	1	1	–	–	–
LIKES	–	1	1	–	–	–	–	–	–
LITTLE	–	1	1	–	–	–	–	–	–
MAC	1	–	1	–	–	–	–	–	–
MACK	2	–	2	–	–	–	–	1	1
MARK	–	–	–	–	–	–	1	–	1
MUD	–	1	1	–	–	–	–	–	–
NEED	–	–	–	–	–	–	–	1	1
NIGHT	1	1	2	1	1	2	3	2	5
NOT	–	–	–	1	–	1	–	–	–
NOT ENOUGH	–	–	–	–	–	–	1	–	1
ORANGE	2	2	4	–	–	–	–	–	–
PACK	–	1	1	–	–	–	–	–	–
PAINT	1	1	2	–	–	–	–	–	–
PAPER	1	1	2	–	1	1	1	–	1
PEN	1	–	1	–	–	–	–	–	–
PENCIL	1	–	1	–	–	–	–	–	–
PERSON	–	–	–	–	–	–	–	1	1
PINK	–	1	1	1	–	1	–	–	–
PIRATE	–	–	–	–	–	–	–	1	1
PLANE	–	–	–	1	–	1	–	–	–

11. BLACK

RESPONSE WORD	1ST M	F	T	3RD M	F	T	5TH M	F	T
PLANET	—	1	1	—	—	—	—	—	—
POCKET	—	1	1	—	—	—	—	—	—
POCKET BOOK	—	1	1	—	—	—	—	—	—
PUPPY	1	—	1	—	—	—	—	—	—
PURPLE	—	2	2	1	—	1	—	2	2
RACK	1	1	2	—	—	—	—	—	—
RAT	—	1	1	—	—	—	—	—	—
RED	3	2	5	3	7	10	7	3	10
RIBBON	1	—	1	—	—	—	—	—	—
RING	—	1	1	—	—	—	—	—	—
ROAD BLOCK	1	—	1	—	—	—	—	—	—
RON	—	—	—	—	—	—	1	—	1
ROOM	1	—	1	—	—	—	—	—	—
ROUND	—	2	2	—	—	—	—	—	—
SACK	2	—	2	1	1	2	—	—	—
SEE	1	1	2	—	—	—	—	—	—
SHACK	1	—	1	—	—	—	—	—	—
SHADE	—	—	—	—	—	—	—	1	1
SHEEP	—	1	1	—	—	—	—	—	—
SHIRT	—	1	1	—	—	—	—	—	—
SHOE	—	2	2	—	1	1	—	—	—
SHOES	—	—	—	—	—	—	—	1	1
SHOES ARE BLACK	—	1	1	—	—	—	—	—	—
SINK	1	—	1	—	—	—	—	—	—
SKY	2	—	2	—	—	—	—	—	—
SNAKE	1	—	1	—	—	—	—	—	—
SOMETHING BLACK ON THE STREET AND THEN	—	1	1	—	—	—	—	—	—
SPAT	1	—	1	—	—	—	—	—	—
SPECK	—	—	—	—	1	1	—	—	—
SPIDER	1	—	1	—	—	—	—	—	—
STACK	—	—	—	1	—	1	—	—	—
STALLION	—	—	—	—	—	—	—	1	1
STORE	—	—	—	—	—	—	1	—	1
STRENGTH	—	—	—	—	—	—	—	1	1
STUFF	1	—	1	—	—	—	—	—	—
SUN	2	—	2	—	—	—	—	—	—
TABLE	—	1	1	—	—	—	—	—	—
TACK	1	—	1	—	—	—	—	—	—
TELEVISION	—	—	—	—	—	—	—	1	1
THEY	—	—	—	—	—	—	1	—	1
TIRE	1	1	2	—	—	—	—	—	—
TRAIN	1	1	2	—	—	—	—	—	—
TRUCK	—	—	—	2	—	2	—	—	—
TRY	—	—	—	1	—	1	—	—	—
WACK	1	1	2	—	—	—	—	—	—
WALL	1	—	1	—	—	—	—	—	—
WASH	—	1	1	—	—	—	—	—	—
WAX	1	—	1	—	—	—	—	—	—
WHACK	—	—	—	2	—	2	—	—	—
WHEN YOU BLACKEN SOMETHING	1	—	1	—	—	—	—	—	—
WHILE	—	—	—	—	1	1	—	—	—
WHITE	16	18	34	65	74	139	61	66	127
WITH	—	—	—	—	1	1	—	—	—
WRITE	—	—	—	—	—	—	1	—	1
YELLOW	2	4	6	7	4	11	2	2	4
YOU COLOR PAPER BLACK	1	—	1	—	—	—	—	—	—
YOUR COLOR	—	1	1	—	—	—	—	—	—

RESPONSE WORD	1ST			3RD			5TH		
	M	F	T	M	F	T	M	F	T

12. BRIGHT

RESPONSE WORD	M	F	T	M	F	T	M	F	T
A LIGHT	—	—	—	—	—	—	1	1	2
BARS	1	—	1	—	—	—	—	—	—
BEAUTIFUL	—	—	—	—	1	1	—	—	—
BED	1	—	1	—	1	1	—	—	—
BEE	1	—	1	—	—	—	—	—	—
BICYCLE	1	—	1	—	—	—	—	—	—
BIKE	1	—	1	—	—	—	—	—	—
BIRD	—	1	1	—	—	—	—	—	—
BITE	—	1	1	1	—	1	—	—	—
BLACK	—	—	—	2	1	3	—	1	1
BLACKBOARD	—	1	1	—	—	—	—	—	—
BLIGHT	1	—	1	—	—	—	—	—	—
BLOND	—	1	1	—	—	—	—	—	—
BLUE	2	1	3	—	—	—	1	—	1
BOOK	2	1	3	—	1	1	—	—	—
BOW	—	1	1	—	—	—	—	—	—
BREAK	1	—	1	—	—	—	—	—	—
BRIGHTER	—	—	—	—	1	1	—	—	—
BRILLIANT	—	—	—	—	—	—	2	2	4
BROKE	—	—	—	—	—	—	1	—	1
BROKEN	—	—	—	—	—	—	—	1	1
BROUGHT	1	—	1	—	—	—	—	—	—
BROWN	2	—	2	—	—	—	—	—	—
CAR	—	1	1	—	—	—	—	—	—
CHAIR	1	—	1	—	—	—	—	—	—
CLEAR	—	—	—	1	2	3	—	—	—
CLEVER	—	—	—	1	1	2	—	—	—
CLOUD	—	—	—	—	—	—	1	—	1
CLOUDY	—	1	1	—	—	—	—	1	1
COLOR	—	—	—	3	2	5	5	6	11
COLORFUL	—	—	—	—	1	1	5	—	5
COLORS	—	—	—	—	—	—	—	1	1
COME	1	—	1	—	—	—	—	—	—
COOL	1	—	1	—	—	—	—	—	—
COUNT	—	1	1	—	—	—	—	—	—
DARK	15	21	36	43	43	86	28	36	64
DAY	1	1	2	2	3	5	3	—	3
DAYLIGHT	1	1	2	—	—	—	—	—	—
DESK	1	—	1	—	—	—	—	—	—
DIGHT	—	1	1	—	—	—	—	—	—
DIM	—	—	—	1	—	1	4	4	8
DOG	2	—	2	1	—	1	—	—	—
DOLL	—	—	—	—	1	1	1	1	2
DONT	—	1	1	—	—	—	—	—	—
DRAWER	1	—	1	—	—	—	—	—	—
DULL	—	—	—	2	4	6	6	6	12
DUMB	—	—	—	—	—	—	1	2	3
EARLY	—	—	—	2	4	6	1	—	1
EAT	—	—	—	—	—	—	1	—	1
EIGHT	1	—	1	—	—	—	—	—	—
FAST	—	1	1	—	—	—	—	—	—
FATHER	—	1	1	—	—	—	—	—	—
FIGHT	1	1	2	—	—	—	—	—	—
FINGERNAILS	—	1	1	—	—	—	—	—	—
FIRE	1	—	1	—	—	—	—	—	—
GARBAGE	—	1	1	—	—	—	—	—	—
GAY	1	—	1	—	2	2	2	—	2
GLAD	—	—	—	—	—	—	—	1	1
GLASS	—	—	—	—	1	1	—	1	—
GLAZE	—	—	—	—	—	—	—	1	1
GOOD	—	1	1	1	1	2	—	—	—
GRAKE	—	—	—	—	—	—	1	—	1
GRASS	—	1	1	—	—	—	—	—	—
GREEN	—	—	—	1	—	1	1	—	1
HAIR	—	1	1	—	—	—	1	—	1
HAIR BARRETTE	—	—	—	—	—	—	—	1	1
HALL	1	—	1	—	—	—	—	—	—
HAPPY	—	—	—	—	1	1	—	1	1
HEIGHT	1	—	1	1	—	1	—	—	—
HERE	1	—	1	—	—	—	—	—	—
IDEAS	—	—	—	—	—	—	—	1	1
IN SUN	1	—	1	—	—	—	—	—	—

12. BRIGHT

RESPONSE WORD	1ST M	F	T	3RD M	F	T	5TH M	F	T
IN THE BRIGHT EVENING	–	1	1	–	–	–	–	–	–
IN THE MORNING	–	1	1	–	–	–	–	–	–
INDIAN	1	–	1	–	–	–	–	–	–
ITS LIGHT OUTSIDE	–	–	–	–	–	–	–	1	1
JANE	1	–	1	–	–	–	–	–	–
KITE	2	2	4	1	–	1	–	–	–
LARGE	–	–	–	–	1	1	–	–	–
LEFT	1	–	1	–	–	–	–	–	–
LETTER	–	–	–	–	–	–	1	–	1
LIGHT	21	16	37	28	41	69	24	30	54
LIGHTLY	–	–	–	1	–	1	–	–	–
LOOK	1	–	1	–	–	–	–	–	–
LOUD	–	–	–	–	–	–	1	1	2
LOW	–	1	1	–	–	–	1	–	1
LY	–	–	–	–	–	–	1	–	1
MAKE	–	1	1	–	–	–	–	–	–
MATE	–	1	1	–	–	–	–	–	–
MIGHT	3	2	5	–	1	1	–	–	–
MIKE	1	–	1	–	–	–	–	–	–
MOON	1	2	3	–	–	–	–	–	–
MORNING	3	4	7	2	2	4	–	–	–
MUSIC	–	–	–	–	–	–	1	–	1
MY	1	–	1	–	–	–	–	–	–
NAME	–	–	–	–	–	–	1	–	1
NICE	–	–	–	–	–	–	–	1	1
NIG	–	–	–	–	–	–	1	–	1
NIGHT	–	2	2	3	–	3	1	1	2
NOON	–	–	–	1	–	1	–	–	–
NOT BRIGHT	2	–	2	–	–	–	–	–	–
NOT DARK	–	–	–	–	–	–	1	–	1
NOT DULL	–	–	–	–	–	–	1	–	1
NOT DUMB	–	–	–	–	–	–	–	1	1
NUMBER	1	–	1	–	–	–	–	–	–
ON THE BALL	–	–	–	–	–	–	1	–	1
ORANGE	2	–	2	–	–	–	–	–	–
OUT	–	1	1	1	–	1	–	–	–
OUTSIDE	–	1	1	–	–	–	–	–	–
PAINT	–	–	–	–	–	–	1	–	1
PEANUT	–	1	1	–	–	–	–	–	–
PENCIL	2	–	2	–	2	2	–	–	–
PIGHT	–	1	1	–	–	–	–	–	–
PIN	1	–	1	–	–	–	–	–	–
POCKETBOOK	–	1	1	–	–	–	–	–	–
PRETTY	1	1	2	–	1	1	1	1	2
PRINT	–	–	–	1	–	1	1	–	1
PURPLE	–	–	–	–	–	–	1	–	1
RABBITS ARE BRIGHT	–	1	1	–	–	–	–	–	–
RAIL	1	–	1	–	–	–	–	–	–
RAIN	–	1	1	–	–	–	–	–	–
REAL BRIGHT	–	1	1	–	–	–	–	–	–
RED	–	–	–	–	–	–	2	4	6
RIDING	1	–	1	–	–	–	–	–	–
RIGHT	2	4	6	2	1	3	–	1	1
RIPE	–	–	–	–	1	1	–	–	–
RON	–	–	–	–	–	–	1	–	1
SAD	1	–	1	–	–	–	–	–	–
SAKE	–	–	–	1	–	1	–	–	–
SCALED	–	–	–	–	–	–	1	–	1
SEAT	1	–	1	–	–	–	–	–	–
SHADE	1	–	1	–	–	–	–	–	–
SHARP	–	–	–	–	–	–	–	1	1
SHINE	–	2	2	–	1	1	2	3	5
SHINING	1	–	1	1	–	1	1	–	1
SHINY	–	–	–	5	6	11	5	–	5
SKY	–	3	3	–	1	1	–	–	–
SMALL	1	1	2	–	–	–	–	–	–
SMART	1	–	1	5	–	5	11	5	16
SOFT	–	–	–	–	–	–	–	1	1
SORRY	1	–	1	–	–	–	–	–	–
SPARKLE	–	–	–	1	–	1	–	2	2
SPARKLING	–	–	–	–	–	–	–	1	1
SPILL	–	–	–	–	–	–	1	–	1

RESPONSE WORD	1ST M	1ST F	1ST T	3RD M	3RD F	3RD T	5TH M	5TH F	5TH T

12. BRIGHT

RESPONSE WORD	M	F	T	M	F	T	M	F	T
SPMOT	–	–	–	–	–	–	1	–	1
SPRAY ON SOMEBODY	–	1	1	–	–	–	–	–	–
SPRINKLE	–	1	1	–	–	–	–	–	–
STAR	1	–	1	–	1	1	2	1	3
STARS	1	1	2	–	1	1	–	–	–
STRIKE	1	–	1	–	–	–	–	–	–
STRONG	–	–	–	1	–	1	–	–	–
STUPID	–	–	–	1	–	1	1	2	3
SUM	1	–	1	–	–	–	–	–	–
SUMMER	–	1	1	–	–	–	–	–	–
SUN	19	23	42	13	7	20	6	10	16
SUNDAY	1	–	1	–	–	–	–	–	–
SUNNY	2	3	5	1	–	1	–	3	3
SUNSHINE	–	2	2	2	–	2	–	–	–
SWEET	1	–	1	–	–	–	–	–	–
TABLE	1	1	2	–	–	–	–	–	–
THE	–	1	1	–	–	–	–	–	–
THE CEMENT WILL GET CLEAN AND YOU CAN G.	–	1	1	–	–	–	–	–	–
THE SUN IS BRIGHT	–	–	–	1	–	1	–	–	–
THE SUNS SO BRIGHT	–	1	1	–	–	–	–	–	–
THEN	1	–	1	1	–	1	–	–	–
THEY	1	–	1	–	–	–	–	–	–
THINGS	1	–	1	–	–	–	–	–	–
THOSE	1	–	1	–	–	–	–	–	–
THREE	1	1	2	–	–	–	–	–	–
TIGHT	1	1	2	–	–	–	–	–	–
TIM	–	–	–	–	–	–	–	1	1
TOO BRIGHT	–	1	1	–	–	–	–	–	–
TOOTH PICKS	–	–	–	1	–	1	–	–	–
TREE	1	–	1	–	–	–	–	–	–
TURN	–	1	1	–	–	–	–	–	–
UNBRIGHT	–	–	–	1	–	1	–	–	–
UP	–	1	1	–	–	–	–	–	–
WALL	–	1	1	–	–	–	–	–	–
WALRUS	–	–	–	1	–	1	–	–	–
WARM	–	–	–	–	1	1	–	–	–
WATER	1	–	1	–	–	–	–	–	–
WAY	–	1	1	–	–	–	–	–	–
WHEN YOU BRIGHTEN SOME CLOTHES.	1	–	1	–	–	–	–	–	–
WHITE	1	–	1	1	–	1	–	–	–
WOOD	–	–	–	–	–	–	–	1	1
WORK	–	–	–	1	–	1	–	–	–
WRITE	–	–	–	1	–	1	–	1	1
WRITE IS ON A PENCIL	–	1	1	–	–	–	–	–	–
YELLOW	–	1	1	–	1	1	2	–	2

13. BUG

RESPONSE WORD	M	F	T	M	F	T	M	F	T
A BEE	–	–	–	1	–	1	–	–	–
AMINAL	–	–	–	–	–	–	–	1	1
AN INSECT	–	–	–	–	–	–	–	1	1
ANIMAL	–	–	–	8	7	15	4	7	11
ANT	4	2	6	2	5	7	8	5	13
ANTE	–	–	–	–	–	–	1	–	1
ANTS	–	–	–	–	1	1	–	–	–
ARE DANGEROUS	–	1	1	–	–	–	–	–	–
AT	–	1	1	–	–	–	–	–	–
AWFUL	–	–	–	–	–	–	1	–	1
BACK	–	1	1	–	–	–	–	–	–
BALL	–	1	1	–	–	–	–	–	–
BAR	–	–	–	–	–	–	–	1	1
BED	2	1	3	–	1	1	–	–	–
BEE	5	9	14	12	11	23	4	2	6
BEETLE	–	2	2	5	4	9	7	7	14
BIG	2	–	2	–	1	1	1	–	1
BIKE	–	1	1	–	–	–	–	–	–
BIRD	–	–	–	1	–	1	2	–	2
BIT	2	1	3	–	–	–	–	1	1
BITE	2	1	3	–	–	–	–	–	–

13. BUG

RESPONSE WORD	1ST M	F	T	3RD M	F	T	5TH M	F	T
BITES	1	–	1	–	1	1	–	–	–
BLACK	–	1	1	–	–	–	1	1	2
BOAT	2	–	2	–	–	–	–	–	–
BOOK	2	–	2	–	–	–	–	–	–
BOTHER	–	–	–	–	–	–	–	1	1
BRIGHT	–	–	–	–	–	–	–	1	1
BROWN	1	–	1	–	–	–	–	–	–
BUD	1	–	1	–	–	–	–	–	–
BUG	–	–	–	–	–	–	–	1	1
BUGGY	1	1	2	2	–	2	1	–	1
BUGS CRAWL	1	–	1	–	–	–	–	–	–
BUS	–	1	1	1	1	2	–	–	–
BUTTER	1	–	1	–	–	–	–	–	–
BUTTERFLY	5	4	9	1	2	3	1	4	5
CAR	–	–	–	–	1	1	–	–	–
CAT	1	–	1	–	1	1	–	1	1
CATCH	4	–	4	–	–	–	–	–	–
CHAIR	1	–	1	–	–	–	–	–	–
CLEAN	–	1	1	–	–	–	–	–	–
CLIMB	–	1	1	–	–	–	–	–	–
CLIMBING	–	–	–	–	1	1	–	–	–
CLOG	1	–	1	–	–	–	–	–	–
CLOSE	–	–	–	–	–	–	1	–	1
COAT	1	–	1	1	–	1	–	–	–
COLLAR	–	1	1	–	–	–	–	–	–
COTTON	–	–	–	–	1	1	–	–	–
COULD FALL ON THE FLOOR	–	1	1	–	–	–	–	–	–
CRACK	1	–	1	–	–	–	–	–	–
CRAWL	5	1	6	1	1	2	–	1	1
CRAWLING	–	–	–	1	–	1	–	–	–
CRAWLS	1	–	1	–	–	–	–	–	–
CRAWLS ON THE FLOOR	–	1	1	–	–	–	–	–	–
CREATURE	–	–	–	–	–	–	1	–	1
CRICKET	–	–	–	–	–	–	–	1	1
CUD	–	1	1	–	–	–	–	–	–
CUP	–	–	–	–	1	1	–	–	–
DADDY LONG LEG	–	–	–	–	1	1	–	–	–
DEAD	–	–	–	1	–	1	–	–	–
DIDNT	–	–	–	1	–	1	–	–	–
DIRTY	1	–	1	–	1	1	–	–	–
DOG	1	–	1	1	–	1	2	–	2
DONT PLAY AROUND AND YOU MIGHT BUST A J	–	1	1	–	–	–	–	–	–
DUG	2	1	3	–	–	–	–	1	1
EAT YOUR LEG	–	1	1	–	–	–	–	–	–
FLIES	2	1	3	–	–	–	–	–	–
FLIES AROUND	1	–	1	–	–	–	–	–	–
FLY	11	22	33	16	20	36	9	12	21
GASOLINE STATION	1	–	1	–	–	–	–	–	–
GEED	–	–	–	–	–	–	1	–	1
GET OFF ME	1	–	1	–	–	–	–	–	–
GLUB	1	–	1	–	–	–	–	–	–
GO	–	1	1	–	–	–	–	–	–
GOES	–	1	1	–	–	–	–	–	–
GRASS	1	–	1	–	–	–	–	1	1
GRASSHOPPER	–	1	1	1	–	1	–	1	1
HARMLESS	–	–	–	–	–	–	–	1	1
HER	–	–	–	–	1	1	–	–	–
HIT	1	–	1	–	–	–	–	–	–
HIVE	–	–	–	–	–	–	1	–	1
HORSE	1	3	4	–	–	–	–	–	–
HOUSE	1	–	1	1	–	1	–	–	–
HUB	1	–	1	–	–	–	–	–	–
HUG	3	1	4	1	–	1	1	–	1
HURT	1	1	2	–	–	–	–	–	–
I DONT	–	–	–	–	1	1	–	–	–
INCAH	–	–	–	–	–	–	1	–	1
INSECK	–	–	–	–	–	–	1	–	1
INSECT	16	18	34	63	56	119	74	67	141
INSECTS	–	–	–	4	2	6	–	–	–
IT	1	–	1	–	–	–	–	–	–
ITCH	–	1	1	–	–	–	–	–	–

RESPONSE WORD	1ST			3RD			5TH		
	M	F	T	M	F	T	M	F	T

13. BUG

RESPONSE WORD	1ST M	F	T	3RD M	F	T	5TH M	F	T
JAPANESE BEETLE	–	–	–	–	–	–	1	–	1
JUG	1	1	2	–	–	–	–	1	1
KIDS	1	–	1	–	–	–	–	–	–
KILL	2	1	3	–	–	–	–	–	–
KILLER	1	–	1	–	–	–	–	–	–
KNIT	–	–	–	–	–	–	1	–	1
LADYBIRD	1	–	1	–	–	–	–	–	–
LADYBUG	1	1	2	–	–	–	–	–	–
LARGE	–	–	–	–	–	–	1	–	1
LEGS	–	–	–	–	1	1	–	–	–
LETS CATCH FLIES	–	1	1	–	–	–	–	–	–
LISTEN	–	–	–	–	–	–	–	1	1
LITTLE	3	2	5	–	–	–	–	1	1
LITTLE CREATURE	–	–	–	–	–	–	1	–	1
LOG	–	–	–	1	–	1	–	–	–
LOSE	–	1	1	–	–	–	–	–	–
LOVE	1	–	1	–	–	–	–	–	–
LUG	–	1	1	–	–	–	–	–	–
LUNCH	–	–	–	–	–	–	1	–	1
MAN	1	1	2	–	–	–	–	–	–
ME	4	–	4	–	–	–	–	–	–
MILK	–	1	1	–	–	–	–	–	–
MOP	–	2	2	–	–	–	–	–	–
MOSQUITO	–	1	1	1	3	4	–	–	–
MOTH	–	1	1	3	3	6	2	3	5
MOTHER	–	1	1	–	–	–	–	–	–
MOVE	–	1	1	–	–	–	–	–	–
MUG	2	1	3	1	1	2	–	–	–
NOISE	–	–	–	–	1	1	–	–	–
NOVE	–	–	–	–	–	–	1	–	1
NOW	–	1	1	–	–	–	–	–	–
NUG	–	1	1	–	–	–	–	–	–
OUT	–	–	–	–	–	–	–	1	1
OUTSIDE	–	–	–	–	–	–	–	1	1
PEACH	–	–	–	1	–	1	–	–	–
PESTY ANIMAL	–	–	–	–	–	–	–	1	1
PIG	2	–	2	1	–	1	–	–	–
PUG	1	–	1	–	–	–	–	–	–
PURSE	–	1	1	–	–	–	–	–	–
RAG	1	–	1	–	–	–	–	–	–
RAT	–	–	–	–	–	–	1	–	1
RED	–	1	1	–	–	–	–	–	–
RIDE FAST	1	–	1	–	–	–	–	–	–
ROACH	1	2	3	–	–	–	1	2	3
ROACHES	–	–	–	1	–	1	–	–	–
ROAD	–	–	–	–	1	1	–	–	–
ROSE	–	1	1	–	–	–	–	–	–
RUG	1	1	2	1	–	1	1	3	4
RUSH	–	–	–	–	–	–	–	1	1
SAILBOAT	–	1	1	–	–	–	–	–	–
SCARE	–	1	1	–	–	–	–	–	–
SCAT	1	–	1	–	–	–	–	–	–
SEAT	1	–	1	–	–	–	–	–	–
SHIRT	1	–	1	–	–	–	–	–	–
SICK	1	–	1	–	–	–	–	–	–
SICKNESS	–	–	–	–	–	–	1	–	1
SIMPLE	–	1	1	–	–	–	–	–	–
SIT	–	–	–	–	1	1	–	–	–
SLEEVE	–	1	1	–	–	–	–	–	–
SMALL	–	–	–	–	2	2	–	–	–
SNUG	1	–	1	–	–	–	–	–	–
SOMETHING THAT CRAWLS	–	–	–	–	–	–	–	1	1
SONGS	–	1	1	–	–	–	–	–	–
SPIDER	6	7	13	2	3	5	2	2	4
SPRAY	1	1	2	–	–	–	–	–	–
SQUITO	–	–	–	–	1	1	–	–	–
STOP	–	1	1	–	–	–	–	–	–
STROLLER	–	1	1	–	–	–	–	–	–
SUG	–	–	–	1	–	1	–	–	–
SUGAR	–	1	1	–	–	–	–	–	–
SWATTER	1	–	1	–	–	–	–	–	–

RESPONSE WORD	1ST			3RD			5TH		
	M	F	T	M	F	T	M	F	T

13.   BUG

RESPONSE WORD	M	F	T	M	F	T	M	F	T
SWIM	–	1	1	–	–	–	–	–	–
TED	–	1	1	–	1	1	–	–	–
TERMITE	–	1	1	–	–	–	–	–	–
THERES A BUG IN THE BACK YARD	–	1	1	–	–	–	–	–	–
THIS	1	–	1	–	–	–	–	–	–
THUNDER	–	1	1	–	–	–	–	–	–
TICK	1	–	1	–	–	–	–	–	–
TRY	1	–	1	1	–	1	–	–	–
TULIP	–	1	1	–	–	–	–	–	–
VOLKSWAGON	1	–	1	–	–	–	–	–	–
WALK	–	2	2	–	–	–	–	–	–
WALKING UP THE GRASS	1	–	1	–	–	–	–	–	–
WALKS	–	–	–	1	–	1	–	–	–
WALL	–	1	1	–	–	–	–	–	–
WASP	–	–	–	1	–	1	–	–	–
WATER	1	1	2	–	–	–	–	–	–
WATER BUG	–	–	–	–	–	–	1	–	1
WEED	–	–	–	–	–	–	1	–	1
WHEN YOU BUST SOMETHING	1	–	1	–	–	–	–	–	–
WHITE	–	1	1	–	–	–	–	–	–
WING	–	1	1	–	–	–	–	–	–
WINGS	2	–	2	–	–	–	–	–	–
WOOD	–	–	–	–	–	–	–	1	1
WORM	1	–	1	–	–	–	1	3	4

14.   BUTTERFLY

RESPONSE WORD	M	F	T	M	F	T	M	F	T
A BUTTERFLY FLIES IN THE AIR	–	1	1	–	–	–	–	–	–
A DOG	1	–	1	–	–	–	–	–	–
A DOOR	1	–	1	–	–	–	–	–	–
A MOTH	–	–	–	1	–	1	–	–	–
AIRPLANE	1	–	1	–	–	–	–	–	–
ANIMAL	–	2	2	9	12	21	7	12	19
ANT	–	1	1	–	1	1	–	1	1
ANTS	–	1	1	–	–	–	–	–	–
BANG	1	–	1	–	–	–	–	–	–
BEAR	–	–	–	1	–	1	–	–	–
BEAUTIFUL	–	–	–	–	2	2	2	1	3
BEE	6	4	10	3	1	4	–	2	2
BEES	–	2	2	–	–	–	–	–	–
BEETLE	–	–	–	–	–	–	1	–	1
BELL	1	–	1	–	–	–	–	–	–
BETTER	–	–	–	1	–	1	–	–	–
BIRD	5	6	11	8	13	21	4	8	12
BIRDS	–	1	1	–	–	–	–	–	–
BLACK	2	1	3	–	–	–	2	–	2
BLUE	–	–	–	–	2	2	–	–	–
BOOKS	–	2	2	–	–	–	–	–	–
BOTTLE	–	–	–	1	–	1	1	–	1
BOY	1	–	1	–	–	–	–	–	–
BREAD	1	–	1	–	–	–	–	–	–
BROKEN	1	–	1	–	–	–	–	–	–
BUB	–	–	–	–	–	–	1	–	1
BUG	3	1	4	10	11	21	11	11	22
BUTTER	12	10	22	7	5	12	4	–	4
BUTTERBALL	–	–	–	–	1	1	–	–	–
BUTTERCUP	–	1	1	2	–	2	–	–	–
BUTTERFINGERS	–	–	–	–	–	–	–	1	1
BUTTERFLY	–	1	1	–	–	–	–	–	–
BY	–	1	1	–	–	–	–	–	–
CAN	–	1	1	–	–	–	–	–	–
CAN FLY	1	1	2	–	–	–	–	–	–
CAT	1	1	2	–	–	–	–	–	–
CATCH	2	4	6	–	–	–	–	–	–
CATERPILLAR	2	1	3	7	4	11	4	–	4
CATERPILLAR GROWN UP	–	–	–	–	–	–	–	1	1
CAUGHT	2	–	2	–	–	–	–	–	–
CHALK	1	–	1	–	–	–	–	–	–

RESPONSE WORD	1ST M	F	T	3RD M	F	T	5TH M	F	T

14. BUTTERFLY

RESPONSE WORD	1ST M	F	T	3RD M	F	T	5TH M	F	T
COAT	1	–	1	–	–	–	–	–	–
COCOON	1	1	2	2	2	4	7	4	11
COLOR	–	–	–	1	–	1	–	1	1
COLORFUL	–	–	–	–	–	–	–	1	1
COLORS	–	1	1	–	2	2	–	1	1
CREATURE	–	–	–	1	1	–	–	–	–
CUP	–	–	–	–	1	1	–	–	–
CUTE	–	1	1	–	–	–	–	–	–
DAN	1	–	1	–	–	–	–	–	–
DEAD	–	2	2	–	–	–	1	–	1
DIRTY	–	1	1	–	–	–	–	–	–
DOG	–	–	–	1	–	1	1	–	1
DOOR	1	1	2	–	–	–	–	–	–
DOWN	–	–	–	1	–	1	–	–	–
DUCK	–	–	–	–	1	1	–	–	–
FIND	–	–	–	1	–	1	–	–	–
FLIES	6	1	7	2	1	3	1	–	1
FLIES AROUND	1	–	1	–	–	–	–	–	–
FLIES AWAY	–	1	1	–	–	–	–	–	–
FLIES IN SKY	–	1	1	–	–	–	–	–	–
FLIES IN THE AIR	–	1	1	–	–	–	–	–	–
FLOPPING	1	–	1	–	–	–	–	–	–
FLOWER	1	1	2	–	5	5	–	–	–
FLOWERS	2	1	3	–	–	–	1	1	2
FLUTTER	–	–	–	–	–	–	–	1	1
FLY	28	33	61	32	24	56	9	14	23
FLY AWAY	–	1	1	–	–	–	–	–	–
FLY BIRD	1	–	1	–	–	–	–	–	–
FLY IN THE AIR	1	–	1	–	–	–	–	–	–
FLYING	–	2	2	2	–	2	–	1	1
FLYING IN THE AIR	2	–	2	–	–	–	–	–	–
FLYING OBJECT	–	–	–	–	–	–	–	1	1
FOLD	1	–	1	–	–	–	–	–	–
FOOD	–	–	–	–	–	–	1	–	1
GO	–	1	1	–	–	–	–	–	–
GOODBYE	1	–	1	–	–	–	–	–	–
GRASS	–	–	–	–	–	–	1	1	2
GRASSHOPPER	–	–	–	–	1	1	–	–	–
GROUND	–	–	–	1	–	1	–	–	–
HANDLE	1	1	2	–	–	–	–	–	–
HAVE WINGS	–	1	1	–	–	–	–	–	–
HI	–	–	–	–	–	–	–	1	1
HONEY	–	–	–	–	1	1	–	–	–
HUTTERFLY	1	–	1	–	–	–	–	–	–
INCEAH	–	–	–	–	–	–	1	–	1
INCECK	–	–	–	–	–	–	1	–	1
INCUER	–	–	–	–	–	–	1	–	1
INSECT	2	2	4	21	17	38	44	39	83
INSECTS	–	–	–	2	1	3	–	–	–
JET	1	–	1	–	–	–	–	–	–
JULY	–	–	–	–	–	–	1	–	1
KILL	–	1	1	–	–	–	–	–	–
KITCHEN	–	1	1	–	–	–	–	–	–
LEAVES	–	1	1	–	–	–	–	–	–
LETS GO CATCH BUTTERFLIES	–	1	1	–	–	–	–	–	–
LIGHT	1	1	2	–	–	–	–	–	–
LINDA	1	–	1	–	–	–	–	–	–
LITTLE	–	–	–	1	–	1	–	–	–
LOW	–	1	1	–	–	–	–	–	–
MADE	–	–	–	1	–	1	–	–	–
MAKES	1	–	1	–	–	–	–	–	–
MAMMAL	–	–	–	–	1	1	–	–	–
MANY	1	–	1	–	–	–	–	–	–
MATCH	1	–	1	–	–	–	–	–	–
MIGHT LOSE HIS WINGS AND HE CAN T FLY	–	1	1	–	–	–	–	–	–
MILK	–	–	–	–	–	–	–	1	1
MIX	–	1	1	–	–	–	–	–	–
MOTH	5	3	8	6	5	11	12	7	19
MOTHER	1	–	1	–	–	–	–	–	–
MUTTERFLY	1	–	1	–	–	–	–	–	–

RESPONSE WORD	1ST			3RD			5TH		
	M	F	T	M	F	T	M	F	T

14. BUTTERFLY

RESPONSE WORD	M	F	T	M	F	T	M	F	T
NEST	–	1	1	–	–	–	–	–	–
NET	3	1	4	1	4	5	3	2	5
NO	–	1	1	–	–	–	–	–	–
NO RESPONSE	–	–	–	1	–	1	–	–	–
NOT MANY	–	–	–	–	–	–	–	1	1
NUTTERFLY	–	1	1	–	–	–	–	–	–
ONCE	1	–	1	–	–	–	–	–	–
ORANGE	–	–	–	–	1	1	1	–	1
OWL	–	1	1	–	–	–	–	–	–
PEPPER	–	1	1	–	–	–	–	–	–
PERTLY	–	1	–	–	–	–	1	–	1
PICTURE	–	1	1	–	–	–	–	–	–
PIE	–	–	–	–	–	–	–	1	1
PIN	–	–	–	–	–	–	–	1	1
PINK	–	–	–	1	–	1	–	1	1
POOL	1	–	1	–	–	–	–	–	–
PRETTY	–	2	2	3	8	11	4	7	11
PUFF	1	–	1	–	–	–	–	–	–
PUSSY CAT	–	–	–	–	–	–	1	–	1
QUIET	–	–	–	–	–	–	–	1	1
RADIO	–	1	1	–	–	–	–	–	–
RAINBOW	1	–	1	–	–	–	–	–	–
READ	–	–	–	1	–	1	–	–	–
RED	1	–	1	–	–	–	–	–	–
REFRIGERATOR	–	1	1	–	–	–	–	–	–
ROAD	1	–	1	–	–	–	–	–	–
RUTTERFLY	–	1	1	–	–	–	–	–	–
SAD	–	1	1	–	–	–	–	–	–
SAW	–	1	1	–	–	–	–	–	–
SCOTCH	–	1	1	–	–	–	–	–	–
SEE	1	–	1	–	–	–	–	–	–
SKY	1	1	2	–	–	–	–	–	–
SOMETHING THAT FLIES	–	–	–	–	–	–	–	1	1
SOMETHING THAT HAS WINGS	–	–	–	–	–	–	1	–	1
SPOT	–	1	1	–	–	–	–	–	–
SPRING	–	–	–	–	–	–	–	1	1
STAIRS	–	–	–	1	–	1	–	–	–
STICK	–	1	1	–	–	–	–	–	–
STING	–	1	1	–	–	–	–	–	–
SUN	–	1	1	–	–	–	–	–	–
SUTTERFLY	1	–	1	–	–	–	–	–	–
TABLE	1	–	1	–	–	–	–	–	–
THIRTEEN	–	1	1	–	–	–	–	–	–
TIGER	–	1	1	–	–	–	–	–	–
TO	–	–	–	–	–	–	1	–	1
TO FLY	–	1	1	–	–	–	–	–	–
TOOTH BRUSH	1	–	1	–	–	–	–	–	–
TRASH	–	1	1	–	–	–	–	–	–
TURN	1	–	1	–	1	1	–	–	–
UP	–	–	–	–	1	1	–	–	–
WAY	–	–	–	1	–	1	–	–	–
WEB	–	–	–	–	1	1	–	–	–
WHEN YOURE MAKING SOME BUTTER	1	–	1	–	–	–	–	–	–
WHITE	–	–	–	–	1	1	1	–	1
WILD	–	1	1	–	–	–	–	–	–
WIND	1	–	1	–	–	–	–	–	–
WING	4	2	6	3	2	5	3	3	6
WINGS	5	4	9	3	2	5	1	5	6
WORM	1	–	1	–	1	1	–	1	1
YELLOW	2	1	3	1	3	4	3	3	6
YELLOW BUTTERFLY	–	–	–	–	1	1	–	–	–
YOLLOW	–	–	–	–	–	–	1	–	1
YOU	–	–	–	1	–	1	–	–	–

RESPONSE WORD	1ST			3RD			5TH		
	M	F	T	M	F	T	M	F	T

15. CARRY

RESPONSE WORD	1ST M	1ST F	1ST T	3RD M	3RD F	3RD T	5TH M	5TH F	5TH T
A	1	–	1	–	–	–	–	–	–
A BABY	1	2	3	–	–	–	–	–	–
A BABY CARRIAGE	–	–	–	1	–	1	–	–	–
A BAG HOME FROM THE STORE	–	1	1	–	–	–	–	–	–
A BAG OF GROCERIES	1	–	1	–	–	–	–	–	–
A BASKET	1	–	1	–	–	–	–	–	–
A BOX	1	–	1	–	–	–	–	–	–
A PACK	–	–	–	1	–	1	–	–	–
A TRUCK CARRYING FOOD	1	–	1	–	–	–	–	–	–
ACROSS	–	–	–	–	–	–	–	1	1
AIRRY	–	1	1	–	–	–	–	–	–
ARITHMETIC	–	–	–	2	–	2	–	–	–
ARM BAG	1	–	1	–	–	–	–	–	–
ARMS	–	1	1	–	–	–	–	–	–
ATE	–	–	–	–	1	1	–	–	–
AWAY	–	–	–	–	1	1	1	–	1
BABY	9	19	28	2	12	14	–	5	5
BABY BUGGY	–	1	1	–	–	–	–	–	–
BACK	–	2	2	–	1	1	–	2	2
BAG	1	5	6	1	2	3	1	2	3
BAGS	–	–	–	1	–	1	–	1	1
BALL	–	–	–	1	–	1	–	–	–
BARRY	1	–	1	–	–	–	–	–	–
BASKET	1	–	1	1	2	3	1	2	3
BASKETS FROM STORE	–	1	1	–	–	–	–	–	–
BERRY	–	–	–	–	–	–	1	–	1
BIKE	1	–	1	1	–	1	–	–	–
BIRD	1	–	1	–	–	–	–	–	–
BIRD THAT CARRIES ITS BABY	–	1	1	–	–	–	–	–	–
BLACK	–	–	–	1	–	1	1	–	1
BLOCKS	1	–	1	–	–	–	–	–	–
BOOK	1	1	2	–	2	2	1	–	1
BOOKS	1	–	1	–	3	3	2	1	3
BOUGHT	–	–	–	–	–	–	1	–	1
BOWL	–	–	–	–	1	1	–	–	–
BOX	2	–	2	–	1	1	–	–	–
BOXES	1	–	1	–	–	–	–	–	–
BOY	1	–	1	–	–	–	–	–	–
BRAVE	–	–	–	–	1	1	–	–	–
BREAK	–	1	1	–	–	–	–	–	–
BRING	–	–	–	5	5	10	2	2	4
BROKE	–	–	–	–	–	–	–	1	1
BROUGHT	–	–	–	–	–	–	–	1	1
BUNDLE	–	–	–	2	1	3	1	1	2
BURDEN	–	–	–	–	–	–	1	–	1
BURY	1	–	1	1	–	1	–	–	–
BUY	–	1	1	–	2	2	–	–	–
CAKE	–	–	–	–	–	–	–	1	1
CAN	1	–	1	–	–	–	–	–	–
CANDLE	1	–	1	–	–	–	–	–	–
CANE	–	–	–	1	–	1	–	–	–
CAR	1	–	1	2	1	3	1	1	2
CAREFUL	1	–	1	–	1	1	–	–	–
CARING	–	–	–	–	1	1	–	–	–
CARRIAGE	4	7	11	–	1	1	–	1	1
CARRIED	1	–	1	3	1	4	–	1	1
CARROT	7	8	15	–	–	–	–	1	1
CARROTS	–	3	3	–	–	–	–	–	–
CARRY	–	1	1	–	–	–	1	–	1
CARRYING	–	–	–	–	–	–	2	–	2
CARRYING ANYTHING	1	–	1	–	–	–	–	–	–
CARRYING IT TO THE CAR	–	1	1	–	–	–	–	–	–
CART	1	–	1	–	–	–	1	–	1
CARTON	–	–	–	–	1	1	–	–	–
CARTONS	–	1	1	–	–	–	–	–	–
CASE	–	1	1	–	–	–	–	–	–
CAT	–	2	2	–	–	–	–	–	–
CATCH	–	–	–	1	–	1	–	–	–
CAUGHT	–	–	–	1	–	1	–	–	–
CELERY	–	1	1	–	–	–	–	–	–

RESPONSE WORD	1ST M	F	T	3RD M	F	T	5TH M	F	T

15. CARRY

RESPONSE WORD	1ST M	F	T	3RD M	F	T	5TH M	F	T
CLEAR	–	–	–	–	1	1	–	–	–
CLOSED	1	–	1	–	–	–	–	–	–
CLOTHESPIN BASKET	–	1	1	–	–	–	–	–	–
COME	2	–	2	1	–	1	–	–	–
COME HERE (NAME)	–	1	1	–	–	–	–	–	–
CONTAIN	–	–	–	–	–	–	1	–	1
CRIB	–	–	–	1	–	1	–	–	–
CUP	–	–	–	–	–	–	–	1	1
DESK	–	1	1	–	–	–	–	–	–
DO NOT	–	–	–	–	–	–	–	1	1
DO NOT CARRY	1	–	1	–	–	–	–	–	–
DOESNT CARRY	–	–	–	1	–	1	–	–	–
DOG	1	–	1	1	–	1	1	1	2
DOLL	1	–	1	–	–	–	–	–	–
DOLL BABY	–	1	1	–	–	–	–	–	–
DONT	–	–	–	1	–	1	–	–	–
DONT CARRY	–	1	1	2	2	4	–	–	–
DOOR	–	1	1	–	–	–	–	–	–
DOWN	1	–	1	–	1	1	1	3	4
DRAG	1	–	1	4	1	5	2	3	5
DRAGGED	–	–	–	2	–	2	–	–	–
DROP	1	2	3	10	11	21	4	14	18
DROPPED	–	–	–	1	–	1	–	1	1
DUMP	–	1	1	–	–	–	–	–	–
EAT	1	–	1	–	–	–	1	–	1
FAIRY	–	1	1	–	–	–	–	–	–
FAST	1	–	1	1	–	1	–	–	–
FEED	1	–	1	–	–	–	–	–	–
FINGERNAIL	1	–	1	–	–	–	–	–	–
FISH	1	–	1	–	–	–	–	–	–
FIVE	–	–	–	–	–	–	1	–	1
FLAG	1	–	1	–	1	1	–	–	–
FLOOR	1	1	2	–	–	–	–	–	–
FOOD	1	1	2	–	1	1	1	–	1
FOOT	–	–	–	–	1	1	–	–	–
FOR	–	–	–	–	1	1	–	–	–
FRIGHT	–	–	–	–	–	–	1	–	1
FURNITURE	1	–	1	–	–	–	–	–	–
GASOLINE	1	–	1	–	–	–	–	–	–
GET	1	–	1	–	–	–	–	–	–
GIRL	–	1	1	–	–	–	–	–	–
GO	–	2	2	1	–	1	–	–	–
GROCERIES	–	2	2	1	1	2	–	1	1
HAIR	–	1	1	–	–	–	–	–	–
HAND	1	–	1	–	–	–	–	–	–
HANDLE	–	1	1	1	2	3	–	1	1
HANDS	–	–	–	–	1	1	–	–	–
HARD	–	1	1	–	–	–	–	–	–
HARRY	1	–	1	1	–	1	–	–	–
HAUL	–	–	–	–	–	–	2	1	3
HAVE	–	–	–	–	–	–	2	–	2
HEAVE	–	–	–	–	–	–	1	–	1
HEAVY	4	5	9	12	4	16	8	9	17
HELD	–	–	–	–	–	–	1	–	1
HELP	–	1	1	–	–	–	–	1	1
HELP ME	1	–	1	–	–	–	–	–	–
HERE	1	–	1	–	–	–	–	–	–
HIM	–	1	1	1	–	1	–	–	–
HOLD	–	1	1	11	18	29	29	33	62
HOLD IT	–	–	–	–	1	1	–	–	–
HOLD ON	–	–	–	–	–	–	1	–	1
HOLD SOMETHING	–	–	–	–	–	–	1	–	1
HOLDING	–	–	–	–	–	–	1	–	1
HOME	1	–	1	–	1	1	–	1	1
HORSE	1	–	1	–	–	–	–	1	1
HORSES	–	–	–	1	–	1	–	–	–
HOT	–	–	–	–	1	1	–	–	–
HOUSE	1	–	1	–	–	–	–	–	–
HURRY	–	–	–	1	1	2	1	1	2
I CAN CARRY MY BABY	–	1	1	–	–	–	–	–	–
I CARRIED A CHAIR	–	–	–	1	–	1	–	–	–
INCARRY	–	–	–	–	–	–	–	1	1

RESPONSE WORD	1ST M	F	T	3RD M	F	T	5TH M	F	T

15. CARRY

RESPONSE WORD	1ST M	F	T	3RD M	F	T	5TH M	F	T
INDIAN STOMP	1	–	1	–	–	–	–	–	–
ISNT	–	–	–	1	–	1	–	–	–
IT	1	–	1	–	1	1	1	–	1
ITSELF	1	–	1	–	–	–	–	–	–
JACKET	1	–	1	–	–	–	–	–	–
JET	–	1	1	–	–	–	–	–	–
KAREN	1	1	2	–	–	–	–	–	–
KITTEN	–	1	1	–	–	–	–	–	–
LABOR	–	–	–	–	1	1	–	–	–
LADY	–	–	–	–	–	–	–	1	1
LAMP	–	–	–	1	–	1	–	–	–
LARRY	–	–	–	1	–	1	1	1	2
LAY	–	–	–	–	–	–	1	–	1
LAY DOWN	1	–	1	–	–	–	–	–	–
LEAVE	–	–	–	1	–	1	–	–	–
LEAVES	–	1	1	–	–	–	–	–	–
LESTER	–	–	–	1	–	1	–	–	–
LETS GO CARRY SOME CARROTS	–	1	1	–	–	–	–	–	–
LIFT	1	–	1	5	3	8	4	4	8
LIFTED UP	–	–	–	–	–	–	1	–	1
LIKE	–	–	–	–	1	1	–	–	–
LOAD	–	–	–	–	–	–	2	3	5
LUGGAGE	–	1	1	1	1	2	–	–	–
LUNCH	–	–	–	–	1	1	–	–	–
MACHINE	1	–	1	–	–	–	–	–	–
MAIL	1	–	1	–	–	–	–	–	–
MAN	–	–	–	–	1	1	–	1	1
MARRY	3	3	6	1	1	2	–	–	–
MARY	1	1	2	–	–	–	–	–	–
ME	2	3	5	2	3	5	1	–	1
ME HOME	–	1	1	–	–	–	–	–	–
MILK	–	–	–	1	–	1	–	–	–
MINE	–	1	1	–	–	–	–	–	–
MOST	–	–	–	–	1	1	–	–	–
MOTHER	1	1	2	1	–	1	–	–	–
MOTHER CARRIES HER BABY IN THE CARRIAGE	–	1	1	–	–	–	–	–	–
MOVE	–	–	–	1	–	1	2	–	2
MY	1	–	1	–	–	–	–	–	–
NAME	–	–	–	–	–	–	–	1	1
NARRY	–	–	–	1	–	1	–	–	–
NO	1	–	1	1	1	2	–	–	–
NOBODY	1	–	1	–	–	–	–	–	–
NOT	–	1	1	–	1	1	–	–	–
NOT CARRY	1	2	3	2	3	5	1	–	1
NOTHING	–	–	–	1	–	1	–	–	–
NOW	–	1	1	–	–	–	–	–	–
OLD	–	–	–	–	1	1	–	–	–
ON	2	1	3	–	–	–	2	2	4
ORANGE	2	–	2	–	–	–	–	–	–
OUT	–	–	–	–	–	–	2	1	3
OVER	–	–	–	1	–	1	–	1	1
PACK	–	–	–	–	–	–	3	–	3
PACKAGE	1	1	2	–	–	–	1	1	2
PACKAGES	–	–	–	–	1	1	–	–	–
PAPER	–	1	1	–	–	–	–	–	–
PARRY	1	–	1	–	–	–	–	–	–
PEOPLE	–	–	–	–	–	–	–	1	1
PERSON	–	–	–	–	–	–	–	2	2
PICK	–	1	1	1	–	1	–	–	–
PICK UP	–	–	–	4	1	5	2	1	3
PILE	1	–	1	–	–	–	–	–	–
PILES	–	1	1	–	–	–	–	–	–
PIPE	1	–	1	–	–	–	–	–	–
PLANE	1	–	1	–	–	–	1	–	1
PLAY	–	–	–	1	–	1	–	–	–
PLAYPEN	1	–	1	–	–	–	–	–	–
POCKETBOOK	1	–	1	–	–	–	–	–	–
PONY EXPRESS	–	–	–	–	–	–	1	–	1
PULL	–	–	–	2	2	4	1	–	1
PUSH	–	–	–	1	–	1	–	1	1

RESPONSE WORD	1ST M	1ST F	1ST T	3RD M	3RD F	3RD T	5TH M	5TH F	5TH T

15. CARRY

RESPONSE WORD	M	F	T	M	F	T	M	F	T
PUT DOWN	1	–	1	–	2	2	–	–	–
RABBIT	–	1	1	–	–	–	–	1	1
RE-CARRY	–	–	–	–	–	–	1	–	1
RIDE	–	1	1	1	–	1	1	1	2
RING	1	1	2	–	–	–	–	–	–
ROCK	–	–	–	–	–	–	1	–	1
ROCKED	–	–	–	1	–	1	–	–	–
ROOM	1	–	1	–	–	–	–	–	–
RUN	–	1	1	–	1	1	1	–	1
RUNNING	–	–	–	1	–	1	–	–	–
SALAD	1	–	1	–	–	–	–	–	–
SAT	–	1	1	–	1	1	–	–	–
SCARE	–	–	–	1	–	1	–	–	–
SHIP	–	–	–	–	–	–	1	–	1
SING	–	1	1	–	1	1	–	–	–
SLED	–	–	–	1	–	1	–	–	–
SLOW	–	–	–	1	–	1	–	1	1
SLOWLY	–	–	–	1	–	1	–	–	–
SOFA	–	1	1	–	–	–	–	–	–
SOFT	–	1	1	1	–	1	–	–	–
SOMEBODY CARRYING SOMETHING	–	1	1	–	–	–	–	–	–
SOMEONE	–	–	–	1	–	1	–	–	–
SOMETHING	3	2	5	–	2	2	–	1	1
SON	1	–	1	–	–	–	–	–	–
SQUIRREL	1	–	1	–	–	–	–	–	–
STOP	–	1	1	1	–	1	–	–	–
STORE	–	1	1	–	1	1	–	–	–
STRAW	–	1	1	–	1	1	–	–	–
STROLLER	–	1	1	–	–	–	–	–	–
STRONG	–	–	–	–	–	–	1	–	1
STUFF	1	–	1	1	–	1	–	–	–
SUITCASE	–	–	–	–	–	–	2	–	2
SWEATER	–	1	1	–	–	–	–	–	–
TABLE	1	1	2	–	–	–	–	–	–
TAKE	–	1	1	–	3	3	8	4	12
TAKE ALONG	–	–	–	–	–	–	–	1	1
TAKE IT	1	–	1	–	–	–	–	–	–
TAKEN	–	–	–	–	–	–	1	–	1
TAKES	–	–	–	1	–	1	–	–	–
TAKING	–	–	–	–	–	–	1	–	1
TALK	1	–	1	–	–	–	–	–	–
TANY	–	1	1	–	–	–	–	–	–
TARRY	–	1	1	1	–	1	–	–	–
THAT	–	–	–	1	1	2	–	–	–
THE BABY	–	–	–	–	1	1	–	–	–
THE BAG	1	–	1	–	–	–	–	–	–
THE BAGGAGE	1	–	1	–	–	–	–	–	–
THE SACK	1	–	1	–	–	–	–	–	–
THEM	–	–	–	–	–	–	1	–	1
THESE	–	–	–	–	1	1	–	–	–
THING	–	–	–	–	1	1	–	–	–
THINGS	1	–	1	–	–	–	1	–	1
TIRED	1	–	1	–	–	–	–	–	–
TO HAVE SOMETHING IN YOU HANDS OR ARMS	–	–	–	–	–	–	–	1	1
TOM	1	–	1	–	–	–	–	–	–
TOOK	–	–	–	–	–	–	1	–	1
TOOKED	–	–	–	–	–	–	1	–	1
TOUR	1	–	1	–	–	–	–	–	–
TRANSPORT	–	–	–	–	–	–	1	–	1
TRAVEL	–	–	–	–	–	–	1	–	1
TRAY	–	–	–	1	–	1	–	–	–
TROT	–	–	–	–	1	1	–	–	–
TRUCK	2	–	2	–	1	1	–	–	–
UNCARRY	–	–	–	–	1	1	–	1	1
UNLOAD	–	–	–	1	–	1	–	–	–
US	1	–	1	–	–	–	–	–	–
VERY	–	–	–	–	–	–	1	–	1
WAGON	2	–	2	–	–	–	–	–	–
WALK	–	1	1	6	5	11	8	8	16
WALKING	–	1	1	–	–	–	–	–	–

RESPONSE WORD	1ST M	F	T	3RD M	F	T	5TH M	F	T
15. CARRY									
WALL	1	–	1	–	–	–	–	–	–
WALLET	1	–	1	–	–	–	–	–	–
WARRY	1	–	1	–	–	–	–	–	–
WATER	–	1	1	1	–	1	–	–	–
WEIGHT	–	–	–	1	–	1	–	–	–
WHEN YOU CARRY SOMETHING	1	–	1	–	–	–	–	–	–
WHERE	–	1	1	–	–	–	–	–	–
WIDE	–	–	–	–	1	1	–	–	–
WITH	–	–	–	–	–	–	–	1	1
WOOD	–	–	–	–	–	–	1	–	1
WORK	–	–	–	–	–	–	1	–	1
WORRY	–	–	–	1	–	1	–	–	–
YOU	–	–	–	–	1	1	–	–	–
YOU TAKE IT	1	–	1	–	–	–	–	–	–
YOUR BABY DOLL	–	–	–	–	–	–	–	1	1
YOUR BERRY	1	–	1	–	–	–	–	–	–
16. CHAIR									
A RECORD PLAYER	–	1	1	–	–	–	–	–	–
AIR	–	1	1	2	1	3	–	1	1
AN	–	–	–	–	1	1	–	–	–
BABY CHAIR	1	–	1	–	–	–	–	–	–
BARE	1	1	2	–	–	–	–	–	–
BATHTUB	1	–	1	–	–	–	–	–	–
BEAN	–	1	1	–	–	–	–	–	–
BEAR	4	5	9	1	–	1	1	–	1
BED	2	–	2	1	2	3	1	–	1
BEDROOM	1	–	1	–	–	–	–	–	–
BENCH	1	–	1	1	2	3	–	1	1
BOOK	–	1	1	–	–	–	–	–	–
BOOKS	–	1	1	–	–	–	–	–	–
BOX	–	1	1	–	–	–	–	–	–
BOY	1	–	1	–	–	–	–	–	–
BREAK	–	1	1	–	–	–	–	–	–
BREAK DOWN	1	–	1	–	–	–	–	–	–
BROKE	1	–	1	–	–	–	–	–	–
CAKE	1	–	1	–	–	–	–	–	–
CAN	–	–	–	–	1	1	–	–	–
CARE	3	4	7	1	–	1	–	–	–
CHAIRS	–	–	–	1	–	1	–	–	–
CHARLES	1	–	1	–	–	–	–	–	–
CHEER	–	–	–	–	1	1	–	–	–
CHERRY	–	–	–	1	–	1	–	–	–
CHERRY PIE	–	1	1	–	–	–	–	–	–
CHILDREN	–	1	1	–	–	–	–	–	–
CHRISTMAS	–	1	1	–	–	–	–	–	–
CHUG	1	–	1	–	–	–	–	–	–
CLOTH	–	–	–	–	1	1	–	–	–
COLORED	–	1	1	–	–	–	–	–	–
COLORING BOARD	1	–	1	–	–	–	–	–	–
COME	1	–	1	–	–	–	–	–	–
COUCH	4	1	5	6	4	10	2	–	2
CUSHION	–	–	–	–	–	–	–	1	1
DARE	–	2	2	–	–	–	–	–	–
DESK	5	4	9	10	19	29	16	21	37
DESKS	–	–	–	1	–	1	–	–	–
DONT TURN YOUR MOTHERS CHAIRS UP	–	1	1	–	–	–	–	–	–
DOOR	–	1	1	1	1	2	–	–	–
DOWN	–	–	–	–	2	2	–	–	–
DRAWER	–	1	1	–	–	–	–	–	–
EAR	–	–	–	1	–	1	–	–	–
EAT	–	–	–	–	–	–	1	–	1
EYES	1	–	1	–	–	–	–	–	–
FLOOR	1	–	1	2	1	3	2	–	2
FOOT	–	–	–	–	1	1	–	–	–
FOR YOU TO SET ON	–	1	1	–	–	–	–	–	–
FOUR LEGS	–	–	–	1	–	1	–	–	–
FURNITURE	–	1	1	5	1	6	1	2	3
GIRL	–	1	1	1	–	1	–	–	–

RESPONSE WORD	1ST M	F	T	3RD M	F	T	5TH M	F	T

16.   CHAIR

RESPONSE WORD	1ST M	F	T	3RD M	F	T	5TH M	F	T
GIVE BACK	1	–	1	–	–	–	–	–	–
GLASSES	1	–	1	–	–	–	–	–	–
GREAT	–	–	–	–	–	–	1	–	1
GREEN	1	–	1	–	–	–	–	–	–
HAIR	2	4	6	2	1	3	1	1	2
HE	1	–	1	–	–	–	–	–	–
HERE	1	–	1	–	–	–	–	–	–
HOOD	1	–	1	–	–	–	–	–	–
HOUSE	1	–	1	–	–	–	–	–	–
IM SITTING IN A CHAIR	–	1	1	–	–	–	–	–	–
INSTRUMENT	–	–	–	–	–	–	–	1	1
KEER	–	–	–	1	–	1	–	–	–
KING	–	–	–	–	–	–	–	1	1
KITE	1	–	1	–	–	–	–	–	–
KNEE	–	–	–	–	–	–	1	–	1
LAIR	1	1	2	–	–	–	–	–	–
LEG	–	–	–	–	–	–	2	1	3
LEGS	–	1	1	4	1	5	1	1	2
LIFT	–	–	–	–	–	–	1	–	1
LIVING ROOM	–	1	1	–	–	–	–	–	–
LIVING ROOM CHAIR	–	–	–	–	1	1	–	–	–
LONG	–	–	–	1	–	1	–	–	–
MAN	1	1	2	–	–	–	–	1	1
MARE	3	–	3	1	–	1	–	–	–
MAYOR	1	–	1	–	–	–	–	–	–
MOTHER	–	1	1	–	–	–	–	–	–
MRS	1	–	1	–	–	–	–	–	–
NICE	–	1	1	–	–	–	–	–	–
PAIL	–	1	1	–	–	–	–	–	–
PAIR	–	–	–	–	–	–	1	1	2
PALE	1	–	1	–	–	–	–	–	–
PAPER	–	–	–	1	–	1	–	–	–
PEAR	–	1	1	–	–	–	–	–	–
PEOPLE	1	–	1	–	2	2	–	–	–
PEPSI	1	–	1	–	–	–	–	–	–
PERSON	–	–	–	1	–	1	–	2	2
PICNIC	1	–	1	–	–	–	–	–	–
PLAY	1	–	1	–	–	–	–	–	–
QUARE	1	–	1	–	–	–	–	–	–
RED	–	–	–	–	–	–	1	–	1
REST	–	–	–	–	–	–	–	3	3
ROCK	2	3	5	–	–	–	–	–	–
ROCKING	1	–	1	–	1	1	–	–	–
ROCKING CHAIR	1	1	2	–	–	–	–	–	–
ROMANS	–	–	–	–	–	–	–	1	1
ROOM	–	–	–	–	–	–	–	1	1
RUG	1	–	1	1	–	1	–	–	–
S	1	–	1	–	–	–	–	–	–
SAT	–	–	–	–	–	–	1	–	1
SEAT	1	1	2	14	9	23	15	11	26
SEATED	–	–	–	–	–	–	–	1	1
SEE	–	1	1	–	–	–	–	–	–
SELFISH	–	–	–	–	1	1	–	–	–
SET	–	1	1	–	2	2	–	1	1
SIT	35	35	70	40	43	83	44	29	73
SIT DOWN	5	3	8	–	1	1	–	1	1
SIT DOWN IN THIS CHAIR	1	–	1	–	–	–	–	–	–
SIT IN	–	–	–	1	–	1	–	–	–
SIT ON	–	–	–	2	–	2	–	1	1
SIT ON IT	–	1	1	–	–	–	–	–	–
SITTING	2	–	2	1	1	2	1	–	1
SLIPPER	1	–	1	–	–	–	–	–	–
SOFA	–	2	2	1	–	1	–	–	–
SOFT	–	–	–	–	–	–	–	1	1
SOMEBODY	–	1	1	–	–	–	–	–	–
SOMEBODY SITS DOWN IN	1	–	1	–	–	–	–	–	–
SOME SITTING ON THE CHAIR	–	1	1	–	–	–	–	–	–
SOMETHING TO SIT ON	–	–	–	–	–	–	1	–	1
SOMETHING YOU WOULD SIT ON	–	–	–	–	–	–	–	1	1
STAND	–	–	–	1	–	1	–	1	1

RESPONSE WORD	1ST M	1ST F	1ST T	3RD M	3RD F	3RD T	5TH M	5TH F	5TH T

16.   CHAIR

RESPONSE WORD	1ST M	1ST F	1ST T	3RD M	3RD F	3RD T	5TH M	5TH F	5TH T
STAR	–	1	1	–	–	–	–	–	–
STE	–	–	–	–	–	–	1	–	1
STOLE	–	–	–	–	–	–	–	1	1
STOOL	–	1	1	6	5	11	3	1	4
STRING	1	–	1	–	–	–	–	–	–
STUDIO COUCH	–	–	–	–	1	1	–	–	–
STURDY	–	–	–	–	–	–	1	–	1
TABLE	22	36	58	23	30	53	34	48	82
TAKE	–	–	–	–	1	1	–	–	–
THE	1	–	1	–	–	–	–	–	–
THING	–	–	–	–	–	–	1	–	1
THING THAT YOU SIT IN	–	–	–	–	–	–	–	1	1
THINGS	–	1	1	–	–	–	–	–	–
THREE	–	1	1	–	–	–	–	–	–
TOLIAN	–	–	–	–	–	–	1	–	1
TOUCH	–	–	–	1	–	1	–	–	–
TOYS	1	–	1	–	–	–	–	–	–
TREAT	–	1	1	–	–	–	–	–	–
UP	1	–	1	–	–	–	–	–	–
WE SIT	1	–	1	–	–	–	–	–	–
WHAT YOU SIT IN	1	–	1	–	–	–	–	–	–
WHEN YOURE SITTING DOWN IN A CHAIR	1	–	1	–	–	–	–	–	–
WHERE	1	1	2	–	–	–	–	–	–
WHITE	–	–	–	1	–	1	–	–	–
WIGGLE	1	–	1	–	–	–	–	–	–
WINDOW	–	–	–	–	1	1	–	–	–
WOOD	–	1	1	1	1	2	4	1	5
WOODEN	–	–	–	–	–	–	–	1	1
WORDS	1	–	1	–	–	–	–	–	–
YOU SIT IN	–	–	–	1	–	1	–	–	–

17.   CLEAN

RESPONSE WORD	1ST M	1ST F	1ST T	3RD M	3RD F	3RD T	5TH M	5TH F	5TH T
APPLE	1	–	1	–	–	–	–	–	–
AT THE CLEANERS	1	–	1	–	–	–	–	–	–
BABY	1	–	1	–	–	–	–	–	–
BATH	1	–	1	1	1	2	–	1	1
BATH TUB	1	1	2	–	–	–	–	–	–
BATHE	–	–	–	–	–	–	1	–	1
BATHTUB	–	–	–	–	1	1	–	–	–
BEAN	2	–	2	–	–	–	–	–	–
BEAUTIFUL	–	–	–	1	1	2	–	–	–
BEING	1	–	1	–	–	–	–	–	–
BING	–	1	1	–	–	–	–	–	–
BIRD	–	1	1	–	–	–	–	–	–
BLANKET	1	–	1	–	–	–	–	–	–
BOWL	–	–	–	1	–	1	–	–	–
BOX	1	–	1	–	–	–	–	–	–
BRACELET	–	1	1	–	–	–	–	–	–
BREAN	1	–	1	–	–	–	–	–	–
BRIGHT	1	–	1	1	–	1	–	1	1
BROOM	–	4	4	–	–	–	–	–	–
BRUSH	1	1	2	–	–	–	–	–	–
BUTTER	–	–	–	–	–	–	–	1	1
CAN	1	–	1	–	–	–	–	–	–
CAR	1	–	1	1	–	1	–	–	–
CARELESS	–	–	–	1	–	1	–	–	–
CASE	–	1	1	–	–	–	–	–	–
CHAIR	–	2	2	2	1	3	–	–	–
CLEAN UP THINGS	1	–	1	–	–	–	–	–	–
CLEANER	–	–	–	1	–	1	–	–	–
CLEANERS	2	–	2	–	–	–	–	–	–
CLEANEST	–	–	–	–	1	1	–	–	–
CLEANING	–	1	1	–	–	–	–	–	–
CLEANLINESS	–	–	–	–	–	–	1	2	3
CLEANS	–	1	1	–	–	–	–	–	–
CLEAR	–	–	–	2	1	3	8	3	11
CLEVELAND	1	–	1	–	–	–	–	–	–
CLOTH	–	1	1	–	–	–	–	–	–
CLOTHES	4	4	8	–	–	–	1	2	3

RESPONSE WORD	1ST M	F	T	3RD M	F	T	5TH M	F	T

17. CLEAN

RESPONSE WORD	1ST M	F	T	3RD M	F	T	5TH M	F	T
CLOUD	1	–	1	–	–	–	–	–	–
CLUM	–	1	1	–	–	–	–	–	–
CLUTTER	–	–	–	–	–	–	–	1	1
COAT	2	–	2	–	–	–	–	–	–
CREEKS	1	–	1	–	–	–	–	–	–
CUP	1	–	1	–	–	–	–	–	–
CUT	–	–	–	1	–	1	–	–	–
DADDY	1	–	1	–	–	–	–	–	–
DEAN	–	1	1	–	–	–	–	–	–
DEAR	–	–	–	–	–	–	1	–	1
DESK	–	–	–	2	1	3	–	–	–
DIAPERS	–	1	1	–	–	–	–	–	–
DING	1	–	1	–	–	–	–	–	–
DIRT	–	–	–	1	2	3	4	2	6
DIRTY	16	13	29	68	66	134	61	61	122
DISH	1	–	1	–	–	–	–	–	–
DISHES	–	–	–	–	–	–	1	1	2
DITY	–	–	–	–	–	–	1	–	1
DO	1	–	1	–	–	–	–	–	–
DONT	–	–	–	–	1	1	–	–	–
DOOR	–	2	2	–	1	1	–	–	–
DRAWER	–	2	2	–	–	–	–	–	–
DRESS	1	1	2	–	1	1	–	1	1
DRITY	–	–	–	–	–	–	1	–	1
DRY CLEANERS	1	–	1	–	–	–	–	–	–
DURTY	–	–	–	–	–	–	–	1	1
DUST	1	4	5	1	2	3	2	6	8
DUSTY	–	–	–	–	–	–	1	–	1
DUTY	–	–	–	–	–	–	1	–	1
FACE	1	–	1	1	–	1	1	–	1
FILTHY	–	–	–	–	–	–	1	1	2
FINISH	–	–	–	–	–	–	1	–	1
FINISHED	–	–	–	–	1	1	–	–	–
FLOOR	6	2	8	1	–	1	–	–	–
FLOORS	–	1	1	1	–	1	–	–	–
FOOD	2	–	2	–	–	–	–	–	–
FRESH	1	–	1	–	–	–	1	–	1
FURNITURE	–	1	1	–	2	2	–	–	–
GARBAGE CAN	1	–	1	–	–	–	–	–	–
GOOD	2	–	2	1	–	1	–	–	–
HAND	1	1	2	1	–	1	–	–	–
HANDS	1	–	1	–	1	1	2	1	3
HANDSOME	–	–	–	–	–	–	1	–	1
HAPPY	–	–	–	–	–	–	1	–	1
HAT	1	–	1	–	–	–	–	–	–
HE	1	–	1	–	–	–	–	–	–
HEALTHY	–	–	–	2	–	2	–	–	–
HELP	–	–	–	–	1	1	–	–	–
HERE	–	–	–	–	1	1	–	–	–
HOME	–	–	–	–	–	–	–	1	1
HOUSE	10	19	29	4	11	15	2	3	5
HOUSEWORK	–	1	1	–	1	1	–	–	–
HURRY	–	–	–	–	1	1	–	–	–
ICE CREAM	1	–	1	–	–	–	–	–	–
IMMACULATE	–	–	–	1	–	1	–	–	–
IN GREEN	–	1	1	–	–	–	–	–	–
JEAN	–	–	–	–	1	1	–	–	–
JUST GO CLEAN THE FLOOR	–	1	1	–	–	–	–	–	–
KEEP YOUR HOUSE CLEAN	–	1	1	–	–	–	–	–	–
KIDS	–	1	1	–	–	–	–	–	–
KITCHEN	1	–	1	–	–	–	–	–	–
KNOCKED	1	–	1	–	–	–	–	–	–
LEAN	–	–	–	1	–	1	–	–	–
LIGHT	–	–	–	–	1	1	–	–	–
LIKE	–	–	–	–	–	–	–	1	1
LOOKS CLEAN	1	–	1	–	–	–	–	–	–
MAID	–	–	–	–	–	–	1	–	1
MAKE	–	–	–	1	–	1	–	–	–
MAN	1	–	1	1	–	1	–	–	–
ME	1	–	1	–	–	–	–	–	–
MEAN	4	2	6	–	–	–	–	–	–
MESS	–	1	1	–	–	–	–	–	–

RESPONSE WORD	1ST M	F	T	3RD M	F	T	5TH M	F	T

17. CLEAN

RESPONSE WORD	1ST M	F	T	3RD M	F	T	5TH M	F	T
MESSED	–	–	–	1	–	1	–	–	–
MESSY	–	1	1	–	1	1	–	1	1
MILK	1	–	1	–	–	–	–	–	–
MOP	2	1	3	–	–	–	1	–	1
MOTHER	–	1	1	–	–	–	–	1	1
MR CLEAN	1	–	1	–	–	–	–	–	–
MY HOUSE IS CLEAN	–	1	1	–	–	–	–	–	–
NEAT	–	1	1	1	2	3	3	13	16
NEVER	–	–	–	–	–	–	1	–	1
NICE	1	2	3	3	5	8	–	–	–
NOT CLEAN	–	–	–	–	2	2	–	1	1
NOT DIRTY	–	–	–	–	1	1	9	2	11
NOT DRY	–	–	–	–	–	–	–	1	1
OFF TABLE	1	–	1	–	–	–	–	–	–
OUT	–	–	–	–	2	2	1	–	1
PAINT	–	1	1	–	–	–	–	–	–
PAN	–	1	1	–	–	–	–	–	–
PANTS	1	–	1	–	–	–	–	–	–
PAPER	–	1	1	–	–	–	–	–	–
PEAN	–	1	1	–	–	–	–	–	–
PICK UP	–	–	–	–	–	–	–	1	1
PLACE	–	–	–	1	–	1	–	–	–
PLATE	2	–	2	–	–	–	–	–	–
PLAY	–	–	–	–	–	–	1	–	1
PLEAN	1	–	1	–	–	–	–	–	–
POLISH	–	–	–	1	–	1	1	–	1
POLISHED	–	–	–	–	–	–	–	1	1
PRETTY	–	3	3	2	5	7	–	–	–
PRETTY HOUSE	1	–	1	–	–	–	–	–	–
PURE	–	–	–	–	–	–	1	–	1
RAIN	–	1	1	–	–	–	–	–	–
RAINBOW	–	1	1	–	–	–	–	–	–
RED	1	–	1	–	–	–	–	–	–
REMOVE DUST	–	–	–	–	–	–	–	1	1
ROOM	–	–	–	–	1	1	–	1	1
RUG	–	–	–	–	–	–	1	–	1
SANITARY	–	–	–	–	1	1	2	2	4
SCRUB	–	2	2	–	–	–	1	–	1
SHES CLEANING	1	–	1	–	–	–	–	–	–
SHINE	–	–	–	–	–	–	–	1	1
SHINY	–	–	–	1	1	2	1	–	1
SHOE	1	–	1	–	–	–	–	–	–
SING	–	–	–	–	1	1	–	–	–
SINK	2	1	3	–	–	–	–	1	1
SOAP	1	–	1	1	1	2	3	2	5
SORE	–	–	–	–	1	1	–	–	–
SPARKLE	–	–	–	1	–	1	–	–	–
SPIC AND SPAN	–	–	–	–	–	–	1	–	1
STARS	–	1	1	–	–	–	–	–	–
STOP	–	–	–	–	–	–	–	1	1
SUDS	–	1	1	–	–	–	–	–	–
SWEEP	–	1	1	2	–	2	–	–	–
TABLE	4	3	7	2	1	3	–	1	1
TAILOR	–	1	1	–	–	–	–	–	–
TAUGHT	1	–	1	–	–	–	–	–	–
TEETH	1	1	2	3	–	3	–	–	–
THE FLOOR	2	–	2	–	–	–	–	–	–
THE HOUSE	3	3	6	–	–	–	–	–	–
THEM	–	–	–	1	–	1	–	–	–
THIS	–	–	–	–	1	1	–	–	–
THROW	–	–	–	1	–	1	–	–	–
TIDY	–	–	–	2	3	5	1	2	3
TIDY UP	–	–	–	–	–	–	1	–	1
TO WASH	–	–	–	–	–	–	–	1	1
TOWEL	–	1	1	–	–	–	–	1	1
UNCLEAN	–	–	–	–	–	–	–	2	2
UNDIRTY	–	–	–	–	–	–	–	1	1
UP	1	1	2	2	2	4	–	–	–
UP HOUSE	–	1	1	–	–	–	–	–	–
UP THE CAR	–	1	1	–	–	–	–	–	–
UP THE TABLE	1	–	1	–	–	–	–	–	–
US	–	1	1	–	–	–	–	–	–

RESPONSE WORD	1ST M	F	T	3RD M	F	T	5TH M	F	T

17. CLEAN

RESPONSE WORD	1ST M	F	T	3RD M	F	T	5TH M	F	T
VACUUM	–	1	1	–	–	–	–	1	1
VACUUM CLEANER	4	7	11	–	–	–	–	–	–
VEEN	–	1	1	–	–	–	–	–	–
VERY	–	1	1	–	–	–	–	–	–
WAIT	–	1	1	–	–	–	–	–	–
WALL	–	1	1	–	–	–	–	–	–
WASH	4	7	11	9	6	15	10	6	16
WASH HANDS AND FACE	1	–	1	–	–	–	–	–	–
WASH MY HANDS	–	–	–	–	–	–	1	–	1
WASHED	–	–	–	–	1	1	–	–	–
WATER	1	1	2	1	–	1	2	–	2
WE CLEAN OUR HOUSE	–	1	1	–	–	–	–	–	–
WEAN	–	1	1	1	–	1	–	–	–
WHEN YOU WASH YOUR CLOTHES IN CLEAN WAT	1	–	1	–	–	–	–	–	–
WHEN YOURE CLEANING THE RUG	1	–	1	–	–	–	–	–	–
WHENEVER SOMEONE TAKES A BATH AND THEYR	–	1	1	–	–	–	–	–	–
WHITE	1	1	2	2	2	4	2	–	2
WINDOW	1	–	1	–	–	–	–	–	–
WINDOWS	1	–	1	–	–	–	–	–	–
WINTER	1	–	1	–	–	–	–	–	–
WIPE	–	–	–	–	–	–	1	1	2
WIPE OFF	–	–	–	–	–	–	–	1	1
WOMAN	–	1	1	–	–	–	–	–	–
WORK	1	2	3	–	–	–	–	3	3
YES	–	–	–	1	–	1	–	–	–
YOU	3	–	3	–	–	–	–	–	–
YOU CLEAN THE HOUSE UP	–	–	–	1	–	1	–	–	–
YOU CLEAN YOUR CLOTHES	1	–	1	–	–	–	–	–	–
YOUR FLOOR	–	1	1	–	–	–	–	–	–
YOUR HANDS	–	1	1	–	–	–	–	–	–
YOUR HOUSE	–	–	–	1	–	1	–	–	–
YOUR SHOES	–	–	–	1	–	1	–	–	–
YOURSELF	1	–	1	–	–	–	–	–	–

18. COCOON

RESPONSE WORD	1ST M	F	T	3RD M	F	T	5TH M	F	T
A BIRDS NEST	–	–	–	–	1	1	–	–	–
A BUTTERFLY	–	1	1	–	–	–	–	1	1
A LITTLE NEST	–	–	–	–	–	–	–	1	1
ACORN	–	–	–	–	–	–	1	–	1
AIRPLANE	1	–	1	–	–	–	–	–	–
AM	–	–	–	–	–	–	–	1	1
AN ANIMAL	–	–	–	–	–	–	1	–	1
ANIMAL	4	5	9	13	27	40	20	31	51
ANIMALS	–	1	1	–	–	–	–	1	1
ANT	–	–	–	1	–	1	–	1	1
ANTS	–	–	–	–	–	–	–	1	1
APPLE	–	1	1	–	1	1	–	–	–
BABOON	2	–	2	–	–	–	–	–	–
BABY	–	3	3	–	–	–	–	1	1
BABY COCOON	1	–	1	–	–	–	–	–	–
BALLOON	–	–	–	–	2	2	–	–	–
BASKET	–	–	–	–	1	1	–	–	–
BAT	–	1	1	–	–	–	–	–	–
BATTLE	1	–	1	–	–	–	–	–	–
BE	–	1	1	–	–	–	–	–	–
BEAR	–	1	1	–	–	–	1	–	1
BEAVER DAM	1	–	1	–	–	–	1	–	1
BED	–	–	–	–	–	–	1	–	1
BEE	1	–	1	–	–	–	–	–	–
BEES	–	–	–	2	–	2	–	–	–
BIRD	5	1	6	3	6	9	1	1	2
BLUE	–	2	2	–	–	–	–	–	–
BOAT	1	–	1	2	–	2	1	2	3
BOOKS	1	1	2	–	–	–	–	–	–
BOON	1	1	2	–	–	–	–	–	–
BORN	–	–	–	2	–	2	–	–	–
BOT	–	–	–	–	–	–	1	–	1

RESPONSE WORD	1ST			3RD			5TH		
	M	F	T	M	F	T	M	F	T

18. COCOON

RESPONSE WORD	M	F	T	M	F	T	M	F	T
BROWN	–	–	–	1	–	1	–	–	–
BRUSH	1	–	1	–	–	–	–	–	–
BUG	–	1	1	1	4	5	2	3	5
BUILDING	–	1	1	–	–	–	1	–	1
BUNNY RABBIT	–	1	1	–	–	–	–	–	–
BUTTERFLY	5	5	10	27	18	45	20	17	37
CA	–	1	1	–	–	–	–	–	–
CADAY	–	1	1	–	–	–	–	–	–
CAN	2	–	2	–	1	1	–	–	–
CAP	–	–	–	1	–	1	–	–	–
CAR	–	–	–	1	–	1	1	–	1
CASE	–	–	–	–	–	–	1	–	1
CAT	2	1	3	–	–	–	–	1	1
CATERPILLAR	6	5	11	9	9	18	10	14	24
CATERPILLAR NEST	–	–	–	–	–	–	–	1	1
CATERPILLARS	1	–	1	–	–	–	–	1	1
CATERPILLARS NEST	–	–	–	–	–	–	–	1	1
CATHY	1	–	1	–	–	–	–	–	–
CHAIR	1	1	2	1	–	1	–	–	–
CHARACTER	–	–	–	–	1	1	–	–	–
CHAROON	–	1	1	–	–	–	–	–	–
CHINA	1	–	1	–	–	–	–	–	–
CHOCOLATE	–	–	–	1	–	1	–	–	–
CHRISTMAS	–	–	–	–	1	1	1	–	1
CLOTEN	–	–	–	–	–	–	1	–	1
CLOTHES LOCKER	1	–	1	–	–	–	–	–	–
COCOANUT	–	2	2	–	–	–	–	–	–
COCOON	1	–	1	–	–	–	1	–	1
COLD	–	2	2	–	–	–	–	–	–
COLOR	–	–	–	1	–	1	–	–	–
COMB	1	–	1	–	–	–	–	–	–
COME	2	2	4	–	–	–	–	–	–
COME HERE	1	–	1	–	–	–	–	–	–
COMOON	–	1	1	–	–	–	–	–	–
CONE	3	1	4	1	–	1	–	–	–
COO-COO	–	1	1	–	–	–	–	1	1
COOCOO BIRD	1	–	1	–	–	–	–	–	–
COOCOO CLOCK	1	–	1	–	–	–	–	–	–
COOK	1	3	4	–	1	1	–	–	–
COOKIE	1	3	4	1	–	1	–	–	–
COOKIES	–	1	1	–	–	–	–	–	–
COOKY	–	1	1	–	–	–	–	–	–
COON	5	3	8	4	2	6	1	3	4
COON IN THE TREE	1	–	1	–	–	–	–	–	–
COONS COULD MAKE NOISE	–	1	1	–	–	–	–	–	–
COOP	–	–	–	1	–	1	–	–	–
COTTON	–	–	–	–	1	1	–	–	–
COTTON BALL	–	–	–	1	–	1	–	–	–
COVER	–	–	–	–	–	–	1	–	1
COW	–	–	–	1	–	1	–	–	–
COWARD	–	–	–	1	–	1	–	–	–
CUB	–	–	–	–	1	1	–	–	–
CUCKOO	1	1	2	–	–	–	–	–	–
CUCUMBER	1	–	1	–	–	–	–	–	–
CUE	–	–	–	–	–	–	–	1	1
CUP	1	–	1	–	–	–	–	–	–
CUT	–	1	1	–	–	–	–	–	–
DEE	1	–	1	–	–	–	–	–	–
DEER	1	1	2	–	–	–	–	–	–
DESK	–	1	1	–	–	–	–	–	–
DIE	–	1	1	–	–	–	–	–	–
DOG	–	–	–	–	–	–	2	–	2
DONT GO IN THE WOOD CAUSE A SNAKE MIGHT	–	1	1	–	–	–	–	–	–
DOOR	1	1	2	–	–	–	–	–	–
DRESS	–	1	1	–	–	–	–	–	–
EAGLE	–	1	1	–	–	–	–	–	–
ELEPHANT	1	–	1	–	–	–	–	–	–
ESKIMO	–	–	–	–	–	–	–	1	1
FAST	1	1	2	–	–	–	–	–	–
FOUR LEGS	–	–	–	1	–	1	–	–	–
FRUIT	1	–	1	–	–	–	–	–	–

RESPONSE WORD	1ST M	F	T	3RD M	F	T	5TH M	F	T

18. COCOON

RESPONSE WORD	1ST M	F	T	3RD M	F	T	5TH M	F	T
FUNNY	–	–	–	–	1	1	–	–	–
FUR	–	–	–	–	1	1	1	–	1
FURROW	–	–	–	–	–	–	1	–	1
FUZZ	–	–	–	1	–	1	–	–	–
FUZZY	1	–	1	–	–	–	–	–	–
GABOON	–	1	1	–	–	–	–	–	–
GARDEN	–	1	1	–	–	–	–	–	–
GET	1	–	1	–	–	–	–	–	–
GIRAFFE	–	–	–	–	1	1	–	–	–
GIRL	–	1	1	–	–	–	–	–	–
GLASSES	–	1	1	–	–	–	–	–	–
GLOOM	1	–	1	–	–	–	–	–	–
GO	1	–	1	–	–	–	–	1	1
GOAT	–	2	2	–	–	–	–	–	–
GOES IN WATER	–	1	1	–	–	–	–	–	–
GOING	–	–	–	–	1	1	–	1	1
GOOD	1	1	2	–	–	–	–	1	1
GOOGOO	–	–	–	1	–	1	–	–	–
GOON	1	–	1	–	–	–	–	–	–
GOSMOON	1	–	1	–	–	–	–	–	–
GRASSHOPPER	–	1	1	–	–	–	–	–	–
GUN	1	–	1	–	–	–	–	–	–
HAIR	–	1	1	1	–	1	–	–	–
HAND LOTION	–	1	1	–	–	–	–	–	–
HARD	–	–	–	–	–	–	–	1	1
HATCH	–	–	–	1	–	1	–	–	–
HEAD	–	–	–	–	–	–	1	–	1
HEAR	–	1	1	–	–	–	–	–	–
HERE	–	1	1	–	–	–	–	–	–
HIVE	–	–	–	–	–	–	1	–	1
HOLE	1	–	1	–	–	–	–	–	–
HOME	–	–	–	1	1	2	1	2	3
HONEY	–	–	–	–	–	–	–	1	1
HOON	1	–	1	–	–	–	–	–	–
HORSE	1	–	1	–	–	–	–	–	–
HOT	–	1	1	–	–	–	1	–	1
HOUSE	–	2	2	2	–	2	1	2	3
HUNTS	–	–	–	1	–	1	–	–	–
HURT	–	–	–	1	–	1	–	–	–
I LIKE RACCOONS	–	1	1	–	–	–	–	–	–
ICE CREAM	1	2	3	1	–	1	1	–	1
ICE CREAM CONE	1	–	1	–	–	–	–	–	–
INSECT	–	–	–	1	1	2	3	2	5
INSECT HOME	–	–	–	–	1	1	–	–	–
INSECTS	–	–	–	1	–	1	–	–	–
ITS IN THE WOODS	–	1	1	–	–	–	–	–	–
KEY	2	–	2	–	–	–	–	–	–
KILLING	1	–	1	–	–	–	–	–	–
LACOON	–	1	1	–	–	–	–	–	–
LAGOON	1	–	1	–	–	–	–	–	–
LEAF	–	–	–	1	–	1	–	1	1
LIGHT	1	–	1	–	–	–	–	–	–
LIKE	–	1	1	–	–	–	–	–	–
LION	2	–	2	–	–	–	–	–	–
LOOK	–	1	1	–	–	–	–	–	–
LOOK AT ANIMALS	1	–	1	–	–	–	–	–	–
LOON	1	–	1	–	–	–	1	–	1
LOUD	–	–	–	–	1	1	–	–	–
MACOON	–	–	–	1	–	1	–	–	–
MALOONED	–	1	1	–	–	–	–	–	–
METAL	–	–	–	–	–	–	–	1	1
MI–MI	1	–	1	–	–	–	–	–	–
MIGHT	–	–	–	–	1	1	–	–	–
MILK	–	–	–	–	–	–	1	–	1
MISSISSIPPI	–	–	–	–	–	–	1	–	1
MOKY	–	–	–	–	–	–	1	–	1
MOLE	1	–	1	–	–	–	–	–	–
MONEY	–	–	–	–	–	–	–	1	1
MONKEY	1	–	1	–	1	1	–	1	1
MOON	9	3	12	2	–	2	1	1	2
MOOSE	–	1	1	–	–	–	–	–	–
MOSTLY	–	–	–	–	1	1	–	–	–

RESPONSE WORD	1ST			3RD			5TH		
	M	F	T	M	F	T	M	F	T

18.   COCOON

RESPONSE WORD	M	F	T	M	F	T	M	F	T
MOTH	–	–	–	–	4	4	6	5	11
MOTHER	1	–	1	–	–	–	–	–	–
MOUSE	2	–	2	–	1	1	–	1	1
NATIVE	–	–	–	–	–	–	1	–	1
NEAR	–	1	1	–	–	–	–	–	–
NEST	2	–	2	4	1	5	7	7	14
NET	–	–	–	1	–	1	1	–	1
NEXT	–	–	–	–	1	1	–	–	–
NO RESPONSE	1	–	1	–	–	–	–	–	–
NOISE	1	–	1	–	1	1	–	–	–
NOT	–	1	1	–	–	–	–	–	–
NOT COCOON	1	–	1	–	–	–	–	–	–
NOTHING	–	1	1	–	–	–	–	–	–
NOW	–	–	–	1	–	1	–	–	–
NUT	–	1	1	–	–	–	–	–	–
OH	–	1	1	–	–	–	–	–	–
OPPOSSUM	–	–	–	1	–	1	–	–	–
ORANGE	–	1	1	–	–	–	–	–	–
OUT OF	–	–	–	1	–	1	–	–	–
OWL	2	2	4	–	1	1	–	–	–
PANTS	–	–	–	–	1	1	–	–	–
PET	1	–	1	–	–	–	–	–	–
PICTURE	–	–	–	–	1	1	–	–	–
PINE CONE	–	1	1	–	–	–	–	–	–
PLACE	–	–	–	–	–	–	1	–	1
PLEASE	1	–	1	–	–	–	–	–	–
PLUG	1	–	1	–	–	–	–	–	–
POFFUM	–	1	1	–	–	–	–	–	–
POON	1	–	1	–	–	–	–	–	–
POSSUM	–	–	–	–	–	–	–	1	1
PRAYING MANTIS	–	–	–	–	–	–	1	–	1
PRAYING-MANTIS	–	–	–	1	–	1	–	–	–
PRESENT	–	–	–	–	–	–	1	–	1
PRETTY	1	–	1	–	–	–	1	–	1
PUPA	–	–	–	–	–	–	–	1	1
RABBIT	1	1	2	2	1	3	–	1	1
RACCOON	8	10	18	14	22	36	6	6	12
RACOON	–	–	–	–	–	–	6	8	14
RAN AWAY	–	–	–	–	1	1	–	–	–
RAT	1	2	3	2	2	4	1	–	1
RECEIVE	–	1	1	–	–	–	–	–	–
RINK	1	–	1	–	–	–	–	–	–
ROCK	–	1	1	–	–	–	–	–	–
ROOM	1	–	1	1	–	1	–	–	–
ROPE	1	–	1	–	–	–	–	–	–
ROUND	–	–	–	1	–	1	–	–	–
RUN	–	–	–	1	–	1	–	–	–
SCHOOL	1	–	1	–	–	–	–	–	–
SEAGULL	–	–	–	1	–	1	–	–	–
SEECOON	–	–	–	1	–	1	–	–	–
SEED	–	–	–	–	–	–	–	1	1
SHELL	–	–	–	–	1	1	–	–	–
SHELTER	–	–	–	1	–	1	–	–	–
SHOON	–	–	–	–	–	–	1	–	1
SILK	–	–	–	–	–	–	1	2	3
SILK WORM	–	–	–	1	–	1	2	–	2
SILKWORM	–	–	–	–	1	1	1	–	1
SIT	–	–	–	–	–	–	1	–	1
SKIN	–	–	–	–	–	–	–	1	1
SKYSCRAPER	1	–	1	–	–	–	–	–	–
SLIMY	–	–	–	–	–	–	1	–	1
SMALL	–	–	–	–	1	1	–	–	–
SNAKE	–	–	–	–	1	1	1	–	1
SOFT	–	–	–	–	1	1	–	–	–
SOME	–	1	1	–	–	–	–	–	–
SOME ANIMAL I THINK	–	–	–	1	–	1	–	–	–
SOMETHING	–	1	1	–	–	–	–	–	–
SOMETHING THAT CATERPILLARS SLEEP IN	–	–	–	–	–	–	1	–	1
SOON	1	1	2	1	–	1	–	–	–
SOUNDS LIKE FUN	–	–	–	–	1	1	–	–	–
SPIDER	–	–	–	1	–	1	1	2	3

RESPONSE WORD	1ST M	1ST F	1ST T	3RD M	3RD F	3RD T	5TH M	5TH F	5TH T

18. COCOON

RESPONSE WORD	1ST M	1ST F	1ST T	3RD M	3RD F	3RD T	5TH M	5TH F	5TH T
SQUIRREL	–	–	–	2	–	2	1	–	1
STABLE	1	–	1	–	–	–	–	–	–
STONE	–	–	–	–	1	1	–	–	–
STRIPED	–	–	–	–	–	–	1	–	1
SUN	–	1	1	–	–	–	–	–	–
SWEATER	–	1	1	–	–	–	–	–	–
SWEET	–	–	–	–	–	–	1	–	1
TABLE	–	1	1	–	–	–	–	–	–
TAIL	–	1	1	–	–	–	–	–	–
TALE	–	–	–	–	1	1	–	–	–
TENT	–	–	–	1	–	1	–	–	–
THE	–	–	–	–	1	1	–	–	–
THE COON PLAY	–	1	1	–	–	–	–	–	–
THIN	–	–	–	–	–	–	1	–	1
THING	–	–	–	–	1	1	1	–	1
TICK	–	1	1	–	–	–	–	–	–
TIGER	1	–	1	–	–	–	–	–	–
TO	–	–	–	–	–	–	1	–	1
TRAIL	1	–	1	–	–	–	–	–	–
TRAIN	–	1	1	–	–	–	–	–	–
TREE	2	4	6	1	–	1	2	–	2
TREES	–	–	–	–	–	–	–	1	1
TWO COCOONS	–	–	–	1	–	1	–	–	–
UP IN THE TREE	–	1	1	–	–	–	–	–	–
WAGON	–	1	1	–	–	–	–	–	–
WALK	–	–	–	–	1	1	–	–	–
WALL	–	–	–	–	1	1	–	–	–
WARM	1	–	1	–	1	1	–	–	–
WASP	–	–	–	–	–	–	1	–	1
WATCH OUT	–	1	1	–	–	–	–	–	–
WATER	–	1	1	1	–	1	–	–	–
WEB	–	–	–	–	1	1	–	–	–
WHEN YOURE COOKING SOMETHING.	1	–	1	–	–	–	–	–	–
WHERE A BUTTERFLY COMES OUT OF	–	–	–	1	–	1	–	–	–
WHITE	–	1	1	–	–	–	–	–	–
WINTER HOME OF A CATERPILLAR.	–	–	–	–	–	–	–	1	1
WOODS	–	–	–	–	–	–	1	–	1
WOOL	–	–	–	–	–	–	1	–	1
WORM	–	1	1	4	1	5	3	2	5
WORMS	1	–	1	–	–	–	–	–	–
YOU	–	–	–	–	–	–	–	1	1

19. COLD

RESPONSE WORD	1ST M	1ST F	1ST T	3RD M	3RD F	3RD T	5TH M	5TH F	5TH T
A BAD COLD	–	1	1	–	–	–	–	–	–
AGO	–	–	–	–	–	–	–	1	1
AIR	1	–	1	–	–	–	–	1	1
ANTARCTIC	–	–	–	–	–	–	1	–	1
AT	–	–	–	1	–	1	–	–	–
BAD	–	–	–	1	–	1	1	–	1
BAD TASK	1	–	1	–	–	–	–	–	–
BATH	–	–	–	–	–	–	–	1	1
BEAR	1	–	1	–	–	–	–	1	1
BITTER	–	–	–	–	–	–	–	1	1
BLUE	–	1	1	–	–	–	–	–	–
BOLD	1	2	3	–	–	–	–	–	–
BOOK	1	–	1	–	–	–	–	–	–
BOOKS	–	1	1	–	–	–	–	–	–
BOY	–	1	1	–	–	–	–	–	–
BREEZE	–	–	–	1	–	1	–	–	–
BUSH	1	–	1	–	–	–	–	–	–
BUTTON	–	1	1	–	–	–	–	–	–
CAR	1	1	2	–	–	–	–	–	–
CHARCOAL	–	–	–	1	–	1	–	–	–
CHILLY	1	–	1	2	3	5	2	2	4
COAL	–	1	1	–	–	–	–	2	2
COAL CAR	1	–	1	–	–	–	–	–	–
COAL YOU PUT IN FURNACES	–	–	–	1	–	1	–	–	–

RESPONSE WORD	1ST M	F	T	3RD M	F	T	5TH M	F	T
					19. COLD				
COAT	2	7	9	–	1	1	1	–	1
COATS	1	–	1	–	–	–	–	–	–
COL	–	–	–	–	–	–	1	–	1
COME	1	1	2	–	–	–	–	–	–
COME OUT THE STOVE	–	1	1	–	–	–	–	–	–
COOK	–	1	1	–	–	–	–	–	–
COOL	2	–	2	–	–	–	–	2	2
COPPER	–	1	1	–	1	1	–	–	–
CORN	1	–	1	–	–	–	–	1	1
COUGH	2	–	2	1	1	2	–	1	1
COULD	–	–	–	–	1	1	–	–	–
CREAM	–	1	1	–	–	–	1	–	1
DAY	1	–	1	–	–	–	–	–	–
DAYS	1	–	1	–	–	–	–	–	–
DIRFT	–	–	–	–	–	–	–	1	1
DOCTOR	–	–	–	–	–	–	1	–	1
DOLD	–	1	1	–	–	–	–	–	–
DOOR	–	1	1	–	–	–	–	–	–
EVENING	–	1	1	–	–	–	–	–	–
FAN	1	–	1	1	–	1	–	–	–
FAST	–	–	–	–	1	1	–	–	–
FEVER	–	–	–	1	–	1	1	–	1
FLOWER	–	1	1	–	–	–	–	–	–
FOOD	1	–	1	–	–	–	–	–	–
FREEZE	1	1	2	3	2	5	5	1	6
FREEZING	1	3	4	8	5	13	7	6	13
FROST	–	–	–	–	–	–	1	–	1
FROZE	1	2	3	–	–	–	–	–	–
FROZEN	–	–	–	–	1	1	2	–	2
FUNNY	–	1	1	–	–	–	–	–	–
GLOVES	1	–	1	–	–	–	–	–	–
GO IN HOUSE	–	1	1	–	–	–	–	–	–
GOLD	1	–	1	–	–	–	–	–	–
GOOD	–	–	–	–	1	1	–	–	–
GRIPPE	–	–	–	–	–	–	–	1	1
HAIR	1	–	1	–	–	–	–	–	–
HAT	–	1	1	–	–	–	–	–	–
HATS	–	1	1	–	–	–	–	–	–
HED	–	–	–	–	–	–	1	–	1
HOLD	3	–	3	–	–	–	–	1	1
HOT	38	36	74	64	75	139	59	60	119
ICE	6	2	8	7	3	10	4	4	8
ICEBOX	1	–	1	1	–	1	1	–	1
ICY	–	–	–	–	–	1	1	1	2
IM COLD	1	–	1	–	–	–	–	–	–
IN	1	–	1	–	–	–	–	–	–
IN THE COLD AIR	–	1	1	–	–	–	–	–	–
INK	–	1	1	–	–	–	–	–	–
IT	–	–	–	1	–	1	–	–	–
IT MIGHT BE TOO COLD FOR YOU TO GO OUTS	–	1	1	–	–	–	–	–	–
ITS COLD AT THE SOUTH POLE	–	1	1	–	–	–	–	–	–
JACKET	2	1	3	–	–	–	–	–	–
LAWN	–	1	1	–	–	–	–	–	–
MALLARD	1	–	1	–	–	–	–	–	–
MAN	1	–	1	–	–	–	–	–	–
ME	–	–	–	1	–	1	1	–	1
MILK	1	–	1	–	–	–	–	–	–
MIND	1	–	1	–	–	–	–	–	–
MITTENS	–	1	1	–	–	–	–	–	–
MOLD	3	–	3	–	–	–	–	–	–
MOMMY IT IS TOO COLD OUTSIDE	–	1	1	–	–	–	–	–	–
MONDAY	–	–	–	–	–	–	–	1	1
NICE	–	1	1	–	–	–	–	–	–
NIGHT	–	1	1	–	–	–	–	2	2
NIGHT TIME	1	–	1	–	–	–	–	–	–
NOLD	–	1	1	1	–	1	–	–	–
NOSE	–	–	–	–	–	–	–	1	1
NOT WARM	–	–	–	1	1	2	3	1	4
OLD	–	–	–	1	2	3	–	–	–

RESPONSE WORD	1ST			3RD			5TH		
	M	F	T	M	F	T	M	F	T

19. COLD

RESPONSE WORD	M	F	T	M	F	T	M	F	T
OUT	1	1	2	-	-	-	-	-	-
OUTSIDE	1	-	1	-	-	-	-	-	-
PEPPER	-	1	1	-	-	-	-	-	-
PUMPKIN	1	-	1	-	-	-	-	-	-
PUT ON A COAT	-	-	-	-	-	-	-	1	1
REAL	-	1	1	-	-	-	-	-	-
REFRIGERATOR	1	-	1	-	-	-	1	-	1
ROCK	-	-	-	-	-	-	1	-	1
ROLLED	-	1	1	-	-	-	-	-	-
SHEEP	1	1	2	1	-	1	-	-	-
SHIVER	-	1	1	-	-	-	2	1	3
SHIVERING	1	-	1	-	-	-	-	2	2
SHORT	1	-	1	-	-	-	-	-	-
SICK	-	1	1	-	1	1	-	1	1
SICKNESS	-	-	-	-	-	-	1	-	1
SKY	1	-	1	-	-	-	-	-	-
SNEEZE	-	1	1	1	3	4	-	-	-
SNOW	2	1	3	2	-	2	1	3	4
SOFT	-	-	-	-	1	1	-	-	-
SOLD	1	-	1	-	-	-	-	-	-
STAY	1	-	1	-	-	-	-	-	-
STEM	-	-	-	1	-	1	-	-	-
STUFF	1	-	1	-	-	-	-	-	-
SUMMER	1	-	1	-	-	-	-	-	-
SUN	1	1	2	-	1	1	-	-	-
SUNNY	-	2	2	-	-	-	-	-	-
TAN	-	1	1	-	-	-	-	-	-
TELEVISION	-	1	1	-	-	-	-	-	-
THIS COULD BE A COLD WINTER	-	1	1	-	-	-	-	-	-
TOO	-	1	1	-	-	-	-	-	-
TOO COLD WATER	-	1	1	-	-	-	-	-	-
TRAIN	1	-	1	-	-	-	-	-	-
TREE	2	-	2	-	-	-	-	-	-
TURTLES	1	-	1	-	-	-	-	-	-
VERY	-	1	1	1	1	2	-	-	-
WARM	10	17	27	29	29	58	29	30	59
WATER	6	3	9	-	-	-	2	-	2
WEATHER	3	3	6	-	1	1	-	-	-
WELL	-	-	-	1	-	1	-	-	-
WERM	-	-	-	-	-	-	1	-	1
WET	-	-	-	1	-	1	-	-	-
WHEN YOURE FREEZING SOMETHING IN THE RE.	1	-	1	-	-	-	-	-	-
WHITE	1	-	1	-	-	-	-	-	-
WIND	1	3	4	-	-	-	1	2	3
WINDY	1	3	4	1	-	1	1	-	1
WINTER	7	9	16	5	5	10	6	7	13
WITH	1	-	1	-	-	-	-	-	-
WORM	-	-	-	-	-	-	-	1	1
YOU ARE	1	-	1	-	-	-	-	-	-
YOU GET COLD AND YOU PUT YOUR COAT ON	1	-	1	-	-	-	-	-	-

20. COLOR

RESPONSE WORD	M	F	T	M	F	T	M	F	T
A COLORING BOOK	1	-	1	-	-	-	-	-	-
A CRAYON OR PAINT	-	-	-	-	-	-	-	1	1
A LITTLE GIRL OR BOYS COLRING IN THE CO.	-	1	1	-	-	-	1	-	1
ABSTRACT	-	1	1	-	-	-	-	-	-
BABY	-	1	1	-	-	-	1	-	1
BEAUTIFUL	-	-	-	-	1	1	1	-	1
BELL	-	-	-	1	-	1	-	-	-
BIG	1	-	1	-	-	-	-	-	-
BIRD	1	-	1	-	-	-	-	1	1
BLACK	5	2	7	16	10	26	17	8	25
BLACK AND WHITE	-	-	-	-	-	-	2	-	2
BLANKET	-	-	-	1	-	1	-	1	1
BLUE	10	10	20	20	17	37	14	20	34
BLUE AND RED	-	1	1	-	-	-	-	-	-

20. COLOR

RESPONSE WORD	1ST M	F	T	3RD M	F	T	5TH M	F	T
BOOK	1	2	3	–	1	1	–	1	1
BOOKS	1	–	1	–	–	–	–	–	–
BOWER	1	–	1	–	–	–	–	–	–
BRIGHT	–	–	–	2	2	4	2	5	7
BROWN	5	2	7	8	5	13	7	7	14
BUCKET	1	–	1	–	–	–	–	–	–
BUT	–	–	–	–	–	–	1	–	1
BUTHER	–	–	–	–	1	1	–	–	–
BUTTER	1	–	1	–	–	–	–	–	–
BUTTERFLY	–	1	1	–	–	–	–	–	–
CAR	–	1	1	–	1	1	–	–	–
CAT	1	–	1	–	–	–	–	–	–
CEMENT	1	–	1	–	–	–	–	–	–
CHAIR	–	–	–	–	–	–	2	–	2
CHANGE	–	–	–	–	–	–	–	1	1
CLOTH	–	–	–	–	–	–	1	–	1
CLOTHES LINE	1	–	1	–	–	–	–	–	–
COAT	1	–	1	–	–	–	–	–	–
COLD	1	–	1	–	–	–	–	–	–
COLOR	–	–	–	–	1	1	–	–	–
COLORED PERSON	–	–	–	1	–	1	–	–	–
COLORING	–	2	2	1	–	1	1	–	1
COLORING BOOK	–	2	2	–	–	–	–	–	–
COLORING BOOKS	–	1	1	–	–	–	–	–	–
COLORS	–	–	–	–	–	–	1	–	1
COME	1	1	2	–	–	–	–	–	–
COMIC BOOK	–	1	1	–	–	–	–	–	–
COVER	–	–	–	–	–	–	–	1	1
COW	–	1	1	–	–	–	–	–	–
CRANAROLY	–	–	–	–	–	–	–	1	1
CRAYON	10	14	24	6	11	17	5	11	16
CRAYONS	6	4	10	3	–	3	–	–	–
CROWN	–	–	–	1	1	2	–	–	–
CUT	–	1	1	–	–	–	–	–	–
DARK	–	–	–	1	–	1	–	–	–
DESIGN	–	–	–	–	–	–	–	1	1
DESK	–	2	2	–	–	–	–	–	–
DEVER	–	1	1	–	–	–	–	–	–
DID	–	1	1	–	–	–	–	–	–
DIFFERENT	–	1	1	1	–	1	–	–	–
DIFFERENT COLOR	–	–	–	–	1	1	–	–	–
DISH	1	–	1	–	–	–	–	–	–
DO	–	–	1	–	–	–	–	–	–
DONT COLOR	1	–	1	–	–	–	1	–	1
DRAW	1	2	3	–	2	2	1	3	4
EXCITING	–	–	–	–	–	–	1	–	1
FACE	1	–	1	–	–	–	–	–	–
FAST	–	1	1	–	–	–	–	–	–
FEATHER	–	1	1	–	–	–	–	–	–
FILL IN	–	–	–	–	–	–	–	1	1
FLAG	–	–	–	–	–	–	–	1	1
FLAVOR	–	1	1	1	–	1	–	–	–
FLESH	–	–	–	–	1	1	–	–	–
FLOOR	–	–	–	1	–	1	–	–	–
FORM	–	1	1	–	1	1	–	–	–
FULL	–	–	–	–	1	1	–	–	–
FUN	–	–	–	1	–	1	–	–	–
GAY	–	–	1	–	–	–	1	–	1
GLASS	1	–	1	–	–	–	–	–	–
GO	1	1	2	–	–	–	–	–	–
GOLD	–	–	–	1	2	3	1	–	1
GOOD	–	1	1	–	–	–	–	–	–
GRASS	–	–	–	–	1	1	–	–	–
GRAY	–	–	–	–	1	1	1	3	4
GREEN	5	8	13	11	5	16	10	7	17
GREY	–	–	–	–	–	–	–	1	1
GUARD	–	–	–	–	–	–	1	–	1
HAIR	1	–	1	–	–	–	–	–	–
HE	–	1	1	–	–	–	–	–	–
HEDGES	1	–	1	–	–	–	–	–	–
HELP	1	–	1	–	–	–	–	–	–
HER	–	–	–	1	–	1	–	–	–

RESPONSE WORD	1ST M	F	T	3RD M	F	T	5TH M	F	T

20. COLOR

RESPONSE WORD	1ST M	F	T	3RD M	F	T	5TH M	F	T
HIGH	–	–	–	–	–	–	1	–	1
HOT	1	–	1	–	–	–	–	–	–
I COLOR PRETTY, MOMMY	–	1	1	–	–	–	–	–	–
I LIKE TO COLOR	–	1	1	–	–	–	–	–	–
IN SCHOOL WITH YOUR COLORING BOOK.	–	1	1	–	–	–	–	–	–
IT	–	2	2	–	1	1	–	–	–
IT RED	–	–	–	–	1	1	–	–	–
LETS GO AND COLOR IN THE COLORING BOOK.	–	1	1	–	–	–	–	–	–
LETS WATCH TV	–	1	1	–	–	–	–	–	–
LIKE A CRAYON	–	–	–	–	–	–	–	1	1
LINE	1	–	1	1	–	1	–	–	–
LOVELY	–	–	–	–	–	–	1	–	1
MAKE BEAUTIFUL	–	–	–	–	–	–	1	–	1
ME GRAY	1	–	1	–	–	–	–	–	–
MEDICINE	–	–	–	–	–	–	1	–	1
MIX	–	–	–	–	–	–	–	1	1
MOLOR	–	–	–	–	1	1	–	–	–
MOTHER	2	1	3	1	–	1	–	–	–
MULLER	2	–	2	–	–	–	–	–	–
MY	–	1	1	–	–	–	–	–	–
NEAT	2	–	2	–	–	–	–	–	–
NICE	–	–	–	1	–	1	–	–	–
NOLLOR	–	1	1	–	–	–	–	–	–
NOT COLOR	1	–	1	1	–	1	–	–	–
NOT TO COLOR	–	–	–	1	–	1	–	–	–
OLOR	1	–	1	–	–	–	–	–	–
ORANGE	3	1	4	1	3	4	3	1	4
OTHER COLORS	1	–	1	–	–	–	–	–	–
PAGE	1	–	1	–	–	–	–	–	–
PAINT	1	3	4	1	–	1	2	3	5
PAINTS	–	–	–	–	–	–	–	1	1
PAPER	3	4	7	–	1	1	–	–	–
PAPERS	1	–	1	–	–	–	–	–	–
PASTE	–	3	3	–	–	–	–	–	–
PENCIL	1	–	1	–	1	1	–	–	–
PICTURE	8	7	15	3	1	4	–	2	2
PICTURES	3	1	4	–	–	–	–	1	1
PINK	1	1	2	2	4	6	–	1	1
PLAIN	1	–	1	–	–	–	–	–	–
POLOR	2	–	2	–	–	–	–	–	–
PRETTY	–	3	3	6	2	8	–	2	2
PURPLE	1	1	2	2	3	5	3	4	7
PUTTY	1	–	1	–	–	–	–	–	–
RAINBOW	–	1	1	–	–	–	–	–	–
READ	1	–	1	–	–	–	–	–	–
RECOLOR	–	–	–	–	–	–	1	–	1
RED	16	18	34	21	32	53	32	27	59
RIGHT	1	–	1	–	–	–	–	–	–
ROLOR	1	1	2	–	–	–	–	–	–
SAFE	–	–	–	–	1	1	–	–	–
SANTA CLAUS PICTURES	–	1	1	–	–	–	–	–	–
SCHOOL	1	–	1	–	–	–	–	–	–
SEE	–	1	1	–	–	–	–	–	–
SELL	–	–	–	–	–	–	–	1	1
SHADE	–	–	–	–	–	–	–	4	4
SHAPE	–	1	1	–	–	–	1	–	1
SHIRT	1	–	1	–	–	–	–	–	–
SHIRTS	–	–	–	1	–	1	–	–	–
SINK	–	–	–	–	–	–	1	–	1
SMELLER	1	–	1	–	–	–	–	–	–
SMOTHER	1	–	1	–	–	–	–	–	–
SOFT	–	–	–	–	–	–	1	–	1
SOMETHING	–	–	–	1	1	2	–	–	–
SOMETHING RED	1	–	1	–	–	–	–	–	–
SONG	–	–	–	–	1	1	–	–	–
SPEAK	–	–	–	–	1	1	–	–	–
SPEAKER	–	–	–	–	1	1	–	–	–
SPOON	–	–	–	1	–	1	–	–	–
STUFF	1	–	1	–	–	–	–	–	–
TASTE	–	–	–	–	–	–	–	1	1

RESPONSE WORD	1ST M	F	T	3RD M	F	T	5TH M	F	T
20. COLOR									
THE	–	–	–	–	–	–	1	–	1
THING	–	–	–	–	–	–	2	–	2
THINGS	–	1	1	–	2	2	–	–	–
THIS	1	–	1	–	–	–	–	–	–
TIME TO COLOR	–	–	–	1	–	1	–	–	–
TONE	–	–	–	–	–	–	–	1	1
TRUCK	1	–	1	–	–	–	–	–	–
TV	1	–	1	1	–	1	–	1	1
WALL	1	–	1	–	–	–	–	–	–
WARM	–	–	–	1	–	1	–	–	–
WATER	1	–	1	–	–	–	–	–	–
WHAT COLOR IS MY SKIRT	–	1	1	–	–	–	–	–	–
WHEN YOURE COLORING A PAGE	1	–	1	–	–	–	–	–	–
WHITE	–	4	4	4	3	7	3	4	7
WORD	–	–	–	–	1	1	1	–	1
WORK	–	–	–	–	1	1	–	–	–
WRITE	1	1	2	–	3	3	–	–	–
WRITING	–	2	2	–	–	–	–	–	–
WULLERD	–	–	–	1	–	1	–	–	–
YELLOW	4	3	7	10	9	19	12	10	22
YOU LIKE	1	–	1	–	–	–	–	–	–
YOU PAINT	–	–	–	1	–	1	–	–	–
YOUR PICTURE	–	1	1	–	–	–	–	–	–
21. DARK									
A DOG	–	1	1	–	–	–	–	–	–
AFRAID	–	1	1	–	–	–	–	–	–
AND	1	–	1	–	–	–	–	–	–
AT NIGHT TIME	–	1	1	–	–	–	–	–	–
ATE	–	–	–	1	–	1	–	–	–
BARK	3	1	4	–	2	2	–	–	–
BASEMENT	1	–	1	–	–	–	–	–	–
BED	1	3	4	–	–	–	1	–	1
BEING IN THE DARK	1	–	1	–	–	–	–	–	–
BERRY	1	–	1	–	–	–	–	–	–
BLACK	5	2	7	7	8	15	13	12	25
BLUE	–	2	2	–	–	–	–	–	–
BOARD	2	–	2	–	–	–	–	–	–
BOOK	–	1	1	–	–	–	–	–	–
BRIGHT	1	–	1	1	–	1	2	3	5
BROWN	–	–	–	1	–	1	–	–	–
BROWN FLOOR IN THE HOUSE	1	–	1	–	–	–	–	–	–
BY	–	–	–	1	–	1	–	–	–
CAN	1	–	1	–	–	–	1	–	1
CANT SEE	1	–	1	2	1	3	2	–	2
CART	–	1	1	–	–	–	–	–	–
CAT	–	–	–	–	–	–	1	–	1
CLOTHING	1	–	1	–	–	–	–	–	–
CLOUDS	2	–	2	–	–	–	–	–	–
CLOUDY	–	–	–	1	–	1	–	–	–
COAL	1	–	1	–	–	–	–	–	–
COLD	1	1	2	–	–	–	–	1	1
COLOR	–	–	–	–	–	–	1	–	1
COME	1	–	1	–	–	–	–	–	–
DART	2	–	2	–	–	–	–	–	–
DAWN	–	–	–	1	–	1	–	–	–
DAY	1	3	4	–	4	4	2	1	3
DAYLIGHT	–	1	1	–	–	–	–	–	–
DEED	–	1	1	–	–	–	–	–	–
DESK	1	–	1	–	–	–	–	–	–
DOG	3	2	5	–	–	–	1	–	1
DONT BE SCARED OF THE DARK	–	1	1	–	–	–	–	–	–
DONT GO OUT	1	–	1	–	–	–	–	–	–
DONT GO OUTSIDE	–	1	1	–	–	–	–	–	–
DOOR	1	–	1	–	–	–	–	–	–
DOWN	1	–	1	–	–	–	–	–	–
DREARY	–	–	–	–	–	–	–	1	1
DRUM	–	–	–	–	1	1	–	–	–

21. DARK

RESPONSE WORD	1ST			3RD			5TH		
	M	F	T	M	F	T	M	F	T
EARLY	—	—	—	1	—	1	—	—	—
FLASHLIGHT	1	—	1	—	—	—	—	—	—
FLOOR	—	—	—	—	—	—	1	—	1
GARK	—	1	1	—	—	—	1	—	1
GHOST	—	—	—	—	1	1	1	—	1
GIRL	—	—	—	—	1	1	—	—	—
GLOOM	—	—	—	—	—	—	1	1	2
GO TO BED	—	1	1	—	—	—	—	—	—
GOOD	—	1	1	—	—	—	—	—	—
GUN	—	1	1	—	—	—	—	—	—
HALLOWEEN	—	1	1	—	—	—	—	—	—
HANDS	1	—	1	—	—	—	—	—	—
HARK	—	2	2	—	—	—	—	—	—
HAUNTED	1	—	1	—	—	—	—	—	—
HEAD	1	—	1	—	—	—	—	—	—
HEAVY	—	—	—	—	—	—	—	1	1
HERE	—	—	—	—	—	—	1	—	1
HOUSE	2	—	2	—	—	—	—	—	—
IN	—	1	1	—	—	—	—	—	—
ITS DARK AT NIGHT	—	1	1	—	—	—	—	—	—
JENNY	1	—	1	—	—	—	—	—	—
JUNGLE	—	—	—	—	—	—	1	—	1
LARK	2	2	4	—	—	—	—	—	—
LIGHT	40	45	85	89	96	185	87	93	180
LIGHTS	—	—	—	—	1	1	—	—	—
LIKE THERES A DARK HOUSE	—	—	—	—	—	—	—	1	1
LOCKER	1	—	1	—	—	—	—	—	—
LOUD	—	—	—	1	—	1	—	—	—
LOW	—	—	—	—	—	—	—	1	1
MAN	1	1	2	1	—	1	—	1	1
MARK	3	2	5	1	1	2	—	1	1
MIDNIGHT	—	1	1	—	2	2	1	—	1
MOON	1	9	10	1	—	1	—	1	1
MOON COMES OUT	—	1	1	—	—	—	—	—	—
MORNING	3	5	8	3	3	6	—	—	—
MORNING TIME	1	—	1	1	—	1	—	—	—
NARK	—	—	—	1	—	1	—	—	—
NIGHT	12	13	25	17	14	31	12	16	28
NIGHT TIME	—	1	1	—	—	—	—	—	—
NO LIGHT	—	—	—	1	—	1	—	—	—
NO SUN	—	—	—	—	—	—	1	—	1
NOT AFRAID	1	—	1	—	—	—	—	—	—
NOT LIGHT	—	—	—	—	—	—	1	1	2
NOT SEE	—	1	1	—	—	—	—	—	—
NOTHING	—	—	—	1	—	1	—	—	—
OUT	—	2	2	—	—	—	—	—	—
OUTSIDE	2	1	3	—	—	—	—	—	—
PARK	—	1	1	—	—	—	—	—	—
PLAY IN DARK	1	—	1	—	—	—	—	—	—
POKE	1	—	1	—	—	—	—	—	—
PUMPKIN	1	—	1	—	—	—	—	—	—
QUIET	—	—	—	1	—	1	—	—	—
REAL DARK	1	—	1	—	—	—	—	—	—
REAL DARK OUT	1	—	1	—	—	—	—	—	—
ROOM	2	—	2	—	—	—	—	—	—
RUNS OUT	—	1	1	—	—	—	—	—	—
SAIL	1	—	1	—	—	—	—	—	—
SCALED	—	—	—	—	—	—	1	—	1
SCARED	—	—	—	—	—	—	1	—	1
SCARY	—	—	—	2	1	3	1	—	1
SEE	1	—	1	1	—	1	—	—	—
SHADOWY	—	—	—	—	—	—	—	1	1
SHARP	—	—	—	—	—	—	1	1	1
SHORT	—	—	—	—	—	—	—	—	—
SIGHT	—	—	—	1	—	1	—	—	—
SKY	—	2	2	—	—	—	—	—	—
SLEEP	1	3	4	1	—	1	—	—	—
SLEEPY	—	1	1	—	—	—	—	—	—
SORT	—	1	1	—	—	—	—	—	—
SPACE	—	—	—	—	—	—	—	1	1
SPARK	2	—	2	—	—	—	—	—	—
SPOOKY	1	—	1	1	—	1	1	1	2

RESPONSE WORD	1ST M	F	T	3RD M	F	T	5TH M	F	T

21. DARK

RESPONSE WORD	M	F	T	M	F	T	M	F	T
STAN	1	–	1	–	–	–	–	–	–
STAR	3	–	3	–	–	–	–	–	–
STARS	1	2	3	–	1	1	–	1	1
SUN	4	5	9	2	–	2	–	–	–
SUNSHINE	1	–	1	–	–	–	–	–	–
SWEATER	–	1	1	–	–	–	–	–	–
TABLE	1	–	1	–	–	–	–	–	–
THARD	1	–	1	–	–	–	–	–	–
THE SUN MAKES IT GET DARK	1	–	1	–	–	–	–	–	–
THOUGHT	–	–	–	–	1	1	–	–	–
THROW	1	–	1	–	–	–	–	–	–
TIME	1	–	1	–	–	–	–	–	–
TRAIN	–	1	1	–	–	–	–	–	–
TREE	1	–	1	–	–	–	–	–	–
TWO	–	1	1	–	–	–	–	–	–
UNBRIGHT	–	–	–	–	–	–	–	1	1
UP	–	1	1	–	–	–	–	–	–
WALK	–	1	1	–	–	–	–	–	–
WALKING	1	–	1	–	–	–	–	–	–
WATER	–	–	–	–	–	–	1	–	1
WHEN ITS REAL DARK	1	–	1	–	–	–	–	–	–
WHEN THE DARK COMES THE DOGS BARK	–	1	1	–	–	–	–	–	–
WHITE	–	–	–	1	2	3	1	–	1
WINDOW	–	1	1	–	–	–	–	–	–
WIRES	–	1	1	–	–	–	–	–	–
WITHOUT ANY LIGHT	–	–	–	–	–	–	1	–	1
WITHOUT LIGHT	–	–	–	–	–	–	1	–	1

22. DECEIVE

RESPONSE WORD	M	F	T	M	F	T	M	F	T
A DOG	1	–	1	–	–	–	–	–	–
A MESSAGE	1	–	1	–	–	–	–	–	–
AFTER	–	–	–	1	–	1	–	–	–
AGAINST	–	–	–	–	–	–	1	3	4
ALONE	–	–	–	–	1	1	–	–	–
ALOUD	–	–	–	–	–	–	–	1	1
AND	–	–	–	1	–	1	–	–	–
ANGRY	–	–	–	–	–	–	–	1	1
ANIMAL	–	–	–	–	–	–	1	–	1
ANSWER	–	–	–	–	1	1	1	–	1
ARE	–	1	1	–	1	1	–	–	–
ARMY	–	–	–	1	–	1	–	–	–
AROUND	–	–	–	–	–	–	–	1	1
ASK FOR	–	–	–	–	1	1	–	–	–
AVENGE	–	–	–	1	–	1	–	–	–
AWAY	–	–	–	1	–	1	–	1	1
B C	1	–	1	–	–	–	–	–	–
BABY	1	–	1	–	–	–	–	–	–
BAD	1	–	1	4	–	4	2	–	2
BADGE	–	1	1	–	–	–	–	–	–
BAT	–	1	1	–	–	–	–	–	–
BE	–	2	2	–	–	–	1	–	1
BEAUTIFUL	–	–	–	–	1	1	–	–	–
BEAVER	–	1	1	–	–	–	–	–	–
BECEIVE	–	–	–	1	–	1	–	1	1
BEE	–	–	–	–	–	–	–	1	1
BEES	–	–	–	–	1	1	–	–	–
BEGIN	–	–	–	1	–	1	–	–	–
BEHIND	–	–	–	1	–	1	–	–	–
BETRAY	–	–	–	–	–	–	1	–	1
BIG	–	–	–	1	–	1	–	–	–
BIRD	–	–	–	2	–	2	–	–	–
BLACKMAIL	–	–	–	–	–	–	–	1	1
BLUE	–	–	–	1	–	1	–	–	–
BOARD	–	1	1	–	–	–	–	–	–
BOOK	–	1	1	–	1	1	–	–	–
BOSTON	1	–	1	–	–	–	–	–	–
BOX	1	–	1	–	–	–	–	–	–
BOY	–	2	2	–	1	1	–	–	–

RESPONSE WORD	1ST			3RD			5TH		
	M	F	T	M	F	T	M	F	T

22. DECEIVE

RESPONSE WORD	M	F	T	M	F	T	M	F	T
BRICKS	1	–	1	–	–	–	–	1	–
BRING	–	–	–	–	2	2	–	1	1
BROUGHT	–	–	–	–	–	–	1	–	1
BUD	1	–	1	–	–	–	–	–	–
BUG	–	–	–	–	1	1	–	–	–
BUT	–	–	–	1	–	1	–	–	–
CAKE	–	1	1	–	–	–	–	–	–
CAME	1	–	1	–	–	–	–	–	–
CAMP	1	–	1	–	–	–	–	–	–
CAN	–	1	1	–	–	–	–	–	–
CANT THINK	–	–	–	–	–	–	1	–	1
CAR	1	–	1	–	–	–	–	–	–
CAT	1	3	4	–	1	1	1	–	1
CEILING	–	–	–	–	1	1	–	–	–
CEIVE	–	–	–	–	1	1	–	3	3
CHAIR	–	1	1	–	1	1	1	–	1
CHALK	1	–	1	–	–	–	–	–	–
CHECK	–	–	–	–	–	–	–	1	1
CHILDREN	–	1	1	–	–	–	–	–	–
CHOSE	–	–	–	–	–	–	–	1	1
CHRISTMAS	–	1	1	–	–	–	–	–	–
CHRISTMAS SEAL	1	–	–	–	1	1	–	–	–
CITY	1	–	1	1	–	1	–	–	–
CLEAN	–	–	–	–	1	1	1	–	1
COLD	–	–	–	–	1	1	–	–	–
COLOR	–	1	1	–	–	–	–	–	–
COLORS	1	–	1	–	–	–	–	–	–
COME	1	2	3	–	1	1	1	1	2
CONFUSE	–	–	–	–	–	–	1	–	1
COP	–	–	–	–	–	–	1	–	1
COUGH	–	–	–	–	1	1	–	–	–
CREAM	–	–	–	1	–	1	–	–	–
CRIB	–	–	–	–	–	–	1	–	1
CROOK	–	–	–	1	–	1	–	–	–
CRUEL	–	–	–	–	1	1	–	–	–
CURTAIN	1	–	1	–	–	–	–	–	–
D	–	1	1	2	–	2	–	–	–
DANGER	1	–	1	–	–	–	–	–	–
DANNY	–	1	1	–	–	–	–	–	–
DARK TIME	1	–	1	–	–	–	–	–	–
DAVID	1	–	1	–	–	–	–	–	–
DAWN	–	–	–	1	–	1	–	–	–
DE	–	–	–	1	1	2	–	–	–
DEAD	–	–	–	–	1	1	–	–	–
DEBROCK	–	1	1	–	–	–	–	–	–
DECAVER	–	–	–	–	–	–	1	–	1
DECAY	–	1	1	–	–	–	–	–	–
DECEIVED	–	–	–	–	–	–	–	1	1
DECEIVER	–	–	–	1	–	1	–	1	1
DECEIVING	–	–	–	–	–	–	–	1	1
DECEMBER	1	1	2	–	1	1	–	–	–
DECENT	–	–	–	1	–	1	–	–	–
DECIDE	–	–	–	3	4	7	–	1	1
DECRIAT	–	–	–	1	–	1	1	–	1
DEER	–	–	–	1	–	1	–	–	–
DEFEND	1	1	2	–	–	–	–	–	–
DELIVER	–	–	–	1	2	3	–	1	1
DEMEVE	–	1	1	–	–	–	–	–	–
DENISE	–	1	1	–	–	–	–	–	–
DEREIVE	1	–	1	–	–	–	–	–	–
DERIVE	–	1	1	–	–	–	–	–	–
DESCRIBE	–	–	–	1	3	4	–	–	–
DESEE HIM	–	–	–	1	–	1	–	–	–
DID NOT	–	–	–	1	–	1	–	–	–
DID SOMETHING	–	–	–	1	–	1	–	–	–
DIDNT	–	–	–	1	–	1	–	–	–
DIE	1	–	1	–	–	–	–	–	–
DIES	–	1	1	–	–	–	–	–	–
DIFFERENCE	–	1	1	–	–	–	–	–	–
DIFFERENT	–	–	–	1	–	1	–	–	–
DIRT	1	–	1	–	–	–	–	–	–
DISAGREE	–	–	–	–	1	1	–	2	2

22.   DECEIVE

RESPONSE WORD	1ST M	1ST F	1ST T	3RD M	3RD F	3RD T	5TH M	5TH F	5TH T
DISCOVER	–	–	–	–	1	1	–	–	–
DISDECEIVE	–	–	–	–	1	1	1	–	1
DISEASE	1	1	2	–	1	1	–	1	1
DISLIKE	–	–	–	–	1	1	–	1	1
DISOBEY	–	–	–	–	2	2	1	2	3
DIVE	–	–	–	1	–	1	–	–	–
DIVEN	–	–	–	–	1	1	1	–	1
DIVIDE	–	–	–	1	1	2	–	–	–
DO IT	–	–	–	–	–	–	1	–	1
DO NOT DECEIVE	1	–	1	–	–	–	–	–	–
DOCTOR	–	1	1	–	–	–	–	–	–
DOESNT	–	–	–	1	–	1	–	–	–
DOG	–	–	–	–	1	1	1	–	1
DONE	1	–	1	–	–	–	–	–	–
DONT	–	–	–	1	–	1	–	1	1
DONT CATCH GERMS	–	1	1	–	–	–	–	–	–
DONT DECEIVE	1	–	1	1	–	1	–	–	–
DONT GET IT	–	–	–	–	–	–	1	–	1
DONT KNOW	1	–	1	–	–	–	–	–	–
DONT WANT IT	–	–	–	–	–	–	1	–	1
DOOR	3	1	4	–	1	1	–	1	1
DOUGH	–	1	1	–	–	–	–	–	–
DOWN	1	1	2	–	1	1	–	–	–
DRAIN	1	–	1	–	–	–	–	–	–
DRAWER	1	–	1	–	–	–	–	–	–
DRESS	–	1	1	–	–	–	–	–	–
DRIVE	–	–	–	–	1	1	–	–	–
DUCK	–	–	–	1	1	2	–	–	–
E	1	–	1	–	–	–	–	–	–
END	–	1	1	–	–	–	–	–	–
EUGINE	–	–	–	–	–	–	1	–	1
EVE	–	2	2	–	–	–	–	–	–
EVEN	–	–	–	–	–	–	1	–	1
EVENING	–	–	–	–	1	1	–	–	–
EVIL	–	–	–	–	–	–	–	2	2
EXCITED	–	–	–	–	–	–	1	–	1
EYES	–	–	–	–	1	1	–	–	–
FAN	–	–	–	–	–	–	1	–	1
FAR	–	–	–	–	–	–	–	1	1
FAST	–	–	–	1	–	1	–	–	–
FEGER	–	–	–	–	–	–	1	–	1
FENCE	1	–	1	–	–	–	–	–	–
FETCH	1	–	1	–	–	–	–	–	–
FIND	–	1	1	–	1	1	2	1	3
FIND OUT	–	–	–	1	–	1	–	–	–
FLOOR	–	–	–	1	–	1	–	–	–
FLOWER	1	–	1	–	–	–	–	–	–
FLOWERS	–	–	–	–	1	1	–	–	–
FOOL	–	–	–	–	–	–	1	–	1
FOR	–	–	–	–	–	–	–	1	1
FORGET	–	–	–	–	–	–	1	2	3
FORSAKE	–	–	–	–	–	–	1	–	1
FOUND	–	–	–	–	–	–	–	1	1
GARBAGE CAN	1	–	1	–	–	–	–	–	–
GARDEN	–	1	1	–	–	–	–	–	–
GAVE	–	–	–	–	1	1	–	–	–
GENTLE	–	–	–	–	–	–	–	1	1
GERM	–	–	–	–	–	–	–	1	1
GET	–	–	–	5	4	9	6	1	7
GETTING	–	–	–	–	–	–	1	–	1
GIFT	–	–	–	1	–	1	–	1	1
GIFTS	–	–	–	1	–	1	–	–	–
GIVE	–	–	–	6	4	10	4	3	7
GIVE AWAY	–	–	–	1	–	1	–	–	–
GIVE BACK	–	–	–	1	–	1	–	–	–
GIVE PEOPLE SOMETHING	–	–	–	1	–	1	–	–	–
GIVEN	–	–	–	–	–	–	–	1	1
GIVING	1	–	1	–	–	–	–	–	–
GO	1	2	3	1	1	2	1	–	1
GO AGAINST	–	–	–	–	–	–	1	–	1
GO BACK	1	–	1	–	–	–	–	–	–
GOING OUT FOR DINNER	–	1	1	–	–	–	–	–	–

RESPONSE WORD	1ST M	F	T	3RD M	F	T	5TH M	F	T

22. DECEIVE

RESPONSE WORD	1ST M	F	T	3RD M	F	T	5TH M	F	T
GONE	1	–	1	–	–	–	–	–	–
GOOD	2	3	5	1	–	1	–	–	–
GOT	–	–	–	1	–	1	–	–	–
GRACEFUL	–	–	–	–	1	1	–	–	–
GRASS	–	2	2	–	1	1	–	–	–
GREEN	–	–	–	1	–	1	–	–	–
GROW	1	–	1	–	–	–	–	–	–
GUESS	–	–	–	–	1	1	–	–	–
GUN	–	–	–	–	–	–	–	1	1
HAPPY	–	–	–	–	–	–	–	1	1
HARD	–	–	–	–	–	–	–	1	1
HARD HEADED	–	–	–	–	–	–	1	–	1
HAT	–	1	1	–	–	–	–	–	–
HATE	–	–	–	–	–	–	1	1	2
HAVE	–	–	–	–	1	1	1	–	1
HEADACHE	–	1	1	–	–	–	–	–	–
HEAR	–	1	1	–	–	–	–	–	–
HEARD	–	–	–	–	1	1	–	–	–
HEAVE	1	–	1	–	–	–	–	–	–
HI-FI	1	–	1	–	–	–	–	–	–
HIM	–	–	–	–	1	1	1	–	1
HOT	–	1	1	–	–	–	–	–	–
HUNT	–	–	–	–	–	–	1	–	1
HURT	–	–	–	–	–	–	–	1	1
I	1	–	1	–	–	–	–	–	–
I CANT THINK OF ANYTHING	–	–	–	–	–	–	1	–	1
I DECEIVE	–	–	–	1	–	1	–	–	–
I DECEIVE A LETTER	–	–	–	–	1	1	–	–	–
I DECEIVED IT	1	–	1	–	–	–	–	–	–
I DONT KNOW	–	–	–	1	1	2	2	1	3
I DONT KNOW WHAT IT MEANS	–	–	–	–	–	–	–	1	1
INCEIVED	–	–	–	–	–	–	–	1	1
INDEED	–	–	–	–	–	–	1	–	1
IT	–	–	–	–	1	1	–	–	–
IT TO HER	–	–	–	–	1	1	–	–	–
IVE	–	–	–	1	–	1	–	–	–
JOYCE	–	–	–	–	–	–	–	1	1
JUMP	–	–	–	–	1	1	–	–	–
KEEN	1	–	1	–	–	–	–	–	–
KEEP	–	–	–	–	–	–	1	–	1
KITTEN	1	1	2	–	–	–	–	–	–
LAUGH	–	–	–	1	–	1	–	–	–
LEARN	–	1	1	–	–	–	1	–	1
LEAVE	5	1	6	–	1	1	2	–	2
LEND	–	–	–	1	–	1	1	–	1
LET	–	1	1	–	–	–	–	3	3
LET DOWN	–	–	–	–	–	–	–	3	3
LETTER	3	2	5	–	4	4	–	1	1
LETTERS	–	1	1	–	–	–	–	–	–
LIE	–	–	–	–	–	–	2	–	2
LIED	–	–	–	–	–	–	–	1	1
LIGHT	–	–	–	–	1	1	–	–	–
LIGHTS	–	–	–	1	1	2	–	–	–
LIKE	–	–	–	1	–	1	–	1	1
LINE	–	–	–	–	–	–	–	1	1
LISTEN	–	–	–	–	1	1	–	–	–
LITTLE	–	–	–	–	1	1	–	–	–
LOOK	1	–	1	–	–	–	1	–	1
LOW	–	–	–	–	1	1	–	–	–
MADESE	–	–	–	1	–	1	–	–	–
MAIL	–	1	1	3	–	3	–	1	1
MAILBOX	–	2	2	–	–	–	–	–	–
MAMA	1	–	1	–	–	–	–	–	–
MAN	–	1	1	–	–	–	1	–	1
MANY	–	–	–	–	1	1	–	–	–
MASK	–	–	–	1	–	1	–	–	–
ME	3	1	4	1	–	1	–	1	1
MEAL	–	–	–	–	1	1	–	–	–
MEAN	–	–	–	1	1	2	–	2	2
MEANING	–	–	–	–	–	–	1	–	1
MEEVE	1	–	1	–	–	–	–	–	–

RESPONSE WORD	1ST M	F	T	3RD M	F	T	5TH M	F	T

22. DECEIVE

RESPONSE WORD	1ST M	F	T	3RD M	F	T	5TH M	F	T
MEIVE	2	1	3	–	–	–	–	–	–
MESSAGE	–	–	–	–	1	1	1	–	1
MESSAGES	–	–	–	–	1	1	–	–	–
MIRROR	–	–	–	1	1	2	–	–	–
MISBEHAVE	–	–	–	–	–	–	1	–	1
MISCHIEF	–	–	–	–	–	–	1	–	1
MISCHIEVOUS	–	–	–	1	–	1	–	–	–
MISS	–	–	–	1	–	1	–	–	–
MODEL	–	–	–	–	–	–	1	–	1
MOTHER	–	1	1	–	–	–	–	–	–
MOUSE	1	–	1	–	–	–	–	–	–
MR	–	–	–	–	–	–	1	–	1
MUST	–	–	–	1	–	1	–	–	–
MY	–	1	1	–	–	–	1	–	1
MY LETTER	–	1	1	–	–	–	–	–	–
NICE	1	1	2	–	–	–	–	–	–
NIGHTS	–	–	–	–	–	–	–	1	1
NO	1	1	2	1	1	2	–	1	1
NO RESPONSE	3	–	3	–	–	–	2	4	6
NOT	–	1	1	–	2	2	3	3	6
NOT DECEIVE	3	–	3	3	1	4	–	–	–
NOT DECEIVED	–	–	–	–	–	–	1	–	1
NOT GET	–	–	–	–	–	–	1	–	1
NOT OBEY	–	–	–	–	–	–	–	1	1
NOT RECEIVING	–	–	–	–	–	–	1	–	1
NOTE	–	–	–	–	1	1	–	–	–
NOTHING	–	1	1	–	–	–	–	1	1
NOVEMBER	–	1	1	–	–	–	–	–	–
NOW	2	–	2	–	–	–	–	–	–
OBEY	–	–	–	–	–	–	–	1	1
OH	1	–	1	–	–	–	–	–	–
OKAY	–	–	–	–	–	–	–	1	1
ON	–	–	–	–	–	–	–	1	1
ONCE	–	–	–	1	–	1	–	–	–
ONE	1	1	2	–	–	–	–	–	–
PACKAGE	1	1	2	–	–	–	–	–	–
PAPER	–	–	–	–	1	1	–	–	–
PASS	–	–	–	–	–	–	–	1	1
PAST	–	–	–	–	–	–	1	–	1
PASTE	–	–	–	1	–	1	–	–	–
PEEVE	–	1	1	–	–	–	–	–	–
PEOPLE	–	–	–	–	–	–	–	1	1
PERSON	–	–	–	–	–	–	1	–	1
PICTURE	1	–	1	–	–	–	–	1	1
PIPE	1	–	1	–	–	–	–	–	–
PISTOL	–	1	1	–	–	–	–	–	–
PLANE	–	–	–	1	–	1	–	–	–
PLAY	–	–	–	–	1	1	–	–	–
PLEASE	–	1	1	–	–	–	–	–	–
POCKETBOOK	1	–	1	–	–	–	–	–	–
POISON	–	1	1	–	–	–	–	–	–
POLE	1	–	1	–	–	–	–	–	–
POLICE CAR	–	–	–	1	–	1	–	–	–
PRESENT	–	2	2	–	2	2	–	–	–
PRESS	1	–	1	–	–	–	–	–	–
PRETEND	–	–	–	–	1	1	–	–	–
PROMISE	–	–	–	–	–	–	–	1	1
PROTOVIAN	1	–	1	–	–	–	–	–	–
PROUD	–	–	–	–	1	1	–	–	–
PULL	–	1	1	–	–	–	–	–	–
QUIET	–	1	1	1	–	1	–	–	–
QUIT	–	–	–	–	–	–	1	–	1
RAIN	1	–	1	–	–	–	–	–	–
READ	–	–	–	–	–	–	1	–	1
REALLY	–	–	–	–	–	–	–	1	1
RECEIVE	3	3	6	15	11	26	25	24	49
RECEIVED	–	1	1	1	–	1	2	4	6
RECEIVER	–	1	1	–	–	–	–	–	–
RECESS	1	–	1	–	–	–	–	–	–
RECEVE	–	–	–	–	–	–	1	–	1
RECIEVE	–	–	–	–	–	–	1	–	1
RECITE	–	–	–	–	1	1	–	–	–

RESPONSE WORD	1ST M	F	T	3RD M	F	T	5TH M	F	T

22.   DECEIVE

RESPONSE WORD	M	F	T	M	F	T	M	F	T
RECOGNIZE	-	-	-	-	1	1	-	1	1
RECTANGLE	-	-	-	-	1	1	-	-	-
RED	-	1	1	-	-	-	1	-	1
REIVE	-	-	-	-	-	-	-	1	1
RELIEF	-	-	-	-	-	-	1	-	1
REMEMBER	-	-	-	-	1	1	-	-	-
RENT	-	-	-	-	-	-	1	-	1
RETREAT	-	-	-	-	-	-	1	-	1
RETURN	-	1	1	1	2	3	-	1	1
REWARD	-	-	-	-	-	-	1	-	1
RIDE	-	1	1	-	-	-	-	-	-
RING	1	-	1	-	-	-	-	-	-
ROT	-	-	-	-	-	-	1	-	1
RUN	-	-	-	1	-	1	-	-	-
SAID	-	1	1	-	1	1	-	-	-
SAW	-	1	1	-	-	-	-	-	-
SAY	1	-	1	-	-	-	-	-	-
SCHOOL	1	-	1	1	-	1	-	-	-
SEA	1	1	2	-	-	-	-	-	-
SEASON	-	-	-	1	-	1	-	-	-
SEE	4	11	15	-	2	2	-	1	1
SEE SOMETHING	-	1	1	-	-	-	-	-	-
SEED	1	1	2	2	-	2	-	-	-
SEEDS	-	1	1	-	-	-	-	-	-
SEEN	-	-	-	1	-	1	-	-	-
SEEVE	1	-	1	-	1	1	-	1	1
SEIZE	1	-	1	-	-	-	-	-	-
SELL	-	-	-	1	-	1	-	-	-
SELL THEM	-	1	1	-	-	-	-	-	-
SEND	-	-	-	-	1	1	1	1	2
SENT SOMETHING	-	-	-	1	-	1	-	-	-
SERVE	1	-	1	-	-	-	-	-	-
SHIRT	-	-	-	-	1	1	-	-	-
SHOES	1	1	2	-	-	-	-	-	-
SHOW	-	-	-	-	-	-	-	1	1
SICK	-	1	1	2	3	5	-	-	-
SINK	-	1	1	-	-	-	-	-	-
SIP	1	-	1	-	-	-	-	-	-
SKIRT	-	1	1	-	-	-	-	-	-
SLY	-	-	-	-	-	-	-	1	1
SNEEZE	-	1	1	-	1	1	-	-	-
SOMEBODY SAYS IT	-	1	1	-	-	-	-	-	-
SOMEONE SPEAKS	-	1	1	-	-	-	-	-	-
SOMETHING	1	2	3	2	2	4	2	-	2
SPOOKY	-	-	-	1	-	1	-	-	-
STAY AND BE UNDER THE COVER	-	1	1	-	-	-	-	-	-
STEAL	1	-	1	-	-	-	1	-	1
STEVE	-	1	1	-	-	-	-	-	-
STUDY	-	-	-	-	-	-	-	1	1
STUFF	1	-	1	1	-	1	-	-	-
SUGAR	1	-	1	-	-	-	-	-	-
SURPRISE	1	-	1	-	-	-	-	-	-
T	1	-	1	-	-	-	-	-	-
T V	-	-	-	-	-	-	1	-	1
TABLE	1	-	1	1	-	1	-	-	-
TAKE	-	1	1	2	-	2	-	3	3
TAKE AWAY	-	-	-	-	-	-	-	1	1
TAKE IT	1	-	1	-	-	-	-	-	-
TAKE SOMETHING FROM SOMEBODY	-	-	-	1	-	1	-	1	1
TALK	-	-	-	2	2	4	-	1	1
TEACH	-	-	-	-	-	-	-	1	1
TEASE	-	-	-	-	-	-	-	1	1
TELEPHONE	-	3	3	-	-	-	-	-	-
TELEVISION	2	1	3	-	-	-	-	-	-
TENNESSEE	1	-	1	-	-	-	-	-	-
THANKS	-	-	-	-	1	1	-	-	-
THE	1	-	1	-	-	-	-	-	-
THEM	-	-	-	-	-	-	1	1	2
THESE	1	-	1	-	-	-	-	-	-
THEY	-	-	-	-	1	1	-	-	-

RESPONSE WORD	1ST M	F	T	3RD M	F	T	5TH M	F	T

22.   DECEIVE

RESPONSE WORD	1ST M	F	T	3RD M	F	T	5TH M	F	T
THIEF	–	–	–	1	–	1	–	–	–
THING	–	–	–	–	1	1	–	–	–
THINK	1	–	1	–	–	–	–	–	–
THIS MORNING	–	–	–	1	–	1	–	–	–
THOUGHT	–	–	–	–	1	1	–	–	–
TO GIVE	–	–	–	–	–	–	1	–	1
TO GIVE A PRESENT	–	–	–	1	–	1	–	–	–
TO HAVE	–	–	–	–	–	–	–	1	1
TO LET DOWN	–	–	–	–	–	–	–	1	1
TOGETHER	–	–	–	1	1	2	–	1	1
TOP	–	–	–	1	–	1	–	–	–
TOWN	–	–	–	1	–	1	–	–	–
TRADE	1	–	1	–	–	–	1	–	1
TRAIN	–	–	–	1	–	1	–	–	–
TRAITOR	–	–	–	–	–	–	1	–	1
TREAT	–	–	–	–	1	1	–	–	–
TREE	2	–	2	–	–	–	–	1	1
TREES	–	1	1	–	–	–	–	–	–
TRICK	–	–	–	–	–	–	2	–	2
TURN	–	–	–	–	–	–	1	–	1
TURNED	–	–	–	–	1	1	–	–	–
TURTLE	–	–	–	–	–	–	1	–	1
UNCEIVE	–	–	–	–	–	–	–	1	1
UNDECEIVE	2	–	2	–	1	1	1	1	2
UNDER	–	1	1	–	–	–	–	1	1
UNDERESTIMATE	–	–	–	–	–	–	1	–	1
UNDERMINE	–	–	–	–	–	–	1	–	1
UNHAPPY	–	–	–	–	1	1	–	–	–
UNKIND	–	–	–	–	–	–	–	1	1
UP	–	1	1	–	–	–	–	–	–
WALL	–	1	1	1	–	1	–	–	–
WALLET	1	–	1	–	–	–	–	–	–
WALLS	–	1	1	–	–	–	–	–	–
WAS GIVEN	–	–	–	–	–	–	–	1	1
WASHINGTON	1	–	1	–	–	–	–	–	–
WATER	1	2	3	–	–	–	1	–	1
WE ARE TOGETHER	–	1	1	–	–	–	–	–	–
WEATHER	1	–	1	–	–	–	–	–	–
WEAVE	1	–	1	–	–	–	–	–	–
WEB	–	–	–	–	–	–	1	–	1
WHAT	–	–	–	–	–	–	1	–	1
WHAT THE PLANT GROWS	–	1	1	–	–	–	–	–	–
WHEN YOU DECEIVE SOMETHING	1	–	1	–	–	–	–	–	–
WHITE	1	–	1	–	–	–	–	–	–
WHY	1	–	1	–	–	–	–	–	–
WILD	–	–	–	–	1	1	–	–	–
WINDOW	1	–	1	–	–	–	–	–	–
WING	–	–	–	–	1	1	–	–	–
WINS	–	–	–	1	–	1	–	–	–
WINTER	–	2	2	–	–	–	–	–	–
WISE	–	–	–	–	–	–	–	1	1
WORD	–	–	–	–	1	1	–	–	–
WORDS	–	–	–	1	–	1	–	–	–
WORK	–	–	–	–	1	1	–	–	–
WOULDNT	–	–	–	–	–	–	1	–	1
YES	1	–	1	–	–	–	–	–	–
YOU	–	–	–	–	1	1	–	–	–
YOU DECEIVE A LETTER	–	–	–	–	–	–	–	1	1
YOUR EYES CAN SEE	–	1	1	–	–	–	–	–	–
YUM	–	–	–	1	–	1	–	–	–
ZEBRA	1	–	1	–	–	–	–	–	–
ZS	–	–	–	–	1	1	–	–	–

RESPONSE WORD	1ST M	1ST F	1ST T	3RD M	3RD F	3RD T	5TH M	5TH F	5TH T

23. ENJOY

RESPONSE WORD	1ST M	1ST F	1ST T	3RD M	3RD F	3RD T	5TH M	5TH F	5TH T
A CIGARETTE	1	–	1	–	–	–	–	–	–
AFTER	–	1	1	–	–	–	–	–	–
AHOY	1	–	1	–	–	–	–	–	–
ALMOND JOY	1	–	1	–	–	–	–	–	–
ANIMALS	–	–	–	–	–	–	–	1	1
ARE	–	1	1	–	–	–	–	–	–
AWFUL	–	–	–	–	1	1	–	–	–
BAD	–	–	–	–	–	–	1	–	1
BAD TIME	1	–	1	–	–	–	–	–	–
BEAR	–	1	1	–	–	–	–	–	–
BEAUTIFUL	–	1	1	–	–	–	–	–	–
BECAUSE	–	–	–	2	–	2	–	–	–
BEER	1	–	1	–	–	–	–	–	–
BETTER	–	1	1	–	–	–	–	–	–
BLACK	2	–	2	–	–	–	–	–	–
BLINDS	–	1	1	–	–	–	–	–	–
BLUE	1	–	1	–	–	–	–	–	–
BORE	–	–	–	–	–	–	1	–	1
BOX	–	–	–	–	1	1	–	–	–
BOY	5	3	8	–	–	–	–	1	1
BUCKET OF WATER	1	–	1	–	–	–	–	–	–
BUILDING	1	–	1	–	–	–	–	–	–
BUT	1	–	1	–	–	–	–	–	–
CAKE	–	2	2	–	–	–	–	–	–
CANDY	1	–	1	–	–	–	–	1	1
CHAIR	–	1	1	–	–	–	–	–	–
CHEERFUL	–	–	–	–	1	1	–	–	–
CHILDREN	–	1	1	–	–	–	–	–	–
CHRISTMAS	–	1	1	–	1	1	–	1	1
COLD EGG	1	–	1	–	–	–	–	–	–
COLORING	–	–	–	1	–	1	–	–	–
COME	–	1	1	–	–	–	–	–	–
COMPANY	1	–	1	–	–	–	–	–	–
COY	1	1	2	–	–	–	–	–	–
CRADLE	–	1	1	–	–	–	–	–	–
CRY	–	–	–	2	–	2	–	–	–
CUP	1	–	1	–	–	–	–	–	–
CUT	–	1	1	–	–	–	–	–	–
DAY	1	–	1	–	–	–	–	–	–
DELIGHT	–	–	–	–	1	1	–	1	1
DESK	–	–	–	–	1	1	–	–	–
DID	–	1	1	–	–	–	–	–	–
DID NOT	–	–	–	–	–	–	1	–	1
DIDNT ENJOY	–	–	–	–	1	1	–	–	–
DINNER	–	1	1	–	–	–	–	–	–
DISAPPOINTED	–	–	–	–	–	–	1	–	1
DISENJOY	–	–	–	1	–	1	1	–	1
DISLIKE	–	–	–	2	–	2	1	1	2
DOG	1	1	2	–	–	–	1	–	1
DONE	–	1	1	–	–	–	–	–	–
DONS	–	–	–	–	–	–	1	–	1
DONT	–	–	–	1	–	1	–	–	–
DONT ENJOY	4	1	5	1	1	2	–	1	1
DOOR	1	–	1	–	–	–	–	–	–
DRINK	1	1	2	–	–	–	–	–	–
DRINKS	–	1	1	–	–	–	–	–	–
EATING	–	2	2	–	–	–	–	–	–
EITHER	–	–	–	–	1	1	–	–	–
EN	–	–	–	1	–	1	–	–	–
ENJOYED MY FAMILY	–	1	1	–	–	–	–	–	–
ENJOYING SOMETHING	–	1	1	–	–	–	–	–	–
ENPOY	1	–	1	1	–	1	–	–	–
ENTERTAIN	–	–	–	–	1	1	–	1	1
ENTERTAINMENT	–	–	–	–	–	–	–	1	1
EVEN	–	–	–	–	–	–	–	1	1
EVENING	–	–	–	–	1	1	–	–	–
EVERYTHING	1	–	1	–	–	–	–	–	–
EXCITED	–	–	–	–	1	1	–	–	–
EXCITEMENT	–	–	–	–	–	–	1	1	2
FABULOUS	–	–	–	–	–	–	–	1	1
FAIR	–	1	1	–	–	–	–	–	–
FASCINATE	–	–	–	–	–	–	1	–	1

RESPONSE WORD	1ST M	F	T	3RD M	F	T	5TH M	F	T

23.   ENJOY

RESPONSE WORD	1ST M	F	T	3RD M	F	T	5TH M	F	T
FAST	1	–	1	–	–	–	–	–	–
FATHER	1	–	1	–	–	–	–	–	–
FAVORITE	–	–	–	–	1	1	–	–	–
FIND	–	–	–	–	–	–	1	–	1
FIRST	–	1	1	–	–	–	–	–	–
FLOOR	–	–	–	1	–	1	–	–	–
FOOD	2	–	2	–	1	1	–	–	–
FOOTBALL GAMES	1	–	1	–	–	–	–	–	–
FOR	–	1	1	–	–	–	–	–	–
FRIENDS	1	–	1	–	–	–	–	–	–
FUN	11	11	22	21	17	38	24	26	50
FUNNY	–	–	–	1	–	1	–	–	–
GAME	–	1	1	–	1	1	–	–	–
GAMES	–	–	–	–	1	1	–	–	–
GAY	–	–	–	–	1	1	–	–	–
GIVE	–	–	–	–	1	1	–	–	–
GLAD	–	–	–	–	–	–	3	1	4
GLASSES	1	–	1	–	–	–	–	–	–
GO	–	1	1	–	–	–	1	–	1
GOING	1	–	1	–	–	–	–	–	–
GOING OUT	–	1	1	–	–	–	–	–	–
GOOD	–	2	2	3	2	5	1	–	1
GOOD TIME	–	–	–	2	1	3	4	1	5
HALL	–	–	–	1	–	1	–	–	–
HAPPEN	–	1	1	–	–	–	1	–	1
HAPPILY	–	–	–	–	1	1	–	1	1
HAPPINESS	–	–	–	–	2	2	–	–	–
HAPPY	1	4	5	20	18	38	19	26	45
HAPPY TIME	–	–	–	–	1	1	–	–	–
HATE	–	–	–	2	–	2	2	3	5
HAVE	–	2	2	–	–	–	–	1	1
HAVE FUN	–	2	2	3	–	3	1	2	3
HAZEL	–	–	–	–	–	–	1	–	1
HERE	1	–	1	–	–	–	–	–	–
HORSE	–	1	1	–	–	–	–	–	–
HOUSE	–	2	2	–	–	–	–	–	–
HOY	1	–	1	–	–	–	–	–	–
I ENJOYED LUNCH	–	1	1	–	–	–	–	–	–
I HATE THIS	–	1	1	–	–	–	–	–	–
I LIKE	–	–	–	1	–	1	–	–	–
ICE CREAM	1	–	1	–	–	–	–	–	–
IN	1	1	2	1	1	2	–	–	–
INDIAN	–	1	1	–	–	–	–	–	–
INDIANS	1	–	1	–	–	–	–	–	–
INSOFTED	–	–	–	–	1	1	–	–	–
INTERESTING	–	–	–	–	–	–	1	–	1
INVITED	–	–	–	–	1	1	–	–	–
IT	1	3	4	2	–	2	–	–	–
JACK	–	1	1	–	–	–	–	–	–
JELLO	1	–	1	–	–	–	–	–	–
JETS	1	–	1	–	–	–	–	–	–
JOHN	1	–	1	–	–	–	–	–	–
JOIN IN WITH ME	1	–	1	–	–	–	–	–	–
JOIN UP	1	–	1	–	–	–	–	–	–
JOY	–	–	–	5	4	9	4	9	13
JOY LIQUID	1	–	1	–	–	–	–	–	–
JOYCE	–	1	1	–	–	–	–	–	–
JOYFUL	–	–	–	–	1	1	1	–	1
JOYOUS	–	–	–	–	–	–	–	1	1
JOYS	1	–	1	–	–	–	–	–	–
JUMP	–	1	1	–	–	–	–	–	–
LADY	–	1	1	–	–	–	–	–	–
LAUGH	–	–	–	–	2	2	3	1	4
LAUGHING	–	–	–	–	1	1	–	–	–
LEARN	–	1	1	–	–	–	–	–	–
LIE	1	–	1	–	–	–	–	–	–
LIFE	1	1	2	2	–	2	–	1	1
LIGHT	1	–	1	–	1	1	–	–	–
LIKE	4	1	5	14	17	31	29	29	58
LIKE IT	–	2	2	1	–	1	–	–	–
LIKE YOU ENJOY A PICNIC	–	–	–	–	–	–	–	1	1
LISTEN	1	–	1	–	–	–	–	–	–

RESPONSE WORD	1ST M	F	T	3RD M	F	T	5TH M	F	T

23.   ENJOY

RESPONSE WORD	1ST M	F	T	3RD M	F	T	5TH M	F	T
LIVE	–	–	–	1	–	1	–	–	–
LIVING	–	1	1	–	–	–	–	–	–
LOOK	–	–	–	1	–	1	1	–	1
LOVE	1	–	1	–	1	1	1	2	3
LOVELY	–	–	–	–	1	1	–	–	–
LUCKY	–	–	–	1	–	1	–	–	–
LUNCH	1	–	1	–	–	–	–	–	–
MAY	–	–	–	–	–	–	1	–	1
ME	6	1	7	1	–	1	–	–	–
MEAL	–	1	1	–	–	–	–	–	–
MIGHT BE YOUR MOTHERS BIRTHDAY	–	1	1	–	–	–	–	–	–
MIST	–	–	–	1	–	1	–	–	–
MOST	–	–	–	1	–	1	–	–	–
MOTHER	–	3	3	–	–	–	–	–	–
MOY	2	–	2	–	–	–	–	–	–
MUCH	–	–	–	–	2	2	–	–	–
MUSIC	–	1	1	1	2	3	2	–	2
NATURE	–	1	1	–	–	–	–	–	–
NEVER	–	–	–	–	3	3	–	–	–
NICE	–	1	1	1	3	4	–	–	–
NO	1	–	1	–	–	–	–	–	–
NOISE	–	–	–	–	–	–	1	–	1
NOT	–	–	–	–	2	2	–	–	–
NOT ENJOY	–	1	1	5	6	11	6	3	9
NOT ENJOYING	–	–	–	1	–	1	1	–	1
NOT INJOY	–	–	–	–	–	–	1	–	1
NOT LIKE	–	–	–	–	–	–	1	–	1
NOT LIKE IT	–	–	–	1	–	1	–	–	–
NOT TO ENJOY	–	–	–	–	–	–	1	–	1
OATMEAL	1	–	1	–	–	–	–	–	–
OFTEN	–	–	–	1	–	1	–	–	–
OK	–	–	–	1	–	1	–	–	–
OUTSIDE	–	1	1	–	–	–	–	–	–
OWNING	–	–	–	1	–	1	–	–	–
PAGES	–	1	1	–	–	–	–	–	–
PAPER	2	1	3	–	–	–	–	–	–
PARTIES	1	–	1	–	–	–	–	–	–
PARTY	2	4	6	2	1	3	1	–	1
PARTY-POOPER	–	–	–	1	–	1	–	–	–
PENCIL	1	–	1	–	–	–	–	–	–
PENJOY	1	–	1	–	–	–	–	–	–
PEOPLE	4	1	5	1	1	2	–	–	–
PERFECT	–	–	–	–	–	–	1	–	1
PICTURES	1	–	1	–	–	–	–	–	–
PIN	1	–	1	–	–	–	–	–	–
PINK	–	1	1	–	–	–	–	–	–
PLAY	1	1	2	–	1	1	2	–	2
PLAYFUL	–	–	–	1	–	1	–	–	–
PLEASANT	–	1	1	2	2	4	2	3	5
PLEASED	–	–	–	–	–	–	–	1	1
PLEASURE	–	–	–	–	–	–	5	2	7
POOR	–	–	–	1	–	1	–	–	–
POY	–	1	1	–	–	–	–	–	–
PRESENT	–	–	–	1	–	1	–	–	–
PROGRAMS	–	–	–	1	–	1	–	–	–
PUT IN SINK	1	–	1	–	–	–	–	–	–
RATHER	–	1	1	–	–	–	–	–	–
RED	–	2	2	–	–	–	–	–	–
REJOY	–	1	1	–	–	–	–	–	–
RELAX	–	1	1	1	–	1	1	1	2
REST	–	1	1	–	–	–	–	–	–
RIDE	–	1	1	–	–	–	–	–	–
RIDES	–	1	1	–	–	–	–	–	–
ROOF	–	–	–	–	1	1	–	–	–
RUNNING	–	1	1	–	–	–	–	–	–
SAD	1	–	1	1	3	4	2	4	6
SANDWICH	–	–	–	1	–	1	–	–	–
SCHOOL	–	1	1	–	–	–	–	–	–
SCISSORS	1	–	1	–	–	–	–	–	–
SEE	–	1	1	–	1	1	–	–	–
SELF	–	1	1	–	1	1	–	–	–

RESPONSE WORD	1ST M	F	T	3RD M	F	T	5TH M	F	T

23. ENJOY

RESPONSE WORD	1ST M	F	T	3RD M	F	T	5TH M	F	T
SHOE	-	-	-	1	-	1	-	-	-
SHOES	1	-	1	-	-	-	-	-	-
SING	-	1	1	-	-	-	-	-	-
SIT	-	2	2	-	-	-	-	-	-
SIX	-	-	-	-	1	1	-	-	-
SLEEP	-	1	1	-	-	-	-	-	-
SMOOTH	1	-	1	-	-	-	-	-	-
SOAP SUDS	1	-	1	-	-	-	-	-	-
SOFT	-	1	1	-	2	2	-	-	-
SOME FUN	-	-	-	1	-	1	-	-	-
SOME WAY	-	-	-	-	1	1	-	-	-
SOMETHING	1	1	2	1	1	2	-	-	-
SONNY	-	-	-	-	1	1	-	-	-
SORRY	1	-	1	-	1	1	-	-	-
SOUND	-	1	1	-	-	-	-	-	-
SPOON	1	-	1	-	-	-	-	-	-
STORE	-	1	1	-	-	-	-	-	-
SUPPER	1	-	1	1	-	1	-	-	-
SURPRISE	-	-	-	-	1	1	-	-	-
TABLE	-	-	-	1	-	1	-	-	-
TELEVISION	2	1	3	-	-	-	-	1	1
TELL	-	-	-	1	-	1	-	-	-
TERRIBLE	-	-	-	-	1	1	-	-	-
THANK YOU	-	1	1	-	-	-	-	-	-
THANKSGIVING	-	-	-	-	-	-	-	1	1
THAT	1	1	2	1	1	2	-	-	-
THE CAKE	-	-	-	1	-	1	-	-	-
THE FOOD	1	-	1	-	-	-	-	-	-
THE FUN	1	-	1	-	-	-	-	-	-
THE GAME	-	1	1	-	-	-	-	-	-
THE HOUSE	-	1	1	-	-	-	-	-	-
THE PARTY	1	1	2	-	-	-	-	-	-
THE SHOW	1	-	1	-	-	-	-	-	-
THE WORLD	1	-	1	-	-	-	-	-	-
THE ZOO	-	-	-	-	1	1	-	-	-
THING	-	-	-	1	-	1	-	-	-
THINGS	1	-	1	-	-	-	-	-	-
THINK	-	-	-	-	1	1	-	-	-
THIS	2	-	2	-	1	1	-	-	-
TIME	1	-	1	1	-	1	-	-	-
TO APPRECIATE	-	-	-	-	-	-	-	1	1
TO LIKE IT	-	-	-	-	-	-	-	1	1
TOYS	2	-	2	-	-	-	-	-	-
TREE	1	-	1	-	-	-	-	-	-
TRIP	-	1	1	-	2	2	-	-	-
TRUCK	1	-	1	-	-	-	-	-	-
TV	-	1	1	1	-	1	-	-	-
UNDER	-	-	-	-	1	1	-	-	-
UNDERLINE	-	-	-	1	-	1	-	-	-
UNENJOY	-	-	-	-	-	-	-	1	1
UNENJOYABLE	-	-	-	-	-	-	1	-	1
UNHAPPY	-	1	1	2	-	2	1	3	4
UNJOY	-	-	-	1	1	2	-	1	1
UNTIL	-	-	-	-	1	1	-	-	-
US	2	-	2	2	-	2	-	-	-
VACATION	-	2	2	-	-	-	-	-	-
VERY MUCH	-	-	-	-	-	-	1	-	1
WALL	-	1	1	-	-	-	-	-	-
WASHING MACHINE	1	-	1	-	-	-	-	-	-
WATER	2	-	2	-	-	-	-	-	-
WHAT YOU LIKE	1	-	1	-	-	-	-	-	-
WHEN YOU JOIN SOMETHING	1	-	1	-	-	-	-	-	-
WHENEVER SOMEONE ENJOYS THEIR RIDE	-	1	1	-	-	-	-	-	-
WHISKEY	1	-	1	-	-	-	-	-	-
WHITE	1	-	1	-	-	-	-	-	-
WIND	1	-	1	-	-	-	-	-	-
WONDERFUL	1	-	1	-	1	1	1	-	1
WORK	1	-	1	-	-	-	-	-	-
WOULD LIKE TO JOIN	1	-	1	-	-	-	-	-	-
YOU	1	2	3	-	-	-	-	-	-
YOUR CAKE	-	1	1	-	-	-	-	-	-

RESPONSE WORD	1ST M	F	T	3RD M	F	T	5TH M	F	T
23. ENJOY									
YOUR FAMILY	1	–	1	–	–	–	–	–	–
YOUR FOOD	–	1	1	–	–	–	–	–	–
YOUR FUN	–	–	–	–	1	1	–	–	–
YOUR PARTY	–	1	1	–	–	–	–	–	–
YOURSELF	1	2	3	1	–	1	–	–	–
YOURSELF PLAYING	–	1	1	–	–	–	–	–	–
24. EXAMINE									
A DOCTORS EXAMINE YOU	–	–	–	1	–	1	–	–	–
A HEAD	–	1	1	1	–	1	–	–	–
ABSENT	–	1	1	1	–	1	–	–	–
ACAMINE	–	1	1	–	–	–	–	–	–
AGE	1	–	1	–	–	–	–	–	–
AID	–	1	1	–	–	–	–	–	–
AMINE	–	1	1	–	–	–	–	1	1
ARE YOU OPERATING ON MY FRIEND	–	1	1	–	–	–	–	–	–
ARITHMETIC	–	–	–	–	–	–	–	1	1
ARMY	–	–	–	1	–	1	–	–	–
ASK	–	1	1	–	1	1	–	–	–
AWSER	–	–	–	–	–	–	1	–	1
BABY	–	1	1	–	–	–	–	–	–
(BE) SUMMARIED	1	–	1	–	–	–	–	–	–
BED	–	1	1	–	–	–	–	–	–
BIG	–	1	1	–	–	–	–	–	–
BIRD	–	1	1	–	–	–	–	–	–
BLACK	1	–	1	–	–	–	–	–	–
BOARD	1	–	1	–	–	–	–	–	–
BODY	2	–	2	1	–	1	–	–	–
BONES	1	–	1	–	–	–	–	–	–
BOOK	–	–	–	–	–	–	1	2	3
BOX	2	–	2	–	–	–	–	–	–
BOY	–	1	1	–	–	–	–	–	–
BUS	–	–	–	–	1	1	–	–	–
CABIN	1	–	1	–	–	–	–	–	–
CACLAMINE	–	1	1	–	–	–	–	–	–
CAMINE	1	–	1	–	–	–	–	–	–
CAN	–	3	3	–	–	–	–	–	–
CANDLE	–	1	1	–	–	–	–	–	–
CANDY	–	–	–	1	–	1	–	–	–
CAR	2	–	2	–	–	–	–	–	–
CARMEN	–	1	1	–	–	–	–	–	–
CAT	1	–	1	–	1	1	–	–	–
CEZAMINE	1	–	1	–	–	–	–	–	–
CHAIR	2	–	2	1	–	1	–	–	–
CHEAKUP	–	–	–	–	–	–	1	–	1
CHECK	–	–	–	2	8	10	11	16	27
CHECK UP	1	–	1	2	–	2	–	3	3
CHECK-UP	1	–	1	–	2	2	2	–	2
CHECKED	–	–	–	–	1	1	–	–	–
CHILDREN	1	–	1	–	–	–	–	–	–
CLAP	1	–	1	–	–	–	–	–	–
CLEAR	–	–	–	1	–	1	–	–	–
CLOTHES	1	–	1	–	–	–	–	–	–
COLD	1	1	2	–	–	–	–	–	–
COLOR	–	1	1	–	–	–	–	–	–
COME	–	1	1	–	–	–	–	–	–
COW	1	1	2	–	–	–	–	–	–
CROSS EXAMINE	–	–	–	–	–	–	1	–	1
CROSS-EXAMINE	–	–	–	–	–	–	1	–	1
CUP	–	–	–	–	1	1	–	–	–
CURTAINS	1	–	1	–	–	–	–	–	–
DO	–	–	–	–	–	–	2	–	2
DO NOT CRY	–	1	1	–	–	–	–	–	–
DOCTOR	14	16	30	20	11	31	6	14	20
DOCTOR CHECKS YOU	–	–	–	1	–	1	–	–	–
DOCTORS	1	–	1	–	3	3	–	–	–
DOCTORS AND GET CUT OPEN	1	–	1	–	–	–	–	–	–
DOG	1	2	3	–	2	2	–	–	–
DONT	–	–	–	1	–	1	–	–	–

RESPONSE WORD	1ST			3RD			5TH		
	M	F	T	M	F	T	M	F	T

24.　EXAMINE

RESPONSE WORD	M	F	T	M	F	T	M	F	T
DOOR	3	1	4	–	–	–	–	–	–
DOWN	1	–	1	–	–	–	–	–	–
DRESSER	–	1	1	–	–	–	–	–	–
EARS	–	–	–	1	–	1	–	–	–
EAT	1	–	1	–	–	–	–	–	–
EDAMIN	–	1	1	–	–	–	–	–	–
EGG	3	–	3	–	–	–	–	–	–
ELEVEN	–	–	–	–	–	–	1	–	1
EVANINE	–	–	–	–	–	–	1	–	1
EX	–	–	–	–	1	1	–	–	–
EXAM	–	1	1	1	1	2	–	–	–
EXAMERATE	–	–	–	–	–	–	1	–	1
EXAMINATION	1	–	1	1	–	1	2	2	4
EXAMINATIONS	–	–	–	1	–	1	1	2	3
EXAMINE	–	–	–	–	1	1	–	–	–
EXAMINED	1	1	2	–	–	–	–	–	–
EXAMMED	–	–	–	1	–	1	–	–	–
EXAMPLE	–	–	–	1	–	1	–	–	–
EXCAMIN	–	–	–	–	–	–	–	1	1
EXCUSE	–	–	–	–	–	–	1	–	1
EXPERIMENT	–	–	–	2	–	2	1	–	1
EXPLAIN	–	–	–	–	2	2	–	–	–
EXPLORE	1	–	1	1	–	1	–	1	1
EXPRESS	–	–	–	1	–	1	–	–	–
EYE	–	2	2	–	1	1	–	–	–
EYES	8	8	16	6	12	18	3	4	7
FAMINE	1	1	2	–	–	–	–	–	–
FAST	1	–	1	–	1	1	1	–	1
FATHER	1	–	1	–	–	–	–	–	–
FIND OUT	–	–	–	–	–	–	1	–	1
FINK	–	1	1	–	–	–	–	–	–
FISH	–	–	–	2	–	2	–	–	–
FIX	–	–	–	2	1	3	–	–	–
FLOOR	1	1	2	–	1	1	–	–	–
FLY	–	1	1	–	–	–	–	–	–
GAMBLING	1	–	1	–	–	–	–	–	–
GAMIT	–	–	–	1	–	1	–	–	–
GET	–	–	–	–	–	–	–	1	1
GIRL	1	–	1	–	2	2	–	–	–
GLASSES	–	–	–	–	3	3	–	–	–
GO	–	2	2	–	–	–	1	1	2
GOOD	–	–	–	–	1	1	1	–	1
GRASS	–	–	–	1	–	1	–	–	–
HAIR	–	–	–	–	1	1	–	–	–
HAM	–	1	1	1	–	1	–	–	–
HAMMER	2	–	2	–	–	–	–	–	–
HANDS	–	–	–	1	–	1	1	–	1
HAPPENED	–	–	–	1	–	1	–	–	–
HAPPY	1	–	1	1	–	1	–	–	–
HAT	1	–	1	–	–	–	–	1	1
HAVE	–	–	–	–	–	–	–	1	1
HAYSTACK	–	1	1	–	–	–	–	–	–
HE	–	–	–	1	–	1	–	–	–
HEAD	–	1	1	1	–	1	–	–	–
HEAR	–	–	–	–	1	1	–	–	–
HEART	1	–	1	–	–	–	–	–	–
HELP	–	2	2	–	1	1	–	–	–
HER	–	–	–	–	–	–	–	1	1
HERE	–	1	1	–	–	–	1	–	1
HIGH SCHOOL	–	–	–	–	–	–	–	1	1
HIM	1	–	1	1	1	2	2	–	2
HORSE	1	–	1	–	–	–	–	–	–
HOSPITAL	–	2	2	2	–	2	–	–	–
HOUSE	1	–	1	–	–	–	–	–	–
HURT	–	2	2	–	1	1	–	–	–
I	–	–	–	–	–	–	1	–	1
I DON'T KNOW	–	–	–	–	1	1	–	–	–
I LOVE YOU	1	–	1	–	–	–	–	–	–
ICE CREAM	1	–	1	–	–	–	–	–	–
ICK	–	1	1	–	–	–	–	–	–
IN	–	1	1	–	1	1	–	–	–
INCENSE	–	–	–	–	1	1	–	–	–

RESPONSE WORD	1ST			3RD			5TH		
	M	F	T	M	F	T	M	F	T

24. EXAMINE

RESPONSE WORD	M	F	T	M	F	T	M	F	T
INQUIRE	–	–	–	–	–	–	–	1	1
INSECT	–	–	–	1	–	1	–	1	1
INSPECT	–	–	–	1	–	1	–	1	1
INSTRUCTIONS	–	–	–	–	–	–	–	1	1
INTURASTING	–	–	–	–	–	–	1	–	1
INVENT	–	1	1	–	1	1	–	–	–
IS	–	1	1	–	–	–	–	–	–
IT	–	2	2	–	–	–	1	–	1
KILL	–	1	1	–	–	–	–	–	–
KNEE	–	–	–	1	–	1	–	–	–
LABORATORY	–	1	1	–	–	–	–	–	–
LADY	–	–	–	–	–	–	1	–	1
LAMB	–	1	1	–	–	–	–	1	1
LAMIM	1	–	1	–	–	–	–	–	–
LEG	–	1	1	–	–	–	–	–	–
LETS LOOK AT	–	1	1	–	–	–	–	–	–
LETTER	–	1	1	–	–	–	–	–	–
LIKE	1	1	2	–	–	–	–	–	–
LINE	1	–	1	–	–	–	–	–	–
LOBBY	–	1	1	–	–	–	–	–	–
LOOK	1	1	2	3	4	7	18	15	33
LOOK AROUND	–	–	–	–	1	1	–	–	–
LOOK AT	1	–	1	4	–	4	3	4	7
LOOK FOR	–	–	–	1	–	1	–	–	–
LOOK OVER	–	–	–	2	1	3	7	9	16
MACHINE	1	–	1	–	–	–	–	–	–
MAN	4	1	5	1	–	1	1	–	1
MANINE	1	–	1	–	–	–	–	–	–
MAP	1	–	1	–	–	–	–	–	–
ME	3	2	5	3	1	4	1	1	2
MEASURE	–	–	–	–	–	–	–	1	1
MEDICINE	–	1	1	–	–	–	–	–	–
MICROSCOPE	–	–	–	–	–	–	1	–	1
MINE	–	–	–	–	–	–	1	1	2
MINER	–	–	–	–	–	–	1	–	1
MITTENS	1	–	1	–	–	–	–	–	–
MOTHER	–	–	–	1	–	1	–	–	–
MOUSE	–	–	–	–	–	–	1	–	1
MOUTH	1	–	1	–	–	–	–	–	–
NATION	–	–	–	–	–	–	–	1	1
NEEDLE	3	3	6	–	5	5	–	1	1
NO RESPONSE	1	–	1	–	–	–	–	–	–
NOSE	–	1	1	–	–	–	–	–	–
NOT	–	1	1	–	–	–	1	–	1
NOT EXAMINE	–	1	1	3	1	4	–	–	–
NOT EXAMINED	1	–	1	1	–	1	1	–	1
NOT TO EXAMINE	–	–	–	1	–	1	–	–	–
NOVEMBER	1	–	1	–	–	–	–	–	–
NOW	2	1	3	–	–	–	1	–	1
NURSE	–	–	–	–	2	2	–	–	–
OFFICE	–	1	1	–	–	–	–	–	–
OPERATE	–	–	–	8	10	18	5	–	5
OPERATING	1	–	1	–	–	–	–	–	–
OPERATION	1	1	2	4	4	8	1	1	2
ORANGE	1	1	2	–	–	–	–	–	–
OUT	–	1	1	–	–	–	–	–	–
PASS	–	–	–	–	–	–	1	–	1
PATCH	1	–	1	–	–	–	–	–	–
PATIENT	–	–	–	1	–	1	–	1	1
PEAR	–	–	–	–	1	1	–	–	–
PEOPLE	2	1	3	1	2	3	–	1	1
PEPER	–	–	–	–	–	–	–	1	1
PERSON	–	–	–	1	–	1	–	–	–
PHYSICAL	–	–	–	–	1	1	–	–	–
PICNIC TABLE	1	–	1	–	–	–	–	–	–
PIG	–	1	1	–	–	–	–	–	–
PIN	1	–	1	–	–	–	–	–	–
PLEASE	1	–	1	–	–	–	–	–	–
POLICE	1	–	1	–	–	–	–	–	–
POLIO	–	1	1	–	–	–	–	–	–
PRAY	–	–	–	–	–	–	–	1	1
PROPECK	–	–	–	–	–	–	–	1	1

RESPONSE WORD	1ST M	1ST F	1ST T	3RD M	3RD F	3RD T	5TH M	5TH F	5TH T

24. EXAMINE

RESPONSE WORD	1ST M	F	T	3RD M	F	T	5TH M	F	T
RAT	–	1	1	–	–	–	–	–	–
RE-EXAMINE	–	–	–	–	–	–	1	–	1
READ	–	–	–	–	1	1	–	–	–
REAL SICK	1	–	1	–	–	–	–	–	–
REEXAMINE	–	–	–	1	–	1	–	–	–
RING	–	1	1	–	–	–	–	–	–
ROY	–	–	–	–	–	–	–	1	1
RUN	–	1	1	–	–	–	–	–	–
SALMON	–	1	1	1	–	1	–	–	–
SCAT	–	–	–	1	–	1	–	–	–
SCIENCE	–	–	–	–	1	1	–	–	–
SCREAM	–	–	–	1	–	1	–	–	–
SEE	–	2	2	1	1	2	2	1	3
SHADOW	–	1	1	–	–	–	–	–	–
SHEP	–	–	–	–	1	1	–	–	–
SHOE	–	1	1	–	–	–	–	–	–
SHORT	–	1	1	–	–	–	–	–	–
SHOT	1	1	2	–	1	1	–	1	1
SHOULDER	1	–	1	–	–	–	–	–	–
SICK	–	2	2	1	2	3	–	1	1
SICK PERSON	1	–	1	–	–	–	–	–	–
SING	–	2	2	–	–	–	–	–	–
SOMETHING	–	1	1	–	–	–	1	1	2
SQUARE	–	–	–	–	1	1	–	–	–
STAR	–	1	1	–	–	–	–	–	–
STAY	1	–	1	–	–	–	–	–	–
STICK	–	1	1	–	–	–	–	–	–
STOP	–	1	1	–	–	–	–	–	–
STORY	–	–	–	–	1	1	–	–	–
STOVE	1	–	1	–	–	–	–	–	–
STUDY	–	–	–	1	–	1	1	–	1
SUSAN	–	1	1	–	–	–	–	–	–
SWIM	–	–	–	–	1	1	–	–	–
SWING	–	–	–	1	–	1	–	–	–
TABLE	–	2	2	–	–	–	–	–	–
TAKE	–	–	–	1	1	1	1	–	1
TAKE A GOOD LOOK AT	–	–	–	–	1	1	–	–	–
TAKE OVER	–	–	–	–	1	1	–	–	–
TAM	–	1	1	–	–	–	–	–	–
TAN-EN	1	–	1	–	–	–	–	–	–
TEETH	–	–	–	1	1	2	–	1	1
TELEVISION	–	1	1	–	–	–	–	–	–
TELL	–	–	–	2	–	2	–	–	–
TEST	1	1	2	13	13	26	26	22	48
TEST ON	–	–	–	–	–	–	–	1	1
TEST YOUR EYES	–	1	1	–	–	–	–	–	–
TESTED	–	–	–	–	–	–	1	–	1
THE	–	1	1	–	–	–	1	–	1
THE CHILDREN	1	–	1	–	–	–	–	–	–
THE GIRL	–	1	1	–	–	–	–	–	–
THE MEN GET MASKS ON AND OPERATE ON THE	1	–	1	–	–	–	–	–	–
THEY	–	–	–	–	1	1	–	–	–
THINK	1	–	1	1	–	1	–	1	1
TIES	1	–	1	–	–	–	–	–	–
TIP	1	–	1	–	–	–	–	–	–
TO	–	1	1	–	–	–	–	–	–
TO LOOK OVER	–	–	–	–	–	–	1	–	1
TRAILER	1	–	1	–	–	–	–	–	–
TREATMENT	–	–	–	–	–	–	–	1	1
TREES	–	–	–	–	–	–	–	1	1
UNDRESS	–	–	–	–	1	1	–	–	–
UNEXAMINE	1	–	1	1	1	2	2	1	3
UNEXAMINED	–	–	–	–	–	–	–	1	1
UNXAMINE	1	–	1	–	–	–	–	–	–
US	1	–	1	1	–	1	–	–	–
VACCINATION	–	–	–	1	–	1	1	1	1
WAIT	–	–	–	–	–	–	1	–	1
WALLET	1	–	1	–	–	–	–	–	–
WASAMINED	–	1	1	–	–	–	–	–	–
WATCH	–	–	–	1	–	1	–	–	–
WEAK	–	1	1	–	–	–	–	–	–

RESPONSE WORD	1ST M	F	T	3RD M	F	T	5TH M	F	T

24.   EXAMINE

RESPONSE WORD	1ST M	F	T	3RD M	F	T	5TH M	F	T
WHEN YOU EXAMINE SOMETHING.	1	–	1	–	–	–	–	–	–
WHY	1	–	1	–	–	–	–	–	–
WILD	1	–	1	–	–	–	–	–	–
WINDOW	1	–	1	–	–	–	–	–	–
WOLF	–	–	–	–	1	1	–	–	–
WOMAN	–	–	–	1	–	1	–	–	–
WOODS	–	1	1	–	–	–	–	–	–
WORK	–	1	1	–	1	1	–	2	2
WORKER	–	–	–	–	–	–	1	–	1
WRITE	–	–	–	–	–	–	1	–	1
X	–	1	1	–	–	–	–	–	–
X-RAY	–	1	1	7	6	13	6	4	10
X-RAYED	–	–	–	–	–	–	–	1	1
X-RAYS	–	–	–	–	1	1	–	–	–
XAMINE	–	1	1	–	–	–	–	1	1
YOU	2	3	5	1	1	2	1	–	1
YOUR	1	–	1	–	–	–	–	–	–
YOUR BRAIN	1	–	1	–	–	–	–	–	–
YOUR EYES	–	–	–	–	–	–	–	1	1
ZOO	1	–	1	1	–	1	–	–	–

25.   FLOWER

RESPONSE WORD	1ST M	F	T	3RD M	F	T	5TH M	F	T
A PLANT	–	–	–	–	–	–	1	1	2
A WHITE FLOWER	–	–	–	1	–	1	–	–	–
ALIVE	–	–	–	–	–	–	1	–	1
BAKING	–	–	–	–	–	–	1	–	1
BEAUTIFUL	–	–	–	–	1	1	3	2	5
BED	–	–	–	1	–	1	–	1	1
BEE	3	3	6	1	1	2	7	2	9
BEES	1	–	1	–	–	–	–	–	–
BELLS	–	–	–	1	–	1	–	–	–
BIG	–	1	1	–	–	–	–	–	–
BIRD	–	1	1	–	–	–	–	1	1
BLACK-EYE-SUSAN	–	–	–	1	–	1	–	–	–
BLACK-EYED SUSAN	–	–	–	–	–	–	–	1	1
BLACKEYED SUSAN	–	–	–	–	–	–	1	–	1
BLOOM	2	–	2	3	3	6	1	2	3
BLOOMING OBJECT	–	–	–	–	–	–	–	1	1
BLOOMS	1	–	1	–	–	–	–	–	–
BLOSSOM	–	–	–	3	3	6	1	1	2
BLOVER	–	1	1	–	2	2	–	1	1
BLUE	1	–	1	–	2	2	–	1	1
BLUW	–	–	–	–	–	–	1	–	1
BOTTLE	1	–	1	–	–	–	–	–	–
BOWER	–	2	2	–	–	–	–	–	–
BOWL	–	1	1	–	–	–	–	–	–
BOX	–	–	–	–	–	–	1	–	1
BRANCH	–	–	–	1	–	1	–	–	–
BREAD	–	–	–	1	–	1	–	–	–
BUD	–	–	–	5	2	7	3	6	9
BUDS	–	–	–	–	1	1	–	–	–
BUG	1	–	1	–	–	–	1	1	2
BUMBLE BEE	1	–	1	–	–	–	–	–	–
BUSH	2	–	2	2	2	4	1	1	2
BUTTERCUP	–	–	–	1	1	2	–	1	1
BUTTERFLY	4	–	4	1	1	2	–	1	1
BUY	–	–	–	–	–	–	–	1	1
BUZZ	–	–	–	1	–	1	–	–	–
CAN	–	–	–	–	–	–	1	–	1
CARNATION	–	–	–	–	–	–	–	1	1
CAT	–	2	2	–	–	–	–	–	–
CEP	1	–	1	–	–	–	–	–	–
CHICKEN	–	1	1	–	–	–	–	–	–
CHRYSANTHEMUM	–	–	–	1	–	1	1	–	1
CLOUD	–	–	–	–	1	1	–	–	–
COLLER	–	–	–	–	–	–	1	–	1
COLOR	–	–	–	–	1	1	2	–	2
COLORS	–	–	–	–	1	1	–	–	–

RESPONSE WORD	1ST M	F	T	3RD M	F	T	5TH M	F	T

25. FLOWER

RESPONSE WORD	1ST M	F	T	3RD M	F	T	5TH M	F	T
CORN	–	1	1	–	–	–	–	–	–
COUER	–	–	–	–	–	–	1	–	1
COUGH	1	–	1	–	–	–	–	–	–
COW	–	1	1	–	–	–	–	–	–
COWER	1	1	2	–	–	–	–	–	–
CROWER	1	–	1	–	–	–	–	–	–
CURTAINS	–	1	1	–	–	–	–	–	–
DAISY	1	2	3	4	2	6	5	7	12
DANDELION	–	1	1	–	–	–	–	–	–
DAY	–	–	–	–	–	–	1	–	1
DEAD	1	–	1	1	–	1	–	–	–
DIED	1	–	1	–	–	–	–	–	–
DIG IN IT	–	1	1	–	–	–	–	–	–
DIRT	2	1	3	–	–	–	1	–	1
DO IT	–	1	1	–	–	–	–	–	–
DO SMELL GOOD	–	1	1	–	–	–	–	–	–
DOE	–	–	–	–	–	–	1	–	1
DOOR	–	1	1	–	–	–	–	–	–
DOUGH	–	2	2	–	–	–	–	1	1
DRESS	–	1	1	–	–	–	–	–	–
DYER	–	1	1	–	–	–	–	–	–
EAT	1	–	1	–	–	–	1	–	1
FALL	–	1	1	–	–	–	–	–	–
FAMILY	–	1	1	–	–	–	–	–	–
FATHER	1	–	1	–	–	–	–	–	–
FED	–	1	1	–	–	–	–	–	–
FLOP	–	1	1	–	–	–	–	–	–
FLOUR	–	–	–	–	1	1	1	1	2
FLOW	–	–	–	–	–	–	1	–	1
FLOWER	1	–	1	–	–	–	–	1	1
FLU	1	–	1	–	–	–	–	–	–
FLY	2	1	3	2	–	2	–	–	–
FOR	–	–	–	–	–	–	1	–	1
FORSYTHIA	–	–	–	1	–	1	–	–	–
FROG	–	–	–	–	1	1	–	–	–
FUNNY	–	–	–	1	–	1	–	–	–
GAME	1	–	1	–	–	–	–	–	–
GARBAGE CAN	–	1	1	–	–	–	–	–	–
GARDEN	2	6	8	7	6	13	2	6	8
GARDENIA	–	–	–	–	–	–	2	–	2
GARDENS	–	1	1	–	–	–	–	–	–
GET	–	1	1	–	–	–	–	–	–
GIRLS	–	–	–	–	1	1	1	–	1
GOOD	–	–	–	–	1	1	–	–	–
GOOD SMELLING	–	1	1	–	–	–	–	–	–
GRASS	5	10	15	4	4	8	2	2	4
GRAY	–	–	–	1	–	1	–	–	–
GREEN	–	2	2	–	–	–	1	–	1
GROUND	1	1	2	–	2	2	–	–	–
GROW	6	4	10	2	1	3	2	1	3
GROWER	1	–	1	–	–	–	–	–	–
GROWS	3	1	4	1	1	2	–	–	–
HAT	1	–	1	–	1	1	–	–	–
HAVE	–	1	1	–	–	–	–	–	–
HER	–	–	–	3	1	4	–	–	–
HERE	–	1	1	–	–	–	–	–	–
HIS	–	–	–	1	–	1	–	–	–
HONEY	1	2	3	3	1	4	–	–	–
HOUR	–	–	–	1	–	1	–	–	–
HOUSE	1	–	1	–	–	–	–	–	–
HOWARD	1	–	1	–	–	–	–	–	–
HOWER	2	–	2	–	–	–	–	–	–
INSECT	–	–	–	–	2	2	–	1	1
INSECTS	–	–	–	1	–	1	–	–	–
INSIDE	–	–	–	–	1	1	–	–	–
IS PRETTY	–	1	1	–	–	–	–	–	–
IT	1	–	1	–	–	–	–	–	–
ITEM	–	–	–	1	–	1	–	–	–
LAMP	–	1	1	–	–	–	–	–	–
LEAF	4	6	10	–	1	1	–	1	1
LEAVE	–	–	–	–	1	1	–	–	–
LEAVES	2	1	3	–	–	–	–	2	2

RESPONSE WORD	1ST M	F	T	3RD M	F	T	5TH M	F	T

25. FLOWER

RESPONSE WORD	1ST M	F	T	3RD M	F	T	5TH M	F	T
LILAC	–	–	–	–	–	–	–	1	1
LITTLE	–	1	1	–	–	–	–	–	–
LONG	–	–	–	1	–	1	–	–	–
LOOK	–	–	–	1	–	1	–	–	–
LOOK AT THAT FLOWER THATS GROWING IN TH.	–	1	1	–	–	–	–	–	–
LOUD	1	–	1	–	–	–	–	–	–
LOWER	–	1	1	1	–	1	–	–	–
LUNCH	1	–	1	–	–	–	–	–	–
MAKE	–	–	–	–	1	1	–	–	–
MAN	2	–	2	–	–	–	–	–	–
MARIGOLD	–	–	–	–	–	–	–	1	1
ME	–	–	–	1	–	1	–	–	–
MOUER	1	–	1	–	1	1	–	–	–
MOWER	1	–	1	–	–	–	–	–	–
NICE	1	–	1	–	–	–	–	–	–
NO	1	–	1	–	–	–	–	–	–
NOT	–	–	–	–	–	–	1	–	1
ONE	1	–	1	–	–	–	–	–	–
ORANGE	1	–	1	–	–	–	–	–	–
OUTSIDE	–	1	1	–	–	–	–	–	–
PANSY	–	–	–	–	1	1	–	–	–
PERFUME	–	–	–	–	–	–	–	1	1
PERSON	–	–	–	–	–	–	–	1	1
PETTER	–	–	–	–	–	–	1	–	1
PETUNIA	–	–	–	1	–	1	1	–	1
PICK	1	2	3	1	–	1	–	–	–
PINK	–	–	–	2	8	10	–	–	–
PIT	1	–	1	–	–	–	–	–	–
PLANT	3	2	5	15	10	25	20	17	37
PLANTS	–	–	–	–	1	1	–	–	–
POLICEMAN	–	1	1	–	–	–	–	–	–
POT	1	2	3	4	5	9	–	3	3
POWDER	–	–	–	–	–	–	2	–	2
POWDERY	–	–	–	1	–	1	–	–	–
POWER	1	–	1	1	–	1	–	–	–
POWERED	–	1	1	–	–	–	–	–	–
PRETTY	2	12	14	16	20	36	9	20	29
PULL	–	–	–	–	1	1	–	–	–
PULLED OFF	1	–	1	–	–	–	–	–	–
PURPLE	–	–	–	–	–	–	–	1	1
PURSE	1	–	1	–	–	–	–	–	–
PUSSY-WILLOW	–	–	–	1	–	1	–	–	–
RAIN	3	1	4	–	1	1	–	–	–
RED	1	–	1	2	–	2	2	–	2
RIDE	–	1	1	–	–	–	–	–	–
ROBIN	–	–	–	–	1	1	–	–	–
ROSE	6	12	18	14	22	36	23	23	46
ROSEBUD	–	–	–	–	–	–	1	–	1
ROSES	2	1	3	2	2	4	–	1	1
ROUND	–	–	–	–	–	–	–	1	1
ROW	1	–	1	–	–	–	–	–	–
ROWER	–	1	1	–	–	–	–	–	–
SALT	–	–	–	–	–	–	1	–	1
SEE	–	1	1	–	–	–	–	–	–
SEED	–	1	1	1	1	2	3	–	3
SHEEP	–	–	–	1	–	1	–	–	–
SHOWER	1	–	1	1	–	1	–	–	–
SLEPT	1	–	1	–	–	–	–	–	–
SLOW	–	–	–	–	–	–	1	–	1
SMELL	3	4	7	2	5	7	4	3	7
SMELL FLOWER	–	1	1	–	–	–	–	–	–
SMELL GOOD	1	–	1	–	–	–	–	–	–
SMELLS	1	1	2	–	–	–	–	1	1
SMELLS GOOD	3	–	3	–	–	–	–	–	–
SMOKE	1	–	1	–	–	–	–	–	–
SNAKE	–	–	–	–	–	–	1	–	1
SNAKE FLOWER	–	–	–	1	–	1	–	–	–
SOUR	1	1	2	1	–	1	–	1	1
SPELLING	1	–	1	–	–	–	–	–	–
SPRAY	1	–	1	–	–	–	–	–	–
SPRING	–	–	–	–	–	–	2	2	4

RESPONSE WORD	1ST			3RD			5TH		
	M	F	T	M	F	T	M	F	T

25. FLOWER

RESPONSE WORD	M	F	T	M	F	T	M	F	T
STANDS	1	–	1	–	–	–	–	–	–
STAR	1	–	1	–	–	–	–	–	–
STEM	1	4	5	–	2	2	1	4	5
STINKY SMELL	–	–	–	–	–	–	1	–	1
STRAWBERRY	1	–	1	–	–	–	–	–	–
SUN	2	–	2	–	–	–	1	1	2
SUNFLOWER	–	–	–	–	–	–	1	1	2
SWEET	–	–	–	4	2	6	1	3	4
THERE IS A WILD FLOWER	–	–	–	–	–	–	–	1	1
THING	–	–	–	1	–	1	–	–	–
THUMB	–	1	1	–	–	–	–	–	–
TIGER LILY	–	–	–	–	–	–	1	–	1
TOWER	1	1	2	–	–	–	–	1	1
TOY STORE	1	–	1	–	–	–	–	–	–
TREE	6	1	7	1	1	2	–	1	1
TULIP	2	–	2	3	3	6	2	2	4
VASE	–	–	–	–	–	–	1	1	2
WARM	–	–	–	–	–	–	1	1	2
WAS	–	–	–	–	1	1	–	–	–
WATER	7	5	12	1	–	1	–	–	–
WATER THE FLOWERS	–	1	1	–	–	–	–	–	–
WATERING CAN	–	1	1	–	–	–	–	–	–
WEED	1	1	2	1	1	2	4	–	4
WEEDS	–	–	–	–	1	1	–	–	–
WHALE	1	–	1	–	–	–	–	–	–
WHEN YOURE WATERING THE FLOWERS	1	–	1	–	–	–	–	–	–
WHENEVER MOTHER BUYS SOME FLOUR	–	1	1	–	–	–	–	–	–
WHITE	–	–	–	1	–	1	–	–	–
WIND	–	–	–	–	1	1	–	–	–
YARD	–	–	–	–	1	1	–	–	–
YELLOW	–	–	–	1	–	1	3	–	3
YOU GET A FLOWER PETAL IN YOUR HAIR	–	1	1	–	–	–	–	–	–
YOU PICK THEM AND PUT THEM IN THE HOUSE	1	–	1	–	–	–	–	–	–
YOU RE	1	–	1	–	–	–	–	–	–

26. FLY

RESPONSE WORD	M	F	T	M	F	T	M	F	T
A BIRD COULD BE FLYING UP IN THE AIR	–	1	1	–	–	–	–	–	–
A BIRD FLIES	–	1	1	–	–	–	–	–	–
A BUG	–	–	–	1	–	1	–	–	–
A FLY	1	–	1	–	–	–	–	–	–
A KITE	–	1	1	–	–	–	–	–	–
ABOVE	–	–	–	–	–	–	–	1	1
AIR	2	1	3	3	3	6	2	4	6
AIRPLANE	6	1	7	2	4	6	8	6	14
AN INSECT	–	–	–	–	–	–	–	1	1
ANIMAL	–	1	1	1	–	1	–	2	2
ANT	–	1	1	–	–	–	–	–	–
AROUND THE CORNER	–	1	1	–	–	–	–	–	–
AWAY	1	1	2	2	–	2	–	–	–
BABY	1	–	1	–	–	–	–	–	–
BATHTUB	1	–	1	–	–	–	–	–	–
BEE	4	3	7	3	5	8	1	3	4
BEETLE	–	1	1	–	1	1	–	–	–
BERRY	1	–	1	–	–	–	–	–	–
BIG	–	–	–	–	1	1	–	–	–
BIRD	15	28	43	9	23	32	11	19	30
BIRD FLIES	–	1	1	–	–	–	–	–	–
BIRDS	1	–	1	1	–	1	1	1	2
BIRDS FLY	–	1	1	–	–	–	–	–	–
BLACK	–	1	1	–	–	–	–	–	–
BLY	–	–	–	–	–	–	1	–	1
BOARD	–	1	1	–	–	–	–	–	–
BOAT	1	–	1	–	1	1	–	–	–
BOTHER	–	–	–	–	–	–	1	–	1
BOY	–	2	2	–	–	–	–	–	–

26. FLY

RESPONSE WORD	1ST			3RD			5TH		
	M	F	T	M	F	T	M	F	T
BUG	4	7	11	10	14	24	9	9	18
BUGS CAN FLY	-	1	1	-	-	-	-	-	-
BUMBLEBEE	1	-	1	-	-	-	-	-	-
BUMBLEBEES	1	-	1	-	-	-	-	-	-
BUTTER	-	-	-	-	1	1	-	-	-
BUTTERFLY	9	9	18	7	1	8	-	1	1
BUY	-	2	2	1	-	1	-	-	-
BUZZ	3	-	3	-	1	1	1	-	1
BUZZES	1	-	1	-	-	-	-	-	-
BY	1	4	5	5	-	5	-	-	-
CAKE	-	1	1	-	-	-	-	-	-
CAN MOVE	1	-	1	-	-	-	-	-	-
CAR	1	1	2	-	-	-	-	-	-
CAREFUL	-	1	1	-	-	-	-	-	-
CAT	1	-	1	-	-	-	-	-	-
CATCH	-	1	1	-	-	-	-	-	-
CLOCK	-	1	1	-	-	-	-	-	-
COW	1	-	1	-	-	-	-	-	-
CRAWL	-	-	-	1	-	1	-	-	-
CRY	1	-	1	-	-	-	-	-	-
CYE	1	-	1	-	-	-	-	-	-
DECEMBER	-	1	1	-	-	-	-	-	-
DIE	-	1	1	1	-	1	-	-	-
DIRT	1	-	1	-	-	-	1	-	1
DONT FLY	-	-	-	1	-	1	-	-	-
DOWN	1	5	6	5	3	8	-	-	-
DRAG	-	1	1	-	-	-	1	-	1
EAR	-	1	1	-	-	-	-	-	-
EYE	-	-	-	1	-	1	-	-	-
FALL	-	1	1	1	-	1	-	-	-
FAST	2	3	5	3	2	5	3	1	4
FATHER	1	-	1	-	-	-	-	-	-
FEE	-	-	-	-	-	-	1	-	1
FENCE	1	-	1	-	-	-	-	-	-
FISH	-	1	1	1	1	2	-	-	-
FIVE	-	-	-	1	-	1	-	-	-
FLEE	-	1	1	-	1	1	1	-	1
FLEW	-	-	-	1	2	3	-	3	3
FLIES	1	-	1	-	-	-	-	-	-
FLIES AROUND	1	-	1	-	-	-	-	-	-
FLIES FLY AROUND	1	-	1	-	-	-	-	-	-
FLOOR	-	1	1	-	-	-	-	-	-
FLOPPING	1	-	1	-	-	-	-	-	-
FLOW	-	1	1	-	-	-	-	-	-
FLOWER	1	-	1	-	1	1	-	-	-
FLOWERS	1	-	1	-	-	-	-	-	-
FLY AWAY	1	-	1	-	-	-	-	-	-
FLYER	-	1	1	-	-	-	-	-	-
FLYING	-	-	-	1	-	1	-	-	-
FOOD	1	-	1	-	-	-	-	-	-
FOUR	-	2	2	-	-	-	-	-	-
FOX	-	-	-	-	1	1	-	-	-
GET THAT FLY OUT OF THE HOUSE.	1	-	1	-	-	-	-	-	-
GIRL	-	1	1	-	-	-	-	-	-
GIVE	1	-	1	-	-	-	-	-	-
GLIDE	-	-	-	-	-	-	1	1	2
GO	-	2	2	3	3	6	-	-	-
GO ON THE GROUND	1	-	1	-	-	-	-	-	-
GOOD-BYE	1	-	1	-	-	-	-	-	-
GROUND	-	1	1	3	2	5	1	-	1
GROUNDED	-	-	-	-	-	-	1	-	1
GUY	1	-	1	-	-	-	-	-	-
HAPPY	-	-	-	-	1	1	-	-	-
HELICOPTER	-	1	1	-	-	-	-	-	-
HERE	-	-	-	1	-	1	-	-	-
HIGH	10	1	11	3	5	8	7	6	13
HIGHT	-	-	-	-	-	-	1	-	1
HIT	-	1	1	-	-	-	-	-	-
HORSE	-	-	-	1	-	1	-	-	-
HOUSE	-	1	1	-	-	-	-	-	-
HOW	1	-	1	-	-	-	-	-	-

26. FLY

RESPONSE WORD	1ST			3RD			5TH		
	M	F	T	M	F	T	M	F	T
HURT	–	–	–	–	–	–	1	–	1
ICE	1	–	1	–	–	–	–	–	–
IN	–	1	1	–	–	–	–	–	–
IN THE AIR	1	1	2	–	–	–	1	–	1
INSECT	5	3	8	8	8	16	25	27	52
JET	–	–	–	1	–	1	1	–	1
KEEP	–	–	–	–	–	–	–	1	1
KITE	–	2	2	1	1	2	–	–	–
LAND	–	–	–	3	1	4	2	–	2
LANDED	–	–	–	–	1	1	–	–	–
LANDING	–	–	–	–	–	–	1	–	1
LETS GO CATCH FLIES	–	1	1	–	–	–	–	–	–
LIE	–	–	–	1	–	1	–	2	2
LIGHT	1	–	1	–	–	–	–	–	–
LOOK AT THAT BUG	1	–	1	–	–	–	–	–	–
LOUD	–	–	–	–	–	–	1	–	1
LOW	–	–	–	1	1	2	1	1	2
MIRROR	–	1	1	–	–	–	–	–	–
MOON	–	1	1	–	–	–	–	–	–
MOSQUITO	–	–	–	1	–	1	–	1	1
MOVE	–	–	–	–	–	–	1	–	1
MOVE IN THE AIR	–	–	–	–	–	–	1	–	1
MY	4	–	4	–	1	1	–	1	1
NO	1	–	1	–	–	–	–	–	–
NOT	1	–	1	–	–	–	–	–	–
NOT FLY	1	–	1	2	1	3	–	–	–
NOW	2	–	2	–	–	–	–	–	–
NUMBER	–	–	–	1	–	1	–	–	–
OFF	–	–	–	–	–	–	1	–	1
OFF GROUND	–	–	–	–	–	–	1	–	1
ORANGE	–	1	1	–	–	–	–	–	–
OUT	–	–	–	–	–	–	1	1	2
PAPER	1	–	1	–	–	–	–	–	–
PERSON	–	–	–	–	–	–	–	1	1
PICTURE	1	–	1	–	–	–	–	–	–
PIE	–	1	1	–	–	–	–	–	–
PLANE	1	–	1	3	2	5	4	4	8
PLANT	–	–	–	1	–	1	–	–	–
PLAY	–	–	–	1	–	1	–	–	–
POCKETBOOK	2	–	2	–	–	–	–	–	–
QUIET	–	–	–	–	–	–	1	–	1
RED	1	–	1	–	–	–	–	–	–
RIDE	1	1	2	3	–	3	–	2	2
ROUND	–	–	–	1	–	1	–	–	–
RUN	1	1	2	4	3	7	2	–	2
RYE	–	1	1	–	–	–	–	–	–
SAIL	–	–	–	2	–	2	–	–	–
SHOT	–	–	–	–	–	–	1	–	1
SIGH	1	–	1	–	1	1	–	–	–
SKIP	–	–	–	–	1	1	–	–	–
SKY	–	–	–	–	1	1	3	2	5
SLIDE DOWN A SLIDING BOARD	–	1	1	–	–	–	–	–	–
SLIDE RULE	–	–	–	1	–	1	–	–	–
SLIPPERY	–	–	–	–	–	–	1	–	1
SLOW	3	3	6	–	1	1	1	–	1
SLY	–	–	–	–	1	1	1	1	2
SMASH	1	–	1	–	–	–	–	–	–
SNOW	–	–	–	1	–	1	–	–	–
SOMETHING THAT CAN FLY IN THE AIR	–	–	–	–	–	–	1	–	1
SOUR	–	–	–	–	–	–	–	1	1
SOUTH	–	–	–	–	1	1	–	–	–
SPACE	–	–	–	–	–	–	–	1	1
SPIDER	–	2	2	1	–	1	–	–	–
STAND	–	1	1	–	1	1	–	–	–
START	–	–	–	–	–	–	1	–	1
STOP	1	1	2	–	1	1	–	–	–
STUFF FLIES	1	–	1	–	–	–	–	–	–
STUNG	–	1	1	–	–	–	–	–	–
SUN	–	–	–	–	–	–	1	–	1

RESPONSE WORD	1ST M	F	T	3RD M	F	T	5TH M	F	T

26. FLY

RESPONSE WORD	1ST M	F	T	3RD M	F	T	5TH M	F	T
SWATTER	1	–	1	1	–	1	–	–	–
SWEATER	–	1	1	–	–	–	–	–	–
SWIFT	–	–	–	–	2	2	–	1	1
SWIM	–	–	–	1	1	2	–	1	1
SWING	–	–	–	1	–	1	–	–	–
TABLE	1	1	2	–	–	–	–	–	–
TAKE TO THE AIR	–	–	–	–	–	–	–	1	1
THE FLY	1	–	1	–	–	–	–	–	–
THROUGH AIR	–	–	–	–	–	–	1	–	1
THROUGH THE AIR	–	–	–	–	–	–	–	1	1
TIE	–	–	–	–	1	1	–	–	–
TIME	–	–	–	–	–	–	1	–	1
TO	–	1	1	–	–	–	–	–	–
TO LIE	–	–	–	–	–	–	–	1	1
TRAIN	1	–	1	–	–	–	–	–	–
TRASHCAN	–	1	1	–	–	–	–	–	–
TWO KINDS	–	–	–	–	1	1	–	–	–
UP	2	–	2	–	–	–	1	1	2
UP IN THE AIR	–	–	–	2	–	2	–	–	–
WALK	2	5	7	24	24	48	21	23	44
WALL	–	–	–	–	1	1	–	–	–
WATER	1	–	1	–	–	–	–	–	–
WENT BY	1	–	1	–	–	–	–	–	–
WHEN YOU GO UP IN THE AIR	–	–	–	–	–	–	–	1	1
WHEN YOURE FLYING OUTSIDE	1	–	1	–	–	–	–	–	–
WING	2	2	4	–	3	3	3	2	5
WINGS	4	2	6	2	3	5	4	4	8
YOU	–	1	1	–	–	–	–	–	–
ZOO	–	–	–	–	–	–	1	–	1

27. FRUIT

RESPONSE WORD	1ST M	F	T	3RD M	F	T	5TH M	F	T
A	–	–	–	–	–	–	–	1	1
A HEALTHFUL FOOD THAT YOU EAT	–	–	–	–	–	–	–	1	1
AN APPLE	1	–	1	1	–	1	–	–	–
ANIMAL	–	1	1	–	–	–	–	–	–
APPLE	11	19	30	30	35	65	46	46	92
APPLES	5	–	5	1	2	3	–	1	1
APPLY	–	–	–	–	–	–	1	–	1
BANANA	5	7	12	4	6	10	4	10	14
BANANAS	1	–	1	–	–	–	–	–	–
BANNA	–	–	–	–	–	–	–	1	1
BASKET	1	4	5	–	1	1	–	–	–
BAT	1	–	1	–	–	–	1	–	1
BERRIES	1	–	1	–	–	–	–	–	–
BINGS	–	1	1	–	–	–	–	–	–
BLUE	1	1	2	–	–	–	–	–	–
BOARD	–	–	–	–	–	–	–	–	–
BOOT	3	1	4	1	–	1	1	1	2
BOWL	–	2	2	–	2	2	–	3	3
BOX	1	–	1	–	–	–	–	–	–
BOY	1	–	1	–	–	–	–	–	–
BULLETIN BOARD	1	–	1	–	–	–	–	–	–
CAKE	1	–	1	–	–	–	2	–	2
CARDBOARD	1	–	1	–	–	–	–	–	–
CARROT	–	–	–	–	1	1	–	–	–
CARROTS	–	1	1	–	–	–	–	–	–
CAT	2	–	2	–	–	–	–	–	–
CHAIR	1	–	1	–	–	–	–	–	–
CHERRY	–	1	1	–	–	–	–	–	–
CITRUS	–	–	–	–	–	–	2	2	4
CLOVER	–	1	1	–	–	–	–	–	–
COCKTAIL	1	1	2	1	–	1	4	–	4
COLD	–	1	1	–	–	–	–	–	–
COLOR	1	–	1	1	–	1	–	–	–
CORN	–	1	1	–	–	–	–	–	–
COWS	1	–	1	–	–	–	–	–	–
CUIT	1	–	1	–	–	–	–	–	–

27. FRUIT

RESPONSE WORD	1ST			3RD			5TH		
	M	F	T	M	F	T	M	F	T
CUP	—	—	—	—	—	—	1	—	1
CUTE	—	1	1	—	—	—	1	—	1
DELICIOUS				—	1	1	—	—	—
DESSERT	2	1	3	1	2	3	—	—	—
DINNER	1	—	1	1	1	2	—	—	—
DISH	—	1	1	—	2	2	—	—	—
DOG	—	—	—	—	—	—	1	—	1
DRINK	1	1	2	1	—	1	—	—	—
DUIT	1	1	2						
DUKE	1	—	1						
EARS	—	1	1						
EAT	11	15	26	11	7	18	6	7	13
EGG SALAD	—	1	1						
ENGENE				—	—	—	1	—	1
FESTIVAL	—	—	—	—	—	—	1	—	1
FINED	—	—	—	—	—	—	1	—	1
FISH	1	—	1	—	—	—	—	—	—
FIST									
FLAVOR	—	1	1	—	1	1	—	1	1
FLIP	—	1	1	1	—	1	—	1	1
FLUTE	1	—	1				—	1	1
FOOD	1	4	5	10	10	20	6	8	14
FOODS				—	1	1	—	—	—
FRONT				1	—	1	—	—	—
FRUIT BASKET	—	1	1	—	—	—			
FUN	—	—	—	—	1	1	—	—	—
FUR	1	—	1						
GLASS	—	1	1						
GLASSES	—	1	1						
GO	1	—	1						
GOD	—	1	1						
GOOD	4	3	7	4	5	9	1	4	5
GOOD TO EAT	1	—	1	—	—	—	—	—	—
GRAP							1	—	1
GRAPE	1	1	2	1	1	2	1	1	2
GRAPEFRUIT	—	1	1	1	—	1	1	1	2
GRAPES	2	1	3	1	—	1	—	1	1
GRASS	1	—	1				—	1	1
GROCERY STORE	—	1	1	—	—	—	—	—	—
GROW	1	—	1	—	—	—	—	—	—
GROWS ON TREES	—	—	—	1	—	1	—	—	—
GROWTH							—	1	1
HAIR	—	1	1	—	—	—	—	1	1
HAM									
HOOT	2	—	2						
I									
I LIKE FRUIT	—	1	1						
I LOVE	—	1	1						
I WANT SOME FRUIT FOR LUNCH	—	1	1	—	—	—	—	—	—
ICE CREAM	—	1	1	—	1	1	—	—	—
IN THE MORNING	—	1	1						
INSECT	1	—	1						
INSTRUMENT	—	1	1	—	—	—	—	1	1
JELLO	1	1	2	—	—	—	—	—	—
JELLY	1	—	1	—	2	2	—	—	—
JUICE	3	3	6	1	—	1	—	—	—
JUICY	—	1	1	—	1	1	—	—	—
KER	—	1	1						
KITTEN	1	—	1						
LETS EAT FRUIT	—	1	1						
LIGHT	—	1	1						
LIKE	1	1	2	—	—	—	—	1	1
LIKE APPLES	—	1	1						
LOT	—	—	—	—	—	—	—	1	1
LOVE	—	1	1	—	—	—	—	1	1
MAN	1	—	1	—	—	—	—	—	—
MEAL	—	—	—	—	—	—	—	—	—
MEAT	1	—	1	2	—	2	—	—	—
MELON	1	—	1	—	—	—	—	—	—
MILK	—	1	1	—	—	—	—	—	—

27. FRUIT

RESPONSE WORD	1ST M	F	T	3RD M	F	T	5TH M	F	T
MOON	–	1	1	–	–	–	–	–	–
MOOT	1	–	1	–	–	–	–	–	–
MOTHER	1	–	1	–	–	–	–	–	–
MUSH	1	–	1	–	–	–	–	–	–
MUSIC	1	–	1	1	–	1	–	–	–
NEW	–	–	–	–	1	1	–	–	–
NEWT	–	–	–	1	–	1	–	–	–
NIUT	1	–	1	–	–	–	–	–	–
NUT	–	–	–	–	–	–	1	1	2
ORANGE	8	6	14	12	15	27	16	18	34
ORANGE JUICE	1	1	2	–	–	–	–	–	–
ORANGES	1	1	2	1	2	3	–	–	–
PEACH	–	–	–	2	1	3	2	–	2
PEACHES	1	–	1	–	1	1	–	–	–
PEAR	6	1	7	2	–	2	3	2	5
PEARS	1	–	1	–	–	–	–	–	–
PINEAPPLE	–	4	4	1	1	2	–	–	–
PINK	–	–	–	–	1	1	–	–	–
PIPES	1	–	1	–	–	–	–	–	–
PLANT	–	–	–	–	–	–	2	–	2
PLATE	–	1	1	–	–	–	–	–	–
PLATES	1	–	1	–	–	–	–	–	–
PUIT	1	–	1	–	–	–	–	–	–
PUT IT ON BREAD	1	–	1	–	–	–	–	–	–
PUTE	–	1	1	–	–	–	–	–	–
REFRIGERATOR	–	1	1	–	–	–	–	–	–
RING	–	–	–	–	1	1	–	–	–
RIPE	–	–	–	1	–	1	–	–	–
ROOF	–	1	1	–	–	–	–	–	–
ROOT	1	2	3	–	–	–	–	–	–
SALAD	2	–	2	–	1	1	–	–	–
SAUCE	1	–	1	–	–	–	–	–	–
SHOE	1	–	1	–	–	–	–	–	–
SING	–	1	1	–	–	–	–	–	–
SOME FRUIT THAT YOUR MOTHER FIXES	–	1	1	–	–	–	–	–	–
SOMETHING TO EAT	–	–	–	–	–	–	1	2	3
SOUR	–	–	–	–	1	1	–	–	–
SPOON	–	1	1	–	–	–	–	–	–
STARVED	–	–	–	1	–	1	–	–	–
STICK	–	–	–	–	1	1	–	–	–
SUIT	1	–	1	–	2	2	–	–	–
SUPPER	–	1	1	–	–	–	–	–	–
SWEET	–	1	1	4	1	5	–	–	–
TABLE	–	1	1	–	–	–	–	–	–
TAKE	1	–	1	–	–	–	–	–	–
TASTE	1	–	1	1	–	1	–	–	–
TASTES GOOD	–	1	1	–	–	–	–	–	–
TASTY	–	–	–	–	–	–	–	1	1
THAT	–	–	–	–	1	1	–	–	–
TO	1	–	1	–	–	–	–	–	–
TOOT	2	–	2	1	–	1	–	–	–
TREE	–	–	–	1	1	2	2	2	4
TWO	1	–	1	–	–	–	–	1	1
VEGATABLE	–	–	–	–	–	–	–	1	1
VEGETABLE	4	4	8	29	18	47	27	16	43
VEGETABLES	7	4	11	7	8	15	2	2	4
VEGETBLE	–	–	–	–	–	–	–	1	1
VEGETTABL	–	–	–	–	–	–	1	–	1
VEGTEABLE	–	–	–	–	–	–	1	–	1
VINE	–	1	1	–	–	–	–	–	–
WATERMELON	1	–	1	–	–	–	–	–	–
WHEN YOURE EATING SOME FRUIT	1	–	1	–	–	–	–	–	–
WHO	1	–	1	–	–	–	–	–	–
WOOL	–	–	–	–	–	–	1	–	1
YES	–	1	1	–	–	–	–	–	–
YOU COULD BUY SOME FRUIT	–	1	1	–	–	–	–	–	–
YUM-YUM	–	1	1	–	–	–	–	–	–

RESPONSE WORD	1ST M	F	T	3RD M	F	T	5TH M	F	T

28. GALLOP

RESPONSE WORD	M	F	T	M	F	T	M	F	T
A HORSE	–	–	–	–	–	–	1	–	1
ALONG	–	1	1	1	–	1	–	–	–
AMIAL	–	–	–	–	–	–	–	1	1
AROUND	–	–	–	2	–	2	–	–	–
AWAY	–	2	2	1	3	4	2	1	3
BALLOP	1	–	1	–	–	–	–	–	–
BATH	–	1	1	–	–	–	–	–	–
BICYCLE	1	–	1	–	–	–	–	–	–
BLUE	1	–	1	–	–	–	–	–	–
BOOK	–	1	1	–	–	–	–	–	–
BOTTLE	–	–	–	–	–	–	–	1	1
BOWLING	–	1	1	–	–	–	–	–	–
BOY	1	–	1	1	–	1	–	–	–
BROWN	–	1	1	–	–	–	–	–	–
BUILDING	–	1	1	–	–	–	–	–	–
CAKE	–	–	–	–	1	1	–	–	–
CANTER	–	–	–	–	–	–	1	2	3
CAR	3	–	3	–	–	–	–	–	–
CHAIR	–	1	1	–	–	–	–	–	–
COOK	–	1	1	–	–	–	–	–	–
COWBOY	–	1	1	–	–	–	1	–	1
DANCE	–	1	1	–	–	–	–	–	–
DESK	2	–	2	–	–	–	–	–	–
DOOR	1	–	1	–	–	–	–	–	–
DOWN	–	–	–	–	2	2	–	–	–
DOWN THE RIVER	1	–	1	–	–	–	–	–	–
EAT	–	–	–	–	1	1	1	–	1
FAST	3	4	7	9	3	12	10	1	11
FAST CANTER	–	–	–	–	–	–	–	1	1
FAST TROT	–	–	–	–	–	–	–	1	1
FATHER	1	–	1	–	–	–	–	–	–
FIGHT	1	–	1	–	–	–	–	–	–
FLOWER	–	1	1	–	–	–	–	–	–
FOLLOW	1	–	1	–	–	–	–	–	–
GAFF	–	–	–	1	–	1	–	–	–
GALLANT MEN	1	–	1	1	–	1	–	–	–
GALLON	–	–	–	1	–	1	–	–	–
GALLOPING	1	1	2	3	1	4	1	–	1
GALLOPING ALONG	–	–	–	–	–	–	–	1	1
GALLOPMEN	1	–	1	–	–	–	–	–	–
GAS	1	–	1	–	–	–	–	–	–
GET OUT	1	–	1	–	–	–	–	–	–
GET UP	–	1	1	–	–	–	–	–	–
GIDDY-UP	–	–	–	–	2	2	–	–	–
GIRL	2	–	2	–	–	–	–	–	–
GITTAUP	–	1	1	–	–	–	–	–	–
GITTY-UP	–	–	–	1	–	1	–	–	–
GIVE	–	1	1	–	–	–	–	–	–
GO	–	2	2	3	2	5	2	3	5
GO FAST ON A HORSE	–	–	–	–	–	–	1	–	1
GO THERE	–	–	–	–	1	1	–	–	–
GOING	–	–	–	–	1	1	–	–	–
GROUND	–	–	–	–	–	–	1	–	1
HALLOP	2	–	2	–	–	–	–	–	–
HAT	–	1	1	–	–	–	–	–	–
HEELS	–	–	–	–	1	1	–	–	–
HIM	–	–	–	–	1	1	–	–	–
HOME	–	1	1	–	–	–	–	–	–
HOP	–	–	–	4	5	9	–	8	8
HOP ALONG	–	–	–	–	1	1	–	–	–
HORSE	59	65	124	37	42	79	31	45	76
HORSE SHOES	–	1	1	–	–	–	–	–	–
HURSES	2	2	4	–	2	2	–	–	–
HORSIE	5	6	11	–	1	1	–	–	–
HOURSE	–	–	–	–	–	–	–	1	1
HOW	1	–	1	–	–	–	–	–	–
HURRY UP	–	–	–	1	–	1	–	–	–
INDIAN	–	–	–	1	–	1	–	–	–
JUMP	1	–	1	1	1	2	2	1	3
JUMPING	1	–	1	–	–	–	–	–	–

RESPONSE WORD	1ST M	F	T	3RD M	F	T	5TH M	F	T

28. GALLOP

RESPONSE WORD	1ST M	F	T	3RD M	F	T	5TH M	F	T
JUST GALLOP WITH THE HORSE	–	1	1	–	–	–	–	–	–
LAP	1	–	1	–	–	–	–	–	–
LE	–	–	–	–	–	–	1	–	1
LEGS	–	–	–	–	1	1	–	–	–
LIGHT	1	–	1	1	–	1	–	–	–
LIKE A HORSE	–	1	1	–	–	–	–	–	–
LIKE A HORSE GALLOPS	–	–	–	–	–	–	–	1	1
LIKE RUN	–	–	–	–	–	–	1	–	1
LITTLE GIRL	–	1	1	–	–	–	–	–	–
LONG	1	–	1	–	–	–	–	–	–
LOPE	–	–	–	–	–	–	1	–	1
LOUT	1	–	1	–	–	–	–	–	–
MALLOP	–	1	1	–	–	–	–	–	–
MALOFF	1	–	1	–	–	–	–	–	–
MAN	1	–	1	1	–	1	–	–	–
ME	1	–	1	–	1	1	–	–	–
MEDIUM	–	–	–	–	–	–	–	1	1
MILK	–	1	1	–	1	1	–	–	–
MOVE	–	–	–	–	–	–	2	–	2
MOVEMENT	–	–	–	–	–	–	–	1	1
MUSIC	–	1	1	–	–	–	–	–	–
NALLOW	–	1	1	–	–	–	–	–	–
NO GALLOP	–	–	–	1	–	1	–	–	–
NOT	1	–	1	–	–	–	–	–	–
ON	–	1	1	–	–	–	–	–	–
ON A HORSE	2	–	2	1	–	1	–	–	–
ON HORSE	1	–	1	–	–	–	–	–	–
ON THE HORSE	1	–	1	–	–	–	–	–	–
ORANGE	1	–	1	–	–	–	–	–	–
OUT	–	–	–	–	–	–	–	1	1
OVER	1	–	1	–	–	–	–	–	–
OWL	–	1	1	–	–	–	–	–	–
PACE	–	–	–	–	1	1	–	–	–
PAPER	1	1	2	–	–	–	–	–	–
PEOPLE	1	–	1	–	–	–	–	1	1
PIANO	1	–	1	–	–	–	–	–	–
PIG	–	–	–	–	–	–	1	–	1
PONY	4	–	4	2	1	3	–	2	2
POUND	–	–	–	–	–	–	1	–	1
PRANCE	–	–	–	–	1	1	–	–	–
QUIDE	–	–	–	–	–	–	1	–	1
RACE	–	–	–	–	–	–	–	1	1
RALLA	–	1	1	–	–	–	–	–	–
RAN	–	–	–	–	1	1	1	–	1
RID	–	–	–	–	–	–	1	–	1
RIDE	5	3	8	14	9	23	16	8	24
RIDE A HORSE	1	–	1	–	–	–	–	–	–
RIDE FAST	–	–	–	1	–	1	–	–	–
RIDING	–	–	–	1	1	2	–	–	–
RING	–	1	1	–	–	–	–	–	–
ROCK	–	–	–	1	–	1	–	–	–
ROPE	1	–	1	–	–	–	–	–	–
ROW	–	–	–	1	–	1	–	–	–
RUN	2	3	5	13	19	32	22	11	33
RUN ALONG	–	–	–	–	–	–	1	–	1
RUNNING	–	1	1	–	–	–	–	–	–
SAID	–	1	1	–	–	–	–	–	–
SALLOP	1	–	1	–	1	1	–	–	–
SAT	–	–	–	–	–	–	–	1	1
SEE	–	1	1	–	–	–	–	–	–
SELL IT	1	–	1	–	–	–	–	–	–
SET	–	1	1	–	–	–	–	–	–
SEWED UP	1	–	1	–	–	–	–	–	–
SILLY	1	–	1	–	–	–	–	–	–
SKID	1	–	1	–	–	–	–	–	–
SKIP	1	1	2	–	4	4	1	2	3
SLOW	–	–	–	–	2	2	1	–	1
SLOW GALLOP	–	–	–	1	–	1	–	–	–
SNAKE	–	1	1	–	–	–	–	–	–
SOFT	–	1	1	–	1	1	–	–	–
SOMETHING	–	–	–	1	–	1	–	–	–

RESPONSE WORD	1ST M	F	T	3RD M	F	T	5TH M	F	T

28. GALLOP

RESPONSE WORD	1ST M	F	T	3RD M	F	T	5TH M	F	T
SOUND	–	1	1	–	–	–	–	–	–
SPONGE	–	1	1	–	–	–	–	–	–
START	–	–	–	–	–	–	–	1	1
STEED	–	–	–	–	1	1	–	–	–
STEP	–	–	–	–	1	1	–	–	–
STILL	–	1	1	–	–	–	–	–	–
STOP	–	2	2	–	1	1	2	–	2
STOP GALLOPING	1	–	1	–	–	–	–	–	–
STROLL	–	–	–	1	–	1	–	–	–
SWIFT	–	–	–	1	–	1	2	2	4
TABLE	–	–	–	–	1	1	–	–	–
TERRIFIC	–	–	–	–	–	–	–	1	1
THE RUN OF A HORSE	–	–	–	–	–	–	–	1	1
THERE	1	–	1	–	–	–	–	–	–
TIME TO GO TO WORK	–	1	1	–	–	–	–	–	–
TO	–	–	–	1	–	1	–	–	–
TOGETHER	–	1	1	–	–	–	–	–	–
TRAMP	–	–	–	1	–	1	–	–	–
TRAVEL	–	–	–	–	1	1	1	–	1
TROOT	–	–	–	–	–	–	1	–	1
TROT	2	1	3	18	13	31	26	34	60
TROTTING	–	–	–	1	2	3	1	–	1
TROUT	–	–	–	–	–	–	–	1	1
TRUCK	1	–	1	–	1	1	–	–	–
TRY	–	1	1	–	–	–	–	–	–
UP	–	–	–	1	1	2	–	–	–
WALK	–	1	1	9	4	13	2	3	5
WALK FAST	–	–	–	–	–	–	1	–	1
WALLOP	–	–	–	1	–	1	–	–	–
WENT	–	1	1	–	–	–	–	–	–
WHAT YOU RIDE ON A HORSE	1	–	1	–	–	–	–	–	–
WHEN A HORSE GALLOP	–	1	1	–	–	–	–	–	–
WHEN YOU GALLOP ON A HORSE	1	–	1	–	–	–	–	–	–
WHOA	1	–	1	–	–	–	–	–	–
YELLOW	–	2	2	–	–	–	–	–	–
YOU	1	–	1	–	–	–	–	–	–
YOU GO BUY SOME MILK	–	1	1	–	–	–	–	–	–
YOU HORSEY	–	1	1	–	–	–	–	–	–

29. GENTLY

RESPONSE WORD	1ST M	F	T	3RD M	F	T	5TH M	F	T
A JET	–	1	1	–	–	–	–	–	–
AIRPLANE	2	–	2	1	–	1	–	–	–
ANIMAL	–	1	1	–	–	–	–	–	–
AWAY	–	–	–	–	1	1	–	–	–
AWFUL	–	1	1	–	–	–	–	–	–
AWNING	1	–	1	–	–	–	–	–	–
BABY	3	6	9	1	–	1	–	1	1
BADLY	–	–	–	–	–	–	1	–	1
BE CAREFUL	1	–	1	–	–	–	–	–	–
BE NICE	–	1	1	–	–	–	–	–	–
BECAUSE	–	–	–	1	–	1	–	–	–
BIG	–	1	1	–	–	–	–	–	–
BLANKET	–	–	–	–	1	1	–	–	–
BLOW	–	–	–	–	1	1	–	–	–
BLUE	–	1	1	–	–	–	–	1	1
BOAT	2	–	2	–	–	–	–	–	–
BOOKS	–	1	1	–	–	–	–	–	–
BOW	1	–	1	–	–	–	–	–	–
BOX	1	–	1	–	–	–	–	–	–
BREAD	–	–	–	1	–	1	–	–	–
CAKE	–	1	1	–	–	–	–	–	–
CAL	1	–	1	–	–	–	–	–	–
CALM	1	–	1	1	1	2	–	–	–
CARE	–	–	–	1	–	1	–	–	–
CAREFUL	–	–	–	1	3	4	–	1	1
CAREFULLY	–	–	–	–	1	1	–	1	1
CARRY	1	–	1	–	–	–	–	–	–
CAT	3	1	4	1	–	1	–	–	–
CAT PRESSING PAIN	1	–	1	–	–	–	–	–	–

RESPONSE WORD	1ST M	1ST F	1ST T	3RD M	3RD F	3RD T	5TH M	5TH F	5TH T

29. GENTLY

RESPONSE WORD	1ST M	1ST F	1ST T	3RD M	3RD F	3RD T	5TH M	5TH F	5TH T
CHILDREN	1	–	1	–	–	–	–	–	–
CHIN	–	1	1	–	–	–	–	–	–
CLOCK	–	1	1	–	1	–	–	–	–
CLOWN	–	–	–	–	1	1	–	–	–
COME	–	2	2	–	–	–	–	–	–
COMMON	–	–	–	1	–	1	–	–	–
COUNTRY	–	1	1	–	–	–	–	–	–
COWBOY	1	–	1	–	–	–	–	–	–
CRAYON	–	–	–	1	–	1	–	–	–
DADDY	–	1	1	–	–	–	–	–	–
DELICATE	1	–	1	1	–	1	–	–	–
DENTLY	1	–	1	–	–	–	–	–	–
DO	1	–	1	–	1	1	–	–	–
DOESNT HURT	1	–	1	1	–	1	–	–	–
DOG	3	–	3	–	–	–	–	–	–
DONT PLAY WITH FIRE	–	1	1	–	–	–	–	–	–
DOOR	–	2	2	–	–	–	–	–	–
DOWN THE STAIRS	–	1	1	–	–	–	–	–	–
DOWN THE STREAM	1	–	1	–	–	–	–	–	–
DRINKS MILK	–	1	1	–	–	–	–	–	–
DUCK	–	1	1	–	–	–	–	–	–
EASILY	–	–	–	–	1	1	2	–	2
EASY	–	–	–	3	2	5	5	4	9
EGG	–	1	1	–	–	–	–	–	–
ENJOY	–	–	–	1	–	1	–	–	–
ENTLY	1	–	1	–	–	–	–	–	–
EVER	–	1	1	–	–	–	–	–	–
EYE	1	–	1	–	–	–	–	–	–
FAMILY	–	1	1	–	–	–	–	–	–
FAST	1	1	2	3	–	3	1	–	1
FATHER	–	–	–	–	–	–	2	–	2
FEEL	–	–	–	–	1	1	–	–	–
FENCE	1	–	1	–	–	–	–	–	–
FINE	–	1	1	–	–	–	–	–	–
FLOWERS	1	–	1	–	–	–	–	–	–
FLUFFY	–	–	–	1	–	1	–	–	–
FORGOT	1	–	1	–	–	–	–	–	–
FRIENDLY	–	–	–	–	1	1	–	–	–
FUME	–	–	–	–	1	1	–	–	–
FUN	–	1	1	–	–	–	–	–	–
GAME	–	–	–	–	1	1	–	–	–
GENT	1	–	1	–	1	1	–	–	–
GENTLE	2	1	3	2	2	4	3	1	4
GENTLEMAN	–	–	–	1	–	1	–	–	–
GENTLY	–	–	–	1	–	1	–	1	1
GIRL	1	–	1	1	1	2	1	–	1
GIVE	–	1	1	–	–	–	–	–	–
GO	–	–	–	1	–	1	–	–	–
GO UP STEPS	1	–	1	–	–	–	–	–	–
GOOD	3	3	6	1	–	1	1	1	2
GOTLY	–	–	–	–	–	–	1	–	1
GREEN	–	1	1	–	2	2	–	–	–
GYM	–	1	1	–	–	–	–	–	–
HAND	1	1	2	–	–	–	–	1	1
HANDLE	–	–	–	–	1	1	1	1	2
HANDLY	1	–	1	–	–	–	–	–	–
HAPPENING	–	1	1	–	–	–	–	–	–
HAPPY	–	1	1	1	1	2	–	1	1
HARD	7	11	18	12	15	27	14	7	21
HARDLY	–	–	–	1	2	3	2	1	3
HARMLESS	–	–	–	–	1	1	–	–	–
HARSH	–	–	–	–	–	–	1	–	1
HARSHLY	–	–	–	–	–	–	–	1	1
HAVE	1	–	1	–	–	–	–	–	–
HE	–	–	–	1	–	1	–	1	1
HEAD	–	1	1	–	–	–	–	–	–
HEAVY	–	–	–	–	1	1	–	–	–
HELP	–	–	–	–	1	1	–	–	–
HER	–	–	–	–	–	–	–	1	1
HERE	1	1	2	–	–	–	–	–	–
HILL	–	1	1	–	–	–	–	–	–
HOLD	1	1	2	–	–	–	1	–	1

29. GENTLY

RESPONSE WORD	1ST M	F	T	3RD M	F	T	5TH M	F	T
HOLDING THE BABY	–	1	1	–	–	–	–	–	–
HORSE	–	–	–	–	–	–	1	2	3
HOUSE	–	1	1	–	–	–	–	–	–
HURT	–	–	–	–	–	–	1	1	2
INTERESTING	–	–	–	–	1	1	–	–	–
J	1	–	1	–	–	–	–	–	–
JACK	–	1	1	–	–	–	–	–	–
JACK-IN-A-BOX	–	1	1	–	–	–	–	–	–
JADE	1	–	1	–	–	–	–	–	–
JELLY	–	1	1	–	–	–	–	–	–
JET	6	–	6	2	2	4	–	–	–
JIM	1	–	1	–	–	–	–	–	–
JOE	2	1	3	–	–	–	–	–	–
JOHN	1	–	1	–	–	–	–	–	–
JOURNEY	–	1	1	–	1	1	–	–	–
JUMP	–	1	1	–	–	–	–	–	–
KENTLY	–	–	–	–	–	–	1	–	1
KIND	3	2	5	9	8	17	4	6	10
KINDLY	1	1	2	–	3	3	–	1	1
KISS	–	1	1	–	–	–	–	–	–
KITTEN	–	–	–	–	–	–	–	1	1
LAMB	–	–	–	–	–	–	1	–	1
LAMP	–	–	–	–	–	–	–	1	1
LAUGH	–	–	–	1	–	1	–	–	–
LAX	–	–	–	1	–	1	–	–	–
LIGHT	1	–	1	1	–	1	–	–	–
LIGHTLY	–	–	–	–	–	–	–	1	1
LITTLE	–	–	–	–	–	–	–	1	1
LONG	1	–	1	–	–	–	–	–	–
LOVE	–	–	–	–	–	–	–	1	1
LOVE THIS	–	–	–	–	1	1	–	1	1
LY	–	–	–	–	–	–	–	1	1
MAN	2	–	2	–	1	1	1	–	1
ME	1	–	1	–	–	–	–	–	–
MEAN	–	1	1	–	2	2	1	2	3
MENTLY	2	1	3	–	–	–	–	–	–
MICE	1	–	1	–	–	–	–	–	–
MINE	1	–	1	–	–	–	–	–	–
MOTHER	–	–	–	1	–	1	–	–	–
MOTORCYCLE	1	–	1	–	–	–	–	–	–
MOUNTAIN	–	–	–	1	–	1	–	–	–
NAME	1	–	1	1	–	1	–	–	–
NENTLY	–	1	1	–	–	–	–	–	–
NICE	4	4	8	4	7	11	2	3	5
NICELY	–	–	–	1	3	4	–	1	1
NO RESPONSE	–	–	–	–	–	–	–	1	1
NOISY	–	1	1	–	–	–	–	–	–
NOT	1	1	2	–	–	–	–	–	–
NOT GENTLY	1	–	1	1	–	1	1	–	1
NOT HARD	–	–	–	–	–	–	1	1	2
NOT TO HARM	–	–	–	–	–	–	–	1	1
NOTHING	–	1	1	–	–	–	–	–	–
NOW	1	1	2	–	–	–	–	–	–
OH	–	1	1	–	–	–	–	–	–
OLD	–	–	–	–	–	–	–	1	1
ONE	–	1	1	–	–	–	–	–	–
ORANGE	–	1	1	–	–	–	–	–	–
OUT	–	1	1	–	–	–	–	–	–
OWN	1	–	1	–	–	–	–	–	–
PAIL	1	–	1	–	–	–	–	–	–
PAIR	–	–	–	–	1	1	–	–	–
PAT	1	–	1	–	–	–	–	1	1
PEN	–	1	1	–	–	–	–	–	–
PENNY	–	–	–	–	1	1	–	–	–
PENTLY	–	1	1	–	–	–	–	–	–
PEOPLE	1	–	1	1	–	1	–	1	1
PET	4	1	5	–	–	–	–	1	1
PICTURE	–	1	1	–	–	–	–	–	–
PLAIN	–	–	–	–	1	1	–	–	–
PLAY	–	1	1	–	–	–	–	–	–
PLEASANT	–	–	–	–	1	1	–	–	–
PLEASE	1	–	1	–	–	–	–	–	–

RESPONSE WORD	1ST M	F	T	3RD M	F	T	5TH M	F	T

29. GENTLY

RESPONSE WORD	1ST M	F	T	3RD M	F	T	5TH M	F	T
PRETTY	1	1	2	—	1	1	—	1	1
PUMPKIN	1	—	1	—	—	—	—	—	—
PURR	—	1	1	—	—	—	—	—	—
PUSH	1	—	1	—	—	—	—	—	—
PUT IN WATER	1	—	1	—	—	—	—	—	—
PUT IT ON	—	—	—	1	—	1	—	—	—
QUIET	1	1	2	3	1	4	1	—	1
QUIETLY	—	—	—	1	1	2	—	—	—
RAIN	1	—	1	—	—	—	—	—	—
RETLY	—	1	1	—	—	—	—	—	—
RING	1	—	1	—	—	—	—	—	—
ROUGH	1	1	2	8	1	9	5	8	13
ROUGHLY	1	1	2	—	3	3	6	4	10
ROWING	—	—	—	1	—	1	—	—	—
RUB	—	1	1	—	—	—	—	—	—
RUDELY	—	—	—	—	—	—	1	—	1
RUFF	—	—	—	—	—	—	1	—	1
RUG	—	—	—	—	1	1	—	—	—
RUN SOFT	—	1	1	—	—	—	—	—	—
SAD	—	2	2	—	—	—	—	—	—
SATH	—	—	—	—	—	—	1	—	1
SAWL	—	—	—	—	—	—	1	—	1
SAY	—	—	—	—	—	—	—	1	1
SEE	—	1	1	—	—	—	—	—	—
SENTLY	1	—	1	—	—	—	—	—	—
SETTLE DOWN	—	1	1	—	—	—	—	—	—
SHADE	—	1	1	—	—	—	—	—	—
SHOF	—	—	—	—	—	—	1	—	1
SHOT	1	—	1	—	—	—	—	—	—
SIT	2	1	3	—	—	—	—	—	—
SIT DOWN	1	—	1	—	—	—	—	—	—
SLEEP	2	1	3	1	—	1	—	—	—
SLOW	1	2	3	—	1	1	1	—	1
SLOWLY	1	—	1	1	1	2	—	1	1
SMENTLY	1	—	1	—	—	—	—	—	—
SMOOT	—	—	—	—	—	—	—	1	1
SMOOTH	1	1	2	6	3	9	4	2	6
SMOOTHLY	—	1	1	—	—	—	—	1	1
SMOOTHS	—	—	—	1	—	1	—	—	—
SNOW	—	—	—	—	—	—	1	—	1
SO	—	—	—	—	—	—	1	—	1
SOAP	1	—	1	—	—	—	—	—	—
SOFT	7	10	17	35	30	65	45	46	91
SOFTLY	5	2	7	11	16	27	11	16	27
SOLF	—	—	—	—	—	—	1	—	1
SOON	—	—	—	1	—	1	1	—	1
SOUND	—	1	1	—	—	—	—	—	—
SPOON	—	1	1	—	—	—	—	—	—
SPRING	—	1	1	—	—	—	—	—	—
STAIRS	—	1	1	—	—	—	—	—	—
STRONG	—	—	—	1	—	1	—	—	—
SUN	—	1	1	—	—	—	—	—	—
TABLE	1	—	1	—	—	—	—	—	—
TALK	—	—	—	—	—	—	—	1	1
TALK GENTLY	—	1	1	—	—	—	—	—	—
TAME	—	—	—	—	—	—	1	—	1
TENTLY	—	1	1	—	—	—	—	—	—
THEM	—	1	1	—	—	—	—	—	—
THREE	1	—	1	—	—	—	—	—	—
TIGHT	—	—	—	1	—	1	—	—	—
TIRED	—	—	—	—	1	1	1	—	1
TO	—	—	—	—	1	1	1	—	1
TOMMY	1	—	1	—	—	—	—	—	—
TOUCH	—	—	—	1	—	1	5	2	7
TREATING SOMEBODY GENTLY	—	—	—	1	—	1	—	—	—
TREE	—	1	1	—	—	—	—	—	—
TREES	1	—	1	—	—	—	—	—	—
TRUCK	1	—	1	—	—	—	—	—	—
TURN	—	1	1	—	—	—	—	—	—
UNTRUE	—	—	—	—	—	—	—	1	1
WALK	1	3	4	—	—	—	—	—	—
WATCH	1	—	1	—	—	—	—	—	—

RESPONSE WORD	1ST M	F	T	3RD M	F	T	5TH M	F	T

29. GENTLY

RESPONSE WORD	M	F	T	M	F	T	M	F	T
WHEN YOU GENTLY ON A BED	1	–	1	–	–	–	–	–	–
WHISPER	1	–	1	–	–	–	–	–	–
WILD	–	–	–	–	1	1	–	1	1
WIND	–	1	1	–	–	–	–	–	–
WINDOW	–	1	1	–	–	–	–	–	–
WITH A GEE	1	–	1	–	–	–	–	–	–
WORD	–	1	1	–	–	–	–	–	–
WRITING	–	1	1	–	–	–	–	–	–
YELLOW	–	1	1	–	–	–	–	–	–
YOU	–	1	1	–	–	–	–	–	–
YOU HOLD IT GENTLY	–	–	–	1	–	1	–	–	–
YOU WANT TO PLAY WITH SOMEBODY	–	1	1	–	–	–	–	–	–

30. GIVE

RESPONSE WORD	M	F	T	M	F	T	M	F	T
A	–	–	–	–	1	1	–	–	–
A PRESENT	–	2	2	–	–	–	–	–	–
A TOY	–	–	–	1	–	1	–	–	–
A TURTLE TO FRIEND	–	1	1	–	–	–	–	–	–
AND	–	1	1	–	–	–	–	–	–
ANSWER	–	–	–	–	–	–	–	1	1
APPLE	–	–	–	–	–	–	–	1	1
ARE	1	–	1	–	–	–	–	–	–
AWAY	2	2	4	6	2	8	5	3	8
AWAY THE PROJECTOR	1	–	1	–	–	–	–	–	–
BABY DOLL	–	1	1	–	–	–	–	–	–
BACK	1	3	4	–	1	1	–	1	1
BAD	–	–	–	–	1	1	–	–	–
BALL	–	1	1	–	–	–	–	–	–
BEANS	–	–	–	–	1	1	–	–	–
BELL	1	–	1	–	–	–	–	–	–
BELLS	–	1	1	–	–	–	–	–	–
BELONG	–	–	–	–	1	1	–	1	1
BLUE	–	1	1	–	–	–	–	–	–
BOOK	–	–	–	–	1	1	–	1	1
BOX	2	1	3	–	–	–	–	–	–
BOY	–	–	–	–	–	–	1	–	1
BUG	–	1	1	–	–	–	–	–	–
BUS	1	–	1	–	–	–	–	–	–
BUY	–	–	–	–	–	–	2	1	3
CAKE	–	–	–	–	–	–	1	–	1
CANDY	2	–	2	–	–	–	–	–	–
CAR	1	–	1	–	–	–	–	–	–
CARE	–	–	–	–	–	–	3	–	3
CAT	–	1	1	–	–	–	–	–	–
CHAIR	1	1	2	–	–	–	–	–	–
CHRISTMAS	–	–	–	–	–	–	2	1	3
CLOCK	–	–	–	–	1	1	–	–	–
CLOSET	–	1	1	–	–	–	–	–	–
COAT	1	–	1	–	–	–	–	–	–
CONTRIBUTE	–	–	–	–	–	–	–	1	1
COOKIE	1	–	1	–	–	–	–	–	–
COOKIES	1	–	1	–	1	1	–	–	–
CRIPPLED CHILDREN	–	–	–	–	1	1	–	–	–
DICK	1	–	1	–	–	–	–	–	–
DID NOT	–	–	–	1	–	1	–	–	–
DIRT	2	–	2	–	–	–	–	–	–
DO	1	–	1	1	–	1	–	–	–
DO IT	1	–	1	–	–	–	–	–	–
DOESNT	–	–	–	1	–	1	–	–	–
DOG	–	1	1	–	–	–	–	–	–
DONT	–	–	–	1	2	3	–	1	1
DONT GIVE	1	1	2	–	–	–	–	–	–
DONT GIVE AWAY WHAT BELONGS TO YOU	–	1	1	–	–	–	–	–	–
DOOR	–	1	1	1	–	1	–	–	–
DOUGH	1	–	1	–	–	–	–	–	–
EYE	1	–	1	–	–	–	–	–	–
FAMILY	1	–	1	–	–	–	–	–	–
FIB	–	1	1	–	1	1	–	–	–

RESPONSE WORD	1ST			3RD			5TH		
	M	F	T	M	F	T	M	F	T

30. GIVE

RESPONSE WORD	M	F	T	M	F	T	M	F	T
FIGHT	1	–	1	–	–	–	–	–	–
FIND	–	–	–	1	–	1	–	–	–
FLOWER	1	–	1	–	–	–	–	–	–
FOOD	1	2	3	1	–	1	–	–	–
FOR	1	–	1	–	–	–	–	–	–
FOR YOU	–	1	1	–	–	–	–	–	–
FORGIVE	–	–	–	–	–	–	–	1	1
FOUR	1	–	1	–	–	–	–	–	–
FREE	–	–	–	–	1	1	1	–	1
FUNNY	–	–	–	–	–	–	–	–	–
GAVE	1	1	2	15	39	54	11	12	23
GAVE AWAY	–	–	–	–	–	–	–	1	1
GENEROUS	–	–	–	–	–	–	–	1	1
GENTLE	–	1	1	–	–	–	–	–	–
GET	1	–	1	3	–	3	–	1	1
GET RID OF	–	–	–	1	–	1	–	–	–
GIFT	1	2	3	–	–	–	–	–	–
GIRL	2	–	2	–	–	–	–	–	–
GIVE	–	–	–	–	–	–	–	1	1
GIVE ME MY HAT	1	–	1	–	–	–	–	–	–
GIVE STUFF AWAY	1	–	1	–	–	–	–	–	–
GIVE THE CHILD YOU'RE PLAYING WITH SOME O.	–	1	1	–	–	–	–	–	–
GIVE TO	–	–	–	–	–	–	1	–	1
GIVEN	–	–	–	1	1	2	–	3	3
GIVES	–	1	1	–	–	–	–	–	–
GIVING	–	1	1	1	1	2	–	–	–
GIVING ME	1	–	1	–	–	–	–	–	–
GO	–	1	1	–	–	–	–	–	–
GO AWAY	–	1	1	–	–	–	–	–	–
GOD	1	1	2	–	–	–	–	–	–
GOOD	1	1	2	–	–	–	–	–	–
GOOD WILL	–	–	–	–	–	–	1	–	1
GOT	–	1	1	1	–	1	–	–	–
GRASS	1	–	1	–	–	–	–	–	–
GREEN	–	1	1	–	–	–	1	–	1
GROCERIES	1	–	1	–	–	–	–	–	–
HAD	–	1	1	–	–	–	–	–	–
HAND	–	–	–	1	1	2	3	2	5
HAND OVER	–	–	–	–	–	–	1	–	1
HAND SOMEBODY	–	–	–	–	–	–	1	–	1
HAND SOMETHING	–	–	–	–	–	–	1	–	1
HAND TO	–	–	–	–	–	–	2	–	2
HAND-OVER	–	–	–	–	1	1	–	–	–
HAPPINESS	–	–	–	–	–	–	–	1	1
HARD	1	–	1	–	–	–	–	1	1
HAT	–	–	–	1	–	1	–	–	–
HAVE	1	–	1	1	2	3	4	2	6
HE	–	–	–	1	–	1	–	–	–
HELP	1	–	1	–	1	1	–	2	2
HER	–	–	–	1	–	1	–	–	–
HERE	2	4	6	2	2	4	–	–	–
HILL	–	–	–	1	–	1	–	–	–
HIM	1	–	1	–	1	1	–	–	–
HIS	–	–	–	1	–	1	–	–	–
HIVE	2	–	2	–	1	1	–	–	–
HOUSE	–	1	1	–	–	–	–	–	–
HOW	1	–	1	–	–	–	–	–	–
I	2	–	2	–	–	–	–	–	–
I CAN'T	1	–	1	–	–	–	–	–	–
I HAVE A STICK	–	1	1	–	–	–	–	–	–
ICE CREAM	–	1	1	–	–	–	–	–	–
IN	–	–	–	–	1	1	–	–	–
INDIAN GIVER	–	–	–	–	–	–	1	–	1
INGIVE	–	–	–	–	–	–	–	1	1
IT	1	3	4	–	2	2	1	–	1
IT TO ME	–	–	–	–	1	1	–	–	–
JUMP	–	–	–	–	–	–	–	1	1
KEEP	1	–	1	6	–	6	2	1	3
KEEP IT	–	–	–	1	–	1	–	–	–
KIND	–	–	–	–	–	–	1	–	1
KIND OLD PERSON	–	–	–	–	–	–	–	1	1

30. GIVE

RESPONSE WORD	1ST M	F	T	3RD M	F	T	5TH M	F	T
KITTY	1	–	1	–	–	–	–	–	–
LADDER	–	1	1	–	–	–	–	–	–
LADY	–	1	1	–	–	–	–	–	–
LEND	–	–	–	–	–	–	–	–	–
LET	–	–	–	–	–	–	–	1	1
LET HAVE	–	–	–	–	–	–	–	1	1
LETTER	1	–	1	–	–	–	–	–	–
LIGHT	–	1	1	–	–	–	–	–	–
LIT	–	–	–	1	–	1	–	–	–
LIVE	1	–	1	1	1	2	–	–	–
LUCK	–	1	1	–	–	–	–	–	–
MAN	1	–	1	–	–	–	–	–	–
ME	8	6	14	3	6	9	2	2	4
ME A BOOK	1	–	1	–	–	–	–	–	–
ME A LOLLIPOP	–	1	1	–	–	–	–	–	–
ME A PRESENT	–	1	1	–	–	–	–	–	–
ME IT	1	–	1	–	–	–	–	–	–
ME THAT TOY	1	–	1	–	–	–	–	–	–
ME THAT, ITS MINE	–	1	1	–	–	–	–	–	–
MILK	–	–	–	1	–	1	–	–	–
MINE	–	1	1	–	–	–	–	–	–
MIVE	2	–	2	–	–	–	–	–	–
MONEY	2	2	4	–	–	–	3	1	4
MONEY FOR POOR	1	–	1	–	–	–	–	–	–
MOO COW	1	–	1	–	–	–	–	–	–
MOP	–	1	1	–	–	–	–	–	–
MY	–	1	1	–	–	–	–	–	–
NEVER	–	–	–	–	–	–	1	–	1
NICE	–	–	–	1	2	3	–	1	1
NINE	1	–	1	–	–	–	–	–	–
NIVE	–	1	1	–	–	–	–	–	–
NO	–	1	1	2	–	2	–	–	–
NO RESPONSE	1	–	1	–	–	–	–	–	–
NOT	–	–	–	1	1	2	–	–	–
NOT GIVE	2	2	4	1	2	3	–	–	–
NOT TO GIVE	–	–	–	–	–	–	1	–	1
NOW	–	–	–	1	–	1	–	–	–
OLD	–	1	1	–	–	–	–	–	–
ONE	1	–	1	–	–	–	–	–	–
OTHER	–	–	–	–	–	–	1	–	1
OUT	–	1	1	–	–	–	–	–	–
OUTSIDE	1	–	1	–	–	–	–	–	–
PAPER	–	1	1	–	–	–	–	–	–
PEOPLE	–	1	1	–	1	1	–	–	–
PICTURE	–	1	1	–	–	–	–	–	–
PIPE	1	–	1	–	–	–	–	–	–
PIVE	1	–	1	–	–	–	–	–	–
PLEASE	–	–	–	2	–	2	–	–	–
PLUS	–	1	1	–	–	–	–	–	–
POCKETBOOK	–	1	1	–	–	–	–	–	–
POOR	–	–	–	2	–	2	–	–	–
PRESENT	7	5	12	2	2	4	2	3	5
PRESENTS	2	2	4	–	–	–	–	–	–
PRETTY	–	2	2	–	–	–	–	–	–
PRIZE	–	1	1	–	–	–	–	–	–
PUT IN WATER	1	–	1	–	–	–	–	–	–
RAT	–	–	–	–	–	–	1	–	1
RECEIVE	–	1	1	4	5	9	11	12	23
RECEIVED	–	–	–	–	–	–	1	–	1
RED	1	–	1	–	–	–	–	–	–
RELEASED	–	–	–	–	–	–	–	1	1
RESCE	–	–	–	–	–	–	–	1	1
RESCUE	–	–	–	–	–	–	–	1	1
RESERVE	–	–	–	–	–	–	–	1	1
REST	–	1	1	–	–	–	–	–	–
RESVE	–	–	–	–	–	–	1	–	1
RIB	–	1	1	–	–	–	–	–	–
RIBBON	–	1	1	–	–	–	–	–	–
ROBBER	1	–	1	–	–	–	–	–	–
SAVE	–	–	–	2	1	3	1	2	3
SAY	1	–	1	–	–	–	–	–	–
SCARE-CROW	1	–	1	–	–	–	–	–	–

RESPONSE WORD	1ST			3RD			5TH		
	M	F	T	M	F	T	M	F	T

30. GIVE

RESPONSE WORD	M	F	T	M	F	T	M	F	T
SCHOOL	-	1	1	-	-	-	-	-	-
SEE	-	1	1	-	-	-	-	-	-
SEIVE	-	-	-	-	1	1	-	-	-
SELFISH	-	-	-	-	1	1	-	-	-
SELL	-	1	1	-	-	-	1	2	3
SEND	-	1	1	-	1	1	2	-	2
SET	-	-	-	-	1	1	-	-	-
SHARE	1	1	2	-	-	-	-	1	1
SHE	-	1	1	-	-	-	-	-	-
SHOE	1	-	1	-	-	-	-	-	-
SHOW	-	-	-	-	1	1	-	-	-
SIVE	1	-	1	-	-	-	-	-	-
SOME	-	-	-	1	-	1	-	1	1
SOMEBODY	1	-	1	-	-	-	-	-	-
SOMEONE	-	-	-	-	1	1	-	1	1
SOMETHING	3	5	8	7	1	8	2	2	4
SOMETHING AWAY	1	-	1	-	-	-	-	-	-
SOMETHING TO ANOTHER	-	1	1	-	-	-	-	-	-
SOMETHING TO SOMEBODY	1	-	1	-	-	-	-	-	-
SOMETHING TO SOMEONE	-	-	-	-	-	-	-	1	1
SOMETHING TO THE OTHER PERSON	-	1	1	-	-	-	-	-	-
SONGS	-	1	1	-	-	-	-	-	-
STEAL	-	-	-	-	1	1	-	-	-
STUFF AROUND	-	1	1	-	-	-	-	-	-
SUN	-	1	1	-	-	-	-	-	-
SURPRISE	1	-	1	-	-	-	-	-	-
SWEATER	1	-	1	-	-	-	-	-	-
TACH	-	-	-	-	-	-	1	-	1
TACK	-	-	-	-	-	-	1	-	1
TAKE	2	4	6	32	24	56	54	45	99
TAKE AWAY	-	-	-	-	1	1	-	-	-
TAKE BACK	-	-	-	-	-	-	1	-	1
TEA	-	1	1	-	-	-	-	-	-
THANK	1	-	1	1	2	3	-	1	1
THANK YOU	1	3	4	3	-	3	2	1	3
THANKFUL	-	-	-	-	-	-	-	2	2
THANKS	-	1	1	2	1	3	1	1	2
THAT	-	-	-	1	-	1	-	-	-
THAT TO ME	1	-	1	-	-	-	-	-	-
THE	1	4	5	-	-	-	-	-	-
THE PERSON	1	-	1	-	-	-	-	-	-
THEIR	-	-	-	1	-	1	-	-	-
THEM	-	1	1	5	2	7	-	-	-
THING	-	-	-	-	-	-	-	1	1
THINGS	-	2	2	1	-	1	1	-	1
THINK	-	-	-	-	-	-	-	1	1
THIS	2	-	2	1	1	2	-	-	-
THOUGHFUL	-	-	-	-	-	-	-	1	1
TO	1	3	4	-	1	1	-	1	1
TO GIVE SOMETHING	-	-	-	-	-	-	-	1	1
TO HIM	1	-	1	-	-	-	-	-	-
TO POOR	1	-	1	-	-	-	-	-	-
TO POOR PEOPLE	1	-	1	-	-	-	-	-	-
TO SOMEBODY	-	-	-	1	-	1	-	-	-
TO SOMETHING	-	-	-	-	-	-	-	1	1
TO THE PEACE CORPS	-	-	-	1	-	1	-	-	-
TO THE POOR	-	1	1	-	-	-	-	-	-
TO YOU	1	-	1	-	-	-	-	-	-
TOOK	-	-	-	-	2	2	1	1	2
TOY	-	1	1	1	-	1	1	1	2
TOYS	2	-	2	-	-	-	-	-	-
TRADE	-	-	-	-	1	1	-	1	1
TRADING	-	-	-	1	-	1	-	-	-
UNGIVE	-	-	-	-	1	1	-	-	-
UNICEF	-	-	-	-	-	-	-	1	1
UNITED	-	-	-	1	-	1	-	-	-
UP	4	-	4	-	-	-	-	-	-
US	-	-	-	1	1	2	-	-	-
US SOMEONE	-	1	1	-	-	-	-	-	-
USE	-	-	-	1	-	1	-	-	-

RESPONSE WORD	1ST			3RD			5TH		
	M	F	T	M	F	T	M	F	T

30. GIVE

RESPONSE WORD	M	F	T	M	F	T	M	F	T
VALENTINE	1	–	1	–	–	–	–	–	–
VERY	–	–	–	–	1	1	–	–	–
VISIT	–	–	–	–	1	1	–	–	–
WALL	–	1	1	–	–	–	–	–	–
WAY	1	–	1	–	1	1	–	–	–
WE	–	1	1	–	–	–	–	–	–
WHEN YOU GIVE IT BACK TO SOMEBODY	1	–	1	–	–	–	–	–	–
WHERE	–	–	–	–	1	1	–	–	–
WINDOW	–	1	1	–	–	–	–	–	–
WONT	–	–	–	1	–	1	–	–	–
WORE	1	–	1	–	–	–	–	–	–
WRIVE	–	–	–	1	–	1	–	–	–
YOU	5	5	10	1	1	2	1	–	1
YOU GIVE SOMEBODY	–	1	1	–	–	–	–	–	–
YOUR	1	–	1	–	–	–	–	–	–

31. HAND

RESPONSE WORD	M	F	T	M	F	T	M	F	T
A PART OF YOUR BODY	–	–	–	–	–	–	–	1	1
AND	1	–	1	1	–	1	–	–	–
ANT	–	1	1	–	–	–	–	–	–
ARM	3	10	13	28	24	52	27	30	57
ARMS	–	–	–	1	–	1	–	–	–
AT THE END OF AN ARM	–	–	–	–	–	–	–	1	1
AWAY	–	–	–	1	–	1	–	–	–
BACK	1	–	1	–	–	–	–	–	–
BAG	–	–	–	–	1	1	–	–	–
BAND	2	3	5	1	–	1	2	2	4
BECAUSE	–	–	–	1	–	1	–	–	–
BELL	–	–	–	–	1	1	–	–	–
BELONG TO PERSON	1	–	1	–	–	–	–	–	–
BENCH	1	–	1	–	–	–	–	–	–
BEND	–	–	–	1	–	1	–	–	–
BIRD	1	–	1	–	–	–	–	–	–
BIRTHDAY	–	1	1	–	–	–	–	–	–
BLACK	–	–	–	–	–	–	–	1	1
BLUE	–	1	1	–	–	–	–	–	–
BODY	1	–	1	5	2	7	1	6	7
BONE	–	2	2	–	–	–	–	–	–
BOOK	–	–	–	–	–	–	–	1	1
BOTH	–	–	–	–	–	–	–	1	1
BOX	–	1	1	–	–	–	–	–	–
BRACELET	1	–	1	–	–	–	–	–	–
BROKEN	1	–	1	–	–	–	–	–	–
BURN	–	–	–	–	1	1	–	–	–
CAN	3	2	5	2	–	2	–	–	–
CAN SELL	–	1	1	–	–	–	–	–	–
CAND	1	–	1	–	–	–	–	–	–
CANDY	1	–	1	–	–	–	–	–	–
CANNED	–	1	1	–	–	–	–	–	–
CARRY	–	1	1	–	1	1	–	–	–
CATCH	1	–	1	–	–	–	–	–	–
CHAIR	1	–	1	–	–	–	–	–	–
CHICKEN	–	5	5	–	–	–	–	–	–
CHICKENS	–	1	1	–	–	–	–	–	–
CLAP	1	1	2	–	–	–	–	–	–
CLEAN	–	–	–	1	–	1	–	–	–
CLOCK	1	1	2	–	–	–	–	–	–
COME	–	1	1	–	–	–	–	–	–
COOK	–	1	1	–	–	–	–	–	–
CUFFS	–	–	–	1	–	1	–	–	–
CUT	–	–	–	1	–	1	1	–	1
CUT OFF	1	–	1	–	–	–	–	–	–
DEAD	1	–	1	–	–	–	–	–	–
DEPTH	1	–	1	–	–	–	–	–	–
DISH WATER	–	1	1	–	–	–	–	–	–
DO	–	–	–	1	1	2	–	–	–
DOG	–	–	–	–	2	2	–	1	1
DOING	–	–	–	–	–	–	1	–	1
DON T PUT YOUR HAND IN YOUR FIRE	–	1	1	–	–	–	–	–	–

31. HAND

RESPONSE WORD	1ST M	F	T	3RD M	F	T	5TH M	F	T
DRAGGED	–	1	1	–	–	–	–	–	–
DRESS	–	1	1	–	–	–	–	–	–
EAT	2	–	2	–	–	–	–	–	–
EAT WITH	1	–	1	–	–	–	–	–	–
EGG	1	–	1	–	–	–	–	–	–
FACE	1	1	2	2	4	6	1	1	2
FAN	1	2	3	2	–	2	–	–	–
FEEL	1	–	1	–	–	–	–	–	–
FEET	2	2	4	4	4	8	3	6	9
FIGURE	–	–	–	–	–	–	–	1	1
FIND	–	1	1	1	–	1	–	–	–
FINER	–	–	–	–	–	–	1	–	1
FINGER	4	8	12	11	9	20	10	14	24
FINGERNAIL	1	–	1	–	–	–	–	–	–
FINGERNAILS	2	1	3	1	–	1	–	–	–
FINGERS	9	10	19	7	17	24	23	14	37
FIST	–	–	–	2	–	2	–	–	–
FIX	–	–	–	–	1	1	–	–	–
FLAT	–	–	–	1	–	1	–	–	–
FLESH	–	–	–	–	–	–	2	1	3
FLOOR	–	1	1	1	–	1	–	–	–
FOOD	–	–	–	2	–	2	–	–	–
FOOT	6	7	13	8	9	17	13	14	27
FRIEND	1	–	1	–	–	–	–	1	1
GET	1	–	1	–	–	–	–	–	–
GET ONE A HAND	1	–	1	–	–	–	–	–	–
GET THINGS	1	–	1	–	–	–	–	–	–
GIFT	–	–	–	–	–	–	–	1	1
GIRL	–	–	–	–	–	–	–	1	1
GIT	1	–	1	–	–	–	–	–	–
GIVE	–	–	–	3	2	5	6	1	7
GIVE TO	–	–	–	–	1	1	–	–	–
GIVE YOU A HAND	1	–	1	–	–	–	–	–	–
GLOVE	–	1	1	–	–	–	–	1	1
GLOVES	–	–	–	–	–	–	1	–	1
GRAB	2	–	2	1	–	1	1	–	1
GRASS	1	–	1	–	–	–	–	–	–
GRIP	–	–	–	–	–	–	1	1	2
HAIR	–	3	3	–	–	–	–	–	–
HAM	1	2	3	–	1	1	–	–	–
HAMMER	–	1	1	–	–	–	–	–	–
HAND	–	–	–	–	–	–	1	–	1
HANDLE	–	–	–	–	1	1	1	1	2
HANDSOME	–	–	–	–	–	–	1	–	1
HANDY	–	1	1	–	–	–	–	–	–
HANGER	–	1	1	–	–	–	–	–	–
HARD	1	–	1	–	–	–	–	–	–
HAT	–	1	1	–	–	–	–	–	–
HEAD	2	4	6	8	8	16	4	1	5
HEART	1	–	1	–	1	1	1	1	2
HELP	–	–	–	–	2	2	1	–	1
HEN	1	3	4	1	2	3	–	–	–
HEN HOUSE	–	–	–	1	–	1	–	–	–
HER	–	–	–	–	1	1	–	–	–
HERE	1	2	3	–	1	1	–	–	–
HIDE	–	1	1	–	–	–	–	–	–
HIGH	–	1	1	–	–	–	–	–	–
HIM	–	1	1	–	1	1	–	–	–
HIND	–	–	–	–	–	–	1	–	1
HIS	–	–	–	2	–	2	–	–	–
HOLD	–	1	1	3	1	4	–	2	2
HOLDING	–	–	–	–	1	1	–	–	–
HOUSE	1	1	2	–	–	–	–	1	1
HURT	–	–	–	1	–	1	1	–	1
I WORK WITH	–	1	1	–	–	–	–	–	–
IS	1	–	1	–	–	–	–	–	–
IT	–	–	–	–	–	–	1	–	1
IT TO ME	1	–	1	–	1	1	–	–	–
JILL	–	–	–	–	1	1	–	–	–
JUICE	1	–	1	–	–	–	–	–	–
JUST LIKE CHICKENS	–	1	1	–	–	–	–	–	–

RESPONSE WORD	1ST M	F	T	3RD M	F	T	5TH M	F	T
31. HAND									
KEEP YOUR HANDS OFF SOMEBODY ELSE.	–	–	–	1	–	1	–	–	–
KEND	–	1	1	–	–	–	–	–	–
KETCHUP	1	–	1	–	–	–	–	–	–
KING	1	–	1	–	–	–	–	–	–
KNEE	–	–	–	1	–	1	–	–	–
LAND	–	–	–	1	–	1	–	–	–
LAY	–	–	–	–	1	1	–	–	–
LEFT	1	1	2	1	–	1	–	–	–
LEG	–	1	1	1	1	2	1	–	1
LEGS	–	–	–	–	1	1	1	1	1
LEND	–	–	–	–	–	–	1	–	1
LINE	–	–	–	1	–	1	–	–	–
LOOK	1	–	1	–	–	–	–	–	–
MACHINE	1	–	1	–	–	–	–	–	–
MADE	–	–	–	–	1	1	1	–	1
MAN	7	2	9	3	–	3	–	1	1
MAND	3	–	3	–	–	–	–	–	–
ME	3	2	5	–	–	–	–	–	–
ME IT	1	–	1	–	–	–	–	–	–
MEET	–	–	–	–	1	1	–	–	–
MITTEN	–	1	1	–	–	–	–	–	–
MONEY	1	–	1	–	–	–	–	–	–
MOON	–	1	1	–	–	–	–	–	–
MOVE	–	–	–	–	1	1	–	–	–
MR	–	1	1	–	–	–	–	–	–
MY HAND CLAPS	–	1	1	–	–	–	–	–	–
MY HAND IS COLD	–	1	1	–	–	–	–	–	–
NAN	–	–	–	1	–	1	–	–	–
NECK	–	–	–	1	–	1	–	–	–
NEWSPAPER	–	–	–	–	–	–	–	1	1
NICK	1	–	1	–	–	–	–	–	–
NO	–	–	–	1	–	1	–	–	–
NOT HAND	–	–	–	1	–	1	–	–	–
NOT SELDOM	–	–	–	–	1	1	–	–	–
OFF	2	–	2	–	–	–	2	–	2
ON	1	–	1	–	–	–	–	2	2
OPEN	1	–	1	–	–	–	–	–	–
ORGAN	–	–	–	–	–	–	1	–	1
OUT YOUR FOOD	1	–	1	–	–	–	–	–	–
OVER	–	–	–	–	–	–	–	1	1
PALM	1	–	1	2	2	4	3	4	7
PAN	–	2	2	–	–	–	1	1	2
PAND	–	1	1	–	–	–	–	–	–
PART	–	–	–	–	1	1	1	1	2
PART OF BODY	–	–	–	–	1	1	2	–	2
PART OF THE BODY	–	–	–	–	–	–	2	–	2
PART OF US	–	–	–	1	–	1	–	–	–
PART OF YOUR BODY	–	–	–	–	–	–	–	2	2
PAT	–	1	1	–	–	–	–	–	–
PAW	–	–	–	–	–	–	1	–	1
PEN	1	–	1	–	–	–	1	–	1
PENCIL	–	2	2	–	2	2	–	–	–
PEOPLE	–	1	1	–	–	–	–	–	–
PERSON	–	–	–	2	1	3	–	–	–
PICK	–	1	1	–	–	–	–	–	–
PICK UP	1	–	1	2	–	2	1	–	1
PIG	–	–	–	–	–	–	1	–	1
PINK	–	1	1	–	–	–	–	–	–
PUSH	–	–	–	1	–	1	–	–	–
RECEIVE	–	–	–	–	–	–	–	1	1
RED	–	–	–	–	–	–	1	–	1
REST	–	–	–	–	–	–	1	–	1
RIGE	–	–	–	–	–	–	1	–	1
RIGHT	1	–	1	–	–	–	–	2	2
RIGHT HAND	1	–	1	–	–	–	–	–	–
RING	1	–	1	1	1	2	1	2	3
ROOSTER	2	–	2	–	–	–	–	–	–
RUB A DUB HAMMER	–	1	1	–	–	–	–	–	–
RUBBER BAND	–	–	–	1	–	1	–	–	–
RUN	–	–	–	–	–	–	1	–	1
SAND	2	–	2	–	3	3	–	–	–

RESPONSE WORD	1ST			3RD			5TH		
	M	F	T	M	F	T	M	F	T

31. HAND

RESPONSE WORD	M	F	T	M	F	T	M	F	T
SAW	1	–	1	–	–	–	1	–	1
SET DOWN	–	–	–	1	–	1	–	–	–
SHAKE	2	5	7	2	–	2	–	2	2
SHAKE HANDS	1	1	2	–	–	–	–	–	–
SHAPE	1	–	1	–	–	–	–	–	–
SHEEP	1	–	1	–	–	–	–	–	–
SHOE	–	1	1	–	–	–	–	–	–
SHOULDER	–	–	–	–	–	–	1	–	1
SHOW	1	–	1	–	–	–	–	–	–
SICK	1	–	1	–	–	–	–	–	–
SKIN	–	–	–	–	3	3	–	–	–
SLIDING BOARD	1	–	1	–	–	–	–	–	–
SMALL	–	–	–	–	–	–	–	1	1
SMAND	1	–	1	–	–	–	–	1	1
SOFT	–	–	–	–	1	1	–	1	1
SOME	–	–	–	–	1	1	1	–	1
SPOON	–	–	–	–	1	1	–	–	–
STAIR	–	–	–	–	–	–	–	1	1
STONES	1	–	1	–	–	–	–	–	–
STRONG	–	–	–	–	–	–	1	–	1
SUM	–	–	–	–	–	–	–	1	1
TELEPHONE POLE	1	–	1	–	–	–	–	–	–
THAT	–	–	–	–	1	1	–	–	–
THROW	–	–	–	1	1	2	–	–	–
THROW WITH	1	–	1	–	–	–	–	–	–
THUMB	–	1	1	–	1	1	–	1	1
TO	1	–	1	–	–	–	–	–	–
TO EAT WITH	1	–	1	–	–	–	–	–	–
TO ME	1	–	1	–	–	–	–	–	–
TO WRITE WITH	–	–	–	–	–	–	–	1	1
TOOL	–	–	–	–	–	–	1	–	1
TOUCH	–	1	1	–	1	1	–	–	–
TOUCH SOMETHING WITH YOUR HANDS	1	–	1	–	–	–	–	–	–
TOUCHED	–	–	–	1	–	1	–	–	–
TRADE	–	–	–	1	–	1	–	–	–
TRUCK	1	–	1	–	–	–	–	–	–
TWO	–	–	–	–	1	1	–	–	–
US	1	–	1	–	–	–	–	–	–
USE	1	1	2	1	–	1	–	–	–
WAND	1	–	1	–	–	–	–	–	–
WASH	1	–	1	–	–	–	–	–	–
WASHING THE DISHES WITH YOUR HANDS	1	–	1	–	–	–	–	–	–
WHAT YOU EAT WITH	1	–	1	–	–	–	–	–	–
WHEN YOURE WASHING YOUR HANDS	1	–	1	–	–	–	–	–	–
WHENEVER SOMEONE HOLDS THEIR HAND OUT	–	1	1	–	–	–	–	–	–
WHITE	1	2	3	–	1	1	–	1	1
WINDOW	–	–	–	–	1	1	–	–	–
WITH	1	–	1	–	–	–	1	1	2
WORK	1	–	1	1	2	3	1	1	2
WRIST	1	1	2	–	1	1	2	1	3
WRITE	–	3	3	–	4	4	1	1	2
WRITE WITH	1	1	2	–	–	–	–	–	–
WRITING	–	1	1	1	–	1	1	–	1
YOU PICK UP STUFF WITH	–	–	–	1	–	1	–	–	–
YOUR	–	1	1	1	–	1	–	1	1
YOUR HAND	–	–	–	–	–	–	–	1	1
YOUR HANDS ARE PRETTY	–	1	1	–	–	–	–	–	–
YOURS	–	–	–	–	1	1	–	–	–

RESPONSE WORD	1ST M	F	T	3RD M	F	T	5TH M	F	T

32. HAPPEN

RESPONSE WORD	1ST M	F	T	3RD M	F	T	5TH M	F	T
A HAPPENED	1	–	1	–	–	–	–	–	–
A WHILE	–	–	–	1	–	1	–	–	–
A WRECK	1	–	1	–	–	–	–	–	–
ACCIDENT	2	–	2	–	1	1	3	4	7
ADVENTURE	–	–	–	–	–	–	–	1	1
AFTER	–	–	–	–	2	2	–	–	–
AGAIN	–	1	1	2	–	2	–	2	2
AGO	–	2	2	1	1	2	2	1	3
ALL OF A SUDDEN	–	–	–	1	–	1	–	–	–
ALLONE	–	–	–	–	–	–	–	1	1
ALMOST	–	–	–	–	–	–	–	1	1
ALONG	–	–	–	–	1	1	–	1	1
ALREADY	–	–	–	1	1	2	2	4	6
ALRIGHT	1	–	1	–	–	–	–	–	–
ALWAYS	–	1	1	–	–	–	–	–	–
APPEAR	–	–	–	–	–	–	1	1	2
APPLE	–	–	–	1	–	1	–	–	–
ARITHMETIC	–	–	–	–	–	–	–	1	1
ARM	–	–	–	–	–	–	–	1	1
ASSONANT	–	1	1	–	–	–	–	–	–
ATTEMPT	–	–	–	–	–	–	–	1	1
AUTOMOBILE	–	–	–	–	–	–	1	–	1
BABY	1	–	1	–	–	–	–	–	–
BAD	1	–	1	2	1	3	–	–	–
BATTER	–	–	–	–	1	1	–	–	–
BATTING	–	1	1	–	–	–	–	–	–
BE CAREFUL	–	1	1	–	–	–	–	–	–
BEANS	1	–	1	–	–	–	–	–	–
BEARD	–	–	–	–	1	1	–	–	–
BECAME	–	–	–	–	–	–	–	1	1
BECAUSE	–	–	–	1	–	1	2	–	2
BECOME	–	–	–	–	1	1	–	–	–
BEFORE	–	2	2	–	3	3	–	2	2
BEGAN	–	–	–	1	–	1	–	–	–
BEGIN	–	–	–	–	2	2	1	–	1
BIRD	–	1	1	–	–	–	–	–	–
BIT	–	1	1	–	–	–	–	–	–
BLAME	–	–	–	–	–	–	–	1	1
BLIND	–	1	1	–	–	–	–	–	–
BOOK	–	–	–	–	1	1	–	–	–
BOTTLE	–	1	1	–	–	–	–	–	–
BREAK	–	1	1	–	–	–	–	–	–
BROKE	–	1	1	–	–	–	–	–	–
BROKE DOWN	1	–	1	–	–	–	–	–	–
BUG	–	–	–	–	–	–	1	–	1
BUTTON	–	–	–	1	–	1	–	1	1
CABIN	–	–	–	1	–	1	–	–	–
CAME	–	–	–	–	–	–	–	2	2
CAPPEN	2	1	3	–	–	–	–	–	–
CAPTAIN	–	1	1	1	–	1	–	–	–
CARS COULD CRASH IN TOGETHER	–	1	1	–	–	–	–	–	–
CAT	1	1	2	–	–	–	–	–	–
CAUSE	–	–	–	–	–	–	1	–	1
CEMENT	1	–	1	–	–	–	–	–	–
CHILD	–	1	1	–	–	–	–	–	–
CHILDREN	–	1	1	–	–	–	–	–	–
CHIMNEY	1	–	1	–	–	–	–	–	–
CLOTHES	1	–	1	–	–	–	–	–	–
COLOR	–	1	1	–	–	–	–	–	–
COME	–	–	–	–	–	–	1	–	1
COME ON	1	–	1	–	–	–	–	–	–
COMES	–	–	–	–	–	–	–	1	1
COP	1	–	1	–	–	–	–	–	–
COULDNT	–	–	–	–	1	1	–	–	–
CRASH	1	–	1	–	1	1	–	–	–
CRY	–	–	–	–	2	2	–	1	1
CUT MY KNEE	–	1	1	–	–	–	–	–	–
DAPPEN	–	1	1	–	–	–	–	–	–
DARK	–	–	–	1	–	1	–	–	–
DAY	–	–	–	1	–	1	–	–	–
DEAD	1	1	2	–	–	–	–	–	–

RESPONSE WORD	1ST			3RD			5TH		
	M	F	T	M	F	T	M	F	T

32. HAPPEN

RESPONSE WORD	M	F	T	M	F	T	M	F	T
DESK	1	–	1	–	–	–	–	–	–
DESTRUCTIVE	–	–	–	–	–	–	1	–	1
DICK	–	1	1	–	–	–	–	–	–
DID	1	–	1	4	4	8	11	7	18
DID NOT	–	–	–	1	1	2	–	1	1
DID NOT HAPPEN	1	–	1	–	–	–	1	1	2
DID SOMETHING	–	–	–	–	–	–	2	–	2
DIDNT	–	1	1	9	4	13	3	–	3
DIDNT HAPPEN	3	–	3	8	3	11	3	1	4
DIED	–	–	–	–	–	–	1	–	1
DIG	–	–	–	–	–	–	1	–	1
DINNER	1	–	1	–	–	–	–	–	–
DISHAPPEN	–	–	–	–	–	–	–	1	1
DISTRESS	–	–	–	–	–	–	–	1	1
DO	–	–	–	1	–	1	7	2	9
DOCTOR	–	1	1	–	–	–	–	–	–
DOES	–	–	–	–	–	–	–	1	1
DOESNT HAPPEN	–	1	1	1	–	1	–	–	–
DOG	1	–	1	–	–	–	–	–	–
DONE	–	–	–	3	2	5	4	5	9
DONT	1	–	1	–	3	3	1	–	1
DONT LET THAT HAPPEN AGAIN	–	1	1	–	–	–	–	–	–
DOOR	–	1	1	–	–	–	–	–	–
DRAWER	1	1	2	–	–	–	–	–	–
DREAM	–	–	–	–	–	–	–	1	1
EAT	–	–	–	1	–	1	1	–	1
END	–	–	–	–	1	1	–	–	–
EVENING	–	–	–	–	1	1	–	–	–
EVENT	–	–	–	–	–	–	1	–	1
EVER	–	1	1	–	–	–	–	–	–
EVERYTHING	–	–	–	1	–	1	–	–	–
EXCITE	–	–	–	–	1	1	–	–	–
EXCITED	–	–	–	–	2	2	–	–	–
EXCITEMENT	1	–	1	–	–	–	1	1	2
EXCITING	–	–	–	–	–	–	–	1	1
FAINTING	–	1	1	–	–	–	–	–	–
FAIRY TALE	–	–	–	–	–	–	–	1	1
FALL	1	1	2	–	–	–	–	1	1
FALL DOWN	–	2	2	–	–	–	–	–	–
FAR	–	–	–	1	–	1	1	–	1
FAST	–	–	–	1	–	1	1	1	2
FAT	–	1	1	–	–	–	–	–	–
FELL	1	2	3	–	1	1	–	–	–
FELL DOWN	1	–	1	–	–	–	–	–	–
FIGHT	2	1	3	–	1	1	–	–	–
FIND	–	1	1	1	–	1	1	–	1
FIRE	1	2	3	–	–	–	–	–	–
FIRE HOUSE	1	–	1	–	–	–	–	–	–
FIRE PLUG	1	–	1	–	–	–	–	–	–
FLOWER	–	1	1	–	–	–	–	–	–
FLY	–	–	–	1	–	1	–	–	–
FOOT	1	–	1	–	–	–	–	–	–
FORGET	–	–	–	–	1	1	–	–	–
FORGOT	–	–	–	–	–	–	1	–	1
FOUND OUT	–	–	–	1	–	1	–	–	–
FOX	–	–	–	–	1	1	–	–	–
FUN	–	1	1	–	–	–	–	–	–
GAVE	–	–	–	1	–	1	–	–	–
GET HURT	1	–	1	–	–	–	–	–	–
GIRL	–	–	–	–	1	1	–	–	–
GLASSES	–	1	1	–	–	–	–	–	–
GLAY	–	–	–	–	–	–	–	1	1
GO	1	2	3	–	–	–	–	–	–
GOES	–	–	–	–	–	–	1	–	1
GOING	–	–	–	1	–	1	1	–	1
GOING ON	–	–	–	1	–	1	–	–	–
GOING TO	–	–	–	1	–	1	–	–	–
GONE	–	–	–	–	–	–	–	1	1
GOOD	1	–	1	1	2	3	–	–	–
GUESS WHAT HAPPENED TO ME	–	1	1	–	–	–	–	–	–

32. HAPPEN

RESPONSE WORD	1ST M	F	T	3RD M	F	T	5TH M	F	T
HAD	2	—	2	—	1	1	—	—	—
HALL	—	—	—	—	—	—	1	—	1
HAMMER	1	—	1	—	—	—	—	—	—
HAP	—	—	—	—	1	1	—	—	—
HAPPENED	—	2	2	3	1	4	3	4	7
HAPPENING	—	—	—	1	1	2	1	4	5
HAPPENS	—	2	2	—	—	—	—	—	—
HAPPY	6	10	16	10	7	17	4	7	11
HAT	1	1	2	—	—	—	—	—	—
HAVE	—	1	1	—	—	—	—	—	—
HAVE HAD	—	—	—	1	—	1	—	—	—
HAVE IT	—	—	—	1	—	1	—	—	—
HAVENT HAPPENED	—	—	—	1	—	1	—	—	—
HELP	1	1	2	—	—	—	—	—	—
HELPING	—	—	—	1	—	1	—	—	—
HER	—	—	—	—	—	—	—	1	1
HERE	3	3	6	—	—	—	—	—	—
HIT	—	—	—	—	—	—	—	1	1
HOLLER	1	—	1	—	—	—	—	—	—
HORSE	—	1	1	—	—	—	—	—	—
HOUSE	4	—	4	—	—	—	1	—	1
HOUSE MIGHT GET ON FIRE	—	1	1	—	—	—	—	—	—
HOW	1	—	1	1	—	1	—	—	—
HURT	1	2	3	2	3	5	—	1	1
I	—	1	1	—	—	—	—	—	—
INSIDE	—	—	—	—	—	—	—	1	1
IT	1	1	2	—	—	—	—	—	—
IT DID	—	—	—	—	—	—	1	—	1
IT DID NOT HAPPEN	—	—	—	—	1	1	—	—	—
IT DOES	—	—	—	—	—	—	1	—	1
IT HAPPENED ON THE STREET	—	—	—	1	—	1	—	—	—
IT HAPPENS	—	—	—	—	—	—	1	—	1
JOY	—	—	—	1	—	1	—	—	—
JUMP	—	—	—	—	—	—	—	1	1
JUNGLE	—	1	1	—	—	—	—	—	—
JUST	—	—	—	—	2	2	—	—	—
JUST THEN	—	—	—	1	—	1	—	—	—
KEVIN	1	—	1	—	—	—	—	—	—
KILL	1	1	2	—	—	—	—	—	—
KNOW	1	—	1	—	—	—	—	—	—
LAFF	—	—	—	—	—	—	1	—	1
LAPPEN	2	—	2	—	1	1	—	—	—
LAST	—	—	—	—	1	1	—	—	—
LATER	—	—	—	—	—	—	—	1	1
LET	1	—	1	—	—	—	—	—	—
LIE	—	—	—	—	—	—	1	—	1
LIGHT	1	—	1	—	—	—	—	—	—
LIKE	—	1	1	—	—	—	1	—	1
LINDA	—	—	—	—	—	—	—	1	1
LISTEN	1	—	1	—	—	—	—	—	—
LONG	—	—	—	—	1	1	3	—	3
LONG AGO	—	—	—	—	—	—	1	—	1
LONGER	—	—	—	—	—	—	—	1	1
LOOK	—	1	1	—	—	—	2	—	2
LOOK WHAT	1	—	1	—	—	—	—	—	—
LOUD	—	—	—	1	—	1	—	—	—
MAD	—	1	1	—	1	1	—	—	—
MADE	—	—	—	—	—	—	1	—	1
MAPPEN	1	—	1	—	—	—	—	—	—
MAVEN	1	—	1	—	—	—	—	—	—
MAY	—	1	1	—	—	—	—	—	—
ME	4	—	4	1	—	1	—	—	—
MIGHT	—	—	—	—	—	—	—	1	1
MIGHT GET HURT	1	—	1	—	—	—	—	—	—
MOON	—	1	1	—	—	—	—	—	—
MORNING	—	—	—	1	—	1	—	—	—
MOVE	—	—	—	—	—	—	1	—	1
MOVIE	1	—	1	—	—	—	—	—	—
MURDER	—	—	—	—	—	—	1	—	1
MYSTERY	1	—	1	—	—	—	—	—	—
NAPPEN	—	—	—	1	—	1	—	—	—

RESPONSE WORD	1ST			3RD			5TH		
	M	F	T	M	F	T	M	F	T

32. HAPPEN

RESPONSE WORD	M	F	T	M	F	T	M	F	T
NEVER	–	–	–	–	2	2	2	2	4
NICE	1	–	1	–	–	–	–	–	–
NIGHT	1	–	1	–	1	1	–	–	–
NO	1	1	2	1	–	1	–	–	–
NOT	–	2	2	–	2	2	2	2	4
NOT ANY MORE	–	1	1	–	–	–	–	–	–
NOT HAPPEN	3	3	6	5	6	11	3	2	5
NOT HAPPENED	–	–	–	1	–	1	–	–	–
NOT LONG AGO	–	–	–	–	–	–	1	–	1
NOT ME	1	–	1	–	–	–	–	–	–
NOT NOW	1	–	1	–	–	–	–	–	–
NOTHING	–	–	–	–	–	–	–	3	3
NOW	6	1	7	3	5	8	5	7	12
OCCUR	–	–	–	–	–	–	1	1	2
OFTEN	–	1	1	–	–	–	1	1	2
ON	–	1	1	2	–	2	–	–	–
ON HAPPEN	–	–	–	–	–	–	1	–	1
ONCE	–	1	1	4	3	7	1	5	6
ONE DAY	–	–	–	–	2	2	–	–	–
ONE TIME	–	–	–	–	1	1	–	–	–
OVEN	–	–	–	–	–	–	–	1	1
PANTS	1	–	1	–	–	–	–	–	–
PAPER	–	1	1	–	–	–	–	–	–
PAPPEN	–	1	1	1	–	1	–	–	–
PAST	–	–	–	–	1	1	1	–	1
PEANUT	–	1	1	–	–	–	–	–	–
PEOPLE	–	–	–	–	1	1	–	1	1
PILLS	1	–	1	–	–	–	–	–	–
PIPE	–	1	1	–	–	–	–	–	–
PLAY	–	2	2	1	–	1	–	–	–
POOR	–	–	–	–	1	1	–	–	–
POST	1	–	1	–	–	–	–	–	–
PRETTY	–	–	–	1	–	1	–	–	–
QUICK	–	–	–	1	–	1	–	1	1
QUICKLY	–	–	–	–	–	–	–	1	1
RAPPEN	–	1	1	–	–	–	–	–	–
RE-HAPPEN	–	–	–	–	–	–	1	–	1
RECENTLY	–	–	–	–	–	–	1	1	2
RETREAT	1	–	1	–	–	–	–	–	–
RIBBON	–	–	–	–	1	1	–	–	–
RIGHT AWAY	–	–	–	–	–	–	–	1	1
ROBBRYE	–	–	–	–	–	–	1	–	1
RUN	–	1	1	–	–	–	–	–	–
SAD	–	–	–	–	3	3	–	–	–
SALT	–	1	1	–	–	–	–	–	–
SANTA CLAUS	1	–	1	–	–	–	–	–	–
SAPPEN	1	–	1	–	–	–	–	–	–
SCAPPEN	1	–	1	–	–	–	–	–	–
SCHOOL	1	–	1	–	–	–	–	–	–
SHOE	–	1	1	–	–	–	–	–	–
SHOT	1	–	1	–	–	–	–	–	–
SICK	–	1	1	–	–	–	–	–	–
SNAKE	1	–	1	–	–	–	–	–	–
SOFT	1	–	1	–	1	1	–	–	–
SOMEONE ASKS YOU WHAT HAPPENS	–	1	1	–	–	–	–	–	–
SOMETHIMES IT WILL HAPPEN BEFORE YOU KN	–	–	–	–	–	–	–	1	1
SOMETHING	1	2	3	2	6	8	2	3	5
SOMETHING HAPPEN	1	–	1	–	–	–	–	–	–
SOMETHING HAPPEN TO YOUR BIKE	–	–	–	–	–	–	–	1	1
SOMETHING HAPPENED	2	–	2	1	–	1	–	–	–
SOMETHING HAPPENED IN THE STREET	–	–	–	1	–	1	–	–	–
SOMETHING HAPPENED TO MY KNEE	–	–	–	–	–	–	–	1	1
SOMETIMES	–	–	–	1	–	1	–	1	1
SOON	–	–	–	–	–	–	–	1	1
SORE	–	1	1	–	–	–	–	–	–
START	–	–	–	–	2	2	–	–	–
STONE WALL	1	–	1	–	–	–	–	–	–

32. HAPPEN

RESPONSE WORD	1ST M	F	T	3RD M	F	T	5TH M	F	T
STREETCAR	1	–	1	–	–	–	–	–	–
SUCKER	1	–	1	–	–	–	–	–	–
SUDDEN	–	–	–	1	3	4	3	4	7
SUDDENLY	–	–	–	3	5	8	1	2	3
SUN	–	1	1	–	–	–	–	–	–
SUNDAY	–	–	–	–	1	1	–	–	–
SUPPOSE	–	–	–	–	–	–	1	–	1
SWEATER	–	1	1	–	–	–	–	–	–
TABLE	–	1	1	–	–	–	–	–	–
TAKE PLACE	–	–	–	–	–	–	1	–	1
TALE	–	–	–	–	–	–	1	–	1
TAPPEN	–	1	1	–	–	–	–	–	–
TAPPING	–	–	–	1	–	1	–	–	–
TEETH	–	–	–	–	–	–	–	1	1
TELL	–	1	1	–	–	–	1	–	1
THEN	1	–	1	–	1	1	1	1	2
THERE	–	–	–	1	–	1	–	–	–
THING	–	–	–	2	1	3	2	–	2
THINGS	–	–	–	–	–	–	–	1	1
THINK	–	–	–	1	–	1	–	–	–
THIS	–	1	1	–	–	–	–	–	–
THOUGHT	–	1	1	–	–	–	–	–	–
THREAD	–	–	–	–	1	1	–	–	–
TIME	–	–	–	–	–	–	1	2	3
TIP OVER	–	–	–	1	–	1	–	–	–
TO	4	1	5	4	3	7	2	1	3
TO A HORSE	1	–	1	–	–	–	–	–	–
TO ME	–	1	1	–	–	–	–	–	–
TO YOUR LEG	–	1	1	–	–	–	–	–	–
TODAY	1	–	1	–	3	3	–	1	1
TOGETHER	–	–	–	–	1	1	1	–	1
TOMORROW	–	1	1	1	–	1	–	–	–
TOOK PLACE	–	–	–	–	–	–	–	1	1
TROUBLE	–	–	–	1	–	1	1	–	1
TRUE	–	–	–	–	–	–	–	1	1
UNHAPPEN	1	–	1	3	2	5	6	4	10
UNHAPPENED	–	1	1	–	–	–	1	–	1
UP	1	–	1	–	–	–	–	–	–
US	1	–	1	–	–	–	–	–	–
WALK	1	–	1	–	–	–	–	–	–
WAS	–	–	–	–	–	–	1	–	1
WASNT	–	–	–	–	–	–	1	–	1
WEAPON	1	–	1	–	–	–	–	–	–
WHAT	2	11	13	2	2	4	1	–	1
WHAT HAPPENED	3	1	4	–	–	–	–	–	–
WHAT HAPPENED HERE	–	1	1	–	–	–	–	–	–
WHEN	–	2	2	–	3	3	3	–	3
WHEN YOURE GETTING SOMETHING HAPPEN	1	–	1	–	–	–	–	–	–
WHERE	–	–	–	–	–	–	1	–	1
WHILE	–	–	–	1	–	1	–	1	1
WHO	–	1	1	–	–	–	–	–	–
WHY	1	1	2	–	–	–	–	–	–
WILL	–	–	–	1	1	2	1	–	1
WILL HAPPEN	–	–	–	–	1	1	–	–	–
WINDOW	–	–	–	1	–	1	–	–	–
WING	–	–	–	–	–	–	–	1	1
WITH	1	1	2	–	–	–	–	–	–
WITH ME	1	–	1	–	–	–	–	–	–
WOODS	1	–	1	–	–	–	–	–	–
WORD	–	–	–	–	–	–	–	2	2
WORKS	–	–	–	–	–	–	1	–	1
WORRY	1	–	1	–	–	–	–	–	–
WOULDNT HAPPENED	–	–	–	–	1	1	–	–	–
WRECK	–	–	–	1	–	1	–	–	–
WRONG	1	–	1	1	1	2	–	–	–
YEARS	–	–	–	1	–	1	–	–	–
YESTERDAY	–	1	1	7	2	9	1	–	1
YOU	2	1	3	1	–	1	–	1	1

RESPONSE WORD	1ST			3RD			5TH		
	M	F	T	M	F	T	M	F	T

33. HARD

RESPONSE WORD	M	F	T	M	F	T	M	F	T
A	–	1	1	–	–	–	–	–	–
A HEART TO PUT IN YOUR SOCK	1	–	1	–	–	–	–	–	–
A TOMATO SANDWICH	1	–	1	–	–	–	–	1	1
ARITHMETIC	–	–	–	–	–	–	–	1	1
ATTIC	–	–	–	–	1	1	–	–	–
BAD	–	2	2	1	–	1	–	–	–
BALL	2	1	3	–	–	–	1	–	1
BANG	1	–	1	–	–	–	–	–	–
BAR	2	–	2	–	–	–	–	–	–
BARD	–	1	1	–	–	–	–	–	–
BARK	1	–	1	–	–	–	–	–	–
BAT	1	–	1	–	–	–	–	–	–
BED	–	–	–	–	1	1	–	–	–
BLOW	1	–	1	–	–	–	–	–	–
BOARD	–	1	1	–	–	–	–	–	–
BOAT	1	–	1	–	–	–	–	–	–
BOOK	–	1	1	–	–	–	–	1	1
BOX	1	–	1	–	–	–	–	–	–
BREAD	–	2	2	–	–	–	–	–	–
BRICK	–	–	–	4	–	4	–	–	–
BRICKS	1	1	2	–	–	–	–	–	–
BRITTLE	–	–	–	–	1	1	–	–	–
BUMPY	–	–	–	1	–	1	1	–	1
CANDY	3	3	6	1	–	1	–	–	–
CANT BREAK	–	–	–	–	1	1	–	–	–
CANT DO	–	–	–	1	–	1	1	–	1
CANT EAT	–	1	1	–	–	–	–	–	–
CAR	4	1	5	–	–	–	–	–	–
CARD	2	1	3	1	2	3	–	–	–
CARS	–	1	1	–	–	–	–	–	–
CEMENT	3	–	3	–	1	1	–	–	–
CHAIR	–	1	1	–	1	1	–	1	1
CHALK BOARD	–	1	1	–	–	–	–	–	–
CHIN	–	1	1	–	–	–	–	–	–
CHRISTMAS TREE	1	–	1	–	–	–	–	–	–
CLAY	–	1	1	–	1	1	–	–	–
CLOCK	1	–	1	–	–	–	–	–	–
COMPLICATED	–	–	–	–	–	–	–	1	1
CONCRETE	1	–	1	–	–	–	–	–	–
CORD	–	–	–	1	–	1	–	–	–
CRACK	1	–	1	–	–	–	–	–	–
DESK	–	1	1	–	–	–	–	–	–
DIFFERENT	–	–	–	–	–	–	–	1	1
DIFFICULT	–	–	–	–	–	–	3	2	5
DO	1	–	1	1	1	2	–	–	–
DOG	–	–	–	–	–	–	1	–	1
DOING	1	–	1	–	–	–	–	–	–
DRAWER	1	–	1	–	–	–	–	–	–
EAST	–	–	–	–	–	–	1	–	1
EASY	4	7	11	24	16	40	30	24	54
EGG	–	–	–	–	1	1	1	–	1
FAST	–	1	1	–	1	1	1	–	1
FIGHT	–	–	–	–	–	–	1	–	1
FLOOR	–	1	1	1	–	1	1	–	1
FOOD	1	1	2	–	–	–	–	–	–
FOR	–	1	1	–	–	–	–	–	–
FOR YOU	1	–	1	–	–	–	–	–	–
FOUGHT	–	–	–	–	–	–	1	–	1
FUN	1	–	1	–	–	–	–	–	–
GAME	1	–	1	–	–	–	–	–	–
GIVE ME A CARD	1	–	1	–	–	–	–	–	–
GLASSES	1	–	1	–	–	–	–	–	–
GO TO DO HARD WORK	–	1	1	–	–	–	–	–	–
GOOD	2	–	2	–	1	1	–	–	–
GRASS	–	–	–	1	–	1	–	–	–
HAD	–	–	–	–	1	1	–	–	–
HAMMER	1	–	1	–	–	–	–	–	–
HARDER	–	–	–	–	1	1	–	–	–
HARDLY	–	–	–	–	–	–	–	1	1
HE	1	–	1	–	–	–	–	–	–
HEAD	–	1	1	1	1	2	–	–	–

RESPONSE WORD	1ST			3RD			5TH		
	M	F	T	M	F	T	M	F	T

33. HARD

RESPONSE WORD	M	F	T	M	F	T	M	F	T
HEART	6	3	9	—	—	—	—	—	—
HEAVY	1	—	1	—	1	1	—	—	—
HERD	—	—	—	—	1	1	1	—	1
HERE	—	1	1	—	1	1	—	—	—
HIT	1	—	1	1	—	1	—	—	—
HOLD	1	—	1	—	—	—	—	—	—
HORSE	1	—	1	—	—	—	—	—	—
HURT	2	—	2	1	—	1	—	—	—
ICE	1	1	2	—	—	—	—	—	—
IS SOMEONE	—	1	1	—	—	—	—	—	—
IT IS A HARD BRICK	—	—	—	1	—	1	—	—	—
JOB	—	—	—	—	1	1	—	—	—
K	—	1	1	—	—	—	—	—	—
KICK STAND (ON BIKE)	—	1	1	—	—	—	—	—	—
KIND	—	—	—	—	—	—	—	1	1
KNIFE	—	1	1	—	—	—	—	—	—
LADY	—	1	1	—	—	—	—	—	—
LARGE	1	—	1	1	—	1	—	—	—
LESS	—	—	—	—	—	—	1	—	1
LIGHT	—	1	1	—	1	1	—	—	—
LITTLE	—	1	1	—	—	—	—	—	—
LOOSE	1	1	2	—	—	—	—	—	—
MAN	2	—	2	—	—	—	—	—	—
MARD	2	1	3	—	—	—	—	—	—
MART	2	—	2	—	—	—	—	—	—
ME	2	—	2	—	—	—	—	—	—
MEAN	—	—	—	—	—	—	1	1	2
METAL	—	1	1	—	—	—	1	—	1
MOST	—	1	1	—	—	—	—	—	—
MOVIE	—	1	1	—	—	—	—	—	—
MUSIC	1	—	1	—	—	—	—	—	—
NARD	—	1	1	1	—	1	—	—	—
NICE	—	1	1	—	1	1	—	—	—
NOT EASY	—	—	—	—	—	—	2	2	4
NOT HARD	2	1	3	—	—	—	—	—	—
NOT SOFT	—	—	—	—	—	—	4	2	6
NOW	1	—	1	—	—	—	—	—	—
OPEN	1	—	1	—	—	—	—	—	—
OUT	—	—	—	1	—	1	—	—	—
PAN	—	2	2	—	—	—	—	—	—
PAPER	1	1	2	—	—	—	—	—	—
PARD	1	1	2	—	—	—	—	—	—
PIPE	1	—	1	—	—	—	—	—	—
PLAY	1	1	2	—	—	—	—	—	—
PLAY HARD	—	1	1	—	—	—	—	—	—
POST	—	—	—	—	1	1	—	—	—
PRESENT	—	1	1	—	—	—	—	—	—
PROBLEM	—	—	—	—	—	—	—	1	1
RAIN	—	—	—	—	1	1	—	—	—
RARD	—	1	1	—	—	—	—	—	—
RAT	—	—	—	1	—	1	—	—	—
RIDE	1	—	1	—	—	—	—	—	—
ROCK	9	3	12	11	6	17	6	2	8
ROCKS	—	2	2	—	—	—	—	—	—
ROCKY	—	—	—	—	1	1	—	1	1
ROUGH	1	—	1	2	2	4	1	6	7
RUGGED	—	—	—	—	—	—	—	1	1
S SOUND	1	—	1	—	—	—	—	—	—
SARD	1	—	1	—	1	1	—	—	—
SCARD	1	—	1	—	—	—	—	—	—
SEAT	—	1	1	—	—	—	—	—	—
SEE	—	1	1	—	—	—	—	1	1
SHIRT	1	1	2	—	—	—	—	—	—
SHOFT	—	—	—	—	—	—	1	—	1
SICK	—	—	—	1	—	1	—	—	—
SKY	1	—	1	—	—	—	—	—	—
SLIP	—	1	1	—	—	—	—	—	—
SLOAK	—	—	—	—	—	—	—	1	1
SLOW	—	—	—	—	—	—	—	1	1
SMOOTH	—	—	—	1	—	1	1	—	1
SOFT	24	31	55	68	81	149	64	70	134
SOLID	—	—	—	—	—	—	2	1	3

33. HARD

RESPONSE WORD	1ST			3RD			5TH		
	M	F	T	M	F	T	M	F	T
SOME	1	–	1	–	–	–	–	–	–
SOMEONE	–	–	–	–	–	–	1	–	1
SOMETHING	–	–	–	–	1	1	–	–	–
SOMETHING THATS NOT VERY SOFT	–	–	–	–	–	–	–	1	1
SOUND	–	–	–	–	–	–	–	1	1
STEAL	–	–	–	–	–	–	1	–	1
STEEL	–	–	–	–	–	–	–	1	1
STIFF	–	1	1	–	–	–	1	–	1
STONE	–	1	1	–	–	–	–	–	–
STORE	–	1	1	–	–	–	–	–	–
STRING	–	–	–	–	1	1	–	–	–
STRONG	1	–	1	1	–	1	2	–	2
STUFF	1	–	1	–	–	–	–	–	–
SUN	–	1	1	–	–	–	–	–	–
SURFACE	–	–	–	–	–	–	1	–	1
TABLE	1	3	4	–	1	1	–	–	–
TAFFY	–	–	–	–	–	–	–	1	1
TEAR	–	1	1	–	–	–	–	1	1
TEST	–	–	–	–	1	1	–	1	1
THAT STEAK IS HARD	–	1	1	–	–	–	–	–	–
THATS HARD	1	–	1	–	–	–	–	–	–
THEIR	–	–	–	1	–	1	–	–	–
THEN	–	–	–	–	–	–	–	1	1
THICK	–	–	–	1	–	1	1	2	3
THINGS	–	–	–	1	–	1	–	–	–
THIS IS TOO HARD	–	1	1	–	–	–	–	–	–
THIS IS VERY HARD	–	1	1	–	–	–	–	–	–
TIME	–	1	1	–	–	–	–	–	–
TO	–	1	1	–	–	–	–	–	–
TO DO	1	–	1	–	–	–	–	1	1
TO DO SOMETHING	–	1	1	–	–	–	–	–	–
TO LITTLE CHILDREN	–	1	1	–	–	–	–	–	–
TOO HARD	–	1	1	–	–	–	–	–	–
TOUGH	–	–	–	–	–	–	1	1	2
TRY	–	–	–	–	1	1	–	–	–
TWO	1	–	1	–	–	–	–	1	1
UNEASY	–	–	–	–	–	–	–	1	1
UNSOFT	–	–	–	–	1	1	–	–	–
VACUUM CLEANER	1	–	1	–	–	–	–	–	–
VALENTINE	1	–	1	–	–	–	–	–	–
VERY HARD	–	–	–	1	–	1	–	1	1
WALK	–	–	–	1	–	1	–	–	–
WALL	–	1	1	1	–	1	–	–	–
WARE STORE	–	1	1	–	–	–	–	–	–
WAY	–	1	1	–	–	–	–	–	–
WHEN SOMETHINGS HARD	1	–	1	–	–	–	–	–	–
WHITE	1	–	1	–	–	–	–	–	–
WHY	–	1	1	–	–	–	–	–	–
WINDOW	–	1	1	–	–	–	–	–	–
WOOD	–	1	1	–	–	–	–	2	2
WORDS	–	–	–	1	–	1	–	–	–
WORK	11	12	23	6	4	10	5	2	7
WORK TO DO	–	1	1	–	–	–	–	–	–
WORKING	–	–	–	–	–	–	–	1	1
WRITE ON	–	–	–	1	–	1	–	–	–
WRITING	–	1	1	–	–	–	–	–	–
YOU	1	–	1	–	–	–	–	–	–

RESPONSE WORD		1ST			3RD			5TH	
	M	F	T	M	F	T	M	F	T

34.   HE

RESPONSE WORD	M	F	T	M	F	T	M	F	T
A BIG BOY	–	1	1	–	–	–	–	–	–
A BOY	–	1	1	–	–	–	–	1	1
A MAN	–	–	–	–	–	–	–	1	1
AM	–	1	1	–	–	–	–	–	–
BAD	–	1	1	–	–	–	–	–	–
BE	–	–	–	1	–	1	1	–	1
BEE	1	1	2	–	–	–	–	–	–
BLIND	1	1	2	–	–	–	–	–	–
BLUE	–	1	1	–	–	–	–	–	–
BOAT	–	2	2	1	–	1	–	–	–
BOOK	1	–	1	–	–	–	–	–	–
BOY	2	5	7	10	9	19	20	26	46
CAN	–	5	5	–	–	–	–	–	–
CAN SWIM	1	–	1	–	–	–	–	–	–
CAR	1	–	1	–	–	–	1	–	1
CAT	–	–	–	–	–	–	1	–	1
CLOTHES	–	–	–	–	1	1	–	–	–
COAT	1	–	1	–	–	–	–	–	–
COLD	–	1	1	–	–	–	–	–	–
COMES	2	–	2	–	–	–	–	–	–
CREE	–	1	1	–	–	–	–	–	–
DARK	–	1	1	–	–	–	–	–	–
DESK	–	1	1	–	–	–	–	–	–
DID	–	–	–	–	1	1	–	1	1
DIRT	1	–	1	–	–	–	–	–	–
DOG	–	–	–	–	–	–	1	–	1
DOLL	1	–	1	–	–	–	–	–	–
DONT WAVE YOUR ARM WHEN YOUR MOTHERS GO.	–	1	1	–	–	–	–	–	–
DOOR	2	–	2	–	–	–	–	–	–
DRINK	–	–	–	1	–	1	–	–	–
FATHER	1	1	2	–	–	–	1	–	1
FIRE HYDRANT	1	–	1	–	–	–	–	–	–
FISH	2	–	2	1	–	1	–	–	–
FLOOR	1	–	1	–	–	–	–	–	–
FRIENDLY	–	1	1	–	–	–	–	–	–
GAVE	2	–	2	–	–	–	–	–	–
GENTLEMAN	–	–	–	–	1	1	–	–	–
GENTLY	1	–	1	–	–	–	–	–	–
GIRL	4	2	6	–	2	2	1	–	1
GO	–	–	–	–	1	1	–	–	–
GO OUT	1	–	1	–	–	–	–	–	–
GOING TO A PARTY	–	1	1	–	–	–	–	–	–
GOOD	1	–	1	–	–	–	–	–	–
GRASS	1	–	1	–	–	–	–	–	–
GREEN	–	1	1	–	–	–	–	–	–
HAPPY	1	–	1	–	–	–	–	–	–
HARD	1	–	1	–	–	–	–	–	–
HAS	–	1	1	–	1	1	–	–	–
HAT	–	1	1	–	–	–	–	–	–
HEARD	–	–	–	1	–	–	–	1	1
HEAT	1	1	2	1	–	1	–	–	–
HEAT-FIRE-STOVE	–	1	1	–	–	–	–	–	–
HEE-HEE	–	1	1	–	–	–	–	–	–
HEED	–	1	1	–	–	–	–	–	–
HER	11	16	27	33	35	68	38	34	72
HERE	–	–	–	1	–	1	–	–	–
HERE IS SOMEONE	–	1	1	–	–	–	–	–	–
HILL	–	1	1	–	–	–	–	–	–
HIM	1	1	2	14	18	32	13	13	26
HIS	–	–	–	2	6	8	2	1	3
HOT	1	2	3	–	–	–	–	–	–
HOTNESS	–	1	1	–	–	–	–	–	–
HOUSE	1	1	2	–	–	–	–	–	–
I	2	1	3	–	–	–	–	–	–
IS	4	2	6	2	1	3	2	–	2
IS A BOY	–	–	–	1	–	1	–	–	–
IS HAPPY	1	–	1	–	–	–	–	–	–
IS HERE	1	–	1	–	–	–	–	–	–
IS LIKE YOUR HEATER	–	1	1	–	–	–	–	–	–
KEEPED	1	–	1	–	–	–	–	–	–
KEEVE	–	1	1	–	–	–	–	–	–

RESPONSE WORD	1ST M	1ST F	1ST T	3RD M	3RD F	3RD T	5TH M	5TH F	5TH T

34. HE

RESPONSE WORD	1ST M	F	T	3RD M	F	T	5TH M	F	T
KEY	2	–	2	–	–	–	–	–	–
KID	–	1	1	–	–	–	–	–	–
KNEE	1	–	1	–	–	–	–	–	–
LEAVE	–	1	1	–	–	–	–	–	–
LIGHT	–	1	1	–	–	–	–	–	–
LIGHTS	–	1	1	–	–	–	–	–	–
LIKE	1	–	1	–	–	–	–	–	–
LIKES	1	–	1	–	–	–	–	–	–
LIPS	1	–	1	–	–	–	–	–	–
LOVES	–	1	1	–	–	–	–	–	–
MADE	–	–	–	1	–	1	–	–	–
MAN	4	5	9	5	1	6	4	1	5
MAN OR BOY	–	–	–	–	–	–	–	1	1
MAY	–	1	1	–	–	–	–	–	–
ME	18	12	30	18	7	25	3	4	7
MEANT	–	1	1	–	–	–	–	–	–
MEN	1	–	1	1	–	1	–	–	–
MOTHER	–	1	1	–	–	–	–	1	1
MY DOG	–	–	–	–	–	–	–	1	1
NAME	–	–	–	1	–	1	–	–	–
NAT	–	–	–	–	1	1	–	–	–
OCEAN	1	–	1	–	–	–	–	–	–
OPEN	–	1	1	–	–	–	–	–	–
OUT	1	–	1	–	–	–	–	–	–
PADDLE	–	–	–	1	–	1	–	–	–
PAINT	–	1	1	–	–	–	–	–	–
PANTS	1	–	1	–	–	–	–	–	–
PEA	–	1	1	–	–	–	–	–	–
PEE	–	1	1	–	–	–	–	–	–
PENCIL	1	–	1	–	–	–	–	–	–
PEOPLE	–	1	1	–	–	–	–	–	–
PERSON	–	–	–	2	–	2	6	5	11
PICTURE	1	–	1	–	–	–	–	–	–
PIPE	–	1	1	–	–	–	–	–	–
POOL	–	–	–	–	–	–	1	–	1
PUSH	–	–	–	1	–	1	–	–	–
RIDE	–	1	1	–	–	–	–	–	–
ROCK	1	–	1	–	–	–	–	–	–
ROOSTER	1	–	1	–	–	–	–	–	–
ROPE	1	–	1	–	–	–	–	–	–
SAID	1	–	1	–	–	–	–	–	–
SALLY	1	1	1	–	–	–	–	–	–
SCREECH	–	1	1	–	–	–	–	–	–
SEA	1	–	1	–	–	–	–	–	–
SEE	–	1	1	–	–	–	–	–	–
SEES	–	–	–	–	–	–	1	–	1
SHE	24	28	52	38	51	89	40	50	90
SHELF	1	–	1	–	–	–	–	–	–
SHOELACES	1	–	1	–	–	–	–	–	–
SHOES	1	–	1	–	–	–	–	–	–
SIT DOWN AND PLAY WITH SAND	1	–	1	–	–	–	–	–	–
SOMEBODY	–	–	–	1	–	1	1	–	1
SOMEONE	–	–	–	1	–	1	–	–	–
SWEEP	–	–	–	1	–	1	–	–	–
TABLE	–	1	1	–	–	–	–	–	–
TEA HOUSE	–	1	1	–	–	–	–	–	–
TEN	1	–	1	–	–	–	–	–	–
THE	–	1	1	–	–	–	–	–	–
THEM	–	–	–	–	1	1	–	–	–
TOLD ME TO PLAY	1	–	1	–	–	–	–	–	–
TOM	1	–	1	–	–	–	–	–	–
TV	1	–	1	–	–	–	–	–	–
UNIVERSITY	1	–	1	–	–	–	–	–	–
UNLOCKS THE DOOR	–	1	1	–	–	–	–	–	–
WALK	–	1	1	–	–	–	–	–	–
WALKED	1	–	1	–	–	–	–	–	–
WANTED	1	–	1	–	–	–	–	–	–
WANTS	2	–	2	–	–	–	–	–	–
WAS	1	1	2	–	–	–	1	–	1
WE	3	3	6	2	1	3	2	–	2
WENT	1	–	1	–	–	–	–	–	–

RESPONSE WORD	1ST			3RD			5TH		
	M	F	T	M	F	T	M	F	T

34. HE

RESPONSE WORD	M	F	T	M	F	T	M	F	T
WENT OUTSIDE	–	1	1	–	–	–	–	–	–
WHAT	–	1	1	–	–	–	–	–	–
WHEN YOU HEAR SOMETHING	1	–	1	–	–	–	–	–	–
WHEN YOURE REAL COLD YOU PUT IN HEAT	1	–	1	–	–	–	–	–	–
WHERE	–	1	1	–	1	1	–	–	–
WILL	–	1	1	–	–	–	–	–	–
WITH	1	–	1	–	–	–	–	–	–
YEE	–	–	–	–	1	1	–	–	–
YOU	–	1	1	–	–	–	–	–	–

35. HER

RESPONSE WORD	M	F	T	M	F	T	M	F	T
A GIRL	–	2	2	–	–	–	–	1	1
A GIRL BABY	–	1	1	–	–	–	–	–	–
A PERSON	–	–	–	–	–	–	1	–	1
AND ME	–	1	1	–	–	–	–	–	–
ARMS	1	–	1	–	–	–	–	–	–
BABY	–	–	–	–	1	1	–	–	–
BABY DOLL	–	–	–	–	–	–	–	1	1
BAG	1	–	1	–	–	–	–	–	–
BALL	–	–	–	1	–	1	–	–	–
BED	1	–	1	–	–	–	–	–	–
BELONG	–	–	–	–	–	–	–	1	1
BEND	–	–	–	1	–	1	–	–	–
BERR	–	–	–	–	–	–	–	1	1
BETTER	–	–	–	1	–	1	–	–	–
BILLIE	–	–	–	1	–	1	–	–	–
BIRD	–	2	2	1	1	2	–	–	–
BIRTHDAY	–	1	1	–	–	–	–	–	–
BLUE	1	–	1	–	–	–	–	–	–
BOOK	–	–	–	1	1	2	–	1	1
BOY	–	4	4	–	–	–	–	–	–
BUBBLES	–	–	–	–	–	–	–	1	1
BUNNY	–	1	1	–	–	–	–	–	–
CAN	–	1	1	–	–	–	–	–	–
CAN WORK	1	–	1	–	–	–	–	–	–
CAREFUL	1	–	1	–	–	–	–	–	–
CAT	–	1	1	–	–	–	1	–	1
CHICKEN	–	1	1	–	–	–	–	–	–
CHRISTMAS	–	–	–	1	1	2	–	–	–
CLOCK	–	1	1	–	–	–	–	–	–
COAT	–	1	1	–	–	–	–	–	–
COLOR	1	–	1	–	–	–	–	–	–
COME	–	1	1	–	1	1	–	–	–
COW	–	–	–	1	–	1	–	–	–
CUR	–	–	–	–	1	1	–	–	–
CURTAIN	–	1	1	–	–	–	–	–	–
DID	1	–	1	–	–	–	–	–	–
DIR	–	1	1	–	–	–	–	–	–
DIRT	1	–	1	–	–	–	–	–	–
DISHES	–	1	1	–	–	–	–	–	–
DOG	–	–	–	–	1	1	1	–	1
DOING SOMETHING	–	1	1	–	–	–	–	–	–
DONT	–	–	–	–	1	1	–	–	–
DONT TOUCH THE STICKS OUT THE SHADE	–	1	1	–	–	–	–	–	–
DRESS	2	1	3	–	–	–	–	–	–
EARLINE	–	1	1	–	–	–	–	–	–
FAN	1	–	1	–	–	–	–	–	–
FAST	–	1	1	–	–	–	–	–	–
FATHER	3	–	3	–	–	–	–	–	–
FEMALE	–	–	–	–	–	–	2	–	2
FISH BOWL	1	–	1	–	–	–	–	–	–
FRIEND	–	1	1	–	–	–	–	–	–
FUR	1	–	1	–	–	–	–	–	–
GIRL	9	8	17	13	8	21	18	24	42
GIRL OR WOMAN	–	–	–	–	–	–	–	1	1
GO	–	1	1	–	–	–	–	–	–
GO UPSTAIRS	–	1	1	–	–	–	–	–	–
GOES OUT	1	–	1	–	–	–	–	–	–

35. HER

RESPONSE WORD	1ST M	F	T	3RD M	F	T	5TH M	F	T
GOOD	–	1	1	–	1	1	–	–	–
GREEN	1	2	3	–	–	–	–	–	–
HAD	1	–	1	–	–	–	–	–	–
HAIR	1	–	1	–	–	–	–	–	–
HAPPY	1	–	1	–	–	–	–	–	–
HAS	1	–	1	–	–	–	–	–	–
HE	15	14	29	27	30	57	24	27	51
HEAD	–	–	–	–	1	1	–	–	–
HEAR	–	–	–	–	–	–	–	1	1
HELP	2	–	2	–	–	–	–	–	–
HERB	–	1	1	–	–	–	–	–	–
HERDER	1	–	1	–	–	–	–	–	–
HERE	1	2	3	–	1	1	1	–	1
HERG	1	–	1	–	–	–	–	–	–
HERS	1	–	1	–	–	–	1	–	1
HERSELF	–	1	1	–	–	–	–	–	–
HEX	1	–	1	–	–	–	–	–	–
HIM	19	20	39	41	46	87	45	49	94
HIS	1	–	1	2	1	3	–	4	4
HURT	3	1	4	–	–	–	–	–	–
I	–	1	1	–	–	–	–	–	–
IN	–	1	1	–	–	–	–	–	–
INJURED	–	–	–	–	–	–	1	–	1
IS	2	–	2	–	–	–	–	–	–
IS A LADY	1	–	1	–	–	–	–	–	–
JAKE	1	–	1	–	–	–	–	–	–
JERK	1	–	1	–	–	–	1	–	1
JOAN	–	–	–	–	–	–	1	–	1
KEY	1	–	1	–	–	–	–	–	–
KICKS	1	–	1	–	–	–	–	–	–
KING	–	1	1	–	–	–	–	–	–
KITE	–	–	–	1	–	1	–	–	–
KITTEN	1	1	2	–	–	–	–	–	–
KITTEN IS YELLOW	–	1	1	–	–	–	–	–	–
LADY	–	1	1	1	1	2	1	–	1
LAWN	–	1	1	–	–	–	–	–	–
LIPSTICK	–	1	1	–	–	–	–	–	–
LITTLE BOY	–	1	1	–	–	–	–	–	–
MAKE	1	–	1	–	–	–	–	–	–
MAN	2	1	3	–	1	1	–	–	–
MAN HURT	1	–	1	–	–	–	–	–	–
ME	7	5	12	8	2	10	–	1	1
MEN	–	–	–	1	–	1	–	–	–
MER	3	1	4	–	1	1	–	–	–
MILK	–	1	1	–	–	–	–	–	–
MISS	–	–	–	–	–	–	1	–	1
MOM	–	–	–	–	–	–	–	1	1
MOMMY	–	–	–	–	–	–	–	1	1
MOTHER	–	3	3	–	1	1	1	–	1
MOUTH	–	1	1	–	–	–	–	–	–
MURR	–	–	–	1	–	1	–	–	–
NAME	–	1	1	–	–	–	–	–	–
NEXT DOOR	1	–	1	–	–	–	–	–	–
NICE	–	–	–	–	1	1	–	–	–
NOT	1	–	1	–	–	–	–	–	–
NOT LIKE	1	–	1	–	–	–	–	–	–
NUT	–	–	–	–	–	–	1	–	1
O	1	–	1	–	–	–	–	–	–
OTHER	–	–	–	–	1	1	–	–	–
OUTSIDE	–	1	1	–	–	–	–	–	–
PANTS	1	–	1	–	–	–	–	–	–
PAPER	1	–	1	–	–	–	–	–	–
PEOPLE	–	1	1	–	–	–	–	–	–
PERSON	–	–	–	–	–	–	1	1	2
PIE	–	1	1	–	–	–	–	–	–
PIG	1	–	1	–	–	–	–	–	–
PLAYS	–	1	1	–	–	–	–	–	–
POCKETBOOK	–	1	1	–	–	–	–	–	–
PURR	2	1	3	–	–	–	–	–	–
QUOW	1	–	1	–	–	–	–	–	–
RAIN	–	–	–	–	1	1	–	–	–
RIDE	1	–	1	–	–	–	–	–	–

RESPONSE WORD	1ST			3RD			5TH		
	M	F	T	M	F	T	M	F	T

35. HER

RESPONSE WORD	M	F	T	M	F	T	M	F	T
RIDING A HORSE	–	1	1	–	–	–	–	–	–
RUNS	–	1	1	–	–	–	–	–	–
SAD FACE	–	1	1	–	–	–	–	–	–
SEE	1	–	1	–	1	1	–	–	–
SEE HER	–	1	1	–	–	–	–	–	–
SELF	–	–	–	–	1	1	–	–	–
SHE	7	18	25	33	31	64	36	21	57
SHEEP	–	1	1	–	–	–	–	–	–
SHOES	1	–	1	–	–	–	–	–	–
SIGH	–	–	–	1	–	1	–	–	–
SIR	1	–	1	–	–	–	–	–	–
SISTER	–	–	–	–	–	–	1	–	1
SNORE	1	–	1	–	–	–	–	–	–
SOCKS	1	–	1	–	–	–	–	–	–
SOFT	1	–	1	–	–	–	–	–	–
SOUND	–	–	–	–	–	–	–	1	1
SPOON	–	1	1	–	–	–	–	–	–
STIR	1	–	1	–	–	–	–	–	–
SWEATER	–	1	1	–	–	–	–	–	–
THAT IS HER	–	–	–	1	–	1	–	–	–
THE	–	1	1	–	–	–	–	–	–
THEE	–	1	1	–	–	–	–	–	–
THEM	–	1	1	–	–	–	–	–	–
THERMOMETER	1	–	1	–	–	–	–	–	–
THIS	1	–	1	–	–	–	–	–	–
TOLD ME TO SING	1	–	1	–	–	–	–	–	–
TOY	1	–	1	–	–	–	–	–	–
TRAIN	1	–	1	–	–	–	–	–	–
TURN	1	–	1	–	–	–	–	–	–
UP	1	–	1	–	–	–	–	–	–
WALK	1	–	1	–	–	–	–	–	–
WALL	1	–	1	–	–	–	–	–	–
WANT	1	–	1	–	–	–	–	–	–
WANTS	1	–	1	–	–	–	–	–	–
WENT	1	–	1	–	–	–	–	–	–
WENT OUTSIDE	–	1	1	–	–	–	–	–	–
WERE	1	1	2	–	–	–	–	–	–
WHEN YOURE PUTTING CLOTHES IN THE WASHI	1	–	1	–	–	–	–	–	–
WHERE	–	–	–	1	–	1	–	–	–
WHITE	1	–	1	–	–	–	–	–	–
WIN	1	–	1	–	–	–	–	–	–
WOMAN	–	–	–	1	1	2	1	1	2
WOMEN	–	–	–	–	–	–	–	1	1
YOU	–	2	2	1	1	2	1	–	1
YOUR FACE	–	1	1	–	–	–	–	–	–

36. HIGH

RESPONSE WORD	M	F	T	M	F	T	M	F	T
A HAT	–	1	1	–	–	–	–	–	–
A HIGH WALL	–	1	1	–	–	–	–	–	–
A LITTLE KITTEN MIGHT BE ON TOP OF A RO.	–	1	1	–	–	–	–	–	–
A THING	1	–	1	–	–	–	–	–	–
ABOVE	–	–	–	1	3	4	1	3	4
AIR	2	–	2	–	1	1	–	–	–
AIRPLANE	2	–	2	1	–	1	–	–	–
ANT	–	1	1	–	–	–	–	–	–
BASE	–	–	–	–	–	–	1	–	1
BE	1	1	2	–	–	–	–	–	–
BEE	–	1	1	–	–	–	–	–	–
BEEHIVE	–	1	1	1	–	1	–	–	–
BEES	–	1	1	1	–	1	–	–	–
BEHIND	1	–	1	–	–	–	1	–	1
BELOW	–	–	–	–	–	–	1	–	1
BIG	–	–	–	2	–	2	–	1	1
BIKE	1	–	1	–	–	–	–	1	1
BIRD	–	–	–	–	–	–	–	1	1
BOW	–	1	1	–	–	–	–	–	–
BROUGHT	–	–	–	–	–	–	–	1	1

RESPONSE WORD	1ST			3RD			5TH		
	M	F	T	M	F	T	M	F	T

36.   HIGH

RESPONSE WORD	M	F	T	M	F	T	M	F	T
BUILDING	–	–	–	1	2	3	–	–	–
BUSH	–	1	1	–	–	–	–	–	–
BUY	1	–	1	1	–	1	–	–	–
BY	3	2	5	2	3	5	–	3	3
BYE	–	7	7	5	1	6	–	1	1
CANT REACH	–	–	–	–	–	–	–	1	1
CAR	1	–	1	–	–	–	–	–	–
CAT	–	–	–	–	–	–	1	–	1
CATCH	1	–	1	–	–	–	–	–	–
CEILING	–	1	1	–	–	–	–	–	–
CHAIR	–	1	1	1	–	1	–	–	–
CLIFF	–	1	1	–	–	–	1	–	1
CLOUD	–	1	1	–	–	–	–	–	–
COME OUT	–	1	1	–	–	–	–	–	–
DANGEROUS	–	–	–	–	–	–	–	1	1
DEE-DEE	–	1	1	–	–	–	–	–	–
DESK	–	1	1	–	–	–	–	–	–
DIE	–	1	1	–	–	–	–	–	–
DISAPPEAR	–	–	–	–	–	–	–	1	1
DISTANCE UP	–	–	–	–	–	–	1	–	1
DOG	–	–	–	–	1	1	–	–	–
DONT CLIMB HIGH IN TREE	1	–	1	–	–	–	–	–	–
DONT EAT FAST	1	–	1	–	–	–	–	–	–
DONT LET THEM GET ME	1	–	1	–	–	–	–	–	–
DOOR KNOB	–	1	1	–	–	–	–	–	–
DOWN	5	4	9	3	1	4	–	–	–
EMPIRE STATE BUILDING	–	–	–	–	–	–	1	–	1
FAR	–	–	–	2	–	2	–	–	–
FAR UP	–	–	–	2	–	2	–	–	–
FAST	–	2	2	–	–	–	–	–	–
FATHER	1	–	1	–	–	–	–	–	–
FEVER	–	1	1	–	–	–	–	–	–
FIND	1	1	2	–	–	–	–	–	–
FINE	–	1	1	–	–	–	–	–	–
FLAG	1	–	1	–	–	–	–	–	–
FLICKA	1	–	1	–	–	–	–	–	–
FLY	2	2	4	–	1	1	–	–	–
FOOD	1	–	1	–	–	–	–	–	–
FOUR	1	–	1	–	1	1	–	–	–
FRISKY	–	–	–	–	1	1	–	–	–
GLOW	–	–	–	1	–	1	–	–	–
GO	1	1	2	–	–	–	1	–	1
GO UP HIGH BIRD	–	1	1	–	–	–	–	–	–
GOING DOWN	–	1	1	–	–	–	–	–	–
GOOD-BYE	4	3	7	4	2	6	2	–	2
GOODBYE	–	–	–	–	–	–	1	–	1
GREEN	1	–	1	–	–	–	–	–	–
GUESS	–	1	1	–	–	–	–	–	–
GYM	–	–	–	1	–	1	–	–	–
HAND	1	–	1	–	–	–	–	–	–
HAS	–	–	–	–	1	1	–	–	–
HAVE	1	–	1	–	–	–	–	–	–
HEAT	–	1	1	–	–	–	–	–	–
HEAVEN	–	–	–	1	–	1	1	–	1
HELLO	3	–	3	1	4	5	3	5	8
HERE	2	1	3	–	–	–	–	–	–
HI	2	–	2	–	–	–	–	–	–
HI, JIM	–	–	–	1	–	1	–	–	–
HIBERNATE	–	–	–	1	–	1	–	–	–
HID	–	–	–	1	–	1	–	–	–
HIDE	5	2	7	–	1	1	1	–	1
HIDE AND GO SEEK	–	–	–	1	–	1	–	–	–
HIGH	–	–	–	–	–	–	1	–	1
HIGHER	–	1	1	–	–	–	–	1	1
HILL	1	1	2	–	–	–	–	–	–
HILLS	–	1	1	–	1	1	–	–	–
HIM	–	–	–	–	1	1	–	–	–
HIT	1	–	1	–	–	–	–	–	–
HO	1	–	1	–	–	–	–	–	–
HORSE	–	1	1	–	–	–	–	–	–
HOUSE	–	2	2	–	–	–	–	–	–

RESPONSE WORD	1ST M	F	T	3RD M	F	T	5TH M	F	T

36.   HIGH

RESPONSE WORD	1ST M	F	T	3RD M	F	T	5TH M	F	T
HOW	–	1	1	–	–	–	1	–	1
I	1	1	2	–	–	–	–	–	–
I DONT	–	–	–	1	–	1	–	–	–
ICE CREAM	1	–	1	–	–	–	–	–	–
IM GLAD YOUR HERE	–	1	1	–	–	–	–	–	–
IN	1	–	1	–	–	–	–	–	–
IN A JET	1	–	1	–	–	–	–	–	–
IN SKY	1	–	1	–	–	–	–	–	–
IN THE AIR	–	–	–	1	–	1	1	1	2
IN THE SKY	1	–	1	–	–	–	–	–	–
JEFF	1	–	1	–	–	–	–	–	–
KITCHEN	–	1	1	–	–	–	–	–	–
KITE	–	1	1	–	–	–	–	–	–
LADDER	–	–	–	–	–	–	2	–	2
LARGE	–	–	–	–	–	–	1	–	1
LAUGH	–	–	–	–	–	–	1	–	1
LAW	1	–	1	–	–	–	1	–	1
LIE	–	–	–	1	–	1	–	–	–
LIGHT	3	–	3	–	–	–	–	–	–
LITTLE	–	–	–	–	1	1	1	–	1
LOGE	–	–	–	–	–	–	1	–	1
LONG	–	–	–	3	1	4	–	–	–
LOOK	–	2	2	–	–	–	–	–	–
LOUDER	–	1	1	–	–	–	–	–	–
LOW	26	35	61	80	97	177	82	95	177
LOWER	1	–	1	–	–	–	–	–	–
MAN	1	–	1	–	–	–	–	–	–
ME	1	–	1	–	–	–	–	–	–
MELTING	–	–	–	–	–	–	1	–	1
MILK BOTTLES	1	–	1	–	–	–	–	–	–
MOUNTAIN	1	–	1	–	–	–	4	5	9
MY	4	–	4	–	–	–	–	–	–
NEST	1	–	1	–	2	2	–	–	–
NO	–	1	1	–	–	–	–	–	–
NOT HIGH	–	–	–	–	–	–	1	–	1
NOT LOW	–	–	–	–	–	–	–	1	1
NOT TO	–	1	1	–	–	–	–	–	–
OPEN	–	–	–	1	–	1	–	–	–
PEAK	1	–	1	–	–	–	–	–	–
PIE	2	1	3	–	–	–	–	–	–
PLANE	–	–	–	1	–	1	–	–	–
POLE	1	–	1	–	1	1	–	–	–
RIDE	1	–	1	–	–	–	–	–	–
RYE	–	1	1	–	–	–	–	–	–
SAY HI TO YOUR NEIGHBOR	1	–	1	–	–	–	–	–	–
SCARY	–	–	–	1	–	1	–	–	–
SCHOOL	–	–	–	1	–	1	1	1	2
SEA	–	–	–	–	1	1	–	–	–
SEAT	1	–	1	–	–	–	–	1	1
SEE	2	2	4	–	–	–	–	–	–
SEST	–	–	–	–	–	–	1	–	1
SEVEN FEET	–	–	–	–	–	–	1	–	1
SHAKE	–	–	–	1	–	1	–	–	–
SHAVE	1	–	1	–	–	–	–	–	–
SHED	–	1	1	–	–	–	–	–	–
SHIP	1	–	1	–	–	–	–	–	–
SHORT	–	–	–	–	–	–	1	–	1
SIDE	–	–	–	1	1	2	–	–	–
SIGH	1	–	1	–	1	1	–	–	–
SIGN	1	–	1	–	–	–	–	–	–
SISTER	–	1	1	–	–	–	–	–	–
SKY	5	5	10	4	1	5	3	1	4
SO LONG	1	–	1	–	–	–	–	–	–
SOCKS	–	–	–	–	–	–	–	1	1
SOFA	–	1	1	–	–	–	–	–	–
SOLD	1	–	1	–	–	–	–	–	–
SOMEBODY IS	–	1	1	–	–	–	–	–	–
SPEAKING	–	–	–	–	1	1	–	–	–
SPOT	–	–	–	–	–	–	1	–	1
SPY	–	1	1	–	–	–	–	–	–
STEEP	–	–	–	1	–	1	1	–	1
STREAM	1	–	1	–	–	–	–	–	–

RESPONSE WORD	1ST M	1ST F	1ST T	3RD M	3RD F	3RD T	5TH M	5TH F	5TH T

36. HIGH

RESPONSE WORD	M	F	T	M	F	T	M	F	T
SWING	–	3	3	–	–	–	–	–	–
SWINGING	1	1	1	–	–	–	–	–	–
TALL	1	1	2	3	1	4	11	10	21
TEAPOT	–	1	1	–	–	–	–	–	–
THAT IS HIGH	–	1	1	–	–	–	–	–	–
THE CUPBOARDS TOO HIGH	–	1	1	–	–	–	–	–	–
THERE	–	1	1	–	–	–	–	–	–
THEY	1	–	1	–	–	–	–	–	–
THINGS	1	–	1	–	–	–	–	–	–
TIDE	–	–	–	–	–	–	–	2	2
TO SOMEBODY	1	–	1	–	–	–	–	–	–
TOO HIGH	–	1	1	–	–	–	–	–	–
TOO HIGH FOR ME TO GET UP THERE	–	1	1	–	–	–	–	–	–
TOWER	1	1	2	–	–	–	–	–	–
TREE	1	1	2	1	1	2	–	–	–
TREES	1	1	2	–	–	–	–	–	–
TREETOPS	–	–	–	1	–	1	–	–	–
UNDER	–	1	1	–	–	–	–	–	–
UP	3	4	7	4	5	9	5	3	8
UP HIGH	–	1	1	–	–	–	–	–	–
UP IN THE AIR	1	1	2	–	–	–	–	–	–
UP IN THE MOUNTAINS	1	–	1	–	–	–	–	–	–
UP IN THE SKY	1	1	2	–	–	–	–	–	–
UP IN THE TREE	–	1	1	–	–	–	–	–	–
VERY HIGH	–	–	–	–	–	–	–	1	1
WAVE	–	–	–	–	1	1	–	–	–
WAY	–	–	–	–	1	1	–	–	–
WE	1	–	1	–	–	–	–	–	–
WET	–	1	1	–	–	–	–	–	–
WHEN YOU HIDE UNDER YOUR BED	1	–	1	–	–	–	–	–	–
WHY	1	–	1	–	1	1	–	–	–
WILL	1	–	1	–	–	–	–	–	–
WIND	–	–	–	1	–	1	–	–	–
YES	–	1	1	–	–	–	–	–	–
YOU	–	1	1	–	–	–	–	–	–
YOUR EYES	–	1	1	–	–	–	–	–	–
YOURE HIGH IN THE AIR	1	–	1	–	–	–	–	–	–

37. HIM

RESPONSE WORD	M	F	T	M	F	T	M	F	T
A BOY	–	1	1	2	–	2	1	–	1
A BOY OR MAN	–	–	–	–	–	–	–	1	1
A MAN	–	–	–	–	–	–	–	1	1
A SONG	–	–	–	–	–	–	–	1	1
ALONG	–	1	1	–	–	–	–	–	–
ARE	1	–	1	–	–	–	–	–	–
ATTIC	–	–	–	1	–	1	–	–	–
BABY	1	–	1	–	–	–	–	–	–
BED	1	–	1	–	–	–	–	–	–
BEE	–	–	–	–	1	1	–	–	–
BEEN	–	–	–	1	–	1	–	–	–
BELT	–	1	1	–	–	–	–	–	–
BENT	–	1	1	–	–	–	–	–	–
BIG	1	–	1	–	–	–	1	–	1
BILL	–	–	–	–	–	–	1	–	1
BIM	2	1	3	–	–	–	–	–	–
BOBBY	–	–	–	–	–	–	–	1	1
BOOK	–	1	1	–	–	–	–	–	–
BOOKS	1	–	1	–	–	–	–	–	–
BOY	3	7	10	7	12	19	14	16	30
BOYS	1	–	1	–	–	–	–	–	–
BROTHER	–	–	–	1	–	1	–	–	–
BUILDING	1	–	1	–	–	–	–	–	–
BUY	1	–	1	–	–	–	–	–	–
CAKE	–	1	1	–	–	–	–	–	–
CALL	–	–	–	–	–	–	1	–	1
CAN	–	1	1	–	–	–	–	–	–
CAR	–	1	1	–	–	–	1	–	1
CAT	1	1	2	–	–	–	–	–	–

RESPONSE WORD	1ST M	1ST F	1ST T	3RD M	3RD F	3RD T	5TH M	5TH F	5TH T

37. HIM

RESPONSE WORD	1ST M	F	T	3RD M	F	T	5TH M	F	T
CHICKEN	−	−	−	1	−	1	−	−	−
CLOTHES	−	1	1	−	−	−	−	−	−
COAT	1	−	1	−	−	−	−	−	−
COME	2	1	3	−	−	−	−	−	−
COOKIE	1	−	1	−	−	−	−	−	−
COULD WALK	−	1	1	−	−	−	−	−	−
CURTAINS	1	−	1	−	−	−	−	−	−
DADDY	−	−	−	−	−	−	−	1	1
DAVE	−	−	−	−	−	−	−	1	1
DID	−	−	−	−	−	−	1	−	1
DIM	−	1	1	−	−	−	−	−	−
DIRT	−	−	−	1	−	1	−	−	−
DISSOLVE	1	−	1	−	−	−	−	−	−
DOES SOMETHING	1	−	1	−	−	−	−	−	−
DOG	−	1	1	−	−	−	−	−	−
DOOR	−	1	1	−	−	−	−	−	−
DOORBELL	1	−	1	−	−	−	−	−	−
DRESS	1	4	5	−	−	−	−	2	2
EYES	−	1	1	−	−	−	−	−	−
FAT	−	−	−	−	−	−	−	1	1
FATHER	1	−	1	−	−	−	−	−	−
FELL	−	−	−	−	−	−	1	−	1
FISHING	1	−	1	−	−	−	−	−	−
FIX	−	−	−	−	1	1	−	−	−
FLY	−	1	1	−	−	−	−	−	−
FUN	1	−	1	−	−	−	−	−	−
GIRL	1	−	1	1	−	1	−	−	−
GLENN	1	−	1	−	−	−	−	−	−
GO	−	−	−	1	−	1	−	−	−
GOOD	1	−	1	−	−	−	−	−	−
GREEN	−	−	−	1	−	1	−	−	−
GRIM	1	−	1	−	−	−	−	−	−
GYM	−	−	−	−	−	−	1	−	1
HAIR	1	−	1	−	−	−	−	−	−
HAM	1	−	1	−	−	−	−	−	−
HAND	−	1	1	−	−	−	−	−	−
HANG ME	−	1	1	−	−	−	−	−	−
HAROLD	−	−	−	−	−	−	−	1	1
HAS	1	−	1	−	−	−	−	−	−
HAT	−	1	1	−	−	−	−	−	−
HAT,MAN	1	−	1	−	−	−	−	−	−
HATE	−	−	−	−	1	1	−	−	−
HAW	−	−	−	−	−	−	1	−	1
HE	5	6	11	8	7	15	14	9	23
HE IS	−	−	−	−	1	1	−	−	−
HE IS DOING SOMETHING	−	1	1	−	−	−	−	−	−
HEAR	1	−	1	−	−	−	−	−	−
HEN	1	2	3	−	1	1	−	1	1
HER	10	27	37	48	77	125	70	77	147
HERE	−	3	3	−	−	−	−	−	−
HIGH	1	−	1	−	−	−	−	−	−
HILL	2	−	2	−	−	−	−	−	−
HIM LIKES ME	1	−	1	−	−	−	−	−	−
HIMSELF	−	−	−	1	−	1	−	1	1
HIN	−	1	1	−	−	−	−	−	−
HINT	−	−	−	−	1	1	−	−	−
HIS	−	2	2	2	2	4	1	1	2
HOME	−	1	1	−	−	−	−	−	−
HORSE	1	−	1	−	−	−	−	−	−
HUNDRED	1	−	1	−	−	−	−	−	−
I	1	3	4	−	−	−	−	−	−
IF YOU HAD LONG PANTS THEN YOU COULD GO.	−	1	1	−	−	−	−	−	−
IN	−	−	−	1	−	1	−	−	−
IN DRESS (LIKE HEM)	−	1	1	−	−	−	−	−	−
INDIAN DANCE	1	−	1	−	−	−	−	−	−
INSECT	−	−	−	1	−	1	−	−	−
IS	1	2	3	−	−	−	−	1	1
IS HAPPY	1	−	1	−	−	−	−	−	−
JACK	1	−	1	1	−	1	−	−	−
JIM	1	−	1	−	−	−	−	−	−
KID	−	1	1	1	−	1	1	−	1

RESPONSE WORD	1ST			3RD			5TH		
	M	F	T	M	F	T	M	F	T

37.   HIM

RESPONSE WORD	M	F	T	M	F	T	M	F	T
KIM	1	1	2	1	–	1	–	–	–
KIN	1	2	3	–	–	–	–	–	–
LATE	1	–	1	–	–	–	–	–	–
LIGHT	1	1	2	–	–	–	–	–	–
LIKE A HILL	–	1	1	–	–	–	–	–	–
LIM	–	1	1	–	–	–	–	–	–
LIMB	1	–	1	1	–	1	–	–	–
LITTLE	1	–	1	–	–	–	–	–	–
LOOK	1	–	1	–	–	–	–	–	–
LYNN	–	1	1	–	–	–	–	–	–
MALE	–	–	–	–	–	–	1	–	1
MAN	5	1	6	6	2	8	3	6	9
ME	6	4	10	12	4	16	5	–	5
MEN	–	–	–	1	–	1	–	–	–
MEND	1	–	1	–	–	–	–	–	–
MIDGET	1	–	1	–	–	–	–	–	–
MIN	2	–	2	–	–	–	–	–	–
MINE	–	–	–	1	–	1	–	–	–
MONKEY	–	–	–	–	1	1	–	–	–
NEEDLE	–	–	–	–	1	1	–	–	–
NIM	–	1	1	–	–	–	–	–	–
NOBODY	1	–	1	–	–	–	–	–	–
NOT HIM	2	–	2	–	–	–	–	–	–
NOW	2	–	2	–	–	–	–	–	–
NUMBER	1	–	1	–	–	–	–	–	–
ORANGE	–	1	1	–	–	–	–	–	–
OUT	1	–	1	–	–	–	–	–	–
PANTS	1	–	1	–	–	–	–	–	–
PAPER	–	–	–	1	–	1	–	–	–
PARACHUTE	1	–	1	–	–	–	–	–	–
PERSON	–	–	–	2	–	2	2	–	2
PIG	1	–	1	–	–	–	–	–	–
PIN	2	–	2	–	–	–	–	–	–
PLAYS	–	1	1	–	–	–	–	–	–
PLEASE	1	–	1	–	–	–	–	–	–
POCKETBOOK	1	–	1	–	–	–	–	–	–
RED	–	1	1	–	–	–	–	–	–
RING	1	–	1	–	–	–	–	–	–
ROAD	1	–	1	–	–	–	–	–	–
RUN	–	1	1	–	–	–	–	–	–
RUNNING	–	–	–	–	1	1	–	–	–
SAFETY	–	1	1	–	–	–	–	–	–
SANG	1	–	1	–	–	–	–	–	–
SAW	1	–	1	–	–	–	–	–	–
SEE	–	1	1	–	–	–	–	1	1
SEE HIM	–	1	1	–	–	–	–	–	–
SEW	–	2	2	–	–	–	–	–	–
SHE	5	12	17	17	14	31	5	7	12
SHIRT	–	2	2	–	–	–	–	–	–
SHOE	–	1	1	–	–	–	–	–	–
SHOES	1	–	1	–	–	–	–	–	–
SIM	1	–	1	–	–	–	–	–	–
SING	2	2	4	–	–	–	–	1	1
SKIN	1	–	1	–	–	–	–	–	–
SKIRT	–	1	1	–	2	2	–	1	1
SLOW	–	1	1	–	–	–	–	–	–
SO	1	1	2	–	–	–	–	–	–
SOMEBODY	–	–	–	1	–	1	–	–	–
SOMETHING	–	1	1	–	–	–	–	–	–
SONG	2	–	2	1	3	4	2	3	5
STAND	1	–	1	–	–	–	–	1	1
STEM	–	1	1	–	–	–	–	–	–
STOP	1	–	1	–	–	–	–	–	–
SWING	–	1	1	–	–	–	–	–	–
TALL	–	–	–	1	–	1	–	–	–
TELEPHONE POLE	1	–	1	–	–	–	–	–	–
THAT BOY	–	1	1	–	–	–	–	–	–
THE CLOTHES	1	–	1	–	–	–	–	–	–
THEM	3	–	3	8	2	10	2	1	3
THEN	–	–	–	–	–	–	1	–	1
THEY	–	1	1	–	–	–	1	2	3
THINK	–	–	–	–	1	1	–	–	–

RESPONSE WORD	1ST M	F	T	3RD M	F	T	5TH M	F	T

37. HIM

RESPONSE WORD	1ST M	F	T	3RD M	F	T	5TH M	F	T
TIM	1	3	4	–	–	–	–	–	–
UNCLE	–	–	–	–	1	1	–	–	–
UP	1	–	1	–	–	–	–	–	–
US	2	1	3	–	2	2	6	–	6
VIM	–	1	1	–	–	–	–	–	–
WALL	1	1	2	–	–	–	–	–	–
WANT	1	–	1	–	–	–	–	–	–
WANT TO	–	–	–	1	–	1	–	–	–
WAS	1	–	1	–	–	–	–	–	–
WE	–	–	–	–	1	1	–	–	–
WHAT	1	–	1	–	–	–	–	–	–
WHEN YOU'RE HEMMING SOMETHING	1	–	1	–	–	–	–	–	–
WHENEVER A HEN IS FAT	–	1	1	–	–	–	–	–	–
WHY	–	1	1	–	–	–	–	–	–
WILL	1	–	1	–	–	–	–	–	–
WIN	1	–	1	–	–	–	–	–	–
WIND	–	1	1	–	–	–	–	–	–
WINDOW	1	–	1	–	–	–	–	–	–
WIRE	1	–	1	–	–	–	–	–	–
WOMAN	–	–	–	1	–	1	–	–	–
WORM	1	–	1	–	–	–	–	–	–
YOU	3	1	4	6	1	7	3	1	4

38. INQUIRE

RESPONSE WORD	1ST M	F	T	3RD M	F	T	5TH M	F	T
A	–	–	–	–	–	–	1	–	1
ABILITY	–	–	–	–	–	–	1	–	1
ABLE	–	–	–	–	–	–	–	1	1
ABOUT	–	–	–	–	1	1	–	1	1
ACQUIRE	–	–	–	–	1	1	1	–	1
ADD	–	–	–	–	–	–	1	–	1
ADJUST	–	–	–	–	–	–	1	–	1
ADMIRE	–	1	1	–	–	–	–	–	–
ADULT	–	–	–	1	–	1	–	–	–
ADVISE	–	–	–	–	–	–	–	1	1
AGAIN	–	1	1	–	–	–	–	1	1
AIRPLANE	1	–	1	1	–	1	–	–	–
ALL	–	–	–	–	–	–	1	1	2
ALOT	–	–	–	–	–	–	–	1	1
AND	–	–	–	–	1	1	–	–	–
ANIMAL	–	–	–	1	–	1	–	–	–
ANSWER	–	–	–	–	–	–	1	1	2
ANYTHING	–	–	–	–	–	–	1	–	1
APPLICATION	–	–	–	1	–	1	1	–	1
AQUARIUM	1	–	1	–	–	–	–	–	–
ASK	–	–	–	1	2	3	17	19	36
ASK ABOUT	–	–	–	–	–	–	1	–	1
ASK IT	–	–	–	–	–	–	–	1	1
AUDITORIUM	1	–	1	–	1	1	–	–	–
AUTOMATIC	–	–	–	1	–	1	–	–	–
BALL	1	–	1	–	–	–	–	–	–
BAND	–	1	1	–	2	2	–	–	–
BANJO	–	1	1	–	–	–	–	–	–
BASEBALL	–	–	–	–	–	–	1	–	1
BE QUIET	1	1	2	1	–	1	–	–	–
BE QUIET WHEN YOUR BABYS ASLEEP	–	1	1	–	–	–	–	–	–
BED	1	–	1	–	–	–	–	–	–
BEDROOM	1	–	1	–	–	–	–	–	–
BELLS	–	–	–	1	–	1	–	–	–
BLACK	1	–	1	–	–	–	–	–	–
BLUE	–	–	–	1	1	2	–	–	–
BOAT	–	–	–	1	–	1	–	–	–
BOOK	–	–	–	2	2	4	1	–	1
BOOKCASE	1	–	1	–	–	–	–	–	–
BORED	–	–	–	–	1	1	–	–	–
BOTTOM	–	–	–	1	–	1	–	–	–
BOYS	1	–	1	–	–	–	–	–	–
BRICK	1	–	1	–	–	–	–	–	–
BROWN	–	1	1	–	–	–	–	–	–

RESPONSE WORD	1ST M	1ST F	1ST T	3RD M	3RD F	3RD T	5TH M	5TH F	5TH T

38.   INQUIRE

RESPONSE WORD	1ST M	1ST F	1ST T	3RD M	3RD F	3RD T	5TH M	5TH F	5TH T
BUCKET	1	–	1	–	–	–	–	–	–
BUG	1	–	1	–	–	–	–	–	–
BUILD	–	–	–	1	–	1	–	–	–
BUILDING	1	–	1	–	–	–	–	–	–
BUN	1	–	1	–	–	–	–	–	–
BUTTON	–	1	1	–	1	1	–	–	–
BUY	–	–	–	1	–	1	–	–	–
BUYER	1	–	1	–	–	–	–	–	–
CALL	1	1	2	–	–	–	–	–	–
CAN	1	1	2	–	–	–	–	–	–
CAPABLE	–	–	–	–	–	–	–	1	1
CAR	1	–	1	–	–	–	–	–	–
CAT	–	–	–	–	–	–	–	1	1
CAUGHT	–	–	–	–	1	1	–	–	–
CHAIR	–	–	–	–	1	1	–	–	–
CHOIR	2	4	6	2	2	4	1	5	6
CHOIR-MAN	1	–	1	–	–	–	–	–	–
CHORUS	–	–	–	–	1	1	–	1	1
CHURCH	4	8	12	3	4	7	–	–	–
CHURCH CHOIR	–	1	1	–	–	–	–	–	–
CLASS	1	–	1	–	–	–	–	–	–
CLOCK	–	–	–	–	1	1	–	–	–
CLOWN	–	–	–	–	1	1	–	–	–
CLUB	–	–	–	–	–	–	1	–	1
COARSE	–	–	–	–	–	–	–	1	1
COAT	–	1	1	–	–	–	–	–	–
COLOR	–	1	1	–	–	–	–	–	–
COME	1	–	1	–	–	–	–	1	1
CONDUCT	–	–	–	–	–	–	1	–	1
CONTAINS	–	–	–	–	–	–	1	–	1
CORNER	–	1	1	–	–	–	–	–	–
CORSE	–	–	–	–	–	–	1	–	1
COURSE	–	–	–	–	–	–	–	1	1
CRADLE	–	1	1	–	–	–	–	–	–
CROWD	–	2	2	–	–	–	–	–	–
CRY-BABY	–	1	1	–	–	–	–	–	–
CUP	–	–	–	1	–	1	–	–	–
DANCE	–	–	–	–	1	1	–	–	–
DARK	–	–	–	–	1	1	–	–	–
DECIDE	–	–	–	–	2	2	–	–	–
DEE (SOMEBODYS NAME)	1	–	1	–	–	–	–	–	–
DEPUIRE	–	–	–	–	–	–	–	1	1
DESIRE	–	–	–	–	–	–	1	–	1
DESK	–	1	1	–	–	–	–	–	–
DID NOT	–	–	–	1	–	1	–	–	–
DIE	–	1	1	–	–	–	–	–	–
DISCOVER	–	–	–	–	1	1	–	–	–
DISCUSS	–	–	–	–	–	–	–	1	1
DISINQUIRE	–	–	–	2	–	2	1	–	1
DISQUIRE	–	–	–	–	–	–	1	–	1
DO	–	–	–	1	1	2	5	5	10
DO NOT INQUIRE	1	–	1	–	–	–	–	–	–
DO SOMETHING	–	–	–	–	–	–	–	3	3
DO TO	–	–	–	–	–	–	1	–	1
DOCTOR	–	1	1	–	–	–	–	–	–
DOG	–	–	–	–	–	–	2	–	2
DOING	–	–	–	–	–	–	1	–	1
DOING SOMETHING	–	–	–	–	–	–	–	1	1
DONE	–	–	–	–	–	–	–	1	1
DONT	–	–	–	–	1	1	–	–	–
DONT INQUIRE	–	–	–	1	–	1	–	–	–
DONT KNOW WHAT IT MEANS	–	–	–	–	1	1	–	–	–
DOOR	2	–	2	1	1	2	–	–	–
DOWN	1	–	1	1	–	1	–	1	1
DRESS	–	1	1	–	–	–	–	–	–
EGG	–	1	1	–	–	–	–	–	–
ELECTRIC	–	1	1	–	–	–	–	–	–
ELECTRICITY	1	–	1	–	–	–	–	–	–
ENTIRE	1	–	1	–	–	–	–	–	–
ENVIRONMENT	–	–	–	–	–	–	1	–	1
EVERYTHING	–	–	–	–	–	–	–	1	1
EXAMINE	1	–	1	–	–	–	–	1	1

RESPONSE WORD	1ST M	F	T	3RD M	F	T	5TH M	F	T

38.   INQUIRE

RESPONSE WORD	1ST M	F	T	3RD M	F	T	5TH M	F	T
EXCUSE	–	–	–	–	–	–	1	–	1
EXPLAIN	–	–	–	2	–	2	–	–	–
FACE	–	–	–	–	1	1	–	–	–
FAIL	–	–	–	–	–	–	1	–	1
FAST	–	2	2	–	1	1	1	–	1
FASTER	1	–	1	–	–	–	–	–	–
FAT	–	–	–	1	–	1	–	–	–
FATHER	–	–	–	–	1	1	–	–	–
FIN	1	–	1	–	–	–	–	–	–
FIND	–	–	–	–	–	–	2	–	2
FIRE	1	2	3	2	–	2	–	–	–
FIRES COULD BE DANGEROUS	–	1	1	–	–	–	–	–	–
FIRST	–	–	–	–	1	1	–	–	–
FISH	–	–	–	–	–	–	1	1	2
FLAT	–	–	–	–	–	–	1	–	1
FLOOR	3	1	4	–	–	–	–	–	–
FLOWER	–	–	–	–	–	–	1	–	1
FLY	–	–	–	1	–	1	–	–	–
FOOD	–	–	–	1	–	1	–	–	–
GARDEN	–	1	1	–	–	–	–	–	–
GAVE	–	–	–	1	–	1	–	–	–
GET	1	–	1	–	–	–	–	–	–
GIRL	–	1	1	–	–	–	–	–	–
GIVE	–	–	–	–	–	–	–	1	1
GLASSES	–	1	1	–	–	–	–	–	–
GO	–	1	1	–	–	–	–	1	1
GO DOWN, SALLY	–	1	1	–	–	–	–	–	–
GO IN	1	–	1	–	–	–	–	–	–
GOOD	–	2	2	–	1	1	1	1	2
GREEN	–	–	–	1	–	1	–	–	–
HAIR	–	–	–	–	1	1	–	–	–
HAPPY	1	–	1	–	–	–	1	–	1
HAT	–	1	1	–	–	–	–	–	–
HAVE	–	–	–	–	–	–	–	2	2
HEAD	–	–	–	1	–	1	–	–	–
HEALTH	–	–	–	–	–	–	1	–	1
HELP	–	–	–	–	–	–	1	–	1
HER	–	–	–	–	1	1	–	–	–
HERT	–	–	–	–	–	–	1	–	1
HIGH	–	2	2	–	–	–	–	–	–
HIGHER	1	–	1	–	–	–	–	–	–
HILL	–	–	–	–	1	1	–	–	–
HIM	–	1	1	–	–	–	–	–	–
HIRE	1	–	1	–	–	–	–	–	–
HIS	–	–	–	–	–	–	1	–	1
HOLD	–	–	–	–	–	–	1	–	1
HOUSE	–	–	–	–	1	1	–	–	–
HURTS	1	–	1	–	–	–	–	–	–
HYMN	–	–	–	–	1	1	–	–	–
I DONT KNOW	–	–	–	1	1	2	1	1	2
I WANT TO GO TO CHOIR	–	1	1	–	–	–	–	–	–
ICE CREAM	1	–	1	–	–	–	–	–	–
IN	–	–	–	4	3	7	1	1	2
IN CHURCH	–	1	1	1	–	1	–	–	–
IN MIRE	–	–	–	1	–	1	–	–	–
IN THE CHOIR IN CHURCH	–	1	1	–	–	–	–	–	–
IN THE CHURCH	–	1	1	–	–	–	–	–	–
IN THE HOUSE	–	1	1	–	–	–	–	–	–
IN THE STORE	1	–	1	–	–	–	–	–	–
IN-BIRE	–	–	–	1	–	1	–	–	–
INBIER	–	1	1	–	–	–	–	–	–
INCLUDE	–	–	–	–	–	–	1	–	1
INDICATE	–	–	–	1	–	1	–	–	–
INDIRE	–	1	1	–	–	–	–	–	–
INGREDIENTS	–	–	–	1	–	1	–	–	–
INHERIT	–	–	–	–	–	–	1	–	1
INQUIET	–	–	–	1	–	1	–	–	–
INQUIREATE	–	–	–	–	1	1	–	–	–
INQUIREMENT	–	–	–	–	–	–	–	1	1
INQUIRY	–	–	–	–	–	–	1	1	2
INSIRE	–	1	1	–	–	–	–	–	–
INSIST	–	–	–	–	–	–	1	–	1

RESPONSE WORD	1ST M	F	T	3RD M	F	T	5TH M	F	T

38. INQUIRE

RESPONSE WORD	1ST M	F	T	3RD M	F	T	5TH M	F	T
INSOUR	–	–	–	1	–	1	–	–	–
INSTEAD	–	–	–	–	1	1	–	–	–
INSTRUCTIONS	–	–	–	–	–	–	1	–	1
INSTRUMENTS	–	1	1	–	–	–	–	–	–
INTEREST	–	–	–	–	1	1	–	–	–
INTO	1	–	1	1	–	1	–	–	–
INTRODUCE	–	–	–	–	–	–	1	–	1
INVERNESY	–	1	1	–	–	–	–	–	–
INVITED	–	–	–	–	1	1	–	–	–
IS IT	–	–	–	1	–	1	–	–	–
ISNT	–	–	–	1	–	1	–	–	–
IT	–	1	1	–	–	–	–	2	2
JOB	–	–	–	–	–	–	–	2	2
JOIN	–	–	–	2	1	3	–	–	–
JOINED	–	–	–	–	–	–	1	–	1
JOY	–	–	–	–	–	–	1	–	1
JUMP	–	–	–	–	1	1	–	–	–
KEY	–	1	1	–	–	–	–	–	–
KILL	–	–	–	–	–	–	1	–	1
KNOW	–	–	–	1	–	1	1	–	1
LAID	–	1	1	–	–	–	–	–	–
LAMP	1	–	1	–	–	–	–	–	–
LARGE	–	–	–	–	–	–	1	–	1
LAUGH	–	–	–	–	1	1	–	–	–
LAWN MOWER	–	1	1	–	–	–	–	–	–
LEARN	–	–	–	–	–	–	1	–	1
LET	–	–	–	–	–	–	–	1	1
LETS GO SWIMMING	–	1	1	–	–	–	–	–	–
LIAR	–	2	2	–	–	–	–	–	–
LIER	–	–	–	–	–	–	–	1	1
LIGHT	1	1	2	–	–	–	–	–	–
LIGHTS	1	–	1	–	–	–	–	–	–
LIKE	–	–	–	–	1	1	–	–	–
LISTEN	–	–	–	–	–	–	1	–	1
LOCOMOTIVE	–	–	–	1	–	1	–	–	–
LOUD	–	2	2	–	1	1	–	–	–
LOUDER	1	–	1	–	–	–	–	–	–
LOUDLY	–	–	–	–	1	1	–	–	–
LOVELY	–	1	1	–	–	–	–	–	–
MAKE	–	–	–	–	–	–	–	1	1
MANY	–	–	–	1	–	1	–	–	–
MAPS	–	–	–	1	–	1	–	–	–
MAY	–	–	–	–	–	–	1	–	1
MAYBE	1	–	1	–	–	–	–	–	–
ME	2	–	2	3	–	3	–	–	–
ME AND MY SISTER	–	1	1	–	–	–	–	–	–
MEAN	–	–	–	–	–	–	1	–	1
MENTION	–	–	–	–	–	–	–	1	1
MILK	1	–	1	–	–	–	–	–	–
MIRE	2	–	2	–	–	–	–	–	–
MIRROR	1	–	1	–	–	–	–	–	–
MOM	–	–	–	–	–	–	–	1	1
MONEY	–	–	–	–	–	–	1	–	1
MORE	–	–	–	1	–	1	–	–	–
MOUNTAIN	–	1	1	–	–	–	–	–	–
MOVE	–	–	–	–	–	–	–	1	1
MUSIC	1	–	1	6	2	8	1	1	2
MY	1	–	1	–	–	–	–	–	–
NEED	–	–	–	–	2	2	–	–	–
NEXT	–	–	–	–	1	1	–	–	–
NO	1	1	2	–	–	–	–	–	–
NO RESPONSE	–	–	–	1	1	2	–	1	1
NOQUIRE	–	–	–	–	1	1	–	–	–
NOSY	–	–	–	–	–	–	–	1	1
NOT INQUIRE	2	–	2	6	2	8	4	–	4
NOT WANTED	–	–	–	–	–	–	1	–	1
NOTHING	–	1	1	–	–	–	1	–	1
NOW	–	2	2	–	–	–	–	–	–
OBEY	–	–	–	1	1	2	1	–	1
OCEAN	–	1	1	–	–	–	–	–	–
ONE	–	–	–	1	–	1	–	–	–
ORANGE	1	–	1	–	–	–	–	–	–

RESPONSE WORD	1ST M	F	T	3RD M	F	T	5TH M	F	T

38. INQUIRE

RESPONSE WORD	1ST M	F	T	3RD M	F	T	5TH M	F	T
ORCHESTRA	–	1	1	–	1	1	–	–	–
OUT	1	1	2	1	–	1	–	–	–
OUT A QUIRE	–	1	1	–	–	–	–	–	–
OUT OF CHOIR	–	1	1	1	–	1	–	–	–
OUTQUIRE	1	–	1	1	1	2	–	–	–
OUTSIDE	–	–	–	–	–	–	1	–	1
PAD	–	–	–	–	1	1	–	–	–
PAPER	1	–	1	–	–	–	1	–	1
PEACE	–	1	1	–	–	–	–	–	–
PENCIL	–	3	3	–	–	–	–	–	–
PEOPLE	1	–	1	1	–	1	–	2	2
PERSON	–	–	–	–	–	–	1	–	1
PERSPIRATION	–	–	–	1	–	1	–	–	–
PHONE	–	–	–	–	1	1	–	–	–
PICTURE	1	–	1	–	–	–	–	–	–
PIN	–	–	–	–	–	–	–	1	1
PIRE	1	1	2	–	–	–	–	–	–
PLEASANT	–	–	–	–	–	–	–	1	1
PLEASE	–	1	1	–	–	–	–	–	–
PLIERS	1	–	1	–	–	–	–	–	–
PLUG	1	–	1	–	–	–	–	–	–
PLUG IN THE CORD	1	–	1	–	–	–	–	–	–
POLICE	1	–	1	–	–	–	–	–	–
POSSIBLE	–	–	–	–	–	–	–	1	1
PRACTICE	–	1	1	–	–	–	–	–	–
PRIEST	1	–	1	–	–	–	–	–	–
PROD	–	–	–	–	–	–	1	–	1
PURSE	–	1	1	–	–	–	–	–	–
QUARRY	–	–	–	–	–	–	–	1	1
QUEER	–	–	–	–	1	1	–	1	1
QUIET	12	5	17	6	6	12	1	1	2
QUIETED	1	–	1	–	–	–	–	–	–
QUIRE	1	1	2	1	1	2	2	3	5
QUIREY	–	–	–	–	–	–	1	–	1
QUIT	–	–	–	–	–	–	1	1	1
RABBIT	–	–	–	–	–	–	1	–	1
REAL QUIET	1	–	1	–	–	–	–	–	–
REASON	–	–	–	–	1	1	–	1	1
RECALL	–	–	–	–	–	–	1	–	1
RECEIVE	–	–	–	1	–	1	–	–	–
RED	1	–	1	–	–	–	–	–	–
REMOVE	–	–	–	–	1	1	–	–	–
REPLY	–	–	–	–	–	–	–	3	3
REQUEST	–	–	–	–	–	–	–	3	3
REQUIRE	–	–	–	1	–	1	2	4	6
RESERVE	–	–	–	–	–	–	1	–	1
RESPONSIBLE	–	–	–	–	–	–	1	–	1
RETIRE	–	–	–	1	–	1	–	–	–
RETURN	–	–	–	–	–	–	1	–	1
RIGHT	–	–	–	–	1	1	–	–	–
ROCKS	1	–	1	–	–	–	–	–	–
ROUND	–	1	1	–	–	–	–	–	–
RUBBER	–	1	1	–	–	–	–	–	–
RULES	–	–	–	1	–	1	–	–	–
RUN	–	–	–	1	–	1	–	–	–
SAID	–	–	–	–	–	–	1	–	1
SAME	–	–	–	–	–	–	–	1	1
SAY	–	–	–	1	–	1	1	2	3
SCHOOL	–	1	1	–	1	1	–	1	1
SCIENCE	–	–	–	–	1	1	–	–	–
SEE	1	1	2	–	1	1	–	1	1
SEEM	–	1	1	–	–	–	–	–	–
SENCE	–	–	–	–	–	–	–	1	1
SEND	–	1	1	–	–	–	–	–	–
SHOT	–	–	–	–	1	1	–	–	–
SHOW	–	–	–	–	–	–	1	–	1
SING	5	8	13	10	16	26	–	7	7
SINGER	–	–	–	–	1	1	–	–	–
SINGING	4	2	6	1	4	5	2	–	2
SINGING(CHOIR)	–	1	1	–	–	–	–	–	–
SIRE	2	–	2	1	–	1	–	–	–

RESPONSE WORD		1ST			3RD			5TH	
	M	F	T	M	F	T	M	F	T

38.   INQUIRE

RESPONSE WORD	M	F	T	M	F	T	M	F	T
SISTER	–	–	–	1	–	1	–	–	–
SIT	–	–	–	–	1	1	–	–	–
SKIN	–	1	1	–	–	–	–	–	–
SKIRE	1	–	1	–	–	–	–	–	–
SLEEP	–	1	1	–	–	–	–	–	–
SLEEPY	–	1	1	–	–	–	–	–	–
SLOW	1	1	2	–	–	–	1	–	1
SLOWLY	–	–	–	1	–	1	–	–	–
SO	–	–	–	–	–	–	1	–	1
SOFT	–	–	–	–	2	2	1	–	1
SOME	–	–	–	1	–	1	–	1	1
SOMETHING	1	–	1	2	3	5	2	–	2
SONG	–	1	1	1	2	3	1	–	1
SONGS	–	2	2	–	–	–	–	–	–
SOUND	1	–	1	–	1	1	–	–	–
SOUND ASLEEP	–	1	1	–	–	–	–	–	–
SPEAK	–	–	–	–	1	1	–	1	1
SPEECH	–	–	–	1	–	1	–	–	–
SPOT	–	1	1	–	–	–	–	–	–
SQUARE	–	–	–	–	1	1	–	–	–
STAGE	–	–	–	1	–	1	–	–	–
STEPS	–	–	–	1	–	1	–	–	–
STICK A WIRE	–	1	1	–	–	–	–	–	–
STOP	–	–	–	1	1	2	–	–	–
STUDIO	–	–	–	–	1	1	–	–	–
SUCH	–	–	–	–	–	–	–	1	1
SUGGEST	–	–	–	–	–	–	1	–	1
SWIM	–	–	–	–	1	1	–	–	–
TABLE	–	–	–	–	1	1	–	–	–
TAKE A JOB	–	–	–	–	–	–	–	1	1
TAKE THE RACKET AWAY	1	–	1	2	3	5	2	3	5
TALK	1	–	1	2	3	5	2	3	5
TALKED	–	–	–	1	–	1	1	–	1
TALKING	–	–	–	1	–	1	–	–	–
TALL	–	–	–	–	1	1	1	–	1
TEACHER	–	–	–	–	1	1	1	–	1
TELEPHONE	–	–	–	1	–	1	–	–	–
TELEVISION	1	–	1	–	–	–	–	–	–
TELL	–	–	–	–	1	1	5	7	12
TELL SOMETHING	–	–	–	–	–	–	1	–	1
THANK YOU	1	–	1	–	–	–	–	–	–
THAT	1	–	1	–	1	1	–	–	–
THE	–	–	–	–	–	–	–	1	1
THE BAND	–	–	–	1	–	1	–	–	–
THERE	1	–	1	1	–	1	–	–	–
THEY	–	–	–	–	1	1	–	–	–
THING	–	–	–	1	–	1	–	–	–
THINK	–	–	–	1	–	1	–	1	1
THINKING	1	–	1	–	–	–	–	–	–
THOSE	–	–	–	–	–	–	1	–	1
THOUGH	–	–	–	–	–	–	1	–	1
THOUGHT	–	–	–	–	–	–	1	–	1
TIME	–	–	–	–	1	1	–	–	–
TIRED	–	1	1	–	–	–	–	–	–
TO	1	–	1	–	–	–	–	–	–
TO BE QUIET	–	–	–	1	–	1	–	–	–
TO DO	–	–	–	–	–	–	1	1	2
TO DO IT	–	–	–	–	–	–	–	1	1
TO HAVE	–	–	–	–	–	–	–	1	1
TO INQUIRE	–	–	–	1	–	1	–	–	–
TO QUESTION	–	–	–	–	–	–	–	1	1
TOGETHER	–	–	–	1	–	1	–	1	1
TOMORROW	–	–	–	–	1	1	–	–	–
TRUCK	2	–	2	–	–	–	–	–	–
TRUMPETS	1	–	1	–	–	–	–	–	–
TV	–	1	1	–	–	–	–	–	–
UNACQUIRE	–	–	–	–	–	–	1	–	1
UNDER	–	–	–	–	–	–	–	1	1
UNDERSTAND	–	–	–	–	–	–	1	–	1
UNINQUIRE	1	–	1	–	–	–	2	–	2
UNQUIRE	2	–	2	2	1	3	2	3	5
UP	2	–	2	1	–	1	1	–	1

RESPONSE WORD	1ST M	F	T	3RD M	F	T	5TH M	F	T

38. INQUIRE

RESPONSE WORD	M	F	T	M	F	T	M	F	T
UP CHUCK	–	–	–	1	–	1	–	–	–
WALL	–	1	1	–	–	–	–	–	–
WANT	–	–	–	1	–	1	–	1	1
WARD	–	–	–	–	–	–	–	1	1
WATER	1	1	2	–	–	–	–	–	–
WE SING	1	–	1	–	–	–	–	–	–
WEB	1	–	1	–	–	–	–	–	–
WHAT	–	–	–	–	–	–	1	–	1
WHEEL	1	–	1	–	–	–	–	–	–
WHEN YOURE QUIET	1	–	1	–	–	–	–	–	–
WHERE	–	–	–	–	–	–	1	–	1
WHY IS IT	–	–	–	–	1	1	–	–	–
WIRE	4	6	10	2	1	3	–	–	–
WIRES	1	1	2	–	–	–	–	–	–
WISE	–	1	1	–	–	–	–	–	–
WITH A QUIRE	1	–	1	–	–	–	–	–	–
WITHIN	–	–	–	1	–	1	1	–	1
WOODS	1	–	1	–	–	–	–	–	–
WORD	–	–	–	1	–	1	–	–	–
WORDS	–	–	–	–	1	1	–	–	–
WORK	–	2	2	–	2	2	–	–	–
WORKING	–	–	–	1	–	1	–	–	–
YELLOW	–	–	–	1	–	1	–	–	–
YES	–	–	–	–	–	–	–	1	1
YOU	–	–	–	–	3	3	1	1	2
YOU INQUIRE SOMETHING	–	–	–	–	–	–	–	1	1
YOUR WORK	–	–	–	1	–	1	–	–	–

39. INSECT

RESPONSE WORD	M	F	T	M	F	T	M	F	T
A BEE	–	–	–	1	–	1	–	–	–
A BUG	–	1	1	1	–	1	–	–	–
A CREATURE	–	–	–	–	–	–	–	1	1
A FLY	–	–	–	–	–	–	1	–	1
A HOUSE	1	–	1	–	–	–	–	–	–
A SPIDER	1	–	1	–	–	–	–	–	–
AIR LINER	1	–	1	–	–	–	–	–	–
AMELIA	1	–	1	–	–	–	–	–	–
AN	–	1	1	–	–	–	1	–	1
AN ANIMAL	–	–	–	–	–	–	1	–	1
ANIMAL	–	3	3	11	10	21	11	12	23
ANMLY	–	–	–	–	–	–	1	–	1
ANT	4	2	6	6	5	11	9	8	17
AWAY	–	–	–	–	1	1	–	–	–
BABY	1	–	1	–	–	–	–	–	–
BAD	2	2	4	–	–	–	–	–	–
BED	–	1	1	–	–	–	–	–	–
BEE	10	3	13	4	2	6	4	9	13
BEETLE	–	–	–	1	–	1	1	1	2
BIG	1	1	2	–	1	1	–	–	–
BILLY	–	–	–	–	–	–	1	–	1
BIRD	–	1	1	–	2	2	2	2	4
BIRDS	–	1	1	–	–	–	–	1	1
BITE	3	2	5	1	2	3	–	–	–
BITES	1	–	1	–	–	–	–	–	–
BITS	–	1	1	–	–	–	–	–	–
BLACK WIDOW	–	–	–	–	–	–	1	–	1
BLUE	2	–	2	–	–	–	–	–	–
BOARD	1	–	1	–	–	–	–	–	–
BODY	–	–	–	–	1	1	–	–	–
BOG	–	–	–	1	–	1	–	–	–
BRINSECT	1	–	1	–	–	–	–	–	–
BUG	30	31	61	63	69	132	74	68	142
BUGS	2	–	2	1	3	4	1	1	2
BUTTERFLY	1	–	1	6	3	9	4	5	9
BUY	–	–	–	–	1	1	1	–	1
BUZZ	1	1	2	–	–	–	–	–	–
CAN	–	1	1	–	–	–	–	–	–
CANT CATCH	–	1	1	–	–	–	–	–	–
CAR	1	–	1	–	–	–	–	–	–
CARPET	1	–	1	–	–	–	–	–	–

39. INSECT

RESPONSE WORD	1ST M	1ST F	1ST T	3RD M	3RD F	3RD T	5TH M	5TH F	5TH T
CAT	2	-	2	-	-	-	-	-	-
CATERPILLAR	-	-	-	-	1	1	-	-	-
CHAIR	-	-	-	1	-	1	-	-	-
COCOON	-	-	-	-	-	-	1	-	1
COLD	-	-	-	1	-	1	-	-	-
COMING IN	1	-	1	1	-	1	-	-	-
COULD	-	-	-	1	-	1	-	-	-
CRAWL	1	-	1	-	-	-	-	-	-
CREATURE	-	-	-	-	-	-	2	-	2
DEAD	-	-	-	1	-	1	-	-	-
DESK	2	1	3	-	-	-	-	-	-
DISSECT	-	-	-	-	1	1	-	-	-
DO NOT CRY	-	1	1	-	-	-	-	-	-
DOG	-	-	-	1	-	1	-	-	-
DONT KNOW	-	1	1	-	-	-	-	-	-
DOOR	-	1	1	-	-	-	-	-	-
DOORKNOB	1	-	1	-	-	-	-	-	-
DOORS	-	1	1	-	-	-	-	-	-
DRAW A BUG	1	-	1	-	-	-	-	-	-
DRESS	-	1	1	-	-	-	-	-	-
EAT	-	1	1	-	1	1	-	-	-
ELEPHANT	-	1	1	1	-	1	-	-	-
ERASER	-	1	1	-	-	-	-	-	-
EYE	-	2	2	-	-	-	-	-	-
FAT	-	1	1	-	-	-	-	-	-
FATHER	-	-	-	-	1	1	-	-	-
FEATHER	-	1	1	-	-	-	-	-	-
FISH	3	-	3	1	-	1	-	-	-
FLEE	-	-	-	-	-	-	-	1	1
FLOWER	-	-	-	-	1	1	1	-	1
FLY	10	5	15	15	7	22	7	12	19
FLYSWATTER	1	-	1	-	-	-	-	-	-
FOOD	-	-	-	-	-	-	-	1	1
FOR	-	1	1	-	-	-	-	-	-
FRESH	1	-	1	-	-	-	-	-	-
GLASS	1	-	1	-	-	-	-	-	-
GLASSES	-	2	2	-	-	-	-	-	-
GO	-	1	1	-	-	-	-	-	-
GOING IN	1	-	1	-	-	-	-	-	-
GOOD	1	2	3	-	-	-	-	-	-
GRASSHOPPER	2	1	3	-	-	-	1	-	1
HAIR	-	1	1	-	-	-	-	-	-
HAPPY	1	-	1	-	-	-	-	-	-
HARMFUL	-	-	-	1	-	1	-	-	-
HAT	2	-	2	-	-	-	-	-	-
HEAT	-	-	-	-	-	-	-	1	1
HIMSEF	-	-	-	-	-	-	1	-	1
HORSE	1	-	1	-	-	-	-	-	-
HOUR	1	-	1	-	-	-	-	-	-
HOUSE	1	1	2	-	-	-	-	-	-
HOW	1	-	1	-	-	-	-	-	-
I	-	-	-	-	-	-	1	-	1
ICE CREAM	1	-	1	-	-	-	-	-	-
IMPEK	-	-	-	1	-	1	-	-	-
IN	-	5	5	2	1	3	1	1	2
IN THIRD	1	-	1	-	-	-	-	-	-
INDECK	-	1	1	-	-	-	-	-	-
INFECT	-	1	1	-	-	-	-	-	-
INSECTS	-	-	-	1	-	1	-	-	-
INSIDE	-	-	-	-	1	1	-	-	-
JET	1	-	1	-	-	-	-	-	-
KATYDID	-	-	-	-	-	-	1	-	1
KILL	-	-	-	1	-	1	-	-	-
KIND	-	-	-	-	-	-	1	-	1
KLECT	1	-	1	-	-	-	-	-	-
LADYBUG	-	-	-	-	-	-	-	1	1
LEG	-	1	1	-	-	-	-	-	-
LET	-	1	1	-	-	-	-	-	-
LETS GO OUTSIDE AND CATCH FLIES	2	2	4	-	-	-	-	-	-
LIGHT	2	1	1	-	-	-	-	-	-
LION	-	1	1	-	-	-	-	-	-

39. INSECT

RESPONSE WORD	1ST M	1ST F	1ST T	3RD M	3RD F	3RD T	5TH M	5TH F	5TH T
LITTLE	1	–	1	–	1	1	1	–	1
LITTLE ANT	–	–	–	–	1	1	–	1	1
LIZARD	–	–	–	1	–	1	–	1	1
LOVE	–	–	–	–	–	–	–	1	1
MAMMAL	–	–	–	–	–	–	1	–	1
MAN	–	1	1	–	–	–	1	–	1
MINSECT	1	–	1	–	–	–	–	–	–
MOSQUITO	–	1	1	3	1	4	2	–	2
MOSQUITOS	–	–	–	1	–	1	–	–	–
MOTH	1	–	1	–	–	–	1	1	2
MOUSE	–	–	–	–	–	–	–	1	1
NEST	–	–	–	–	1	1	–	–	–
NET	–	–	–	–	–	–	–	1	1
NICE	–	1	1	–	–	–	–	–	–
NO	1	–	1	–	–	–	–	–	–
NOISE	–	–	–	–	1	1	–	–	–
NOT	–	1	1	–	–	–	–	–	–
NOT INSECT	–	–	–	1	–	1	–	–	–
NOTHING	–	1	1	–	–	–	–	1	1
NOW	1	1	2	–	–	–	–	–	–
NURSE	–	1	1	–	–	–	–	–	–
ONCE	–	–	–	–	1	1	–	–	–
ONE	1	–	1	–	–	–	–	–	–
OUT	–	2	2	–	–	–	–	–	–
OUT IN	–	–	–	1	–	1	–	–	–
OUTSECT	–	1	1	1	–	1	–	–	–
OUTSIDE	1	–	1	–	1	1	–	–	–
OW	–	–	–	–	1	1	–	–	–
PAPER	1	–	1	–	–	–	–	–	–
PECKED	1	–	1	–	–	–	–	–	–
PEOPLE	–	–	–	–	–	–	1	–	1
PERSON	–	–	–	2	–	2	–	–	–
PET	–	1	1	–	–	–	–	–	–
PICK	–	1	1	–	–	–	–	–	–
PICTURE	–	1	1	–	–	–	–	–	–
PIGGY	1	–	1	–	–	–	–	–	–
PINSECT	–	1	1	–	–	–	–	–	–
PLAY	–	1	1	–	–	–	–	–	–
POCKET BOOK	–	1	1	–	–	–	–	–	–
PRIZE	–	1	1	–	–	–	–	–	–
PURPLE	–	1	1	–	–	–	–	–	–
RAID	1	–	1	–	–	–	–	–	–
REMEMBER	–	–	–	–	1	1	–	–	–
REMINDS ME OF WHEN YOURE SICK	1	–	1	–	–	–	–	–	–
REPTILE	–	–	–	–	1	1	–	–	–
RESECT	–	–	–	1	–	1	–	–	–
RIDSECTS	–	1	1	–	–	–	–	–	–
ROACH	–	–	–	–	–	–	1	–	1
ROACHES	–	–	–	1	–	1	–	–	–
ROUGH	–	1	1	–	–	–	–	–	–
SAID	–	–	–	–	1	1	–	–	–
SALT	1	–	1	–	–	–	–	–	–
SAME THING	1	–	1	–	–	–	–	–	–
SAP	1	–	1	–	–	–	–	–	–
SECT	1	–	1	–	1	1	–	1	1
SEE	–	1	1	–	–	–	–	–	–
SHOE	1	–	1	–	–	–	–	–	–
SICK	–	1	1	–	–	–	–	–	–
SIT DOWN	–	1	1	–	–	–	–	–	–
SMALL	–	–	–	–	2	2	–	–	–
SMOOTH	1	–	1	–	–	–	–	–	–
SNAKE	–	–	–	–	1	1	–	–	–
SOME	–	1	1	–	–	–	–	–	–
SOMEONE	–	–	–	–	1	1	–	–	–
SOMETHING	–	–	–	–	–	–	–	1	1
SPDER	–	–	–	–	–	–	1	–	1
SPIDER	2	5	7	–	4	4	2	4	6
SPRAY	2	–	2	–	–	–	–	–	–
SPRING	–	–	–	–	–	–	–	1	1
SQUARE	–	1	1	–	–	–	–	–	–

RESPONSE WORD	1ST M	F	T	3RD M	F	T	5TH M	F	T

39.   INSECT

RESPONSE WORD	1ST M	F	T	3RD M	F	T	5TH M	F	T
SQUIRREL	−	−	−	1	−	1	−	−	−
STACK YOUR THINGS WHEN YOURE GETTING RE	−	1	1	−	−	−	−	−	−
STICK	−	−	−	1	−	1	−	−	−
STORE	1	−	1	−	−	−	−	−	−
STRING	1	−	1	−	−	−	−	−	−
TABLE	1	−	1	−	−	−	−	−	−
TELL	−	1	1	−	−	−	−	1	1
TEMPERATURE	−	−	−	−	1	1	−	−	−
TERMITE	1	−	1	−	−	−	−	−	−
THREE	1	1	2	−	1	1	−	−	−
TOE	1	−	1	−	−	−	−	−	−
TREE	1	−	1	−	−	−	−	−	−
TRIANGLE	−	−	−	−	1	1	−	−	−
TUMMY ACHE	−	1	1	−	−	−	−	−	−
TV	−	1	1	−	−	−	−	−	−
UNTIL	−	−	−	−	1	1	−	−	−
UP	1	−	1	−	−	−	−	−	−
WALL	−	2	2	−	−	−	−	−	−
WASHING THE WINDOWS	−	1	1	−	−	−	−	−	−
WHEN YOU ARE IN SOMETHING	−	1	1	−	−	−	−	−	−
WHENEVER MOTHER IS MAD	−	1	1	−	−	−	−	−	−
WINDOW	−	3	3	−	−	−	−	−	−
WINDOWS	1	−	1	−	−	−	−	−	−
WINE	−	1	1	−	−	−	−	−	−
WITH	−	1	1	−	−	−	−	−	−
WORD	1	−	1	−	−	−	−	−	−
WORM	−	−	−	2	2	4	−	−	−
WRITE	−	−	−	−	1	1	−	−	−
YELLOW	1	1	2	−	−	−	−	−	−
YOU	−	1	1	1	−	1	−	−	−
YOU CATCH SOME GERMS FROM A BUG	−	1	1	−	−	−	−	−	−
YOURS	−	−	−	−	−	−	−	1	1

40.   INTO

RESPONSE WORD	1ST M	F	T	3RD M	F	T	5TH M	F	T
A	1	1	2	−	−	−	−	−	−
A CAR	1	−	1	−	−	−	−	−	−
A HOUSE	2	2	4	1	−	1	−	−	−
A PLANE	−	−	−	1	−	1	−	−	−
AGAIN	−	−	−	1	−	1	−	−	−
AIR	−	−	−	1	−	1	−	−	−
AND ONE	1	−	1	−	−	−	−	−	−
ANIMAL	−	−	−	−	−	−	−	1	1
AROUND	−	−	−	−	−	−	1	−	1
AWNING	1	−	1	−	−	−	−	−	−
BEAR	−	−	−	1	−	1	−	−	−
BED	−	−	−	−	−	−	−	1	1
BEENTO	−	1	1	−	−	−	−	−	−
BETWEEN	−	−	−	−	1	1	−	−	−
BIRD	1	−	1	−	−	−	−	−	−
BLEND	−	−	−	−	1	1	−	−	−
BLUE	−	1	1	−	−	−	−	−	−
BOAT	1	−	1	−	−	−	−	−	−
BOOK	−	1	1	−	−	−	−	−	−
BOX	3	2	5	−	1	1	1	1	2
BOY	−	−	−	−	−	−	−	1	1
BREAK	1	−	1	−	−	−	−	−	−
BROKE	−	−	−	−	1	1	−	−	−
BUCKET	−	−	−	1	−	1	−	−	−
BUILDING	1	−	1	1	−	1	−	−	−
BUTTERFLY	−	−	−	1	−	1	−	−	−
BUTTON	1	−	1	−	−	−	−	−	−
CABIN	1	−	1	−	−	−	−	−	−
CAME IN	−	−	−	−	−	−	−	1	1
CAN	−	1	1	−	1	1	−	−	−
CAR	1	1	2	1	−	1	−	−	−
CAT	−	2	2	−	−	−	−	−	−
CAVE	1	−	1	1	−	1	−	−	−

RESPONSE WORD	1ST M	1ST F	1ST T	3RD M	3RD F	3RD T	5TH M	5TH F	5TH T

40.   INTO

RESPONSE WORD	1ST M	1ST F	1ST T	3RD M	3RD F	3RD T	5TH M	5TH F	5TH T
CHAIR	–	1	1	–	–	–	–	–	–
CHEW	–	1	1	–	–	–	–	–	–
CHURCH	1	–	1	–	–	–	–	–	–
CINTO	1	–	1	–	–	–	–	–	–
CLASS	1	–	1	–	–	–	–	–	–
CLASSROOM	–	–	–	–	1	1	–	–	–
CLIMB	–	–	–	1	–	1	–	–	–
COCOON	–	–	–	1	–	1	–	–	–
COME	–	–	–	–	1	1	–	1	1
COME HERE	–	–	–	–	1	1	–	–	–
COME IN	–	1	1	–	–	–	–	3	3
COMPOUND WORD	–	–	–	1	–	1	–	–	–
CONTAIN	–	–	–	–	–	–	2	–	2
COOKIES	–	1	1	–	–	–	–	–	–
COON	1	1	2	–	–	–	–	–	–
CRAWL	–	–	–	1	–	1	–	–	–
CUCKOO	1	–	1	–	–	–	–	–	–
CUT	–	1	1	–	–	–	–	–	–
DAY	–	–	–	1	–	1	–	–	–
DESK	–	1	1	1	–	1	–	–	–
DIAMOND	–	1	1	–	–	–	–	–	–
DIE	–	–	–	1	–	1	–	–	–
DISHES	1	–	1	–	–	–	–	–	–
DO	–	1	1	–	–	–	–	–	–
DOG	–	2	2	–	–	–	1	–	1
DONT	–	–	–	–	–	–	–	1	1
DONT GO INTO THINGS	–	1	1	–	–	–	–	–	–
DOOR	3	3	6	2	1	3	2	2	4
DOORS	–	1	1	–	–	–	–	–	–
DOWN	1	–	1	–	–	–	–	–	–
DOWN TO	–	1	1	–	–	–	–	–	–
DUEL	–	–	–	–	–	–	1	–	1
EATER	–	1	1	–	–	–	–	–	–
ENGLAND	1	–	1	–	–	–	–	–	–
ENTER	2	2	4	–	–	–	1	3	4
ENTRANCE	–	–	–	–	–	–	1	–	1
FALL	1	–	1	–	–	–	–	–	–
FARM	1	–	1	–	–	–	–	–	–
FATHER	1	–	1	–	–	–	–	–	–
FLINT	–	–	–	–	–	–	1	–	1
FLOOR	1	–	1	–	–	–	–	–	–
FLY	1	–	1	–	–	–	–	–	–
FOO	–	1	1	–	–	–	–	–	–
FOOD	–	1	1	–	–	–	–	–	–
FOR	–	–	–	–	1	1	–	–	–
FUN	1	1	2	–	–	–	–	–	–
GET	–	–	–	–	–	–	1	–	1
GET IN THE HOUSE	1	–	1	–	–	–	–	–	–
GET OUT	1	–	1	–	–	–	–	–	–
GIVE	–	–	–	–	–	–	1	–	1
GLASSES	–	1	1	–	–	–	–	–	–
GO	1	–	1	–	2	2	13	14	27
GO IN	–	–	–	1	–	1	2	3	5
GO INTO	–	–	–	–	–	–	1	–	1
GO INTO A STORE	–	–	–	–	–	–	–	1	1
GO OUT	–	–	–	–	–	–	1	–	1
GO TO	–	–	–	1	–	1	1	–	1
GOING	–	1	1	–	1	1	1	1	2
GOING IN	1	–	1	1	–	1	–	–	–
GOING INTO SOMETHING	–	–	–	–	–	–	1	–	1
GOING OUT	–	–	–	1	–	1	–	–	–
GOOD	1	–	1	–	–	–	–	–	–
GOON	1	–	1	–	–	–	–	–	–
GREAT	–	–	–	–	1	1	–	–	–
HAPPY	1	–	1	–	–	–	–	–	–
HEART	–	1	1	–	–	–	–	–	–
HER	–	–	–	–	1	1	–	–	–
HERE	–	1	1	–	–	–	–	–	–
HIS	1	–	1	–	–	–	–	–	–
HOLE	–	–	–	1	–	1	1	1	1
HOME	–	–	–	–	–	–	1	–	1
HOOD	1	–	1	–	–	–	–	–	–

RESPONSE WORD	1ST			3RD			5TH		
	M	F	T	M	F	T	M	F	T

40.   INTO

RESPONSE WORD	M	F	T	M	F	T	M	F	T
HOT	–	–	–	–	–	–	1	–	1
HOUSE	8	6	14	6	6	12	5	3	8
I	–	–	–	–	1	1	–	–	–
ICE CREAM	1	–	1	–	–	–	–	–	–
IN	5	5	10	9	11	20	5	7	12
IN AND OUT	–	–	–	1	–	1	–	–	–
IN FROM	–	–	–	1	–	1	–	–	–
IN IT	–	–	–	1	–	1	–	–	–
IN MY HOUSE	–	1	1	–	–	–	–	–	–
IN ONE	1	–	1	–	–	–	–	–	–
IN THERE	–	–	–	1	–	1	–	–	–
INDIAN	5	1	6	–	–	–	–	–	–
INDIAN TEPEE	1	–	1	–	–	–	–	–	–
INDIANS	–	1	1	–	–	–	–	–	–
INDOORS	–	1	1	–	–	–	–	–	–
INHALE	–	–	–	1	–	1	–	–	–
INNER TUBE	1	–	1	–	–	–	–	–	–
INSECTS	1	–	1	–	–	–	–	–	–
INSIDE	3	2	5	4	6	10	3	8	11
INTRODUCING	–	1	1	–	–	–	–	–	–
INVERNESY	–	1	1	–	–	–	–	–	–
INWARD	–	–	–	–	–	–	–	1	1
JOIN	–	–	–	–	–	–	4	–	4
JUMP	1	–	1	1	–	1	–	–	–
KEY	–	1	1	–	–	–	–	–	–
KNITTED	1	–	1	–	–	–	–	–	–
KNOB	–	1	1	–	–	–	–	–	–
LATER	–	–	–	–	–	–	1	–	1
LETS GO INTO MY HOUSE	–	1	1	–	–	–	–	–	–
LIGHT	–	1	1	–	–	–	–	–	–
LIKE	–	1	1	–	–	–	–	–	–
LIKE YOU WOULD GO INTO A SCHOOL	–	–	–	–	–	–	–	1	1
LION	–	1	1	–	–	–	–	–	–
LITTLE	–	1	1	–	–	–	–	–	–
ME	1	1	2	–	–	–	–	–	–
MESS	–	1	1	–	–	–	–	–	–
MIDDLE	–	–	–	–	–	–	2	–	2
MIRROR	1	–	1	–	–	–	–	–	–
MOO	2	–	2	–	–	–	–	–	–
NAILS	–	1	1	–	–	–	–	–	–
NO	1	–	1	–	–	–	–	–	–
NOT	–	–	–	–	–	–	–	–	–
NOT INTO	1	–	1	1	1	2	–	–	–
NOW	1	–	1	–	–	–	–	–	–
NURSE	–	1	1	–	–	–	–	–	–
NUT	1	–	1	–	–	–	–	–	–
OFF	–	–	–	–	1	1	–	–	–
ON	–	–	–	–	2	2	–	4	4
ONE	1	2	3	–	–	–	–	–	–
ONTO	–	–	–	1	2	3	1	2	3
OUR HOUSE	1	–	1	–	–	–	–	–	–
OUT	7	10	17	47	61	108	59	52	111
OUT IN	–	–	–	1	–	1	–	–	–
OUT OF	2	2	4	12	6	18	10	6	16
OUT OF IT	1	–	1	–	–	–	–	–	–
OUT SIDE	–	–	–	–	–	–	1	–	1
OUT TO	2	3	5	7	3	10	1	3	4
OUTDOOR	–	–	–	–	1	1	–	–	–
OUTDOORS	–	–	–	1	2	3	–	–	–
OUTSIDE	–	1	1	13	8	21	–	1	1
PAPER	1	2	3	–	–	–	–	–	–
PERSON	–	1	1	–	–	–	–	–	–
PLACE	–	–	–	1	–	1	–	–	–
PLAY WITH	–	1	1	–	–	–	–	–	–
PLEASE	–	1	1	–	–	–	–	–	–
PLUG	–	1	1	–	–	–	–	–	–
POCKETBOOK	1	–	1	–	–	–	–	–	–
PRAYER	–	1	1	–	–	–	–	–	–
PRUNE	1	–	1	–	–	–	–	–	–
PUMPKIN	–	1	1	–	–	–	–	–	–
PUPPY	1	–	1	–	–	–	–	–	–

RESPONSE WORD	1ST			3RD			5TH		
	M	F	T	M	F	T	M	F	T

40. INTO

RESPONSE WORD	M	F	T	M	F	T	M	F	T
PURPLE	–	1	1	–	–	–	–	–	–
PUT	–	–	–	–	–	–	1	1	2
PUT TOGETHER	–	–	–	–	–	–	–	1	1
QUIET	–	–	–	–	1	1	–	–	–
RABBIT	–	1	1	–	–	–	–	–	–
RAIN	–	2	2	–	–	–	–	–	–
RAN	–	–	–	–	1	1	–	–	–
RAT	–	–	–	–	–	–	1	–	1
RED	1	–	1	–	–	–	–	–	–
RING	–	–	–	–	–	–	–	1	1
ROOM	1	–	1	–	–	–	–	–	–
RUN	–	–	–	–	–	–	1	–	1
SAD	–	1	1	–	–	–	–	–	–
SAT	–	–	–	–	–	–	1	–	1
SAW	–	1	1	–	–	–	–	–	–
SAYS TO NEIGHBOR INTO	–	1	1	–	–	–	–	–	–
SCHOOL	–	1	1	–	–	–	1	1	2
SEE	–	1	1	–	–	–	–	–	–
SET TO	1	–	1	–	–	–	–	–	–
SHOP	–	1	1	–	–	–	–	–	–
SIDE	–	–	–	–	–	–	1	–	1
SKELETON	1	–	1	–	–	–	–	–	–
SLIP	–	1	1	–	–	–	–	–	–
SNAKES	1	–	1	–	–	–	–	–	–
SOMETHING	–	2	2	–	1	1	1	–	1
SOMETHING BIG	1	–	1	–	–	–	–	–	–
SPICKET	1	–	1	–	–	–	–	–	–
STABLE	–	1	1	–	–	–	–	–	–
START	–	–	–	–	–	–	1	–	1
STORE	1	1	2	–	–	–	1	–	1
STUFF	1	1	2	–	–	–	–	–	–
SWING	–	1	1	–	–	–	–	–	–
TABLE	–	2	2	–	–	–	–	–	–
THE	2	1	3	–	1	1	–	1	1
THE CAVE	1	–	1	–	–	–	–	–	–
THE HOUSE	–	3	3	1	–	1	–	–	–
THEY	–	–	–	1	–	1	–	–	–
THING	–	–	–	–	–	–	–	1	1
THROUGH	–	–	–	–	–	–	–	1	1
THUNDER	1	–	1	–	–	–	–	–	–
TIGER	1	–	1	–	–	–	–	–	–
TO	7	5	12	3	4	7	1	4	5
TODAY	–	–	–	–	1	1	–	–	–
TOGETHER	–	–	–	–	1	1	1	–	1
TOOTH	1	–	1	–	–	–	–	–	–
TOOTHBRUSH	–	1	1	–	–	–	–	–	–
TOWARD US	–	1	1	–	–	–	–	–	–
TRAIN	1	–	1	–	–	–	–	–	–
TRAP	1	–	1	–	–	–	–	–	–
TRASH	–	–	–	–	1	1	–	–	–
TREE	1	–	1	–	–	–	–	–	–
TREES	–	1	1	–	–	–	–	–	–
TRINTO	1	–	1	–	–	–	–	–	–
TROUBLE	–	1	1	–	–	–	–	–	–
TRUCK	1	–	1	–	–	–	–	–	–
TUBE	–	2	2	–	–	–	–	–	–
TUNE	2	–	2	–	–	–	–	–	–
TUNNEL	–	1	1	–	–	–	–	–	–
UNDER	–	–	–	–	–	–	–	2	2
UNTO	–	–	–	–	1	1	–	2	2
UP	1	–	1	–	–	–	–	–	–
UP INTO	1	–	1	–	–	–	–	–	–
UPON	–	–	–	–	–	–	1	–	1
URN	–	1	1	–	–	–	–	–	–
US	1	–	1	–	–	–	–	–	–
WALK	1	–	1	–	–	–	1	–	1
WALL	1	–	1	–	–	–	–	–	–
WENT TO	–	1	1	–	–	–	–	–	–
WHAT	1	1	2	–	–	–	–	–	–
WHEEL	1	–	1	–	–	–	–	–	–
WHEN YOU'RE INTO SOMETHING.	1	–	1	–	–	–	–	–	–

RESPONSE WORD	1ST M	1ST F	1ST T	3RD M	3RD F	3RD T	5TH M	5TH F	5TH T

40. INTO

RESPONSE WORD	1ST M	1ST F	1ST T	3RD M	3RD F	3RD T	5TH M	5TH F	5TH T
WHITE	–	2	2	–	–	–	–	–	–
WHY	–	1	1	–	–	–	–	–	–
WIDE	1	–	1	–	–	–	–	–	–
WINDOW	–	2	2	–	–	–	–	–	–
WINTER	–	1	1	–	–	–	–	–	–
WITCH	1	–	1	–	–	–	–	–	–
WITH	–	–	–	–	–	–	–	1	1
WITHOUT	–	–	–	1	–	1	–	–	–
WORD	–	–	–	1	–	1	–	–	–
WORK	1	–	1	–	–	–	–	1	1
YARD	–	–	–	–	1	1	–	–	–
YOU	–	1	1	–	–	–	–	–	–
YOU DRAW A BUG	1	–	1	–	–	–	–	–	–
YOUR	–	–	–	1	–	1	–	–	–

41. IT

RESPONSE WORD	1ST M	1ST F	1ST T	3RD M	3RD F	3RD T	5TH M	5TH F	5TH T
A	–	–	–	–	–	–	–	1	1
A THING	–	–	–	–	–	–	3	2	5
ADD	–	–	–	1	–	1	–	–	–
ALWAYS	–	–	–	–	1	1	–	–	–
ANIMAL	1	–	1	–	–	–	2	1	3
ANYTHING	–	–	–	–	1	1	1	–	1
APRIL	–	–	–	–	–	–	1	–	1
ARENT	–	–	–	1	–	1	–	–	–
AT	5	10	15	6	11	17	4	2	6
BALL	–	–	–	2	–	2	–	1	1
BE	–	–	–	–	–	–	1	1	2
BELL	1	–	1	–	–	–	–	–	–
BID	–	–	–	1	–	1	–	–	–
BIRD	–	–	–	–	1	1	–	–	–
BIT	2	3	5	7	1	8	1	1	2
BITE	–	–	–	–	1	1	–	–	–
BLACK	–	–	–	–	1	1	–	–	–
BLIND	–	1	1	–	–	–	–	–	–
BOARD	1	–	1	–	–	–	–	–	–
BOOK	–	1	1	–	1	1	–	–	–
BOY	–	–	–	2	–	2	1	–	1
BROWN	1	–	1	–	–	–	–	–	–
BUG	–	–	–	–	–	–	–	1	1
BUTTER	1	–	1	–	–	–	–	–	–
BUTTERFLY	–	–	–	1	–	1	–	–	–
CAME	1	–	1	–	–	–	–	–	–
CAN	2	4	6	–	1	1	–	–	–
CAR	–	–	–	1	–	1	1	–	1
CARD	–	1	1	–	–	–	–	–	–
CAT	–	1	1	1	2	3	2	1	3
CAUGHT	–	–	–	–	–	–	1	–	1
CHALKBOARD	–	1	1	–	–	–	–	–	–
CHASE	–	–	–	–	1	1	–	–	–
CIGARETTE	1	–	1	–	–	–	–	–	–
CLOTHES	1	–	1	–	–	–	–	–	–
COME	–	2	2	–	–	–	–	–	–
COULD BE A CHAIR, LIKE THAT	–	1	1	–	–	–	–	–	–
COULDNT BE	–	1	1	–	–	–	–	–	–
COUNTRY	–	–	–	1	–	1	–	–	–
COW	–	1	1	–	–	–	–	–	–
CREATURE	–	–	–	–	–	–	–	1	1
CUPBOARD	–	1	1	–	–	–	–	–	–
DEAR	–	–	–	1	–	1	–	–	–
DESK	–	1	1	–	–	–	1	–	1
DID	1	–	1	1	–	1	–	–	–
DIRT	–	–	–	–	–	–	–	1	1
DO	–	–	–	1	–	1	–	–	–
DOES	–	1	1	–	–	–	–	–	–
DOG	1	1	2	–	1	1	–	2	2
DONT	–	–	–	–	1	1	1	–	1
DOOR	–	1	1	–	–	–	–	–	–
DOORKNOB	–	1	1	–	–	–	–	–	–
EARTH	–	–	–	–	–	–	–	1	1

RESPONSE WORD	1ST M	1ST F	1ST T	3RD M	3RD F	3RD T	5TH M	5TH F	5TH T

41. IT

RESPONSE WORD	1ST M	1ST F	1ST T	3RD M	3RD F	3RD T	5TH M	5TH F	5TH T
EASTER	–	1	1	–	–	–	–	–	–
EAT	1	–	1	–	–	–	–	–	–
FALL	1	–	1	1	1	2	–	–	–
FATHER	1	–	1	–	–	–	–	–	–
FIRE	–	–	–	–	–	–	–	1	1
FISH	1	–	1	–	–	–	–	–	–
FIT	–	3	3	–	1	1	2	–	2
FOOD	–	–	–	–	–	–	1	–	1
FREE	–	1	1	–	–	–	–	–	–
GAME	–	–	–	–	–	–	–	1	1
GET	2	3	5	–	–	–	–	1	1
GET IN	–	1	1	–	–	–	–	–	–
GET SOMETHING	1	–	1	–	–	–	–	–	–
GIRL	–	1	1	–	–	–	–	–	–
GIVE	–	–	–	1	–	1	–	–	–
GOOD	1	–	1	–	1	1	–	–	–
HALF A DOLLAR	1	–	1	–	–	–	–	–	–
HAPPENED	1	–	1	–	–	–	–	–	–
HARD	–	–	–	–	–	–	1	–	1
HAS	1	–	1	–	1	1	–	–	–
HAT	1	–	1	–	–	–	–	–	–
HE	–	–	–	1	1	2	1	2	3
HEART	1	–	1	–	–	–	–	–	–
HEATER	1	–	1	–	–	–	–	–	–
HER	–	–	–	1	–	1	1	–	1
HERE	1	–	1	–	–	–	–	–	–
HIDE	–	1	1	–	–	–	–	–	–
HIDE-AND-GO-SEEK-	1	–	1	–	–	–	–	–	–
HIM	–	–	–	1	1	2	2	–	2
HIMSELF	–	–	–	–	–	–	1	–	1
HIS	–	–	–	1	1	2	–	–	–
HIT	3	2	5	2	4	6	1	–	1
HIT IT	1	–	1	–	–	–	–	–	–
HOME	–	1	1	–	–	–	–	–	–
HOT	–	1	1	–	–	–	–	–	–
HOUSE	–	1	1	–	–	–	–	–	–
I	1	–	1	2	–	2	1	1	2
I QUIT IT	1	–	1	–	–	–	–	–	–
IF	–	–	–	–	2	2	1	1	2
IN	1	–	1	2	4	6	4	1	5
IS	22	25	47	23	46	69	26	29	55
IS A BABY BOY	1	–	1	–	–	–	–	–	–
IS COLD	1	–	1	–	–	–	–	–	–
IS GOOD	–	1	1	–	–	–	–	–	–
IS IT	–	–	–	–	1	1	–	–	–
IS NOT	–	–	–	1	–	1	–	–	–
IS NOT HERE	1	–	1	–	–	–	–	–	–
IS NOT YOU	–	1	1	–	–	–	–	–	–
IS SOMETHING	1	–	1	–	–	–	–	1	1
IS THE ONE	–	1	1	–	–	–	–	–	–
IS THE TRAIN	–	–	–	1	–	1	–	–	–
IS WINTER	–	1	1	–	–	–	–	–	–
ISNT	–	–	–	4	1	5	–	–	–
IT	–	–	–	1	–	1	–	–	–
IT IS	–	–	–	1	–	1	1	–	1
IT NEVER	–	1	1	–	–	–	–	–	–
IT WILL	–	–	–	–	–	–	1	–	1
ITCH	–	2	2	–	–	–	–	–	–
ITCHES	–	1	1	–	–	–	–	–	–
ITS	–	–	–	2	1	3	4	2	6
JACKY DAWSON	–	–	–	–	–	–	–	1	1
JIT	1	–	1	–	–	–	–	–	–
KID	–	1	1	–	–	–	–	–	–
KITTEN	–	–	–	–	1	1	–	–	–
KNIT	–	2	2	1	–	1	–	–	–
LEADER	–	1	1	–	–	–	–	–	–
LET	–	–	–	–	1	1	–	–	–
LIKE	1	–	1	–	–	–	–	–	–
LIT	1	–	1	–	–	–	–	–	–
LITTLE	–	1	1	–	–	–	–	–	–
LONG	1	–	1	1	–	1	1	–	1
LOOK	–	1	1	1	–	1	1	–	1

RESPONSE WORD	1ST M	F	T	3RD M	F	T	5TH M	F	T
				41. IT					
LYNN MY SISTER	–	–	–	–	–	–	–	1	1
MAINTAIN	1	–	1	–	–	–	–	–	–
MAN	1	–	1	–	–	–	–	–	–
ME	3	3	6	–	–	–	–	1	1
MEANS	–	–	–	–	1	1	–	–	–
MIGHT HAPPEN	1	–	1	–	–	–	–	–	–
MINE	–	1	1	–	1	1	–	–	–
MIRROR	1	–	1	–	–	–	–	–	–
MIT	2	–	2	–	1	1	–	–	–
MITT	1	–	1	1	1	2	–	–	–
MITTEN	4	–	4	–	–	–	–	–	–
MOVED	–	–	–	–	–	–	–	1	1
MY	–	1	1	–	–	–	–	–	–
NAME	–	–	–	–	–	–	1	–	1
NO	–	1	1	–	–	–	1	–	1
NO RESPONSE	–	–	–	–	–	–	–	1	1
NOISY	1	–	1	–	–	–	–	–	–
NOT	3	3	6	3	2	5	3	5	8
NOT HERE	1	–	1	–	–	–	–	–	–
NOT IT	3	4	7	2	1	3	3	2	5
NOTHING	1	–	1	1	–	1	–	–	–
NOW	1	–	1	1	–	1	–	–	–
NUMBERS	1	–	1	–	–	–	–	–	–
OBJECT	–	–	–	–	–	–	2	1	3
OF	1	–	1	–	–	–	–	–	–
ON	–	–	–	–	–	–	1	1	2
ONCE	–	1	1	–	–	–	–	–	–
OR	–	–	–	–	–	–	1	–	1
OUT	–	–	–	1	3	4	–	–	–
PANTS	–	1	1	–	–	–	–	–	–
PAPER	1	–	1	–	–	–	–	–	–
PASTE	–	1	1	–	–	–	–	–	–
PERSON	1	–	1	–	–	–	–	2	2
PICTURE	1	1	2	–	–	–	–	–	–
PIT	3	2	5	1	–	1	–	1	1
PLAY	–	1	1	–	–	–	–	–	–
PLAYS	–	1	1	–	–	–	–	–	–
POINT	–	–	–	–	–	–	–	1	1
PUT	–	–	–	1	–	1	–	–	–
PUT DOGS IN A TRUCK	1	–	1	–	–	–	–	–	–
QUIET	–	1	1	1	–	1	–	–	–
QUIT	–	–	–	–	–	–	1	–	1
RIT	–	1	1	–	–	–	–	–	–
RUBBERBAND	–	1	1	–	–	–	–	–	–
RUG	–	–	–	1	–	1	–	–	–
RUN	–	1	1	–	–	–	–	–	–
SALT	1	–	1	–	–	–	–	–	–
SAME	–	–	–	–	–	–	1	–	1
SAT	1	–	1	–	–	–	–	–	–
SAUCER	1	–	1	–	–	–	–	–	–
SEE	1	3	4	–	–	–	–	–	–
SEVEN	–	1	1	–	–	–	–	–	–
SHE	–	–	–	1	2	3	2	–	2
SHOES	–	1	1	–	–	–	–	–	–
SIT	1	1	2	3	3	6	1	–	1
SO	–	–	–	1	–	1	–	1	1
SOAP	–	–	–	1	–	1	–	–	–
SODA	1	–	1	–	–	–	–	–	–
SOMEONE	–	–	–	2	–	2	–	–	–
SOMETHING	1	–	1	7	5	12	7	7	14
SOMETIME	–	–	–	1	–	1	–	–	–
SOUP	–	–	–	–	–	–	–	1	1
SOUR	1	–	1	–	–	–	–	–	–
STOP	1	–	1	–	–	–	–	–	–
STOP IT	–	1	1	–	–	–	–	–	–
STUFF	–	–	–	–	–	–	–	1	1
SUGAR	–	1	1	–	–	–	–	–	–
SUPPER	1	–	1	–	–	–	–	–	–
TABLE	–	2	2	–	–	–	–	–	–
TAG	3	1	4	2	–	2	1	1	2
TAGGED	1	–	1	–	–	–	–	–	–
THAT	–	1	1	14	13	27	16	19	35

RESPONSE WORD	1ST M	F	T	3RD M	F	T	5TH M	F	T

41. IT

RESPONSE WORD	M	F	T	M	F	T	M	F	T
THE	1	2	3	1	2	3	1	–	1
THE THING	–	–	–	–	1	1	–	1	1
THEIRS	–	–	–	–	–	–	–	1	1
THEM	–	–	–	–	–	–	–	1	1
THEN	–	–	–	–	–	–	1	1	2
THERE	–	–	–	2	1	3	2	1	3
THEY	–	–	–	1	1	2	1	2	3
THING	–	–	–	5	–	5	17	13	30
THINGS	–	–	–	1	–	1	–	–	–
THIS	1	–	1	1	2	3	–	2	2
THUMB	1	–	1	–	–	–	–	–	–
TO	–	–	–	1	–	1	–	–	–
TO DO IT	–	–	–	–	–	–	–	1	1
TOUCH	–	1	1	–	–	–	–	–	–
TOY	–	1	1	–	–	–	–	–	–
TREE	2	–	2	–	–	–	–	–	–
TRUCK	1	–	1	–	–	–	–	–	–
TWO	–	–	–	1	–	1	–	–	–
UP	2	1	3	–	–	–	–	–	–
US	–	–	–	1	1	2	–	1	1
WAS	3	1	4	3	1	4	5	7	12
WAS A FROG	1	–	1	–	–	–	–	–	–
WASNT	–	–	–	1	–	1	–	–	–
WATER	–	1	1	–	–	–	–	–	–
WE	–	–	–	–	–	–	–	1	1
WENT	1	–	1	–	–	–	–	–	–
WHAT	–	–	–	1	–	1	–	–	–
WHEN YOURE HITTING A BALL	1	–	1	–	–	–	–	–	–
WHERE	–	1	1	–	–	–	–	–	–
WHICH	1	–	1	–	–	–	–	–	–
WILL	1	1	2	–	–	–	–	1	1
WINDSHIELDS	–	1	1	–	–	–	–	–	–
WIT	2	–	2	2	–	2	–	–	–
WORD	–	–	–	1	–	1	–	1	1
WORKS	–	–	–	–	–	–	1	–	1
YOU	2	2	4	1	5	6	2	2	4
YOU READING IN A BOOK	–	1	1	–	–	–	–	–	–
YOUR	–	–	–	–	1	1	–	–	–
YOU RE IT	1	2	3	–	–	–	–	–	–

42. JOIN

RESPONSE WORD	M	F	T	M	F	T	M	F	T
A CLUB	–	–	–	2	–	2	–	–	–
A JOINT	–	1	1	–	–	–	–	–	–
A PARTY	–	3	3	–	–	–	–	–	–
A POOL	1	–	1	–	–	–	–	–	–
AGAIN	–	–	–	1	–	1	–	1	1
AGAINST	–	–	–	1	–	1	–	–	–
AN	1	–	1	–	–	–	–	–	–
AND	1	–	1	–	–	–	–	–	–
APART	–	–	–	2	–	2	–	2	2
APPEAR	–	–	–	–	–	–	1	–	1
APPLICATION	–	–	–	–	–	–	1	–	1
ARMY	1	1	2	2	–	2	4	1	5
ASK	–	–	–	–	–	–	–	1	1
ASKED	–	–	–	–	1	1	–	–	–
ATTEND	–	–	–	–	–	–	–	1	1
AWAY	–	–	–	2	–	2	–	–	–
B	1	–	1	–	–	–	–	–	–
BAD	–	–	–	–	–	–	2	–	2
BASEBALL	–	–	–	–	–	–	1	–	–
BASEFUL	–	–	–	1	–	1	–	–	–
BE WITH	–	–	–	1	–	1	–	–	–
BECOME	–	–	–	1	–	1	–	1	1
BEER	1	–	1	–	–	–	–	–	–
BEGIN	–	–	–	–	3	3	1	–	1
BELL	–	1	1	–	1	1	–	–	–
BELONG	–	–	–	1	–	1	–	2	2
BETTER	–	1	1	–	–	–	–	–	–
BIT	1	–	1	–	–	–	–	–	–

42. JOIN

RESPONSE WORD	1ST M	1ST F	1ST T	3RD M	3RD F	3RD T	5TH M	5TH F	5TH T
BONE	1	–	1	–	–	–	–	–	–
BOOK	–	–	–	–	–	–	1	–	1
BOOKS	–	1	1	–	–	–	–	–	–
BORN	–	1	1	–	1	1	–	–	–
BOTTLE	1	–	1	–	–	–	–	–	–
BOX	1	–	1	–	–	–	–	–	–
BOY	–	1	1	–	1	1	–	–	–
BREAK	1	–	1	1	1	2	1	1	2
BRING	1	–	1	–	–	–	1	–	1
BUNCH	–	–	–	–	1	1	–	–	–
CACTUS	1	–	1	–	–	–	–	–	–
CAKE	–	–	–	–	–	–	–	1	1
CAME	–	–	–	–	1	1	–	–	–
CAMP	–	1	1	–	–	–	–	–	–
CAN	–	1	1	–	–	–	–	–	–
CAR	–	–	–	–	–	–	–	1	1
CARD	–	1	1	–	–	–	–	–	–
CHAIR	–	1	1	–	–	–	–	–	–
CHICKEN	1	–	1	–	–	–	–	–	–
CHOIR	–	1	1	–	–	–	–	–	–
CHURCH	–	–	–	–	–	–	–	1	1
CIRCLE	1	1	2	–	–	–	–	1	1
CIRCUS	–	–	–	1	2	3	–	1	1
CLAP	–	–	–	–	1	1	–	1	1
CLASS	–	1	1	–	–	–	–	–	–
CLOB	–	–	–	–	–	–	1	–	1
CLOSE	–	–	–	1	–	1	1	1	1
CLOTHES	1	–	1	–	–	–	1	–	1
CLUB	14	3	17	16	17	33	11	6	17
CLUBS	1	–	1	–	–	–	–	–	–
COAT	1	–	1	–	–	–	–	–	–
COIN	6	5	11	3	–	3	1	1	2
COMBINE	–	–	–	–	–	–	1	–	1
COME	–	1	1	3	5	8	1	2	3
COME (WITH THEM)	–	–	–	–	1	1	–	–	–
COME IN	–	–	–	1	–	1	1	–	1
COMING	–	–	–	1	–	1	–	–	–
COMPANY	1	–	1	–	–	–	–	–	–
CONNECT	–	–	–	–	–	–	2	4	6
CONNECTED	–	–	–	–	–	–	1	–	1
CORN	–	1	1	–	–	–	–	–	–
COUPLE	–	–	–	–	–	–	2	–	2
COUPLES	–	1	1	–	–	–	–	–	–
CRADLE	–	1	1	–	–	–	–	–	–
CRATES	–	–	–	1	–	1	–	–	–
CROSS	–	–	–	–	1	1	–	–	–
CROWD	–	2	2	1	1	2	–	1	1
CUB	–	–	–	–	–	–	–	1	1
CUB SCOUT	–	1	1	–	–	–	–	–	–
CUB SCOUTS	1	–	1	1	–	1	–	–	–
CURTAIN	1	–	1	–	–	–	–	–	–
DANCE	–	1	1	–	–	–	–	–	–
DIAMOND	1	–	1	–	–	–	–	–	–
DISQUALIFY	–	–	–	–	1	1	–	–	–
DOG	4	1	5	–	–	–	–	–	–
DONT	–	1	1	1	–	1	–	–	–
DOOR	–	1	1	–	–	–	–	–	–
EARRINGS	–	1	1	–	–	–	–	–	–
END	–	–	–	1	–	1	–	–	–
ENJOY	–	–	–	1	2	3	–	–	–
ENLIST	–	–	–	–	–	–	1	–	1
ENTER	–	–	–	–	–	–	1	1	2
EVERYBODY	–	–	–	–	1	1	–	–	–
EVERYONE	–	–	–	1	–	1	–	–	–
FASTEN	–	–	–	–	–	–	–	1	1
FATHER	–	1	1	–	–	–	–	–	–
FINE	–	–	–	–	1	1	–	–	–
FIRE	1	–	1	–	–	–	–	–	–
FIRST DAY	–	–	–	–	–	–	–	1	1
FLY	–	–	–	1	–	1	–	–	–
FOIN	–	1	1	–	–	–	–	–	–
FOR	–	–	–	–	–	–	1	–	1

42. JOIN

RESPONSE WORD	1ST M	F	T	3RD M	F	T	5TH M	F	T
FOR DINNER	-	1	1	-	-	-	-	-	-
FRIENDS	1	-	1	-	-	-	-	-	-
FUN	4	6	10	3	2	5	1	2	3
FUNNY	-	-	-	-	-	-	1	-	1
GAME	3	4	7	1	4	5	-	-	-
GANG	1	-	1	4	2	6	1	-	1
GATHER	-	-	-	-	-	-	1	2	3
GATO	-	-	-	-	-	-	1	-	1
GENTLY	-	1	1	-	-	-	-	-	-
GET IN	-	-	-	-	-	-	-	1	1
GET INTO	-	-	-	-	-	-	1	-	1
GET TOGETHER	1	-	1	-	-	-	1	1	2
GETHER	-	-	-	-	1	1	-	2	2
GIRL	-	1	1	2	1	3	-	1	1
GIVE	-	-	-	-	-	-	1	-	1
GLAD	-	-	-	1	-	1	-	-	-
GLASS	-	-	-	-	1	1	-	-	-
GO	-	1	1	3	1	4	-	1	1
GO EVERY DAY	-	-	-	-	1	1	-	-	-
GO IN	-	-	-	-	-	-	-	1	1
GO TO	-	-	-	1	-	1	-	-	-
GO TOGETHER	-	-	-	-	-	-	1	-	1
GOING	-	-	-	-	1	1	-	-	-
GOOD	-	1	1	1	-	1	-	-	-
GOODER	-	-	-	-	1	1	-	-	-
GREEN	-	-	-	-	1	1	-	-	-
GROUP	1	-	1	2	-	2	3	4	7
HAND	-	1	1	-	1	1	-	1	1
HANDS	5	2	7	4	2	6	2	-	2
HAPPEN	1	-	1	-	-	-	-	-	-
HAPPILY	-	1	1	-	-	-	-	-	-
HAPPINESS	-	1	1	-	-	-	-	-	-
HAPPY	2	2	4	2	4	6	3	2	5
HAVE	-	-	-	-	1	1	-	-	-
HAVE FUN	-	1	1	-	-	-	-	-	-
HEAD	-	-	-	-	-	-	1	-	1
HEATER	1	-	1	-	-	-	-	-	-
HELP	-	-	-	-	-	-	-	1	1
HERE	-	2	2	-	-	-	-	-	-
HIGH	-	1	1	-	-	-	-	-	-
HIM	-	1	1	-	-	-	-	-	-
HIT	1	-	1	1	-	1	-	-	-
HITCH	-	-	-	1	-	1	1	-	1
HOBBY	1	-	1	-	-	-	-	-	-
HOIN	2	-	2	-	-	-	-	-	-
HOLD	-	1	1	1	3	4	2	3	5
HOLD HANDS	-	-	-	1	-	1	-	-	-
HOLD TOGETHER	-	-	-	-	1	1	-	-	-
HOOK	-	-	-	1	-	1	-	-	-
HOUSE	-	1	1	-	-	-	-	-	-
HOW DO YOU DO	-	1	1	-	-	-	-	-	-
I WOULD LIKE TO JOIN	1	-	1	-	-	-	-	-	-
IN	2	2	4	1	1	2	2	1	3
INVITE	-	-	-	2	-	2	-	1	1
IT	-	1	1	-	-	-	-	-	-
J	1	-	1	-	-	-	-	-	-
JACK	1	1	2	-	-	-	1	-	1
JAIL	1	1	2	-	-	-	-	-	-
JANE	-	1	1	-	-	-	-	-	-
JAR	-	-	-	1	1	2	-	-	-
JAW	-	-	-	-	1	1	-	-	-
JAY	-	-	-	1	-	1	-	-	-
JELLO	-	1	1	-	-	-	-	-	-
JEWELRY	-	1	1	-	-	-	-	-	-
JOANNE	1	-	1	-	-	-	-	-	-
JOB	-	-	-	-	3	3	-	-	-
JOE	1	-	1	-	-	-	-	-	-
JOHN	-	-	-	-	1	1	2	-	2
JOIN	-	-	-	-	-	-	-	1	1
JOIN THINGS	1	-	1	-	-	-	-	-	-
JOINED	-	-	-	1	-	1	2	-	2
JOINING	-	-	-	1	-	1	-	-	-

42. JOIN

RESPONSE WORD	1ST M	F	T	3RD M	F	T	5TH M	F	T
JOINING SOMETHING	–	1	1	–	–	–	–	–	–
JOINT	1	1	2	–	1	1	–	–	–
JOKE	–	–	–	1	–	1	–	–	–
JOSEPH	1	–	1	–	–	–	–	–	–
JOY	2	2	4	–	5	5	2	3	5
JOYCE	–	1	1	–	–	–	–	–	–
JOYFUL	–	–	–	–	1	1	–	–	–
JUDGE	–	–	–	–	1	1	–	–	–
KEEP	–	–	–	–	–	–	1	–	1
KICKED OUT	–	–	–	–	–	–	1	–	1
KITTY CAT	–	1	1	–	–	–	–	–	–
LAMP	–	1	1	–	–	–	–	–	–
LEAGUE	–	–	–	–	–	–	–	1	1
LEARN	–	1	1	–	–	–	–	–	–
LEAVE	–	–	–	–	2	2	–	1	1
LET	–	–	–	–	1	1	–	–	–
LIGHT	–	1	1	–	–	–	–	1	1
LIKE	–	1	1	–	1	1	–	–	–
LIKE YOU JOIN A LINE	–	–	–	–	1	1	–	–	–
LINE	–	1	1	–	–	–	–	–	–
LINK	–	–	–	–	–	–	1	–	1
LITTLE	–	1	1	–	–	–	–	–	–
LONG	–	–	–	–	1	1	–	–	–
LOOSE	–	–	–	–	–	–	–	1	1
LOVELY	–	–	–	–	1	1	–	–	–
MADE	–	–	–	–	1	1	–	–	–
MAKE	–	–	–	–	–	–	–	1	1
MAN	1	–	1	–	–	–	1	–	1
MARRIED	–	–	–	–	–	–	–	1	1
ME	4	4	8	1	–	1	–	–	–
MEET	–	–	–	1	1	2	–	1	1
MEETING	–	1	1	–	–	–	1	–	1
MEMBER	–	–	–	–	1	1	2	2	4
MENTER	–	–	–	–	–	–	1	–	1
MERRY	–	–	–	–	–	–	–	1	1
MET	–	–	–	1	1	2	–	–	–
MILK	1	–	1	–	–	–	–	–	–
MINE	1	–	1	–	–	–	–	–	–
MISS	–	–	–	–	–	–	1	–	1
MIX	–	–	–	–	–	–	–	1	1
MOIN	1	–	1	–	–	–	–	–	–
MOON	2	–	2	–	–	–	–	–	–
MOTHERS AND FATHERS	–	1	1	–	–	–	–	–	–
MOUSE	1	–	1	–	–	–	–	–	–
MY FAMILY	–	1	1	–	–	–	–	–	–
MY NAME	–	–	–	1	–	1	–	–	–
MY PARTY	–	1	1	–	–	–	–	–	–
NAVY	1	–	1	1	–	1	1	1	2
NECKLACE	–	1	1	–	–	–	–	–	–
NEVER	–	–	–	1	–	1	–	–	–
NICE	–	–	–	–	1	1	–	–	–
NO	1	–	1	–	–	–	–	–	–
NO RESPONSE	–	–	–	–	–	–	1	1	2
NOJOIN	–	–	–	1	–	1	–	–	–
NOT	1	–	1	–	–	–	–	1	1
NOT JOIN	–	–	–	2	1	3	–	1	1
NOT JOINED	1	–	1	–	–	–	–	–	–
NOTHING	–	–	–	–	–	–	1	–	1
NOW	1	–	1	1	–	1	–	–	–
ON	–	–	–	2	–	2	–	–	–
OUT	–	1	1	–	–	–	1	1	2
OWN	–	–	–	–	–	–	1	–	1
PAIN	1	–	1	–	–	–	–	–	–
PARADE	–	–	–	–	1	1	–	–	–
PART	–	–	–	1	–	1	–	1	1
PARTICIPATE	–	–	–	–	–	–	1	1	2
PARTY	5	6	11	–	–	–	–	1	1
PEOPLE	1	1	2	1	–	1	–	–	–
PERSON	–	–	–	1	–	1	1	–	1
PLACE	–	–	–	–	1	1	1	–	1
PLANS	1	1	2	1	1	2	1	–	1
PLAY	1	1	2	1	1	2	1	–	1

RESPONSE WORD	1ST M	1ST F	1ST T	3RD M	3RD F	3RD T	5TH M	5TH F	5TH T

42. JOIN

RESPONSE WORD	M	F	T	M	F	T	M	F	T
PLEASE	1	–	1	–	–	–	–	–	–
POIN	1	1	2	–	–	–	–	–	–
POOL	–	1	–	–	–	–	–	1	1
POTTY	–	1	1	–	–	–	–	–	–
POUND	–	1	1	–	–	–	–	–	–
PURPLE	–	1	1	–	–	–	–	–	–
PUT IN WATER	1	–	1	–	–	–	–	–	–
PUT OUT	–	–	–	–	1	1	–	–	–
PUT TOGETHER	–	–	–	1	1	2	3	1	4
QUIT	–	–	–	3	–	3	4	4	8
QUITE	–	–	–	–	–	–	–	1	1
RECEIVE	–	–	–	1	–	1	–	–	–
REJOIN	–	–	–	–	–	–	2	3	5
RETIRE	–	–	–	–	–	–	–	1	1
RIDE	–	1	1	–	–	–	–	–	–
RING	1	–	1	–	–	–	–	–	–
ROIN	–	1	1	–	–	–	–	–	–
ROOF	1	–	1	–	–	–	–	–	–
SAD	–	–	–	1	–	1	–	–	–
SANTA	–	1	1	–	–	–	–	–	–
SCHOOL	1	1	2	–	–	–	–	–	–
SCOUTS	–	–	–	–	–	–	–	1	1
SEPARATE	–	–	–	–	–	–	1	–	1
SHOIN	1	–	1	–	–	–	–	–	–
SIGN	–	–	–	1	–	1	1	–	1
SIGN OUT	–	–	–	1	–	1	–	–	–
SIGN UP	1	–	1	–	–	–	–	–	–
SLED	–	–	–	–	1	1	–	–	–
SOFT	–	1	1	–	–	–	–	–	–
SOIN	1	–	1	1	–	1	–	–	–
SOMEONE	1	–	1	–	–	–	–	–	–
SOMETHING	3	2	5	–	–	–	–	1	1
SONG	–	–	–	1	–	1	–	–	–
SPREAD	–	1	1	–	–	–	–	–	–
START	–	–	–	–	1	1	–	1	1
STARTED	–	–	–	–	–	–	–	1	1
STAY	–	–	–	–	2	2	–	1	1
STEP	–	–	–	–	1	1	–	–	–
STICK	–	–	–	1	–	1	–	–	–
STORE	–	2	2	–	–	–	–	–	–
SUDS	1	–	1	–	–	–	–	–	–
TABLE	–	1	1	–	–	–	–	–	–
TASTE	–	–	–	–	–	–	1	–	1
TEACHER	1	–	1	–	–	–	–	–	–
TEETH	–	–	–	–	1	1	–	–	–
TERRIBLE	–	–	–	–	–	–	1	–	1
THE	1	–	1	–	–	–	–	–	–
THE ARMY	1	–	1	–	–	–	–	–	–
THE FUN	1	–	1	–	–	–	–	–	–
THE GAME	–	–	–	1	–	1	–	–	–
THE OTHER BOYS	1	–	1	–	–	–	–	–	–
THE PARTY	1	2	3	–	–	–	–	–	–
THEM	–	–	–	–	–	–	1	1	2
THEY	–	–	–	–	1	1	–	–	–
THINK	1	–	1	–	–	–	–	–	–
THIS	–	1	1	–	–	–	–	–	–
THREE	–	1	1	–	–	–	–	–	–
TO	–	–	–	–	–	–	1	–	1
TO ANOTHER CAR	1	–	1	–	–	–	–	–	–
TO ENTER	–	–	–	–	–	–	–	1	1
TO GO IN WITH	–	–	–	–	–	–	–	1	1
TO UNITE	–	–	–	–	–	–	–	1	1
TOGATHER	–	–	–	–	–	–	–	1	1
TOGETHER	1	3	4	19	24	43	37	35	72
TOM	–	1	1	–	–	–	–	–	–
TOOTH	–	–	–	1	–	1	–	–	–
TREE	–	1	1	–	–	–	–	–	–
UNCONNECTED	–	–	–	1	–	1	–	–	–
UNHOOK	–	–	–	–	–	–	1	–	1
UNION	–	–	–	–	–	–	1	–	1
UNITED	–	–	–	–	–	–	–	1	1
UNJOIN	1	–	1	3	3	6	–	3	3

RESPONSE WORD	1ST M	F	T	3RD M	F	T	5TH M	F	T

42.   JOIN

RESPONSE WORD	1ST M	F	T	3RD M	F	T	5TH M	F	T
UNJOINED	–	–	–	1	–	1	–	–	–
UP	–	1	1	1	–	1	–	–	–
US	–	2	2	–	–	–	–	–	–
VISIT	–	–	–	–	1	1	–	–	–
WALL	1	–	1	–	–	–	–	–	–
WATER	1	–	1	–	–	–	–	–	–
WENT	–	1	1	–	–	–	–	–	–
WHY	1	–	1	–	–	–	–	–	–
WINDOW	2	–	2	–	1	1	–	–	–
WITH	–	2	2	1	–	1	–	–	–
WITH ME	1	–	1	–	–	–	–	–	–
WITH PEOPLE	–	1	1	–	–	–	–	–	–
YOU	1	1	2	–	–	–	–	–	–
YOUR LIFE	–	1	1	–	–	–	–	–	–

43.   LISTEN

RESPONSE WORD	1ST M	F	T	3RD M	F	T	5TH M	F	T
AND	–	1	1	1	–	1	–	–	–
ANGRY	–	–	–	1	–	1	–	–	–
ANSWER	–	–	–	1	–	1	1	1	2
ARE	–	1	1	–	–	–	–	–	–
ASK	–	–	–	–	1	1	–	–	–
AT ME	–	1	1	–	–	–	–	–	–
ATTENTION	–	–	–	3	–	3	2	4	6
ATTRACTIVE	–	–	–	–	–	–	1	–	1
BABY	1	–	1	–	–	–	–	–	–
BAD	2	1	3	–	1	1	–	–	–
BAD GIRLS	–	1	1	–	–	–	–	–	–
BANG	1	–	1	–	–	–	–	–	–
BAT	1	–	1	–	–	–	–	–	–
BE GOOD	1	–	1	–	–	–	–	–	–
BE QUIET	3	–	3	–	–	–	–	–	–
BECAUSE	1	–	1	–	–	–	–	–	–
BED	–	–	–	–	1	1	–	–	–
BEHAVE	–	1	1	–	2	2	–	–	–
BELL	–	1	1	–	–	–	–	–	–
BICYCLE	1	–	1	–	–	–	–	–	–
BIRD	–	1	1	–	1	1	–	–	–
BISTEN	1	1	2	–	–	–	–	–	–
BORE	1	–	1	–	–	–	–	–	–
BOX	1	–	1	–	–	–	–	–	–
BOY	1	–	1	–	–	–	–	–	–
BRAIN	1	–	1	–	–	–	–	–	–
BRICK	–	1	1	–	–	–	–	–	–
CANT LISTEN	–	–	–	–	–	–	1	–	1
CAR	1	–	1	–	–	–	–	–	–
CAREFUL	1	1	2	2	2	4	–	2	–
CAREFULLY	1	3	4	1	4	5	–	2	2
CARRY ON	–	1	1	–	–	–	–	–	–
CAT	2	–	2	–	–	–	1	–	1
CATCH	1	–	1	–	–	–	–	–	–
CHAIR	–	1	1	–	–	–	–	–	–
CHAIRS	1	–	1	–	–	–	–	–	–
CLEAR	–	–	–	1	–	1	–	–	–
CLOSELY	–	–	–	–	1	1	–	–	–
CONCENTRATE	–	–	–	–	–	–	1	–	1
CONTENT	–	–	–	–	–	–	1	–	1
COOKIE	1	–	1	–	–	–	–	–	–
DEAF	–	1	1	–	–	–	–	–	–
DESK	1	–	1	–	–	–	–	–	–
DID NOT	–	–	–	1	–	1	–	–	–
DIRECTIONS	1	–	1	2	–	2	2	2	4
DISTURB	–	–	–	–	–	–	1	–	1
DIT	1	–	1	–	–	–	–	–	–
DO	–	–	–	–	1	1	–	–	–
DOG	1	1	2	1	1	2	–	–	–
DONT	–	1	1	2	2	4	2	–	2
DONT LISTEN	2	–	2	4	1	5	4	2	6
DOOR	–	1	1	–	–	–	–	–	–
DOWN	–	1	1	–	–	–	–	–	–
DREAM	–	–	–	–	1	1	–	–	–

RESPONSE WORD	1ST M	1ST F	1ST T	3RD M	3RD F	3RD T	5TH M	5TH F	5TH T

43. LISTEN

RESPONSE WORD	1ST M	1ST F	1ST T	3RD M	3RD F	3RD T	5TH M	5TH F	5TH T
DRESSER	–	1	1	–	–	–	–	–	–
EAR	1	–	1	1	1	2	3	3	6
EARS	1	1	2	–	1	1	3	–	3
EAT	1	–	1	–	–	–	–	–	–
ELEPHANT	–	1	1	–	–	–	–	–	–
ENJOY	1	–	1	–	–	–	–	–	–
FATHER	1	1	2	–	–	–	–	–	–
FLAG	1	–	1	–	–	–	–	–	–
FLOOR	–	–	–	1	–	1	–	–	–
FOLLOW	–	–	–	–	–	–	–	1	1
FOLLOW DIRECTION	–	–	–	–	–	–	–	1	1
FOOD	1	–	1	–	–	–	–	–	–
FORGET	–	–	–	2	–	2	–	–	–
FORGOT	–	–	–	–	1	1	–	–	–
GLISTEN	1	–	1	–	–	–	–	–	–
GO	–	–	–	–	1	1	–	–	–
GO DOWNSTAIRS	–	1	1	–	–	–	–	–	–
GOOD	–	1	1	2	2	4	–	–	–
GOOD BYE	–	–	–	1	–	1	–	–	–
GREEN	–	1	1	–	–	–	–	–	–
GROCERY STORE	1	–	1	–	–	–	–	–	–
GROWL	1	–	1	–	–	–	–	–	–
HARD	1	–	1	1	1	2	–	–	–
HAT	1	–	1	–	–	–	–	–	–
HEAD	–	–	–	–	–	–	1	–	1
HEAR	14	19	33	42	42	84	55	68	123
HEARD	–	–	–	1	–	1	3	4	7
HEARING	–	–	–	1	–	1	–	1	1
HEAT	–	1	1	–	–	–	–	–	–
HER	–	–	–	–	–	–	–	1	1
HERE	2	5	7	–	1	1	2	–	2
HIM	1	–	1	1	–	1	–	–	–
HISTEN	1	–	1	–	–	–	–	–	–
HOME	1	–	1	–	–	–	–	–	–
I	–	1	1	–	–	–	–	–	–
I WILL LISTEN TO YOU	–	1	1	–	–	–	–	–	–
IGNORE	–	–	–	–	–	–	1	1	2
IM NOT GOING TO LISTEN	1	–	1	–	–	–	–	–	–
IN	1	–	1	1	–	1	–	–	–
IT	–	–	–	1	–	1	–	–	–
KEEP CARE	–	1	1	–	–	–	–	–	–
KEEP QUIET	–	–	–	1	–	1	–	–	–
KISSING	–	–	–	–	–	–	–	1	1
KISTEN	1	–	1	–	–	–	–	–	–
KNOW	–	–	–	1	–	1	–	–	–
LEARN	–	–	–	2	1	3	2	2	4
LIKE	1	–	1	–	–	–	–	–	–
LIKE YOU LISTEN TO SOMETHING	–	1	1	–	–	–	–	1	1
LINE	–	1	1	–	–	–	–	–	–
LIS	–	1	1	–	–	–	–	–	–
LIST	2	–	2	1	–	1	–	–	–
LISTEN TO A RECORD	–	1	1	–	–	–	–	–	–
LISTENER	–	–	–	–	1	1	–	–	–
LISTENING	–	–	–	–	–	–	–	1	1
LOOK	–	1	1	1	–	1	–	2	2
LOUD	1	3	4	–	1	1	–	1	1
LOVE	1	–	1	–	–	–	–	–	–
MAKE	–	–	–	–	–	–	1	–	1
MAN	1	–	1	–	1	1	–	–	–
ME	–	1	1	1	2	3	–	–	–
MISS	–	1	1	–	–	–	–	–	–
MISSEN	2	–	2	–	–	–	–	–	–
MISTEN	1	–	1	–	1	1	–	–	–
MOMMY	–	1	1	–	–	–	–	–	–
MOTHER	–	1	1	–	–	–	–	–	–
MOVIES	–	1	1	–	–	–	–	–	–
MR	–	–	–	1	–	1	–	–	–
MUSIC	1	1	2	–	–	–	3	–	3
NEAR	–	1	1	–	–	–	–	–	–
NEEDLE	1	–	1	–	–	–	–	–	–
NEVER LISTEN	–	–	–	–	1	1	–	–	–

RESPONSE WORD	1ST M	1ST F	1ST T	3RD M	3RD F	3RD T	5TH M	5TH F	5TH T

43. LISTEN

RESPONSE WORD	M	F	T	M	F	T	M	F	T
NEXT DOOR NEIGHBOR	–	1	1	–	–	–	–	–	–
NO	1	–	1	–	–	–	1	–	1
NO NOISE	–	–	–	–	–	–	–	1	1
NOISE	2	2	4	2	2	4	–	–	–
NOISY	1	–	1	2	1	3	2	–	2
NOT	–	–	–	–	1	1	2	–	2
NOT LISTEN	2	1	3	3	7	10	4	3	7
NOT LISTENING	–	1	1	–	–	–	–	–	–
NOT ROUGH	1	–	1	–	–	–	–	–	–
NOTHING	–	–	–	–	1	1	–	–	–
NOW	4	2	6	2	2	4	–	–	–
NUMBERS	–	–	–	–	–	–	1	–	1
OBEY	–	–	–	4	3	7	5	1	6
OBSERVE	–	–	–	–	–	–	–	1	1
OKAY	–	–	–	–	–	–	1	–	1
OUT	–	2	2	–	–	–	–	1	1
PAPER	2	–	2	–	–	–	–	–	–
PARAGRAPH	–	–	–	–	–	–	1	–	1
PARAKEET	1	–	1	–	–	–	–	–	–
PAY ATTENTION	–	1	1	3	4	7	2	3	5
PAYATENSION	–	–	–	–	–	–	–	1	1
PENCIL	–	1	1	–	–	–	–	–	–
PEOPLE	–	–	–	1	–	1	–	–	–
PERMISSION	1	–	1	–	–	–	–	–	–
PIG	–	1	1	–	–	–	–	–	–
PISSEN	–	–	–	1	–	1	–	–	–
PISTEN	–	1	1	–	–	–	–	–	–
PLAY	–	–	–	1	–	1	–	–	–
PLEASE	–	–	–	–	–	–	–	1	1
PLUG	–	–	–	–	–	–	–	1	1
PONY	1	–	1	–	–	–	–	–	–
POT	–	–	–	–	1	1	–	–	–
QUIET	3	9	12	14	14	28	9	4	13
QUIETLY	2	3	5	1	1	2	1	–	1
QUIT	–	–	–	–	–	–	1	–	1
QUITE	–	–	–	–	–	–	1	–	1
RADIO	–	1	1	–	–	–	–	–	–
RE-LISTEN	–	–	–	–	–	–	1	–	1
READ	–	1	1	–	1	1	2	1	3
RECORDS	–	1	1	–	–	–	–	–	–
REMEMBER	–	–	–	1	–	1	–	–	–
REMIND	–	–	–	1	–	1	–	–	–
RISSEN	–	1	1	–	–	–	–	–	–
RISTEN	1	–	1	–	–	–	–	–	–
SAD	–	–	–	–	1	1	–	–	–
SAG	–	–	–	–	–	–	–	1	1
SAID	–	1	1	–	–	–	–	1	1
SCHOOL	–	–	–	–	–	–	–	1	1
SCHOOL TEACHER	–	1	1	–	–	–	–	–	–
SCRATCH	1	–	1	–	–	–	–	–	–
SCREAM	–	–	–	1	–	1	–	–	–
SECRET	–	1	1	–	–	–	–	–	–
SEE	–	1	1	–	–	–	–	–	–
SHOE	1	–	1	–	–	–	–	–	–
SILENCE	–	–	–	–	–	–	–	1	1
SING	–	1	1	–	–	–	–	–	–
SISTER	–	1	1	–	–	–	–	–	–
SIT	–	1	1	–	–	–	–	–	–
SIT DOWN AND WRITE YOUR NUMBERS	–	1	1	–	–	–	–	–	–
SLOW	–	–	–	–	1	1	–	–	–
SMOOTH	1	–	1	–	–	–	–	–	–
SOMEBODY	–	–	–	1	–	1	–	–	–
SOMEBODY LISTEN	–	1	1	–	–	–	–	–	–
SOMETHING	–	1	1	–	1	1	–	–	–
SOUND	1	3	4	1	3	4	–	1	1
SPEAK	–	–	–	–	1	1	3	–	3
SPOKE	1	–	1	–	–	–	–	–	–
STOP	–	2	2	1	–	1	–	1	1
STUDY	–	–	–	–	–	–	1	1	2
TAKE AWAY	–	1	1	–	–	–	–	–	–
TALK	2	–	2	6	5	11	3	7	10

RESPONSE WORD	1ST M	F	T	3RD M	F	T	5TH M	F	T

43.   LISTEN

RESPONSE WORD	1ST M	F	T	3RD M	F	T	5TH M	F	T
TEACH	—	—	—	1	—	1	—	—	—
TEACHER	2	1	3	1	1	2	1	1	2
TELL	—	—	—	2	1	3	1	2	3
TEND	—	—	—	—	—	—	1	—	1
THAT	1	—	1	—	1	1	—	—	—
THINK	—	1	1	—	—	—	1	—	1
THIS	—	1	1	—	—	—	—	—	—
TO	8	3	11	2	4	6	1	—	1
TO GO HOME	—	1	1	—	—	—	—	—	—
TO HEAR	—	—	—	—	—	—	1	—	1
TO ME	4	4	8	—	1	1	—	—	—
TO MOTHER	2	—	2	—	—	—	—	—	—
TO MUSIC	1	—	1	—	—	—	—	—	—
TO PAY ATTENTION	—	—	—	—	—	—	—	1	1
TO SOMETHING	1	—	1	—	—	—	—	—	—
TO STOP	—	—	—	—	—	—	—	1	1
TO TEACHER	1	—	1	—	—	—	—	—	—
TO TEACHERS	1	—	1	—	—	—	—	—	—
TO THAT	1	—	1	—	—	—	—	—	—
TO THE BIRDS	1	—	1	—	—	—	—	—	—
TO THE NOISE	1	—	1	—	—	—	—	—	—
TO THE TEACHER	—	1	1	1	—	1	—	—	—
TO WHAT SHE SAYING	—	1	1	—	—	—	—	—	—
TO WHAT YOU HEAR	1	—	1	—	—	—	—	—	—
TO WHAT YOUR MOTHER SAY	1	—	1	—	—	—	—	—	—
TO WHAT YOUR TEACHER SAYS OR YOU MIGHT	—	1	1	—	—	—	—	—	—
TO YOU	—	1	1	—	—	—	—	—	—
TO YOUR MOTHER	2	—	2	—	—	—	—	—	—
TO YOUR TEACHER	1	1	2	—	—	—	—	—	—
TOM	2	—	2	—	—	—	—	—	—
TRAIN	—	1	1	—	—	—	—	1	1
TREE	1	—	1	—	—	—	—	—	—
TV	—	—	—	—	1	1	—	—	—
UNDERSTAND	—	—	—	—	1	1	1	—	1
UNLISTED	—	—	—	—	1	1	—	1	1
UNLISTEN	—	—	—	—	1	1	—	1	1
UNLISTENING	—	—	—	1	—	1	—	—	—
US	—	—	—	1	—	1	—	—	—
WALK	1	—	1	—	—	—	—	—	—
WALL	1	—	1	—	—	—	—	—	—
WANT TO	—	—	—	1	—	1	—	—	—
WATCH TV	—	1	1	—	—	—	—	—	—
WATCHING	—	—	—	—	—	—	1	—	1
WELL	—	—	—	—	—	—	—	1	1
WHAT I SAY	—	1	1	—	—	—	—	—	—
WHEN SOMEONE WANTS YOU TO LISTEN TO HIM	—	1	1	—	—	—	—	—	—
WHEN YOU LISTEN TO SOMEBODY	1	—	1	—	—	—	—	—	—
WITH	1	—	1	—	—	—	—	—	—
WORDS	—	—	—	1	—	1	1	—	1
WORK	—	1	1	—	—	—	—	—	—
YELL	—	—	—	1	1	2	—	—	—
YES	—	1	1	1	—	1	—	—	—
YOU	—	3	3	—	—	—	—	—	—

44.   LONG

RESPONSE WORD	1ST M	F	T	3RD M	F	T	5TH M	F	T
A GREAT DEAL	—	—	—	—	—	—	1	—	1
A LAWN YOU MOW	—	—	—	1	—	1	—	—	—
A LONG, BIG BOARD	1	—	1	—	—	—	—	—	—
ACRE	—	—	—	1	—	1	—	—	—
AGO	—	2	2	—	1	1	—	1	1
AIR	—	—	—	1	—	1	—	—	—
ALLIGATOR	1	—	1	—	—	—	—	—	—
ALWAYS	—	—	—	1	—	1	—	1	1
AWAY	1	—	1	—	—	—	—	—	—
BABY DOLL	—	1	1	—	—	—	—	—	—
BAD	1	—	1	—	—	—	—	—	—
BANANA	—	—	—	—	—	—	1	—	1

RESPONSE WORD	M	1ST F	T	M	3RD F	T	M	5TH F	T

44. LONG

RESPONSE WORD	M	1ST F	T	M	3RD F	T	M	5TH F	T
BARN	–	1	1	1	–	1	–	–	–
BATHROOM	–	1	1	–	–	–	–	–	–
BEANS	–	1	1	–	–	–	–	–	–
BEARD	1	–	1	–	–	–	–	–	–
BEFORE	–	–	–	–	1	1	–	–	–
BELL	1	–	1	–	–	–	–	–	–
BELONG	2	–	2	–	1	–	–	–	–
BERMUDAS	–	–	–	–	1	1	–	–	–
BIG	5	1	6	3	2	5	1	1	2
BOARD	1	1	2	–	–	–	1	–	1
BOAT	1	–	1	1	–	1	–	–	–
BONG	–	–	–	–	–	–	–	1	1
BORING	–	–	–	–	1	1	–	1	1
BOY	–	–	–	–	1	1	–	–	–
BREATHE	–	–	–	2	–	2	–	–	–
BROAD	–	–	–	–	–	–	1	–	1
BROWN	1	–	1	–	–	–	–	–	–
BUILDING	1	–	1	–	–	–	1	–	1
BUS	1	–	1	–	–	–	–	–	–
BY	1	–	1	–	1	1	–	–	–
BYE	–	1	1	–	–	–	–	–	–
CABBAGE	–	–	–	1	–	1	–	–	–
CALL	–	1	1	–	–	–	–	–	–
CAR	–	–	–	–	–	–	1	–	1
CHAIR	–	2	2	–	–	–	–	–	–
CHALK	1	–	1	–	–	–	–	–	–
CLOTHES	–	1	1	–	–	–	–	–	–
COAT	–	1	1	–	–	–	–	–	–
COME	–	1	1	–	–	–	–	–	–
CORN	1	1	2	–	–	–	–	–	–
CUPBOARD	–	1	1	–	–	–	–	–	–
CUT	2	3	5	–	–	–	–	–	–
CUT A EDGE OFF	–	1	1	–	–	–	–	–	–
DAYS	–	1	1	–	–	–	–	–	–
DESK	1	–	1	–	–	–	–	–	–
DID	–	1	1	–	–	–	–	–	–
DISTANCE	1	–	1	–	1	1	–	–	–
DONG	1	–	1	–	–	–	–	–	–
DONT	–	–	–	–	1	1	–	–	–
DOOR	–	1	1	–	–	–	–	–	–
DRESS	–	3	3	–	–	–	–	–	–
DRIVE	–	–	–	–	–	–	1	–	1
DUCK	–	1	1	–	–	–	–	–	–
FALL	–	–	–	1	–	1	–	–	–
FANG	–	1	1	–	–	–	–	–	–
FAR	–	–	–	5	–	5	1	1	2
FAST	–	1	1	1	2	3	–	–	–
FAT	–	1	1	–	–	–	–	–	–
FEET	–	–	–	–	–	–	1	–	1
FIRE	1	–	1	–	–	–	–	–	–
FOR	–	–	–	1	–	1	–	–	–
FROG	1	–	1	–	–	–	–	–	–
FUNNING	–	1	1	–	–	–	–	–	–
GIRL	–	1	1	–	–	–	–	–	–
GO	–	–	–	–	1	1	–	1	1
GONE	1	–	1	–	–	–	–	–	–
GOOD	1	1	2	–	–	–	1	–	1
GOOD LENGTH	–	–	–	–	–	–	1	–	1
GRASS	8	3	11	5	2	7	3	2	5
GREEN	–	1	1	–	1	1	–	–	–
HAIR	1	5	6	1	–	1	–	1	1
HALL	1	–	1	–	–	–	–	–	–
HAND	1	–	1	–	–	–	–	–	–
HANG	–	1	1	–	–	–	–	–	–
HANGER	–	1	1	–	–	–	–	–	–
HAT	1	–	1	–	–	–	–	–	–
HAY	–	–	–	–	1	1	–	–	–
HEAD	–	1	1	–	–	–	–	–	–
HEATER	1	–	1	–	–	–	–	–	–
HER	1	–	1	–	–	–	–	–	–
HERE	–	1	1	1	–	1	–	–	–
HIGH	–	–	–	1	–	1	1	1	2

RESPONSE WORD	1ST M	F	T	3RD M	F	T	5TH M	F	T
44. LONG									
HOME	1	–	1	–	–	–	–	–	–
HORSE	–	–	–	–	–	–	1	–	1
HOSE	1	–	1	–	–	–	–	–	–
HOUSE	–	1	1	–	–	–	–	–	–
I AM SIX	1	–	1	–	–	–	–	–	–
I CAN STAY HERE LONG	–	1	1	–	–	–	–	–	–
I WANT TO STAY UP LONG	–	1	1	–	–	–	–	–	–
ICE	–	–	–	–	1	1	–	–	–
ICE CREAM	1	–	1	–	–	–	–	–	–
JOURNEY	–	–	–	–	–	–	1	1	2
JUICE	1	–	1	–	–	–	–	–	–
KEEP	–	1	1	–	–	–	–	–	–
LARGE	1	1	2	–	3	3	2	1	3
LAST	1	–	1	–	–	–	–	–	–
LAWN	1	1	2	–	–	–	–	–	–
LAWN MOWER	2	5	7	–	–	–	–	–	–
LEG	–	1	1	–	1	1	–	–	–
LEGS	1	–	1	–	–	–	–	–	–
LENGTH	–	–	–	2	1	3	2	2	4
LIGHT	–	–	–	1	1	2	–	1	1
LIMB	–	1	1	–	–	–	–	–	–
LINE	–	–	–	1	–	1	–	1	1
LITTLE	1	4	5	1	2	3	–	–	–
LOCKERS	1	–	1	–	–	–	–	–	–
LOG	–	–	–	–	2	2	1	1	2
LONGER	–	–	–	–	–	–	1	1	2
LONGMOWER	–	1	1	–	–	–	–	–	–
LONGS	1	–	1	–	–	–	–	–	–
LOVE	1	–	1	–	–	–	–	–	–
LOW	1	1	2	–	–	–	–	1	1
MAIL BOX	1	–	1	–	–	–	–	–	–
MAN	1	–	1	–	–	–	–	–	–
MILE	–	–	–	–	–	–	3	–	3
MONG	1	–	1	–	–	–	–	–	–
NARROW	–	–	–	–	–	–	2	4	6
NEVER	–	–	–	–	–	–	–	1	1
NEW	–	1	1	–	–	–	–	–	–
NOT SHORT	–	–	–	–	–	–	1	2	3
NOW	–	1	1	–	–	–	–	–	–
ORANGE	–	1	1	–	–	–	–	–	–
PAPER	–	1	1	–	–	–	–	–	–
PAWN	–	–	–	–	1	1	–	–	–
PENCIL	–	1	1	–	–	–	–	–	–
PEOPLE	2	–	2	–	–	–	–	–	–
PERSON	1	–	1	–	–	–	–	–	–
PICTURE	1	–	1	–	–	–	–	–	–
PLANE	–	–	–	–	–	–	1	–	1
POLES	–	–	–	–	–	–	1	–	1
POND	–	1	1	–	–	–	–	1	1
REAL	–	1	1	–	–	–	–	–	–
RIDE	3	2	5	–	–	–	–	–	–
RING	–	2	2	–	–	–	1	–	1
RIVER	–	–	–	–	–	–	1	–	1
ROAD	–	–	–	–	1	1	–	–	–
ROOM	1	–	1	–	–	–	–	–	–
ROPE	2	1	3	1	1	2	2	–	2
ROUND	1	–	1	–	–	–	1	1	2
RULER	–	–	–	–	–	–	–	1	1
SAD	–	–	–	1	–	1	–	–	–
SCISSORS	–	1	1	–	–	–	–	–	–
SENTENCE	1	–	1	1	–	1	–	–	–
SHONG	–	–	–	–	–	–	1	–	1
SHORT	26	30	56	85	92	177	80	84	164
SHORTER	–	–	–	1	–	1	–	–	–
SHOT	–	–	–	–	–	–	1	–	1
SIDEWALK	2	–	2	–	–	–	–	–	–
SIGHT	–	–	–	–	–	–	1	–	1
SINK	–	1	1	–	–	–	–	–	–
SKINNY	–	1	1	1	1	2	–	–	–
SKYSCRAPER	1	–	1	–	–	–	–	–	–
SLIM	–	–	–	–	1	1	–	–	–

RESPONSE WORD	1ST			3RD			5TH		
	M	F	T	M	F	T	M	F	T

44.   LONG

RESPONSE WORD	M	F	T	M	F	T	M	F	T
SLOW	2	–	2	–	1	2	–	2	2
SMALL	2	1	3	1	1	2	–	3	3
SNAKE	1	–	1	1	–	1	–	–	–
SNAKES	1	–	1	–	–	–	–	–	–
SOFT	–	–	–	–	1	1	–	–	–
SOMEBODY LONG	–	1	1	–	–	–	–	–	–
SOMETHING VERY LONG	–	–	–	–	–	–	–	1	1
SONG	1	–	1	–	–	–	–	–	–
SONT	–	–	–	–	–	–	1	–	1
SOON	1	–	1	–	–	–	–	–	–
SORT	–	1	1	–	–	–	–	–	–
SPONG	–	–	–	1	–	1	–	–	–
SPRING	1	–	1	–	–	–	–	–	–
SQUARE	–	–	–	–	1	1	–	–	–
STATION WAGON	1	–	1	–	–	–	–	–	–
STAY	–	1	1	–	–	–	–	–	–
STEADY	–	–	–	–	–	–	–	1	1
STICK	3	–	3	–	–	–	–	–	–
STRAIGHT	1	–	1	1	–	1	–	1	1
STRETCH	1	–	1	3	1	4	2	1	3
STRING	2	1	3	–	–	–	–	–	–
STRIP	–	–	–	1	–	1	–	–	–
TABLE	2	–	2	–	1	1	–	–	–
TAIL	1	2	3	–	–	–	–	1	1
TALK	–	1	1	–	–	–	–	–	–
TALL	–	–	–	1	1	2	1	–	1
TELEVISION	–	1	1	–	–	–	–	–	–
THIN	–	–	–	–	–	–	2	–	2
THROAT	–	–	–	–	–	–	–	1	1
TIGHT	–	–	–	–	1	1	–	–	–
TIME	–	2	2	1	2	3	3	1	4
TO WANT SOMETHING BADLY	–	–	–	–	–	–	–	1	1
TONG	2	–	2	–	–	–	–	–	–
TONSILS	–	–	–	1	–	1	–	–	–
TOO LONG	–	1	1	–	–	–	–	–	–
TRAILER	1	–	1	–	–	–	–	–	–
TRAIN	–	–	–	–	1	1	1	–	1
TREE	1	–	1	–	1	1	–	1	1
TREES	–	1	1	–	–	–	–	–	–
TRIP	1	1	2	–	–	–	–	–	–
TRUCK	1	–	1	–	–	–	–	–	–
TUNNEL	1	–	1	–	–	–	–	–	–
TYPE	1	–	1	–	–	–	–	–	–
UNSHORT	–	–	–	–	–	–	1	–	1
UP	–	1	1	–	–	–	–	–	–
WAGON	–	1	1	–	–	–	–	–	–
WAIT	–	–	–	–	–	–	–	1	1
WAITED	1	–	1	–	–	–	–	–	–
WALK	1	1	2	–	–	–	–	1	1
WALL	–	2	2	–	–	–	–	–	–
WATCH	–	2	2	–	–	–	–	–	–
WATER	–	1	1	–	–	–	–	–	–
WAY	–	3	3	1	1	2	1	–	1
WENT	–	1	1	–	–	–	–	–	–
WHAT YOU CUT DOWN	1	–	1	–	–	–	–	–	–
WHEN YOURE LAWNING THE GRASS	1	–	1	–	–	–	–	–	–
WHENEVER SOMEONE TAKES YOU ALONG	–	1	1	–	–	–	–	–	–
WHILE	–	–	–	–	–	–	–	1	1
WIDE	1	1	2	2	3	5	6	6	12
WITH	–	–	–	1	–	1	–	–	–
WOOD	2	–	2	–	–	–	2	1	3
WORD	–	–	–	–	–	–	–	1	1
WOULD	–	–	–	–	1	1	–	–	–
WRONG	–	1	1	–	–	–	–	–	–
YARD	–	–	–	1	–	1	–	1	1
YARDSTICK	–	–	–	–	–	–	1	–	1
YEAR	–	–	–	1	–	1	1	–	1
YELLOW	–	–	–	1	–	1	–	–	–
YOU	1	–	1	–	–	–	–	–	–
YOU COULD GO OUTSIDE AND PLAY IN THE FI	–	1	1	–	–	–	–	–	–

RESPONSE WORD	1ST M	1ST F	1ST T	3RD M	3RD F	3RD T	5TH M	5TH F	5TH T

45. LOUD

RESPONSE WORD	M	F	T	M	F	T	M	F	T
AIRPLANE	3	–	3	–	–	–	–	–	–
ALLOW	1	–	1	–	–	–	–	–	–
ALLOWED TO TAKE A DOLLAR	–	–	–	1	–	1	–	–	–
ANGEL	–	–	–	1	–	1	–	–	–
BABY	1	–	1	–	–	–	–	–	–
BANG	–	–	–	–	–	–	–	1	1
BE QUIET	1	–	1	–	–	–	–	–	–
BELL	–	1	1	–	–	–	–	–	–
BIG	1	–	1	1	–	1	–	–	–
BIG NOISE	–	–	–	–	–	–	1	–	1
BLARE	–	–	–	–	–	–	1	–	1
BOAT	–	1	1	–	–	–	–	–	–
BOWED	–	1	1	–	–	–	–	–	–
BOYS	–	1	1	1	–	1	–	–	–
CALL	–	–	–	–	–	–	2	–	2
CAR	1	–	1	–	–	–	–	1	1
CAT	1	–	1	–	–	–	–	–	–
CHAIR	1	1	2	–	–	–	–	–	–
CHALK BOARD	2	–	2	–	–	–	–	–	–
CIRLE	–	–	–	–	1	1	–	–	–
CLEAR	–	1	1	7	4	11	3	1	4
CLEARLY	–	–	–	–	1	1	–	–	–
CLOUD	1	2	3	2	–	2	–	–	–
COUNTRY	–	–	–	1	–	1	–	–	–
COW	–	2	2	–	–	–	–	–	–
CRASS	1	–	1	–	–	–	–	–	–
CREAM	–	–	–	1	–	1	–	–	–
CROWD	1	1	2	–	–	–	1	–	1
CRY	–	–	–	–	1	1	–	–	–
CRYING	1	–	1	–	–	–	–	–	–
DESK	1	–	1	–	–	–	–	–	–
DIG	1	–	1	–	–	–	–	–	–
DIGGING	–	–	–	–	–	–	1	–	1
DOG	1	1	2	–	–	–	–	–	–
DONT HOLLER LOUD	–	1	1	–	–	–	–	–	–
DONT TALK LOUD	1	–	1	–	–	–	–	–	–
DONT TALK OUT LOUD	–	1	1	–	–	–	–	–	–
DOOR	–	1	1	–	–	–	–	–	–
DOWN	–	2	2	–	–	–	–	–	–
DRUM	–	–	–	–	1	1	–	–	–
DULL	–	–	–	1	–	1	–	–	–
EAR	–	–	–	–	–	–	1	–	1
EASY	1	–	1	1	1	2	–	–	–
FALL	–	–	–	–	1	1	–	–	–
FATHER	1	–	1	–	–	–	–	–	–
FIRE	1	–	1	–	–	–	–	–	–
FLOOR	1	–	1	–	–	–	–	–	–
FLOWER	1	–	1	–	–	–	–	–	–
FLOWERS	–	1	1	–	–	–	–	–	–
FUR	–	–	–	–	–	–	1	–	1
GATE	–	–	–	–	1	1	–	–	–
GO	–	–	–	–	1	1	–	–	–
GOOD	1	–	1	–	–	–	–	–	–
GROUD	–	1	1	–	–	–	–	–	–
HANDLE	1	–	1	–	–	–	–	–	–
HARD	–	–	–	2	2	4	–	1	1
HARDER	1	–	1	–	–	–	–	–	–
HARSH	–	–	–	–	–	–	1	–	1
HEAR	2	2	4	2	1	3	–	–	–
HEARD	–	–	–	1	–	1	–	1	1
HIGH	–	–	–	1	–	1	2	1	3
HIGH TUNE	–	–	–	–	–	–	1	–	1
HIGHT	–	–	–	–	–	–	1	1	2
HOLLAR	1	–	1	–	1	1	2	–	2
HOLLER	5	4	9	–	1	1	1	1	2
HOLLERED	–	–	–	–	–	–	1	–	1
HOLLERING	1	–	1	–	–	–	–	–	–
HOUSE	–	1	1	–	–	–	–	–	–
HOW	2	–	2	–	–	–	–	–	–
HOWL	–	1	1	1	–	1	–	–	–
HURTS EARS	1	–	1	–	–	–	–	–	–
HUSH	–	1	1	–	–	–	–	–	–

RESPONSE WORD	1ST M	F	T	3RD M	F	T	5TH M	F	T

45. LOUD

RESPONSE WORD	1ST M	F	T	3RD M	F	T	5TH M	F	T
JAIL	–	–	–	1	–	1	–	–	–
LADDER	–	3	3	–	–	–	–	–	–
LARGE	–	1	1	–	1	1	1	–	1
LAY DOWN	–	–	–	–	–	–	–	1	1
LEAF	–	–	–	–	2	2	–	–	–
LETS SING LOUD	–	1	1	–	–	–	–	–	–
LIGHT	–	–	–	1	–	1	–	–	–
LIGHTLY	–	1	1	–	–	–	–	–	–
LITTLE	–	–	–	1	–	1	–	–	–
LOG	1	–	1	–	–	–	–	–	–
LOUDER	–	–	–	1	1	2	–	–	–
LOUDLY	1	–	1	–	–	–	–	2	2
LOUNGE	–	1	1	–	–	–	–	–	–
LOUNGE CHAIR	1	–	1	–	–	–	–	–	–
LOVE	1	–	1	–	–	–	–	–	–
LOW	9	9	18	5	10	15	7	6	13
LYING	1	–	1	–	–	–	–	–	–
MAN	2	1	3	–	–	–	–	–	–
MONEY	1	–	1	–	–	–	–	–	–
MOON	–	1	1	–	–	–	–	–	–
MOSTLY	–	–	–	–	1	1	–	–	–
MOUD	1	–	1	–	–	–	–	–	–
MOUSE	1	–	1	–	–	–	–	–	–
MOUTH	4	2	6	1	2	3	1	1	2
MOW	1	–	1	–	–	–	–	–	–
MUSIC	1	–	1	–	–	–	1	–	1
NAVY	–	–	–	1	–	1	–	–	–
NO	–	1	1	–	–	–	–	–	–
NOISE	5	5	10	5	10	15	14	11	25
NOISY	1	3	4	10	11	21	9	12	21
NOIZE	–	–	–	–	–	–	1	–	1
NOSEY	–	–	–	–	–	–	1	–	1
NOT LOUD	–	1	1	2	–	2	1	–	1
NOT NOISY	–	–	–	–	–	–	–	1	1
NOT QUIET	–	–	–	–	1	1	–	–	–
NOT SOFT	–	–	–	–	–	–	–	1	1
OPEN	–	1	1	–	–	–	–	–	–
OUT	–	1	1	–	–	–	–	–	–
OUTSTANDING	–	–	–	–	–	–	1	–	1
OW	1	–	1	–	–	–	–	–	–
PAGE	–	–	–	–	–	–	1	–	1
PEOPLE	–	–	–	–	–	–	–	1	1
PEOPLE TALK LOUD	1	–	1	–	–	–	–	–	–
PIANO	–	1	1	–	–	–	–	–	–
PICTURE	1	1	2	–	–	–	–	–	–
PLAY LOUD	1	–	1	–	–	–	–	–	–
POUD	–	1	1	–	–	–	–	–	–
PROUD	1	–	1	–	–	–	–	–	–
PUPPY	1	–	1	–	–	–	–	–	–
PURPLE	–	1	1	–	–	–	–	–	–
QUIET	14	16	30	25	13	38	6	8	14
QUIETLY	–	–	–	1	–	1	–	–	–
QUITE	–	–	–	–	–	–	1	–	1
RADIO	–	–	–	–	–	–	–	1	1
READ	–	1	1	–	–	–	–	–	–
REAL LOUD	1	–	1	–	–	–	–	–	–
RING	–	1	1	–	–	–	–	–	–
ROAR	–	–	–	1	–	1	–	–	–
ROUD	–	–	–	–	–	–	1	–	1
SAY LOUD	–	1	1	–	–	–	–	–	–
SCREAM	2	8	10	2	3	5	2	3	5
SCREAMING	2	–	2	–	–	–	–	1	1
SEE	1	–	1	–	–	–	–	–	–
SHOF	–	–	–	–	–	–	1	–	1
SHORT	–	–	–	–	1	1	–	–	–
SHOUT	5	5	10	9	2	11	8	6	14
SHOUTED	–	–	–	–	1	1	–	–	–
SHUT UP	1	–	1	–	–	–	–	–	–
SILENT	–	–	–	1	4	5	1	–	1
SING	–	1	1	–	–	–	–	–	–
SLOW	–	5	5	–	–	–	–	–	–
SMALL	–	–	–	–	1	1	–	–	–

RESPONSE WORD	1ST M	F	T	3RD M	F	T	5TH M	F	T

45. LOUD

RESPONSE WORD	1ST M	F	T	3RD M	F	T	5TH M	F	T
SMOOTH	1	–	1	–	–	–	–	–	–
SMOUD	1	–	1	–	–	–	–	–	–
SOFT	15	19	34	35	51	86	50	60	110
SOFTLY	1	1	2	2	1	3	2	4	6
SOLID	–	–	–	–	1	1	–	–	–
SOMEBODY LOUD	–	1	1	–	–	–	–	–	–
SOUD	–	–	–	–	1	1	–	–	–
SOUND	1	–	1	1	1	2	1	1	2
SPEAK	–	–	–	2	–	2	1	–	1
SPEAKER	–	–	–	–	–	–	1	–	1
SPEECH	–	–	–	–	–	–	–	2	2
SQUARE	–	–	–	1	–	1	–	–	–
STAND	–	–	–	–	–	–	1	–	1
STOP	–	2	2	–	–	–	–	–	–
STRAIN	–	–	–	–	–	–	–	1	1
SUN	2	–	2	–	–	–	–	–	–
SWOUD	1	–	1	–	–	–	–	–	–
TABLE	–	1	1	–	–	–	–	–	–
TAKE	–	–	–	–	–	–	1	–	1
TALK	3	1	4	1	1	2	–	6	6
TALK LOUDLY	–	1	1	–	–	–	–	–	–
TALKER	–	–	–	1	–	1	–	–	–
TALKING	1	–	1	–	–	–	1	–	1
TALKING OUT	1	–	1	–	–	–	–	–	–
TALKS	–	–	–	–	1	1	–	–	–
TEASE	1	–	1	–	–	–	–	–	–
THE	–	–	–	–	–	–	1	–	1
THIS	–	–	–	1	–	1	–	–	–
TOAST	1	–	1	–	–	–	–	–	–
TOO	–	1	1	–	–	–	–	–	–
TRAIN	–	–	–	1	–	1	–	–	–
TREE	1	–	1	–	–	–	–	–	–
TREES	1	–	1	–	–	–	–	–	–
TRUCK	1	–	1	–	–	–	–	–	–
US	–	–	–	–	–	–	–	1	1
VOICE	2	–	2	2	1	3	–	–	–
WE	–	1	1	–	–	–	–	–	–
WHENEVER SOMEONE HOLLERS	–	1	1	–	–	–	–	–	–
WHISPER	–	1	1	1	–	1	–	–	–
WILL	1	–	1	–	–	–	–	–	–
WIND	1	–	1	–	–	–	–	–	–
WIRE	–	–	–	–	1	1	–	–	–
WOUD	–	1	1	–	–	–	–	–	–
YELL	–	6	6	2	–	2	3	2	5
YELLOW	–	1	1	–	–	–	–	1	1
YOU CAN HOLLER	1	–	1	–	–	–	–	–	–

46. LOUDLY

RESPONSE WORD	1ST M	F	T	3RD M	F	T	5TH M	F	T
ALOUD	–	–	–	1	–	1	–	1	1
AWAY	–	–	–	–	1	1	–	–	–
BAD	1	–	1	–	–	–	–	–	–
BAND	–	1	1	–	–	–	–	–	–
BE QUIET	1	–	1	–	–	–	–	–	–
BELL	–	1	1	–	–	–	–	–	–
BICYCLE	–	1	1	–	–	–	–	–	–
BIRD	–	1	1	–	–	–	–	–	–
BOLDLY	–	–	–	–	–	–	–	1	1
BOY	1	–	1	–	1	1	–	–	–
BOYS	1	–	1	–	–	–	–	–	–
BRICKS	1	–	1	–	–	–	–	–	–
CAN	–	1	1	–	–	–	–	–	–
CARS	1	–	1	–	–	–	–	–	–
CEILING	–	1	1	–	–	–	–	–	–
CHALKBOARD	1	–	1	–	–	–	–	–	–
CLEAR	–	1	1	1	1	2	1	–	1
CLEARLY	–	–	–	3	1	4	4	1	5
CLOTHES	–	1	1	–	–	–	–	–	–
CLOUD	–	1	1	1	–	1	–	1	1
CLOUDS	–	1	1	–	–	–	–	–	–
COAT HANGER	1	–	1	–	–	–	–	–	–

RESPONSE WORD	1ST M	F	T	3RD M	F	T	5TH M	F	T

46. LOUDLY

RESPONSE WORD	1ST M	F	T	3RD M	F	T	5TH M	F	T
COME	1	–	1	–	–	–	–	–	–
COUDLY	–	–	–	–	1	1	–	–	–
COUNTRY	–	–	–	–	1	1	–	–	–
CRY	–	–	–	–	–	–	1	1	2
DEAF	–	–	–	–	–	–	–	1	1
DOG	–	1	1	–	–	–	1	–	1
DONT	–	1	1	–	–	–	–	–	–
DONT MAKE THE TEACHER HOWL AT YOU	–	1	1	–	–	–	–	–	–
DONT SHOUT	1	–	1	–	–	–	–	–	–
DONT TALK LOUD	1	–	1	–	–	–	–	–	–
DOOR	–	1	1	–	–	–	–	–	–
DOWN	2	–	2	–	–	–	–	–	–
EARDRUM	–	–	–	–	–	–	1	–	1
FACK	–	–	–	–	–	–	1	–	1
FAR	–	–	–	1	–	1	–	–	–
FAST	1	1	2	–	1	1	–	–	–
FAT	–	1	1	–	–	–	–	–	–
FLOWER	2	1	3	–	–	–	–	–	–
FLY	–	1	1	–	–	–	–	–	–
GAS	1	–	1	–	–	–	–	–	–
GENTLY	–	–	–	1	2	3	–	–	–
GIRL	–	1	1	–	–	–	–	–	–
GLASSES	–	2	2	–	–	–	–	–	–
GOBBLE	–	1	1	–	–	–	–	–	–
GOOD	–	–	–	–	–	–	1	–	1
GRAY	–	–	–	1	–	1	–	–	–
HAND	2	–	2	–	–	–	–	–	–
HANDLE	1	–	1	–	–	–	–	–	–
HARD	–	–	–	–	2	2	1	–	1
HAT	–	1	1	–	–	–	–	–	–
HEAR	2	5	7	1	–	1	–	2	2
HEARD	–	–	–	1	–	1	–	–	–
HELLO	1	–	1	–	–	–	–	–	–
HERE	–	1	1	–	–	–	–	–	–
HIGH	–	–	–	1	–	1	1	1	2
HIGH TUNE	–	–	–	–	–	–	1	–	1
HIGHLY	–	–	–	–	–	–	1	–	1
HOLLAR	1	–	1	–	–	–	1	–	1
HOLLER	3	1	4	1	2	3	–	1	1
HOLLER OUT	–	1	1	–	–	–	–	–	–
HOLLER OUT LOUD	–	1	1	–	–	–	–	–	–
HOLLERING	1	–	1	–	–	–	–	–	–
HOTTER	1	–	1	–	–	–	–	–	–
HOUDLY	2	–	2	–	–	–	–	–	–
HOUSE	–	1	1	–	–	–	–	–	–
HURRY	–	–	–	–	1	1	–	–	–
HUSH	–	1	1	–	–	–	–	–	–
I	1	–	1	–	–	–	–	–	–
I TALK	–	1	1	–	–	–	–	–	–
LADY	1	–	1	–	–	–	–	–	–
LAUGH	–	1	1	–	–	–	–	–	–
LAY	–	1	1	–	–	–	–	–	–
LEAF	–	1	1	–	1	1	–	–	–
LETS SING LOUD	–	1	1	–	–	–	–	–	–
LIBRARY	–	–	–	–	1	1	–	–	–
LIGHTLY	–	1	1	1	–	1	–	–	–
LIKE	–	–	–	1	–	1	–	–	–
LITTLE	–	–	–	1	–	1	–	–	–
LIVELY	–	1	1	–	–	–	–	–	–
LOFTLY	–	1	1	–	–	–	–	–	–
LONG	–	–	–	–	1	1	–	1	1
LOT OF NOISE	–	–	–	–	–	–	–	–	–
LOUD	7	3	10	4	2	6	4	3	7
LOUD MAN	1	–	1	–	–	–	–	–	–
LOUD MOUTH	1	–	1	–	–	–	–	–	–
LOUD NOISE	–	–	–	–	–	–	1	–	1
LOUD WITH MY BOY FRIENDS	–	–	–	1	–	1	–	–	–
LOUDER	1	–	1	–	–	–	–	–	–
LOW	3	3	6	4	5	9	4	–	4
LOWER	–	–	–	–	–	–	–	1	1
LOWLY	–	–	–	1	2	3	3	1	4

RESPONSE WORD	1ST			3RD			5TH		
	M	F	T	M	F	T	M	F	T

46. LOUDLY

RESPONSE WORD	M	F	T	M	F	T	M	F	T
MAN	1	–	1	–	–	–	–	–	–
ME	–	1	1	–	–	–	1	–	1
MEGAPHONE	–	–	–	–	–	–	–	1	1
MILK	–	1	1	–	–	–	–	–	–
MOUDLY	1	–	1	–	–	–	–	–	–
MOUTH	2	1	3	1	2	3	–	–	–
MOVE	1	–	1	–	–	–	–	–	–
MUSIC	–	–	–	–	–	–	–	1	1
NEWS	–	–	–	–	–	–	–	1	1
NOICE	–	–	–	–	–	–	1	–	1
NOISE	–	1	1	4	3	7	10	9	19
NOISES	–	–	–	–	–	–	1	–	1
NOISILY	–	–	–	–	1	1	2	2	4
NOISY	1	–	1	13	9	22	10	8	18
NOT	1	–	1	–	–	–	–	–	–
NOT LIGHT	–	–	–	–	–	–	–	1	1
NOT LOUDLY	–	–	–	2	–	2	–	–	–
NOT QUIET	–	–	–	–	–	–	–	1	1
NOT SLOW	–	–	–	–	–	–	–	1	1
NOT SO LOUD	–	–	–	–	1	1	–	–	–
NOT SOFT	–	–	–	–	–	–	1	2	3
OCEAN	1	–	1	–	–	–	–	–	–
OUT	1	–	1	–	–	–	–	–	–
PEOPLE	–	–	–	–	–	–	–	1	1
PILLOW	1	–	1	–	–	–	–	–	–
POCKETBOOK	1	–	1	–	–	–	–	–	–
POUD	–	1	1	–	–	–	–	–	–
POUDLY	2	–	2	–	–	–	–	–	–
POUND	–	1	1	–	–	–	–	–	–
POW	1	–	1	–	–	–	–	–	–
PRETTY	1	–	1	1	–	1	–	–	–
QUEIT	–	–	–	–	–	–	–	1	1
QUIET	7	7	14	10	5	15	3	5	8
QUIETLY	3	4	7	2	6	8	3	3	6
QUITE	–	–	–	–	–	–	1	–	1
RADIO	–	–	–	–	–	–	1	–	1
REAL LOUD	2	2	4	–	–	–	–	–	–
ROAR	–	–	–	1	–	1	–	–	–
ROUDLY	–	1	1	–	–	–	–	–	–
SAD	1	–	1	–	–	–	–	–	–
SADDENING	–	–	–	1	–	1	–	–	–
SAFELY	–	–	–	–	–	–	1	–	1
SAND	1	–	1	–	–	–	–	–	–
SAY	–	1	1	–	–	–	–	–	–
SAY OUT LOUD	–	1	1	–	–	–	–	–	–
SCREAM	6	6	12	3	6	9	5	2	7
SCREAMED	–	–	–	–	–	–	1	–	1
SCREAMER	1	–	1	–	–	–	–	–	–
SCREAMING	–	–	–	–	–	–	–	1	1
SCREECH	–	–	–	–	–	–	1	–	1
SEAT	1	–	1	–	–	–	–	–	–
SEE	–	1	1	–	–	–	–	–	–
SHOE	–	2	2	–	–	–	–	–	–
SHOFTLEY	–	–	–	–	–	–	1	–	1
SHORT	–	–	–	–	2	2	–	–	–
SHORTLY	–	–	–	1	–	1	1	–	1
SHOULY	–	–	–	–	–	–	1	–	1
SHOUT	3	1	4	4	5	9	7	6	13
SHOUTED	–	–	–	–	1	1	1	–	1
SHOUTING	–	–	–	2	–	2	1	–	1
SHUT	–	–	–	–	–	–	1	–	1
SILENCE	–	–	–	1	–	1	–	–	–
SILENT	–	–	–	–	–	–	–	1	1
SILENTLY	–	–	–	–	1	1	1	–	1
SING	–	1	1	–	–	–	–	–	–
SING LOUD	–	1	1	–	–	–	–	–	–
SKEEP	–	–	–	–	–	–	–	1	1
SLOW	2	5	7	2	2	4	–	–	–
SLOWLY	4	4	8	5	3	8	1	1	2
SMOOTH	–	–	–	1	–	1	–	1	1
SMOOTHLY	–	–	–	1	–	1	–	1	1
SNIVELY	1	–	1	–	–	–	–	–	–

RESPONSE WORD	1ST			3RD			5TH		
	M	F	T	M	F	T	M	F	T

46. LOUDLY

RESPONSE WORD	M	F	T	M	F	T	M	F	T
SOFT	4	4	8	9	12	21	12	14	26
SOFTEN	–	–	–	1	–	1	–	–	–
SOFTER	1	–	1	1	1	2	–	–	–
SOFTLY	18	22	40	39	45	84	39	52	91
SOLD	–	–	–	–	1	1	–	–	–
SOLID	–	–	–	–	1	1	–	–	–
SOMEONE SPEAKING LOUD	–	1	1	–	–	–	–	–	–
SOTFLY	–	–	–	1	–	1	–	–	–
SOUDLY	1	–	1	–	–	–	–	–	–
SOUND	1	–	1	–	–	–	1	1	2
SOUNDLY	–	1	1	–	–	–	–	–	–
SOVELY	1	–	1	–	–	–	–	–	–
SPEAK	2	–	2	–	1	1	1	1	2
SPEAKER	1	–	1	–	1	1	–	–	–
STOP	–	1	1	–	–	–	1	–	1
SWEATER	–	–	–	1	–	1	–	–	–
SWEEP	–	1	1	–	–	–	–	–	–
TAKE	1	–	1	–	–	–	–	–	–
TALK	3	2	5	–	2	2	–	2	2
TALK LOUD	1	1	2	1	–	1	–	–	–
TALK LOUDLY	1	1	2	–	–	–	–	–	–
TALKING	–	–	–	1	–	1	–	–	–
TELL	–	–	–	1	–	1	–	–	–
TO SHOUT LOUD	–	–	–	–	–	–	–	1	1
TOUDLY	–	1	1	–	–	–	–	–	–
TRASH CAN	1	–	1	–	–	–	–	–	–
TREE	1	–	1	–	–	–	–	–	–
UGLY	–	–	–	–	1	1	–	–	–
UNALLOWED	–	–	–	–	–	–	1	–	1
UNLOUD	–	1	1	–	–	–	–	–	–
UNSOFT	–	–	–	–	–	–	–	1	1
VACUUM CLEANER	1	–	1	–	–	–	–	–	–
VERY LOUD	–	–	–	1	–	1	–	–	–
VOICE	1	–	1	1	–	1	–	–	–
WALL	1	–	1	–	–	–	–	–	–
WATER	1	4	5	–	–	–	–	–	–
WAVES	1	–	1	–	–	–	–	–	–
WE	–	1	1	–	–	–	–	–	–
WE HEAR YOU	–	1	1	–	–	–	–	–	–
WE PLAY	1	–	1	–	–	–	–	–	–
WHEN YOURE SCREAMING	1	–	1	–	–	–	–	–	–
WHISPER	–	1	1	1	–	1	–	–	–
WHITE	1	–	1	–	–	–	–	–	–
WIDE	–	–	–	1	–	1	–	–	–
WINDOW	1	–	1	–	–	–	–	–	–
WITCH	1	–	1	–	–	–	–	–	–
WOUDLY	–	1	1	–	–	–	–	–	–
YELL	–	5	5	2	2	4	2	–	2
YELLOW	–	1	1	–	–	–	–	–	–
YOU	–	–	–	–	–	–	–	1	1

47. MAINTAIN

RESPONSE WORD	M	F	T	M	F	T	M	F	T
A DOG	–	1	1	–	–	–	–	–	–
A DRESS	–	1	1	–	–	–	–	–	–
A PILL	1	–	1	–	–	–	–	–	–
A SHOW	–	1	1	–	–	–	–	–	–
ABLE	–	–	–	–	–	–	–	1	1
ACT	–	–	–	2	1	3	1	–	1
ACTION	–	–	–	1	–	1	–	–	–
ACTRESS	–	–	–	–	1	1	–	–	–
ADD	–	–	–	2	–	2	–	–	–
ALL GONE	–	–	–	–	–	–	1	–	1
ANIMAL	–	–	–	1	2	3	1	1	2
ANIMALS	–	–	–	–	1	1	–	–	–
ANYTHING	–	–	–	1	1	2	–	–	–
ANYTIME	–	–	–	1	–	1	–	–	–
APPLE	–	–	–	–	–	–	–	1	1
ARE	–	–	–	–	–	–	–	1	1
ARITHMETIC	–	–	–	–	–	–	–	1	1
AROUND	–	–	–	–	1	1	–	–	–

RESPONSE WORD	1ST M	1ST F	1ST T	3RD M	3RD F	3RD T	5TH M	5TH F	5TH T

47. MAINTAIN

RESPONSE WORD	1ST M	1ST F	1ST T	3RD M	3RD F	3RD T	5TH M	5TH F	5TH T
ARTICLE	−	−	−	−	−	−	1	−	1
ASH TRAY	1	−	1	−	−	−	−	−	−
ATTEND	−	−	−	−	−	−	1	−	1
AWFUL	−	−	−	−	−	−	−	1	1
BAD	1	1	2	−	−	−	−	−	−
BAGS	1	−	1	−	−	−	−	−	−
BAIT	1	−	1	−	−	−	−	−	−
BAKING SODA	−	−	−	−	1	1	−	−	−
BALL	−	−	−	1	−	1	−	−	−
BASIS	−	−	−	−	−	−	−	1	1
BAT	1	−	1	−	−	−	−	−	−
BAY	−	−	−	−	1	1	−	−	−
BE CAREFUL	−	−	−	−	1	1	−	−	−
BE QUIET	−	−	−	1	−	1	−	−	−
BEANS	−	1	1	−	−	−	−	−	−
BEARD	−	1	1	−	−	−	−	−	−
BEAUTIFUL	−	−	−	−	1	1	−	−	−
BECAUSE	−	−	−	1	−	1	−	1	1
BECOME	−	−	−	−	−	−	−	1	1
BEGIN	−	−	−	1	3	4	−	1	1
BEHAVE	−	−	−	1	−	1	−	−	−
BEHIND	−	−	−	2	−	2	−	−	−
BELL	−	−	−	−	−	−	1	−	1
BELONG	−	−	−	1	−	1	−	−	−
BIG	1	−	1	−	−	−	−	−	−
BIG HILL	−	−	−	−	−	−	2	−	2
BING	1	−	1	−	−	−	−	−	−
BIRD	−	−	−	−	−	−	−	1	1
BLEND	−	−	−	−	−	−	1	−	1
BLOOD	−	−	−	−	−	−	−	1	1
BOAT	−	−	−	2	−	2	−	−	−
BODY	1	−	1	−	−	−	−	−	−
BOOK	−	1	1	1	2	3	−	1	1
BOOK TAG	1	−	1	−	−	−	−	−	−
BOOT	−	−	−	−	−	−	−	1	1
BOTTLE	−	1	1	−	1	1	−	−	−
BOX	1	1	2	−	−	−	−	−	−
BOY	−	1	1	−	−	−	−	−	−
BRING	−	−	−	−	−	−	−	1	1
BULLETIN BOARD	−	−	−	1	−	1	−	−	−
BUTTER	−	−	−	−	1	1	−	−	−
BUTTERFLY	1	−	1	−	−	−	−	−	−
BUTTON	−	−	−	−	−	−	−	1	1
CABINET	2	−	2	−	−	−	−	−	−
CAME	1	1	2	−	−	−	−	−	−
CAN	3	6	9	−	4	4	−	−	−
CANDYCANE	1	−	1	−	−	−	−	−	−
CANE	2	2	4	1	1	2	−	−	−
CANS	−	−	−	−	1	1	−	−	−
CANT TAIN	1	−	1	−	−	−	−	−	−
CANTEEN	1	−	1	1	−	1	−	−	−
CAR	3	−	3	−	−	−	−	−	−
CARBON DIOXIDE	−	−	−	−	−	−	−	1	1
CAT	−	−	−	−	−	−	2	−	2
CATCH	1	−	1	−	−	−	−	−	−
CHAIR	−	1	1	−	1	1	−	−	−
CHAMPAGNE	1	1	2	−	−	−	−	−	−
CHANGE	−	1	1	−	−	−	−	−	−
CHICKEN	−	−	−	−	−	−	1	−	1
CHURCH	−	1	1	−	−	−	−	−	−
CLIMBER	−	−	−	−	−	−	1	−	1
CLOCK	−	1	1	1	−	1	−	−	−
CLUB	−	−	−	−	−	−	1	−	1
COLLECT	−	−	−	−	−	−	1	−	1
COLOR	−	1	1	−	−	−	−	−	−
COME	−	1	1	−	3	3	1	1	2
COMPLETE	−	−	−	−	−	−	−	1	1
CONTAIN	−	−	−	1	4	5	6	3	9
CONTAINER	−	1	1	2	2	4	−	1	1
CONTAINS	−	−	−	−	−	−	−	1	1
CONTINUE	−	−	−	−	−	−	1	−	1
COUNTRY	−	−	−	−	1	1	−	−	−

RESPONSE WORD	1ST M	F	T	3RD M	F	T	5TH M	F	T

47.   MAINTAIN

RESPONSE WORD	1ST M	F	T	3RD M	F	T	5TH M	F	T
CRAB	–	–	–	–	1	1	–	–	–
CRADLE	1	–	1	–	–	–	–	–	–
CRANE	–	–	–	1	–	1	–	–	–
CUP	1	–	1	–	1	1	–	–	–
CUPBOARD	1	–	1	–	–	–	–	–	–
DEPEND	–	–	–	–	1	1	–	–	–
DESCRIBE	–	–	–	–	1	1	–	–	–
DESK	–	–	–	–	–	–	1	–	1
DISLIKE	–	–	–	–	–	–	1	–	1
DIVIDE	–	–	–	–	1	1	–	–	–
DO	–	–	–	1	1	2	2	1	3
DO NOT MAINTAIN	–	–	–	–	1	1	–	–	–
DO SOMETHING	–	–	–	–	–	–	2	–	2
DOCTOR	–	–	–	–	1	1	–	–	–
DOESNT	–	–	–	1	–	1	–	–	–
DOG	2	–	2	–	2	2	1	–	1
DONT HAVE	–	–	–	–	–	–	1	–	1
DONT MAINTAIN	–	–	–	1	–	1	–	–	–
DOOR	1	3	4	–	–	–	–	–	–
DRAINER	–	–	–	–	1	1	–	–	–
DRESS	–	–	–	–	–	–	–	1	1
DRUM	–	1	1	1	–	1	–	–	–
DUST	–	1	1	–	–	–	–	–	–
DYING	1	–	1	–	–	–	–	–	–
EAT	2	1	3	–	–	–	–	–	–
EATING	–	1	1	–	–	–	–	–	–
ELAINE	1	–	1	–	–	–	–	–	–
EMPTY	–	–	–	1	2	3	1	–	1
EMTY	–	–	–	–	–	–	–	1	1
ENJOY	–	–	–	–	1	1	–	–	–
ENTERTAIN	–	1	1	1	1	2	1	2	3
ENTERTAINMENT	–	–	–	–	–	–	–	1	1
ESPECIAL	–	–	–	–	1	1	–	–	–
EVERT	–	–	–	–	–	–	–	1	1
EVERYTHING	–	–	–	–	1	1	–	–	–
EXIT	–	–	–	–	1	1	–	–	–
EXPERIENCE	–	–	–	2	–	2	–	–	–
EXPLANATION	–	–	–	–	–	–	–	1	1
EYES	1	–	1	–	1	1	–	–	–
FACE	1	–	1	–	–	–	–	–	–
FAIN	–	1	1	–	–	–	–	–	–
FAINT	–	1	1	–	–	–	–	–	–
FAST	–	–	–	–	–	–	1	–	1
FASTER	–	–	–	–	–	–	–	2	2
FATHER	1	–	1	–	–	–	–	1	1
FAYTAIN	–	–	–	1	–	1	–	–	–
FENCE	–	1	1	–	–	–	–	–	–
FIGURE	–	1	1	–	–	–	–	–	–
FILL	1	–	1	1	1	2	–	–	–
FINANCIAL	–	–	–	1	–	1	–	–	–
FINISH	–	–	–	–	–	–	1	–	1
FIRE HYDRANT	–	1	1	–	–	–	–	–	–
FIRECRACKER	–	1	1	–	–	–	–	–	–
FISH	–	–	–	1	–	1	–	–	–
FIX	–	–	–	1	1	2	1	–	1
FLOOR	–	–	–	1	–	1	–	–	–
FLYING	–	–	–	1	–	1	–	–	–
FOOD	–	–	–	–	–	–	–	2	2
FOOT	1	–	1	–	–	–	–	–	–
FOREST	–	–	–	1	–	1	–	–	–
FORGET	–	–	–	–	–	–	1	–	1
FORGOT	–	–	–	–	1	1	–	–	–
FOUNTAIN	–	–	–	–	–	–	1	–	1
FREQUENT	–	–	–	–	–	–	–	1	1
GAIN	–	–	–	1	–	1	1	–	1
GAS	2	–	2	1	1	2	–	–	–
GASOLINE	–	–	–	1	–	1	–	–	–
GENTLE	–	–	–	1	–	1	–	–	–
GET	1	–	1	–	1	1	1	4	5
GET MORE	–	–	–	1	–	1	–	–	–
GIRL	–	–	–	–	1	1	1	–	1
GIVE	–	–	–	2	–	2	2	–	2

RESPONSE WORD	1ST M	F	T	3RD M	F	T	5TH M	F	T

47.   MAINTAIN

RESPONSE WORD	1ST M	F	T	3RD M	F	T	5TH M	F	T
GIVE IN	–	–	–	–	–	–	–	1	1
GLASS	1	1	2	1	–	1	–	1	–
GLASSES	–	1	1	–	–	–	–	–	–
GLOVE	–	1	1	–	–	–	–	–	–
GO	–	–	–	–	–	–	1	–	1
GO HOME	1	–	1	–	–	–	–	–	–
GO ON	–	–	–	–	–	–	1	–	1
GOAT	–	1	1	–	–	–	1	–	1
GOLD	–	–	–	–	–	–	1	–	1
GOOD	3	2	5	1	–	1	1	–	1
GRAIN	1	–	1	–	–	–	–	–	–
GRASS	1	1	2	1	–	1	–	–	–
GREEN	–	–	–	1	–	1	–	–	–
GROUP	–	–	–	1	–	1	–	–	–
GUESS	–	1	1	–	–	–	–	1	1
GUN	1	–	1	–	–	–	–	–	–
HAIN	1	–	1	–	–	–	–	–	–
HAIR	–	1	1	–	–	–	–	–	–
HANG	–	1	1	–	–	–	–	–	–
HAPPEN	–	–	–	–	–	–	–	1	1
HAPPY	–	–	–	1	–	1	–	–	–
HAS	–	–	–	–	–	–	1	–	1
HAT	–	1	1	–	–	–	–	–	–
HAVE	–	–	–	2	–	2	4	4	8
HAY	1	–	1	–	–	–	–	–	–
HEADACHE	–	1	1	–	–	–	–	–	–
HELL	–	–	–	–	–	–	1	–	1
HEN	1	–	1	–	–	–	–	–	–
HER	–	–	–	1	–	1	–	–	–
HERE	–	1	1	1	–	1	–	–	–
HIDE	–	–	–	1	–	1	–	–	–
HIE	–	–	–	–	–	–	1	–	1
HIGH	–	–	–	–	–	–	1	2	3
HIGHT	–	–	–	–	–	–	1	–	1
HILL	–	–	–	–	–	–	2	3	5
HILLY	–	–	–	–	–	–	1	–	1
HOLD	–	–	–	3	1	4	8	6	14
HOLDER	–	–	–	–	1	1	–	–	–
HOLDS	–	–	–	–	1	1	1	–	1
HOME	–	–	–	–	1	1	–	–	–
HORSE	2	–	2	–	–	–	1	–	1
HOUSE	2	1	3	–	–	–	–	–	–
I	–	1	1	–	–	–	–	–	–
I CANT THINK	–	–	–	–	–	–	–	1	1
I DONT KNOW	–	–	–	–	1	1	1	1	2
I DONT KNOW WHAT IT MEANS.	–	–	–	–	–	–	1	–	1
IDEA	–	–	–	–	–	–	–	1	1
ILLUSTRATE	–	–	–	–	1	1	–	–	–
IN	–	1	1	–	1	1	–	2	2
IN YOUR DESK	–	–	–	1	–	1	–	–	–
INFORMATION	–	–	–	–	–	–	–	1	1
INGREDIENTS	–	–	–	1	–	1	1	2	3
INSIDE	–	–	–	–	–	–	1	–	1
INTAIN	–	–	–	1	–	1	1	1	2
INTEREST	–	–	–	–	–	–	1	–	1
INTO	–	–	–	–	–	–	1	–	1
INVENT	–	–	–	–	–	–	–	1	1
ISLAND	–	–	–	1	–	1	–	–	–
IT	–	–	–	1	1	2	1	–	1
JANE	–	1	1	–	–	–	–	–	–
JAR	1	–	1	–	–	–	–	1	1
JOB	–	–	–	–	–	–	–	1	1
JOIN	–	–	–	1	–	1	–	1	1
JUICE	2	–	2	–	–	–	–	1	1
JUICY	–	–	–	1	–	1	–	–	–
KEEP	–	–	–	–	1	1	7	6	13
KEEP DOING	–	–	–	–	–	–	–	1	1
KEEP GOING	–	–	–	–	–	–	1	–	1
KEEP ORDER	–	–	–	–	–	–	1	–	1
KEEP UP	–	–	–	–	–	–	3	–	3
KEEP-UP	–	–	–	–	–	–	–	1	1

47. MAINTAIN

RESPONSE WORD	1ST M	1ST F	1ST T	3RD M	3RD F	3RD T	5TH M	5TH F	5TH T
KEPT	-	-	-	-	1	1	-	-	-
KITE	1	-	1	-	-	-	-	-	-
KNEW	-	-	-	1	-	1	-	-	-
LAMP	-	1	1	-	-	-	-	-	-
LAST	-	1	1	-	-	-	-	-	-
LEAD	-	-	-	1	-	1	-	-	-
LEMONADE	-	-	-	1	-	1	-	-	-
LETS TRAIN A HORSE	-	1	1	-	-	-	-	-	-
LETTER	-	-	-	-	1	1	-	-	-
LIGHT	-	4	4	-	1	1	-	-	-
LIKE	1	-	1	-	-	-	-	-	-
LIKE GOING OUT FOR SWIMMING	1	-	1	-	-	-	-	-	-
LION	1	-	1	2	1	3	-	-	-
LISTEN	-	-	-	1	2	3	-	-	-
LOCKER	-	-	-	-	1	1	-	-	-
LYING	-	1	1	-	-	-	-	-	-
MADE	-	1	1	-	-	-	-	1	1
MAGIC	-	1	1	-	-	-	-	-	-
MAID	-	1	1	-	-	-	-	-	-
MAIN	2	3	5	2	2	4	2	5	7
MAIN BRAIN	-	-	-	-	-	-	1	-	1
MAIN TENT	-	-	-	1	-	1	-	-	-
MAINBAIN	-	1	1	-	-	-	-	-	-
MAINE	-	-	-	1	-	1	-	-	-
MAINLY	-	-	-	-	-	-	-	1	1
MAINSHAIN	1	-	1	-	-	-	-	-	-
MAINTAIN	-	-	-	-	1	1	1	-	1
MAKE	-	-	-	-	1	1	-	1	1
MAKING	1	-	1	-	-	-	-	-	-
MAN	3	2	5	2	2	4	-	-	-
MANAGE	-	-	-	-	-	-	1	-	1
MANE	-	-	-	-	1	1	-	-	-
MANGER	-	1	1	-	-	-	-	-	-
MANTAN ROBIN	-	1	1	-	-	-	-	-	-
MATION	-	-	-	-	-	-	1	-	1
MAY	1	-	1	-	-	-	-	-	-
MAYBE	-	-	-	1	-	1	-	-	-
MAYONNAISE	-	1	1	-	-	-	-	-	-
ME	1	1	2	2	-	2	-	-	-
MEAN	2	-	2	-	1	1	-	-	-
MEAT	-	-	-	1	-	1	-	-	-
MEDICINE	-	-	-	-	1	1	-	-	-
MEDICINE MAKES YOU BETTER	-	1	1	-	-	-	-	-	-
MEETING	-	-	-	-	-	-	-	2	2
MILE	-	-	-	-	-	-	-	1	1
MILK	1	2	3	-	2	2	-	-	-
MINK	-	1	1	-	-	-	-	-	-
MITTEN	-	-	-	-	1	1	-	-	-
MIX	-	-	-	2	-	2	-	-	-
MOMMY	-	1	1	-	-	-	-	-	-
MONEY	1	-	1	-	-	-	-	-	-
MONKEY	-	-	-	-	1	1	-	-	-
MOTHER	1	1	2	-	-	-	-	-	-
MOUNTAIN	-	-	-	-	1	1	-	1	1
MUSIC	-	-	-	1	-	1	-	-	-
MY	1	-	1	-	-	-	-	-	-
NAME	-	1	1	1	-	1	-	1	1
NEATNESS	-	-	-	-	-	-	-	1	1
NECKLACE	1	-	1	-	-	-	-	-	-
NIGHT	-	-	-	-	-	-	-	1	1
NINETEEN	-	-	-	1	-	1	-	-	-
NO RESPONSE	-	-	-	1	-	1	2	1	3
NONE	-	-	-	-	-	-	-	1	1
NOT MAINTAIN	2	-	2	4	2	6	3	1	4
NOT QUIET	-	-	-	1	-	1	-	-	-
NOTHING	-	-	-	2	-	2	2	-	2
NOW	-	1	1	-	-	-	-	-	-
NUTRITION	-	-	-	1	-	1	-	-	-
OBJECT	-	-	-	1	-	1	-	-	-
OBTAIN	-	-	-	-	-	-	1	-	1

RESPONSE WORD	1ST M	F	T	3RD M	F	T	5TH M	F	T

47. MAINTAIN

RESPONSE WORD	1ST M	F	T	3RD M	F	T	5TH M	F	T
ODOR	–	–	–	–	1	1	–	–	–
OF	–	–	–	1	–	1	–	–	–
OFF	–	–	–	–	1	1	–	–	–
OFFICE	–	–	–	–	–	–	1	–	1
ONE	1	–	1	–	–	–	–	–	–
ORDER	–	1	1	–	1	1	–	–	–
OWL	–	–	–	–	1	1	–	–	–
PAIN	2	1	3	–	2	2	–	–	–
PAINT	–	2	2	–	–	–	–	–	–
PAN	1	–	1	–	–	–	–	–	–
PAPER	2	1	3	–	–	–	1	–	1
PAY	–	–	–	1	–	1	–	–	–
PEN	–	–	–	–	–	–	1	–	1
PEOPLE	1	–	1	–	1	1	–	–	–
PEPPER	1	–	1	–	–	–	–	–	–
PERFUME	–	1	1	–	–	–	–	–	–
PERSON	–	–	–	–	–	–	1	–	1
PICTURE	–	–	–	1	–	1	–	–	–
PIG	–	1	1	–	–	–	1	–	1
PIPE	1	–	1	–	–	–	–	–	–
PLACE	–	–	–	1	–	1	–	–	–
PLAYGROUND	–	–	–	1	–	1	–	–	–
PLUS	–	–	–	1	–	1	–	–	–
POLES	–	1	1	–	–	–	–	–	–
POOR	–	–	–	–	–	–	–	1	1
POSSESS	–	–	–	–	–	–	–	1	1
POUR STUFF IN	1	–	1	–	–	–	–	–	–
POWDER	1	–	1	–	–	–	–	–	–
PRESSED	1	–	1	–	–	–	–	–	–
PRETEND	–	–	–	–	1	1	–	–	–
PUPPY	–	1	1	–	–	–	–	–	–
PURPLE	–	1	1	–	–	–	–	–	–
PUT	1	–	1	–	–	–	–	–	–
PUT TOGETHER	–	–	–	–	1	1	–	–	–
QUEST	–	–	–	–	1	1	–	–	–
QUESTION	–	1	1	–	–	–	–	–	–
QUIET	–	1	1	–	–	–	–	–	–
RAIN	–	1	1	1	–	1	1	–	1
RAINTAIN	–	1	1	–	–	–	–	–	–
RANGE	–	–	–	–	–	–	1	–	1
RATAINED	–	1	1	–	–	–	–	–	–
RATHER	–	–	–	–	–	–	–	1	1
REACH	–	–	–	–	–	–	1	–	1
REASON	–	–	–	–	–	–	1	–	1
RECEIVE	–	–	–	1	–	1	2	1	3
REDUCE	–	–	–	–	–	–	1	–	1
REFRIGERATOR	1	–	1	–	–	–	–	–	–
REGAIN	–	–	–	1	–	1	–	–	–
RELY	1	–	1	–	–	–	–	–	–
REMAIN	–	–	–	–	–	–	1	–	1
REMAINTAIN	–	–	–	–	–	–	1	–	1
REMEMBER	–	–	–	3	–	3	–	–	–
REPORT CARD	–	–	–	–	–	–	1	–	1
REQUIRE	–	–	–	–	–	–	1	–	1
RESTORE	1	–	1	–	–	–	–	–	–
RETAIN	–	–	–	3	1	4	–	1	1
RETURN	–	–	–	–	–	–	1	–	1
RIDE	1	–	1	–	–	–	–	–	–
ROCK	–	–	–	–	–	–	1	–	1
ROUGH	–	–	–	–	1	1	–	–	–
RUN	–	–	–	–	1	1	–	–	–
RUT	1	–	1	–	–	–	–	–	–
SAINTAIN	1	–	1	–	–	–	–	–	–
SAINTLIKE	–	–	–	–	1	1	–	–	–
SALT	1	–	1	–	–	–	–	1	1
SAME THING	–	–	–	–	–	–	1	–	1
SAND	1	–	1	–	–	–	–	–	–
SAT	–	–	–	1	–	1	–	–	–
SAVE	–	1	1	–	–	–	–	1	1
SCREEN	1	1	1	–	–	–	–	–	–
SEE	1	1	2	–	1	1	–	–	–
SEND	–	–	–	–	–	–	1	–	1

RESPONSE WORD	1ST M	F	T	3RD M	F	T	5TH M	F	T

47. MAINTAIN

RESPONSE WORD	1ST M	F	T	3RD M	F	T	5TH M	F	T
SERVE	–	–	–	–	1	1	–	–	–
SEVEN	1	–	1	–	–	–	–	–	–
SHOES	1	–	1	–	–	–	–	–	–
SHOW	–	–	–	–	3	3	–	1	1
SIZE	–	–	–	1	–	1	–	–	–
SLOW	–	–	–	–	–	–	–	1	1
SODA	–	–	–	1	–	1	–	–	–
SOFT	1	–	1	–	1	1	–	–	–
SOLD	–	–	–	–	1	1	–	–	–
SOME	–	1	–	–	–	–	–	1	1
SOME MILK	–	1	1	–	–	–	–	–	–
SOMETHING	–	3	3	–	–	–	2	1	3
SOMETHING YOU COULD DRINK	–	1	1	–	–	–	–	–	–
SPAIN	–	2	2	–	–	–	–	–	–
SPEAK	–	–	–	–	1	1	–	–	–
SPEED	–	–	–	–	–	–	–	1	1
SPICKS	–	–	–	–	–	–	–	1	1
SPINACH	1	–	1	–	–	–	–	–	–
SPOONS	–	–	–	1	–	1	–	–	–
STAND TAIN	1	–	1	–	–	–	–	–	–
STAY	–	–	–	–	1	1	–	–	–
STEET	–	–	–	–	–	–	–	1	1
STOP	–	–	–	–	–	–	2	–	2
STUDY	–	–	–	1	–	1	–	–	–
STUFF	–	–	–	–	1	1	–	–	–
SUGAR	1	–	1	2	1	3	–	–	–
SUPPLY	–	–	–	–	1	1	–	–	–
TABLE	–	2	2	–	1	1	1	1	2
TAIN	1	1	2	2	2	4	1	7	8
TAINER	–	–	–	1	–	1	–	–	–
TAINT	–	–	–	1	–	1	–	–	–
TAKE	1	–	1	–	–	–	–	1	1
TAME	2	1	3	–	2	2	–	1	1
TAME A LION	1	–	1	–	–	–	–	–	–
TAMING THE LION	–	–	–	–	1	1	–	–	–
TAND	–	–	–	–	–	–	–	1	1
TANGERINE	1	–	1	–	–	–	–	–	–
TANK	1	–	1	–	–	–	–	–	–
TEA	–	–	–	–	1	1	–	–	–
TEACHER	–	–	–	–	–	–	–	1	1
TEED	–	1	1	–	–	–	–	–	–
THAT	1	–	1	–	3	3	–	–	–
THE	1	–	1	–	–	–	–	–	–
THE CLASS	–	1	1	–	–	–	–	–	–
THEY	–	1	1	–	–	–	–	–	–
THINK	–	–	–	1	–	1	–	–	–
THINKER	1	–	1	–	–	–	–	–	–
THIS	–	1	1	–	–	–	–	–	–
THOSE	–	–	–	–	–	–	1	–	1
THREE	–	1	1	–	–	–	–	–	–
TIGERS	–	1	1	–	–	–	–	–	–
TILE	–	–	–	–	1	1	–	–	–
TO DO SOMETHING	–	–	–	–	–	–	–	1	1
TO GET	–	–	–	–	–	–	1	–	1
TO HAVE	–	–	–	–	–	–	–	1	1
TO KEEP	–	–	–	–	–	–	1	–	1
TODAY	–	–	–	–	1	1	–	–	–
TOGETHER	–	–	–	–	1	1	–	1	1
TOMATOES	–	1	1	–	–	–	–	–	–
TOO	–	–	–	–	–	–	1	–	1
TOP	–	–	–	1	–	1	–	1	1
TRAIN	–	1	1	–	–	–	1	1	2
TRASHCAN	–	1	1	–	–	–	–	–	–
TRAVEL	–	–	–	–	–	–	–	1	1
TRIM	–	–	–	–	–	–	1	–	1
TRUE	–	–	–	–	–	–	1	–	1
TRY	–	–	–	–	1	1	–	–	–
TURTLE	–	–	–	–	–	–	–	1	1
TWIST	–	–	–	–	–	–	–	1	1
UNDER	–	–	–	1	–	1	–	2	2
UNDERSTAND	–	–	–	–	–	–	1	–	1

RESPONSE WORD	1ST M	F	T	3RD M	F	T	5TH M	F	T

47. MAINTAIN

RESPONSE WORD	1ST M	F	T	3RD M	F	T	5TH M	F	T
UNMAINTAIN	2	1	3	–	1	1	1	–	1
UNTAIN	–	–	–	2	1	3	–	–	–
UP	–	–	–	1	–	1	–	–	–
USE	–	–	–	1	–	1	–	–	–
VAIN	–	1	1	–	–	–	–	–	–
WAIT	–	1	1	–	–	–	–	–	–
WALL	1	–	1	–	1	1	–	1	1
WALLS	–	–	–	–	1	1	–	–	–
WANT	–	1	1	–	–	–	–	1	1
WASHER	1	–	1	–	–	–	–	–	–
WATER	6	2	8	2	1	3	1	–	1
WAY	–	–	–	–	1	1	–	–	–
WE	1	1	2	–	–	–	–	–	–
WHAT	–	–	–	–	1	1	–	–	–
WHEN YOU MAINTAIN SOMETHING	1	–	1	–	–	–	–	–	–
WHENEVER YOUR MOTHER SAYS MAINTAIN	–	1	1	–	–	–	–	–	–
WHERE	–	1	1	–	–	–	–	–	–
WHISKEY	–	1	1	–	–	–	–	–	–
WHITE	1	–	1	–	–	–	–	–	–
WHY	1	–	1	–	–	–	–	–	–
WILD	–	–	–	1	–	1	–	–	–
WINDOW	–	1	1	–	–	–	–	–	–
WINE	–	1	1	–	–	–	–	–	–
WINK	–	1	1	–	–	–	–	–	–
WIRE	1	–	1	–	–	–	–	–	–
WITH	–	–	–	–	–	–	–	1	1
WITHSTAND	–	1	1	–	–	–	–	–	–
WORD	–	–	–	–	–	–	–	1	1
WORDS	–	–	–	–	–	–	–	1	1
YELLOW	1	–	1	–	–	–	–	–	–
YES	–	–	–	1	–	1	–	–	–
YOU	–	1	1	2	1	3	–	–	–
YOU COULD GO SOMEWHERE AND WATCH A CLOW	–	1	1	–	–	–	–	–	–
YOU TAME DOGS	1	–	1	–	–	–	–	–	–
ZOO	–	–	–	–	1	1	–	–	–

48. MAN

RESPONSE WORD	1ST M	F	T	3RD M	F	T	5TH M	F	T
A HUMAN	–	–	–	–	–	–	–	1	1
A PERSON	–	–	–	–	–	–	–	1	1
AND	1	–	1	–	–	–	–	–	–
ARM	1	–	1	–	–	–	–	–	–
ATLE	–	–	–	–	–	–	1	–	1
BAG	–	1	1	–	–	–	–	–	–
BAN	1	1	2	–	–	–	–	–	–
BAND	1	–	1	1	–	1	–	–	–
BEAST	–	–	–	–	–	–	1	–	1
BED	–	1	1	–	–	–	–	–	–
BIG	–	–	–	1	–	1	–	–	–
BOOK	–	–	–	–	1	1	–	–	–
BOSS	1	–	1	–	–	–	–	–	–
BOY	4	5	9	13	6	19	7	4	11
BOYS	–	–	–	1	–	1	–	–	–
BURDEN	–	–	–	–	–	–	1	–	1
CAME	–	–	–	–	–	–	1	–	1
CAN	5	4	9	1	3	4	–	–	–
CAR	2	1	3	1	–	1	–	–	–
CAT	–	1	1	–	–	–	1	–	1
CAUSE	1	–	1	–	–	–	–	–	–
CAVE MAN	–	–	–	–	–	–	1	–	1
CHALK	1	–	1	–	–	–	–	–	–
CHILD	1	–	1	–	–	–	–	–	–
CHILDREN	–	–	–	1	–	1	–	–	–
CLOTHES	2	3	5	–	–	–	–	–	–
COAT	1	–	1	–	–	–	–	–	–
COMING TO YOUR HOUSE	–	1	1	–	–	–	–	–	–
COWBOY	–	1	1	–	–	–	–	–	–
DADDY	–	–	–	–	–	–	–	1	1

RESPONSE WORD	1ST M	F	T	3RD M	F	T	5TH M	F	T

48. MAN

RESPONSE WORD	1ST M	F	T	3RD M	F	T	5TH M	F	T
DANCE	1	–	1	–	–	–	–	–	–
DOG	1	–	1	–	–	–	2	1	3
DONT LET A MAN SHOOT YOU	–	1	1	–	–	–	–	–	–
DOOR	–	1	1	–	–	–	–	–	–
FAN	2	2	4	1	1	2	1	–	1
FATHER	5	8	13	4	1	5	4	3	7
FEMALE	–	–	–	1	–	1	–	–	–
FINGERS	1	–	1	–	–	–	–	–	–
FLOWER	–	–	–	1	–	1	–	–	–
FOOTBALL PLAYER	–	–	–	–	–	–	–	1	1
FRIEND	1	–	1	–	–	–	–	–	–
FURNACE	1	–	1	–	–	–	–	–	–
GAN	–	–	–	1	–	1	–	–	–
GENTLEMAN	–	–	–	–	–	–	1	1	2
GIRL	3	7	10	2	1	3	3	1	4
GLAD	–	–	–	1	–	1	–	–	–
GO TO WORK	1	–	1	–	–	–	–	–	–
GO WITH	1	–	1	–	–	–	–	–	–
GOES TO WORK	–	1	1	–	–	–	–	–	–
GROWN UP	–	–	–	–	–	–	1	1	2
GROWN-UP	1	–	1	–	–	–	–	–	–
GROWNUP	–	–	–	–	–	–	1	1	2
GUN	1	1	2	–	–	–	–	–	–
GUY	–	–	–	–	–	–	1	–	1
HAN	1	–	1	–	1	1	–	–	–
HAND	9	3	12	–	–	–	2	–	2
HANG	–	1	1	–	–	–	–	–	–
HAT	4	4	8	–	1	1	–	–	–
HAVE	1	–	1	–	–	–	–	–	–
HAVE HANDS	–	1	1	–	–	–	–	–	–
HE	1	2	3	–	1	1	2	2	4
HE COULD WORK	–	1	1	–	–	–	–	–	–
HE GETS IN THE CAR AND HE DRIVES IT	1	–	1	–	–	–	–	–	–
HE IS TALL	1	–	1	–	–	–	–	–	–
HEAD	–	1	1	–	–	–	–	–	–
HELP	1	–	1	–	–	–	–	–	–
HEN	1	–	1	1	–	1	–	–	–
HER	–	1	1	–	–	–	–	–	–
HERE	–	1	1	–	–	–	–	–	–
HIM	–	–	–	1	–	1	1	–	1
HUMAN	–	–	–	1	–	1	5	–	5
HUMAN BEING	–	–	–	–	–	–	1	–	1
HUSBAND	–	–	–	–	2	2	–	2	2
IS GROWN	1	–	1	–	–	–	–	–	–
IT	–	–	–	–	–	–	1	–	1
ITS A REAL MAN	1	–	1	–	–	–	–	–	–
JET	1	–	1	–	–	–	–	–	–
KIDS	–	–	–	1	–	1	–	–	–
KISS	–	1	1	–	–	–	–	–	–
KNIFE	–	–	–	–	–	–	1	–	1
LADDY	–	–	–	–	–	–	–	1	1
LADY	10	17	27	10	16	26	4	12	16
LAMB	–	–	–	–	–	–	–	1	1
LAMP	–	1	1	–	–	–	–	–	–
LANTERN	1	–	1	–	–	–	–	–	–
LARGE	–	–	–	–	–	–	1	–	1
LIGHT BULB	–	–	–	1	–	1	–	–	–
LITTLE	1	–	1	–	–	–	–	–	–
LIVING	–	–	–	–	1	1	–	–	–
LOOK	1	–	1	–	–	–	–	–	–
LOTS OF MEN	1	–	1	–	–	–	–	–	–
MAD	3	1	4	–	–	–	–	–	–
MADE	–	–	–	–	1	1	–	–	–
MAIL	–	–	–	–	–	–	1	–	1
MALE	1	–	1	–	–	–	5	2	7
MAN	–	–	–	–	–	–	–	1	1
MAN-MADE	–	–	–	1	–	1	–	–	–
MANS HAT	–	1	1	–	–	–	–	–	–
MARRIED	–	1	1	–	1	1	–	–	–
MAY	–	1	1	–	–	–	–	–	–
ME	–	–	–	1	–	1	–	–	–

RESPONSE WORD	1ST M	F	T	3RD M	F	T	5TH M	F	T

48. MAN

RESPONSE WORD	1ST M	F	T	3RD M	F	T	5TH M	F	T
MEN	2	3	5	10	15	25	7	5	12
MILK	1	–	1	–	–	–	–	–	–
MIRROR	1	–	1	–	–	–	–	–	–
MISS	–	1	1	–	–	–	–	–	–
MISTER	–	1	1	–	–	–	–	–	–
MONEY	1	1	2	–	–	–	–	–	–
MONKEY	–	1	1	–	–	–	–	–	–
MOTHER	1	8	9	1	3	4	–	–	–
MR	–	–	–	–	–	–	–	1	1
MY DADDY	–	–	–	1	–	1	–	–	–
NAME	1	–	1	–	–	–	–	–	–
NAN	–	1	1	–	1	1	–	–	–
NEW	–	–	–	1	–	1	–	–	–
NICE	–	–	–	–	2	2	–	–	–
OFFICE	–	1	1	–	–	–	–	–	–
OLD	1	–	1	1	–	1	–	–	–
OUT	–	1	1	–	–	–	1	–	1
PAN	–	3	3	–	–	–	–	–	–
PANTS	1	1	2	–	–	–	1	–	1
PARSON	–	–	–	1	–	1	–	–	–
PARTY	–	1	1	–	–	–	–	–	–
PEN	1	–	1	–	–	–	–	–	–
PEOPLE	–	2	2	4	2	6	1	–	1
PERSON	1	–	1	7	4	11	8	9	17
PICTURE	–	1	1	–	–	–	–	–	–
PRUNE	–	1	1	–	–	–	–	–	–
PUSSY CAT	1	–	1	–	–	–	–	–	–
RAN	–	1	1	–	–	–	–	–	–
RANDY	1	–	1	–	–	–	–	–	–
RANNED	–	–	–	1	–	1	–	–	–
RIDES	1	–	1	–	–	–	–	–	–
ROOSTER	1	–	1	–	–	–	–	–	–
RUN	–	–	–	1	–	1	–	1	1
SAD	–	–	–	1	–	1	–	–	–
SAM	1	–	1	–	–	–	–	–	–
SAND	1	1	2	1	–	1	–	–	–
SEE	1	–	1	–	–	–	–	–	–
SELL	1	–	1	–	–	–	–	–	–
SHE	1	–	1	–	–	–	–	1	1
SNAN	1	–	1	–	–	–	–	–	–
SODA	1	–	1	–	–	–	–	–	–
SOLDIER	–	1	1	–	–	–	–	–	–
SONG	–	–	–	–	1	1	–	–	–
STRANGE	–	–	–	–	–	–	–	1	1
STRONG	–	1	1	1	–	1	3	1	4
STUBBORN	–	–	–	–	–	–	–	1	1
SUBMARINE	–	–	–	1	–	1	–	–	–
SUIT	–	–	–	–	–	–	–	1	1
TALL	–	–	–	3	1	4	–	3	3
TAN	2	–	2	–	–	–	–	–	–
THAT WORKS	–	–	–	–	–	–	–	1	1
THE FATHER	–	1	1	–	–	–	–	–	–
THEM	–	–	–	–	1	1	–	–	–
TIE	2	–	2	–	–	–	–	–	–
TOGETHER	–	–	–	1	–	1	–	–	–
TWO LEGS	1	–	1	–	–	–	–	–	–
WALK	1	–	1	–	–	–	–	–	–
WALKED	1	–	1	–	–	–	–	–	–
WALKING	1	–	1	–	–	–	–	–	–
WALKS	1	–	1	–	–	–	–	–	–
WALL	–	1	1	–	–	–	–	–	–
WATCH	1	–	1	–	–	–	–	–	–
WEM	–	–	–	–	–	–	1	–	1
WHENEVER THEY WORK	–	1	1	–	–	–	–	–	–
WHITE	1	–	1	–	–	–	–	–	–
WIFE	1	1	2	1	–	1	1	2	3
WOMAN	14	22	36	54	68	122	59	68	127
WOMEN	–	–	–	1	4	5	7	8	15
WORK	8	4	12	2	1	3	–	–	–
WRITING	–	1	1	–	–	–	–	–	–
WRONG	1	–	1	–	–	–	–	–	–
YOU BE MAD	1	–	1	–	–	–	–	–	–

RESPONSE WORD	1ST M	F	T	3RD M	F	T	5TH M	F	T

49. MIX

RESPONSE WORD	1ST M	F	T	3RD M	F	T	5TH M	F	T
A CAKE	–	–	–	–	–	–	1	–	1
A CAKE MIX UP	1	–	1	–	–	–	–	–	–
A PIE	1	–	1	–	–	–	–	–	–
ADD	–	–	–	2	–	2	–	1	1
ALLOW	–	–	–	–	–	–	1	–	1
BABY	1	–	1	–	–	–	–	–	–
BAKE	–	1	1	–	–	–	–	1	1
BANANA	–	1	1	–	–	–	–	–	–
BATTER	2	1	3	2	2	4	1	1	2
BE	–	1	1	–	–	–	–	–	–
BEAT	–	–	–	–	–	–	–	1	1
BEATER	2	3	5	–	–	–	–	–	–
BEATERS	–	–	–	–	–	–	1	–	1
BEST	–	–	–	1	–	1	–	–	–
BIRD	–	2	2	–	–	–	–	–	–
BISQUICK	–	–	–	–	–	–	–	1	1
BITE	–	–	–	–	–	–	1	–	1
BITS	–	1	1	–	–	–	–	–	–
BIX	–	2	2	–	–	–	–	–	–
BLACK	1	–	1	–	–	–	–	–	–
BLEND	–	–	–	1	2	3	5	6	11
BLENDED	–	–	–	1	–	1	–	–	–
BLOOD	1	–	1	–	–	–	–	–	–
BLUE	–	–	–	–	–	–	–	1	1
BOWL	1	3	4	–	1	1	–	3	3
BOX	–	1	1	–	–	–	–	–	–
BREAD	1	1	2	–	–	–	1	–	1
BROKE	–	–	–	1	–	1	–	–	–
BROWN	–	–	–	–	1	1	–	–	–
BUTTER	4	2	6	–	–	–	–	–	–
BUTTER AND MILK	–	–	–	–	–	–	1	–	1
BUTTON	1	–	1	–	–	–	–	–	–
CABINET	1	–	1	–	–	–	–	–	–
CAKE	21	21	42	22	20	42	13	19	32
CAKEMIX	–	–	–	1	–	1	–	–	–
CAKES	–	1	1	–	–	–	–	–	–
CAN	–	1	1	–	–	–	–	–	–
CANDY	1	–	1	–	–	–	–	–	–
CAR	–	–	–	–	–	–	1	–	1
CARRY	–	–	–	1	–	1	–	–	–
CAT	1	1	2	–	1	1	–	–	–
CEILING	1	–	1	–	–	–	–	–	–
CEMENT	–	–	–	3	–	3	1	–	1
CEREAL	–	–	–	–	1	1	–	–	–
CHEF	–	–	–	–	–	–	1	–	1
CHEMICALS	–	–	–	–	–	–	1	–	1
CHICK	1	–	1	–	–	–	–	–	–
CHOCOLATE	–	–	–	–	1	1	–	1	1
CLOCK	–	1	1	–	–	–	–	–	–
CLOUDS	–	1	1	–	–	–	–	–	–
COAT	–	–	–	–	1	1	–	–	–
COFFEE	1	–	1	–	–	–	–	–	–
COLER	–	–	–	–	–	–	1	–	1
COLOR	–	–	–	–	–	–	2	4	6
COLORS	–	–	–	1	–	1	2	–	2
COMBINATION	–	–	–	1	–	1	–	–	–
COMBINE	–	–	–	–	–	–	2	–	2
COMBINED	–	–	–	–	–	–	1	–	1
COMPARE	–	–	–	–	–	–	1	1	2
CONTAIN	–	–	–	–	–	–	1	1	2
COOK	3	1	4	–	2	2	–	2	2
COOKIE	–	1	1	–	–	–	–	–	–
COW	1	–	1	–	–	–	–	–	–
CREAM	1	–	1	–	1	1	–	–	–
CREAM MIX	–	–	–	–	1	1	–	–	–
CUP	2	–	2	–	–	–	–	–	–
DID	–	–	–	–	1	1	–	–	–
DID NOT	–	–	–	–	–	–	–	1	1
DIFFERENT	–	–	–	–	1	1	1	2	3
DISH	–	–	–	–	1	1	–	–	–
DISSOLVE	–	–	–	–	–	–	–	1	1
DISTURB	–	–	–	–	–	–	1	–	1

49. MIX

RESPONSE WORD	1ST M	1ST F	1ST T	3RD M	3RD F	3RD T	5TH M	5TH F	5TH T
DIVIDE	–	–	–	1	2	3	–	–	–
DIX	3	–	3	1	–	1	–	–	–
DOESNT MIX	–	–	–	1	–	1	–	–	–
DOG	–	1	1	–	–	–	–	–	–
DONE	–	–	–	1	–	1	–	–	–
DONT	–	–	–	–	1	1	–	–	–
DONT MIX	–	–	–	1	–	1	–	–	–
DOOR	–	1	1	–	–	–	–	–	–
DOUGH	2	1	3	1	1	2	–	1	1
DOUGH TOGETHER	–	–	–	1	1	2	–	–	–
DRINK	–	1	1	1	1	2	–	1	1
DRINKS	1	–	1	–	1	1	–	–	–
EAR	–	–	–	–	1	1	–	–	–
EAT	–	2	2	1	–	1	–	–	–
EGG	–	–	–	1	–	1	–	–	–
EGGS	1	–	1	1	–	1	–	1	1
ELECTRIC	1	–	1	–	–	–	–	–	–
EXAM	–	1	1	–	–	–	–	–	–
FAST	–	–	–	–	–	–	1	–	1
FEATHERS	–	–	–	–	–	–	1	–	1
FINISH	–	–	–	–	1	1	–	–	–
FIX	–	2	2	10	9	19	5	5	10
FIXTURE	–	–	–	2	–	2	–	–	–
FLOUR	2	3	5	4	4	8	1	–	1
FLOUR AND SALT	–	–	–	1	–	1	–	–	–
FLOWER	–	–	–	–	2	2	–	–	–
FOOD	1	3	4	1	2	3	1	–	1
FOR ME	1	–	1	–	–	–	–	–	–
FORMULA	–	–	–	2	–	2	1	–	1
FROSTING	1	–	1	–	–	–	–	–	–
FRUIT	1	–	1	–	–	–	–	1	1
GARDEN	–	1	1	–	–	–	–	–	–
GATHER	–	–	–	–	–	–	–	1	1
GETHER	–	–	–	–	–	–	1	–	1
GLOVES	1	1	2	–	–	–	–	–	–
GLUE	–	–	–	–	–	–	1	–	1
GO	1	–	1	–	–	–	–	–	–
GOOD	1	–	1	–	–	–	–	–	–
GRASS	1	–	1	–	–	–	–	–	–
GRIND	–	–	–	–	–	–	1	–	1
HALLOWEEN	–	–	–	1	–	1	–	–	–
HALLS	1	–	1	–	–	–	–	–	–
HEAD	1	–	1	–	–	–	–	–	–
HELP	1	–	1	–	–	–	–	–	–
HER	–	–	–	–	1	1	–	–	–
HIM	–	–	–	–	1	1	–	–	–
HIX	2	–	2	–	–	–	–	–	–
HOE	1	–	1	–	–	–	–	–	–
HORSE	–	–	–	–	1	1	–	–	–
HOT	1	–	1	–	1	1	–	–	–
ICE	1	–	1	–	–	–	–	–	–
ICING	1	2	3	–	–	–	–	–	–
IN	–	2	2	–	–	–	–	–	–
INGREDIENTS	–	–	–	–	–	–	2	2	4
IT	1	1	2	1	–	1	–	–	–
JELLO	–	–	–	–	–	–	1	–	1
JUICE	–	–	–	1	–	1	–	–	–
JUNK	–	–	–	–	1	1	–	–	–
KICK	–	–	–	1	–	1	–	–	–
KICKS	1	–	1	–	–	–	–	–	–
KILL IT	–	1	1	–	–	–	–	–	–
KIND	–	–	–	1	–	1	–	–	–
KITTENS	1	–	1	–	–	–	–	–	–
KIX	–	1	1	–	–	–	–	–	–
KNACK	1	–	1	–	–	–	–	–	–
LEAF	–	1	1	–	–	–	–	–	–
LIKE	–	1	1	–	–	–	–	–	–
LIX	–	1	1	–	–	–	–	–	–
LUMPY	–	1	1	–	–	–	–	–	–
LUNCH MEAT	–	–	–	1	–	1	–	–	–
MAKE	1	–	1	3	4	7	2	1	3
MATCH	–	–	–	–	1	1	–	–	–

RESPONSE WORD	1ST M	1ST F	1ST T	3RD M	3RD F	3RD T	5TH M	5TH F	5TH T

49.   MIX

RESPONSE WORD	1ST M	1ST F	1ST T	3RD M	3RD F	3RD T	5TH M	5TH F	5TH T
MAX	–	–	–	1	–	1	–	–	–
ME	2	–	2	–	–	–	–	–	–
MICK	–	–	–	1	–	1	–	–	–
MILK	–	2	2	1	3	4	–	–	–
MILKSHAKE	1	–	1	–	–	–	–	–	–
MINK STOLE	–	1	1	–	–	–	–	–	–
MISTER	1	–	1	–	–	–	–	–	–
MITTEN	–	3	3	–	–	–	–	–	–
MITTENS	–	2	2	–	–	–	–	–	–
MIX UP	–	–	–	–	–	–	–	1	1
MIX-UP	–	–	–	–	–	–	1	–	1
MIXCHURE	–	–	–	–	–	–	1	–	1
MIXED	–	–	–	–	–	–	3	–	3
MIXED UP	–	1	1	1	–	1	–	–	–
MIXED UP SOMETHING	1	–	1	–	–	–	–	–	–
MIXER	1	5	6	1	1	2	–	–	–
MIXING	2	2	4	1	–	1	1	2	3
MIXTURE	1	–	1	–	3	3	–	1	1
MOON	1	–	1	–	–	–	–	–	–
MOTHER	1	1	2	–	–	–	–	–	–
MOTHER MIXES FOOD	–	1	1	–	–	–	–	–	–
MOTHERS	–	–	–	1	–	1	–	–	–
MOUSE	2	–	2	–	–	–	–	–	–
MR	–	–	–	–	1	1	–	–	–
NAME	–	–	–	–	1	1	–	–	–
NEST	1	–	1	–	–	–	–	–	–
NET	1	–	1	–	–	–	–	–	–
NO	–	–	–	1	–	1	–	–	–
NO MIX	1	–	1	–	–	–	–	–	–
NONE	–	–	–	1	–	1	–	–	–
NOT	–	–	–	1	1	2	–	–	–
NOT HER	–	–	–	–	1	1	–	–	–
NOT MIX	–	–	–	–	–	–	1	–	1
NOT MIXED	1	–	1	2	–	2	–	1	1
NOT NIX	–	–	–	–	–	–	1	–	1
NUMBERS	–	–	–	–	–	–	1	1	2
OIL	–	–	–	–	–	–	–	1	1
ONE	–	–	–	–	–	–	–	1	1
OUT	–	–	–	1	–	1	–	–	–
PACKAGE	–	1	1	–	–	–	–	–	–
PAINT	1	–	1	–	1	1	1	–	1
PANCAKE	–	–	–	–	1	1	1	–	1
PANCAKES	–	3	3	–	–	–	1	–	1
PART	–	–	–	–	–	–	1	–	1
PEPPER	–	–	–	–	1	1	–	–	–
PICTURE	–	–	–	–	1	1	–	–	–
PIG	–	–	–	–	–	–	1	–	1
PIX	–	1	1	–	–	–	–	–	–
PLAYPEN	–	–	–	1	–	1	–	–	–
POTATO	–	–	–	–	1	1	–	–	–
POTATOES	–	–	–	–	–	–	1	–	1
POUR	–	–	–	–	–	–	–	1	1
POWDER	–	–	–	1	–	1	–	1	1
POWDERED	–	–	–	1	–	1	–	–	–
PREPARE	–	–	–	1	–	1	2	–	2
PUDDING	1	3	4	1	–	1	–	–	–
PULL	–	1	1	–	–	–	–	–	–
PUMP	1	–	1	–	–	–	–	–	–
PUNCH	–	–	–	–	–	–	1	–	1
PUT	–	–	–	1	–	1	2	1	3
PUT TOGETHER	–	–	–	1	2	3	8	7	15
QUICK	–	–	–	1	–	1	–	–	–
RECIPE	–	–	–	–	–	–	1	–	1
RED	–	–	–	–	–	–	–	1	1
REPLACE	–	–	–	–	–	–	–	1	1
RIDE	–	1	1	–	–	–	–	–	–
RING	–	1	1	–	–	–	–	–	–
RIX	–	1	1	–	–	–	–	–	–
ROAD	1	–	1	–	–	–	–	–	–
SAFETY	–	1	1	–	–	–	–	–	–
SALAD	–	–	–	–	–	–	–	1	1
SALT	–	–	–	1	–	1	–	–	–

RESPONSE WORD	1ST			3RD			5TH		
	M	F	T	M	F	T	M	F	T

49. MIX

RESPONSE WORD	M	F	T	M	F	T	M	F	T
SAME	–	–	–	–	–	–	–	1	1
SAUERKRAUT	–	1	1	–	–	–	–	1	1
SCRABBLE	–	–	–	1	–	1	–	–	–
SCRAMBLE	–	–	–	–	–	–	2	–	2
SEE	–	1	1	1	–	1	–	–	–
SEPARATE	–	–	–	–	–	–	1	2	3
SHACK	–	–	–	–	–	–	–	1	1
SHAKE	–	–	–	2	–	2	–	–	–
SIGH	–	–	–	1	–	1	–	–	–
SIX	–	–	–	1	1	2	–	–	–
SLICKS	–	–	–	1	–	1	–	–	–
SODA	–	1	1	–	–	–	–	–	–
SOFT	–	–	–	1	–	1	–	–	–
SOLID	–	–	–	–	–	–	–	1	1
SOME DOUGH	–	1	1	–	–	–	–	–	–
SOME PUDDING	–	1	1	–	–	–	–	–	–
SOME STUFF	–	–	–	–	1	1	–	–	–
SOMETHING	1	1	2	–	1	1	–	1	1
SOMETHING IN A BOWL	–	–	–	–	1	1	–	–	–
SOMETHING TOGETHER	–	–	–	1	–	1	–	–	–
SOUP	2	1	3	–	–	–	–	–	–
SOUR	–	–	–	1	–	1	–	–	–
SPOON	2	3	5	–	4	4	1	1	2
STAPER	–	–	–	–	–	–	–	1	1
START	–	–	–	–	–	–	1	–	1
STAY	–	–	–	–	–	–	1	–	1
STEAR	–	–	–	–	–	–	1	–	1
STER	–	1	1	–	–	–	1	–	1
STEW	–	1	1	–	–	–	–	–	–
STICKS	1	–	1	2	–	2	–	–	–
STIR	3	6	9	15	22	37	20	27	47
STOP	–	–	–	–	1	1	–	–	–
STOP SIGN	1	–	1	–	–	–	–	–	–
STORE	1	–	1	–	–	–	–	–	–
STRA	–	–	–	–	–	–	1	–	1
STUFF	2	–	2	–	–	–	–	1	1
STUFF UP	1	–	1	–	–	–	–	–	–
SUGAR	–	1	1	–	1	1	–	–	–
SUPPER	–	–	–	–	1	1	–	–	–
SWING	1	–	1	–	–	–	–	–	–
SWIRL	–	–	–	–	–	–	1	–	1
SYRUP	1	1	2	–	–	–	–	–	–
TABLE	1	1	2	–	–	–	–	–	–
TAKE	–	–	–	–	1	1	–	–	–
TAKEN	–	–	–	1	–	1	–	–	–
TASTE	–	1	1	1	–	1	–	–	–
TATOES	–	1	1	–	–	–	–	–	–
TELEPHONE	1	–	1	–	–	–	–	–	–
THAT	1	1	2	–	–	–	–	–	–
THE PIE	1	–	1	–	–	–	–	–	–
THINGS	–	–	–	–	2	2	1	–	1
TICK	–	–	–	–	1	1	–	–	–
TICKS	1	2	3	–	–	–	–	–	–
TICS	1	–	1	–	–	–	–	–	–
TIX	1	1	2	–	–	–	–	–	–
TO	–	–	–	1	–	1	–	–	–
TO BLEND	–	–	–	–	–	–	–	1	1
TODAY	–	–	–	–	2	2	–	–	–
TOGATHER	–	–	–	–	–	–	1	–	1
TOGETHER	–	1	1	5	4	9	13	18	31
TORNADO	–	1	1	–	–	–	–	–	–
TREE	–	–	–	–	1	1	–	–	–
TURN	–	–	–	2	1	3	–	–	–
TWO	–	–	–	–	–	–	–	1	1
UGLY	–	–	–	–	–	–	1	–	1
UNMIX	–	–	–	1	2	3	2	2	4
UNMIXED	2	–	2	–	–	–	1	–	1
UP	3	2	5	3	1	4	2	–	2
US	1	–	1	–	–	–	–	–	–
VICKS	1	–	1	–	–	–	–	–	–
WAKE	1	–	1	–	–	–	–	–	–
WASHING MACHINE	1	–	1	–	–	–	–	–	–

RESPONSE WORD	1ST			3RD			5TH		
	M	F	T	M	F	T	M	F	T

49. MIX

RESPONSE WORD	M	F	T	M	F	T	M	F	T
WATER	1	1	2	–	2	2	–	–	–
WHAT YOU MAKE CAKE WITH	1	–	1	–	–	–	–	–	–
WHEN YOURE MAKING SOMETHING	1	–	1	–	–	–	–	–	–
WHIP	–	–	–	–	–	–	–	1	1
WHITE	–	1	1	1	–	1	–	–	–
WICKS	1	–	1	–	–	–	–	–	–
WITCH	–	–	–	–	–	–	1	–	1
YELLOW	1	–	1	–	–	–	–	–	–
YOU COULD BAKE A CAKE	–	1	1	–	–	–	–	–	–
YOU MAKE KOOL-AID	–	1	1	–	–	–	–	–	–
YOU MIX MUD	–	–	–	–	–	–	–	1	1

50. MOTH

RESPONSE WORD	M	F	T	M	F	T	M	F	T
A BOSS OF ME	–	1	1	–	–	–	–	–	–
A CREATURE THATLL FLY, HAS A FURRY BODY	–	–	–	–	–	–	–	1	1
A MOTH THAT FLIES IN THE AIR AND GETS	1	–	1	–	–	–	–	–	–
A PUPPET	1	–	1	–	–	–	–	–	–
AIR	–	1	1	1	–	1	–	–	–
ALOT	–	–	–	–	–	–	1	–	1
AN	–	1	1	–	–	–	–	1	1
AN INSECT	–	–	–	–	–	–	–	1	1
ANIMAL	–	–	–	–	3	3	11	2	13
ANT	–	–	–	–	–	–	1	1	2
ANYTHING	–	–	–	1	–	1	–	–	–
ARTH	1	–	1	–	–	–	–	–	–
ATE	–	–	–	–	–	–	–	1	1
BAD	–	–	–	–	1	1	–	–	–
BAG	–	–	–	–	1	1	–	–	–
BAKE	–	1	1	–	–	–	–	–	–
BALL	4	5	9	11	10	21	4	9	13
BALLS	2	–	2	1	1	2	–	1	1
BAT	–	–	–	1	–	1	–	–	–
BEAUTIFUL	–	–	–	–	1	1	–	–	–
BECAUSE	1	–	1	–	–	–	–	–	–
BED	–	–	–	–	–	–	–	1	1
BEE	–	2	2	2	–	2	–	–	–
BIG	–	1	1	–	–	–	–	–	–
BIRD	–	–	–	1	2	3	2	–	2
BITE	1	1	2	–	–	–	–	–	–
BOOK	–	1	1	–	–	–	–	–	–
BOTH	1	1	2	–	–	–	–	–	–
BOTTLE	1	–	1	–	–	–	–	–	–
BROOM	–	1	1	–	–	–	–	1	1
BROWN	–	–	–	–	–	–	1	–	1
BUCKET	1	1	2	–	–	–	–	–	–
BUG	5	5	10	8	9	17	17	29	46
BUGS	–	–	–	–	1	1	–	1	1
BUILDING	–	1	1	–	–	–	–	–	–
BUTTERFLY	8	8	16	23	25	48	23	20	43
CAN	–	2	2	–	–	–	–	–	–
CANDY	–	1	1	–	1	1	–	–	–
CAR	2	–	2	–	–	–	–	–	–
CAT	–	–	–	–	–	–	1	–	1
CATCH	2	–	2	–	–	–	–	–	–
CATCHED	–	–	–	1	–	1	–	–	–
CATERPILLAR	–	–	–	–	1	1	1	–	1
CHAIR	1	1	2	–	–	–	–	–	–
CHECK	–	1	1	–	1	1	–	–	–
CIGARETTE	1	–	1	–	–	–	–	–	–
CLEAN THE FLOOR	1	–	1	–	–	–	–	–	–
CLOSET	–	1	1	1	–	1	1	–	1
CLOTH	9	7	16	3	3	6	1	3	4
CLOTHES	1	1	2	1	5	6	1	3	4
CLOTHING	–	–	–	1	–	1	–	–	–
COAT	–	2	2	1	–	1	–	–	–
COCOON	–	–	–	1	1	2	3	–	3

RESPONSE WORD	1ST M	F	T	3RD M	F	T	5TH M	F	T

50. MOTH

RESPONSE WORD	1ST M	F	T	3RD M	F	T	5TH M	F	T
COKE	–	–	–	–	1	1	–	–	–
COLLECTION	–	–	–	–	–	–	1	–	1
COOKIES	1	–	1	–	–	–	–	–	–
COTTON	–	–	–	–	2	2	–	–	–
COUGH	2	3	5	–	1	1	1	–	1
COW	1	–	1	–	1	1	–	–	–
CRAB	–	–	–	1	–	1	–	–	–
CRICKET	–	–	–	1	–	1	–	–	–
CUP	–	–	–	–	1	1	–	–	–
CUPBOARD	–	–	–	1	–	1	–	–	–
CURTAINS	–	1	1	–	–	–	–	–	–
DEERS	1	–	1	–	–	–	–	–	–
DESK	1	–	1	–	–	–	–	–	–
DIRT	–	1	1	–	–	–	–	–	–
DIRTY	–	–	–	1	–	1	–	–	–
DOFF	1	–	1	–	–	–	–	–	–
DOOR	2	–	2	–	1	1	–	–	–
DUST	–	1	1	1	–	1	1	–	1
EAR	–	–	–	–	–	–	1	1	2
EAT	–	–	–	1	1	2	2	–	2
EAT CLOTHES	–	–	–	–	–	–	–	1	1
EATEN	–	–	–	–	–	–	–	1	1
EATS CLOTHES	1	–	1	1	–	1	–	–	–
EGGS	–	1	1	1	–	1	–	–	–
FALL	–	1	1	–	–	–	–	–	–
FAR AWAY	–	–	–	1	–	1	–	–	–
FINGERS	1	–	1	–	–	–	–	–	–
FLAKY	–	–	–	–	–	–	1	–	1
FLEA	–	–	–	–	–	–	1	–	1
FLIES	1	–	1	2	–	2	1	–	1
FLOOR	–	1	1	–	–	–	–	–	–
FLOWER	1	–	1	2	1	3	–	1	1
FLUFF	–	–	–	1	–	1	–	–	–
FLY	12	12	24	18	10	28	4	8	12
FLYING	1	–	1	1	1	2	–	–	–
FOFF	–	1	1	–	–	–	–	–	–
FOOD	–	–	–	–	–	–	1	–	1
GET IN YOUR HOUSE	1	–	1	–	–	–	–	–	–
GET INTO CLOTHES	–	–	–	–	–	–	1	–	1
GIRL	1	1	2	2	–	2	–	–	–
(GIRL S NAME)	–	–	–	–	1	1	–	–	–
GOLF	–	–	–	–	1	1	–	–	–
GOLFT	1	–	1	–	–	–	–	–	–
GOOD	1	–	1	–	–	–	1	–	1
GOTH	1	1	2	–	–	–	–	–	–
GRASS	–	3	3	1	1	2	1	1	2
GRASSHOPPER	–	–	–	–	–	–	1	–	1
GREEN	–	–	–	–	2	2	–	–	–
GROUND	–	–	–	–	1	1	–	1	1
GROW	–	1	1	–	–	–	–	–	–
HAIR	1	–	1	–	–	–	–	–	–
HAND	1	–	1	–	–	–	–	–	–
HAY	–	1	1	–	–	–	–	–	–
HEAT	2	–	2	–	–	–	–	–	–
HERE	1	–	1	–	–	–	–	–	–
HOLE	–	–	–	–	1	1	–	2	2
HOLES	–	–	–	–	1	1	1	–	1
HOME	–	1	1	–	–	–	–	–	–
HOSS	1	–	1	–	–	–	–	–	–
HOTH	1	–	1	–	–	–	–	–	–
HUNGRY	–	–	–	–	1	1	–	–	–
IN	2	–	2	–	–	–	–	–	–
IN WATER	–	–	–	–	–	–	1	–	1
IN YOUR HAND	1	–	1	–	–	–	–	–	–
INSECT	3	2	5	17	15	32	27	26	53
INSECT WITH WINGS	–	–	–	–	–	–	–	1	1
INSECTS	–	–	–	1	–	1	2	–	2
IT	–	–	–	1	–	1	–	–	–
IT IS	1	–	1	–	–	–	–	–	–
JUMP UP	–	1	1	–	–	–	–	–	–
JUST	–	–	–	–	1	1	–	–	–
KITCHEN	–	1	1	–	–	–	–	–	–
KITTY	1	–	1	–	–	–	–	–	–

RESPONSE WORD	1ST M	1ST F	1ST T	3RD M	3RD F	3RD T	5TH M	5TH F	5TH T
				50.	MOTH				
LAKE	–	–	–	1	–	1	–	–	–
LAUGH	1	–	1	–	–	–	–	–	–
LEAF	1	–	1	–	–	–	–	–	–
LIGHT	1	1	2	1	2	3	1	2	3
LIKE A MOTH IS IN YOUR HOUSE.	–	–	–	–	–	–	–	1	1
LIKE POWDER	–	–	–	–	1	1	–	–	–
LIVE	–	1	1	–	–	–	–	–	–
LOOK	–	2	2	–	–	–	–	–	–
LOSS	–	–	–	–	1	1	–	–	–
LOST	1	–	1	–	–	–	–	–	–
MAD	1	–	1	–	–	–	–	–	–
MALL	–	1	1	–	–	–	–	–	–
MAPLE	–	1	1	–	–	–	–	–	–
MARK	–	–	–	–	–	–	–	1	1
MARTHA	–	1	1	–	–	–	–	–	–
MERRANTILLISUM	–	–	–	–	–	–	1	–	1
MERTHER	–	–	–	–	–	–	1	–	1
MIDDLE	–	1	1	–	–	–	–	–	–
MIKE	1	–	1	–	–	–	–	–	–
MIST	1	–	1	–	–	–	–	–	–
MO	–	–	–	–	–	–	1	–	1
MONTH	–	–	–	–	–	–	1	–	1
MOP	3	4	7	–	–	–	1	–	1
MORN	–	–	–	–	–	–	1	–	1
MOSQUITO	–	–	–	1	2	3	1	–	1
MOSS	1	1	2	–	–	–	–	1	1
MOTHBALL	–	2	2	1	1	2	–	–	–
MOTHER	1	1	2	–	–	–	–	–	–
MOTHS	1	–	1	–	–	–	–	–	–
MOUSE	–	–	–	–	–	–	–	1	1
MOUTH	–	–	–	–	1	1	1	–	1
MOVE	–	–	–	–	–	–	–	1	1
MR MAZOFF	–	1	1	–	–	–	–	1	1
MUD	–	–	–	–	–	–	–	1	1
MUFFIN	1	–	1	–	–	–	–	–	–
MUMPS	–	–	–	1	–	1	–	–	–
MUSCLE	–	1	1	–	–	–	–	–	–
NAME	–	–	–	–	1	1	–	–	–
NEST	–	2	2	1	–	1	–	–	–
NET	1	2	3	–	–	–	–	–	–
NO RESPONSE	–	1	1	–	–	–	–	–	–
NORTH	1	–	1	–	1	1	–	1	1
NOT	1	–	1	–	–	–	–	–	–
NOT MOTH	1	–	1	1	–	1	–	–	–
NOTH	–	1	1	1	–	1	–	–	–
OFF	–	1	1	1	–	1	–	–	–
OFTEN	–	–	–	–	1	1	–	–	–
OLD	–	–	–	–	1	1	–	–	–
OPEN	–	–	–	–	–	–	1	–	1
PAN	1	–	1	–	–	–	–	–	–
PAPER	1	–	1	–	1	1	–	–	–
PEAT MOSS	1	–	1	–	–	–	–	–	–
PENCIL	1	–	1	–	–	–	–	–	–
PEOPLE	–	–	–	–	–	–	–	1	1
PEPPER	–	1	1	–	–	–	–	–	–
PINOCCHIO	–	1	1	–	–	–	–	–	–
PLAY	–	1	1	–	–	–	–	–	–
PLAY BALL	–	1	1	–	–	–	–	–	–
POTH	1	1	2	–	–	–	–	–	–
PUFF	–	1	1	–	–	–	1	–	1
RABBIT	–	1	1	–	–	–	–	–	–
RACOON	–	–	–	–	1	1	–	–	–
RAG	–	1	1	–	–	–	–	–	–
RAKE	–	1	1	–	–	–	–	–	–
RAT	–	–	–	–	–	–	1	–	1
RED	1	–	1	–	1	1	–	–	–
RICH	1	–	1	–	–	–	–	–	–
RIDE	–	1	1	–	–	–	–	–	–
RING	–	1	1	–	–	–	–	–	–
ROUND	–	–	–	–	1	1	–	–	–
RUST	1	–	1	–	–	–	–	–	–

RESPONSE WORD	1ST			3RD			5TH		
	M	F	T	M	F	T	M	F	T

50. MOTH

RESPONSE WORD	M	F	T	M	F	T	M	F	T
SEE	–	–	–	1	–	1	–	–	–
SHOES	1	–	1	–	–	–	–	–	–
SMALL	–	–	–	–	1	1	–	–	–
SMELL	–	–	–	–	2	2	–	–	–
SMOOTH	1	–	1	–	–	–	–	–	–
SNOFF	1	–	1	–	–	–	–	–	–
SOFF	–	–	–	–	1	1	–	–	–
SOFT	4	1	5	3	2	5	–	1	1
SOMEONE TO GO	–	1	1	–	–	–	–	–	–
SOMETHING	–	–	–	–	–	–	–	1	1
SOTH	1	–	1	–	–	–	–	–	–
SOUGHT	–	1	1	–	–	–	–	–	–
SPANKY	–	1	1	–	–	–	–	–	–
SPIDER	1	1	2	–	–	–	–	1	1
STING	–	–	–	1	1	2	–	–	–
STORE	–	–	–	–	–	–	1	–	1
SUGAR	–	–	–	1	–	1	–	–	–
SUN	1	–	1	–	–	–	–	–	–
SWEEP	–	1	1	1	–	1	–	–	–
SWIMMING POOL	–	1	1	–	–	–	–	–	–
TALK	2	3	5	–	–	–	1	–	1
TALL	1	–	1	–	–	–	–	–	–
TEETH	–	–	–	–	–	–	1	2	3
THE	1	–	1	–	–	–	–	–	–
THERES A MOTH IN THE BACK YARD	–	1	1	–	–	–	–	–	–
THICK	–	–	–	–	–	–	1	–	1
THREAD	–	–	–	1	–	1	–	–	–
TIME	–	–	–	–	–	–	1	–	1
TOWEL	1	1	2	–	–	–	–	–	–
TOY	1	–	1	1	–	1	–	–	–
TREE	1	–	1	–	–	–	–	1	1
TRUCK	–	–	–	1	–	1	–	–	–
TWO	–	1	1	–	–	–	–	–	–
UNMOTH	–	–	–	–	–	–	1	–	1
UNTIL	–	–	–	1	–	1	–	–	–
USE IT WHEN YOU STORE THINGS	–	1	1	–	–	–	–	–	–
WALK	–	1	1	–	–	–	–	–	–
WALL	–	–	–	–	–	–	1	–	1
WAPE	–	–	–	–	1	1	–	–	–
WASH	–	–	–	1	–	1	–	–	–
WASP	–	1	1	–	1	1	–	–	–
WATER	–	2	2	–	1	1	–	–	–
WEB	–	1	1	–	–	–	–	–	–
WEEDS	–	–	–	1	–	1	–	–	–
WEST	–	–	–	–	–	–	1	–	1
WHAT	–	–	–	–	1	1	–	–	–
WHEN YOURE MOPPING SOMETHING	1	–	1	–	–	–	–	–	–
WHENEVER YOUR MOTHER OR FATHER SAYS IT	–	1	1	–	–	–	–	–	–
WHITE	1	–	1	2	1	3	1	4	5
WHO	–	–	–	1	–	1	–	–	–
WING	1	–	1	1	–	1	1	–	1
WINGS	–	–	–	–	1	1	–	1	1
WIRE	–	1	1	–	–	–	–	–	–
WITCH DOCTOR	–	–	–	1	–	1	–	–	–
WITH	1	–	1	–	–	–	–	–	–
WOOL	1	–	1	1	–	1	–	1	1
WOOL-EATER	1	–	1	–	–	–	–	–	–
WORK	–	1	1	–	–	–	–	–	–
YEAR	–	–	–	–	–	–	2	2	4
YOU	1	–	1	–	–	–	–	–	–
YOU DRINK MILK	1	–	1	–	–	–	–	–	–
YOUR ARM	–	1	1	–	–	–	–	–	–

RESPONSE WORD	1ST M	1ST F	1ST T	3RD M	3RD F	3RD T	5TH M	5TH F	5TH T

51. MOVE

RESPONSE WORD	1ST M	1ST F	1ST T	3RD M	3RD F	3RD T	5TH M	5TH F	5TH T
A BED	1	–	1	–	–	–	–	–	–
A VAN	–	–	–	–	–	–	1	–	1
ABLE	–	–	–	1	–	1	–	–	–
ACTION	–	–	–	2	1	3	1	2	3
ALONG IN A CAR	–	–	–	–	–	–	–	1	1
ANIMAL	–	3	3	–	–	–	–	–	–
ANOTHER PLACE	–	–	–	–	–	–	1	–	1
AROUND	2	1	3	–	1	1	–	–	–
AWAY	1	4	5	2	8	10	2	2	4
BABY	–	1	1	–	–	–	–	–	–
BACK	1	–	1	–	–	–	–	1	1
BAD	–	1	1	–	–	–	–	–	–
BALL	–	1	1	–	2	2	–	–	–
BE QUIET	–	1	1	–	–	–	–	–	–
BEAR	1	–	1	–	–	–	–	–	–
BIRD	2	–	2	–	–	–	–	–	–
BLOW	–	–	–	1	–	1	–	–	–
BOARD	–	1	1	–	–	–	–	–	–
BOO	–	1	1	–	–	–	–	–	–
BOVE	1	–	1	–	–	–	–	–	–
BOY	1	–	1	–	–	–	–	–	–
BRACE	–	1	1	–	–	–	–	–	–
BUG	1	–	1	1	–	1	–	–	–
BULGE	–	–	–	–	–	–	1	–	1
BULLDOZER	1	–	1	–	–	–	–	–	–
CANT MOVE	–	–	–	–	1	1	–	–	–
CAR	8	4	12	1	1	2	4	–	4
CARAVAN	–	–	–	–	–	–	1	–	1
CAT	–	–	–	–	–	–	–	1	1
CHAIR	1	1	2	–	–	–	–	–	–
CHANGE	–	–	–	–	–	–	1	1	2
CHEWING GUM	1	–	1	–	–	–	–	–	–
CHIV	1	–	1	–	–	–	–	–	–
CHUCK	–	–	–	–	1	1	–	–	–
CLOTH	–	1	1	–	–	–	–	–	–
CLOTHES	1	–	1	–	–	–	–	–	–
COAT	1	–	1	–	–	–	–	–	–
COME	–	1	1	–	1	1	–	–	–
COOVE	1	–	1	–	–	–	–	–	–
COUCH	–	1	1	–	–	–	–	–	–
COW	–	3	3	–	–	–	–	–	–
CROCODILE	1	–	1	–	–	–	–	–	–
CROSS	–	–	–	1	–	1	–	–	–
DAY	–	1	1	–	–	–	–	–	–
DESK	–	–	–	–	1	1	1	–	1
DO	–	1	1	–	1	1	–	–	–
DOG	–	2	2	–	–	–	–	–	–
DOLL	–	1	1	–	–	–	–	–	–
DONT	1	1	2	2	2	4	–	–	–
DONT MOVE	1	2	3	1	1	2	–	–	–
DOOR	1	–	1	–	–	–	–	–	–
DOWN	1	–	1	–	–	–	–	1	1
DUVE	1	–	1	–	–	–	–	–	–
ELEPHANT	–	1	1	–	–	–	–	–	–
EYE	–	1	1	–	–	–	–	–	–
EYES	–	1	1	–	–	–	–	–	–
FACE	–	1	1	–	–	–	–	–	–
FAST	3	7	10	6	3	9	5	4	9
FEET	1	–	1	1	–	1	–	–	–
FLAT TOWER	1	–	1	–	–	–	–	–	–
FLOOR	–	1	1	–	–	–	–	–	–
FOOD	–	1	1	–	–	–	–	1	1
FREQUENTLY	–	–	–	–	–	–	–	1	1
FROM ONE PLACE TO ANOTHER	–	–	–	–	–	–	1	–	1
FROM THE CHAIR	1	–	1	–	–	–	–	–	–
FUNNY	–	1	1	–	–	–	–	–	–
FURNITURE	–	–	–	3	5	8	1	1	2
GET OUT OF MY WAY	1	–	1	–	–	–	–	–	–
GET OUT OF PLACE	–	–	–	–	–	–	–	1	1
GIT	1	–	1	–	–	–	–	–	–
GLOVES	–	1	1	–	–	–	–	–	–

51. MOVE

RESPONSE WORD	1ST M	1ST F	1ST T	3RD M	3RD F	3RD T	5TH M	5TH F	5TH T
GO	4	6	10	15	6	21	22	10	32
GO AWAY	-	-	-	-	-	-	-	2	2
GOING	-	-	-	4	-	4	1	2	3
GOING SOMEPLACE	-	-	-	-	-	-	1	-	1
GOOD	-	1	1	-	-	-	-	-	-
GOOVE	1	-	1	-	-	-	-	-	-
GREEN	1	-	1	-	-	-	-	-	-
GROVE	-	-	-	1	-	1	-	-	-
HAND	1	1	2	-	-	-	-	-	-
HAT	1	-	1	-	-	-	-	-	-
HAUL	-	-	-	-	-	-	1	-	1
HERE	-	-	-	1	1	2	-	-	-
HIGH HEELS	-	1	1	-	-	-	-	-	-
HIS CHAIR	1	-	1	-	-	-	-	-	-
HOLLER	1	-	1	-	-	-	-	-	-
HOME	-	-	-	1	-	1	1	1	2
HOOVE	1	-	1	-	-	-	-	-	-
HOUSE	1	4	5	3	2	5	4	3	7
I	-	1	1	-	-	-	-	-	-
IN	-	-	-	-	-	-	1	-	1
INDIAN	-	-	-	-	-	-	-	1	1
IT	1	2	3	-	1	1	-	-	-
IT IN	-	-	-	1	-	1	-	-	-
KOOVE	1	-	1	-	-	-	-	-	-
LEAVE	-	-	-	-	-	-	-	1	1
LEFT	-	-	-	-	-	-	-	1	1
LEGS	1	-	1	2	3	5	-	-	-
LETS GO MOVE	-	1	1	-	-	-	-	-	-
LETTER	1	-	1	-	-	-	-	-	-
LIE	-	1	1	-	-	-	-	-	-
LIGHT	-	-	-	1	1	2	-	-	-
LIKE	-	1	1	-	-	-	-	-	-
LIVE	-	-	-	1	1	2	-	-	-
LOCK	-	1	1	-	-	-	-	-	-
LONG	-	-	-	1	-	1	-	-	-
LOOK	-	-	-	-	1	1	-	-	-
M-	-	-	-	-	1	1	-	-	-
MAILBOX	-	1	1	-	-	-	-	-	-
MAKE	-	-	-	-	-	-	-	1	1
MAMMAL	-	-	-	-	1	1	-	-	-
MAN	-	-	-	-	-	-	-	1	1
ME	1	1	2	1	-	1	-	-	-
MISS HAN	-	1	1	-	-	-	-	-	-
MOO	1	2	3	-	-	-	-	-	-
MOODY	-	-	-	1	-	1	-	-	-
MOOED	1	-	1	-	-	-	-	-	-
MOON	2	4	6	-	-	-	-	-	-
MOPY	1	-	1	-	-	-	-	-	-
MOTHER	1	-	1	-	-	-	-	-	-
MOTION	-	-	-	-	-	-	2	5	7
MOTORCYCLE	1	-	1	-	-	-	-	-	-
MOUTH	-	1	1	-	-	-	-	-	-
MOVED	-	-	-	-	-	-	1	1	2
MOVEIN	-	-	-	-	-	-	1	-	1
MOVER	-	-	-	-	-	-	1	-	1
MOVIE	-	2	2	-	1	1	-	-	-
MOVING	1	1	2	3	-	3	1	1	2
MOVING MAN	1	1	2	-	-	-	-	-	-
MOVING TRUCK	1	-	1	-	-	-	-	-	-
MOVINGMAN	1	-	1	-	-	-	-	-	-
NEW	-	-	-	-	1	1	-	-	-
NEXT	-	-	-	1	-	1	-	-	-
NICE	-	1	1	-	-	-	-	-	-
NOT	-	-	-	1	1	2	-	-	-
NOT MOVE	-	-	-	3	2	5	1	1	2
NOTHING	-	-	-	-	1	1	-	-	-
NUMBER SEVEN	1	-	1	-	-	-	-	-	-
O K	1	-	1	-	-	-	-	-	-
ON	1	-	1	-	1	1	-	-	-
OUT	-	2	2	-	1	1	-	1	1
OUT OF MY WAY	1	-	1	-	-	-	-	-	-
OUT OF THE WAY BROTHER	-	1	1	-	-	-	-	-	-

RESPONSE WORD	1ST M	F	T	3RD M	F	T	5TH M	F	T

51. MOVE

RESPONSE WORD	M	F	T	M	F	T	M	F	T
OUTSIDE	–	–	–	–	1	1	–	–	–
OVER	–	–	–	1	1	2	–	–	–
PARALYZE	–	–	–	–	–	–	1	–	1
PENCIL	1	–	1	–	–	–	–	–	–
PEOPLE	1	3	4	–	–	–	–	1	1
PERSON	–	–	–	–	1	1	–	–	–
PIANO	2	–	2	–	–	–	–	1	1
PICTURE	1	–	1	–	–	–	1	1	2
PLACE	–	–	–	–	2	2	1	4	5
PLACE TO PLACE	–	–	–	–	–	–	1	–	1
POLE	1	–	1	–	–	–	–	–	–
PRACTICE	1	–	1	–	–	–	–	–	–
PROVE	–	–	–	–	–	–	–	1	1
PUMP	–	–	–	–	–	–	–	1	1
PUSH	–	–	–	2	1	3	3	1	4
PUT IN ANOTHER PLACE	–	–	–	–	–	–	–	1	1
QUICK	–	1	1	–	–	–	2	–	2
QUICKLY	–	–	–	1	–	1	–	2	2
QUIET	–	–	–	–	–	–	–	1	1
RAPIDLY	–	–	–	1	–	1	–	–	–
REMOVE	–	–	–	–	2	2	1	–	1
REPLACE	–	–	–	–	–	–	–	2	2
RIDE	2	3	5	–	–	–	–	–	–
ROOM	–	–	–	1	–	1	–	–	–
ROW	–	–	–	–	–	–	–	1	1
RUE	–	1	1	–	–	–	–	–	–
RUN	1	1	2	3	6	9	6	2	8
RUNNING	–	–	–	–	1	1	–	–	–
SCARED	–	–	–	–	–	–	–	1	1
SCREEN	–	1	1	–	–	–	–	–	–
SELL	–	–	–	–	1	1	–	–	–
SHELF	1	–	1	–	–	–	–	–	–
SHOE	–	–	–	1	1	2	–	–	–
SHOVE	–	–	–	–	–	–	–	1	1
SILENT	–	–	–	–	–	–	–	1	1
SILENTLY	–	–	–	–	1	1	–	–	–
SIT	–	–	–	1	–	1	1	1	2
SLIDE	–	–	–	–	1	1	–	–	–
SLIP	1	–	1	–	–	–	–	–	–
SLOW	5	–	5	4	3	7	2	1	3
SLOWLY	2	–	2	2	1	3	–	–	–
SMOOTH	1	–	1	1	1	2	–	1	1
SODA	–	1	1	–	–	–	–	–	–
SOF	–	–	–	1	–	1	–	–	–
SOFT	1	2	3	–	1	1	–	–	–
SOFTLY	–	1	1	–	–	–	–	–	–
SOMETHING	–	1	1	–	1	1	–	–	–
SOMETIMES	–	–	–	1	–	1	–	–	–
SOVE	–	–	–	–	1	1	–	–	–
SPEED	–	–	–	–	–	–	–	1	1
SPOT	1	–	1	–	–	–	–	–	–
SQUIRREL	1	–	1	–	–	–	–	–	–
STAND	–	1	1	2	3	5	–	3	3
STAND STILL	–	1	1	1	1	2	2	–	2
STARS	–	1	1	–	–	–	–	–	–
START	–	–	–	–	–	–	–	1	1
STARTED	–	–	–	–	–	–	–	1	1
STATION WAGON	1	–	1	–	–	–	–	–	–
STATIONARY	–	–	–	–	–	–	1	–	1
STATUE	1	–	1	–	–	–	–	–	–
STAY	2	–	2	12	14	26	11	16	27
STAY HERE	–	1	1	1	–	1	–	–	–
STAY STILL	–	–	–	–	–	–	1	–	1
STEAL	1	–	1	–	2	2	–	–	–
STEP	–	–	–	2	–	2	–	–	–
STIFF	–	1	1	–	–	–	–	1	1
STILL	2	7	9	13	17	30	12	11	23
STING	1	1	2	–	–	–	–	–	–
STIR	–	–	–	–	–	–	–	1	1
STIRRING	–	–	–	–	1	1	–	–	–
STOP	10	3	13	11	7	18	12	7	19
STOP MOVING AROUND	–	1	1	–	–	–	–	–	–

51. MOVE

RESPONSE WORD	1ST M	F	T	3RD M	F	T	5TH M	F	T
STOPPED	−	−	−	−	1	1	−	−	−
STOPS	−	−	−	−	−	−	1	−	1
STRAIGHT	−	1	1	−	−	−	−	−	−
SUDDEN	−	−	−	−	−	−	−	1	1
SUN	2	−	2	−	−	−	−	−	−
SWIFTLY	−	−	−	−	−	−	2	−	2
SWIM	−	1	1	−	1	1	−	−	−
TABLE	2	1	3	1	1	2	−	−	−
TABLES AND STUFF	−	1	1	−	−	−	−	−	−
TAKE	−	−	−	2	1	3	6	1	7
TAKE ALONG	−	−	−	−	−	−	−	1	1
TAKE AWAY	−	−	−	−	−	−	−	2	2
TAKE FROM ONE PLACE TO ANOTHER	−	−	−	−	−	−	−	1	1
THEM	−	−	−	−	1	1	−	−	−
THEN	−	−	−	−	1	1	−	−	−
THERE	1	−	1	1	−	1	−	−	−
THINGS	−	1	1	−	−	−	−	−	−
THROW	−	−	−	1	−	1	−	−	−
TO A HOUSE	−	−	−	1	−	1	−	−	−
TO ACTION	−	−	−	−	−	−	−	1	1
TO ANOTHER HOUSE	−	1	1	−	−	−	1	−	1
TO LEAVE	−	−	−	−	−	−	−	1	1
TOP	−	−	−	1	−	1	−	−	−
TOWARD	−	−	−	−	−	−	−	1	1
TOWEL	−	1	1	−	−	−	−	−	−
TOYS	2	−	2	−	−	−	−	−	−
TRAVEL	−	−	−	−	−	−	2	−	2
TRUCK	3	3	6	3	−	3	3	2	5
TRUE	1	−	1	−	−	−	−	−	−
TRUTH	1	−	1	−	−	−	−	−	−
TURTLE	1	−	1	−	−	−	−	1	1
UNMOVE	−	−	−	−	1	1	−	−	−
VAN	−	−	−	1	−	1	−	−	−
WALK	3	2	5	3	4	7	7	12	19
WALK AWAY	−	−	−	−	−	−	−	1	1
WALKING	−	−	−	−	1	1	−	−	−
WALL	−	1	1	−	−	−	−	−	−
WE MOVING	−	1	1	−	−	−	−	−	−
WHAT	−	1	1	−	−	−	−	−	−
WHAT YOU PUT IN GLASS	1	−	1	−	−	−	−	−	−
WHEELS	1	−	1	−	−	−	1	−	1
WHEN YOURE MOVING	1	−	1	−	−	−	−	−	−
WHENEVER SOMEONE MOVES	−	1	1	−	−	−	−	−	−
WHERE A CAR IS MOVING	−	−	−	1	−	1	−	−	−
WHO	1	−	1	−	−	−	−	−	−
WHY	−	−	−	1	−	1	−	−	−
WIGGLE	1	−	1	−	1	1	−	−	−
WITH THEIR LEGS	−	1	1	−	−	−	−	−	−
WOOD	−	−	−	−	−	−	1	−	1
WOOVE	1	−	1	−	−	−	−	−	−
WORK	1	−	1	−	−	−	−	−	−
WRITE	−	−	−	−	−	−	−	1	1
YOU	2	2	4	−	−	−	−	−	−
YOUR HAND	1	−	1	−	−	−	−	−	−
YOUR HEAD	−	1	1	−	−	−	−	−	−
YOURSELF	1	−	1	−	−	−	−	−	−
YOUVE	−	1	1	−	−	−	−	−	−

52. MUSIC

RESPONSE WORD	1ST M	F	T	3RD M	F	T	5TH M	F	T
A COURSE IN SCHOOL	-	-	-	-	-	-	-	1	1
AMUSE	-	1	1	-	-	-	-	-	-
ANIMALS	-	-	-	-	1	1	-	-	-
ARITHMETIC	-	-	-	1	-	1	-	-	-
ART	-	1	1	3	1	4	1	-	1
BALLET	-	-	-	-	-	-	-	1	1
BAND	4	2	6	3	-	3	3	-	3
BANJO	1	-	1	1	-	1	-	-	-
BEAT	-	-	-	-	-	-	-	1	1
BELL	1	-	1	1	-	1	-	-	-
BLACK	1	-	1	-	-	-	-	-	-
BLOW	-	-	-	-	1	1	-	-	-
BOAT	1	-	1	-	-	-	-	-	-
BOOK	-	2	2	-	-	-	-	-	-
BOX	1	-	1	-	-	-	-	-	-
BREAD	-	1	1	-	-	-	-	-	-
BUSIC	1	-	1	-	-	-	-	-	-
CAME	-	-	-	-	1	1	-	-	-
CAR	1	-	1	-	-	-	-	-	-
CATCH	1	-	1	-	-	-	-	-	-
CHAIR	-	1	1	-	-	-	-	-	-
CHILDREN	-	-	-	-	1	1	-	-	-
CHOIR	-	-	-	1	1	2	1	-	1
CHORUS	-	-	-	-	-	-	1	1	2
CHURCH	1	-	1	-	-	-	2	-	2
CLARINET	-	-	-	-	-	-	2	-	2
CLASS	-	-	-	-	-	-	1	-	1
COMPOSERS	-	-	-	-	-	-	-	1	1
COURA	-	-	-	-	-	-	-	1	1
DANCE	2	2	4	2	1	3	-	1	1
DANCING	-	1	1	2	2	4	-	1	1
DO	-	1	1	-	-	-	-	-	-
DOING	-	-	-	1	-	1	-	-	-
DOOR	2	1	3	-	-	-	-	-	-
DRUM	-	-	-	3	2	5	2	-	2
DRUMS	-	1	1	-	-	-	-	-	-
DRUSIC	-	1	1	-	-	-	-	-	-
DUSIC	1	-	1	-	-	-	-	-	-
ENCHANT	-	-	-	-	-	-	1	-	1
ENJOYMENT	-	-	-	-	-	-	1	-	1
ENTERTAINMENT	-	-	-	-	1	1	1	-	1
FATHER OR BIG CHILD PLAYS MUSIC ON A PI.	-	1	1	-	-	-	-	-	-
FLANNEL	1	-	1	-	-	-	-	-	-
FLUTE	-	-	-	1	3	4	-	-	-
FOR	1	-	1	-	-	-	-	-	-
FOR YOU	1	-	1	-	-	-	-	-	-
FUN	1	1	2	-	-	-	3	-	3
FUNNY	-	1	1	-	-	-	-	-	-
GAY	-	-	-	-	-	-	1	-	1
GENTLE	-	-	-	1	-	1	-	-	-
GO	-	1	1	-	-	-	-	-	-
GOOD	-	1	1	2	-	2	1	-	1
GUITAR	1	-	1	-	-	-	1	-	1
GYM	-	1	1	-	-	-	-	-	-
HAMMER	-	1	1	-	-	-	-	-	-
HARP	1	1	2	-	-	-	-	-	-
HAVE	-	1	1	-	-	-	-	-	-
HEAR	-	1	1	-	-	-	2	3	5
HEARD	-	-	-	-	-	-	-	1	1
HER	-	1	1	-	-	-	-	-	-
HIM	-	-	-	1	-	1	-	-	-
HOBBY	-	-	-	1	-	1	-	-	-
HOLE IN THE GROUND	1	-	1	-	-	-	-	-	-
HORN	2	-	2	3	-	3	1	1	2
HORSE	-	-	-	1	-	1	-	-	-
HUSIC	2	-	2	-	-	-	-	-	-
HYMN	-	-	-	1	-	1	-	-	-
I LIKE MUSIC CAUSE IT SOUNDS PRETTY.	-	1	1	-	-	-	-	-	-
INK	-	1	1	-	-	-	-	-	-
INSTRUMENT	1	-	1	7	6	13	7	11	18

RESPONSE WORD	1ST M	F	T	3RD M	F	T	5TH M	F	T

52.   MUSIC

RESPONSE WORD	1ST M	F	T	3RD M	F	T	5TH M	F	T
INSTRUMENTS	1	3	4	–	2	2	2	6	8
IS GOOD	–	1	1	–	–	–	–	–	–
IS NOT	–	–	–	1	–	1	–	–	–
JOE	–	–	–	–	–	–	1	–	1
JOYFUL	–	–	–	–	–	–	1	–	1
JUSIC	1	–	1	–	–	–	–	–	–
JUST SING SONGS WITH THE MUSIC	–	1	1	–	–	–	–	–	–
KEYS	–	–	–	–	1	1	–	–	–
KITCHEN	1	–	1	–	–	–	–	–	–
KUSIC	1	–	1	–	–	–	–	–	–
LEARN	1	1	2	–	–	–	–	–	–
LESSON	–	–	–	–	–	–	1	–	1
LESSONS	–	–	–	–	–	–	1	–	1
LIKE MUSIC	1	–	1	–	–	–	–	–	–
LIKE PLAYING PIANO	–	1	1	–	–	–	–	–	–
LINES	–	1	1	–	–	–	–	–	–
LISTEN	1	2	3	4	1	5	–	1	1
LOUD	3	2	5	3	5	8	–	–	–
LOUD MUSIC	1	–	1	–	–	–	–	–	–
LOUDLY	–	–	–	–	1	1	–	–	–
LOUDNESS	1	–	1	–	–	–	–	–	–
LOVE	1	–	1	–	–	–	–	–	–
LOVELY	–	–	–	–	1	1	–	1	1
MACHINE	–	–	–	–	1	1	–	–	–
MAN	3	–	3	–	–	–	–	–	–
MARK	1	–	1	–	–	–	–	–	–
MARY	1	–	1	–	–	–	–	–	–
ME	1	–	1	–	–	–	–	–	–
MELODY	–	–	–	1	–	1	1	–	1
MIDDLE	1	–	1	–	–	–	–	–	–
MOON	–	1	1	–	–	–	–	–	–
MOTH	1	–	1	–	–	–	–	–	–
MOVE	–	–	–	1	–	1	–	–	–
MUSE	–	1	1	–	–	–	–	–	–
MUSIC ROOM	1	–	1	–	–	–	–	–	–
MUSIC TEACHER	–	1	1	–	–	–	–	–	–
NEW	1	–	1	–	–	–	–	–	–
NEWS	–	–	–	1	–	1	1	–	1
NICE	–	1	1	–	3	3	1	–	1
NO	–	–	–	–	–	–	1	–	1
NO MUSIC	–	–	–	2	1	3	–	–	–
NO RESPONSE	1	–	1	–	–	–	–	–	–
NOICE	–	–	–	–	–	–	1	–	1
NOISE	1	1	2	6	4	10	7	5	12
NOISES	–	–	–	1	–	1	–	–	–
NOISY	1	1	2	–	–	–	–	–	–
NOT MUSIC	1	–	1	–	–	–	–	1	1
NOTE	–	1	1	–	–	–	1	–	1
NOTES	1	–	1	2	–	2	6	7	13
NOW	–	–	–	–	1	1	–	–	–
NUN	–	1	1	–	–	–	–	–	–
ORCHESTRA	1	–	1	–	–	–	1	–	1
ORGAN	–	1	1	–	–	–	–	–	–
OVER	–	–	–	1	–	1	–	–	–
PEANO	–	–	–	–	–	–	1	–	1
PERIOD	–	–	–	–	–	–	–	1	1
PIANO	17	21	38	4	11	15	6	11	17
PIANO MUSIC	1	–	1	–	–	–	–	–	–
PLAY	5	7	12	4	7	11	1	3	4
PLAY PIANO	1	1	2	–	–	–	–	–	–
PLAY SOME	1	–	1	–	–	–	–	–	–
PLAYING	–	–	–	–	–	–	–	1	1
PLAYS	–	1	1	–	–	–	–	–	–
PLEASANT	–	–	–	–	–	–	1	1	2
PRACTICE	–	–	–	–	1	1	–	–	–
PRETTY	5	–	5	2	5	7	3	3	6
PUZZLE	1	–	1	–	–	–	–	–	–
QUIET	1	4	5	1	1	2	–	–	–
RADIO	1	1	2	–	–	–	2	–	2
RECORD	2	3	5	1	1	2	1	1	2
RECORD PLAYER	2	3	5	2	1	3	–	–	–

RESPONSE WORD	1ST M	F	T	3RD M	F	T	5TH M	F	T

52. MUSIC

RESPONSE WORD	1ST M	F	T	3RD M	F	T	5TH M	F	T
RECORDS	–	1	1	–	–	–	–	–	–
RED	–	–	–	1	1	2	–	–	–
RHYTHM	–	–	–	1	–	1	–	1	1
ROCK	–	–	–	–	–	–	–	1	1
ROCK AND ROLL	–	–	–	–	–	–	1	1	2
ROOM	–	1	1	–	–	–	–	–	–
RUN	–	1	1	–	–	–	–	–	–
RUSIC	–	1	1	–	–	–	–	–	–
SALLFT	–	–	–	–	–	–	1	–	1
SANG	1	–	1	–	–	–	1	–	1
SAXOPHONE	–	–	–	–	–	–	1	–	1
SCALE	–	–	–	–	1	1	–	–	–
SCHOOL	1	–	1	–	–	–	–	–	–
SHOES	–	1	1	–	–	–	–	–	–
SHOWS	–	1	1	–	–	–	–	–	–
SILENCE	–	–	–	–	–	–	–	1	1
SING	11	21	32	15	21	36	11	17	28
SINGING	2	5	7	5	4	9	4	3	7
SNUSIC	1	–	1	–	–	–	–	–	–
SOCK	1	–	1	–	–	–	–	–	–
SOFT	–	–	–	–	1	1	2	3	5
SOFTLY	–	–	–	–	–	–	–	1	1
SOMEONE PLAYING AN INSTRUMENT	–	–	–	–	–	–	–	1	1
SOND	–	–	–	–	–	–	1	–	1
SONG	1	5	6	12	16	28	13	12	25
SONGS	–	2	2	4	5	9	1	5	6
SORRY	–	–	–	–	1	1	–	–	–
SOUND	3	–	3	8	13	21	17	16	33
SOUNDS	–	–	–	2	2	4	2	1	3
SPELL	–	1	1	–	–	–	–	–	–
SUBJECT	–	–	–	–	–	–	1	–	1
SUSIC	–	–	–	1	–	1	–	–	–
SUSIE	–	–	–	–	1	1	–	–	–
SWEET	–	–	–	–	–	–	1	2	3
SYMPHONY	–	–	–	–	–	–	1	1	2
TABLE	–	1	1	–	–	–	–	–	–
TAKE MUSIC	1	–	1	–	–	–	–	–	–
TALK	–	2	2	3	–	3	1	1	2
TALKING	–	–	–	1	–	1	–	–	–
TEACH	–	–	–	1	–	1	–	–	–
TEACHER	11	2	13	3	–	3	1	2	3
THERE	1	–	1	–	–	–	–	–	–
THEY ARE PLAYING MUSIC	–	–	–	1	–	1	–	–	–
THING	–	–	–	1	–	1	–	–	–
THINGS	–	1	1	–	–	–	–	–	–
THOSE	1	–	1	–	–	–	–	–	–
TIME	1	–	1	–	–	–	–	–	–
TO PLAY	–	1	1	–	–	–	–	–	–
TODAY	–	–	–	1	–	1	–	–	–
TOMORROW	–	–	–	–	1	1	–	–	–
TONE	–	–	–	1	1	2	–	–	–
TOO	–	–	–	1	–	1	–	–	–
TROMBONE	–	–	–	1	–	1	–	–	–
TRUE	1	–	1	–	–	–	–	–	–
TRUMPET	–	–	–	–	1	1	8	–	8
TUBA	–	–	–	–	–	–	1	–	1
TUNE	–	–	–	4	1	5	1	–	1
TUSIC	1	–	1	–	–	–	–	–	–
TV	1	–	1	–	–	–	–	–	–
VIOLIN	2	–	2	1	–	1	–	1	1
VIOLINS	–	–	–	–	–	–	–	1	1
VOICE	–	–	–	–	–	–	1	–	1
WE	–	1	1	–	–	–	–	–	–
WHEN YOURE SINGING	1	–	1	–	–	–	–	–	–
WHISTLE	–	–	–	–	1	1	–	–	–
WINDER	1	–	1	–	–	–	–	–	–
WINDOW	1	–	1	–	–	–	–	–	–
WONDERFUL	–	–	–	–	–	–	–	1	1
YANKEE DOODLE	–	1	1	–	–	–	–	–	–
YOU	–	1	1	–	–	–	–	1	1

RESPONSE WORD		1ST			3RD			5TH	
	M	F	T	M	F	T	M	F	T

53. NEEDLE

RESPONSE WORD	M	F	T	M	F	T	M	F	T
A LITTLE NEEDLE	–	1	1	–	–	–	–	–	–
A PIN	–	–	–	–	–	–	1	–	1
A THREAD AND NEEDLE	–	–	–	1	–	1	–	–	–
ARM	1	1	2	1	–	1	–	–	–
BAND	–	–	–	1	–	1	–	–	–
BE	–	–	–	–	–	–	1	–	1
BE WILD LIKE	–	1	1	–	–	–	–	–	–
BEAR	–	–	–	1	–	1	–	–	–
BEAT	1	1	2	–	–	–	–	–	–
BEEDLE	–	1	1	–	–	–	–	1	1
BEETLE	3	1	4	4	–	4	1	–	1
BEETLES AND FLOWERS	1	–	1	–	–	–	–	–	–
BEG	–	–	–	–	1	1	–	–	–
BETTER	–	–	–	–	1	1	–	–	–
BETTLE	–	1	1	–	–	–	–	–	–
BLACK	1	–	1	–	–	–	–	–	–
BOAT	1	–	1	–	–	–	–	–	–
BOBBYPIN	1	–	1	–	–	–	–	–	–
BOOSTER SHOT	–	1	1	–	–	–	–	–	–
BOX	2	–	2	–	–	–	1	–	1
BOY	2	1	3	–	–	–	–	–	–
BRACELET	–	1	1	–	–	–	–	–	–
BREAD	–	–	–	–	1	1	–	–	–
CAN	–	1	1	–	–	–	–	–	–
CANDY	1	–	1	–	1	1	–	–	–
CAT	–	1	1	1	–	1	–	–	–
CATCH	1	–	1	–	–	–	–	–	–
CHAIR	1	–	1	–	–	–	–	–	–
CHEATING	1	–	1	–	–	–	–	–	–
CLOTHES	–	1	1	–	–	–	–	1	1
CLOTHES PIN	1	–	1	–	–	–	–	–	–
CLOUDS	1	–	1	–	–	–	–	–	–
COME	1	–	1	–	–	–	–	–	–
COTTON	–	2	2	–	2	2	–	2	2
CREEDLE	1	–	1	–	–	–	–	–	–
DESK	1	–	1	–	–	–	–	–	–
DO HURT ME	–	1	1	–	–	–	–	–	–
DOCTOR	6	1	7	2	4	6	4	3	7
DOG	1	–	1	–	–	–	–	–	–
DONT CRY	–	1	1	–	–	–	–	–	–
DONT HURT YOURSELF	–	1	1	–	–	–	–	–	–
DONT PLAY WITH THE NEEDLE CAUSE YOU MIG	–	1	1	–	–	–	–	–	–
DOOR	–	–	–	1	–	1	–	–	–
DRESS	–	–	–	1	–	1	–	–	–
EAT	–	–	–	–	1	1	–	–	–
EMBROIDERY	–	–	–	–	–	–	–	1	1
EYE	–	1	1	–	–	–	2	5	7
FISHING	–	–	–	–	1	1	–	–	–
FOOD	–	–	–	–	–	–	1	–	1
FOR	–	1	1	–	–	–	–	–	–
FORK	1	–	1	–	–	–	–	–	–
FOUR	–	1	1	–	–	–	–	–	–
FRIEND	–	–	–	1	–	1	1	–	1
GEEDLE	–	–	–	1	–	1	–	–	–
GET	–	–	–	–	1	1	–	–	–
GET DOWN	–	–	–	–	–	–	1	–	1
GET NEEDLES	1	–	1	–	–	–	–	–	–
GET STUCK WITH A PIN	–	1	1	–	–	–	–	–	–
GIRL	–	1	1	–	–	–	–	–	–
GLASSES	1	1	2	–	–	–	–	–	–
HAPPY	1	–	1	–	–	–	–	–	–
HARED	–	–	–	–	–	–	1	–	1
HART	–	–	–	–	–	–	1	–	1
HAYSTACK	–	–	–	–	–	–	5	–	5
HEATER	1	–	1	–	–	–	–	–	–
HEEDLE	1	–	1	–	–	–	–	–	–
HEEL	–	–	–	–	1	1	–	–	–
HER	–	1	1	–	–	–	–	–	–
HIM	–	–	–	1	–	1	–	–	–
HOUSE	–	–	–	1	–	1	–	–	–
HURT	4	4	8	7	6	13	3	5	8

RESPONSE WORD	1ST			3RD			5TH		
	M	F	T	M	F	T	M	F	T

53. NEEDLE

RESPONSE WORD	M	F	T	M	F	T	M	F	T
HURTS	3	1	4	–	–	–	–	–	–
INK	1	–	1	–	–	–	–	–	–
INSTRUMENT	–	–	–	–	–	–	–	1	1
IS A HORSE	1	–	1	–	–	–	–	–	–
JAG	–	1	1	–	–	–	–	–	–
KID	1	–	1	–	–	–	–	–	–
KNEEL	–	1	1	–	–	–	–	–	–
KNEES	–	1	1	–	–	–	–	–	–
KNIFE	–	1	1	–	–	–	–	–	–
KNITTING	–	1	1	–	–	–	1	1	2
LEG	1	–	1	–	–	–	–	–	–
LITTLE NEEDLE	1	–	1	–	–	–	–	–	–
LOCKER	1	–	1	–	–	–	–	–	–
LOOK OUT	–	–	–	1	–	1	–	–	–
MEAL	1	–	1	–	–	–	–	–	–
MEAN	–	1	1	–	–	–	–	–	–
MEAT	–	1	1	–	–	–	–	–	–
MEDICINE	1	–	1	5	2	7	–	1	1
MEED	–	–	–	–	–	–	1	–	1
MEEDLE	1	–	1	–	–	–	–	–	–
METAL	–	–	–	2	–	2	–	–	–
NAIL	–	–	–	–	1	1	–	–	–
NEAT	–	3	3	–	–	–	–	–	–
NEED	–	–	–	–	–	–	2	–	2
NELOR	–	–	–	–	–	–	1	–	1
NICE	–	–	–	–	1	1	–	–	–
NO	1	–	1	1	–	1	–	–	–
NO NEEDLE	1	–	1	–	–	–	–	–	–
NO NEEDLES	–	–	–	1	–	1	–	–	–
NOODLE	1	–	1	–	–	–	–	–	–
NOSE	1	–	1	–	–	–	–	–	–
NOT	1	–	1	–	–	–	–	–	–
NURSE	1	1	2	–	–	–	–	–	–
OBJECT	–	–	–	–	–	–	1	–	1
OPERATION	–	–	–	–	–	–	1	–	1
OUCH	3	1	4	1	2	3	2	1	3
OW	–	1	1	–	–	–	–	1	1
PAPER	–	–	–	1	–	1	–	–	–
PATIENT	–	–	–	1	–	1	–	–	–
PEAL	–	1	1	–	–	–	–	–	–
PEEDLE	–	–	–	–	1	1	–	–	–
PEN	1	–	1	–	3	3	2	–	2
PENCIL	–	–	–	–	1	1	–	–	–
PENICILLIN	1	–	1	–	–	–	–	–	–
PILL	–	–	–	–	–	–	1	–	1
PIN	6	15	21	36	29	65	26	14	40
PINCH	1	1	2	–	–	–	–	–	–
PINS	–	1	1	–	–	–	–	–	–
POINT	1	2	3	–	–	–	3	3	6
POLIO	–	–	–	–	1	1	–	–	–
POLIO SHOT	–	1	1	–	–	–	–	–	–
PRICK	–	–	–	–	–	–	1	1	2
PRICKLY	1	–	1	–	–	–	–	–	–
PUNCH	–	1	1	–	–	–	–	–	–
PUSH	–	1	1	–	–	–	–	–	–
PUT IN ARM TO GET VACCINATED	1	–	1	–	–	–	–	–	–
PUT THREAD IN A NEEDLE	–	1	1	–	–	–	–	–	–
QUIET	–	–	–	–	1	1	–	–	–
REEDLE	–	1	1	1	–	1	–	–	–
RIBBON	–	1	1	–	–	–	–	–	–
RING	–	–	–	1	–	1	–	–	–
SADDLE	1	–	1	–	–	–	–	–	–
SCHOOL	1	–	1	–	–	–	–	–	–
SCISSORS	1	–	1	–	–	–	–	–	–
SEED	–	–	–	1	–	1	–	–	–
SEEDLE	1	1	2	–	–	–	–	–	–
SEW	9	11	20	2	4	6	4	12	16
SEW WITH	–	1	1	–	–	–	–	–	–
SEWING	1	1	2	–	4	4	–	3	3
SEWING MACHINE	3	–	3	–	–	–	–	–	–
SEWING NEEDLE	1	–	1	–	–	–	–	–	–

RESPONSE WORD	1ST M	F	T	3RD M	F	T	5TH M	F	T

53. NEEDLE

RESPONSE WORD	1ST M	F	T	3RD M	F	T	5TH M	F	T
SHARP	6	2	8	10	7	17	25	9	34
SHARP-POINTED INTRUMENT	-	-	-	-	-	-	-	1	1
SHOT	13	9	22	7	6	13	5	3	8
SHOTS	1	-	1	-	-	-	-	-	-
SIT	-	-	-	-	-	-	-	1	1
SLOPPY	-	-	-	1	-	1	-	-	-
SOMETHING LITTLE AND SHARP	-	-	-	-	-	-	-	1	1
SPOOL	-	1	1	-	-	-	-	-	-
STERPER	-	-	-	-	-	-	-	1	1
STICK	3	5	8	4	-	4	1	5	6
STICK IT ARM	1	-	1	-	-	-	-	-	-
STICKER	-	-	-	1	-	1	-	-	-
STICKS	1	-	1	-	-	-	-	-	-
STING	-	-	-	1	-	1	-	1	1
STRING	-	2	2	-	2	2	-	1	1
STUNG	1	-	1	-	-	-	-	1	1
TABLE	1	1	2	-	-	-	-	-	-
TACK	-	-	-	-	-	-	-	1	1
TEEDLE	-	1	1	-	-	-	-	-	-
TELEVISION	-	1	1	-	-	-	-	-	-
TERRIBLE	-	-	-	1	-	1	-	-	-
THAT YOU SEW WITH	-	-	-	-	-	-	-	1	1
THE	-	-	-	-	-	-	1	-	1
THEM	-	-	-	-	1	1	-	-	-
THIMBLE	-	-	-	-	-	-	1	-	1
THING	-	-	-	-	-	-	1	-	1
THING THAT YOU SEW WITH	-	-	-	1	1	2	-	1	1
THORN	-	-	-	-	-	-	-	-	-
THREAD	17	27	44	36	51	87	31	55	86
THRED	-	-	-	-	-	-	1	-	1
THRID	-	-	-	-	-	-	1	-	1
THROUGH	1	-	1	-	-	-	-	-	-
TICKLE	-	-	-	1	-	1	-	-	-
TOP	-	-	-	-	-	-	1	-	1
TRASH CAN	-	1	1	-	-	-	-	-	-
TREAD	-	-	-	-	-	-	1	1	2
USE	-	-	-	1	-	1	-	-	-
VACCINATION	-	1	1	-	-	-	1	-	1
W	-	1	1	-	-	-	-	-	-
WALL	-	-	-	-	1	1	-	-	-
WANT	1	-	1	-	-	-	-	1	1
WEEDLE	1	-	1	-	-	-	-	-	-
WHAT I HATE	1	-	1	-	-	-	-	-	-
WHAT YOU GET IN YOUR ARM	-	1	1	-	-	-	-	-	-
WHEN YOURE STICKING A NEEDLE IN SOMEBOD.	1	-	1	-	-	-	-	-	-
WOOL	1	-	1	-	-	-	-	-	-
WORK	-	-	-	-	1	1	-	-	-
YARN	-	-	-	-	-	-	1	-	1
YES	-	1	1	-	-	-	-	-	-
YOU	-	-	-	-	-	-	-	1	1
YOUR DRESS	-	1	1	-	-	-	-	-	-

54. NET

RESPONSE WORD	1ST M	F	T	3RD M	F	T	5TH M	F	T
A FISHING NET	-	-	-	1	-	1	-	-	-
A HAIRNET OR A FISHING NET	-	-	-	-	-	-	-	1	1
AND	-	1	1	-	-	-	-	-	-
ANIMAL	-	1	1	-	-	-	-	1	1
ANNETTE	-	1	1	-	-	-	-	-	-
AT	-	1	1	-	-	-	-	-	-
AWAY	-	-	-	-	1	1	-	-	-
BABY	1	-	1	-	-	-	-	-	-
BACKYARD	-	1	1	-	-	-	-	-	-
BADMINTON	1	-	1	-	-	-	-	1	1
BAG	-	1	1	1	1	2	-	2	2
BAIT	-	-	-	-	-	-	1	-	1
BALL	-	1	1	-	1	1	-	1	1
BASKET	-	-	-	1	5	6	3	-	3

RESPONSE WORD	1ST			3RD			5TH		
	M	F	T	M	F	T	M	F	T

54.   NET

RESPONSE WORD	M	F	T	M	F	T	M	F	T
BASKETBALL	–	–	–	–	–	–	1	–	1
BASKETBALL NET	–	1	1	–	–	–	–	–	–
BAT	–	1	1	1	–	1	–	1	1
BED	1	–	1	1	1	2	–	1	1
BEE HOUSE	–	1	1	–	–	–	–	–	–
BEES	–	–	–	–	1	1	–	–	–
BERNETTE	–	1	1	–	–	–	–	–	–
BET	2	4	6	4	4	8	1	1	2
BIG	–	2	2	1	1	2	1	–	1
BIKE	–	1	1	1	–	1	–	–	–
BIRD	6	10	16	–	–	–	–	–	–
BIRD NEST	–	–	–	1	–	1	–	–	–
BIRD NET	–	2	2	–	–	–	–	–	–
BIRDS NEST	–	1	1	–	–	–	–	–	–
BIT	–	–	–	1	–	1	–	–	–
BLACK	–	–	–	–	1	1	–	–	–
BLUE	–	–	–	1	–	1	–	–	–
BOARD	1	–	1	–	–	–	–	–	–
BOAT	2	–	2	–	1	1	–	–	–
BOATS	–	–	–	–	1	1	–	–	–
BOOK	–	–	–	–	1	1	–	–	–
BOX	–	1	1	–	–	–	–	–	–
BRAT	–	1	1	–	–	–	–	–	–
BROTHER	–	1	1	–	–	–	–	–	–
BROWN	–	1	1	–	–	–	–	–	–
BUD	–	–	–	–	1	1	–	1	1
BUG	–	–	–	–	–	–	–	1	1
BURN	–	–	–	1	–	1	–	–	–
BUTTERFLY	5	2	7	2	4	6	3	1	4
BUTTON	1	–	1	–	–	–	–	–	–
CAGE	–	1	1	–	1	1	4	1	5
CAN	–	1	1	–	–	–	–	–	–
CAR	1	–	1	–	–	–	–	–	–
CARROT	–	1	1	–	–	–	–	–	–
CAT	3	1	4	–	–	–	–	–	–
CATCH	12	7	19	18	14	32	13	11	24
CATCH A BUTTERFLY	–	1	1	–	–	–	–	–	–
CATCH A FISH	–	1	1	–	–	–	–	–	–
CATCH FISH IN IT	–	–	–	–	–	–	1	–	1
CATCH THE FISHES	–	1	1	–	–	–	–	–	–
CATCH WITH	–	–	–	–	–	–	–	1	1
CATCHING	–	1	1	–	–	–	–	–	–
CATFISH	–	1	1	–	–	–	–	–	–
CAUGHT	1	1	2	1	–	1	–	2	2
CAUGHT A FISH WITH A NET	–	1	1	–	–	–	–	–	–
CEILING	1	–	1	–	–	–	–	–	–
CHAIR	–	–	–	1	–	1	–	–	–
CHATE	–	–	–	–	–	–	–	1	1
CIRCLE	–	–	–	–	–	–	–	1	1
CIRCUS	–	–	–	2	–	2	–	1	1
CLOTH	–	–	–	2	–	2	–	–	–
CLOTHES	–	1	1	–	–	–	–	–	–
COAT	–	–	–	–	–	–	–	1	1
COUCH	1	–	1	–	–	–	–	–	–
COVER	–	–	–	–	1	1	–	–	–
CRAB	4	–	4	1	3	4	–	–	–
CRABS	1	–	1	1	–	1	–	–	–
CRET	1	1	2	–	–	–	–	–	–
CURLERS	–	1	1	–	–	–	–	–	–
DARN	–	–	–	–	–	–	–	1	1
DID	–	1	1	–	–	–	–	–	–
DIRTY	–	–	–	–	–	–	1	–	1
DOG	–	1	1	–	–	–	1	–	1
DOGCATCHERS CATCH DOGS IN A NET	–	1	1	–	–	–	–	–	–
DRAB	–	–	–	–	1	1	–	–	–
DRAG	–	–	–	1	–	1	1	–	1
DRINK	–	–	–	1	–	1	–	–	–
ELEPHANT	–	1	1	–	–	–	–	–	–
EVER	–	1	1	–	–	–	–	–	–
FALL	–	–	–	2	–	2	2	–	2
FELT	–	–	–	–	–	–	–	1	1

RESPONSE WORD	1ST			3RD			5TH		
	M	F	T	M	F	T	M	F	T

54. NET

RESPONSE WORD	M	F	T	M	F	T	M	F	T
FET	1	–	1	–	–	–	–	–	–
FIGHT	–	–	–	–	1	1	–	–	–
FIREMAN	–	–	–	–	–	–	2	–	2
FIREMEN	1	–	1	–	–	–	–	–	–
FISH	22	16	38	29	31	60	41	42	83
FISH CATCH	–	–	–	1	–	1	–	–	–
FISH CATCHING	–	–	–	–	–	–	–	1	1
FISH NET	1	–	1	–	–	–	–	1	1
FISHER	–	–	–	–	–	–	–	1	1
FISHERMAN	–	1	1	3	–	3	2	–	2
FISHERMEN	–	–	–	–	–	–	–	1	1
FISHES	–	–	–	1	–	1	–	–	–
FISHHOOK	–	–	–	1	–	1	–	–	–
FISHING	3	–	3	2	2	4	5	3	8
FISHING LINE	–	–	–	–	–	–	–	1	1
FISHING NET	1	–	1	3	–	3	–	–	–
FISHING POLE	1	–	1	–	–	–	–	–	–
FISHING ROD	2	–	2	–	–	–	–	–	–
FLASHLIGHT	–	–	–	1	–	1	–	–	–
FLIES	–	–	–	1	–	1	–	1	1
FLY	–	2	2	–	–	–	1	–	1
FOOD	1	–	1	–	–	–	–	–	–
FOOT	1	–	1	–	–	–	–	–	–
FOR	1	–	1	–	1	1	–	–	–
FRED	–	1	1	–	–	–	–	–	–
FREE	1	–	1	–	–	–	–	–	–
FRET	–	1	1	–	–	–	–	–	–
GAME	–	–	–	–	–	–	–	1	1
GET	1	1	2	1	–	1	–	–	–
GIRL	–	–	–	–	–	–	1	–	1
GO	–	–	–	–	–	–	–	1	1
GOAL	1	–	1	–	–	–	–	–	–
GOOD	–	–	–	–	–	–	1	1	2
GRAB	1	–	1	–	–	–	–	–	–
HAIR	2	4	6	–	6	6	–	9	9
HAIRNET	–	1	1	–	–	–	–	–	–
HAND	1	–	1	–	–	–	–	–	–
HAPPEN	–	1	1	–	–	–	–	–	–
HAT	2	1	3	–	1	1	1	2	3
HEAD	1	1	2	–	–	–	–	1	1
HER	–	1	1	–	–	–	–	–	–
HET	1	–	1	–	–	–	–	–	–
HIM	–	–	–	1	–	1	–	–	–
HIT	–	–	–	1	1	2	–	–	–
HOLD	–	–	–	–	–	–	1	–	1
HOLDS	–	–	–	1	–	1	1	–	1
HOLES	–	–	–	–	1	1	–	2	2
HOOK	–	–	–	–	–	–	–	1	1
HOUSE	–	–	–	1	–	1	–	–	–
INSECT	–	–	–	1	–	1	–	–	–
IS A BIRD WHERE HE SITS DOWN	1	–	1	–	–	–	–	–	–
JET	2	–	2	–	–	–	–	–	–
JUMP	–	–	–	1	–	1	–	–	–
KET	–	1	1	–	–	–	–	–	–
KNIT	–	1	1	3	–	3	–	1	1
KNIT SOMETHING	–	–	–	–	–	–	–	1	1
KNITTED	–	–	–	1	–	1	–	–	–
KNITTING	–	1	1	–	–	–	–	–	–
LET	2	1	3	–	1	1	–	–	–
LETS GO FISHING	–	1	1	–	–	–	–	–	–
LIGHT	1	–	1	–	–	–	–	–	–
LIKE	–	1	1	–	–	–	–	–	–
LIKE A BIRD NEST	–	1	1	–	–	–	–	–	–
LINE	–	–	–	–	–	–	–	1	1
MAKE	–	–	–	–	1	1	–	–	–
MAKING	–	–	–	–	–	–	1	–	1
MAN	–	–	–	1	–	1	–	–	–
MATERIAL	–	–	–	–	1	1	–	1	1
MATTRESS	1	–	1	–	–	–	–	–	–
ME	–	–	–	2	–	2	–	–	–
MEANT SOMETHING	1	–	1	–	–	–	–	–	–

RESPONSE WORD	1ST M	F	T	3RD M	F	T	5TH M	F	T

54.   NET

RESPONSE WORD	1ST M	F	T	3RD M	F	T	5TH M	F	T
MEAT	–	–	–	1	1	2	–	1	1
MEND	–	–	–	–	–	–	–	1	1
MESS	1	–	1	–	–	–	–	–	–
MET	2	–	2	2	2	4	1	1	2
MISS	–	–	–	–	1	1	–	–	–
MOON	–	1	1	–	–	–	–	–	–
MOVIE	1	–	1	–	–	–	–	–	–
NAME	–	1	1	–	–	–	–	–	–
NAP	–	1	1	–	–	–	–	–	–
NEAT	–	–	–	–	–	–	1	3	4
NECK	–	1	1	–	–	–	–	–	–
NEEDLE	–	–	–	1	2	3	2	–	2
NEST	2	1	3	2	5	7	1	2	3
NESTY	–	–	–	–	1	1	1	–	1
NET	–	–	–	–	1	1	–	–	–
NETHER	1	–	1	–	–	–	–	–	–
NETS	–	–	–	–	–	–	1	–	1
NETWORK	–	–	–	–	–	–	1	–	1
NEW	1	–	1	–	1	1	–	–	–
NEXT	–	–	–	–	1	1	–	1	1
NO	1	–	1	–	–	–	–	–	–
NOT	–	3	3	–	–	–	–	–	–
NOT NET	1	–	1	–	–	–	–	–	–
NOW	–	1	1	–	–	–	–	–	–
NYLON	–	–	–	–	–	–	–	1	1
OFFICE	–	1	1	–	–	–	–	–	–
ON SOMEBODY	–	1	1	–	–	–	–	–	–
ONE	–	1	1	–	–	–	–	–	–
PEN	–	1	1	–	–	–	–	–	–
PEOPLE	–	–	–	1	–	1	–	–	–
PET	1	1	2	2	1	3	3	1	4
PICTURE	1	–	1	1	–	1	–	–	–
PIN	–	–	–	–	1	1	–	–	–
PIT	–	1	1	1	–	1	–	–	–
POLE	–	1	1	1	–	1	1	–	1
POLICE	–	–	–	–	–	–	1	–	1
RAT	–	–	–	–	1	1	–	–	–
RED	1	–	1	1	–	1	–	–	–
ROD	–	–	–	–	2	2	–	1	1
ROOM	–	1	1	–	–	–	–	–	–
ROOSTER	1	–	1	–	–	–	–	–	–
ROPE	–	–	–	2	2	4	6	4	10
SACK	–	–	–	1	–	1	–	–	–
SAIL	–	–	–	–	1	1	–	–	–
SAILOR	–	–	–	–	–	–	–	1	1
SCARF	1	–	1	–	–	–	–	–	–
SCOOP	–	–	–	–	–	–	1	–	1
SCREEN	–	–	–	–	–	–	1	1	2
SEA	–	–	–	–	1	1	–	–	–
SEAT COVER	–	1	1	–	–	–	–	–	–
SEINE	–	–	–	1	–	1	–	–	–
SENT	–	–	–	–	1	1	–	–	–
SET	–	–	–	1	5	6	2	–	2
SEW	–	2	2	–	2	2	1	1	2
SHIRT	1	–	1	–	–	–	–	–	–
SHOOTING	1	–	1	–	–	–	–	–	–
SIN	–	–	–	–	1	1	–	–	–
SING	–	1	1	–	–	–	–	–	–
SIT	–	–	–	–	1	1	–	–	–
SKY	1	–	1	–	–	–	–	–	–
SLOPY	–	–	–	–	–	–	1	–	1
SNET	1	–	1	–	–	–	–	–	–
SO	–	–	–	–	–	–	1	–	1
SOMEBODY	1	–	1	–	–	–	–	–	–
SOMEONE	–	–	–	–	1	1	–	–	–
SOMETHING TO CATCH A FISH	–	–	–	–	–	–	1	–	1
SOMETHING TO CATCH FISH IN	–	–	–	–	–	–	–	1	1
SOW	–	–	–	–	–	–	1	–	1
SPET	–	1	1	–	–	–	–	–	–
SPIDER	1	–	1	–	–	–	–	–	–

RESPONSE WORD	1ST			3RD			5TH		
	M	F	T	M	F	T	M	F	T

54. NET

RESPONSE WORD	M	F	T	M	F	T	M	F	T
STARS	–	2	2	–	–	–	–	–	–
STICK	–	1	1	–	–	–	–	–	–
STING	–	–	–	1	1	2	1	–	1
STONE	1	–	1	–	–	–	–	–	–
STORE IT AGAIN	–	–	–	1	–	1	–	–	–
STREING	–	–	–	–	–	–	1	–	1
STRING	–	–	–	6	5	11	5	3	8
STRINGS	–	–	–	–	2	2	1	–	1
STRINGY	–	–	–	–	–	–	2	–	2
STUCK	–	–	–	–	1	1	–	–	–
SWEATER	–	1	1	–	–	–	–	–	–
SWING	–	–	–	–	–	–	–	1	1
TABLE	1	–	1	–	–	–	–	–	–
TED	–	–	–	–	–	–	1	1	2
TELL	–	–	–	1	–	1	–	–	–
TEN	–	–	–	–	1	1	–	–	–
TENNIS	–	–	–	–	–	–	1	–	1
TENT	1	–	1	1	2	3	–	–	–
THANK YOU	1	–	1	–	–	–	–	–	–
THAT GOES ON MOTHERS HAT	–	1	1	–	–	–	–	–	–
THAT THEY CATCH FISH IN	1	–	1	–	–	–	–	–	–
THE	–	–	–	–	–	–	1	–	1
THEM	1	–	1	–	–	–	1	1	2
THING	–	–	–	–	–	–	1	1	2
THING USED FOR CATCHING FISH	–	–	–	–	–	–	1	1	2
THREAD	–	1	1	–	1	1	–	2	2
THREE	1	–	1	–	–	–	–	–	–
THROW	–	1	1	–	–	–	–	–	–
TIGER	1	1	2	–	–	–	–	–	–
TITY	–	–	–	–	–	–	1	–	1
TO CATCH A FLY	1	–	1	–	–	–	–	–	–
TO PUT NUMBERS DOWN	1	–	1	–	–	–	–	–	–
TRAMPOLINE	–	–	–	1	–	1	–	–	–
TRAP	–	–	–	2	–	2	–	–	–
TRAPEZE	1	–	1	–	–	–	–	–	–
TRASH CAN	–	1	1	–	–	–	–	–	–
TREE	–	1	1	1	–	1	–	–	–
TRUCK	1	–	1	–	–	–	–	–	–
UGLY	–	–	–	–	–	–	–	1	1
UN-NET	–	1	1	–	–	–	–	–	–
UNNET	–	1	1	–	–	–	–	–	–
WAIT	–	–	–	1	–	1	–	–	–
WALL	1	–	1	–	1	1	–	–	–
WATER	–	–	–	1	–	1	–	–	–
WEAVE	–	–	–	1	–	1	1	1	2
WEB	1	–	1	1	–	1	1	–	1
WET	1	1	2	2	1	3	2	2	4
WHEN YOU ANNEX SOMETHING	1	–	1	–	–	–	–	–	–
WHITE	–	1	1	–	–	–	–	–	–
WHY	1	–	1	–	–	–	–	–	–
WINDOW	1	1	2	–	–	–	–	–	–
WING	–	–	–	–	–	–	1	–	1
WIPE YOUR MOUTH	–	1	1	–	–	–	–	–	–
WIRE	–	–	–	1	–	1	1	–	1
WOOL	1	1	2	–	–	–	–	–	–
WOVEN	–	–	–	1	–	1	–	–	–
YARN	–	–	–	–	–	–	–	1	1
YOU	–	–	–	1	–	1	–	1	1
YOU COULD CATCH FISHES	–	1	1	–	–	–	–	–	–
YOU PUT IT IN THE WATER	1	–	1	–	–	–	–	–	–

RESPONSE WORD	1ST			3RD			5TH		
	M	F	T	M	F	T	M	F	T

55. NEVER

RESPONSE WORD	M	F	T	M	F	T	M	F	T
AGAIN	7	9	16	10	15	25	8	6	14
AGO	-	-	-	-	1	1	-	-	-
ALL	-	-	-	-	1	1	-	-	-
ALL TIMES	-	-	-	1	-	1	-	-	-
ALMOST	-	-	-	-	-	-	1	-	1
ALWAYS	6	5	11	20	21	41	23	26	49
ALWAYS DONT	-	-	-	-	1	1	-	-	-
ANY	-	-	-	-	1	1	-	-	-
ANYTHING	-	-	-	-	1	1	-	-	-
APPLE	-	-	-	-	1	1	-	-	-
AT ALL	-	1	1	-	-	-	-	-	-
ATE	1	-	1	-	-	-	-	-	-
AVER	-	-	-	-	-	-	1	-	1
AWAY	1	-	1	1	-	1	-	1	1
BABY	-	1	1	-	-	-	-	-	-
BAD	-	2	2	1	-	1	-	-	-
BAG	1	-	1	-	-	-	-	-	-
BALL	-	1	1	-	-	-	-	-	-
BE	1	-	1	-	-	-	-	-	-
BECAUSE	-	1	1	1	1	2	1	-	1
BED	-	-	-	-	-	-	-	1	1
BEEF	1	-	1	-	-	-	-	-	-
BEFORE	-	1	1	2	5	7	2	3	5
BEGIN	-	-	-	-	1	1	-	-	-
BEVER	1	-	1	-	-	-	-	-	-
BICYCLE	1	-	1	-	-	-	-	-	-
BIG	1	-	1	-	-	-	-	-	-
BIRD	-	1	1	-	-	-	-	-	-
BOAT	-	1	1	-	-	-	-	-	-
BOOK	-	2	2	-	-	-	-	-	-
BOY	-	-	-	-	-	-	1	-	1
BUGGY	1	-	1	-	-	-	-	-	-
BURN	1	-	1	-	-	-	-	-	-
BUTTERFLY	-	1	1	-	-	-	-	-	-
BUTTON	1	-	1	-	-	-	-	-	-
BUZZ	-	1	1	-	-	-	-	-	-
CAME	-	-	-	1	-	1	-	-	-
CAME BACK	1	-	1	-	-	-	-	-	-
CAN	-	2	2	3	-	3	-	1	1
CANT	-	-	-	1	1	2	2	1	3
CATCH	1	-	1	-	-	-	-	-	-
CHAIR	-	1	1	-	-	-	-	-	-
CHOO-CHOO TRAIN	1	-	1	-	-	-	-	-	-
CLOSE MY EYES	1	-	1	-	-	-	-	-	-
CLUTCH	-	1	1	-	-	-	-	-	-
COAT	-	-	-	-	1	1	-	-	-
COME	-	4	4	-	1	1	-	1	1
COME BACK	1	1	2	-	-	-	-	-	-
COME IN	1	-	1	-	-	-	-	-	-
COULD	-	1	1	-	-	-	-	-	-
COULDNT	-	-	-	-	-	-	-	1	1
CRAWL	1	-	1	-	-	-	-	-	-
CROSS	-	1	1	-	1	1	-	-	-
CRY	1	-	1	-	-	-	-	-	-
CUP	-	-	-	1	-	1	-	-	-
DARE	1	-	1	-	-	-	-	-	-
DEAD	-	1	1	-	-	-	-	-	-
DESK	1	2	3	-	-	-	-	-	-
DEVER	1	1	2	-	-	-	-	-	-
DID	-	-	-	1	1	2	1	-	1
DIDNT	-	-	-	-	3	3	1	2	3
DIE	-	2	2	-	-	-	-	2	2
DO	5	1	6	4	3	7	-	2	2
DO EVERYTHING	1	-	1	-	-	-	-	-	-
DO IT	2	-	2	1	1	2	-	-	-
DO IT AGAIN	1	-	1	1	-	1	-	-	-
DO NOT	-	-	-	1	-	1	1	-	1
DO NOT DO IT AGAIN	-	-	-	-	-	-	1	-	1
DO NOT TOUCH A MATCH	1	-	1	-	-	-	-	-	-
DO NOTHING	-	1	1	-	-	-	-	-	-
DO SOMETHING	-	-	-	-	-	-	-	1	1
DO THAT	-	-	-	1	-	1	-	-	-

RESPONSE WORD	1ST			3RD			5TH		
	M	F	T	M	F	T	M	F	T

55. NEVER

RESPONSE WORD	M	F	T	M	F	T	M	F	T
DO THAT AGAIN	–	1	1	–	–	–	–	–	–
DO THAT NO MORE	–	1	1	–	–	–	–	–	–
DOESNT HAPPEN	–	–	–	–	–	–	1	–	1
DOG	1	–	1	–	–	–	–	–	–
DON	–	–	–	1	–	1	–	1	1
DONE	–	–	–	1	–	1	–	–	–
DONT	1	2	3	3	8	11	3	5	8
DONT COME BACK	–	1	1	–	–	–	–	–	–
DONT DO IT ANYMORE	1	–	1	–	–	–	–	–	–
DONT DO NOTHING	–	1	1	–	–	–	–	–	–
DONT NEVER GET INTO DANGEROUS THINGS	–	1	1	–	–	–	–	–	–
DONT NEVER RUN AWAY	–	1	1	–	–	–	–	–	–
DOOR	1	1	2	–	–	–	–	–	–
DOWN	–	–	–	–	1	1	–	–	–
DRESS	–	–	–	1	–	1	–	–	–
EARTH	–	–	–	–	–	–	–	1	1
EASY	–	1	1	–	–	–	–	–	–
EAT	–	–	–	–	–	–	1	–	1
END	–	–	–	–	1	1	1	–	1
ENTHER	–	–	–	–	1	1	–	1	1
EVEN	–	–	–	–	1	1	–	1	1
EVER	14	14	28	28	19	47	28	30	58
EVER FIGHT	–	1	1	–	–	–	–	–	–
EVERY	–	–	–	–	–	–	2	–	2
FAMILY	1	–	1	–	–	–	–	–	–
FAR	–	1	1	–	–	–	–	–	–
FARTHER	–	–	–	–	–	–	–	1	1
FAST	–	–	–	–	–	–	1	–	1
FATHER	–	2	2	–	–	–	–	–	–
FEATHER	–	1	1	–	–	–	–	–	–
FIGHT	1	1	2	–	–	–	–	–	–
FIRST TIME	–	–	–	–	–	–	1	–	1
FISH	–	–	–	1	–	1	–	–	–
FLIES	–	–	–	–	1	1	–	–	–
FLOOR	1	–	1	–	–	–	–	–	–
FLOWERS	1	–	1	–	–	–	–	–	–
FLY	–	1	1	–	–	–	1	–	1
FOREVER	–	–	–	2	–	2	1	–	1
FORGET	–	–	–	–	–	–	1	–	1
FORGOT	–	–	–	–	1	1	–	–	–
FREQUENT	–	–	–	–	–	–	–	1	1
FUTURE	–	–	–	–	–	–	–	1	1
GET MARRIED	–	–	–	1	–	1	–	–	–
GIVE	–	1	1	–	–	–	–	–	–
GO	–	4	4	4	3	7	1	–	1
GO AWAY	1	3	4	–	–	–	–	–	–
GO HOME	–	1	1	–	–	–	–	–	–
GO IN FRONT OF CAR	–	1	1	–	–	–	–	–	–
GO OUT	–	3	3	–	–	–	–	–	–
GOING TO	–	1	1	–	–	–	–	–	–
GOOD WORK	1	–	1	–	–	–	–	–	–
GRASS	1	–	1	–	–	–	–	–	–
GRASSHOPPER	1	–	1	–	–	–	–	–	–
GRAY	1	–	1	–	–	–	–	–	–
HAD	–	1	1	–	2	2	–	–	–
HAPPEN	–	1	1	2	1	3	1	1	2
HAPPENED	1	–	1	–	–	–	–	–	–
HAPPENING	–	–	–	–	–	–	–	1	1
HAPPENS	2	–	2	–	–	–	–	–	–
HAPPENS AGAIN	1	–	1	–	–	–	–	–	–
HARDLY	–	–	–	–	1	1	2	2	4
HAVE	1	–	1	–	–	–	–	–	–
HE	–	–	–	–	–	–	–	1	1
HER	–	–	–	–	1	1	–	–	–
HERE	1	–	1	–	1	1	–	–	–
HEVER	2	–	2	–	–	–	–	–	–
HIM	1	–	1	–	–	–	–	–	–
HIT ME	1	–	1	–	–	–	–	–	–
HOP	–	1	1	–	–	–	–	–	–
HORSE	–	–	–	–	1	1	–	–	–
HOT	–	–	–	–	–	–	1	–	1

453

55. NEVER

RESPONSE WORD	1ST M	1ST F	1ST T	3RD M	3RD F	3RD T	5TH M	5TH F	5TH T
I GO	–	1	1	–	–	–	–	–	–
I NEVER HAD A RING BEFORE	–	–	–	–	–	–	–	1	1
I WILL	–	–	–	1	–	1	–	2	2
IMPOSSIBLE	–	–	–	1	–	1	–	–	–
IN	–	1	1	1	–	1	–	–	–
INK	–	1	1	–	–	–	–	–	–
INTERESTING	–	–	–	1	–	1	–	–	–
IT	–	–	–	2	–	2	–	–	–
IT FLIES	1	–	1	–	–	–	–	–	–
IT IS NEVER DONE	–	–	–	–	–	–	1	–	1
JACKET	1	–	1	–	–	–	–	–	–
JOIN	–	–	–	–	–	–	–	1	1
JUMP	1	–	1	–	–	–	–	–	–
JUST NEVER	–	–	–	–	–	–	–	1	1
KEVER	1	–	1	–	–	–	–	–	–
KILL	–	1	1	–	–	–	–	–	–
KING	–	1	1	–	–	–	–	–	–
LAND	4	–	4	–	–	–	–	–	–
LEAF	–	–	–	–	1	1	–	–	–
LET	–	–	–	–	–	–	1	–	1
LETS	–	–	–	–	–	–	1	–	1
LEVER	1	–	1	–	–	–	–	–	–
LIE	–	2	2	–	–	–	–	–	–
LIKE	–	1	1	–	–	–	–	–	–
LISTEN	–	–	–	1	–	1	–	–	–
LIVER	–	2	2	–	–	–	–	–	–
LONG	–	–	–	–	–	–	1	–	1
LOUD	–	1	1	–	–	–	–	–	–
MAN	–	1	1	–	–	–	–	–	–
MATCHES	–	–	–	1	1	2	–	–	–
MAY	–	1	1	–	–	–	–	–	–
MAYBE	–	–	–	–	–	–	–	1	1
ME	1	1	2	–	–	–	–	–	–
MEET	1	–	1	–	–	–	–	–	–
MEVER	1	–	1	–	–	–	–	–	–
MOON	1	–	1	–	–	–	–	–	–
MOSTLY	–	–	–	–	1	1	–	–	–
MUSIC	1	–	1	–	–	–	–	–	–
NEAR	–	–	–	1	2	3	–	–	–
NEITHER	–	–	–	–	–	–	–	1	1
NERVOUS	1	–	1	–	–	–	–	–	–
NEST	2	–	2	1	–	1	–	–	–
NEV	–	–	–	1	–	1	–	–	–
NEVER	–	1	1	–	–	–	1	–	1
NEVER AT ALL	–	–	–	–	–	–	1	–	1
NEVER, NEVER	–	–	–	–	1	1	–	–	–
NEW	–	1	1	–	–	–	–	–	–
NIGHT	–	1	1	–	–	–	–	–	–
NINE	–	1	1	–	–	–	–	–	–
NO	2	3	5	1	1	2	4	6	10
NO ONE	–	–	–	1	–	1	–	–	–
NO TIME	–	–	–	1	–	1	–	1	1
NOT	1	–	1	1	2	3	11	7	18
NOT AGAIN	–	–	–	1	–	1	–	2	2
NOT ALLOWED	–	–	–	1	–	1	1	–	1
NOT ALWAYS	–	–	–	–	–	–	1	–	1
NOT ANY TIME	–	–	–	–	–	–	1	1	2
NOT AT ALL	–	–	–	1	–	1	1	2	3
NOT DO	–	–	–	1	–	1	–	2	2
NOT EVER	–	–	–	–	1	1	–	2	2
NOT HAPPENED	–	–	–	–	–	–	1	–	1
NOT HAPPY	–	–	–	–	–	–	1	1	1
NOT LET	–	–	–	–	–	–	1	–	1
NOT NEVER	–	–	–	1	–	1	1	–	1
NOT OFTEN	–	–	–	–	–	–	1	–	1
NOT PERMITTED	–	–	–	–	–	–	1	–	1
NOT TO DO	–	–	–	–	–	–	–	1	1
NOTHING	–	–	–	1	1	2	–	1	1
NOW	1	2	3	3	1	4	3	1	4
NOWHERE	–	–	–	–	1	1	–	–	–

55.   NEVER

RESPONSE WORD	1ST			3RD			5TH		
	M	F	T	M	F	T	M	F	T
OFTEN	–	–	–	1	1	2	–	1	1
ONCE	1	–	1	1	1	2	–	1	1
OUT	–	–	–	–	–	–	–	1	1
PAPER	1	–	1	–	–	–	–	–	–
PEOPLE	–	–	–	–	–	–	1	–	1
PEVER	1	–	1	–	–	–	–	–	–
PIG	–	–	–	–	–	–	1	–	1
PLAY	–	1	1	–	–	–	–	–	–
PLAY WITH PEOPLE WHO HAVE COMPANY	–	1	1	–	–	–	–	–	–
PLUCK	–	1	1	–	–	–	–	–	–
PONY	–	1	1	–	–	–	–	–	–
POTATOES	1	–	1	–	–	–	–	–	–
PULL	1	–	1	–	–	–	–	–	–
RAIN	–	1	1	–	–	–	–	–	–
REVER	–	1	1	–	–	–	–	–	–
RIGHT	–	–	–	1	–	1	–	–	–
RIVER	–	1	1	–	–	–	–	–	–
ROACH	1	–	1	–	–	–	–	–	–
ROCK	1	–	1	–	–	–	–	–	–
SABLE	1	–	1	–	–	–	–	–	–
SCRATCH	–	1	1	–	–	–	–	–	–
SEE	1	1	2	1	–	1	1	–	1
SEE YOU	–	–	–	1	–	1	–	–	–
SEEN	1	–	1	–	1	1	1	1	2
SELDOM	–	–	–	1	–	1	–	2	2
SHIRT	–	–	–	–	1	1	–	–	–
SHOOT A PERSON	1	–	1	–	–	–	–	–	–
SHORT	–	–	–	–	–	–	–	1	1
SHOULDNT	–	–	–	–	–	–	1	–	1
SIGN	1	–	1	–	–	–	–	–	–
SMEVER	1	–	1	–	–	–	–	–	–
SOFT	–	1	1	–	–	–	–	–	–
SOMETIME	–	–	–	1	–	1	–	–	–
SOMETIMES	1	–	1	–	–	–	1	–	1
SOON	–	–	–	1	1	2	–	1	1
SPEAK	–	1	1	–	–	–	–	–	–
SPEAK TO YOU AGAIN	1	–	1	–	–	–	–	–	–
STATUE OF LIBERTY	–	–	–	1	–	1	–	–	–
STAY	1	–	1	1	–	1	–	–	–
STERDO	–	–	–	–	–	–	1	–	1
STOP	–	2	2	–	–	–	–	–	–
STORY	–	–	–	–	1	1	–	–	–
SUPPOSE	–	1	1	–	1	1	–	–	–
TELL	–	1	1	1	1	2	–	–	–
THEN	–	–	–	–	1	1	–	–	–
THERE	–	1	1	–	–	–	1	–	1
THEY	–	1	1	–	–	–	–	–	–
THROW STUFF	1	–	1	–	–	–	–	–	–
TO	1	–	1	–	–	–	–	–	–
TO DO WHATS WRONG	1	–	1	–	–	–	–	–	–
TODAY	–	–	–	–	1	1	1	–	1
TOUCH	2	–	2	1	–	1	–	–	–
TOUCH FIRE	1	–	1	–	–	–	–	–	–
TOUCH THAT STOVE, ITS HOT	–	1	1	–	–	–	–	–	–
TOYS	1	–	1	–	–	–	–	–	–
TREE	–	–	–	–	1	1	–	–	–
TRUE	–	–	–	–	1	1	1	–	1
UN-NEVER	–	–	–	–	1	1	–	–	–
UNABLE	–	–	–	–	–	–	–	1	1
UNDONE	–	–	–	–	–	–	–	1	1
VERY OFTEN	–	–	–	–	–	–	1	–	1
WALL	–	1	1	–	–	–	–	–	–
WANTS	1	–	1	–	–	–	–	–	–
WAS	–	1	1	–	–	–	–	–	–
WAY	–	–	–	–	1	1	–	–	–
WE	2	–	2	–	–	–	–	–	–
WEATHER	–	–	–	1	–	1	–	–	–
WEVER	–	–	–	1	–	1	–	–	–
WHEN	–	–	–	–	1	1	–	–	–
WHEN YOU NEVER GIVE NOTHING TO SOMEBODY	1	–	1	–	–	–	–	–	–

RESPONSE WORD	1ST			3RD			5TH		
	M	F	T	M	F	T	M	F	T

55. NEVER

RESPONSE WORD	M	F	T	M	F	T	M	F	T
WHENEVER	–	–	–	–	1	1	–	–	–
WHENEVER SOMEONE NEVER GOES ANYWHERE	–	1	1	–	–	–	–	–	–
WHERE	1	–	1	–	–	–	–	–	–
WHY	1	–	1	–	–	–	1	–	1
WILL	1	–	1	3	2	5	3	2	5
WINDOW	1	–	1	–	–	–	–	–	–
WINDOWS	–	1	1	–	–	–	–	–	–
WON	–	–	–	1	–	1	–	–	–
WONT	–	–	–	3	–	3	4	1	5
WONT DO IT	–	–	–	1	–	1	–	–	–
WONT DO NOTHING	–	–	–	–	1	1	–	–	–
WORK	1	–	1	–	–	–	–	–	–
WOULD	–	–	–	1	–	1	–	–	–
WOULDNT	–	–	–	–	–	–	–	2	2
YEARS	–	–	–	–	–	–	1	–	1
YELLOW	1	1	2	–	–	–	–	–	–
YES	4	–	4	–	–	–	–	–	–
YET	–	–	–	–	2	2	–	–	–
YOU	–	2	2	–	1	1	–	–	–
YOU NEVER DO SOMETHING BAD	1	–	1	–	–	–	–	–	–
ZOO	–	–	–	–	1	1	–	–	–

56. OBEY

RESPONSE WORD	M	F	T	M	F	T	M	F	T
A	–	–	–	1	–	1	–	–	–
A BED	–	1	1	–	–	–	–	–	–
AH	–	1	1	–	–	–	–	–	–
AIR	1	–	1	–	–	–	–	–	–
ALWAYS	–	–	–	–	–	–	1	–	1
ANGRY	–	–	–	–	1	1	–	1	1
ANNOY	–	–	–	–	–	–	–	1	1
ANOTHER	–	–	–	1	–	1	–	–	–
ARCHITECT	–	–	–	–	1	1	–	–	–
ARE	–	1	1	–	–	–	–	–	–
AS TOLD	–	–	–	–	–	–	–	1	1
ASK	–	–	–	–	1	1	–	–	–
AUNT	1	–	1	–	–	–	–	–	–
AWAY	1	–	1	–	–	–	–	–	–
BABY	–	1	1	–	–	–	–	–	–
BABY DOLL	–	1	1	–	–	–	–	–	–
BAD	2	7	9	3	4	7	2	2	4
BAG	–	1	1	–	–	–	–	–	–
BATH YOURSELF AND THEN GO TO SCHOOL	–	1	1	–	–	–	–	–	–
BAY	–	2	2	1	–	1	–	1	1
BE GOOD	1	–	1	3	1	4	–	–	–
BED	2	1	3	–	–	–	–	–	–
BEDROOM	–	1	1	–	–	–	–	–	–
BEG	1	–	1	–	–	–	–	–	–
BEHAVE	–	–	–	1	2	3	5	2	7
BELIEVE	–	–	–	1	–	1	–	–	–
BELLOW	–	–	–	–	–	–	–	1	1
BIG	–	1	1	–	–	–	–	1	1
BOAT	1	–	1	–	–	–	–	–	–
BOOK-BAG	1	–	1	–	–	–	–	–	–
BOW	–	–	–	–	1	1	–	–	–
BOY	1	–	1	–	–	–	–	–	–
BRAT	–	–	–	–	–	–	1	–	1
BUG	1	–	1	–	–	–	–	–	–
BUY	–	1	1	–	–	–	–	–	–
CAFETERIA	–	–	–	1	–	1	–	–	–
CAKE	–	–	–	–	–	–	–	1	1
CANT	–	–	–	–	–	–	–	1	1
CAT	–	1	1	–	–	–	1	–	1
CHAIR	–	1	1	–	–	–	–	–	–
CHESAPEAKE	–	–	–	1	–	1	–	–	–
CHILDREN	–	2	2	–	–	–	–	–	–
CHRISTMAS	–	–	–	–	1	1	–	–	–
CHRISTMAS TREE	1	–	1	–	–	–	–	–	–

RESPONSE WORD		1ST			3RD			5TH	
	M	F	T	M	F	T	M	F	T

56. OBEY

RESPONSE WORD	M	F	T	M	F	T	M	F	T
CHUND	–	–	–	–	–	–	1	–	1
CLOTHES HANGER	–	–	–	1	–	1	–	–	–
COAT	1	–	1	–	–	–	–	–	–
COBEY	1	–	1	–	–	–	–	–	–
COME	1	1	2	1	–	1	1	–	1
COMMAND	–	–	–	–	–	–	6	4	10
CORRECT	–	–	–	1	–	1	–	–	–
COW	–	1	1	–	–	–	–	–	–
CRADLE	–	1	1	–	–	–	–	–	–
CRAMP	–	–	–	1	–	1	–	–	–
CRUEL	–	–	–	2	–	2	–	–	–
DAD	–	–	–	–	–	–	1	–	1
DAY	–	–	–	–	–	–	–	1	1
DESIRE	–	–	–	–	–	–	–	1	1
DIDNT	–	–	–	1	1	2	–	–	–
DINNER	1	–	1	–	–	–	–	–	–
DIRT	–	–	–	–	1	1	–	–	–
DISCIPLINE	–	–	–	–	–	–	1	–	1
DISCOVER	–	–	–	–	1	1	–	–	–
DISOBEDIENT	–	–	–	1	–	1	–	–	–
DISOBEY	1	1	2	6	11	17	27	28	55
DO	–	–	–	5	8	13	8	5	13
DO AS TOLD	–	–	–	–	–	–	1	–	1
DO IT	–	–	–	1	–	1	–	–	–
DO NOT	–	–	–	1	2	3	–	–	–
DO NOT LISTEN	–	–	–	1	–	1	–	–	–
DO NOT OBEY	–	–	–	1	1	2	–	–	–
DO RIGHT	–	–	–	–	–	–	–	1	1
DO THINGS YOU SHOULD	1	–	1	–	–	–	–	–	–
DO WHAT SOMEBODY SAYS	–	–	–	–	–	–	1	–	1
DO WHAT SOMEONE SAYS	–	–	–	–	1	1	–	–	–
DOESNT OBEY	–	–	–	1	–	1	–	–	–
DOG	–	2	2	–	–	–	–	–	–
DOLL	–	1	1	–	–	–	–	–	–
DONT	1	2	3	2	2	4	–	–	–
DONT OBEY	3	1	4	4	–	4	2	–	2
DOOR	–	–	–	–	1	1	–	–	–
ENJOY	–	–	–	–	1	1	–	–	–
FALL	1	–	1	–	–	–	–	–	–
FATHER	1	–	1	1	–	1	–	–	–
FENCES	–	1	1	–	–	–	–	–	–
FEY	–	1	1	–	–	–	–	–	–
FIGHT	–	–	–	–	1	1	–	–	–
FINE	–	1	1	–	–	–	–	–	–
FIRE	–	–	–	–	–	–	1	–	1
FOLLOW	–	–	–	1	1	2	2	6	8
FOLLOW DIRECTIONS	–	–	–	–	1	1	–	–	–
FORGET	–	–	–	–	2	2	–	–	–
FRIEND	–	–	–	–	1	1	–	–	–
GAY	1	–	1	–	1	1	–	–	–
GIRL	–	–	–	–	1	1	–	–	–
GIVEN	–	1	1	–	–	–	–	–	–
GLORY	–	–	–	–	1	1	–	–	–
GLOVE	–	1	1	–	–	–	–	–	–
GO	–	1	1	–	1	1	–	1	1
GO BACK	1	–	1	–	–	–	–	–	–
GO ON	–	–	–	–	–	–	1	–	1
GO STRAIGHT	–	–	–	–	–	–	1	–	1
GO TO SLEEP	–	1	1	–	–	–	–	–	–
GOD	–	1	1	–	–	–	–	–	–
GOOD	2	–	2	8	10	18	4	5	9
GOODBY	–	–	–	–	–	–	1	–	1
GREEN	1	–	1	–	1	1	–	–	–
GROWN-UPS	–	1	1	–	–	–	–	–	–
HAPPINESS	–	–	–	–	–	–	–	1	1
HAPPY	1	–	1	–	–	–	–	1	1
HATE	–	–	–	–	–	–	–	1	1
HAY	2	–	2	–	–	–	–	–	–
HEAR	–	–	–	1	–	1	–	–	–
HELP	–	1	1	–	1	1	–	–	–
HER	–	–	–	–	1	1	–	–	–
HERE	–	–	–	–	1	1	–	–	–

RESPONSE WORD	1ST			3RD			5TH		
	M	F	T	M	F	T	M	F	T

56.   OBEY

RESPONSE WORD	M	F	T	M	F	T	M	F	T
HONEST	–	–	–	–	–	–	1	–	1
HONOR	–	–	–	–	–	–	1	–	1
HOUSE	–	–	–	–	1	1	–	–	–
I BAY	–	1	1	–	–	–	–	–	–
IBEY	–	–	–	–	1	1	–	–	–
IMMEDIATE	–	–	–	1	–	1	–	–	–
INK	–	1	1	–	–	–	–	–	–
INSTRUCTIONS	–	–	–	–	–	–	1	2	3
JOB	–	–	–	–	1	1	–	–	–
KILL IT	–	1	1	–	–	–	–	–	–
KIND	–	1	1	–	–	–	–	–	–
KNOW	–	–	–	–	1	1	–	–	–
LAID	–	–	–	1	–	1	–	–	–
LAP	1	–	1	–	–	–	–	–	–
LAW	5	3	8	9	2	11	3	2	5
LAWS	–	2	2	1	2	3	–	–	–
LAY	–	2	2	–	–	–	–	–	–
LEARN	–	–	–	–	1	1	1	–	1
LET	1	–	1	–	–	–	–	–	–
LETTER	1	–	1	–	–	–	–	–	–
LIKED	1	–	1	–	–	–	–	–	–
LISEN	–	–	–	–	–	–	1	–	1
LISTEN	3	1	4	11	12	23	23	27	50
LISTEN TO	–	–	–	–	1	1	1	–	1
LISTENED	–	–	–	–	1	1	–	–	–
LOVE	–	1	1	–	–	–	–	–	–
LOW	1	–	1	–	–	–	–	–	–
MADE	1	–	1	–	–	–	–	–	–
MAKE	1	–	1	–	–	–	–	–	–
MAKE UP	–	1	1	–	–	–	–	–	–
MANNERS	1	–	1	–	–	–	1	–	1
MASTER	–	–	–	1	–	1	–	–	–
MAY	–	1	1	1	1	2	–	–	–
ME	7	5	12	1	3	4	–	1	1
MILK	1	–	1	–	–	–	–	–	–
MIND	–	2	2	2	3	5	2	3	5
MOMMY	–	2	2	–	–	–	–	–	–
MOTHER	3	7	10	3	1	4	1	1	2
MOTHER AND FATHER	1	–	1	–	–	–	–	–	–
MUST	–	–	–	1	–	1	–	–	–
NAME	–	–	–	1	–	1	–	–	–
NAMES	1	–	1	–	–	–	–	–	–
NAUGHTY	–	–	–	–	–	–	–	1	1
NAY	–	1	1	–	–	–	–	–	–
NECKLACE	1	–	1	–	–	–	–	–	–
NEST	–	1	1	–	–	–	–	–	–
NICE	–	–	–	–	1	1	–	1	1
NO	–	2	2	1	1	2	–	–	–
NO RESPONSE	2	–	2	–	–	–	–	–	–
NOBEY	–	1	1	–	–	–	–	–	–
NOT	2	1	3	1	2	3	1	1	2
NOT LISTEN	–	–	–	1	–	1	–	–	–
NOT OBEY	5	4	9	4	5	9	6	2	8
NOT TO DO SOMETHING BAD	1	–	1	–	–	–	–	–	–
NOTE	1	–	1	–	–	–	–	–	–
NOTHING	–	–	–	–	1	1	–	–	–
NOTOBEY	–	–	–	–	–	–	1	–	1
NOW	1	1	2	–	–	–	1	–	1
NUMBERS	1	–	1	–	–	–	–	–	–
O	–	1	1	–	–	–	–	–	–
O SAY	–	–	–	1	–	1	–	–	–
O-WHERE	–	1	1	–	–	–	–	–	–
OBEDIENCE	–	–	–	–	–	–	–	1	1
OBEDIENT	–	–	–	1	1	2	3	3	6
OBEYED ORDERS	–	–	–	–	1	1	–	–	–
OH	–	1	1	–	–	–	–	–	–
OKAY	5	–	5	2	–	2	1	1	2
OLD	–	–	–	–	1	1	–	–	–
OLD MAID	1	–	1	–	–	–	–	–	–
OMAY	1	–	1	–	–	–	–	–	–
ONE	1	–	1	–	–	–	–	–	–
OPEN	1	–	1	–	–	–	–	–	–

RESPONSE WORD	1ST			3RD			5TH		
	M	F	T	M	F	T	M	F	T

56. OBEY

RESPONSE WORD	M	F	T	M	F	T	M	F	T
ORDER	1	–	1	5	3	8	3	2	5
ORDERS	3	2	5	5	4	9	–	–	–
OSANK	–	1	1	–	–	–	–	–	–
OSTRICH	1	–	1	–	–	–	–	–	–
OTHERS	–	–	–	–	1	1	–	–	–
OWE	–	1	1	–	–	–	–	–	–
PARENTS	1	2	3	–	–	–	1	1	2
PASTE	–	1	1	–	–	–	–	–	–
PAY	1	–	1	–	–	–	–	–	–
PAY ATTENTION	–	–	–	–	1	1	–	1	1
PEOPLE	1	1	2	–	–	–	–	–	–
PERSON	–	–	–	–	–	–	–	1	1
PLACE	–	–	–	–	–	–	1	–	1
PLEASE	–	1	1	–	–	–	–	–	–
POCKETBOOK	–	1	1	–	–	–	–	–	–
POLICE	1	–	1	–	–	–	–	–	–
POLICEMAN	–	–	–	–	–	–	1	–	1
PROMISE	1	–	1	–	–	–	–	–	–
RAISE	1	–	1	–	–	–	–	–	–
REJECT	–	–	–	–	–	–	–	1	1
RESPECT	–	–	–	1	–	1	–	2	2
RIDE	–	1	1	–	–	–	–	–	–
RIGHT	–	–	–	1	1	2	–	1	1
ROBEY	–	1	1	–	–	–	–	–	–
ROOM	1	–	1	1	1	2	3	3	6
RULE	1	2	3	–	–	–	–	–	–
RULES	8	8	16	10	7	17	5	5	10
SAFETY	1	–	1	–	–	–	1	2	3
SAFETY LAWS	–	–	–	1	–	1	–	–	–
SAFETY RULES	1	–	1	–	–	–	–	–	–
SAID	–	1	1	–	–	–	–	–	–
SASS	–	–	–	–	–	–	–	1	1
SAY	–	–	–	–	–	–	1	–	1
SEE	–	2	2	–	2	2	–	–	–
SERVE	–	1	1	–	–	–	–	–	–
SHIP	–	1	1	–	–	–	–	–	–
SHUT	–	–	–	1	–	1	–	–	–
SING	–	1	1	–	–	–	–	–	–
SLAY	–	1	1	–	–	–	–	–	–
SLOW	–	–	–	–	–	–	1	–	1
SNOW	–	1	1	–	–	–	–	–	–
SNOWMAN	–	1	1	–	–	–	–	–	–
SOAP THAT YOU PUT IN WATER	1	–	1	–	–	–	–	–	–
SOFTLY	–	–	–	–	–	–	–	1	1
SOMEBODY	–	1	1	–	–	–	–	–	–
SOMEONE	–	–	–	–	1	1	–	–	–
SOMETHING	2	–	2	1	–	1	–	–	–
SORRY	–	–	–	–	1	1	–	–	–
SPANK	–	–	–	1	–	1	–	–	–
STOOP	–	1	1	–	–	–	–	–	–
STOP	1	–	1	1	–	1	–	–	–
STREET	–	1	1	–	–	–	–	–	–
STRICT	–	–	–	1	–	1	–	–	–
STUFF	1	–	1	–	–	–	–	–	–
SUNDAY	–	1	1	–	–	–	–	–	–
SUNG	1	–	1	–	–	–	–	–	–
SUPPER	–	1	1	–	–	–	–	–	–
SWIM	–	1	1	–	–	–	–	–	–
TALK	–	–	–	–	–	–	1	–	1
TALLY	1	–	1	–	–	–	–	–	–
TAN	–	–	–	–	–	–	1	–	1
TAUGHT	–	–	–	1	1	2	–	1	1
TEACHER	–	–	–	1	1	2	–	1	1
TEATHER	–	–	–	–	–	–	1	–	1
TELEPHONE POLE	1	–	1	–	–	–	–	–	–
TELEVISION	1	–	1	–	–	–	–	–	–
TELL	–	–	–	–	–	–	1	–	1
THE	–	–	–	1	–	1	–	–	–
THE LAW	3	–	3	1	2	3	–	–	–
THE LAWS	–	–	–	1	–	1	–	–	–
THE LORD	–	1	1	–	–	–	–	–	–

RESPONSE WORD	1ST M	F	T	3RD M	F	T	5TH M	F	T
56. OBEY									
THE RULES	–	1	1	–	1	1	–	1	1
THE TRAFFIC LAWS	–	–	–	1	–	1	–	–	–
THEY	–	–	–	–	–	–	1	–	1
THINGS	1	–	1	–	1	1	–	–	–
THINK	1	–	1	1	1	2	–	1	1
TO DO WHAT IS RIGHT	–	–	–	–	–	–	1	–	1
TO DO WHAT SOMEBODY SAYS	–	–	–	–	–	–	–	1	1
TO MIND	–	–	–	–	–	–	–	1	1
TO OBEY	–	–	–	1	–	1	–	–	–
TODAY	1	–	1	–	–	–	–	–	–
TOLD	–	–	–	–	1	1	–	–	–
TRAFFIC	1	–	1	–	–	–	–	–	–
TRUST	–	–	–	2	1	3	–	–	–
UNBEYED	–	–	–	1	–	1	–	–	–
UNDERSTAND	1	–	1	1	1	2	–	–	–
UNOBEY	1	–	1	–	–	–	–	–	–
US	1	–	1	–	–	–	–	–	–
WASH	1	–	1	–	–	–	–	–	–
WASH THE DISHES	1	–	1	–	–	–	–	–	–
WATER	–	–	–	–	–	–	–	1	1
WE	1	–	1	–	–	–	–	–	–
WHAT	–	1	1	–	–	–	–	–	–
WHEN YOU OBEY SOMETHING	1	–	1	–	–	–	–	–	–
WHITE	1	–	1	–	–	–	–	–	–
WINDOW	1	–	1	–	–	–	–	–	–
WITH YOUR FATHER	–	1	1	–	–	–	–	–	–
WONDERFUL	–	–	–	–	1	1	–	–	–
WORD	1	–	1	–	–	–	–	–	–
WRITING	1	–	1	–	–	–	–	–	–
WRONG	–	–	–	1	–	1	–	–	–
YELLOW	–	1	1	–	–	–	–	–	–
YOU	1	1	2	2	–	2	–	–	–
YOU OBEY SOMEONE	–	1	1	–	–	–	–	–	–
YOUR FATHER	–	1	1	–	–	–	–	–	–
YOUR MOMMY	–	1	1	–	–	–	–	–	–
YOUR MOTHER	2	5	7	–	–	–	–	–	–
YOURE TOO OLD	1	–	1	–	–	–	–	–	–
57. OCEAN									
A BODY OF WATER	–	–	–	–	1	1	–	1	1
AIR	–	–	–	–	1	1	–	–	–
ATLANTIC	–	–	–	–	–	–	2	1	3
ATLANTIC CITY	1	–	1	–	–	–	–	–	–
BAY	–	–	–	3	4	7	6	6	12
BEACH	1	1	2	–	1	1	–	1	1
BED	–	2	2	–	–	–	–	–	–
BIG BODY OF WATER	–	–	–	–	–	–	1	–	1
BLUE	1	2	3	3	1	4	3	1	4
BLUES	–	–	–	–	–	–	1	–	1
BOARD	1	–	1	–	–	–	–	–	–
BOAT	9	7	16	2	1	3	–	–	–
BOATS	–	1	1	–	–	–	–	1	1
BOCEAN	–	2	2	–	–	–	–	–	–
BODY OF WATER	–	–	–	–	–	–	–	3	3
BOTTOM	–	–	–	–	–	–	1	–	1
BRACKISH	–	–	–	–	–	–	–	1	1
BRICKS	–	–	–	1	–	1	–	–	–
BUT	1	–	1	–	–	–	–	–	–
CANDY	–	1	1	–	–	–	–	–	–
CAT	1	–	1	–	–	–	–	–	–
CITY	8	6	14	4	5	9	–	–	–
CLEAN	–	–	–	–	–	–	–	1	1
CLOCK	–	1	1	–	–	–	–	–	–
CLOSION	1	–	1	–	–	–	–	–	–
COCEAN	1	–	1	–	–	–	–	–	–
COKE	1	–	1	–	–	–	–	–	–
CORNER	–	–	–	1	–	1	–	–	–
CUPBOARD	1	–	1	–	–	–	–	–	–
DEEP	–	–	–	1	1	2	–	1	1
DIE IN IT	–	1	1	–	–	–	–	–	–

RESPONSE WORD	1ST			3RD			5TH		
	M	F	T	M	F	T	M	F	T

57. OCEAN

RESPONSE WORD	M	F	T	M	F	T	M	F	T
DOOR KNOB	–	1	1	–	–	–	–	–	–
DRESS	–	1	1	–	–	–	–	–	–
DRIFTING WATER	–	–	–	–	–	–	–	1	1
DUCKS SWIM IN THE OCEAN	–	1	1	–	–	–	–	–	–
DUMPED	1	–	1	–	–	–	–	–	–
EATER	–	–	–	–	–	–	1	1	2
EMPTY	1	–	1	–	–	–	–	–	–
FACED	–	–	–	1	–	1	–	–	–
FAN	–	1	1	–	–	–	–	–	–
FINGERNAIL	–	1	1	–	–	–	–	–	–
FISH	5	1	6	2	–	2	2	3	5
FISHING	–	–	–	–	–	–	–	–	–
FLOOR	–	1	1	–	–	–	1	–	1
FULL	1	–	1	–	–	–	–	–	–
FUN	–	–	–	1	–	1	–	–	–
GENTLY	–	1	1	–	–	–	–	–	–
GLASSES	1	–	1	–	–	–	–	–	–
GO SWIMMING WHEN ITS HOT	–	1	1	–	–	–	–	–	–
GOOD	–	1	1	–	–	–	–	–	–
GRANDPARENTS	1	–	1	–	–	–	–	–	–
GRASS	1	–	1	–	–	–	–	–	–
GREEN	–	–	–	–	1	1	–	–	–
GROCEAN	1	–	1	–	–	–	–	–	–
HILL	–	1	1	–	–	–	–	–	–
HIM	1	–	1	–	–	–	–	–	–
I LIKE THE OCEAN	–	1	1	–	–	–	–	–	–
ICE CREAM	1	–	1	–	–	–	–	–	–
IN THE SEA	1	–	1	–	–	–	–	–	–
INK	–	1	1	–	–	–	–	–	–
IS LIKE WATER	–	1	1	–	–	–	–	–	–
IS SEA	–	1	1	–	–	–	–	–	–
ISLAND	–	–	–	–	–	–	–	–	1
LAKE	1	–	1	4	1	5	7	3	10
LAND	–	1	1	3	1	4	1	–	1
LETS GO FISHING	–	1	1	–	–	–	–	–	–
LETS GO TO THE OCEAN	–	1	1	–	–	–	–	–	–
LIGHT	–	1	1	–	–	–	–	–	–
LIKE	1	–	1	–	–	–	–	–	–
LINER	5	2	7	–	–	–	1	2	3
LIPS	–	1	1	–	–	–	–	–	–
LOTION	–	1	1	–	–	–	–	–	–
MARTINS	1	–	1	–	–	–	–	–	–
MOON	–	3	3	–	–	–	–	–	–
MOTION	4	1	5	–	2	2	–	–	–
MUD	–	–	–	–	–	–	1	–	1
NOT OCEAN	–	1	1	–	–	–	–	–	–
OCEAN CITY	2	–	2	–	–	–	–	1	1
OPEN	–	1	1	–	–	–	–	–	–
PEOPLE	1	–	1	–	–	–	–	–	–
PHONE	–	1	1	–	–	–	–	–	–
PICTURE	1	–	1	–	–	–	–	–	–
PIER	–	–	–	–	1	1	–	–	–
PIN	1	–	1	–	–	–	–	–	–
PLAYING IN	1	–	1	–	–	–	–	–	–
POCEAN	1	–	1	–	–	–	–	–	–
POND	1	–	1	1	–	1	–	–	–
POTIENT	1	–	1	–	–	–	–	–	–
POTION	1	–	1	1	–	1	–	–	–
PRETTY	–	–	–	–	1	1	–	–	–
RIVE	–	–	–	–	–	–	1	–	1
RIVER	2	7	9	15	17	32	8	15	23
ROAR	–	–	–	–	1	1	–	–	–
ROCEAN	–	1	1	–	–	–	–	–	–
ROCK	–	1	1	–	–	–	–	–	–
ROUGH	–	1	1	1	–	1	2	–	2
SAIL	1	–	1	–	–	–	–	–	–
SALT	1	1	2	–	–	–	–	1	1
SALT WATER	1	1	2	–	1	1	–	–	–
SALTY	1	–	1	–	1	1	–	–	–
SALTY WATER	1	–	1	–	–	–	–	–	–
SAND	3	2	5	1	–	1	–	–	–
SEA	13	15	28	53	60	113	41	54	95

RESPONSE WORD	1ST			3RD			5TH		
	M	F	T	M	F	T	M	F	T

57.   OCEAN

RESPONSE WORD	M	F	T	M	F	T	M	F	T
SEA SHELL	1	–	1	–	–	–	–	–	–
SEA SHELLS	2	1	3	–	–	–	–	–	–
SEAT BELTS	1	–	1	–	–	–	–	–	–
SEE THE WATER	–	1	1	–	–	–	–	–	–
SEE-SAW	1	–	1	–	–	–	–	–	–
SEVEN	1	–	1	–	–	–	–	–	–
SHAMPOO	–	1	1	–	–	–	–	–	–
SHELL	–	1	1	–	1	1	–	–	–
SHELLS	1	3	4	–	–	–	–	–	–
SHIP	1	–	1	–	1	1	2	1	3
SHOE	–	1	1	–	–	–	–	–	–
SHORE	–	–	–	–	–	–	1	–	1
SHORT	–	–	–	–	–	–	–	1	1
SING	–	1	1	–	–	–	–	–	–
SKIP	–	–	–	–	1	1	–	–	–
SKY	–	–	–	–	–	–	–	1	1
SOFT	2	–	2	–	–	–	1	–	1
START	1	–	1	–	–	–	–	–	–
STEAM	1	–	1	–	–	–	–	–	–
STREAM	2	–	2	4	–	4	2	1	3
SUMMER	–	–	–	–	–	–	–	1	1
SUN	1	–	1	–	–	–	–	–	–
SWIM	4	3	7	2	1	3	–	2	2
SWIMMING	1	1	2	–	–	–	–	–	–
SWIMMING POOL	1	–	1	–	–	–	–	–	–
SWIMS	–	1	1	–	–	–	–	–	–
TABLE	–	1	1	–	–	–	–	–	–
THEY	–	–	–	–	–	–	1	–	1
THIS	1	–	1	–	–	–	–	–	–
UP	1	–	1	–	–	–	–	–	–
USUAL	–	–	–	–	1	1	–	–	–
VOYAGE	–	1	1	–	–	–	–	–	–
WAGON	1	–	1	–	–	–	–	–	–
WALL	–	1	1	–	–	–	–	–	–
WATER	22	31	53	32	29	61	49	31	80
WATERY	–	1	1	–	–	–	–	–	–
WAVE	1	2	3	1	–	1	–	–	–
WAVES	2	3	5	3	2	5	1	4	5
WAVY	–	–	–	–	–	–	1	–	1
WET	–	–	–	–	–	–	1	–	1
WHAT YOU PUT IN WATER	1	–	1	–	–	–	–	–	–
WHAT YOU PUT ON	–	1	1	–	–	–	–	–	–
WHEN YOURE FISHING	1	–	1	–	–	–	–	–	–
WHERE YOU HAVE SOMETHING	–	1	1	–	–	–	–	–	–
WHICH THE SHIPS FLOAT THRU	–	–	–	1	–	1	–	–	–
WHITE	1	–	1	–	–	–	–	–	–
WIDE	–	–	–	–	2	2	–	–	–
YOU	–	1	1	–	1	1	–	–	–
YOU SWIM AT	1	–	1	–	–	–	–	–	–

58.   OFF

RESPONSE WORD	M	F	T	M	F	T	M	F	T
A BOAT	1	–	1	–	–	–	–	–	–
A STREET	–	1	1	–	–	–	–	–	–
AGAIN	1	–	1	–	–	–	–	–	–
AID	1	–	1	–	–	–	–	–	–
AIR	1	–	1	–	–	–	–	–	–
AIRPLANE	1	1	2	–	–	–	–	–	–
ALL THE WAY	–	–	–	–	1	1	–	–	–
AN AIRPLANE	–	1	1	–	–	–	–	–	–
AND	–	1	1	–	–	–	–	–	–
AUTUMN	–	1	1	–	–	–	–	–	–
AWAY	–	2	2	–	–	–	–	–	–
BALL	–	–	–	1	–	1	–	–	–
BE	–	1	1	–	–	–	–	–	–
BED	1	–	1	–	–	–	–	–	–
BICYCLE	–	–	–	–	–	–	–	1	1
BIKE	1	1	2	–	–	–	–	–	–
BIRD	1	–	1	–	–	–	1	–	1

58. OFF

RESPONSE WORD	1ST M	1ST F	1ST T	3RD M	3RD F	3RD T	5TH M	5TH F	5TH T
BLACKBOARD	–	1	1	–	–	–	–	–	–
BLUE	–	–	–	–	–	–	1	–	1
BOAT	1	–	1	–	–	–	–	–	–
BOFF	–	1	1	–	–	–	–	–	–
BORDER	–	–	–	1	–	1	–	–	–
BOUGHTS	–	1	1	–	–	–	–	–	–
BOX	1	–	1	–	–	–	–	–	–
BUS	1	–	1	–	–	–	–	–	–
BY	–	1	1	–	–	–	–	–	–
CAKE	–	1	1	–	–	–	–	–	–
CAR	3	3	6	–	–	–	–	–	–
CAT	1	–	1	–	–	–	–	–	–
CAUSE	–	–	–	1	–	1	–	–	–
CHAIR	–	1	1	–	–	–	–	–	–
CHALK	–	1	1	–	–	–	–	–	–
CHALK BOARD	1	–	1	–	–	–	–	–	–
CLIFF	1	–	1	–	–	–	–	–	–
CLIP	–	–	–	–	1	1	–	–	–
CLOSET	1	–	1	–	–	–	–	–	–
CLOTH	–	1	1	–	–	–	–	–	–
CLOTHES	–	–	–	–	1	1	–	–	–
CLOVER	1	–	1	–	–	–	–	–	–
COAT	1	–	1	–	–	–	–	–	–
COME	–	1	1	–	–	–	–	–	–
COOKIE	1	1	2	–	–	–	–	–	–
COUGH	3	–	3	–	–	–	–	–	–
COURSE	1	–	1	–	–	–	–	–	–
CROSS	1	1	2	–	–	–	–	–	–
DARK	–	–	–	–	–	–	1	–	1
DAY	–	1	1	–	1	1	–	–	–
DESK	1	–	1	–	–	–	–	–	–
DID	1	–	1	–	–	–	–	–	–
DISTANCE	1	–	1	–	–	–	–	–	–
DIVING BOARD	1	–	1	–	–	–	–	–	–
DOFF	1	2	3	–	–	–	–	–	–
DOG	1	–	1	–	–	–	–	–	–
DOLL	–	1	1	–	–	–	–	–	–
DONT TURN IT ON	–	1	1	–	–	–	–	–	–
DOOR	–	1	1	–	–	–	–	–	–
DOWN	2	1	3	1	4	5	1	1	2
EASY-OFF	1	–	1	–	–	–	–	–	–
FALL	–	–	–	1	–	1	–	2	2
FAN	–	2	2	–	–	–	–	–	–
FAST	1	1	2	–	–	–	–	–	–
FATHER	–	1	1	–	–	–	–	–	–
FELL	–	1	1	1	–	1	1	–	1
FIRE	–	–	–	1	–	1	–	–	–
FOOD	1	–	1	–	–	–	–	–	–
FURNACE	1	–	1	–	–	–	–	–	–
GERMS	1	–	1	–	–	–	–	–	–
GET	1	–	1	–	–	–	2	–	2
GET OFF	1	–	1	–	–	–	–	–	–
GET OFF THE SLIDE	1	–	1	–	–	–	–	–	–
GO	1	4	5	–	3	3	1	4	5
GO BACK ON THE ROAD	1	–	1	–	–	–	–	–	–
GO OFF	1	–	1	–	–	–	–	–	–
GOES	–	1	1	–	–	–	–	–	–
GOLF	–	1	1	–	–	–	–	–	–
GONE	–	1	1	2	–	2	–	1	1
GOOD BYE	–	–	–	1	–	1	–	–	–
GRASS	1	–	1	–	–	–	–	–	–
GROUND	1	–	1	–	–	–	–	–	–
HAT	–	1	1	–	–	–	–	–	–
HEAT	–	1	1	–	–	–	–	–	–
HERE	3	–	3	–	1	1	–	–	–
HOFF	–	1	1	–	–	–	–	–	–
HOME	1	–	1	–	–	–	–	–	–
HOOK	–	–	–	1	–	1	–	–	–
I GO	1	–	1	–	–	–	–	–	–
ICE CREAM	1	–	1	–	–	–	–	–	–
IF	–	–	–	1	–	1	–	–	–
IN	1	2	3	2	1	3	5	1	6

RESPONSE WORD	1ST			3RD			5TH		
	M	F	T	M	F	T	M	F	T

58. OFF

RESPONSE WORD	M	F	T	M	F	T	M	F	T
INTO	–	–	–	1	–	1	–	–	–
IT	–	1	1	–	–	–	–	–	–
JANITOR	1	–	1	–	–	–	–	–	–
JET	–	–	–	–	1	1	–	–	–
JUMP	1	–	1	1	–	1	–	–	–
JUMP OFF THE GROUND	–	–	–	–	–	–	–	1	1
KEEP OFF	–	–	–	1	–	1	–	–	–
KING	1	–	1	–	–	–	–	–	–
LEAVES	1	–	1	–	–	–	–	–	–
LIGHT	5	1	6	–	2	2	2	–	2
LIGHTS	–	–	–	–	1	1	–	–	–
LIGHTS GOING OFF	1	–	1	–	–	–	–	–	–
LIGHTS OFF	1	–	1	–	–	–	–	–	–
LIKE IF YOU TURN OFF SOMETHING	–	–	–	1	–	1	–	–	–
LIPS	–	1	1	–	–	–	–	–	–
LOFF	2	–	2	–	–	–	–	–	–
LOST	1	–	1	1	–	1	–	–	–
MOFF	–	–	–	–	1	1	–	–	–
MONEY	1	–	1	–	–	–	–	–	–
MOSS	1	1	2	1	–	1	–	–	–
MOTH	1	1	2	–	–	–	–	–	–
MOUNTAIN	1	–	1	–	–	–	–	–	–
MUFF	–	1	1	–	–	–	–	–	–
MY DADDY WENT OFF THE TRAIN	–	1	1	–	–	–	–	–	–
NEW	–	–	–	–	1	1	–	–	–
NOFF	1	–	1	–	–	–	–	–	–
NOFT	1	–	1	–	–	–	–	–	–
NOT ON	–	–	–	1	2	3	9	6	15
NOW	–	1	1	–	–	–	–	–	–
OCCUR	–	–	–	–	–	–	1	–	1
OF	3	–	3	3	–	3	1	2	3
OF IT	–	1	1	–	–	–	–	–	–
OF THE MERRY GO ROUND	–	1	1	–	–	–	–	–	–
OFF	1	–	1	–	–	–	–	–	–
OFF MY SWING	1	–	1	–	–	–	–	–	–
OFFICE	–	1	1	–	–	–	–	–	–
OFFICE MAN COULD COME AND FIX YOUR SCRE	–	1	1	–	–	–	–	–	–
OFTEN	–	–	–	–	1	1	–	1	1
ON	36	43	79	103	110	213	99	110	209
OR	–	–	–	–	1	1	–	–	–
ORANGE	1	–	1	–	–	–	–	–	–
OUT	–	1	1	2	2	4	2	1	3
OUTNESS	–	–	–	–	–	–	–	1	1
OVER	–	–	–	1	–	1	–	–	–
PAPER	–	–	–	–	–	–	1	–	1
PEOPLE	–	–	–	–	–	–	–	1	1
PICTURE	1	–	1	–	–	–	–	–	–
PLAY	–	1	1	–	–	–	–	–	–
PLAYGROUND	–	1	1	–	–	–	–	–	–
POFF	–	1	1	–	–	–	–	–	–
PROPERTY	1	–	1	–	–	–	–	–	–
PUFF	1	–	1	–	–	–	–	–	–
PURPLE	–	1	1	–	–	–	–	–	–
RADIO	–	–	–	1	–	1	–	–	–
RAISIN	–	–	–	1	–	1	–	–	–
RED	2	–	2	–	–	–	–	–	–
ROCK	1	–	1	–	–	–	–	–	–
ROCKET	1	–	1	–	–	–	–	–	–
ROOSTER	1	–	1	–	–	–	–	–	–
ROUGH	–	1	1	–	–	–	–	–	–
RUB	–	–	–	–	–	–	–	1	1
SAW	–	1	1	–	–	–	–	–	–
SEA-SAWS	–	1	1	–	–	–	–	–	–
SEE	–	2	2	–	–	–	–	–	–
SHUT	1	–	1	–	–	–	1	–	1
SIDELINES	–	–	–	–	–	–	–	1	1
SING	–	1	1	–	–	–	–	–	–
SISTER	–	–	–	–	1	1	–	–	–
SOFT	2	–	2	1	1	2	–	–	–

RESPONSE WORD	1ST M	F	T	3RD M	F	T	5TH M	F	T

58. OFF

RESPONSE WORD	1ST M	F	T	3RD M	F	T	5TH M	F	T
SOMEWHERE	–	1	1	–	–	–	–	–	–
SPIGOT	–	–	–	1	–	1	–	–	–
STAPLER	–	1	1	–	–	–	–	–	–
START	–	–	–	–	–	–	1	–	1
STAY	–	–	–	–	–	–	1	–	1
STICK	–	1	1	–	–	–	–	–	–
STOP	–	–	–	–	–	–	2	–	2
STOVE	–	1	1	1	–	1	–	1	1
SUN	–	1	1	–	–	–	–	–	–
SWITCH	–	–	–	1	1	2	–	–	–
TABLE	–	–	–	–	–	–	1	–	1
TAKE	–	–	–	1	–	1	1	–	1
TALK	–	–	–	–	–	–	–	1	1
THE	–	–	–	–	–	–	1	–	1
THE CAR	1	–	1	–	–	–	–	–	–
THE ROAD	1	1	2	–	–	–	–	–	–
THE STEP	–	–	–	1	–	1	–	–	–
THE SWING	–	1	1	–	–	–	–	–	–
THE TRACK	–	1	1	–	–	–	–	–	–
THE WATER	–	1	1	–	–	–	–	–	–
THE WATER IS OFF	–	1	1	–	–	–	–	–	–
THE WAY	–	1	1	–	–	–	–	–	–
THEY	1	–	1	–	–	–	–	–	–
THING	–	–	–	1	–	1	–	–	–
THIS	1	–	1	–	–	–	–	–	–
TILT	–	–	–	–	–	–	1	–	1
TRACK	–	–	–	–	–	–	3	–	3
TREE	–	1	1	–	–	–	–	–	–
TURN	–	1	1	–	–	–	–	–	–
TURN IT OFF	1	–	1	–	–	–	–	–	–
TURN OFF	1	1	2	–	–	–	–	–	–
TURN OFF THE WASHING MACHINE	1	–	1	–	–	–	–	–	–
TURN WATER	1	–	1	–	–	–	–	–	–
TURNED OFF	–	–	–	–	–	–	–	1	1
TWO ONE	–	1	1	–	–	–	–	–	–
UNDER	–	1	1	–	–	–	–	1	1
US	–	1	1	–	1	1	–	–	–
WATER	1	–	2	–	–	–	–	1	1
WE GO	1	–	1	–	–	–	–	–	–
WHENEVER YOUR MOTHER SAYS IT OR SOMETHI	–	1	1	–	–	–	–	–	–
WHITE	1	–	1	–	–	–	–	–	–
WHO	–	–	–	–	1	1	–	–	–
WIN	1	–	1	–	–	–	–	–	–
WIND	–	1	1	–	–	–	–	–	–
WINDOW	1	–	1	–	–	–	–	–	–
WORK	–	2	2	–	–	–	–	–	–
WRONG	–	–	–	1	–	1	–	–	–
YELLOW	–	1	1	–	–	–	–	–	–
YOU	–	1	1	1	–	1	–	–	–
YOU GET OFF	–	1	1	–	–	–	–	–	–
YOU GO ON BUS	–	1	1	–	–	–	–	–	–
YOURE GOING OFF A RIDGE	–	–	–	–	–	–	–	1	1
ZOO	–	1	1	–	–	–	–	–	–

59. ON

RESPONSE WORD	1ST M	F	T	3RD M	F	T	5TH M	F	T
A BIKE	–	–	–	–	–	–	1	–	1
A BOARD	–	1	1	–	–	–	–	–	–
A BOAT	–	1	1	–	–	–	–	–	–
A CLIFF	–	–	–	–	–	–	–	1	1
AFTER	–	–	–	–	1	1	–	–	–
AGAIN	1	–	1	–	–	–	–	–	–
AGO	–	–	–	–	1	1	–	–	–
AIRPLANE	1	–	1	–	–	–	–	–	–
ALARM	1	–	1	–	–	–	–	–	–
ALWAYS	–	1	1	–	–	–	–	–	–
ANIMAL	–	–	–	1	–	1	–	–	–
ARE	–	1	1	–	–	–	–	–	–
AWNING	–	1	1	–	–	–	–	–	–

RESPONSE WORD	1ST M	F	T	3RD M	F	T	5TH M	F	T

59. ON

RESPONSE WORD	1ST M	F	T	3RD M	F	T	5TH M	F	T
BABY	1	–	1	–	–	–	–	–	–
BABY DOLL	–	1	1	–	1	1	–	–	–
BACK	–	–	–	–	1	1	–	–	–
BALL	1	–	1	–	–	–	–	–	–
BAWN	–	1	1	–	1	1	–	–	–
BEGIN	–	–	–	–	1	1	–	–	–
BELL	1	–	1	–	–	–	–	–	–
BIG	–	–	–	–	–	–	–	1	1
BIKE	–	1	1	–	–	–	1	–	1
BOARD	–	1	1	–	–	–	–	–	–
BOAT	1	1	2	–	–	–	–	–	–
BODY	–	–	–	–	–	–	1	–	1
BOTTOM	–	–	–	–	–	–	1	–	1
BOX	–	1	1	–	–	–	–	–	–
BRICK	1	–	1	–	–	–	–	–	–
BRIDGE	1	–	1	–	–	–	–	–	–
BUS	1	–	1	–	–	–	–	–	–
BY	–	–	–	–	1	1	–	–	–
CALM	1	–	1	–	–	–	–	–	–
CAMERA	–	1	1	–	–	–	–	–	–
CAN	–	1	1	–	–	–	–	–	–
CAR	–	2	2	–	–	–	–	–	–
CHAIR	1	1	2	1	1	2	1	–	1
CHON	1	–	1	–	–	–	–	–	–
CLOSE	–	1	1	–	–	–	–	–	–
CLOTHES	1	2	3	–	1	1	–	–	–
COIN	1	–	1	–	–	–	–	–	–
COLD	–	1	1	–	–	–	–	–	–
COME	–	3	3	–	–	–	1	–	1
CON	3	–	3	–	–	–	–	–	–
CONTINUE	–	–	–	–	1	1	–	–	–
COOK	–	1	1	–	–	–	–	–	–
CORN	1	2	3	–	–	–	–	–	–
CRY	1	–	1	–	–	–	–	–	–
CUT	1	–	1	–	–	–	–	–	–
DARK	–	–	–	–	–	–	1	–	1
DAY	–	1	1	–	1	1	–	–	–
DESK	–	–	–	–	–	–	1	–	1
DOG	–	1	1	–	–	–	–	–	–
DOING	–	–	–	–	–	–	1	–	1
DON	–	1	1	–	–	–	–	–	–
DONT	–	1	1	–	–	–	–	–	–
DOWN	1	–	1	1	–	1	–	–	–
EASY	–	–	–	–	1	1	–	–	–
FARM	–	–	–	–	–	–	1	–	1
FAST	–	3	3	–	1	1	–	–	–
FAWN	–	1	1	–	1	1	–	–	–
FINE	–	–	–	–	1	1	–	–	–
FISH	–	–	–	1	–	1	1	–	1
FLOOR	1	–	1	1	–	1	1	1	2
FLY	1	–	1	–	–	–	1	–	1
FON	–	1	1	–	–	–	–	–	–
FOOD	–	–	–	–	–	–	–	1	1
FORWARD	–	–	–	–	–	–	1	–	1
FOUR	–	1	1	–	–	–	–	–	–
GARBAGE CAN	1	–	1	–	–	–	–	–	–
GET	–	–	–	–	–	–	1	–	1
GET GOING	1	–	1	–	–	–	–	–	–
GET ON	–	–	–	–	1	1	–	–	–
GET ON MY SCOOTER	–	1	1	–	–	–	–	–	–
GET ON THERE	1	–	1	–	–	–	–	–	–
GO	1	2	3	8	4	12	5	8	13
GO ON	1	–	1	–	–	–	–	–	–
GOES TODAY	–	1	1	–	–	–	–	–	–
GOING	–	–	–	1	–	1	1	–	1
GONE	2	1	3	–	–	–	–	–	–
GRACE	1	–	1	–	–	–	–	–	–
GRASS	1	–	1	–	–	–	–	–	–
GROUND	–	1	1	–	–	–	–	–	–
HAIR	–	1	1	–	–	–	–	–	–
HE	–	–	–	–	1	1	–	–	–
HELP	–	1	1	–	–	–	–	–	–

RESPONSE WORD	1ST			3RD			5TH		
	M	F	T	M	F	T	M	F	T

59. ON

RESPONSE WORD	M	F	T	M	F	T	M	F	T
HERE	2	—	2	—	—	—	—	—	—
HIGH	—	—	—	—	1	1	1	—	1
HOOK	1	—	1	—	—	—	—	—	—
HORSE	—	—	—	1	1	2	—	—	—
HOUSE	—	1	1	—	—	—	1	—	1
I	2	1	3	—	—	—	—	—	—
I AM	—	—	—	—	1	1	—	—	—
I WILL TURN ON THE TELEVISION	—	1	1	—	—	—	—	—	—
ICE CREAM	1	—	1	—	—	—	—	—	—
IN	2	4	6	2	1	3	1	3	4
INTO	—	—	—	—	1	1	—	—	—
IRONING BOARD	1	—	1	—	—	—	—	—	—
IT	—	1	1	2	1	3	1	—	1
JUMP	—	—	—	—	—	—	1	—	1
KEEP ON	1	—	1	—	—	—	—	—	—
KNOW	—	—	—	—	1	1	—	—	—
LAWN	1	2	3	—	—	—	—	—	—
LEG	—	—	—	—	1	1	1	—	1
LIGHT	4	—	4	1	1	2	1	—	1
LIKE AN AIRPLANE FLYING IN THE AIR	1	—	1	—	—	—	—	—	—
LIKE IF YOU TURN ON SOMETHING.	—	—	—	1	—	1	—	—	—
LISTEN	1	—	1	—	—	—	—	—	—
LITTLE	—	1	1	—	—	—	—	—	—
LIVE	—	1	1	—	—	—	—	—	—
LONG	1	1	2	1	—	1	—	1	1
LOW	—	—	—	1	—	1	—	—	—
MAN	—	—	—	—	—	—	1	—	1
MAWN	1	—	1	—	—	—	—	—	—
ME	4	1	5	—	—	—	—	—	—
METAL	1	—	1	—	—	—	—	—	—
MIRROR	1	1	2	—	—	—	—	—	—
MISSED	1	—	1	—	—	—	—	—	—
MON	1	—	1	—	—	—	—	—	—
MOON	—	1	1	—	—	—	—	—	—
MOTHER MIGHT CUT ON THE TV AND YOU COUL.	—	1	1	—	—	—	—	—	—
MOTORCYCLE	1	—	1	—	—	—	—	—	—
MOVIE	1	—	1	—	—	—	—	—	—
MY	—	1	1	1	1	2	—	—	—
NAIL	—	—	—	—	—	—	—	1	1
NEAR	—	—	—	1	—	1	—	—	—
NEVER	—	1	1	—	—	—	—	—	—
NO	—	2	2	4	3	7	—	—	—
NOT ON	—	—	—	2	1	3	—	—	—
NOW	1	2	3	1	2	3	1	—	1
NUGGET	1	—	1	—	—	—	—	—	—
O	1	—	1	—	—	—	—	—	—
OF	—	—	—	2	—	2	—	1	1
OFF	23	35	58	79	84	163	73	74	147
ON	—	—	—	—	—	—	1	—	1
ON AND ON	—	1	1	—	—	—	—	—	—
ON IT	—	—	—	—	—	—	—	1	1
ON TOP	—	—	—	—	—	—	—	1	1
OP	—	—	—	—	—	—	1	—	1
ORANGE	2	1	3	—	—	—	—	—	—
OUT	1	—	1	4	—	4	3	—	3
OVER	—	—	—	—	2	2	4	3	7
PART	—	—	—	—	—	—	1	—	1
PAUSE	—	—	—	—	—	—	—	1	1
PAWN	—	1	1	—	—	—	—	—	—
PEN	1	—	1	—	—	—	—	—	—
PIER	1	—	1	—	—	—	—	—	—
PIPE	1	—	1	—	—	—	—	—	—
PLACE	—	—	—	—	—	—	—	1	1
PLANE	—	1	1	—	—	—	—	—	—
PLAYGROUND	—	—	—	—	—	—	—	1	1
POND	2	—	2	—	—	—	—	—	—
PONY	—	1	1	—	—	—	—	—	—
POUNCE	—	—	—	—	—	—	1	—	1

RESPONSE WORD	1ST M	F	T	3RD M	F	T	5TH M	F	T

59. ON

RESPONSE WORD	1ST M	F	T	3RD M	F	T	5TH M	F	T
PROPERTY	–	–	–	–	–	–	–	1	1
PURPLE	–	1	1	–	–	–	–	–	–
PUT	–	1	1	–	–	–	–	–	–
RADIO	1	–	1	–	–	–	–	–	–
RIDE	–	–	–	–	–	–	1	–	1
RIDING	–	–	–	–	–	–	1	–	1
ROAD	–	–	–	1	1	2	–	–	–
ROCK	–	–	–	1	–	1	–	–	–
SAT	–	–	–	1	–	1	–	–	–
SCARE	–	–	–	1	–	1	–	–	–
SCAT	–	–	–	1	–	1	–	–	–
SCHOOL	–	–	–	–	1	1	–	–	–
SEATED	–	–	–	–	–	–	–	1	1
SEE	–	1	1	–	–	–	–	–	–
SETTING	–	–	–	–	–	–	–	1	1
SHIP	1	–	1	–	–	–	–	–	–
SHOW	2	–	2	–	–	–	–	–	–
SIT	–	–	–	–	–	–	1	1	2
SITTING ON	–	–	–	–	–	–	–	1	1
SIX	–	–	–	–	–	–	1	–	1
SOMEBODY ON	–	1	1	–	–	–	–	–	–
SOMEONE EATS ALL THEIR DESSERT	–	1	1	–	–	–	–	–	–
SOMETHING	1	1	2	1	1	2	–	–	–
SOMETHING YOU COULD EAT	–	1	1	–	–	–	–	–	–
SONG	1	–	1	–	1	1	–	–	–
SQUASH	–	–	–	1	–	1	–	–	–
STAND	–	–	–	–	–	–	1	–	1
START	–	–	–	1	–	1	–	–	–
STARTED	–	–	–	1	–	1	–	–	–
STOOL	–	–	–	1	–	1	–	–	–
STOP	2	2	4	1	–	1	1	1	2
STOP IT	–	1	1	–	–	–	–	–	–
STOVE	–	1	1	–	–	–	–	1	1
SURPRISE	–	–	–	1	–	1	–	–	–
SWING	1	–	1	–	–	–	–	–	–
SWITCH	1	–	1	–	–	–	1	1	2
T V	–	1	1	–	–	–	–	–	–
TABLE	–	1	1	–	1	1	1	3	4
TAKE	–	1	1	–	–	–	–	–	–
TELEVISION	–	1	1	–	–	–	–	–	–
THAT	–	–	–	–	1	1	–	–	–
THE	4	–	4	–	–	–	–	–	–
THE CAR	1	–	1	1	–	1	–	–	–
THE GRASS	–	1	1	–	–	–	–	–	–
THE LINES	–	1	1	–	–	–	–	–	–
THE MOTOR GOES ON	1	–	1	–	–	–	–	–	–
THE MOUNTAIN	1	–	1	–	–	–	–	–	–
THE OPPOSITE OF OFF	–	–	–	–	–	–	–	1	1
THE ROAD	1	–	1	–	–	–	–	–	–
THE WATER	–	–	–	1	–	1	–	–	–
THEN	–	–	–	1	–	1	–	–	–
THERE	2	–	2	3	–	3	–	2	2
THEY	–	–	–	–	1	1	–	–	–
THOSE	–	1	1	–	–	–	–	–	–
THOUGHT	–	1	1	–	–	–	–	–	–
TIRE	1	–	1	–	–	–	–	–	–
TO	–	–	–	–	2	2	–	1	1
TODAY	–	–	–	–	1	1	–	–	–
TOP	–	–	–	4	5	9	9	11	20
TOP OF	–	–	–	–	–	–	1	1	2
TOUCH	–	–	–	–	–	–	1	–	1
TRACK	–	–	–	1	1	2	–	–	–
TRAIL	1	–	1	–	–	–	–	–	–
TRAIN	2	–	2	–	1	1	1	–	1
TRAIN STATION	–	–	–	–	–	–	–	1	1
TRAMPOLINE	1	–	1	–	–	–	–	–	–
TRASHCAN	–	1	1	–	–	–	–	–	–
TREE	1	–	1	–	1	1	1	–	1
TRUCK	1	–	1	–	–	–	–	–	–
TURN	1	1	2	1	1	2	–	1	1
TURN EVERYTHING ON	1	–	1	–	–	–	–	–	–

RESPONSE WORD	1ST M	F	T	3RD M	F	T	5TH M	F	T

59. ON

RESPONSE WORD	1ST M	F	T	3RD M	F	T	5TH M	F	T
TURN IT OFF	1	–	1	–	–	–	–	–	–
TURN IT ON	–	1	1	–	–	–	–	–	–
TURN ON	1	1	2	–	–	–	–	–	–
TURNED IT ON	1	–	1	–	–	–	–	–	–
TV	–	1	1	–	–	–	–	–	–
UNDER	1	–	1	–	–	–	–	2	2
UP	–	2	2	–	–	–	2	1	3
UPON	–	–	–	–	–	–	2	7	9
VON	–	1	1	–	–	–	–	–	–
WALK	–	1	1	–	–	–	–	–	–
WALK ON TO THE PLAYGROUND	1	–	1	–	–	–	–	–	–
WARM	1	–	1	–	–	–	–	–	–
WASHING MACHINE	1	–	1	–	–	–	–	–	–
WATER	–	1	1	–	–	–	–	–	–
WAYS	–	–	–	–	–	–	–	1	1
WE	–	1	1	–	–	–	–	–	–
WE GO	–	1	1	–	–	–	–	–	–
WHATS GOING ON	1	–	1	–	–	–	–	–	–
WHEN YOURE ON SOMETHING	1	–	1	–	–	–	–	–	–
WHERE	–	1	1	–	–	–	–	–	–
WHICH	1	–	1	–	–	–	–	–	–
WINDOW	–	–	–	–	1	1	–	–	–
WITH	1	–	1	1	–	1	–	–	–
WITH THE SHOW	1	–	1	–	–	–	–	–	–
WITH THE STOVE	1	–	1	–	–	–	–	–	–
WORD	1	–	1	–	–	–	–	–	–
WORKING	–	–	–	–	–	–	1	–	1
YAWN	1	–	1	–	–	–	–	–	–
YOU	–	1	1	–	–	–	–	–	–

60. ONCE

RESPONSE WORD	1ST M	F	T	3RD M	F	T	5TH M	F	T
A	1	1	2	–	–	–	1	–	1
A DAY	1	–	1	1	–	1	–	–	–
A HILL	1	–	1	–	–	–	–	–	–
A LOT OF TIMES	–	–	–	–	1	1	–	–	–
A TIME	–	–	–	–	2	2	–	1	1
A TOY	1	–	1	–	–	–	–	–	–
A YEAR	1	–	1	–	2	2	–	–	–
AFTER	–	–	–	–	2	2	–	–	–
AGAIN	4	3	7	5	5	10	4	6	10
AGAINST	–	–	–	–	–	–	–	1	1
AGO	–	–	–	2	1	3	5	3	8
ALL	–	–	–	1	–	1	1	–	1
ALL THE TIME	–	–	–	1	–	1	–	–	–
ALONDTIME	–	–	–	–	–	–	1	–	1
ALONG	–	–	–	–	1	1	–	–	–
ALREADY	–	–	–	–	–	–	–	1	1
ALWAYS	–	–	–	1	3	4	1	2	3
ANIMAL	1	–	1	–	–	–	–	–	–
ANOTHER	–	–	–	2	2	4	–	–	–
APONE	–	–	–	–	–	–	2	–	2
APPLE	–	2	2	–	1	1	–	–	–
APPLES	–	1	1	–	–	–	–	–	–
AT	–	–	–	–	1	1	–	–	–
AT A TIME	–	–	–	1	–	1	–	–	–
AT ONCE	–	–	–	1	–	1	–	–	–
AT ONCED	–	–	–	1	–	1	–	–	–
AWAY	–	–	–	–	1	1	–	–	–
BABY	1	–	1	–	–	–	–	–	–
BACK	–	–	–	–	–	–	–	1	1
BALL	1	1	2	–	–	–	–	–	–
BALL COURT	1	–	1	–	–	–	–	–	–
BANANA	1	–	1	–	–	–	–	–	–
BEEN	–	–	–	1	–	1	–	–	–
BEETLE	–	–	–	–	–	–	1	–	1
BEFORE	–	4	4	4	2	6	2	2	4
BEG	–	1	1	–	–	–	–	–	–
BEGINNING	–	–	–	–	1	1	–	–	–
BEGINNING OF SOMETHING	–	–	–	–	–	–	1	–	1

RESPONSE WORD	1ST			3RD			5TH		
	M	F	T	M	F	T	M	F	T

60.   ONCE

	M	F	T	M	F	T	M	F	T
BIRD	1	1	2	–	–	–	–	–	–
BLACK	–	1	1	–	–	–	–	–	–
BOOK	1	–	1	–	–	–	–	–	–
BOWLING PIN	1	–	1	–	–	–	–	–	–
BOX	1	–	1	–	–	–	–	1	–
BOY	1	–	1	–	–	–	–	1	1
BOYS	–	–	–	–	–	–	1	–	1
BUMPS	–	1	1	–	–	–	–	–	–
BUNCE	–	1	1	–	–	–	–	–	–
BUNCH	–	–	–	1	–	1	–	–	–
CAKE	–	–	–	1	–	1	–	–	–
CAME	–	–	–	–	–	–	1	–	1
CANES	1	–	1	–	–	–	–	–	–
CAPITAL	1	–	1	–	–	–	–	–	–
CAT	1	–	1	–	–	–	–	–	–
CLOCK	1	–	1	–	–	–	–	–	–
COLOR	1	–	1	–	–	–	–	–	–
COME	–	2	2	1	1	2	–	–	–
COME WITH ME	1	1	2	–	–	–	–	–	–
CONCE	–	1	1	–	–	–	–	–	–
CONDY	–	1	1	–	–	–	–	–	–
COOK	–	1	1	–	–	–	–	–	–
COOKIE	1	–	1	–	–	–	–	–	–
COULD	–	–	–	–	1	1	–	–	–
COUNT BY ONES	1	–	1	–	–	–	–	–	–
CRIPPLED	–	1	1	–	–	–	–	–	–
DAY	2	–	2	1	1	2	1	2	3
DAYS	1	–	1	–	–	–	–	–	–
DESK	–	–	–	1	–	1	–	–	–
DID	–	–	–	1	1	2	–	–	–
DIDNT	–	–	–	1	–	1	–	–	–
DO	–	–	–	–	–	–	–	1	1
DO SOMETHING	–	1	1	–	–	–	–	–	–
DOCTOR	1	–	1	–	–	–	–	–	–
DOG	–	–	–	–	–	–	1	–	1
DONCE	–	1	1	–	–	–	–	–	–
DONE IT	–	–	–	–	1	1	–	–	–
DOOR	1	1	2	–	–	–	–	–	–
DOWN	–	–	–	–	–	–	1	–	1
EVER	–	1	1	–	1	1	–	1	1
FAIRY TALE	–	–	–	–	–	–	–	3	3
FALSE	–	–	–	1	–	1	–	–	–
FATHER	–	–	–	1	–	1	–	–	–
FEW	–	–	–	–	–	–	–	1	1
FIND	–	1	1	–	–	–	–	–	–
FIRST	–	–	–	2	3	5	1	3	4
FOOD	1	–	1	–	–	–	–	–	–
FOR	–	–	–	1	–	1	–	–	–
FOR ALL	–	–	–	–	–	–	–	1	1
FOUR	–	1	1	–	–	–	–	–	–
FUN	–	1	1	–	–	–	–	–	–
GENTLY	–	–	–	–	–	–	1	–	1
GIVE	–	–	–	–	–	–	1	1	2
GLASSES	–	1	1	–	–	–	–	–	–
GO	–	–	–	–	–	–	1	–	1
GO OUTSIDE	–	1	1	–	–	–	–	–	–
GOOD	1	–	1	–	–	–	–	–	–
GOT	–	–	–	1	–	1	–	–	–
GRASS	–	2	2	–	–	–	–	–	–
GUNCE	1	–	1	–	–	–	–	–	–
HAD	1	1	2	–	–	–	–	–	–
HAIR	–	–	–	–	1	1	–	–	–
HAPPEN	–	–	–	–	2	2	1	1	2
HAPPENED	–	–	–	–	–	–	–	2	2
HAS	–	–	–	–	1	1	1	–	1
HEAR	–	–	–	1	–	1	–	–	–
HEATER	1	–	1	–	–	–	–	–	–
HER	–	1	1	–	–	–	–	–	–
HERE	3	1	4	–	–	–	–	–	–
HIM	–	1	1	–	–	–	–	–	–
HISTORY	–	–	–	–	–	–	–	1	1
HUNCE	1	1	2	–	–	–	–	–	–

RESPONSE WORD	1ST M	F	T	3RD M	F	T	5TH M	F	T

60. ONCE

RESPONSE WORD	M	F	T	M	F	T	M	F	T
I	1	2	3	–	–	–	–	–	–
I ONCE	–	–	–	1	–	1	–	–	–
I SAW YOU	–	1	1	–	–	–	–	–	–
I SEE YOU	1	–	1	–	–	–	–	–	–
I WANT A BOOK	1	–	1	–	–	–	–	–	–
I WANT MY MOTHER	–	1	1	–	–	–	–	–	–
IN A WHILE	1	–	1	–	–	–	–	–	–
IS	–	–	–	–	1	1	–	–	–
JUMP OVER THE ROPE ONE TIME	–	1	1	–	–	–	–	–	–
JUNK	1	–	1	–	–	–	–	–	–
KEEPS	–	–	–	1	–	1	–	–	–
LADY	–	1	1	–	–	–	–	–	–
LAMP	1	–	1	–	–	–	–	–	–
LAST	1	–	1	3	4	7	–	–	–
LEARN	–	1	1	–	–	–	–	–	–
LETS PLAY HOUSE	–	1	1	–	–	–	–	–	–
LIGHT	1	–	1	–	–	–	–	–	–
LIKE	1	1	2	–	–	–	–	–	–
LONG	–	1	1	1	–	1	–	2	2
LONG AGO	–	–	–	–	1	1	–	–	–
LONG TIME	–	–	–	–	–	–	–	1	1
LONG TIME AGO	–	–	–	–	–	–	1	1	2
LOOK	–	1	1	–	–	–	–	–	–
MANY	–	–	–	–	–	–	1	–	1
ME	1	2	3	–	1	1	–	–	–
MIX	–	–	–	–	–	–	–	1	1
MONTHS	1	–	1	–	–	–	–	–	–
MORE	–	1	1	1	–	1	1	–	1
MOUSE	–	1	1	–	–	–	–	–	–
MOVIE	1	–	1	–	–	–	–	–	–
MUNCE	2	–	2	–	–	–	–	–	–
MY DADDY	–	1	1	–	–	–	–	–	–
NAME TAG	1	–	1	–	–	–	–	–	–
NEVER	1	1	2	3	1	4	2	3	5
NEW	–	–	–	–	2	2	–	–	–
NEXT	–	–	–	–	1	1	–	–	–
NOBODY	–	–	–	–	–	–	1	–	1
NONE	–	–	–	–	–	–	1	–	1
NOT	2	–	2	–	–	–	–	–	–
NOT AGAIN	–	–	–	1	–	1	–	–	–
NOT OFTEN	–	–	–	–	–	–	–	1	1
NOTHING	–	1	1	–	–	–	–	–	–
NOW	1	2	3	2	1	3	4	6	10
NUMBERS	–	–	–	1	–	1	–	–	–
NUTS	–	–	–	1	–	1	–	–	–
OFTEN	–	–	–	–	2	2	–	2	2
ON TIME	–	–	–	–	–	–	1	–	1
ONE	5	5	10	9	11	20	13	6	19
ONE DAY	–	–	–	1	–	1	1	–	1
ONE STEP	1	–	1	–	–	–	–	–	–
ONE TIME	2	1	3	4	1	5	5	6	11
ONE TIME ONLY	–	–	–	1	–	1	–	–	–
ONLY	–	–	–	–	1	1	1	–	1
OTHER	1	–	1	–	1	1	–	–	–
OTHERS	–	–	–	1	–	1	–	–	–
OVER	1	–	1	–	1	1	–	–	–
PEOPLE	1	–	1	–	–	–	–	–	–
PERIOD	–	–	–	–	–	–	1	–	1
PICTURE	–	1	1	1	–	1	–	–	–
PLEASE	1	–	1	–	–	–	–	–	–
POCKET	–	1	1	–	–	–	–	–	–
POCKETBOOK	1	1	2	–	–	–	–	–	–
POUND	–	1	1	–	–	–	–	–	–
PUNTS	–	1	1	–	–	–	–	–	–
QUIT	–	–	–	–	–	–	1	–	1
RAILING	–	1	1	–	–	–	–	–	–
RIGHT	–	–	–	–	–	–	–	1	1
RIGHT NOW	1	–	1	–	–	–	–	–	–
SATURDAY	–	1	1	–	–	–	–	–	–
SAY	–	1	1	–	–	–	–	–	–
SECOND	–	–	–	2	1	3	–	–	–

RESPONSE WORD	1ST M	F	T	3RD M	F	T	5TH M	F	T

60. ONCE

RESPONSE WORD	1ST M	F	T	3RD M	F	T	5TH M	F	T
SED	-	-	-	-	-	-	-	1	1
SEE	-	2	2	-	-	-	-	-	-
SENT SOMETHING	1	-	1	-	-	-	-	-	-
SHORT	-	-	-	-	1	1	-	-	-
SINGLE	-	-	-	1	-	1	1	-	1
SMALL	-	-	-	-	1	1	-	-	-
SOCK	-	1	1	-	-	-	-	-	-
SOME	-	1	1	-	-	-	-	-	-
SOMEONE SPEAKS AND SAYS SOMETHING	-	1	1	-	-	-	-	-	-
SOMETHING	2	2	4	-	-	-	-	-	-
SOMETIME	-	-	-	-	2	2	-	1	1
SONCE	-	1	1	-	-	-	-	-	-
STOP	-	1	1	-	-	-	-	-	-
STOP HERE	-	1	1	-	-	-	-	-	-
STORES	-	1	1	-	-	-	-	-	-
STORY	-	-	-	-	-	-	4	1	5
SWEATER	1	-	1	-	-	-	-	-	-
SWIFT	-	-	-	1	-	1	-	-	-
SWING	1	-	1	-	-	-	-	-	-
TABLE	1	-	1	-	-	-	-	-	-
TAKE	-	-	-	-	1	1	-	-	-
TALE	-	-	-	-	-	-	-	2	2
TALK	-	-	-	1	-	1	-	-	-
TELL	-	-	-	-	-	-	1	-	1
TEN	-	-	-	-	-	-	1	-	1
THAT	-	-	-	-	1	1	-	-	-
THE	-	-	-	1	-	1	-	-	-
THEN	1	-	1	1	3	4	1	-	1
THERE	2	2	4	1	3	4	1	-	1
THERE WAS A BOAT	1	-	1	-	-	-	-	-	-
THEY	-	-	-	-	1	1	-	-	-
THINK	-	-	-	-	1	1	-	-	-
TIE	-	1	1	-	-	-	-	-	-
TIME	6	6	12	8	9	17	7	12	19
TIME AGO	-	-	-	1	-	1	-	-	-
TOOTH	-	1	1	-	-	-	-	-	-
TOY	-	-	-	1	-	1	-	-	-
TRAP DOOR	1	-	1	-	-	-	-	-	-
TRY	-	1	1	-	-	-	-	-	-
TWICE	17	16	33	31	29	60	44	42	86
TWICED	-	-	-	-	1	1	-	-	-
TWICETT	-	-	-	1	-	1	-	-	-
TWISE	-	-	-	-	-	-	-	1	1
TWO	8	11	19	6	1	7	1	2	3
TWO TIMES	3	-	3	-	-	-	-	1	1
TWOS	-	1	1	-	-	-	-	-	-
UP	-	-	-	-	1	1	-	-	-
UPON	2	-	2	6	10	16	8	11	19
UPON A TIME	3	1	4	1	1	2	3	-	3
US	1	-	1	-	-	-	-	-	-
USUALLY	1	-	1	-	-	-	-	-	-
VUNCE	-	1	1	-	-	-	-	-	-
WALK	1	-	1	-	-	-	-	-	-
WANT	1	4	5	2	1	3	-	-	-
WANT SOMETHING	1	-	1	-	-	-	-	-	-
WANT TO	-	-	-	1	-	1	-	-	-
WANTED	-	1	1	-	-	-	-	1	1
WANTS TO	-	-	-	1	-	1	-	-	-
WANTS TO SEE SOMETHING	-	1	1	-	-	-	-	-	-
WAS	-	-	-	1	1	2	2	-	2
WATER	-	1	1	-	-	-	-	-	-
WE	-	1	1	-	-	-	-	-	-
WENT	-	-	-	1	1	2	-	-	-
WHAT	2	-	2	-	-	-	-	-	-
WHAT IN THE WORLD	1	-	1	-	-	-	-	-	-
WHATS	-	-	-	1	-	1	-	-	-
WHEEL	-	-	-	-	1	1	-	-	-
WHEELS	1	-	1	-	-	-	-	-	-
WHEN	-	-	-	2	-	2	1	-	1
WHEN YOU OWE	-	1	1	-	-	-	-	-	-
WHEN YOU WANT SOMETHING	1	-	1	-	-	-	-	-	-

RESPONSE WORD	1ST M	F	T	3RD M	F	T	5TH M	F	T

60. ONCE

RESPONSE WORD	1ST M	F	T	3RD M	F	T	5TH M	F	T
WHERE	1	–	1	–	2	2	–	–	–
WHICH	–	–	–	1	–	1	–	–	–
WHITE	–	1	1	–	–	–	–	–	–
WHOA	–	1	1	–	–	–	–	–	–
WHY DONT YOU GO OUTSIDE	–	1	1	–	–	–	–	–	–
WINDOW	1	–	1	–	–	–	–	–	–
WITH	1	–	1	–	–	–	–	–	–
WORK	1	–	1	–	–	–	–	–	–
WOULD	–	–	–	1	–	1	–	–	–
WRITE DOWN A WORD	1	–	1	–	–	–	–	–	–
WUNT	–	1	1	–	–	–	–	–	–
YEAR	–	–	–	–	2	2	–	–	–
YOU	2	1	3	–	–	–	1	–	1

61. PLEASANT

RESPONSE WORD	1ST M	F	T	3RD M	F	T	5TH M	F	T
ABSENT	–	–	–	–	–	–	2	–	2
AFTERNOON	–	–	–	1	–	1	–	–	–
AGAIN	–	–	–	–	1	1	–	–	–
AGAINST	–	–	–	–	–	–	–	1	1
AGGRAVATING	–	–	–	–	–	–	–	1	1
ALL RIGHT	–	–	–	1	–	1	–	–	–
ALONE	–	–	–	1	–	1	–	–	–
ALWAYS	–	–	–	1	–	1	–	–	–
AND	–	–	–	1	–	1	–	–	–
ANGRY	–	–	–	1	–	1	–	1	1
ANYTHING	–	–	–	1	–	1	–	–	–
AT HOME	1	–	1	–	–	–	–	–	–
AWFUL	1	–	1	2	2	4	1	–	1
BAD	1	–	1	1	1	2	1	–	1
BALL	1	–	1	–	–	–	–	–	–
BATHROOM	–	1	1	–	–	–	–	–	–
BE	–	1	1	–	–	–	–	–	–
BE GOOD	–	1	1	–	–	–	–	–	–
BE PLEASANT	2	–	2	–	–	–	–	–	–
BEAUTIFUL	–	–	–	3	–	3	–	1	1
BED	–	1	1	–	–	–	–	–	–
BEING PLEASANT	–	1	1	–	–	–	–	–	–
BEND	–	1	1	–	–	–	–	–	–
BIRD	–	1	1	1	–	1	–	1	1
BIRTHDAY	–	1	1	–	–	–	1	–	1
BITTER	–	–	–	–	–	–	2	–	2
BLOOD	–	2	2	–	–	–	–	–	–
BOYS	–	1	1	–	–	–	–	–	–
BUGGY	–	–	–	–	–	–	–	1	1
CABINS	–	1	1	–	–	–	–	–	–
CAKE	–	–	–	1	–	1	–	–	–
CALENDAR	–	1	1	–	–	–	–	–	–
CAME	–	–	–	–	–	–	1	–	1
CAN	1	2	3	–	–	–	–	–	–
CAR	1	–	1	–	–	–	–	–	–
CAREFUL	–	–	–	1	–	1	–	–	–
CAT	–	–	–	–	–	–	1	–	1
CEASANT	–	1	1	–	–	–	–	–	–
CHAIR	–	1	1	–	–	–	–	–	–
CHALKBOARD	1	1	2	–	–	–	–	–	–
CHEASANT	1	–	1	–	–	–	–	–	–
CHEERFUL	–	–	–	–	1	1	–	–	–
CHILD	1	–	1	–	–	–	–	–	–
CHILDREN ARE	1	–	1	–	–	–	–	–	–
CHRISTMAS	1	–	1	–	–	–	–	–	–
CLOTHES	–	–	–	–	1	1	–	–	–
CLOVER	1	–	1	–	–	–	–	–	–
COAT	1	–	1	–	–	–	–	–	–
COLD	1	–	1	–	–	–	–	–	–
COLOR	–	1	1	–	–	–	–	–	–
COME	2	–	2	–	1	1	–	–	–
COMFORTABLE	–	–	–	–	–	–	3	–	3
CONVENIENT	–	–	–	1	–	1	–	–	–
COOL	–	–	–	–	1	1	–	–	–

RESPONSE WORD	1ST M	F	T	3RD M	F	T	5TH M	F	T

61.   PLEASANT

RESPONSE WORD	1ST M	F	T	3RD M	F	T	5TH M	F	T
CROWS	1	—	1	—	—	—	—	—	—
CURTAIN	1	—	1	—	—	—	—	—	—
CUT	—	1	1	—	—	—	—	—	—
DAY	2	2	4	1	1	2	—	—	—
DAYS	—	—	—	—	1	1	—	—	—
DEER	1	—	1	—	—	—	—	—	—
DELEASANT	—	1	1	—	—	—	—	—	—
DELIGHT	—	—	—	—	—	—	—	1	1
DELIGHTFUL	—	—	—	—	—	—	—	1	1
DESIGN	—	—	—	—	1	1	—	—	—
DICK	1	—	1	—	—	—	—	—	—
DIRT	—	1	1	—	—	—	—	—	—
DIRTY	—	—	—	1	—	1	—	—	—
DISTURB	—	—	—	—	2	2	—	—	—
DO PLEASANT THINGS	1	—	1	—	—	—	—	—	—
DOG	—	—	—	—	1	1	—	—	—
DONE	—	1	—	—	—	—	1	—	1
DONT WORK ME	—	1	1	—	—	—	—	—	—
DOOR	1	—	1	1	—	1	—	—	—
DREAM	—	—	—	2	1	3	—	—	—
DREAMING	—	—	—	1	—	1	—	—	—
DREAMS	4	4	8	1	—	1	—	—	—
EACH PRESENT	1	—	1	—	—	—	—	—	—
EASY	—	—	—	1	—	1	1	1	2
EAT	—	—	—	—	—	—	—	1	1
EATING	—	—	—	—	1	1	—	—	—
ENJOY	—	—	—	1	—	1	3	1	4
ENJOYABLE	—	—	—	—	1	1	—	2	2
ENJOYED	—	—	—	—	—	—	—	1	1
ENJOYING	1	—	1	1	—	1	—	—	—
FALL	1	—	1	1	—	1	—	—	—
FAST	—	1	1	—	—	—	1	—	1
FEELING	1	—	1	—	—	—	—	—	—
FENCE	—	1	1	1	—	1	—	—	—
FINE	1	—	1	—	—	—	1	—	1
FLESH	1	—	1	—	—	—	—	—	—
FLOOR	—	1	1	—	—	—	—	—	—
FLOWER	1	—	1	—	—	—	—	—	—
FOOTBALL	—	1	—	—	—	—	—	1	1
FOREVER	—	1	1	—	—	—	—	—	—
FRECKLES	1	—	1	—	—	—	—	—	—
FRIENDLY	—	—	—	1	—	1	—	—	—
FUN	—	3	3	1	1	2	2	2	4
FUTURE	—	—	—	—	—	—	—	1	1
GAME	—	1	1	—	1	1	—	—	—
GAY	—	—	—	—	—	—	1	1	2
GENTLE	1	1	2	—	1	1	1	—	1
GENTLY	—	—	—	1	—	1	1	—	1
GIFT	—	—	—	—	1	1	—	—	—
GIRL	—	2	2	1	—	1	—	1	1
GIVE	1	—	1	—	—	—	1	—	1
GIVING	—	—	—	—	—	—	—	1	1
GLAD	1	—	1	1	—	1	—	1	1
GLAD TO SEE YOU	—	2	2	—	—	—	—	1	1
GO	—	—	—	—	—	—	—	—	—
GOOD	2	2	4	4	4	8	3	4	7
GOOD NATURED	—	—	—	—	—	—	—	1	1
GOOD TIME	—	—	—	—	—	—	—	1	1
GORGEOUS	—	1	1	—	—	—	—	—	—
GRACEFUL	—	—	—	—	1	1	—	—	—
GREEDY	—	—	—	1	1	2	—	—	—
GREEN	1	1	2	—	—	—	1	—	1
HAPPEN	—	—	—	—	1	1	1	—	1
HAPPY	3	4	7	7	10	17	21	20	41
HARD	—	1	1	2	—	2	—	1	1
HARSH	—	—	—	—	—	—	1	1	2
HATE	—	—	—	1	—	1	—	—	—
HATEFUL	—	—	—	—	—	—	1	—	1
HAVE	—	—	—	—	1	1	—	—	—
HAWAII	—	—	—	—	—	—	1	—	1
HEAR	—	—	—	—	—	—	—	1	1
HEASANT	1	—	1	—	—	—	—	—	—

RESPONSE WORD	1ST M	1ST F	1ST T	3RD M	3RD F	3RD T	5TH M	5TH F	5TH T

61. PLEASANT

RESPONSE WORD	1ST M	1ST F	1ST T	3RD M	3RD F	3RD T	5TH M	5TH F	5TH T
HEATER	1	–	1	–	–	–	–	–	–
HEAVEN	1	–	1	–	–	–	–	–	–
HELP	1	–	1	–	–	–	–	–	–
HER	–	–	–	1	–	1	–	–	–
HERE	–	2	2	1	–	1	–	–	–
HIGH	–	1	1	–	–	–	–	–	–
HORRIBLE	1	–	1	–	1	1	1	1	2
ICE CREAM	1	–	1	–	–	–	1	–	1
IDEA	1	–	1	–	–	–	–	–	–
IM PLEASANT TO YOU	1	–	1	–	–	–	–	–	–
IN THE HOUSE	–	1	1	–	–	–	–	–	–
ISNT IT	–	1	1	–	–	–	–	–	–
JEWELRY	1	–	1	–	–	–	–	–	–
JIM	1	–	1	–	–	–	1	–	1
JOLLY	–	–	–	–	–	–	–	1	1
JOY	–	–	–	–	–	–	–	1	1
JOYFUL	–	–	–	–	–	–	–	1	1
KIND	–	2	2	1	1	2	1	2	3
KINDLY	–	–	–	–	2	2	–	–	–
LADDER	–	1	1	–	–	–	–	–	–
LAMP	–	1	1	–	–	–	–	–	–
LESSENT	1	–	1	–	–	–	–	–	–
LETS BE NICE	–	1	1	–	–	–	–	–	–
LIE	–	1	1	–	–	–	–	–	–
LIKE	3	1	4	–	2	2	–	–	–
LITTLE	–	1	1	–	–	–	–	–	–
LIVE HAPPILY EVER AFTER	1	–	1	–	–	–	–	–	–
LIVING	7	1	8	5	3	8	1	–	1
LOOK	1	–	1	–	–	–	–	–	–
LOVE	–	–	–	–	1	1	1	–	1
LOVELY	–	–	–	–	–	–	–	1	1
MAD	2	1	3	2	–	2	–	1	1
MANY	–	–	–	1	–	1	–	–	–
MARRIED	–	–	–	1	–	1	–	–	–
ME	1	1	2	1	–	1	–	–	–
MEAN	–	–	–	–	1	1	1	–	1
MEDICINE	1	–	1	–	–	–	–	–	–
MORNING	3	–	3	–	–	–	–	–	–
MOSTLY	–	–	–	–	1	1	–	–	–
MUSIC	1	–	1	–	–	–	1	–	1
MY	–	1	1	–	–	–	–	–	–
NAME	1	–	1	–	–	–	–	–	–
NASTY	–	–	–	–	–	–	2	–	2
NENT	–	–	–	–	–	–	1	–	1
NICE	5	6	11	23	29	52	32	28	60
NICE TIME	–	–	–	1	–	1	–	–	–
NIGHT	–	1	1	–	–	–	–	–	–
NOISY	–	2	2	1	2	3	2	1	3
NOT	1	1	2	–	2	2	–	–	–
NOT PLEASANT	4	–	4	4	3	7	1	–	1
NOTHING	–	1	1	–	1	1	–	–	–
NOW	1	–	1	–	–	–	–	–	–
OFF	–	–	–	–	1	1	–	–	–
OKAY	–	–	–	–	1	1	–	1	1
ONE	–	–	–	1	–	1	–	–	–
PAPER	2	–	2	–	–	–	–	–	–
PARTY	–	–	–	–	1	1	–	–	–
PATSY	–	1	1	–	–	–	–	–	–
PEACE	–	–	–	–	–	–	–	1	1
PEACEFUL	–	–	–	1	2	3	–	2	2
PEASANT	2	–	2	–	–	–	–	–	–
PEOPLE	2	–	2	–	1	1	–	–	–
PHEASANT	2	2	4	1	–	1	–	1	1
PHONE	–	1	1	–	–	–	–	–	–
PIANO	–	1	1	–	–	–	–	–	–
PICNIC	–	–	–	–	–	–	1	–	1
PIG	–	–	–	–	1	1	–	–	–
PLAIN	1	1	2	–	–	–	–	–	–
PLANE	–	–	–	–	1	1	–	–	–
PLAY	3	4	7	2	–	2	–	–	–
PLAYING	–	–	–	1	–	1	–	–	–
PLEASANTLY	–	1	1	–	–	–	–	–	–

RESPONSE WORD	1ST M	F	T	3RD M	F	T	5TH M	F	T

61. PLEASANT

RESPONSE WORD	1ST M	F	T	3RD M	F	T	5TH M	F	T
PLEASE	2	2	4	3	4	7	2	1	3
PLEASED	–	–	–	–	–	–	–	1	1
PLEASING	–	1	1	–	–	–	–	–	–
PLEASURE	–	–	–	–	–	–	2	–	2
POCKET BOOK	–	1	1	–	–	–	–	–	–
POLITE	–	1	1	1	4	5	1	–	1
PONY	1	–	1	–	–	–	–	–	–
PRESENT	4	9	13	2	–	2	–	–	–
PRESIDENT	–	–	–	–	1	1	–	–	–
PRETTY	–	–	–	1	1	2	–	2	2
QUAINT	–	–	–	–	1	1	–	–	–
QUET	–	–	–	–	–	–	–	1	1
QUIET	1	1	2	–	5	5	2	1	3
RAIN	1	–	1	–	–	–	–	–	–
RAISE	–	–	–	–	–	–	1	–	1
RAT	–	–	–	–	–	–	1	–	1
REALX	–	–	–	–	–	–	1	–	1
REASANT	–	1	1	–	–	–	–	–	–
RELAX	–	–	–	–	–	–	1	–	1
RELIEF	–	–	–	–	–	–	1	–	1
RIGHT	1	–	1	–	–	–	–	–	–
RIVER	–	1	1	–	–	–	–	–	–
ROUGH	–	–	–	1	–	1	–	–	–
RUDE	–	–	–	2	–	2	–	1	1
SAD	–	–	–	–	1	1	2	1	3
SAFE	–	–	–	–	–	–	–	1	1
SCISSORS	1	–	1	–	–	–	–	–	–
SEASANT	–	–	–	1	–	1	–	–	–
SECRET	–	–	–	–	–	–	–	1	1
SEE	–	1	1	–	–	–	–	–	–
SEEMS LIKE BET	–	1	1	–	–	–	–	–	–
SHADE	1	–	1	–	–	–	–	–	–
SHEET	–	–	–	1	–	1	–	–	–
SILENT	–	–	–	–	1	1	–	–	–
SIT DOWN	1	–	1	–	–	–	–	–	–
SKY	–	1	1	–	–	–	–	–	–
SMALL	–	–	–	–	–	–	1	1	1
SNOW	–	–	–	–	–	–	–	1	1
SOFT	–	1	1	3	–	3	1	–	1
SOMETIMES ITS NOT PLEASANT	1	–	1	–	–	–	–	–	–
SONG	–	1	1	–	–	–	–	–	–
SOUR	–	–	–	–	–	–	1	–	1
SPRING	–	1	1	–	–	–	–	–	–
STARS	–	1	1	–	–	–	–	–	–
STATE	–	1	1	–	–	–	–	–	–
STREET	–	–	–	4	2	6	–	–	–
SUN	–	1	1	–	–	–	–	–	–
SURPRISE	–	–	–	2	–	2	–	–	–
SWEET	–	–	–	2	1	3	2	4	6
TABLE	1	–	1	–	–	–	–	1	1
TEACHER	1	–	1	–	–	–	–	–	–
TEASANT	–	1	1	–	–	–	–	–	–
TERRIBLE	–	2	2	2	–	2	–	2	2
THANK	–	–	–	1	2	3	–	–	–
THANK YOU	–	–	–	1	2	3	–	–	–
THANKFUL	–	–	–	–	1	1	–	–	–
THE	–	1	1	–	–	–	–	–	–
THE CLOUDS	1	–	1	–	–	–	–	–	–
THING	–	–	–	–	–	–	1	1	2
THINGS	–	–	–	–	1	1	–	–	–
THREE	–	1	1	–	–	–	–	–	–
THRILLING	–	–	–	1	–	1	–	–	–
THROUGH	–	1	1	–	–	–	–	–	–
THUMB	1	–	1	–	–	–	–	–	–
TIME	5	2	7	2	3	5	–	–	–
TIMES	1	–	1	1	–	1	–	–	–
TO	–	–	–	–	1	1	–	–	–
TO SEE YOU	1	1	2	–	–	–	–	–	–
TODAY	1	–	1	–	1	1	–	–	–
TOGETHER	–	–	–	–	1	1	–	–	–

RESPONSE WORD	1ST M	1ST F	1ST T	3RD M	3RD F	3RD T	5TH M	5TH F	5TH T

61. PLEASANT

RESPONSE WORD	1ST M	F	T	3RD M	F	T	5TH M	F	T
TREE	1	–	1	–	–	–	–	–	–
TROUBLE	–	–	–	–	–	–	–	1	1
TRUCK	1	–	1	–	–	–	–	–	–
TURKEY	–	–	–	–	–	–	–	1	1
TWO	1	–	1	–	–	–	–	–	–
UNGRATEFUL	–	–	–	–	–	–	–	1	1
UNHAPPY	–	–	–	–	1	1	1	1	2
UNPLEASANT	1	5	6	12	11	23	18	22	40
US	1	1	2	–	–	–	–	–	–
VEREY HAPPY	–	–	–	–	–	–	1	–	1
VOICE	–	–	–	1	–	1	–	–	–
WALK	2	1	3	–	–	–	–	–	–
WALTZ	–	1	1	–	–	–	–	–	–
WE	–	1	1	–	–	–	–	–	–
WE SIT	1	–	1	–	–	–	–	–	–
WEATHER	–	1	1	–	–	–	–	–	–
WELL	–	1	1	–	–	–	–	–	–
WESSENT	–	1	1	–	–	–	–	–	–
WHEN YOU RE PRESENT YOU GO SOMEWHERE ELSE.	1	–	1	–	–	–	–	–	–
WHITE	–	1	1	–	–	–	–	–	–
WINTER	1	–	1	–	–	–	–	–	–
WITH ME	1	–	1	–	–	–	–	–	–
WONDERFUL	1	–	1	–	–	–	–	1	1
WRITING	–	–	–	–	1	1	–	–	–
YOU COULD GIVE A PERSON A PRESENT.	–	1	1	–	–	–	–	–	–
YOU HAVE A PLEASANT EVENING.	–	1	1	–	–	–	–	–	–
YOURE A PLEASANT GIRL	–	–	–	–	–	–	–	1	1
YOURS	1	–	1	–	–	–	–	–	–

62. PREPARE

RESPONSE WORD	1ST M	F	T	3RD M	F	T	5TH M	F	T
A PEAR	–	–	–	–	1	1	–	–	–
A TREE	1	–	1	–	–	–	–	–	–
ADD	1	–	1	–	–	–	–	–	–
AGAIN	–	–	–	–	–	–	–	1	1
ALWAYS	–	–	–	–	1	1	–	–	–
AMMUNITION	–	–	–	1	–	1	–	–	–
ANIMAL	–	1	1	1	–	1	–	–	–
ANIMALS	–	–	–	1	–	1	–	–	–
ANNOUNCED	–	–	–	1	–	1	–	–	–
ANYTHING	–	–	–	–	–	–	–	1	1
APPLE	3	2	5	–	1	1	–	–	–
APPLES	–	1	1	–	–	–	–	–	–
ARE	–	1	1	–	–	–	–	–	–
ARITHMETIC	–	–	–	–	–	–	–	1	1
ARMS	–	1	1	–	–	–	–	–	–
ARRANGE	–	–	–	–	–	–	1	–	1
AWAY	–	–	–	–	1	1	–	–	–
BABY	1	–	1	–	–	–	–	–	–
BALL	–	–	–	1	–	1	–	–	–
BE GOOD TO YOUR MOMMY	–	1	1	–	–	–	–	–	–
BE READY	–	–	–	2	–	2	1	–	1
BE SURE	–	–	–	–	–	–	1	–	1
BEAR	1	–	1	–	–	–	–	–	–
BECARE	1	–	1	–	–	–	–	–	–
BEFORE	–	–	–	–	–	–	1	1	2
BEGIN	–	–	–	–	–	–	–	1	1
BETWEEN	–	–	–	–	–	–	–	1	1
BEWARE	–	–	–	–	–	–	1	–	1
BIKE	–	1	1	–	–	–	–	–	–
BIRD	–	–	–	–	1	1	1	–	1
BOOK	–	–	–	–	1	1	–	–	–
BOOKS	–	–	–	–	2	2	–	–	–
BOY	–	1	1	–	–	–	–	–	–
BREAKFAST	–	–	–	1	–	1	–	–	–
BROKE	–	–	–	–	–	–	1	1	2
BROKEN	1	–	1	–	–	–	–	–	–

RESPONSE WORD	1ST M	F	T	3RD M	F	T	5TH M	F	T
				62. PREPARE					
BRUSH	1	–	1	–	–	–	–	–	–
BUILD	–	1	1	–	1	1	–	–	–
BUNNY	–	1	1	–	–	–	–	–	–
BUTTON	–	1	1	–	–	–	–	–	–
CABIN	–	1	1	–	–	–	–	–	–
CAKE	–	2	2	–	–	–	–	–	–
CAR	3	2	5	1	–	1	–	–	–
CARE	2	1	3	–	–	–	–	–	–
CARPENTER	–	–	–	–	1	1	–	–	–
CHAIR	3	1	4	–	–	–	–	–	–
CLEAN	–	–	–	1	–	1	–	–	–
CLOCK	1	–	1	–	–	–	–	–	–
CLOTHES	–	1	1	–	1	1	–	–	–
COAL	1	–	1	–	–	–	–	–	–
COAT	–	–	–	–	1	1	–	–	–
COLD	2	–	2	1	–	1	–	–	–
COMING	–	–	–	1	–	1	–	–	–
COOK	–	–	–	–	–	–	1	2	3
COT	–	–	–	–	–	–	1	–	1
CRASH	–	–	–	1	–	1	–	–	–
CREEK	–	–	–	–	1	1	–	–	–
DECORATE	–	–	–	–	–	–	–	1	1
DELIVERY TRUCK	1	–	1	–	–	–	–	–	–
DEPARE	–	1	1	–	–	–	–	–	–
DESAIRED	–	–	–	1	–	1	–	–	–
DID	–	–	–	1	–	1	–	1	1
DINNER	6	4	10	2	1	3	–	1	1
DISH	–	–	–	–	–	–	–	1	1
DISPREPARE	–	–	–	–	–	–	–	2	2
DO	–	–	–	1	–	1	2	–	2
DO AGAIN	–	–	–	–	–	–	1	–	1
DO IT OVER	–	–	–	–	1	1	–	–	–
DO NOT PREPARE	1	–	1	–	–	–	–	–	–
DOES	–	–	–	–	–	–	–	1	1
DOG	1	–	1	–	–	–	1	–	1
DONE	–	–	–	1	–	1	–	–	–
DONT	1	1	2	1	1	2	–	–	–
DONT PREPARE	–	1	1	1	–	1	–	–	–
DOOR	1	–	1	–	–	–	–	–	–
DOOR HANDLE	1	–	1	–	–	–	–	–	–
DRESS	–	2	2	–	–	–	1	–	1
DUCK	1	–	1	–	–	–	–	–	–
E-PAIR	–	1	1	–	–	–	–	–	–
EAT	1	2	3	–	–	–	–	–	–
ELEPHANT	–	1	1	–	–	–	–	–	–
EMPTY	–	–	–	–	–	–	1	–	1
ENDS	–	1	1	–	–	–	–	–	–
EVERY	–	–	–	–	1	1	–	–	–
FAIR	–	–	–	–	–	–	1	–	1
FARMER	1	–	1	–	–	–	–	–	–
FATHER	1	–	1	–	–	–	–	1	1
FEAST	–	–	–	–	1	1	–	1	1
FEED	–	–	–	1	–	1	–	1	1
FIGHT	–	–	–	1	–	1	1	–	1
FILL	–	–	–	–	–	–	–	1	1
FIND	1	–	1	–	–	–	–	–	–
FINISH	–	–	–	–	–	–	1	1	2
FINISHED	–	–	–	–	–	–	2	–	2
FIRE	–	–	–	1	–	1	1	–	1
FIRST	–	–	–	1	–	1	1	–	1
FISH	2	–	2	19	13	32	22	10	32
FIX	–	–	–	–	1	1	–	1	1
FIXED	–	3	3	–	–	–	–	–	–
FLOOR	8	–	8	1	–	1	1	1	2
FOOD	–	–	–	1	–	1	–	1	1
FOR	–	–	–	1	–	1	–	–	–
FOR A JUMP	1	–	1	–	–	–	–	–	–
FOR CHRISTMAS	1	–	1	–	–	–	–	–	–
FOR LANDING	–	–	–	1	1	2	–	–	–
FORGOT	–	–	–	1	–	1	–	–	–
FOWL	1	–	1	–	–	–	–	–	–
FREEZING									

RESPONSE WORD	1ST M	F	T	3RD M	F	T	5TH M	F	T

62.　PREPARE

RESPONSE WORD	1ST M	F	T	3RD M	F	T	5TH M	F	T
FRONT	–	–	–	–	1	1	–	–	–
FROZEN	1	–	1	–	–	–	–	–	–
FRUIT	1	1	2	–	–	–	–	–	–
FURNITURE	–	1	1	–	–	–	–	–	–
GARE	1	–	1	–	–	–	–	–	–
GAS STATION	–	–	–	1	3	4	1	–	1
GET	–	–	–	1	3	4	–	1	1
GET READY	–	1	1	6	6	12	14	19	33
(GET) READY	–	–	–	–	–	–	1	–	1
GET SET	–	–	–	–	1	1	1	2	3
GETTING READY	–	–	–	–	1	1	–	–	–
GIRL	–	1	1	–	–	–	–	–	–
GIVE	–	–	–	1	1	2	–	–	–
GLOVE	–	–	–	–	1	1	–	–	–
GO	1	–	1	1	1	2	–	–	–
GOOD	2	2	4	–	–	–	–	–	–
GOT	–	–	–	–	1	1	–	–	–
GRASSHOPPER	–	1	1	–	–	–	–	–	–
GREEN	1	–	1	1	–	1	–	–	–
GUN	1	–	1	–	–	–	–	–	–
HAD	–	–	–	–	–	–	1	–	1
HAIR	1	–	1	1	1	2	–	–	–
HAPPEN	–	–	–	1	1	2	–	1	1
HAPPY	1	–	1	–	–	–	–	–	–
HAT	–	–	–	–	1	1	–	–	–
HAVE	–	–	–	–	–	–	–	2	2
HAVE IT	–	–	–	1	–	1	–	–	–
HEAD	1	–	1	–	–	–	–	–	–
HER	–	–	–	–	2	2	–	–	–
HIM	–	1	1	2	–	2	–	–	–
HOT	1	1	2	–	–	–	–	–	–
HOUSE	–	2	2	–	–	–	–	–	–
HUNCH	–	1	1	–	–	–	–	–	–
HUNTING	–	–	–	–	–	–	–	1	1
I	–	1	1	–	1	1	–	–	–
ICE CREAM	1	–	1	–	–	–	–	–	–
ICE CREAM TRUCK	–	1	1	–	–	–	–	–	–
IMPREPARED	–	–	–	–	–	–	–	1	1
INQUIRE	–	–	–	–	–	–	–	1	1
IRON	1	–	1	–	–	–	–	–	–
IRRIGATE	–	–	–	1	–	1	–	–	–
IS	1	–	1	–	–	–	1	–	1
IT	–	2	2	–	–	–	–	–	–
KITCHEN	1	–	1	–	–	–	–	–	–
LAZY	–	–	–	–	1	1	–	–	–
LEAF	–	–	–	–	1	1	–	–	–
LESSON	–	–	–	–	–	–	–	1	1
LET	–	–	–	–	–	–	–	1	1
LIGHT	1	2	3	2	2	4	–	–	–
LIKE	–	–	–	–	1	1	–	–	–
LIKE A REPAIR MAN WHENEVER SOMETHINGS B.	–	1	1	–	–	–	–	–	–
LIKE YOU REPAIR A TYPEWRITER	–	–	–	1	–	1	–	–	–
LISTEN	–	–	–	–	–	–	–	1	1
LITTLE	–	–	–	–	–	–	–	1	1
LUNCH	1	–	1	–	2	2	–	1	1
MACHINE	–	–	–	–	1	1	–	–	–
MAD	1	–	1	1	–	1	–	–	–
MADE FOR	–	–	–	1	–	1	–	–	–
MAKE	–	1	1	–	1	1	5	1	6
MAKE READY	–	–	–	–	–	–	1	2	3
MAN	3	2	5	–	2	2	–	–	–
MARE	1	2	3	–	–	–	–	–	–
MAY PARE	–	–	–	–	1	1	–	–	–
MAYBE	–	–	–	–	–	–	1	–	1
ME	–	1	1	–	1	1	–	–	–
MEMARE	1	–	1	–	–	–	–	–	–
MEND	–	–	–	–	3	3	–	–	–
MOLDY	1	–	1	–	–	–	–	–	–
MONEY	1	–	1	–	–	–	–	–	–
MORE	1	–	1	–	–	–	–	1	1
MORNING	–	–	–	–	–	–	–	1	1

RESPONSE WORD	1ST M	F	T	3RD M	F	T	5TH M	F	T

62.   PREPARE

RESPONSE WORD	1ST M	F	T	3RD M	F	T	5TH M	F	T
MOVE	–	–	–	1	–	1	–	–	–
MY SHOES	1	–	1	–	–	–	–	–	–
NARRLED	–	1	1	–	–	–	–	–	–
NEAT	–	–	–	–	–	–	2	–	2
NEW	2	–	2	–	1	1	–	1	1
NICE	–	3	3	–	1	1	–	–	–
NO	–	1	1	–	–	–	1	–	1
NOT	–	1	1	2	1	3	–	1	1
NOT BEING PREPARED	–	1	1	–	–	–	–	–	–
NOT PREPARE	1	–	1	6	4	10	2	–	2
NOT PREPARED	2	1	3	3	3	6	2	–	2
NOT READY	–	–	–	–	1	1	–	1	1
NOT REPAIR	–	–	–	1	–	1	–	–	–
NOTHING	–	1	1	–	–	–	–	–	–
NOW	1	–	1	–	–	–	2	–	2
NUT	–	–	–	1	–	1	–	–	–
OH CARE	1	–	1	–	–	–	–	–	–
OUT	–	1	1	–	–	–	1	–	1
PACK	1	–	1	–	–	–	1	–	1
PACKAGE	–	1	1	–	–	–	–	–	–
PAIL	–	1	1	–	1	1	–	–	–
PAIR	2	2	4	2	1	3	–	1	1
PANTS	1	–	1	–	–	–	–	–	–
PAPE	–	–	–	–	–	–	1	–	1
PAPERS	1	–	1	–	–	–	–	–	–
PARE	1	1	2	–	2	2	2	1	3
PARED	–	1	1	–	–	–	–	–	–
PATSY	–	1	1	–	–	–	–	–	–
PAY	–	–	–	1	–	1	–	–	–
PEAR	2	6	8	–	1	1	1	1	2
PEARLS	–	–	–	–	1	1	–	–	–
PEARS	2	2	4	–	–	–	–	–	–
PENCIL LEAD	–	1	1	–	–	–	–	–	–
PICKLE	–	1	1	–	1	1	–	–	–
PICTURE	–	–	–	2	–	2	–	1	1
PLAN	–	–	–	1	–	1	–	–	–
PLAY	1	–	1	–	–	–	–	–	–
PLEPARE	1	–	1	–	–	–	–	–	–
POCKETBOOK	1	–	1	–	–	–	–	–	–
PONY	–	–	–	1	1	2	1	–	1
PRE	–	1	1	–	–	–	–	–	–
PREACHER	–	1	1	–	–	–	–	1	1
PREMARE	–	1	1	–	–	–	–	–	–
PREPARATION	–	1	1	–	–	–	–	1	1
PRETTY	–	1	1	–	–	–	–	–	–
PURPLE	–	1	1	–	–	–	–	1	1
QUESTION	–	1	1	–	–	–	–	–	–
QUIET	–	1	1	–	–	–	–	–	–
RAIN	–	–	–	1	–	1	–	–	–
RAINCOAT	1	–	1	–	–	–	1	–	1
READ	–	1	1	17	21	38	30	29	59
READY	–	–	–	–	1	1	–	–	–
READY FOR SOMETHING	–	–	–	1	–	1	–	–	–
READY TO	–	–	–	–	–	–	–	1	1
READY TO DO	–	1	1	–	–	–	–	–	–
RED	1	–	1	–	–	–	1	–	1
REFRIGERATOR	–	–	–	–	–	–	–	–	–
RELAX	–	–	–	1	–	1	1	–	1
REMEMBER	1	1	2	2	2	4	2	2	4
REPAIR	–	1	1	–	–	–	–	–	–
REPAIR MAN	–	1	1	–	–	–	–	–	–
REPAIR MY TIRE	–	1	1	–	–	–	–	–	–
REPAIR THIS BIKE	–	–	–	1	–	1	–	–	–
REPAIRED ALREADY	–	–	–	–	–	–	1	–	1
REPAIRING	–	–	–	–	–	–	–	1	1
SAILT	1	–	1	–	–	–	–	–	–
SALE	1	–	1	–	1	1	–	–	–
SAW	1	–	1	1	–	1	–	1	1
SCHOOL	1	–	1	1	–	1	–	–	–
SCHOOL SUPPLIES	1	–	1	–	–	–	–	–	–
SCREW	1	1	2	–	–	–	–	–	–
SEE									

62. PREPARE

RESPONSE WORD	1ST M	F	T	3RD M	F	T	5TH M	F	T
SEND	–	–	–	–	–	–	–	–	–
SERVE	–	–	–	1	1	2	–	1	1
SET	–	–	–	1	–	1	1	2	3
SET UP	–	–	–	–	–	–	1	–	1
SEWER PIPE	1	–	1	–	–	–	–	–	–
SHOE	1	1	2	–	–	–	–	–	–
SHOES	1	1	2	–	–	–	–	–	–
SHOOT	–	–	–	1	–	1	–	–	–
SHOP	1	–	1	–	–	–	–	–	–
SINK	–	1	1	–	–	–	–	–	–
SLOW	–	–	–	–	1	1	–	–	–
SMOOKE	–	–	–	–	–	–	–	1	1
SNOW	–	–	–	2	–	2	–	–	–
SOFTLY	–	1	1	–	–	–	–	–	–
SOME	1	1	2	–	–	–	–	–	–
SOMETHING	1	2	3	–	–	–	1	–	1
SOMETHING YOU EAT	1	–	1	–	–	–	–	–	–
SOMETHINGS PAIRED ON YOUR CHAIRS.	–	1	1	–	–	–	–	–	–
SONGS	–	1	1	–	–	–	–	–	–
SOUR	–	–	–	–	–	–	–	1	1
START	–	–	–	–	–	–	1	1	2
STOP	1	–	1	–	–	–	–	–	–
STORE	–	1	1	–	3	3	–	–	–
STORES	–	1	1	–	–	–	–	–	–
STORM	–	1	1	–	–	–	–	–	–
STRONG	–	1	1	–	–	–	–	–	–
STUDY	–	–	–	–	–	–	2	–	2
STUFF	1	–	1	–	–	–	–	–	–
SUMMER	–	1	1	–	–	–	–	–	–
SUN	–	1	1	–	1	1	–	–	–
SUPPER	1	–	1	2	1	3	1	1	2
SUPPRESSED	–	–	–	1	–	1	–	–	–
SWEATER	1	1	2	–	–	–	–	–	–
TABLE	1	–	1	–	1	1	1	1	2
TAKE	–	–	–	2	–	2	–	–	–
TAKE OFF	–	–	–	1	–	1	–	–	–
TEAR	–	1	1	–	–	–	–	–	–
TELEVISION	–	1	1	–	–	–	–	–	–
THAT	1	1	2	–	–	–	–	–	–
THE	1	–	1	–	–	–	–	–	–
THE BUSTED CAR	1	–	1	–	–	–	–	–	–
THE MILK	–	–	–	1	–	1	–	–	–
THEM	–	–	–	–	1	1	–	–	–
THERE	–	1	1	–	–	–	–	1	1
THEY	–	–	–	–	1	1	–	–	–
TO	1	–	1	–	–	–	–	–	–
TO DO	–	–	–	–	–	–	–	1	1
TO FIX	–	–	–	–	–	–	–	1	1
TO GO TO THE CITY	1	–	1	–	–	–	–	–	–
TO START	–	–	–	–	–	–	–	1	1
TO WAR	1	–	1	–	–	–	–	–	–
TOGETHER	–	–	–	–	1	1	1	–	1
TOOL	1	–	1	–	–	–	–	–	–
TOY	–	–	–	–	1	1	–	–	–
TOYS	–	1	1	–	–	–	–	–	–
TRACK	–	1	1	–	–	–	–	–	–
TRIP	–	–	–	–	1	1	–	–	–
TRUCK	1	–	1	1	–	1	–	–	–
TURN ON	–	1	1	–	–	–	–	–	–
UNABLE	–	–	–	–	–	–	–	1	1
UNDER	–	1	1	–	2	2	–	–	–
UNDERSTAND	–	–	–	–	–	–	1	–	1
UNLECTION	–	–	–	–	1	1	–	–	–
UNPACKING	1	–	1	–	–	–	–	–	–
UNPARE	–	–	–	–	–	–	–	1	1
UNPERPAR	–	–	–	–	–	–	1	–	1
UNPREPARE	2	1	3	1	3	4	2	4	6
UNPREPARED	–	2	2	4	–	4	4	3	7
WALK	–	–	–	1	–	1	–	–	–
WALL	–	1	1	–	–	–	–	–	–
WAR	–	–	–	3	–	3	1	–	1

RESPONSE WORD	1ST M	F	T	3RD M	F	T	5TH M	F	T

62. PREPARE

RESPONSE WORD	M	F	T	M	F	T	M	F	T
WARM	–	1	1	–	–	–	–	–	–
WARM-UP	–	–	–	–	–	–	–	1	1
WASH	–	1	1	–	–	–	–	–	–
WASHING MACHINE	1	–	1	–	–	–	–	–	–
WATER	1	1	2	–	1	1	–	–	–
WE	1	–	1	1	–	1	–	–	–
WEAR	–	–	–	1	–	1	–	–	–
WEATHER	–	–	–	–	2	2	–	–	–
WEDDING	–	–	–	–	1	1	–	–	–
WHEN YOU REPAIR SOMETHING	1	–	1	–	–	–	–	–	–
WHITE	–	1	1	–	–	–	–	–	–
WIND	–	1	1	–	–	–	–	–	–
WINDOW	–	1	1	–	–	–	–	–	–
WINTER	1	–	1	–	1	1	–	–	–
WINTER CLOTHES	–	1	1	–	–	–	–	–	–
WITH	–	1	1	–	–	–	–	–	–
WORD	–	–	–	–	–	–	–	1	1
WORK	1	1	2	1	1	2	–	3	3
WORRY	1	–	1	–	–	–	–	–	–
WRENCHES	1	–	1	–	–	–	–	–	–
WRITE	–	–	–	–	1	1	–	–	–
YESTERDAY	–	–	–	1	–	1	–	–	–
YOU	–	1	1	1	–	1	–	–	–
YOU COULD STAY IN THE HOUSE AND EAT A P.	–	1	1	–	–	–	–	–	–
YOUR	1	–	1	–	–	–	–	–	–
YOUR BICYCLE	–	–	–	–	–	–	–	1	1

63. PRETTY

RESPONSE WORD	M	F	T	M	F	T	M	F	T
A PRETTY DOG OR PRETTY GIRL	–	1	1	–	–	–	–	–	–
ALL DRESSED UP	–	1	1	–	–	–	–	–	–
APPLE	1	–	1	–	–	–	–	–	–
AT	1	–	1	–	–	–	–	–	–
AWFUL	2	3	5	2	1	3	–	1	1
BABY	1	–	1	–	–	–	–	–	–
BAD	–	–	–	–	1	1	1	–	1
BASKET	–	1	1	–	–	–	–	–	–
BEAUTIFUL	3	3	6	44	57	101	39	39	78
BEAUTY	–	–	–	–	1	1	–	1	1
BEETLE	–	1	1	–	–	–	–	–	–
BETTY	–	–	–	–	–	–	–	1	1
BIRD	2	–	2	–	–	–	–	–	–
BOOK	1	–	1	–	–	–	–	–	–
BOOKS	1	–	1	–	–	–	–	–	–
BOX	1	–	1	–	–	–	–	–	–
BOY	1	–	1	–	–	–	–	–	–
BRACELET	–	1	1	–	–	–	–	–	–
BREAKFAST	1	–	1	–	–	–	–	–	–
BROWN	–	1	1	–	–	–	–	–	–
BUBBLE GUM	1	–	1	–	–	–	–	–	–
BULLY	–	1	1	–	–	–	–	–	–
BUTTERFLY	–	–	–	–	–	–	–	1	1
CAR	1	–	1	–	–	–	–	–	–
CARD	1	–	1	–	–	–	–	–	–
CHITTY	1	–	1	–	–	–	–	–	–
CITY	–	–	–	–	1	1	–	–	–
CLEAN	1	–	1	1	–	1	–	–	–
CLOTHES	1	1	2	–	–	–	–	–	–
COAT	–	1	1	–	–	–	–	–	–
COLOR	–	–	–	–	–	–	1	–	1
COW	1	–	1	–	–	–	–	–	–
CREW	1	–	1	–	–	–	–	–	–
CURTY	–	–	–	1	–	1	–	–	–
CUTE	–	2	2	4	4	8	7	1	8
DAD	1	–	1	–	–	–	–	–	–
DARK	1	–	1	–	–	–	–	–	–
DIAMOND	–	1	1	–	–	–	–	–	–
DID	1	–	1	–	–	–	–	–	–

RESPONSE WORD	1ST M	F	T	3RD M	F	T	5TH M	F	T

63. PRETTY

RESPONSE WORD	1ST M	F	T	3RD M	F	T	5TH M	F	T
DIFFERENT	–	–	–	1	–	1	–	–	–
DIRTY	–	1	1	–	–	–	–	–	–
DOG	1	–	1	–	–	–	–	–	–
DOLL	1	–	1	–	–	–	–	–	–
DOLLS	–	1	1	–	–	–	–	–	–
DORIS DAY	–	–	–	–	–	–	–	1	1
DRESS	7	13	20	2	4	6	3	2	5
DREST	–	–	–	–	–	–	–	1	1
DUMB	–	–	–	–	–	–	1	–	1
EDUGY	–	–	–	–	–	–	–	1	1
EGGAN	–	–	–	–	–	–	–	1	1
EVEING	–	–	–	–	–	–	–	1	1
EVIL	–	–	–	1	–	1	–	–	–
FANCY	–	–	–	–	–	–	–	1	1
FISH	–	1	1	–	–	–	–	–	–
FLOWER	6	5	11	1	4	5	3	–	3
FLOWERS	3	2	5	–	–	–	1	–	1
FLUFFY	–	–	–	1	–	1	–	–	–
FOOTBALL	–	–	–	–	–	–	–	1	1
GAY	–	–	–	–	–	–	–	1	1
GHOST	1	–	1	–	–	–	–	–	–
GIRL	10	9	19	4	2	6	4	6	10
GIRLS	1	–	1	–	–	–	1	–	1
GLASSES	–	1	1	–	–	–	–	–	–
GO	–	1	1	–	–	–	–	–	–
GOLD	–	1	1	–	–	–	–	–	–
GOOD	6	2	8	2	1	3	3	–	3
GOOD LOOKING	–	–	–	–	–	–	1	–	1
GORGEOUS	–	1	1	1	–	1	–	–	–
GRASS	–	1	1	–	–	–	–	–	–
GRITTY	1	–	1	–	–	–	–	–	–
HAIR	4	1	5	–	–	–	–	1	1
HANDLE	1	1	2	–	–	–	–	–	–
HANDSOME	1	–	1	2	–	2	2	3	5
HAPPY	–	–	–	2	2	4	–	–	–
HARD	–	–	–	–	–	–	1	–	1
HAT	–	1	1	–	–	–	–	–	–
HEART	1	–	1	–	–	–	–	–	–
HIGH	1	–	1	–	–	–	–	–	–
HIGH HEELS	–	1	1	–	–	–	–	–	–
HIM	–	1	1	–	–	–	–	–	–
HOG	–	–	–	–	–	–	1	–	1
HORRIBLE	–	3	3	–	1	1	–	–	–
HOT	–	–	–	1	–	1	–	–	–
HOUSE	1	2	3	–	–	–	–	–	–
IN BED	–	1	1	–	–	–	–	–	–
IT	1	–	1	1	–	1	–	–	–
KISS	1	–	1	–	–	–	–	–	–
KITTEN	–	1	1	–	–	–	–	–	–
KITTY	–	1	1	–	–	–	–	–	–
LADY	1	4	5	–	1	1	–	–	–
LIGHT	–	–	–	1	–	1	–	–	–
LIKE	–	2	2	–	–	–	–	–	–
LITTLE	–	1	1	–	–	–	–	–	–
LITTY	1	–	1	–	–	–	–	–	–
LOOK	–	1	1	–	–	–	–	–	–
LOOKING	1	–	1	–	–	–	–	–	–
LOOKS	–	–	–	–	–	–	1	–	1
LOVELY	1	2	3	4	–	4	4	3	7
MAGNIFICENT	–	–	–	–	–	–	1	–	1
MAKE-UP	–	–	–	–	–	–	1	–	1
MAN	2	1	3	–	–	–	–	–	–
MANY	–	1	1	–	–	–	–	–	–
MAY	1	–	1	–	–	–	–	–	–
MITTY	1	–	1	–	–	–	–	–	–
MOTHER	–	2	2	–	–	–	1	–	1
MURTY	2	–	2	–	–	–	–	–	–
MUSIC	1	–	1	–	–	–	–	–	–
NEAT	–	–	–	–	–	–	–	1	1
NERTTY	–	1	1	–	–	–	–	–	–
NEWSPAPER	1	–	1	–	–	–	–	–	–
NICE	5	6	11	9	4	13	9	8	17

RESPONSE WORD	1ST			3RD			5TH		
	M	F	T	M	F	T	M	F	T

63. PRETTY

RESPONSE WORD	M	F	T	M	F	T	M	F	T
NO	–	1	1	–	–	–	–	–	–
NOISE	1	–	1	–	–	–	–	–	–
NOT	–	1	1	–	–	–	–	–	–
NOT PRETTY	3	1	4	2	–	2	1	–	1
NOT UGLY	–	–	–	–	–	–	–	1	1
NUDDY	1	–	1	–	–	–	–	–	–
OLD	–	–	–	–	1	1	1	–	1
ORANGE	1	–	1	–	–	–	–	–	–
OUT	1	–	1	–	–	–	–	–	–
PAPER	1	1	2	–	–	–	–	–	–
PARTY	–	–	–	–	1	1	–	–	–
PATTY	–	1	1	–	–	–	–	–	–
PEN	1	–	1	–	–	–	–	–	–
PENCIL	–	1	1	–	–	–	–	–	–
PEOPLE	1	–	1	–	–	–	–	–	–
PERFUME	1	–	1	–	–	–	–	–	–
PERSON	–	–	–	–	–	–	1	–	1
PIG	–	–	–	–	–	–	1	–	1
PIN	–	–	–	1	–	1	–	–	–
PITY	–	1	1	–	–	–	–	–	–
PLACE	–	–	–	–	1	1	–	–	–
PLAY	–	1	1	–	–	–	–	–	–
POLITE	–	–	–	–	1	1	–	–	–
PONY	1	–	1	–	–	–	–	–	–
POTATOES	1	–	1	–	–	–	–	–	–
PRETTIER THAN YOU	–	1	1	–	–	–	–	–	–
PRINCESS	–	1	1	–	–	–	–	–	–
PUFF	1	–	1	–	–	–	–	–	–
PUT	1	–	1	–	–	–	–	–	–
QUEEN	1	–	1	–	–	–	–	–	–
QUIT	–	–	–	–	–	–	1	–	1
REAL PRETTY	–	1	1	–	–	–	–	–	–
RED	1	–	1	–	–	–	1	–	1
RIBBONS	–	1	1	–	–	–	–	–	–
RING	–	1	1	1	–	1	–	–	–
RITTY	–	1	1	–	–	–	–	–	–
SAD	2	–	2	–	–	–	–	–	–
SCHOOL	1	–	1	–	–	–	–	–	–
SCREEN	–	1	1	–	–	–	–	–	–
SEE	–	1	1	–	–	–	–	–	–
SEXY	1	–	1	–	–	–	–	–	–
SHE	1	–	1	–	–	–	–	–	–
SHEEP	1	–	1	–	–	–	–	–	–
SHINY	–	1	1	–	–	–	–	–	–
SHOES	–	–	–	–	–	–	–	1	1
SITTING	1	–	1	–	–	–	–	–	–
SKIRTY	1	–	1	–	–	–	–	–	–
SMART	–	–	–	–	–	–	1	–	1
SOFT	–	–	–	–	–	–	1	–	1
SOON	–	–	–	–	1	1	–	–	–
SPRING	–	–	–	–	–	–	1	–	1
STOP	1	–	1	–	–	–	–	–	–
SWEET	–	–	–	1	–	1	1	1	2
TABLE	–	1	1	–	–	–	–	–	–
TERRIBLE	–	1	1	1	–	1	–	–	–
THATS PRETTY	1	–	1	–	–	–	–	–	–
THEY	–	–	–	–	1	1	–	–	–
THINGS	1	–	1	1	1	2	–	–	–
TOGETHER	–	–	–	–	1	1	–	–	–
TRAIN	1	–	1	–	–	–	–	–	–
UGLEY	–	–	–	–	–	–	1	–	1
UGLY	10	20	30	43	46	89	39	59	98
ULDY	–	–	–	–	–	–	1	–	1
UNGY	–	–	–	–	–	–	1	–	1
UNPRETTY	–	–	–	–	1	1	–	–	–
US	–	–	–	1	–	1	–	–	–
VERY PRETTY	–	1	1	–	–	–	–	–	–
WAY	–	–	–	–	1	1	–	–	–
WHALING	1	–	1	–	–	–	–	–	–
WHEN YOU DRESS UP AND YOURE PRETTY	1	–	1	–	–	–	–	–	–
WHISTLE	–	1	1	–	–	–	–	–	–

RESPONSE WORD	1ST M	1ST F	1ST T	3RD M	3RD F	3RD T	5TH M	5TH F	5TH T

63. PRETTY

RESPONSE WORD	1ST M	1ST F	1ST T	3RD M	3RD F	3RD T	5TH M	5TH F	5TH T
WIFE	1	–	1	–	–	–	–	–	–
WISE	–	–	–	–	–	–	1	–	1
WOMAN	–	–	–	–	–	–	–	1	1
WONDERFUL	–	–	–	1	–	1	1	1	2
YELLOW	–	1	1	–	–	–	–	–	–
YOU	1	2	3	2	–	2	–	–	–
YOU ARE	2	–	2	–	–	–	–	–	–
YOU ARE PRETTY	2	2	4	–	–	–	–	–	–
YOU ARE REAL PRETTY	1	–	1	–	–	–	–	–	–
YOU COULD BE DRESSED UP AND YOU COULD G.	–	1	1	–	–	–	–	–	–
YOUNG	–	–	–	2	–	2	–	–	–
YOURE A PRETTY GIRL	–	1	1	–	–	–	–	–	–
YOURE PRETTY	1	1	2	–	–	–	–	–	–

64. QUIET

RESPONSE WORD	1ST M	1ST F	1ST T	3RD M	3RD F	3RD T	5TH M	5TH F	5TH T
ABLE TO HEAR SOMEBODY	1	–	1	–	–	–	–	–	–
AGAIN	–	–	–	–	–	–	–	1	1
B	–	1	1	–	–	–	–	–	–
BABY	1	2	3	–	–	–	1	1	2
BE	3	5	8	–	1	1	–	–	–
BE GOOD	1	–	1	–	–	–	–	–	–
BE QUIET	10	2	12	1	2	3	–	–	–
BE QUIET CAUSE MY BABY IS ASLEEP.	–	1	1	–	–	–	–	–	–
BE QUIET FOR YOUR SISTERS ARE SLEEPING	–	1	1	–	–	–	–	–	–
BE QUIET WHEN YOUR MOTHER OR FATHERS AS	–	1	1	–	–	–	–	–	–
BE STILL	–	–	–	–	–	–	1	–	1
BED	1	–	1	–	–	–	–	–	–
BEHAVE	–	–	–	1	–	1	–	–	–
BIG	–	–	–	–	–	–	1	–	1
BITE	–	–	–	–	–	–	–	1	1
BOARD	–	1	1	–	–	–	–	–	–
BOOK	1	1	2	–	–	–	–	–	–
BOX	1	–	1	–	–	–	–	–	–
BOY	1	–	1	–	–	–	–	–	–
BREEZE	–	–	–	–	–	–	1	–	1
BROWN	–	–	–	–	1	1	–	–	–
BUIET	–	1	1	–	–	–	–	–	–
BUY IT	1	–	1	–	–	–	–	–	–
CALM	–	–	–	1	1	2	–	–	–
CAME	–	–	–	–	–	–	1	–	1
CARE	–	–	–	–	–	–	1	–	1
CAT	–	–	–	–	–	–	–	1	1
CHOIR	–	–	–	1	–	1	–	–	–
CHURCH	–	–	–	–	–	–	1	–	1
CLASS	1	–	1	–	–	–	–	–	–
CLOCK	–	1	1	–	–	–	–	–	–
COAT	1	–	1	–	–	–	–	–	–
COME	–	–	–	–	–	–	1	–	1
COME DOWN	–	1	1	–	–	–	–	–	–
COW	1	–	1	–	–	–	–	–	–
DAY	1	–	1	1	–	1	–	–	–
DEAD	–	1	1	–	–	–	–	–	–
DESK	1	3	4	1	–	1	–	–	–
DOESNT	–	–	–	1	–	1	–	–	–
DOESNT MAKE NOISE	–	–	–	1	1	1	–	–	–
DOG	1	–	1	–	1	1	1	–	1
DONT	1	–	1	1	–	1	–	–	–
DONT BE	1	–	1	–	–	–	–	–	–
DONT HOLLER	1	–	1	–	–	–	–	–	–
DONT TALK	1	1	2	1	2	3	–	–	–
DONT YELL	–	1	1	–	–	–	–	–	–
DOWN	7	5	12	–	–	–	–	1	1
DR. KIT	–	1	1	–	–	–	–	–	–
EAT AT THE TABLE, DONT PLAY	–	1	1	–	–	–	–	–	–
EVIL	–	–	–	–	1	1	–	–	–

RESPONSE WORD	1ST			3RD			5TH		
	M	F	T	M	F	T	M	F	T

64. QUIET

RESPONSE WORD	M	F	T	M	F	T	M	F	T
FALL	1	–	1	–	–	–	–	–	–
FAST	1	–	1	–	–	–	–	–	–
FLIP	–	1	1	–	–	–	–	–	–
FLOOR	–	–	–	–	1	1	–	–	–
FROG	–	–	–	1	–	1	–	–	–
FRY	–	1	1	–	–	–	–	–	–
GENTLY	–	–	–	–	1	1	–	–	–
GIRAFFE	1	–	1	–	–	–	–	–	–
GLASS	–	–	–	–	1	1	–	–	–
GO	–	–	–	1	–	1	–	1	1
GO ON	–	–	–	–	–	–	–	1	1
GOOD	1	–	1	1	1	2	–	–	–
GRASS	–	1	1	–	–	–	–	–	–
HAPPY	–	1	1	–	–	–	–	–	–
HE	1	–	1	–	–	–	–	–	–
HEAD	1	–	1	–	–	–	–	–	–
HEAR	2	–	2	–	–	–	–	–	–
HERE	1	–	1	–	–	–	–	–	–
HIGH	1	–	1	–	–	–	–	–	–
HIGHER	1	–	1	–	–	–	–	–	–
HIGHET	1	–	1	–	–	–	–	–	–
HOLLER	–	1	1	–	–	–	–	–	–
HORSE	–	1	1	–	–	–	–	–	–
HOSPITAL	–	–	–	–	–	–	1	–	1
HOUSE	4	2	6	1	–	1	–	–	–
HUSH	–	–	–	–	1	1	–	–	–
I SIT	–	1	1	–	–	–	–	–	–
JACKET	1	–	1	–	–	–	–	–	–
JUMP	1	–	1	–	–	–	–	–	–
KIDS	1	–	1	–	–	–	–	–	–
KING	–	–	–	–	–	–	–	1	1
KNOB	1	–	1	–	–	–	–	–	–
LAID	1	–	1	–	1	1	–	–	–
LAW	–	–	–	–	–	–	–	1	1
LESS	–	1	1	–	–	–	–	–	–
LIBRARY	–	–	–	–	–	–	–	1	1
LIGHT	–	1	1	–	–	–	–	–	–
LIKE BE QUIET	–	–	–	–	–	–	–	1	1
LION	1	–	1	–	–	–	–	–	–
LISTEN	–	–	–	–	2	2	–	–	–
LISTENING	–	1	1	–	–	–	–	–	–
LITTLE DRUM	–	1	1	–	–	–	–	–	–
LOAD	–	2	2	–	1	1	–	–	–
LOD	–	–	–	–	–	–	–	1	1
LOUAD	–	–	–	–	–	–	1	–	1
LOUD	23	25	48	47	45	92	44	43	87
LOUDER	–	–	–	–	–	–	–	1	1
LOUDLY	4	1	5	3	–	3	2	–	2
LOW	–	–	–	–	1	1	–	1	1
MAD	–	–	–	–	–	–	1	–	1
MAN	1	–	1	–	–	–	–	–	–
ME	–	–	–	1	–	1	–	–	–
MIET	2	–	2	–	–	–	–	–	–
MORNING	–	1	1	–	–	–	–	–	–
MOUSE	2	–	2	–	–	–	–	–	–
MOUTH	–	2	2	–	–	–	–	1	1
MUSIC	–	–	–	–	–	–	1	–	1
NAUGHTY	–	–	–	–	–	–	1	–	1
NEWSPAPER	–	1	1	–	–	–	–	–	–
NICE	–	–	–	1	–	1	–	–	–
NIET	–	2	2	–	–	–	–	–	–
NIGHT	–	1	1	–	–	–	–	–	–
NO	–	1	1	–	–	–	–	–	–
NO NOISE	–	–	–	–	–	–	2	3	5
NO SOUND	–	–	–	–	–	–	–	1	1
NO WORDS	–	–	–	–	–	–	1	–	1
NOIESY	–	–	–	–	–	–	1	–	1
NOISE	–	4	4	7	8	15	6	6	12
NOISELESS	–	–	–	–	–	–	1	–	1
NOISILY	–	1	1	1	–	1	–	1	1
NOISY	7	11	18	30	28	58	26	22	48
NOIZE	–	–	–	–	–	–	1	–	1

64. QUIET

RESPONSE WORD	1ST M	F	T	3RD M	F	T	5TH M	F	T
NOSE	–	–	–	–	–	–	–	1	1
NOT	1	1	2	–	–	–	1	1	2
NOT A SOUND	–	–	–	1	–	1	–	–	–
NOT LOUD	–	–	–	–	–	–	1	2	3
NOT NOISEY	–	–	–	–	–	–	–	1	1
NOT NOISY	1	–	1	–	–	–	6	3	9
NOT QUIET	–	–	–	1	–	1	–	–	–
NOT SPEAKING	–	–	–	1	–	1	1	–	1
NOT TALK	–	–	–	–	–	–	–	2	2
NOT TALKED	–	–	–	1	–	1	–	–	–
NOT TALKING	–	–	–	1	1	2	–	–	–
NOW	2	–	2	–	–	–	2	–	2
OFTEN	–	–	–	–	–	–	1	–	1
ORANGE	1	–	1	–	–	–	–	–	–
OTHER	–	–	–	–	1	1	–	–	–
OUT	1	–	1	–	–	–	–	–	–
PAPER	–	1	1	–	–	–	–	1	1
PEACE	–	2	2	1	1	2	–	1	1
PEACEABLE	–	–	–	1	–	1	–	–	–
PEACEFUL	–	–	–	–	2	2	–	4	4
PEOPLE	1	1	2	–	–	–	1	1	2
PIET	–	–	–	1	–	1	–	–	–
PILER	1	–	1	–	–	–	–	–	–
PIN	–	1	1	–	–	–	–	–	–
PLAY WITH WAGON	1	–	1	–	–	–	–	–	–
PLEASANT	–	–	–	1	1	2	–	–	–
POLITE	–	–	–	–	–	–	1	–	1
POOR	1	–	1	–	–	–	–	–	–
PUDDING	1	–	1	–	–	–	–	–	–
PUT HEAD DOWN	–	1	1	–	–	–	–	–	–
QUAIL	–	–	–	1	–	1	–	–	–
QUARTER	–	–	–	–	1	1	–	–	–
QUICK	–	–	–	–	1	1	1	–	1
QUIT	–	–	–	–	–	–	–	1	1
QUITE	–	–	–	1	–	1	–	–	–
READ	1	–	1	–	–	–	–	–	–
READY	–	1	1	–	–	–	–	–	–
REAL QUIET	1	–	1	–	–	–	–	–	–
RED	1	–	1	–	–	–	1	–	1
ROOM	–	–	–	–	–	–	1	–	1
SAY NOTHING	–	–	–	1	–	1	–	–	–
SCREENDOOR	–	1	1	–	–	–	–	–	–
SET	–	1	1	–	–	–	–	–	–
SHH–	–	1	1	–	–	–	–	–	–
SHHH	–	–	–	–	1	1	–	–	–
SHOTUP	–	–	–	–	–	–	1	–	1
SHOUT	1	–	1	2	–	2	–	1	1
SHOUTED	–	–	–	–	1	1	–	–	–
SHUT	–	2	2	1	1	2	–	–	–
SHUT UP	–	–	–	1	–	1	–	1	1
SIET	1	–	1	–	–	–	–	–	–
SILENCE	–	1	1	–	–	–	3	3	6
SILENT	–	–	–	3	2	5	7	3	10
SILENTLY	–	–	–	–	1	1	–	–	–
SIT QUIET	1	1	2	–	–	–	–	–	–
SKIRT	–	–	–	–	1	1	–	–	–
SLEEP	4	2	6	–	–	–	–	–	–
SLEEPING	2	–	2	–	–	–	–	–	–
SLEEPY	–	1	1	–	–	–	–	–	–
SLOW	–	–	–	–	1	1	–	–	–
SLOWLY	–	–	–	–	1	1	–	–	–
SNEAK	–	1	1	–	–	–	–	–	–
SOFT	1	–	1	1	5	6	3	9	12
SOFTLY	2	3	5	1	3	4	2	2	4
SOMEONE IS REAL QUIET	–	1	1	–	–	–	–	–	–
SONG	–	1	1	–	–	–	–	–	–
SOUND	–	–	–	2	5	7	2	1	3
SOUNDLESS	–	–	–	–	1	1	1	–	1
SOUR	–	1	1	–	–	–	–	–	–
SPEAKLESS	–	–	–	–	–	–	–	1	1
SPEECHLESS	–	–	–	–	–	–	1	–	1
SPOON	–	1	1	–	–	–	–	–	–

RESPONSE WORD	1ST M	F	T	3RD M	F	T	5TH M	F	T

64.　QUIET

RESPONSE WORD	M	F	T	M	F	T	M	F	T
SSH	1	–	1	–	–	–	–	–	–
STEP	–	–	–	1	–	1	–	–	–
STICKS	–	1	1	–	–	–	–	–	–
STILL	–	–	–	3	–	3	1	1	2
STOCKINGS	–	1	1	–	–	–	–	–	–
STOP	–	–	–	–	–	–	–	1	1
STORM	–	–	–	–	–	–	1	–	1
STOVE	–	1	1	–	–	–	–	–	–
TABLE	2	2	4	–	–	–	–	–	–
TALK	4	1	5	5	7	12	–	6	6
TALK SOFT	–	–	–	–	1	1	–	–	–
TALKING	–	–	–	1	–	1	1	–	1
TEETH	1	1	2	–	–	–	–	–	–
TEST	–	–	–	1	–	1	–	–	–
TIE IT	–	1	1	–	–	–	–	–	–
TIME	–	1	1	–	–	–	–	–	–
TIP-TOEING	1	–	1	–	–	–	–	–	–
TIRED	–	–	–	1	–	1	–	–	–
TORN	–	1	1	–	–	–	–	–	–
TOWEL	1	–	1	–	–	–	–	–	–
TREE	1	–	1	–	–	–	–	–	–
UNLOUD	–	–	–	–	–	–	1	1	2
UP	–	1	1	–	–	–	–	–	–
UP TO BED THE CHILDREN GO	–	1	1	–	–	–	–	–	–
VERY	–	1	1	–	–	–	–	–	–
WALL	–	1	1	–	–	–	–	–	–
WE SIT	1	–	1	–	–	–	–	–	–
WERE	–	–	–	–	–	–	1	–	1
WHEN YOURE QUIET IN THE HOUSE	1	–	1	–	–	–	–	–	–
WHISPER	–	1	1	2	1	3	–	–	–
WIFE	1	–	1	–	–	–	–	–	–
WILL	1	–	1	–	–	–	–	–	–
WINDOW	1	–	1	–	–	–	–	–	–
WYET	–	1	1	–	–	–	–	–	–
YELL	–	–	–	–	–	–	–	1	1
YES	–	1	1	–	–	–	–	–	–
YOU	–	1	1	–	–	–	–	–	–

65.　RESTORE

RESPONSE WORD	M	F	T	M	F	T	M	F	T
A BALL	1	–	1	–	–	–	–	–	–
A BOOK	–	–	–	–	–	–	–	1	1
A STORE YOU SELL THINGS FROM	–	–	–	1	–	1	–	–	–
AGAIN	–	–	–	1	–	1	3	1	4
ALL THINGS	1	–	1	–	–	–	–	–	–
ANIMALS	–	–	–	–	1	1	–	–	–
APARTMENT	–	–	–	1	–	1	–	–	–
APPLE	1	–	1	1	1	2	–	–	–
APPLES	1	–	1	–	–	–	–	–	–
AVAILABLE	–	–	–	–	–	–	1	–	1
AWAY	–	–	–	–	1	1	1	1	2
AWFUL	–	–	–	1	–	1	–	–	–
BABY	–	2	2	–	–	–	–	–	–
BACK	–	–	–	1	–	1	1	–	1
BACK ROOM	–	–	–	–	–	–	1	–	1
BAKERY	–	1	1	–	–	–	–	–	–
BASEMENT	–	–	–	–	2	2	–	–	–
BAT	1	–	1	–	–	–	–	–	–
BED	–	1	1	–	–	–	–	–	–
BEFORE	–	–	–	–	1	1	–	1	1
BELONG	–	–	–	1	–	1	–	–	–
BESTORE	1	–	1	–	–	–	–	–	–
BETTER	1	–	1	–	–	–	–	–	–
BIG	–	–	–	–	–	–	–	1	1
BIRTH	–	1	1	–	–	–	1	–	1
BIT	–	1	1	–	–	–	–	–	–
BLOOD	1	–	1	–	–	–	–	–	–
BOOK	3	3	6	–	–	–	–	1	1

RESPONSE WORD	1ST M	1ST F	1ST T	3RD M	3RD F	3RD T	5TH M	5TH F	5TH T

65.   RESTORE

RESPONSE WORD	1ST M	1ST F	1ST T	3RD M	3RD F	3RD T	5TH M	5TH F	5TH T
BOOKS	1	1	2	–	–	–	–	–	–
BOUGHT	–	–	–	–	1	1	–	–	–
BOX	1	–	1	–	1	1	–	–	–
BOXES	1	–	1	–	–	–	1	1	2
BOY	–	1	1	–	–	–	–	–	–
BOYS	–	–	–	–	–	–	–	1	1
BRACELET	1	–	1	–	–	–	–	–	–
BREAD	–	1	1	–	–	–	–	–	–
BREAK DOWN	–	–	–	–	–	–	1	–	1
BRING BACK	–	–	–	–	–	–	1	3	4
BRING OUT	–	–	–	1	–	1	–	–	–
BUILD	–	–	–	–	–	–	1	–	1
BUY	3	5	8	2	1	3	–	1	1
BUY STUFF	1	–	1	–	–	–	–	–	–
BUY THINGS	1	–	1	–	–	–	–	–	–
CABIN	–	1	1	–	–	–	–	–	–
CABINET	–	1	1	–	1	1	–	–	–
CAME BACK	–	–	–	–	–	–	–	1	1
CANDY	1	2	3	–	–	–	–	–	–
CANNED	–	–	–	–	1	1	–	–	–
CAPTURE	–	–	–	–	–	–	–	1	1
CAR	1	1	2	–	1	1	–	–	–
CARE	–	1	1	–	–	–	–	–	–
CHAIR	1	–	1	–	1	1	–	–	–
CHERRIES	–	–	–	1	–	1	–	–	–
CHICKY	–	–	–	–	–	–	1	–	1
CHILDREN	–	1	1	–	–	–	–	–	–
CHILLY	–	1	1	–	–	–	–	–	–
CHIPMUNK	–	–	–	1	–	1	–	–	–
CLASSROOM	–	–	–	1	–	1	–	–	–
CLOSET	–	–	–	–	–	–	1	–	1
CLOTHES	–	–	–	2	1	3	1	–	1
COLOR	1	–	1	–	–	–	–	–	–
COME	–	–	–	–	1	1	–	1	1
COME IN	1	–	1	–	–	–	–	–	–
COME TO LIFE	–	–	–	–	–	–	1	–	1
CONFIDENCE	–	–	–	–	–	–	1	1	2
COOKIES	–	1	1	–	–	–	–	–	–
CORN	–	1	1	–	–	–	–	–	–
COVER	–	–	–	1	–	1	–	–	–
CURTAIN RODS	–	1	1	–	–	–	–	–	–
DANCE	–	–	–	–	1	1	–	–	–
DESK	1	–	1	–	–	–	–	–	–
DISTORE	–	–	–	–	–	–	–	1	1
DO AGAIN	–	–	–	–	–	–	1	1	2
DOESNT	–	–	–	1	–	1	–	–	–
DOG	–	–	–	1	–	1	1	–	1
DONT RESTORE	–	1	1	1	–	1	–	–	–
DOOR	4	5	9	–	–	–	1	–	1
DRESS	–	–	–	–	1	1	–	–	–
EAR	–	1	1	–	–	–	–	–	–
EAT	2	–	2	–	–	–	2	–	2
EMPTY	–	–	–	–	–	–	1	1	2
EMTY	–	–	–	–	–	–	2	–	2
ENERGY	–	–	–	–	–	–	1	–	1
ESTORE	–	1	1	–	–	–	–	–	–
FACTORY	–	–	–	–	1	1	–	–	–
FAN	1	–	1	–	1	1	–	–	–
FATHER	–	1	1	–	–	–	–	–	–
FIND	–	–	–	1	–	1	–	–	–
FISH	–	–	–	1	–	1	–	–	–
FIX	–	–	–	1	1	2	2	1	3
FLOOR	2	–	2	–	2	2	–	–	–
FLOOR WAXED	–	1	1	–	–	–	–	–	–
FOOD	18	14	32	10	13	23	6	8	14
FOR	1	–	1	1	–	1	–	–	–
FREEZER	–	–	–	1	–	1	–	–	–
FRESH	1	–	1	–	–	–	–	–	–
FRUIT	–	–	–	–	–	–	1	–	1
FULL	–	–	–	1	–	1	–	–	–
FURNACE	1	–	1	–	–	–	–	–	–
FURNITURE	–	1	1	–	1	1	–	–	–

RESPONSE WORD	1ST M	1ST F	1ST T	3RD M	3RD F	3RD T	5TH M	5TH F	5TH T

65.   RESTORE

RESPONSE WORD	M	F	T	M	F	T	M	F	T
GAIN	–	–	–	–	–	–	1	2	3
GATHER	–	–	–	–	1	1	1	–	1
GATHER UP	–	–	–	–	–	–	–	1	1
GEESORD	–	–	–	1	–	1	–	–	–
GET	–	–	–	2	–	2	–	–	–
GET SOMETHING	–	–	–	1	–	1	–	–	–
GIANT	1	–	1	–	–	–	–	–	–
GIVE	–	–	–	1	1	2	1	1	2
GIVE AWAY	–	–	–	1	–	1	–	–	–
GIVE SOMETHING AWAY	–	–	–	1	–	1	–	–	–
GLASSES	1	–	1	–	–	–	–	–	–
GO IN THE STORE	1	–	1	–	–	–	–	–	–
GO OUT	1	–	1	–	–	–	–	–	–
GO TO STORES	–	1	1	–	–	–	–	–	–
GOING TO	1	1	2	–	–	–	–	–	–
GONE	–	1	1	–	–	–	1	–	1
GOODS	–	–	–	–	–	–	1	–	1
GRASS	–	–	–	–	–	–	1	–	1
GREEN	1	–	1	1	–	1	1	–	1
GROCERIES	3	2	5	–	–	–	1	–	1
GROCERY	–	1	1	–	–	–	–	–	–
GROCERY STORE	–	–	–	–	–	–	–	1	1
GROCERY STORY	–	1	1	–	–	–	–	–	–
HAIR	–	–	–	–	1	1	–	–	–
HAND	–	1	1	–	–	–	–	–	–
HARD	–	–	–	–	–	–	–	1	1
HARVEST	–	–	–	–	1	1	–	1	1
HEALTH	–	–	–	–	–	–	–	2	2
HEALTHY	–	1	1	–	–	–	–	2	2
HELP	–	–	–	–	–	–	–	2	2
HIDE	–	–	–	1	–	1	–	–	–
HILL	–	–	–	–	1	1	–	–	–
HOAR	1	–	1	–	–	–	–	–	–
HOLD	–	–	–	–	–	–	1	1	2
HOME	–	1	1	–	–	–	–	–	–
HORE	1	–	1	–	–	–	–	–	–
HOSPITAL	1	–	1	–	–	–	–	–	–
HOUSE	1	2	3	5	1	6	2	–	2
I	–	1	1	–	1	1	–	–	–
I BOUGHT	–	–	–	–	1	1	–	–	–
ICE CREAM	1	–	1	–	–	–	–	–	–
IN	–	–	–	1	–	1	–	–	–
INDOOR	–	–	–	1	–	1	–	–	–
IT	–	–	–	1	1	2	–	–	–
JAR	–	–	–	–	1	1	–	–	–
JARS	–	–	–	–	1	1	–	–	–
JOHN	1	–	1	–	–	–	–	–	–
JOIN	–	–	–	–	–	–	1	–	1
KEEP	–	1	1	11	7	18	19	13	32
KEEP AWAY	–	–	–	1	–	1	–	1	1
KEEP UP	–	–	–	–	–	–	1	–	1
KEPT	–	–	–	–	1	1	1	–	1
LAWNMOWER	–	–	–	–	1	1	–	–	–
LAY AWAY	–	–	–	–	–	–	1	–	1
LEAVE	–	–	–	1	–	1	1	–	1
LEFT OVER	–	–	–	1	–	1	–	–	–
LEFTOVERS	–	–	–	1	–	1	–	–	–
LIFE	–	–	–	2	–	2	1	1	2
LIGHT	1	–	1	–	1	1	–	–	–
LIKE	1	–	1	–	1	1	–	–	–
LIVE	–	–	–	–	–	–	1	1	2
LOAD	–	–	–	–	–	–	–	1	1
LONG	–	–	–	–	–	–	–	1	1
LONG TIME	–	–	–	–	–	–	1	–	1
LUNCH	–	–	–	–	–	–	–	1	1
MAKE	1	–	1	–	–	–	–	–	–
MAN	–	2	2	–	1	1	–	–	–
MANAGER	–	–	–	1	–	1	–	–	–
MAT	1	–	1	–	–	–	–	–	–
ME	1	–	1	–	–	–	–	–	–
MEAT	–	1	1	–	–	–	–	–	–
MEMORY	–	–	–	–	–	–	–	1	1

RESPONSE WORD	1ST M	F	T	3RD M	F	T	5TH M	F	T

65. RESTORE

RESPONSE WORD	1ST M	F	T	3RD M	F	T	5TH M	F	T
MIGHT BE A STORM AND YOU MIGHT BE OUTSI	–	1	1	–	–	–	–	–	–
MIND	–	–	–	–	–	–	–	1	1
MONEY	–	2	2	–	–	–	–	–	–
MONY	–	–	–	–	–	–	–	1	1
MOON	–	1	1	–	–	–	–	–	–
MORE	5	3	8	–	2	2	1	1	2
MOVE	–	–	–	–	1	1	–	–	–
MOVIE	1	–	1	–	–	–	–	–	–
NEST	–	–	–	–	1	1	–	–	–
NEVER	–	–	–	1	–	1	–	–	–
NEW	–	–	–	–	1	1	–	–	–
NO	–	–	–	1	–	1	–	–	–
NO RESTORE	–	–	–	–	1	1	–	–	–
NORR	–	1	1	–	–	–	–	–	–
NOT	–	–	–	1	–	1	–	–	–
NOT RESTORE	3	–	3	2	1	3	2	–	2
NOT RESTORED	–	–	–	2	–	2	–	–	–
NOT STORE	–	–	–	–	1	1	–	–	–
NOT THERE	–	–	–	1	–	1	–	–	–
NOTHING	–	–	–	–	1	1	–	–	–
NUTS	–	–	–	1	–	1	–	–	–
OLD PICTURES	1	–	1	–	–	–	–	–	–
ON STORE	1	–	1	–	–	–	–	–	–
OUT	–	–	–	–	–	–	–	1	1
OUTSIDE	1	–	1	–	–	–	–	–	–
OVER	–	–	–	–	–	–	–	1	1
OVER AGAIN	–	–	–	–	–	–	1	–	1
PACK	–	–	–	1	–	1	2	1	3
PACKAGE	–	–	–	–	1	1	–	1	1
PACKAGES	1	–	1	–	–	–	–	–	–
PAPER	–	–	–	–	1	1	–	–	–
PAT	–	–	–	–	–	–	–	1	1
PEAR	1	–	1	–	–	–	–	–	–
PECK	–	–	–	–	–	–	1	–	1
PENCIL	–	–	–	1	–	1	–	–	–
PEOPLE	–	1	1	–	–	–	–	–	–
PERSON	–	–	–	–	1	1	–	–	–
PEST	–	1	1	–	–	–	–	–	–
PICTURE	–	–	–	–	1	1	–	–	–
PLACE	–	1	1	1	–	1	–	–	–
PLAYPEN	–	–	–	–	1	1	–	–	–
POCKET	–	–	–	1	–	1	–	–	–
POCKET-BOOK	1	–	1	–	–	–	–	–	–
POUR	–	1	1	–	–	–	–	–	–
PRESERVE	–	–	–	–	–	–	–	2	2
PULL AWAY	–	–	–	–	1	1	–	–	–
PUT	1	–	1	1	2	3	2	–	2
PUT AWAY	–	–	–	1	4	5	8	13	21
PUT BACK	–	–	–	1	1	2	1	–	1
PUT BACK AGAIN	–	–	–	–	–	–	1	–	1
PUT INTO	–	–	–	–	–	–	–	1	1
PUT STUFF IN A STORING THING	–	–	–	1	–	1	–	–	–
RAIN	1	–	1	–	–	–	–	–	–
RAKE	1	–	1	–	–	–	–	–	–
RE-DO	–	–	–	–	–	–	–	1	1
REACTIVATE	–	–	–	–	–	–	1	–	1
READ	1	1	2	–	–	–	–	–	–
READY	–	–	–	–	–	–	–	1	1
REBUILD	–	–	–	–	–	–	2	–	2
RECEIVE	–	–	–	–	1	1	–	–	–
RECONSTRUCT	–	–	–	–	–	–	1	–	1
RECREATION	–	–	–	–	–	–	–	1	1
REFRESH	–	–	–	–	–	–	–	1	1
REFRIGERATOR	1	–	1	–	–	–	–	–	–
REGAIN	–	–	–	1	1	2	–	–	–
RELOAD	–	–	–	–	–	–	1	–	1
REMAIN	–	–	–	–	–	–	–	1	1
REMAKE	–	–	–	–	–	–	1	–	1
REMEMBER	–	–	–	1	–	1	–	–	–
REMORE	1	–	1	–	–	–	–	–	–

RESPONSE WORD	1ST M	F	T	3RD M	F	T	5TH M	F	T
				65.	RESTORE				
REMOVE	–	–	–	–	–	–	1	–	1
RENEW	–	–	–	–	–	–	–	1	1
REPAIR	–	–	–	2	1	3	1	–	1
REPAIRED	–	–	–	–	1	1	–	–	–
REPEAT	–	–	–	–	–	–	1	–	1
REPLACE	–	–	–	1	–	1	1	1	2
REPORE	1	–	1	–	–	–	–	–	–
REST	–	–	–	–	–	–	1	–	1
RESTORED	–	–	–	–	–	–	1	–	1
RESTORES	–	1	1	–	–	–	–	–	–
RICKY	1	–	1	–	–	–	–	–	–
ROOM	–	–	–	1	–	1	–	–	–
ROUGHNESS	1	–	1	–	–	–	–	–	–
SAND	–	–	–	–	1	1	–	–	–
SAVE	–	–	–	2	2	4	6	5	11
SAW	–	1	1	–	1	1	–	–	–
SCHOOL	1	–	1	–	–	–	–	–	–
SEAL	–	–	–	–	–	–	1	–	1
SELL	1	2	3	–	–	–	–	–	–
SELL SOME FOOD	–	1	1	–	–	–	–	–	–
SELL STORE	–	–	–	–	–	–	–	1	1
SEND	–	–	–	1	–	1	–	–	–
SHACK	–	–	–	–	1	1	–	–	–
SHARE	–	–	–	1	–	1	–	–	–
SHELF	–	–	–	–	–	–	1	–	1
SHELTER	–	–	–	1	–	1	–	–	–
SHIRT	2	–	2	–	–	–	–	–	–
SHOES	–	1	1	–	–	–	–	–	–
SHOP	1	1	2	–	1	1	–	–	–
SILO	1	–	1	–	–	–	–	–	–
SINK	1	–	1	–	–	–	–	–	–
SLOPPY	–	–	–	1	–	1	–	–	–
SNEEZE	–	1	1	–	–	–	–	–	–
SNORE	1	–	1	–	–	–	–	–	–
SOARING	1	–	1	–	–	–	–	–	–
SODA	–	1	1	–	–	–	–	–	–
SOLDIERS	–	1	1	–	–	–	–	–	–
SOMETHING	–	–	–	1	1	2	–	1	1
STAR	–	1	1	1	–	1	–	–	–
STARE	–	–	–	–	–	–	1	–	1
STASH AWAY	–	–	–	–	1	1	–	–	–
STEWART	1	–	1	–	–	–	–	–	–
STOCK	–	1	1	1	–	1	3	4	7
STOP	–	–	–	–	–	–	1	–	1
STORAGE	–	1	1	–	5	5	1	2	3
STORAGE ROOM	–	–	–	–	1	1	–	1	1
STORE	9	24	33	15	23	38	12	16	28
STORE FOOD	–	1	1	–	–	–	–	–	–
STORE FURNITURE	1	–	1	–	–	–	–	–	–
STORE MAN	–	1	1	–	–	–	–	–	–
STORE OVER AGAIN	–	–	–	–	–	–	–	1	1
STORE SOME FOOD	–	1	1	–	–	–	–	–	–
STORE SOMETHING	–	1	1	–	–	–	–	–	–
STORE THAT YOU BUY FOOD IN	1	–	1	–	–	–	–	–	–
STORE THINGS	–	–	–	1	–	1	–	–	–
STORED	–	–	–	1	–	1	1	1	2
STOREHOUSE	–	–	–	1	–	1	–	–	–
STOREROOM	–	–	–	1	–	1	–	–	–
STORES	–	–	–	–	1	1	–	–	–
STORING	–	–	–	–	–	–	–	2	2
STORM	1	1	2	2	–	2	–	–	–
STORY	–	1	1	–	2	2	–	–	–
STRENGTH	–	–	–	1	–	1	–	–	–
SUGAR	–	–	–	1	–	1	–	–	–
SUPPLY	–	–	–	–	–	–	1	–	1
TABLE	1	–	1	–	–	–	–	1	1
TAKE	–	2	2	–	–	–	–	2	2
TAKE OUT	–	–	–	–	2	2	–	1	1
TAKE TO OTHER PLACES	–	–	–	–	–	–	1	–	1
TALK	–	–	–	1	–	1	–	–	–
TELEVISION	–	1	1	–	–	–	–	–	–

RESPONSE WORD	1ST M	F	T	3RD M	F	T	5TH M	F	T

65. RESTORE

RESPONSE WORD	1ST M	F	T	3RD M	F	T	5TH M	F	T
TEN	–	1	1	–	–	–	–	–	–
TESTING	1	–	–	–	–	–	1	–	1
THAT	1	–	1	–	–	–	–	–	–
THE	–	–	–	1	–	1	–	–	–
THE HOUSE	–	–	–	1	–	1	–	–	–
THE N AND W	–	–	–	1	–	1	–	–	–
THE STORE	–	–	–	1	–	1	–	–	–
THE TABLE	–	1	1	–	–	–	–	–	–
THINGS	1	–	1	2	2	4	–	–	–
THINK	–	–	–	–	–	–	–	2	2
THROW	–	–	–	–	1	1	–	–	–
THROW AWAY FOOD	1	–	1	–	–	–	–	–	–
THROW THAT MEAT AWAY CAUSE ITS POISON	–	1	1	–	–	–	–	–	–
TO	–	–	–	–	1	1	–	–	–
TO BUILD AGAIN	–	–	–	–	–	–	1	–	1
TO KEEP	–	–	–	–	–	–	1	1	2
TO PUT SOMETHING BACK	–	–	–	–	–	–	–	1	1
TO REPLACE THINGS	–	–	–	–	–	–	–	1	1
TO TAKE	–	–	–	–	–	–	1	–	1
TODAY	–	–	–	–	1	1	–	–	–
TOM	1	–	1	–	–	–	–	–	–
TOWERS	1	–	1	–	–	–	–	–	–
TOY	–	–	–	1	–	1	–	–	–
TOY STORE	1	–	1	–	–	–	–	–	–
TOYS	–	2	2	–	–	–	–	–	–
TREE	–	–	–	1	–	1	–	–	–
TRUCK	1	–	1	–	–	–	–	–	–
TRUNK	–	–	–	–	–	–	–	1	1
UNDER	–	–	–	1	1	2	–	–	–
UNDERSTORE	–	–	–	–	–	–	1	–	1
UNPACK	–	1	1	–	–	–	–	–	–
UNRESTORE	–	–	–	–	2	2	1	–	1
UNRESTORED	–	–	–	1	–	1	–	–	–
UNSTORE	–	–	–	2	2	4	1	4	5
UNSTORED	–	–	–	2	–	2	–	–	–
USE	–	–	–	–	1	1	–	–	–
VEGETABLES	1	–	1	–	–	–	–	–	–
WATCH	1	1	2	1	–	1	–	–	–
WE FREE	–	–	–	1	–	1	–	–	–
WEAK	1	–	1	–	–	–	1	–	1
WHAT YOU GET FOOD OUT	1	–	1	–	–	–	–	–	–
WHEN YOU RESTORE SOMETHING	1	–	1	–	–	–	–	–	–
WHENEVER YOUR MOTHER CALLS SOMEONE TO G	–	1	1	–	–	–	–	–	–
WHERE WE STORE FOOD FOR THE WINTER	–	1	1	–	–	–	–	–	–
WHERE YOU GET ALL THE FOOD THAT YOU BUY	1	–	1	–	–	–	–	–	–
WHITE	1	–	1	–	–	–	–	–	–
WILDLIFE	–	–	–	–	–	–	1	–	1
WINDOW	1	–	1	–	–	–	–	–	–
WINE	–	–	–	–	–	–	–	1	1
WINTER	–	1	1	1	–	1	–	–	–
WORN OUT	1	–	1	–	–	–	–	–	–
WREATH	–	–	–	–	1	1	–	–	–
YARD	–	1	1	–	–	–	–	–	–
YES	–	–	–	–	1	1	–	–	–
YOU	–	1	1	–	–	–	–	–	–
YOU MAKE ME NERVOUS	1	–	1	–	–	–	–	–	–

RESPONSE WORD	1ST M	F	T	3RD M	F	T	5TH M	F	T

66.   RIVER

RESPONSE WORD	1ST M	F	T	3RD M	F	T	5TH M	F	T
A STREAM	–	–	–	–	–	–	–	1	1
AWAY	–	1	1	–	–	–	–	–	–
BABY	1	–	1	–	–	–	–	–	–
BANK	–	–	–	2	2	4	2	2	4
BAY	1	1	2	1	3	4	9	7	16
BEACH	–	1	1	–	–	–	–	1	1
BEAR CREEK	–	–	–	1	–	1	–	–	–
BED	–	–	–	–	–	–	1	1	2
BLANKET	1	–	1	–	–	–	–	–	–
BLUE	3	–	3	2	–	2	1	1	2
BOAT	10	10	20	5	2	7	2	3	5
BOATS	4	–	4	–	–	–	–	–	–
BODY OF WATER	–	–	–	–	–	–	3	–	3
BOOK	1	–	1	–	–	–	–	–	–
BOOKS	–	1	1	–	–	–	–	–	–
BOW	–	1	1	–	–	–	–	–	–
BRIDGE	2	–	2	1	1	2	–	–	–
BROOK	–	–	–	–	1	1	1	2	3
CAMEL	1	–	1	–	–	–	–	–	–
CAN	–	1	1	–	–	–	–	–	–
CAN BE A FAST, FLOWING STREAM	–	–	–	–	–	–	–	1	1
CAR	1	2	3	–	–	–	–	–	–
CASTLE	1	–	1	–	–	–	–	–	–
CAT	1	–	1	–	–	–	–	–	–
CATCH	1	–	1	–	–	–	–	–	–
CHAIR	–	1	1	–	–	–	–	–	–
CHIMNEY	–	1	1	–	–	–	–	–	–
CITY	–	–	–	–	2	2	–	–	–
CIVER	–	1	1	–	–	–	–	–	–
CREDIT	–	–	–	–	–	–	1	–	1
CREEK	–	2	2	–	–	–	1	–	1
CRIVER	–	1	1	–	–	–	–	–	–
DAM	1	–	1	–	1	1	–	3	3
DARK	–	1	1	–	–	–	–	–	–
DEEP	1	–	1	1	1	2	1	1	2
DEER	–	2	2	–	–	–	–	–	–
DESERT	–	–	–	–	1	1	–	–	–
DIBBER	–	1	1	–	–	–	–	–	–
DIVER	1	1	2	–	–	–	–	–	–
DOLL	–	–	–	–	1	1	–	–	–
DONT FALL	–	1	1	–	–	–	–	–	–
DOWN	1	–	1	–	–	–	–	–	–
DROWN	1	–	1	–	–	–	–	–	–
DRY	–	–	–	–	–	–	1	–	1
EVER	–	1	1	–	–	–	–	–	–
FALL	–	2	2	1	–	1	1	–	1
FIELD	–	1	1	–	–	–	–	–	–
FIELDS	–	1	1	–	–	–	–	–	–
FISH	6	2	8	2	1	3	1	–	1
FISH SWIM IN THE RIVER	–	1	1	–	–	–	–	–	–
FISHES SWIM IN THE RIVER	–	1	1	–	–	–	–	–	–
FLOAT	2	–	2	1	–	1	–	–	–
FLOATING	1	–	1	–	–	–	–	–	–
FLOOR	1	–	1	–	–	–	–	–	–
FLOW	–	1	1	1	–	1	3	3	6
GHOST	1	–	1	–	–	–	–	–	–
GIVER	3	–	3	–	–	–	–	–	–
GLASSES	–	1	1	–	–	–	–	–	–
GO	–	–	–	1	–	1	–	–	–
GO OVER	–	1	1	–	–	–	–	–	–
GOING	1	–	1	–	–	–	–	–	–
GOTS A WATER IN IT	1	–	1	–	–	–	–	–	–
GREEN	–	1	1	–	–	–	–	–	–
HAIR	–	–	–	–	1	1	–	–	–
HAT	1	–	1	–	–	–	–	–	–
HIVER	1	–	1	–	–	–	–	–	–
HOUSE	–	1	1	–	–	–	1	–	1
ICE	1	–	1	–	–	–	1	–	1
INK	–	1	1	–	–	–	–	–	–
IS	1	–	1	–	–	–	–	–	–
IS GOING DOWN THE STREAM	1	–	1	–	–	–	–	–	–

66. RIVER

RESPONSE WORD	1ST M	1ST F	1ST T	3RD M	3RD F	3RD T	5TH M	5TH F	5TH T
JEEP	–	–	–	–	–	–	1	–	1
JUMP	1	–	1	–	–	–	–	–	–
KILL	–	1	1	–	–	–	–	–	–
KIVER	1	–	1	–	–	–	–	–	–
LAKE	9	7	16	13	27	40	14	22	36
LAND	1	–	1	3	–	3	2	–	2
LARGE STREAM	–	–	–	–	–	–	1	–	1
LIGHT	1	–	1	–	–	–	–	1	1
LIVER	2	1	3	–	–	–	–	–	–
LONG	–	1	1	–	–	–	–	–	–
LOOK AT THAT BOAT IN THE RIVER.	1	–	1	–	–	–	–	–	–
MEADOW	–	–	–	–	1	1	–	–	–
MEAT	–	–	–	–	–	–	1	–	1
MIGHT BE BREAKING	–	1	1	–	–	–	–	–	–
MISSISSIPPI	–	–	–	–	–	–	1	1	2
MIVER	–	–	–	–	1	1	–	–	–
MIX	–	–	–	1	–	1	–	–	–
MOON	–	1	1	–	–	–	–	–	–
MOSTLY	–	–	–	–	1	1	–	–	–
MOUNTAINS	–	–	–	1	–	1	–	–	–
NEVER	1	–	1	–	–	–	–	–	–
NIGHT	–	1	1	–	–	–	–	–	–
NILE	–	–	–	1	–	1	1	1	2
OCEAN	3	11	14	16	17	33	7	15	22
OUT	1	–	1	–	–	–	–	–	–
OVER	–	1	1	1	1	2	–	–	–
PAINT	1	–	1	–	–	–	–	–	–
PALM	–	–	–	–	1	1	–	–	–
PAPER	1	–	1	–	–	–	–	–	–
PIVER	1	–	1	–	–	–	–	–	–
POCKETBOOK	1	–	1	–	–	–	–	–	–
POND	1	4	5	3	3	6	–	–	–
PUDDLE	–	–	–	1	–	1	–	–	–
PULL	–	–	–	–	1	1	–	–	–
QUIVER	–	–	–	–	–	–	–	1	1
RAN	1	–	1	–	–	–	–	–	–
RED	1	–	1	–	1	1	–	–	–
RIB	–	1	1	–	–	–	–	–	–
RIBBON	–	1	1	–	–	–	–	–	–
RIDE	1	1	2	–	–	–	–	–	–
RIVER	–	–	–	–	–	–	1	–	1
ROAD	1	–	1	–	–	–	–	–	–
ROCK	–	–	–	–	–	–	–	1	1
ROOM	1	–	1	–	–	–	–	–	–
ROW	–	2	2	–	–	–	–	–	–
SAIL	1	–	1	–	–	–	–	–	–
SAILBOAT	–	1	1	–	–	–	–	–	–
SEA	3	6	9	3	8	11	5	5	10
SHEET	–	1	1	–	–	–	–	–	–
SHIP	1	–	1	–	–	–	–	–	–
SHOES	–	–	–	1	–	1	–	–	–
SHORE	–	1	1	–	–	–	1	1	2
SIDE	–	–	–	–	2	2	–	–	–
SILVER	–	–	–	1	–	1	–	–	–
SIT	–	–	–	–	–	–	1	–	1
SIVER	1	–	1	1	–	1	–	–	–
SNIVER	1	–	1	–	–	–	–	–	–
SPIGOT	–	1	1	–	–	–	–	–	–
STEAM	–	–	–	1	–	1	1	1	2
STONE	1	–	1	–	–	–	–	–	–
STONES	–	1	1	–	–	–	–	–	–
STOP	1	–	1	–	–	–	–	–	–
STREAM	13	6	19	34	27	61	37	35	72
STREAMING	1	–	1	–	–	–	–	–	–
STREM	–	–	–	–	–	–	1	–	1
SUN	–	–	–	–	–	–	1	–	1
SWAMP	–	–	–	–	–	–	–	1	1
SWAN	–	1	1	–	–	–	–	–	–
SWIM	3	4	7	3	2	5	2	1	3
SWIMMING	–	1	1	–	1	1	–	–	–
TABLE	1	–	1	–	–	–	–	–	–

RESPONSE WORD	1ST M	F	T	3RD M	F	T	5TH M	F	T

66. RIVER

RESPONSE WORD	1ST M	F	T	3RD M	F	T	5TH M	F	T
TAKE SWIM IN IT	1	–	1	–	–	–	–	–	–
THROUGH	2	–	2	–	–	–	–	–	–
TO SWIM	–	1	1	–	–	–	–	1	1
VALLEY	–	1	1	1	1	2	–	1	1
WALK	–	–	–	1	–	1	–	–	–
WALLS	–	1	1	–	–	–	–	–	–
WANT	–	1	1	–	–	–	–	–	–
WATER	21	31	52	34	27	61	31	26	57
WATERFALL	2	–	2	–	–	–	–	–	–
WAVE	–	1	1	1	–	1	–	–	–
WHEN YOURE GOING SWIMMING	1	–	1	–	–	–	–	–	–
WIDE	–	–	–	–	–	–	1	–	1
WIND	–	1	1	–	–	–	–	–	–
WOOD	1	–	1	1	1	2	–	–	–
WOODS	–	–	–	–	–	–	–	1	1
YOU COULD WALK ON	–	1	1	–	–	–	–	–	–

67. ROUGH

RESPONSE WORD	1ST M	F	T	3RD M	F	T	5TH M	F	T
AND READY	1	1	2	–	–	–	–	–	–
ANIMAL COOKIE	–	1	1	–	–	–	–	–	–
ANIMLE	–	–	–	–	–	–	–	1	1
AWFUL	–	–	–	–	–	–	–	1	1
BAD	–	2	2	–	3	3	1	1	2
BAKING SODA	–	–	–	1	–	1	–	–	–
BARE	–	–	–	–	1	1	–	–	–
BARK	1	4	5	–	1	1	–	–	–
BE CAREFUL	1	–	1	–	–	–	–	–	–
BEAR	–	1	1	–	–	–	–	–	–
BEAT	–	–	–	–	1	1	–	–	–
BED	–	–	–	–	1	1	–	–	–
BIRD	–	1	1	–	–	–	–	–	–
BITE	–	–	–	1	–	1	–	–	–
BLACK	1	–	1	–	–	–	–	–	–
BLUE	–	1	1	–	–	–	–	–	–
BOARD	–	1	1	–	–	–	–	–	–
BOBBY	–	1	1	–	–	–	–	–	–
BOUGH	–	1	1	–	–	–	–	–	–
BOW-WOW	–	1	1	–	–	–	–	–	–
BOX	1	–	1	–	–	–	–	–	–
BOY	1	2	3	–	1	1	–	–	–
BOYS	1	–	1	–	–	–	–	–	–
BRAIL	–	–	–	–	–	–	–	1	1
BRUSH	–	1	1	–	–	–	–	–	–
BRUTE	–	–	–	–	–	–	1	–	1
BUFF	2	1	3	–	–	–	–	–	–
BUFFALO	–	1	1	–	–	–	–	–	–
BUG	–	–	–	–	–	–	–	1	1
BUMPPITY	–	–	–	–	–	–	1	1	1
BUMPY	–	–	–	6	2	8	3	3	6
CAGE	–	–	–	–	–	–	–	1	1
CAKE	–	1	1	–	–	–	–	–	–
CALM	1	1	2	–	–	–	–	–	–
CAN	–	2	2	–	–	–	–	–	–
CAT	–	1	1	–	–	–	–	–	–
CEMENT	1	–	1	–	–	–	–	–	–
CHILD	–	1	1	–	–	–	–	–	–
CLIFT	–	–	–	–	–	–	1	–	1
COAL	–	–	–	1	–	1	–	–	–
COARSE	–	–	–	–	–	–	–	1	1
COLD	–	–	–	–	–	–	1	–	1
COMB	–	–	–	–	1	1	–	–	–
COUGH	1	–	1	–	–	–	–	–	–
COW	1	–	1	1	–	1	–	–	–
CRUFF	–	–	–	1	–	1	–	–	–
CUFF	1	1	2	–	1	1	–	–	–
DARK	–	–	–	–	1	1	–	–	–
DAY	–	1	1	–	–	–	–	–	–
DEER	–	1	1	–	–	–	–	–	–
DINGY	–	–	–	–	1	1	–	–	–

RESPONSE WORD	1ST M	F	T	3RD M	F	T	5TH M	F	T

67. ROUGH

RESPONSE WORD	1ST M	F	T	3RD M	F	T	5TH M	F	T
DIRT	–	1	1	–	–	–	–	–	–
DIRT ROAD	1	–	1	–	–	–	–	–	–
DOG	11	13	24	2	1	3	2	1	3
DOG BARK	1	–	1	–	–	–	–	–	–
DONT FIGHT	–	1	1	–	–	–	–	–	–
DONT GET ROUGH WITH A DOG BECAUSE	–	1	1	–	–	–	–	–	–
DONT PLAY ROUGH	1	1	2	–	–	–	–	–	–
DULL	–	1	1	–	–	–	–	–	–
EASIER	–	–	–	–	–	–	–	1	1
EASY	4	3	7	4	1	5	2	3	5
EDGE	–	–	–	–	–	–	1	–	1
FALL	1	–	1	–	–	–	–	–	–
FAN	1	–	1	–	–	–	–	–	–
FAST	1	1	2	–	–	–	–	–	–
FATHER	1	1	2	–	–	–	–	–	–
FIGHT	7	8	15	8	2	10	2	1	3
FIGHT ROUGH	1	–	1	–	–	–	–	–	–
FIGHTER	1	–	1	–	–	–	–	–	–
FIGHTING	2	1	3	–	–	–	–	–	–
FINGERNAIL	–	1	1	–	–	–	–	–	–
FIVE	1	–	1	–	–	–	–	–	–
FLAT	–	–	–	1	–	1	1	–	1
FLOUR	–	–	–	–	–	–	1	–	1
FOOD	–	–	–	–	–	–	1	–	1
FOOTBALL	1	1	2	1	–	1	–	1	1
FOOTBALL GAME	1	–	1	–	–	–	–	–	–
FUFF	–	1	1	–	–	–	–	–	–
FUN	–	–	–	–	1	1	–	–	–
GARBAGE CAN	–	1	1	–	–	–	–	–	–
GENTLE	1	–	1	4	5	9	2	2	4
GENTLY	–	–	–	2	2	4	–	–	–
GLASS	1	–	1	–	–	–	–	–	–
GO	1	1	2	–	–	–	–	–	–
GOOD	–	1	1	–	–	–	–	–	–
GRASS	–	1	1	–	–	–	1	–	1
GROUND	–	1	1	–	–	–	–	–	–
GROWL	–	–	–	–	1	1	–	–	–
GRUFF	–	–	–	–	–	–	–	1	1
HAND	1	–	1	–	–	–	–	–	–
HANDS	–	1	1	–	–	–	–	–	–
HAPPY	1	–	1	–	–	–	–	–	–
HARD	4	7	11	15	29	44	20	39	59
HEAVY	–	–	–	–	1	1	–	–	–
HELP	–	1	1	–	–	–	–	–	–
HEND	–	–	–	–	–	–	1	–	1
HILL	–	–	–	1	–	1	1	–	1
HILLS	1	–	1	–	–	–	1	–	1
HILLY	–	–	–	–	–	–	1	–	1
HIT	2	–	2	–	–	–	–	–	–
HOLDING ON	–	1	1	–	–	–	–	–	–
HORSE	1	–	1	–	–	–	–	–	–
HOUGH	1	–	1	–	–	–	–	–	–
HOUSE	3	–	3	–	–	–	–	–	–
HURT	2	–	2	1	3	4	–	–	–
HURTS	1	–	1	–	–	–	–	1	1
ITCHY	–	–	–	–	–	–	–	1	1
JAGGED	–	–	–	–	–	–	1	–	1
JUMP	1	–	1	–	–	–	–	–	–
KINCE	1	–	1	–	–	–	–	–	–
KIND	–	–	–	–	1	1	–	–	–
LIGHT	–	–	–	1	–	1	–	–	–
LONG	–	–	–	1	–	1	–	–	–
LOUD	–	–	–	–	1	1	–	–	–
LUMPY	–	–	–	–	1	1	–	–	–
MAD	–	–	–	2	–	2	–	–	–
MAN	1	–	1	–	–	–	–	–	–
MEAN	–	1	1	1	–	1	2	–	2
MINE	1	–	1	–	–	–	–	–	–
MOON	–	–	–	–	–	–	1	–	1
MOUNTAIN	–	–	–	–	–	–	2	–	2
MRS	–	–	–	1	–	1	–	–	–

RESPONSE WORD	1ST M	F	T	3RD M	F	T	5TH M	F	T

67. ROUGH

RESPONSE WORD	1ST M	F	T	3RD M	F	T	5TH M	F	T
MUFF	1	–	1	1	–	1	–	–	–
MUSCLES	1	–	1	–	–	–	–	–	–
MY BROTHER IS ROUGH	–	1	1	–	–	–	–	–	–
NAUGHTY	1	–	1	–	–	–	–	–	–
NEAT	–	–	–	1	–	1	–	–	–
NICE	–	2	2	–	2	2	–	–	–
NOT	–	2	2	–	–	–	–	–	–
NOT ROUGH	2	1	3	3	2	5	–	–	–
NOT SMOOTH	–	–	–	–	–	–	4	2	6
NOT SOFT	–	–	–	1	–	1	–	2	2
NOUGH	–	1	1	1	–	1	–	–	–
OCEAN	–	1	1	1	–	1	–	–	–
ON	1	–	1	–	–	–	–	–	–
ON A CAR	–	1	1	–	–	–	–	–	–
ON SOMEBODY	–	1	1	–	–	–	–	–	–
ORE	–	–	–	–	–	–	1	–	1
PAINT	–	1	1	–	1	1	–	–	–
PAPER	–	1	1	–	–	–	1	–	1
PIECE	1	–	1	–	–	–	–	–	–
PLAY	1	3	4	–	5	5	–	–	–
PLAY ROUGH	1	–	1	–	–	–	–	–	–
PLAYING	–	1	1	–	–	–	–	–	–
PLEASANT	1	–	1	–	–	–	–	–	–
POLE	1	–	1	–	–	–	–	–	–
POST	1	–	1	–	–	–	–	–	–
POWDER	–	1	1	–	–	–	–	–	–
PRUFF	–	1	1	–	–	–	–	–	–
PUFF	1	–	1	–	–	–	–	–	–
PUNCH YOU IN THE NOSE	1	–	1	–	–	–	–	–	–
RACCOON	–	–	–	–	–	–	1	–	1
RAN	–	–	–	1	–	1	–	–	–
RASSLE	–	1	1	–	–	–	–	–	–
READY	4	–	4	2	1	3	1	–	1
REAL TOUGH	–	–	–	–	–	–	–	1	1
RED	–	–	–	–	1	1	–	–	–
RESTLESS	–	–	–	–	1	1	–	–	–
RIDE	1	–	1	–	–	–	–	–	–
RIGHT	1	–	1	–	–	–	–	–	–
ROAD	–	–	–	1	–	1	1	2	3
ROCK	–	–	–	1	–	1	1	–	1
ROCKS	1	2	3	–	–	–	–	–	–
ROCKY	–	–	–	1	–	1	–	–	–
ROUGH	–	–	–	–	–	–	1	–	1
ROUGHLY	–	1	1	–	–	–	–	–	–
ROUGHTEN	–	–	–	–	1	1	–	–	–
ROUTE	–	–	–	–	–	–	1	–	1
RUFF	–	–	–	–	–	–	1	–	1
RUFFLE	–	1	1	–	–	–	–	–	–
RUG	–	1	1	–	–	–	–	–	–
RUGGED	–	–	–	–	–	–	2	–	2
RUN	1	2	3	–	1	1	–	–	–
SAD	–	–	–	–	1	1	–	–	–
SCRATCH	–	1	1	–	–	–	–	–	–
SCRATCHY	–	–	–	–	–	–	1	–	1
SCUSS	–	–	–	1	–	1	–	–	–
SHARP	–	–	–	–	–	–	–	1	1
SHORT	–	–	–	–	–	–	1	–	1
SIDEWALK	1	–	1	–	–	–	–	–	–
SIT DOWN	–	1	1	–	–	–	–	–	–
SKIN	–	1	1	–	–	–	–	–	–
SMOOTH	3	6	9	18	15	33	38	37	75
SMOTH	–	–	–	–	–	–	1	–	1
SNUFF	1	–	1	–	–	–	–	–	–
SOFT	5	5	10	22	26	48	14	18	32
SOFTER	1	–	1	–	–	–	–	–	–
SOLVE	–	1	1	–	–	–	–	–	–
SOMEBODY ROUGH	–	1	1	–	–	–	–	–	–
SOMETHING IS ROUGH	–	1	1	–	–	–	–	–	–
SOUGH	1	–	1	–	–	–	–	–	–
STEAL	1	–	1	–	–	–	–	–	–
STEEL	–	–	–	1	–	1	–	–	–
STICK	1	–	1	–	–	–	–	–	–

RESPONSE WORD	1ST			3RD			5TH		
	M	F	T	M	F	T	M	F	T

67.   ROUGH

RESPONSE WORD	M	F	T	M	F	T	M	F	T
STILL	-	-	-	-	1	1	-	-	-
STONE	-	1	1	1	-	1	-	-	-
STONY	-	-	-	-	-	-	1	-	1
STOP	1	-	1	-	-	-	-	-	-
STRAIGHT	-	-	-	-	-	-	-	1	1
STRONG	-	-	-	1	-	1	1	3	4
STUFF	-	-	-	1	-	1	-	-	-
SWEATER	1	1	2	-	-	-	-	-	-
TABLE	1	-	1	-	-	-	-	-	-
TANGLE	-	1	1	-	-	-	-	-	-
TENDER	-	-	-	-	1	1	-	-	-
TERRIBLE	-	-	-	-	1	1	-	-	-
THAT IS TOO ROUGH	1	-	1	-	1	1	-	-	-
THIN	-	-	-	-	1	1	-	-	-
THOUGHT	-	-	1	-	-	-	1	-	1
TOO ROUGH	1	-	1	-	-	-	-	-	-
TOUGH	11	7	18	17	7	24	10	9	19
TRUCK	1	-	1	-	-	-	-	-	-
TUMBLE	-	-	-	1	-	1	1	-	1
TURN	-	-	-	-	1	1	-	-	-
UNCOMFORTABLE	-	-	-	-	-	-	1	-	1
UNSMOOTH	-	-	-	-	-	-	-	2	2
WAGON	1	-	1	-	-	-	-	-	-
WALL	-	2	2	1	-	1	-	-	-
WATER	-	2	2	1	2	3	1	-	1
WAVES	-	-	-	2	-	2	-	-	-
WAY	-	-	-	-	1	1	-	-	-
WE REALLY GET ROUGH	-	1	1	-	-	-	-	-	-
WEAK	1	-	1	-	-	-	1	-	1
WEEK	-	-	-	-	-	-	1	-	1
WHEN YOURE ROUGHING SOMETHING.	1	-	1	-	-	-	-	-	-
WHERE	-	-	-	-	1	1	-	-	-
WHILE	-	-	-	-	-	-	1	-	1
WHY	1	-	1	-	-	-	-	-	-
WILD	-	-	-	-	3	3	-	-	-
WILL	-	-	-	1	-	1	-	-	-
WIND	1	-	1	-	-	-	-	-	-
WINDOW	-	1	1	-	-	-	-	-	-
WOLF	1	-	1	-	-	-	-	-	-
WOMAN	1	-	1	-	-	-	-	-	-
WOOD	-	-	-	-	-	-	1	-	1
WOOL	1	-	1	-	-	-	-	-	-
WORK	2	-	2	-	-	-	-	-	-
WRESTLE	1	-	1	2	1	3	-	-	-
YES	-	-	-	1	-	1	-	-	-
YOU	-	-	-	1	1	2	-	-	-
YOU FIGHT ROUGH	1	-	1	-	-	-	-	-	-
YOU TOO ROUGH HITTING ME	1	-	1	-	-	-	-	-	-
YOURE TOO ROUGH	-	1	1	-	-	-	-	-	-
66	-	-	-	-	-	-	1	-	1

68.   RUN

RESPONSE WORD	M	F	T	M	F	T	M	F	T
A MOVEMENT	-	-	-	-	-	-	1	-	1
ACROSS	-	-	-	-	-	-	1	-	1
ACTION	-	-	-	1	-	1	-	2	2
AIRPLANE	1	-	1	-	-	-	-	-	-
AND PLAY	3	-	3	-	-	-	-	-	-
APPLE	-	-	-	-	-	-	-	1	1
AWAY	1	2	3	-	1	1	-	1	1
BABY	1	-	1	-	-	-	-	-	-
BASEBALL	1	-	1	-	-	-	-	-	-
BICYCLE	1	-	1	-	-	-	-	-	-
BIRD	-	1	1	-	-	-	-	-	-
BLOCK	1	-	1	-	-	-	-	-	-
BOY	2	1	3	-	1	1	-	1	1
BOYS RUN	1	1	2	-	-	-	-	-	-
BREATH	-	1	1	-	-	-	-	-	-
BUD	-	-	-	-	1	1	-	-	-
BUN	3	2	5	-	1	1	-	-	-

RESPONSE WORD	1ST M	F	T	3RD M	F	T	5TH M	F	T

68.   RUN

RESPONSE WORD	M	F	T	M	F	T	M	F	T
CAN	1	–	1	–	1	1	–	–	–
CAR	1	1	2	–	1	1	–	–	–
CAT	3	–	3	–	–	–	1	–	1
CATCH	1	1	2	–	–	–	–	–	–
CHAIRS	1	–	1	–	–	–	–	–	–
CHILDREN	–	1	1	–	–	–	–	–	–
COME	–	7	7	–	–	–	–	–	–
COW	1	–	1	–	–	–	–	–	–
CUN	–	1	1	–	–	–	–	–	–
DESK	–	–	–	–	1	1	–	–	–
DICK	–	1	1	–	–	–	–	–	–
DOG	1	–	1	–	–	–	–	–	–
DONT RUN	1	–	1	–	–	–	–	–	–
DOOR	1	–	1	–	–	–	–	–	–
DOWN	1	–	1	–	–	–	1	–	1
EXERCISE	–	–	–	1	–	1	–	2	2
FALL	4	1	5	1	–	1	–	–	–
FAST	21	25	46	33	27	60	32	35	67
FAST RACE	–	–	–	–	–	–	–	1	1
FAST WALK	–	–	–	–	–	–	1	–	1
FASTER	–	–	–	–	1	1	–	–	–
FASTER SPEED THAN WALK	–	–	–	–	1	1	–	1	1
FEET	–	–	–	–	1	1	1	1	2
FOOTBALL	–	–	–	–	–	–	–	1	1
FOR	1	–	1	–	–	–	–	–	–
FUL	–	–	–	–	–	–	1	–	1
FUN	6	2	8	1	4	5	2	–	2
GALLOP	–	1	1	–	–	–	2	–	2
GENTLY	–	1	1	–	–	–	–	–	–
GET	1	1	2	–	–	–	–	–	–
GO	2	2	4	1	1	2	3	2	5
GO FAST	1	–	1	–	–	–	–	–	–
GO RUN	–	1	1	–	–	–	–	–	–
GOING	–	–	–	–	–	–	1	–	1
GONE	1	–	1	–	–	–	–	–	–
GOOD	1	–	1	–	–	–	–	–	–
GRASS	–	1	1	–	–	–	–	–	–
GRUNT	–	1	1	–	–	–	–	–	–
GUN	2	1	3	–	1	1	–	–	–
HELP	–	1	1	–	–	–	–	–	–
HERE	1	–	1	–	–	–	–	–	–
HOLE	1	–	1	–	–	–	–	–	–
HOME	2	–	2	–	–	–	–	–	–
HOME-RUN	–	–	–	1	–	1	–	–	–
HOP	–	–	–	1	1	2	–	1	1
HORSE	1	–	1	–	–	–	–	–	–
HOUSE	–	1	1	–	–	–	–	–	–
HUN	1	–	1	–	–	–	–	–	–
HURRY	–	–	–	2	1	3	–	–	–
HURRY UP TO SCHOOL	–	1	1	–	–	–	–	–	–
JANE	1	–	1	–	–	–	–	–	–
JUMP	8	14	22	3	6	9	4	7	11
KEN	1	–	1	–	–	–	–	–	–
LEGS	–	–	–	–	–	–	2	1	3
LETS HAVE SOME FUN	–	1	1	–	–	–	–	–	–
LIKE	–	1	1	–	–	–	–	–	–
LIKE YOURE RUNNING	–	–	–	–	–	–	–	1	1
LOCKER	1	–	1	–	–	–	–	–	–
MAIL	–	–	–	–	1	1	–	–	–
MAN	1	1	2	–	–	–	1	–	1
MOTION	–	–	–	–	–	–	1	–	1
MOVE	–	–	–	–	–	–	4	–	4
MOVE OVER	–	–	–	–	–	–	1	–	1
MOVEMENT	–	–	–	–	–	–	1	–	1
MUN	2	–	2	1	–	1	–	–	–
NO RESPONSE	–	–	–	–	–	–	–	1	1
NOT RUN	–	–	–	1	–	1	–	1	1
NOT WALK	–	–	–	–	–	–	–	1	1
NOW	1	–	1	–	–	–	–	–	–
OF	–	–	–	–	–	–	1	–	1
ON	–	1	1	–	–	–	–	–	–
ONCE	–	–	–	–	1	1	–	–	–

RESPONSE WORD	1ST			3RD			5TH		
	M	F	T	M	F	T	M	F	T

68.   RUN

RESPONSE WORD	M	F	T	M	F	T	M	F	T
PAN	1	–	1	–	–	–	–	–	–
PERSON	1	–	1	–	–	–	–	–	–
PIG	–	–	–	–	–	–	1	–	1
PLAY	4	13	17	5	4	9	2	1	3
PUMPKIN	1	–	1	–	–	–	–	–	–
PUN	–	1	1	–	–	–	–	–	–
QUICK	–	–	–	–	1	1	–	–	–
RACE	1	–	1	1	1	2	1	3	4
RAG	1	–	1	–	–	–	–	–	–
RAIN	–	–	–	–	1	1	–	–	–
RAN	3	4	7	19	18	37	14	15	29
RANNED	–	–	–	1	–	1	–	–	–
REAL FAST	1	–	1	–	–	–	–	–	–
RED	–	–	–	–	1	1	–	–	–
RIDE	1	–	1	–	–	–	–	–	–
RIN	–	–	–	–	–	–	1	–	1
ROBERT	–	1	1	–	–	–	–	–	–
ROBIN	–	1	1	–	–	–	–	–	–
RUN	–	–	–	1	–	1	–	–	–
RUNNER	–	–	–	–	–	–	1	–	1
RUNNING	1	1	2	3	1	4	–	–	–
SAT	1	–	1	–	–	–	–	–	–
SEVEN	–	1	1	–	–	–	–	–	–
SHOE	–	1	1	–	–	–	–	–	–
SHOES	3	–	3	–	–	–	–	–	–
SIT	–	–	–	–	–	–	–	1	1
SKIP	2	2	4	–	8	8	2	3	5
SLOW	2	2	4	5	–	5	3	1	4
SLOWLY	1	–	1	–	–	–	–	–	–
SNUN	1	–	1	–	–	–	–	–	–
SOMEBODYS RUNNING	–	1	1	–	–	–	–	–	–
SOMEONE RUNNING	–	–	–	–	–	–	–	1	1
SPEED	–	1	1	–	–	–	1	–	1
SPORTS	–	–	–	–	–	–	–	1	1
SPREAD LEGS	–	1	1	–	–	–	–	–	–
SPUN	–	1	1	–	–	–	–	–	–
START	–	–	–	–	1	1	–	–	–
STICK	–	1	1	–	–	–	–	–	–
STOP	2	4	6	3	5	8	3	3	6
SUN	1	1	2	3	–	3	–	1	1
SWIFTLY	–	–	–	–	–	–	2	2	4
SWIM	1	–	1	–	–	–	–	–	–
TABLE	–	1	1	–	–	–	–	–	–
THE	–	–	–	–	–	–	1	–	1
TO	–	1	1	–	–	–	–	–	–
TO NEIGHBOR	1	–	1	–	–	–	–	–	–
TO SCHOOL	–	1	1	–	–	–	–	–	–
TO THE STORE	1	–	1	–	–	–	–	–	–
TONGUE	1	–	1	–	–	–	–	–	–
TROT	–	–	–	–	1	1	1	2	3
TRYING TO BEAT SOMEBODY TO RUN	–	1	1	–	–	–	–	–	–
TUN	–	1	1	–	–	–	–	–	–
UP	–	1	1	–	–	–	–	–	–
WAGON	–	1	1	–	–	–	–	–	–
WALK	17	15	32	51	45	96	44	45	89
WALKED	–	–	–	–	–	–	1	1	2
WALKING	–	–	–	1	1	2	–	–	–
WHEN	–	–	–	1	1	2	–	–	–
WHENEVER A PERSON RUNS	–	1	1	–	–	–	–	–	–
WITH	–	1	1	–	–	–	–	–	–
WITH FRIEND	1	–	1	–	–	–	–	–	–
WOMAN	–	1	1	–	–	–	–	–	–
WORK	–	1	1	–	–	–	–	–	–
YOU RUN	1	–	1	–	–	–	–	–	–
YOURE RUNNING HOME	–	1	1	–	–	–	–	–	–

69. SAD

RESPONSE WORD	1ST M	F	T	3RD M	F	T	5TH M	F	T
AD	1	–	1	–	–	–	–	–	–
ADD	1	–	1	–	–	–	–	1	1
ANGRY	–	–	–	–	1	1	–	–	–
ASK	–	–	–	–	1	1	–	1	1
AT SOMEONE	–	1	1	–	–	–	–	–	–
AWFUL	–	–	–	–	–	–	–	1	1
BABY	1	–	1	–	–	–	–	–	–
BACK	1	–	1	–	–	–	–	–	–
BAD	7	1	8	6	2	8	2	–	2
BAWL	1	–	1	–	–	–	–	–	–
BE QUIET	1	–	1	–	–	–	–	–	–
BEACH	2	–	2	–	–	–	–	–	–
BED	–	1	1	–	–	–	–	–	–
BEND	–	1	1	–	–	–	–	–	–
BILL	1	–	1	–	–	–	–	–	–
BLACK	1	–	1	–	–	–	–	–	–
BOY	1	–	1	1	–	1	–	–	–
BRICKS	1	–	1	–	–	–	–	–	–
BROTHER	–	–	–	–	–	–	1	–	1
BUCKET	–	1	1	–	–	–	–	–	–
BY	–	–	–	1	–	1	1	–	1
CAN	1	1	2	–	–	–	1	–	1
CAT	–	1	1	–	–	–	–	–	–
CHAIR	–	–	–	1	–	1	–	–	–
CHOO-CHOO TRAIN	1	–	1	–	–	–	–	–	–
CLOWN	–	–	–	–	–	–	1	–	1
COAT	1	–	1	–	–	–	–	–	–
COUGH	1	–	1	–	–	–	–	–	–
CRAYON	1	–	1	–	–	–	–	–	–
CRIED	1	1	2	–	–	–	–	–	–
CRY	4	13	17	3	2	5	4	2	6
CRYING	4	2	6	2	3	5	–	2	2
CURLING	1	–	1	–	–	–	1	–	1
CUT	–	–	–	–	–	–	1	–	1
DAD	–	–	–	–	1	1	–	–	–
DID	–	–	–	1	2	3	–	–	–
DIRT	1	–	1	–	–	–	–	–	–
DOG	1	–	1	–	–	–	–	–	–
DOLL	1	–	1	–	–	–	–	–	–
DONT	–	1	1	–	–	–	–	–	–
DONT CRY	–	1	1	–	–	–	–	–	–
DONT FEEL GOOD	–	1	1	–	–	–	–	–	–
DOWN	2	–	2	–	–	–	–	–	–
DROOPY	–	–	–	–	–	–	–	1	1
EMOTIONAL UPSET	–	–	–	–	–	–	–	1	1
ENJOY	–	–	–	–	–	–	2	–	2
FACE	1	3	4	–	1	1	–	–	–
FAN	–	–	–	1	–	1	–	–	–
FATHER	–	1	1	–	–	–	–	–	–
FAUCET	1	–	1	–	–	–	–	–	–
FEEL	1	–	1	–	–	–	–	–	–
FEEL BAD	–	1	1	2	–	2	–	–	–
FIND	–	1	1	–	–	–	–	–	–
FIRE	1	–	1	–	–	–	–	–	–
FLOOR	1	–	1	–	–	–	1	–	1
FROWN	–	–	–	–	–	–	1	–	1
FUNNY	2	1	3	–	–	–	–	–	–
FUNNY FACE	–	1	1	–	–	–	–	–	–
GAD	–	–	–	1	–	1	–	–	–
GAY	–	–	–	1	–	1	–	1	1
GIRL	–	2	2	–	1	1	–	–	–
GLAD	4	2	6	1	5	6	2	2	4
GLASS	1	–	1	–	–	–	–	–	–
GLOOMY	–	–	–	–	–	–	–	1	1
GO HOME	–	1	1	–	–	–	–	–	–
GO ON TRIP	–	1	1	–	–	–	–	–	–
GOAT	–	1	1	–	–	–	–	–	–
GOOD	–	–	–	–	1	1	–	1	1
GRASS	–	1	1	–	–	–	–	–	–
GRATEFUL	–	–	–	–	–	–	1	–	1
GRIM	–	–	–	–	–	–	1	–	1
HAD	4	–	4	–	–	–	–	–	–

RESPONSE WORD	1ST M	1ST F	1ST T	3RD M	3RD F	3RD T	5TH M	5TH F	5TH T

69. SAD

RESPONSE WORD	M	F	T	M	F	T	M	F	T
HAP	1	–	1	–	–	–	–	–	–
HAPPEN	–	–	–	–	–	–	1	–	1
HAPPY	29	38	67	96	93	189	81	81	162
HIM	–	–	–	–	1	1	–	–	–
HOUSE	–	1	1	–	–	–	–	–	–
HURT FEELINGS	1	–	1	–	–	–	–	–	–
I AM	–	1	1	–	–	–	–	–	–
IM	1	–	1	–	–	–	–	–	–
IM SAD	–	1	1	–	–	–	–	–	–
IM SAD BECAUSE MY SISTER RAN AWAY	–	1	1	–	–	–	–	–	–
INK	–	1	1	–	–	–	–	–	–
IS	–	1	1	–	–	–	–	–	–
JUMP	1	–	1	–	–	–	–	–	–
LEE	–	1	1	–	–	–	–	–	–
LONELY	–	–	–	–	–	–	–	3	3
LOOKING	1	–	1	–	–	–	–	–	–
MAC	–	1	1	–	–	–	–	–	–
MAD	15	10	25	7	10	17	5	6	11
MAN	3	2	5	–	–	–	–	–	–
MAYBE	1	–	1	–	–	–	–	–	–
ME	2	–	2	–	–	–	–	–	–
MEAN	–	2	2	–	1	1	–	1	1
MOON	–	1	1	–	–	–	–	–	–
MOTHER	–	3	3	–	–	–	–	–	–
NICE	1	1	2	–	–	–	–	–	–
NICK	–	1	1	–	–	–	–	–	–
NO	1	–	1	–	–	–	–	–	–
NO MONEY	1	–	1	–	–	–	–	–	–
NOISE	1	–	1	–	–	–	–	–	–
NOT HAPPY	–	–	–	3	–	3	7	4	11
NOT SAD	–	1	1	–	–	–	–	–	–
ONELY	1	–	1	–	–	–	–	–	–
PAD	1	1	2	–	–	–	–	–	–
PAIN	1	–	1	–	–	–	–	–	–
PEN	–	1	1	–	–	–	–	–	–
PEOPLE	4	–	4	1	–	1	–	–	–
PERSON	1	–	1	–	–	–	–	–	–
PICTURE	1	–	1	–	–	–	–	–	–
PLAY	–	2	2	–	–	–	–	–	–
POOR	1	–	1	–	–	–	–	–	–
POTATO SALAD	–	1	1	–	–	–	–	–	–
PUT IT ON BREAD	1	–	1	–	–	–	–	–	–
QUIET	–	–	–	–	–	–	1	–	1
RAD	–	2	2	–	–	–	–	–	–
REAL SAD	–	1	1	–	–	–	–	–	–
REFRIGERATOR	–	1	1	–	–	–	–	–	–
RING	1	–	1	–	–	–	–	–	–
ROCK	–	–	–	1	–	1	–	–	–
SACK	1	–	1	–	–	–	1	–	1
SADLY	–	–	–	–	1	1	–	–	–
SAID	1	2	3	–	1	1	–	–	–
SAND	–	1	1	–	–	–	–	–	–
SATIN	–	1	1	–	–	–	–	–	–
SAW	–	1	1	–	–	–	–	–	–
SAY	–	–	–	–	3	3	1	–	1
SEA	–	1	1	–	–	–	–	–	–
SEAT	–	1	1	–	–	–	–	–	–
SEE	–	2	2	–	–	–	–	–	–
SET	1	–	1	–	–	–	–	–	–
SEW	1	–	1	–	–	–	–	–	–
SHOES	–	1	1	–	–	–	–	–	–
SHOVEL	–	1	1	–	–	–	–	–	–
SILVER	–	–	–	–	1	1	–	–	–
SIT	–	1	1	–	–	–	–	–	–
SKY	1	–	1	–	–	–	–	–	–
SMALL	–	–	–	–	–	–	1	–	1
SMILE	–	1	1	–	–	–	–	–	–
SOFT	–	–	–	–	–	–	–	1	1
SOMEBODY SAD	–	1	1	–	–	–	–	–	–
SORRY	–	–	–	–	–	–	1	–	1
SOUP	1	–	1	–	–	–	–	–	–

RESPONSE WORD	1ST M	F	T	3RD M	F	T	5TH M	F	T

69. SAD

RESPONSE WORD	1ST M	F	T	3RD M	F	T	5TH M	F	T
SPOKE	-	-	-	-	1	1	-	-	-
SQUARE	-	1	1	-	-	-	-	-	-
STAND	-	-	-	1	-	1	-	-	-
SUN	1	-	1	-	-	-	-	-	-
SWEATER	-	1	1	-	-	-	-	-	-
TALK	-	-	-	-	1	1	-	2	2
TALL	-	-	-	-	1	1	-	-	-
TERRIBLE	-	1	1	-	-	-	-	-	-
TOM	1	-	1	-	-	-	-	-	-
TREE	1	-	1	-	-	-	-	-	-
UNHAPPY	3	-	3	9	5	14	20	28	48
UNPLEASANT	-	-	-	-	-	-	-	1	1
UNSAD	-	-	-	1	-	1	-	-	-
US	1	-	1	-	-	-	-	-	-
VOICE	-	-	-	-	1	1	-	-	-
WALK	-	1	1	-	-	-	-	-	-
WALL	-	1	1	-	-	-	-	-	-
WET	-	-	-	-	-	-	1	-	1
WHEN ITS SAD AND YOURE CRYING	1	-	1	-	-	-	-	-	-
WHEN YOURE CRYING	-	-	-	1	-	1	-	-	-
WHENEVER SOMEONE IS SAD	-	1	1	-	-	-	-	-	-
WHY	1	-	1	-	-	-	-	-	-
WORD	-	-	-	-	-	-	1	-	1
WORRIED	-	-	-	-	1	1	1	-	1
YOU	-	1	1	-	-	-	-	-	-
YOU MIGHT BE SAD TO GO ANYWHERE	-	1	1	-	-	-	-	-	-
YOUR FACE IS SAD	-	1	1	-	-	-	-	-	-

70. SALT

RESPONSE WORD	1ST M	F	T	3RD M	F	T	5TH M	F	T
A SPICE	-	-	-	-	-	-	-	1	1
AND PEPPER	-	1	1	-	-	-	-	-	-
APPLE	-	2	2	-	-	-	-	-	-
BAD TASTING	-	1	1	1	-	1	-	-	-
BAKE	-	1	1	-	-	-	-	-	-
BAKING	-	-	-	-	-	-	1	-	1
BALL	1	-	1	-	-	-	-	-	-
BALT	-	1	1	-	-	-	-	-	-
BED	1	1	2	-	-	-	-	-	-
BITTER	-	-	-	-	2	2	1	1	2
BOLT	-	-	-	-	-	-	-	1	1
BOOK	-	1	1	-	-	-	-	-	-
BOUGHT	1	1	2	-	-	-	-	-	-
BREAD	1	-	1	-	-	-	-	-	-
BURN	-	-	-	-	-	-	1	-	1
BUTTER	2	1	3	-	-	-	1	-	1
CAKE	-	1	1	-	-	-	-	-	-
CALT	1	-	1	-	-	-	-	-	-
CAN	2	-	2	-	-	-	-	-	-
CAR	-	1	1	-	-	-	-	-	-
CATSUP	1	-	1	-	-	-	-	-	-
CELERY	1	-	1	-	-	-	1	-	1
CEREAL	1	-	1	-	-	-	-	-	-
CHICKEN	-	-	-	-	1	1	-	-	-
COAT	1	-	1	-	1	1	-	-	-
COFFEE	-	-	-	-	-	-	1	1	2
COLTHERS	-	-	-	-	-	-	-	1	1
COOKIE	-	1	1	-	-	-	1	-	1
CORN ON THE COB	-	-	-	-	1	1	-	-	-
COTTON	-	-	-	-	1	1	-	1	1
CRYSTALS	-	-	-	-	-	-	-	1	1
CUP	1	1	2	-	-	-	-	-	-
DEER	-	-	-	-	-	-	-	1	1
DINNER	1	1	2	-	-	-	-	-	-
DRINK	1	1	2	-	-	-	-	-	-
DRY	-	-	-	1	1	2	2	1	3
EAT	3	1	4	-	-	-	3	-	3
EGG	2	2	4	-	-	-	-	2	2
EGGS	-	-	-	1	-	1	-	-	-

RESPONSE WORD	1ST			3RD			5TH		
	M	F	T	M	F	T	M	F	T

70. SALT

RESPONSE WORD	M	F	T	M	F	T	M	F	T
FAR	1	–	1	–	–	–	–	–	–
FISH	–	–	–	–	–	–	–	1	1
FLAVOR	–	–	–	–	–	–	–	1	1
FLOUR	–	–	–	3	3	–	2	1	3
FOOD	–	2	2	3	3	6	5	11	16
GAME	1	–	1	–	–	–	–	–	–
GARGLE	–	1	1	1	–	1	–	–	–
GIVE	1	–	1	–	–	–	–	–	–
GLASS	1	–	1	2	–	2	–	–	–
GOOD	–	–	–	–	–	–	2	1	3
GRAIN	1	–	1	–	–	–	2	–	2
HALT	1	–	1	–	–	–	–	–	–
HAMBURGER	1	–	1	–	–	–	–	–	–
HARD	–	–	–	–	2	2	1	–	1
HATT	1	–	1	–	–	–	–	–	–
HAVE	–	–	–	–	–	–	1	–	1
HELP	–	–	–	–	–	–	1	–	1
HORRIBLE	–	–	–	–	1	1	–	–	–
HORSE	–	1	1	–	–	–	–	–	–
HOT	–	5	5	–	–	–	1	–	1
HUNGRY	–	1	1	–	–	–	–	–	–
I LIKE	–	1	1	–	–	–	–	–	–
I LIKE SALT	–	1	1	–	–	–	–	–	–
I WANT SALT	–	1	1	–	–	–	–	–	–
I WANT SALT ON MY POTATO	–	1	1	–	–	–	–	–	–
INGREDIENT	–	–	–	–	–	–	1	–	1
INGREDIENTS	–	–	–	–	–	–	1	–	1
IODIZED	–	–	–	–	1	1	–	1	1
IS	–	–	–	–	1	1	–	–	–
IS GOOD FOR YOU	1	–	1	–	–	–	–	–	–
IT	1	–	1	–	–	–	–	–	–
ITS TOO SALT	–	1	1	–	–	–	–	–	–
JANE	–	1	1	–	–	–	–	–	–
LIGHTS	–	1	1	–	–	–	–	–	–
LOW	–	–	–	–	–	–	–	1	1
MAD	–	–	–	–	–	–	1	–	1
MALT	2	–	2	–	1	1	–	–	–
MASHED POTATOES	1	–	1	–	–	–	–	–	–
MAT	1	–	1	–	–	–	–	–	–
MEAT	–	–	–	1	–	1	1	–	1
MILK	–	–	–	–	–	–	1	–	1
MINE	–	–	–	–	–	–	3	1	4
MINERAL	–	–	–	1	–	1	1	1	2
MOIST	–	–	–	–	–	–	–	1	1
MUCH	–	–	–	–	1	1	–	–	–
MY MEAT	1	–	1	–	–	–	–	–	–
NALT	–	1	1	–	–	–	–	–	–
NINE	–	1	1	–	–	–	–	–	–
NOT SWEET	–	–	–	–	–	–	1	–	1
NOW	–	–	–	1	–	1	–	–	–
OCEAN	1	–	1	1	3	4	2	2	4
ON	–	1	1	–	–	–	–	–	–
ON BACON AND EGGS	1	–	1	–	–	–	–	–	–
ON BREAD	1	–	1	–	–	–	–	–	–
ON FOOD	1	–	1	–	–	–	–	–	–
ON MY FOOD	1	–	1	–	–	–	–	–	–
ORANGE JUICE	1	–	1	–	–	–	–	–	–
PALT	1	–	1	–	–	–	–	–	–
PAN	–	2	2	–	–	–	–	–	–
PANE	–	–	–	–	–	–	1	–	1
PAPER	–	–	–	–	–	–	1	–	1
PEP	–	–	–	–	–	–	1	–	1
PEPER	–	–	–	–	–	–	–	1	1
PEPPER	56	68	124	78	81	159	56	69	125
PERRY	–	–	–	–	–	–	–	1	1
PICTURES	1	–	1	–	–	–	–	–	–
PINK	–	–	–	1	–	1	–	–	–
PIPE	1	–	1	–	–	–	–	–	–
PIPER	–	–	–	–	–	–	1	–	1
PLATE	–	2	2	–	–	–	–	–	–
POPCORN	1	–	1	–	–	–	–	–	–
POPSICLE	–	–	–	1	–	1	–	–	–

RESPONSE WORD	1ST			3RD			5TH		
	M	F	T	M	F	T	M	F	T

70. SALT

RESPONSE WORD	M	F	T	M	F	T	M	F	T
POTATO	–	–	–	–	–	–	1	–	1
POTATOES	2	–	2	–	–	–	–	–	–
POUR IN	1	–	1	–	–	–	–	–	–
PUMPKIN	–	1	1	–	–	–	–	–	–
PUT	1	–	1	–	–	–	–	–	–
PUT ON	–	–	–	–	1	1	–	–	–
PUT ON FOOD	–	–	–	–	–	–	–	1	1
RIVER	–	–	–	–	–	–	–	1	1
ROCK	–	–	–	–	–	–	1	–	1
ROUGH	–	–	–	–	1	1	–	–	–
RUNNING	–	–	–	1	–	1	1	–	1
SALTINES	–	–	–	1	–	1	–	–	–
SALTY	3	1	4	–	2	2	–	1	1
SAND	–	–	–	–	1	1	–	–	–
SAND DUST	–	1	1	–	–	–	–	–	–
SANDWICH	1	–	1	–	–	–	–	–	–
SAW	2	1	3	–	–	–	–	–	–
SAW DRIVER	–	1	1	–	–	–	–	–	–
SEA	1	–	1	2	–	2	–	1	1
SEA WATER	–	–	–	–	1	1	1	–	1
SEASON	–	–	–	–	–	–	1	–	1
SEASONING	–	–	–	–	1	1	1	2	3
SHAKE	–	1	1	–	1	1	–	–	–
SHAKER	–	1	1	–	–	–	–	–	–
SHORER	–	–	–	–	–	–	1	–	1
SINK	1	–	1	–	–	–	–	–	–
SIR	1	–	1	–	–	–	–	–	–
SLUG	–	–	–	1	–	1	–	–	–
SOFT	–	1	1	2	–	2	–	–	–
SOMETHING	–	1	1	–	–	–	–	–	–
SOMETHING TO PUT ON A FOOD	–	–	–	–	–	–	1	–	1
SOUR	–	1	1	2	3	5	2	1	3
SPICE	–	–	–	1	1	2	–	2	2
SPICES	–	–	–	–	1	1	–	–	–
SPOT	1	–	1	–	–	–	–	–	–
STEAK	–	–	–	–	–	–	1	–	1
STRONG	1	–	1	–	–	–	–	–	–
STUFF	–	–	–	1	–	1	–	–	–
SUE	1	–	1	–	–	–	–	–	–
SUGAR	1	5	6	9	9	18	12	5	17
SWEAT	–	–	–	–	–	–	–	1	1
SWEET	–	2	2	3	2	5	2	1	3
TABLE	–	–	–	1	1	2	–	–	–
TABLET	–	–	–	–	–	–	1	–	1
TAFFY	–	–	–	–	1	1	–	–	–
TASTE	–	–	–	–	1	1	–	2	2
TEAM	–	–	–	1	–	1	1	–	1
TELL	–	–	–	–	–	–	1	–	1
TERRIBLE	–	–	–	–	1	1	–	–	–
TEST	–	–	–	–	–	–	–	1	1
THIRSTY	1	1	2	1	–	1	–	1	1
THROW UP	1	–	1	–	–	–	–	–	–
TIM	–	1	1	–	–	–	–	–	–
TO PUT ON YOUR FOOD	–	1	1	–	–	–	–	–	–
TOMATO	1	–	1	–	–	–	–	–	–
TREE	1	–	1	–	–	–	–	–	–
USE	–	–	–	1	–	1	–	–	–
VEGETABLES	1	–	1	–	–	–	–	–	–
WALL	1	–	1	–	–	–	–	–	–
WALT	–	1	1	–	–	–	–	–	–
WATER	11	4	15	19	11	30	10	15	25
WE PUT ON THE COOKIES	1	–	1	–	–	–	–	–	–
WHAT YOU PUT ON FOOD	1	1	2	–	–	–	–	–	–
WHEN YOURE SALTING SOMETHING	1	–	1	–	–	–	–	–	–
WHENEVER SOMEONE POURS SOME SALT ON THE	–	1	1	–	–	–	–	–	–
WHITE	–	2	2	2	2	4	3	2	5
WIGHT	–	–	–	–	–	–	1	–	1
WOOD	1	–	1	–	–	–	–	–	–
WWIN	–	–	–	–	–	–	1	–	1

RESPONSE WORD	1ST M	F	T	3RD M	F	T	5TH M	F	T

70.　SALT

RESPONSE WORD	1ST M	F	T	3RD M	F	T	5TH M	F	T
YOU MIGHT HAVE A SORE THROAT AND DRINK	–	1	1	–	–	–	–	–	–
YOU PUT ON FOOD	–	–	–	1	–	1	–	–	–

71.　SELDOM

RESPONSE WORD	1ST M	F	T	3RD M	F	T	5TH M	F	T
A CELL	–	–	–	1	–	1	–	–	–
ACID	–	–	–	1	–	1	–	–	–
AGE	–	–	–	–	1	1	–	–	–
ALL GONE	–	1	1	–	1	1	–	–	–
ALL THE TIME	–	–	–	–	–	–	1	–	1
ALMOST	–	–	–	–	–	–	1	–	1
ALMOST NEVER	–	–	–	–	–	–	1	3	4
ALWAYS	–	1	1	9	6	15	9	10	19
AND	–	1	1	–	–	–	–	–	–
APPLE	–	–	–	–	1	1	–	–	–
APPLES	–	–	–	1	–	1	–	–	–
ARE	–	–	–	–	1	1	–	–	–
ARM	1	–	1	–	–	–	–	–	–
BABY	–	1	1	–	–	–	–	–	–
BACON	1	–	1	–	–	–	–	–	–
BAD	1	–	1	–	–	–	–	–	–
BAG	–	–	–	1	–	1	–	–	–
BARELY	–	–	–	–	–	–	1	–	1
BARGAIN	–	–	–	–	–	–	1	–	1
BARN	1	–	1	–	–	–	–	–	–
BARS	–	–	–	1	–	1	–	–	–
BASEMENT	–	–	–	–	1	1	–	–	–
BE	–	1	1	–	–	–	–	–	–
BEAN	–	–	–	1	–	1	–	–	–
BECOME	–	–	–	–	–	–	–	1	1
BEGIN	1	–	1	–	–	–	–	–	–
BEGINNING	–	–	–	–	1	1	–	–	–
BEHAVE	–	–	–	–	–	–	1	–	1
BELDOM	–	1	1	–	–	–	–	–	–
BELL	–	1	1	–	–	–	–	–	–
BERRY	1	–	1	–	–	–	–	–	–
BILL	1	–	1	–	–	–	–	–	–
BIRD	–	1	1	–	–	–	–	–	–
BLOCKS	–	1	1	–	–	–	–	–	–
BOAT	–	–	–	1	–	1	–	–	–
BOOK	–	–	–	1	–	1	–	–	–
BOX	1	–	1	–	–	–	–	–	–
BOY	–	1	1	–	–	–	–	–	–
BREAK	1	–	1	–	–	–	–	1	1
BROWN	–	–	–	–	1	1	–	–	–
BUG	1	–	1	–	–	–	–	–	–
BULDOM	–	1	1	–	–	–	–	–	–
BUTTER	–	1	1	–	–	–	–	–	–
BUTTERFLY	–	–	–	–	1	1	–	–	–
BUTTON	1	–	1	–	–	–	–	–	–
BUY	–	–	–	1	–	1	–	1	1
BUYING	–	–	–	1	–	1	–	–	–
CANDLES	–	1	1	–	–	–	–	–	–
CANDY	–	1	1	–	–	–	–	–	–
CANS	1	–	1	–	–	–	–	–	–
CARE	–	–	–	1	–	1	–	–	–
CAREFUL	–	–	–	–	1	1	–	–	–
CARROT	–	1	1	–	–	–	–	–	–
CARS	1	–	1	–	–	–	–	–	–
CAT	1	–	1	–	1	1	–	–	–
CATCH	–	1	1	–	–	–	1	–	1
CELERY	4	3	7	–	–	–	–	–	–
CELLAR	–	2	2	1	–	1	1	–	1
CHAIR	–	2	2	–	–	–	–	–	–
CHIMNEY	1	–	1	–	–	–	–	–	–
CIDER	–	1	1	–	–	–	–	–	–
CLOCK	–	–	–	1	–	1	–	–	–
CLOSET	–	1	1	–	–	–	–	–	–
CLOTH ON BOAT	–	–	–	–	–	–	–	1	1
COAT	1	–	1	–	–	–	–	–	–

RESPONSE WORD	1ST M	F	T	3RD M	F	T	5TH M	F	T

71. SELDOM

RESPONSE WORD	1ST M	F	T	3RD M	F	T	5TH M	F	T
COLUMN	–	–	–	–	1	1	–	–	–
COME	–	–	–	–	2	2	–	–	–
COME HERE	–	–	–	–	1	1	–	–	–
COOK	–	1	1	–	–	–	–	–	–
COOKOO	1	–	1	–	–	–	–	–	–
COUNTRY	1	–	1	–	–	–	–	–	–
CRAZY	–	1	1	–	–	–	–	–	–
CROSS	1	–	1	1	–	1	–	–	–
CUP	–	–	–	–	1	1	–	–	–
DANCE	1	–	1	–	–	–	–	–	–
DAY	–	–	–	–	1	1	–	–	–
DEEP	–	–	–	1	–	1	–	–	–
DELAY	1	–	1	–	–	–	–	–	–
DESK	–	–	–	–	1	1	–	–	–
DID NOT SELL THEM	–	–	–	1	–	1	–	–	–
DIFFERENT	–	–	–	–	1	1	1	–	1
DINNER	1	–	1	–	–	–	–	–	–
DISHES	–	1	1	–	–	–	–	–	–
DO	–	–	–	–	–	–	1	–	1
DO SOMETHING	–	–	–	–	–	–	1	–	1
DOG	–	–	–	2	1	3	–	–	–
DOING	–	–	–	1	–	1	–	–	–
DONT	–	–	–	1	–	1	–	–	–
DONT SELDOM	1	–	1	1	–	1	–	–	–
DOOR	3	–	3	–	1	1	–	–	–
DOOR KNOB	–	1	1	–	–	–	–	–	–
DOOR KNOBBLE	1	–	1	–	–	–	–	–	–
DOORBELL	–	–	–	1	–	1	–	–	–
DOWN	–	1	1	–	–	–	–	–	–
DRESS	–	1	1	–	–	–	–	–	–
DRINK	2	2	4	–	–	–	–	–	–
DRUM	–	1	1	–	–	–	–	–	–
DRYER	–	1	1	–	–	–	–	–	–
DUCKS	1	–	1	–	–	–	–	–	–
DUMB	–	–	–	–	1	1	–	–	–
DUMMY	1	–	1	–	–	–	–	–	–
EGGS	1	–	1	–	–	–	–	–	–
EMPTY	–	–	–	–	–	–	1	–	1
EVER	–	–	–	–	1	–	1	4	5
EVERYTHING	–	–	–	–	1	1	–	–	–
EVERYTIME	–	–	–	1	–	1	–	–	–
EYES	1	–	1	–	–	–	–	–	–
FACE	–	1	1	–	–	–	–	–	–
FAIR	–	1	1	–	–	–	–	–	–
FAN	–	1	1	–	–	–	–	–	–
FATHER	2	1	3	–	–	–	–	–	–
FEET	1	–	1	1	–	1	–	–	–
FELT	–	–	–	–	1	1	–	–	–
FENCE	1	–	1	–	–	–	–	–	–
FEW	–	–	–	–	–	–	2	2	4
FEW TIMES	–	–	–	–	–	–	1	–	1
FEWER	–	–	–	–	–	–	1	–	1
FIND	–	–	–	1	–	1	–	–	–
FINGER	–	1	1	–	–	–	–	–	–
FIRE	–	–	–	1	–	1	–	–	–
FISH	–	–	–	–	–	–	1	1	2
FLAKY	–	–	–	–	1	1	–	–	–
FLAT	–	–	–	–	1	1	–	–	–
FLOOR	–	1	1	–	–	–	–	1	1
FLOWERS	–	1	1	–	–	–	–	–	–
FOOD	–	2	2	–	1	1	–	–	–
FOR	–	–	–	–	–	–	1	–	1
FREE	–	–	–	–	–	–	1	–	1
FREEDOM	1	–	1	3	1	4	–	–	–
FREQUENTLY	–	–	–	–	1	1	–	1	1
FROG	–	1	1	–	–	–	–	–	–
FROM	1	–	1	–	–	–	–	–	–
FRUIT	–	–	–	1	–	1	–	–	–
FRY	–	–	–	–	–	–	1	–	1
FUNNY	1	–	1	–	–	–	–	–	–
GENTLE	–	1	1	–	–	–	–	–	–
GIRL	–	–	–	–	1	1	–	–	–

RESPONSE WORD	1ST M	1ST F	1ST T	3RD M	3RD F	3RD T	5TH M	5TH F	5TH T

71. SELDOM

RESPONSE WORD	1ST M	F	T	3RD M	F	T	5TH M	F	T
GIVE	–	1	1	1	–	1	–	–	–
GLASSES	–	–	–	–	1	1	–	–	–
GOES IN WATER	–	1	1	–	–	–	–	–	–
GOOD	1	1	2	1	–	1	–	–	–
GRASS	–	–	–	1	–	1	–	–	–
GREEN	1	–	1	–	–	–	–	–	–
GRELLDOM	1	–	1	–	–	–	–	–	–
GROCERIES	1	–	1	–	–	–	–	–	–
GROWD	–	–	–	–	–	–	–	1	1
GUM	1	–	1	–	–	–	–	–	–
HAIR	1	–	1	–	1	1	1	–	1
HALLY	–	–	–	–	–	–	1	–	1
HAND	–	2	2	–	–	–	–	–	–
HANDLE	–	1	1	–	–	–	–	–	–
HAPPEN	–	–	–	–	–	–	1	–	1
HAPPENED	–	–	–	–	–	–	–	1	1
HAPPENS	3	–	3	–	–	–	–	1	1
HAPPY	–	–	–	–	–	–	1	1	2
HARD	–	–	–	1	1	2	–	1	1
HARDLY	–	–	–	1	2	3	7	6	13
HARDLY EVER	–	–	–	1	1	2	1	–	1
HAVE	1	–	1	1	–	1	–	–	–
HE	1	–	1	–	–	–	–	–	–
HE SELL THE CHICKEN	–	–	–	1	–	1	–	–	–
HEALTH	1	–	1	–	–	–	–	–	–
HEARD	–	–	–	5	4	9	4	3	7
HEARD ONCE IN A WHILE	–	–	–	–	–	–	–	1	1
HELD	–	1	1	–	–	–	–	–	–
HELDEN	–	1	1	–	–	–	–	–	–
HELDOM	1	–	1	–	1	1	–	–	–
HELL	1	–	1	–	–	–	–	–	–
HELP	1	1	2	–	–	–	–	–	–
HENNY	–	–	–	–	–	–	–	1	1
HER	–	–	–	–	1	1	–	–	–
HERE	1	–	1	1	–	1	–	–	–
HIM	–	–	–	1	–	1	–	–	–
HIT	1	–	1	–	–	–	–	–	–
HOME	1	–	1	–	–	–	–	–	–
HOPE	–	–	–	–	1	1	–	–	–
HORSE	–	1	1	–	–	–	–	–	–
HOT	1	–	1	1	–	1	1	–	1
HOUSE	–	–	–	2	–	2	–	–	–
HUNGRY FOR FOOD	–	1	1	–	–	–	–	–	–
HURRY	–	–	–	1	1	2	–	–	–
I CANT THINK	–	–	–	–	1	1	–	–	–
IN	–	–	–	1	–	1	–	–	–
IN THE CELLAR ITS DARK	–	1	1	–	–	–	–	–	–
INK	–	1	1	–	–	–	–	–	–
INSELDOM	–	–	–	–	–	–	–	1	1
IRRESPONSIBLE	–	–	–	–	–	–	–	1	1
IS HEARD	–	1	1	–	–	–	–	–	–
IT	–	1	1	–	2	2	–	–	–
JAIL	1	–	1	–	1	1	–	–	–
KELDOM	1	1	2	–	–	–	–	–	–
KELLING	1	–	1	–	–	–	–	–	–
KIND	–	–	–	–	1	1	–	–	–
KINGDOM	–	–	–	1	–	1	–	–	–
KITTEN	1	–	1	–	–	–	–	–	–
KLEENEX	–	1	1	–	–	–	–	–	–
LAST	–	–	–	1	–	1	–	–	–
LAY	1	–	1	–	–	–	–	–	–
LESS	–	1	1	–	–	–	–	–	–
LET	1	–	1	–	–	–	–	–	–
LETS GO FOR A RIDE	1	–	1	–	–	–	–	–	–
LIGHT	2	–	2	1	1	2	–	–	–
LIPS	–	1	1	–	–	–	–	–	–
LISTEN	–	–	–	–	1	1	–	–	–
LITTLE	–	–	–	1	–	1	–	–	–
LIVE	–	1	1	–	–	–	–	–	–
LOCK	1	–	1	–	–	–	–	–	–
LOG	–	1	1	–	–	–	–	–	–
LONELY	–	–	–	–	1	1	–	–	–

RESPONSE WORD	1ST M	1ST F	1ST T	3RD M	3RD F	3RD T	5TH M	5TH F	5TH T

71.   SELDOM

RESPONSE WORD	M	F	T	M	F	T	M	F	T
LONESOME	–	1	–	–	–	–	–	1	1
LONGDOM	–	1	1	–	–	–	–	–	–
LOVE	–	1	1	–	–	–	–	–	–
MAINTAIN	1	–	1	–	–	–	–	1	1
MATTER	–	–	–	1	–	1	–	–	–
MAY	–	1	1	–	–	–	–	–	–
MEAT	1	1	2	–	–	–	–	–	–
MELDOM	1	2	3	1	1	2	–	–	–
MELLON	–	–	–	–	–	–	–	1	1
MELTED	1	–	1	–	–	–	–	–	–
MELTING	1	–	1	–	–	–	–	–	–
MELTOM	–	–	–	–	1	1	–	–	–
MEN	–	–	–	–	1	1	–	–	–
MILK	1	–	1	–	–	–	–	–	–
MIX	1	–	1	–	–	–	–	–	–
MOLDY	–	–	–	1	–	1	–	–	–
MOM	–	–	–	–	–	–	–	1	1
MONEY	1	–	1	–	–	–	–	–	–
MORE	1	–	1	–	–	–	–	–	–
MOSTLY	–	–	–	–	1	1	–	1	1
MOTHER	1	1	2	–	–	–	–	–	–
NAME	–	–	–	1	2	3	–	–	–
NEARLY	–	–	–	1	–	1	–	–	–
NEVER	–	–	–	1	2	3	12	15	27
NEW	–	–	–	–	1	1	–	–	–
NICE	–	1	1	1	–	1	–	–	–
NO RESPONSE	–	–	–	–	2	2	–	–	–
NOISE	–	–	–	–	–	–	–	1	1
NOT	–	–	–	–	1	1	2	–	2
NOT ABLE	–	–	–	–	–	–	1	–	1
NOT ALWAYS	–	–	–	–	1	1	3	–	3
NOT AT ALL	–	–	–	–	–	–	1	–	1
NOT HEAR	–	–	–	1	–	1	–	–	–
NOT LOUD	–	–	–	1	–	1	–	–	–
NOT MUCH	–	–	–	–	1	1	2	–	2
NOT OFTEN	–	–	–	–	1	1	5	4	9
NOT RECENTLY	–	–	–	–	–	–	–	1	1
NOT SELDOM	1	–	1	4	3	7	–	–	–
NOT TOO MANY TIMES	–	–	–	–	–	–	1	–	1
NOT TOO OFTEN	1	–	1	–	–	–	–	–	–
NOT USUALLY	–	–	–	1	–	1	–	–	–
NOT VERY MUCH	–	–	–	1	–	1	–	–	–
NOT VERY OFTEN	–	–	–	–	1	1	2	2	4
NOTALWAYS	–	–	–	–	–	–	–	1	1
NOTHING	–	–	–	–	–	–	1	–	1
NOW	–	–	–	2	–	2	–	–	–
OFER	–	–	–	–	–	–	1	–	1
OFF	–	–	–	–	–	–	1	–	1
OFFEND	–	–	–	–	–	–	1	–	1
OFFER	–	–	–	1	–	1	–	–	–
OFTEN	–	–	–	7	14	21	26	28	54
ONCE IN A WHILE	–	–	–	–	–	–	1	1	2
ONCE IN AWHILE	–	–	–	1	2	3	–	–	–
OTHER	–	–	–	1	–	1	–	–	–
OVEN	–	–	–	–	–	–	1	–	1
PAINT	–	1	1	–	–	–	–	–	–
PAPER	–	1	1	–	1	1	–	–	–
PEACH	–	–	–	1	–	1	–	–	–
PEACHES	1	–	1	–	–	–	–	–	–
PELDOM	–	1	1	2	–	2	–	–	–
PENCIL	–	–	–	–	1	1	–	–	–
PEOPLE	–	–	–	–	–	–	–	1	1
PERSON	–	–	–	–	–	–	–	1	1
PICTURE	–	–	–	–	1	1	–	–	–
PIPE	–	–	–	1	–	1	–	–	–
PLAY	–	–	–	2	–	2	–	–	–
PLEASANT	–	–	–	–	–	–	–	1	1
POLICEMAN	–	–	–	–	1	1	–	–	–
PRAY	–	1	1	–	–	–	–	–	–
PRETTY	–	–	–	–	2	2	–	1	1
PROBLEM	–	–	–	–	1	1	–	–	–
PUMPKIN	–	1	1	–	–	–	–	–	–

RESPONSE WORD	1ST M	F	T	3RD M	F	T	5TH M	F	T
71. SELDOM									
QUICKLY	–	–	–	–	–	–	–	1	1
QUIET	–	–	–	–	1	1	–	1	1
RAIN	1	–	1	–	–	–	–	–	–
RARE	–	–	–	–	–	–	1	1	2
RARELY	–	–	–	–	1	1	–	1	1
RING	1	1	2	–	–	–	–	–	–
RUBBER BAND	1	–	1	–	–	–	–	–	–
SAIL	1	1	2	–	–	–	–	–	–
SAILING	1	–	1	–	–	–	–	–	–
SALAD	1	–	1	–	–	–	–	–	–
SALE	1	–	1	–	–	–	1	–	1
SALON	–	1	1	–	–	–	–	–	–
SALT	1	1	2	–	1	1	–	–	–
SAME	–	–	–	–	–	–	–	1	1
SAW	1	2	3	–	–	–	–	–	–
SAWMILL	1	–	1	–	–	–	–	–	–
SAY	–	1	1	–	–	–	–	–	–
SCRATCHING	1	–	1	–	–	–	–	–	–
SEA	1	–	1	–	–	–	–	–	–
SEE	–	–	–	1	1	2	–	–	–
SELD	–	–	–	–	–	–	–	1	1
SELDOMLY	–	–	–	–	1	1	–	–	–
SELF	–	–	–	1	1	2	–	–	–
SELFISH	–	1	1	–	–	–	–	–	–
SELL	7	11	18	9	6	15	1	3	4
SELL DONUTS	–	1	1	–	–	–	–	–	–
SELL DRESS WHAT IS TOO SMALL	–	1	1	–	–	–	–	–	–
SELL FOOD	–	2	2	–	–	–	–	–	–
SELL HIM	–	–	–	1	–	1	–	–	–
SELL HORSES	1	–	1	–	–	–	–	–	–
SELL SOMETHING	1	–	1	1	–	1	–	–	–
SELL THEM	3	1	4	–	–	–	–	–	–
SELLER	1	1	2	–	–	–	–	–	–
SELLING	3	3	6	1	–	1	–	–	–
SELLING THEM	1	–	1	–	–	–	–	–	–
SETTING	1	–	1	–	–	–	–	–	–
SETTLE	–	–	–	–	1	1	–	–	–
SEW	1	–	1	–	–	–	–	–	–
SEWING MACHINE	–	1	1	–	–	–	–	–	–
SHE	1	–	1	–	–	–	–	–	–
SHOES	–	–	–	1	1	2	–	–	–
SHOOTING	–	–	–	–	1	1	–	–	–
SHORT	–	–	–	–	–	–	–	1	1
SHOULD	–	–	–	–	1	1	–	–	–
SILBY	–	1	1	–	–	–	–	–	–
SILENT	–	–	–	–	–	–	–	1	1
SILLY	–	–	–	–	1	1	–	–	–
SILVER	–	–	–	1	–	1	–	–	–
SILVERWARE	1	–	1	–	–	–	–	–	–
SING	–	1	1	–	–	–	–	–	–
SINK	–	1	1	–	–	–	–	–	–
SISTER	–	–	–	–	–	–	–	1	1
SIT	1	–	1	–	1	1	–	–	–
SIX	–	–	–	1	–	1	–	–	–
SKELETON-MASK	–	1	1	–	–	–	–	–	–
SLAB	–	–	–	–	–	–	1	–	1
SOAP	–	1	1	–	–	–	–	–	–
SOFT	–	1	1	–	2	2	–	1	1
SOLD	–	1	1	1	–	1	–	1	1
SOLD IN (I DONT THINK I KNOW IT)	–	–	–	–	–	–	–	1	1
SOLD OUT	–	–	–	1	–	1	–	–	–
SOLID	–	–	–	1	–	1	1	–	1
SOME	–	–	–	1	1	2	1	–	1
SOMETHING	1	1	2	3	2	5	–	2	2
SOMETIME	–	–	–	2	1	3	–	–	–
SOMETIMES	1	1	2	4	1	5	7	6	13
SOUGHT	1	–	1	–	–	–	–	–	–
SOUND	–	–	–	–	1	1	–	–	–
SOUP	1	–	1	–	–	–	–	–	–
SOUR	–	1	1	–	2	2	–	–	–

71. SELDOM

RESPONSE WORD	1ST M	1ST F	1ST T	3RD M	3RD F	3RD T	5TH M	5TH F	5TH T
SPOT	-	-	-	1	-	1	-	-	-
STEAL	-	-	-	1	-	1	-	-	-
STOP	-	1	1	-	-	-	-	-	-
STORE	-	2	2	-	-	-	-	-	-
SUN	-	2	2	-	-	-	-	-	-
SUSAN	1	-	1	-	-	-	-	-	-
SWIM	1	-	1	1	-	1	1	-	1
TAKE	1	-	1	-	-	-	-	-	-
TALK	-	-	-	-	1	1	-	-	-
TAME SOMETHING	-	-	-	-	1	1	-	-	-
TEETH	-	1	1	-	-	-	-	-	-
TELDOM	1	-	1	-	-	-	-	-	-
TEN	-	-	-	1	-	1	-	-	-
TEST	-	-	-	1	-	1	-	-	-
THANK	-	-	-	-	1	1	-	-	-
THAT	1	-	1	1	-	1	-	-	-
THE	-	-	-	-	-	-	1	-	1
THE UNITED NATION	1	-	1	-	-	-	-	-	-
THEM	-	1	1	-	1	1	-	-	-
THERE	-	-	-	1	-	1	1	-	1
THING	-	-	-	-	1	1	-	-	-
THINGS	1	-	1	-	-	-	-	-	-
TO	1	-	1	1	-	1	-	-	-
TOES	-	1	1	-	-	-	-	-	-
TOGETHER	-	-	-	-	-	-	1	-	1
TOO	-	-	-	-	-	-	1	-	1
TOY	-	1	1	-	-	-	-	-	-
TOYS	-	1	1	-	-	-	-	-	-
TRICYCLE	1	-	1	-	-	-	-	-	-
UNDER	-	-	-	1	-	1	-	1	1
UNLIKELY	-	-	-	-	-	-	1	-	1
UNOFTEN	-	-	-	-	-	-	2	-	2
UNSELDOM	1	-	1	-	-	-	2	-	2
UNUSUAL	-	-	-	1	-	1	3	-	3
UNUSUALLY	-	-	-	-	-	-	2	-	2
USE	-	-	-	-	-	-	-	1	1
USED	-	-	-	1	-	1	2	2	-
USUALLY	1	-	1	1	2	3	2	2	4
VEGETALBE	-	-	-	-	-	-	-	1	1
VEREY OFFTEN	-	-	-	-	-	-	1	-	1
VERY	-	1	1	-	-	-	-	2	2
VERY LITTLE	-	-	-	-	1	1	-	-	-
VERY OFTEN	-	-	-	-	-	-	-	1	1
VERY SELDOM	-	-	-	-	-	-	1	-	1
WALL	-	2	2	-	-	-	-	-	-
WANT	-	1	1	-	-	-	-	-	-
WATER	-	1	1	-	1	1	-	-	-
WE	-	-	-	-	1	1	-	-	-
WELDEN	-	1	1	-	-	-	-	-	-
WELDOM	-	-	-	1	-	1	-	-	-
WELL	-	1	1	1	1	2	-	-	-
WHAT	1	-	1	-	-	-	-	-	-
WHAT YOU MAKE A SANDWICH	1	-	1	-	-	-	-	-	-
WHEEL	-	1	1	-	-	-	-	-	-
WHEN	1	-	1	-	-	-	-	1	1
WHEN YOU FELL	1	-	1	-	-	-	-	-	-
WHENEVER YOUR MOTHER CALLS HER NEIGHBOR	-	1	1	-	-	-	-	-	-
WOOD	-	1	1	-	-	-	-	-	-
WORK	1	-	1	-	-	-	-	1	1
WRITE	-	-	-	-	-	-	-	1	1
YAWN	-	-	-	-	1	1	-	-	-
YES	1	-	1	-	-	-	-	-	-
YOU	-	-	-	-	1	1	-	-	-
YOU COULD GO TO THE MOVIES	-	1	1	-	-	-	-	-	-
YOU HEAR A STORY	-	-	-	-	-	-	-	1	1
YOURS	-	-	-	1	-	1	-	-	-

RESPONSE WORD	1ST M	F	T	3RD M	F	T	5TH M	F	T
					72.	SELL			
A BOOK	–	–	–	–	–	–	–	1	1
A CELL WHERE YOU KEEP PEOPLE	–	–	–	1	–	1	–	–	–
AFTER	–	1	1	–	–	–	–	–	–
AGAIN	–	–	–	–	–	–	–	1	1
AIR	1	–	1	–	–	–	–	–	–
APPLE	3	1	4	–	–	–	–	–	–
APPLES	1	1	2	–	1	1	1	–	1
ARE	–	1	1	–	–	–	–	–	–
AWAY	–	–	–	1	1	2	–	–	–
BACK	–	1	1	–	–	–	–	–	–
BAKER	–	1	1	–	–	–	–	–	–
BALL	1	–	1	–	–	–	–	–	–
BALLS	1	–	1	–	–	–	1	–	1
BANANAS	2	–	2	–	–	–	–	–	–
BARGAIN	–	–	–	–	–	–	1	1	2
BARS	1	–	1	–	–	–	–	–	–
BASEMENT	1	–	1	–	–	–	–	–	–
BED	–	–	–	1	–	1	–	–	–
BEE	1	–	1	–	–	–	1	1	2
BELL	3	2	5	4	5	9	3	1	4
BELONG	–	–	–	–	1	1	–	1	1
BIG	–	–	–	–	1	1	–	–	–
BIKE	1	–	1	–	–	–	1	–	1
BIRD	–	–	–	–	–	–	–	1	1
BITE	1	–	1	–	–	–	–	–	–
BLACK	–	–	–	–	–	–	1	–	1
BLOCK	–	–	–	–	1	1	–	–	–
BOAT	–	–	–	–	1	1	–	–	–
BOOK	1	–	1	–	–	–	–	–	–
BOOTS	–	–	–	–	1	1	–	–	–
BOUGHT	–	–	–	–	4	4	3	1	4
BOX	–	1	1	–	–	–	–	–	–
BOY	–	–	–	1	1	2	–	–	–
BRACELET	–	1	1	–	–	–	–	–	–
BREAD	–	1	1	–	1	1	–	–	–
BROUGHT	–	–	–	–	–	–	–	2	2
BRUSH	–	1	1	–	–	–	–	–	–
BRUSHES	–	–	–	–	–	–	–	1	1
BUG	–	1	1	–	1	1	–	–	–
BUNS	–	–	–	–	1	1	–	–	–
BUP	–	–	–	–	–	–	–	1	1
BUY	–	3	3	26	13	39	45	37	82
BUYING	–	–	–	–	–	–	1	–	1
BY	–	–	–	–	–	–	2	–	2
CABBAGE	–	–	–	–	1	1	–	–	–
CAGE	–	–	–	2	1	3	–	–	–
CAKES OR YO-YOS	1	–	1	–	–	–	–	–	–
CALL	1	–	1	–	–	–	–	–	–
CAN	–	–	–	–	1	1	–	–	–
CANDY	–	4	4	1	–	1	1	–	1
CANT	–	1	1	–	–	–	–	–	–
CAR	2	–	2	–	–	–	1	–	1
CARROT	–	1	1	–	–	–	–	–	–
CAT	1	1	2	–	–	–	–	–	–
CATS	1	1	1	–	–	–	–	–	–
CELERY	2	2	4	–	–	–	–	–	–
CELL	–	–	–	–	–	–	–	1	1
CELLAR	4	1	5	–	2	2	1	–	1
CHAIN	–	–	–	–	1	1	–	–	–
CHAIRS	–	1	1	–	–	–	–	–	–
CHEESE	1	–	1	–	–	–	–	–	–
CHICKEN	–	–	–	–	–	–	–	1	1
CHICKENS	1	–	1	–	–	–	–	–	–
CHILDREN	–	1	1	–	–	–	–	–	–
CLASS	1	–	1	–	–	–	–	–	–
CLOTHES	1	1	2	–	–	–	–	1	1
COAT	–	–	–	–	1	1	–	–	–
COMIC BOOKS	–	1	1	–	–	–	–	–	–
CONTAINER	–	–	–	–	–	–	1	–	1
COOKIES	–	1	1	–	2	2	–	–	–
COUGH	–	1	1	–	–	–	–	–	–

RESPONSE WORD	1ST			3RD			5TH		
	M	F	T	M	F	T	M	F	T

72. SELL

RESPONSE WORD	M	F	T	M	F	T	M	F	T
COVERS	1	–	1	–	–	–	–	–	–
CUP	–	1	1	–	–	–	–	–	–
DELL	–	1	1	–	1	1	–	–	–
DINING ROOM	1	–	1	–	1	1	–	–	–
DINNER	–	–	–	–	1	1	–	–	–
DO	1	–	1	–	–	–	–	–	–
DO NOT SELL	–	–	–	1	1	2	–	–	–
DOCTOR	–	–	–	1	–	1	–	–	–
DOESNT SELL	–	–	–	1	–	1	–	–	–
DOG	1	2	3	–	1	1	–	–	–
DONATE	–	–	–	–	–	–	1	–	1
DONT	–	–	–	1	1	2	–	–	–
DONT SELL	1	–	1	2	–	2	–	–	–
DONUTS	–	1	1	–	–	–	–	–	–
DOOR	1	–	1	–	–	–	–	–	–
DOWN	1	–	1	–	1	1	–	–	–
DRESS	–	2	2	–	–	–	–	–	–
DRINK	–	1	1	–	–	–	–	–	–
E	1	1	2	–	–	–	–	–	–
EAT	–	1	1	1	–	1	–	–	–
ELF	–	1	1	–	–	–	–	–	–
FAST	–	2	2	–	–	–	–	–	–
FATHER	–	–	–	–	–	–	1	–	1
FELL	–	–	–	3	1	4	–	1	1
FITTED	1	–	1	–	–	–	–	–	–
FIX	–	–	–	–	1	1	1	–	1
FLOAT	–	–	–	–	–	–	–	1	1
FOOD	5	11	16	–	2	2	1	2	3
FOOLED	–	1	1	–	–	–	–	–	–
FOR	2	–	2	–	–	–	–	–	–
FOR SALE	1	–	1	–	1	1	–	–	–
FREE	–	–	–	–	1	1	–	–	–
FRUIT	5	2	7	1	–	1	–	1	1
GARBAGE CAN	1	–	1	–	–	–	–	–	–
GAS	–	–	–	–	–	–	1	–	1
GAVE	–	–	–	1	1	2	–	2	2
GET	–	–	–	1	–	1	1	1	2
GET RID OF	–	–	–	–	–	–	–	2	2
GET RID OF SOMETHING	–	–	–	–	–	–	1	–	1
GET SOME FOOD	–	1	1	–	–	–	–	–	–
GIVE	–	2	2	8	8	16	8	5	13
GIVE AWAY	–	–	–	1	3	4	1	5	6
GIVE FOR MONEY	–	–	–	–	–	–	1	–	1
GIVE OUT	–	–	–	–	–	–	–	1	1
GIVE STUFF	–	–	–	–	1	1	–	–	–
GIVING	–	–	–	–	1	1	–	–	–
GLASS	1	–	1	–	–	–	–	–	–
GO	1	1	2	1	1	2	–	1	1
GOLD	1	–	1	–	–	–	–	–	–
GOLDFISH	–	–	–	–	1	1	–	–	–
GOOD	1	–	1	–	–	–	–	–	–
GOODS	–	–	–	–	–	–	–	1	1
GREEN	–	1	1	–	–	–	–	–	–
GRELL	1	–	1	–	–	–	–	–	–
GROCERIES	–	3	3	–	–	–	–	–	–
GROUND	–	1	1	–	–	–	–	–	–
HAIR	–	1	1	–	–	–	–	1	1
HAND	–	–	–	–	–	–	1	–	1
HARD	–	–	–	–	–	–	–	1	1
HAT	–	–	–	–	–	–	–	1	1
HATS	–	1	1	–	–	–	–	–	–
HAVE	–	–	–	–	2	2	1	–	1
HEART	1	–	1	–	–	–	–	–	–
HELL	1	1	2	–	–	–	–	–	–
HELP	1	1	2	–	–	–	–	–	–
HER	–	–	–	1	–	1	–	–	–
HIGH	–	1	1	–	–	–	–	–	–
HIM	–	–	–	1	1	2	–	–	–
HUMAN	–	–	–	–	–	–	–	1	1
I SELL FRUIT	–	1	1	–	–	–	–	–	–
I SELL THINGS	–	1	1	–	–	–	–	–	–
ICE CREAM	–	1	1	–	–	–	–	–	–

72. SELL

RESPONSE WORD	1ST M	F	T	3RD M	F	T	5TH M	F	T
INSECT	–	–	–	–	–	–	–	1	1
IT	–	3	3	–	1	1	–	–	–
JAIL	2	1	3	4	–	4	3	2	5
JAIL (USED CELL)	–	–	–	–	–	–	1	–	1
JAIL CELL	–	–	–	1	–	1	–	–	–
JELL	–	–	–	–	–	–	1	–	1
JUMP	1	–	1	–	–	–	–	–	–
KALL	–	1	1	–	–	–	–	–	–
KEEP	2	1	3	1	3	4	4	5	9
KELL	1	1	2	–	–	–	–	–	–
KEY	–	–	–	–	–	–	1	–	1
KITCHEN	1	–	1	–	–	–	–	–	–
LEAVE	1	1	2	–	–	–	–	–	–
LELL	2	–	2	–	–	–	–	–	–
LEMONADE	–	–	–	1	–	1	–	–	–
LET	–	–	–	–	1	1	–	–	–
LET ME BE BY MYSELF	–	1	1	–	–	–	–	–	–
LIGHT	1	–	1	–	–	–	–	–	–
LINE	1	–	1	–	–	–	–	–	–
LOT	–	–	–	–	–	–	1	–	1
LOW	–	2	2	–	–	–	–	–	–
MADE	–	–	–	1	–	1	–	–	–
MAIL	–	–	–	–	1	1	–	–	–
MAKE	1	–	1	–	–	–	1	–	1
MAKE A LIVING	–	–	–	1	–	1	–	–	–
MAKE THE LEAF	1	–	1	–	–	–	–	–	–
MAN	–	–	–	–	1	1	1	–	1
MARKET	1	–	1	–	–	–	–	1	1
ME	–	–	–	–	2	2	–	–	–
ME A DOG	1	–	1	–	–	–	–	–	–
MEAT	–	–	–	1	–	1	–	–	–
MELL	1	1	2	–	1	1	–	–	–
MELT	1	–	1	–	–	–	–	–	–
MERCHANDISE	–	–	–	–	–	–	1	–	1
MERCHANT	–	–	–	–	1	1	–	–	–
METAL	1	–	1	–	–	–	–	–	–
MILK	2	–	2	–	–	–	–	–	–
MONEY	2	1	3	2	2	4	6	4	10
MOTHER FIXES SOME CELERY	–	1	1	–	–	–	–	–	–
MY	–	1	1	–	–	–	–	–	–
MY COOKIES	–	1	1	–	–	–	–	–	–
NAIL	–	1	1	–	–	–	–	–	–
NEEDLE	–	–	–	–	–	–	–	1	1
NEWS	–	–	–	–	1	1	–	–	–
NIOL	–	–	–	1	–	1	1	–	1
NO	–	–	–	1	1	2	–	–	–
NOT	–	1	1	–	–	–	–	–	–
NOT SELL	1	2	3	1	2	3	–	1	1
NOW	1	–	1	–	–	–	–	–	–
OUT	–	1	1	1	–	1	–	–	–
OUT OF ORDER	–	–	–	1	–	1	–	–	–
OWN	–	–	–	1	–	1	–	–	–
PAID	–	–	–	–	2	2	–	–	–
PAN	1	–	1	–	–	–	–	–	–
PAPER	1	2	3	2	–	2	–	–	–
PAY	–	–	–	–	1	1	–	–	–
PEANUTS	–	1	1	–	–	–	–	–	–
PEARS	–	–	–	–	–	–	–	1	1
PEDDLE	–	–	–	–	–	–	1	–	1
PEDDLER	–	–	–	–	1	1	–	–	–
PELL	1	–	1	1	1	2	–	–	–
PEPPER	–	1	1	–	–	–	–	–	–
PILL	–	–	–	1	–	1	–	–	–
PINEAPPLE	–	–	–	–	–	–	–	1	1
PLANKTON	–	–	–	–	–	–	1	–	1
PLAY	1	1	2	–	–	–	–	–	–
POCKET BOOK	1	–	1	–	–	–	–	–	–
POLL	–	–	–	–	–	–	1	–	1
PORE	–	–	–	–	–	–	–	1	1
PRICE	–	–	–	–	1	1	2	–	2
PRICED	–	–	–	–	–	–	–	1	1
PRISON	–	–	–	1	–	1	–	1	1

| RESPONSE | | 1ST | | | 3RD | | | 5TH | |
WORD	M	F	T	M	F	T	M	F	T

72.   SELL

RESPONSE WORD	M	F	T	M	F	T	M	F	T
PRISONER	–	–	–	1	–	1	–	–	–
PRODUCE	–	–	–	–	–	–	1	–	1
PURCHASE	–	–	–	–	1	1	–	1	1
RECEIVE	–	–	–	–	1	1	–	1	1
RENT	–	–	–	–	–	–	1	1	2
ROOM	–	1	1	–	–	–	–	–	–
SAIL	–	1	1	–	1	1	–	1	1
SALAD	1	–	1	–	–	–	–	–	–
SALAD DRESSING	1	–	1	–	–	–	–	–	–
SALARY	1	–	1	–	–	–	–	–	–
SALE	–	–	–	1	2	3	6	6	12
SALESMAN	–	–	–	1	–	1	1	–	1
SALT	1	–	1	–	1	1	–	–	–
SAT	1	–	1	–	–	–	–	–	–
SAVE	–	–	–	–	–	–	1	–	1
SAW	1	2	3	–	–	–	–	–	–
SEA	1	–	1	–	–	–	–	1	1
SEAL	–	–	–	–	–	–	–	1	1
SEE	1	–	1	1	1	2	–	–	–
SEED	–	–	–	–	–	–	–	1	1
SELF	–	1	1	–	–	–	–	–	–
SELFISH	–	1	1	–	–	–	–	–	–
SELL	–	–	–	1	–	1	1	–	1
SELL SOMETHING	–	–	–	1	–	1	–	–	–
SELLDER	1	–	1	–	–	–	–	–	–
SELLER	–	–	–	–	–	–	–	1	1
SELLING	–	–	–	1	–	1	2	–	2
SEND	–	–	–	1	1	2	–	–	–
SEW	–	1	1	–	–	–	1	–	1
SEWING	–	–	–	–	1	1	–	–	–
SEWING MACHINE	–	1	1	–	–	–	–	–	–
SHARE	–	–	–	–	1	1	–	–	–
SHELF	1	–	1	–	–	–	–	–	–
SHELL	–	–	–	1	1	2	1	3	4
SIGN	–	1	1	–	–	–	–	–	–
SILL	–	–	–	–	1	1	–	–	–
SINK	2	1	3	–	–	–	–	–	–
SIT	–	1	1	–	–	–	–	–	–
SKIN	–	–	–	–	–	–	1	–	1
SLIP	1	–	1	–	–	–	–	–	–
SMELL	–	–	–	1	–	1	–	–	–
SNOW	–	–	–	–	1	1	–	–	–
SOAP	–	1	1	–	–	–	–	–	–
SOLD	–	–	–	19	12	31	9	16	25
SOLD IT	–	–	–	1	–	1	–	–	–
SOME FOOD	–	1	1	–	–	–	–	–	–
SOMETHING	3	4	7	1	3	4	–	1	1
SON	–	1	1	–	–	–	–	–	–
SOUP	1	–	1	–	–	–	–	–	–
SOUR	2	–	2	–	–	–	–	–	–
SPELL	–	–	–	–	–	–	1	–	1
SPIDER	–	–	–	1	–	1	1	–	1
STABLE	–	–	–	–	–	–	1	–	1
STAR	–	1	1	–	–	–	–	–	–
STARE	–	1	1	–	–	–	–	–	–
STORE	2	2	4	2	7	9	–	3	3
STRING	–	–	–	–	–	–	1	–	1
STUFF	1	–	1	2	–	2	–	–	–
SUE	1	–	1	–	–	–	–	–	–
SUGAR	–	–	–	1	–	1	–	–	–
SWEATER	1	–	1	–	–	–	–	–	–
TABLE	1	–	1	–	–	–	–	–	–
TELL	–	–	–	1	1	2	–	1	1
THAT	1	–	1	1	–	1	–	–	–
THE	2	–	2	1	–	1	–	–	–
THE FOOD	–	1	1	–	–	–	–	–	–
THE WINDOW SILL	–	–	–	–	1	1	–	–	–
THEM	–	–	–	1	–	1	1	–	1
THINGS	3	2	5	8	2	10	–	–	–
THIS	1	1	2	–	–	–	–	–	–
TO ME	–	–	–	1	–	1	–	–	–
TOWN	–	1	1	–	–	–	–	–	–

RESPONSE WORD	1ST			3RD			5TH		
	M	F	T	M	F	T	M	F	T

72. SELL

RESPONSE WORD	M	F	T	M	F	T	M	F	T
TOY	1	1	2	–	–	–	1	–	1
TOYS	2	2	4	–	–	–	–	–	–
TRAIN	–	1	1	–	–	–	–	–	–
TREE	–	–	–	1	–	1	–	–	–
TRUCK	2	–	2	–	–	–	–	–	–
UNSELL	1	–	1	–	1	1	–	–	–
UP	1	–	1	–	–	–	–	–	–
VEGETABLES	–	–	–	–	1	1	–	–	–
WALL	–	2	2	–	–	–	–	–	–
WANT	–	–	–	1	–	1	–	–	–
WATER	–	–	–	1	1	2	–	–	–
WAVE	–	–	–	1	–	1	–	–	–
WEAR	–	–	–	–	–	–	–	1	1
WELL	–	2	2	2	3	5	1	1	2
WHAT YOU PUT IN WATER	1	–	1	–	–	–	–	–	–
WHEEL	1	–	1	–	–	–	–	–	–
WHEN YOURE SELLING NEWSPAPER	1	–	1	–	–	–	–	–	–
WINDOW	–	–	–	1	–	1	–	1	1
WINDOW SILL	–	–	–	–	–	–	–	1	1
WINDOWS	1	–	1	–	–	–	–	–	–
WORK	1	–	1	–	–	–	–	–	–
YELL	–	–	–	1	1	2	–	–	–
YELLOW	1	–	1	–	–	–	–	–	–
YOU	–	1	1	–	–	–	–	–	–
YOU COULD SELL SOME FRUIT	–	1	1	–	–	–	–	–	–
YOUR	1	–	1	–	–	–	–	–	–

73. SHE

RESPONSE WORD	M	F	T	M	F	T	M	F	T
A GIRL	–	1	1	–	–	–	–	2	2
A LADY	–	–	–	–	–	–	1	–	1
ALLEY	1	–	1	–	–	–	–	–	–
AN	–	1	1	–	–	–	–	–	–
ANIMAL	–	–	–	–	–	–	1	–	1
ANIMALS	1	–	1	–	–	–	–	–	–
ARE	–	1	1	–	–	–	–	–	–
BAA	–	1	1	–	–	–	–	–	–
BAD	–	1	1	–	–	–	–	–	–
BASKET	–	1	1	–	–	–	–	–	–
BED	1	–	1	1	–	1	–	–	–
BOY	–	2	2	2	1	3	1	1	2
BROWN	–	–	–	–	1	1	–	–	–
BUDDY	–	1	1	–	–	–	–	–	–
BUDS	–	–	–	–	1	1	–	–	–
CAN	1	3	4	–	–	–	–	–	–
CAT	–	–	–	–	1	1	–	–	–
CHALKBOARD	–	1	1	–	–	–	–	–	–
CHEESE	–	1	1	–	–	–	–	–	–
COAT	–	1	1	–	–	–	–	–	–
COLOR	–	–	–	–	1	1	–	–	–
COME	1	1	2	–	–	–	–	–	–
COVER	–	1	1	1	–	1	–	–	–
COW	1	–	1	–	–	–	–	–	–
CREED	1	–	1	–	–	–	–	–	–
DEE	–	1	1	–	–	–	–	–	–
DEEP	–	1	1	–	–	–	–	–	–
DID	1	–	1	1	–	1	1	–	1
DOCTOR	1	–	1	–	–	–	–	–	–
DOES SOMETHING	1	1	2	–	–	–	–	–	–
DOG	–	1	1	–	–	–	–	–	–
DONT PULL ON YOUR MOTHERS CURTAIN	–	1	1	–	–	–	–	–	–
DOOR	–	3	3	–	–	–	–	–	–
DOWN	1	1	2	–	–	–	–	–	–
DRESS	1	–	1	–	–	–	–	–	–
EAT	1	–	1	–	–	–	–	–	–
EATS	–	1	1	–	–	–	–	–	–
FAINTED	1	–	1	–	–	–	–	–	–
FAMILY	–	1	1	–	–	–	–	–	–

RESPONSE WORD	1ST			3RD			5TH		
	M	F	T	M	F	T	M	F	T

73.   SHE

RESPONSE WORD	M	F	T	M	F	T	M	F	T
FEMALE	–	–	–	–	–	–	2	–	2
FUR	1	–	1	–	–	–	–	–	–
GAVE	–	1	1	–	–	–	–	–	–
GET	–	–	–	–	–	–	1	–	1
GIRL	6	9	15	17	8	25	24	21	45
GO	–	1	1	–	–	–	–	–	–
GOOD	2	–	2	–	–	–	–	–	–
GOOD NIGHT	–	1	1	–	–	–	–	–	–
GRASS	1	–	1	–	–	–	–	–	–
HAD	2	–	2	–	–	–	–	–	–
HAIR	1	–	1	–	–	–	–	–	–
HAM	1	–	1	–	–	–	–	–	–
HAND	1	–	1	–	1	1	–	–	–
HANDLE	1	–	1	–	–	–	–	–	–
HAS	1	2	3	1	1	2	–	–	–
HAS TO COME IN	–	1	1	–	–	–	–	–	–
HAT	1	–	1	–	–	–	–	–	–
HAVE	–	1	1	–	–	–	–	–	–
HE	28	32	60	47	58	105	45	63	108
HEARD	–	–	–	1	–	1	–	–	–
HEEP	1	–	1	–	–	–	–	–	–
HELPS YOU	–	1	1	–	–	–	–	–	–
HER	3	6	9	25	30	55	36	25	61
HERE	–	1	1	–	–	–	–	–	–
HIM	6	6	12	21	25	46	18	18	36
HIS	1	–	1	1	1	2	–	–	–
I	1	–	1	–	–	–	–	–	–
IN BED	–	1	1	–	–	–	–	–	–
IS	4	3	7	1	1	2	1	–	1
IS A GIRL	–	–	–	1	–	1	–	1	1
IS A LADY	1	–	1	–	–	–	–	–	–
IS GOOD	–	1	1	–	–	–	–	–	–
IS HAPPY	1	–	1	–	–	–	–	–	–
IS LIKE A BEE	–	1	1	–	–	–	–	–	–
IS MAD	1	–	1	–	–	–	–	–	–
IT	–	–	–	–	–	–	1	–	1
KEY	–	1	1	–	–	–	–	–	–
KNEW	–	–	–	1	–	1	–	–	–
LADY	2	–	2	1	1	2	–	–	–
LAMB	1	1	2	1	1	2	–	–	–
LAMP	1	–	1	–	–	–	–	–	–
LAY	1	–	1	–	–	–	–	–	–
LEE	2	1	3	–	–	–	–	–	–
LIBRARY	1	–	1	–	–	–	–	–	–
LIGHT	–	1	1	–	–	–	–	–	–
LIKE	2	–	2	–	–	–	–	–	–
LITTLE BABY THAT IS A SHE BABY	–	1	1	–	–	–	–	–	–
LONG HAIR	1	–	1	–	–	–	–	–	–
LOOK	–	–	–	1	–	1	–	–	–
LOUD	–	1	1	–	–	–	–	–	–
LOVES	–	1	1	–	–	–	–	–	–
MACHINE	2	–	2	–	–	–	–	–	–
MAN	3	1	4	–	–	–	–	–	–
MARRIED	1	–	1	–	–	–	–	–	–
ME	10	3	13	9	3	12	1	3	4
MINE	1	–	1	–	–	–	–	–	–
MOCK	–	1	1	–	–	–	–	–	–
MOTHER	1	–	1	–	–	–	1	–	1
MOVIE	–	1	1	–	–	–	–	–	–
MY	–	1	1	–	–	–	–	–	–
NAME	–	1	1	–	–	–	–	–	–
NANCY	–	–	–	–	–	–	–	1	1
NO	–	1	1	–	–	–	–	–	–
NO RESPONSE	–	1	1	–	–	–	–	–	–
NOT	1	–	1	–	–	–	–	–	–
PAPER	–	1	1	–	–	–	–	–	–
PEAT	1	1	2	–	–	–	–	–	–
PEEK	–	1	1	–	–	–	–	–	–
PERSON	–	–	–	–	1	1	2	1	3
PET	1	–	1	–	–	–	–	–	–
PLAY	–	–	–	–	–	–	–	1	1

RESPONSE WORD	1ST			3RD			5TH		
	M	F	T	M	F	T	M	F	T

73. SHE

RESPONSE WORD	M	F	T	M	F	T	M	F	T
PLAYS	-	1	1	-	-	-	-	-	-
PRETTY	1	-	1	-	-	-	-	-	-
QUEEN	1	-	1	-	-	-	-	1	1
RAG	1	-	1	-	-	-	-	-	-
REE	-	1	1	-	-	-	-	-	-
SAID	-	-	-	1	-	1	-	-	-
SAT	1	-	1	-	-	-	-	-	-
SAT DOWN	-	1	1	-	-	-	-	-	-
SEE	-	1	1	-	-	-	-	1	1
SHE	-	-	-	-	-	-	1	-	1
SHEEP	6	8	14	2	-	2	-	-	-
SHEEP DOG	-	1	1	-	-	-	-	-	-
SHEET	4	1	5	-	-	-	-	1	1
SHELL	-	1	1	-	-	-	-	-	-
SHOE	1	1	2	-	-	-	-	-	-
SHOES	1	-	1	-	-	-	-	-	-
SHORT	-	-	-	1	-	1	-	-	-
SHY	1	-	1	-	-	-	-	-	-
SIDEWALK	1	-	1	-	-	-	-	-	-
SING	1	1	2	-	-	-	-	-	-
SLEEP	-	-	-	-	1	1	-	-	-
SNAR	-	-	-	-	-	-	1	-	1
TELL	-	-	-	1	-	1	-	-	-
THATS A SHE-MOOSE	-	1	1	-	-	-	-	-	-
THEY	-	-	-	-	1	1	-	-	-
TIP	1	-	1	-	-	-	-	-	-
WANTS	2	-	2	-	-	-	-	-	-
WAS	1	-	1	-	1	1	-	-	-
WE	1	1	2	1	-	1	-	-	-
WENT	1	-	1	1	-	1	-	-	-
WHAT	-	-	-	-	-	-	1	-	1
WHAT YOU PUT ON A BED	1	-	1	-	-	-	-	-	-
WHEN YOU SEE SOMETHING	1	-	1	-	-	-	-	-	-
WILL	-	1	1	-	1	1	-	-	-
WINDOW	1	-	1	-	-	-	-	-	-
WOMAN	-	-	-	1	-	1	1	-	1
WOOL	2	-	2	-	-	-	-	-	-
WORK	-	2	2	-	-	-	-	-	-
YOU	-	2	2	-	-	-	-	-	-

74. SHEEP

RESPONSE WORD	M	F	T	M	F	T	M	F	T
A ANIMAL	-	-	-	1	-	1	-	1	1
A PET	-	1	1	-	-	-	-	-	-
AN ANIMAL	-	-	-	-	-	-	1	-	1
AN ANIMAL THAT IS SHEARED	-	-	-	-	-	-	-	1	1
ANIMAL	1	2	3	16	13	29	27	23	50
ANIMALS	-	1	1	2	1	3	2	1	3
ANIMLAL	-	-	-	-	-	-	1	-	1
ASLEEP	-	-	-	-	-	-	1	-	1
AT	1	-	1	-	-	-	-	-	-
AWAKE	-	-	-	-	-	-	-	1	1
BAA	1	1	2	1	-	1	-	2	2
BAA GOES HER SHEEP	-	1	1	-	-	-	-	-	-
BAA-BAA	-	1	1	-	-	-	-	-	-
BABY	1	-	1	-	-	-	-	-	-
BAD	-	1	1	-	-	-	-	-	-
BARN	-	1	1	-	-	-	-	-	-
BEACH	-	-	-	-	-	-	1	-	1
BEAD	-	1	1	-	-	-	-	-	-
BED	1	-	1	-	-	-	-	1	1
BEEP	3	1	4	1	-	1	1	1	2
BEET	1	-	1	-	-	-	-	-	-
BLACK	1	-	1	1	-	1	-	-	-
BLANKET	-	1	1	-	-	-	-	-	-
BLOUSE	-	-	-	-	1	1	-	-	-
BOAT	-	-	-	1	-	1	-	-	-
BOOK	1	-	1	-	-	-	-	-	-
BOUGHT	-	1	1	-	-	-	-	-	-
BOY	-	-	-	-	1	1	-	-	-

RESPONSE WORD	1ST			3RD			5TH		
	M	F	T	M	F	T	M	F	T

74. SHEEP

RESPONSE WORD	M	F	T	M	F	T	M	F	T
BROWN	–	–	–	–	1	1	–	–	–
BULL	2	–	2	2	–	2	1	–	1
BUNK	1	–	1	–	–	–	–	–	–
BUS	1	–	1	–	–	–	–	–	–
BY	1	–	1	–	–	–	–	–	–
CALF	–	–	–	2	–	2	–	–	–
CALM	1	–	1	–	–	–	–	–	–
CAMEL	–	–	–	–	1	1	–	–	–
CAMELS	–	–	–	1	–	1	–	–	–
CAR	1	–	1	–	–	–	–	–	–
CARROT	1	–	1	–	–	–	–	–	–
CAT	1	–	1	–	3	3	–	1	1
CATTLE	1	1	2	1	6	7	5	3	8
CHALK	–	1	1	–	–	–	–	–	–
CHASE	1	–	1	–	–	–	–	–	–
CHERRIES	–	–	–	–	1	1	–	–	–
CLOTHES	–	–	–	–	1	1	–	–	–
CLOTHING	–	–	–	1	–	1	–	–	–
COAT	–	–	–	–	1	1	–	–	–
COLCK	–	–	–	–	–	–	–	1	1
COME	–	1	1	–	–	–	–	–	–
COMES	–	–	–	–	–	–	1	–	1
COTTON	–	–	–	–	1	1	2	–	2
COUNT	–	–	–	–	–	–	–	1	1
COW	3	4	7	8	7	15	2	4	6
COWS	1	–	1	–	–	–	1	–	1
CRAWLS	1	–	1	–	–	–	–	–	–
CREEP	1	–	1	–	–	–	–	–	–
CROWD	–	–	–	1	–	1	–	–	–
DEEP	–	1	1	–	–	–	–	–	–
DOG	3	4	7	7	5	12	11	7	18
DONKEY	–	–	–	–	1	1	–	–	–
DRAINK	–	–	–	–	–	–	–	1	1
DUCK	1	–	1	–	–	–	–	–	–
EWE	–	–	–	–	–	–	–	2	2
FALL	1	–	1	–	–	–	–	–	–
FARM	–	1	1	–	–	–	1	–	1
FARMER	1	–	1	–	–	–	–	–	–
FAWN	–	1	1	–	–	–	–	–	–
FIELD	–	–	–	1	–	1	–	1	1
FISH	–	1	1	–	–	–	–	–	–
FLOCK	–	–	–	–	2	2	–	2	2
FLOOR	–	1	1	–	–	–	–	–	–
FLOWER	1	–	1	–	–	–	–	–	–
FLUFFY	–	–	–	1	–	1	–	–	–
FOX	1	1	2	–	2	2	–	–	–
FUR	3	3	6	1	2	3	–	1	1
FURRY	–	–	–	–	–	–	1	–	1
GIRL	1	–	1	–	–	–	1	–	1
GO	–	1	1	–	–	–	–	–	–
GOAT	3	–	3	3	4	7	12	6	18
GOATS	–	–	–	–	–	–	3	–	3
GOD	–	–	–	–	–	–	–	1	1
GRASS	–	1	1	1	1	2	–	–	–
HACHET	1	–	1	–	–	–	–	–	–
HAIR	2	1	3	1	2	3	–	–	–
HAT	1	–	1	–	–	–	–	–	–
HAVE HORNS	–	1	1	–	–	–	–	–	–
HAY	–	–	–	–	1	1	–	–	–
HAYSTACK	–	1	1	–	–	–	–	–	–
HE	1	1	2	1	–	1	1	–	1
HEAP	–	2	2	–	–	–	–	–	–
HEAR	–	–	–	1	–	1	–	–	–
HEARD	–	–	–	–	–	–	1	–	1
HEEP	2	–	2	–	–	–	–	–	–
HELP	1	–	1	–	–	–	–	–	–
HEN	–	1	1	–	–	–	–	–	–
HER	–	1	1	–	–	–	–	–	–
HERD	–	–	–	2	3	5	3	5	8
HERE	1	–	1	–	–	–	–	–	–
HIM	–	–	–	–	1	1	1	–	1
HORSE	1	2	3	2	3	5	–	–	–

74. SHEEP

RESPONSE WORD	1ST M	1ST F	1ST T	3RD M	3RD F	3RD T	5TH M	5TH F	5TH T
HORSES	-	-	-	-	1	1	-	1	1
HOUSE	-	-	-	2	-	2	-	1	1
I WANT TO KEEP A SHEEP	1	-	1	-	-	-	-	-	-
IS WHITE	1	-	1	-	-	-	-	-	-
KEEP	1	2	3	-	-	-	2	1	3
KEEP THE SHEEP	-	1	1	-	-	-	-	-	-
KILL	1	-	1	-	-	-	-	-	-
LAMB	17	27	44	30	33	63	18	35	53
LAMBS	-	-	-	1	1	2	-	1	1
LAMP	-	2	2	-	1	1	-	4	4
LEAP	1	1	2	1	-	1	-	-	-
LEAVES	1	-	1	-	-	-	-	-	-
LEG	-	1	1	-	-	-	-	-	-
LIGHT	1	-	1	-	-	-	-	-	-
LIMB	-	1	1	-	-	-	-	-	-
LITTLE SHEEP	2	-	2	-	-	-	-	-	-
MAN	-	1	1	1	1	2	-	-	-
MANY	1	-	1	-	-	-	-	-	-
MARY	1	1	2	-	-	-	-	-	-
ME	1	-	1	1	-	1	-	-	-
MEADOW	3	2	5	1	1	2	1	-	1
MEAT	2	2	4	-	-	-	-	-	-
MEEP	1	-	1	-	-	-	-	-	-
MILK	-	-	-	-	1	1	-	-	-
MITTENS	-	1	1	-	-	-	-	-	-
MOCK	-	1	1	-	-	-	-	-	-
MOO COW	1	-	1	-	-	-	-	-	-
MOON	1	-	1	-	-	-	-	-	-
MOUSE	-	1	1	-	-	-	-	-	-
MRS	-	-	-	1	-	1	-	-	-
NEEP	-	1	1	-	-	-	-	-	-
NO RESPONSE	-	1	1	-	-	-	-	-	-
NOT SHEEP	1	-	1	-	-	-	-	-	-
NUMBER	-	1	1	-	-	-	-	-	-
PAPER	-	-	-	-	-	-	-	1	1
PASTURE	-	1	1	-	1	1	1	1	2
PEEP	2	-	2	2	-	2	1	-	1
PEOPLE	1	-	1	-	-	-	-	-	-
PEP	-	-	-	-	-	-	1	-	1
PET	1	-	1	-	-	-	-	-	-
PIG	-	-	-	1	1	2	-	1	1
PILLOW	-	1	1	-	-	-	-	-	-
PILLOWCASE	-	1	1	-	-	-	-	-	-
PIRATE	1	-	1	-	-	-	-	-	-
POCKET BOOK	-	1	1	-	-	-	-	-	-
POLL	-	-	-	-	-	-	1	-	1
RABBIT	-	-	-	-	1	1	-	-	-
RAM	-	-	-	1	-	1	2	1	3
RAT	-	-	-	-	1	1	-	-	-
REAL	1	-	1	-	-	-	-	-	-
REAP	-	1	1	-	-	-	-	-	-
RIVER	1	-	1	-	-	-	-	-	-
RUG	-	1	1	-	-	-	-	-	-
SALLY	-	1	1	-	-	-	-	-	-
SCHOOL	-	1	1	-	-	-	-	-	-
SEA	-	1	1	-	-	-	-	-	-
SEE	-	2	2	-	-	-	-	1	1
SHAIR	-	-	-	-	-	-	1	-	1
SHE	2	6	8	1	2	3	-	-	-
SHEEP DOG	1	-	1	-	-	-	1	-	1
SHEEPHERDER	-	1	1	1	-	1	1	1	1
SHEET	2	-	2	1	1	2	-	1	1
SHEPHERD	-	3	3	-	1	1	6	2	8
SHEPHERDS	-	-	-	-	-	-	1	-	1
SHIRT	-	1	1	-	-	-	-	-	-
SHOE	-	1	1	-	-	-	-	-	-
SHOES	-	1	1	-	-	-	-	-	-
SHOW	1	-	1	-	-	-	-	-	-
SIGNED	1	-	1	-	-	-	-	-	-
SILK	-	-	-	-	1	1	-	-	-
SKEEP	-	1	1	-	-	-	-	-	-

RESPONSE WORD	1ST M	1ST F	1ST T	3RD M	3RD F	3RD T	5TH M	5TH F	5TH T

74.   SHEEP

RESPONSE WORD	M	F	T	M	F	T	M	F	T
SKIP	–	–	–	–	1	1	–	–	–
SLEEP	3	–	3	4	4	8	4	1	5
SMALL	–	–	–	–	–	–	–	1	1
SOFT	–	–	–	2	–	2	1	–	1
SOUP	1	–	1	–	–	–	–	–	–
SOW	–	–	–	–	–	–	–	1	1
SPEED	–	–	–	–	–	–	1	–	1
STARS	–	1	1	–	–	–	–	–	–
STOLE	2	–	2	–	–	–	–	–	–
SWEATER	–	–	–	–	–	–	1	–	1
SWEEP	1	–	1	–	–	–	–	–	–
TABLE	2	–	2	–	–	–	–	–	–
THEM	–	–	–	–	1	1	–	–	–
THEY	–	1	1	–	–	–	–	–	–
TIN	1	–	1	–	–	–	–	–	–
TORN	–	1	1	–	–	–	–	–	–
TREE	–	1	1	–	–	–	–	–	–
WAKE	–	–	–	1	–	–	–	1	1
WALL	–	–	–	1	–	1	1	–	1
WATCH DOG	1	–	1	–	–	–	–	–	–
WATER	1	–	1	–	–	–	–	–	–
WEEP	2	–	2	1	–	1	–	–	–
WHEAT	–	1	1	–	–	–	–	–	–
WHILE THE MEN WASH THE SHEEP	1	–	1	–	–	–	–	–	–
WHITE	5	4	9	2	6	8	3	4	7
WHITE SHEEP	1	1	2	–	–	–	–	–	–
WHITE WOOL	–	1	1	–	–	–	–	–	–
WIGHT	–	–	–	–	–	–	1	–	1
WINDOW	–	1	1	–	–	–	–	–	–
WIPE	1	–	1	–	–	–	–	–	–
WOBBLE	1	–	1	–	–	–	–	–	–
WOLF	1	1	2	3	1	4	3	1	4
WOOD	1	–	1	–	–	–	–	–	–
WOOF	–	1	1	–	–	–	–	–	–
WOOL	9	7	16	23	12	35	6	13	19
WOOLLY	–	–	–	–	2	2	1	–	1
WOOLY	1	–	1	–	–	–	–	–	–
YOU	–	1	1	–	–	–	–	–	–
YOU GO BAA	–	1	1	–	–	–	–	–	–

75.   SHORT

RESPONSE WORD	M	F	T	M	F	T	M	F	T
A DOLL BABY	–	1	1	–	–	–	–	–	–
ARMS	–	–	–	–	–	–	1	1	1
BABY	1	–	1	–	–	–	1	1	2
BAD	–	1	1	–	–	–	–	–	–
BECAUSE	–	–	–	1	–	1	–	–	–
BEGIN	–	1	1	–	–	–	–	–	–
BESIDE	–	–	–	1	–	1	–	–	–
BIG	7	13	20	6	4	10	2	1	3
BIGGER	–	1	1	–	–	–	–	–	–
BLACKBOARD	1	–	1	–	–	–	–	–	–
BLOUSE	–	1	1	–	–	–	–	–	–
BOARD	1	–	1	–	–	–	–	–	–
BOAT	–	1	1	–	–	–	–	–	–
BOOK	–	–	–	–	–	–	–	1	1
BORT	1	1	2	–	–	–	–	–	–
BOX	1	–	1	–	–	–	–	–	–
BOY	2	–	2	–	–	–	–	–	–
BUTTER	–	1	1	–	–	–	–	–	–
CAKE	1	–	1	–	–	–	–	–	–
CAN	1	1	2	–	–	–	–	–	–
CAR	1	–	1	–	–	–	–	–	–
CAT	1	–	1	–	1	1	–	1	1
CAUGHT	–	–	–	–	–	–	–	1	1
CHALK BOARD	1	–	1	–	–	–	–	–	–
CLOTHES	–	2	2	–	–	–	–	–	–
COME	–	–	–	–	1	1	–	–	–
COOK	–	1	1	–	–	–	–	–	–
CORE	1	–	1	–	–	–	–	–	–

75. SHORT

RESPONSE WORD	1ST M	1ST F	1ST T	3RD M	3RD F	3RD T	5TH M	5TH F	5TH T
CORNER	—	1	1	—	—	—	—	—	—
COT	—	1	1	—	—	—	—	—	—
COW	—	—	—	—	1	1	—	—	—
CUT	—	2	2	—	—	—	—	—	—
CUTS	—	1	1	—	—	—	—	—	—
DESK	1	1	2	—	—	—	—	—	—
DISTANCE	—	1	1	1	—	1	—	—	—
DOG	1	1	2	—	—	—	—	—	—
DONT WEAR THOSE SHORTS WHEN ITS REAL CO	—	1	1	—	—	—	—	—	—
DOOR	1	—	1	—	—	—	—	—	—
DOOR KNOB	—	1	1	—	—	—	—	—	—
DOWN	—	1	1	—	—	—	—	—	—
DRESS	—	4	4	—	1	1	—	—	—
FALL	—	—	—	1	—	1	—	—	—
FAST	—	—	—	—	—	—	1	1	2
FAT	1	—	1	—	—	—	—	1	1
FIGHT	—	—	—	—	1	1	—	—	—
FLY	—	—	—	1	—	1	—	—	—
FOOT	1	—	1	—	—	—	—	—	—
FORK	1	—	1	—	—	—	—	—	—
FUN	—	—	—	—	—	—	1	—	1
GIRL	—	1	1	—	—	—	—	—	—
GO	—	—	—	—	—	—	—	1	1
GOOD	1	—	1	—	—	—	—	—	—
HAIR	2	2	4	—	—	—	—	—	—
HALF	1	—	1	—	—	—	—	—	—
HAND	1	—	1	—	—	—	—	—	—
HEARD	—	—	—	—	—	—	—	1	1
HERE	—	2	2	—	—	—	—	—	—
HIGH	1	2	3	1	—	1	1	1	2
HIM	—	—	—	—	—	—	—	1	1
HORT	2	—	2	—	—	—	—	—	—
HOUSE	—	1	1	—	—	—	—	—	—
I HAVE SHORTS ON	—	1	1	—	—	—	—	—	—
IN	1	—	1	—	1	1	—	—	—
INCH	—	—	—	—	—	—	2	—	2
LARGE	—	—	—	—	2	2	—	—	—
LEGS	—	1	1	—	—	—	—	—	—
LENGTH	—	—	—	—	—	—	1	1	2
LIGHT	1	—	1	—	—	—	—	—	—
LIKE SHORTS YOU WEAR	—	1	1	—	—	—	—	—	—
LITTLE	4	10	14	7	10	17	4	4	8
LOND	—	—	—	—	—	—	1	—	1
LONG	28	19	47	80	79	159	61	69	130
LONT	—	—	—	—	—	—	1	—	1
LOTS	—	1	1	—	—	—	—	—	—
LOUD	—	—	—	—	—	—	1	—	1
LOW	—	1	1	—	—	—	1	—	1
MAN	6	1	7	—	3	3	1	—	1
ME	—	—	—	—	1	1	1	—	1
MEDIUM	—	—	—	—	1	1	—	—	—
MOMMY	—	—	—	—	—	—	—	1	1
MORT	4	1	5	—	—	—	—	—	—
MOTHER	1	—	1	—	—	—	—	—	—
MOUNTAIN	1	—	1	—	—	—	—	—	—
NAME	1	—	1	—	—	—	—	—	—
NICE	—	—	—	—	1	1	—	—	—
NOT LONG	—	—	—	—	—	—	1	3	4
NOT TALL	—	—	—	—	—	—	1	1	2
NOT TALL ENOUGH	—	—	—	—	—	—	1	—	1
NOW	—	1	1	—	—	—	—	—	—
OUT	—	—	—	—	—	—	1	1	2
OVERALLS	1	—	1	—	—	—	—	—	—
PANT	—	1	1	—	—	—	—	—	—
PANTS	13	6	19	2	—	2	—	—	—
PAPER	—	1	1	—	—	—	—	—	—
PEOPLE	1	—	1	—	—	—	—	1	1
PERSON	1	—	1	—	—	—	—	—	—
PLAY	1	1	2	—	—	—	—	—	—
POCKETBOOK	1	1	2	—	—	—	—	—	—

RESPONSE WORD	1ST M	F	T	3RD M	F	T	5TH M	F	T

75. SHORT

RESPONSE WORD	1ST M	F	T	3RD M	F	T	5TH M	F	T
POLE	1	–	1	–	–	–	–	–	–
PORT	2	2	4	–	–	–	–	–	–
PUNK	–	–	–	–	–	–	1	–	1
PUPPY	2	–	2	–	–	–	–	–	–
PUT IT ON	1	–	1	–	–	–	–	–	–
QUART	1	–	1	–	–	–	–	–	–
QUIET	–	–	–	1	–	1	–	–	–
RACOON	–	–	–	1	–	1	–	–	–
REAL	–	1	1	–	–	–	–	–	–
RED	–	1	1	–	–	–	–	–	–
RIBBON	–	–	–	–	–	–	–	1	1
RUN	–	–	–	–	1	1	–	–	–
SECOND	–	–	–	–	–	–	1	–	1
SHIFT	–	1	1	–	–	–	–	–	–
SHIRT	–	1	1	–	–	–	–	–	–
SHOE	1	–	1	–	–	–	–	–	–
SHORT	–	1	1	–	–	–	–	–	–
SHORTENING	1	–	1	–	–	–	–	–	–
SHORTIES	1	–	1	–	–	–	–	–	–
SHORTLY	–	1	1	–	–	–	–	–	–
SHORTS	2	4	6	–	–	–	–	–	–
SHORTS YOU WEAR	–	1	1	–	–	–	–	–	–
SHORTY	2	1	3	–	–	–	–	–	–
SHRIMP	–	–	–	1	–	1	1	–	1
SITTING	1	–	1	–	–	–	–	–	–
SKINNY	1	3	4	1	–	1	–	–	–
SKIRT	–	1	1	–	–	–	–	–	–
SLEEVE	–	–	–	–	–	–	1	–	1
SMALL	5	6	11	14	17	31	14	15	29
SNOW	–	1	1	–	–	–	–	–	–
SOMEBODY SHORT	–	1	1	–	–	–	–	–	–
SOMETHING	–	–	–	–	–	–	1	–	1
SORT	1	–	1	1	–	1	–	–	–
SQUIRR	–	–	–	1	–	1	–	–	–
SQUIRT	–	–	–	1	–	1	–	–	–
STOCKY	–	1	1	–	–	–	–	–	–
STOP	1	–	1	–	–	–	–	–	–
STORE	–	–	–	1	–	1	–	–	–
STOUT	–	–	–	–	–	–	–	1	1
STRING	–	–	–	1	–	1	–	–	–
STRIP	–	–	–	1	–	1	–	–	–
STUBBY	–	–	–	–	–	–	3	1	4
SUMMER	1	–	1	–	–	–	–	–	–
TABLE	–	1	1	–	–	–	–	–	–
TAIL	1	1	2	–	1	1	–	–	–
TALL	7	6	13	15	12	27	33	29	62
THIN	–	1	1	–	–	–	–	–	–
THINGS	1	–	1	–	–	–	–	–	–
TIME	–	–	–	–	–	–	–	1	1
TINY	–	–	–	–	1	1	–	–	–
TO	–	1	1	–	–	–	–	–	–
TOO	–	1	1	–	–	–	–	–	–
TOO TIGHT	–	1	1	–	–	–	–	–	–
TREE	1	–	1	–	–	–	–	–	–
TRIP	–	1	1	–	–	–	–	–	–
TURN	1	1	2	–	–	–	–	–	–
TURTLE	–	–	–	–	–	–	–	1	1
US	–	1	1	–	–	–	–	–	–
WARD	–	–	–	–	–	–	1	–	1
WART	–	1	1	1	–	1	–	–	–
WATER	1	–	1	–	–	–	–	–	–
WAY	–	1	1	–	–	–	–	–	–
WE	–	–	–	–	1	1	–	–	–
WEAR OUTSIDE IN SUMMER	1	–	1	–	–	–	–	–	–
WHEEL	–	1	1	–	–	–	–	–	–
WHEN YOU SHORTEN SOMETHING	1	–	1	–	–	–	–	–	–
WIDE	–	–	–	1	–	1	–	–	–
WING	1	–	1	–	–	–	–	–	–
WINGS	1	–	1	–	–	–	–	–	–
WORM	1	–	1	–	–	–	–	–	–

RESPONSE WORD	1ST			3RD			5TH		
	M	F	T	M	F	T	M	F	T

76. SINCE

RESPONSE WORD	1ST M	F	T	3RD M	F	T	5TH M	F	T
A NUMBER	1	–	1	–	–	–	–	–	–
ABLE	–	–	–	1	–	1	–	–	–
AFTER	–	–	–	4	2	6	3	1	4
AGAIN	–	–	–	1	–	1	–	3	3
AGO	–	–	–	1	1	2	4	2	6
ALONG TIME	–	–	–	–	–	–	1	–	1
ALREADY	–	–	–	–	–	–	–	1	1
ALWAYS	–	–	–	1	–	1	–	4	4
AND	–	1	1	–	–	–	–	–	–
ANOTHER	–	–	–	1	–	1	–	–	–
ANTS	–	–	–	–	1	1	–	–	–
ANYTHING	–	–	–	–	1	1	–	–	–
ARE	–	1	1	–	1	1	–	–	–
AWAY	–	1	1	–	1	1	–	–	–
BABY	1	–	1	–	–	–	–	–	–
BACK	–	–	–	–	1	1	–	–	–
BASKET	1	–	1	–	–	–	–	–	–
BAT	–	1	1	–	–	–	–	–	–
BE	1	–	1	–	–	–	–	–	–
BEADS	–	–	–	–	1	1	–	–	–
BECAUSE	–	1	1	1	3	4	1	2	3
BEETLES	1	–	1	–	–	–	–	–	–
BEFORE	1	–	1	1	3	4	6	3	9
BEGIN	1	–	1	1	–	1	1	2	3
BEHAVE	–	1	1	–	–	–	–	–	–
BESIDE	–	–	–	1	–	1	–	–	–
BETTER	–	1	1	–	–	–	–	–	–
BETWEEN	–	–	–	–	–	–	1	–	1
BIG	1	–	1	–	–	–	–	–	–
BINCE	–	2	2	–	–	–	–	–	–
BIRD	1	1	2	–	–	–	–	–	–
BIRDIE	1	–	1	–	–	–	–	–	–
BLACKBOARD	–	1	1	–	–	–	–	–	–
BOARD	–	1	1	–	–	–	–	–	–
BOAT	–	1	1	–	–	–	–	–	–
BOOK	–	–	–	1	–	1	–	–	–
BOX	1	–	1	–	–	–	–	–	–
BOY	–	–	–	2	–	2	1	–	1
BRACELET	–	1	1	–	–	–	–	–	–
BRAIN	1	–	1	2	2	4	1	1	2
BRAINS	–	–	–	1	1	2	1	1	1
BROTHER	–	–	–	–	–	–	1	–	1
BROWN	1	–	1	–	–	–	–	–	–
BUG	–	1	1	–	–	–	–	–	–
BUGS	1	–	1	–	–	–	–	–	–
BUREAU	–	1	1	–	–	–	–	–	–
BUSHES	1	–	1	–	–	–	–	–	–
BUTTERFLY	1	–	1	–	–	–	–	–	–
BUYING	–	–	–	1	–	1	–	–	–
CAME	–	–	–	1	–	1	–	–	–
CAN	1	–	1	–	–	–	–	–	–
CAR	–	–	–	–	1	1	–	–	–
CAT	–	–	–	1	–	1	–	–	–
CAUSE	–	1	1	–	–	–	–	–	–
CEILING	1	–	1	–	–	–	–	–	–
CENT	1	–	1	–	2	2	–	–	–
CENTS	–	1	1	3	1	4	–	–	–
CHAIR	1	–	1	–	–	–	–	–	–
CHALK	–	1	1	–	–	–	–	–	–
CHANGE	–	–	–	2	–	2	–	–	–
CHECK	–	–	–	–	–	–	1	–	1
CINCH	–	1	1	–	–	–	–	–	–
CINCINNATI	1	–	1	–	–	–	–	–	–
CINDY	–	1	1	–	–	–	–	–	–
CLIMB ON IT	–	1	1	–	–	–	–	–	–
CLOCK	–	–	–	–	1	1	–	–	–
CLOSE	–	–	–	1	–	1	–	–	–
COLD	–	1	1	–	–	–	–	–	–
COME BACK	–	–	–	1	–	1	–	–	–
COMMON	–	–	–	–	–	–	1	1	2
COMPASS	1	–	1	–	1	1	–	–	–
COW	–	–	–	–	1	1	–	–	–

RESPONSE WORD	1ST			3RD			5TH		
	M	F	T	M	F	T	M	F	T

76.   SINCE

RESPONSE WORD	M	F	T	M	F	T	M	F	T
CRAYON	1	–	1	–	–	–	–	–	–
CRAZY	–	1	1	–	–	–	–	1	1
CRINKS	–	1	1	–	–	–	–	–	–
CUZ	1	–	1	–	–	–	–	–	–
DAY	1	–	1	–	2	2	–	–	–
DEBT	–	1	1	–	–	–	–	–	–
DENSE	1	–	1	–	–	–	–	–	–
DESERT	–	–	–	–	–	–	1	–	1
DESK	1	–	1	–	–	–	–	–	–
DID	–	–	–	–	1	1	–	–	–
DIDNT DO IT	–	–	–	1	–	1	–	–	–
DIME	–	–	–	–	1	1	–	–	–
DISOBEY	–	–	–	–	1	1	–	–	–
DO	–	–	–	–	–	–	–	1	1
DO NOT SINCE	1	–	1	–	–	–	–	–	–
DOESNT	–	1	1	–	–	–	–	–	–
DOG	2	1	3	–	–	–	1	1	2
DOG SMELLED	1	–	1	–	–	–	–	–	–
DOLLAR	2	–	2	–	–	–	–	–	–
DONT PAY ANY ATTENTION CAUSE HES SILLY	–	1	1	–	–	–	–	–	–
DONT RUN	1	–	1	–	–	–	–	–	–
DOOR	2	1	3	–	–	–	–	–	–
DOWN	–	–	–	–	–	–	–	1	1
DOWN IN	–	–	–	–	–	–	1	–	1
DUCK	–	1	1	–	–	–	–	–	–
DUMB	1	–	1	–	–	–	1	–	1
DURING	–	–	–	–	–	–	–	1	1
EAT	–	–	–	–	–	–	1	–	1
EIGHT CENTS	1	–	1	–	–	–	–	–	–
END	–	–	–	–	1	1	–	–	–
ENOUGH	–	–	–	–	1	1	–	–	–
EVENING	–	–	–	–	1	1	–	–	–
EVER	–	1	1	1	4	5	5	4	9
EVER SINCE	–	1	1	1	–	1	–	1	1
EVERYONE	–	–	–	1	–	1	–	–	–
EXAMINE	–	–	–	–	–	–	–	1	1
FAIR	–	1	1	–	–	–	–	–	–
FALL	–	1	1	–	–	–	–	–	–
FAR	–	1	1	–	–	–	–	–	–
FENCE	3	2	5	–	–	–	1	1	2
FENCE COULD STAND UP	–	1	1	–	–	–	–	–	–
FIRST	–	–	–	–	1	1	–	–	–
FIVE PENNIES	–	1	1	–	–	–	–	–	–
FLOOR	1	–	1	–	–	–	–	–	–
FLOWER	1	–	1	–	–	–	–	–	–
FLY	3	1	4	–	–	–	–	–	–
FOOD	–	–	–	–	–	–	1	–	1
FOR A LONG TIME	–	–	–	1	–	1	–	–	–
FOREVER	–	–	–	–	–	–	–	2	2
FROM	–	–	–	–	–	–	1	3	4
FROM THEN	–	–	–	1	–	1	–	–	–
FROM THEN ON	–	–	–	–	–	–	1	–	1
FROM THEN TO NOW	–	–	–	–	–	–	–	1	1
FRUIT	–	–	–	1	–	1	–	–	–
GALE	–	–	–	–	1	1	–	–	–
GET	–	1	1	–	–	–	–	–	–
GET SOME SENSE IN YOU	1	–	1	–	–	–	–	–	–
GLASSES	1	–	1	–	–	–	–	–	–
GO	–	1	1	–	–	–	–	–	–
GOING OUT	–	1	1	–	–	–	–	–	–
GOING TO	–	–	–	1	–	1	–	–	–
GONE	–	–	–	–	–	–	1	–	1
GOOD	2	2	4	1	–	1	–	–	–
GRASS	–	–	–	1	–	1	–	–	–
GREEN	1	–	1	–	–	–	–	–	–
GREW UP	1	–	1	–	–	–	–	–	–
HAPPEN	–	–	–	1	–	1	1	–	1
HAPPY	1	–	1	1	–	1	–	1	1
HAT	1	–	1	–	–	–	–	–	–
HE	–	–	–	–	–	–	1	–	1
HEAD	1	–	1	1	1	2	–	–	–

76. SINCE

RESPONSE WORD	1ST M	F	T	3RD M	F	T	5TH M	F	T
HEARING	–	–	–	–	1	1	–	1	1
HEAVEN	1	–	1	–	1	1	–	–	–
HENCE	1	–	1	2	–	2	–	–	–
HERE	1	1	2	1	–	1	–	–	–
HIM	–	–	–	1	–	1	–	–	–
HINCE	1	–	1	–	–	–	–	–	–
HOPES	–	1	1	–	–	–	–	–	–
HOUSE	–	1	1	–	–	–	–	–	–
HOW	–	2	2	–	–	–	–	–	–
HOW LONG	–	–	–	–	–	–	1	–	1
HUMOR	1	–	1	1	–	1	–	–	–
I	3	3	6	–	2	2	–	–	–
I CAME HOME	1	–	1	–	–	–	–	–	–
I CANT THINK	–	–	–	–	–	–	–	1	1
I DONT KNOW	–	–	–	1	–	1	–	–	–
I HAD IT SINCE I WAS A BOY	–	–	–	1	–	1	–	–	–
I SAW YOU LEAVE	–	1	1	–	–	–	–	–	–
I WAS	–	–	–	1	–	1	–	–	–
IN	1	–	1	–	–	–	–	–	–
IN YOU	–	1	1	–	–	–	–	–	–
INK	–	1	1	–	–	–	–	–	–
IT	1	–	1	2	–	2	–	–	–
IT HAPPENED	–	–	–	1	–	1	–	–	–
IVE	–	–	–	1	–	1	–	–	–
JULY	–	–	–	–	–	–	–	1	1
KINCE	2	–	2	–	–	–	–	–	–
LAST	–	–	–	–	2	2	5	1	6
LAST NIGHT	–	–	–	–	1	1	–	–	–
LAST TIME	–	–	–	–	1	1	–	1	1
LAST WEEK	–	–	–	–	1	1	–	–	–
LATE	–	–	–	–	1	1	–	–	–
LATER	–	–	–	–	1	1	–	–	–
LIGHT	1	2	3	–	–	–	–	–	–
LISTEN	2	–	2	–	–	–	–	–	–
LONG	–	–	–	2	3	5	3	5	8
LONG AGO	–	–	–	1	–	1	6	–	6
LONG TIME	–	–	–	–	–	–	3	1	4
LONG, NOW	–	–	–	–	–	–	–	1	1
LOOK	–	–	–	–	–	–	–	2	2
LYNCH	–	–	–	1	–	1	–	–	–
MACHINE	1	–	1	–	–	–	–	–	–
MAD	–	–	–	–	1	1	–	–	–
MAKE	1	–	1	–	–	–	–	1	1
MANNERS	–	1	1	–	–	–	1	–	1
MARCH	–	–	–	–	–	–	1	–	1
MASK	–	1	1	–	–	–	–	–	–
ME	1	1	2	–	1	1	–	–	–
MEN	–	1	1	–	–	–	–	–	–
MILL	–	–	–	–	–	–	1	–	1
MIN	1	–	1	1	–	1	–	–	–
MINCE	4	1	5	1	–	1	–	–	–
MIND	–	–	–	–	2	2	4	–	4
MINE	–	–	–	–	1	1	–	1	1
MONDAY	–	–	–	–	–	–	–	1	1
MONEY	3	2	5	3	4	7	2	–	2
MONTHS	–	–	–	–	1	1	1	–	1
MORNING	–	–	–	–	–	–	1	–	1
MOTHER	–	1	1	–	–	–	–	–	–
MOUSE	–	–	–	–	–	–	–	1	1
MY	–	1	1	–	–	–	–	–	–
MY DADDY GOT SICK	–	1	1	–	–	–	–	–	–
NAME	–	–	–	–	–	–	1	–	1
NEVER	–	–	–	2	4	6	3	4	7
NEXT	–	–	–	1	–	1	–	–	–
NICE	–	1	1	–	–	–	–	–	–
NICKEL	–	–	–	2	–	2	–	–	–
NICKLE	–	–	–	1	–	1	–	–	–
NIGHT	–	–	–	–	–	–	1	–	1
NINCE	–	1	1	1	–	1	–	–	–
NO	1	–	1	–	–	–	1	–	1
NO RESPONSE	–	–	–	–	–	–	–	1	1

RESPONSE WORD	1ST			3RD			5TH		
	M	F	T	M	F	T	M	F	T

76. SINCE

RESPONSE WORD	M	F	T	M	F	T	M	F	T
NO SENSE	—	1	1	—	—	—	—	—	—
NONSENSE	—	—	—	—	—	—	—	1	1
NOSE	—	—	—	—	—	—	1	—	1
NOSINCE	—	—	—	—	—	—	—	1	1
NOT	—	—	—	1	1	2	—	1	1
NOT SEND	—	—	—	—	—	—	—	1	1
NOT SINCE	4	—	4	1	3	4	—	1	1
NOTICE	—	—	—	1	1	—	—	—	—
NOW	3	3	6	8	3	11	5	3	8
ODD	—	—	—	—	1	1	—	—	—
OFTEN	—	—	—	—	—	—	—	2	2
ONCE	1	—	1	—	1	1	4	1	5
ONE	—	1	1	—	—	—	—	—	—
ORANGE	—	—	—	—	1	1	—	—	—
PAN	—	1	1	—	—	—	—	—	—
PAPER	—	—	—	1	—	1	—	—	—
PAST	—	—	—	—	—	—	2	5	7
PEAR	—	—	—	1	—	1	—	—	—
PENCE	—	—	—	1	—	1	—	—	—
PENNIES	1	—	1	—	—	—	—	—	—
PENNY	1	—	1	1	—	1	—	1	1
PEOPLE	—	—	—	—	1	1	—	—	—
PIANO	—	—	—	—	—	—	—	1	1
PICTURE	1	—	1	1	—	1	—	—	—
PINCE	1	—	1	—	—	—	—	—	—
PLAY	—	1	1	—	—	—	—	—	—
POND	—	—	—	—	1	1	—	—	—
PURPLE	1	—	1	—	—	—	—	—	—
RADIO	—	1	1	—	—	—	—	—	—
RAIN	—	—	—	—	1	1	—	—	—
RAT	—	1	1	—	—	—	—	—	—
READ	—	—	—	—	—	—	—	1	1
RECIFT	—	—	—	—	—	—	—	1	1
RECOVER	—	—	—	—	1	1	—	—	—
RED	—	1	1	—	—	—	—	—	—
RENCE	—	1	1	—	—	—	—	—	—
RETURN	—	—	—	—	—	—	1	—	1
RINSE	1	—	1	—	—	—	—	—	—
RUBBER	1	—	1	—	—	—	—	—	—
RUN	—	2	2	1	—	1	—	1	1
SAD	—	—	—	—	1	1	—	—	—
SAID	1	—	1	—	—	—	—	—	—
SAND	1	1	2	—	—	—	—	—	—
SAT	1	—	1	—	—	—	—	—	—
SAW	—	1	1	1	—	1	—	—	—
SCHOOL	—	—	—	—	—	—	—	1	1
SCIENCE	—	—	—	—	1	1	—	1	1
SCISSORS	—	1	1	—	—	—	—	—	—
SCOUT	—	—	—	—	—	—	1	—	1
SEA	2	—	2	—	—	—	—	—	—
SEE	1	2	3	—	—	—	—	1	1
SEEM	—	—	—	1	—	1	—	1	1
SEEN	—	—	—	1	1	2	—	—	—
SENDS	—	—	—	—	1	1	—	—	—
SENSE	2	—	2	2	1	3	1	2	3
SENT	1	1	2	—	—	—	—	1	1
SENTENCE	—	1	1	—	1	1	—	—	—
SET	—	1	1	—	—	—	—	—	—
SEW	1	—	1	—	—	—	—	—	—
SHORT	—	—	—	—	1	1	—	—	—
SICK	—	—	—	—	1	1	—	—	—
SIDEWALK	1	—	1	—	—	—	—	—	—
SIFT	—	1	1	—	—	—	—	—	—
SIGN	—	—	—	—	—	—	1	—	1
SIN	1	1	2	1	1	2	1	—	1
SINCE WE STARTED	—	—	—	—	—	—	1	—	1
SING	—	3	3	—	—	—	—	—	—
SINGING	1	—	1	—	—	—	—	—	—
SINK	1	—	1	—	—	—	—	—	—
SIR	—	1	1	—	—	—	—	—	—
SISTER	—	1	1	—	—	—	—	—	—
SIT	—	—	—	1	—	1	—	—	—

76. SINCE

RESPONSE WORD	1ST M	1ST F	1ST T	3RD M	3RD F	3RD T	5TH M	5TH F	5TH T
SITTING	–	–	–	–	1	1	–	–	–
SKY	1	–	1	–	–	–	–	–	–
SMART	–	1	1	1	–	1	2	–	2
SMELL	–	–	–	–	–	–	3	2	5
SO	–	1	1	–	–	–	–	–	–
SO ON	–	–	–	–	1	1	–	–	–
SOME TIME AGO	1	–	1	–	–	–	–	–	–
SOMEONE	1	–	1	–	–	–	–	–	–
SOMETHING	1	2	3	–	–	–	–	–	–
SOMETHING PAST	–	–	–	–	–	–	–	1	1
SOMETHING THATS BEEN STARTED AND STILL	–	–	–	–	–	–	1	–	1
SOON	–	1	1	–	–	–	–	2	2
SOUGHT	–	1	1	–	–	–	–	–	–
START	–	–	–	–	–	–	3	–	3
STARTED	–	–	–	–	–	–	1	–	1
STILL	–	1	1	–	–	–	1	–	1
STOLE	1	–	1	–	–	–	–	–	–
STORE	–	1	1	–	–	–	–	–	–
STUDY	–	–	–	–	–	–	–	1	1
SUBJECT	–	–	–	–	–	–	1	–	1
SUCH	–	–	–	–	1	1	–	–	–
SUMMERY	–	–	–	–	–	–	1	–	1
SUN	1	1	2	–	–	–	–	–	–
TABLE	1	2	3	1	–	1	–	–	–
TAKER	–	–	–	–	–	–	1	–	1
TALK	–	1	1	–	–	–	–	–	–
TASTE	–	–	–	1	–	1	–	–	–
TEST	–	–	–	–	–	–	–	1	1
THAT	–	–	–	1	–	1	–	–	–
THAT HAPPENED	1	–	1	–	–	–	–	–	–
THAT TIME	–	–	–	1	–	1	–	–	–
THAT WAS SO LONG	–	1	1	–	1	1	–	–	–
THE DAY	–	–	–	–	1	1	–	–	–
THEN	3	4	7	14	14	28	17	12	29
THEN AFTER	–	–	–	–	–	–	–	1	1
THEN ON	–	–	–	–	–	–	1	–	1
THEY	–	–	–	–	–	–	–	1	1
THINGS	–	–	–	–	–	–	1	–	1
THINK	–	–	–	1	–	1	1	–	1
THOUGHT	–	–	–	–	–	–	–	1	1
THUMB	–	–	–	–	1	1	–	–	–
TILL	–	–	–	–	1	1	–	–	–
TIME	–	–	–	1	1	2	4	2	6
TO	1	–	1	–	–	–	–	–	–
TODAY	–	–	–	2	3	5	–	3	3
TOMORROW	–	–	–	1	–	1	–	–	–
TOUCH	–	–	–	–	1	1	–	1	1
TRAIN	–	–	–	–	1	1	–	–	–
TREES	1	–	1	–	–	–	–	–	–
TRUCK	–	1	1	–	–	–	1	–	1
TRUE	–	–	–	–	1	1	–	–	–
TUESDAY	–	–	–	–	1	1	–	–	–
TURN	1	–	1	–	–	–	–	–	–
TWICE	–	–	–	–	–	–	–	1	1
TWO CENTS	–	1	1	–	–	–	–	–	–
TWO HUNDRED YEARS AGO	–	1	1	–	–	–	1	–	1
UNDERSTAND	–	–	–	–	1	1	–	–	–
UNHAPPY	–	–	–	1	1	2	–	–	–
UNSINCE	–	–	–	–	–	–	1	1	2
UNTIL	–	–	–	–	–	–	1	–	1
USUALLY	–	–	–	–	–	–	1	–	1
WARNING	–	1	1	–	–	–	–	–	–
WAS	–	–	–	1	1	2	–	–	–
WAY	2	2	4	–	–	–	–	–	–
WE	–	1	1	–	–	–	–	–	–
WE CANT GO	1	–	1	–	–	–	–	–	–
WE HAVE TREES	–	–	–	–	–	1	1	–	1
WEATHER	–	–	–	1	–	1	1	–	1
WENT	–	1	1	–	–	–	–	–	–
WHAT	3	5	8	11	14	25	4	11	15
WHEN									

RESPONSE WORD	1ST			3RD			5TH		
	M	F	T	M	F	T	M	F	T

76. SINCE

RESPONSE WORD	M	F	T	M	F	T	M	F	T
WHEN YOURE SITTING SOMETHING.	1	–	1	–	–	–	–	–	–
WHENEVER SOMEBODY SAYS SINCE YOURE GOOD	–	1	1	–	–	–	–	–	–
WHILE	–	–	–	1	–	1	–	2	2
WHY	–	1	1	–	–	–	–	–	–
WILL	1	–	1	–	–	–	–	–	–
WINDOW	–	1	1	–	–	–	–	–	–
WONDER	–	–	–	–	1	1	–	–	–
WOOD	1	–	1	–	–	–	–	–	–
WORD	1	–	1	–	–	–	–	–	–
WORDS	–	–	–	–	–	–	1	–	1
WORK	–	–	–	–	–	–	–	1	1
YEAR	–	–	–	–	–	–	–	1	1
YESTERDAY	–	–	–	7	4	11	–	3	3
YET	–	–	–	–	–	–	–	1	1
YOU	2	4	6	2	3	5	–	–	–
YOU GOT SENSE	–	–	–	1	–	1	–	–	–
YOU LOST YOUR SENSE	1	–	1	–	–	–	–	–	–
YOU MIGHT GET UNCONSCIOUS.	–	1	1	–	–	–	–	–	–
YOU WENT	1	–	1	–	–	–	–	–	–
YOU WERE HERE	–	1	1	–	–	–	–	–	–
ZIN	–	1	1	–	–	–	–	–	–
ZINCE	–	1	1	–	–	–	–	–	–

77. SIT

RESPONSE WORD	M	F	T	M	F	T	M	F	T
ALL	–	1	1	–	–	–	–	–	–
AT	–	–	–	–	–	–	–	1	1
BATTLE	–	1	1	–	–	–	–	–	–
BEAD	1	–	1	–	–	–	–	–	–
BENCH	–	1	1	–	–	–	–	1	1
BIT	1	2	3	2	–	2	–	–	–
BLANKET	–	1	1	–	–	–	–	–	–
BOOK	–	1	1	–	–	–	–	1	1
BOOKS	–	1	1	–	–	–	–	–	–
C	1	–	1	–	–	–	–	–	–
CAT	–	2	2	–	–	–	–	–	–
CATCH	1	–	1	–	–	–	–	–	–
CHAIR	20	22	42	21	15	36	22	18	40
CHOSE	1	–	1	–	–	–	–	–	–
CLOCK	–	1	1	–	–	–	–	–	–
CLOSE	1	–	1	–	–	–	–	–	–
COMFORTABLE	–	–	–	1	–	1	–	–	–
DIP	–	1	1	–	–	–	–	–	–
DO	–	–	–	1	–	1	–	–	–
DOG	1	–	1	–	1	1	–	–	–
DOLL	1	–	1	–	–	–	–	–	–
DOOR	–	1	1	–	1	1	–	–	–
DOWN	51	47	98	31	33	64	32	22	54
DOWN AND HAVE SOME SODA	–	1	1	–	–	–	–	–	–
DOWN IN A CHAIR	1	–	1	–	–	–	–	–	–
DOWN ON THE FURNITURE	1	–	1	–	–	–	–	–	–
DOWN PLEASE	–	1	1	–	–	–	–	–	–
DRINKING FOUNTAIN	–	–	–	1	–	1	–	–	–
DRUM	–	1	1	–	–	–	–	–	–
EAT	–	–	–	1	–	1	1	–	1
FAN	1	–	1	–	–	–	–	–	–
FELL	–	–	–	–	–	–	1	–	1
FIGHT	–	–	–	–	–	–	1	–	1
FLOOR	1	–	1	–	1	1	–	–	–
FOR	1	–	1	–	–	–	–	–	–
FOUND	–	1	1	–	–	–	–	–	–
GET	1	–	1	–	–	–	–	–	–
GET UP	1	–	1	–	–	–	–	–	–
GET UP ON MY LAP, DOG	–	1	1	–	–	–	–	–	–
GO	–	–	–	1	–	1	–	–	–
GO SIT DOWN AND LOOK AT TV	–	1	1	–	–	–	–	–	–
HANGER	–	1	1	–	–	–	–	–	–

RESPONSE WORD	1ST M	F	T	3RD M	F	T	5TH M	F	T

77. SIT

RESPONSE WORD	1ST M	F	T	3RD M	F	T	5TH M	F	T
HARD	—	—	—	1	—	1	—	—	—
HE	—	—	—	—	—	—	—	1	1
HEAD	1	—	1	—	—	—	—	—	—
HER	—	—	—	—	—	—	—	1	1
HERE	1	2	3	—	—	—	—	—	—
HIT	3	—	3	1	1	2	1	—	1
I WILL SIT BESIDE YOU	—	1	1	—	—	—	—	—	—
IN	1	1	2	1	1	2	1	—	1
IN CHAIR	1	—	1	—	—	—	—	—	—
IN FRONT	—	—	—	1	—	1	—	—	—
IN YOUR CHAIR	—	1	1	—	—	—	—	—	—
IT	—	—	—	2	—	2	—	—	—
ITS READY TO BREAK DOWN	1	—	1	—	—	—	—	—	—
KICK	1	—	1	—	—	—	—	—	—
KIT	—	—	—	1	—	1	—	—	—
KNEEL	—	—	—	—	—	—	—	1	1
KNIT	—	—	—	—	—	—	—	1	1
KNIVES	—	—	—	—	—	—	—	1	1
LADDER	—	1	1	—	—	—	—	—	—
LANGUAGE	—	—	—	—	—	—	—	1	1
LAY	—	—	—	1	—	1	2	1	3
LIKE	1	—	1	—	—	—	—	—	—
LONG	—	—	—	—	1	1	—	—	—
MINT	1	—	1	—	—	—	—	—	—
MIT	—	—	—	—	1	1	—	—	—
MITT	1	—	1	—	—	—	—	—	—
MITTEN	—	1	1	—	—	—	—	—	—
MONEY	—	—	—	1	—	1	—	—	—
MOTHER	—	1	1	—	—	—	—	—	—
NAIL	—	1	1	—	—	—	—	—	—
NOT MOVE	—	—	—	—	—	—	1	—	1
NOT SIT	—	1	1	—	1	1	1	—	1
OF	—	—	—	—	—	—	1	—	1
OFF	—	—	—	1	—	1	—	—	—
OH	—	—	—	—	1	1	—	—	—
ON	—	—	—	2	—	2	2	3	5
ON A HASSOCK	1	—	1	—	—	—	—	—	—
ON CHAIR	1	—	1	—	—	—	—	—	—
ON IT	—	—	—	—	—	—	1	—	1
OUT	1	—	1	—	—	—	—	—	—
PAID	—	—	—	1	—	1	—	—	—
PEACE	—	1	1	—	—	—	—	—	—
PICTURE	—	1	1	—	—	—	—	—	—
PICTURES	1	—	1	—	—	—	—	—	—
PIN	1	—	1	—	—	—	—	—	—
PIT	1	—	1	—	—	—	—	—	—
PLACE	—	—	—	—	—	—	—	1	1
POOL	1	—	1	—	—	—	—	—	—
POSITION	—	—	—	—	—	—	—	1	1
POSTURE	—	—	—	—	—	—	—	1	1
PUT	—	1	1	—	—	—	—	—	—
QUIET	2	3	5	—	—	—	—	—	—
QUIETLY	2	1	3	—	—	—	—	—	—
READ	2	—	2	—	—	—	—	—	—
RELAX	—	—	—	—	—	—	1	—	1
REST	—	—	—	—	—	—	3	—	3
REST ON SOMETHING	—	—	—	—	—	—	1	—	1
RING	1	—	1	—	—	—	—	—	—
RIT	—	2	2	—	—	—	—	—	—
ROOM	2	—	2	—	—	—	—	—	—
RUN	—	—	—	—	1	1	—	—	—
SAND	—	—	—	—	—	—	—	—	—
SAT	2	4	6	11	24	35	10	12	22
SEAT	1	1	2	2	2	4	2	3	5
SEAT BELT	1	—	1	—	—	—	—	—	—
SEATS	—	—	—	—	1	1	—	—	—
SEE	—	1	1	—	—	—	—	—	—
SET	1	—	1	—	—	—	4	6	10
SET THE TABLE	—	1	1	—	—	—	—	—	—
SETTING	—	—	—	1	—	1	—	—	—
SHOES	—	1	1	—	—	—	—	—	—
SITTING	—	—	—	—	—	—	1	—	1

RESPONSE WORD	1ST M	F	T	3RD M	F	T	5TH M	F	T

77. SIT

RESPONSE WORD	1ST M	F	T	3RD M	F	T	5TH M	F	T
SITTING DOWN	–	–	–	–	–	–	–	1	1
SKINNY	1	–	1	–	–	–	–	–	–
SLATE	–	–	–	–	–	–	1	–	1
SLEEP	1	–	1	–	–	–	–	–	–
SOUP	1	–	1	–	–	–	–	–	–
SQUAT	–	–	–	–	–	–	1	–	1
STAD	–	–	–	–	–	–	1	–	1
STAND	8	8	16	42	44	86	41	54	95
STAND UP	1	2	3	–	–	–	–	–	–
STANDING	1	–	1	1	–	1	–	–	–
STAY	–	–	–	–	–	–	1	1	2
STAYED	–	–	–	1	–	1	–	–	–
STILL	–	–	–	1	–	1	–	1	1
STOOD	–	–	–	–	–	–	1	–	1
STOOL	1	–	1	–	–	–	1	–	1
STRAIGHT	–	–	–	1	1	2	–	–	–
SUSAN	1	–	1	–	–	–	–	–	–
TABLE	–	1	1	–	–	–	–	–	–
TALK	1	–	1	–	–	–	–	–	–
THAW	–	1	1	–	–	–	–	–	–
THING	–	1	1	–	–	–	–	–	–
THROW UP	1	–	1	1	–	1	–	–	–
TIGHT	–	–	–	1	–	1	–	–	–
TO MOVE TO A POSITION	–	–	–	–	–	–	–	1	1
TOOLS	1	–	1	–	–	–	–	–	–
UP	2	6	8	6	6	12	4	3	7
WAIT	–	–	–	–	1	1	–	–	–
WALK	1	1	2	–	1	1	1	1	2
WAS	–	–	–	–	1	1	–	–	–
WATCH	–	–	–	–	1	1	–	1	1
WHEN YOURE SITTING DOWN IN A CHAIR	1	–	1	–	–	–	–	–	–
WHENEVER SOMEONE WANTS YOU TO SIT	–	1	1	–	–	–	–	–	–
WHIT	–	–	–	1	–	1	–	–	–
WITH	–	1	1	–	–	–	–	–	–
WITH ME	1	–	1	–	–	–	–	–	–
YES	–	1	1	1	–	1	–	–	–

78. SLOW

RESPONSE WORD	1ST M	F	T	3RD M	F	T	5TH M	F	T
ACTION	1	–	1	–	1	1	–	–	–
AIRPLANE	1	–	1	–	–	–	–	–	–
AIRPLANE MIGHT RUN OUT OF GAS AND GO SL	–	1	1	–	–	–	–	–	–
ANT	1	–	1	–	–	–	–	–	–
BACK ROOM	1	–	1	–	–	–	–	–	–
BAD	1	–	1	–	1	1	–	–	–
BALL	–	1	1	–	–	–	–	–	–
BE SLOW WHEN HUSBAND DRIVES	–	1	1	–	–	–	–	–	–
BEADS	1	–	1	–	–	–	–	–	–
BICYCLE	–	–	–	–	1	1	–	–	–
BIKE	1	–	1	–	–	–	1	–	1
BIRD	1	–	1	–	–	–	–	–	–
BITE	1	–	1	–	–	–	–	–	–
BLIND	1	–	1	–	–	–	–	–	–
BLOW	1	–	1	–	–	–	–	–	–
BOAT	1	–	1	–	–	–	–	–	–
BOOK	–	1	1	–	–	–	–	–	–
BOW	–	1	1	–	–	–	–	–	–
BUSH	1	–	1	–	–	–	–	–	–
CAN	–	1	1	–	–	–	–	–	–
CAR	4	5	9	–	–	–	2	–	2
COOKIE	1	–	1	–	–	–	–	–	–
CORN	–	–	–	1	–	1	–	–	–
COW	1	–	1	–	–	–	–	–	–
CRAWL	1	–	1	–	–	–	–	1	1
DINOSAUR	–	–	–	1	–	1	–	–	–
DOESNT GO FAST	–	–	–	1	–	1	–	–	–
DOG	–	–	–	–	1	1	1	–	1

RESPONSE WORD	1ST M	F	T	3RD M	F	T	5TH M	F	T

78. SLOW

RESPONSE WORD	1ST M	F	T	3RD M	F	T	5TH M	F	T
DONT	–	–	–	–	1	1	–	–	–
DOOR	–	1	1	–	–	–	–	–	–
DOWN	4	3	7	–	–	–	1	2	3
DRAG	–	–	–	–	–	–	–	1	1
DRAGS	–	–	–	–	–	–	1	–	1
DRAWER	1	–	1	–	–	–	–	–	–
DRIVE	–	2	2	–	–	–	–	–	–
DRIVING	1	–	1	–	–	–	–	–	–
DRY	–	1	1	–	–	–	–	–	–
ELEPHANT	–	1	1	–	–	–	–	–	–
FAST	49	51	100	111	110	221	98	105	203
FASTER	1	–	1	–	–	–	–	–	–
FAT	–	–	–	–	–	–	1	–	1
FEET	1	–	1	–	–	–	–	–	–
FIVE	–	1	1	–	–	–	–	–	–
GIRL	–	–	–	–	1	1	–	–	–
GLASSES	–	1	1	–	–	–	–	–	–
GO	4	5	9	2	2	4	–	–	–
GO SLOW	–	1	1	–	–	–	–	–	–
GO VERY SLOW	–	–	–	–	–	–	–	1	1
GO, SALLY	1	–	1	–	–	–	–	–	–
GOING	–	1	1	–	–	–	–	–	–
GOING SLOW	1	–	1	1	–	1	–	–	–
GOOD-BYE	1	–	1	–	–	–	–	–	–
GUESS	–	1	1	–	–	–	–	–	–
HAIR	–	1	1	–	–	–	–	–	–
HALLS	1	–	1	–	–	–	–	–	–
HAT	1	–	1	–	–	–	–	–	–
HIGH	–	1	1	–	–	–	–	–	–
HO	1	–	1	–	–	–	–	–	–
HOLLER	1	–	1	–	–	–	–	–	–
HORSE	1	–	1	–	–	–	–	–	–
HOW	1	–	1	–	–	–	–	–	–
HURRY	–	–	–	–	1	1	–	–	–
HURRY UP	–	1	1	–	–	–	–	–	–
IN YOUR CAR	1	–	1	–	–	–	–	–	–
JET	1	–	1	–	–	–	–	–	–
JIM	1	–	1	–	–	–	–	–	–
JOY	–	–	–	–	–	–	1	–	1
KNOW	–	1	1	–	–	–	–	–	–
LAWNMOWER	1	–	1	–	–	–	–	–	–
LAZY	–	–	–	1	1	2	–	–	–
LETS GO HORSEBACK RIDING	–	1	1	–	–	–	–	–	–
LIGHT	–	2	2	–	–	–	–	–	–
LIKE RUN SLOW	–	1	1	–	–	–	–	–	–
LITTLE	–	3	3	–	1	1	–	–	–
LONG	–	–	–	–	1	1	–	1	1
LOUD	–	–	–	–	1	1	–	–	–
LOW	2	1	3	2	–	2	–	1	1
LUG	–	–	–	–	1	1	–	–	–
MASON	–	1	1	–	–	–	–	–	–
ME	–	–	–	1	–	1	–	–	–
MEDIUM-NOT FAST	–	–	–	–	1	1	–	–	–
MO	1	–	1	–	–	–	–	–	–
MOTION	1	–	1	1	–	1	–	–	–
MOUSE	–	1	1	–	–	–	–	–	–
MOVE	–	–	–	–	–	–	1	–	1
MOW	2	–	2	–	1	1	–	–	–
MUSIC	–	–	–	–	–	–	1	–	1
MY SISTER IS SMALL	–	1	1	–	–	–	–	–	–
NICE	–	1	1	–	–	–	–	–	–
NO	–	2	2	–	–	–	–	–	–
NO RESPONSE	–	–	–	–	–	–	–	1	1
NOT FAST	1	1	2	6	2	8	6	7	13
NOT LAST	–	–	–	–	–	–	1	–	1
NOW	–	2	2	–	–	–	–	–	–
OH	1	–	1	–	–	–	–	–	–
OK	2	–	2	–	–	–	–	–	–
ONE	–	–	–	–	1	1	–	–	–
OUT	–	–	–	–	–	–	–	1	1
PLEASANT	–	–	–	–	–	–	1	–	1
PLEASE	1	–	1	–	–	–	–	–	–

RESPONSE WORD	1ST			3RD			5TH		
	M	F	T	M	F	T	M	F	T

78. SLOW

RESPONSE WORD	M	F	T	M	F	T	M	F	T
POKE	3	1	4	–	–	–	–	1	1
POKE ALONG	–	–	–	–	–	–	1	–	1
POKEY	–	–	–	–	–	–	–	2	2
POTATO SALAD	–	1	1	–	–	–	–	–	–
PRECIPITATION	–	–	–	–	–	–	1	–	1
PUSH HANDLE	1	–	1	–	–	–	–	–	–
QUIET	–	–	–	–	1	1	–	–	–
QUIETLY	–	–	–	–	1	1	–	–	–
RAN	1	–	1	–	–	–	–	–	–
RIDE	1	1	2	–	–	–	–	–	–
ROW	–	1	1	–	–	–	–	–	–
RUM	–	–	–	–	–	–	1	–	1
RUN	1	–	1	–	–	–	2	1	3
RUNNING	1	–	1	–	–	–	–	–	–
SALLY	1	–	1	–	–	–	–	–	–
SAW	1	–	1	–	–	–	–	–	–
SCHOOL	–	–	–	1	–	1	–	–	–
SECOND	1	–	1	–	–	–	–	–	–
SHADE	–	–	–	–	–	–	–	1	1
SHIRT	1	–	1	–	–	–	–	–	–
SHORT	–	–	–	–	–	–	–	1	1
SIGN	1	–	1	–	–	–	–	–	–
SILENTLY	–	–	–	–	1	1	–	–	–
SKIP	–	–	–	–	1	1	–	–	–
SLED	1	7	8	–	–	–	–	–	–
SLED RIDE	1	–	1	–	–	–	–	–	–
SLEEP	–	1	1	–	–	–	–	–	–
SLEIGH	–	1	1	–	–	–	–	–	–
SLIDE	1	–	1	–	–	–	–	–	–
SLIPPER	–	1	1	–	–	–	–	–	–
SLOPE	–	1	1	–	–	–	–	–	–
SLOW BOY	1	–	1	–	–	–	–	–	–
SLOW POKE	–	1	1	–	–	–	–	–	–
SLOWLY	–	1	1	1	–	1	–	–	–
SLOWPOKE	1	2	3	–	–	–	–	–	–
SLUG	1	–	1	–	–	–	–	–	–
SMOOTH	–	–	–	–	–	–	1	–	1
SNOW	–	1	1	–	–	–	–	–	–
SOFT	–	1	1	–	–	–	–	–	–
SOMEBODY	–	1	1	–	–	–	–	–	–
SOMEONE IS SLOW	–	1	1	–	–	–	–	–	–
SPELLING	–	–	–	–	–	–	–	1	1
START	–	–	–	–	–	–	1	–	1
STEADILY	–	–	–	–	–	–	–	1	1
STEADY	–	–	–	–	–	–	–	1	1
STOP	1	2	3	3	1	4	1	1	2
TAKES A LONG TIME	–	–	–	–	–	–	1	–	1
TARDY	–	–	–	–	–	–	1	–	1
TEETER-TOTTER	1	–	1	–	–	–	–	–	–
TEETH	–	1	1	–	–	–	–	–	–
THINGS	1	–	1	–	–	–	–	–	–
TIME	–	–	–	1	–	1	–	–	–
TOO LOUD	1	–	1	–	–	–	–	–	–
TRASH CAN	–	1	1	–	–	–	–	–	–
TULLER	–	–	–	–	–	–	1	–	1
TURTLE	1	–	1	4	1	5	10	4	14
VERY	–	–	–	–	2	2	–	–	–
WAGON	–	1	1	–	–	–	–	–	–
WALK	4	8	12	1	3	4	2	3	5
WALK SLOW	1	–	1	–	–	–	–	–	–
WALKER	–	1	1	–	–	–	–	–	–
WALKING	1	–	1	–	–	–	–	1	1
WALKING SLOW	–	–	–	1	–	1	–	–	–
WASH	–	1	1	–	–	–	–	–	–
WATER	–	–	–	–	1	1	1	–	1
WATERS	–	–	–	–	–	–	–	1	1
WHAT	1	–	1	–	–	–	–	–	–
WHEN YOURE GOING SLOW OUTSIDE	1	–	1	–	–	–	–	–	–
WHITE	–	1	1	–	–	–	–	–	–
WHOA	1	–	1	–	–	–	–	–	–
WINDOW	1	–	1	–	–	–	–	–	–

RESPONSE WORD	1ST			3RD			5TH		
	M	F	T	M	F	T	M	F	T

78. SLOW

RESPONSE WORD	1ST			3RD			5TH		
YOU	1	–	1	1	–	1	–	–	–

79. SLOWLY

RESPONSE WORD	1ST			3RD			5TH		
ACCURATE	–	–	–	–	–	–	–	1	1
ALMOST STOPPED	–	–	–	–	–	–	1	–	1
BALL	–	1	1	–	–	–	1	–	1
BIKE	–	2	2	–	–	–	1	–	1
BIRD	–	1	1	–	–	–	1	–	1
BITE	1	–	1	–	–	–	–	–	–
BOARD	–	1	1	–	–	–	–	–	–
BOAT	1	–	1	–	–	–	1	–	1
BOOKS	1	–	1	–	–	–	–	–	–
BOWLING	1	–	1	–	–	–	–	–	–
BRICK	1	–	1	–	–	–	–	–	–
BUCKET	–	1	1	–	–	–	–	–	–
BUTTERFLY	–	1	1	–	–	–	–	–	–
CALL	1	–	1	–	–	–	–	–	–
CAN	–	2	2	–	–	–	–	–	–
CAR	9	2	11	–	–	–	1	–	1
CAR GOING	1	–	1	–	–	–	–	–	–
CAR IS GOING SLOWLY	1	–	1	–	–	–	–	–	–
CAR MIGHT RUN OUT OF GAS AND YOU MIGHT	–	1	1	–	–	–	–	–	–
CAREFULLY	–	–	–	–	1	1	1	–	1
CARS GO SLOW	–	1	1	–	–	–	–	–	–
CAT	–	1	1	–	–	–	–	–	–
CATCH	–	–	–	1	–	1	–	–	–
CATECHISM	–	–	–	–	1	1	–	–	–
CHAIR	1	–	1	–	–	–	–	–	–
CLOCK	–	1	1	–	–	–	–	–	–
COATS	–	1	1	–	–	–	–	–	–
COLD	–	–	–	–	–	–	–	1	1
COME	–	–	–	–	2	2	–	–	–
COWLY	1	–	1	–	–	–	–	–	–
CRAWL	–	–	–	–	1	1	–	1	1
CREEP	–	–	–	–	–	–	–	1	1
DESK	1	–	1	–	–	–	–	–	–
DOWN	3	–	3	–	–	–	–	–	–
DRIVE	–	3	3	–	–	–	–	–	–
DRIVE SLOW	–	1	1	–	–	–	–	–	–
DRSE	–	–	–	–	–	–	1	–	1
DRY	–	–	–	–	–	–	1	–	1
EAGLE	1	–	1	–	–	–	–	–	–
FACT	–	–	–	–	–	–	1	–	1
FAIN	–	–	–	–	–	–	1	–	1
FAST	43	40	83	69	78	147	59	68	127
FASTER	4	1	5	12	9	21	7	4	11
FASTLY	3	7	10	22	9	31	17	15	32
FEW	–	–	–	–	–	–	1	–	1
FIFTEEN	1	–	1	–	–	–	–	–	–
FINGER	1	–	1	–	–	–	–	–	–
FIVE	–	1	1	–	–	–	–	–	–
FLASH	–	–	–	1	–	1	–	–	–
FLOAT	1	–	1	–	–	–	–	–	–
FLOATING	–	–	–	–	1	1	–	–	–
FLY	–	–	–	–	–	–	1	–	1
FOOD	1	–	1	–	–	–	–	–	–
FOOT	–	–	–	–	–	–	–	1	1
GENTLY	–	–	–	–	1	1	–	1	1
GIRL	–	–	–	–	1	1	–	–	–
GIT	1	–	1	–	–	–	–	–	–
GLASSES	1	1	2	–	–	–	–	–	–
GO	1	5	6	2	–	2	–	1	1
GO FAST	–	–	–	–	1	1	–	–	–
GO SALLY	1	–	1	–	–	–	–	–	–
GO-LY	1	–	1	–	–	–	–	–	–
GOING	–	1	1	–	–	–	–	–	–
GOING SLOW	–	–	–	1	–	1	–	–	–
HAIR	–	1	1	–	–	–	–	–	–
HARD	–	–	–	–	1	1	–	1	1

RESPONSE WORD	1ST M	F	T	3RD M	F	T	5TH M	F	T

79. SLOWLY

RESPONSE WORD	1ST M	F	T	3RD M	F	T	5TH M	F	T
HAT	−	1	1	−	−	−	−	−	−
HIGHER	−	1	1	−	−	−	−	1	1
HOLEY	−	1	1	−	−	−	−	−	−
HOLY	1	−	1	−	−	−	−	−	−
HOWLY	1	−	1	−	−	−	−	−	−
HURRIEDLY	−	−	−	−	−	−	1	−	1
HURRY UP	−	1	1	−	−	−	−	−	−
ICE CREAM CONE	1	−	1	−	−	−	−	−	−
INK	−	1	1	−	−	−	−	−	−
JUMP	−	−	−	−	1	1	−	−	−
KITTEN	−	1	1	−	−	−	−	−	−
LANGUAGE	−	−	−	−	−	−	1	−	1
LAZILY	−	−	−	−	1	1	−	−	−
LAZY	−	−	−	−	−	−	1	−	1
LETS SLOW DOWN	−	1	1	−	−	−	−	−	−
LISTEN	−	−	−	−	1	1	−	−	−
LITTLE	−	1	1	−	−	−	−	−	−
LONG	−	−	−	−	−	−	2	−	2
LONGLY	−	−	−	−	1	1	−	−	−
LOW	−	−	−	1	−	1	1	−	1
LOWLY	1	−	1	−	−	−	−	−	−
MAN	−	1	1	−	−	−	−	−	−
ME	1	−	1	1	−	1	−	−	−
MEND	−	1	1	−	−	−	−	−	−
MERRILY	1	−	1	−	−	−	−	−	−
MIKE	1	−	1	−	−	−	−	−	−
MOLELY	1	−	1	−	−	−	−	−	−
MOUSE	−	1	1	−	−	−	−	−	−
MOUWLY	1	−	1	−	−	−	−	−	−
MOVE	−	1	1	1	1	2	−	−	−
MOVING	−	−	−	−	−	−	−	1	1
MOWLY	−	−	−	−	1	1	−	−	−
NEST	−	1	1	−	−	−	−	−	−
NICE	−	−	−	−	1	1	−	−	−
NICELY	−	−	−	−	1	1	−	−	−
NO	−	1	1	−	−	−	−	−	−
NO RESPONSE	−	1	1	−	−	−	−	1	1
NORMAN	−	1	1	−	−	−	−	−	−
NOT FAST	1	−	1	3	1	4	8	7	15
NOT HARD	−	−	−	−	−	−	−	1	1
NOT QUICK	−	−	−	−	−	−	−	1	1
NOT RAPIDLY	−	−	−	−	−	−	1	−	1
NOT VERY FAST	−	−	−	−	−	−	1	−	1
NOW	−	1	1	−	−	−	−	−	−
ORANGE	1	−	1	−	−	−	−	−	−
OUT	1	−	1	−	−	−	−	−	−
PAINT	−	−	−	1	−	1	−	−	−
PAPER	2	−	2	−	−	−	−	−	−
PEOPLE	−	1	1	−	1	1	−	−	−
POKEY	1	−	1	−	−	−	−	−	−
PORCH	1	−	1	−	−	−	−	−	−
POWLY	−	2	2	−	−	−	−	−	−
QUICK	−	−	−	−	−	−	−	1	1
QUICKER	−	−	−	−	1	1	−	−	−
QUICKLY	−	−	−	−	−	−	4	3	7
QUIET	1	−	1	−	−	−	−	−	−
QUIETLY	−	−	−	−	1	1	−	1	1
RAN	−	−	−	−	1	1	−	−	−
REAL SLOW	1	−	1	−	−	−	−	−	−
RIDE	−	1	1	−	−	−	−	−	−
RIDE IN CAR	−	1	1	−	−	−	−	−	−
ROWLY	−	1	1	−	−	−	−	−	−
RUN	3	1	4	−	−	−	−	−	−
RUN SLOW	−	1	1	−	−	−	−	−	−
SAST	−	−	−	−	−	−	1	−	1
SEA	1	−	1	−	−	−	−	−	−
SHORT	−	−	−	1	−	1	−	−	−
SHORTLY	−	−	−	−	1	1	−	−	−
SIDE	−	1	1	−	−	−	−	−	−
SIGN	1	−	1	−	−	−	−	−	−
SINK	−	1	1	−	−	−	−	−	−
SISTER	−	1	1	−	−	−	−	−	−

RESPONSE WORD	1ST			3RD			5TH		
	M	F	T	M	F	T	M	F	T

79. SLOWLY

RESPONSE WORD	M	F	T	M	F	T	M	F	T
SIT	–	–	–	–	1	1	–	–	–
SLED	–	3	3	–	–	–	–	–	–
SLIPPERY	1	–	1	–	–	–	–	–	–
SLOW	1	2	3	9	6	15	7	4	11
SLOW DOWN	1	2	3	–	–	–	–	–	–
SLOW MOTION	1	–	1	–	–	–	–	–	–
SLOW THINGS	1	–	1	–	–	–	–	–	–
SMALL	–	–	–	1	–	1	–	–	–
SNAIL	–	–	–	–	1	1	–	–	–
SNAKE	1	–	1	–	–	–	–	–	–
SNOW	–	1	1	1	–	1	–	–	–
SO LATE	–	1	1	–	–	–	–	–	–
SOAP	–	1	1	–	–	–	–	–	–
SOFT	–	–	–	1	1	2	–	2	2
SOFTLY	–	1	1	–	3	3	–	2	2
SOMETHING	1	–	1	–	–	–	–	–	–
SPEEDING	–	–	–	1	–	1	–	–	–
STEADILY	–	–	–	–	–	–	–	1	1
STEP	–	–	–	1	–	1	–	–	–
STILL	–	–	–	1	–	1	–	–	–
STOP	1	3	4	1	–	1	2	1	3
STOP FOR A RED LIGHT	–	–	–	–	–	–	–	1	1
STUBBORN	–	–	–	–	–	–	–	1	1
SUN	–	1	1	–	–	–	–	–	–
SWIFTLY	–	–	–	1	–	1	2	1	3
TAIL	1	–	1	–	–	–	–	–	–
TARDY	–	–	–	–	–	–	1	–	1
TEETH	–	1	1	–	–	–	–	–	–
TEN	1	–	1	–	–	–	–	–	–
THEY DRIVE	1	–	1	–	–	–	–	–	–
TO	–	–	–	–	–	–	1	–	1
TROT	–	–	–	–	–	–	1	–	1
TURN	1	1	2	–	–	–	–	–	–
TURTLE	1	–	1	2	2	4	5	6	11
UNFAST	–	–	–	–	–	–	–	1	1
VERY	–	–	–	–	1	1	–	–	–
WAGON	1	–	1	–	–	–	–	–	–
WAIT SLOWLY	–	1	1	–	–	–	–	–	–
WALK	13	13	26	5	5	10	4	5	9
WALK SLOW	1	1	2	–	–	–	–	–	–
WALKED	–	–	–	–	–	–	–	1	1
WALKER	–	–	–	1	–	1	–	–	–
WALKING	1	–	1	–	–	–	1	1	2
WALKING ALONG	–	1	1	–	–	–	–	–	–
WALL	–	1	1	–	–	–	–	–	–
WANDER	–	–	–	–	–	–	1	–	1
WATER	–	1	1	–	–	–	–	–	–
WE WALK	1	–	1	–	–	–	–	–	–
WERE GOING SLOWLY	1	–	1	–	–	–	–	–	–
WET	1	–	1	–	–	–	–	–	–
WHEN YOU'RE WALKING YOU GO SLOW	1	–	1	–	–	–	–	–	–
WHENEVER SOMEONE IS SLOW	–	1	1	–	–	–	–	–	–
WIND	1	–	1	–	–	–	–	–	–
WOMAN	–	–	–	–	–	–	–	1	1

80. SMOOTH

RESPONSE WORD	M	F	T	M	F	T	M	F	T
A BABYS SMOOTH	–	–	–	1	–	1	–	–	–
ALE	1	–	1	–	–	–	–	–	–
ANGRY	–	1	1	–	–	–	–	–	–
ARM	–	1	1	–	–	–	–	–	–
BABY	–	2	2	–	–	–	–	–	–
BARK	–	–	–	–	–	–	1	–	1
BED	2	2	4	1	–	1	–	1	1
BEE	1	–	1	–	–	–	–	–	–
BIG	1	–	1	–	–	–	–	–	–
BLANKET	1	1	2	–	–	–	–	–	–
BOOK	–	–	–	–	1	1	–	–	–
BOOTH	1	1	2	–	–	–	–	–	–
BOTH	–	1	1	–	–	–	–	–	–

RESPONSE WORD	1ST M	1ST F	1ST T	3RD M	3RD F	3RD T	5TH M	5TH F	5TH T

80. SMOOTH

RESPONSE WORD	M	F	T	M	F	T	M	F	T
BREAD	1	2	3	1	–	1	–	–	–
BRICK	1	–	1	1	–	1	–	–	–
BRIGHT	–	1	1	–	1	1	–	–	–
BUMP	1	–	1	–	–	–	–	–	–
BUMPETY	–	1	1	–	–	–	–	–	–
BUMPIDY	1	–	1	–	–	–	–	–	–
BUMPITY	1	–	1	–	–	–	–	–	–
BUMPS	1	–	1	–	–	–	–	–	–
BUMPY	3	1	4	7	6	13	5	2	7
BUTTERFLY	–	1	1	–	–	–	–	–	–
BUTTON	–	1	1	–	–	–	–	–	–
CAKE	1	2	3	1	–	1	–	–	–
CALM	–	–	–	–	–	–	–	1	1
CAN	–	1	1	–	–	–	–	–	–
CANDY	1	–	1	–	–	–	–	–	–
CAT	1	2	3	–	1	1	–	1	1
CEMENT	1	–	1	–	–	–	–	–	–
CHAIN	–	–	–	–	–	–	1	–	1
CHILDREN	–	1	1	–	–	–	–	–	–
CLEAN HOUSE	1	–	1	–	–	–	–	–	–
CLEAR	–	–	–	1	1	2	–	–	–
CLEVER	–	–	–	1	–	1	–	–	–
CLOTH	1	–	1	1	–	1	–	–	–
CLOTHES	–	–	–	–	1	1	–	–	–
COMFORTABLE	–	1	1	–	–	–	–	–	–
COO	–	–	–	1	–	1	–	–	–
COOL	1	1	2	–	–	–	–	–	–
COOTH	–	1	1	–	1	1	–	–	–
COTTON	–	–	–	–	1	1	–	–	–
COUGH	–	–	–	1	–	1	–	–	–
COVER	–	–	–	–	1	1	–	–	–
CRAMP	–	–	–	1	–	1	–	–	–
CREAM	–	1	1	–	–	–	–	–	–
CUE	1	–	1	–	–	–	–	–	–
CURTAINS	–	1	1	–	1	1	–	–	–
DESK	–	–	–	–	1	1	–	–	–
DOESNT HURT FEET	1	–	1	–	–	–	–	–	–
DOG	1	–	1	–	–	–	–	–	–
DOOR	–	2	2	–	–	–	–	–	–
DOOR KNOB	–	1	1	–	–	–	–	–	–
DOOTH	–	1	1	–	–	–	–	–	–
DOWN	–	–	–	–	–	–	1	1	2
DUST	–	–	–	–	–	–	–	1	1
DUST PAN	–	1	1	–	–	–	–	–	–
EASY	–	2	2	–	1	1	–	1	1
ENVELOPE	1	–	1	–	–	–	–	–	–
EVEN	–	–	–	–	–	–	–	2	2
EYES	–	–	1	–	–	–	–	1	1
FACE	1	–	1	–	–	–	–	–	–
FAIL	–	–	–	–	1	1	–	–	–
FAST	3	1	4	–	–	–	1	1	2
FEATHER	1	–	1	–	–	–	–	–	–
FINE	–	–	–	–	–	–	–	1	1
FISH	2	–	2	–	–	–	–	–	–
FLAT	3	1	4	6	1	7	4	2	6
FLOOR	1	–	1	–	–	–	–	–	–
FLUFFY	–	–	–	–	1	1	1	1	2
FOOD	–	–	–	1	–	1	–	–	–
FORK	–	1	1	–	–	–	–	–	–
FRESH	–	–	–	1	–	1	–	–	–
FUR	–	2	2	–	1	1	–	–	–
GENTLE	–	–	–	3	1	4	2	2	4
GENTLY	1	1	2	1	1	2	–	2	2
GET	–	–	–	1	–	1	–	–	–
GLASSES	1	–	1	–	–	–	–	–	–
GOOD	1	1	2	1	–	1	1	–	1
GOOTH	1	–	1	–	–	–	–	–	–
GRACE	–	–	–	1	–	1	–	–	–
GRASS	–	–	–	–	1	1	–	–	–
GROUND	–	1	1	–	–	–	–	–	–
HAED	–	–	–	–	–	–	1	–	1
HAIR	1	–	1	–	1	1	1	–	1

RESPONSE WORD	1ST M	F	T	3RD M	F	T	5TH M	F	T

80. SMOOTH

RESPONSE WORD	1ST M	F	T	3RD M	F	T	5TH M	F	T
HAND	1	1	2	–	–	–	–	–	–
HANDS	1	–	1	–	–	–	–	–	–
HARD	13	13	26	20	30	50	13	19	32
HE	–	–	–	1	–	1	–	–	–
HEAVY	–	1	1	–	–	–	–	–	–
HILLY	–	–	–	–	–	–	1	–	1
HOOVE	1	1	2	–	–	–	–	–	–
ICE	1	–	1	–	–	–	–	–	–
ICE CREAM	–	–	–	–	–	–	–	1	1
ICING	1	–	1	–	–	–	–	–	–
INK	–	1	1	–	–	–	–	–	–
JAGGED	–	–	–	–	–	–	1	–	1
JAR	1	–	1	–	–	–	–	–	–
KOOVE	1	–	1	–	–	–	–	–	–
LAND	1	–	1	–	–	–	–	–	–
LANDING	–	–	–	–	–	–	1	–	1
LAY	1	–	1	–	–	–	–	–	–
LETTERS	1	–	1	–	–	–	–	–	–
LEVEL	–	–	–	–	–	–	2	–	2
LIGHT	1	1	2	1	–	1	–	–	–
LIKE	–	1	1	–	–	–	–	–	–
LITTLE	–	1	1	–	–	–	–	–	–
LONG	–	–	–	–	–	–	1	–	1
LOSE	–	–	–	1	–	1	–	–	–
LOUD	1	–	1	–	–	–	–	–	–
LUMPY	–	–	–	1	1	2	–	–	–
MACHINE	–	1	1	–	–	–	–	–	–
MAD	–	–	–	–	1	1	–	–	–
MASK	–	1	1	–	–	–	–	–	–
MICE	–	–	–	–	–	–	1	–	1
MONKEY	–	1	1	–	–	–	–	–	–
MOON	–	–	–	1	–	1	–	–	–
MOTOR	1	–	1	–	–	–	–	–	–
MOVE	3	1	4	–	–	–	–	–	–
NAPKIN	1	–	1	–	–	–	–	–	–
NICE	2	–	2	1	–	1	1	1	2
NO	–	1	1	–	–	–	–	–	–
NOT	–	–	–	–	–	–	1	–	1
NOT BUMPY	–	–	–	–	–	–	1	–	1
NOT HARD	–	–	–	1	–	1	–	–	–
NOT ROUGH	–	–	–	–	–	–	6	3	9
NOT SMOOTH	1	–	1	–	–	–	–	–	–
NOTE	1	–	1	–	–	–	–	–	–
NUMBER SIX	1	–	1	–	–	–	–	–	–
NUMBERS	1	–	1	–	–	–	–	–	–
OOO	1	–	1	–	–	–	–	–	–
OPEN MY LOCKER	–	1	1	–	–	–	–	–	–
PAPER	1	–	1	–	–	–	–	–	–
PART	1	–	1	–	–	–	–	–	–
PEANUT BUTTER	–	–	–	–	–	–	1	1	2
PENCIL	1	–	1	–	–	–	–	–	–
PIE	1	–	1	–	–	–	–	–	–
PILLOW	1	2	3	–	–	–	–	1	1
PLANE	–	–	–	–	–	–	–	1	1
PLAY	–	1	1	–	–	–	–	–	–
POWDER	–	–	–	1	–	1	–	–	–
QUIETLY	1	–	1	–	–	–	–	–	–
RAFE	–	–	–	–	–	–	1	–	1
REFRIGERATOR	1	–	1	–	–	–	–	–	–
RIDE SMOOTH	1	–	1	–	–	–	–	–	–
RIDING	1	–	1	–	–	–	–	–	–
ROAD	2	–	2	–	–	–	1	–	1
ROCK	–	–	–	1	–	1	1	–	1
ROCKET RODE	1	–	1	–	–	–	–	–	–
ROCKS	–	–	–	–	1	1	–	–	–
ROCKY	–	–	–	–	2	2	–	–	–
ROUGH	6	9	15	24	15	39	47	44	91
ROUGHLY	–	–	–	–	1	1	–	1	1
ROUH	–	–	–	–	–	–	1	–	1
RUDE	1	1	2	–	–	–	–	–	–
RUFF	–	–	–	–	–	–	1	–	1
RUG	1	–	1	–	–	–	–	–	–

RESPONSE WORD	1ST M	F	T	3RD M	F	T	5TH M	F	T

80. SMOOTH

RESPONSE WORD	1ST M	F	T	3RD M	F	T	5TH M	F	T
RUGGED	–	1	–	–	–	–	–	1	1
RUN	–	1	1	–	–	–	–	–	–
RUN TRACTOR	–	1	1	–	–	–	–	–	–
RUNNER	–	–	–	1	–	1	–	–	–
SAND	1	–	1	–	–	–	–	–	–
SCAR	–	–	–	–	–	–	1	–	1
SEAT	1	–	1	–	–	–	–	–	–
SHINY	–	1	1	1	1	2	–	–	–
SILK	–	–	–	–	–	–	1	2	3
SKIM	–	–	–	–	–	–	–	1	1
SKIN	1	–	1	–	–	–	–	1	1
SKY	–	1	1	–	–	–	–	–	–
SLAT	1	–	1	–	–	–	–	–	–
SLEEK	–	–	–	–	–	–	1	–	1
SLICK	–	–	–	1	–	1	1	–	1
SLIPPERY	–	–	–	1	1	2	–	–	–
SLOW	–	1	1	–	–	–	–	–	–
SMOKE	–	–	–	1	–	1	–	–	–
SMOOD	1	–	1	–	–	–	–	–	–
SMOOTHING OUT	1	–	1	–	–	–	–	–	–
SMOOTHLY	–	4	4	1	2	3	–	1	1
SNOW	1	1	2	–	–	–	1	–	1
SOFT	12	20	32	39	49	88	26	36	62
SOFTLY	–	–	–	–	3	3	1	–	1
SOLID	–	–	–	–	1	1	–	–	–
SOMEBODY IS	–	1	1	–	–	–	–	–	–
SOMETHING LIKE A TABLE THAT HAS BEEN VA	–	–	–	–	–	–	–	1	1
SONG	–	1	1	–	–	–	–	–	–
SONGS	–	1	1	–	–	–	–	–	–
SOOTHE	–	–	–	1	–	1	–	–	–
SOOVE	1	–	1	–	–	–	–	–	–
SPOON	–	–	–	–	1	1	–	–	–
SPREAD	–	–	–	–	1	1	–	1	1
STEADY	–	–	–	–	1	1	–	–	–
STING	1	–	1	–	–	–	–	–	–
STOP	–	1	1	–	–	–	–	–	–
STRAIGHT	–	1	1	2	3	5	2	1	3
STREAM	–	–	–	–	–	–	–	1	1
SUN	–	1	1	–	–	–	–	–	–
SURFACE	–	–	–	1	1	2	1	–	1
SUSAN	1	–	1	–	–	–	–	–	–
SWIMMING POOL	–	1	1	–	–	–	–	–	–
TABLE	3	3	6	–	–	–	–	–	–
TABLE CLOTH	–	1	1	–	–	–	–	–	–
TALK SMOOTHLY	–	1	1	–	–	–	–	–	–
TAR	1	–	1	–	–	–	–	–	–
TENDER	–	–	–	–	–	–	1	–	1
TEXTURE	–	–	–	–	–	–	1	–	1
THAT IS SMOOTH	–	1	1	–	–	–	–	–	–
THE DESK IS VERY SMOOTH	–	1	1	–	–	–	–	–	–
THE WALLS ARE SMOOTH	–	–	–	1	–	1	–	–	–
THIN	–	–	–	–	–	–	–	1	1
THIS	1	–	1	–	–	–	–	–	–
TIRES MAKE CAR RUN SMOOTH	–	–	–	1	–	1	–	–	–
TOP	–	–	–	–	–	–	–	1	1
TOUGH	–	–	–	1	1	2	1	–	1
TOWELS	1	–	1	–	–	–	–	–	–
TWO	1	1	2	–	–	–	–	–	–
USE	1	–	1	–	–	–	–	–	–
WALK	–	1	1	–	–	–	–	–	–
WALL	1	–	1	–	1	1	–	–	–
WASHRAG	–	1	1	–	–	–	–	–	–
WATCH	1	–	1	–	–	–	–	–	–
WATER	–	2	2	1	–	1	–	–	–
WAX	–	–	–	–	–	–	1	–	1
WET	–	1	1	–	–	–	–	–	–
WETTER	–	1	1	–	–	–	–	–	–
WHAT	–	–	–	1	–	1	–	–	–
WHAT YOU PUT IN WATER	1	–	1	–	–	–	–	–	–
WHEN YOU SMOOTH A RUG	1	–	1	–	–	–	–	–	–

RESPONSE WORD	1ST M	F	T	3RD M	F	T	5TH M	F	T

80. SMOOTH

RESPONSE WORD	1ST M	F	T	3RD M	F	T	5TH M	F	T
WHENEVER SOMEONE IS SMOOTH	—	1	1	—	—	—	—	—	—
WHITE	1	—	1	—	—	—	—	—	—
WHOSE	1	—	1	—	—	—	—	—	—
WINDOW	—	—	—	1	—	1	—	—	—
WINDOWS WALLS	1	—	1	—	—	—	—	—	—
WOOD	—	2	2	—	—	—	—	—	—
WOOL	1	—	1	—	—	—	—	—	—
WRITE	—	1	1	—	—	—	—	—	—
WRITING	1	1	2	—	—	—	—	—	—
YOU	—	1	1	—	—	—	—	—	—
YOUR CAKE	—	1	1	—	—	—	—	—	—
YOUR HAIR MIGHT BE SMOOTH	—	1	1	—	—	—	—	—	—
YOUR HAND	1	—	1	—	—	—	—	—	—

81. SOMETIMES

RESPONSE WORD	1ST M	F	T	3RD M	F	T	5TH M	F	T
A	1	—	1	—	—	—	—	—	—
A CAR	1	—	1	—	—	—	—	—	—
A COUPLE	—	—	—	—	—	—	1	—	1
A LITTLE BIT	—	—	—	—	1	1	—	—	—
A LOT OF TIMES	—	—	—	—	1	1	—	—	—
ABLE	—	—	—	2	—	—	—	1	1
AFTER	—	—	—	2	2	4	—	—	—
AFTERNOON	—	—	—	—	1	1	—	—	—
AGAIN	—	1	1	1	—	1	—	1	1
AGO	—	1	1	1	—	1	1	—	1
ALL	—	—	—	—	—	—	4	—	4
ALL THE TIME	1	—	1	9	5	14	8	5	13
ALL THE TIMES	1	—	1	2	2	4	—	1	1
ALL TIME	—	—	—	—	—	—	1	—	1
ALL TIMES	—	—	—	—	2	2	2	3	5
ALLOWANCE	—	1	1	—	—	—	—	—	—
ALLWAYS	—	—	—	—	—	—	1	—	1
ALMOST	—	—	—	—	—	—	1	3	4
ALONG	—	—	—	—	—	—	—	1	1
ALSO	—	—	—	—	—	—	1	—	1
ALWAYS	3	3	6	29	35	64	28	27	55
AND	—	1	1	—	—	—	—	—	—
ANN	1	—	1	—	—	—	—	—	—
ANOTHER TIME	—	—	—	—	1	1	—	—	—
ANY	—	—	—	—	—	—	—	1	1
ANY TIME	—	—	—	1	1	2	—	—	—
ANYONE	—	—	—	—	—	—	1	—	1
ANYTHING	—	1	1	—	—	—	—	—	—
ANYTIME	—	—	—	2	2	4	—	1	1
ANYWHERE	—	—	—	1	—	1	1	—	1
APPLE	1	—	1	—	—	—	—	—	—
ARE	1	—	1	—	—	—	—	—	—
AT	1	—	1	—	—	—	—	—	—
AWAY	—	—	—	1	1	2	—	—	—
BAD	1	—	1	—	—	—	—	1	1
BALL	—	—	—	1	1	2	—	—	—
BARN	—	1	1	—	—	—	—	—	—
BECAUSE	—	—	—	1	1	2	—	—	—
BEFORE	—	1	1	2	3	5	—	—	—
BEGIN	—	—	—	—	1	1	—	—	—
BELONG	1	—	1	—	—	—	—	—	—
BIMES	1	—	1	—	—	—	—	—	—
BIRD	—	1	1	—	—	—	—	1	1
BIRTHDAY	1	—	1	—	—	—	—	—	—
BLACKBOARD	—	1	1	—	—	—	—	—	—
BLUE	—	1	1	—	—	—	—	—	—
BOBBY	—	—	—	—	—	—	—	1	1
BRING	—	—	—	—	1	1	—	—	—
BUS	1	—	1	—	—	—	—	—	—
BUTTON	1	1	2	—	—	—	—	—	—
CAN	—	2	2	—	—	—	—	—	—
CAN GO	1	—	1	—	—	—	—	—	—
CAN I	—	1	1	—	—	—	—	—	—

RESPONSE WORD	1ST			3RD			5TH		
	M	F	T	M	F	T	M	F	T

81. SOMETIMES

RESPONSE WORD	M	F	T	M	F	T	M	F	T
CAR	1	–	1	–	–	–	–	–	–
CHAIR	1	–	1	–	–	–	–	–	–
COLOR	–	1	1	–	–	–	–	–	–
COME	1	–	1	–	2	2	–	–	–
COME HERE	1	1	2	–	–	–	–	–	–
COMETIMES	1	–	1	–	–	–	–	–	–
COMPOUND	–	–	–	1	–	1	–	–	–
COULD BE SOME	–	1	1	–	–	–	–	–	–
COUPLE OF TIMES	–	–	–	1	–	1	–	–	–
CRUMTIMES	–	1	1	–	–	–	–	–	–
CUPBOARD	–	1	1	–	–	–	–	–	–
CURTAIN	1	–	1	–	–	–	–	–	–
DAY	–	–	–	1	2	3	–	–	–
DAY TIME	–	–	–	1	–	1	–	–	–
DEFFENCT	–	–	–	–	–	–	1	–	1
DESK	1	–	1	–	–	–	–	–	–
DIDNT	–	–	–	1	–	1	–	–	–
DIRT	–	1	1	–	–	–	–	–	–
DISH	–	1	1	–	–	–	–	–	–
DO	1	1	2	–	–	–	–	1	1
DO IT	1	–	1	–	–	–	–	1	1
DO IT NOT VERY OFTEN	–	–	–	–	–	–	–	1	1
DO SOMETHING	–	1	1	–	–	–	–	–	–
DOG	1	–	1	–	–	–	2	–	2
DONT	1	–	1	–	–	–	–	–	–
DONT HAVE TO	–	1	1	–	–	–	–	–	–
DOOR	–	1	1	–	1	1	–	1	1
EAT	1	–	1	–	–	–	–	1	1
EGGS	1	–	1	–	–	–	–	–	–
EVEN	–	–	–	1	–	1	1	–	1
EVER	–	–	–	1	–	1	–	1	1
EVER TIME	–	–	–	1	–	1	–	–	–
EVERY NOW AND THEN	–	–	–	–	–	–	1	–	1
EVERY TIME	–	–	–	2	–	2	2	–	2
EVERYBODY	–	–	–	1	–	1	–	–	–
EVERYTHING	–	–	–	–	–	–	–	1	1
EVERYTIME	–	–	–	2	1	3	2	–	2
EYE	–	2	2	–	–	–	–	–	–
FACE	–	1	1	–	–	–	–	–	–
FEW	–	–	–	–	–	–	–	1	1
FEW TIMES	–	–	–	–	–	–	1	–	1
FIRE	–	1	1	–	–	–	–	–	–
FIRE DRILL	1	–	1	–	–	–	–	–	–
FOREVER	–	–	–	–	–	–	1	–	1
FORGET	1	–	1	–	–	–	–	–	–
FOUR	1	–	1	–	–	–	–	–	–
FRIGHTENED	–	–	–	1	–	1	–	–	–
FUM	–	1	1	–	–	–	–	–	–
FUN TIMES	–	1	1	–	–	–	–	–	–
GAME	–	–	–	–	1	1	–	–	–
GARBAGE CAN	–	1	1	–	–	–	–	–	–
GET HURT	1	–	1	–	–	–	–	–	–
GIRL	–	–	–	–	–	–	1	–	1
GLAD	1	–	1	–	–	–	–	–	–
GO	1	3	4	–	–	–	–	–	–
GOOD	1	–	1	1	–	1	–	–	–
GREEN	1	–	1	–	–	–	–	–	–
HAPPY	1	–	1	–	–	–	–	–	–
HARDLY	–	–	–	1	–	1	–	–	–
HARRIS	1	–	1	–	–	–	–	–	–
HAVE	–	1	1	–	–	–	–	–	–
HAVE TROUBLE	–	–	–	1	–	1	–	–	–
HELPING	1	–	1	–	–	–	–	–	–
HERE	1	3	4	–	–	–	–	–	–
HIM	–	1	1	–	–	–	–	–	–
HIMES	1	–	1	–	–	–	–	–	–
HOUSE	2	–	2	–	–	–	–	–	–
HOUSES	–	1	1	–	–	–	–	–	–
HUMTIMES	1	–	1	–	–	–	–	–	–
I	6	5	11	–	1	1	1	–	1
I AM HERE	–	1	1	–	–	–	–	–	–
I CAN WORK	1	–	1	–	–	–	–	–	–

RESPONSE WORD	1ST M	1ST F	1ST T	3RD M	3RD F	3RD T	5TH M	5TH F	5TH T

81. SOMETIMES

RESPONSE WORD	1ST M	1ST F	1ST T	3RD M	3RD F	3RD T	5TH M	5TH F	5TH T
I DO	1	–	1	–	–	–	–	–	–
I DO SO MUCH	–	1	1	–	–	–	–	–	–
I GET MAD	1	–	1	–	–	–	–	–	–
I GO	1	–	1	–	–	–	–	–	–
I GO AWAY	–	–	–	1	–	1	–	–	–
I GO TO THE STORE	–	1	1	–	–	–	–	–	–
I PLAY	–	1	1	–	–	–	–	–	–
I SEE YOU	–	1	1	–	–	–	–	–	–
I THINK	1	–	1	–	–	–	–	–	–
I WILL	1	–	1	–	–	–	–	–	–
IM	–	–	–	1	–	1	–	–	–
IN	2	1	3	–	–	–	–	–	–
IRREGULAR	–	–	–	–	–	–	–	1	1
IT	1	1	2	–	–	–	–	–	–
IT HAPPENS ONCE IN A WHILE	–	–	–	–	–	–	1	–	1
ITS	–	–	–	–	–	–	1	–	1
ITS RAINING	–	1	1	–	–	–	–	–	–
KIND	–	–	–	1	–	1	–	–	–
LADY	–	–	–	–	1	1	–	–	–
LAST YEAR	–	1	1	–	–	–	–	–	–
LATER	–	–	–	–	1	1	–	1	1
LETS GO GET IN THE POOL AND SWIM AROUND	–	1	1	–	–	–	–	–	–
LETTER	–	–	–	1	–	1	–	–	–
LITILE	1	–	1	–	–	–	–	1	1
LOCKER	1	–	1	–	–	–	–	–	–
LONG	–	–	–	1	–	1	1	–	1
LONG AGO	–	–	–	–	–	–	1	–	1
LOTS	–	–	–	1	–	1	–	–	–
MAGNIFY	–	–	–	–	–	–	1	–	1
MAKE	1	–	1	–	–	–	–	–	–
MAKE UP YOUR MIND	–	1	1	–	–	–	–	–	–
MANY	–	–	–	–	–	–	2	–	2
MAYBE	–	1	1	1	4	5	5	5	10
ME	1	2	3	–	–	–	–	–	–
MILK	–	1	1	–	–	–	–	–	–
MOST	–	–	–	1	1	2	1	1	2
MOST OF THE TIME	1	–	1	1	–	1	–	1	1
MOST TIMES	–	–	–	1	–	1	–	1	1
MOSTLY	1	–	1	–	1	1	–	–	–
MOTHER	–	2	2	–	–	–	–	–	–
MOVE	–	1	1	–	–	–	–	–	–
MUMTIMES	1	–	1	–	–	–	–	–	–
MUNTIMES	1	–	1	–	–	–	–	–	–
MY	1	–	1	–	–	–	–	–	–
NEAR	–	1	1	–	–	–	–	–	–
NEEDLE	1	–	1	–	–	–	–	–	–
NEVER	1	4	5	3	1	4	6	6	12
NICE	–	1	1	–	–	–	–	–	–
NILL	–	–	–	–	–	–	1	–	1
NO	1	–	1	–	1	1	–	–	–
NO MORE	–	1	1	–	–	–	–	–	–
NO RESPONSE	–	1	1	–	–	–	–	–	–
NO TIME	1	–	1	2	–	2	–	–	–
NO TIMES	1	–	1	–	2	2	–	–	–
NOT	–	1	1	–	1	1	–	1	1
NOT ALL THE TIME	–	–	–	–	–	–	1	1	2
NOT ALWAYS	–	–	–	–	2	2	5	8	13
NOT MANY	–	–	–	–	–	–	1	–	1
NOT MUCH	–	–	–	–	–	–	1	–	1
NOT OFTEN	–	–	–	–	–	–	–	1	1
NOT SOMETIMES	4	–	4	–	1	1	–	–	–
NOT TOO MUCH	–	–	–	–	1	1	–	–	–
NOT YOURS	–	1	1	–	–	–	–	–	–
NOTHING	–	–	–	1	1	2	1	–	1
NOW	–	–	–	2	2	4	1	–	1
NUMBERS	1	–	1	–	–	–	–	–	–
OFTEN	–	–	–	4	3	7	6	15	21
ONCE	1	–	1	2	3	5	5	10	15
ONCE BEFORE	–	1	1	–	–	–	–	–	–
ONCE IN A WHILE	–	–	–	1	1	2	3	2	5

RESPONSE WORD	1ST M	F	T	3RD M	F	T	5TH M	F	T

81. SOMETIMES

RESPONSE WORD	1ST M	F	T	3RD M	F	T	5TH M	F	T
ONCE IN A-WHILE	–	–	–	–	–	–	2	–	2
ONCE IN AWHILE	–	–	–	1	–	1	–	–	–
ONE	1	1	2	–	1	1	–	1	1
ONE A DAY	–	–	–	–	1	1	–	–	–
ONE DAY	1	–	1	–	–	–	–	–	–
ONE TIME	–	1	1	1	–	1	–	–	–
ONETIMES	–	1	1	1	–	1	–	–	–
ONLY	–	–	–	–	–	–	–	1	1
ORANGE	1	–	1	–	–	–	–	–	–
OTHER	–	–	–	–	1	1	–	–	–
OTHER TIMES	–	–	–	2	3	5	–	–	–
OTHERS	–	1	1	–	–	–	–	–	–
OUT	–	1	1	–	–	–	–	–	–
OWL	–	–	–	–	–	–	1	–	1
PAD	1	–	1	–	–	–	–	–	–
PENCIL	–	1	1	–	–	–	–	–	–
PEOPLE	2	–	2	1	–	1	–	1	1
PEPPER	–	1	1	–	–	–	–	–	–
PINEAPPLE	–	1	1	–	–	–	–	–	–
PLAY	3	2	5	–	–	–	–	–	–
PLAY BALL	–	1	1	–	–	–	–	–	–
PLENTY	–	–	–	–	–	–	1	–	1
POINT	1	–	1	–	–	–	–	–	–
POMTIMES	–	1	1	–	–	–	–	–	–
PUT IN WATER	1	–	1	–	–	–	–	–	–
RAIN	–	1	1	–	–	–	–	–	–
REASON	–	–	–	–	–	–	1	–	1
RIDE	1	–	1	–	–	–	–	–	–
RIDE A BIKE	1	–	1	–	–	–	–	–	–
ROAD	–	1	1	–	–	–	–	–	–
ROCK	–	1	1	–	–	–	–	–	–
SAD	–	–	–	–	1	1	–	–	–
SCARECROW	1	–	1	–	–	–	–	–	–
SCHOOL	1	–	1	–	–	–	–	–	–
SEAT	1	–	1	–	–	–	–	–	–
SEE	1	3	4	–	–	–	–	–	–
SEE-SAW	–	1	1	–	–	–	–	–	–
SELDOM	–	–	–	1	–	1	1	1	2
SENT	–	1	1	–	–	–	–	–	–
SHIRT	–	–	–	–	–	–	–	1	1
SHOPPING	1	–	1	–	–	–	–	–	–
SLOW	–	1	1	–	–	–	–	1	1
SOME	–	4	4	5	–	5	1	2	3
SOME BETTER	–	–	–	1	–	1	–	–	–
SOME OTHER TIME	–	–	–	1	–	1	–	–	–
SOMEDAY	–	–	–	–	2	2	–	–	–
SOMEDAYS	–	–	–	–	1	1	–	–	–
SOMEKIMES	–	–	–	1	–	1	–	2	3
SOMEONE	–	–	–	5	4	9	1	2	3
SOMETHING	3	4	7	3	9	12	9	7	16
SOMETHING HAPPENS	1	–	1	–	–	–	–	–	–
SOMETHINGS	2	–	2	2	–	2	1	–	1
SOMETIME	–	–	–	–	1	1	–	–	–
SOMETIMES	–	–	–	–	1	–	1	–	1
SOMETIMES SOMETHING HAPPEN TO YOU.	1	–	1	–	–	–	–	–	–
SOMEWHERE	–	–	–	6	4	10	1	3	4
SOON	–	–	–	–	–	–	–	1	1
SPRING	–	–	–	–	1	1	–	–	–
SUMMER	2	2	4	1	–	1	–	–	–
SUN	4	7	11	–	–	–	–	–	–
TABLE	–	1	1	–	–	–	–	–	–
TELEPHONE	1	–	1	–	–	–	–	–	–
THANKSGIVING	–	1	1	–	–	–	–	–	–
THAT	–	1	1	–	–	–	–	–	–
THE	–	1	1	–	–	–	–	–	–
THEM	–	–	–	1	–	1	–	–	–
THEN	1	1	2	–	–	–	–	–	–
THEY PLAY	1	–	1	–	–	–	–	–	–
THING	–	–	–	1	1	2	1	–	1
THINGS	–	–	–	–	–	–	–	1	1
THINK	1	–	1	–	–	–	–	–	–

RESPONSE WORD	1ST			3RD			5TH		
	M	F	T	M	F	T	M	F	T

81. SOMETIMES

RESPONSE WORD	M	F	T	M	F	T	M	F	T
TIME	1	–	1	2	3	5	–	–	–
TIMES	–	1	1	1	1	2	4	3	7
TIMES AGO	–	–	–	–	–	–	1	–	1
TIMMY	1	–	1	–	–	–	–	–	–
TODAY	1	–	1	2	–	2	–	1	1
TOGETHER	–	–	–	–	–	–	1	–	1
TOMORROW	–	–	–	–	1	1	–	1	1
TONNORA	–	–	–	–	–	–	1	–	1
TRACK	–	–	–	1	–	1	–	–	–
TRASH CAN	–	–	–	1	–	1	–	–	–
TUMTIMES	–	1	1	–	–	–	–	–	–
U WILL	1	–	1	–	–	–	–	–	–
USUAL	–	–	–	–	–	–	–	2	2
USUALLY	–	–	–	1	–	1	1	2	3
VERY OFTEN	–	–	–	–	–	–	1	–	1
WANT IT	–	–	–	1	–	1	1	–	1
WARMER	1	–	1	–	–	–	–	–	–
WAS	–	1	1	–	–	–	–	–	–
WATER	–	2	2	–	–	–	–	–	–
WE	3	1	4	1	1	2	1	–	1
WE DO SOMETHING	1	–	1	–	–	–	–	–	–
WE LIKE TO COME OUTSIDE	–	1	1	–	–	–	–	–	–
WE MEET	1	–	1	–	–	–	–	–	–
WE PLAY	–	1	1	–	–	–	–	–	–
WE TALK	1	–	1	–	–	–	–	–	–
WE WANT	1	–	1	–	–	–	–	–	–
WENT	–	1	1	–	–	–	–	–	–
WHAT	1	1	2	–	–	–	–	–	–
WHAT YOU MEAN	–	1	1	–	–	–	–	–	–
WHEN	–	1	1	1	4	5	1	1	2
WHEN ITS SUMMERTIME	1	–	1	–	–	–	–	–	–
WHENEVER YOUR MOTHER SAYS SOMETIMES DO	–	1	1	–	–	–	–	–	–
WHERE	–	1	1	–	–	–	–	–	–
WINTER	–	1	1	–	–	–	–	–	–
WONDER	–	–	–	–	1	1	–	–	–
WORK	–	–	–	–	1	1	–	–	–
WORRY	1	–	1	–	–	–	–	–	–
WRITE	–	1	1	–	–	–	–	–	–
YARD	1	–	1	–	–	–	–	–	–
YESTERDAY	–	–	–	–	1	1	–	–	–
YOU	5	2	7	1	1	2	1	–	1
YOU GO FAST	1	–	1	–	–	–	–	–	–
YOU HEAR A STORY	–	–	–	–	–	–	–	1	1
YOU MAY	1	–	1	–	–	–	–	–	–
YOU MAY EAT YOUR LUNCH	–	1	1	–	–	–	–	–	–

82. SOUR

RESPONSE WORD	M	F	T	M	F	T	M	F	T
A PEAR IS SOUR	–	1	1	–	–	–	–	–	–
APPLE	2	1	3	1	2	3	1	–	1
AWFUL	–	–	–	2	2	4	3	3	6
BAD	–	–	–	1	3	4	3	–	3
BAD TASTE	1	–	1	–	–	–	1	–	1
BAD, TASTY	–	–	–	–	1	1	–	–	–
BATHTUB	–	1	1	–	–	–	–	–	–
BELCH	–	–	–	–	1	1	–	–	–
BET	–	–	–	–	–	–	1	–	1
BIRD	–	1	1	–	–	–	–	–	–
BITTER	4	2	6	14	11	25	29	22	51
BITTER TASTE	–	–	–	1	–	1	–	–	–
BLTY	–	–	–	–	–	–	1	–	1
BOOK	–	1	1	–	–	–	–	1	1
BOTTLE	–	1	1	–	–	–	–	–	–
BOUR	–	1	1	–	–	–	1	–	1
BOWER	–	2	2	–	–	–	–	–	–
BOWLING PIN	1	–	1	–	–	–	–	–	–
BREAD	–	1	1	–	–	–	–	–	–
BROWN	–	1	1	–	–	–	–	–	–
BURREL	–	1	1	–	–	–	–	–	–
BUTTERMILK	–	1	1	–	1	1	–	–	–

RESPONSE WORD	1ST M	1ST F	1ST T	3RD M	3RD F	3RD T	5TH M	5TH F	5TH T

82.   SOUR

RESPONSE WORD	1ST M	1ST F	1ST T	3RD M	3RD F	3RD T	5TH M	5TH F	5TH T
CABBAGE	—	1	1	—	—	—	—	—	—
CAKE	—	1	1	—	—	—	—	—	—
CAN	—	1	1	—	—	—	—	—	—
CARROT	—	1	1	—	—	—	—	—	—
CAT	—	—	—	—	—	—	1	—	1
CELERY	1	1	2	—	—	—	—	—	—
CHAIR	—	1	1	—	—	—	—	—	—
CHIMNEY	1	—	1	—	—	—	—	—	—
CLOCK	—	1	1	—	—	—	—	—	—
COLD	1	—	1	—	—	—	—	—	—
COOK	—	1	1	—	—	—	—	—	—
COOKIE	—	1	1	—	—	—	—	—	—
COW	—	1	1	—	—	—	—	—	—
COWER	—	1	1	—	—	—	—	—	—
CREAM	1	1	2	2	1	3	—	4	4
CROUR	—	1	1	—	—	—	—	—	—
CROWD	—	2	2	—	1	1	—	1	1
CUP	—	—	—	—	1	1	—	—	—
CUT	—	—	—	—	—	—	1	—	1
DIRT	1	—	1	—	—	—	—	—	—
DOESNT TASTE GOOD	—	1	1	1	—	1	—	1	1
DONT EAT	—	1	1	—	—	—	—	—	—
DONT EAT IT	—	1	1	—	—	—	—	—	—
DONT GO IN THE CELLAR CAUSE MIGHT BE SU.	—	1	1	—	—	—	—	—	—
DONT TASTE GOOD	1	—	1	—	—	—	—	—	—
DONT WANT THIS	1	—	1	—	—	—	—	—	—
DOOR	—	—	—	—	—	—	—	1	1
DOORKNOB	—	—	—	1	—	1	—	—	—
DRAWER	1	—	1	—	—	—	—	—	—
DRESS	—	1	1	—	—	—	—	—	—
DRESSING	—	—	—	—	1	1	—	—	—
DRINK	—	2	2	1	—	1	—	—	—
DRINK JUICE	1	—	1	—	—	—	—	—	—
DRY	—	—	—	2	—	2	—	—	—
EARTH	—	—	—	—	—	—	1	—	1
EASY	—	1	1	—	—	—	—	—	—
EAT	1	1	2	—	—	—	—	—	—
EATING	—	1	1	—	—	—	—	—	—
EGG	—	—	—	—	—	—	1	—	1
EGGS	1	—	1	—	—	—	—	—	—
ENTER	—	1	1	—	—	—	—	—	—
FAST	—	—	—	—	—	—	1	—	1
FELL	—	—	—	—	—	—	1	—	1
FINGER	1	—	1	—	—	—	—	—	—
FIRE	1	—	1	—	—	—	—	—	—
FIRSH	—	—	—	—	1	1	—	1	1
FISH	—	—	—	—	1	1	—	1	1
FLOWER	3	1	4	—	—	—	—	1	1
FOOD	3	3	6	—	—	—	—	1	1
FORK	—	1	1	—	—	—	—	—	—
FRESH	—	1	1	5	1	6	2	—	2
FRUIT	—	—	—	1	—	1	—	—	—
FURNITURE	1	—	1	—	—	—	—	—	—
GET	1	—	1	—	—	—	—	—	—
GLASS	—	2	2	—	—	—	—	—	—
GOOD	3	7	10	9	13	22	2	1	3
GRAPE	—	—	—	—	—	—	2	—	2
GRAPEFRUIT	1	—	1	—	1	1	2	—	2
GRAPES	1	—	1	—	2	2	3	1	4
GREAT	—	—	—	—	—	—	1	—	1
GUN	—	—	—	1	—	1	—	—	—
HARD	—	1	1	1	—	1	—	—	—
HARSH	—	—	—	—	—	—	1	1	2
HATE IT	1	—	1	—	—	—	—	—	—
HEARD	—	—	—	—	—	—	—	1	1
HOLE	—	—	—	—	—	—	1	—	1
HORSE	—	—	—	1	—	1	—	—	—
HOUR	—	—	—	—	1	1	—	—	—
HOUSE	—	—	—	1	—	1	—	—	—
HOWER	—	1	1	—	—	—	—	—	—
HURT	—	—	—	—	—	—	3	3	6

82. SOUR

RESPONSE WORD	1ST M	1ST F	1ST T	3RD M	3RD F	3RD T	5TH M	5TH F	5TH T
ICE	–	–	–	1	–	1	–	–	–
IS FLOWERS	1	–	1	–	–	–	–	–	–
IT	–	–	–	1	–	1	–	–	–
JET	1	–	1	–	1	–	–	–	–
JUICE	2	4	6	–	1	1	–	–	–
JUICY	1	–	1	2	–	2	–	–	–
KETCHUP	1	–	1	–	–	–	–	–	–
KIND OF	–	1	1	–	–	–	–	–	–
KOOL-ADE	–	1	1	–	–	–	–	–	–
KRAUT	13	7	20	4	4	8	–	–	–
LEAVES	–	1	1	–	–	–	–	–	–
LEMON	4	9	13	8	4	12	4	7	11
LIKE	–	1	1	–	–	–	–	–	–
LIME	1	–	1	–	–	–	–	–	–
LOUDER	1	–	1	–	–	–	–	–	–
LOUSY	–	–	–	–	–	–	–	1	1
LUNCH	–	1	1	–	–	–	–	–	–
MALLARD	1	–	1	–	–	–	–	–	–
MAR	–	–	–	–	–	–	1	–	1
ME	1	–	1	–	–	–	–	–	–
MELT	1	–	1	–	–	–	–	–	–
MILK	7	14	21	8	4	12	5	4	9
MIX	–	–	–	–	–	–	1	–	1
MOM	–	–	–	–	–	–	1	–	1
MOSTY	–	–	–	1	–	1	–	–	–
MOUR	2	–	2	–	–	–	–	–	–
MOWER	1	–	1	–	–	–	–	–	–
MUSHY	–	–	–	–	–	–	1	–	1
NICE	–	–	–	2	–	2	–	–	–
NIGHT	–	–	–	–	1	1	–	–	–
NO GOOD	–	1	1	1	–	1	–	–	–
NO GOOD TO DRINK	1	–	1	–	–	–	–	–	–
NOT	–	2	2	–	–	–	1	–	1
NOT GOOD	1	–	1	–	2	2	1	1	2
NOT RIPE	–	–	–	1	–	1	–	–	–
NOT SOUR	1	3	4	2	3	5	–	–	–
NOT SWEET	–	–	–	–	–	–	4	1	5
NOUR	1	–	1	–	–	–	–	–	–
ONION	2	1	3	–	–	–	1	–	1
OOO	–	–	–	–	–	–	–	1	1
OOU	–	1	1	–	–	–	–	1	1
ORANGE	3	–	3	1	–	1	1	–	1
ORANGE JUICE	–	1	1	1	–	1	–	–	–
ORANGE JUICE IS SOUR	–	–	–	–	–	–	–	1	1
ORANGES	1	1	2	–	–	–	–	–	–
OUCH	–	–	–	–	–	–	–	1	1
OUR	–	–	–	–	–	–	1	–	1
PAN	–	–	–	–	1	1	–	–	–
PEANUT BUTTER	1	–	1	–	–	–	–	–	–
PEN	–	1	1	1	–	1	–	–	–
PEPPER	1	–	1	–	–	–	–	–	–
PICKLE	1	1	2	2	3	5	1	1	2
PICKLES	1	–	1	–	1	1	1	–	1
PIPE	1	–	1	–	–	–	–	–	–
PIPER	–	–	–	–	–	–	–	1	1
PLAIN	–	–	–	–	–	–	–	1	1
PLAY	1	–	1	–	–	–	–	–	–
POCKETBOOK	1	–	1	–	–	–	–	–	–
POT	1	–	1	–	–	–	–	–	–
POUR	–	–	–	–	–	–	–	1	1
POWER	1	–	1	1	–	1	–	–	–
PUSS	3	1	4	–	–	–	–	–	–
RAIN	–	–	–	–	–	–	1	–	1
RAT	–	1	1	–	–	–	–	–	–
RED APPLE	–	–	–	1	–	1	–	–	–
RENKY	–	–	–	–	1	1	–	–	–
RICE	–	–	–	1	–	1	–	–	–
RICH	–	–	–	–	1	1	–	–	–
RIN	–	–	–	–	–	–	1	–	1
RIPE	–	–	–	–	1	1	1	–	1
ROTTEN	1	–	1	–	1	1	1	1	2
ROUR	–	1	1	–	–	–	–	–	–

RESPONSE WORD	1ST			3RD			5TH		
	M	F	T	M	F	T	M	F	T

82.   SOUR

RESPONSE WORD	M	F	T	M	F	T	M	F	T
SADDLE	1	—	1	—	—	—	—	—	—
SALAD	3	—	3	—	—	—	—	—	—
SALLY	—	1	1	—	—	—	—	—	—
SALT	1	1	2	1	—	1	—	1	1
SANDWISH	—	—	—	—	—	—	—	1	1
SAUERKRAUT	—	2	2	—	1	1	—	—	—
SAURKRAUT	1	—	1	—	—	—	—	—	—
SAY	—	—	—	—	—	—	—	1	1
SCAT	—	—	—	1	—	1	—	—	—
SEA	1	—	1	—	—	—	—	—	—
SEAP	—	—	—	—	—	—	1	—	1
SEE	1	—	1	—	—	—	—	—	—
SEEWEL	—	—	—	—	—	—	1	—	1
SELL	1	—	1	—	—	—	—	—	—
SELLING	1	—	1	—	—	—	—	—	—
SHADE	—	—	—	—	—	—	—	1	1
SHOE	1	—	1	—	—	—	—	—	—
SHOWER	—	—	—	1	—	1	—	—	—
SICK	1	—	1	—	—	—	—	—	—
SIDEWALK	—	1	1	—	—	—	—	—	—
SIGN	—	1	1	—	—	—	—	—	—
SKY	—	1	1	—	—	—	—	—	—
SMELLY	—	—	—	—	—	—	—	1	1
SNEE	1	—	1	—	—	—	—	—	—
SO	—	1	1	—	—	—	—	—	—
SOFT	1	—	1	1	1	2	—	—	—
SOLD	—	1	1	—	—	—	—	—	—
SOME GRAPES ARE SOUR	—	1	1	—	—	—	—	—	—
SOMETHING	1	—	1	—	—	—	—	—	—
SOMETHING IS SOUR JUST LIKE ORANGE	—	1	1	—	—	—	—	—	—
SORE	—	—	—	—	—	—	1	—	1
SOUP	1	—	1	—	1	1	—	—	—
SOUR	1	—	1	—	—	—	—	—	—
SOURED	2	—	2	—	—	—	—	—	—
SPAGHETTI	—	1	1	—	—	—	—	—	—
SPOILED	—	—	—	—	1	1	—	—	—
SQUINTING	—	—	—	—	—	—	—	1	1
STALE	—	—	—	—	1	1	1	—	1
STATE	—	—	—	—	1	1	—	—	—
STOP	—	1	1	—	—	—	—	—	—
STREAM	—	1	1	—	—	—	—	—	—
STRONG	—	—	—	—	2	2	—	1	1
STUFF	1	—	1	—	—	—	—	—	—
SUGAR	—	1	1	—	1	1	1	1	2
SUN	1	1	2	—	—	—	—	—	—
SWEAT	—	—	—	—	—	—	—	1	1
SWEET	10	8	18	46	50	96	37	60	97
TASTE	1	—	1	3	5	8	3	—	3
TASTE GOOD	1	—	1	—	—	—	—	—	—
TASTY	—	—	—	1	—	1	—	2	2
TERRIBLE	—	—	—	2	—	2	2	—	2
THAT	1	—	1	—	—	—	—	—	—
THATS SOUR	1	—	1	—	—	—	—	—	—
THE	—	—	—	—	1	1	—	—	—
THE MOON	1	—	1	—	—	—	—	—	—
THING	—	—	—	—	1	1	—	—	—
TICKLE	—	1	1	—	—	—	—	—	—
TOO SOUR	—	1	1	—	—	—	—	—	—
UGLY	—	—	—	1	—	1	—	—	—
UNCLE	—	1	1	—	—	—	—	—	—
UNHAPPY	—	—	—	—	—	—	—	1	1
UNSWEET	—	—	—	—	—	—	1	1	2
UNTASTY	—	—	—	—	—	—	—	1	1
VINEGAR	3	—	3	—	1	1	—	—	—
WARM	1	—	1	—	—	—	—	—	—
WASH	1	—	1	—	—	—	—	—	—
WE DONT LIKE IT	1	—	1	—	—	—	—	—	—
WET	—	—	—	—	—	—	1	—	1
WHEN YOU SOUR A GLASS OF WATER	1	—	1	—	—	—	—	—	—
WHITE	—	1	1	—	—	—	—	—	—

RESPONSE WORD	1ST M	F	T	3RD M	F	T	5TH M	F	T

82. SOUR

RESPONSE WORD	1ST M	F	T	3RD M	F	T	5TH M	F	T
WOOD	1	–	1	–	–	–	–	–	–
WORD	–	–	–	–	1	1	–	–	–
YELLOW	–	–	–	–	–	–	–	1	1

83. SQUARE

RESPONSE WORD	1ST M	F	T	3RD M	F	T	5TH M	F	T
A BLOCK	–	–	–	1	–	1	–	–	–
A BOX	–	1	1	–	–	–	1	–	1
A SHAPE	–	–	–	–	–	–	–	1	1
AWAY	–	1	1	–	–	–	–	–	–
BALL	1	–	1	–	–	–	–	–	–
BASEBALL	–	–	–	–	–	–	–	1	1
BASIN	–	1	1	–	–	–	–	–	–
BEAR	1	1	2	–	–	–	–	–	–
BEATNIK TERM	–	–	–	–	–	–	1	–	1
BED	1	–	1	–	–	–	–	–	–
BICYCLE	1	–	1	–	–	–	–	–	–
BIG	–	1	1	1	1	2	–	1	1
BLACK	–	–	–	–	1	1	–	1	1
BLACKBOARD	–	1	1	–	–	–	–	–	–
BLARE	–	–	–	–	1	1	–	–	–
BLOCK	6	7	13	10	12	22	10	10	20
BLOCKS	–	1	1	1	–	1	–	–	–
BOARD	1	–	1	1	–	1	–	–	–
BOAT	1	–	1	–	–	–	–	–	–
BOOK	–	1	1	1	–	1	–	–	–
BOX	21	13	34	13	18	31	12	19	31
BOXES	–	1	1	–	–	–	–	–	–
BRIGHT	1	–	1	–	–	–	–	–	–
BROWN	–	1	1	–	–	–	–	–	–
BUILDING	1	–	1	–	–	–	–	–	–
BY	1	–	1	–	–	–	–	–	–
CAKE	–	2	2	–	–	–	–	–	–
CANDY	–	1	1	–	–	–	–	–	–
CAR	1	–	1	–	1	1	–	–	–
CARE	2	1	3	–	–	–	–	–	–
CHAIR	1	–	1	–	–	–	–	–	–
CHECKERS	–	1	1	–	–	–	–	–	–
CIRCLE	9	11	20	20	25	45	17	36	53
CIRCLED	–	–	–	–	–	–	–	1	1
CIRCLES	–	–	–	–	–	–	1	–	1
CLOCK	–	1	1	–	–	–	–	–	–
COAT	–	1	1	–	–	–	–	–	–
COMES IN A SQUARE	–	1	1	–	–	–	–	–	–
CONMER	–	–	–	–	–	–	–	1	1
CORNER	–	–	–	–	1	1	–	1	1
CORNERS	1	–	1	1	–	1	–	–	–
CUT A BOARD IN HALF	1	–	1	–	–	–	–	–	–
DAMPED	–	–	–	–	1	1	–	–	–
DANCE	1	2	3	–	1	1	–	–	–
DARE	–	1	1	–	–	–	–	–	–
DAY	–	–	–	1	–	1	–	–	–
DESK	–	1	1	–	–	–	–	–	–
DIAMOND	1	–	1	–	–	–	–	–	–
DOLL	–	–	–	–	1	1	–	–	–
DONT EAT TOO MUCH	–	1	1	–	–	–	–	–	–
DOOR	–	1	1	–	–	–	1	–	1
DUMB	–	–	–	–	–	–	1	–	1
DUMPLING	–	1	1	–	–	–	–	–	–
EAT	–	–	–	–	–	–	1	–	1
EIGHT	–	1	1	–	–	–	–	–	–
EQUAL	–	–	–	1	1	2	–	–	–
EVEN	–	–	–	–	1	1	–	2	2
FAIR	1	1	2	–	–	–	1	–	1
FALL	–	1	1	–	–	–	–	–	–
FIGHT	1	–	1	–	–	–	–	–	–
FIN	–	–	–	–	–	–	–	1	1
FINSH	–	–	–	1	3	4	2	–	2
FLAT	–	–	–	1	3	4	2	–	2
FLOOR	1	–	1	–	–	–	–	–	–
FOR CAT	1	–	1	–	–	–	–	–	–

83. SQUARE

RESPONSE WORD	1ST M	F	T	3RD M	F	T	5TH M	F	T
FOUR EVEN ENDS	-	-	-	-	1	1	-	-	-
FOUR SIDES	-	-	-	-	-	-	1	-	1
FRACTIONS	-	-	-	-	-	-	1	-	1
GEOMETRY	-	-	-	-	-	-	-	1	1
GET IN A BOX AND PLAY HOUSE WITH IT	-	1	1	-	-	-	-	-	-
GLASS	1	-	1	-	-	-	-	-	-
GO	-	1	1	-	-	-	1	-	1
GOLD	-	1	1	-	-	-	-	-	-
GROUND HOG	-	-	-	-	-	-	-	1	1
HAIR	8	1	9	-	-	-	-	1	1
HALF	-	1	1	-	-	-	-	-	-
HARD	-	-	-	-	1	1	1	-	1
HAVE	-	1	1	-	-	-	-	-	-
HEAD	-	-	-	-	-	-	1	-	1
HEART	-	-	-	-	1	1	-	-	-
HERE	-	-	-	1	-	1	-	-	-
HIM	-	-	-	-	-	-	-	1	1
HOLD	1	-	1	-	-	-	-	-	-
HOLE	1	-	1	-	-	-	-	-	-
HOUSE	2	2	4	-	1	1	-	1	1
I	1	-	1	-	-	-	-	-	-
I HAVE A SQUARE BLOCK	-	1	1	-	-	-	-	-	-
IN	-	-	-	-	-	-	1	-	1
IS	1	1	2	-	-	-	-	-	-
IS A BOX	1	-	1	-	-	-	-	-	-
JACK-IN-THE-BOX	1	-	1	-	-	-	-	-	-
LARGE	-	1	1	1	2	3	-	-	-
LAYER	1	-	1	-	-	-	-	-	-
LEAVES	1	-	1	-	-	-	-	-	-
LETS BUILD WITH BLOCKS	-	1	1	-	-	-	-	-	-
LIGHT	1	-	1	-	-	-	-	-	-
LIKE A BOX	-	1	1	-	-	-	-	-	-
LIKE A KITE	-	-	-	1	-	1	-	-	-
LIKE BREAD	-	1	1	-	-	-	-	-	-
LINE	-	-	-	1	-	1	-	-	-
LINES	-	-	-	2	-	2	-	-	-
LITTLE	3	3	6	1	-	1	-	-	-
LOCK	-	-	-	-	-	-	-	1	1
LONG	-	-	-	2	-	2	-	1	1
LOOK	-	1	1	-	-	-	-	-	-
LOOK DOWN	1	-	1	-	-	-	-	-	-
MAKE	-	-	-	1	-	1	-	-	-
MAN	-	-	-	-	1	1	-	-	-
MARE	1	1	2	1	1	2	-	-	-
MARRY	1	-	1	-	-	-	-	-	-
MASS	1	-	1	-	-	-	-	-	-
MAVE	1	-	1	-	-	-	-	-	-
MAYOR	1	-	1	-	-	-	-	-	-
ME	1	-	1	-	-	-	-	-	-
MEAL	-	-	-	-	-	-	1	-	1
MEASURE	-	-	-	-	1	1	1	-	1
MEN	-	-	-	-	1	1	1	-	1
MIDDLE	1	-	1	-	-	-	-	-	-
MILK	1	-	1	-	-	-	-	-	-
MOTORCYCLE	1	-	1	-	-	-	-	-	-
MOUSE	1	-	1	-	-	-	-	-	-
MOUTH	-	1	1	-	-	-	-	-	-
NAIRE	-	1	1	-	-	-	-	-	-
NICE	-	1	1	-	-	-	-	-	-
NOT	-	2	2	-	-	-	-	-	-
NOT ROUND	-	-	-	1	-	1	1	1	2
NOW	-	-	-	-	-	-	-	1	1
NUT	-	-	-	1	-	1	2	1	3
O	1	-	1	-	-	-	-	-	-
OBJECT	-	-	-	-	-	-	1	1	2
OVAL	-	-	-	-	-	-	2	1	3
PAIR	1	3	4	1	-	1	-	-	-
PAN	-	-	-	-	-	-	1	-	1
PAPER	1	1	2	-	-	-	-	-	-
PEAR	-	1	1	-	-	-	-	-	-
PEOPLE	-	-	-	-	-	-	-	2	2

RESPONSE WORD	1ST M	F	T	3RD M	F	T	5TH M	F	T

83. SQUARE

RESPONSE WORD	1ST M	F	T	3RD M	F	T	5TH M	F	T
PICTURE	1	–	1	–	–	–	–	–	–
PIECE	1	–	1	–	1	1	–	–	–
PIN	–	1	1	–	–	–	–	–	–
PLAY SQUARES	1	–	1	–	–	–	–	–	–
PRESENT	1	–	1	–	–	–	–	–	–
PURPLE	–	–	–	–	–	–	–	1	1
RECTANGLE	3	–	3	10	7	17	–	9	9
RED	1	–	1	–	–	–	–	–	–
RIDING	1	–	1	–	–	–	–	–	–
ROND	–	–	–	–	–	–	1	–	1
ROOM	–	–	–	–	–	–	–	1	1
ROPE	–	1	1	–	–	–	–	–	–
ROUND	8	14	22	34	31	65	42	21	63
SALE	1	–	1	–	–	–	–	–	–
SAW	1	–	1	–	–	–	–	–	–
SCAT	1	–	1	–	–	–	–	–	–
SEWING MACHINE	–	1	1	–	–	–	–	–	–
SHAPE	–	–	–	3	4	7	8	1	9
SHAPES	1	1	2	–	1	1	–	–	–
SHOE	–	–	–	–	1	1	–	–	–
SHOOK	1	–	1	–	–	–	–	–	–
SICK	1	–	1	–	–	–	–	–	–
SIDE	1	–	1	–	–	–	–	–	–
SIDES	–	–	–	–	–	–	2	–	2
SIMPLE	–	–	–	1	–	1	–	–	–
SIX	1	–	1	–	–	–	–	–	–
SIZE	–	–	–	1	–	1	–	–	–
SMALL	1	1	2	–	–	–	–	1	1
SNAKE	–	1	1	–	–	–	–	–	–
SOMEONE	–	–	–	–	–	–	–	1	1
SOMETHING	–	–	–	–	–	–	1	–	1
SOMETHING SQUARE	–	–	–	–	–	–	–	1	1
SOUP	1	–	1	–	–	–	–	–	–
SQUASH	–	1	1	–	–	–	–	–	–
SQUIRE	–	1	1	–	–	–	1	–	1
SQUIRREL	2	3	5	2	–	2	–	–	–
SQUIRT	–	1	1	–	–	–	–	–	–
STORY	–	–	–	–	1	1	–	–	–
STRAIGHT	–	–	–	–	–	–	–	1	1
STRAW	–	1	1	–	–	–	–	–	–
SUSAN	–	1	1	–	–	–	–	–	–
SWEAR	1	–	1	–	–	–	–	–	–
TABLE	–	–	–	–	2	2	–	–	–
TAIL	–	1	1	–	–	–	–	–	–
TEAR	–	1	1	–	–	–	–	–	–
TELEPHONE POLE	1	–	1	–	–	–	–	–	–
TEN	–	1	1	–	–	–	–	–	–
THE	1	–	1	–	–	–	–	–	–
THERE	–	–	–	1	–	1	–	–	–
THICK	–	–	–	–	–	–	1	–	1
THIN	–	1	1	1	–	1	–	–	–
THING	–	–	–	1	–	1	–	–	–
TILE	–	–	–	–	1	1	–	–	–
TOWN	–	–	–	1	–	1	–	1	1
TREE	–	1	1	–	–	–	–	–	–
TREES	–	1	1	–	–	–	–	–	–
TRIANGE	–	–	–	–	–	–	1	–	1
TRIANGLE	6	9	15	18	13	31	13	10	23
TRIANGLE SHAPE	–	–	–	–	–	–	1	–	1
TRIANGULAR	–	–	–	1	–	1	1	–	1
TRUCK	1	–	1	–	–	–	–	–	–
UNEVEN	–	–	–	–	–	–	1	–	1
WATER	–	–	–	–	–	–	1	–	1
WEAR	1	–	1	1	–	1	–	–	–
WHENEVER MOTHER IS MAD	–	1	1	–	–	–	–	–	–
WHERE	1	3	4	–	–	–	1	–	1
WIDE	–	1	1	–	2	2	–	2	2
WINDOW	–	1	1	–	–	–	–	–	–
WITH	1	–	1	–	–	–	–	–	–
WRONG	–	1	1	–	–	–	–	–	–
YARD	1	–	1	–	–	–	–	–	–
YELLOW	–	1	1	–	–	–	–	–	–

RESPONSE WORD	1ST			3RD			5TH		
	M	F	T	M	F	T	M	F	T

83. SQUARE

RESPONSE WORD	M	F	T	M	F	T	M	F	T
YOU	1	–	1	–	–	–	–	1	1
YOU BE IN A SQUARE	1	–	1	–	–	–	–	–	–
YOUR	–	–	–	–	–	–	1	–	1

84. SWIFT

RESPONSE WORD	M	F	T	M	F	T	M	F	T
A BOAT GOES SWIFTING ALONG.	–	–	–	1	–	1	–	–	–
AIR	2	–	2	–	–	–	–	–	–
AIRPLANE FLIES	1	–	1	–	–	–	–	–	–
ANTS	–	–	–	–	–	–	–	1	1
AROUND	1	–	1	–	1	1	–	–	–
ARROW	–	–	–	–	1	1	–	–	–
AWAY	–	1	1	1	–	1	–	–	–
BABY	–	–	–	1	–	1	–	–	–
BACK AND FORTH	–	–	–	–	–	–	–	1	1
BAD	–	–	–	–	1	1	1	–	1
BALL	–	1	1	–	–	–	–	–	–
BE SWIFT	1	–	1	–	–	–	–	–	–
BEACH	–	1	1	–	–	–	–	–	–
BEAT	–	1	1	–	–	–	–	–	–
BELL	–	1	1	–	–	–	–	–	–
BELT	1	–	1	–	–	–	–	–	–
BIFT	1	–	1	–	–	–	–	–	–
BIKES	1	–	1	–	–	–	–	–	–
BIRD	1	–	1	–	1	1	1	1	2
BIT	–	1	1	–	–	–	–	–	–
BITE	–	1	1	–	–	–	–	–	–
BLACK	–	–	–	–	1	1	–	–	–
BOAT	–	–	–	–	–	–	–	1	1
BOOK	–	–	–	–	1	1	–	–	–
BOY	–	1	1	2	1	3	–	–	–
BRAVE	–	–	–	1	–	1	–	–	–
BREAD	1	2	3	–	1	1	–	–	–
BREEZE	–	–	–	–	–	–	–	3	3
BRIEF	–	–	–	–	–	–	–	1	1
BROOM	3	2	5	1	1	2	–	–	–
BUGS	–	–	–	–	1	1	–	–	–
CAKE	1	1	2	–	–	–	–	–	–
CAME	–	–	–	–	1	1	–	–	–
CAN	1	1	2	–	–	–	–	–	–
CANNED	–	1	1	–	–	–	–	–	–
CAR	1	2	3	1	–	1	–	–	–
CAREFUL	–	–	–	–	1	1	–	–	–
CAT	–	1	1	–	–	–	–	–	–
CAUGHT	1	–	1	–	–	–	–	–	–
CHAIR	–	1	1	–	1	1	–	–	–
CHANGE	–	–	–	–	–	–	1	–	1
CHEAP	–	–	–	–	–	–	1	–	1
CHEESE	1	1	2	6	1	7	–	–	–
CHIMNEY	1	–	1	–	–	–	1	–	1
CLEAN	–	–	–	–	1	1	–	–	–
CLEVER	–	–	–	–	1	1	–	–	–
CLOTHES	–	1	1	–	–	–	–	–	–
COLD	1	–	1	–	–	–	–	–	–
COME WITH ME	–	1	1	–	–	–	–	–	–
COUNT	–	1	1	–	–	–	–	–	–
COURT	–	–	–	–	1	1	–	–	–
CREAM	1	–	1	–	–	–	–	–	–
DASH	–	–	–	1	–	1	–	–	–
DEAR	–	1	1	–	–	–	–	–	–
DEPEND	–	–	–	–	1	1	–	–	–
DIDNT	1	1	2	–	–	–	–	–	–
DIRTY	–	1	1	–	–	–	–	–	–
DIST	–	1	1	–	–	–	–	–	–
DIVING BOARD	–	1	1	–	–	–	–	–	–
DO	–	–	–	–	1	1	–	–	–
DOG	2	–	2	–	–	–	–	–	–
DONT BE BAD CAUSE YOUR MOTHER MIGHT BE.	–	1	1	–	–	–	–	–	–
DOOR	2	–	2	–	–	–	–	–	–

RESPONSE WORD	1ST M	F	T	3RD M	F	T	5TH M	F	T

84. SWIFT

RESPONSE WORD	1ST M	1ST F	1ST T	3RD M	3RD F	3RD T	5TH M	5TH F	5TH T
DOWN	–	1	1	–	–	–	–	–	–
DOWN MOUNTAIN	1	–	1	–	–	–	–	–	–
DRAFT	–	1	1	–	–	–	–	–	–
DRAWN	–	1	1	–	–	–	–	–	–
DRESS	1	–	1	–	–	–	–	–	–
DRIFT	1	–	1	–	–	–	–	–	–
DUST	–	1	1	–	–	–	–	–	–
DUST MOP	–	1	1	–	–	–	–	–	–
EASY	1	–	1	–	–	–	2	2	4
EMPIRE	–	–	–	1	–	1	–	–	–
EYE	–	1	1	–	–	–	–	–	–
FAIR	–	1	1	–	–	–	–	–	–
FAMILY	–	–	–	1	–	1	–	–	–
FAN	1	–	1	–	–	–	–	–	–
FAST	5	4	9	29	18	47	81	64	145
FASTEST	–	–	–	1	–	1	–	–	–
FIERCE	–	–	–	1	–	1	–	–	–
FIRE	–	–	–	1	–	1	–	–	–
FISH	1	–	1	–	–	–	–	–	–
FIVE	1	–	1	–	–	–	–	–	–
FLOAT	–	–	–	–	1	1	–	1	1
FLOOR	–	–	–	–	1	1	–	–	–
FLOW	–	–	–	–	–	–	–	1	1
FLOWER	–	–	–	1	–	1	–	–	–
FLY	1	1	2	1	1	2	–	2	2
FOOT	–	–	–	–	1	1	–	–	–
FUN	–	–	–	–	–	–	–	1	1
GENTLE	1	–	1	–	–	–	–	–	–
GENTLY	–	–	–	–	3	3	1	1	2
GIANT	–	1	1	–	–	–	–	–	–
GIFT	3	–	3	–	–	–	–	–	–
GLAD	–	–	–	–	–	–	1	–	1
GLADE	–	–	–	–	–	–	–	1	1
GLASSES	1	–	1	–	–	–	–	–	–
GLIDE	–	–	–	–	–	–	1	–	1
GO	1	1	2	1	3	4	–	1	1
GO BACK	–	1	1	–	–	–	–	–	–
GOOD	–	–	–	–	2	2	–	–	–
GRADUALLY	–	–	–	–	1	1	–	–	–
GROUND	–	–	–	–	1	1	–	–	–
HAIR CUT	–	–	–	1	–	1	–	–	–
HANDY	–	–	–	–	1	1	–	–	–
HARD	–	2	2	1	–	1	4	1	5
HARD TO STAND UP	–	–	–	–	1	1	–	–	–
HAT	1	–	1	–	–	–	–	–	–
HER	–	–	–	1	2	3	–	–	–
HERE	–	1	1	–	–	–	–	–	–
HILL	–	2	2	–	–	–	–	1	1
HIM	–	–	–	1	–	1	–	–	–
HIS	–	–	–	1	–	1	–	–	–
HISS	1	–	1	–	–	–	–	–	–
HIT	–	1	1	1	1	2	–	–	–
HOME	–	1	1	–	–	–	–	–	–
HORSE	1	–	1	1	–	1	–	–	–
HOUSE	–	1	1	–	–	–	–	–	–
HOW	1	–	1	1	–	1	–	–	–
I	–	1	1	–	–	–	–	–	–
ICE CREAM	1	–	1	–	–	–	–	–	–
IF	–	–	–	1	1	2	–	–	–
IM GOING TO SWEEP MOMS FLOOR.	–	1	1	–	–	–	–	–	–
INDIAN	–	–	–	–	–	–	–	1	1
INK	1	–	1	–	–	–	–	–	–
IS	–	3	3	1	–	1	–	–	–
IT	–	2	2	–	1	1	–	–	–
JIMMY	1	–	1	–	–	–	–	–	–
JUST WHENEVER YOUR MOTHER SAYS IT	–	1	1	–	–	–	–	–	–
KICK	–	–	–	–	–	–	–	1	1
KID	–	1	1	–	–	–	–	–	–
KIFT	–	1	1	–	–	–	–	–	–
LAKE	–	–	–	–	–	–	–	1	1

RESPONSE WORD	1ST M	F	T	3RD M	F	T	5TH M	F	T

84. SWIFT

RESPONSE WORD	M	F	T	M	F	T	M	F	T
LAST NAME	–	–	–	–	1	1	–	–	–
LAW	–	1	1	–	–	–	–	–	–
LAYER	–	–	–	–	–	–	1	–	1
LEVEL	–	–	–	–	–	–	1	–	1
LIFT	3	1	4	–	2	2	–	1	1
LIGHT	1	3	4	1	–	1	–	2	2
LIGHT BULB	1	–	1	–	–	–	–	–	–
LIGHTNING	1	–	1	–	–	–	–	–	–
LIKE MAGIC	–	–	–	1	–	1	–	–	–
LIKE THE WIND	–	1	1	–	–	–	–	–	–
LILT	–	–	–	–	–	–	–	1	1
LONG	–	–	–	1	1	2	–	–	–
LOVE	1	1	2	–	–	–	–	–	–
MAN	–	–	–	–	–	–	1	–	1
MASH	–	–	–	–	1	1	–	–	–
ME	2	–	2	–	–	–	–	–	–
MEAN	–	1	1	–	1	1	–	–	–
MIFF	2	–	2	–	–	–	–	–	–
MIFT	1	3	4	1	–	1	–	–	–
MILK	–	1	1	–	–	–	–	–	–
MISSED	–	–	–	1	–	1	–	–	–
MIST	1	–	1	–	–	–	–	–	–
MIX	–	–	–	1	–	1	–	–	–
MIXED	1	–	1	–	–	–	–	–	–
MOSTLY	–	–	–	–	1	1	–	–	–
MOTHER	–	1	1	–	–	–	–	–	–
MOTOR	1	–	1	–	–	–	–	–	–
MOUSE	1	–	1	–	–	–	–	–	–
MOVE	–	–	–	–	–	–	–	1	1
MUSIC	–	–	–	–	–	–	1	–	1
MY	–	1	1	–	–	–	–	–	–
MY ARM	–	–	–	1	–	1	–	–	–
MY TABLE	–	1	1	–	–	–	–	–	–
NICE	1	–	1	–	1	1	–	–	–
NIGHT	–	–	–	1	1	2	–	–	–
NO	–	–	–	–	1	1	–	–	–
NOT SWIFT	2	–	2	4	–	4	–	–	–
OCEAN	1	1	2	–	–	–	–	–	–
ON	1	–	1	–	–	–	–	1	1
PADDLE	–	1	1	–	–	–	–	–	–
PAIL	–	–	–	1	–	1	–	–	–
PENCIL	1	–	1	–	–	–	–	–	–
PIFF	1	–	1	–	–	–	–	–	–
PIT	1	–	1	–	–	–	–	–	–
PITCHER	1	–	1	–	–	–	–	–	–
POND	–	–	–	–	1	1	–	–	–
PRETTY	–	1	1	–	–	–	–	–	–
PULL	–	1	1	–	–	–	–	–	–
PUMPKIN	1	–	1	–	–	–	–	–	–
PUSH	–	1	1	–	–	–	–	–	–
PUT IN GLASS	1	–	1	–	–	–	–	–	–
QUICK	–	–	–	–	1	1	4	3	7
QUICKLY	–	–	–	–	1	1	–	7	7
RAT	1	–	1	–	–	–	–	–	–
RED	–	1	1	–	–	–	–	–	–
RIDE	–	–	–	1	–	1	–	1	1
RIFT	–	1	1	–	–	–	–	–	–
RIFTS	–	1	1	–	–	–	–	–	–
RIP	–	1	1	–	–	–	–	–	–
RIPPING	–	1	1	–	–	–	–	–	–
RIVER	–	–	–	–	–	–	1	1	2
ROOF	1	–	1	–	–	–	–	–	–
ROUGH	–	–	–	1	–	1	3	1	4
ROUND	–	–	–	–	1	1	–	–	–
RUN	–	1	1	1	1	2	3	–	3
RUNNER	–	–	–	1	–	1	–	–	–
RUNNING	–	–	–	1	1	2	–	–	–
SAD	–	–	–	–	1	1	–	–	–
SAID	1	–	1	–	–	–	–	–	–
SCHOOL	–	1	1	–	–	–	–	–	–
SEA	2	–	2	1	1	2	1	1	2
SEE	–	1	1	–	–	–	–	–	–

RESPONSE WORD	1ST			3RD			5TH		
	M	F	T	M	F	T	M	F	T

84. SWIFT

RESPONSE WORD	M	F	T	M	F	T	M	F	T
SHAKE	–	–	–	–	1	1	–	–	–
SHAVE	–	–	–	1	–	1	–	–	–
SHIFT	–	1	1	–	1	1	–	–	–
SHOES	–	1	1	–	–	–	–	–	–
SHORT	–	–	–	–	–	–	1	–	1
SIFT	–	1	1	–	–	–	–	–	–
SLOW	2	–	2	6	4	10	9	10	19
SLOWLY	–	–	–	–	1	1	–	–	–
SMALL	1	–	1	–	–	–	–	–	–
SMART	–	–	–	–	–	–	2	–	2
SMELL	–	–	–	–	1	1	–	2	2
SMIFF	–	–	–	–	1	1	–	–	–
SMITH	–	1	1	–	1	1	–	–	–
SMOOTH	1	2	3	4	2	6	7	5	12
SMOOTHLY	–	–	–	–	–	–	–	2	2
SMOTH	–	–	–	–	–	–	1	–	1
SNEEZE	–	1	1	–	–	–	–	–	–
SNIFF	1	–	1	1	–	1	–	–	–
SNIFFED	–	–	–	3	1	4	–	–	–
SNOW	–	–	–	2	–	2	–	–	–
SOFT	6	1	7	8	6	14	2	4	6
SOFTLY	–	–	–	–	1	1	–	–	–
SOMEONE	–	1	1	–	–	–	–	–	–
SOMETHING AWAY	–	–	–	–	–	–	–	1	1
SOMETHING ON	–	1	1	–	–	–	–	–	–
SPIT	–	1	1	–	–	–	–	–	–
SPLASH	–	–	–	–	1	1	–	–	–
STEADY	–	–	–	1	–	1	–	–	–
STIFF	1	–	1	–	1	1	–	–	–
STILL	–	–	–	1	–	1	–	–	–
STOP	–	–	–	–	1	1	–	–	–
STOP SIGN	1	–	1	–	–	–	–	–	–
STRAIGHT	–	1	1	–	–	–	–	1	1
STRONG	–	–	–	–	–	–	–	1	1
STURDY	–	–	–	1	–	1	–	–	–
SURE	–	–	–	–	1	1	–	–	–
SWAFT	–	–	–	–	–	–	–	1	1
SWAM	1	–	1	1	–	1	–	–	–
SWAP	–	–	–	–	1	1	–	–	–
SWAY	–	–	–	–	1	1	–	–	–
SWAYED	–	–	–	–	2	2	–	–	–
SWEAT	–	–	–	1	–	1	–	–	–
SWEATER	1	2	3	–	1	1	–	–	–
SWEEP	1	2	3	2	1	3	–	1	1
SWEEP AROUND	–	1	1	–	–	–	–	–	–
SWEET	1	–	1	–	–	–	–	–	–
SWERE	–	1	1	–	–	–	–	–	–
SWIFF	–	–	–	1	–	1	–	–	–
SWIFTER	–	–	–	–	1	1	–	–	–
SWIFTING	1	–	1	–	–	–	–	–	–
SWIFTLY	–	1	1	1	1	2	2	1	3
SWIM	3	6	9	3	6	9	–	–	–
SWIMMING	–	–	–	1	–	1	–	1	1
SWING	1	1	2	–	4	4	–	1	1
SWING AROUND	1	–	1	–	–	–	–	–	–
SWIPE	–	–	–	1	–	1	–	–	–
SWIRL	–	–	–	–	1	1	–	–	–
SWISH	–	–	–	1	2	3	–	–	–
SWISH-SWASH	–	–	–	1	–	1	–	–	–
SWISHED	–	–	–	–	1	1	–	–	–
SWISHING	–	–	–	1	–	1	–	–	–
SWISS	–	–	–	–	–	–	–	1	1
SWISS CHEESE	–	1	1	–	–	–	–	–	–
SWITCH	2	–	2	1	1	2	–	–	–
SWITCH ON	1	–	1	–	–	–	–	–	–
SWITCH THE KEY	1	–	1	–	–	–	–	–	–
SWITCHER	1	–	1	–	–	–	–	–	–
SWOOPED	–	–	–	–	–	–	1	–	1
SWORD	1	–	1	–	1	1	–	–	–
TABLE	–	1	1	–	–	–	–	–	–
TAIL	–	–	–	1	–	1	–	–	–
TAKE	–	–	–	1	–	1	–	–	–

RESPONSE WORD	1ST			3RD			5TH		
	M	F	T	M	F	T	M	F	T

84. SWIFT

RESPONSE WORD	M	F	T	M	F	T	M	F	T
THE	—	1	1	1	—	1	—	1	1
THE BIRD	1	—	1	—	—	—	—	—	—
THE GROUND	—	1	1	—	—	—	—	—	—
THE HILL IS SWIFT	—	1	1	—	—	—	—	—	—
THEN	—	—	—	—	1	1	—	—	—
THEY	1	—	1	—	—	—	—	—	—
THIFT	—	—	—	—	1	1	—	—	—
THINGS	—	1	1	—	—	—	—	—	—
THINK	1	—	1	—	—	—	—	—	—
THIS	1	1	2	—	—	—	—	—	—
THROUGH	—	1	1	—	—	—	—	—	—
THROW	—	—	—	—	3	3	—	—	—
TO	1	—	1	—	—	—	—	—	—
TOM	—	—	—	—	1	1	—	—	—
TOOK	—	—	—	1	—	1	—	—	—
TOWEL	1	—	1	—	—	—	—	—	—
TRADE	—	—	—	—	1	1	—	—	—
TRUCK	1	—	1	—	—	—	—	—	—
TURN OVER	1	—	1	—	—	—	—	—	—
UNSWIFT	—	—	—	—	1	1	1	—	1
VACUUM CLEANER	1	—	1	—	—	—	—	—	—
VERY FAST	—	—	—	—	—	—	1	—	1
WALK	—	—	—	1	—	1	—	—	—
WATER	2	2	4	1	—	1	1	—	1
WAVE	1	—	1	1	—	1	—	—	—
WAVES	1	—	1	1	—	1	—	—	—
WAYS	1	1	2	—	—	—	—	—	—
WE	1	—	1	—	1	1	—	—	—
WHALES	—	1	1	—	—	—	—	—	—
WHAT	—	1	1	—	—	—	—	—	—
WHEN	2	—	2	—	1	1	—	—	—
WHEN YOURE SWITCHING THINGS	1	—	1	—	—	—	—	—	—
WHICH	—	—	—	—	1	1	—	—	—
WHIFF	—	—	—	1	—	1	—	—	—
WHIP	1	1	2	1	—	1	—	—	—
WHIP IT	1	—	1	—	—	—	—	—	—
WHISK	—	1	1	—	—	—	—	—	—
WHITE	1	—	1	—	—	—	—	—	—
WIFF	1	—	1	—	1	1	—	—	—
WIFT	—	—	—	—	1	1	1	—	1
WILD	—	—	—	—	1	1	—	—	—
WIND	1	4	5	3	1	4	—	—	—
WINDOW	—	—	—	—	1	1	—	—	—
WING	—	1	1	—	—	—	—	—	—
WINGS	—	—	—	—	1	1	—	—	—
WISH	—	—	—	1	—	1	—	—	—
WITH	3	3	6	2	—	2	—	—	—
WOLF	—	—	—	1	—	1	—	—	—
WRITE	—	—	—	—	1	1	—	—	—
YOU	—	1	1	—	—	—	—	—	—
YOUR HAND	1	—	1	—	—	—	—	—	—

85. TABLE

RESPONSE WORD	M	F	T	M	F	T	M	F	T
ABLE	—	1	1	1	2	3	—	—	—
BABY	—	—	—	1	—	1	—	—	—
BAD	—	—	—	—	—	—	1	—	1
BED	1	—	1	—	—	—	—	—	—
BED TRAY	—	—	—	—	—	—	—	1	1
BENCH	—	—	—	1	1	2	1	—	1
BIG	1	—	1	—	—	—	—	—	—
BLACK	1	—	1	—	—	—	—	—	—
BLUE	—	1	1	—	—	—	—	—	—
BOY	1	—	1	—	—	—	—	—	—
BROWN	—	1	1	3	1	4	1	1	2
BUCCANEERS	1	—	1	—	—	—	—	—	—
CABLE	1	—	1	—	—	—	1	—	1
CAN	1	—	1	—	—	—	—	—	—
CAR	—	1	1	—	—	—	—	—	—
CARE	1	—	1	—	—	—	—	—	—

RESPONSE WORD	1ST M	F	T	3RD M	F	T	5TH M	F	T

85. TABLE

RESPONSE WORD	1ST M	F	T	3RD M	F	T	5TH M	F	T
CAREFULLY	—	—	—	—	1	1	—	—	—
CAT				3	—	3	1	—	1
CEILING	1	—	1	—	—	—	—	—	—
CHAIR	44	57	101	64	81	145	67	74	141
CHAIR WITH TABLE	—	1	1	—	—	—	—	—	—
CHAIRS	3	3	6	2	2	4	2	4	6
CLOTH	1	—	1	3	1	4	2	6	8
CONTENTS	—	—	—	—	—	—	—	1	1
COUCH	—	—	—	—	1	1	—	—	—
COUGH	—	—	—	—	—	—	—	2	2
COUNTER	—	—	—	1	—	1	—	—	—
COVER	—	—	—	—	—	—	—	1	1
CUP	—	—	—	—	1	1	—	—	—
CUPS AND SAUCERS	—	—	—	1	—	1	—	—	—
DARK	—	1	1	—	—	—	—	—	—
DESK	3	3	6	9	8	17	10	7	17
DINING ROOM TABLE	—	—	—	—	1	1	—	—	—
DINNER	1	2	3	—	4	4	3	2	5
DINNER TABLE	1	—	1	—	—	—	—	—	—
DISH	—	1	1	4	—	4	1	—	1
DISHES	1	3	4	1	1	2	—	1	1
DOG	1	—	1	—	—	—	—	—	—
DOWN	1	—	1	—	—	—	—	—	—
DRESS	—	1	1	—	—	—	—	—	—
EAT	7	11	18	9	4	13	8	10	18
EAT OFF OF	1	—	1	—	—	—	—	—	—
EAT ON	2	—	2	1	—	1	—	—	—
EAT ON THE TABLE	1	—	1	—	—	—	—	—	—
EATING	1	—	1	1	—	1	—	—	—
EATING IN	1	—	1	—	—	—	—	—	—
EATING ON THE TABLE	—	1	1	—	—	—	—	—	—
EGG	—	—	—	—	—	—	1	—	1
EIGHT	—	1	1	—	—	—	—	—	—
F	1	—	1	—	—	—	—	—	—
FISH	1	—	1	1	—	1	—	—	—
FIX	—	1	1	—	—	—	—	—	—
FLAT	—	—	—	1	2	3	1	—	1
FLOOR	—	—	—	1	—	1	—	3	3
FOOD	4	2	6	3	4	7	11	2	13
FOR YOU TO EAT ON	—	1	1	—	—	—	—	—	—
FORK	—	—	—	—	—	—	—	1	1
FORKS	—	—	—	1	—	1	—	—	—
FOUR LEGS	—	—	—	—	—	—	2	—	2
FUNNY	—	1	1	—	—	—	—	—	—
FURNITURE	—	—	—	3	2	5	1	2	3
GLABLE	1	—	1	—	—	—	—	—	—
GLASS	—	—	—	1	1	2	—	—	—
GLASSES	—	1	1	—	—	—	—	—	—
GRASS	—	1	1	—	—	—	—	—	—
HABLE	2	1	3	—	—	—	—	—	—
HARD	1	—	1	—	—	—	—	1	1
HAT	1	—	1	—	—	—	—	—	—
HOLDER	—	—	—	—	—	—	1	—	1
HOUSE	1	3	4	1	—	1	2	—	2
I SIT	—	1	1	—	—	—	—	—	—
KITCHEN	—	—	—	—	1	1	1	—	1
KITTEN	1	—	1	—	—	—	—	—	—
KNEE	—	1	1	—	—	—	—	—	—
LABEL	1	2	3	—	1	1	—	—	—
LAMP	—	—	—	—	—	—	3	—	3
LEG	2	1	3	—	5	5	3	—	3
LEGS	2	—	2	2	2	4	1	3	4
LIKE A BIG, BIG TYPEWRITER	1	—	1	—	—	—	—	—	—
LINE	—	—	—	1	—	1	—	—	—
LITTLE	1	—	1	—	—	—	—	—	—
LONG	1	—	1	—	—	—	—	—	—
MABLE	6	1	7	1	1	2	—	1	1
MAD	—	1	1	—	—	—	—	—	—
MANNERS	—	1	1	—	—	—	—	—	—
MARBLE	2	—	2	—	—	—	—	—	—
MILK	—	—	—	1	—	1	—	—	—

RESPONSE WORD	1ST			3RD			5TH		
	M	F	T	M	F	T	M	F	T

85. TABLE

RESPONSE WORD	M	F	T	M	F	T	M	F	T
MITTENS	1	–	1	–	–	–	–	–	–
MOTHER	–	–	–	1	–	1	–	–	–
MOUTH	–	1	1	–	–	–	–	–	–
OFF	–	–	–	–	–	–	1	–	1
ON	1	–	1	–	–	–	–	–	–
ONE	1	–	1	–	–	–	–	–	–
OVER	–	–	–	1	–	1	–	–	–
PABLE	–	1	1	–	–	–	–	–	–
PAPER	1	–	1	–	–	–	–	–	–
PEOPLE	1	–	1	–	–	–	–	–	–
PLACE FOR SITTING THINGS	–	–	–	–	–	–	–	1	1
PLATE	–	2	2	1	–	1	–	4	4
PLATES	–	–	–	1	–	1	–	1	1
POCKETBOOK	–	1	1	–	–	–	–	–	–
PUMPKIN	1	–	1	–	–	–	–	–	–
PURPLE	–	–	–	–	–	–	1	–	1
PUT	–	–	–	1	1	2	1	–	1
RABLE	–	2	2	–	–	–	–	–	–
READY TO BREAK DOWN	1	–	1	–	–	–	–	–	–
REFRIGERATOR	–	1	1	–	–	–	–	–	–
ROUND	–	–	–	–	1	1	–	–	–
SABLE	1	–	1	–	–	–	–	–	–
SALT	1	–	1	–	–	–	–	–	–
SCABLE	1	–	1	–	–	–	–	–	–
SEAT	2	–	2	1	–	1	–	–	–
SEE	1	–	1	–	–	–	–	–	–
SET	–	1	1	–	1	1	–	–	–
SET FOOD	–	1	1	–	–	–	–	–	–
SHELF	–	1	1	–	–	–	–	–	–
SHINY LEGS	–	–	–	–	–	–	–	1	1
SHOES	1	–	1	–	–	–	–	–	–
SHORT	–	–	–	–	–	–	1	–	1
SHORT TABLE	–	–	–	1	–	1	–	–	–
SILVER	–	–	–	–	–	–	–	1	1
SING	–	–	–	–	1	1	–	–	–
SINK	–	–	–	1	–	1	–	–	–
SIT	4	4	8	1	–	1	1	1	2
SITTING AT	–	1	1	–	–	–	–	–	–
SKIRT	–	1	1	–	–	–	–	–	–
SOMETHING	–	–	–	–	1	1	–	–	–
SOMETHING YOU EAT ON	–	–	–	–	–	–	–	1	1
SPOON	–	1	1	–	–	–	1	–	1
STEEL	–	–	–	–	1	1	–	–	–
STOOL	–	–	–	1	–	1	–	–	–
SUPPER	–	–	–	1	–	1	1	–	1
T	1	–	1	–	–	–	–	–	–
TABLE	–	–	–	–	1	1	–	–	–
TABLECLOTH	1	1	2	–	2	2	–	–	–
TABLES	–	1	1	–	–	–	–	–	–
TAKE	1	–	1	–	–	–	–	–	–
TAME	–	1	1	–	–	–	–	–	–
TEA	–	1	1	–	–	–	–	–	–
TED	–	1	1	–	–	–	–	–	–
TENT	1	–	1	–	–	–	–	–	–
THE	1	–	1	–	1	1	–	–	–
THING WHERE YOU PUT STUFF	–	–	–	–	–	–	–	1	1
THINGS	–	–	–	–	1	1	–	–	–
THIS	–	–	–	1	–	1	–	–	–
TIM	1	–	1	–	–	–	–	–	–
TIME	1	–	1	–	–	–	–	–	–
TOP	1	1	2	–	–	–	2	2	4
TREE	–	1	1	–	–	–	–	–	–
TWO	1	–	1	–	–	–	–	–	–
UNDER	–	–	–	–	1	1	–	–	–
USE	–	–	–	–	–	–	–	1	1
USE CHAIR	–	–	–	1	–	1	–	–	–
VASE	–	1	1	–	–	–	–	–	–
WE HAVE A TABLE AT HOME	–	1	1	–	–	–	–	–	–
WEATHER	–	1	1	–	–	–	–	–	–
WHAT YOU EAT ON	1	–	1	–	–	–	–	–	–

RESPONSE WORD	1ST M	1ST F	1ST T	3RD M	3RD F	3RD T	5TH M	5TH F	5TH T

85. TABLE

RESPONSE WORD	1ST M	1ST F	1ST T	3RD M	3RD F	3RD T	5TH M	5TH F	5TH T
WHAT YOU SET THE TABLE WITH	-	1	1	-	-	-	-	-	-
WHEN YOURE WASHING THE TABLE OFF	1	-	1	-	-	-	-	-	-
WHENEVER YOUR MOTHER PUTS A PICNIC TABL	-	1	1	-	-	-	-	-	-
WHITE	-	-	-	1	-	1	1	-	1
WINDOW	2	-	2	-	-	-	-	-	-
WITH	1	-	1	-	-	-	-	-	-
WOOD	2	-	2	4	1	5	5	1	6
WOODEN	-	-	-	-	-	-	-	1	1
WRITE	-	1	1	-	-	-	-	1	1
YOU EAT ON	-	1	1	1	-	1	-	-	-

86. TALL

RESPONSE WORD	1ST M	1ST F	1ST T	3RD M	3RD F	3RD T	5TH M	5TH F	5TH T
A MAN IS TALL	-	-	-	1	-	1	-	-	-
ALL	-	-	-	1	-	1	-	-	-
AT	1	-	1	-	-	-	-	-	-
AT ALL	-	-	-	-	1	-	-	1	1
AUNT	-	-	-	-	1	1	-	-	-
BALL	-	-	-	1	-	1	-	1	1
BASKETBALL	-	-	-	-	-	-	-	1	1
BATHROOM	-	1	1	-	-	-	-	-	-
BICYCLE	1	-	1	-	-	-	-	-	-
BIG	10	8	18	6	8	14	5	4	9
BIG MAN	1	-	1	-	-	-	-	-	-
BLACK	-	1	1	-	-	-	-	-	-
BOARD	-	-	-	1	-	1	-	-	-
BOW	1	-	1	-	-	-	-	-	-
BOY	3	1	4	-	-	-	-	1	1
BROTHER	-	-	-	-	-	-	-	1	1
BUILDING	2	-	2	-	-	-	1	-	1
CALL	1	-	1	1	1	2	1	1	2
CHILDREN	-	1	1	-	-	-	-	-	-
CLOTHES	-	1	1	-	-	-	-	-	-
CRAWL	-	-	-	1	-	1	-	-	-
CUP	1	-	1	-	-	-	-	-	-
CURTAINS	1	-	1	-	-	-	-	-	-
DAD	-	1	1	-	-	-	-	-	-
DARK	-	-	-	1	-	1	-	-	-
DIRTY	-	-	-	-	-	-	1	-	1
DOG	-	1	1	-	-	-	2	-	2
DOLL	-	1	1	-	-	-	-	-	-
DOOR	1	-	1	-	-	-	-	-	-
EAR	1	-	1	-	-	-	-	-	-
ELBOWS	1	-	1	-	-	-	-	-	-
FALL	-	-	-	-	-	-	1	-	1
FAR UP	-	-	-	1	-	1	-	-	-
FAT	1	1	2	-	1	1	2	-	2
FATHER	1	2	3	-	-	-	-	-	-
FIRE	-	1	1	-	-	-	-	-	-
FIST	-	-	-	-	-	-	-	1	1
FLY	-	1	1	-	-	-	-	-	-
GIANT	1	-	1	-	1	1	-	-	-
GIRAFFE	-	-	-	-	1	1	-	-	-
GIRL	-	1	1	-	1	1	1	-	1
GLASSES	-	2	2	-	-	-	-	-	-
GRASS	-	-	-	1	-	1	-	-	-
GREAT	-	-	-	-	-	-	1	-	1
GROW	-	1	1	-	-	-	-	-	-
HAIR	-	1	1	-	-	-	-	-	-
HALL	3	2	5	-	-	-	-	-	-
HAMMER	1	-	1	-	-	-	-	-	-
HANDSOME	1	-	1	1	-	1	3	-	3
HELP	1	-	1	-	-	-	-	-	-
HIGH	1	3	4	14	5	19	8	9	17
HIGHT	-	-	-	-	-	-	1	-	1
HIT	1	-	1	-	-	-	-	-	-
HIVES	1	-	1	-	-	-	-	-	-
HOUSE	-	-	-	-	-	-	1	1	2

RESPONSE WORD	1ST M	1ST F	1ST T	3RD M	3RD F	3RD T	5TH M	5TH F	5TH T

86. TALL

RESPONSE WORD	1ST M	F	T	3RD M	F	T	5TH M	F	T
HUGE	–	–	–	–	–	–	1	1	2
I	1	–	1	–	–	–	–	–	–
I AM TALL	–	1	1	–	–	–	–	–	–
IT	1	1	2	–	–	–	1	–	1
KID	1	–	1	–	–	–	–	–	–
LADY	–	1	1	–	–	–	–	–	–
LALL	1	–	1	–	–	–	–	–	–
LARGE	–	1	1	2	1	3	7	1	8
LAW	–	1	1	–	–	–	–	–	–
LENGTH	–	–	–	–	–	–	–	1	1
LIGHT	1	–	1	–	–	–	–	–	–
LINE	–	–	–	1	–	1	–	–	–
LISTEN	–	–	–	1	–	1	–	–	–
LITTLE	12	17	29	7	8	15	2	1	3
LOG	1	1	2	–	–	–	–	–	–
LONG	3	2	5	3	6	9	2	7	9
LOUD	–	–	–	–	–	–	–	1	1
LOW	5	1	6	1	4	5	1	1	2
MALK	1	–	1	–	–	–	–	–	–
MALL	–	1	1	–	–	–	–	–	–
MAN	17	9	26	3	2	5	3	2	5
ME	1	–	1	–	–	–	–	–	–
MELL	1	–	1	–	–	–	–	–	–
MEN	–	1	1	–	–	–	–	1	1
MOLLY	1	–	1	–	–	–	–	–	–
MOUNTAIN	–	–	–	–	–	–	1	–	1
MOUSE	–	–	–	–	1	1	–	–	–
MY FATHER IS TALL	–	1	1	–	–	–	–	–	–
MY SISTER DEBORAH	1	–	1	–	–	–	–	–	–
NALL	–	1	1	–	–	–	–	–	–
NOT SHORT	–	–	–	–	–	–	1	2	3
NOW	–	1	1	–	–	–	–	–	–
PALL	–	1	1	–	–	–	–	–	–
PAPER	–	1	1	–	–	–	–	–	–
PAUL	1	–	1	–	–	–	–	–	–
PAUL BUNYAN	–	–	–	–	–	–	–	1	1
PERSON	1	–	1	–	–	–	–	1	1
POCKETBOOK	–	1	1	–	–	–	–	–	–
SAID	–	–	–	–	–	–	–	1	1
SALL	1	1	2	–	1	1	–	–	–
SALLY	–	1	1	–	–	–	–	–	–
SALT	–	1	1	–	–	–	–	–	–
SAW	–	1	1	–	–	–	–	–	–
SEE	–	1	1	–	–	–	–	–	–
SET	1	–	1	–	–	–	–	–	–
SHINING	1	–	1	–	–	–	–	–	–
SHORT	19	15	34	64	65	129	68	74	142
SINK	–	1	1	–	–	–	–	–	–
SIT	–	–	–	–	–	–	1	–	1
SIX FOOT	–	–	–	–	–	–	–	1	1
SKINNY	–	–	–	2	1	3	1	–	1
SKYSCRAPER	–	–	–	–	–	–	1	–	1
SMALL	11	19	30	20	25	45	12	15	27
SMOOTH	–	–	–	–	1	1	–	–	–
SOMEONES BIG AND TALL	–	1	1	–	–	–	–	–	–
SOMETHING TALL	–	–	–	–	–	–	–	1	1
SOUND	–	–	–	1	–	1	1	–	1
SPEAK	–	–	–	1	–	1	1	–	1
SQUIRT	–	–	–	1	–	1	–	–	–
STICK	–	–	–	1	–	1	–	–	–
STOUT	–	–	–	–	–	–	1	–	1
STRAIGHT	–	–	–	–	1	1	–	–	–
STRONG	1	–	1	–	–	–	–	–	–
SUN	–	1	1	–	–	–	–	–	–
SWISH	–	–	–	–	–	–	–	1	1
T V	–	1	1	–	–	–	–	–	–
TABLE	–	1	1	–	1	1	1	–	1
TABLES	1	–	1	–	–	–	–	–	–
TAIL	–	–	–	–	–	–	1	–	1
TALE	–	–	–	1	–	1	1	–	1
TALK	2	2	4	–	1	1	–	–	–
TALKING	–	1	1	–	–	–	–	–	–

RESPONSE WORD	1ST M	F	T	3RD M	F	T	5TH M	F	T

86. TALL

RESPONSE WORD	1ST M	F	T	3RD M	F	T	5TH M	F	T
TALLER	–	1	1	1	–	1	–	–	–
TARZAN	1	–	1	–	–	–	–	–	–
TATTLE-TALE	1	–	1	–	–	–	–	–	–
THAN YOU	–	1	1	–	–	–	–	–	–
THE	–	1	1	–	–	–	–	1	1
THIN	1	–	1	1	–	1	2	2	4
TILE ON THE FLOOR	1	–	1	–	–	–	–	–	–
TILL	–	–	–	–	–	–	1	–	1
TOU TALL	–	1	1	–	–	–	–	–	–
TOOLS	1	–	1	–	–	–	–	–	–
TOP	1	–	1	–	–	–	–	–	–
TORE	–	–	–	–	1	1	–	–	–
TOY	2	1	3	–	–	–	–	–	–
TREE	1	4	5	–	–	–	–	3	3
TREES	–	–	–	–	1	1	–	–	–
TROUSER	1	–	1	–	–	–	–	–	–
UP	–	–	–	–	1	1	–	–	–
VALL	–	1	1	–	–	–	–	–	–
WALL	1	1	2	–	–	–	–	–	–
WATCH	1	–	1	–	–	–	–	–	–
WAUGG	–	1	1	–	–	–	–	–	–
WEATHER	–	1	1	–	–	–	–	–	–
WHAT YOU RIDE IN	1	–	1	–	–	–	–	–	–
WHEN YOURE GROWING	1	–	1	–	–	–	–	–	–
WHY	–	1	1	–	–	–	–	–	–
WINDOW	–	1	1	–	–	–	–	–	–
WORD	1	–	1	–	–	–	–	–	–
WORDS	–	1	1	–	–	–	–	–	–
WRITE	–	1	1	–	–	–	–	–	–
YOU	1	–	1	1	–	1	1	–	1
YOU COULD SING A SONG	–	1	1	–	–	–	–	–	–
YOURE BIG	–	1	1	–	–	–	–	–	–

87. TELL

RESPONSE WORD	1ST M	F	T	3RD M	F	T	5TH M	F	T
ABOUT	1	–	1	–	2	2	–	–	–
ACHE	1	–	1	–	–	–	–	–	–
AGO	–	–	–	–	1	1	–	–	–
ANSWER	–	1	1	2	1	3	1	2	3
APARTMENT	1	–	1	–	–	–	–	–	–
APOSTROPHE	–	–	–	–	1	1	–	–	–
ASK	–	2	2	22	10	32	8	8	16
ASKED	–	–	–	1	1	2	–	–	–
AT	–	–	–	–	1	1	–	–	–
BECAUSE	–	–	–	1	–	1	–	–	–
BED	1	–	1	–	–	–	–	–	–
BELL	1	1	2	1	1	2	4	2	6
BELT	1	–	1	–	–	–	–	–	–
BIG	–	–	–	–	–	–	1	–	1
BLAME	–	–	–	–	1	1	–	–	–
BLUE	1	–	1	1	–	1	–	–	–
BOW	1	–	1	–	–	–	–	–	–
BOY	–	–	–	1	–	1	–	–	–
BUG	–	1	1	–	–	–	–	–	–
BUILDING	1	–	1	–	–	–	–	–	–
CALL	–	–	–	–	–	–	2	4	6
CAT	–	1	1	–	–	–	–	–	–
CHILDREN	–	–	–	–	1	1	–	–	–
CITY	–	–	–	–	1	1	–	–	–
COMMAND	–	–	–	–	–	–	1	–	1
COW	1	1	2	–	–	–	–	–	–
CURTAIN	1	–	1	–	–	–	–	–	–
DECIDE	–	–	–	–	1	1	–	–	–
DEFIDE	–	–	–	–	–	–	1	–	1
DESCRIBE	–	–	–	–	1	1	–	–	–
DESK	1	–	1	–	–	–	–	–	–
DICK	1	–	1	–	–	–	–	–	–
DICTATE	–	–	–	–	–	–	1	–	1
DIDNT	–	–	–	–	1	1	–	–	–
DO	–	–	–	1	–	1	–	–	–
DO NOT	1	1	2	–	–	–	–	–	–

RESPONSE WORD	1ST M	F	T	3RD M	F	T	5TH M	F	T

87. TELL

RESPONSE WORD	1ST M	F	T	3RD M	F	T	5TH M	F	T
DOG	1	–	1	–	–	–	–	–	–
DOLLY	–	1	1	–	–	–	–	–	–
DONT	1	–	1	1	5	6	1	1	2
DONT BE A TELL A TALE	–	1	1	–	–	–	–	–	–
DONT TELL	–	1	1	1	2	3	–	1	1
DONT TELL ON ME	–	1	1	–	–	–	–	–	–
DOOR	–	1	1	–	–	–	–	–	–
DRY	1	–	1	1	–	1	–	–	–
DUCK	1	–	1	–	–	–	–	–	–
EAR	1	–	1	–	–	–	–	–	–
EVERYTHING	–	–	–	1	–	1	–	–	–
EXPLAIN	–	–	–	–	–	–	–	1	1
EYE	–	1	1	–	–	–	–	–	–
FACE	1	–	1	–	–	–	–	–	–
FALL	–	–	–	–	–	–	1	–	1
FAST	–	1	1	–	–	–	–	–	–
FAT	–	–	–	–	–	–	1	–	1
FATHER	2	–	2	–	–	–	–	–	–
FELL	–	–	–	3	2	5	1	–	1
FIB	–	–	–	1	–	1	–	1	1
FOF	–	1	1	–	–	–	–	–	–
FOOT	–	–	–	–	1	1	–	–	–
FORETELL	–	–	–	–	–	–	1	–	1
FORGET	–	–	–	1	–	1	–	–	–
FORGOT	–	–	–	1	–	1	–	–	–
FROG	–	–	–	–	1	1	–	–	–
GIRL	–	1	1	–	–	–	–	–	–
GIVE	–	–	–	–	–	–	1	1	2
GIVE AWAY	–	–	–	–	1	1	–	–	–
GO	1	1	2	–	–	–	1	–	1
GOSSIP	–	–	–	–	–	–	1	1	2
GRASS	–	1	1	–	–	–	–	–	–
GREEN	–	–	–	–	1	1	–	–	–
GUESS	1	–	1	–	–	–	–	–	–
HANGER	1	–	1	–	–	–	–	–	–
HAT	1	–	1	–	–	–	–	–	–
HAUL	–	–	–	1	–	1	–	–	–
HEAR	2	2	4	1	1	2	2	4	6
HEARD	–	–	–	–	–	–	–	1	1
HELL	2	–	2	–	–	–	–	–	–
HER	1	1	2	–	–	–	–	1	1
HILL	1	–	1	–	–	–	–	–	–
HIM	–	–	–	1	2	3	1	–	1
HOTEL	–	–	–	1	–	1	–	–	–
IT	1	4	5	–	–	–	–	–	–
KEEP	–	–	–	–	–	–	–	2	2
KELL	1	–	1	–	–	–	–	–	–
KNOW	–	–	–	–	1	1	–	1	1
LANTERN	1	–	1	–	–	–	–	–	–
LAY	–	–	–	–	–	–	–	1	1
LELL	2	–	2	–	–	–	–	–	–
LESSON	–	–	–	–	–	–	1	–	1
LIE	–	–	–	1	–	1	1	–	1
LIGHT	–	1	1	–	–	–	–	–	–
LIKE	–	–	–	–	1	1	–	–	–
LISTEN	–	2	2	3	3	6	4	7	11
LONG	–	–	–	1	–	1	–	–	–
LOOK	–	1	1	–	–	–	–	–	–
MAIL	–	1	1	–	–	–	–	–	–
MAKE	1	1	2	–	–	–	–	–	–
MAN	–	1	1	–	–	–	–	–	–
ME	7	16	23	6	6	12	–	8	8
ME A QUESTION	1	–	1	–	–	–	–	–	–
ME A SECRET	–	1	1	–	–	–	–	–	–
ME SOMETHING	2	–	2	–	–	–	–	–	–
ME THE TRUTH	–	1	1	–	–	–	–	–	–
ME WHAT	–	1	1	–	–	–	–	–	–
ME WHAT TO DO	1	–	1	–	–	–	–	–	–
MELL	3	2	5	–	–	–	–	–	–
MELON	–	1	1	–	–	–	–	–	–
MEN	1	–	1	–	–	–	–	–	–
MINE	1	–	1	–	–	–	–	–	–

RESPONSE WORD	1ST			3RD			5TH		
	M	F	T	M	F	T	M	F	T

87. TELL

RESPONSE WORD	M	F	T	M	F	T	M	F	T
MOM	–	1	1	–	–	–	–	–	–
MOMMY	1	–	1	–	–	–	–	–	–
MOTEL	1	–	1	–	–	–	–	–	–
MOTHER	2	6	8	–	1	1	–	–	–
MOUTH	–	–	–	1	–	1	–	–	–
MOVE	–	–	–	–	–	–	1	–	1
MUSIC	–	–	–	–	1	1	–	–	–
MUSNT TELL	–	1	1	–	–	–	–	–	–
MUST	–	–	–	1	–	1	–	–	–
NELL	–	–	–	1	–	1	–	–	–
NO	–	1	1	1	–	1	–	–	–
NOT	–	1	1	1	–	1	1	1	2
NOT TALL	–	–	–	–	–	–	1	–	1
NOT TELL	4	–	4	5	3	8	2	1	3
NOT TO	–	–	–	–	–	–	–	1	1
NOT TO TELL	–	1	1	–	–	–	–	–	–
NOTHING	1	–	1	1	–	1	–	–	–
NOW	–	2	2	–	–	–	2	–	2
OF	–	–	–	1	–	1	–	–	–
OFF	–	–	–	–	1	1	–	–	–
OKAY	1	–	1	–	–	–	–	–	–
ON ME	1	–	1	–	–	–	–	–	–
ON SOMEONE	2	–	2	–	–	–	–	–	–
ON YOU	2	–	2	–	–	–	–	–	–
ONE	–	–	–	1	–	1	–	–	–
OUR MOTHER	–	1	1	–	–	–	–	–	–
OVER	–	–	–	–	–	–	–	1	1
PAPER	2	–	2	–	–	–	–	–	–
PEA	–	1	1	–	–	–	–	–	–
PELL	1	–	1	–	–	–	–	–	–
PEOPLE	–	1	1	1	–	1	–	2	2
PEOPLE THINGS	–	1	1	–	–	–	–	–	–
PHONE	–	–	–	1	–	1	–	–	–
PLACED	–	–	–	1	–	1	–	–	–
PLAY	–	–	–	1	–	1	–	–	–
PURSE	–	1	1	–	–	–	–	–	–
PUT IN WATER	1	–	1	–	–	–	–	–	–
QUESTION	–	–	–	–	–	–	3	–	3
QUIET	–	–	–	–	–	–	2	–	2
QUIETLY	–	–	–	–	1	1	–	–	–
RAIL	–	1	1	–	–	–	–	–	–
RAT	–	–	–	1	–	1	–	–	–
RE-TELL	–	–	–	–	–	–	1	–	1
READ	–	–	–	–	–	–	1	–	1
RECEIVE	–	–	–	–	–	–	1	–	1
RECITE	–	–	–	–	–	–	–	1	1
REPORT	–	–	–	–	1	1	–	–	–
RETELL	–	–	–	–	–	–	–	1	1
RING	–	1	1	–	–	–	–	–	–
ROAD	–	–	–	–	1	1	–	–	–
RUNNING AWAY	1	–	1	–	–	–	–	–	–
SAD	–	–	–	–	–	–	–	1	1
SAID	–	1	1	–	–	–	2	1	3
SAY	1	–	1	5	7	12	9	10	19
SAY SOMETHING	–	–	–	–	–	–	1	–	1
SECRET	5	3	8	1	2	3	5	3	8
SEE	–	–	–	1	–	1	1	–	1
SEEDS	1	–	1	–	–	–	–	–	–
SELL	–	–	–	–	2	2	5	2	7
SENT	–	–	–	–	–	–	1	–	1
SHARE	–	–	–	1	–	1	–	–	–
SHELL	–	–	–	1	–	1	–	–	–
SHOES	–	1	1	–	–	–	–	–	–
SHOUT	–	–	–	1	–	1	–	–	–
SHOW	3	2	5	2	3	5	1	–	1
SHOW AND TELL	–	1	1	–	1	1	–	–	–
SHUT UP	–	–	–	–	–	–	–	1	1
SISTER	1	–	1	–	–	–	–	–	–
SLEEP	–	–	–	1	–	1	–	–	–
SMELL	–	–	–	1	–	1	–	–	–
SOLD	–	–	–	–	–	–	1	–	1
SOMEBODY	–	3	3	–	–	–	2	1	3

RESPONSE WORD	1ST			3RD			5TH		
	M	F	T	M	F	T	M	F	T

87. TELL

RESPONSE WORD	M	F	T	M	F	T	M	F	T
SOMEONE	–	–	–	2	–	2	–	–	–
SOMEONE TELLING YOU SOMETHING.	–	1	1	–	–	–	–	–	–
SOMETHING	3	6	9	3	7	10	–	4	4
SON	1	–	1	–	–	–	–	–	–
SOUND	–	–	–	1	–	1	–	–	–
SPEAK	–	–	–	2	3	5	6	5	11
SPELL	–	–	–	–	–	–	1	1	2
SQUEAL	–	–	–	–	–	–	–	1	1
STAR	1	–	1	–	–	–	–	–	–
STARS	–	1	1	–	–	–	–	–	–
STATEMENT	–	–	–	–	–	–	1	–	1
STORIES	1	1	2	2	1	3	–	–	–
STORY	3	3	6	5	9	14	6	8	14
T	1	–	1	–	–	–	–	–	–
TAIL	–	–	–	–	–	–	1	–	1
TAKE	1	–	1	1	–	1	–	–	–
TALE	1	1	2	–	–	–	–	–	–
TALK	–	–	–	11	13	24	21	15	36
TALK TO	–	–	–	–	2	2	–	–	–
TALKING	–	1	1	1	1	2	–	–	–
TALL	–	–	–	1	2	3	–	–	–
TALLY	–	1	1	–	–	–	–	–	–
TATTLE	–	1	1	–	–	–	3	5	8
TATTLER	–	–	–	1	–	1	–	–	–
TATTLETALE	6	6	12	1	–	1	3	–	3
TEACHER	–	2	2	–	–	–	1	–	1
TELEPHONE	1	–	1	–	–	–	–	–	–
TELESCOPE	1	–	1	–	–	–	–	–	–
TELEVISION	–	1	1	–	–	–	–	–	–
TELL	–	–	–	1	–	1	–	–	–
TELL IT LOW	1	–	1	–	–	–	–	–	–
TELL TALE	–	1	1	–	–	–	–	–	–
TELLING	1	–	1	1	1	2	–	–	–
TELLING ON YOU	1	–	1	–	–	–	–	–	–
TELLING SOMEONE	–	–	–	–	1	1	–	1	1
TELLS	–	–	–	–	1	1	–	–	–
TENT	1	–	1	–	–	–	–	–	–
THE	1	1	2	–	–	–	–	–	–
THE PEOPLE SOMETHING	–	1	1	–	–	–	–	–	–
THE STREET	–	–	–	1	–	1	–	–	–
THE TEACHER	–	1	1	–	–	–	–	–	–
THEM	–	–	–	1	–	1	–	–	–
THEN	–	1	1	–	–	–	–	–	–
THEY	–	–	–	–	1	1	–	–	–
THINGS	1	–	1	–	1	1	–	–	–
THINK	–	–	–	–	–	–	1	–	1
THINKING	–	–	–	1	–	1	–	–	–
THIS	–	–	–	1	–	1	–	–	–
TIME	2	1	3	–	–	–	–	–	–
TO	1	–	1	–	–	–	–	–	–
TO SAY SOMETHING TO SOMEONE.	–	–	–	–	–	–	–	1	1
TOE	1	–	1	–	–	–	–	–	–
TOLD	2	3	5	6	12	18	7	18	25
TOLLED	–	–	–	–	–	–	1	–	1
TOWN	1	–	1	–	–	–	–	–	–
TOYS	–	1	1	–	–	–	–	–	–
TRAIN STATION	–	–	–	–	–	–	–	1	1
TRUCK	1	–	1	–	–	–	–	–	–
TV	1	–	1	–	–	–	–	–	–
UNBELIEVE	–	–	–	–	–	–	1	–	1
UNTELL	–	–	–	1	1	2	–	–	–
UNTIL	–	–	–	–	1	1	–	1	1
US	3	–	3	–	–	–	–	–	–
VILLAGE	–	–	–	–	–	–	1	–	1
VOICE	–	1	1	–	–	–	–	–	–
WASH	1	1	2	–	–	–	–	–	–
WATER	–	1	1	–	–	–	–	–	–
WELL	1	1	2	7	3	10	2	–	2

RESPONSE WORD	1ST M	1ST F	1ST T	3RD M	3RD F	3RD T	5TH M	5TH F	5TH T

87. TELL

RESPONSE WORD	1ST M	1ST F	1ST T	3RD M	3RD F	3RD T	5TH M	5TH F	5TH T
WENT	1	–	1	–	–	–	–	–	–
WHALE	–	–	–	–	–	–	1	–	1
WHAT	1	4	5	–	–	–	–	–	–
WHAT HAPPENED	–	–	–	–	–	–	1	–	1
WHAT I HAVE	–	1	1	–	–	–	–	–	–
WHAT YOU IN SCHOOL	1	–	1	–	–	–	–	–	–
WHAT YOU WANT	1	–	1	–	–	–	–	–	–
WHEEL	–	1	1	–	–	–	–	–	–
WHEN YOU TELL ON SOMETHING	1	–	1	–	–	–	–	–	–
WHISPER	1	–	1	1	2	3	–	1	1
WHISPERING	–	–	–	–	1	1	–	–	–
WHITE	–	–	–	–	1	1	–	–	–
WHO	1	1	2	–	–	–	–	–	–
WILL	–	–	–	–	–	–	1	–	1
WILLIAM	1	–	1	–	–	–	–	1	1
WINDOW	–	1	1	–	–	–	–	–	–
WOOD	–	1	1	–	–	–	–	–	–
WORDS	–	–	–	–	–	–	–	1	1
WRITE	–	1	1	–	–	–	–	–	–
YELL	–	–	–	1	–	1	1	1	2
YOU	6	5	11	1	2	3	–	1	1
YOU TELL ME	–	–	–	1	–	1	–	–	–
YOUR MOTHER	1	–	1	–	–	–	–	–	–

88. THEM

RESPONSE WORD	1ST M	1ST F	1ST T	3RD M	3RD F	3RD T	5TH M	5TH F	5TH T
A FEW	–	–	–	–	–	–	1	–	1
A LOT OF PEOPLE	–	–	–	–	–	–	–	1	1
A NUMBER	–	–	–	–	1	1	–	–	–
AFTER	–	–	–	1	–	1	–	–	–
AIM	1	–	1	–	–	–	–	–	–
ALL	1	2	3	–	–	–	1	1	2
AND	–	1	1	–	–	–	–	–	–
AND I WENT TO A PICNIC	–	–	–	–	–	–	–	1	1
ANIMALS	–	–	–	–	–	–	–	1	1
ANOTHER	–	–	–	1	–	1	–	–	–
ANOTHER FAMILY	–	–	–	–	–	–	–	1	1
ARE	2	3	5	1	1	2	–	–	–
ARE MAD	1	–	1	–	–	–	–	–	–
ARENT	–	1	1	–	–	–	–	–	–
AWAY	–	1	1	–	–	–	–	–	–
BAD	1	–	1	–	–	–	–	–	–
BANDAID	–	1	1	–	–	–	–	–	–
BE	–	–	–	–	1	1	–	–	–
BEES	–	–	–	–	–	–	–	1	1
BEN	–	1	1	–	–	–	–	–	–
BETTER	–	1	1	–	–	–	–	–	–
BLUE	1	–	1	–	–	–	–	–	–
BOARD	–	1	1	–	–	–	–	–	–
BONNET	–	–	–	–	1	1	–	–	–
BOOKS	1	–	1	–	–	–	–	–	–
BOTH	–	–	–	–	1	1	–	1	1
BOX	–	1	1	–	–	–	–	–	–
BOYS	–	–	–	1	1	2	–	1	1
BOYS AND GIRLS	–	1	1	–	–	–	–	–	–
BUTTON	1	–	1	–	–	–	–	–	–
CAN	3	3	6	–	–	–	–	–	–
CAR	–	1	1	–	–	–	1	–	1
CAT	–	–	–	–	–	–	1	–	1
CATCH	1	–	1	–	–	–	–	–	–
CHAIR	1	–	1	–	–	–	–	–	–
CHILDREN	–	2	2	2	2	4	1	1	2
CLOTHESBASKET	–	1	1	–	–	–	–	–	–
COLTS	–	–	–	–	–	–	–	1	1
COME	4	3	7	–	–	–	–	–	–
COUNT	–	–	–	–	–	–	–	1	1
COUPLE	–	–	–	1	–	1	–	–	–
COW	1	–	1	1	–	1	–	–	–
CREW	–	–	–	–	–	–	1	–	1
CURTAIN	1	–	1	–	–	–	–	–	–

RESPONSE WORD	1ST M	F	T	3RD M	F	T	5TH M	F	T
				88.	THEM				
DAY	—	—	—	—	1	1	—	—	—
DESK	—	1	1	—	—	—	—	—	—
DETERGENT	—	—	—	1	—	1	—	—	—
DID	2	—	2	1	—	1	—	—	—
DO	—	—	—	—	—	—	1	—	1
DO SOMETHING	1	—	1	—	—	—	—	—	—
DOCTORS	1	—	1	—	—	—	—	—	—
DOING SOMETHING	—	1	1	—	—	—	—	—	—
DONT	—	1	1	—	—	—	—	—	—
DONT GO OUTSIDE WHEN ITS TOO DAMP	—	1	1	—	—	—	—	—	—
DOOR	—	2	2	—	—	—	—	—	—
DRESS	—	1	1	—	—	—	—	—	—
EAT	1	—	1	—	—	—	—	—	—
EM	1	—	1	—	—	—	—	—	—
END	—	—	—	—	—	—	—	1	1
EVERYBODY	—	—	—	—	—	—	1	—	1
FAMILY	1	1	2	—	—	—	—	—	—
FATHER	—	1	1	—	—	—	—	—	—
FENCE	1	—	1	—	—	—	—	—	—
FINGERNAIL	—	1	1	—	—	—	—	—	—
FLAG	1	—	1	—	—	—	—	—	—
FLOOR	1	—	1	—	—	—	—	—	—
GIRL	—	1	1	—	—	—	—	—	—
GIRLS	1	—	1	—	1	1	—	—	—
GO	2	1	3	—	—	—	—	—	—
GO GET THEM	1	—	1	—	—	—	—	—	—
GOING	—	1	1	1	—	1	—	—	—
GONE	—	1	1	—	—	—	—	—	—
GOT	1	—	1	—	—	—	—	—	—
GRANDMA + GRANDPA	—	1	1	—	—	—	—	—	—
GROUP	—	—	—	—	1	1	2	4	6
HAND	—	1	1	—	—	—	—	—	—
HANDLE	—	1	1	—	—	—	—	—	—
HAPPENED	1	—	1	—	—	—	—	—	—
HAPPENS	1	—	1	—	—	—	—	—	—
HAVE	1	1	2	—	—	—	1	—	1
HE	1	—	1	2	6	8	3	—	3
HE IS DEAD	1	—	1	—	—	—	—	—	—
HE OR SHE	—	—	—	—	1	1	—	—	—
HELP	—	1	1	—	—	—	1	—	1
HEM	3	—	3	1	—	1	—	—	—
HER	1	1	2	2	3	5	3	3	6
HERE	2	2	4	—	1	1	—	—	—
HIM	3	5	8	16	9	25	4	—	4
HIS	—	—	—	1	—	1	—	—	—
HIT	1	—	1	—	—	—	—	—	—
HOW ABOUT THEM	—	1	1	—	—	—	—	—	—
HURT	—	1	1	—	—	—	—	—	—
I	1	—	1	—	1	1	—	—	—
I THEM	—	—	—	1	—	1	—	—	—
IN A TIRE	—	—	—	1	—	1	—	—	—
INK	—	1	1	—	—	—	—	—	—
IS	1	—	1	—	—	—	—	—	—
IT	—	—	—	—	—	—	—	1	1
KEM	1	—	1	—	—	—	—	—	—
KEN	—	1	1	—	—	—	—	—	—
KIDS	1	1	2	1	—	1	—	—	—
KNOW THEM	—	—	—	1	—	1	—	—	—
LADY	1	1	2	—	—	—	—	—	—
LAST	—	1	1	1	—	1	—	—	—
LEM	—	1	1	—	—	—	—	—	—
LEMONADE	—	1	1	—	—	—	—	—	—
LETS	—	—	—	—	1	1	—	—	—
LETS GO HAVE SOME FUN	—	1	1	—	—	—	—	—	—
LIGHT	1	—	1	1	—	1	—	—	—
LIKE	1	—	1	—	—	—	—	—	—
LIMB	—	1	1	—	—	—	—	—	—
LINE	—	1	1	—	—	—	—	—	—
LOOK	1	—	1	—	—	—	—	—	—
LOT	—	—	—	—	—	—	1	—	1
LOTS	1	—	1	—	—	—	—	—	—

88. THEM

RESPONSE WORD	1ST M	F	T	3RD M	F	T	5TH M	F	T
MANY	–	–	–	1	–	1	–	–	–
ME	6	6	12	4	4	8	3	2	5
MEAN	–	–	–	1	–	1	–	1	1
MEM	3	–	3	–	–	–	–	–	–
MEN	1	1	2	–	–	–	–	–	–
MILL	1	–	1	–	–	–	–	–	–
MIND	–	–	–	1	–	1	–	–	–
MINE	–	1	1	–	–	–	–	–	–
MITTEN	–	1	1	–	–	–	–	–	–
MORE	–	–	–	–	–	–	–	1	1
MOTHER	2	2	4	–	–	–	1	–	1
NOBODY	–	–	–	1	–	1	–	–	–
NOT	–	1	1	–	–	–	1	–	1
NOT HUNGRY	–	1	1	–	–	–	–	–	–
NOT THEM	1	–	1	1	1	2	–	–	–
NOTHING	–	1	1	–	–	–	–	–	–
NOW	–	–	–	1	1	2	–	2	2
NUMBER	2	–	2	–	–	–	–	–	–
NURSE	–	1	1	–	–	–	–	–	–
OH	1	–	1	–	–	–	–	–	–
ONE	1	–	1	–	1	1	–	–	–
OTHER PEOPLE	–	–	–	–	–	–	–	1	1
OTHERS	–	–	–	2	1	3	–	–	–
OUR	–	–	–	2	–	2	–	–	–
OVER THE RIVER	1	–	1	–	–	–	–	–	–
PAPER	1	–	1	–	–	–	–	–	–
PEN	–	2	2	–	–	–	–	–	–
PEOPLE	5	5	10	10	12	22	21	13	34
PERSON	1	–	1	1	–	1	1	1	2
PICTURE	–	1	1	–	–	–	–	–	–
PIN	–	1	1	–	–	–	–	–	–
PLAY	–	2	2	–	–	–	–	–	–
PLEASE	1	–	1	–	–	–	–	–	–
POCKETBOOK	–	1	1	–	–	–	–	–	–
POLITE	–	1	1	–	–	–	–	–	–
PRETTY	1	–	1	–	–	–	–	–	–
QUESTION	–	–	–	1	–	1	–	–	–
RAIL	1	–	1	–	–	–	–	–	–
RECORD	–	1	1	–	–	–	–	–	–
REMIND ME OF PEOPLE	–	–	–	–	–	–	–	1	1
RIDE	3	2	5	–	–	–	–	–	–
RIND	–	1	1	–	–	–	–	–	–
RING	–	2	2	–	–	–	–	–	–
RIVER	–	–	–	1	–	1	–	–	–
ROAD	–	–	–	–	1	1	1	–	1
RUN	–	–	–	1	–	1	1	–	1
SAID	–	1	1	–	–	–	–	–	–
SALLS	–	–	–	–	–	–	1	–	1
SAME	–	–	–	1	–	1	–	–	–
SEE	1	1	2	–	–	–	–	–	–
SEE THEM	–	1	1	–	–	–	–	–	–
SEM	–	–	–	–	1	1	–	–	–
SHE	–	1	1	–	1	1	–	–	–
SHERRY,LINDA	–	–	–	–	–	–	–	1	1
SIM	–	–	–	1	–	1	–	–	–
SOME COOKIES	–	1	1	–	–	–	–	–	–
SOMEBODY	1	–	1	1	–	1	–	–	–
SOMEBODY ELSE	–	–	–	1	–	1	–	–	–
SOMEONE	–	–	–	1	1	2	2	1	3
SOMETHING	–	–	–	–	–	–	1	–	1
SOMETHING COULD BE HAPPENING.	–	1	1	–	–	–	–	–	–
SOUP	1	–	1	–	–	–	–	–	–
SPELLING	–	–	–	–	–	–	–	1	1
SPOON	–	1	1	–	–	–	–	–	–
SQUIRREL	1	–	1	–	–	–	–	–	–
STEM	1	–	1	–	–	–	–	–	–
STICKS	1	–	1	–	–	–	–	–	–
STORE	1	–	1	–	–	–	–	–	–
STRING	1	–	1	–	–	–	–	–	–
SUSAN	1	–	1	–	–	–	–	–	–
TABLET	–	1	1	–	–	–	–	–	–

RESPONSE WORD	1ST			3RD			5TH		
	M	F	T	M	F	T	M	F	T

88. THEM

RESPONSE WORD	M	F	T	M	F	T	M	F	T
TAKE	–	–	–	1	–	1	–	–	–
TEAN	–	–	–	–	–	–	1	–	1
TEN	–	1	1	–	–	–	–	–	–
TENT	1	–	1	–	–	–	–	–	–
THAT	–	–	–	1	4	5	–	–	–
THE	2	–	2	1	–	1	1	1	2
THEE	1	–	1	–	–	–	1	–	1
THEIR	1	2	3	4	7	11	5	6	11
THEM	–	1	1	–	–	–	–	–	–
THEN	2	1	3	2	7	9	5	2	7
THEN WHAT HAPPENED	–	1	1	–	–	–	–	–	–
THER	–	–	–	–	–	–	1	–	1
THERE	–	–	–	1	1	2	3	4	7
THESE	1	–	1	–	1	1	1	1	2
THEY	5	6	11	27	27	54	35	46	81
THEY ARE	–	–	–	–	1	1	–	–	–
THEY TOLD ON US	1	–	1	–	–	–	–	–	–
THIN	1	–	1	–	–	–	–	–	–
THINGS	–	–	–	–	–	–	1	–	1
THIS	1	–	1	–	–	–	–	1	1
THOSE	–	–	–	2	3	5	6	4	10
THOSE TWO PEOPLE OVER THERE	–	–	–	–	–	–	1	–	1
THUMB	2	1	3	–	–	–	–	–	–
TIME	–	–	–	1	1	2	–	–	–
TO	–	–	–	1	1	2	–	1	1
TO PEOPLE	–	–	–	–	–	–	–	1	1
TOGETHER	1	–	1	3	1	4	1	1	2
TOILET	–	1	1	–	–	–	1	–	1
TOO	–	–	–	–	–	–	1	–	1
TWO	–	1	1	1	2	3	2	–	2
TYPEWRITER	1	–	1	–	–	–	–	–	–
UP	–	–	–	–	–	–	1	–	1
US	6	6	12	17	16	33	16	17	33
VIM	–	1	1	–	–	–	–	–	–
WALL	1	–	1	–	–	–	–	–	–
WANT	1	–	1	–	–	–	–	–	–
WAS	–	1	1	–	1	1	–	–	–
WAY	–	–	–	–	–	–	–	–	–
WE	6	3	9	3	2	5	–	6	6
WEIGH	–	1	1	–	–	–	–	–	–
WENT	–	–	–	1	1	2	–	–	–
WERE	–	–	–	–	1	1	–	–	–
WHAT YOU PUT IN WATER	1	–	1	–	–	–	–	–	–
WHEN	1	–	1	2	2	4	1	1	2
WHEN YOURE DOING SOMETHING LIKE WASHING	1	–	1	–	–	–	–	–	–
WHERE	–	1	1	–	1	1	1	–	1
WHO	1	–	1	–	–	–	–	2	2
WIG	–	1	1	–	–	–	–	–	–
YOU	2	6	8	2	3	5	2	2	4

89. THEY

RESPONSE WORD	M	F	T	M	F	T	M	F	T
A COUPLE OF PEOPLE	–	–	–	–	–	–	–	1	1
AGE	–	1	1	–	–	–	–	–	–
ALL	1	1	2	–	1	1	2	1	3
ALL WENT HOME	–	1	1	–	–	–	–	–	–
ANGRY	–	–	–	1	–	1	–	–	–
ANOTHER PERSON	–	–	–	–	–	–	–	1	1
ARE	5	6	11	15	8	23	3	1	4
ARE BACK	–	1	1	–	–	–	–	–	–
ARE CHILDREN	–	1	1	–	–	–	–	–	–
ARE COMING	1	–	1	–	–	–	–	–	–
ARE HERE	–	–	–	1	–	1	–	–	–
ARE MAD	1	–	1	–	–	–	–	–	–
ARE NUTS	1	–	1	–	–	–	–	–	–
ARENT	–	–	–	–	1	1	–	–	–
AWAY	–	–	–	1	2	3	–	–	–
BAG	1	–	1	–	–	–	–	–	–
BALL	1	–	1	1	–	1	–	–	–

89. THEY

RESPONSE WORD	1ST M	1ST F	1ST T	3RD M	3RD F	3RD T	5TH M	5TH F	5TH T
BAY	1	–	1	–	–	–	1	1	2
BED	1	1	2	–	1	1	–	–	–
BEG	1	–	1	–	–	–	–	–	–
BELONG	1	–	1	–	–	–	–	–	–
BIG	–	1	1	–	–	–	–	–	–
BLOTS	1	–	1	–	–	–	–	–	–
BOAT	1	–	1	–	–	–	–	–	–
BOB AND JANE	–	–	–	–	–	–	1	–	1
BOOK	–	1	1	–	–	–	–	–	–
BOTH	–	–	–	–	–	–	–	2	2
BOYS AND GIRLS	–	–	–	–	–	–	–	1	1
CAKE	1	–	1	–	–	–	–	–	–
CAME	–	–	–	–	1	1	1	1	2
CAN	2	8	10	1	–	1	1	–	1
CAN MOVE	–	1	1	–	–	–	–	–	–
CAN WORK	1	–	1	–	–	–	–	–	–
CANDY	1	–	1	–	–	–	–	–	–
CAR	1	1	2	–	–	–	–	–	–
CARE	1	–	1	–	–	–	–	–	–
CATCHER	–	1	1	–	–	–	–	–	–
CHAIR	1	1	2	–	–	–	–	–	–
CHALK	1	–	1	–	–	–	–	–	–
CHILDREN	–	1	1	1	2	3	–	–	–
COLD	–	1	1	–	–	–	–	–	–
COME	–	2	2	1	2	3	–	1	1
COMING	–	–	–	–	1	1	–	–	–
COULD	–	–	–	1	–	1	–	–	–
COUPLE	–	–	–	1	–	1	–	–	–
DADDY	–	1	1	–	–	–	–	–	–
DAY	2	1	3	–	–	–	–	–	–
DESK	–	1	1	–	–	–	–	–	–
DID	–	1	1	1	–	1	1	2	3
DID BAD	1	–	1	–	–	–	–	–	–
DIDNT	1	–	1	1	–	1	–	–	–
DO RUN	–	1	1	–	–	–	–	–	–
DOG	–	1	1	–	–	–	–	–	–
DOING SOMETHING	–	1	1	–	–	–	–	–	–
DONT	–	1	1	–	–	–	–	–	–
DOWN	–	–	–	–	1	1	–	–	–
DRESS	–	1	1	–	–	–	–	–	–
DRESSER	–	1	1	–	–	–	–	–	–
DUBY	1	–	1	–	–	–	–	–	–
END	–	1	1	–	–	–	–	–	–
EVERYBODY	–	–	–	1	–	1	–	–	–
FACE	–	1	1	–	–	–	–	–	–
FAINT	–	1	1	–	–	–	–	–	–
FAMILY	–	–	–	1	1	2	–	–	–
FAST	2	–	2	–	–	–	–	–	–
FEET	1	–	1	–	–	–	–	–	–
FLOWER	–	1	1	–	–	–	–	–	–
FOR	–	1	1	–	–	–	–	–	–
FOUND	–	–	–	1	–	1	–	–	–
FUN	–	1	1	–	–	–	–	–	–
GAVE	–	–	–	–	–	–	1	–	1
GIVE	–	–	–	1	–	1	1	–	1
GO	1	–	1	1	1	2	1	–	1
GO AWAY	1	–	1	–	–	–	–	–	–
GOING	–	2	2	–	–	–	–	–	–
GOOD	1	–	1	–	–	–	–	–	–
GOOD BYE	–	1	1	–	–	–	–	–	–
GROUP	–	–	–	–	–	–	–	5	5
HAPPEN	1	–	1	–	–	–	–	–	–
HAPPY DAY	–	1	1	–	–	–	–	–	–
HAVE	1	1	2	1	3	4	1	2	3
HAY	3	2	5	–	–	–	–	–	–
HE	1	1	2	4	7	11	3	–	3
HEAR	2	–	2	–	–	–	–	–	–
HELP	1	–	1	–	–	–	–	–	–
HER	1	–	1	2	–	2	1	–	1
HERE	1	1	2	1	–	1	–	1	1
HEY	–	1	1	–	–	–	–	1	1
HI	–	1	1	–	–	–	–	1	1

RESPONSE WORD	1ST M	F	T	3RD M	F	T	5TH M	F	T

89. THEY

RESPONSE WORD	1ST M	F	T	3RD M	F	T	5TH M	F	T
HIM	–	–	–	10	7	17	4	4	8
HO	–	–	–	–	–	–	2	–	2
HOME	1	–	1	–	–	–	–	–	–
HORSE	–	2	2	–	–	–	–	–	–
HOUSE	1	1	2	–	–	–	–	–	–
HURT	–	1	1	–	–	–	–	–	–
I	–	–	–	–	1	1	–	–	–
IS	2	–	2	–	1	1	–	–	–
JIME	–	–	–	–	–	–	1	–	1
JOIN	–	–	–	1	–	1	–	–	–
K	1	–	1	–	–	–	–	–	–
KEYS	1	–	1	–	–	–	–	–	–
KILL	1	–	1	–	–	–	–	–	–
KITTEN	–	1	1	–	–	–	–	–	–
KNOW	–	–	–	1	–	1	–	–	–
LADY	1	–	1	–	–	–	–	–	–
LAY	2	–	2	–	–	–	–	–	–
LEG	1	–	1	1	–	1	–	–	–
LIGHT	1	–	1	–	–	–	–	–	–
LIKE	–	1	1	1	–	1	–	–	–
LOOK	–	2	2	–	–	–	–	–	–
MADE	–	1	1	1	–	1	–	–	–
MAN	–	1	1	–	–	–	–	–	–
MANY	–	–	–	–	–	–	–	1	1
MARE	1	–	1	–	–	–	–	–	–
MAY	3	3	6	1	1	2	–	1	1
ME	4	2	6	3	2	5	1	1	2
MEN	–	–	–	1	–	1	–	–	–
MICE	–	–	–	–	–	–	–	1	1
MIGHT	1	–	1	–	–	–	–	–	–
MONDAY	–	1	1	–	–	–	–	–	–
MONEY	1	–	1	–	–	–	–	–	–
MORE THAN	–	–	–	–	1	1	–	–	–
MORE THAN ONE	–	–	–	–	–	–	–	1	1
MORNING	1	–	1	–	–	–	–	–	–
MOST	–	–	–	1	–	1	–	–	–
MOTHER	–	1	1	–	–	–	–	–	–
MOTHERED	–	1	1	–	–	–	–	–	–
MOVE	–	1	1	–	–	–	–	–	–
NAY	–	1	1	–	–	–	–	–	–
NEW	–	1	1	–	–	–	–	–	–
NICE	1	2	3	–	–	–	–	–	–
NO ONE	–	–	–	1	–	1	–	–	–
NOT ONE	–	–	–	–	–	–	–	1	1
OBEY	1	1	2	–	–	–	–	–	–
OCEAN	–	–	–	–	–	–	–	1	1
ONE	3	1	4	–	–	–	–	–	–
ONE PERSON	–	1	1	–	–	–	–	–	–
OTHER PEOPLE	–	–	–	1	–	1	–	–	–
PAINT	–	1	1	–	–	–	–	–	–
PAPER	1	–	1	–	–	–	–	–	–
PAY	1	–	1	2	–	2	–	–	–
PEOPLE	6	–	6	12	10	22	20	19	39
PEOPLES	–	1	1	–	–	–	–	–	–
PERSON	–	–	–	2	–	2	1	–	1
PERSONS	1	–	1	–	–	–	–	–	–
PICTURE	–	–	–	1	–	1	–	–	–
PICTURES	–	1	1	–	–	–	–	–	–
PINE NEEDLE	1	–	1	–	–	–	–	–	–
PIPE	1	–	1	–	–	–	–	–	–
PLAY	2	2	4	–	–	–	–	–	–
PLENTY	–	–	–	–	1	1	–	–	–
POCKET BOOK	–	–	–	–	1	1	–	–	–
PUSH	1	–	1	–	–	–	–	–	–
RAN	1	–	1	–	–	–	–	–	–
RED	1	–	1	–	–	–	–	–	–
RIDE	–	2	2	–	–	–	–	–	–
ROOF	–	1	1	–	–	–	–	–	–
ROOSTER	1	–	1	–	–	–	–	–	–
RUN	–	–	–	–	1	1	–	–	–
SAID	1	–	1	1	–	1	–	–	–
SAY	1	–	1	–	–	–	–	–	–

89. THEY

RESPONSE WORD	1ST M	1ST F	1ST T	3RD M	3RD F	3RD T	5TH M	5TH F	5TH T
SEE	–	2	2	–	–	–	–	–	–
SHE	–	1	1	1	–	1	–	1	1
SINGLE	–	1	1	–	–	–	–	–	–
SKATE	1	–	1	–	–	–	–	–	–
SLEEP	1	–	1	–	–	–	–	–	–
SMOKE	1	–	1	–	–	–	–	–	–
SNOW	–	1	1	–	–	–	–	–	–
SOME	–	1	1	–	–	–	–	–	–
SOMEBODY	1	–	1	1	–	1	–	–	–
SOMEONE	–	–	–	1	1	2	2	–	2
SOUND	1	–	1	–	–	–	–	–	–
SPEED	1	–	1	–	–	–	–	–	–
STAY	–	–	–	1	–	1	1	–	1
SUMMER	–	–	–	–	1	1	–	–	–
SUMMERTIME	1	–	1	–	–	–	–	–	–
SUN	–	2	2	–	–	–	–	–	–
SWAY	1	–	1	–	–	–	–	–	–
SWIM	–	1	1	–	–	–	–	–	–
SWORD	1	–	1	–	–	–	–	–	–
TABLE	2	2	4	–	1	1	–	–	–
TALL	–	1	1	–	–	–	–	–	–
THAT	–	–	–	2	–	2	–	1	1
THE	2	5	7	5	1	6	–	2	2
THEIR	–	–	–	6	8	14	4	2	6
THEIRS	1	–	1	–	–	–	–	–	–
THEM	1	3	4	16	38	54	51	54	105
THEN	1	2	3	1	2	3	3	1	4
THERE	–	–	–	1	1	2	1	2	3
THESE	–	–	–	–	1	1	–	1	1
THEY	–	–	–	–	–	–	–	1	1
THINK	–	–	–	1	–	1	–	–	–
THIS	1	–	1	–	–	–	–	–	–
THOUGHT	–	–	–	–	1	1	–	–	–
THREW ROCKS	1	–	1	–	–	–	–	–	–
TIME	–	–	–	–	–	–	–	1	1
TO	–	–	–	–	1	1	–	–	–
TODAY	–	2	2	–	–	–	–	–	–
TOGETHER	1	–	1	–	–	–	3	–	3
TOLD	–	1	1	–	–	–	–	–	–
TOLD ME TO GO	1	–	1	–	–	–	–	–	–
TOM	–	–	–	–	–	–	1	–	1
TWO	–	–	–	2	1	3	–	–	–
TWO PEOPLE	–	1	1	–	–	–	–	–	–
US	3	2	5	8	6	14	7	10	17
VERY GOOD	–	1	1	–	–	–	–	–	–
WALK	–	1	1	–	–	–	–	–	–
WANT	2	–	2	–	–	–	–	–	–
WANT SOMETHING	1	–	1	–	–	–	–	–	–
WANTED	1	–	1	–	–	–	–	–	–
WATER	1	–	1	–	–	–	1	–	1
WAY	–	2	2	2	3	5	1	–	1
WE	3	5	8	6	6	12	12	12	24
WELL	1	–	1	–	–	–	–	–	–
WENT	4	1	5	3	1	4	–	–	–
WENT OUTSIDE	1	1	2	–	–	–	–	–	–
WENT TO THE STORE	–	–	–	–	–	–	–	1	1
WERE	–	1	1	1	5	6	4	–	4
WHAT YOU PUT IN WATER	1	–	1	–	–	–	–	–	–
WHEN	–	–	–	1	1	2	–	–	–
WHEN YOUR DANCING	1	–	1	–	–	–	–	–	–
WHENEVER YOURE PLAYING AND YOUR MOTHER	–	1	1	–	–	–	–	–	–
WHO	1	–	1	–	–	–	–	–	–
WHY	–	–	–	1	–	1	–	–	–
WILL	2	3	5	–	3	3	–	–	–
WINDOW	1	–	1	–	–	–	–	–	–
WITH	–	–	1	1	–	1	–	–	–
WOULDNT	1	–	1	–	–	–	–	–	–
YOU	1	5	6	–	–	–	2	–	2

RESPONSE WORD	1ST			3RD			5TH		
	M	F	T	M	F	T	M	F	T

90.   THIRSTY

RESPONSE WORD	M	F	T	M	F	T	M	F	T
A GLASS	1	–	1	–	–	–	–	–	–
AGAIN	–	1	1	–	–	–	–	–	–
APPETITE	–	–	–	–	–	–	1	–	1
BA-BA	–	–	–	–	1	1	–	1	1
BEG	–	–	–	–	1	1	–	–	–
BIRSTY	–	1	1	–	–	–	–	–	–
BOWL	–	1	1	–	–	–	–	–	–
BOWL OF SOUP	–	1	1	–	–	–	–	–	–
BUS	–	1	1	–	–	–	–	–	–
BUTTER FACTORIES	1	–	1	–	–	–	–	–	–
CAT	1	–	1	–	–	–	–	–	–
CHEERRYFUL	–	–	–	–	–	–	–	1	1
COKE	–	–	–	–	–	–	–	1	1
COLD	–	–	–	1	–	1	–	–	–
CRY	1	–	1	–	–	–	–	–	–
CUP	–	3	3	–	–	–	–	–	–
DAY	–	–	–	2	1	3	2	–	2
DESK	–	1	1	–	–	–	–	–	–
DETERMINED	–	–	–	–	–	–	–	1	1
DINNER	1	–	1	–	–	–	–	–	–
DIRSTY	–	1	1	–	–	–	–	–	–
DOG	–	1	1	–	–	–	–	–	–
DOLL	–	1	1	–	–	–	–	–	–
DONE	–	1	1	–	–	–	–	–	–
DRANK	–	–	–	–	1	1	1	–	1
DRINK	30	37	67	32	40	72	22	26	48
DRINK OF WATER	4	3	7	–	–	–	–	–	–
DRINK WATER	2	–	2	–	–	–	–	–	–
DRINKING	–	–	–	2	1	3	–	–	–
DROWN	–	–	–	1	–	1	–	–	–
DRY	2	–	2	6	7	13	18	17	35
FALL	–	–	–	–	–	–	–	1	1
FAMISHED	–	–	–	1	–	1	–	–	–
FAST	–	–	–	1	–	1	–	–	–
FATIGUE	1	–	1	–	–	–	–	–	–
FIRST	–	1	1	–	–	–	–	–	–
FOR	1	–	1	–	–	–	–	–	–
FOR WATER	1	1	2	–	–	–	–	1	1
FOUNTAIN	1	–	1	–	–	–	–	–	–
FRIDAY	1	–	1	2	2	4	1	–	1
FULL	–	1	1	2	2	4	4	2	6
FUNNY	1	–	1	–	–	–	–	–	–
GET A DRINK	1	–	1	–	–	–	–	–	–
GET A DRINK OF WATER	1	–	1	1	–	1	–	–	–
GLASS	5	4	9	2	–	2	–	–	–
GLASS OF WATER	1	–	1	–	–	–	–	–	–
H	1	–	1	–	–	–	–	–	–
HANDY	–	–	–	–	1	1	–	–	–
HAPPY	–	–	–	–	–	–	1	–	1
HARD	–	–	–	–	–	–	–	1	1
HARN	–	–	–	–	–	–	1	–	1
HAT	1	–	1	–	–	–	–	–	–
HEALTH	–	–	–	1	–	1	–	–	–
HELP	1	–	1	–	–	–	–	–	–
HIRSY	1	–	1	–	–	–	–	–	–
HOT	1	1	2	3	7	10	–	2	2
HUNGRY	7	16	23	25	27	52	17	21	38
I AM	–	1	1	–	1	1	–	–	–
I AM THIRSTY	–	1	1	–	–	–	–	–	–
I AM VERY THIRSTY	–	1	1	–	–	–	–	–	–
I WANT A DRINK OF WATER	1	1	2	–	–	–	–	–	–
I WANT SOMETHING TO DRINK.	–	1	1	–	–	–	–	–	–
IM THIRSTY	1	–	1	–	–	–	–	–	–
IN THE MIDDLE OF THE NIGHT.	–	1	1	–	–	–	–	–	–
KITE	–	–	–	1	–	1	–	–	–
LETTERS	1	–	1	–	–	–	–	–	–
LIGHT	1	–	1	–	–	–	–	–	–
MAY I HAVE A GLASS OF WATER.	–	1	1	–	–	–	–	–	–
MEN	–	–	–	–	–	–	1	–	1

RESPONSE WORD	1ST M	F	T	3RD M	F	T	5TH M	F	T

90. THIRSTY

RESPONSE WORD	1ST M	F	T	3RD M	F	T	5TH M	F	T
MILK	2	5	7	1	3	4	–	–	–
MIRSTY	3	–	3	–	1	1	–	–	–
MONEY	1	–	1	–	–	–	–	–	–
MOSSTY	1	–	1	–	–	–	–	–	–
MOUTH DRY	1	–	1	–	–	–	–	–	–
MUCH	1	–	1	–	–	–	–	–	–
NAIL	1	–	1	–	–	–	–	–	–
NECKLACE	1	–	1	–	–	–	–	–	–
NEEDFUL	–	–	–	–	–	–	1	–	1
NEEDS WATER	–	–	–	–	–	–	–	1	1
NET	–	1	1	–	–	–	–	–	–
NO	–	–	–	–	–	–	1	–	1
NOT	1	–	1	1	1	2	–	–	–
NOT THIRSTY	3	2	5	8	4	12	4	2	6
NOW	–	–	–	1	–	1	–	–	–
OLD	–	–	–	–	–	–	–	2	2
PEAR	1	–	1	–	–	–	–	–	–
PERSON	–	–	–	–	–	–	1	–	1
PIECE OF GRASS	1	–	1	–	–	–	–	–	–
PINEAPPLE	1	–	1	–	–	–	–	–	–
PIRSTY	–	1	1	1	–	1	–	–	–
PIRT	1	–	1	–	–	–	–	–	–
PLEASE	1	–	1	–	–	–	–	–	–
QUIRSTY	1	–	1	–	–	–	–	–	–
REAL THIRSTY	–	1	1	–	–	–	–	–	–
REFRESHMENTS	–	–	–	–	1	1	–	–	–
SATURDAY	–	1	1	–	–	–	–	–	–
SEA	1	–	1	–	–	–	–	–	–
SELF	–	–	–	–	1	1	–	–	–
SICK	–	1	1	–	–	–	–	–	–
SODA	–	–	–	1	1	2	–	–	–
SOUND	1	–	1	–	–	–	–	–	–
STAND	–	1	1	–	–	–	–	–	–
STARVED	–	–	–	–	–	–	1	–	1
STAY DOWN	–	–	–	–	1	1	–	–	–
STEEP	–	–	–	–	–	–	1	–	1
SUNDAY	–	–	–	–	–	–	1	–	1
SUPPER	–	1	1	–	–	–	–	–	–
TAKE A DRINK OF WATER	–	1	1	–	–	–	–	–	–
TEA	–	1	1	–	–	–	–	–	–
THE	–	–	–	–	–	–	1	–	1
THERN	–	1	1	–	–	–	–	–	–
THEY	–	–	–	–	–	–	1	–	1
THIRST	–	–	–	1	1	2	–	–	–
THROATS DRY	–	–	–	–	–	–	1	–	1
THURSDAY	1	–	1	–	–	–	–	1	1
TIN	–	1	1	–	–	–	–	–	–
TIRED	–	1	1	1	2	3	–	1	1
TOO THIRSTY	1	–	1	–	–	–	–	–	–
TURKEY	1	–	1	–	–	–	–	–	–
UNIT	–	–	–	–	–	–	–	1	1
UNTHIRSTY	–	–	–	1	1	2	4	–	4
UP	–	–	–	–	1	1	–	–	–
WAIT	–	1	1	–	–	–	–	–	–
WANT	–	1	1	–	–	–	–	1	1
WANT A DRINK	–	–	–	1	–	1	–	–	–
WANT A DRINK OF WATER	–	1	1	–	–	–	–	–	–
WANT FOR WATER	–	–	–	–	–	–	–	1	1
WANTING WATER	–	–	–	–	–	–	1	–	1
WARM	–	1	1	–	–	–	–	–	–
WATER	40	28	68	38	31	69	48	53	101
WATER BOY	–	–	–	–	–	–	–	1	1
WATER FOUNTAIN	–	–	–	1	–	1	–	–	–
WEDNESDAY	–	1	1	–	–	–	2	–	2
WET	–	–	–	2	–	2	3	–	3
WHEN YOU WANT SOME WATER	1	–	1	–	–	–	–	–	–
WHENEVER SOMEONE IS THIRSTY	–	1	1	–	–	–	–	–	–
WINDOW	–	1	1	–	–	–	–	–	–
WORSTY	–	1	1	–	–	–	–	–	–
YOU COULD BE THIRSTY AND YOU COULD ASK.	–	1	1	–	–	–	–	–	–

RESPONSE WORD	1ST M	F	T	3RD M	F	T	5TH M	F	T

90. THIRSTY

RESPONSE WORD	1ST M	F	T	3RD M	F	T	5TH M	F	T
YOU WANT SOMETHING TO DRINK.	–	–	–	–	–	–	–	1	1

91. UP

RESPONSE WORD	1ST M	F	T	3RD M	F	T	5TH M	F	T
A BIRD FYING IN THE AIR	1	–	1	–	–	–	–	–	–
ABOVE	–	–	–	–	1	1	1	–	1
AIR	–	–	–	–	–	–	1	1	2
AIRPLANE	5	–	5	1	–	1	2	–	2
APPLE	1	–	1	–	–	–	1	–	1
AWAY	1	–	1	–	–	–	–	–	–
BALLOON	1	–	1	–	–	–	–	–	–
BED	–	1	1	–	–	–	–	–	–
BIG	–	1	1	–	–	–	–	–	–
BIRD	2	1	3	–	–	–	–	–	–
BIRD IS UP IN THE AIR	–	1	1	–	–	–	–	–	–
BOOKS	–	1	1	–	–	–	–	–	–
BUB	1	–	1	–	–	–	–	–	–
BUCKING BRONCO	1	–	1	–	–	–	–	–	–
BUNNY	–	1	1	–	–	–	–	–	–
CAR	–	1	1	–	–	–	–	–	–
CLIMB	–	–	–	1	–	1	1	1	2
CLOUD	–	1	1	–	–	–	–	–	–
CLOUDS	–	–	–	–	–	–	1	–	1
COME	–	–	–	–	–	–	1	–	1
CROW	–	1	1	–	–	–	–	–	–
CUP	1	–	1	–	1	1	–	–	–
DO	–	–	–	–	–	–	1	–	1
DOORKNOB	–	1	1	–	–	–	–	–	–
DOWN	65	79	144	123	123	246	102	112	214
DUP	1	1	2	–	–	–	–	–	–
EAT	1	–	1	–	–	–	–	–	–
ELEVATOR	4	–	4	–	–	–	–	1	1
FAST	1	–	1	1	–	1	–	–	–
FLY	3	1	4	2	1	3	–	–	–
GAME	–	1	1	–	–	–	–	–	–
GET UP	1	–	1	–	–	–	–	–	–
GLASS	–	1	1	–	–	–	–	–	–
GO	4	1	5	1	–	1	–	–	–
GO UP HILL	1	–	1	–	–	–	–	–	–
GO UP IN THE ATTIC	1	–	1	–	–	–	–	–	–
GOES	2	–	2	–	–	–	–	–	–
GOING	1	–	1	–	–	–	–	–	–
GOING UP	1	–	1	–	–	–	–	–	–
GROUND	–	–	–	–	–	–	1	–	1
HAYLOFT	–	–	–	–	–	–	–	1	1
HEAVEN	–	–	–	–	–	–	1	–	1
HELP	–	1	1	–	–	–	–	–	–
HIGH	3	3	6	5	8	13	10	6	16
HIGH INTO SKY	–	1	1	–	–	–	–	–	–
HILL	–	–	–	–	–	–	1	–	1
HOUSE	–	1	1	–	–	–	–	–	–
HOW	–	1	1	–	–	–	–	–	–
IN A BOOK	1	–	1	–	–	–	–	–	–
IN SKY	1	–	1	–	–	–	–	–	–
IN THE AIR	3	–	3	1	–	1	1	2	3
IN THE SKY	2	–	2	–	–	–	–	1	1
INNER	–	–	–	–	–	–	1	–	1
JUMP	2	3	5	–	–	–	1	–	1
KITE	–	–	–	1	–	1	–	1	1
KITY	–	–	–	–	–	–	–	1	1
LADDER	1	–	1	–	–	–	–	–	–
LADDERS COULD GO UP	–	1	1	–	–	–	–	–	–
LETS GO DOWN THE HILL	–	1	1	–	–	–	–	–	–
LIGHT	1	–	1	–	–	–	–	–	–
LITTLE	–	1	1	–	–	–	–	–	–
LOOK	1	1	2	–	–	–	–	–	–
LOOK UP	–	1	1	–	–	–	–	–	–
LOOK UP IN THE AIR	–	1	1	–	–	–	–	–	–
LOW	–	–	–	–	–	–	–	1	1
LUP	1	–	1	–	–	–	–	–	–

RESPONSE WORD	1ST M	F	T	3RD M	F	T	5TH M	F	T

91. UP

RESPONSE WORD	1ST M	F	T	3RD M	F	T	5TH M	F	T
ME	1	–	1	–	–	–	–	–	–
MINE	1	–	1	–	–	–	–	–	–
MOON	–	1	1	–	–	–	–	–	–
MOUNTAIN	–	–	–	–	–	–	1	–	1
MY	–	–	–	–	–	–	1	–	1
NOT DOWN	–	–	–	–	–	–	–	2	2
NOW	1	–	1	–	–	–	–	–	–
NUFF	1	–	1	–	–	–	–	–	–
O	–	1	1	–	–	–	–	–	–
ON	–	–	–	–	1	1	1	–	1
ORANGE	–	–	–	1	–	1	1	–	1
OUT	–	–	–	–	–	–	1	–	1
OVEN	1	–	1	–	–	–	–	–	–
OVER	–	–	–	1	–	1	–	–	–
PLANE	1	–	1	–	–	–	1	–	1
POCKET-BOOK	1	–	1	–	–	–	–	–	–
PUP	–	1	1	–	–	–	–	1	1
RAISE	–	–	–	–	–	–	1	–	1
REAL UP	1	–	1	–	–	–	–	–	–
RIDE	–	1	1	–	–	–	–	–	–
RISE	–	–	–	–	–	–	1	–	1
ROAD	1	–	1	–	–	–	–	–	–
ROCKET	–	1	1	–	–	–	1	–	1
SEE	–	–	–	–	–	–	1	–	1
SKY	–	4	4	–	1	1	2	2	4
SLOWLY	1	–	1	–	–	–	–	–	–
SOMEBODY MIGHT DIE,THEN THEY GO UP TO H.	–	1	1	–	–	–	–	–	–
SPACE	–	–	–	–	–	–	–	1	1
STAIRS	3	4	7	2	2	4	–	–	–
STAND	–	1	1	–	–	–	–	–	–
STEEP	–	–	–	–	–	–	1	–	1
STEP	–	–	–	–	–	–	–	1	1
STEPS	1	1	2	–	–	–	–	–	–
SUP	1	–	1	–	–	–	–	–	–
SUSIE	–	–	–	–	–	–	–	1	1
TAKE IT	–	–	–	–	–	–	1	–	1
TALL	–	–	–	–	–	–	–	1	1
THE	–	1	1	–	–	–	–	–	–
THE HILL	–	1	1	–	–	–	–	–	–
THE SUN IS UP IN THE SKY	–	1	1	–	–	–	–	–	–
TO YOUR BEDROOM	–	1	1	–	–	–	–	–	–
TOWARD	–	–	–	–	–	–	–	1	1
TOWN	–	–	–	–	–	–	1	–	1
TREE	1	2	3	–	–	–	–	1	1
TRUCK	1	–	1	–	–	–	–	–	–
UNDER	–	–	–	–	1	1	–	–	–
UP, TIM	–	1	1	–	–	–	–	–	–
UPWARD	–	–	–	–	–	–	–	2	2
UPWARDS	–	–	–	–	–	–	1	–	1
US	–	–	–	–	1	1	–	–	–
VERY HIGH	–	–	–	1	–	1	–	–	–
WAKE	–	1	1	–	–	–	–	–	–
WALL	1	–	1	–	–	–	–	–	–
WAY UP	1	–	1	–	–	–	–	–	–
WE GO	1	–	1	–	–	–	–	–	–
WENT	–	1	1	–	–	–	–	–	–
WHAT	1	1	2	–	–	–	–	–	–
WHAT COMES UP, MUST COME DOWN.	1	–	1	–	–	–	–	–	–
WHEN YOURE GOING UP A HILL	1	–	1	–	–	–	–	–	–
WHITE	1	–	1	–	–	–	–	–	–
WINDOW	–	1	1	–	–	–	–	–	–
WORD	1	–	1	–	–	–	–	–	–
WRUP	–	1	1	–	–	–	–	–	–
YOU GO	–	1	1	–	–	–	–	–	–

RESPONSE WORD	1ST			3RD			5TH		
	M	F	T	M	F	T	M	F	T

92. US

RESPONSE WORD	M	F	T	M	F	T	M	F	T
A BLUE WALL	1	–	1	–	–	–	–	–	–
ALL	1	–	1	–	2	2	1	–	1
AM	1	–	1	–	–	–	–	–	–
ANIMAL	–	1	1	–	–	–	–	–	–
ANT	–	1	1	–	–	–	–	–	–
ANYONE	–	–	–	–	1	1	–	–	–
ARE GONNA GO TO THE STORE.	–	1	1	–	–	–	–	–	–
ARM	–	–	–	–	–	–	1	–	1
AS	–	–	–	–	1	1	–	–	–
AT	1	–	1	–	–	–	–	–	–
AWAY	–	–	–	–	1	1	–	–	–
BAG	1	–	1	–	–	–	–	–	–
BLUE	–	1	1	–	–	–	–	–	–
BOAT	1	–	1	–	–	–	–	–	–
BOOK	1	–	1	–	–	–	–	–	–
BOTH	–	–	–	–	–	–	1	2	3
BOYS	–	–	–	1	–	1	1	1	2
BUS	6	4	10	2	1	3	1	1	2
CAN	1	2	3	–	–	–	–	–	–
CAT	–	1	1	–	–	–	–	–	–
CHAIR	–	1	1	–	–	–	–	–	–
CHILDREN	–	–	–	–	1	1	–	–	–
COLD	–	–	–	1	–	1	–	–	–
COME	–	3	3	–	–	–	–	–	–
COUSINS	1	–	1	–	–	–	–	–	–
CUSS	3	–	3	–	–	–	–	–	–
DAN	–	–	–	–	–	–	1	–	1
DO	1	–	1	–	–	–	–	–	–
DO YOUR WORK	–	1	1	–	–	–	–	–	–
DOG	1	–	1	–	–	–	–	–	–
DUS	3	–	3	–	–	–	–	–	–
DUST	1	–	1	–	1	1	–	–	–
EAT	–	1	1	–	–	–	–	–	–
EVERYBODY	–	–	–	–	–	–	1	–	1
EVERYONE	–	–	–	–	–	–	–	1	1
EYES	1	–	1	–	–	–	–	–	–
FACE	1	–	1	–	–	–	–	–	–
FAMILY	1	1	2	1	1	2	–	–	–
FENCE	2	–	2	–	–	–	–	–	–
FINE	1	–	1	–	–	–	–	–	–
FLOOR	1	–	1	–	–	–	–	–	–
FLUSS	–	–	–	1	–	1	–	–	–
FLY	–	1	1	–	–	–	–	–	–
FRIENDS	–	1	1	–	–	–	–	–	–
FUSS	2	–	2	–	1	1	–	–	–
GAME	1	–	1	–	–	–	–	–	–
GET SOME KIDS AND PLAY WITH THEM.	–	1	1	–	–	–	–	–	–
GIRL	–	–	–	1	–	1	1	–	1
GIRLS	–	–	–	–	–	–	–	1	1
GIVE	–	1	1	–	–	–	–	–	–
GLAD	–	–	–	–	–	–	–	1	1
GO	1	4	5	1	–	1	–	–	–
GO OUTSIDE	1	–	1	–	–	–	–	–	–
GO TO BED	1	–	1	–	–	–	–	–	–
GOD	–	1	1	–	–	–	–	–	–
GOING	–	–	–	1	–	1	–	–	–
GOOD	–	2	2	–	–	–	–	–	–
GRASS	1	–	1	–	–	–	–	–	–
GUS	1	1	2	–	1	1	–	–	–
HAD A PARTY	–	1	1	–	–	–	–	–	–
HAIR	–	1	1	–	–	–	–	–	–
HAPPY	1	–	1	–	–	–	–	–	–
HAVE	2	1	3	–	–	–	–	–	–
HE	–	–	–	1	–	1	1	–	1
HELP	–	–	–	–	1	1	–	–	–
HER	1	–	1	–	–	–	–	1	1
HERE	–	4	4	–	–	–	–	–	–
HIM	–	–	–	2	6	8	2	1	3
HIS	–	–	–	1	1	2	–	1	1
HOME	–	1	1	–	–	–	–	–	–

RESPONSE WORD	1ST			3RD			5TH		
	M	F	T	M	F	T	M	F	T

92. US

RESPONSE WORD	M	F	T	M	F	T	M	F	T
HON	–	–	–	–	–	–	1	–	1
HOUSE	2	–	2	–	–	–	–	–	–
HUS	1	–	1	–	–	–	–	–	–
I	–	1	1	–	3	3	–	–	–
ICE	1	–	1	–	–	–	–	–	–
ICE CREAM	1	–	1	–	–	–	–	–	–
IN	–	1	1	–	–	–	–	–	–
IS OURSELVES	–	1	1	–	–	–	–	–	–
JOIN	1	–	1	–	–	–	–	–	–
JUST	–	–	–	1	–	1	1	–	1
KEEP	–	–	–	–	1	1	–	–	–
KEY	1	–	1	–	–	–	–	–	–
KID	–	1	1	–	–	–	–	–	–
KIDS	1	–	1	1	–	1	1	–	1
KILL	–	1	1	–	–	–	–	–	–
LET US GO OUTSIDE	–	1	1	–	–	–	–	–	–
LIGHT	–	–	–	–	–	–	1	–	1
LIKE TWO OF US	–	–	–	–	–	–	–	1	1
LOT	–	1	1	–	–	–	1	–	1
MAY	–	1	1	–	–	–	–	–	–
ME	10	10	20	15	10	25	12	11	23
MESS	1	–	1	–	–	–	–	–	–
MOON	1	–	1	–	–	–	–	–	–
MORE	–	–	–	–	–	–	–	1	1
MORE THAN ONE	–	–	–	–	–	–	–	1	1
MOTHER	1	–	1	–	–	–	–	–	–
MOVIES	–	–	–	–	–	–	–	1	1
MOW	–	–	–	–	–	–	1	–	1
MUS	1	–	1	2	–	2	–	–	–
MUSS	1	2	3	–	–	–	–	–	–
MUST	1	–	1	5	–	5	–	–	–
MY	–	1	1	–	–	–	–	–	–
MY OWN	1	–	1	–	–	–	–	–	–
NEAR	–	–	–	1	–	1	–	–	–
NEVER	–	–	–	–	–	–	–	1	1
NICE	–	–	–	1	–	1	–	–	–
NIGHT	–	–	–	1	–	1	–	–	–
NOBODY	–	–	–	1	–	1	–	–	–
NOT	1	–	1	–	–	–	–	–	–
NOT US–	1	–	1	–	–	–	–	–	–
NOW	2	1	3	–	–	–	–	–	–
NUS	–	1	1	–	–	–	–	–	–
NUSS	–	–	–	1	–	1	–	–	–
ON	1	–	1	–	–	–	–	–	–
ONE	–	–	–	–	–	–	1	–	1
OTHER	–	–	–	–	1	1	–	–	–
OTHERS	–	–	–	1	1	2	–	–	–
OUR	–	–	–	1	–	1	–	–	–
OUR FRIENDS	1	–	1	–	–	–	1	–	1
PAIR	–	–	–	–	–	–	1	–	1
PAPER	–	–	–	1	1	2	–	–	–
PEOPLE	7	9	16	9	7	16	14	6	20
PERSON	1	–	1	–	–	–	–	–	–
PERSONS	–	–	–	–	–	–	–	1	1
PIG	–	–	–	–	–	–	1	–	1
PLAY	–	6	6	–	–	–	–	–	–
PLAYING	–	1	1	–	–	–	–	–	–
PURSE	–	1	1	–	–	–	–	–	–
PUS	2	–	2	–	–	–	–	–	–
PUSS	–	–	–	–	1	1	–	–	–
RAT	1	–	1	–	–	–	–	–	–
ROAD	1	–	1	–	–	–	–	–	–
RUN	2	–	2	–	1	1	–	–	–
RUS	–	1	1	–	–	–	–	–	–
RUST	–	1	1	–	1	1	–	–	–
SAID	–	–	–	–	1	1	–	–	–
SAME	–	–	–	–	–	–	–	1	1
SANTA	–	1	1	–	–	–	–	–	–
SCHOOL	–	1	1	–	–	–	–	–	–
SCRAM	1	–	1	–	–	–	–	–	–
SEE	1	2	3	1	–	1	–	–	–
SHE	–	–	–	1	–	1	–	–	–

RESPONSE WORD	1ST			3RD			5TH		
	M	F	T	M	F	T	M	F	T

92. US

RESPONSE WORD	M	F	T	M	F	T	M	F	T
SHOE	-	1	1	-	-	-	-	-	-
SKIRT	-	1	1	-	-	-	-	-	-
SLEEP	1	-	1	-	-	-	-	-	-
SOMEONE	-	-	-	1	-	1	-	-	-
SON	-	1	1	-	-	-	-	-	-
SORT OF LIKE YOU AND ME	-	-	-	1	-	1	-	-	-
STAY IN	1	-	1	-	-	-	-	-	-
STOP	-	1	1	-	-	-	-	-	-
SUN	1	2	3	-	-	-	-	-	-
TABLE	1	1	2	-	-	-	-	-	-
TALKING	1	-	1	-	-	-	-	-	-
TEACH	-	1	1	-	-	-	-	-	-
THAT	1	-	1	-	1	1	-	-	-
THEM	5	5	10	18	22	40	24	19	43
THEN	2	1	3	-	-	-	-	-	-
THEY	-	3	3	6	4	10	8	7	15
THING	-	-	-	-	-	-	-	-	-
THIS	1	-	1	-	-	-	-	-	-
THREE	-	-	-	1	-	1	-	-	-
THUS	-	2	2	-	-	-	-	-	-
TO	-	-	-	-	-	-	1	-	1
TOGETHER	1	-	1	3	6	9	5	5	10
TOP	-	1	1	-	-	-	-	-	-
TRAIN	1	-	1	-	-	-	-	-	-
TREE	2	-	2	-	-	-	-	-	-
TRUCK	-	-	-	-	-	-	1	-	1
TUSK	-	-	-	-	-	-	2	-	2
TWO	-	-	-	-	2	2	4	-	4
TWO PEOPLE	-	1	1	1	-	1	1	3	4
UP	1	-	1	-	-	-	-	-	-
US	-	-	-	-	-	-	1	-	1
USE	-	-	-	-	2	2	-	-	-
WALL	-	1	1	-	-	-	-	-	-
WANT	1	-	1	1	-	1	-	-	-
WATER	-	-	-	-	-	-	-	1	1
WE	13	13	26	12	17	29	22	37	59
WE HELP	-	1	1	-	-	-	-	-	-
WENT	1	-	1	-	-	-	-	-	-
WHAM	1	-	1	-	-	-	-	-	-
WHAT	-	1	1	-	-	-	-	-	-
WHEN YOURE US YOU GO SOMEWHERE ELSE	1	-	1	-	-	-	-	-	-
WHITE	-	1	1	-	-	-	-	-	-
WHY DONT WE HAVE SOME FUN.	-	1	1	-	-	-	-	-	-
WILL	-	1	1	1	-	1	-	-	-
WITH	-	1	1	1	-	1	-	1	1
WOMAN	1	-	1	-	-	-	-	-	-
WORK	1	-	1	-	-	-	1	-	1
YELLOW	-	-	-	-	-	-	-	1	1
YOU	10	14	24	40	38	78	24	31	55
YOU AND ME	1	1	2	-	-	-	-	1	1
YOU DRINK	1	-	1	-	-	-	-	-	-
YOU RE TOGETHER	-	1	1	-	-	-	-	-	-
YOUR.	-	-	-	-	1	1	-	-	-
YOUSE	-	-	-	-	1	1	-	-	-

93. USUALLY

RESPONSE WORD	M	F	T	M	F	T	M	F	T
A LOT	-	-	-	-	2	2	-	-	-
ACCIDENT HAPPENED	1	-	1	-	-	-	-	-	-
AFTER	1	-	1	1	-	1	-	-	-
AGAIN	-	-	-	1	-	1	-	-	-
AGO	-	1	1	-	-	-	-	-	-
AIR	1	-	1	-	-	-	-	-	-
ALL	-	-	-	-	-	-	-	1	1
ALL THE TIME	-	-	-	-	1	1	1	2	3
ALMOST	-	-	-	2	2	4	1	2	3
ALMOST ALWAYS	-	-	-	-	-	-	1	-	1
ALMOST EVERYTIME	-	-	-	-	1	1	-	-	-
ALWAY	-	-	-	-	-	-	-	1	1

RESPONSE WORD	1ST M	1ST F	1ST T	3RD M	3RD F	3RD T	5TH M	5TH F	5TH T

93. USUALLY

RESPONSE WORD	M	F	T	M	F	T	M	F	T
ALWAYS	–	–	–	15	14	29	12	10	22
ANIMAL	–	1	1	–	–	–	–	–	–
ANYTHING	–	–	–	1	–	1	–	–	–
ANYWAY	–	1	1	–	–	–	–	–	–
ANYWHERE	–	–	–	–	–	–	1	–	1
ARE	–	1	1	–	–	–	–	–	–
ARM	–	–	–	–	1	1	–	–	–
AS	–	1	1	–	–	–	–	–	–
BABY	1	–	1	–	–	–	–	–	–
BAD	2	1	3	–	1	1	1	–	1
BAKING SODA	–	–	–	1	–	1	–	–	–
BALL	–	–	–	–	1	1	–	–	–
BARE	–	–	–	–	–	–	–	1	1
BEAR	–	1	1	–	–	–	–	–	–
BEHIND	–	–	–	1	–	1	–	–	–
BETTER	–	–	–	1	–	1	–	–	–
BIG	–	–	–	–	–	–	1	–	1
BIRD	–	1	1	–	–	–	–	–	–
BLACKBOARD	–	–	–	–	1	1	–	–	–
BLOCKS	–	1	1	–	–	–	–	–	–
BOARD	–	–	–	–	1	1	–	–	–
BOATS	1	–	1	–	–	–	–	–	–
BOOKSHELF	–	1	1	–	–	–	–	–	–
BOOM	1	–	1	–	–	–	–	–	–
BOONILY	1	–	1	–	–	–	–	–	–
BOX	–	2	2	1	–	1	–	–	–
BRAIN	1	–	1	–	–	–	–	–	–
BROOM	–	1	1	–	–	–	–	–	–
BRUSH	1	1	2	–	–	–	–	–	–
BRUSUALLY	–	1	1	–	–	–	–	–	–
BUTTERFLY	1	–	1	–	–	–	–	–	–
BUTTON	1	–	1	–	–	–	–	–	–
CABINS	–	1	1	–	–	–	–	–	–
CAN	–	2	2	–	–	–	–	–	–
CAP	–	1	1	–	–	–	–	–	–
CAR	2	–	2	–	–	–	–	–	–
CAT	–	–	–	–	–	–	1	–	1
CEREAL	1	–	1	–	–	–	–	–	–
CERTAIN	–	–	–	1	–	1	–	–	–
CHAIR	1	2	3	–	–	–	1	–	1
CLEAN	–	2	2	1	–	1	1	–	1
CLEAN UP	–	1	1	–	–	–	–	–	–
CLEANING	–	1	1	–	–	–	–	–	–
CLOSE	1	1	2	–	–	–	–	–	–
COAT	1	–	1	–	–	–	–	–	–
COKE	1	–	1	–	–	–	–	–	–
COMB	–	1	1	–	–	–	–	–	–
COME THERE	–	–	–	–	1	1	–	–	–
COMMON	–	–	–	1	–	1	3	2	5
COOK	1	1	2	–	–	–	–	–	–
COW	1	–	1	–	–	–	–	–	–
CUPBOARD	–	1	1	–	–	–	–	–	–
CUSUALLY	1	–	1	–	–	–	–	–	–
DARK	–	1	1	–	–	–	–	–	–
DAY	–	1	1	–	1	1	–	–	–
DESK	–	1	1	–	–	–	–	–	–
DID	–	–	–	–	–	–	–	1	1
DIFFERENT	–	–	–	–	2	2	1	1	2
DIRT	–	–	–	–	1	1	–	–	–
DIRTY	–	1	1	–	–	–	–	–	–
DO	1	4	5	–	–	–	2	2	4
DO SOMETHING	2	–	2	–	–	–	–	–	–
DOES	–	–	–	1	–	1	–	–	–
DOESNT	–	–	–	–	1	1	–	–	–
DOG	–	2	2	–	–	–	–	–	–
DOLL	–	1	1	–	–	–	–	–	–
DONE	–	–	–	1	–	1	–	1	1
DONT	–	1	1	–	–	–	–	–	–
DOOR	1	1	2	1	–	1	–	–	–
DOWN	–	1	1	–	1	1	–	–	–
DRAW	–	–	–	–	–	–	1	–	1
DRESS	–	1	1	–	–	–	–	–	–

RESPONSE WORD		1ST			3RD			5TH	
	M	F	T	M	F	T	M	F	T

93.   USUALLY

RESPONSE WORD	M	F	T	M	F	T	M	F	T
DRINK	1	–	1	–	–	–	–	–	–
DRY	1	–	1	–	–	–	–	–	–
DUMB	–	–	–	–	–	–	1	–	1
EARLY	–	–	–	–	1	1	–	–	–
EAT	–	–	–	–	–	–	1	–	1
ENJOIN	–	–	–	1	–	1	–	–	–
EVER	–	–	–	–	–	–	–	1	1
EVERY	–	–	–	–	–	–	1	–	1
EVERY DAY	–	–	–	–	–	–	1	–	1
EVERY ONCE IN AWHILE	–	–	–	1	–	1	–	–	–
EVERY TIME	–	–	–	–	–	–	–	1	1
EVERYTIME	–	1	1	–	–	–	–	–	–
EXPECTED	–	–	–	–	–	–	1	–	1
FACE	–	–	–	–	–	–	1	–	1
FAIR	–	2	2	–	–	–	–	–	–
FAMILIAR	–	–	–	–	–	–	–	1	1
FAST	–	1	1	–	–	–	–	–	–
FIGHT	–	–	–	–	–	–	–	1	1
FINALLY	–	–	–	1	1	2	–	–	–
FINE	–	–	–	1	1	2	–	–	–
FIRE	–	–	–	–	–	–	1	–	1
FIRE ESCAPE	–	1	1	–	–	–	–	–	–
FIRST	–	–	–	1	–	1	–	–	–
FLOOR	2	–	2	–	–	–	–	–	–
FLOWERS	–	1	1	–	–	–	–	–	–
FOOD	–	–	–	1	–	1	–	–	–
FORGET	–	1	1	–	–	–	–	–	–
FOUND	–	–	–	–	1	1	–	–	–
FREQUENTLY	–	–	–	–	1	1	–	–	–
FRIEND	–	–	–	–	1	1	–	–	–
FUN	1	–	1	–	–	–	–	–	–
GENERALLY	–	–	–	–	–	–	1	1	2
GENEROUS	–	–	–	–	–	–	–	1	1
GIVE	–	–	–	–	1	1	–	–	–
GLASSES	1	–	1	–	–	–	–	–	–
GO	–	2	2	–	–	–	–	–	–
GO HOME	–	1	1	–	–	–	–	–	–
GO OUTSIDE	1	–	1	–	–	–	–	–	–
GO THERE	–	1	1	–	–	–	–	–	–
GO TO SCHOOL	1	–	1	–	–	–	–	–	–
GOES TO THE STORE	1	–	1	–	–	–	–	–	–
GOING OUT	1	–	1	–	–	–	–	–	–
GOOD	1	1	2	–	–	–	–	–	–
GOOSEL	1	–	1	–	–	–	–	–	–
GRASS	1	–	1	–	–	–	1	–	1
GROUND	–	–	–	1	–	1	–	–	–
HAIR	–	1	1	–	–	–	–	–	–
HAPPEN	–	2	2	1	–	1	4	1	5
HAPPENED	–	–	–	–	–	–	–	1	1
HAPPENING	–	–	–	–	–	–	–	1	1
HAPPENINGS	–	–	–	–	–	–	1	–	1
HAPPENS	2	–	2	1	–	1	–	–	–
HARD	–	–	–	1	1	2	–	–	–
HARDLY	–	–	–	–	–	–	1	–	1
HAT	3	–	3	–	–	–	–	–	–
HAVE	–	1	1	2	–	2	–	–	–
HAVE TO	1	–	1	–	–	–	–	–	–
HEAD	1	–	1	–	–	–	–	–	–
HEALTHY	–	1	1	–	–	–	–	–	–
HEATER	1	–	1	–	–	–	–	–	–
HELP	4	1	5	–	1	1	–	–	–
HER	–	–	–	1	–	1	–	–	–
HERE	–	2	2	–	2	2	–	–	–
HI	–	–	–	–	–	–	–	1	1
HOME	1	1	2	–	–	–	–	–	–
HOMEWORK	–	–	–	1	–	1	–	–	–
HORN	1	–	1	–	–	–	–	–	–
HOUSE	1	1	2	1	1	2	–	–	–
HOW	–	–	–	1	–	1	–	–	–
I	3	2	5	–	1	1	–	–	–
I AM GOOD	–	–	–	–	–	–	–	1	1
I DO	1	–	1	–	–	–	–	–	–

	1ST			3RD			5TH		
RESPONSE WORD	M	F	T	M	F	T	M	F	T

93. USUALLY

RESPONSE WORD	M	F	T	M	F	T	M	F	T
I DONT CARE	–	1	1	–	–	–	–	–	–
I GO OUTSIDE	–	–	–	1	–	1	–	–	–
I SIT IN CHURCH	–	1	1	–	–	–	–	–	–
I THINK	1	–	1	–	–	–	–	–	–
I WANT	1	–	1	–	–	–	–	–	–
I WILL SEE YOU	–	1	1	–	–	–	–	–	–
IM GOOD	–	1	1	–	–	–	–	–	–
IS IT SUPPOSED TO BE	1	–	1	–	–	–	–	–	–
IS NOT	–	–	–	1	–	1	–	–	–
IT	–	–	–	1	–	1	–	–	–
IT HAPPENED	1	–	1	–	–	–	–	–	–
KIDS	–	1	1	–	–	–	–	–	–
KITTY CAT	1	–	1	–	–	–	–	–	–
KUSUALLY	1	–	1	–	–	–	–	–	–
LAST	–	–	–	1	–	1	–	–	–
LATER	–	1	1	–	–	–	–	–	–
LAY IN THE BED	1	–	1	–	–	–	–	–	–
LIGHT	1	–	1	–	–	–	–	–	–
LIKE	1	2	3	–	–	–	–	–	–
LIKELY	–	–	–	–	–	–	1	–	1
LISTEN	–	–	–	2	–	2	–	–	–
LONESOME	–	–	–	–	1	1	–	–	–
LONG	–	–	–	1	–	1	–	–	–
LOOK	1	–	1	–	–	–	–	–	–
LOOSE	–	1	1	–	–	–	–	–	–
LOSE	–	–	–	1	–	1	–	–	–
LOVE	1	–	1	–	–	–	–	–	–
MAN	1	–	1	–	–	–	–	–	–
MAT	1	–	1	–	–	–	–	–	–
MAYBE	–	1	1	–	–	–	2	1	3
ME	4	–	4	1	–	1	–	1	1
MEN	1	–	1	1	–	1	–	–	–
MEWS	–	–	–	1	–	1	–	–	–
MILK	–	1	1	–	–	–	–	–	–
MOMMY	1	–	1	–	–	–	–	–	–
MOO	1	–	1	–	–	–	–	–	–
MORNING	–	–	–	1	–	1	–	–	–
MOST	–	2	2	1	2	3	5	1	6
MOST OF THE TIME	–	–	–	1	3	4	6	6	12
MOST TIMES	–	–	–	–	1	1	1	–	1
MOSTLY	–	1	1	–	2	2	4	1	5
MOSTLY HEARD	–	–	–	–	–	–	–	1	1
MOTHER	–	1	1	–	–	–	–	–	–
MOVE	1	–	1	–	–	–	–	–	–
MOVIES	–	–	–	1	–	1	–	–	–
MUCH	–	–	–	1	–	1	–	–	–
MUSEDLY	1	–	1	–	–	–	–	–	–
MUSUALLY	1	–	1	–	1	1	–	–	–
MY	–	1	1	–	–	–	–	–	–
NAME	–	1	1	–	–	–	–	–	–
NAP	–	1	1	–	–	–	–	–	–
NATURAL	–	–	–	–	–	–	–	1	1
NECESSARY	–	–	–	–	–	–	1	–	1
NEVER	–	3	3	4	5	9	3	2	5
NEVER HAPPENS	–	–	–	1	–	1	–	–	–
NICE	–	2	2	1	–	1	–	–	–
NO	1	2	3	–	1	1	–	–	–
NORMAL	–	–	–	–	–	–	1	–	1
NOT	3	–	3	4	3	7	4	1	5
NOT ALL THE TIME	–	–	–	–	–	–	1	–	1
NOT ALWAYS	–	–	–	1	–	1	1	–	1
NOT ALWAYS USUALLY	1	–	1	–	–	–	–	–	–
NOT MUCH	–	–	–	1	–	1	–	–	–
NOT OFTEN	–	–	–	2	–	2	1	2	3
NOT USUALLY	2	1	3	5	6	11	2	–	2
NOT VERY OFTEN	–	–	–	1	–	1	1	–	1
NOW	1	1	2	2	3	5	1	–	1
ODD	–	–	–	–	–	–	–	1	1
OFFTEN	–	–	–	–	–	–	1	–	1
OFTEN	1	1	2	7	8	15	22	24	46
ON TIME	–	–	–	–	1	1	–	–	–
ONCE IN A WHILE	–	–	–	–	–	–	2	–	2

RESPONSE WORD	1ST M	F	T	3RD M	F	T	5TH M	F	T

93. USUALLY

RESPONSE WORD	M	F	T	M	F	T	M	F	T
ORANGE	1	–	1	–	–	–	–	–	–
P	–	–	–	1	–	1	–	–	–
PADDLE	1	–	1	–	–	–	–	–	–
PEE	–	1	1	–	–	–	–	–	–
PENCIL	1	–	1	–	–	–	–	–	–
PERHAPS	–	–	–	–	1	1	–	–	–
PICTURE	1	–	1	–	–	–	–	–	–
PINK	–	–	–	–	1	1	–	–	–
PLAY	1	–	1	1	–	1	–	–	–
PLAY WITH DOG	–	–	–	1	–	1	–	–	–
PLEASE	–	1	1	–	–	–	–	–	–
POSSIBLE	–	1	1	–	–	–	–	1	1
PRETTY	–	–	–	1	–	1	–	1	1
PROBABLY	–	–	–	1	–	1	–	1	1
QUICK	–	–	–	1	–	1	–	–	–
QUIET	–	–	–	–	1	1	–	–	–
RAIN	1	–	1	–	–	–	–	–	–
RATTLELY	–	–	–	–	1	1	–	–	–
READY	–	–	–	–	–	–	1	1	2
RECEIVE	–	–	–	–	–	–	1	–	1
RECENTLY	–	–	–	–	–	–	1	–	1
REGULAR	–	–	–	–	1	1	–	–	–
REGULARLY	–	–	–	–	1	1	–	1	1
RESUALLY	–	1	1	–	–	–	–	–	–
RIGHT	–	–	–	1	–	1	1	–	1
ROUND	–	–	–	–	1	1	–	–	–
RUSUALLY	1	–	1	–	–	–	–	–	–
SAME	–	–	–	–	–	–	2	2	4
SAVE TIME	–	–	–	–	–	–	1	–	1
SCHOOL	–	–	–	–	–	–	–	1	1
SELDOM	–	–	–	1	1	2	–	1	1
SET	–	–	–	–	1	1	–	–	–
SHOE	1	–	1	–	–	–	–	–	–
SHORT	–	–	–	–	–	–	–	2	2
SILENT	–	–	–	–	1	1	–	–	–
SING	1	–	1	–	–	–	–	–	–
SNAG	–	–	–	–	–	–	1	–	1
SNOW	1	–	1	–	–	–	–	–	–
SOFT	–	1	1	–	2	2	–	–	–
SOFTLY	–	–	–	–	1	1	–	–	–
SOME	–	–	–	–	1	1	–	–	–
SOMETHING	1	4	5	–	1	1	–	–	–
SOMETIME	–	–	–	3	–	3	1	–	1
SOMETIMES	4	5	9	14	12	26	4	21	25
SOON	–	–	–	–	2	2	–	–	–
SOOTHELY	1	–	1	–	–	–	–	–	–
SOUND	–	–	–	–	1	1	–	–	–
SPECIAL	–	1	1	–	–	–	–	–	–
SQUIRREL	–	1	1	–	–	–	–	–	–
STANGE	–	–	–	–	–	–	1	–	1
STOP	–	–	–	1	–	1	–	–	–
STORE	1	–	1	–	1	1	1	–	1
SUALLY	–	–	–	1	–	1	–	–	–
SURE	–	–	–	1	–	1	–	–	–
SUSUALLY	1	–	1	1	–	1	–	–	–
SWEEP	1	–	1	1	–	1	–	–	–
TABLE	1	–	1	1	–	1	–	–	–
THAT	–	–	–	–	1	1	–	–	–
THE	–	1	1	–	–	–	1	–	1
THEN	–	–	–	1	–	1	–	–	–
THINGS	1	–	1	–	1	1	–	–	–
THINGS HAPPEN	1	–	1	–	–	–	–	–	–
THINK	–	2	2	–	2	2	–	1	1
THINKING	–	–	–	1	–	1	–	–	–
TIME	–	–	–	–	–	–	1	–	1
TIMES	1	–	1	–	–	–	–	–	–
TODAY	–	–	–	–	1	1	–	–	–
TOYS	1	–	1	–	–	–	–	–	–
TRUCK	1	–	1	1	–	1	–	–	–
UALLY	–	–	–	–	–	–	–	1	1
UNDER	–	–	–	–	1	1	–	–	–

RESPONSE WORD	1ST M	F	T	3RD M	F	T	5TH M	F	T

93. USUALLY

RESPONSE WORD	1ST M	F	T	3RD M	F	T	5TH M	F	T
UNDERSTOOD	–	–	–	–	1	1	–	–	–
UNHAPPY	–	–	–	–	2	2	–	1	1
UNSELFISH	–	–	–	1	–	1	–	–	–
UNTIL	–	–	–	1	2	3	–	–	–
UNUALLY	–	–	–	–	–	–	–	1	1
UNUSALLY	–	–	–	–	–	–	–	1	1
UNUSUAL	–	–	–	–	4	4	2	5	7
UNUSUALLY	1	1	2	6	3	9	16	14	30
UP	–	–	–	1	–	1	–	–	–
US	2	–	2	1	–	1	1	–	1
USE	3	3	6	6	2	8	1	3	4
USE YOUR HEAD	–	1	1	–	–	–	–	–	–
USE YOUR SOAP	1	–	1	–	–	–	–	–	–
USE YOUR WATCH	1	–	1	–	–	–	–	–	–
USEAL	–	–	–	–	–	–	–	1	1
USED TO CLEAN UP THE HOUSE	–	1	1	–	–	–	–	–	–
USING	–	–	–	1	–	1	–	–	–
USUAL	–	–	–	–	1	1	–	1	1
VERY OFTEN	–	–	–	–	–	–	1	–	1
VOWEL RULE	–	–	–	–	1	1	–	1	1
WARM	–	–	–	–	1	1	–	–	–
WASH	1	4	5	–	–	–	–	–	–
WASH CLOTH	–	1	1	–	–	–	–	–	–
WASH THE DISHES	1	–	1	–	–	–	–	–	–
WATER	–	1	1	–	–	–	–	–	–
WE DO THAT	1	–	1	–	–	–	–	–	–
WE GO	–	–	–	–	1	1	–	–	–
WE PLAY	1	–	1	–	–	–	–	–	–
WE PLAY OUTSIDE	1	–	1	–	–	–	–	–	–
WE WASH	1	–	1	–	–	–	–	–	–
WET	–	1	1	–	–	–	–	–	–
WHAT	1	1	2	–	–	–	–	–	–
WHEN YOURE USING SOMETHING	1	–	1	–	–	–	–	–	–
WHENEVER YOUR MOTHER SAYS WE WILL USUAL	–	1	1	–	–	–	–	–	–
WHY	–	1	1	–	–	–	–	–	–
WITCH	1	–	1	–	–	–	–	–	–
WON	–	–	–	1	–	1	–	–	–
WOOD	–	1	1	–	–	–	–	–	–
WORD	–	–	–	–	–	–	–	1	1
WORK	2	2	4	–	–	–	–	–	–
WORKING	–	1	1	–	–	–	–	–	–
YET	–	–	–	–	1	1	–	–	–
YOU	3	1	4	1	1	2	–	–	–
YOU COULD USE THE BATHROOM	–	1	1	–	–	–	–	–	–
YOU DO	1	–	1	–	–	–	–	–	–
YOU GROW UP AND BE IN THE 4TH GRADE	–	1	1	–	–	–	–	–	–
YOU MAY CALL SOMEBODY	–	1	1	–	–	–	–	–	–
YOU WRITE	1	–	1	–	–	–	–	–	–
YOURE USUALLY DOING SOMETHING	–	1	1	–	–	–	–	–	–
YOUTH	–	–	–	–	1	1	–	–	–

94. WILD

RESPONSE WORD	1ST M	F	T	3RD M	F	T	5TH M	F	T
A BIG SUN	–	1	1	–	–	–	–	–	–
AFRICA	–	–	–	–	1	1	–	–	–
ALONE	–	–	–	–	–	–	–	1	1
AMENE	–	–	–	–	–	–	1	–	1
AN ANIMAL	–	–	–	–	–	–	–	1	1
AND	–	1	1	–	–	–	–	1	1
ANGRY	–	–	–	–	1	1	–	1	1
ANIMAL	15	19	34	16	23	39	24	15	39
ANIMALS	6	8	14	5	4	9	1	–	1
ANIMLE	–	–	–	–	–	–	–	1	1
ART	1	–	1	–	–	–	–	–	–
BAD	–	2	2	–	1	1	–	–	–

RESPONSE WORD	1ST			3RD			5TH		
	M	F	T	M	F	T	M	F	T

94. WILD

RESPONSE WORD	M	F	T	M	F	T	M	F	T
BAG	–	–	–	–	–	–	–	1	1
BAIL	–	–	–	–	–	–	–	1	1
BALL	–	2	2	–	–	–	–	–	–
BEAR	6	4	10	3	1	4	1	–	1
BEARS ARE WILD	–	1	1	–	–	–	–	–	–
BEAST	3	1	4	4	1	5	2	3	5
BEHAVED	–	–	–	–	1	1	–	–	–
BIRD	–	2	2	2	1	3	1	1	2
BIRDS	–	1	1	–	–	–	–	–	–
BLEW	–	–	–	–	–	–	–	1	1
BOARD	–	1	1	–	–	–	–	–	–
BOAT	1	–	1	–	–	–	–	–	–
BOY	–	1	1	1	–	1	–	1	1
BOYS	–	1	1	–	–	–	–	–	–
BUFFALO	2	–	2	1	–	1	–	–	–
BULL	4	2	6	–	–	–	–	–	–
CALM	2	–	2	1	2	3	–	6	6
CAN	1	–	1	–	–	–	–	–	–
CAR	1	–	1	–	–	–	–	–	–
CAT	2	5	7	2	3	5	–	–	–
CATS	–	–	–	–	1	1	–	–	–
CHAIR	1	–	1	1	–	1	1	–	1
CHILD	1	–	1	2	–	2	–	–	–
CIVILIZED	–	–	–	1	–	1	–	–	–
COAT	1	–	1	–	–	–	–	–	–
COME	–	–	–	1	–	1	–	–	–
COOKIE	1	–	1	–	–	–	–	–	–
COW	1	2	3	–	–	–	–	–	–
COWED	1	–	1	–	–	–	–	–	–
COWT	–	1	1	–	–	–	–	–	–
CRAZY	–	–	–	2	1	3	3	2	5
CREASY	–	–	–	–	–	–	1	–	1
DANGEROUS	2	–	2	1	1	2	–	–	–
DEAD	1	–	1	–	–	–	–	–	–
DEER	–	1	1	–	–	–	1	1	2
DOCTOR	1	–	1	–	–	–	–	–	–
DOG	2	–	2	1	1	2	–	–	–
DOMESTIC	–	–	–	–	–	–	–	1	1
DONT	–	1	1	–	–	–	–	–	–
DONT BE	1	–	1	–	–	–	–	–	–
DONT GET ON	–	1	1	–	–	–	–	–	–
DONT PLAY WITH DOGS CAUSE THE DOGS MIGH.	–	1	1	–	–	–	–	–	–
DOOR	1	–	1	–	–	–	–	–	–
DRESS	–	1	1	–	–	–	–	–	–
DUCK	1	1	2	1	–	1	–	–	–
DUCKS	1	1	2	–	–	–	–	–	–
EASY	–	1	1	–	1	1	–	–	–
ELEPHANT	1	1	2	–	–	–	1	–	1
FAIRY	–	1	1	–	–	–	–	–	–
FAN	1	–	1	–	–	–	–	–	–
FAST	–	–	–	–	2	2	–	–	–
FAWN	–	–	–	–	1	1	–	–	–
FENCE	–	–	–	–	1	1	–	–	–
FEROCIOUS	–	–	–	2	1	3	1	–	1
FIERCE	–	–	–	–	2	2	1	3	4
FIGHT	–	–	–	–	–	–	–	1	1
FILE	1	–	1	–	–	–	–	–	–
FINGER	–	1	1	–	–	–	–	–	–
FISH	–	1	1	–	–	–	–	–	–
FLOOR	–	1	1	–	–	–	–	–	–
FLOWER	–	1	1	1	–	1	–	2	2
FLOWERS	–	–	–	–	1	1	–	–	–
FOLLOW	–	–	–	–	1	1	–	–	–
FOOTBALL	–	1	1	–	–	–	–	–	–
FOREST	–	–	–	–	–	–	–	1	1
FOX	1	–	1	–	1	1	1	1	2
FREE	–	–	–	–	–	–	1	–	1
FRIEND	–	–	–	–	–	–	1	–	1
FRONTIER	–	–	–	–	–	–	–	1	1
FURIOUS	–	1	1	–	–	–	–	1	1
GAME	–	–	–	1	–	1	–	–	–

RESPONSE WORD	1ST			3RD			5TH		
	M	F	T	M	F	T	M	F	T

94.   WILD

RESPONSE WORD	M	F	T	M	F	T	M	F	T
GEESE	–	–	–	–	–	–	–	2	2
GENTLE	–	1	1	3	2	5	2	4	6
GENTLY	–	–	–	2	–	2	–	–	–
GIANT	–	–	–	1	–	1	–	–	–
GIRL	–	1	1	–	–	–	–	–	–
GLORY	–	–	–	–	–	–	1	–	1
GOOD	–	2	2	–	1	1	–	–	–
GORILLA	1	–	1	–	–	–	–	–	–
GREEN	1	–	1	1	–	1	–	–	–
GROW	–	–	–	–	–	–	–	1	1
HANGER	–	1	1	–	–	–	–	–	–
HARD	–	1	1	–	3	3	–	2	2
HERD	–	–	–	–	–	–	–	1	1
HILD	2	1	3	–	–	–	–	–	–
HOLLER	–	1	1	–	–	–	1	–	1
HORSE	11	6	17	2	7	9	1	3	4
HORSES	–	–	–	–	3	3	–	–	–
HOUND	–	–	–	–	1	1	–	–	–
HOUSE	2	–	2	–	–	–	–	–	–
HOW	–	–	–	–	–	–	–	1	1
HUSH	–	–	–	–	1	1	–	–	–
I	–	1	1	–	–	–	–	1	1
IMPATIENT	–	–	–	–	–	–	–	1	1
IN THE JUNGLE	1	–	1	–	–	–	–	–	–
INDIAN	–	–	–	–	1	1	–	–	–
INDIANS	1	–	1	–	–	–	–	1	1
INTERESTING	–	–	–	1	–	1	–	–	–
JUMPY	–	–	–	–	–	–	–	1	1
JUNGLE	1	1	2	1	–	1	1	–	1
KEY	–	1	1	–	–	–	–	–	–
KILL	–	–	–	–	1	1	–	–	–
KIND	–	–	–	2	–	2	–	–	–
KINDLY	–	–	–	–	1	1	–	–	–
LADY	1	–	1	–	–	–	–	–	–
LIFE	–	–	–	1	1	2	–	–	–
LIGHT	1	–	1	–	1	1	–	–	–
LINE	–	1	1	–	–	–	–	–	–
LION	7	4	11	1	1	2	3	1	4
LIONS	–	2	2	–	–	–	–	1	1
LITTLE	–	1	1	–	–	–	–	–	–
LOOK	–	–	–	1	–	1	–	–	–
LOOSE	–	–	–	–	1	1	2	–	2
LOUD	–	1	1	–	–	–	–	–	–
LOW	–	–	–	–	1	1	–	–	–
MAD	–	–	–	–	–	–	2	1	3
MAN	3	–	3	–	–	–	–	1	1
MANGER	–	1	1	–	–	–	–	–	–
ME	1	1	2	–	–	–	–	–	–
MEAN	–	1	1	2	2	4	3	2	5
METAL	–	–	–	–	–	–	1	–	1
MICE	–	–	–	–	1	1	–	–	–
MILD	1	–	1	2	–	2	–	–	–
MOUSE	1	–	1	–	–	–	–	–	–
MOUTH	1	–	1	–	–	–	–	–	–
MOVE	–	–	–	–	–	–	1	–	1
NAP	–	–	–	1	–	1	–	–	–
NEAR	–	–	–	1	–	1	–	–	–
NICE	–	–	–	2	3	5	–	1	1
NIGHT	–	–	–	1	–	1	–	–	–
NO	–	1	1	–	–	–	–	–	–
NOISY	–	–	–	–	1	1	–	–	–
NOT	–	2	2	–	–	–	–	–	–
NOT TAME	–	–	–	–	–	–	4	3	7
NOT TAMED	–	–	–	–	–	–	–	1	1
NOT TAUGHT	–	–	–	1	–	1	–	–	–
NOT TRAINED	–	–	–	–	–	–	–	1	1
NOT WILD	6	2	8	6	4	10	–	1	1
NOW	–	1	1	1	2	3	1	–	1
OFTEN	–	–	–	–	1	1	–	–	–
OLD	–	1	1	–	–	–	–	–	–
OPEN	–	–	–	–	1	1	–	–	–
PAINT	1	–	1	–	–	–	–	–	–

RESPONSE WORD	1ST M	1ST F	1ST T	3RD M	3RD F	3RD T	5TH M	5TH F	5TH T

94. WILD

RESPONSE WORD	1ST M	1ST F	1ST T	3RD M	3RD F	3RD T	5TH M	5TH F	5TH T
PAPER	–	1	1	–	–	–	–	–	–
PEOPLE	–	–	–	1	–	1	–	–	–
PET	1	–	1	3	1	4	1	–	1
PICTURE	–	–	–	1	–	1	–	–	–
PIG	–	–	–	–	–	–	–	1	1
PLANT	–	–	–	–	–	–	1	–	1
PONY	–	–	–	1	–	1	–	–	–
POPPED	–	1	1	–	–	–	–	–	–
RABBIT	1	–	1	1	–	1	–	–	–
RAMBUNCTIOUS	–	–	–	–	–	–	–	1	1
RAMPAGE	–	–	–	–	–	–	1	–	1
RAT	1	1	2	–	–	–	–	–	–
RECKLESS	–	–	–	–	1	1	–	–	–
RED	–	–	–	1	1	2	–	–	–
RILD	–	1	1	–	–	–	–	–	–
ROUGH	1	–	1	–	1	1	–	1	1
RUN	2	–	2	1	–	1	–	–	–
RUNNING	–	–	–	–	1	1	–	–	–
SAT	–	1	1	–	–	–	–	–	–
SAVAGE	–	–	–	–	–	–	1	–	1
SCARE	–	–	–	–	–	–	–	1	1
SCARED	–	–	–	1	1	2	1	–	1
SCARES	–	–	–	1	–	1	–	–	–
SCAREY	–	1	1	–	–	–	–	–	–
SCREAM	–	–	–	–	–	–	1	–	1
SHARP	1	–	1	–	–	–	–	–	–
SHOOTING	–	–	–	1	–	1	–	–	–
SILD	1	–	1	1	1	2	–	–	–
SINK	–	1	1	–	–	–	–	–	–
SLOW	1	–	1	–	–	–	–	–	–
SMOOTH	–	–	–	–	1	1	–	–	–
SNAKE	–	1	1	–	–	–	1	–	1
SNILD	1	–	1	–	–	–	–	–	–
SNOL	–	–	–	–	–	–	1	–	1
SOFT	1	2	3	2	2	4	–	–	–
SOFTLY	–	–	–	1	–	1	–	–	–
SPASE	–	–	–	–	–	–	1	–	1
STALLION	–	–	–	3	–	3	–	–	–
STAMPEDE	1	–	1	–	–	–	–	–	–
STOP	–	2	2	–	–	–	–	–	–
STRAIGHT	–	–	–	–	–	–	–	1	1
STRANGE	–	–	–	–	–	–	–	2	2
STRANGER	–	–	–	–	1	1	–	–	–
STRONG	–	–	–	–	1	1	–	–	–
SWELL	–	1	1	–	–	–	–	–	–
TABLE	1	–	1	–	–	–	–	–	–
TAIM	–	–	–	–	–	–	–	1	1
TAM	–	–	–	–	–	–	–	1	1
TAME	5	3	8	25	19	44	41	40	81
TAMED	2	1	3	1	1	2	5	1	6
TEAM	–	–	–	–	–	–	–	2	2
TELEVISION	–	1	1	–	–	–	–	–	–
TEME	–	–	–	–	–	–	1	–	1
THE	–	–	–	1	–	1	–	–	–
THING	–	–	–	1	–	1	–	–	–
THINGS	1	–	1	–	–	–	–	–	–
THINK	–	–	–	–	1	1	–	–	–
TIGER	1	2	3	–	–	–	–	2	2
TILE	–	–	–	–	–	–	1	–	1
TILED	–	1	1	–	–	–	–	–	–
TIME	–	–	–	–	–	–	1	–	1
TINY	–	–	–	–	–	–	1	–	1
TO	–	–	–	–	–	–	1	–	1
TOY	–	–	–	–	–	–	1	–	1
TRAIN	–	1	1	1	4	5	1	–	1
TRAINED	–	–	–	4	–	4	1	–	1
TREE	–	–	–	–	1	1	–	–	–
TROLLEY CAR	1	–	1	–	–	–	–	–	–
TURKEY	1	–	1	–	–	–	–	–	–
UNBEHAVE	–	–	–	–	1	1	–	–	–
UNCIVILIZED	–	–	–	–	–	–	1	–	1
UNHAPPY	–	–	–	–	2	2	–	–	–

RESPONSE WORD	1ST			3RD			5TH		
	M	F	T	M	F	T	M	F	T

94. WILD

RESPONSE WORD	M	F	T	M	F	T	M	F	T
UNTAME	–	–	–	–	–	–	2	3	5
UNTAMED	–	–	–	–	–	–	1	1	2
UNWILD	–	–	–	–	1	1	1	2	3
VICIOUS	–	–	–	–	–	–	1	–	1
WAIT	–	–	–	–	–	–	–	1	1
WAITING	–	–	–	1	–	1	–	–	–
WALL	–	1	1	–	–	–	–	–	–
WATER	–	–	–	1	–	1	–	–	–
WHAT	–	1	1	–	–	–	–	–	–
WHEN YOU GO MAD YOU CAN BE WILD	–	–	–	–	–	–	–	1	1
WHEN YOURE BITING SOMEBODY	1	–	1	–	–	–	–	–	–
WHERE	–	1	1	–	–	–	–	–	–
WHINE	–	1	1	–	–	–	–	–	–
WHOA	1	–	1	–	–	–	–	–	–
WHY	1	1	2	–	–	–	–	–	–
WIDE	–	–	–	–	1	1	1	–	1
WIFE	–	–	–	1	–	1	–	–	–
WIGGLE	–	–	–	–	1	1	–	–	–
WILDLY	–	–	–	1	–	1	–	–	–
WILL	–	1	1	–	–	–	–	–	–
WIND	–	1	1	–	–	–	2	–	2
WING	–	–	–	–	–	–	–	1	1
WIRE	1	–	1	–	–	–	–	–	–
WITH	1	–	1	–	–	–	–	–	–
WOLF	–	1	1	–	1	1	–	1	1
WOODS	–	–	–	–	–	–	1	–	1
WORK	3	1	4	–	–	–	–	–	–
WORLD	–	–	–	–	–	–	1	–	1
WOW	–	–	–	1	–	1	–	–	–
WRESTLING	1	–	1	–	–	–	–	–	–
WRONG	–	–	–	1	–	1	–	–	–
YOU	–	–	–	1	–	1	–	–	–
YOU ARE	–	1	1	–	–	–	–	–	–
YOU WILD	–	1	1	–	–	–	–	–	–

95. WING

RESPONSE WORD	M	F	T	M	F	T	M	F	T
A BIRD MIGHT NOT HAVE A WING AND THEN HE	–	1	1	–	–	–	–	–	–
A BIRDIE	1	–	1	–	–	–	–	–	–
A BIRDS WING	–	1	1	–	–	–	–	–	–
AFTER	–	–	–	1	–	1	–	–	–
AIR	–	–	–	–	–	–	1	1	2
AIRPLANE	6	–	6	2	–	2	4	3	7
AIRPLANE WING	–	–	–	1	–	1	–	–	–
ANGEL	–	3	3	–	1	1	1	1	2
ANGELS HAVE WINGS	–	1	1	–	–	–	–	–	–
ANGLE	–	–	–	–	–	–	–	1	1
ANIMAL	–	–	–	1	1	2	1	1	2
ARM	–	1	1	3	7	10	3	2	5
ARMS	–	–	–	–	–	–	1	–	1
ART	–	–	–	–	1	1	–	–	–
BAD	–	1	1	–	–	–	–	–	–
BAG	1	1	2	–	–	–	–	–	–
BALL	–	–	–	1	–	1	–	–	–
BAT	–	–	–	–	–	–	1	–	1
BATHTUB	–	1	1	–	–	–	–	–	–
BEAK	1	–	1	–	–	–	1	1	2
BED	–	1	1	–	–	–	–	–	–
BEE	–	–	–	–	–	–	1	–	1
BILL (OF A BIRD)	–	–	–	–	1	1	–	–	–
BING	–	1	1	1	–	1	1	–	1
BIRD	19	23	42	25	30	55	37	55	92
BIRDIE	2	–	2	–	–	–	–	–	–
BIRDS	1	–	1	1	–	1	2	1	3
BIRDS WING	1	–	1	–	–	–	–	–	–
BLACK	–	1	1	–	–	–	–	–	–
BLOG	–	–	–	–	–	–	1	–	1
BLUE	–	–	–	–	–	–	–	1	1

95. WING

RESPONSE WORD	1ST M	F	T	3RD M	F	T	5TH M	F	T
BOARD	-	1	1	-	-	-	-	-	-
BOAT	-	-	-	-	-	-	-	1	1
BODY	-	-	-	-	1	1	2	1	3
BOOKS	-	1	1	-	-	-	-	-	-
BREAST	1	-	1	1	-	1	-	-	-
BREEZE	-	-	-	1	1	2	-	-	-
BRING	1	-	1	-	-	-	-	-	-
BROKE	-	-	-	-	-	-	1	1	2
BROKEN	1	-	1	-	1	1	-	-	-
BUCKET	-	-	-	-	1	1	-	-	-
BUG	-	-	-	-	1	1	-	-	-
BUTTERFLIES	1	1	2	-	-	-	-	-	-
BUTTERFLY	-	1	1	1	-	1	1	1	2
CAME	-	-	-	-	-	-	1	-	1
CANT	-	-	-	1	-	1	-	-	-
CHAIR	1	-	1	-	-	-	-	-	-
CHICKEN	-	1	1	1	1	2	1	-	1
CLING	1	-	1	-	-	-	-	-	-
CLOTHES	-	-	-	1	-	1	-	-	-
CLOUDY	-	1	1	-	-	-	-	-	-
COLD	-	1	1	-	-	-	-	-	-
COLONY	-	-	-	-	1	1	-	-	-
COME HERE	1	-	1	-	-	-	-	-	-
DEBT	-	1	1	-	-	-	-	-	-
DID	-	1	1	-	-	-	-	-	-
DIND	-	-	-	-	-	-	1	-	1
DING	3	-	3	1	-	1	1	-	1
DOG	1	1	2	1	-	1	1	-	1
DOLL	-	1	1	-	1	1	-	-	-
DOWN	-	1	1	-	-	-	-	-	-
DRUM	1	-	1	-	-	-	-	-	-
ELECTRICITY	1	-	1	-	-	-	-	-	-
FAST	1	-	1	-	2	2	-	-	-
FATHER	-	1	1	-	-	-	-	-	-
FEATHER	3	3	6	4	5	9	6	3	9
FEATHERS	-	-	-	1	-	1	4	1	5
FEET	-	-	-	1	-	1	-	-	-
FELL OFF	1	-	1	-	-	-	-	-	-
FEREN	-	-	-	-	1	1	-	1	1
FIELD	-	-	-	-	1	1	-	-	-
FINE	1	-	1	-	1	1	-	-	-
FING	-	-	-	1	-	1	-	-	-
FLAP	-	-	-	1	-	1	-	-	-
FLIES	-	1	1	-	-	-	-	-	-
FLING	1	-	1	-	-	-	-	-	-
FLOWERS	-	1	1	-	-	-	-	-	-
FLY	29	34	63	59	51	110	35	39	74
FLY BIRD	1	-	1	1	-	1	-	-	-
FLYING	-	1	1	1	-	1	-	2	2
FOOT	-	-	-	-	-	-	1	2	3
FOOTBALL	-	-	-	-	-	-	1	-	1
GAME	-	-	-	-	1	1	-	-	-
GING	-	-	-	-	1	1	-	-	-
GIRL	-	-	-	-	1	1	-	-	-
HAIR	-	-	-	-	2	2	-	-	-
HAND	-	-	-	1	1	2	-	-	-
HANDS	-	-	-	1	-	1	-	-	-
HAVE	-	-	-	-	1	1	-	-	-
HAVE FUN	-	1	1	-	-	-	-	-	-
HAWK	-	-	-	1	-	1	-	-	-
HEAD	1	-	1	1	-	1	-	-	-
HELP	-	1	1	-	-	-	-	-	-
HELPS BIRDS	1	-	1	-	-	-	-	-	-
HI	-	-	-	-	-	-	1	-	1
HING	1	-	1	-	-	-	-	-	-
HIT	-	-	-	-	-	-	1	-	1
HOME	1	-	1	-	-	-	-	-	-
HORSE	-	-	-	-	-	-	1	1	2
HURT	-	-	-	-	-	-	1	-	1
IS A BIRD	1	-	1	-	-	-	-	-	-
JIMMY	-	1	1	-	-	-	-	-	-
KIND	-	-	-	1	-	1	-	-	-

95. WING

RESPONSE WORD	1ST M	F	T	3RD M	F	T	5TH M	F	T
KING	5	4	9	–	–	–	–	–	–
KINK	1	–	1	–	–	–	–	–	–
KITE	1	–	1	–	–	–	–	–	–
LADY	1	–	1	–	–	–	–	–	–
LEAF	–	–	–	1	1	2	–	–	–
LEG	–	–	–	1	–	1	1	–	1
LETTER	–	1	1	–	–	–	–	–	–
LIE	–	1	1	–	–	–	–	–	–
LIGHT	2	–	2	–	–	–	–	–	–
LING	1	–	1	–	–	–	–	–	–
LONG	–	–	–	–	–	–	1	–	1
LOST	–	1	1	1	–	1	–	–	–
ME	–	–	–	1	–	1	–	–	–
MEAT	–	–	–	–	1	1	1	–	1
MING	–	1	1	–	1	1	–	–	–
MONDAY	–	1	1	–	–	–	–	–	–
NECKLACE	1	–	1	–	–	–	–	–	–
NO WING	1	–	1	–	–	–	–	–	–
NO WINGS	–	–	–	–	1	1	–	–	–
NOT WING	1	–	1	–	–	–	–	–	–
NUMBER	–	1	1	–	–	–	–	–	–
OF A BIRD	–	–	–	–	–	–	–	1	1
OF BIRD	–	–	–	–	–	–	–	1	1
OF THE BIRD	1	–	1	–	–	–	–	–	–
ON A BUMBLEBEE	–	1	1	–	–	–	–	–	–
ON AN AIRPLANE	1	1	2	–	–	–	–	–	–
ON IT	1	–	1	–	–	–	–	–	–
ONE	–	1	1	–	–	–	–	–	–
ORANGE	1	–	1	–	–	–	–	–	–
ORGAN	–	–	–	–	–	–	1	–	1
PART	–	–	–	1	–	1	2	1	3
PART OF A BIRDS BODY	–	–	–	–	–	–	1	–	1
PART OF A BODY	–	–	–	–	–	–	–	1	1
PART OF AN AIRPLANE	–	–	–	–	–	–	1	–	1
PART OF BIRD	–	–	–	–	–	–	1	–	1
PART OF THE BODY OF A BIRD	–	–	–	–	–	–	–	1	1
PAST	–	1	1	–	–	–	–	–	–
PAY	–	–	–	–	1	1	–	–	–
PEOPLE	1	–	1	1	–	1	–	–	–
PIN	–	–	–	1	–	1	–	–	–
PING	–	1	1	–	–	–	–	–	–
PLANE	–	–	–	1	–	1	2	2	4
PLAY	–	1	1	–	–	–	–	–	–
PLAY ON	1	–	1	–	–	–	–	–	–
PRETTY	–	1	1	–	–	–	–	–	–
PROPELLER	1	–	1	–	–	–	–	–	–
RING	1	2	3	2	–	2	1	1	2
ROPE	–	1	1	–	–	–	–	–	–
RUDDER	–	–	–	1	–	1	–	–	–
RUN	1	–	1	–	–	–	–	–	–
SANG	–	–	–	–	–	–	–	1	1
SCHOOL	–	1	1	–	–	–	–	–	–
SEE	–	–	–	–	1	1	–	–	–
SHE WILL	–	1	1	–	–	–	–	–	–
SHOOT	1	–	1	–	–	–	–	–	–
SHORT	–	–	–	–	–	–	–	1	1
SIDEWALK	–	1	1	–	–	–	–	–	–
SING	3	3	6	7	4	11	3	2	5
SKY	–	–	–	–	–	–	–	1	1
SLIDE	1	–	1	–	–	–	–	–	–
SODA	1	–	1	–	–	–	–	–	–
SOFT	–	–	–	–	1	1	–	–	–
SOMETHING	–	1	1	–	–	–	–	–	–
SOMETHING ON A BIRD	–	–	–	–	–	–	–	1	1
SPIDER	–	1	1	–	–	–	–	–	–
SPRING	–	–	–	1	–	1	–	–	–
STING	1	–	1	–	–	–	–	–	–
SWING	9	9	18	1	3	4	3	2	5
TABLE	2	–	2	–	–	–	–	–	–
TAIL	–	–	–	2	2	4	2	–	2
TEACHER	–	–	–	–	–	–	2	1	3

RESPONSE WORD	1ST M	1ST F	1ST T	3RD M	3RD F	3RD T	5TH M	5TH F	5TH T

95. WING

RESPONSE WORD	1ST M	1ST F	1ST T	3RD M	3RD F	3RD T	5TH M	5TH F	5TH T
THE	—	1	1	—	—	—	—	1	1
THIGH	—	—	—	—	—	—	—	—	—
THING	1	—	1	1	2	3	1	—	1
TING	—	—	—	—	—	—	—	—	—
TO A BIRD	—	1	1	—	—	—	—	—	—
TREE	—	1	1	—	—	—	—	—	—
TURKEY	1	—	1	—	—	—	—	—	—
TV	1	—	1	—	—	—	—	—	—
TWO WINGS	—	—	—	1	—	1	—	—	—
UP	—	1	1	—	—	—	—	—	—
WAG	—	—	—	1	—	1	—	—	—
WAGON	—	1	1	—	—	—	—	—	—
WAITING	—	—	—	—	1	1	—	—	—
WALK	1	—	1	1	1	2	—	—	—
WANT	1	—	1	—	—	—	—	—	—
WATER	—	—	—	1	—	1	—	—	—
WE	—	1	1	—	1	1	—	—	—
WELL	—	1	1	—	—	—	—	—	—
WHAT	2	—	2	—	—	—	—	—	—
WHEN YOURE WINGING SOMETHING	1	—	1	—	—	—	—	—	—
WHITE	—	—	—	—	1	1	—	—	—
WHY	—	1	1	—	1	1	—	—	—
WIGGLE	—	—	—	—	1	1	—	—	—
WIND	2	1	3	—	1	1	1	1	2
WINDY	—	—	—	—	1	1	2	1	3
WING	—	—	—	—	—	—	—	—	—
WINGS	—	3	3	—	—	—	—	—	—
WORK	1	—	1	—	—	—	—	—	—
YELLOW	1	—	1	—	1	1	—	—	—
YOU	—	—	—	—	—	—	—	—	—

96. YELLOW

RESPONSE WORD	1ST M	1ST F	1ST T	3RD M	3RD F	3RD T	5TH M	5TH F	5TH T
A COLOR	—	—	—	1	—	1	1	2	3
AIRPLANE	1	—	1	—	—	—	—	—	—
BALL	1	1	2	—	—	—	—	—	—
BALLOON	—	—	—	—	—	—	4	—	4
BANANA	—	2	2	—	—	—	—	—	—
BANANAS	—	1	1	—	1	1	—	—	—
BEAUTIFUL	—	—	—	—	1	1	—	—	—
BEE	1	1	2	—	—	—	—	—	—
BELLOW	1	—	1	—	—	—	—	—	—
BIRD	2	—	2	1	—	1	—	—	—
BLACK	6	6	12	19	9	28	8	6	14
BLOND	—	—	—	—	1	1	—	—	—
BLUE	11	15	26	13	16	29	6	11	17
BRIGHT	1	2	3	—	4	4	1	3	4
BROWN	1	1	1	7	6	13	6	8	14
BUBBLE	—	1	1	—	—	—	—	—	—
BUSY	—	1	1	—	—	—	—	—	—
BUTTER	1	—	1	—	—	—	—	—	—
BUTTERFLY	4	—	4	1	1	2	—	4	4
CAKE	1	—	1	—	—	—	—	—	—
CALL IT A COLOR	1	—	1	—	—	—	—	—	—
CAR	1	—	1	1	1	2	1	—	1
CAROL	—	1	1	1	—	1	—	—	—
CAT	1	—	1	—	—	—	—	—	—
CATCH	—	—	—	—	—	—	1	—	1
CHALK	—	—	—	—	—	—	3	—	3
CHICKEN	—	—	—	—	—	—	1	—	1
CLEAR	—	—	—	—	—	—	—	—	—
CLOCK	1	—	1	—	—	—	—	—	—
COAT	—	1	1	—	—	—	1	—	1
COLAR	—	—	—	—	—	—	—	—	—
COLOR	7	10	17	33	32	65	52	61	113
COLOR THE WORD	—	1	1	—	—	—	—	—	—
COLOR YOUR PICTURE	—	1	1	—	—	—	—	—	—
COUCH	1	—	1	—	—	—	—	—	—
COWARD	—	—	—	—	1	1	—	—	—
CRAYON	7	3	10	3	2	5	—	4	4

96. YELLOW

RESPONSE WORD	1ST			3RD			5TH		
	M	F	T	M	F	T	M	F	T
CRAYONING	–	1	1	–	–	–	–	–	–
CRY	–	1	1	–	–	–	–	–	–
CURTAIN	1	–	1	–	–	–	–	–	–
DID	–	1	1	–	–	–	–	–	–
DOG	–	1	1	–	–	–	–	–	–
DOOR	–	–	–	1	–	1	–	–	–
DRESS	–	2	2	–	1	1	–	–	–
DUCK	1	2	3	–	–	–	–	–	–
EASTER	–	–	–	–	–	–	1	–	1
EAT YOUR JELLO AND GET THE COLORS YOU W	1	–	1	–	–	–	–	–	–
FARBLE	1	–	1	–	–	–	–	–	–
FELLOW	1	1	2	1	–	1	–	2	2
FENCE	1	–	1	–	–	–	–	–	–
FLAG	1	–	1	–	–	–	–	–	–
FLOWER	2	2	4	–	–	–	1	1	2
FLOWERS	1	1	2	–	–	–	–	1	1
FLY	–	–	–	1	–	1	–	–	–
GLASS	1	–	1	–	–	–	–	–	–
GOLD	–	–	–	–	1	1	–	1	1
GRAPEFRUITS	–	1	1	–	–	–	–	–	–
GRASS	–	–	–	–	–	–	1	–	1
GREEN	13	9	22	12	14	26	13	11	24
GREY	1	–	1	–	–	–	–	–	–
GROUND	–	1	1	–	–	–	–	–	–
HAIR	1	–	1	–	–	–	–	–	–
HAY	1	–	1	–	–	–	–	–	–
HELLO	1	1	2	–	–	–	–	–	–
HOUSE	2	–	2	–	–	–	–	–	–
I	–	1	1	–	–	–	–	–	–
I HAVE A YELLOW BLOUSE	–	1	1	–	–	–	–	–	–
I PRETEND IS WHITE	–	1	1	–	–	–	–	–	–
IS ME	1	–	1	–	–	–	–	–	–
JACKET	–	–	–	1	–	1	–	–	–
JELLO	2	1	3	–	–	–	–	–	–
KELLOW	1	–	1	–	–	–	–	–	–
KLEENEX	1	–	1	–	–	–	–	–	–
LADDER	–	1	1	–	–	–	–	–	–
LEAVES	1	1	2	1	–	1	–	–	–
LEMON	–	–	–	–	–	–	1	–	1
LIGHT	–	2	2	2	1	3	1	1	2
LIGHT COLOR	1	–	1	1	–	1	–	–	–
LIKE YOURE YELLOW	–	–	–	1	–	1	–	1	1
LOCKERS	1	–	1	–	–	–	–	1	1
LONG	–	–	–	1	–	1	–	–	–
MARGARINE	–	–	–	–	–	–	–	1	1
MELLOW	1	1	2	–	–	–	–	–	–
MINE	–	1	1	–	–	–	–	–	–
O	–	1	1	–	–	–	–	–	–
OPPOSITE	–	–	–	–	1	1	–	–	–
ORANGE	8	9	17	6	8	14	3	4	7
ORANGISH YELLOW	–	–	–	1	–	1	–	–	–
ORGAN	1	–	1	–	–	–	–	–	–
OVEN	1	–	1	–	–	–	–	–	–
PALE	–	–	–	–	–	–	1	–	1
PAN	–	1	1	–	–	–	–	–	–
PAPER	–	2	2	1	–	1	–	–	–
PEAR	1	1	2	–	–	–	–	–	–
PELLOW	1	–	1	–	–	–	–	–	–
PENCIL	–	–	–	–	–	–	1	1	2
PENT	–	–	–	–	–	–	1	–	1
PIANO	2	–	2	–	–	–	–	–	–
PIECE OF PAPER	1	–	1	–	–	–	–	–	–
PILLOW	–	–	–	–	–	–	–	–	–
PINK	2	–	2	6	3	9	1	2	3
PLAY	–	3	3	–	1	1	1	–	1
PRETTY	–	–	–	–	1	1	–	–	–
PRIMARY COLOR	–	1	1	–	–	–	1	–	1
PURPLE	1	4	5	3	3	6	3	2	5
RED	11	13	24	14	16	30	12	6	18
RING	–	1	1	–	–	–	–	–	–
RINK	–	–	–	–	–	–	1	–	1

RESPONSE WORD	1ST M	F	T	3RD M	F	T	5TH M	F	T

96.   YELLOW

RESPONSE WORD	1ST M	F	T	3RD M	F	T	5TH M	F	T
ROCK	1	–	1	–	–	–	–	–	–
SALLY	1	–	1	–	–	–	–	–	–
SAY	–	–	–	–	–	–	1	–	1
SCARED	–	–	–	–	–	–	1	–	1
SCREEN	–	1	1	–	–	–	–	–	–
SEAT	1	–	1	–	–	–	–	–	–
SHADE	–	–	–	–	1	1	–	–	–
SHOE	–	–	–	–	–	–	–	1	1
SHOES	–	1	1	–	–	–	–	–	–
SILVER	1	–	1	–	1	1	–	–	–
SING	–	1	1	–	–	–	–	–	–
SKIRT	–	1	1	–	–	–	–	–	–
SKY	–	1	1	–	–	–	–	–	–
SOFT	1	–	1	–	–	–	–	–	–
SUN	4	2	6	–	2	2	3	4	7
TABLE	1	1	2	–	–	–	2	–	2
TEETH	–	1	1	–	–	–	–	–	–
THE SUN IS YELLOW	–	1	1	–	–	–	–	–	–
THINK	1	–	1	–	–	–	–	–	–
THIS	1	–	1	–	–	–	–	–	–
TOWN	–	1	1	–	–	–	–	–	–
TRUCK	1	–	1	–	–	–	–	–	–
TURQUOISE	–	–	–	–	–	–	1	–	1
WALL	1	–	1	–	–	–	–	–	–
WALLS	–	–	–	–	1	1	–	–	–
WHEN YOU COLORING SOMETHING YELLOW	1	–	1	–	–	–	–	–	–
WHITE	3	8	11	8	9	17	5	2	7
WOOL	1	–	1	–	–	–	–	–	–
YELL	–	1	1	1	–	1	–	–	–
YOU	1	–	1	–	1	1	–	–	–
YOUR DRESS IS YELLOW	–	1	1	–	–	–	–	–	–
ZEBRA	–	–	–	–	1	1	–	–	–

Index

WORD ASSOCIATIONS OF YOUNG CHILDREN

by Doris R. Entwisle

designer:	Athena Blackorby
typesetter:	Baltimore Type and Composition Corporation
typefaces:	(text) Baskerville, (display) Bodoni
printer:	Universal Lithographers, Inc.
paper:	Pinnacle Opaque Offset
binder:	Moore & Co., Inc.
cover material:	Columbia Riverside Linen

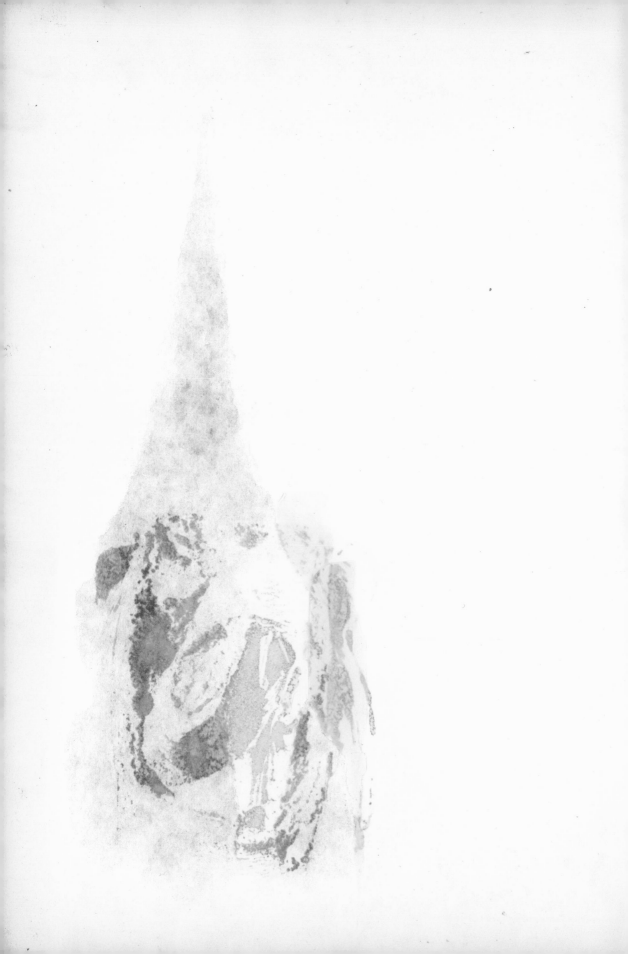